Antique Trader®

POTTERY & PORCELAIN
CERAMICS

PRICE GUIDE

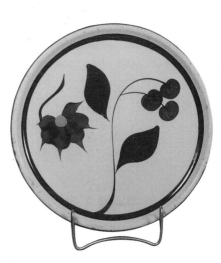

Edited by
Kyle Husfloen

Published by

kp **krause publications**

An Imprint of F+W Publications

700 East State Street • Iola, WI 54990-0001
715-445-2214 • 888-457-2873

Our toll-free number to place an order or obtain
a free catalog is (800) 258-0929.

Library of Congress Catalog Number: ISSN 1547-643X

ISBN 13-digit: 978-0-89689-418-1
ISBN 10-digit: 0-89689-418-5

Designed by Wendy Wendt
Edited by Kyle Husfloen

Printed in China

TABLE OF CONTENTS

Introduction

Over 35 years ago, The Antique Trader produced its first general price guides covering all types of antiques and collectibles. Since the founding of our Antique Trader Books division in 1994, we have greatly expanded our offerings in the category of price guides, as well as other specialized references for the collecting field.

The first new product in our expanded price guide lineup was *Antique Trader Books Pottery & Porcelain — Ceramics Price Guide*, released in early 1994. This well-illustrated reference covered all major categories of pottery and porcelain, foreign and domestic, and was well received by the collecting community. The popularity of this guide has led to further editions and we're pleased to present here the all new fifth edition. Although similar in format to our earlier editions, we greatly expanded the number of ceramics categories included. All of our listings are new or updated with many contributions by leading authorities in specific ceramics fields. Highlighting the listings are even more quality all-color photographs that add to this guide's usefulness and eye appeal. As in the earlier editions, this guide covers ceramics produced as far back as the eighteenth century in Europe, but also includes expanded sections on popular twentieth century American chinawares and pottery. Whatever segment of the vast ceramics market you find most appealing, we'll have information included here.

We always pride ourselves on providing the most accurate and detailed descriptions possible for each item included. Each category also begins with a brief introductory paragraph and, in most sections, sketches of typical manufacturers' marks found on the pieces.

Ceramics, like most collecting specialties, has a vocabulary all its own. To give you a better understanding of terms used throughout this guide, we begin with a general introduction to the collecting of ceramics followed by several pages of sketches showing a wide variety of pieces and forms you will find listed. The sketches include brief notes on the forms and body parts which will make it easier to study and use our guide. As an additional reference source we are including, at the conclusion of our price listings, a Glossary of Selected Ceramics Terms followed by several special Appendices covering individual collecting groups, museums of interest and references to pottery and porcelain marks. Since English ceramics of the nineteenth and early twentieth century make up quite a large portion of collectible ceramic wares found in this country, we also include an appendix explaining the unique system of English Registry Marks.

My staff and I have put many hours of effort into producing an attractive and useful guide, and it took many hands and hearts to produce the volume you now hold. A special note of thanks goes to our many special contributors for preparing a variety of categories covering some of today's most popular and collectible ceramics. You will find a complete listing of these special contributors on page 6. Their efforts have assured that we are presenting a well rounded and comprehensive guide.

I sincerely hope that all who add *Antique Trader Books Pottery & Porcelain—Ceramics Price Guide 5th Edition* to their library will find it handy, easy to use and authoritative. Use it as a guide in your collecting pursuits and it should serve you well. If you have special comments or questions, we'll be happy to answer your inquiries. Enjoy this guide and may it bring you new knowledge and appreciation of your ceramic treasures and those waiting your discovery.

Kyle Husfloen, Editor

Photography Credits

There are many other companies and individuals I must also thank. Among the photographers who have contributed to this edition are: Charles Casad, Monticelo, Ill.; Neva Colbert, St. Clairsville, Ohio; Susan N. Cox, El Cajon, Calif., Susan Eberman, Bedford, Ind., Mary Ann Johnston, New Cumberland, West Virginia; Ann Kerr, Sidney, Ohio; Vivian Kromer, Bakersfield, Calif., and Pat McPherson, Ramona, Calif.

For other photographers, artwork, data or permission to photograph in their shops, we sincerely express appreciation to the following auctioneers, galleries, individuals and shops: Alderfers, Hatfield, Pa.; Charlton Hall Galleries, Columbia, S.C.; Christie's, New York, N.Y.; Cincinnati Art Galleries, Cincinnati, Ohio; Copake Country Auction, Copake, N.Y.; William Doyle Galleries, New York, N.Y.; Early Auction Company, Milford, Ohio; Garth's Auctions, Delaware, Ohio; Glass-Works Auctions, East Greenville, Pa. and Green Valley Auctions, Mt. Crawford, Va.

Also to Harris Auction Center, Marshalltown, Iowa; Jackson's International Auctioneers, Cedar Falls, Iowa; James D. Julia, Fairfield, Maine; McMasters Harris Auctions, Cambridge, Ohio; Neal Auction Company, New Orleans, La.; New Orleans Auction Galleries, New Orleans, La.; Northwest Auctions, Portsmouth, N.H.; Dave Rago Arts & Crafts, Lambertville, N.J.; Seeck Auctions, Mason City, Iowa; Skinner, Inc., Bolton, Mass.; Treadway Gallery, Cincinnati, Ohio; Bruce & Vicki Waasdorf, Clarence, N.Y.; and Wood Auctions, Douglass, Kan.

ON THE COVER: Upper left - Ceramic Arts Studio of Madison "Rhumba Dancers" figures, $80-120; Right - Nippon porcelain whiskey jug and stopper, $770; Lower left - Willow Wares - Blue Willlow Sauce Tureen, $125-150.

Special Contributors

ABC Plates

Joan M. George, Ed.D
67 Stevens Ave.
Old Bridge, NJ 08857
e-mail: drjgeorge@nac.net

Abingdon

Elaine Westover
210 Knox Highway 5
Abingdon, IL 61410-9332

American Painted Porcelain

Dorothy Kamm
10786 Grey Heron Ct.
Port St. Lucie, FL 34986
e-mail: dorothykamm@adelphia.net

Amphora-Tepliz

Les and Irene Cohen
Pittsburgh, PA 15235

Amphora Collectors International
21 Brooke Dr.
Elizabethtown, PA 17022
email: www.tombeaz@comcast.net

Belleek (American)

Peggy Sebek, ISA, AAA
3255 Glencairn Rd.
Shaker Heights, OH 44122
e-mail: pegsebek@earthlink.net

Belleek (Irish)

Del E. Domke
16142 N.E. 15th St.
Bellevue, WA 98008-2711
(425) 746-6363
Fax: (425) 746-6363
e-mail: delyicious@comcast.net
Web site: The Beauty and Romance of
Irish Belleek

Blue and White Pottery

Steve Stone
12795 W. Alameda Pkwy.
Lakewood, CO 80225
e-mail: Sylvanlvr@aol.com

Blue Ridge Dinnerwares

Marie Compton
M & M Collectibles
1770 S. Randall Rd., #236
Geneva, IL. 60134-4646
ebay name: brdoll

Blue Willow (see Willow Wares)

Ceramic Arts Studio of Madison

Tim Holthaus
CAS Collectors Association
P.O. Box 46
Madison, WI 53701-0046
e-mail: CAScollectors@Ameritech.net

Donald-Brian Johnson
3329 South 56th St., #611
Omaha, NE 68106
email: donaldbrian@webtv.net

Clarice Cliff Designs

Laurie Williams
Rabbitt Antiques and Collectibles
(408) 248-1260
email: rabbitt3339@yahoo.com

Cowan

Tim and Jamie Saloff
P.O. Box 339
Edinboro, PA 16412
e-mail: tim.saloff@verizon.net

Czech Pottery

Cheryl Goyda
Box 137
Hopeland, PA 17533
e-mail: Mzczech@aol.com

Doulton & Royal Doulton
- Bunnykins

Reg. G. Morris
2050 Welcome Way
The Villages, FL 32162
e-mail: modexmin@comcast.net

Other

Louise Irvine
England - (020) 8876-7739
email: louiseirvine@blueyonder.co.uk

Pascoe and Company
253 SW 22nd Ave.
Miami, FL 33135
email: sales@pascoeandcompany.com

Fiesta

Mick and Lorna Chase
Fiesta Plus
380 Hawkins Crawford Rd.
Cookeville, TN 38501
(931) 372-8333
email: fiestaplus@yahoo.com
Web: www.fiestaplus.com

Florence Ceramics

David G. Miller
1971 Blue Fox Dr.
Lansdale, PA 19446-5505
(610) 584-6127

Florence Ceramics Collectors Society
e-mail: FlorenceCeramics@aol.com

Flow Blue

K. Robert and Bonne Hohl
47 Fawn Dr.
Reading, PA 19607

Geisha Girl Porcelain

Elyce Litts
P.O. Box 394
Morris Plains, NJ 07950
(908) 964-5055
e-mail: memories@worldnet.att.net

Hall China

Marty Kennedy
4711 S.W. Brentwood Rd.
Topeka, KS 66606
(785) 554-5837
(785) 273-4981
e-mail: martykennedy@cox.net
Web site: http://www.inter-services.com/
HallChina

Harker Pottery

William A. and Donna J. Gray
2 Highland Colony
East Liverpool, OH 43920-1871
e-mail: harkermate@comcast.net

Haviland

Nora Travis
13337 E. South St.
Cerritos, CA 90701
(714) 521-9283
e-mail: Travishrs@aol.com

Head Vase Planters

Maddy Gordon
P.O. Box 83H
Scarsdale, NY 10583-8583

Hull

Joan Hull
1376 Nevada SW
Huron, SD 57350

Hull Pottery Association
11023 Tunnel Hill N.E.
New Lexington, OH 43764

Ironstone

Bev Dieringer
P.O. Box 536
Redding Ridge, CT 06876
e-mail: dieringer1@aol.com

Jewel Tea - Autumn Leaf

Jo Cunningham
535 E. Normal
Springfield, MO 65807-1659
(417) 831-1320
e-mail: hlresearcher@aol.com

Kitchen Collectibles

Cow Creamers:

LuAnn Riggs
1781 Lindberg Dr.
Columbia, MO 65201
e-mail: artichokeannies@bessi.net

Egg Cups:

Joan M. George, Ed.D
67 Stevens Ave.
Old Bridge, NJ 08857
e-mail: drjgeorge@nac.net

Napkin Dolls, Reamers:

Bobbie Zucker Bryson is the co-author,
with Deborah Gillham and Ellen
Bercovici, of the pictorial price guide
*Collectibles for the Kitchen, Bath &
Beyond, 2nd Edition*, published by
Krause Publications. It covers a broad
range of collectibles including napkin
dolls, stringholders, pie birds, figural
egg timers, razor blade banks, whimsical
whistle milk cups and laundry sprinkler
bottles. Bryson can be contacted via e-
mail at Napkindoll@aol.com

String Holders, Egg Timers, Pie Birds:

Ellen Bercovici
360-11th Ave. So.
Naples, FL 34102

Limoges

Debby DuBay, Ret. USAF
Limoges Antiques Shop
20 Post Office Avenue
Andover, MA 01810
(978) 470-8773
e-mail: dlimoges@flash.net
Web: www.limogesantiques.com <http://
www.limogesantiques.com>

Lotus Ware

William A. and Donna J. Gray
2 Highland Colony
East Liverpool, OH 43920-1871
email: harkermate@comcast.net

Majolica

Michael G. Strawser Auctions
P.O. Box 332
Wolcottville, IN 46795
(260) 854-2859
Web: www.majolicaauctions.com <http://
www.majolicaauctions.com>

Mettlach

Gary Kirsner
Glentiques, Ltd.
1940 Augusta Terrace
P.O. Box 8807
Coral Springs, FL 33071
e-mail: gkirsner@myacc.net

Andre Ammelounx
P.O. Box 136
Palatine, IL 60078
(847) 991-5927

Morton Potteries

Burdell Hall
201 W. Sassafras Dr.
Morton, IL 61550
(309) 263-2988
e-mail: bnbhall@mtco.com

Nippon

Jackson's International Auctioneers &
Appraisers
2229 Lincoln St.
Cedar Falls, IA 50613
(319) 277-2256
(319) 277-1252 (fax)
Web: www.jacksonsauction.com <http://
www.jacksonauction.com>

Noritake

Janet and Tim Trapani
7543 Northport Dr.
Boynton Beach, FL 33437
e-mail: ttrapani1946@yahoo.com

Old Ivory

Alma Hillman
197 Coles Corner Rd.
Winterport, ME 04496
e-mail: oldivory@adelphia.net

Oyster Plates

Michael G. Strawser Auctions
P.O. Box 332
Wolcottville, IN 46795
(260) 854-2859
Web: www.majolicaauctions.com <http://
www.majolicaauctions.com>

Pennsbury Pottery

Mark and Ellen Supnick
7725 NW 78th Ct.
Tamarac, FL 33321
email: Saturdaycook@aol.com

Phoenix Bird Porcelain

Joan Collett Oates
1107 Deerfield St.
Marshall, MI 49068
e-mail: koates120@earthlink.net

Purinton Pottery

Sharon Dahlhauser
212 N. Jones
Algona, IA 50511
email: csdahl@connect.com

Quimper

Sandra V. Bondhus
16 Salisbury Way
Farmington, CT 06032
email: nbondhus@pol.net

Red Wing

Gail Peck
2121 Pearl St.
Fremont, NE 68025
email: gpeckl@neb.rr.com

Royal Bayreuth

Mary McCaslin
6887 Black Oak Ct. E.
Avon, IN 46123
(317) 272-7776
e-mail: maryjack@indy.rr.com

Royal Copley

Donald-Brian Johnson
3329 South 56th St., #611
Omaha, NE 68106
email: donaldbrian@webtv.net

R.S. Prussia

Mary McCaslin
6887 Black Oak Ct. E.
Avon, IN 46123
(317) 272-7776
e-mail: maryjack@indy.rr.com

Russel Wright Designs

Kathryn Wiese
Retrospective Modern Design
P.O. Box 305
Manning, IA 51455
e-mail: retrodesign@earthlink.net

Shawnee

Linda Guffey
2004 Fiat Ct.
El Cajon, CA 92019-4234
e-mail: Gufantique@aol.com

Shelley China

Mannie Banner
126 S.W. 15th St.
Pembroke Pines, FL 33027
(954) 443-2933

Steins

Gary Kirsner
Glentiques, Ltd.
1940 Augusta Terrace
P.O. Box 8807
Coral Springs, FL 33071
e-mail: gkirsner@myacc.net

Andre Ammelounx
P.O. Box 136
Palatine, IL 60078
(847) 991-5927

Torquay Pottery

Judy Wucherer
Transitions of Wales, Ltd.
P.O. Box 1441
Brookfield, WI 53045

North American Torquay Society
R.J. Lookabill, Membership
email: membership@torquayus.org

Uhl Pottery

Lloyd Martin
1582 Gregory Lane
Jasper, IN 47546
e-mail: nlmartin@insightbb.com

Vernon Kilns

Pam Green
You Must Remember This
P.O. Box 822

Hollis, NH 03049
e-mail: ymrt@aol.com
Web: www.ymrt.com <http://www.ymrt.
com>

Warwick

John Rader Sr.
780 S. Village Dr., Apt. 203
St. Petersburg, FL 33716
(727) 570-9906

Watt Pottery

William Hill
W223 N2493 Glenwood Lane
Waukesha, WI 53186
e-mail: wmhill2@yahoo.com <mailto:
wmhill2@yahoo.com>

Willow Wares

Jeff Siptak
4013 Russellwood Dr.
Nashville, TN 37204
e-mail: WillowWare@aol.com

Zeisel (Eva) Designs

Pat Moore
695 Monterey Blvd., Apt. 203
San Francisco, CA 94124
e-mail: ezcclub@pacbell.net

Kathryn Wiese
Retrospective Modern Design
P.O. Box 305
Manning, IA 51455
email: retrodesign@earthlink.net

Zsolnay

Federico Santi / John Gacher
The Drawing Room Antiques
152 Spring St.
Newport, RI 02840
(401) 841-5060
email: drawrm@hotmail.com
Web: www.drawrm@hotmail.com

Collecting Guidelines

Whenever I'm asked about what to collect, I always stress that you should collect what you like and want to live with. Collecting is a very personal matter and only you can determine what will give you the most satisfaction. With the wide diversity of ceramics available, everyone should be able to find a topic they will enjoy studying and collecting.

One thing that every collector should keep in mind is that to get the most from their hobby they must study it in depth, read everything they can get their hands on, and purchase the best references available for their library. New research material continues to become available for collectors and learning is an ongoing process.

It is also very helpful to join a collectors' club where others who share your enthusiasm will support and guide your learning. Fellow collectors often become your best friends and sources for special treasures to add to your collection. Dealers who specialize in a ceramics category are always eager to help educate and support collectors and many times they become a mentor for a novice who is just starting out on the road to the "advanced collector" level.

With the very ancient and complex history of ceramic wares, it's easy to understand why becoming educated about your special interest is of paramount importance. There have been collectors of pottery and porcelain for centuries, and for nearly as long collectors have had to be wary of reproductions or "reissues." In Chinese ceramics, for instance, it has always been considered perfectly acceptable to copy as closely as possible the style and finish of earlier ceramics and even mark them with period markings on the base. The only problem arises when a modern collector wants to determine whether their piece, "guaranteed" antique, was produced over two hundred years ago or barely a century ago.

With European and, to some extent, American wares, copying of earlier styles has also been going on for many decades. As far back as the mid-nineteenth century, "copies" and "adaptions" of desirable early wares were finding their way onto the collector market. By the late nineteenth century, in particular, revivals of eighteenth century porcelains and even some early nineteenth century earthenwares were available, often sold as decorative items and sometimes clearly marked. After a hundred years, however, these early copies can pose a real quagmire for the unwary.

Again, education is the key. As you're building your store of knowledge and experience, buy with care from reliable sources.

Another area that calls for special caution on the part of collectors, especially the tyro, is that of damaged and repaired pieces. A wise collector will always buy the best example they can find and it is a good policy to save up to buy one extra fine piece rather than a handful of lesser examples. You never want to pass up a good buy. But, in the long run, a smaller collection of choice pieces will probably bring you more satisfaction (and financial reward) than a large collection of moderate quality.

Purchasing a damaged or clearly repaired piece is a judgment only the collector can make. In general I wouldn't recommend it unless the piece is so unique that another example is not likely to come your way in the near future. For certain classes of expensive and rare ceramics, especially early pottery that has seen heavy use, a certain amount of damage may be inevitable and more acceptable. The sale price, however, should reflect this fact.

Restoration of pottery and porcelain wares has been a fact of life for many decades. Even in the early nineteenth century before good glues were available, "make-do" repairs were sometimes done to pieces using small metal staples and today some collectors seek out these quaint examples of early recycling. Since the early twentieth century, glue and repainting have been common methods used to mask damages to pottery and porcelain and these repairs can usually be detected today with a strong light and the naked eye.

The problem in recent decades has been the ability of restorers to completely mask any sign of previous damages using more sophisticated repair methods. There is nothing wrong with a quality restoration of a rare piece as long as the eventual purchaser is completely aware such work has been done.

It can take more than the naked eye and a strong light to detect some invisible repairs today and that's where the popular "black light," using ultraviolet rays, can be of help. Many spots of repair will fluoresce under the "black light." I understand, however, that newer glues and paints are becoming available which won't show up under the black light. The key then, especially for the beginner, is know your ceramic or your seller and be sure you have a money-back guarantee when making a major purchase.

I certainly don't want to sound too downbeat and discourage anyone from pursuing what can be a wonderfully fun and fulfilling hobby, but starting from a position of strength, with confidence and education, will certainly pay off in the long run for every collector.

Ceramics, in addition to their beauty and charm, also offer the collecting advantage of durability and low maintenance. It's surprising how much pottery and porcelain from two centuries ago is still available to collect. There were literally train cars full of it produced and sold by the late nineteenth century, and such wares are abundantly available and often reasonably priced. Beautiful dinnerwares and colorful vases abound in the marketplace and offer exciting collecting possibilities. They look wonderful used on today's dining tables or gracing display shelves.

A periodic dusting and once-a-year washing in mild sudsy, warm water is about all the care they will require. Of course, it's not recommended you put older pottery and porcelains in your dishwasher where rattling and extremely hot water could cause damage. Anyway, it's more satisfying to hold a piece in your hand in warm soapy water in a rubber dishpan (for added protection) and caress it carefully with a dishrag. The tactile enjoyment of a ceramic piece brings a new dimension to collecting and this sort of tender loving care can be nearly as satisfying as just admiring a piece in a china cabinet or on a shelf.

Whatever sort of pottery or porcelain appeals to you most, whether it be eighteenth century Meissen or mid-twentieth century California-made pottery, you can take pride in the fact that you are carrying on a collecting tradition that goes back centuries when the crowned heads of Europe first began vying for the finest and rarest ceramics with which to accent their regal abodes.

Kyle Husfloen, Editor

Typical Ceramic Shapes

The following line drawings illustrate typical shapes found in pottery and porcelain pitchers and vases. These forms are referred to often in our price listings.

Pitcher - Barrel-shaped

Pitcher - Jug-type

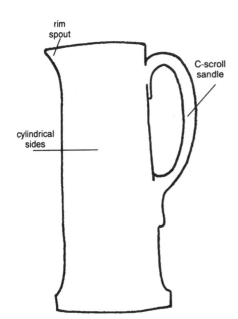

Pitcher - Tankard-type with cylindrical sides, C-scroll handle, and rim spout.

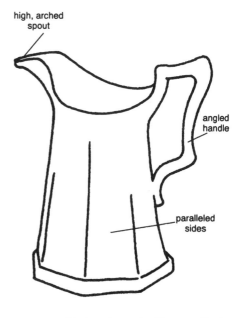

Pitcher - Tankard-type with panelled (octagonal) sides, angled handle and high, arched spout.

Vases

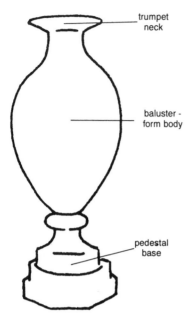

Vase - Baluster-form body with trumpet neck on a pedestal base.

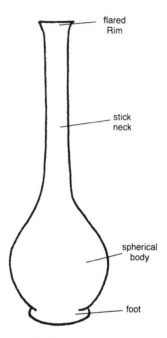

Vase - Bottle-form — Spherical footed body tapering to a tall stick neck with flared rim.

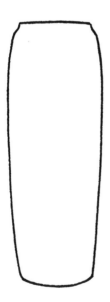

Vase - Cylindrical

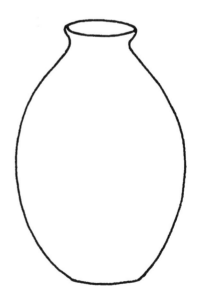

Vase - Ovoid body, tapering to a short, flared neck.

Vases (Continued)

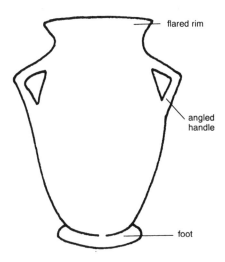

Vase - Ovoid, footed body with
        flared rim & angled handles.

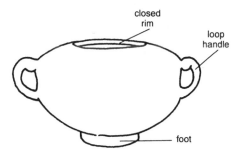

Vase - Pillow-shaped with molded rim;
        on knob feet.

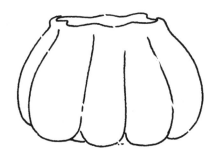

Vase or bowl vase - Spherical, footed
        body with closed rim and loop
        handles.

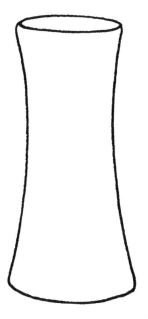

Vase - Waisted cylindrical form.

Vase - Squatty bulbous body
        with lobed sides.

ABC Plates

These children's plates were popular in the late 19th and early 20th centuries. An alphabet border was incorporated with nursery rhymes, maxims, scenes or figures in an apparent attempt to "spoon feed" a bit of knowledge at mealtime. An important reference book in this field is A Collector's Guide to ABC Plates, Mugs and Things *by Mildred L. and Joseph P. Chalala (Pridemark Press, Lancaster, Pennsylvania, 1980).*

Letter "A" ABC Plate

"A, Apple, Ape, Air," 6" d., black transfer w/color added to an apple and ape w/large "A" in center & words "Apple, Ape, Air" above picture, red line on rim, probably part of a series (ILLUS.) **$225**

Girl with Alphabet Book ABC Plate

ABCs, 4 3/4" d., purple transfer of small girl reading alphabet book to dog in doghouse, letters "N," "S" & "Z" reversed (ILLUS.) **$200**

"Baked Taters All Hot" ABC Plate

"Baked Taters All Hot," 7 1/8" d., blue transfer of man & woman dressed for the cold selling potatoes at a stove on the street (ILLUS.).. **$155**

"Band of Hope" ABC Plate

"Band of Hope - The Sabbath Keepers," 6" d., center illustration of congregation filing into church over "Rise early and thankfully put up your prayer - Be at school in good time and be diligent there," color has been added (ILLUS.)....... **$225**

"Base Ball Caught on the Fly" Plate

"Base Ball Caught on the Fly," 6 3/16" d., from the "American Sports" series, black transfer of a baseball game in action showing a fielder catching the ball (ILLUS., previous page) **$650**

"Base Ball Running to First Base," 6 1/4" d., from "American Sports" series, illustration of field w/several boys playing baseball, crazing, small rim flake **$650**

"Base Ball Striker & Catcher" Plate

"Base Ball Striker and Catcher," 7 1/8" d., from the "American Sports" series, green transfer of a batter ("striker") & catcher (ILLUS.).. **$650**

"The Beggar's Petition" ABC Plate

"Beggar's Petition (The)" 7 1/4" d., black transfer w/some color added of young girl giving something to a begging dog (ILLUS.).. **$225**

Bird, 7 1/4" d., brown transfer of titmouse in branches & print alphabet, marked "England" **$150**

"C, Cow, Cat, Clown," 5 1/4" d., black & white, large letter "C" surrounded by images of cow, cat & clown, part of alphabet series (ILLUS., top next column)............... **$275**

Letter "C" ABC Plate

"Canotiers - Boatmen" ABC Plate

"Canotiers - Boatmen," 6 3/4" d., blue transfer w/slight color added of two young boys dressed as sailors w/a large oar (ILLUS.) **$175**

Children at Lunch ABC Plate

Children at lunch, 8 3/8" d., sepia transfer w/colors added of two children sitting at table, two more children carrying food to the table (ILLUS.) **$175**

"Commander A.H. Foote" ABC Plate

"Commander A.H. Foote," 5 1/8" d., black transfer portrait, no mark (ILLUS.) **$300**

"Contemplation" ABC Plate

"Contemplation," 6 5/16" d., from the "Flowers that Never Fade" series, transfer w/color added, "Lord, what is life? - Tis like a flow'r. That blossoms & is gone! We see it flourish for an hour. With all its beauty on" & related illustration of young girls looking at a flower (ILLUS.) **$250**

ABC Plate from "Conundrum" Series

Conundrum, 6 1/8" d., from "Conundrum" series, "What fruit does our sketch represent?" under illustration of two figures sitting at table piled high, both waving spoons, one rubbing his stomach (ILLUS.) **$250**
Cricket game, 7 1/4" d., brown transfer of cricket game in progress **$175**

"Crusoe Finding the Foot Prints"

"Crusoe Finding the Foot Prints," 8" d., from "Robinson Crusoe" series, Brownhills Pottery Company, sepia transfer w/color added of Robinson Crusoe discovering Friday's footprints, letters printed in sepia around edge of plate (ILLUS.) **$175**

"Diamond" Series ABC Plate

Diamond, 7 5/8" d., from "Diamond" series, center diamond shows man & horse, four sepia pictures surrounding center diamond illustrate the rest of the story, also known as a comic book of the 1800s (ILLUS.) **$175**
"England's Hope. Prince of Wales," 7" d., black transfer of image of young prince astride pony, black lines around edge (ILLUS., top next page) **$500**

"England's Hope" ABC Plate

"Exhibition Prize Rabbits" ABC Plate

"Exhibition Prize Rabbits," black transfer of long-eared rabbits, writing under picture hard to decipher (ILLUS.)................... **$275**

"The Favourite Rabbits" ABC Plate

"Favourite Rabbits (The)," 5" d., one of a series, black & white, "How joyous at each sunshine hour - I haunted ev'ry green retreat - of forest, garden, heath & bower - Their cell to store with clover sweet" surrounds center illustration of girl in period dress feeding pet rabbits, older plate (ILLUS.)... **$300**

"Federal Generals" ABC Plate

"Federal Generals," 6" d., black transfer showing four Civil War generals on horseback (ILLUS.).................................... **$500**

"The Finding of Moses" ABC Plate

"Finding of Moses (The)" from the "Bible Pictures" series, multicolor scene of two women finding Moses in the bulrushes, letters & floral decorations in space not taken up by center scene (ILLUS.) **$275**
"Franklin's Proverbs," 5" d., "Keep thy shop and thy shop will keep thee" over center illustration of merchant................... **$175**
"Franklin's Proverbs" 7" d., "Keep thy shop and thy shop will keep thee" around colorful central transfer of merchant in front of shop, J. & G. Meakin, 1851 .... **$175**

"Gathering Cotton" ABC Plate

"Gathering Cotton," 6" d., black transfer w/color added of two slaves picking cotton (ILLUS.)... **$275**

George Washington ABC Plate

George Washington, 7 1/2" d., black portrait of George Washington, same as picture used on one-dollar bill (ILLUS.) **$600**

ABC Plate, "The Lord's Prayer" series

"Give Us This Day Our Daily Bread," 6 1/4" d., from "The Lord's Prayer" series, blue transfer picture of old man w/a cane receiving food from children (ILLUS.).......... **$225**

"The Gleaners" ABC Plate

"Gleaners (The)," 5 5/8" d., illustration of woman w/bundle on her head walking across bridge w/two children (ILLUS.) **$175**

"The Graces" ABC Plate

"Graces (The)," 7 1/4" d., black transfer of three girls in period dress embracing, red luster rim (ILLUS.).................................... **$300**

"The Guardian" ABC Plate

"Guardian (The)," 7 1/4" d., brown transfer w/color added of sleeping girl guarded by large dog (ILLUS., bottom previous page) .. **$225**
Hens & rooster, 6 1/2" d., colorful transfer of rooster & hens, pale blue embossed alphabet border, probably Germany **$85**

"Highland Dance" ABC Plate

"Highland Dance," 5 1/2" d., black transfer w/color added of several people dancing (ILLUS.).. **$175**

"The Irish Jig" ABC Plate

"Irish Jig (The)," 6 1/4" d., pink transfer of a girl dancing, "The Irish Jig" printed at top (ILLUS.)... **$200**

"John Gilpin" ABC Plate

"John Gilpin Pursued as a Highwayman," 6 1/4" d., black print w/slightly painted details, one of a series showing the humorous anniversary adventures of a 19th c. draper, illustrations based on Cruikshank's published in 1828 (ILLUS.)............. **$250**

Kite ABC Plate

Kite, 5 1/8" d., black transfer w/colors added of three boys holding a large yellow kite (ILLUS.).. **$225**

"Leopard and the Fox" ABC Plate

"Leopard and the Fox," 6 1/2" d., part of early "Aesop Fables" series, black & white, center w/illustration of leopard & fox in wooded setting, large letters around rim (ILLUS.).. **$275**

"The Lion" ABC Plate

"Lion (The)," 7 5/16" d., from the "Wild Animals" series, Brownhills Pottery Company, sepia transfer w/color added (ILLUS., previous page) **$325**

"The Little Jockey" ABC Plate

"Little Jockey (The)" 7" d., center illustration of child in dress & plumed hat riding on the back of a large dog, large black letters on rim (ILLUS.) **$350**

"The Little Play-fellows" ABC Plate

"Little Play-fellows (The)," 5 1/2" d., black transfer of young boy w/hoop or net & two girls w/wheelbarrow (ILLUS.) **$350**
"Little Red Riding Hood," 8 3/16" d., from the "Nursery Tales" series, multicolor transfer in reserve of Little Red Riding Hood & the wolf, scattered alphabet to the side, Staffordshire **$325**
"Little strokes fell great Oaks," 8 1/4" d., black transfer w/red, yellow & green illustration of man w/ax standing by felled tree, Staffordshire...................................... **$150**
"London Dogseller," 7 1/8" d., black transfer w/color added of man in period dress holding two dogs in his arms & one on a leash, w/small dog in back pocket.............. **$175**

Boys Playing Marbles ABC Plate

Marbles, 6 3/16" d., blue transfer of three boys in period clothes playing marbles, red lines around rim (ILLUS.).................... **$250**
"Marine Railway Station, Manhatton [sic] Beach Hotel," 7" d., illustration of station in center, Staffordshire............................... **$135**

"The Milk Girl" ABC Plate

"Milk Girl (The)," 5 1/2" d., black transfer of girl carrying bowl, another woman milking a cow in a field (ILLUS.)............................. **$350**
Musicians, 6" d., mulberry transfer of two children playing stringed instruments, made for H.C. Edmeston, England **$175**

"My Face is My Fortune" ABC Plate

"My Face is My Fortune," 6 3/4" d., blue & white transfer picture of a sitting bulldog (ILLUS., previous page) **$175**

"The Nurse" ABC Plate

"Nurse (The)" 5 1/2" d., black transfer of nicely dressed woman sitting on the front lawn of a large house, two children hugging her, two black lines outlining edge of plate (ILLUS.) **$350**

Piano ABC Plate

Piano, 5 7/8" d., black transfer w/color added of girl in blue dress on tiptoes at a piano w/"The pretty child on tiptoe stands - to reach the piano with her hands" underneath, Elsmore & Forster (ILLUS.)............. **$200**

"Playing at Lovers" ABC Plate

"Playing at Lovers," 5 1/2" d., black transfer w/colors added of a boy & a girl dressed as adults (ILLUS.) **$175**

Riddle ABC Plate

Riddle, 6 1/16" d., blue transfer w/riddle "I ever live man's unrelenting foe - mighty in mischief though I'm small in size - And he at last that seems to lay me low - My food and habitation both supplies" and answer ("Worm") printed around center illustration of two girls playing a game w/hoops & sticks (ILLUS.) **$250**

"Rupert and Spot," multicolor image of young boy on hands & knees being watched over by a big dog in center, letters in black around image, Roman numerals up to XII & decorative border around letters **$325**

Sign Language ABC Plate with Owls

Sign language, 6 1/2" d., center w/illustration of schoolmaster owl at desk, little owls in attendance, circled by illustrations of hand signs & letters, red line around rim (ILLUS.)... **$300**

Sign Language ABC Plate

Sign language, 7" d., illustrations of hands forming letters of sign language in boxes in the middle of the plate, h.p. ("hand painted") flowers on rim, extremely rare (ILLUS.)... **$600**

Children Sledding ABC Plate

Sledding, 7 3/8" d., center illustration of children & toy bears sledding, circled by printed letters of the alphabet in addition to the embossed letters on the rim (ILLUS.).......... **$250**

"Soldier Tired" ABC Plate

"Soldier Tired," 7 1/4" d., black transfer of sleeping boy in dress w/a sword & hat nearby guarded by a dog (ILLUS.)............ **$300**

"The Sponge Bath" ABC Plate

"Sponge Bath (The)," 7 7/8" d., black & white, image of young boy bathing in large tub, laughing as he pulls fully clothed child into the water, large printed letters on rim (ILLUS.)............................... **$175**

"Thames Tunnel" ABC Plate

"Thames Tunnel," 5 1/4" d., black transfer picture illustrating the opening of the Tunnel in London, 1843, w/people in period dress (ILLUS.).. **$225**

"Turk" ABC Plate

"Turk," 7 1/4" d., from the "Nations of the World" series, Brownhills Pottery Company, transfer w/polychrome highlights depicts woman in costume, letters to the side rather than in circle on rim of plate (ILLUS., previous page) **$225**

Girls Holding Umbrella ABC Plate

Umbrella, 7" d., black transfer w/color added of two girls under an umbrella, an old woman & other children watching from a doorway (ILLUS.) **$250**

"Union Troops" ABC Plate

"Union Troops in Virginia," 6 1/8" d., black transfer w/color highlights of a large number of soldiers in formation (ILLUS.) ... **$600**

"Victoria Regina" ABC Plate

"Victoria Regina," 5 1/16" d., black transfer of portrait of Queen Victoria as a young woman over words "Born 25 of May 1818. Proclaimed 20 of June 1837" (ILLUS.)..... **$1,000**

"Whom Are You For" ABC Plate

"Whom are you for," 5 1/8" d., center picture of a field sentry w/bayonet stopping two solders, colors added (ILLUS.)............ **$250**

"William Penn" ABC Plate

"William Penn," 7 1/2" d., pink transfer portrait, no mark (ILLUS.)............................... **$450**

Woman Riding Spotted Horse Plate

Woman riding, 5 3/16" d., center illustration of woman balancing large basket on her head & riding on spotted horse (ILLUS., previous page) **$175**

Abingdon

From about 1934 until 1950, Abingdon Pottery Company, Abingdon, Illinois, manufactured decorative pottery, mainly cookie jars, flowerpots and vases. Decorated with various glazes, these items are becoming popular with collectors who are especially attracted to Abingdon's novelty cookie jars.

Also see Antique Trader Pottery & Porcelain Ceramics Price Guide, 4th Edition.

Abingdon Mark

Abingdon Leaf Ashtray

Ashtray, Leaf, in the shape of a maple leaf, white interior, black exterior, No. 660, 1948-50, 5 1/2" d. (ILLUS.) **$35**

Abingdon Ashtrays

Ashtray, New Mode, round, divided in half by ridge to hold cigarettes, rectangular

base, pink, No. 456, 1939-48, 5 3/4" d. (ILLUS. left).. **$30**

Abingdon Octagonal Ashtray

Ashtray, octagonal, turquoise, No. 551, 1941-46, 7 x 7" (ILLUS.) **$50**

Ashtray, round, black w/black donkey standing on top, No. 510, 1940-41, 5 1/2" d. (ILLUS. left, w/elephant ashtray, bottom of page)... **$150**

Abingdon Round Ashtray

Ashtray, round, turquoise, No. 555, 1941-46, 8" d. (ILLUS.) **$25**

Ashtray, round, white, No. 334 (ILLUS. right, w/New Mode ashtray) **$30**

Ashtray, round, white w/black elephant standing on top w/trunk raised, No. 509, 1940-41, 5 1/2" d. (ILLUS. right, w/donkey ashtray) **$150**

Abingdon Donkey & Elephant Ashtrays

Abingdon Russian Dancer Bookends

Bookends, figures of Russian dancers w/arms crossed at chest, fez-type hats, rectangular bases, white, No. 321, 1934-40, 6 1/2" h. (ILLUS., top of page) **$250-300**

Bookends, model of Scottie dog, No. 650, 7 1/2" h., pr. **$300-400**

Bookends, model of sea gull, spread wings, No. 305, ivory glaze, 1934-1942, 6" h., pr. (ILLUS. left w/model of sea gull, page 32) **$150-165**

Cactus Bookends/Planters

Bookends/planters, model of cactus, No. 374, 1936-8, 7" h., pr. (ILLUS.) **$125**

Bookends/planters, model of dolphin, No. 444D, blue glaze, 5 3/4" h., pr. **$80**

Abingdon Chinese Bowl

Bowl, 9 x 11" oval, Chinese, gently flaring body on short rectangular feet, white floral decoration on white ground, No. 345, 1935-37 (ILLUS.) **$200**

Bowl, 9 x 14" rectangular, turquoise, Han patt., No. 523, 1940 (ILLUS., bottom of page) **$40**

Abingdon Han Bowl

Abingdon Salad Bowl & Candleholders

Bowl, salad, 10" d., 5" h., Rope patt., scalloped rim, ropetwist foot, turquoise, No. 313, 1934-36 (ILLUS. center w/Quatrain candleholders)... **$75**

Candleholder, double, No. 479, Scroll patt., 4 1/2" h. **$15**

Bamboo Candleholders & Console Plate

Candleholders, Bamboo patt., No. 716, pr. (ILLUS. left & right w/console plate)............. **$50**

Candleholders, Quatrain patt., quatrefoil shapes w/center hole for candle, turquoise, No. 360, 1935-36, pr. (ILLUS. w/Rope salad bowl, top of page)................. **$75**

Candleholders, Sunburst, in the form of three ribbed connected semicircles, rose, No. 447, 1938, 8" l., pr. (ILLUS. right & left w/window box, bottom of page)............. **$80**

Console bowl, No. 532, Scroll patt., 14 1/2" l. **$20**

Console plate, Bamboo patt., No. 715, 10 1/2" d.   (ILLUS.   w/candleholders, above) **$125**

Cookie jar, Baby, No. 561, 11" h. **$750-1,000**

Cookie jar, Bo Peep, No. 694D, 1950, 12" h. **$375**

Abingdon Shell Candleholder

Candleholder, double, Shell line, green, No. 505, 1940-49, 4" h., pr. (ILLUS.) **$25**

Sunburst Candleholders & Window Box

Little Ol' Lady Cookie Jars

Abingdon Choo Choo Cookie Jar

Cookie jar, Choo Choo, No. 651D, 1948-50, 7 1/2" h. (ILLUS.) **$225**
Cookie jar, Clock, No. 563, 9" h. **$130**

Abingdon Daisy Cookie Jar

Cookie jar, Daisy, No. 677, 1949-50, 8" h. (ILLUS.)... **$95**

Fat Boy Cookie Jar

Cookie jar, Fat Boy, No. 495, 1940-46, 8 1/4" h. (ILLUS.) **$500-700**
Cookie jar, Floral/Plaid, No. 697, 8 1/2" h. **$150-250**
Cookie jar, Hippo, No. 549, plain & decorated, 8" h.. **$250-550**
Cookie jar, Humpty Dumpty, No. 663, 10 1/2" h... **$275**
Cookie jar, Little Girl, No. 693, 9 1/2" h. **$200-225**
Cookie jar, Little Ol' Lady, No. 471, 9" h., various decorations, each (ILLUS. of three, top of page)............................. **$200-300**
Cookie jar, Miss Muffet, No. 662D, 11" h. **$275**
Cookie jar, Money Bag, No. 588D, 7 1/2" h. ... **$100**

Abingdon Display Sign

Mother Goose Cookie Jar

Cookie jar, Mother Goose, No. 695D, 1950,
12" h. (ILLUS.) **$425**

Wigwam Cookie Jar

Cookie jar, Wigwam, No. 665D, 11" h.
(ILLUS.).. **$750-1,000**
Display sign, marked "Abingdon" (ILLUS.,
top of page).. **$300**

Pineapple Cookie Jar

Cookie jar, Pineapple, No. 664, 1949-50,
10 1/2" h. (ILLUS.) **$200**
Cookie jar, Pumpkin, No. 674D, 8" h. **$550**
Cookie jar, Three Bears, No. 696D,
8 3/4" h.. **$200**
Cookie jar, Windmill, No. 678, 10 1/2" h. **$500**
Cookie jar, Witch, No. 692, 11 1/2" h. **$1,200**

Scarf Dancer Figure

Figure, Scarf Dancer, No. 3902, 13" h.
(ILLUS.).. **$800 up**

Abingdon Flower Boat & Fruit Boat

Various Abingdon Flowerpots

Flower boat, Fern Leaf, oblong ribbed leaf shape, pink, No. 426, 1937-38, 13 x 4" (ILLUS. left w/fruit boat, top of page) **$100**

Flowerpots, Nos. 149 to 152, floral decoration, 3 to 6" h., each (ILLUS. of three, second from top) **$15-30**

Fruit boat, Fern Leaf, oblong ribbed leaf shape, white, No. 432, 1938-39, 6 1/2 x 15" (ILLUS. right w/flower boat) **$100**

Lamp base, No. 254, draped shaft, 13" h. (ILLUS.)... **$200**

Two Abingdon Mantel Pieces

Mantel pieces, cov., handled, bird & floral decoration on white ground, No. KR22, rare, each (ILLUS. of two)........................... **$65**

Model of heron, No. 574, tan glaze, 5 1/4" h. **$68**

Model of peacock, No. 416, turquoise glaze, 7" h. **$96**

Abingdon Lamp Base

Abingdon Gull Figurine & Bookends

Abingdon Penguin Figurines

Model of penguin, black, wearing top hat, No. 573, 5" h. (ILLUS.) **$65**
Model of penguin, white, 3" h. **$50**
Model of sea gull, w/spread wings, No. 562, 1942, 5" h. (ILLUS. right w/book ends, top of page) **$50-75**
Model of swan, No. 661, 3 3/4" h. **$150**

Grecian Pitcher & Vase

Pitcher, 15" h., Grecian patt., No. 613 (ILLUS. right w/vase) **$150**

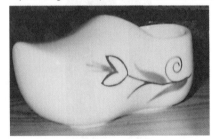

Abingdon Dutch Shoe Planter

Planter, Dutch shoe, stylized tulip decoration on white ground, No. 655D, 1948, 5" l. (ILLUS.) **$125**
Planter, model of a puppy, No. 652D, 6 3/4" l. **$75**

Abingdon Planter

Planter, short foot, flared sides rising to scroll ends, white, No. 476, 10" w., 3" h. (ILLUS., top of page)................................ **$30**

String holder, Chinese head, No. 702, 5 1/2" h... **$500**

Vase, 3 1/2" h., No. A1, whatnot type............ **$100**

Vase, 4 1/2" h., No. C1, whatnot type **$100**

Vase, 5" h., No. B1, whatnot type.................. **$100**

Vase, 5" h., white floral decoration on blue ground, small handles, No. 567D, 1942-46 (ILLUS. right w/window box No. 570D) **$40**

Vase, 5 1/2" h., No. 142, Classic line **$40**

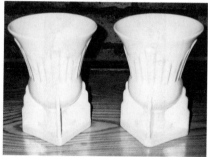

Abingdon Capri Vases

Vase, 5 3/4" h., Capri, urn form w/quatrefoil bases, white, No. 351, 1935-37, each (ILLUS. of two) **$125**

Abingdon Cattail Vase

Vase, 6 1/4" h., vertical ribs, three h.p. cat-tails, No. 152 (ILLUS.).................................... **$35**

Vase, 7" h., No. 171, Classic line **$40**

Vase, 7 1/4" h., Fern Leaf, ribbed leaf-style sides flaring to bowl-style opening, green, No. 423, 1937-38 (ILLUS. right w/taller Fern Leaf vase)............................. **$100**

Figural Blackamoor Vase

Vase, 7 1/2" h., figure of Blackamoor, No. 497D (ILLUS.)... **$150**

Abingdon Delta Vase

Vase, 8" h., Delta, handles, ribbed base, rose, No. 108, 1938-39 (ILLUS.).................. **$40**

Abingdon Gamma Vase

Vase, 8" h., Gamma, short bulbous base connected to tall slightly flaring lobed neck by applied side handles, turquoise, No. 107, 1938-39 (ILLUS.) **$40**

Vase, 8" h., No. 132, Classic line **$40**

Abingdon Scroll Vase

Vase, 8" h., Scroll, bulbous body, neck w/four handles tapers out at top, green, No. 417, 1937-38 (ILLUS.) **$125**

Vase, 8" h., Wreath, circular on ribbed ogee base, leaf garland, bow & star decoration, pink, No. 467, 1938-39 .... **$95**

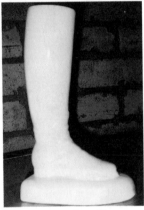

Abingdon Boot Vase

Vase, 8" h., model of a boot, white, No. 584, 1947 (ILLUS.) **$45**

Abingdon Swedish Vase

Vase, 8 1/4" h., Swedish, handled, white, No. 314, 1934-36 (ILLUS.) **$85**

Abingdon Fern Leaf Vases

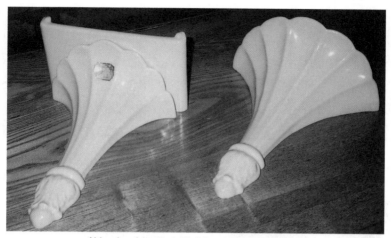

Abingdon Acanthus Wall Bracket & Wall Pocket

Vase, 10 1/4" h., Fern Leaf, tall ribbed leaf-shape sides taper out to top opening, blue, No. 422, 1937-39 (ILLUS. left w/smaller Fern Leaf vase, bottom previous page) **$95**

Lung Pattern Vase

Vase, 11" h., Lung patt., No. 302 (ILLUS.) **$225**
Vase, 15" h., floor-type, Grecian patt., No. 603 (ILLUS. left w/pitcher) **$150**
Wall bracket, Acanthus, pink, No. 589, 1947, 7" h. (ILLUS. left w/wall pocket, top of page) **$65**
Wall pocket, Acanthus, pink, No. 648, 1948, 8 3/4" h. (ILLUS. right w/wall bracket, top of page) **$65**
Wall pocket, figural butterfly, No. 601, 8 1/2" h. **$150**
Wall pocket, figural Dutch boy, No. 489, 10" h. **$150**
Wall pocket, figural Dutch girl, No. 490, 10" h. **$150**

Abingdon Wall Pockets

Wall pocket, Leaf, overlapping pink veined leaves, No. 724, 1950, scarce, 10 x 5 1/2" (ILLUS. top w/Triad wall pocket) **$75**

Double Trumpet Wall Pocket

Abingdon Window Box & Vase

Wall pocket, Morning Glory, double trumpet form, No. 375, 1936-40, 6 1/2" h. (ILLUS., previous page).. **$45-55**

Morning Glory Wall Pocket

Wall pocket, Morning Glory, trumpet form, pink, No. 377, 1936-50, 7 1/2" h. (ILLUS.)..... **$35**

Wall pocket, Triad, in the form of three pink connected flowerpots, No. 640, 1940, 5 1/2 x 8" (ILLUS. bottom w/Leaf wall pocket) **$40-50**

Window box, oblong, scalloped rim, white floral decoration on blue ground, No. 570D, 1942-46, 10" l. (ILLUS. left w/vase No. 567D, top of page)............................... **$35**

Window box, Sunburst, in the form of three connected ribbed semicircles, rose, No. 448, 1938-39, 9" l. (ILLUS. center w/Sunburst candleholders, top of page)................ **$85**

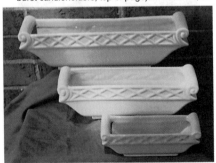

Various Sized Window Boxes

Window boxes, No. 477, 13 1/2" l., No. 476, 10 1/2" l., No. 475, 7" l., each (ILLUS.) **$25-35**

American Painted Porcelain

During the late Victorian era, American artisans produced thousands of hand-painted porcelain items including tableware, dresser sets, desk sets, and bric-a-brac. These pieces of porcelain were imported and usually bear the marks of foreign factories and countries. To learn more about identification, evaluation, history and appraisal, the following books and newsletter by Dorothy Kamm are recommended: American Painted Porcelain: Collector's Identification & Value Guide, Comprehensive Guide to American Painted Porcelain, *and* Dorothy Kamm's Porcelain Collector's Companion.

Berry spoon holder, pierced handles, decorated w/two clusters of blackberries, light blue border, burnished gold rim & handles, marked "Bavaria," ca. 1894-1914, 4 5/8 x 10" **$65**

Bonbon Box with Peacock Decor

Bonbon box, cov., round, low domed cover decorated w/a conventional design of three intertwined peacocks, baby blue base, burnished gold rims & feet, opal luster interior, marked "T&V Limoges - France," 1892-1907 (ILLUS.) **$125**

Bonbon dish, round w/gold upright ring handles, decorated w/clusters of currants on a multicolored ground, an inner border band w/gilded outlines of spider webs & currant clusters, burnished gold rim, signed "I.A. Johnson, 1915" & marked "UNO-IT - Favorite - Bavaria," 6 3/8" d. **$55**

Celery Dish with Daisy Border

Bouillon cup & saucer, decorated w/a curvilinear geometric design in burnished gold outlined in dark blue, burnished gold rims & handles, marked "T & V - Limoges - France," ca. 1892-1907 .... **$30**

Small Footed Bowl

Bowl, 5 1/2" d., 2 3/4" h., pedestal foot, decorated w/a conventional border in moss, yellow, orange & burnished gold on an ivory ground, dark green base, burnished bold rim & band, marked w/"La Seynie - P and P - Limoges - France," 1903-17 (ILLUS.).................................... **$50**

Bowl, 7 1/2" d., cereal, decorated w/a border design of daisy clusters on an ivory ground, light blue border & burnished gold rim, marked "HR - Hutschenreuther - Selb - Bavaria," ca. 1905-18 .... **$38**

Bowl, 8 3/4" w., square fruit-type, decorated on the interior w/geraniums on a polychrome ground, on the exterior w/scrolls on a graduated green ground, burnished gold rim, ca. 1880-1900 .... **$85**

Butter dish, cover & liner, decorated on the domed cover & dished base w/clusters of pink roses & greenery on a pale pink & green ground, burnished gold rim & handle, signed "R.O. BRIGGS, AUSTIN, IL (?)," marked w/crowned double-headed eagle & "MZ - Austria," 1884-1909 .... **$75**

Butter tub, round, decorated w/forget-me-nots on an ivory ground, burnished gold rim & handles, signed "Tossy," marked "T

& V - Limoges - France," ca. 1892-1917 (no pierced insert)..................................... **$50**

Cake plate, pierced rim handles, scalloped edge, decorated w/a four-panel design w/conventional-style flowers in each panel, burnished gold border outlines, dotted grounds & rim, signed w/illegible cipher & marked "HR - Charlotte - Bavaria," ca. 1887+, 9 1/8" d... **$95**

Individual Cake Plate with Wild Roses

Cake plate or cookie tray, individual size, paneled sides, open handles, decorated w/a cluster of pink wild roses on a multi-colored pastel ground, signed "R.J. '30" (ILLUS.)... **$35**

Celery dish, long narrow shallow boat-form w/squared ends, decorated w/a paneled design of daisies & leaves on a pastel polychrome ground, ivory center, signed "Weiler," 1900-20, 5 3/4 x 12 3/4" (ILLUS., top of page) **$67**

Chocolate cup & saucer, decorated w/yellow primrose on a shaded yellow brown ground, burnished gold rims, cup base & handle, signed "A. Brown," marked "Haviland - Limoges - France," ca. 1894-1931 ..... **$35**

Chocolate pot, cov., decorated w/cluster of pink roses on a pastel polychrome ground, burnished gold knob & handle, signed "M.H. Dorothy," marked "GDA - France," ca. 1900-41................................. **$225**

Decorated Creamer & Covered Sugar

Coffeepot, cov., decorated w/a conventional-style dandelion design, burnished gold rims, spout interior, upper lip & handles, signed "M. Lamour," marked "J. & C. Bavaria," ca. 1902, 10" h............. **$250**

Morning Glory-decorated Compote

Compote, 8 7/8" d., 4 1/4" h., open, wide shallow round flaring bowl raised on a flaring pedestal base, the interior decorated w/a cluster of pink & white morning glories, rim & foot decorated w/bands of conventional pink butterflies, burnished gold rim & foot, signed "CL April 13th, 188(1)," marked "CFH" (ILLUS. of interior).............. **$200**

Cracker & cheese dish, decorated w/a conventional Chinese-style floral design, an opal lustre ground, burnished gold borders & rims, illegible signature, marked w/a wreath & star & "R.S. Tillowitz - Silesia," ca. 1920-38, 8 1/2" d. **$125**

Cracker jar, cov., decorated w/white wild roses on a pastel polychrome ground w/burnished gold handles, signed "A.S.S.," marked "Royal" & wreath w/"O. & E.G.," 1898-1918 .... **$70**

Creamer & cov. sugar bowl, each w/a tapering cylindrical form, the base decorated w/a conventional blue & green floral border on a burnished gold band, ivory ground, burnished gold lips, spout, rims & handles, signed "Helen Hurley," 1900-20, pr. (ILLUS., top of page) **$70**

Creamer & open sugar bowl, decorated w/yellow roses on a light green border band, burnished gold borders, rims, base rims & handles, creamer marked w/a bird & "C.T. - Altwasser - Silesia," marked "KPM," ca. 1909-1930, pr............................ **$55**

Cup, after dinner size, decorated w/panels of Japanese-style medallions in antique green & bright gold on a dull red ground, signed "MA 12/92" (no saucer) **$20**

Breakfast Cup & Saucer with Clover

Cup & saucer, breakfast-size, decorated w/a clover design on a light blue ground, burnished gold rims & handle, signed "A. H. h.," ca. 1880s-90s (ILLUS.) **$65**

Cup & Saucer with Celtic Border

Cup & saucer, cylindrical cup w/angled handle, decorated w/a conventional Celtic border design in celadon, light blue border, ivory center & interior, burnished gold rims & handle, signed "L.E.S.," marked w/a crown in double circle & "Victoria Austria," 1900-20, the set (ILLUS.) **$45**

Cup & Saucer with Floral Border

Cup & saucer, decorated w/pink roses on a pastel polychrome ground, opal lustre interior, burnished gold rims & handle, marked "Favorite - Bavaria," ca. 1908-18, the set **$35**

Cup & saucer, tapering cylindrical cup w/angled handle, decorated w/a conventional blue floral garland border design, burnished gold rims & handle, signed "Jane Bent Telin," marked "Favorite Bavaria,"1910-25, the set (ILLUS., top of page) **$40**

Fern pot, decorated w/pink wild roses on a graduated green ground, signed "B.E. Miehling 99," marked "Elite" in a shield & "Limoges - France," 1899, 7 1/2" d., 4 3/4" h. **$250**

Gold-decorated Hair Receiver

Hair receiver, cov., squatty round form on three gold curved legs, decorated w/a conventional rose design in burnished gold, burnished gold rim & feet, signed "Ferver," ca. 1900-10, 3 7/8" d., 3 1/4" h. (ILLUS.).. **$50**

Decorated Hairpin Box

Hairpin box, cov., oval, decorated w/a conventional-style rose, leaf & stem border on a burnished gold ground, ivory top, light blue base, marked "Favorite - Bavaria," ca. 1908-1915, 1 1/2 x 4 1/2", 1 3/4" h. (ILLUS.) **$30**

Handkerchief box, cov., decorated w/peach-tinged yellow roses on a pastel polychrome ground, signed "WSO - 1913," marked "D. & Co. - France," 5 1/4" sq., 3" h. **$95**

Honey dish, on three ball feet, decorated w/pink clover & wheat sheaves, light grey border, white enamel trim, burnished gold rim, marked "Bavaria," ca. 1891-1914, 7 1/8" d..................................... **$45**

Ice-cream bowl, decorated w/a winter scene w/burnished gold border & rim, signed "F.L. Hey," marked "CFH - GDM," ca. 1920-30, 6 3/4 x 10 5/8", 2 3/16" h.. **$125**

Jelly tray, round, individual size, decorated w/a conventional border design in greens, blue, yellow & burnished gold, outlined in black, burnished gold rim & handles, signed "LMC," marked "Made in Japan," ca. 1925, 7 1/8" d.......................... **$35**

Lobster or shrimp salad bowl, decorated w/border clusters of seashells & seaweed, white enamel trim, pale polychrome ground colors on exterior, burnished gold rim, marked "H and Co. - Limoges - France," ca. 1888-1896, 7 3/4 x 10 1/2"... **$150**

Luncheon set: 7 1/2" d. plate, cup & saucer; decorated in a conventional-style floral border w/white enameled flower centers & burnished gold rims & handle, marked "Germany," ca. 1914-18, the set $55

Mayonnaise bowl & underplate, decorated w/clusters of forget-me-nots on a pale blue border, ivory ground, burnished gold rims & feet, signed "AG," marked "Stouffer," 1906-1914, bowl 4 1/2" d., underplate 5 7/16" d., 2 pcs. $40

Muffin dish, cov., round, decorated w/pink wild roses & greenery on a pastel polychrome ground, burnished gold rim & handles, signed "E. Starer," marked "J & C - 'Louise' - Bavaria," ca. 1902, 9 1/4" d., 4" h. $325

Mug, decorated w/colorful yellow & yellowish red gooseberries on a polychrome ground, marked w/a crown & two shields w/"Vienna - Austria," ca. 1900-15, 4 3/4" h. $65

Mustard jar w/attached underplate & cover, decorated w/conventional-style water lilies on a light blue & burnished gold ground, burnished gold handle & rims, marked "D. & Co. - France," ca. 1879-1900, 3" h. $45

Napkin ring, decorated w/forget-me-nots, white enamel trim & burnished gold rims, signed "Luken," ca. 1895-1926, 2" d. $20

Napkin ring, half moon-shape, decorated w/a purple columbine on an ivory ground, ca. 1880-1915, 2 1/2" w. $25

Nut bowl, decorated in polychrome colors w/a squirrel, acorns & oak leaves on a branch, opal lustre interior, burnished gold feet & fluted rim, signed "Mrs. O.C. Oakes," 1900-20 .... $100

Olive dish, ring-handled, decorated w/heliotrope, w/etched & burnished gold border & burnished gold handle, marked "T & V - Limoges - France," ca. 1892-1907, 7 3/8" d. $50

Perfume with Honeysuckle Decor

Perfume bottle w/original gold stopper, ovoid body w/a short neck & large ball stopper, decorated w/a conventional design of honeysuckle in matte bronze greens, outlined in burnished gold, on a matte pale green ground, burnished gold lip & stopper, signed "M.L. Cushman" & "CFH/GDM," 1882-1890, 4 3/4" h. (ILLUS.)....................................... $95

Perfume Bottle with Daisy Decoration

Perfume bottle w/original gold stopper, squatty bulbous base tapering to a tall slender cylindrical neck, decorated around the lower body w/daisies & leaves on an ivory ground, burnished gold rim & stopper, marked w/a wreath & "O. & E.G. - Royal - Austria," 1898-1918, 4 3/4" h. (ILLUS.)... $75

Decorated Orange Cups

Orange cups, footed, decorated w/designs of orange blossoms on light blue & yellow grounds, embellished w/white & yellow enamel, burnished gold rim, base band, foot & prongs, signed "CKI," marked "T & V - France - Deposé," ca. 1900-15, 3 1/4" d., 2 3/4" h., pr. (ILLUS.) $130

Pin Tray with Moth Decoration

Pin tray, oval, decorated w/a border design of four blue & burnished gold moths, connected by a burnished gold & black band, ivory ground, burnished gold rim, signed "E. Arrindell - 1-2/18," marked w/a crown & double-headed eagle & "MZ - Austria," 1918 (ILLUS.).. **$50**

Pitcher, 9 3/4" h., claret-type, decorated w/a conventional Art Nouveau-style floral design outlined in gold, burnished gold handle & edges, signed "V.B. Chase," ca. 1890-1914... **$70**

Pitcher, 5 3/4" h., lemonade, bulbous body, decorated w/currants on a polychrome ground, ca. 1900-1920.............................. **$250**

Pitcher, 5 3/4" h., lemonade-type, decorated w/clusters of purple grapes on an ivory ground, antique green beaded handle & border band at top, ca. 1900-16 .... **$250**

Pitcher & underplate, 3 3/8" h. milk-type pitcher, 5 1/4" d. plate, decorated w/conventionalized orange blossoms w/burnished gold borders, rims, spout & handle, signed "J.M. Cliffe, 11/28" & marked "Japan," the set **$35**

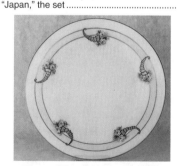

Coupe Plate with Cornucopias

Plate, 6 3/4" d., coupe-style, decorated w/a border design of pink roses in burnished gold cornucopias, interspersed on a pink band, ivory ground, burnished gold rim & banding, marked w/a crown & scepter & "Silesia," ca. 1900-20 (ILLUS.)..................... **$25**

Plate, 7 3/4" d., round w/lightly scalloped rim, decorated w/multicolored pansies & greenery & burnished gold scrolls, ivory center, lavender rim border, burnished gold rim band, signed "BS" & marked "J&C - Louise - Bavaria," ca. 1902+ (ILLUS., top next column) **$50**

Plate Decorated with Pansies

Plate with Well-painted Nasturtiums

Plate, 8 3/4" d., decorated w/orange nasturtiums, green leaves & light green scrolls accented w/gilded dots, burnished gold border band & rim, signed "G. Leykauf - 1908," marked "J.P.L. - France" (ILLUS.) **$275**

Tulip-decorated Plate

Powder Puff Box & Pin Tray

Plate, 8 1/4" d., decorated w/large red tulips & green leaves on a shaded rust to cream ground w/burnished gold rim, marked w/a bird & "Altwasser - Germany," ca. 1909-34 (ILLUS., previous page) **$45**

Poppy-decorated Plate

Plate, 8 3/4" d., decorated w/large orange poppies & green leaves on a shaded green ground, burnished gold rim, stamped on bottom "J. Lycett - St. Louis, Mo. - The Odeon," ca. 1900-15 (ILLUS.) **$50**

Plate, 5 1/4 x 9 1/2", salad-type, crescent-shaped, decorated w/multicolored sweet peas on a pale violet & green ground, burnished gold rim, ca. 1900-24 .... **$42**

Hand-painted Pomade Jar

Pomade jar, cov., small cylindrical form, decorated w/a conventional geometric design in baby blue & burnished gold outlined in brown, marked "W. G. & Co. - Limoges - France," ca. 1901, 2 1/2" d., 1 1/2" h. (ILLUS.) **$35**

Powder puff box & pin tray, round box w/domed cover & gold scroll loop finial, oblong lobed tray, each decorated w/a conventional dark bluish violet floral & pale green leaf border design w/burnished gold rims & vines outlined in black, on a pale pecan background, ivory ground, burnished gold finial, pin tray marked "GDA - France," box marked "T&V Limoges - France," 1900-20, tray 4 1/2 x 5 5/8", box 4 7/8" d., the set (ILLUS., top of page) .. **$100**

Punch cups, decorated w/clusters of forget-me-nots, opal lustre interiors, burnished gold stems & rims, marked w/"Royal," a wreath & "O. & E.G.," 1898-1918, 4" h., set of 5 .... **$125**

Pretty Painted Relish Pot

Relish pot, cov., ovoid body w/small inset domed cover w/gold loop handle, gold side handle, decorated w/a conventional design of fruits & flowers in polychrome colors, yellow enamel accents, baby blue ground, burnished gold rim & handles, signed "L Hogue," marked in a circle "K&L - Germany," 1915-30, 3 5/8" h. (ILLUS.) **$30**

Salt dips, cauldron-shaped, decorated w/pink roses on a pale blue & yellow

Lovely Egg-shaped Tea Set with Vines of Pink Roses

ground, burnished gold rims & ball feet, signed "P. Putzki," marked w/a crown, double-head eagle & "MZ - Austria," ca. 1884-1909, set of 6 .... **$120**

Decorated Nippon Porcelain Shakers

Salt & pepper shakers, decorated w/delicate panels of conventional-style hawthorn berries & leaves on an opal lustre ground, burnished gold tops & branch-shaped borders, signed "A.E.F.," marked "Noritake Nippon," 1914-21, 2 1/2" h., pr. (ILLUS.)... **$55**

Salt & Peppers with Blue Insects

Salt & pepper shakers, tapering square form w/domed gold top, white ground decorated w/a conventional design of

blue-winged insects, burnished gold tops, 1905-20, 3" h., pr. (ILLUS.)................ **$50**

Sandwich tray, double pierced handles, decorated w/a polychrome conventional design, burnished gold rim & handles, marked w/a crown & crossed scepters w/"Rosenthal - Bavaria," 1908-25, 10" l. ... **$110**

Sherbet, decorated w/daisies on an ivory ground, mother-of-pearl lustre interior, burnished gold border, rim & foot, signed "M. Paddock," marked "Epiag - Czechoslovakia," ca. 1920-39, 3 1/8" h. **$50**

Soup plates, flanged rim decorated w/three clusters of seashells & seaweed on a very pale polychrome ground, burnished gold rims, signed "ALB," marked "H. & Co. - Haviland - Limoges - France," 1876-1879, 9" d., pr. **$55**

Sugar shaker, decorated w/Art Nouveau-style florals & squiggling border band in burnished gold, burnished gold pierced top, signed "E.C.R.," ca. 1905-15, 2 3/4" d., 4 1/2" h. **$120**

Syrup jug, cov., decorated w/pink & ruby roses on a polychrome ground, burnished gold handle, knob & rims, opal lustre spout interior, marked "ADK - France," ca. 1891-1910, 4" h. (missing underplate).. **$35**

Table top centerpiece, decorated w/a cluster of daisies on a pastel polychrome ground, burnished gold rim, signed "E. Miller," marked "T & V - Limoges - France," ca. 1892-1907, 11 5/8" d. **$90**

Tea set: cov. teapot, cov. sugar bowl & creamer; each w/an upright egg-form body raised on four gilt scroll feet, gold loop handles, each h.p. w/a continuous design of leafy vines & pink roses, delicate gold trim bands, made for iced tea, blanks marked "Favorite, Bavaria," early 20th c., the set (ILLUS., top of page)............... **$200-300**

American Painted Willets Belleek Tea Set

Tea set: cov. teapot, cov. sugar bowl & creamer; footed wide flattened cylindrical bodies, flat covers w/gold peg finials, angular gold handles, each decorated w/burnished gold designs of stylized floral roundels alternating w/gold panels, artist-signed "MSF," Willets Belleek blanks, ca. 1880-1909, the set (ILLUS.) **$300-400**

American Painted Porcelain Tea Set with Gold Bands & Pink Roses

Tea set: cov. teapot, cov. sugar bowl, creamer & round undertray; bulbous bodies w/low domed covers & angular gold handle, each h.p. w/pastel blue border bands above arched angular gold bands separated by delicate pink rose clusters, artist-signed "C.E. Tolehard 1914," MZ Austria factory mark, tray 11 1/4" d., the set (ILLUS.) **$300-400**

Lovely American-painted Porcelain Teapot & Creamer

Teapot & sugar bowl, teapot & matching cov. sugar bowl, each w/a round foot & knop stem below the bulbous ovoid body tapering to a flat rim & domed cover w/molded upright gold finial, serpentine spout & ornate gold scroll handles, the cover & upper body painted in pale green around the upper third above an undulating band of delicate gold scrolls & pink roses & green leafy stems on the lower white body, gold base bands, artist initials, unmarked blanks, ca. 1880-1910, teapot 6 1/4" h., 2 pcs. (ILLUS., top of page) **$100-150**

Toast set: plate & cup; 9 3/16 w. plate decorated w/conventional-style strawberries on an ivory ground, opal lustre cup interior, burnished gold borders, rims & handle, ca. 1925-30, 2 pcs. **$75**

Toothpick holder, decorated w/double violets on a pastel ivory & green ground, burnished gold rim, signed "Wats" & "Pitkin & Brooks Studio," marked "T & V - Limoges - France," 1903-10, 2 3/4" h. **$55**

Tumbler, decorated w/ruby roses on a polychrome ground, burnished gold rim, illegible signature, marked "La Seynie - PP - Limoges - France," ca. 1903-17, 3 3/8" h. **$35**

Vase, 7 7/8" h., bulbous baluster-form w/wide flared neck, decorated w/two Art Deco-style floral panels in lustre & burnished gold, gold center band & base & neck bands, signed "M.D.P. 1920," marked w/a shield & "Thomas" (ILLUS., next column) **$125**

Vase, 7" h., bulbous base tapering to a tall slender neck, two-handled, decorated w/pink & yellow roses on a pastel polychrome ground, burnished gold rim, accents & handle, ca. 1900-20 .... **$65**

Art Deco Design Painted Vase

Jewelry

American painted porcelain jewelry comprises a unique category. While the metallic settings and porcelain medallions were inexpensive, the painted decoration was a work of fine art. The finished piece possessed greater intrinsic value than costume jewelry of the same period because it was a one-of-a-kind creation, but one that was not as expensive as real gold and sterling silver settings and precious and semiprecious jewels. Note that signatures are rare, backstamps lacking.

Dorothy Kamm

Bar pin, decorated w/pink roses & greenery, brass-plated bezel, ca. 1880s, 7/16 x 1 1/2" **$30**

Bar pin, decorated w/pink roses on a pale green ground, burnished gold tips & brass-plated bezel, ca. 1900-1915, 2 5/8" w. **$50**

Belt Buckle Brooch with Portrait

Belt buckle brooch, oval, decorated w/a profile of a woman wearing a pink top & white shawl, pink roses in her curly brown hair, black choker at her neck, burnished gold rim, gold-plated bezel, signed "M.e.M.," 1900-17, 1 7/8 x 2 3/8" (ILLUS.)... **$175**

Belt Buckle Brooch with Pansy

Belt buckle brooch, oval, decorated w/a white pansy, accented w/white enamel, on a burnished gold ground, gold-plated bezel, 1900-17, 1 11/16 x 2 1/4" (ILLUS.) **$75**

Art Nouveau Florals on Belt Brooch

Belt buckle brooch, oval, decorated w/an Art Nouveau-style water lily design outlined w/raised paste, petals filled in w/lavender enamel, burnished green & gold background, gold-plated bezel, 1900-17, 1 7/8 x 2 5/8" (ILLUS.) **$150**

Bachelor Buttons on Belt Brooch

Belt buckle brooch, oval, decorated w/blue bachelor buttons & greenery on a polychrome ground, irregular burnished gold border outlined in black, gold-plate bezel, 1900-17, 1 7/8 x 2 5/8" (ILLUS.) **$115**

Belt buckle brooch, oval, decorated w/roses & greenery on a polychrome ground, burnished gold scalloped border outlined in black, gold-plated bezel, 1900-17, 1 15/16 x 2 11/16" **$125**

Brooch, decorated w/violets on a light yellow brown ground w/raised paste scrolled border covered w/burnished gold & burnished gold rims, gold-plated bezel, ca. 1890-1920, 1 1/2" d. **$65**

Brooch, diamond-shaped, decorated w/a water lily & waterscape w/white enamel highlights, sky & clouds in background, burnished gold rim, gold-plated bezel, ca. 1930s-1940s, 7/8" sq. **$50**

Heart-shaped Brooch with Roses

Brooch, heart-shaped, decorated w/a pink & a ruby rose w/leaves on a polychrome ground, white enamel accents, burnished gold rim, gold-plated bezel, 7/8 x 7/8" (ILLUS.) **$50**

Brooch, horseshoe shape, decorated w/pink & ruby roses on a green & yellow ground, white enamel highlights & bur-

nished gold tips, ca. 1880s-1915,
1 1/4 x 1 1/2" **$85**

Forget-me-nots on Long Oval Brooch

Brooch, long oval, decorated w/forget-me-nots & leaves on a pastel polychrome ground, white enamel highlights, burnished gold rim, gold-plated bezel, 1 x 1 3/4" (ILLUS.)...................................... **$45**

Brooch, lozenge shape, decorated w/forget-me-nots on a pink & pale yellow ground w/white enamel highlights & burnished gold rim, brass-plated bezel, ca. 1890-1920, 7/8 x 1 5/8" **$50**

Brooch, oval, decorated w/a conventional-style Colonial dame in light blue & yellow w/opal lustre background & burnished gold rim, brass-plated bezel, ca. 1915-25, 1 5/8 x 2 1/8" **$60**

Brooch, oval, decorated w/a conventional-style lavender iris & green leaves outlined in black on a yellow lustre ground w/white enamel highlights on petal edges & yellow enamel highlights on flower centers, burnished gold rim, gold-plated bezel, ca. 1900-20, 1 5/8 x 2 1/8" **$80**

Pink Rose on Oval Brooch

Brooch, oval, decorated w/a large pink rose & green leaves on a light blue ground, burnished gold rim, gold-plated bezel, 1 1/8 x 1 3/8" (ILLUS.)................................ **$45**

Brooch, oval, decorated w/a sunset landscape scene w/house by stream, trees in background, burnished gold rim, gold-plated bezel, 1 1/2 x 1 15/16" **$175**

Brooch, oval, decorated w/a tropical Florida scene, burnished gold border & brass-plated bezel, ca. 1920s, 1 1/2 x 2" **$85**

Florida River Landscape on Brooch

Brooch, oval, decorated w/a tropical river landscape in polychrome colors, signed on the lower left "OC" (Olive Commons, Coconut Grove, Florida), gold-plated bezel, ca. 1920s, 1 3/8 x 1 1/4" (ILLUS.) ... **$125**

Art Nouveau Maiden on Brooch

Brooch, oval, decorated w/an Art Nouveau maiden's portrait surrounded by forget-me-nots on an ivory ground, white enamel highlights, framed by burnished gold raised paste scrolls & dots, gold-plated bezel, 1 1/4 x 1 5/8" (ILLUS.)...................... **$95**

Brooch, oval, decorated w/forget-me-nots on a pale yellow center w/pale blue border, gold-plated bezel, signed "A. Jibbing," ca. 1900-20, 1 3/8 x 1 1/2" **$75**

Brooch, oval, decorated w/pink & white & ruby roses & green leaves on a rich blue ground w/white enamel highlights, burnished gold border & rim, gold-plated bezel, ca. 1940s, 1 1/2 x 2" **$65**

Brooch, rectangular, decorated w/a tropical scene of palm tree in white on a platinum ground, painted by Olive Commons, Miami, Florida, sterling silver bezel, ca. 1920s-1940s, 3/4 x 1" **$110**

Brooch, round, decorated w/a conventional-style trillium w/raised paste & burnished gold pistols & burnished gold background, brass-plated bezel, ca. 1910-15, 1 9/16" d. **$55**

Brooch/pendant, heart shape, decorated w/daisies on a light shading to dark blue ground, gold-plated bezel, ca. 1900-20, 1 13/16 x 2" **$55**

Brooches, oval, decorated w/forget-me-nots on a pale pink & blue ground w/white enamel highlights on petal edges, burnished gold rims, gold-plated bezels, gold wear, ca. 1900-20, 13/16 x 1", pr. **$75**

Brooches with Pink & Ruby Roses

Brooches, round, decorated w/pink & ruby roses & green leaves on a polychrome ground, burnished gold rim, gold-plated bezel, 7 /8" d., pr. (ILLUS.) **$75**

Cuff pin, rectangular, decorated w/a purple iris outlined & bordered in burnished gold, brass-plated bezel, ca. 1900-15, 1/4 x 1 1/16" **$25**

Cuff Pins with Forget-me-nots

Cuff pins, rectangular, decorated w/forget-me-nots on a burnished gold ground, gold-plated bezel, ca. 1900-15, 1/4 x 1 1/4", pr. (ILLUS.) **$45**

Flapper pin, oval, decorated w/a stylized, elegant red-haired woman wearing blue dress & fur stole, pink flower & large comb in her hair, white ground w/burnished gold border, gold-plated bezel, ca. 1922-30, 1 11/16 x 2 1/8" **$135**

Flapper pin, oval, decorated w/bust of stylized red-haired flapper on a pastel polychrome ground, burnished gold rim & brass-plated bezel, ca. 1924-28, 1 5/8 x 2 1/8" **$125**

Handy pin, crescent shape, asymmetrically decorated w/a purple pansy on an ivory ground, burnished gold tip & brass-plated bezel, ca. 1880-1915, 2" w **$35**

Handy pin, crescent-shaped, decorated w/forget-me-nots & leaves on a burnished gold ground, gold-plated bezel, ca. 1890-1915, gold wear, 1 13/16" w **$30**

Handy pin, crescent-shaped, decorated w/pink & ruby roses & green leaves on an ivory ground, w/white enamel highlights

& one burnished gold tip, gold-plated bezel, ca. 1890-1915, 2 3/16" w. **$45**

Hatpin, circular head, decorated w/a conventional geometric design in raised paste dots & scrolls, covered w/burnished gold, turquoise enamel jewels, cobalt blue flat enamel, gold-plated bezel, ca. 1905-20, 1" d., 6 3/8" shaft **$110**

Hatpin, circular head, decorated w/pink roses & greenery on a pale blue & yellow ground, burnished gold border, gold-plated bezel, ca. 1890-1920, some gold wear, 1" d., 7 3/4" shaft **$125**

Hatpin Head with Wild Roses

Hatpin, circular head, decorated w/pink wild roses & greenery on a yellow ground, burnished gold rim, gold-plated filigree setting, head 1 1/16" d., shaft 9" l. (ILLUS. of head) **$125**

Hatpin Head with Ruby Roses

Hatpin, circular head, decorated w/ruby roses & green leaves, embellished w/burnished gold scrolls, gold-plated bezel, head 1 3/8" d., shaft 7 3/4" l. (ILLUS. of head) **$125**

Pendant, decorated w/a purple pansy w/white enamel center accents & burnished gold border, gold-plated bezel, ca. 1880s-1914, 1" d. **$60**

Pendant, oval, decorated w/forget-me-nots on a pastel polychrome ground w/white enamel highlights & burnished gold rim, gold-plated bezel, ca. 1900-25, 1 1/4 x 1 3/4" **$65**

Scarf pin, medallion-shaped, decorated w/violets, brass-plated bezel & shank, ca. 1880-1920, medallion 1 1/4" d., shank 3" l. **$75**

Shirtwaist Buttons with Pinwheels

Shirtwaist Button with Clover Leaf

Shirtwaist button, oval w/shank, decorated w/a three-leaf clover in green on a yellow & brown ground, burnished gold rim, 7/8 x 1 1/16" (ILLUS.)............................ **$25**

Shirtwaist Button with Flower

Shirtwaist button, round w/eye, decorated w/a conventional stylized long blossom flanked by pointed oval leaves in pale yellow, dark blue & black on a burnished gold ground, 1 1/16" d. (ILLUS.) **$35**

Unusual Portrait Shirtwaist Button

Shirtwaist button, round w/shank, decorated w/the bust portrait of a young blonde-haired girl, wearing a pale blue dress, against a shaded yellow to black ground, 1 3/8" d. (ILLUS.) **$90**

Shirtwaist buttons, heart-shaped, decorated w/pink roses, raised paste scrolled border covered w/burnished gold, ca. 1890-1910, 1 1/8 x 1 3/16", pr. **$85**

Shirtwaist buttons, round, each decorated w/a geometric pinwheel design in light blue, black & gold trimmed w/burnished gold dots & a center turquoise "jewel," on a burnished gold ground, two 1" d., three 7/8" d., the set (ILLUS., top of page)... **$125**

Shirtwaist set: oval brooch & pr. of oval cuff links; decorated w/blue forget-me-nots on an ivory background w/white enamel highlights, brass-plated mounts, ca. 1900-10, brooch w/burnished gold free-form border & rim, 1 3/8 x 1 3/4", cuff links w/burnished gold rims, 13/16 x 1 1/16", the set... **$250**

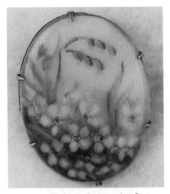

Brooch from Shirtwaist Set

Shirtwaist set: oval brooch & two round buttons w/shank; each decorated w/for-get-me-nots & greenery on a pastel poly-chrome ground, burnished gold rim, gold-plated bezel, brooch 1 1/4 x 1 3/4", but-tons 15/16" d., the set (ILLUS. of brooch) **$90**

Shirtwaist set: oval cuff links & three round buttons w/shanks; decorated w/clusters of violets on pale yellow ground, bur-nished gold rim, gold-plated bezel on cuff links, ca. 1900-15, cuff links 3/4 x 1 1/4", buttons 1 1/4" d., the set **$175**

Watch chatelaine, oval, decorated w/a woman wearing a rose-colored bodice, light shading to dark warm green ground, set in gold-plated rim w/twisted gold edge, ca. 1880s, 1 1/8 x 1 3/8" **$175**

Amphora - Teplitz

In the late 19th and early 20th centuries numerous potteries operated in the vicinity of Teplitz in the Bohemian region of what was Austria but is now the Czech Republic. They included Amphora, RStK, Stellmacher, Ernst Wahliss, Paul Dachsel, Imperial and lesser-known potteries such as Johanne Maresh, Julius Dressler, Bernard Bloch and Heliosine.

The number of collectors in this category is growing while availability of pieces is shrinking. Prices for better, rarer pieces, including those with restoration, are continuing to appreciate.

The price ranges presented here are retail. They presume mint or near mint condition or, in the case of very rare damaged pieces, proper resto-ration. They reflect such variables as rarity, design, quality of glaze, size and the intangible "in-vogue factor." They are the prices that knowl-edgeable sellers will charge and knowledgeable collectors will pay.

Various Amphora-Teplitz Factory Marks

Bowl, 10 1/4" w., 5 1/4" h., consisting of two wonderfully detailed high-glazed fish swimming around the perimeter, each executed in the Art Nouveau style w/flow-ing fins & tails, tentacles drip from their mouths, high-relief w/gold & reddish highlights, rare theme, impressed in ovals "Amphora" & "Austria" w/a crown **$3,800-4,200**

Bowl, 14 1/2" w., 4 3/8" h., an exotic Paul Dachsel design of calla lilies growing out of stems which originate at the bottom & gracefully extend around the sides to fully developed calla lilies at each end, in the center on each side are several "jewels" w/abstract leaves of high-glazed green w/gold overtones, mottled texture w/"jew-eled" greenish gold embellishments, stamped over glaze w/intertwined "PD - Turn-Teplitz," handwritten over glaze "0/45" (ILLUS., bottom of page) .... **$10,500 - 11,000**

Exotic Paul Dachsel Bowl

Bust of a Sultry Princess

Bust of a woman, perhaps Sarah Bernhardt in the role of a sultry princess, magnificently finished w/plentiful gold & bronze glazes without excessive fussiness, mounted on a base featuring a maiden on a horse in a forest setting, the bust seemingly supported by stag horns protruding from each side, impressed "Amphora" & "Austria" in a lozenge w/a crown, "1431" & "A" in blue, 13 1/2" w., 18 1/4" h. (ILLUS.) **$4,000-5,000**

Bust of Richard Wagner

Bust of Richard Wagner, the somber looking composer mounted on a pedestal emblazoned "Wagner" on the front, the head w/a beautiful soft flesh-toned Amphora glaze, the pedestal w/a shriveled tan & white glaze w/shades of olive green highlights, one of a rare series of composers, impressed "Amphora" & "Austria" in ovals w/a crown, a circle w/"Imperial

Amphora" & "250 -1," 19 3/4" h. (ILLUS.)
.... **$5,000-5,500**

Rare Amphora Candlestick

Candlestick, rare Amphora piece w/many of its special characteristics including jewels, spider webs, butterflies & wonderful soft muted Amphora glazes w/reds, blues & gold, a large handle extends from near the top of the socket, four smaller handles extend up & outward from the base, eleven jewels of various sizes & colors, impressed "Amphora" in an oval & a crown & "28," 14" h. (ILLUS.) **$7,000-7,500**

Centerpiece, an expansive bowl w/a "jeweled" effect along the rim, supported by two seated male lions w/fine details, a round base w/a "jeweled" effect, the underside of the bowl suggests a tropical jungle, a better example of a design featuring animals supporting a bowl, multicolored "jewels," lion in a natural brownish glaze, stamped "Amphora - Made in Czecho-slovakia" in an oval, "734 - 261" in black ink, 12" w., 9 5/8" h. **$2,500-3,000**

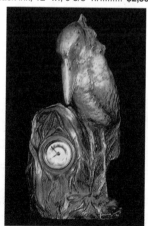

Fantasy Stork Clock

Clock, table model, a fantasy stork, similar to Martin Bros. birds, stands next to a clock dial framed by Art Nouveau-style leaves, fine detailing, soft brownish tan glaze, rare, raised rectangle w/factory logo & "AK-Turn," impressed "319," 13" h. (ILLUS.) **$7,500-8,000**

Amphora Teplitz Ewer

Ewer, an Art Nouveau design w/extraordinary detail combining a reticulated handle suggesting Paul Dachsel & varied circles on the body suggesting Gustav Klimt, a reticulated top, many "jewels" of different colors & sizes randomly located over the body suggesting a spectrum of stars in the Milky Way, unusual gold bud spout, high-glazed blue garlands randomly draped about the body, heavy gold trim on the upper part of the handle, top & spout, a subdued gold trim extends down the handle to & around the bottom where there is an abstract tree design, very difficult to produce, rare, impressed "Amphora" in a circle & "40 -537," 14" h. (ILLUS.)...................................... **$9,500-10,000**

Figure group, a small fine scenic figural group w/a rooster & hen perched side by side overlooking a pond, a small gold frog climbing into the pond, gives a barnyard feeling, soft muted shades of tan w/highlights of gold, a realistic theme & valuable because of the small size, impressed "Amphora" in an oval & illegible numbers, 6 1/2" w., 7 3/4" h. **$1,250-1,300**

Unique Figural Humidor

Humidor, cov., figural, a fantasy piece featuring a large globe representing the world being shot from a tiny cannon & caught by a jester lying on his back, the jester reputedly represents a prime minister of the time, a hat at the top of the globe forms the handles, soft muted grey Amphora glaze, rare, impressed "Amphora" in an oval & "4216," 14" w., 9" h. (ILLUS.).. **$7,500-8,500**

Indian Heads Amphora Humidor

Humidor, cov., figural, a massive Native American theme composed of three Indian heads w/high-glazed pink & green feathered headdresses, "jeweled" & draping beaded necklaces on two, a draping necklace of animal teeth on the third, high-glaze green & cobalt blue finial handle on a decorative mixed glazed top, basic color of Campina brown w/much contrasting high-glaze in green, pink, brown & blue, rare, impressed ovals w/"Amphora" & "Austria," a crown & "Imperial - Amphora - Turn" in a circle & "S-1633-46," 10 1/2" h. (ILLUS.)........ **$5,500-6,500**

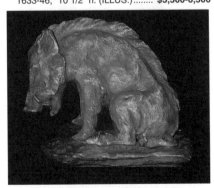

Amphora Model of a European Boar

Model of a boar, seated European boar leaning to one side as though attempting to rest from a hunter's pursuit, finished in brownish gold glaze, very lifelike, rare, impressed "Amphora" & "Austria" in oval, a crown, #8236/36 & artist's mark "H" in gold, 10" h. (ILLUS.)...................... **$3,000-3,500**

Large Model of a Crowing Rooster

Model of a rooster, larger-than-life crowing rooster designed by Berwiel & glazed in mottled golden brown, this example found in Germany, another reported to be in a Scandinavian art museum, incised "Berwiel 08" on the side, impressed "Amphora" & "Austria" in oval, a crown, "Imperial - Amphora - Turn" in a circle & 8237/37, 26" h. (ILLUS.) **$10,500-11,000**

Unusual Amphora Lamp - Vase

Oil lamp-vase, a massive tiered form w/a swelled shoulder & wide flat-topped lower section decorated w/a variety of multicolored "jewels" w/a removable lamp font insert, rare, impressed "Amphora" & "Austria" in ovals & "8796/52," 12 1/2" h. (ILLUS.)...................................... **$9,500-10,000**

Plaque, a large oval shape centered by an Art Nouveau woman in high relief attired in a luminescent pink dress blowing a double-horned musical instrument and seated on a rocky ledge, the border of the plaque consisting of garlands of flowers

& leaves in high relief, especially the buds, basic color of seafoam green, the surrounding florals in greens & tans, impressed "Ernst Wahliss," 17 x 19 1/2" **$3,000-3,500**

Plaque with Art Nouveau Woman

Plaque, terra cotta rectangular form depicting a very stylized beautifully coifed Art Nouveau woman in profile in high relief, her unique elegance suggesting a woman of high social stature, the borders garlanded leaves & buds in high relief, organic mossy shades of green, soft purples, tans & warm browns, impressed marks "Ernst Wahliss - Made in Austria - Turn - Wien - 157," 11 3/4 x 17" (ILLUS.) **$2,500-3,500**

Amphora King Tut Teapot with Lady

Teapot, cov., King Tut Series, flared foot & ovoid body tapering to a flat mouth, C-form handle from rim to shoulder, angled short shoulder spout w/arched brace to rim, incised & decorated on one side w/standing woman wearing a long blue robe w/a diadem on her head, holding a long staff in one arm & a small jug in the other hand, against a pebbled rose red ground w/stylized blue flowerheads, white & blue zigzag foot band, the reverse side decorated w/squares in a rectangle w/a larger flower matching the two on the other side, marked "Made in Czech-Slovakia - Amphora" in double inked ovals, impressed numbers "12315 - 5" & "1661" painted in underglaze, ca. 1918-39, 8 1/4" h. (ILLUS.) **$195**

Amphora Russian Folk Art Teapot

Teapot, cov., Russian Folk Art Series, tall ovoid form w/flared foot & flat rim, arched C-form handle from rim to shoulder, short angled shoulder spout w/an arched brace to the rim, decorated on center front w/a large stylized bust portrait of a Russian cleric w/black beard & brown & blue hat, the portrait enclosed by a ring of blue stars & blue dots w/other bands of dots & teardrops about the top & base, all against a tan ground, the reverse w/a design of multiple triangles enclosed w/a ring of stars, impressed "Austria - Amphora" in ovals & "11892,47 - G" plus a crown, ca. 1907-08, 8 1/4" h. (ILLUS.) **$295**

Blue & Cream Amphora Teapot

Teapot, cov., wide squatty bulbous body tapering sharply to a small cylindrical neck bulbed at the top w/an arched handle

from the back of the neck to the shoulder & a double-arch bracket from the neck to the tip of the long angled straight spout, the center of the side w/a large almond-shaped reserve w/a dark blue ground decorated w/three stylized Macintosh Roses & flanked by a dark blue band continuing up the spout that is decorated w/a dark blue band decorated w/small yellow flower clusters, neck in blue w/matching florals, blue handle & brackets, the background of the body in creamy mottled white ground decorated w/scattered small yellow blossoms, similar to designs by Paul Dachsel, ca. 1906-07, impressed "Austria" & "Amphora" in ovals & a crown, impressed numbers "3974," overall 8" h. (ILLUS.) **$695**

Vase, 5 3/4" h., figural, elegantly executed Paul Dachsel creation w/a greenish cast & numerous vertical ribs extending up from the base, four intertwined gold-bodied dragonflies form a reticulated top, immediately below a series of smaller dragonflies encircle the vase, two multilayered handles within handles complete the design, stamped over glaze w/intertwined "PD - Turn - Teplitz," impressed "104" **$3,500-4,000**

Fine Figural Vase with Maiden

Vase, 7" h., figural, demure, elegant wonderfully detailed young woman seated & reaching down to retrieve a flower, against an upright flowering vine-covered wall, mixed iridescent colors of blue, magenta, silver, purple & gold all w/a bronze-like finish, a top-of-the-line creation of Ernst Wahliss, marked "EW - Turn - Vienna - Made in Austria" & an incised "I" & 4838/8/360/7 (ILLUS.) **$3,000-3,500**

Vase, 7 1/2" h., a playful expression of Amphora w/a pink snake draped around the body of the bulbous vase & extending to the top where its delicate tongue protrudes, a subtle leaf design extends around the bottom, the pink color of the snake distinguishes this piece from more drab versions, impressed in ovals "Amphora" & "Austria," & "4114 - 52"... **$2,500-3,000**

Vase, 7 3/4" h., round bulbous shape, decorated w/a profile of a young girl w/long flowing brownish hair full of numerous multicolored high-glazed flowers w/gold touches, all surrounded by a brownish tan forest scene, finely executed, impressed "Amphora - 663," overglaze red mark "RStK - Turn - Teplitz - Made in Austria"... **$2,500-3,000**

Vase, 8 3/4" h., four-paneled high-shouldered squared form w/a front-faced Mucha-style Art Nouveau princess portrait, elaborate gold enameling against a landscape decorated w/blue & purple trees w/gold highlights above a base decorated w/Paul Dachsel-style abstract red flowers in a green base, impressed "Amphora" in oval & "579-40," red "RStK Austria" overglaze mark, artist mark "Fr" in gold overglaze.............................. **$4,000-4,500**

Paul Dachsel Forest Scene Vase

Vase, 9" h., a bulbous Paul Dachsel forest scene w/reticulated gold top & varied reddish mushrooms in high relief encircling the bottom, a production mold but h.p. to produce a uniquely different forest scene, stamped over the glaze w/intertwined "PD - Turn - Teplitz," impressed "1106 - 2," blue overglaze "094" (ILLUS.)
.... **$4,000-4,500**

Rare Amphora Cat Head Vase

Vase, 9" h., wide bulbous tapering form, rare form suggesting an inverted Tiffany lamp shade, four large Persian cat heads molded in full relief & projecting from the sides w/a forest of abstract trees w/160-170 opal-like translucent "jewels" symbolizing fruits, the jewels in various sizes & shades of opal blue mounted in gold surrounds, heavy gold rim, the tree branches extending to the jewels on a background of Klimt-like subtle gold circles, holes behind the jewels permit candlelight or an electric bulb to illuminate the jewels, cat heads finished in a soft pinkish gold w/traces of green & gold highlights on the ears, impressed "Amphora - Austria" in a lozenge, a crown & "8183 - 28" (ILLUS.)........................... **$25,000+**

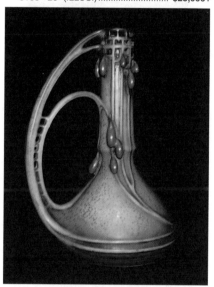

Abstract Paul Dachsel Vase

Vase, 9 7/8" h., a Paul Dachsel abstract design w/a reticulated geometric top & a reticulated handle within a reticulated handle sweeping in an arc from the top to the bottom w/abstract tendrils extending around the bottom of the body & back of the handles, several high-glazed green pods resembling teardrops of various sizes hang from the abstract handle, vines & a center funnel, the top rim & top of handle finished in gold, rare, stamped over glaze w/intertwined "PD - Turn - Teplitz" (ILLUS.).. **$7,000-7,500**

Vase, 10" h., a Paul Dachsel abstract architectural style w/a geometric design consisting of a rounded bottom from which four handles begin flush & extend to the top of the rim where they flare open, each handle suggests an abstract candelabrum w/charcoal flames rising from each, finished in iridescent gunmetal grey w/charcoal black sheen touches, gold wash on top, modern in all respects even though produced in the 1904-10 period, rare form, stamped over glaze w/intertwined "PD - Turn - Teplitz," impressed "1049"... **$8,500-9,000**

Vase, 10 5/8" h., figural, in the form of a prancing male lion, snarling open mouth, standing on a broad base narrowing at the top, numerous concentric circles form bands around the top & bottom, lion reflects an iridescent gold, green & rose combination of color, body of base in metallic green w/undertones of blues & splotches of reds, impressed "Amphora" & "Austria" in oval, a crown & "500-52," handwritten in black ink over glaze "CB - 613417," estimated value without jewels, $1,500-2,000, value w/jewels........ **$3,500-4,500**

Vase with Persian Cat Heads

Vase, 11" h., four gold Persian cat heads adorn a center-pillared body w/four surrounding gold "jeweled" arms extending from each cat head to the base, metallic blue w/a gold wash, cobalt blue "jewels," rare design, more common versions have cabochons instead of animal heads, marked "Amphora" & "Austria" in ovals, a crown & impressed "Imperial" circle mark & "11677 - 51" (ILLUS.)................. **$6,500-7,000**

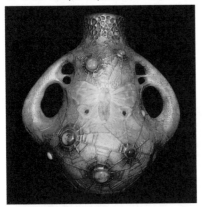

Ornate Jeweled Art Nouveau Vase

Vase, 11 1/4" h., tapering lobed ovoid form of exceptional Art Nouveau design w/numerous "jewels," spider webs & two but-

terflies w/heavy pierced extended handles suggesting a larger butterfly, 17 "jewels" in varying sizes & colors, red abstract circles drape from the gold-edged top, soft muted tan, red, blue & green glazes w/gold iridescence, impressed "Amphora" & "Austria" in ovals, a crown & "8551-42," red "RStK Austria" overglaze mark (ILLUS.)............................... **$9,000-9,500**

Czech Vase with Figural Dragon

Vase, 12" h., a wonderful & colorful dragon hugs the circumference of the top w/its huge, detailed wings draping along the sides, detailed claw-like feet decorated in two glazes, one predominately blue, the other predominately tan, a Czechoslovakian creation w/no Austrian counterpart, stamped over the glaze "Amphora - Made in Czech-slovakia" in an oval (ILLUS.) **$6,000**

Amphora Figural Cockatoo Vase

Vase, 12" h., figural, three standing cockatoos, fully feathered, extend around the body of the vase, their plumes rising over the rim, very detailed w/glossy glaze,

subtle color mix of blues, greens & tans w/brown streaks, semi-rare, impressed "Amphora" & "Austria" in ovals, a crown & Imperial circle & "11986 - 56" (ILLUS.)
.... **$4,500-5,000**

Vase, 12 3/4" h., elegant form consisting of four beautifully veined tall leaves forming the funnel of the vase w/the stem of each leaf forming a handle extending into the bottom, each stem issues an additional flat leaf extending across the bottom, leaves finished in a mottled orange w/touches of greens & yellows w/gold overtones (although marked by Ernst Wahliss the design indicates the work of Paul Dachsel who worked at various Amphora factories), rare, stamped over glaze "EW" red mark, impressed "9491," "9786a - 10" in ink over the glaze
.... **$8,000-8,500**

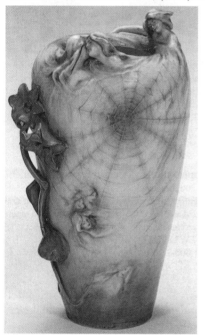

Teplitz Vase with Spider Web & Maidens

Vase, 12 3/4" h., tall ovoid body in creamy white decorated around the sides w/a gold spider web & molded around the closed rim w/emerging heads of Art Nouveau maidens w/other maiden heads around the sides, a large gold flower vine up one side, Teplitz mark, base drilled, ca. 1900 (ILLUS.) **$863**

Dachsel "Enchanted Forest" Vase

Vase, 13" h., wide-shouldered tapering cylindrical body, a fantasy design by Paul Dachsel worthy of the description "enchanted forest," the design consists of slender molded abstract trees extending from the narrow base to the bulbous top, lovely heart-shaped leaves extend in clusters from the various branches, trees in muted green, the leaves in pearlized off-white w/gold framing, the symbolic sky in rich red extending between the trees from the bottom to the top, rare, intertwined "PD" mark rubbed off (ILLUS.)
.... **$9,500-10,000**

Vase, 14" h., figural, a fantasy dragon featuring two flaring wings, one extending practically from the top to the bottom of the body, the other well above & beyond the rim, creature w/a convoluted tail, spine & teeth, the head w/open mouth positioned at top of the vase, bluish green gold iridescence, glazes vary from a flat tan to a variety of very iridescent colors, made in 14" & 17" size, impressed "Amphora" in oval, illegible numbers, large size w/better glazes, $6,500, 14" size w/drab glazes **$9,500-10,000**

Vase, 14 5/8" h., a figural fantasy piece, a different variety of dragon vase but not highly glazed, the dragon is mostly brown but it features a well-defined head, body, clawed feet & tail, a snake tongue drapes from the mouth, hideously beautiful, the body contrasts nicely w/the metallic greenish blue iridescence of the mottled background, found in various glazes, impressed "Amphora" & "Austria" in oval, a crown & "C 4543" **$3,500-4,000**

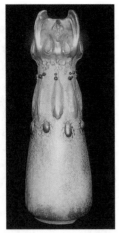

Tall Amphora Vase with Insects

Vase, 14 3/4" h., tall gently tapering ovoid body w/a swelled top, decorated w/eight three-dimensional iridescent indigo blue insects of varying sizes crawling up the side toward a series of leaves adorned w/berries, above the berries is a four-handled 3" h. heavily gilded top, the rest of the body in iridescent light blue w/gold highlights, rare, impressed "Amphora" & "Austria" in ovals, a crown & 3987/58 (ILLUS.) **$9,000-9,500**

Flower-decorated Art Nouveau Vase

Vase, 15" h., bulbous squatty base tapering to a slender neck w/fanned rim, unique Art Nouveau design w/an open flower blossom tinged in gold at the top, two curved vine handles extend from the neck to the base, the base relief-molded w/detailed leaves, found in numerous color variations & glazes, the most magnificent being a bronze glaze, value depends on the glaze w/bronze being the rarest, impressed "Amphora" & "Austria" in oval, a crown & 3852/42 (ILLUS.) **$4,500-5,500**

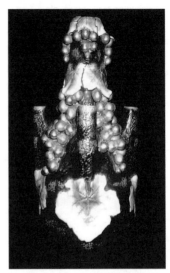

Amphora Vase with Golden Grapes

Vase, 15 1/2" h., cascades of golden grapes stream down on all sides between four funnel necks, the central funnel projecting skyward, this funnel design suggests Paul Dachsel, especially desirable because the piece is viewable from any angle, metallic purplish glaze w/metallic gold highlights containing numerous little gold circles, marked "Amphora" & "Austria" in ovals, a crown & "3680" (ILLUS.)
.... **$4,000-4,500**

Rare Jeweled Amphora Vase

Vase, 16" h., bulbous ovoid body tapering to a slender flaring lobed reticulated neck, outswept loop handles at the lower sides, shimmering burnished gold ground w/red touches, adorned randomly w/twenty large variously colored 'jewels,' one handle in red, the other in gold, overall molded vertical ribbing, rare form, impressed

"Amphora" in an oval, crown, old "RStK" mark & "3349" (ILLUS.) **$15,000-18,000**

Tall Heliosine Ware Art Nouveau Vase

Vase, 16" h., tall elegant Heliosine Ware piece w/a striking Art Nouveau design, two curved slender handles swoop gracefully from the top rim to the bottom w/a slender central shaft, a wide array of iridescent metallic glazes, an increasingly popular line, marked "Heliosine Ware - Austria" & impressed "21020 -D" (ILLUS.) **$2,500-3,000**

Amphora Vase with Figural Pheasant

Vase, 16 1/4" h., figural, a footed wide squatty base mounted w/the model of a long-tailed realistic exotic pheasant beside a tall swelled cylindrical neck molded w/gilt veins up to the widely fanned compressed mouth, shaded green, blue & yellow w/heavy gold trim, Amphora mark, Model 4272 - 52, ca. 1904 (ILLUS.) **$1,434**

Rare Amphora Octopus Vase

Vase, 16 1/2" h., a massive fantasy piece w/a large golden iridescent octopus around the bottom, its tentacles extending around the sides & up to the top where they grab a large swimming sea horse, a particularly rare style of octopus w/only one known at present, impressed "Amphora" & "Austria" in ovals, a crown & "4597 - 50" (ILLUS.) .... **$21,000+**

Vase, 16 1/2" h., fine Paul Dachsel creation in an undulating freeform design consisting of several abstract trees extending from the bottom to the top where a branch wraps around the top & then down dividing into other branches w/a series of red-glazed leaves, numerous white "jewels" suggesting seeds & seed pods attached to the branches & trunks, red leaves w/gold-tinged ends, very rare form, stamped over the glaze w/intertwined "PD - Turn - Teplitz," impressed "1115".............. **$9,000-9,500**

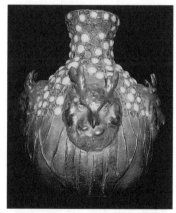

Rare Large Vase with Owl Heads

Vase, 16 3/4" h., wide bulbous body w/small shoulder handles, tapering to a short flaring neck, the design suggests an ominous nightfall w/four dark owl heads peering from among tree branches w/150 or so translucent 'jewel-like' leaves, when a candle is placed inside it softly lights these jewels, rare form recently discovered in Europe, impressed "Amphora" & "Austria" in ovals, a crown, incised "D" & 8180 (ILLUS.)...................................... **$35,000+**

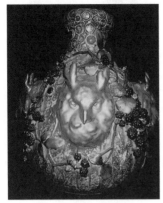

Rare Owl Head Vase

Vase, 17" h., massive bulbous bottle-form w/four finely detailed gold-finished owl heads projecting from the sides surrounded by brambles, leaves & many clusters of berries & numerous "jewels" of various sizes & colors interspersed among the brambles, unusual & complicated design, some similar pieces w/other animal heads exist but few survive intact, rare, impressed "Amphora" in oval, a crown & "8160" (ILLUS.) .... **$25,000+**

Vase, 17 1/8" h., tall Art Nouveau form gradually tapering to a narrower top, the bottom w/seven delicate female heads w/long flowing hair emerging from a swirling ocean, tan w/highlights of gold & green, a similar example found in a Berlin museum, marks include a raised Art Nouveau girl's head & "Amphora" in a raised rectangle, red "RStK Austria" mark over the glaze, impressed illegible numbers, handwritten "1081 - L - 372" over the glaze........ **$7,000-7,500**

Rare Reticulated Amphora Vase

Vase, 17 1/2" h., an important reticulated piece composed of a basket-like vase within a vase elaborately entwined w/swooping gold handles joined in the middle, numerous varied colored "jewels" around the sides, viewed through the reticulation a high-glazed blue swirly design w/gold highlights is seen, the exterior w/a metallic bluish green w/gold wash & gold highlights, high-glazed gold rim, only one known so far, impressed "Amphora" & "Austria" in ovals, a crown & "3791-45" (ILLUS.)................... **$25,000-30,000**

Rare Tall Triangular Amphora Vase

Vase, 17 1/2" h., tall tapering triangular ovoid body w/a flared rim, iridescent & heavily gilded w/multiple 'jewels' on each panel, rich magenta glaze blends into each gilded panel, rarely seen shape, impressed "Amphora" & "Austria" in oval, 8658/55 (ILLUS.)...................... **$14,500-15,000**

Amphora Vase with Coiling Beast

Vase, 18 1/4" h., a fantasy piece w/a coiling beast not really a dragon, snake or octopus but w/characteristics of each, finished in a golden color w/gold highlights, the head extends above the top, the body entwines down around the sides, mottled metallic purplish blue background, impressed "Amphora" & "Austria" in ovals, a crown & "4539-50," values vary w/the glaze (ILLUS., previous page)..... **$9,500-10,000**

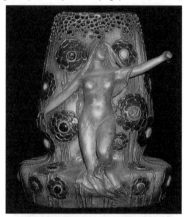

Rare Large Figural Amphora Vase

Vase, 18 1/4" h., figural, a massive Art Nouveau form featuring an elegant woman wearing a diaphanous gown & standing in front of the body of the vase, her extended hand holding a 'jewel' like those adorning the sides of the piece, reticulated top finished in rich gold, impressed "Amphora - Austria" in a lozenge, 8171 (ILLUS.)..................................... **$45,000-50,000**

Vase, 20" h., footed tall wide cylindrical body w/squatty bulbous base & closed-in rim, mottled mauve glaze w/relief-molded dragon figure in yellow, tan & gilt glaze conforming entirely around body & rim, minor restorations to chips, impressed "AMPHORA" in a lozenge, a crown & "4548 50".................................. **$12,500-13,000**

Tall Vase with Pine Cones

Vase, 20" h., tall slightly tapering cylindrical form w/a widely flared base, boldly molded pine cones hang around the top section from symbolic green trees divided by red indented vertical panels, a Paul Dachsel Secessionist design, rare, stamped over the glaze w/intertwined "PD - Turn - Teplitz" & impressed "2038 - 6" (ILLUS.) **$19,500-20,000**

Massive Amphora Mermaid Vase

Vase, 21" h., 18" w., figural, a wide squatty bulbous base centered by a tall neck, Art Nouveau style w/a mermaid clinging to the top rim, her well-defined body extends down along the side, applied berries, vines & leaves complete the decoration, finished in a matte tan w/gold wash & highlights, bluish berries, red stems, greenish red leaves & a high-glazed gold rim, important & very rare, would be rare even without the applied foliage, impressed "Amphora" in oval & "07 - 7 - 3" (ILLUS.).................................... **$22,500-23,000**

Tall Amphora Portrait Vase

Vase, 21 1/2" h., portrait-type, a very large profiled Sarah Bernhardt portrait inspired by Gustav Klimt featuring a majestic bird headdress w/eleven "jewels" of various sizes & colors, the figure w/long flowing hair streaming from under the headdress to her shoulders, below her neck is a jeweled butterfly, on one side a golden sun rises from the ocean emitting numerous golden rays, bluish green metallic background w/heavy gold detail, impressed "Amphora" & "Austria" in a lozenge, a crown & "02047 - 28" (ILLUS.) .. **$30,000-32,000**

Tall Amphora Vase with Bats

Vase, 21 1/2" h., tall bottle-form w/swarms of gold bats feeding on golden fruits around the reticulated top, they are about to be joined by other bats flying up the sides, tall graceful form w/the rounded base encircled by golden lily pad leaves w/the stems extending up the sides on an eggshell off-white ground, impressed "Amphora" in oval, red "Austria RStK" mark over glaze, impressed "41 - 668" & "750 - 1029" in ink (ILLUS.)....... **$15,500-16,000**

Somber, Eerie Dragon Vase

Vase, 22" h., figural, a somber swampy-green dragon encircles the tall body several times, its wings spread like a cobra's hood, leering down hungrily at a frog restrained by his tail at the base, this piece can be found finished in other colors including red & tan, impressed "Amphora" & "Austria" in ovals, a crown & "4536 - 6" (ILLUS.).................................... **$11,000-12,000**

Unusual Vase with Figural Bear

Vase, 23 1/2" h., figural, a squatty bulbous base w/flattened shoulder mounted w/a huge gilded bear licking his extended paws, decorated w/a variety of subtle colors & circles, rare subject matter, found in South America, impressed "Amphora" & "Austria" in ovals & 4509, also in overglaze red "RSstK - Turn - Teplitz - Made in Austria" (ILLUS.) .... **$16,000+**

Vases, 10 1/2" h., footed bulbous ovoid body tapering to a slender cylindrical neck w/a flattened disk rim, painted in shades of purple, pink, green, blue, black & gilt w/the bust of a young maiden wearing a voluminous hood surmounted by a Byzantine crown surrounded by a gilt aura, a lower border of roses, the crown & roses w/applied bosses, one printed w/mark "Turn - Teplitz - Bohemia - R.St. - Made in Austria," the other impressed "Amphora," each impressed "2014 -28," pr... **$14,000**

Vases, 19 1/2" h., tapering cylindrical form w/cushion foot & spiky rim, applied w/a realistically modeled octopus capturing a crab, covered in a sponged blue, white & yellow glaze, the creatures in beige & burnt orange, printed in blue "AMPHORA - Made in Czecho-Slovakia" & impressed numbers, pr.............................. **$11,000-12,000**

Arequipa

Dr. Philip King Brown established The Arequipa Sanitorium in Fairfax, California, in the early years of the 20th century. In 1911 he set up a pottery at the facility as therapy for his female tuberculosis patients since he had been impressed with the success of the similar Marblehead pottery in Massachusetts.

The first art director was the noted ceramics designer Frederick H. Rhead who had earlier been art director at the Roseville Pottery.

In 1913 the pottery was separated from the medical facility and incorporated as The Arequipa Potteries. Later that year Rhead and his wife, Agnes, one of the pottery instructors, left Arequipa and Albert L. Solon took over as the pottery director. The corporation was dissolved in 1915 and the pottery closed in 1918 although the sanitorium remained in operation until 1957.

Arequipa Marks

Bowl, 6 1/2" d., 2 1/4" h., wide flat bottomed form w/squatty bulbous incurved sides w/a wide flat mouth, embossed w/eucalyptus branches under a dark matte green & blue glaze, stamped mark, incised "KH - 11" **$880**

Arequipa Bowl with Seashells

Bowl, 8 1/2" d., 2 1/4" h., wide flat-bottomed shallow shape w/incurved sides applied w/two seashells on the shoulder in a blue crystalline matte glaze, impressed "Arequipa California" logo & "703- 12," light crazing, few pinpoint open bubbles (ILLUS.) **$875**

Vase, 3 1/4" h., 3" d., miniature, simple wide ovoid form w/closed rim, decorated in squeeze-bag w/stylized leaves in a fine organic matte green w/small red circles, against a matte yellow ground, incised mark "?27 - Arequipa - California - 1912" **$6,325**

Vase, 3 1/2" h., 2 1/2" d., miniature, simple ovoid body w/closed rim, decorated in squeeze-bag w/a rim band of holly leaves & red berries against a matte, mottled greenish blue ground, by Frederick Rhead, white & brown glaze mark **$6,325**

Vase, 4 1/4" h., 7" d., footed wide squatty bulbous form w/the wide shoulder tapering to a short flared neck, enamel-deco-

rated w/a plant w/white berries against a semi-matte greyish blue ground, rare early mark, incised "AP - 1911" **$660**

Vase, 4 3/4" h., 3 1/4" d., swelled cylindrical body w/a narrow rounded shoulder to the short, wide neck, smooth matte leathery dark green glaze, incised "3 - Arequipa - Cal." **$358**

Unusual Black-glazed Arequipa Vase

Vase, 4 3/4" h., 3 3/4" d., bulbous body tapering to a short cylindrical neck w/flat rim, carved w/an abstract leaf-like design, covered in a gunmetal black glaze, incised mark w/tree, minor flat stilt-pull chip (ILLUS.) **$3,819**

Vase, 6" h., 3 1/4" d., simple ovoid body w/wide incurved rim, decorated w/incised abstract leaves in a flowing, glossy dark blue against a turquoise ground, restoration to small inner rim chip, Frederick Rhead period, signed in ink "Arequipa California - 1912 - 463 - 4" **$2,420**

Vase, 6 1/4" h., 5" d., bulbous shouldered ovoid body w/a wide flat rim, decorated in squeezebag w/stylized yellow flowers over large, bright green leaves w/blue veins, from the Frederick Rhead period, blue ink mark "Arequipa - California," ca. 1911-12, minute glaze nick on raised point **$9,350**

Vase, 7" h., 4" d., simple ovoid body decorated in squeezebag w/stylized leaves in brown on a matte feathered green ground, a dark green drip down from each leaf, fine glaze nicks on rim, Rhead period, ca. 1912, blue enamel mark **$3,740**

Vase, 7 1/2" h., 4" d., bulbous base below tapering cylindrical sides, decorated in squeezebag w/a wreath of heart-shaped leaves under a fine leathery pea green matte glaze, Frederick Rhead period, marked in ink "Arequipa California 1913 - 2123 - 123" **$1,980**

Vase, 11" h., 6 1/4" d., baluster-form w/a short flaring neck, hand-cut w/large upright bell-shaped flowers around the sides & small daisy-like blossom heads around the neck, clear brown glossy glaze, die-stamped mark & "403-22 -WI" .. **$770**

Banko Ware

These collectible Japanese pottery wares were produced for domestic use and also exported in the late 19th and early 20th century. Pieces are finely detailed and composed of very thin clays in various colors including white, marbleized, grey, brown and tapestry. Traditional as well as whimsical pieces were produced, especially teapots. Banko Ware pieces generally have impressed markings on the base or handle. Decorative details could be painted, incised or applied in low or high relief.

Banko "1000 Treasures" Teapot

Teapot, cov., grayware, squatty bulbous body applied w/brightly enameled "1000 Treasures" design in high relief, twisted brown & grey clay rope w/bows applied around the rim & flaring crimped neck, inset cover w/knob finial, includes Banko tea infuser inside, marked w/impressed round Banko signature, Japan, ca. 1900, 4 1/2" l., 4" h. (ILLUS.) **$135**

Banko Ware Figural Bird Teapot

Teapot, cov., figural, model of a peacock, the cover in the top of the back, brightly enameled, beige clay, impressed "Made in Japan" mark, ca. 1920, 6 1/2" l., 4 1/2" h. (ILLUS.) **$200**

Teapot, cov., figural, model of an elephant w/a seated rider atop the cover, grey clay w/brightly enameled blanket on the back, unmarked, Japan, pictured in a dated 1916 Vantine's catalog, 6" l., 6" h. (ILLUS., top of next page)... **$200**

Banko Teapot with Cranes & Flowers

Teapot, cov., grayware, squatty bulbous body enameled w/flying cranes & flowers, twisted brown & grey clay applied handle & rope around the crimped flaring neck, inset cover w/knob finial, unsigned, Japan, ca. 1900, 4 1/2" l., 3" h. (ILLUS.)...... **$50**

Rare Banko Cottage-shaped Teapot

Teapot, cov., figural, modeled as a thatched roof cottage, top of roof forming the cover, applied in relief w/flowers, trimmed w/bright enamels on the grey clay ground, fine woven brass wire bail handle, two impressed signatures on the base, Japan, ca. 1900, 5 1/2" l., 3 1/2" h. (ILLUS.)... **$400**

Banko Teapot with Grapes & Birds

Teapot, cov., grayware, squatty bulbous body w/short spout, low domed cover w/twisted applied handle w/further handles flanking the wide mouth, decorated overall w/hand-applied grapes & leaves & brightly enameled w/birds & flowers, impressed artist's signature, Japan, ca. 1900, 5" l., 3 1/2" h. (ILLUS.) **$150**

Colorful Elephant & Rider Banko Teapot

Large "Marquetry" Banko Teapot

Small Banko "Marquetry" Teapot

Teapot, cov., marquetry-style, tapestry finish, large spherical body w/a wide flat mouth, woven bamboo swing bail handle, the shoulder trimmed w/large applied green enameled leaves, the body composed of small squares of multicolored clay pressed together to form a checkerboard design, the clays being tinted, not painted on the surface, apparently unmarked, Japan, ca. 1900, 6" l., 5" h. (ILLUS.) **$140**

Teapot, cov., marquetry-style, tapestry finish, squatty bulbous body w/a wide flared mouth w/an applied tan rope tied in bows under the handle holds, fine braided wire bail handle, the body composed of small squares of multicolored clay pressed together to form a checkerboard design, the clays being tinted, not painted on the surface, Japan, ca. 1900, 4" l., 3" h. (ILLUS., next column) **$100**

Miniature Swirled Clay Banko Teapot

Teapot, cov., miniature, brown & tan swirled clay, hand-formed squatty bulbous body w/an applied rope & bows below the crimped flaring rim, inset cover w/knob finial, enameled floral decoration on the sides, original woven rattan

bail handle, Japan, ca. 1900, 3 1/2" l.,
2 1/2" h. (ILLUS.) $60

Banko Teapot with Swirled Clays

Teapot, cov., swirled blue & grey clay, tapestry finish, nearly spherical body w/a wide flat mouth, inset domed cover w/applied twig & flower finial, the sides applied w/enameled flowers & branches, wrapped rattan bail handle, marked "Made in Japan," ca. 1920s, 4 1/2" l., 3 1/2" h. (ILLUS.) $60

Bauer

The Bauer Pottery was moved to Los Angeles, California, from Paducah, Kentucky, in 1909 in the hope that the climate would prove beneficial to the principal organizer, John Andrew Bauer, who suffered from severe asthma. Flowerpots made of California adobe clay were the first production at the new location, but soon they were able to resume production of stoneware crocks and jugs, the mainstay of the Kentucky operation. In the early 1930s, Bauer's colorfully glazed earthen dinnerwares, especially the popular Ring-Ware pattern, became an immediate success. Sometimes confused with its imitator, Fiesta Ware (first registered by Homer Laughlin in 1937), Bauer pottery is collectible in its own right and is especially popular with West Coast collectors. Bauer Pottery ceased operation in 1962.

Bauer Mark

Baking dish, cov., individual, Ring-Ware patt., green or yellow, 4" d., each................ $40
Batter bowl, Ring-Ware patt., green, 1 qt. $125

Beater pitcher, Ring-Ware patt., red, 1 qt. $85
Bowl, batter, Ring-Ware, large................. $75-100
Bowl, berry, 5 1/2" d., Ring-Ware patt., delphinium $30
Bowl, berry, 5 1/2" d., Ring-Ware patt., yellow... $25
Bowl, soup, cov., 5 1/2" d., lug handles, Ring-Ware patt., orange, green, ivory or cobalt blue, each...................................... $90
Bowl, 13" d., Cal-Art line, green..................... $35
Bowl, 15" d., wide low sides, white & brown speckled glaze, No. 149........................... $95
Butter dish, cov., round, Ring-Ware patt., red... $155
Cake plate, Monterey patt., yellow................ $185
Candleholders, spool-shaped, Ring-Ware patt., jade green, pr.................................. $130
Casserole, w/holder, Ring-Ware, 5 1/2" h. $60-75
Casserole, cov., individual, Ring-Ware patt., cobalt blue, 5 1/2" d. $300
Casserole, cov., individual, Ring-Ware patt., ivory, 5 1/2" d. $300
Casserole, cov., individual, Ring-Ware patt., orange/red, 5 1/2" d. $200
Coffee carafe, cov., Ring-Ware patt., copper handle, delph blue $250
Coffee carafe, cov., Ring-Ware patt., copper handle, orange/red............................ $150
Console set: bowl & pr. of three-light candlesticks; Cal-Art line, pink, semi-matte finish, 3 pcs. $145
Cookie jar, cov., Monterey Moderne patt., chartreuse.. $100
Cookie jar, pastel Kitchenware.............. $100-150
Creamer, midget, Monterey patt., orange/red $20
Creamer & cov. sugar bowl, Ring-Ware patt., ivory, pr. $150
Creamer & cov. sugar bowl, Ring-Ware patt., orange, pr.. $75
Cup & saucer, demitasse, Ring-Ware patt., yellow.. $125
Cup & saucer, Monterey Moderne patt. $20-30
Cup & saucer, Ring-Ware patt., yellow $45-50
Custard cup, Ring-Ware $15-25
Flowerpot, Ring-Ware patt., cobalt blue......... $45
Flowerpot, Speckleware, flesh pink, 8 1/4" d., 6 1/2" h. $40
Gravy boat, Monterey Moderne patt., pink...... $40
Gravy boat, Monterey patt......................... $30-40
Gravy boat, Ring-Ware patt., burgundy........ $145
Jug, ball-shape, La Linda patt................... $40-50
Mixing bowl, Atlanta line, No. 24, cobalt blue $100
Mixing bowl, nesting-type, Ring-Ware patt., No. 18, chartreuse $75
Mixing bowl, nesting-type, Ring-Ware patt., No. 36, ivory... $55
Mixing bowl, speckled, 1950s, 6" h........... $15-20
Mug, barrel-shaped, Ring-Ware patt., jade green or yellow, each............................... $150
Oil jar, #122, 20" h. $750-100
Oil jar, No. 100, orange, 16" h. $1,000
Oil jar, No. 100, cobalt blue, 22" h. $1,700
Oil jars, No. 100, white, 12" h., pr. $3,000
Pie plate, Ring-Ware patt., green $45
Pitcher, Ring-Ware patt., orange, 1 qt. $85
Pitcher, Ring-Ware patt., delph blue, 2 qt. $200

Bauer "Aladdin Lamp" Teapot

Pitcher, cov., jug-type, ice water, Monterey patt., turquoise **$325**
Pitcher, water, w/ice lip, Monterey patt., green **$125**
Planter, model of a swan, chartreuse, medium **$95**
Plate, chop-type, Ring-Ware, 15" d. **$75-100**
Plate, luncheon-type, Ring-Ware **$20-25**
Plate, 5" d., bread & butter, Ring-Ware patt., green **$15**
Plate, salad, 7 1/2" d., Ring-Ware patt., yellow **$30**
Plate, 9" d., Ring-Ware patt., grey **$65**
Plate, 10 1/2" d., dinner, Ring-Ware patt., cobalt or delph blue, each **$95**
Plate, 10 1/2" d., dinner, Ring-Ware patt., jade green, orange or yellow, each **$85**
Plate, chop, 12" d., Ring-Ware patt., burgundy **$150**
Plate, chop, 12" d., Ring-Ware patt., white **$230**
Plate, chop, 14" d., Ring-Ware patt., yellow **$125**
Plate, chop, Monterey Moderne patt., yellow **$45**
Plate, grill, Monterey Moderne patt., chartreuse **$35**
Plate, luncheon, Ring-Ware patt., yellow **$40**
Punch bowl, Ring-Ware patt., three-footed, cobalt blue, 14" d. **$850**
Punch bowl, Ring-Ware patt., three-footed, jade green, 14" d. **$550**
Punch cup, Ring-Ware patt., delph, cobalt blue, green, yellow or burgundy, each **$35**
Refrigerator set, stacking, Ring-Ware, 4 pcs. **$250-350**
Relish dish, divided, Ring-Ware patt., cobalt blue. **$195**
Salt & pepper shakers, beehive-shaped, Ring-Ware patt., orange/red, pr. **$60**
Salt & pepper shakers, Ring-Ware patt., black, pr. **$85**
Shakers, La Linda patt., old style **$20-25**
Sugar bowl, cov., demitasse, Ring-Ware patt., burgundy **$60**
Sugar bowl, Monterey patt. **$20-25**
Sugar shaker, Ring-Ware patt., jade green... **$350**
Syrup pitcher, Ring-Ware patt., cobalt blue .. **$285**
Teapot, cov., Aladdin Lamp-shape, tan glaze (ILLUS., top of page) **$80-120**
Teapot, cov., Ring-Ware patt., burgundy, 2-cup size **$325**

Teapot, cov., Ring-Ware patt., yellow, 2-cup size **$125**
Teapot, cov., Ring-Ware patt., yellow, 6-cup size **$100-150**
Teapot, Ring-Ware, 6 cup capacity **$100-150**
Teapot, cov., Ring-Ware patt., orangish red, 2-cup size **$125**
Tumbler, Ring-Ware patt., green, large **$45-65**
Tumbler, Ring-Ware patt., delphinium, small **$40**
Vase, 8" h., Billy-type **$50-75**
Vase, 4 1/4" h., bulbous, Fred Johnson Artware line, jade green **$65**
Vase, 8" h., Hi-Fire line, deep trumpet-shaped form w/widely flaring sides fluted on the exterior, yellow **$90**
Vase, 8" h., ovoid base w/widely flared rim, twist shoulder handles, orange, Matt Carlton Artware line **$650**
Vase, 10 1/2" h., cylindrical, Ring-Ware patt., delph blue **$95**
Vase, 13" h., ovoid base w/widely flared rim, twist shoulder handles, jade green, Matt Carlton Artware line **$1,200**
Vase, 24" h., Rebekah, tall slender baluster-form w/loop handles near the short flaring neck, jade green, Matt Carlton Artware line **$2,500**

Belleek

American Belleek
Marks:

American Art China Works - R&E, 1891-95

AAC (superimposed), 1891-95

American Belleek Company - Company name, banner & globe

Ceramic Art Company - CAC palette, 1889-1906

Colombian Art Pottery - CAP, 1893-1902

Cook Pottery - Three feathers w/"CHC," 1894-1904

Coxon Belleek Pottery - "Coxon Belleek" in a shield, 1926-1930

Gordon Belleek - "Gordon Belleek," 1920-28

Knowles, Taylor & Knowles - "Lotusware" in a circle w/a crown, 1891-96

Lenox China - Palette mark, 1906-1924

Ott & Brewer - crown & shield, 1883-1893

Perlee - "P" in a wreath, 1925-1930

Willets Manufacturing Company - Serpent mark, 1880-1909

Cook Pottery - Three feathers w/"CHC"

Baskets and Bowls

Lenox, bowl, 10 1/2" d., 3" h., h.p. Art Deco cameos of tulips accented w/heavy gold, artist-signed "Clara May," dated "22," palette mark $325

Lenox, fernery, h.p. violets on a bowl-shaped base on shell gilded feet, artist palette mark, 7" d., 6" h. $500

Ott and Brewer, basket, applied floral & leaf decoration, crown & sword mark, 6 x 8", 3" h. $600

Ott and Brewer, bowl, h.p. flowers on a cream ground w/gilded thistle handles, crown & sword mark.................................... $500

Ott and Brewer, tazza, hand-decorated w/twig feet & gilt paste ferns, crown, sword & O.B. mark, 8" d............................ $900

Handpainted Bowl with Gilt Trim

Willets, bowl, ovoid form w/small h.p. sprays of flowers over entire outside, gilding on ruffled rim, foot & handles, serpent mark (ILLUS.).................................... $600

Willets, bowl, 6 1/4" d., 5" h., h.p. apple blossoms, leaves & twigs accented w/heavy gold, artist-signed "ES James," serpent mark $650

Willets, bowl, 6 1/2" d., 3" h., handled, h.p. delicate floral sprays, ruffled top trimmed w/gold, gilt shaped handles, serpent mark $425

Ruffled Rim Bowl with Gold Accents

Willets, bowl, 7" d., 3" h., ovoid form h.p. w/decoration of roses, heavy gold accents on ruffled rim, foot & two applied handles, serpent mark (ILLUS.)................ $625

Willets, bowl, fruit, 10" d., 4" h., deep scalloped rim, h.p. inside & out w/images of grapes & foliage, highlighted w/heavy gold $700

Candlesticks and Lamps

Lenox, candlestick lamps, hexagonal inverted tulip shaped shades, h.p. roses joined by green swags & gilding, artist-signed "Trezisc," palette mark, shades 6" d., overall 18" h., pr............................... $560

Lenox, candlesticks, black w/Art Deco-style enameled flowers accented w/raised gold, palette mark, 8 1/4" h., pr................. $225

Cups and Saucers

Ceramic Art Company, cabinet cup, on square footed base, enameled pink & gold saucer, 3 3/4" h. $125

Ceramic Art Company Cabinet Cup

Ceramic Art Company, cabinet cup, no saucer, delicately enameled fretwork on footed base, CAC palette mark, 3 3/4" h. (ILLUS.).. $75

Ceramic Art Company, cup & saucer, "Tridacna" body shape, cream-colored exterior, blue lustre interior w/gold handle & trim, CAC palette mark, saucer 5 1/4" d. $225

Ceramic Art Company, demitasse cup & saucer, decorated w/scenes of elves & pixies inspired by illustrator Palmer Cox, CAC palette mark, saucer 4" d. $750

Coxon Belleek, demitasse cup & saucer, h.p. "Boulevard" patt. gold around the rim of the cup & saucer, saucer 5" d. $125

Lenox, bouillon cup & saucer, cream-colored body w/gold banding around top of cup & saucer, palette mark, saucer 6" d. $125

Cup with Sterling Holder & Saucer

Lenox, demitasse cup & saucer, colored porcelain w/double gold rim & pink border w/enameled flowers, hammered sterling holder & saucer, palette mark, 2 1/2" d. saucer (ILLUS.).. **$95**

Art Deco Silver Overlay Cup, Saucer

Lenox, demitasse cup & saucer, cov., sterling silver overlay of Art Deco design w/orange & green enameling, silver overlay around rim of cup & octagonal saucer, palette mark, 4 1/2" w. saucer (ILLUS.) **$75**

Demitasse Cup & Saucer with Holder

Lenox, demitasse cup & saucer, cream-colored porcelain w/double gold bands, flared rim, sterling saucer & reticulated

holder w/angled handle, palette mark, 2" h. cup, 2 3/4" d. saucer (ILLUS.) **$75**

Lenox, demitasse cup & saucer, filigree sterling silver overlay on two sides of the cup & around the rim of the cup & saucer, palette mark, saucer 1 1/2" d. **$75**

Morgan, cup & saucer, h.p. in the "Orient" patt., urn mark, saucer 5 1/4" d................. **$200**

Morgan, demitasse cup & saucer, w/heavy gold embossed rims & handle, footed cup, 2 3/4" d. x 1 7/8" h. cup **$125**

Ott and Brewer, cup & saucer, "Tridacna" body shape, cream-colored exterior, blue lustre interior w/gold handle & rim, crown & sword mark, saucer 5 1/4" d. **$225**

Willets, bouillon cup & saucer, h.p. flowers w/gold trim, serpent mark, saucer 5 1/2" d. **$225**

Willets, bouillon cup & saucer, "Tridacna" body patt., pearlized pale blue exterior & white interior, serpent mark, 6 1/2" d. saucer **$200**

Pink Luster Bouillon Cup & Saucer

Willets, bouillon cup & saucer, "Tridacna" body patt., pink luster finish interior, cream color exterior w/gold trim & double handles, serpent mark, 3 1/2" d. cup, 5 1/4" d. saucer (ILLUS.) **$200**

Willets, cup & saucer, coffee-size, cream-colored fluted body w/gold handle & trim, serpent mark, saucer 5 1/2" d. **$175**

Willets, demitasse cup & saucer, fluted white body w/purple monogram "W," outlined in gold w/gold-flecked purple dragon-shaped handle, serpent mark, saucer 4" d... **$110**

Jars and Boxes

Ceramic Art Company, box, cov., lid w/ruffled edge, h.p. w/violets & foliage, accented w/gold, CAC palette mark, 1 3/4" h., 3 7/8" w....................................... **$295**

Lidded Dresser Jar

Ceramic Art Company, dresser jar, cov., hand-decorated w/gold paste roses & stripes, CAC palette mark, 3 1/2" d., 5" h. (ILLUS.) **$195**

Knowles, Taylor & Knowles Lotus Ware, rose jar, cov., "Orleans," body & lid w/ornately patterned & pierced overall design **$3,200**

Lenox, condiment jar & cover, tapering hexagonal form w/domed cover, white ground w/blue jewel beading w/gold paste swags, sterling finial, palette mark, 4 1/2" w., 5 1/2" h. **$275**

Morgan Covered Mustard

Morgan, mustard, cov., h.p. cobalt band w/Deco-style enameled basket of fruit on front, gold-colored finial on lid w/opening for spoon, 5" h., 4" d. (ILLUS.) **$150**

Ott and Brewer, cracker jar & cover, hand-decorated w/gold paste flowers & gold handles, sword & crown mark, 5" d., 7" h. **$475**

Ott and Brewer, dresser jar, cov., cylindrical form, h.p. w/illustration of geisha, gold accents on lid, sword & crown mark, 5 1/2" h., 3 1/2" d. (ILLUS., top next column) **$450**

Geisha Dresser Jar

Willets, humidor, cov., h.p. college crest on one side & painting of cigarettes & matches on other, serpent mark, 5 1/2" h., 4 1/4" w. **$375**

Mugs

Ceramic Art Company, Art Deco design w/heavy gold accents, CAC palette mark, 7" h. **$200**

Baluster-form Mug

Ceramic Art Company, baluster-form, h.p. overall w/flowers & foliage on green ground, artist signed, CAC palette mark, 6" h. (ILLUS.) **$175**

Ceramic Art Company, h.p. chrysanthemums & leaves, artist-signed in gold "A.B. Wood," CAC palette mark, 5 1/2" h. .. **$175**

Ceramic Art Company, h.p. design of grapes of various colors & grapevines, accented w/heavy gold on a pink pastel body, artist-signed "KR" & dated 1904, CAC palette mark, 6" h. **$225**

Ceramic Art Company, h.p. peasant women in the Delft style of monochromatic blue on white, CAC palette mark, 5 1/2" h. **$175**

Ceramic Art Company, h.p. scene of children flying kites, artist-signed "CHT," CAC palette mark, 4 3/4" h., 5 1/4" d. **$225**

Mug with Blackberries

Ceramic Art Company, ovoid form w/h.p. blackberries & foliage on pastel pink ground, CAC palette mark, 5" h. (ILLUS.) .. **$175**

Ceramic Art Company, portrait-type, h.p. "Colonial Drinkers," artist-signed by Fred Little, CAC palette mark, 5" h. **$150**

Ceramic Art Company, portrait-type, h.p. portrait of a Native American Chief, CAC palette mark, 6" h. **$1,100**

Ceramic Art Company, portrait-type, h.p. portrait of an old man w/a stein seated at a table, artist-signed "E.D. Westphal," CAC palette mark, 5 3/4" h. **$175**

Stein-type Mug with Grape Design

Ceramic Art Company, stein-type, h.p. all over w/images of grapes & foliage on blue & purple ground, CAC palette mark, 7 1/2" h. (ILLUS.) **$225**

Lenox, h.p. bird decoration, palette mark, 4 1/4" h. **$110**

Lenox, h.p. heavy enameled flowers in the Art Deco style, artist-signed "HRM," palette mark, 7" h. **$150**

Lenox, h.p. off-white & multicolored poppies on a soft cream matte ground accented w/gold & a gold curved handle, palette mark, 7" h. **$150**

Lenox, h.p. w/intense green leaves & berries on a rust & brown ground, palette mark, 5" h. **$125**

Mug with Plum Decoration

Lenox, ovoid shape, w/h.p. Deco-style blue plums & foliage in cream panel around top, lower mug solid green, palette mark, 4 1/2" h. (ILLUS.) **$75**

Rust Mug with Grape Decoration

Willets, cylindrical shape flaring at base, decorated w/h.p. grapes & foliage on a rust ground, serpent mark, 5 1/2" h. (ILLUS.) **$175**

Willets, goblet, toasting-type, "Aforetone," h.p., artist-signed "E.S. Wright," dated "1903," serpent mark, 5" d., 11" h. **$225**

Willets, h.p. blackberries & foliage on a pastel ground, serpent mark, 4 1/2" h. **$125**

Willets Belleek Mug with Monk

Willets, h.p. scene of a monk w/a wine cask, deep maroon base & handle, serpent mark, 6" h. (ILLUS.) **$150**

Orange Mug with Currants

Willets, ovoid form, h.p. orange currants & green leaves on orange ground, serpent mark, 5" h. (ILLUS.) **$125**

Art Nouveau-style Mug

Willets, ovoid form w/Art Nouveau-style h.p. hearts & whiplash decoration in pale lilac, serpent mark, 4" h. (ILLUS.) **$85**

Mug with Handpainted Cherries

Willets, slightly tapering cylindrical form w/panel at base w/raised design, decorated w/cherries, h.p. & marked "D'Arcy's Hand Painted," serpent mark, 5 1/2" h. (ILLUS.)... **$150**

Willets, small h.p. bunches of grapes & foliage all around, heavy gilded handle & rim, serpent mark, 4 1/2" h........................ **$175**

Mug with Rose Swags & Gilding

Willets, tall cylindrical form w/slightly flaring base, applied handle, h.p. rose swags on cream ground, heavy gilding on rim, handle & raised leaf design around base, serpent mark, 5 1/2" h. (ILLUS.) **$175**

Mug with Design of Ripe Plums

Willets, tall cylindrical form w/slightly flaring base, applied handle, h.p. all over w/images of ripe plums & foliage, artist-signed, additional "Darcy's Hand Painted, #6007," serpent mark, 5 1/2" h. (ILLUS.).................. **$200**

Willets Mug with Peaches

Willets, tall, slightly ovoid form w/h.p. decoration of peaches & foliage on deep orange ground, serpent mark, 5 3/4" h. (ILLUS.) **$125**

Artist-signed Mug

Willets, tapering cylindrical form w/gilt handle, h.p. w/grape foliage on lilac band on paler ground, artist signed "M. Schaffer '10," serpent mark, 6" h. (ILLUS.) **$125**

Pitchers, Creamers and Ewers

Ceramic Art Company, cider pitcher, h.p. all around w/large pink roses & leaves, accented w/gold, beaded gold handle, CAC palette mark, 8" h., 6" d., ... **$400**

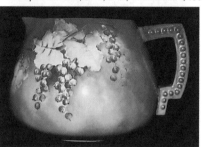

Cider Pitcher with Currants

Ceramic Art Company, cider pitcher, h.p. orange & currants & pale green leaves, 8" h., 6" d., CAC palette mark (ILLUS.)...... **$400**

Ceramic Art Company, creamer, footed swan-form, gold highlights, artist-signed "ES," dated "1903," CAC palette mark, 3 1/2" h.. **$225**

Ceramic Art Company, pitcher, 6 1/2" h., tankard-type, h.p. grapes, leaves & vines on rust ground, heavy gold accents, CAC palette mark **$800**

Water Lily Cider Pitcher

Lenox, cider pitcher, h.p. overall w/water lilies & leaves, artist-signed, 6 1/2" h., palette mark (ILLUS.)...................................... **$450**

Lenox Silver Overlay Creamer

Lenox, creamer, cream-colored body w/swags of silver overlay, 5 1/4" h., palette mark (ILLUS.).. **$75**

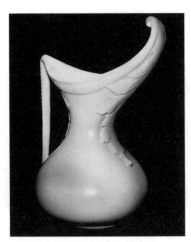

American Belleek Ewer

Lenox, ewer, cream-colored body w/design of flowing colors in yellow, green & mauve, 5 1/2" h., 3 1/2" d., palette mark (ILLUS.)... $295

Lenox, lemonade pitcher, w/h.p. lemons & foliage over entire body, artist-signed, 10 1/2" h., palette mark $450

Lenox, pitcher, 9" h., jug-type, handled, h.p. w/an overall floral design, trimmed in gold, palette mark...................................... $500

Lenox, pitcher, 14" h., tankard-type, h.p. grapes, leaves & vines, embossed handle trimmed in gold, palette mark.............. $650

Ott and Brewer, creamer, cream-colored, hand-decorated w/gold paste foliage & an applied gilded thistle handle, crown & sword mark, 3 1/2" h. $400

Ott and Brewer, ewer, shaped form w/raised gold paste stylized leaf decoration on a matte ground, cactus-shaped handle, crown & sword mark, 8" h., 7 1/2" d.. $1,200

Willets, apple cider pitcher, decorated w/h.p. apples & foliage on purple to pale ground, 6" h.. $550

Willets Creamer

Willets, creamer, thin porcelain w/arched, ruffled spout & forked handle, delicate h.p. pink blossoms & green leaves, 3 1/2" h., 3" d. (ILLUS.)................. $125

Willets, pitcher, 7" h., jug-shaped, h.p. large poppies w/soft gold-accented foliage & handle, artist-signed "A.B. Julia," dated "1910," serpent mark...................... $250

Willets Jug with Cavalier

Willets, pitcher, 8" h., jug-type, handled wide ovoid form w/short neck, h.p. scene of a bearded cavalier seated at a table w/a wine jug & goblet, serpent mark, (ILLUS.)... $500

Willets, pitcher, 10 1/2" h., tankard-type, h.p. fruit decoration all over, artist-signed, serpent mark $750

Willets, pitcher, 11 1/4" h., tankard-type, dragon-handled, h.p. w/wisteria, artist-signed $900

Willets, pitcher, 15" h., tankard-type, h.p. blackberries, leaves & vines on light green matte ground, artist-signed "Fisher," serpent mark...................................... $825

Willets, pitcher, 15" h., tankard-type, h.p. w/berries all around................................. $825

Plates and Platters

Gordon Belleek, plate, 8" d., decorated w/birds, heavy enameling & gold trim $75

Lenox, plate, 7 1/2" d., cream-colored w/sterling silver overlay of festoons of ribbons, silver around outer rim, palette mark $40

Lenox, plate, 7 1/2" d., h.p. medallions surrounded & connected by heavy silver overlay by the Rockwell Silver Company, palette mark... $65

Lenox, plate, 8" d., h.p. w/a few flowers, palette mark... $50

Lenox, platter, 16 1/2" l., Art Deco design w/h.p. border & solid handles w/gold trim, palette mark... $130

Morgan, plate, 10 1/2" d., decorated w/intricate enameled design of fruit, flowers & birds $175

Morgan, plate, 10 5/8" d., Orient, Deco-style h.p. enamel decoration...................... $125

Ott and Brewer, plate, 8 1/2" d., scalloped rim w/h.p. ferns in pink, dark green, mauve & light green, crown & sword mark... $125

Salt Dips

Scalloped-rim Salt Dip

Ceramic Art Pottery, h.p. violets & leaves, scalloped gold rim, CAC palette mark, 1 1/2" d. (ILLUS.) **$50**

Lenox, h.p. w/a soft pink ground & small purple blossoms & green leaves w/gold trim, palette mark, 1 1/4" d., set of 12 .... **$250**

Artist-signed Lenox Salt Dip

Lenox, h.p. w/a stylized band & blossom design, signed by E. Sweeny, palette mark, 1 1/2" d. (ILLUS.) **$35**

Footed Lenox Salt Dip

Lenox, three-footed, lustre body, gold-trimmed feet & scalloped rim, palette mark, 1 1/4" d. (ILLUS.) **$35**

Willets Salt with Lustre Exterior

Willets, pink lustre exterior, cream-colored interior, serpent mark, 2" d. (ILLUS.) **$35**

Footed Willets Salt Dip

Willets, three-footed, lustre exterior w/gold rim & feet, serpent mark, 3" d. (ILLUS.) **$25**

Sets

Lenox, cider set: pitcher & six cups; h.p. red apples, leaves & stems in an overall design, palette mark, cups 5" h., pitcher 6" h., the set **$750**

Lenox, coffee set: pedestal-based cov. coffeepot, cov. sugar & creamer; h.p. flowers in gold shields w/heavy gold accents, artist-signed "Kaufman," palette mark, the set **$1,200**

Lenox, creamer & cov. sugar bowl, pedestal base, urn-form bodies, cream ground w/hand-decorated Art Deco design of enameled beading & gold paste, palette mark, 7" h., pr. (ILLUS., below)................. **$400**

Lenox Creamer & Sugar Bowl

Creamer & Sugar in Sterling Holders

Silver Overlay Creamer & Sugar

Lenox Rose-decorated Tea Set

Lenox, creamer & open sugar, cream color porcelain inserts w/flaring rims in sterling silver reticulated footed holders, palette mark, 3 1/2" h. creamer, 2 1/2" h. sugar, pr. (ILLUS., top of page)............................. **$200**

Lenox, creamer & open sugar, cream color w/silver overlay of flying geese, trees & foliage, palette mark, 3" h., pr. (ILLUS., middle of page) **$225**

Lenox, salt & pepper shakers, h.p. w/small sprays of flowers, palette mark, 2 1/2" h., pr. **$95**

Lenox, tea set: cov. teapot, cov. sugar bowl & creamer; each w/a pedestal base & square foot, boat-shaped body w/angled handle, h.p. w/pink roses & blue blossoms w/green leaves, gold handles & finial, palette mark, teapot 11" l., the set (ILLUS., third set of photos)..................................... **$950**

Vases

Ceramic Art Chrysanthemums Vase

Ceramic Art Company, 7 1/2" h., ovoid body w/short neck & flared rim, h.p. chrysanthemums on a light green matte ground w/gold trim & gold on neck & neck rim, artist-signed "DeLan," CAC palette mark (ILLUS.) **$625**

Vase with Jonquil Decoration

Ceramic Art Company, 8 1/4" h., cylindrical body tapering to small 4 1/2" top opening, h.p. w/large yellow jonquils & leaves all around, on a pale blue ground, some gold highlights, CAC palette mark (ILLUS.) **$975**

Ceramic Art Company, 10" h., w/h.p. roses & gold embellishments, CAC palette mark **$700**

Ceramic Art Company, 10 1/2" h., ovoid body w/narrow waisted neck opening to flaring rim, h.p. w/large pink roses on a lavender ground, high glaze, CAC palette mark **$800**

Ceramic Art Company, 10 1/2" h., pearshaped body w/short neck opening w/slightly flaring rim, h.p. w/large pink roses on a green ground, high glaze, CAC palette mark **$800**

Artist-signed Vase with Flowers

Ceramic Art Company, 13" h., ovoid body w/short narrow neck & flaring rim, decorated w/h.p. orange flowers & green leaves on pale green & cream ground, artist-signed, CAC palette mark (ILLUS.) **$900**

Ceramic Art Company, 16" h., 7" d., portrait-type, cylindrical, h.p. Art Nouveaustyle standing woman w/flowing hair, CAC palette mark **$1,400**

Ceramic Art Company, 17" h., w/h.p. wisteria decoration, artist-signed, CAC palette mark **$1,200**

Knowles, Taylor and Knowles Lotus Ware, 8" h., 5" d., front h.p. w/a scene of a Victorian woman standing by a beehive looking up at two flying cherubs, the back w/a bouquet of flowers, applied "fishnet" work on body **$1,400**

Lenox, 9" h., hexagonal shape, Art Deco style design, a pale blue paneled rim w/stylized rose sprays, palette mark, ... **$275**

Basket-style Lenox Vase

Lenox, basket-style, w/scalloped rim & foot, h.p. w/Deco-style baskets of flowers & gold highlights on white ground, palette mark (ILLUS., previous page) **$125**

Early Lenox Urn-shaped Vase

Lenox, 8" h., urn-shaped on a flaring pedestal & square foot, swan's-neck handles, white ground h.p. w/a central floral medallion on the front & back, early wreath mark (ILLUS.).. **$200**

Lenox, 8" h., 3" d., h.p. flowers w/fine gilding, signed "Valborg, 1905," fluted top w/attached handle to side of tilted bowl, palette mark **$650**

Lenox, 8" h., 5" d., bulbous body, h.p. floral decoration in mint condition, palette mark .. **$510**

Lenox, 9 1/2" h., 3" d., cylindrical, h.p. bird on branch w/flowers, palette mark **$450**

Lenox, 10 1/4" h., ovoid body tapering to short, wide, flared neck, h.p. decoration of open roses, leaves & petals on mauve matte ground, palette mark **$550**

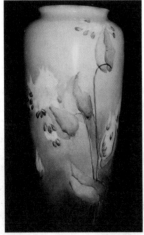

Lenox Vase with Blossom Seeds

Lenox, 10 1/4" h., tapering cylindrical body w/a short wide flared neck, h.p. w/open

seed pods w/white & brown seeds & green leaves, shaded brown to cream ground, palette mark (ILLUS.)................... **$575**

Lenox, 10 1/4" h., 3" d., cylindrical, decorated w/a stylized bird highlighted in gold, artist-signed "E.R. Martin," palette mark **$325**

Lenox, 11 1/2" h., 5 1/2" d., impressionistic h.p. decoration w/gold trim, palette mark **$400**

Lenox, 12 1/2" h., ovoid body tapering to a short flared neck, h.p. w/large chrysanthemums w/soft gold highlights, palette mark.. **$625**

Lenox Vase with Landscape Band

Lenox, 13" h., cylindrical w/slightly incurved rim, a wide rim band h.p. w/a stylized country landscape & gold border, the lower body w/a pale ground h.p. overall w/diamond devices, palette mark (ILLUS.)........ **$525**

Lenox, 15 1/2" h., cylindrical, h.p. Oriental women, trees & foliage, palette mark......... **$350**

Lenox, 18 1/2" h., decorated w/h.p. roses accented w/gold, heavily gilded shaped handles, palette mark............................. **$2,500**

Willets Gourd-style Vase

Willets, 7" h., gourd-type, w/h.p. flowers & foliage on white ground, serpent mark (ILLUS.)... **$325**

Willets Vase with a Tiger

Willets, 9" h., 4" d., baluster-form w/flared foot & rim, dark green ground decorated w/a h.p. tiger on one side, serpent mark (ILLUS.).. **$900**
Willets, 10" h., bulbous form w/all over floral decoration, artist-signed, dated 1905, serpent mark... **$1,200**
Willets, 10" h., 3" d., cylindrical, h.p. design of three Japanese women in kimonos on a pale green ground, serpent mark............ **$450**
Willets, 10" h., 8" d., bulbous body w/a short pinched neck & fluted rim, h.p. overall w/large pastel roses & foliage, serpent mark **$500**

Willets Vase with Birds & Wisteria

Willets, 10 1/2" h., 6" d., ovoid form w/h.p. decoration of birds & wisteria, serpent mark (ILLUS.)...................................... **$800**

Willets, 10 1/2" h., 6" d., h.p. Pickard decoration of a full-length Art Nouveau woman w/flowing hair & gown on a pink lustre ground, serpent mark............................. **$1,400**
Willets, 11" h., h.p. chrysanthemums accented w/gold on white ground, serpent mark... **$665**
Willets, 11" h., 6 1/2" d., bulbous shape w/a short, small neck w/fluted rim, h.p. w/flowers & heavy gold paste accents, serpent mark... **$900**
Willets, 11 1/2" h., cylindrical, h.p. w/large roses of different shades of pink w/green leaves & gold trim, serpent mark **$625**
Willets, 12" h., tapering from a small top to a flared bottom, h.p. clusters of roses, artist-signed "M.A. Minor - 1902," serpent mark **$1,200**
Willets, 13" h., 6" d., bulbous form w/a short flared neck, h.p. overall w/pink, red & white roses w/soft gold highlights, serpent mark... **$1,400**
Willets, 13" h., 9" d., bulbous shape w/a short pinched neck w/fluted rim, h.p. overall w/pink, red & white roses, serpent mark... **$1,500**
Willets, 13 3/4" h., 8" d., undecorated, urn-shaped w/curved applied handles, serpent mark... **$125**
Willets, 15 1/2" h., waisted cylindrical form, h.p. overall w/hyacinths w/gold accents, artist-signed "E. Miler," serpent mark... **$900**
Willets, 15 1/2" h., 3" d., h.p. large flowers, artist-signed "J. Brauer," serpent mark **$900**
Willets, 15 1/2" h., 4" d., cylindrical w/flared bottom & flared scalloped top, h.p. completely w/pink & red roses on a soft pastel pink ground, serpent mark **$1,200**

Miscellaneous
Ceramic Art Company, loving cup, h.p. images of grapes & foliage, gilded rim, base & handles, topped w/figural children's heads, serpent mark, 8 1/4" h., 6 1/4" d.
.... **$2,000**
Knowles, Taylor & Knowles Lotus Ware rose bowl, 5" d., 6" h., "Columbia," raised cameo-style flowers w/gold branching ornamentation **$760**
Knowles, Taylor & Knowles Lotus Ware rose bowl, 7" d., 7 1/2" h., cov., h.p. ornately patterned pierced cover & handles, applied gilded roses & "jewels"....... **$2,500**

Lenox Teapot with Roses Decoration

Lenox, teapot, cov., pedestal base on square foot, boat-shaped body w/angled handle, h.p. sprays of pink & white roses w/green leaves, gold band trim, palette mark, 10" l., 8" h. (ILLUS., previous page) **$300**

Lenox, ice bucket, h.p. w/Deco-style basket of flowers, palette mark, 5 1/2" h., 6 1/4" w. **$225**

Lenox, toothpick holder, h.p. ravens sitting on pine branches, straight sides, palette mark, 2 1/4" h. **$150**

Willets, chalice, decorated overall w/white dogwood blossoms & foliage ona darker green ground, serpent mark, 11" h. **$575**

Willets, dresser tray, thin ruffled rim, h.p. sprays of cosmos, serpent mark, 8 x 11" ... **$495**

Willets, jardiniere, overall h.p. forest scene, serpent mark, 8" d., 6 1/2" h. **$600**

Three-handled Loving Cup

Willets, loving cup, three-handled ovoid form on pedestal base, decorated w/h.p. chrysanthemums & foliage in teal on white ground, serpent mark, 5 1/2" d., 8" h. (ILLUS.) **$125**

Willets Sherbet in Holder

Willets, sherbet, porcelain insert in sterling silver reticulated holder w/pedestal base, serpent mark, 3 1/2" d., 3 3/4" h. (ILLUS.)..... **$75**

Irish Belleek

Belleek china has been made in Ireland's County Fermanagh for many years. It is exceedingly thin porcelain. Several marks were used, including a hound and harp (1865-1880), and a hound, harp and castle (1863-1891). A printed hound, harp and castle with the words "Co. Fermanagh Ireland" constitutes the mark from 1891. The earliest marks were printed in black followed by those printed in green. In recent years the marks appear in gold.

The item identification for the following listing follows that used in Richard K. Degenhardt's reference "Belleek - The Complete Collector's Guide and Illustrated Reference," first and second editions. The Degenhardt illustration number (D...) appears at the end of each listing. This number will be followed in most cases by a Roman numeral "I" to indicate a first period black mark while the Roman numeral "II" will indicate a second period black mark. In the "Baskets" section an Arabic number "1" indicates an impressed ribbon mark with "Belleek" while the numeral "2" indicates the impressed ribbon with the words "Belleek - Co. Fermanagh." Both these marks were used in the first period, 1865-1891. Unless otherwise noted, all pieces here will carry the black mark. A thorough discussion of the early Belleek marks is found in this book as well as at the Web site: http://members.aol.com/delyicious/index.html.

Prices for items currently in production may also be located at this site, especially via the 1983 Suggested Retail Price List. Prices given here are for pieces in excellent or mint condition with no chips, cracks, crazing or repairs, although, on flowered items, minimal chips to the flowers is acceptable to the extent of the purchaser's tolerance. Earthenware pieces often exhibit varying degrees of crazing due to the primitive bottle kilns originally used at the pottery.

Basket Ware

Basket, cov., oval, small size (D114-I)........ **$6,000**
Basket, four-lobed form w/widely flared rims, D1693-1 (ILLUS., top next page) **$3,000**

Large Henshall's Twig Basket

Basket, Henshall's Twig Basket, large size, D120-1 (ILLUS.)..................................... **$4,200**

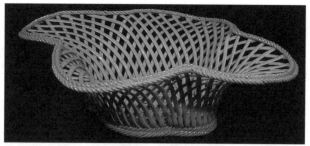

Four-lobed Belleek Basket

Basket, round, center arched handle, flattened rim w/applied colored blossoms, flat rod, D1274-1 (ILLUS.) **$6,200**

Belleek Melvin Basket

Basket, Melvin Basket, painted blossoms, D1690-5 (ILLUS.) **$800**

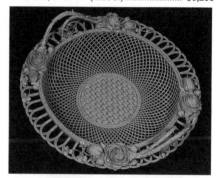

Large Sydenham Twig Basket

Basket, Shamrock basket, three different flowers around the rim, small size, D109-1, each (ILLUS. of two, bottom of page) **$520**

Basket, Sydenham Twig Basket, large size, D108-1 (ILLUS.) **$4,400**

Box, cov., Forget-Me-Not trinket box, flower blossoms on the cover (D111-III) **$600**

Brooch, flowered (D1525-II) **$400**

Round Belleek Handled Basket

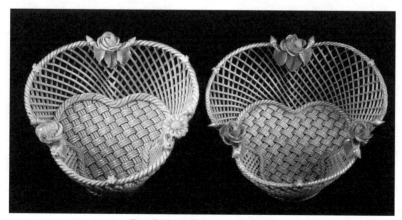

Two Belleek Shamrock Baskets

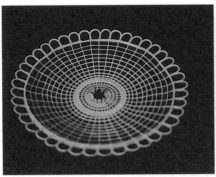

Two Views of the Rare Spider's Web Cake Plate

Cake plate, Spider's Web cake plate, D1279-3 (ILLUS. of plate & close-up of spider, top of page) **$5,400**

Flower bouquet, hand-formed in green ware, features samples of all flower styles used on Belleek wares, mounted in a shadowbox frame, marked with two ribbons & "Belleek (R) Co. Fermanagh," ca. 1955-79 .... **$2,200**

Woven Flowered Jewel Stand

Jewel stand, Woven Flowered Jewel Stand, D1575-II (ILLUS.) **$1,400**

Menu holder, decorated w/applied flowers, various designs, D275-II, each **$600**

Comports & Centerpieces

Very Rare Belleek Frame

Frame, photo or mirror, oblong w/two oval picture openings, ornately applied w/flowers overall, D66-II (ILLUS.) **$6,200**

Unique Belleek Woven Mirror Frame

Frame, woven mirror frame, oval, unique, Second Period Mark II (ILLUS.) **$5,000**

Cherub Candelabra

Candelabra, Cherub Candelabra, w/drip cups, D341-II (ILLUS.) **$6,000**

Bird Nest Stump Vase-Centerpiece

Centerpiece, Bird Nest Stump Vase, w/eggs in nest, D57-II (ILLUS.) **$3,200**

Rare Belleek Bittern Comport

Comport, Bittern Comport, figural tall birds form pedestal, gilt trim, D6-II (ILLUS.)... **$10,000**

Boy on Swan Figural Comport

Comport, Boy on Swan Comport, beetle flys on base, D33-I (ILLUS.) **$10,000**

Belleek Thorn Comport & Top View

Comport, Thorn Comport, D36-II, 4 1/2" h. (ILLUS. of two views) **$1,400**

Belleek Tri Dolphin & Shell Comport

Comport, Tri Dolphin & Shell Pedestal Comport, painted, D1149-I (ILLUS.) **$4,200**

Earthenware

Earthenware Bowl with Inscription

Bowl, deep sides, Celtic inscription that translates "Friendship is Better than Gold," D857-II (ILLUS.) **$400**

Chamber Pot with Gladstone

Chamber pot, printed portrait of William Gladstone on the inside bottom, D2082-I (ILLUS., previous page) **$1,600**
Jelly mold, deep slightly flaring rounded sides, design on the interior (D880-I) **$460**
Mug, cylindrical, scenic transfer-printed decoration (D858-II) **$360**

Belleek Earthenware Decorated Trviet

Trivet, round, decal & hand-painted decoration, D1057-I (ILLUS.) **$800**

Transfer-printed Belleek Plate

Plate, 10" d., black transfer-printed pottery scene in the center, a crest on the flanged rim, D887-I (ILLUS.) **$400**

Hand-painted Earthenware Trivete

Trivet, round, h.p. w/lily-of-the-valley, D1057-I (ILLUS.) **$1,000**

Belleek Earthenware Serving Dish

Serving dish, open, oval, embossed end handles, pedestal base, D915-II (ILLUS.) **$400**
Toothbrush tray, cov., found w/various transfer-printed designs (D932-I) **$440**

Figurines

Belgian Hawkers Figurines

Belgian Hawker, female, fully-decorated, D15-II (ILLUS. right) **$3,000**
Belgian Hawker, male, fully-decorated, D21-II (ILLUS. left) **$3,000**

Floral-decorated Earthenware Tray

Tray, oval, brown transfer-printed floral design, D900-I (ILLUS.) **$400**

Belleek Bust of Clytie

Bust of Clytie, low pedestal base, D14-II (ILLUS.) **$2,200**

Bust & Figure of Lesbie

Bust of Lesbie, trimmed w/flowers & highlighted w/colors, D1651-I (ILLUS. right) .. **$3,600**

Shepherd & Dog Candleholder

Candleholder, figure of a sleeping shepherd & his dog on the rounded base, ring handle, green tint & gilt trim, D1603-I (ILLUS.) **$4,000**

Boy & Girl Figural Candlesticks

Candlestick, boy w/basket on shoulder, fully decorated & pierced, D1126-I (ILLUS. left) **$3,200**
Candlestick, girl w/basket on her shoulder, fully-decorated & pierced, D1137-I (ILLUS. right with Boy candlestick) **$3,200**

Figures of Affection & Meditation

Figure of Affection, fully-decorated, D1134-I (ILLUS. left) **$3,400**

Belleek Figure of a Cavalier

Figure of Cavalier, standing, D22-II
(ILLUS., previous page) **$3,400**

Rare Belleek Crouching Venus Figure

Figure of Crouching Venus, gilt highlights,
D16-I (ILLUS.) **$10,000**

Rare Belleek Figure of Erin

Figure of Erin, standing figure by well, D1-I
(ILLUS.) **$10,000**
Figure of Lesbie, standing, highlighted
w/colors, D1656-I (ILLUS. left with bust of
Lesbie) **$3,600**
Figure of Meditation, fully-decorated, D20-
I (ILLUS. right with Affection) **$3,400**
Model of Horse & Snake, D1139-II **$12,000**

Religious Items & Lithophanes
Figure of the Blessed Virgin Mary, large
size (D1106-II) **$1,800**

Belleek Cherub Head Water Font

Holy water font, Cherub head w/spread
wings, D1110-VI (ILLUS.) **$100**
Holy water font, Coral & Shell (D1111-V) **$100**

Sacred Heart Holy Water Font #4

Holy water font, Sacred Heart font, #4,
D1115-III (ILLUS.) **$260**
Holy water font, Sacred Heart font, #8
(D1114-II) **$320**
Lithophane, Madonna, Child & Angel
(D1544-III) **$3,200**
Lithophane, Madonna, Child & Angel
(D1544-VII) **$600**

Child Looking in Mirror Lithophane

Lithophane, round, child looking in mirror,
D1539-VII (ILLUS.) **$480**

Tea Ware - Common Patterns (Harp, Shamrock, Limpet, Hexagon, Neptune, Shamrock & Tridacna)

Harp Shamrock Butter Plate

Harp Shamrock butter plate, D1356-III
(ILLUS.) **$200**

Belleek Hexagon Breakfast Set

Harp Shamrock Plate for Butter

Harp Shamrock butter plate, D1356-VI (ILLUS.).. **$100**

Belleek Harp Shamrock Teakettle

Harp Shamrock teakettle, overhead handle, large size, gilt trim, D1359-III (ILLUS.) .. **$660**

Hexagon breakfast set: small cov. teapot, open sugar & creamer, two plates & two cups & saucers, h.p. floral decoration, no tray, D396-II (ILLUS., top of page) **$3,200**

Hexagon Pattern Belleek Teapot

Hexagon teapot, cov., large size, D407-II (ILLUS.).. **$600**

Shamrock Souvenir Mug

Mug, cylindrical, Shamrock, souvenir-type, h.p. Irish scene, D216-II (ILLUS.)...... **$300**

Neptune biscuit jar, cov. (D531-II) **$460**

Neptune creamer & open sugar bowl, green tint, pr. (D416-II & D417-II) **$400**

Neptune Pattern Cup & Saucer

Neptune teacup & saucer, green tint, D414-II (ILLUS.).. **$240**

Neptune teapot, cov., medium size, green tint (D415-II).. **$480**

Neptune tray, green tint (D418-II) **$1,200**

Shamrock bread plate, round w/loop handles (D379-III) **$180**

Shamrock egg cup, footed (D389-II) **$120**

Shamrock Marmalades & Mustard

Shamrock marmalade jar, cov., barrrel-shaped, D1561-IV (ILLUS. right with marmalde & mustard)................................. **$100**

Shamrock marmalade jar, cov., cup marmalade, D1323-III (ILLUS. center with mustard & marmalade)............................. **$100**

Shamrock mug, large size, D216-II (ILLUS. right, bottom of page)................................ **$120**

Shamrock mug, Name Mug, impressed reserve for name, small size, D216-II (ILLUS. left, bottom of page)..................... **$140**

Shamrock mustard jar, cov., footed spherical form, D298-III (ILLUS. left with marmalades, top of page) **$100**

Shamrock pitcher, milk, jug-form (D390-II) **$320**

Shamrock teacup & saucer, low shape, D366-III (ILLUS., next column)................... **$160**

Shamrock Low-Shape Cup & Saucer

Shamrock Large & Name Mugs

Tridacna Boat-shaped Creamer

Tridacna creamer, boat-shaped, D247-VI
(ILLUS.).. **$60**

Large Tridacna Gilt-trimmed Sugar

Tridacna sugar bowl, open, gilt-trimmed,
large size, D472-I (ILLUS.)......................... **$440**

Tea Ware - Desirable Patterns (Echinus, Limpet (footed), Grass, Hexagon, Holly, Mask, New Shell & Shell)

Echinus creamer & open sugar bowl,
decorated (D647-I & D648-I), pr.............. **$1,000**
Echinus cup & saucer, egg shell, crested
(D358-I).. **$500**
Echinus egg cup, footed (D666-I)................. **$400**
Echinus teapot, cov., pink tint w/gold trim,
small size (D659-I) **$900**
Grass coffeepot, cov., large size (D1402-I)
.... **$1,600**
Grass creamer & covered sugar bowl,
middle size, D748 & D748-I, pr. **$800**

Grass Egg Cup with Crest

Grass egg cup, footed, crested decoration,
D754-I (ILLUS.)... **$600**
Grass honey pot, cover & stand, model of
a beehive on a low table-form base, the
set (D755-I).. **$1,000**
Grass mustache cup & saucer (D739-I)...... **$620**
Grass teakettle, cov., large size, D751-I
(ILLUS. at right with teapot & tray).......... **$1,000**

Grass Teapot, Kettle & Tray

Grass teapot, cov., small size, D750-I
(ILLUS. left with kettle & tray) **$800**
Grass tray, round, D736-I (ILLUS. with tea-
pot & teakettle)....................................... **$2,000**
Mask powder bowl, small size, D1548-III..... **$160**

Tea Ware - Museum Display Patterns (Artichoke, Chinese, Finner, Five O'Clock, Lace, Ring Handle Ivory, Set #36 & Victoria)

Bone china bread plate, heavy pink
ground & gilt trim, D844-I (ILLUS. left with
teacup & saucer, top next page).............. **$680**
Bone china teacup & saucer, heavy pink
ground & gilt trim, D848-I (ILLUS. right
with bread plate, top next page)............... **$620**
**Chinese creamer w/dragon head spout &
open sugar bowl,** decorated (D485-I &
D486-I), pr.. **$1,400**
Chinese tea urn, figural cover, ornate
winged dragon spout, twisted rope-form
overhead handle, large winged dragon
support on round base w/paw feet, deco-
rated (D482-I)... **$18,000**

Chinese Pattern Teacup & Saucer

Chinese teacup & saucer, decorated,
D483-I (ILLUS.)... **$800**
Chinese teapot, cov., small size, decorated
(D484-I).. **$2,000**

Bone Cchina Bread Plate & Teacup and Saucer

Tea Ware - Museum Display Patterns (Artichoke, Chinese, Finner, Five O'Clock, Lace, Ring Handle Ivory, Set #36 & Victoria)

Lace Pattern Belleek Teapot

Lace teapot, cov., medium size, D800-II (ILLUS.)... **$1,000**
Lace tray, round, decorated (D803-I) **$6,000**
Ring Handle bread plate, Limoges decoration (D824-I) **$1,400**

Tea Ware - Rare Patterns (Aberdeen, Blarney, Celtic (low & tall), Cone, Erne, Fan, Institute, Ivy, Lily (high & low), Scroll, Sydney, Thistle & Thorn)

Aberdeen breakfast set: cov. teapot, creamer, open sugar & cups & saucers; no tray, D494-II (ILLUS., below) **$2,200**

Belleek Aberdeen Pattern Breakfast Tea Set

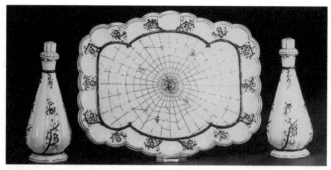

Thorn Brush Tray & Scent Bottles

Celtic Fruit Dish & Vases

Celtic fruit dish, round, D1512-II (ILLUS.
center with Celtic Vases)......................... **$1,200**
Celtic teacup & saucer, low shape, painted
(D1456-III & D1457-III)............................. **$400**
Cone teacup & saucer, pink tint (D432-II) **$440**

Fern Pattern Teacup & Saucer

Fan teacup & saucer, decorated, D694-II
(ILLUS.).. **$600**
Institute plate, 6" d., pink tint (D724-I) **$160**

Institute Decorated Sugar Bowl

Institute sugar bowl, cov., decorated,
D728-I (ILLUS.).. **$600**
Thorn brush tray & scent bottles, tur-
quoise & gilt decoration, D333-I & D335-
I (ILLUS., top of page)............................. **$2,200**
Thorn creamer & open sugar bowl, small
size (D760-I & D761-I), pr. **$1,000**
Thorn teapot, cov., small size, decorated
(D759-I).. **$800**
Thorn tray, oval, decorated (D762-I) **$2,600**

Tea Wares - General

Low Lily Tea Set with Green Tint & Gold Trim

Another Version of the Rare Chinese Tea Urn

Tea set: cov. teapot, open sugar & creamer & two cups & saucers; Low Lily patt., green tint w/gold trim, 2nd period, creamer & open sugar, $400-500; cup & saucer, $260-320; teapot only (ILLUS. of set, bottom of previous page) **$700-800**

Tea urn, Chinese (Dragon) patt., fancy dark pink, black & heavy gold trim, 17" h., 1st period (ILLUS., top of page)...... **$18,000-25,000**

Extremely Rare Decorated Chinese Pattern Tall Tea Urn

Tea urn, Chinese (Dragon) patt., fancy pale pink, black & heavy gold trim, 17" h., 1st period (ILLUS.)
.... **$18,000-25,000**

Grass Pattern Teakettle with Multicolored Decoration

Teakettle, Grass patt., multicolored decoration w/gold, 1st period (ILLUS.)........ **$600-1,000**

Gold-trimmed Ringhandle Teakettle

Teakettle, Ringhandle patt., undecorated except gold trim, 3rd period (ILLUS.) **$1,000-1,400**

Aberdeen Pattern Teapot with Cob Decoration

Teapot, Aberdeen patt., Cob decoration, 2nd period (ILLUS.)............................ **$700-800**

Decorated Artichoke Pattern Teapot

Teapot, Artichoke patt., green decoration w/gold trim, 1st period (ILLUS.) **$800-1,000**
Teapot, Bamboo patt., undecorated, 1st period(ILLUS. right with decorated Echinus teapot) **$800-1,000**

Blarney Pattern Teapot with Green Tint & Gold Trim

Teapot, Blarney patt., green tint & gold trim, 2nd period (ILLUS.)............................. **$700-800**

Rare Chinese Pattern Decorated Teapot

Teapot, Chinese (Dragon) patt., multicolored decoration with gold, 1st period (ILLUS.) **$1,600-2,800**

A Decorated Echinus and Undecorated Bamboo Teapot

Cone Pattern Teapot with Orange Tint & Gold Trim

Teapot, Cone patt., orange tint & gold trim, 2nd period (ILLUS.)............................ **$600-800**

Teapot, Echinus patt., footed, blue & pink decoration w/gold trim, 1st period (ILLUS. left with Bamboo teapot, top of page) **$800-1,200**

Early Echinus Teapot with Pink Tint & Gold Trim

Teapot, Echinus patt., footed, pink tint & gold trim, 1st period (ILLUS.).............. **$700-800**

Teapot, Fan patt., pink tint & gold trim, 2nd period (ILLUS., bottom of page)....... **$600-1,000**

Fan Pattern Teapot with Pink Tint & Gold Trim

Multicolored Finner Pattern Teapot

Teapot, Finner patt., multicolored decoration, 2nd period (ILLUS.) **$1,000-1,400**

5 O'Clock Pattern Teapot with Green Decoration

Teapot, (Five) 5 O'Clock patt., green decoration, note the unique "5 O'clock-shaped" handle (ILLUS.) **$1,200-2,000**

Grass Pattern Teapot with Color Decoration

Teapot, Grass patt., multicolored decoration, 1st period (ILLUS.) **$600-800**

High Lily Teapot with Green Tint

Teapot, High Lily patt., green tint, 2nd period (ILLUS.) **$700-800**

Lace Pattern Teapot with Chocolate & Gold Decoration

Teapot, Lace patt., chocolate decoration & gold trim, 2nd period (ILLUS.) **$1,000-1,400**

Early Undecorated Lace Pattern Teapot

Teapot, Lace patt., undecorated, 1st period (ILLUS.) **$800-900**

Limpet Footed Pink Tint 2nd Period Teapot

Teapot, Limpet patt., footed, pink tint, 2nd period (ILLUS.) **$600-800**
Teapot, Limpet patt., pink tint w/gold trim, 3rd period **$300-400**

Limpet Shape Irish Belleek Teapot

Teapot, Limpet shape, coral-form handle & finial, ca. 1927-41 (ILLUS., previous page) .. **$300**

Low Celtic Pink Tint Teapot

Teapot, Low Celtic patt., pink tint, 3rd period (ILLUS.).. **$800-1,200**

Undecorated Mask Pattern Teapot

Teapot, Mask patt., undecorated, 3rd period (ILLUS.).. **$400-500**

Neptune Pattern Teapot with Pink Tint

Teapot, Neptune patt., pink tint, 2nd period (ILLUS.).. **$400-600**

Ringhandle Teapot with Celtic Decoration

Teapot, Ringhandle patt., Celtic decoration, 3rd period (ILLUS.)........................... **$800-1,000**

Shamrock-Basketweave Teapot with Standard Decoration

Teapot, Shamrock-Basketweave patt., standard decoration, 3rd period (ILLUS.) **$400-500**

Shell Pattern Teapot with Pink & Gold Decoration

Teapot, Shell patt., footed, pink & gold decoration, 1st period (ILLUS.).............. **$800-1,000**

Sydney Pattern Teapot with Pink Tint

Teapot, Sydney patt., pink tint, 2nd period (ILLUS.).. **$600-800**

Early Undecorated Thistle Pattern Teapot

Teapot, Thistle patt., undecorated, 1st period (ILLUS.)...................................... **$600-800**

Gold-trimmed Thorn Pattern Teapot

Teapot, Thorn patt., gold trim, 1st period
(ILLUS.)... **$600-1,000**

Early Tridacna Teapot with Gold Trim

Teapot, Tridacna patt., gold trim, 1st period
(ILLUS.).. **$400-600**

Vases & Spills

Aberdeen vases, left & right, flowered, medium size (D58-II), pr............................. **$1,600**
Celtic Vase-J, D1199-III, each (ILLUS. left & right with Celtic fruit dish)....................... **$460**

Belleek Coral and Shell Vase

Coral and Shell Vase, D133-II (ILLUS.)........ **$880**
Daisy spill, D178-III (ILLUS. right with Shamrock spills, top next page)................ **$220**

Irish Belleek Double Fish Vase

Double Fish vase, painted, D1204-I, 11 1/2" h. (ILLUS.) **$2,400**

Belleek Flowered Spill

Flowered Spill, raised on twig feet, large size, D45-III (ILLUS.) **$380**

Clam Shell & Griffin Belleek Vase

Clam Shell & Griffin vase, pink tint, D140-I (ILLUS.).. **$2,200**

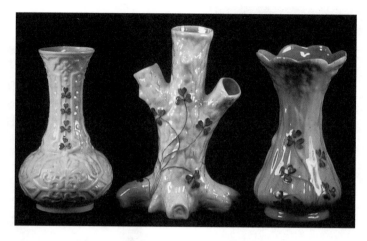

Daisy & Shamrock Spills

Belleek Figural Frog Vase

Frog vase, model of frog w/head up & mouth open, large size, D181-II (ILLUS.) **$1,000**
Ivy Stump spill (D147-I) **$420**

Marine Jug Vase, coral designs, ruffled foot, D134-II (ILLUS.)................................. **$800**
Prince Arthur Vase, flowered (D1218-II) **$920**

Belleek Ram's Head Flower Holder

Ram's Head Flower Holder, figural, D1180-I (ILLUS.).................................... **$1,400**

Belleek Rathmore Flowerpot

Rathmore flowerpot, bulbous w/flaring scalloped rim & applied flowers, D43-II (ILLUS.).. **$2,200**

Belleek Marine Jug Vase

Belleek Ribbon Vase

Ribbon Vase, flowered, D1220-III (ILLUS.) ... **$340**

Seahorse and Shell Flower Holder

Seahorse and Shell flower holder, rectangular base, D129-I (ILLUS.) **$1,200**
Shamrock spill, D191-III (ILLUS. left with Daisy spill) **$220**
Shamrock Tree Stump spill, D1224-III (ILLUS. center with Daisy spill) **$240**

Irish Belleek Specimen Holder

Specimen holder, composed of small ball-shaped vases, large size, D185-I, 5 1/2" h. (ILLUS.) **$1,200**
Triple Fish Vase, painted (D1231-I) **$4,600**

Belleek Typha Jug Spill

Typha Jug Spill, decorated w/shamrocks, D1790-VI (ILLUS.) **$120**

Tea Wares - Miscellaneous
Items produced, but with NO matching tea set pieces.

Cardium on Shell dish, Size 2, pink tint, D261-I (ILLUS. center with Sycamore & Worcester plates, top next page) **$180**
Cleary salt dip, oblong, pink tint & gilt trim (D295-II) **$100**

Decorated Belleek Flask

Flask, ovoid form, gilt Harp, Hound & Castle logo at the center in gold, D1523-I (ILLUS.) **$2,200**

Cadmium on Shell Dish & Sycamore and Worcester Plates

Greek Dessert Plate with Scene

Greek dessert plate, tinted & gilt-trimmed, h.p. center scene titled "Eel Fishery on the Erne," by E. Sheerin, D29-I (ILLUS.)... **$3,600**

Flower-decorated Heart Plate

Heart plate, scalloped edges, Size 2, h.p. flowers, D635-III (ILLUS.)........................... **$120**

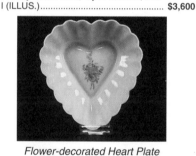

Irish Pot Creamer & Open Sugar Bowl

Irish Pot creamer & open sugar bowl, Size 2, D232-II, pr. (ILLUS.)...................... **$240**

Armorial Souvenir Loving Cup

Loving cup, three-handled, armorial souvenir, D1503-I (ILLUS.)................................ **$400**

Model of Irish Harp

Model of Irish Harp, small size, D77-II (ILLUS.) **$400**

Bowl-shaped Shell Plateau

Ring Handle plate, 6" d., Limoges Decoration, D822-I (ILLUS.) **$600**
Shell creamer, large size (D601-I) **$720**

Shell-shaped Nautilus Creamer

Nautilus creamer, shell-shaped, pink tint, D279-I (ILLUS.) **$600**

Belleek Oblong Shell Jelly

Shell jelly, oblong, painted, D798-I (ILLUS.) **$520**
Shell plateau, bowl-shaped, medium size, D792-I (ILLUS., top of page) **$380**
Swan creamer, figural, large size, D254-III (ILLUS. left, bottom of page) **$320**
Swan creamer, figural, large size, D254-VI (ILLUS. right, bottom of page) **$120**
Sycamore plate, leaf-shaped, Size 2, pink tint, D642-II (ILLUS. right with Cardium on Shell dish, top of page 101) **$120**
Toy creamer & open sugar bowl, Cleary patt. (D249-III), pr. **$160**
Toy creamer & open sugar bowl, Ivy patt., small size (D241-I), pr. **$240**
Triple Shell menu holder, D535-II (ILLUS., top next page) **$400**
Worcester plate, Size 2, D682-II (ILLUS. left with Cardium on Shell dish, top of page 101) **$120**

Ring Handle Decorated Plate

Two Large Swan Creamers

Belleek Triple Shell Menu Holder

Bennington

Bennington wares, which ranged from stoneware to parian and porcelain, were made in Bennington, Vermont, primarily in two potteries, one in which Captain John Norton and his descendants were principals, and the other in which Christopher Webber Fenton (also once associated with the Nortons) was a principal. Various marks are found on the wares made in the two major potteries, including J. & E. Norton, E. & L. P. Norton, L. Norton & Co., Norton & Fenton, Edward Norton, Lyman Fenton & Co., Fenton's Works, United States Pottery Co., U.S.P. and others.

The popular pottery with the mottled brown on yellowware glaze was also produced in Bennington, but such wares should be referred to as "Rockingham" or "Bennington-type" unless they can be specifically attributed to a Bennington, Vermont factory.

Book flask, binding marked "Departed Spirits G," Flint Enamel glaze, 5 1/2" h. **$532**
Book flask, noting lettering on binding, mottled brown & cream Rockingham glaze, 5 3/4" h. **$392**
Flask, in shape of book, flint enamel glaze in light brown & teal green, impressed "Departed Spirits," 7 3/4" h. **$1,265**
Flask, in shape of book, running flint enamel glaze, impressed "Departed Spirits G," 5 5/8" h. **$935**

Bennington Rockingham Oval Frame

Picture frame, oval w/wide ringed rounded sides, overall mottled Rockingham glaze, few underside flakes, mid-19th c., 8 3/4 x 9 3/4" (ILLUS.) **$489**

Pitcher, 9 1/4" h., parian, Waterfall patt., molded in relief as a cylindrical waterfall w/rocks showing through, United States Pottery, 1852-58 .... **$518**
Pitcher, 9 3/8" h., parian, Cascade patt., cylindrical form molded w/an overall waterfall on rocky cliff design, tree branch handle, glazed interior, Bennington relief lozenge mark **$550**
Pitcher, 9 1/2" h., parian, bulbous paneled & deeply waisted form w/a flat rim & wide arched spout, molded overall w/flowering vines w/a vine-wrapped handle, United States Pottery, ca. 1850-58 .... **$518**

Berlin (KPM)

The mark KPM was used at Meissen from 1724 to 1725, and was later adopted by the Royal Factory, Konigliche Porzellan Manufaktur, in Berlin. At various periods it was incorporated with the Brandenburg scepter, the Prussian eagle or the crowned globe. The same letters were also adopted by other factories in Germany in the late 19th and early 20th centuries. With the end of the German monarchy in 1918, the name of the firm was changed to Staatliche Porzellan Manufaktur and though production was halted during World War II, the factory was rebuilt and is still in business. The exquisite paintings on porcelain were produced at the close of the 19th century and are eagerly sought by collectors today.

Centerpiece, in the Vienna style, a deep oval bowl w/serpentine sides pierced at the rim & flanked by large gold scrolling loop handles, the front finely painted w/a Classical view representing the Arts in a garden setting & the reverse depicting Neptune as a child riding a dolphin w/other putti, a gold bead band around the base of the bowl & raised on a deep maroon pedestal w/gilt scroll decoration & an oblong gold foot w/block feet alternating w/dolphin mask feet between gold knobs, titled in German on the bottom, blue sceptre mark, late 19th c., 15" l. (ILLUS., top next page) **$4,183**

Very Rare Berlin Pate-Sur-Pate Charger

Outstanding Ornate Berlin Centerpiece

Charger, pate-sur-pate, round w/a wide dished rim band in white decorated w/ornate gold Art Nouveau floral looping panels w/small forget-me-nots & roses, the wide center w/a celadon green ground painted & hand-tooled in white slip w/a scene of a diaphanously clad Bacchante pouring a vessel of wine into Pan's lips as he kneels beside a tree stump, blue sceptre & iron-red orb marks, ca. 1895, 13 3/4" d. (ILLUS., previous page)......... **$5,378**

ter painted in color w/a bust portrait of a 16th c. lady w/a fancy headdress, signed by Wagner, in a deep square giltwood shadowbox frame lined in red velvet, late 19th c., 16" d. (ILLUS.) **$2,185**

Berlin Charger with Lovely Portrait

Charger, round, the wide border band w/a cobalt blue ground very ornately painted in gold w/alternating panels of a wreath & crown & scrolls in pointed arcs, the cen-

Berlin Model of a Red Squirrel

Model of a squirrel, seated animal in dark brick red holding a brown acorn, on a green & brown stump molded w/acorns & oak leaves, some gold wear, second half 19th c., 10" h. (ILLUS.) **$1,150**

KPM Plaque of "The Sistine Madonna"

Plaque, oval, decorated w/a color copy of "The Sistine Madonna" after Raphael, mounted in an elaborate rectangular giltwood pierce-carved frame composed of scrolling acanthus leaves w/a red velvet liner, fitted in a glazed rectangular shadowbox frame, impressed sceptre & KPM marks, late 19th c., plaque 13 1/2 x 17" (ILLUS.).. **$4,025**

Charming KPM Plaque with Family

Plaque, rectangular, painted w/a winter scene of an elderly grandfather just outside a cottage door & standing holding a small baby w/his little granddaughter nearby, titled "The First Snowfall," impressed sceptre & KPM marks, artist-signed, in a fancy acanthus leaf-carved wooden frame, late 19th c., plaque 7 1/2 x 10" (ILLUS.) **$4,370**

Plaque with Exotic Woman Musician

Plaque, rectangular, finely painted w/the portrait of an exotic raven-haired beauty playing a lyre carved as the head of an Egyptian pharaoh, a brazier at her feet, impressed monogram & sceptre mark, titled on the back, late 19th - early 20th c., mounted in giltwood frame, 6 1/4 x 9 3/8" (ILLUS.).. **$4,183**

Berlin KPM Plaque in Ornate Gilt Frame

Plaque, rectangular, scene of two young women w/long flowing hair & wearing diaphanous gowns holding floral garland above their heads, reverse impressed "KPM" w/scepter, in very ornate gilt wood frame of pierced scroll decoration, 19th c., 7 1/2 x 10" (ILLUS.)............................ **$4,830**

Extraordinary Berlin Plaque with an Elaborate Classical Scene

Plaque, rectangular, a long classical scene depicting the goddess Aurora & her attendants, after a painting by Guido Reni, inscribed & titled on the back along w/a label reading "Painted for Mermood and Jaccurd Jewelry Co., St. Louis," impressed KPM & other marks, artist-signed, mounted in an elaborate reticulated giltwood framed, plaque 8 x 13" (ILLUS.)............ **$10,638**

Most abundant from the Victorian era are figures and groups, but other pieces, from busts to vases, were made by numerous potteries in the United States and abroad. Reproductions have been produced for many years, so care must be taken when seeking antique originals.

Reclining Bisque Bathing Beauty

Bathing beauty figure, nude lady reclining on stomach w/head raised resting on her arms, legs w/painted-on stocking & shoes, original blonde mohair wig w/flowered hat, marked "1740 2/0 B," early 20th c., 4 1/2" l. (ILLUS.)............................ **$400-500**

Bathing beauty figure, seated nude lady wearing lavender high heels & strumming a lute, real wig & turban, marked "Bavaria - 2739 B," early 20th c., 5" l. (ILLUS., top next page) **$625-675**

Large Berlin KPM Bolted Urn

Urn, octagonal stepped base below ringed pedestal supporting baluster-form body w/trumpet neck, two gilt coiled snakeform handles, front w/h.p. decoration of winged cherub among floral bouquet, reverse w/butterflies & florals, marked w/red orb & blue underglaze circle, late 19th c., 18 3/4" h. (ILLUS.).................... **$3,680**

Bisque

Bisque is biscuit china, fired a single time but not glazed. Some bisque is decorated with colors.

Figural Bisque Candlesticks

Rare Bisque Bathing Beauty with Lute

Candlesticks, figural, two-light, an ornate scroll-molded tan base & shaft support-ing lift-off serpentine arms ending in sockets, one base w/a figure of a lady wearing a dark blue & white outfit, the other w/a facing man in a blue & white outfit, each 6" w., 8 1/2" h., pr. (ILLUS., previous page) **$275-300**

Figure Group of Young Couple

Figure group, a young man & woman in 18th c. attire walking & holding a large umbrella, pastel coloring, late 19th c., 6" h. (ILLUS.) **$140-150**

Lovely Bisque Family Group

Figure group, a family group all wearing 18th c. costume, a young man standing close behind & a pretty young woman looking down, a young boy in front reach-ing up to them, finely painted ornate cos-tumes in shades of blue, pink & gold & fine facial features, on a rounded rock-work base, printed anchor mark, late 19th c., some very minor professional repairs, 26" h. (ILLUS.) **$1,955**

Bisque Dutch Girl Figure

Figure of a Dutch girl, seated pose w/hands on her knees, wearing a white bonnet over light brown hair, tinted face & arms, blue dress w/white bodice & trim on sleeves & at waist, unmarked Heubach, 3 1/2 x 5", 6 1/2" h. (ILLUS., previous page) **$200-225**

Charming Victorian Girl by a Fountain

Figure of a Victorian girl, the young blonde-haired girl walking down rocky steps & leaning on a low wall w/a lion head fountain issuing blue water, wearing a short ruffled blue dress, large blue bonnet & blue shoes, carrying a brown basket on her arm, nice coloring, "R" in diamond mark, perhaps Royal Rudolstadt, Germany, ca. 1900, 10" h. (ILLUS.) **$80-100**

Charming Bisque Group of Woman & Goat

Figure of a woman & goat, the woman standing wearing an 18th c. peasant costume in white, blue & pink w/overall tiny painted flowers, holding a sheaf of grain

& looking down at a small goat jumping up to nibble on the flowers gathered in her skirt, on a round socle base decorated w/blue & gold bands & delicate blue & yellow ribbon band, late 19th c., minor repair, 18" h. (ILLUS.) **$374**

Lovely Bisque Baby in Highchair

Figure of baby in highchair, delicate baby wearing a blue-tinted bonnet, pink lace collar & white gown, in a tan-colored wicker highchair, marked w/sunburst trademark of Gebruder Heubach, Germany, late 19th - early 20th c., 8" h. (ILLUS.) **$275-325**

Tall Bisque Figure of Gentleman

Figure of gentleman, young man in gold-trimmed pastel-colored outfit w/white ruffled shirt, holding rose in one hand, on round base modeled to resemble stones or bricks of a courtyard, marked w/blue diamond "R," 20 1/2" h. (ILLUS.) **$104**

Bisque Girl & Boy Figures in Armchairs

Figures, a young girl in a late Victorian outfit w/a light & dark green dress & matching large hat molded in a large tan & green armchair, a matching young boy in fancy green suit & hat also in a large armchair, gold trim, late 19th c., 6 1/4" h., pr. (ILLUS.) **$140-150**

Bisque Children Blowing Soap Bubbles

Figures of children blowing bubbles, girl wearing a cream dress w/pink floral decoration & gold trim at collar & hem, boy w/pink flower-decorated knee breeches & cream shirt w/dotted ruffled neck & cuffs, each holding a bubble pipe to mouth & each sitting on bench that also holds bowl for soapy water, h.p. features, unmarked, Heubach, Germany, ca. 1900, 13" h., pr. (ILLUS.) **$978**

Bisque Figures of Boy & Girl

Figures of boy & girl, the girl wearing yellow skirt w/red bows & white ruffled hem, white blouse, pale blue bodice & overskirt w/white lacy trim, orange shoes, tam-like hat, holding white & orange fan in one hand, the boy in short yellow pants w/white ruffled cuffs, matching yellow jacket, pale blue stockings & shirt, yellow & orange boots, & white hat w/orange trim, standing w/one hand on hip, the other at hat, unmarked, Germany, ca. 1900, 14" h., pr. (ILLUS.) **$201**

Man & Lady in 18th Century Costume

Figures of man & woman, each dressed in colorful 18th c. costume, she wearing a draped windswept dress painted w/tiny flowers & a pink lace-trimmed bodice, a blue bonnet behind her blonde-haired head, he wearing flower-painted knee breeches & vest & ruffled shirt under a pink jacket, holding his black tricorn hat as it blows off his head, each on a round molded base w/gilt scroll trim, Victorian-style, each 18" h., pr. (ILLUS.) **$489**

Bisque Figures of Young Tennis Players

Figures of Man & Woman with Molded Flowers

Figures of man & woman, each dressed in pale green outfit w/peach-colored bows & decorations, the man w/knee breeches & jacket, holding flowers in one hand, a staff in the other, the woman in dress w/laced bodice & elbow-length sleeves, each standing on ornate scroll base that holds trellis-like backdrop w/molded flowers, h.p. features, unmarked, late 19th c., Germany, 16" h., pr. (ILLUS.)........ **$288**

Figures of tennis players, the girl wearing aqua pleated skirt & cream colored blouse w/gold sash belt, white hat w/short aqua brim, holding racket in one hand & ball in the other, the boy wearing aqua knee breeches & matching shirt w/cream colored neckerchief, white hat w/short aqua brim, also holding racket & ball, each on base formed to resemble green grass of playing field, h.p. features, unmarked, Heubach, Germany, 15" h., pr. (ILLUS.) **$748**

Bisque Figures of Young Woman & Man

Bisque Figures of Man & Woman

Figures of man & woman, wearing buff-colored outfits & draping cloaks, h.p. features, each on molded cylindrical base, unmarked, 20 1/2" h., pr. (ILLUS.) **$978**

Figures of young woman & man, each dressed in Renaissance-style costumes in pale pink & cream shades trimmed in white & decorated w/darker peach flowers, each wearing brimmed hat, the woman holding one hand to forehead, the other holding skirt, h.p. features & florals on tinted ground, unmarked, Germany, ca. 1900, 16 1/2" h., pr. (ILLUS.) **$316**

Figures of Woman & Man in Rose Outfits

Figures of young woman & man, the woman wearing rose-colored dress w/gold bodice trimmed in white lace & pale aqua short sleeves, the narrow skirt w/pale aqua bows down front & matching wide sash at waist, white long gloves, pink shoes, elaborately styled powdered hair, the fair-haired man w/long curls, wearing rose-colored short lace-trimmed pants & matching jacket w/gold trim & pale aqua cloak, rose boots, h.p. features, gilt accents, unmarked, Germany, ca. 1900, 16" h., pr. (ILLUS.) **$173**

Fine Heubach Bisque Piano Baby

Piano baby, nude baby seated & leaning forward on his arms, tilted head w/blond-painted hair, blue intaglio eyes, molded red lips & pink cheeks, marked w/sunburst trademark of Gebruder Heubach, late 19th - early 20th c., 6" h. (ILLUS.)
.... **$325-400**

Marked Heubach Seated Piano Baby

Piano baby, seated unjointed figure w/blue intaglio eyes, open-closed mouth w/two upper teeth, molded & painted blonde hair, molded baby dress w/ruffle & green ribbon trim unfastened on right shoulder & falling off left shoulder, reaching for his right foot, overall excellent condition, marked on lower back by the Gebruder Heubach factory, Germany, ca. 1900, 8" h. (ILLUS.) **$413**

Piano baby, unjointed figure of a baby lying on its stomach w/one hand near its mouth & one leg bent up, h.p. blue eyes, open-closed mouth w/two lower teeth, molded & painted brown hair, molded blue dress w/blue flowers & lace edging at the neck, sleeves & hem, minor firing line at back of neck, some paint missing from repair, 17" l. (ILLUS., bottom of page)... **$270**

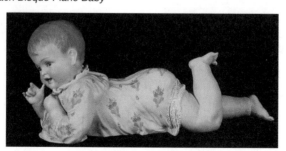

Charming Reclining Piano Baby

Blanc de Chine Mythological Horses

Blanc De Chine

This ware is a fine white Chinese porcelain with a rich clear glaze. It became popular in France in the early 18th century and remained popular in Europe and America through the 19th century. Fine figural pieces are most often found, with the earlier examples bringing the highest prices.

antlers looking back over their shoulders & their razor-like backs & raised tails, raised on fitted carved wood bases, China, 19th c., one w/broken & repaired leg, each 10" l., 13 1/4" h., pr. (ILLUS., top of page)... **$1,150**

Early Chinese Blanc-de-Chine Vases

Vases, 5 1/8" h., footed squatty bulbous lower body molded w/wide lappets & tapering to a tall cylindrical neck flanked by elephant head handles suspending rings, China, 18th c., pr. (ILLUS.) **$311**

Blue Ridge Dinnerwares

The small town of Erwin, Tennessee, was the home of the Southern Potteries, Inc., originally founded by E.J. Owen in 1917 and first called the Clinchfield Pottery.

In the early 1920s Charles W. Foreman purchased the plant and revolutionized the company's output, developing the popular line of handpainted wares sold as "Blue Ridge" dinnerwares. Freehand painted by women from the surrounding hills, these colorful dishes in many patterns continued in production until the plant's closing in 1957.

Guanyin Figures Mounted as Lamps

Figures of Guanyin, each standing gracefully w/flowing gown & one hand out, the other holding a lotus stem, raised on a lotus-trimmed pedestal base, China, 19th c., now mounted as lamps, overall 15" h., 1 pr. (ILLUS.)... **$382**

Model of mythological horses, facing pair of standing animals w/mascaron heads &

Blue Ridge Dinnerwares Mark

Ashtray, individual, Tralee Rose patt. $15
Bonbon, shell-shaped, flat, Nove Rose patt. $75

Shell-shaped Blue Ridge Bowl

Bowl, 9" d., Belvedere patt., deep shell shape, in shades of blue & red (ILLUS.) $75
Bowl, 6" d., berry or cereal, Bountiful patt....... $10
Butter pat/coaster, Lyonnaise patt., 4" d. $100
Cake lifter, Pomona patt., 9" l. $32
Cake tray, maple leaf shape, French Peasant patt. $125
Cake tray, maple leaf shape, Rose of Sharon patt., 10 1/4" l. $75
Cake tray, maple leaf shape, Verna patt......... $75
Candy box, cov., Rose Marie patt. $225
Celery, leaf-shaped, Fruit Fantasy patt., 10 1/2" l. $75
Character jug, American Indian.................... $725
Cigarette box, cov., French Peasant patt...... $150
Coffeepot, cov., ovoid, various floral patterns, 10 1/2" h., each $150
Creamer, Candlewick shape, Cock o' the Walk patt., 7" l. $35
Creamer, Mardi Gras patt. $15
Creamer & cov. sugar bowl, Colonial shape, Garden Lane patt., the set $45
Creamer & cov. sugar bowl, Ridge Daisy patt., pr. $35
Cup, Crab Apple patt.. $9
Cup, Square Dance patt.................................. $79
Cup & saucer, demitasse, china, Rose Marie patt. $85

Gravy boat, Colonial shape, French Peasant patt., 7 1/4" l. $80
Mug, child's, Chanticleer patt. $220
Pie plate, Cassandra patt., wine-colored border.. $30
Pie plate & server, Cross Stitch patt., 2 pcs. $60
Pie server, blue & white lattice design........... $30
Pitcher, 5" h., china, Annett's Wild Rose patt., Antique shape.................................. $85
Pitcher, 6 1/4" h., earthenware, Fairmede Fruits patt., Alice shape (small smear on red line trim)...................................... $150
Pitcher, 7" h., Sculptured Fruit patt.,.............. $50
Pitcher, china, decorated w/grapes, Helen shape... $95
Pitcher, Milady patt...................................... $220
Plate, 6" d., Bluebell Bouquet patt. $8
Plate, 6" sq., "Milkmaid," Provincial Farm Scene, Candlewick shape.......................... $65
Plate, dinner, Chanticleer patt. $38
Relish dish, deep shell-shaped, French Peasant patt.. $150
Salt & pepper shakers, Dogtooth Violet patt., pr... $75
Salt & pepper shakers, figural Mallard hen & drake, pr. $450
Salt & pepper shakers, tall, footed, Ruff Rose patt., brown & green leaves & various floral decorations, 5 1/2" h. pr. $75
Sugar bowl, cov., Nocturne patt. $20

Blue Ridge Adoration Pattern Teapot

Teapot, cov., Ball shape, Adoration patt., 6 3/4" h. (ILLUS.) $150
Teapot, cov., Ball shape, Bluebelle Bouquet patt... $225

Blue Ridge Cherry Pattern Teapot

Teapot, cov., Colonial shape, Cherry patt., 8 3/4" h. (ILLUS.) $175
Tray, Trellis shape, Daffodil patt. $150

Vase in a Boot Shape

Vase, 8" h., boot shape, various floral decorations (ILLUS.) $75
Vase, 5 1/2" h., china, Hampton patt., Hibiscus shape $80
Vase, 9 1/4" h., ruffle-top style, Delphine patt. $50
Vegetable bowl, cov., Mardi Gras patt. $75
Vegetable bowl, open, round, Ridge Daisy patt. $20

Blue & White Pottery

The category of blue and white or blue and grey pottery includes a wide variety of pottery, earthenware and stoneware items widely produced in this country in the late 19th century right through the 1930s. Originally marketed as inexpensive wares, most pieces featured a white or grey body molded with a fruit, flower or geometric design and then trimmed with bands or splashes of blue to highlight the molded pattern. Pitchers, butter crocks and salt boxes are among the numerous items produced, but other kitchenwares and chamber sets are also found. Values vary depending on the rarity of the embossed pattern and the depth of color of the blue trim; the darker the blue, the better. Some entries refer to several different books on Blue and White Pottery. These books are: Blue & White Stoneware, Pottery & Crockery by Edith Harbin (1977, Collector Books, Paducah, KY); Stoneware in the Blue and White by M.H. Alexander (1993 reprint, Image Graphics, Inc., Paducah, KY); and Blue & White Stoneware by Kathryn McNerney (1995, Collector Books, Paducah, KY).

Apple cider cooler, cov., w/spigot, 13" d., 15" h. $425
Bank, miniature, jug-form, stenciled rectangle w/"Money Bank" (ILLUS., top next column) $650
Basin, embossed Bow Tie patt. w/rose decal, Brush-McCoy Pottery Co., basin 15" d. $150
Basin, embossed Apple Blossom patt., Burley-Winter Pottery Co., 9" d. $185
Basin, embossed Apple Blossom patt., Burley-Winter Pottery Co., 14 d. $295

Miniature Blue & White Bank

Wildflower Batter Jar & Pail

Reverse Pyramids-Picket Fence Bowl

Batter jar, cov., stenciled Wildflower patt., Brush-McCoy Pottery Co., small, 6" d., 5 3/4" h. (ILLUS. right with Wildflower batter pail, bottom previous page)............. **$350**

Batter jar, cov., stenciled Wildflower patt., Brush-McCoy Pottery Co., large, 7" d., 8" h. **$400**

Batter pail, bail handle, stenciled Wildflower patt., Brush-McCoy Pottery Co., 4 7/8" h. (ILLUS. left with batter jar, bottom of previous page) **$375**

Advertising Beater Jar

Beater jar, advertising-type, "Stop And Shop at Wagner's Cash Grocery, Kingsley, Iowa," 4 3/4" h. (ILLUS.) **$325**

Bird bath, miniature, embossed birds around base, Western Stoneware Co., 10" h. (ILLUS., top next column) **$3,250**

Bowl, 4" d., 2" h., berry, embossed Flying Bird patt., w/advertising, A.E. Hull Pottery Co... **$450**

Bowl, 4" d., 2" h., berry or cereal, embossed Flying Bird patt., A.E. Hull Pottery Co. **$250**

Bowl, 4 1/2" d., 2 1/2" h., embossed Reverse Pyramids patt., Ruckles Pottery.... **$65-75**

Bowl, 6" to 12" d., embossed Greek Key patt., Red Wing Pottery Co., ranges **$100-170**

Bowl, 7 1/2" d., 2 3/4" h., embossed Apricot with Honeycomb patt., A.E. Hull Pottery Co. **$135**

Miniature Blue & White Bird Bath

Bowl, 7 1/2" d., 5" h., embossed Reverse Pyramids w/Reverse Picket Fence patt., Ruckles Pottery (ILLUS., top of page) **$90-100**

Bowl, 9 1/2" d., 3 3/4" h., embossed Apricot with Honeycomb patt., A.E. Hull Pottery Co. **$150**

Bowl, 9 1/2" d., 5" h., embossed Currants and Diamonds patt.................................. **$230**

Bowl, 10" d., 5" h., embossed Heart Banded patt... **$135**

Bowl, embossed Heart patt........................... **$450**

Bowl, stenciled Nautilus patt., rim handles, A.E. Hull Pottery Co. **$325**

Embossed Venetian Pattern Bowl

Bowl, 7" d., 2 1/2" h., embossed Venetian patt., same as Reverse Pyramids w/Reverse Picket Fence but w/honeycomb at bottom, Roseville Pottery (ILLUS.) **$50**
Bowls, nesting-type, embossed Basketweave patt., depending on size .... **$220+**
Bowls, nesting-type, embossed Zig-Zag patt., depending on size **$100-150**
Bowls, embossed Ringsaround (Wedding Ring) patt., A.E. Hull Pottery Co., six sizes, ranges **$85-225**
Bowls, nesting-type, embossed Cosmos patt., A.E. Hull Pottery Co., depending on size, each **$165-275**

Stenciled Wildflower Bowl

Bowls, nesting-type, stenciled Wildflower patt., Brush-McCoy Pottery Co., 4" to 14" d., depending on size (ILLUS. of 10" d. size) **$150-450**
Brush vase, embossed Bow Tie (Our Lucile) patt., w/rose decal, Brush-McCoy Pottery Co., 5 1/2" h. **$115**
Brush vase, embossed Willow (Basketweave & Morning Glory) patt., Brush-McCoy Pottery Co., small, 4 3/4" h. (ILLUS., top next column) **$325**
Butter crock, cov., advertising-type, 6" d., 6" h. **$100**
Butter crock, cov., embossed Butterfly patt., Nelson McCoy Sanitary Stoneware Co., 10 lb. size, 9 1/2" d., 6" h. **$275**
Butter crock, cov., embossed Daisy and Basketweave patt., 7" d., 6 3/4" h. **$350**
Butter crock, cov., embossed Diffused Blues with Inverted Pyramid Bands patt., 6" d., 4" h. **$150**
Butter crock, cov., embossed Greek Column (Draped Windows) patt., Red Wing Pottery Co. & Nelson McCoy Sanitary Stoneware Co., found in 2, 3, 4 & 5 lb. sizes, ranges **$225-295**

Willow Pattern Brush Vase

Butter crock, cov., embossed Indian Good Luck Sign (Swastika) patt., produced by Nelson McCoy Sanitary Stoneware Co., Robinson-Ransbottom Pottery Co. & The Crooksville Pottery Co., 6 1/4" d., 5 1/4" h. **$175**
Butter crock, cov., embossed Jersey Cow patt., 4" h. **$1,000**

Lovebird Butter Crock

Peacock Butter Crock & Salt Box

Embossed Willow Canisters

Butter crock, cov., embossed Lovebird patt., A.E. Hull Pottery Co., 6" d., 4 34" h. (ILLUS., previous page) **$650**

Butter crock, cov., embossed Peacock patt., w/bail handle, Brush-McCoy Pottery Co., 3 lb., 5" h. (ILLUS. right with Peacock salt box, top of page).................. **$800**

Butter crock, cov., embossed Peacock patt., w/bail handle, Brush-McCoy Pottery Co., 1 lb., 4" h. **$1,250**

Butter crock, cov., embossed Rose & Waffle patt., 5" d., 4 1/2" h.............................. **$300**

Canister, cov., embossed Willow (Basketweave & Morning Glory) patt., "Barley," Brush-McCoy Pottery Co., average 6 1/2 to 7" h., each. **$1,000**

Canister, cov., embossed Willow (Basketweave & Morning Glory) patt., "Cereal," Brush-McCoy Pottery Co., average 5 1/2" to 6 1/2" h. (ILLUS. center row, far left, second from top) **$550**

Canister, cov., embossed Willow (Basketweave & Morning Glory) patt., "Coffee," Brush-McCoy Pottery Co., average 5 1/2 to 6 1/2" h. (ILLUS. middle row, second from left, second from top)............. **$275**

Canister, cov., embossed Willow (Basketweave & Morning Glory) patt., "Crackers" (short), Brush-McCoy Pottery Co., average 5 1/2 to 6 1/2" h., each. (ILLUS. top row, third from right, second from top) .. **$550**

Canister, cov., embossed Willow (Basketweave & Morning Glory) patt., "Crackers" (tall), Brush-McCoy Pottery Co., average 6 1/2 to 7" h., each (ILLUS. top row, third from left, second from top) **$1,000**

Canister, cov., embossed Willow (Basketweave & Morning Glory) patt., "Raisins," Brush-McCoy Pottery Co., average 5 1/2" to 6 1/2" h. (ILLUS. top row, second from right, second from top)............... **$625**

Canister, cov., embossed Willow (Basketweave & Morning Glory) patt., "Rice," Brush-McCoy Pottery Co., average 6 1/2 to 7" h., each.................................. **$1,250**

Canister, cov., embossed Willow (Basketweave & Morning Glory) patt., "Salt," "Beans," or blank, Brush-McCoy Pottery Co., average 5 1/2 to 6 1/2" h., each (ILLUS. of Salt, middle row, center; Beans, top row, far right, second from top).. **$375**

Canister, cov., embossed Willow (Basketweave & Morning Glory) patt., "Sugar," Brush-McCoy Pottery Co., average 5 1/2 to 6 1/2" h. (ILLUS. middle row, second from right, second from top) **$275**

Wildflower Canisters & Spice Jars

Canister, cov., embossed Willow (Basketweave & Morning Glory) patt., "Tea," Brush-McCoy Pottery Co., average 5 1/2 to 6 1/2" h. (ILLUS. middle row, far right, second from top, previous page)............... **$275**

Canister, cov., embossed Willow (Basketweave & Morning Glory) patt., "Tobacco," Brush-McCoy Pottery Co., average 6 1/2 to 7" h., each (ILLUS. top row, far left, second from top, previous page)...... **$1,000**

Stenciled Floral Pattern Canister

Canister, cov., stenciled Floral patt., "Coffee," probably A.E. Hull Pottery Co., 5 7/8" h. (ILLUS.) **$275**

Canister, cov., stenciled Wildflower patt., "Barley," "Cornstarch" or "Grape Nuts," Brush-McCoy Pottery Co., 5 3/4" h., each (ILLUS. second row from bottom with other canisters & spice jars) **$550**

Canister, cov., stenciled Wildflower patt., "Beans," or "Peas," Brush-McCoy Pottery Co., 5 1/2 to 6 1/2", each (ILLUS. of Beans, second row from bottom, top of page)..................................... **$325**

Canister, cov., stenciled Wildflower patt., blank title, Brush-McCoy Pottery Co. (ILLUS. bottom row with other canisters & spice jars, top of page)........................ **$475**

Canister, cov., stenciled Wildflower patt., "Butter," tall w/flared rim, Brush-McCoy Pottery Co., 5 3/5" h. (ILLUS. top row with other canisters & spice jars, top of page).. **$350**

Canister, cov., stenciled Wildflower patt., "Cereal (Sago)," Brush-McCoy Pottery Co., 5 1/2 to 6 1/2" h. (ILLUS. bottom row with canisters & spice jars, top of page).. **$400**

Canister, cov., stenciled Wildflower patt., "Choice Sour Pickles," Brush-McCoy Pottery Co., 12" h...................................... **$850**

Canister, cov., stenciled Wildflower patt., "Coffee," "Rice" or "Tea," 5 1/2 to 6 1/2", each (ILLUS. second, third & bottom rows with canisters & spice jars, top of page).. **$225**

Canister, cov., stenciled Wildflower patt., "Corn Meal" (tall), Brush-McCoy Pottery Co., 10" h. (ILLUS. top row, right, with canisters & spice jars, top of page)........... **$750**

Canister, cov., stenciled Wildflower patt., "Crackers" (tall), Brush-McCoy Pottery Co., 5 1/2 to 6 1/2" h. (ILLUS. top row with canisters & spice jars, top of page) **$700**

Canister, cov., stenciled Wildflower patt., "Currants," Brush-McCoy Pottery Co., 5 1/2 to 6 1/2" (ILLUS. bottom row with canisters & spice jars, top of page)........... **$425**

Embossed GrapeWare Casserole

Canister, cov., stenciled Wildflower patt., "Farina," "Prunes" or "Raisins," Brush-McCoy Pottery Co., 5 1/2 to 6 1/2", each (ILLUS. second row from bottom & bottom row with canisters & spice jars, top of previous page) $375

Canister, cov., stenciled Wildflower patt., "Flour," Brush-McCoy Pottery Co., 5 1/2 to 6 1/2" h. (ILLUS. top row with canisters & spice jars, top of previous page)............ $800

Canister, cov., stenciled Wildflower patt., "Genuine German Dills," Brush-McCoy Pottery Co., 12" h. (ILLUS. top row, far left with canisters & spice jars, top of previous page)... $850

Canister, cov., stenciled Wildflower patt., "Oatmeal," Brush-McCoy Pottery Co., 5 1/2 to 6 1/2", each (ILLUS. second row from bottom with canisters & spice jars, top previous page) $400

Canister, cov., stenciled Wildflower patt., "Sugar," Brush-McCoy Pottery Co., 5 1/2 to 6 1/2" (ILLUS. bottom row, far right, with canisters & spice jars, top previous page).. $250

Canister, cov., stenciled Wildflower patt., "Sugar" (tall), Brush-McCoy Pottery Co., 10" h. (ILLUS. top row, second from left with canisters & spice jars, top previous page).. $500

Canister, cov., stenciled Wildflower patt., "Tapioca," Brush-McCoy Pottery Co., 5 1/2 to 6 1/2" h. (ILLUS. second row from bottom with canisters & spice jars, top previous page) $450

Canister, cov., stenciled Wildflower patt., "Tobacco," Brush-McCoy Pottery Co., 5 1/2 to 6 1/2" h., each $600

Canister, cov., stenciled Wildflower patt., blank, Brush-McCoy Pottery Co., 2 gal. $425

Canister, cov., stenciled Wildflower patt., blank, Brush-McCoy Pottery Co., 3 gal. $525

Canister/cookie jar, cov., embossed Willow (Basketweave & Morning Glory) patt., "Put Your Fist In," Brush-McCoy Pottery Co., average 6 1/2 to 7" h., each. (ILLUS. top row, second from left w/other Willow canisters, top of previous page) $1,000

Casserole, cov., embossed GrapeWare patt., Brush-McCoy Pottery Co. (ILLUS. with extra cover, top of page)................... $425

Apple Blossom Chamber Pot

Chamber pot, cov., embossed Apple Blossom patt., Burley-Winter Pottery Co., 11" d., 6" h. (ILLUS.)................................. $375

Chamber pot, cov., embossed Bow Tie (Our Lucile) patt. w/rose decal, Brush-McCoy Pottery Co., 11" d., 6" h. $225

Chamber pot, cov., embossed Open Rose and Spearpoint Panels patt., A.E. Hull Pottery Co., 9 1/2" d., 6" h. $300

Chamber pot, cov., embossed Willow (Basketweave & Morning Glory) patt., Brush-McCoy Pottery Co., 9 1/2" d., 8" h. (ILLUS. right with Willow slop jar, top of next page) .. $325

Chamber pot, open, embossed Apple Blossom patt., Burley-Winter Pottery Co., 11" d., 6" h. $325

Willow Chamber Pot & Slop Jar

Rare Peacock Coffeepot & Pitcher

Coffeepot, cov., embossed Peacock patt., Brush-McCoy Pottery Co., 6 1/2" d., overall 10 3/4" h. (ILLUS. left with Peacock pitcher, above)............................... **$4,250**

Cold fudge crock, w/tin lid & ladle, marked "Johnson Cold Fudge Crock," various sizes known, 12" d., 13" h. **$300**

Cooking or preserving kettle, cov., bail handle, embossed Peacock patt., Brush-McCoy Pottery Co., 5 qt. **$1,100**

Creamer, ovoid form, stenciled Dutch Boy patt., 4 1/4" h. (ILLUS.) **$225**

Stenciled Dutch Boy Creamer

Rare Anchovies Storage Crock

Decorated Bow Tie Ewer & Basin Set

Crock, anchovies storage-type, swelled cylindrical form, three blue bands around top & bottom, stenciled on the side "A. Rensch & Co. - Anchois (sic) Mustard [over a fish] - Toledo, O.," impressed on the bottom "Burley, Winter & Co. - Crooksville, O.," 10 1/2" h. (ILLUS., previous page)... **$575**

Cup, embossed Paneled Fir Tree patt., Brush-McCoy Pottery Co., 3" d., 3 1/2" h. ... **$175**

Cuspidor, embossed Poinsettia and Basketweave patt., 9 3/4" d., 9" h. **$180**

Cuspidor, embossed Willow (Basketweave & Morning Glory) patt., Brush-McCoy Pottery Co., 7 1/2" d., 5 1/2" h.................... **$185**

Miniature Diffused Blue Cuspidor

Cuspidor, miniature, souvenir-type, Diffused Blue patt., 2" h. (ILLUS.) **$325**

Custard cup, embossed Fishscale patt., A.E. Hull Pottery Co., 2 1/2" d., 5" h. **$125**

Blue & White Ewer & Pitcher

Ewer, embossed Apple Blossom patt., large, Burley-Winter Pottery Co., 12" h. (ILLUS. right with embossed Scrolls & Feathers pitcher)...................................... **$450**

Small-mouthed Apple Blossom Ewer

Ewer, embossed Apple Blossom patt., small mouth, Burley-Winter Pottery Co., 8" h. (ILLUS.)... **$400**

Ewer, embossed Bow Tie (Our Lucile) patt., w/rose decal, Brush-McCoy Pottery Co., 11" h.. **$175**

Ewer, Floral Decal (Memphis patt.), Western Stoneware Co., small, 7" h. **$175**

Ewer & basin set, embossed Apple Blossom patt., Burley-Winter Pottery Co., pr.
.... **$700**

Ewer & basin set, embossed Bow Tie patt. w/Flying Bird decal, Brush-McCoy Pottery Co., basin 15" d., ewer 11" h., pr. (ILLUS., top of page).. **$625**

Cosmos Jardinieres & Pedestals in Cream & Green Spongeware & Blue & White

Match holder, model of a duck, 5 1/2" d.,
5" h. $250

Bow Tie Ewer from Set

Ewer & basin set, embossed Bow Tie patt.
w/stenciled Wildflower decoration,
Brush-McCoy Pottery Co., basin 15" d.,
ewer 11" h., pr. (ILLUS. of ewer only)
.... $625

Ewer & basin set, Floral Decal (Memphis
patt.), Western Stoneware Co., basin
15" d., ewer 11 1/4" h., pr. $365

Foot warmer, signed by Logan Pottery Co.
.... $250

Grease jar, cov., embossed Flying Bird
patt., A.E. Hull Pottery Co., 4" h. $1,100

Iced tea cooler, cov., plain barrel shape,
printed "3 - Iced Tea Cooler," 3 gal.,
11" d., 13" h. $310

Jardiniere & pedestal, embossed Cosmos
patt., possibly Weller or Burley-Winter
Pottery Co., jardiniere 6" h., pedestal
5 1/2" h. (ILLUS. right with green & green
spongeware jardiniere, top of page) $2,000

Figural Rooster Match Holder

Match holder, model of a rooster (ILLUS.)
.... $435

Milk crock, embossed Apricot patt., A.E.
Hull Pottery Co., 10" d., 5" h. $225

Lovebird Pattern Milk Crock

Milk crock, embossed Lovebird patt., w/bail
handle, A.E. Hull Pottery Co., 9" d.,
5 1/2" h. (ILLUS.) $500

Columns & Arches Mug & Pitcher

Mug, embossed Cattail patt., Western Stoneware Co., 3" d., 4" h.......................... **$130**
Mug, embossed Columns and Arches patt., extremely rare, Brush-McCoy Pottery Co., 4 1/2" h. (ILLUS. left with Columns & Arches pitcher, top of page).................... **$650+**
Mug, stenciled Cattail patt., Western Stoneware Co., 3" d., 4" h.................................. **$130**
Mustard jar, cov., Diffused Blue, stenciled "Mustard," 3" d., 4" h............................... **$200**
Pie baker, embossed Loop patt., light blue, unglazed rim & under collar, 8" d. (ILLUS., top next page) **$40**

Embossed Apple Blossom Mug

Mug, embossed Apple Blossom patt., Burley-Winter Pottery Co., 5" h. (ILLUS.) **$750**

Embossed Cattail Advertising Mug

Mug, embossed Cattail patt., w/advertising, Western Stoneware Co., 3" d., 4" h. (ILLUS.) **$275**

Bluebird Decal Hall Boy Pitcher

Pitcher, 9" h., 7" d., Bluebird decal, hall boy-style, Brush-McCoy Pottery Co. (ILLUS.)
.... **$425**
Pitcher, 7" h., 3 1/2" d., Diffused Blue w/rose decal, A.E. Hull Pottery Co............. **$125**
Pitcher, Diffused Blue, plain smooth shape, found in 1/4-, 1/2-, 5/8- & 1-gallon size, smallest is rarest, depending on the size
.... **$150-225**

Embossed Loop Pie Baker

Pitcher, 6 1/2" h., embossed Beaded Swirl patt., A.E. Hull Pottery Co. (ILLUS.).......... **$950**

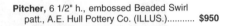

Avenue of Trees Pitcher

Pitcher, 8" h., embossed Avenue of Trees patt. (ILLUS.)... **$325**
Pitcher, embossed Bands and Rivets patt., 1 gal. **$275**
Pitcher, embossed Bands and Rivets patt., 1 pt. **$285**
Pitcher, embossed Bands and Rivets patt., 1/2 gal. **$285**
Pitcher, embossed Bands and Rivets patt., 1/4 gal. **$285**
Pitcher, embossed Bands and Rivets patt., 5/8 gal. **$225**

Small Embossed Butterfly Pitcher

Pitcher, 4 3/4" h., embossed Butterfly patt., Nelson McCoy Sanitary Stoneware Co. (ILLUS.).. **$600**

Beaded Swirl Pattern Pitcher

Embossed Cattails Pitcher

Pitcher, 5 3/4" h., embossed Cattails patt. (ILLUS.).. **$400**

Cherry Cluster & Grape Pattern Pitchers

Embossed Cherry Band Pitcher

Embossed Eagle Pattern Pitcher

Embossed Grape Pattern Pitcher

Pitcher, 9 1/2" h., embossed Cherry Band patt., Red Wing Pottery Co., 8 pt., available in numerous sizes, the smallest being the most valuable, often seen w/printed advertising, which adds **$300** minimum to the value, without advertising (ILLUS.)... **$225-400**

Pitcher, 10" h., 8 1/2" d., embossed Cherry Cluster with Basketweave patt., A.E. Hull Pottery Co. (ILLUS. bottom row, left w/various grape pattern pitchers, top of page).. **$325**

Pitcher, 9" h., embossed Columns and Arches patt., Brush-McCoy Pottery Co. (ILLUS. right with Columns & Arches mug).. **$600**

Pitcher, 8" h., embossed Eagle patt., A.E. Hull Pottery Co. (ILLUS., top next column).. **$650**

Pitcher, 7 1/2" h., embossed Grape patt., Burley-Winter Pottery Co. (ILLUS., bottom next column)..................................... **$1,000**

Graduated Lincoln Head with Log Cabin Pitchers

Grape Cluster & Trellis Pattern Pitcher

Old Fashioned Garden Rose Pitcher

Pitcher, embossed Grape Cluster on Trellis patt., four sizes, 5" to 9 1/2" h., depending on size, each (ILLUS. of....) **$165-245**

Pitcher, 7" h., embossed Grape Cluster on Trellis patt., squat body w/cover, Uhl Pottery Co. **$350**

Pitcher, 7" h., embossed Grape Cluster on Trellis patt., squat body w/no cover, Uhl Pottery Co. **$200**

Pitcher, embossed Grape with Rickrack patt., three sizes, smallest the most valuable, each **$195-325**

Pitcher, embossed Lincoln Head with Log Cabin patt., Uhl Pottery Co., five sizes, one gallon size largest & most valuable, depending on size (ILLUS., top of page) **$575-1,500**

Pitcher, 7" h., 7" d., embossed Old Fashioned Garden Rose patt., Burley-Winter Pottery Co. (ILLUS., top next column) **$500**

Pitcher, 7" h., 7" d., embossed Paul Revere patt., Whites Pottery Co. **$450**

Pitcher, 8 1/2" h., embossed Peacock patt., Brush-McCoy Pottery Co. (ILLUS. right with Peacock coffeepot) **$1,500**

Pitcher, 8" h., embossed Scrolls & Feathers patt. (ILLUS. left with Apple Blossom ewer, pg. 121) **$650**

Pitcher, 8 1/2" h., 6" d., embossed Swan patt., Burley-Winter Pottery Co. **$450**

Pitcher, 9" h., embossed Windmill and Bush patt., J.W. McCoy Pottery Co. & Brush-McCoy Pottery Co. .... **$400+**

Embossed Windy City Pitcher

Pitcher, 8 1/2" h., embossed Windy City patt., Robinson Clay Products Pottery Co. (ILLUS.) **$325**

Pitcher, 7" h., embossed Windmill & Bush patt., J.W. McCoy Pottery Co. & Brush-McCoy Pottery Co. **$250**

Pitcher, 8 1/2" h., Flying Bluebird decal, J.W. McCoy Pottery Co. **$250**

Three Stenciled Blue & White Pitchers

Pitcher, 8" h., stenciled Acorn patt., Brush-McCoy Pottery Co. (ILLUS. center)............ **$300**

Pitcher, 7 3/4" h., stenciled Bow Tie patt., possibly A.E. Hull Pottery Co. (ILLUS.)...... **$175**

Pitcher, 5 3/4" h., stenciled Cattail patt., Brush-McCoy Pottery Co. (ILLUS. left with Acorn pitcher) **$250**

Pitcher, 5" h., stenciled Conifer Tree patt., Brush-McCoy Pottery Co. (ILLUS. right with Acorn pitcher) **$250**

Pitcher, 8 1/2" h., stenciled Dutch Scene (Dutch Landscape) patt. w/two Dutch children **$275**

Pitcher, 6" h., stenciled Wildflower patt., hall boy-type w/waisted body & five stencils per side, Brush-McCoy Pottery Co. (ILLUS. right with other Wildflower hall boy, bottom of page) **$750**

Pitcher, 6 3/4" h., stenciled Wildflower patt., hall boy-type w/cylindrical body & five stencils per side, Brush-McCoy Pottery Co. (ILLUS. left with other Wildflower hall boy, bottom of page) **$550**

Pitcher, 7 1/2" h., 4" d., stenciled Wildflower patt., hall boy-type, Brush-McCoy Pottery Co. **$275**

Stenciled Bow Tie Pitcher

Two Wildflower Hall Boy Pitchers

Three Sizes of Wildflower Rolling Pins

Pitcher, 9" h., 4" d., Swirl patt., Diffused Blue swirled bands up around sides **$275**
Ramekin or nappy, embossed Peacock patt., Brush-McCoy Pottery Co., 4" d. **$300**
Refrigerator jar, cov., Diffused Blue, stenciled "Refrigerator Jar," 3 lb., 7" d., 6 1/2" h. **$325**

Salt box, cov., Blue Band patt., 5" d., 6" h. **$130**

Stenciled Wildflower Roaster

Roaster, cov., stenciled Wildflower patt., Brush-McCoy Pottery Co., 12" d., 8 1/2" h. (ILLUS.) **$450**
Rolling pin, stenciled Wildflower patt., large baker's type, Brush-McCoy Pottery Co., stoneware roller, 3 1/2" d., 14 1/2" l. (ILLUS. bottom with two other Wildflower rolling pins, top of page) **$800**
Rolling pin, stenciled Wildflower patt., lBrush-McCoy Pottery Co., medium size, stoneware roller, 4" d., 12" l. (ILLUS. top with two other Wildflower rolling pins, top of page) **$500**
Rolling pin, stenciled Wildflower patt., Brush-McCoy Pottery Co., small, 3" d., 8" l. (ILLUS. center with two other Wildflower rolling pins, top of page) **$600**
Rolling pin, stenciled Wildflower patt., w/advertising, large baker's type, Brush-McCoy Pottery Co., stoneware roller, 3 1/2" d., 14 1/2" l. **$3,000**

Advertising Hanging Salt Box

Salt box, cov., Diffused Blue patt., Western Stoneware advertising-type, "You Need Salt, We Need You - The Hodgin Store, Whittier, Iowa," 4 1/4" h. (ILLUS.) **$600**
Salt box, cov., embossed Apple Blossom patt., Burley-Winter Pottery Co., 6" d., 4" h. **$400**
Salt box, cov., embossed Basketweave & Grapes, patt., sponged blue decoration, 6" d., 4" h. **$375**
Salt box, cov., embossed Daisy patt., 6" d., 6 1/2" h. **$250**
Salt box, cov., embossed Good Luck Sign (Swastika) patt., Nelson McCoy Sanitary Stoneware Co., Robinson-Ransbottom Pottery Co. & The Crooksville Pottery Co., 6" d., 4" h. **$250**
Salt box, cov., embossed Grape & Waffle patt. **$350**

Salt box, cov., embossed Raspberry patt., Brush-McCoy Pottery Co., 5 1/2" d., 5 1/2" h. $250
Salt box, cov., embossed Waffle patt. $220
Salt box, cov., hanging-type, embossed Peacock patt., Brush-McCoy Pottery Co., 5" d., 4 1/4" h. (ILLUS. left with Peacock butter crock) $225
Salt box, cov., plain $100

Wildflower Salt with Compass Decor

Salt box, cov., stenciled Wildflower patt., hinged wooden cover, compass design around "Salt" on front, J.W. McCoy Pottery Co., 6" d., 4 1/2" h. (ILLUS. with no cover) $300
Sand jar, embossed Polar Bear patt., Uhl Pottery Co., 11" d., 13 1/2" h. $750
Sand jar, embossed Polar Bear patt., Uhl Pottery Co., 12 1/4" d., 14 1/2" h. $1,250
Shaving mug, embossed Rose & Fishscale patt., A. E. Hull Pottery Co., 3/3/4" h. (ILLUS. right with Rose & Fishscale brush vase & soap dish) $750
Shaving mug, scuttle-form, 4" d., 6" h. $1,250

Embossed Apple Blossom Slop Jar

Slop jar, cov., embossed Apple Blossom patt., Burley-Winter Pottery Co., 10" h. (ILLUS.) $350

Slop jar, cov., embossed Rose & Fishscale patt., A.E. Hull Pottery Co., 10" h. $325
Slop jar, cov., embossed Willow (Basketweave & Morning Glory) patt., Brush-McCoy Pottery Co., 9 1/2" d., 12 1/2" h. (ILLUS. left with chamber pot) $350
Soap dish, embossed Cat Head patt., small round style, 3 3/4" d. $155

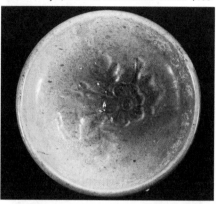

Embossed Flower Cluster Soap Dish

Soap dish, embossed Flower Cluster w/Fishscale patt., small round form, 4 1/2" d., 3/4" h. (ILLUS.) $135
Soap dish, embossed Lion Head patt., small round style, 3 3/4" d. $155

Rectangular Slab Soap with Rose Decal

Soap dish, slab-type, rectangular, Rose Decal decoration, maker unknown, 3 3/4 x 4 5/8" (ILLUS.) $125

Round Flying Blue Bird Slab Soap

Willow Pattern Spice Jars

Soap dish, slab-type, round, Flying Blue Bird decal, maker unknown, 4 5/8" (ILLUS., previous page) **$225**

Soap dish, stenciled Wildflower patt., slab-type, Brush-McCoy Pottery Co., 3 5/8 x 5 1/4", 3/4" thick **$275**

Soap dish, cover & drainer, embossed Rose & Fishscale patt., A.E. Hull Pottery Co., 5 1/4" d., 2" h. (ILLUS. center with Rose & Fishscale brush vase & shaving mug) **$850**

Wildflower/Arches & Columns Soap Dish

Soap dish, cover & drainer, stenciled Wildflower patt. on embossed Arches & Columns shape, Brush-McCoy Pottery Co., 5 1/4" d., 2" h. (ILLUS.) **$600**

Spice jar, cov., embossed Willow (Basketweave & Morning Glory) patt., "Cinnamon," "Nutmeg," "Allspice," "Ginger," "Cloves" & "Pepper," each (ILLUS. of group, top of page) **$250-300**

Two Near Wildflower Spice Jars

Spice jar, cov., stenciled Near Wildflower patt., uncommon design, found in "Allspice," "Pepper," "Cinnamon," "Nutmeg," "Ginger" & "Cloves," possibly by Brush-McCoy or A.E. Hull Pottery Co., 3 3/4" h., each (ILLUS. of Pepper on right) **$500**

Spice jar, cov., stenciled Near Wildflower patt., uncommon design, "Nutmegs" (plural) & "Mustard," possibly by Brush-McCoy or A.E. Hull Pottery Co., 3 3/4" h., each (ILLUS. of Nutmegs on left with Pepper jar) **$700**

Spice jar, cov., stenciled Plume patt., "Nutmeg," A.E. Hull Pottery Co., 4 1/4" h. **$150**

Spice jar, cov., stenciled Snowflake patt., various spices, A.E. Hull Pottery Co., each **$150-225**

Spice jar, cov., stenciled Wildflower patt., "Allspice," "Pepper," "Cinnamon," "Nutmeg," "Cloves" & "Ginger," Brush-McCoy Pottery Co., 3 1/4" h., each (ILLUS. third row from bottom with canisters & spice jars) **$250**

Spice jar, cov., stenciled Wildflower patt., "Allspice," "Pepper," "Cinnamon," "Nutmeg," "Cloves" & "Ginger," Brush-McCoy Pottery Co., very rare size, 2 3/4" h., each (ILLUS. third row from bottom with canisters & spice jars) **$400**

Spice jar, cov., stenciled Wildflower patt., "Nutmegs" (plural) & "Mustard," extremely rare, Brush-McCoy Pottery Co., 3 1/4" h., each (ILLUS. third row from bottom with canisters & spice jars) **$500**

Spice jar, cov., stenciled Wildflower patt., "Nutmegs" (plural) & "Mustard," extremely rare & rare small size, Brush-McCoy Pottery Co., 2 3/4" h., each (ILLUS. third row from bottom with canisters & spice jars) **$800**

Windy City Pattern Stein

Stein, embossed Windy City patt., 5 1/2" h. (ILLUS.) **$165**

Two Blue & White Daffodil Vases

Stewer, cov., embossed Willow (Basketweave & Morning Glory) patt., Brush-McCoy Pottery Co., 2 qt. **$325**
Stewer, cov., embossed Willow (Basketweave & Morning Glory) patt., Brush-McCoy Pottery Co., 4 qt. **$275**
Stewer, cov., stenciled Wildflower patt., Brush-McCoy Pottery Co., 4 qt. **$285**

ets for wire bail handle w/turned wood grip, blue 6" d., 6" h. (ILLUS.) .... **$800+**
Tumbler, stenciled Wildflower patt., tapering cylindrical form, no printed designs inside, 5" h. **$300**

Stenciled Wildflower Tumbler

Tumbler, stenciled Wildflower patt., tapering cylindrical form, printed designs inside, 5" h. (ILLUS.) **$350**
Umbrella stand, embossed Two Stags patt., solid blue, Logan Pottery Co., 21" h. **$1,500**
Vase, 8" h., embossed Daffodil patt., incised on the bottom "WPC" (ILLUS. left with matching larger vase, top of page) **$200**

Blue & White Pottery Teapot

Teapot, cov., Swirl patt., spherical body w/row of relief-molded knobs around the shoulder, inset cover w/knob finial, swan's-neck spout, shoulder loop brack-

Flying Bird Water Set

Tall Diffused Blue Vase

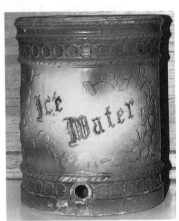

Apple Blossom Water Cooler

Vase, 11" h., Diffused Blue, tall ovoid shape tapering to a low flared neck, unknown maker (ILLUS.).. **$325**

Vase, 12" h., embossed Daffodil patt., incised on the bottom "WPC" (ILLUS. right with smaller vase) **$275**

Vase, Diffused Blue, wide ovoid body w/short flared neck & pointed shoulder handles .... **$300+**

Water cooler, cov., embossed Apple Blossom patt., no/spigot, found in various sizes, Burley-Winter Pottery Co., 13" h. (ILLUS., top next column) **$1,000**

Water cooler, cov., embossed Cupid patt., w/spigot, Western Stoneware, 5 gal.......... **$725**

Water cooler, cov., embossed Polar Bear patt., w/ spigot, Uhl Pottery Co., 10 gal... **$1,250**

Water cooler, cov., embossed Polar Bear patt., w/ spigot, Uhl Pottery Co., 2 gal....... **$600**

Water cooler, cov., embossed Polar Bear patt., w/ spigot, Uhl Pottery Co., 4 gal........ **$725**

Water set: pitcher & six mugs; embossed Flying Bird patt., A.E. Hull Pottery Co., the set (ILLUS., top of page)................. **$2,400**

Other Colors

Jardiniere & pedestal, embossed Cosmos patt., green & cream spongeware, possibly Weller or Burley-Winter Pottery Co., jardiniere 6" h., pedestal 5 1/2" h. (ILLUS. left with Cosmos jardiniere & pedestal, pg. 122).. **$2,500**

Boch Freres

The Belgian firm, founded in 1841 and still in production, first produced stoneware art pottery of mediocre quality, attempting to upgrade their wares through the years. In 1907, Charles Catteau became the art director of the pottery, and slowly the influence of his work was absorbed by the artisans surrounding him. All through the 1920s wares were decorated in distinctive Art Deco designs and are now eagerly sought along with the hand-thrown gourd-form vessels coated with earthtone glazes that were produced during the same time. Almost all Boch Freres pottery is marked, but the finest wares also carry the signature of Charles Catteau in addition to the pottery mark.

Boch Freres Mark

Box, cov., low rectangular form w/rounded corners, decorated w/crossed bands of stylized flowers in turquoise, sapphire blue, yellow & black on a crackled ivory ground, brass hinge & border, base w/circular stamp "Boch F La Louvière," brass stamped "France," ca. 1920s, 4 x 5 1/2", 1 1/2" h. **$288**

Bold Art Deco Boch Freres Box

Box, cov., rounded square w/domed top, colorful Art Deco design w/alternating tapering stripes of black & green up the sides with every other black stripe painted w/a stilized oval & loop design in maroon, orange & yellow, marked "Boch Freres La Louviere," 1930s, 4 5/8" w., 2 7/8" h. (ILLUS.) **$288**
Charger, large round form w/flanged rim, decorated in the center w/a large grazing antelope, the border band w/round geometric devices, in sapphire blue, turquoise green & black on a crackled ivory ground, marked "D943 - Ch. Catteau - 22p C K," ca. 1920s, 14 1/2" d. **$1,150**
Vase, 7" h., bulbous ovoid body tapering sharply to a small neck, decorated w/a repeating floral design of yellow blossoms, bluish green leaves & burgundy berries on branches, on a sapphire blue ground, separated by bands of blue, green, orange & black, circular stamp mark "Boch F La Louvière," ca. 1920s (crazing) **$920**
Vase, 8 1/2" h., ovoid body tapering to a tall slender & slightly tapering neck, decorated w/three stylized flowers & leaves in a basket w/double swag, repeated in three

sections, divided by border of multiple ovals, in yellow, orange, sapphire blue & light blue on an ivory crackled ground, circular mark "Boch F La Louvière," Belgium, ca. 1920s **$403**
Vase, 8 3/4" h., footed ovoid body w/the swelled shoulder tapering to a wide, short flared neck, decorated overall w/large stylized yellow blossoms & leafy vines in yellow, turquoise, sapphire blue, orange & pale green w/blue borders on a crackled ivory ground, partial stamp "Keramis - Made in Belgium - 31," ca. 1920s **$690**
Vase, 8 3/4" h., low footring supporting a wide bulbous cylindrical body w/a wide rounded shoulder centering a thick molded rim band, decorated w/a wide center band featuring a continuous row of large upright stylized penguin-like birds in black against a yellow ground, black borders at the base & top, signed & stamped "Ch. Catteau - Keramis - Made in Belgium - Grès Keramis - 1059 C," ca. 1928-29 .... **$6,600**
Vase, 9" h., wide ovoid body w/a wide rounded shoulder centering a short cylindrical neck, decorated w/a continuous band of large grazing antelope in sapphire blue, turquoise, bluish green & black on a crackled ivory ground, marked "Boch F La Louvière - D943 - 13 - 1291," ca. 1925 .... **$1,265**

Boch Catteau Vase with Two Antelope

Vase, 9 1/4" h., bulbous ovoid body w/a short cylindrical neck, a Charles Catteau design w/a grazing antelope on each side painted in shades of blue & black against a white crackled ground, marked "D 943 made in Belgium," 1930s (ILLUS.).......... **$1,265**
Vase, 9 1/4" h., very wide bulbous ovoid body tapering to a short cylindrical neck, decorated w/symmetrical stylized floral reserve in sapphire blue, bluish green & orange on a crackled white ground, stamped "Keramis - Made in Belgium - D60 - R V Larouche Belge - 1293," ca. 1920s **$805**
Vase, 9 1/2" h., bulbous ovoid body tapering to a tiny cylindrical neck, decorated w/a white central band painted w/large styl-

ized black bears against a white band w/narrower brown upper & lower bands trimmed w/black banding & zigzag lines, signed & stamped "Ch. Catteau - D. 1487 - Keramis - Made in Belgium - Grès Keramis - 996 C".. **$5,100**

Vase, 10 1/2" h., flat-bottomed wide ovoid body w/a small cupped neck, decorated w/large brown & black flying bats against a greenish grey sky w/dark grey clouds, design 1378, signed & impressed "D. 1378 - Ch. Catteau - Made in Belgium - Grès Keramis - 1053 C.," ca. 1929 (drilled).............................. **$3,840**

Vase, 10 1/2" h., simple ovoid body tapering to a flat molded mouth, decorated w/four large repeating stylized swirled sunburst flowers in sections separated by a wavy line w/alternating oval dots, in turquoise, yellow & sapphire blue on an ivory crackled ground, turquoise border bands, stamped & signed "Boch F La Louvière - D889 - CT - K 899," ca. 1920s **$575**

Vase, 10 1/2" h., simple ovoid form w/a footring & rim ring, decorated w/wide color vertical bands of stylized tulips & flowers w/leaves in yellow, sapphire blue, green & brown on an ivory crackled ground, sapphire blue bands, marked "Keramis - Made in Belgium - D2779 - 9 - 899," ca. 1920s **$690**

Vase, 12 1/2" h., stoneware, tall simple ovoid form w/a thick short rolled neck, a wide central band decorated in black & cream w/a row of large stylized birds, the upper & lower bands in black w/cream fishscale designs, designed by Charles Catteau, signed "Ch. Catteau - D. 1026A" & incised "Gres Keramis" w/wolf mark & "Keramis - Made in Belgium," original retailer's sticker, ca. 1925......................... **$3,300**

Vase, 13 1/2" h., wide ovoid body tapering to a wide cupped neck, decorated w/a wide central band of stylized antelope in dark blue & black grazing on blue & green grass at the bottom & w/leaves & geometric designs around the top, against a crackle-glazed white ground, signed & stamped "Ch. Catteau - Boch Frs. - La Louvière - Made in Belgium - Fabrication Belgique - 911," ca. 1924 .... **$6,000**

Rare Boch Fres. Penguin Vase

Vase, 14 1/2" h., 13 1/2" d., wide bulbous body w/a small molded mouth, decorated w/a tall band of stylized penguins in black & light green against a white crackle ground, a wide geometric base band composed of black & light green triangles, black in mark & number "D 1104," ca. 1930 (ILLUS.)........................ **$9,400**

Vase, 16" h., tall baluster form w/a cylindrical short neck, decorated w/a wide band of gazelle in dark blue, purple & black among stylized foliage against a creamy white ground, the neck & lower body w/overall geometric ring designs in matching colors, designed by Charles Catteau, signed "Ch. Catteau - D. 943," stamped "Keramis - Made in Belgium - 24," inscribed "762"................................. **$3,300**

Vase, 19 1/4" h., large ovoid form w/a heavy rolled rim, the body painted w/large stylized exotic birds among large rounded blossoms & leafy branches w/berries in greenish yellow on a dark brown ground w/black base & rim bands, designed by Jules-Ernest Chaput, signed, ca. 1930 . **$12,000**

Vase, 19 1/2" h., large, tall ovoid form tapering to a tiny neck w/deeply rolled rim, wide vertical bands of stylized creamy white blossom clusters & green scrolls alternating w/narrow creamy white zigzag stripes, stamped & signed "Ch. Catteau - D. 1003 - Boch Frs. - La Louvière - Made in Belgium - Fabrication Belgique - Grès Keramis - 961 - V.," ca. 1925 .... **$6,000**

Vases, 11 1/2" h., ovoid body tapering to a short cylindrical neck w/molded rim, decorated w/two large stylized standing birds w/extended wings among leafy vines, in sapphire blue, blue, bluish green & pale green on an ivory crackled ground, striped border bands, stamped "Keramis - Made in Belgium - D4507," ca. 1920s, pr... **$920**

Metal-mounted Boch Oxblood Vases

Vases, 11 1/2" h., ovoid oxblood-glazed bodies mounted on a stamped metal foot & fitted w/metal blossom & stem handles flanking the mouth, one marked w/company logo, each drilled in the base, pr. (ILLUS.).. **$375**

Bobcat Mother & Cubs

Boehm Porcelains

Although not antique, Boehm porcelain sculptures have attracted much interest as Edward Marshall Boehm excelled in hard porcelain sculptures. His finest creations, inspired by the beauties of nature, are in the forms of birds and flowers. Since his death in 1969, his work has been carried on by his wife at the Boehm Studios in Trenton, New Jersey. In 1971, an additional studio was opened in Malvern, England, where bone porcelain sculptures are produced. We list both limited and non-limited editions of Boehm.

Bobcat with Cubs, the mother cat on a large tree stump holding one cub in her mouth, the other climbing up to her, rockwork base, marked & numbered under base, 14" l., 9" h. (ILLUS., top of page)...... **$863**

Lighter Grey Catbird with Hyacinths

Catbird with Hyacinths, a light grey bird w/wings down, perched in front of large white & lavender hyacinth blossoms, marked & numbered on base 483, 14 1/2" h. (ILLUS.) **$748**

Dark Catbird with Hyacinths

Catbird with Hyacinths, large dark grey bird w/one wing open, beside tall white & lavender hyacinth blossoms, marked & numbered on base 483, 14" h. (ILLUS.)
.... **$690**

Flamingo on Nest with Chick

Flamingo, nesting bird w/head curved down to feed a chick peeking out from under wing, Audubon Society edition, marked & numbered on base 40316-98, 14 1/2" l., 13 1/4" h. (ILLUS.) **$2,875**

Boehm Red-Winged Blackbirds

Boehm Green Jays on Berried Branches

Green Jays, each perched on a rustic branch w/orange berries, marked & numbered on the base 486, one 12" w. x 19" h., the other 10" w. x 14 1/2" h., pr. (ILLUS.) **$1,955**

Red-Winged Blackbirds, a male & female each modeled on cattails, marked & numbered on base #426, very good condition, 15 1/2" h., the pair (ILLUS., next column) **$2,530**

Varied Bunting, small bird perched at the base of a tall stem of orange bell-shaped blossoms, marked & numbered on the base 481, three flower buds detached, 23 1/2" h. (ILLUS., bottom next column) **$2,185**

A Varied Bunting on Large Flower

Wood Thrushes on Flowering Branches

Wood Thrushes, a male & female perched on white-flowered branches, the female feeding a nest of chicks, the male w/head up singing, ca. 1965, marked & numbered on the bases 485, each 15" h., pr. (ILLUS.)... **$3,680**

Boehm Whooping Crane in Flight

Whooping Crane in flight, large black & white bird, Audubon Society edition, marked & numbered 40254 on base, 18 1/2" h. (ILLUS.) **$1,380**

Cambridge Art Pottery

The Cambridge Art Pottery was incorporated in Cambridge, Ohio, in 1900 and began production of artwares in early 1901. Its earliest lines, Terrhea and Oakwood, were slip-decorated glossy-glazed wares similar to the products of other Ohio potteries of that era.

In 1902 it began production of an earthenware cooking ware line called Guernsey that featured a dark brown exterior and porcelain white lining. This eventually became its leading seller, and in 1909 the name of the firm was changed to The Guernsey Earthenware Company to reflect this fact. In 1907 the company introduced a matte green-glazed art line it called Otoe, but all production of its art pottery lines ceased in 1908. The company eventually became part of The Atlas Globe China Company, which closed in 1933.

Cambridge Oakwood Line Cruet

Cruet, Oakwood line, footed bulbous body tapering to a tall cylindrical neck w/wide spout, small looped shoulder handle, streaky mottled tan & green to dark brown & brick red glossy glaze, impressed on the bottom "Oakwood 34," 5 1/4" h. (ILLUS.) **$70**

Cambridge Oakwood Line Vase

Vase, 7 3/4" h., Oakwood line, simple baluster-form body tapering to a small flaring neck, overall drippy black, brown & yellow glaze, marked on base "Oakwood - 200," bruise at rim, stilt pull on base (ILLUS.)........ **$81**

Canton

This ware has been decorated for nearly two centuries in factories near Canton, China. Intended for export sale, much of it was originally inexpensive blue-and-white hand-decorated ware. Late-18th- and early-19th-century pieces are superior to later ones and fetch higher prices.

Basket & undertray, flaring oval basket w/reticulated sides, on a matching oval undertray, 19th c., 10 1/4" l., 3 3/4" h., 2 pcs. (minor edge chips)............................. **$805**
Bowl, 9" d., round, w/scalloped edge............. **$523**

Fine Canton Lobe-edged Bowl

Bowl, 9" d., 4 1/2" h., serpentine four-lobed rim, 19th c. (ILLUS.)................................ **$1,035**

Nicely Scalloped Canton Bowl

Bowl, 9 1/2" d., 4 1/2" h., squared body w/flaring scalloped rim, interior bottom scene, 19th c. (ILLUS.)........................... **$1,208**
Bowl, 8 1/4 x 10", lobed shape, orange peel glaze, ... **$330**
Container, cov., round w/two wire bale handles, lid w/flat wafer finial, 6 3/4" d., 3 1/4" h... **$990**
Creamer, "bullnose" spout w/flared rim, orange peel glaze, 3 3/4" h. **$220**
Creamer, helmet-shaped w/angled branch handle, 4" h.. **$495**
Creamer, squat body w/high handle, 3 1/4" h... **$220**
Fruit basket & undertray, deep oval reticulated basket w/gently flaring sides & flanged rim, in a deep matching undertray w/reticulated flanged rim, 19th c., basket 8 5/8" l., 4 1/2" h., undertray 9 7/8" l., 2 pcs. **$1,150**
Hot water plate, rounded slightly paneled rim, edge spout opening, 19th c., 9 1/2" d... **$303**
Pitcher, 6" h., bulbous body w/high, thin handle w/molded fan end & exaggerated slope to spout, orange peel glaze............. **$880**
Pitcher, 4 1/2" h., jug-form w/double twisted strap handle, 19th c. **$605**
Platter, 11 1/2" l., oblong w/canted corners, 19th c.. **$413**
Platter, 13 x 16", octagonal w/dark slate blue & white decoration (some firing imperfections in glaze)................................. **$330**

Large Oblong Canton Platter

Platter, 14 1/2 x 17", oblong w/dished sides, 19th c. (ILLUS.) **$805**
Platter, 14 x 17 1/2" rounded octagonal shape, medium blue decoration of a bridge, pagodas & an island, orange peel glaze **$495**

Large Canton Platter

Canton Covered Warming Dish

Platter, 16 x 18 3/4", oblong w/angled corners, 19th c. (ILLUS., previous page) **$1,150**
Platter & strainer, 13 3/4 x 17 1/8", deep oval form, oblong w/canted corners, 19th c., 2 pcs. (minor glaze irregularities, color variations).. **$978**
Serving bowl, oblong octagonal form, 11 x 13 1/2"... **$880**
Serving dish, square w/lobed corners, orange peel glaze, 8 1/2" sq.......................... **$440**
Sugar bowl, cov., cup-shaped w/double, intertwined handles w/applied decorative ends, fruit finial, 3 7/8" d., 4 1/2" h., minor flakes on foot **$523**
Teapot, cov., canister-shaped body & intertwined, reeded handle w/ornate, applied floral ends, fruit finial, straight spout, 5 1/2" h., some rim flakes **$908**
Teapot, cov., cylindrical body tapering in at top, intertwined handle w/decorative ends, fruit finial on lid, curved spout, 6 3/4" h. **$578**

Large Canton Covered Tureen

Tureen, cov., footed deep oblong base w/boar's head end handles, low domed cover w/large center handle & a butterfly design edge band, 19th c., 9 1/2 x 11 1/2", 9" h. (ILLUS.) **$550**

Canton Tureen with Boar Head Handles

Tureen, cov., footed flaring oval shaped w/figural boar head end handles, low

domed cover w/stem finial, 19th c., 8 1/2 x 10", 6 1/2" h. (ILLUS.) **$978**
Tureen, cov., footed oblong body w/animal head end handles, 10 x 12", 8" h. **$1,540**
Vegetable bowl, open, oblong w/cut corners, 9 3/4 x 11 1/2"................................. **$605**

Large Canton Covered Vegetable

Vegetable dish, cov., rectangular w/flaring sides & cut-corners, low domed cover w/figural nut finial, 19th c., 8 1/2 x 9 3/4", 4 1/2" h. (ILLUS.) **$690**
Warming dish, cov., high base w/blue & white design on interior, lid has fruit finial, 9 3/8" d., 5" h. **$660**
Warming dish, cov., shallow oblong base w/angled corners & filling hole at one end, domed cover w/nut-like finial, 19th c., 9 3/4 x 15" (ILLUS., top of page)....... **$1,265**
Water bottle, ovoid, w/long neck, white ground w/hint of blue, darker blue design of buildings w/hills, 7 5/8" h., short hairlines at lip.. **$688**

Capo-di-Monte

Production of porcelain and faience began in 1736 at the Capo-di-Monte factory in Naples. In 1743 King Charles of Naples established a factory there that made wares with relief decoration. In 1759 the factory was moved to Buen Retiro near Madrid, operating until 1808. Another Naples pottery was opened in 1771 and operated until 1806 when its molds were acquired by the Doccia factory of Florence, which has since made reproductions of original Capo-di-Monte pieces with the "N" mark beneath a crown. Some very early pieces are valued in the thousands of dollars but the subsequent productions are considerably lower.

Bowl, 8 3/4" d., wide shallow form w/upright sides molded in relief w/a continuous colorful scene of frolicking bacchantes in a landscape, molded lappets around the bottom, the interior & scalloped rim painted w/foliate scrolls & sprays, 19th c.......... **$431**

Casket, cov., rectangular w/high domed hinged cover, on leafy scroll tab feet, the cover & sides decorated w/colorful relief-molded panels of putti around the sides & a scene of Psyche w/putti on the cover, 19th c., 9 1/2" l., 7 1/2" h. **$518**

Dessert service: twelve 7 3/4" d. dessert plates, eight teacups & seven saucers; each plate painted w/a crested coat-of-arms trimmed in gilt, the border molded in low relief w/mythological figures at leisure pursuits, the bases marked w/blue crowned "N" mark & museum accession numbers & two w/gilt inscription "A Madame la Comtesse de Spilinbergo," late 19th - early 20th c., the set..................... **$1,410**

Ornate Colorful Capo-de-Monte Ewer

Ewer, fancy baroque style w/a square foot supporting a figural dolphin stem below the campana urn-form body molded around the bottom w/masks & scrolls below relief-molded classical figures, the wide shoulder molded w/colorful scrolls & leaves, the figure of a seated man at the top w/his arms around the arched spout, a C-scroll ornate handle from his shoulder to his lower back, overall colorful enamels, blue Crown N mark, first half 20th c., 8 1/2" h. (ILLUS.).......................... **$294**

Capo-di-Monte Mug with Figures

Mug, cylindrical sides molded in relief w/a continous band of satyrs & semi-nude men & women w/grapes, flowering branch handle, gilt trim, blue Crown N mark, early 20th c., 4 3/4" h. (ILLUS.)........ **$115**

Pitcher, 9" h., cylindrical w/enameled relief-molded figural w/a gilt background, scrolled handles, underglaze-blue mark, 19th c. **$288**

Plaques, oblong octagonal form, each decorated in color w/a Classical battle scene, in molded octagonal frames, 19th c., 5 1/2 x 6 12", pr. **$920**

Ornate Capo-di-Monte Stein

Stein, cov., tall cylindrical body molded in relief w/a battle scene w/warriors & horses decorated in bright enamels, domed cover w/figural seated lion finial, elephant head handle, blue Crown N mark, first half 20th c., 8" h. (ILLUS.)....................... **$147**

Urns, cov., a stepped square base supporting a short pedestal below the tall slightly flaring cylindrical body w/molded lion mask side handles & a high stepped cover w/pineapple finial, decorated w/molded low-relief Bacchic putti riding a goat & a donkey decorated in color, gold trim, 20th c., 12" h., pr. **$353**

Wall plaque, teardrop shield-form, a large central scroll-framed landscape scene of warriors w/horses, border cartouches w/military trophies & a grotesque head at the top, in a tooled leather frame, wear, late 19th c., 27" h. **$863**

Carlton Ware

The Staffordshire firm of Wiltshaw & Robinson, Stoke-on-Trent, operated the Carlton Works from about 1890 until 1958, producing both earthenwares and porcelain. Specializing in decorative items like vases and teapots, it became well known for its lustre-finished wares, often decorated in the Oriental taste. The trademark Carlton Ware was incorporated into its printed mark. Since 1958, a new company, Carlton Ware Ltd., has operated the Carlton Works at Stoke.

Long Oval Carlton Ware Bowl

Harebell Pattern Carlton Posy Bowl

Bowl, 9" d., 3 1/2" h., posy-type, Harebell patt., a wide angled rim around a small cylindrical well, blue background painted w/pink bellflowers & other yellow & purple flowers & green, yellow, black & gold leaves (ILLUS.) **$400-425**

Bowl, 7 1/8 x 12 1/4", 3 1/4" h., long oval form w/scalloped sides & squared end handles, Art Deco style decoration w/a large stylized tree in blue w/green leaves & red blossoms, shaded pale yellow to black ground & lustred brick red end handles, ca. 1930s (ILLUS., top of page) **$300-350**

ground decorated w/elaborate gold & light blue Chinese landscapes w/temples, bowl 8 3/4" d., 4" h., jars 4 1/2" d., 9 1/4" h., set of 3 (ILLUS. of part) **$950**

Carlton Ware Tobacco Humidor

Humidor, cov., spherical body w/wide, short cylindrical neck, dark orange background w/a large black reserve painted w/colorful birds & leafy trees & grasses, gold trim, flat brass cover w/disk finial, 4 1/2" d., 4 1/4" h. (ILLUS.) **$300-350**

Carlton Rouge Royale Pitcher

Pitcher, 6 3/4" h., 5" d., Rouge Royale line, flaring gold foot below the ovoid body

Bowl & Jar from Garniture set

Garniture set: two cov. jars & large bowl, "Kang Hsi" patt., each w/a dark blue

decorated w/an iridescent deep red ground w/a large flying bird & trees & branches in the background, overall gold trim & squared gold handle, mother-of-pearl interior (ILLUS.).......................... **$500-550**

Carlton Ware Potpourri Jar

Potpourri jar, cov., wide ovoid body w/a fitted domed cover, yellow ground decorated w/a large cartouche-form black reserve painted in color w/a Chinese landscape w/temples, trees & figures, heavy gold trim, smaller scene on reverse & on the cover, 7 1/2" d., 9 3/4" h. (ILLUS.).. **$400-450**

Carlton Ware Persian Pattern Vase

Vase, cov., 6 5/8" h., 3 1/4" d., footed ovoid body w/a wide, low pagoda-form cover, Persian patt., dark blue ground decorated in color w/an Islamic landscape w/figures in the foreground & a mosque in the distance, gold trim (ILLUS.)................ **$300-350**

Carlton Temple Jar-form Vase

Vase, cov., 8 3/4" h., 3 1/2" d., temple-jar form, the body background in sponged blue painted w/a large black & white tree w/large pink blossoms & green leaves, gold trim, domed cover w/figural gold foo dog finial (ILLUS.) **$350-375**

Carlton Persian Vase with Landscape

Vase, 10 1/2" h., 4 3/4" d., Persian patt., footed ovoid body w/a narrow shoulder to the short flared neck, dark blue ground decorated in color w/a continuous Islamic landscape w/a garden pavilion & figures surrounded by trees, flowers, birds & animals, gold trim (ILLUS.) **$350-400**

Ceramic Arts Studio of Madison

During its 15 years of operation, Ceramic Arts Studio of Madison, Wisconsin, was one of the nation's most prolific producers of figurines, shakers, and other decorative ceramics. The Stu-

dio began in 1940 as the joint venture of potter Lawrence Rabbitt and entrepreneur Reuben Sand. Early products included hand-thrown bowls, pots, and vases, exploring the potential of Wisconsin clay. However, the arrival of Betty Harrington in 1941 took CAS in a new direction, leading to the type of work it is best known for. Under Mrs. Harrington's artistic leadership, the focus was changed to the production of finely sculpted decorative figurines. Among the many subjects covered were adults in varied costumes and poses, charming depictions of children, fantasy and theatrical figures, and animals. The inventory soon expanded to include figural wall plaques, head vases, salt-and-pepper shakers, self-sitters, and "snuggle pairs".

Metal display accessories complementing the ceramics were produced by another Reuben Sand firm, Jon-San Creations, under the direction of Zona Liberace (stepmother of the famed pianist). Mrs. Liberace also served as the Studio's decorating director.

During World War II, Ceramic Arts Studio flourished, since the import of decorative items from overseas was suspended. In its prime during the late 1940s, CAS produced over 500,000 pieces annually, and employed nearly 100 workers.

As primary designer, the talented Betty Harrington is credited with creating the vast majority of the 800-plus designs in the Studio inventory--a remarkable achievement for a self-taught artist. The only other CAS designer of note was Ulle Cohen ("Rebus"), who contributed a series of modernistic animal figurines in the early 1950s.

The popularity of Ceramic Arts Studio pieces eventually resulted in many imitations of lesser quality. After World War II, lower-priced imports began to flood the market, forcing the Studio to close its doors in 1955. An attempt to continue the enterprise in Japan, using some of the Madison master molds as well as new designs, did not prove successful. An additional number of molds and copyrights were sold to Mahana Imports, which released a series of figures based on the CAS originals. Both the Ceramic Arts Studio-Japan and Mahana pieces utilized a clay much whiter and more lightweight than that of Madison pieces. Additionally, their markings differ from the "Ceramic Arts Studio, Madison Wis." logo, which appears in black on the base of many Studio pieces. However, not all authentic Studio pieces were marked (particularly in pairs); a more reliable indicator of authenticity is the "decorator tick mark". This series of colored dots, which appears at the drain hole on the bottom of every Ceramic Arts Studio piece, served as an in-house identifier for the decorator who worked on a specific piece. The tick mark is a sure sign that a figurine is the work of the Studio.

Ceramic Arts Studio is one of the few figural ceramics firms of the 1940s and '50s which operated successfully outside of the West Coast. Today, CAS pieces remain in high demand, thanks to their skillful design and decoration, warm use of color, distinctively glossy glaze, and highly imaginative and exquisitely realized themes.

Many pieces in the Ceramic Arts Studio inventory were released both as figurines and as salt-and-pepper shakers. For items not specifically noted as shakers in this listing, add 50 percent for the shaker price estimate.

Complete reference information on the Studio can be found in Ceramic Arts Studio: The Legacy of Betty Harrington by Donald-Brian Johnson, Timothy J. Holthaus, and James E. Petzold (Schiffer Publishing Ltd., 2003). The official Ceramic Arts Studio collectors group, "CAS Collectors", publishes a quarterly newsletter, hosts an annual convention, and can be contacted at www.cascollectors.com The Studio also has an official historical site, www.ceramicartsstudio.com. Photos for this category are by John Petzold.

Ceramic Arts Studio Marks

Bedtime Girl

Bedtime Girl, 4 3/4" h. (ILLUS.) **$75-95**
Berty, w/ball, 4 1/2" h. **$240-270**
Betty, sleeping, 5 1/2" l. **$240-270**
Betty & Benny, running bunnies, 3" h., 2 1/4" h., pr. **$260-300**
Birch bark canoe, Indian group, 7 1/2" l.
.... **$100-125**
Blythe, 6 1/2" h. **$150-175**

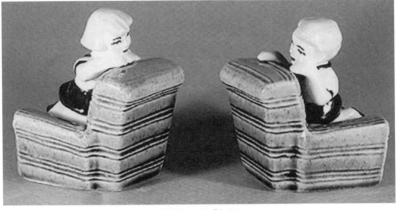

Children in Chairs

Bobby, sitting, 3 1/4" h. $240-270
Boy Doll, 12" h. $1,200-1,400
Boy with Puppy, shelf-sitter, 4 1/4" h. $75-100
Boy with Towel, 5" h. $300-350
Bride & Groom, 4 3/4" h. & 5" h., pr. $250-300
Budgie & Pidgie, parakeets, shelf sitters,
6" h. $100-120
Bunny, Indian group, 1 3/4" h. $35-45
Burmese Chinthe, 5" h. $175-200
Burmese Man & Woman, 4 3/4" h., pr. .. $250-400
Butch & Billy Boxer, 3" l., 2" l. $120-160
Cellist Man, 6 1/2" h. $500-600
Children in Chairs, boy looking over back of
one armchair, girl looking over matching
chair, 1" to 1 1/2" h., each piece (ILLUS.,
top of page) $60-80
Chinese Boy & Girl, 4 1/4" h. & 4" h., pr. ... $30-40
Chinese Lantern Man & Woman wall
plaques, 8" h., pr. $120-140
Chipmunk, Indian group, 2" h. $35-45
Cinderella & Prince, 6 1/2" h., pr. $60-80
Circus Clown & Dog snugglers, 3 3/4" h.
& 2 1/2" h., pr. $150-190
Cocker Spaniel, shelf-sitter, paws over the
edge, 5" l. $80-100
Collie mother, shelf-sitter, 5" h. $75-100
Collie pup sleeping, 2 1/4" l. $50-60

Colonel Jackson, 7 1/4" h. $40-50
Colonial Boy & Girl, 5 1/2" & 5" h., pr. ... $200-250
Colonial Boy & Girl, shelf-sitters, 5" h.,
5 1/4" h., pr. $250-300
Colonial Man & Woman, 6 1/2" h., pr. ... $130-170
Comedy & Tragedy, dark green, 10" h., pr.
.... $160-200
Cowboy, shelf-sitter, 4 1/2" h. $125-150
Cowgirl, shelf-sitter, 4 1/2" h. $125-150
Crocodile & Boy salt & pepper shakers,
4 1/2" l., 3" h., pr. $200-240
Cupid, 5" h. $275-500
Daisy, Ballet Group, standing, 6" h. $260-280
Daisy Donkey, 4 3/4" h. (ILLUS. left with
Elsie Elephant, bottom of page) $85-100
Dawn, 6 1/2" h. $175-200
Dem (donkey) & Rep (elephant) salt &
pepper shakers, 3 3/4" h., pr. $200-250
Drum Girl, 4 1/2" h. $160-180
Drum Girl bank, 4 1/2" h. $220-250
Dutch Dance Boy, 7 1/2" h. $200-250
Dutch Dance Girl, 7 1/2" h. $200-250
Dutch Love Boy & Dutch Love Girl, 5" h.,
pr. $120-140
Egyptian Man, 9 1/2" h. $700-750
Elsie Elephant, 5" h. (ILLUS. right with Don-
key) $85-110

Daisy Donkey & Elsie Elephant

Peter Pan & Wendy

Peter Pan & Wendy, 5 /4" h., pr. (ILLUS.)
.... **$220-270**
Pied Piper, Nursery Rhyme Group, 6 1/4" h... **$200-225**
Pioneer Sam & Pioneer Susie, 5 1/2" h. & 5" h., pr... **$80-100**
Pitcher, 3" h., miniature, relief-molded Adam & Eve decoration, branch handle.. **$40-50**
Polish Boy & Girl, 6 3/4" & 6" h., pr. **$60-80**
Praying Girl, Nursery Rhyme Group, 3" h.
.... **$60-80**

Promenade Man & Woman

Promenade Man, 7 3/4" h. (ILLUS. right)
.... **$100-150**
Promenade Woman, 7 3/4" h. (ILLUS. left with Promenade Man)......................... **$100-150**
Ralph the goat, 4" h. **$75-100**

Rhumba Man & Woman

Rhumba Dancers, man & woman, 7 1/4" h. & 7" h., pr. (ILLUS.).............................. **$80-120**
Rose, Ballet Group, stooping, 5" h. **$260-280**
Running Boy, Nursery Rhyme Group, 3 1/2" h... **$60-80**
Running Girl, Nursery Rhyme Group, 3 1/4" h... **$60-80**

Sad Imp with Spear, 5" h. **$500-550**
Saint George, on charger, 8 1/2" h........... **$145-175**
Sambo & Tiger, tiger 5" l., Sambo 3 1/2" h., pr.. **$500-575**
Santa Claus & evergreen tree salt & pepper shakers, figural, 2 1/4" h. & 2 1/2" h., pr.. **$325-375**
Saucy Squirrel, 2 1/4" h. **$175-350**
Scottie, Sooty, black, 3" h...................... **$45-65**
Scottie, Taffy, brown, 3" h. **$45-65**
Sea gull, Indian group, hooks onto side of canoe, 4" w. wing span **$800-850**
Sea horse & Coral salt & pepper shakers, 3 1/2" h. & 3" h., pr......................... **$100-140**
Seal Mother, 6" l. **$400-450**
Seal Pup, 3" l. **$350-400**
Seal Pup on rock, 5" l. **$450-500**
See No Evil candleholder, 5" h. **$80-100**

Shepherd & Shepherdess

Shepherd & Shepherdess, 8 1/2" h. & 8" h., pr. (ILLUS.)............................... **$180-220**

Skunky Bank

Skunky bank, 4" h. (ILLUS.).................. **$260-280**
Space bowl, 5 1/4" h. **$100-125**
Speak No Evil candleholder, 5" h. **$80-100**
Spring Sue, Four Seasons group, 5" h.
.... **$140-170**

Tembo & Tembino Elephants

Square Dance Boy & Girl

Swedish Dance Couple

Swedish Dance Couple, 6 1/2 & 7" h., pr. (ILLUS.)... $180-240
Swish & Swirl Fish (straight tail/twist tail), 3 1/2", 3".................................... $130-170
Tembo & Tembino Elephant, w/trunk up, 6 3/4" h., w/trunk down, & 2 1/2" h., pr. (ILLUS., top of page)......................... $345-415
Temple Dance Man, 7" h...................... $450-500
Temple Dance Woman, 6 3/4" h............ $450-500
Thai & Thai-Thai salt & pepper shakers, Siamese cats, reclining, 4 1/2" l., 5 1/2" l.
.... $70-90
Thunder Stallion, 5 3/4" h...................... $150-175
Ting-A-Ling & Sung-Tu, 5 1/2" h., 4" h., pr.
.... $50-80
"Toadstool Pixie," elf on mushroom, 4" h.
.... $40-50
Tom Cat, standing, 5" h. $75-95
Tony the Barber bank, bust of man, 4 3/4" h.. $75-100
Tortoise with Cane, 2 1/4" h. $120-140

Square Dance Boy, 6 1/2" h. (ILLUS. left w/girl).. $100-125
Square Dance Girl, 6 1/2" h. (ILLUS. right w/boy)... $100-125
Squeaky Squirrel, 3 1/4" h. $50-70
St. Agnes with Lamb, 6" h. $260-285
Straight Tail Fish salt & pepper shakers, pr.. $160-200
Sultan on Pillow, 4 1/2" h...................... $120-145
Sultan only, 4" h.................................... $130-155
Summer Sally, Four Seasons group, 3 1/2" h... $100-130
Sun-Li & Su-Lin, shelf-sitters, 5 1/2" h., pr.
.... $50-80
Suzette Poodle & Pillow salt & pepper shakers, 3 1/4" h. & 1" sq., pr............. $130-160
Swan Lake Man, 7" h............................. $900-950
Swan Lake Woman, 7" h. $900-950

Chinese Export Dish & Models of Hawks

Chinese Export

Large quantities of porcelain have been made in China for export to America from the 1780s, much of it shipped from the ports of Canton and Nanking. A major source of this porcelain was Ching-te-Chen in the Kiangsi province, but the wares were also made elsewhere. The largest quantities were blue and white. Prices fluctuate considerably depending on age, condition, decoration, etc.

ROSE MEDALLION export wares are listed separately.

Chinese Export Helmet-shape Creamer

Creamer, helmet-shaped, armorial-type, blue band decoration & h.p. blue, red &

gold crest below the spout, ca. 1790, 6 3/4" l., 5 1/2" h. (ILLUS.) **$500**

Dish, squared shape w/lobed corners, decorated w/a h.p. central scene depicting a master w/concubines & servants, floral & butterfly border band, late 18th - early 19th c., 9" w. (ILLUS. right with models of hawks, top of page) **$863**

One of a Pair of Armorial Dishes

Dishes, round, armorial-type, decorated w/two dark blue overglazed bands centering the colorful arms of Oliphant impaling Browne, minor decoration wear, ca. 1790, 6 1/8" d., 1 1/4" h., pr. (ILLUS. of one) **$920**

Models of hawks, colorful perched birds in a muted famille rose palette, late 18th - early 19th c., 10" h., pr. (ILLUS. left with squared dish with scene) **$489**

Early Armorial Plate & Pots de Creme

Plate, 8 3/4" d., armorial-type, wide fancy floral-decorated rim in underglaze-blue, the center painted w/a the large arms of Godfrey w/a Latin motto, hairline in bottom, ca. 1725 (ILLUS. right with pots de creme) **$1,093**

Plates, 10" d., green Fitzhugh patt., ca. 1800, pr. (ILLUS. of one) **$1,150**

Famille Rose Platter with Fighting Dragons

Platter, 13 1/4 x 16 1/8", oval w/flanged rim, famille rose palette, colorful floral border & a central scene of two large iron-red fighting dragons, late 19th c. (ILLUS.) **$403**

Famille Rose Chinese Export Plate

Plate, 9" d., famille rose palette, wide rim painted w/sepia cartouches on a pale rose honeycomb background, centering a scene of a tall vase, table & flowering branch, roughness to glaze on half the rim, minor rim flakes & two small hairlines, ca. 1750 (ILLUS.) **$403**

Blue Fitzhugh Platter

Platter, 17 x 20", oval, blue Fitzhugh patt., 19th c. (ILLUS.) **$770**

One of a Pair of Fitzhugh Pattern Plates

Chinese Export Tea Set for the American Market

Pots de creme, cov., armorial-type, footed bulbous tapering body w/entwined strap handle & domed cover w/pomegranate finial, painted around the rims w/colorful floral band & bearing arms, one w/a hairline, ca. 1800, 3 1/2" h., pr. (ILLUS. left with early armorial plate, previous page) **$633**

Large Chinese Export Soup Tureen

Soup tureen, cov., footed squatty bulbous oval body w/twisted branch end handles, domed cover w/large flower blossom finial, cobalt blue & gilt trim, orange peel glaze, 19th c., 8 x 13 1/2", 11" h. (ILLUS.) **$1,870**

Tea set: cov. teapot, cov. tea caddy, helmet-shaped creamer, cov. cream pot & handleless cup; the oval teapot w/upright sides & a tapering shoulder to the inset cover w/berry finial, the bulbous tapering cream pot w/domed cover, upright flat-sided rectangular tea caddy w/arched shoulder, short neck & domed cap, each piece h.p. on the side in sepia, orange & gold w/a spread-winged American eagle w/shield, made for the American market, late 18th c., teapot 8 1/2" l., the set (ILLUS., top of page) **$5,175**

Tea set: tall tapering cov. teapot, short oval cov. teapot, helmet-shaped creamer, cov. sugar bowl, upright rectangular cov. tea caddy, cake plate & two handleless cups & saucers; each piece h.p. w/a sepia & orange spread-winged eagle & shield, gilt trim, late 18th c., tall teapot 10" h., the set (ILLUS.) **$8,338**

Extensive American-market Chinese Export Tea Set

American-market Chinese Export Tea Set

Tea set: tall tapering cylindrical cov. teapot, short oval cov. teapot & undertray, upright rectangular cov. tea caddy, serving plate, two large handleless tea cups, one smaller tea cup & saucer; each piece h.p. w/an orange & black spread-winged eagle w/an oval medallion decorated w/the initials "SSD," made for the American market, late 18th - early 19th c., tall teapot 9 1/2" h., the set (ILLUS.)................. **$5,000**

Small Chinese Teapot with Piercing

Teapot, cov., a footed spherical double-walled style w/the outer layer pierced overall w/a delicate green vine w/orange blossoms, a light blue shoulder band & the matched domed & pierced cover w/a button finial, a C-form handle & a straight angled silver spout, unmarked, late 18th - early 19th c., chips & repairs on cover, small chip on base rim, 6" h. (ILLUS.)........ **$230**

Teapot, cov., a round foot below a low flaring base below a wide slightly concave body band below a wide slightly rounded shoulder centering a short gold neck, a serpentine spout & C-scroll handle, the high domed cover w/a gold ball finial above a scene of a woman & a cartouche of a man above a band of flowers & birds, the wide shoulder painted overall w/colorful birds, flowers & butterflies, the body band decorated w/continuous scenes of

Colorfully Decorated Chinese Teapot

Chinese ladies, ca. 1840, restoration to rim & spout, chip at pot mouth, wear to cover gilt, 9" h. (ILLUS.)............................ **$690**

Colorful Rose Medallion Teapot

Teapot, cov., Rose Medallion patt., a round flaring foot supporting a wide urn-form body w/a serpentine spout & C-scroll handle, the high domed cover w/a gold ball finial, the cover, shoulder & body all decorated w/h.p. cartouches featuring birds, flowers & butterflies or Chinese figures, gold trim, ca. 1860, 11" l., 10 1/2" h. (ILLUS., previous page) **$920**

Small Famille Rose Teapot

Teapot, cov., Famille Rose palette, footed squatty spherical body w/straight spout & C-form handle, domed flanged cover w/pointed knob finial, h.p. w/Chinese figures in a landscape, 19th c., 5 1/2" h. (ILLUS.) **$288**

American-market Chinese Teapot

Teapot, cov., tall tapering cylindrical body w/a straight angled spout & twisted strap handle, the flanged domed cover w/a knob finial, decorated for the American market w/a rusty orange design of an American eagle w/floral-decorated shield, similar to a design used for the Nichols Family of Salem, Massachusetts, late 18th - early 19th c., two small hairlines w/dings, overall 10" h. (ILLUS.) **$920**

Very Colorful Famille Rose Armorial Tureen

Tureen, cov., armorial-type, Famille Rose palette, footed squatty bulbous oval body w/gilt twisted branch end handles, domed cover w/gilt artichoke finial, decorated w/continuous scenes of Chinese figures in a landscape on the cover, the base painted w/the arms of Grant w/family mottoes, a rim band decorated w/flowers, butterflies & birds, the sides w/a continuous scene of Chinese figures on balconies & in gardens, portions of interior cover rim restored, gilt wear, glaze flaws, ca. 1810, 13 1/2" l., 9" h. (ILLUS.) **$4,140**

Colorful Large Chinese Export Urn

Urn, cov., wide baluster-form body w/foo dog head & ring shoulder handles, domed cover w/figural foo lion finial, famille rose palette, the sides painted w/large reserves w/festival scenes & crowds of Chinese figures, floral background & wide geometric base band, cover finial w/broken tail, second half 19th c., 21" h. (ILLUS.) **$403**

Chinese Export Moon Flask Vase

Vase, 9 1/2" h., moon flask-form, short cylindrical neck flanked by figural red dragon handles above the flattened round sides w/a blue ground ornately decorated w/white floral scrolls, one side w/a large round reserve painted w/a color scene of mounted warriors, the other sides w/a reserve of birds among flowering branches, upright base w/a pink & green geometric design, worn gilt on mouth rim, ca. 1880 (ILLUS.).. **$374**

Chintz China

There are over fifty flower patterns and myriad colors from which Chintz collectors can choose. That is not surprising considering companies in England began producing these showy, yet sometimes muted, patterns in the early part of this century. Public reception was so great that this production trend continued until the 1960s.

Sweet Pea Bowl in Crown Shape

Bowl, Sweet Pea patt., Crown shape, Royal Winton (ILLUS.).. **$750**

Royal Winton Sunshine Butter Pat

Butter pat, Sunshine patt., Royal Winton (ILLUS.).. **$135**

Summertime Cheese Dish

Cheese dish, cov., Summertime patt., Dane shape, Royal Winton (ILLUS.).......... **$350**

Queen Anne Compote

Compote, open, oblong shallow shaped bowl on a flaring rectangular pedestal base, Queen Anne patt., Royal Winton (ILLUS.).. **$225**

Creamer & cov. sugar bowl, Chintz patt., Old Cottage shape, Royal Winton, pr. **$250**

Sunshine Pattern Gravy Boat

Gravy boat & undertray, Sunshine patt., Royal Winton, 2 pcs. (ILLUS.)................... **$295**

Triumph Mustard Jar

Mustard jar, cov., footed barrel shape, Triumph patt., Royal Winton (ILLUS.)........... **$155**

Chintz Majestic Pattern Breakfast Set

Royal Winton Chelsea Pitcher

Pitcher, 3" h., jug-form, miniature milk-type, Chelsea patt., Globe shape, Royal Winton (ILLUS.)... **$110**

Tea set: breakfast set: cov. teapot, cup, creamer, open sugar bowl, toast rack & oblong paneled tray w/end handles; Majestic patt., Countess shape, Royal Winton, the set (ILLUS., top of page)
.... **$1,750-2,000**

Florence Pattern Stacking Tea Set

Tea set: stacking-type, cov. creamer, sugar & teapot; Florence patt., Delamere shape, Royal Winton, the set (ILLUS.)
.... **$1,750-2,000**

DuBarry Pattern Chintz Teapot

Teapot, cov., DuBarry patt., Diamond shape, James Kent, Ltd. (ILLUS.)
.... **$950-1,000**

Joyce-Lynn Ascot Shape Teapot

Teapot, cov., Joyce-Lynn patt., Ascot shape, Royal Winton (ILLUS.) **$1,300-1,500**

Royal Winton Summertime Pattern Teapot

Teapot, cov., Summertime patt., Ajax shape, Royal Winton (ILLUS.).................. **$950**

Royal Winton Silverdale Trivet

Trivet, round, Silverdale patt., Royal Winton (ILLUS.)...................................... **$95**

Clarice Cliff Designs

Clarice Cliff was a designer for A.J. Wilkinson, Ltd., Royal Staffordshire Pottery, Burslem, England when it acquired the adjoining Newport Pottery Company, whose warehouses were filled with undecorated bowls and vases. In about 1925 her flair with the Art Deco style was incorporated into designs appropriately named "Bizarre" and "Fantasque" and the warehouse stockpile was decorated in vivid colors. These hand-painted earthenwares, all bearing the printed signature of designer Clarice Cliff, were produced until World War II and are now finding enormous favor with collectors.

Note: Reproductions of the Clarice Cliff "Bizarre" marking have been appearing on the market recently.

Clarice Cliff Mark

Bowl, 5" d., 3" h., footed flared cylindrical form, Autumn Crocus patt., a yellow band on the inside rim, the exterior w/blue, orange & purple flowers, ca. 1930s (minor glaze scratches)..................................... **$345**

Bowl, 6 1/4" d., octagonal flanged rim on the rounded body, Woodland patt., stylized landscape w/trees in orange, green, black, blue, purple & yellow, marked........ **$550**

Bowl, 6 1/2" d., 3" h., "Bizarre" ware, footed deep slightly flaring sides, Crocus patt., the sides divided into two horizontal bands of color w/a band of small crocus blossoms along the upper half, in orange, blue, purple & green, stamped mark......... **$550**

Bowl, 7 1/2" d., 3 1/8" h., Forest Glen patt., a thin footing below the deep upright round sides curved around the base, a variation w/an orange & brown sky produced in Delicia runnings, mottled orange interior, marked, ca. 1936 (glaze flaking around rim)................................. **$288**

Bowl, 8" d., 3 3/4" h., "Bizarre" ware, deep gently rounded sides tapering to a footring, Original Bizarre patt., a wide band of blocks & triangles around the upper half in blue, orange, ivory & purple, purple band around the bottom section, marked **$500**

Bowl, 8" d., 4 1/4" h., "Bizarre" ware, octagonal, h.p. w/Original Bizarre patt., large crudely painted bands of maroon, dark orange & dark blue diamonds above an ochre base band, ink mark................ **$1,100**

Bowl, 8 3/8" d., 3 1/2" h., round w/deep upright sides, Keyhole patt., a geometric design in yellow, black & green, stamped marks, ca. 1929 (glaze wear)................... **$374**

Bowl, 9" d., deep rounded sides, the upper half w/a wide band in polychrome featuring large stylized cottages w/pointed orange roofs beneath arching trees, lime green banding, marked............................ **$900**

Bowl, 9 1/2" d., 4 1/2" h., orange, green & blue h.p. poppies.................................... **$600**

Butter dish, cov., "Bizarre" ware, short wide cylindrical body w/an inset cover w/large button finial, Secrets patt., decorated w/a stylized landscape in shades of green, yellow & brown w/red-roofed houses on a cream ground, marked, 4" d., 2 5/8" h. **$550**

Candleholders, figural, modeled as a kneeling woman w/her arms raised high holding the candle socket modeled as a basket of flowers, My Garden patt., orange dress & polychrome trim, marked, 7 1/4" h., facing pr. **$1,200**

Candleholders, Fantasque line, cylindrical form w/flared base & rim, Melon patt., decorated w/a band of overlapping fruit in predominantly orange glaze w/yellow, bluish green & brown outline, stamped on base "Hand Painted Fantasque by Clarice Cliff Wilkinson Ltd. England," ca. 1930, minor glaze nicks, two small firing cracks to inside rim of one, 3 1/4" h., pr. **$1,000**

Candlestick, loop-handled, Tonquin patt., red.. **$30**

Two Pairs of Clarice Cliff Candlesticks

Candlesticks, slender baluster-form shaft above a disk foot & w/a wide flattened rim, painted w/bold geometric designs in blue, orange & green, Delicia Citrus patt., brightly painted fruits on a cream ground pr. (ILLUS. left & right) **$2,500**

Candlesticks, squared pedestal foot supporting a tall square tapering shaft & cylindrical socket w/flared rim, decorated in bold geometric designs in orange, cream, green, blue & yellow, pr. (ILLUS. center) **$2,900**

Centerpiece, "Bizarre" ware, model of a stylized Viking longboat, raised on trestle supports & w/a frog insert, glazed in orange, yellow, brown & black on a cream ground, printed factory marks, ca. 1925, restored, 15 3/4" l., 9 5/8" h., 2 pcs. **$1,500**

Rare Crest Pattern Charger

Charger, large round dished form, Crest patt., three large Japanese-style crests in gold, blue, rust red, black & green on a mottled green ground (ILLUS.) **$12,000**

Charger, Taormina patt., round, decorated w/large stylized trees on a cliff top w/the sea in the distance in tones of orange, yellow, green & blue, marked, 17" d. (minor crazing) **$1,093**

Coffee service: cov. coffeepot, creamer, open sugar bowl, five cake plates & six cups & saucers; Ravel patt., creamer & sugar w/pointed conical bodies supported by buttress legs, other serving pieces w/flaring cylindrical bodies, marked, coffeepot 6" h., the set **$1,500**

Condiment set: two jars w/silver-plated lids & a small open bowl fitted in a silver-plated frame w/a looped center handle; each piece h.p. w/stylized red & blue flowers on an ivory ground, marked, tray 4 1/2 x 5", the set (small chip on one piece) **$523**

Cracker jar, cov., "Bizarre" ware, Blue Chintz patt., stylized blue, green & pink blossom forms w/blue border band (ILLUS. center w/plate) **$1,200**

Cracker jar, cov., "Bizarre" ware, bulbous barrel shape w/large side knobs to support the arched woven wicker bail handle, wide flat mouth w/a slightly domed cover centered by a large ball finial, Gayday patt., decorated w/a wide band of large stylized flowers in orange, rust, amethyst, blue & green above a lower band in orange on a cream ground, the cover w/an orange finial & yellow band, 5 7/8" d., 6 1/4" h. (ILLUS. right w/butter dish) **$975**

Delicia Citrus Cracker Jar & Vases

Cracker jar, cov., "Bizarre" ware, squatty kettle-form w/side knobs supporting the swing bail handle, Delicia Citrus patt. (ILLUS. right) **$900**

Cracker jar, cov., Celtic Harvest patt., spherical footed body decorated w/embossed fruit & sheaves of wheat, chromed metal cover, 6 1/2" h. (chrome wear) **$173**

Cup & saucer, "Bizarre" ware, Autumn Crocus patt., Athens shape **$300**

Demitasse set: cov. coffeepot, six demitasse cups & saucers, creamer & open sugar bowl; "Bizarre" ware, Windbells patt., decorated w/a stylized tree on one side, the other w/stylized hollyhocks, small chips to one saucer, 15 pcs. **$3,200**

Dinner service: four dinner plates, thirteen luncheon plates, fifteen soup bowls, eight fruit plates, seven appetizer plates, four dessert plates, seven cups & saucers, cov. sugar, creamer & serving bowl; Biarritz patt., the square plates w/deep rounded wells, the creamer & sugar w/upright flattened round shapes, each decorated w/concentric bands in black, maroon, taupe, gold & yellow on a cream ground, ca. 1929, marked, the set **$2,000**

Figures, "Bizarre" ware, flat cutouts, comprising two groups of musicians & two groups of dancing couples, all highly stylized & glazed in reddish orange, yellow,

lime green, cream & black, printed factory marks, ca. 1925, 5 5/8 to 7" h., 4 pcs.
.... **$35,000**
Jam jar, cov., cylindrical body, Melon patt.,
decorated w/a band of overlapping fruit,
predominantly orange w/yellow, blue &
green w/brown outline, ca. 1930, restora-
tion to rim & side, marked, 4" h. **$690**
Jam pot, cov., "Bizarre" ware, Crocus patt., a
wide shallow base w/low, upright sides fitted w/a shallow, flat-sided cover w/a slightly domed top & flat button finial, the top
decorated w/purple, blue & orange blossoms on an ivory ground, marked, 4" d.,
2 3/4" h. **$550**
Jam pot, cov., Blue Firs patt., flat-sided
round form on small log feet, domed cover w/flat round knob, stylized landscape
w/trees, marked, 4 1/4" h. **$900**
Lemonade set: 8" h. tankard pitcher & four
cylindrical tumblers; each decorated in an
abstract geometric pattern in orange, blue,
purple, green & yellow, marked, the set.... **$1,100**
Pitcher, 5 1/8" h., "Fantasque" line, squared
base w/flattened spherical sides, Autumn
(Balloon Trees) patt. in blue, yellow,
green, orange, black & purple, stamped
on base "Registration Applied For Fantasque Hand Painted Bizarre by Clarice
Cliff Newport Pottery England," ca. 1931,
minor glaze bubbles & nicks **$920**
Pitcher, 5 3/4" h., "Fantasque" line, Melon
patt., wide conical body w/solid triangular
handle, orange & thin black bands flanking a wide central band of stylized mel-
ons in yellow, blue, green & orange,
marked, ca. 1930 (tiny glaze nicks at rim
& base, faint scratch in lower orange
band) **$875**
Pitcher, 6 7/8" h., "Bizarre" ware, flaring cylindrical body w/a wide rim & wide arched
spout opposite an angled handle, Secrets patt., decorated w/a stylized landscape in shades of green, yellow & brown
w/a red-roofed house on a cream ground,
stamped mark **$900**
Pitcher, 7" h., 7" d., "Bizarre" ware, tapering
cylindrical body w/flat rim & wide pointed
spout, flattened angled handle from rim
to base, Sliced Fruit patt., wide band of
abstract fruit in yellow, orange & red,
stamped mark **$1,800**
Pitcher, 9 1/4" h., My Garden patt., wide rim
tapering to a flared base w/embossed
flowers ornamenting the handle in orange, green & brown on a light tan
ground, post-1936.................................... **$288**
Pitcher, 9 3/4" h., 7 3/4" d., jug-type, "Bizarre" ware, Isis shape, Summerhouse
patt., decorated w/trees & gazebos in yellow, green, purple, red & blue against an
ivory ground, marked **$3,900**
Pitcher, 12" h., "Bizarre" ware, Lotus shape,
ringed ovoid body tapering to a wide cylindrical neck, heavy loop handle, Delicia
Citrus patt., large stylized red, yellow &
orange fruits around the top w/green
leaves & streaky green on a cream
ground (ILLUS., top next column) **$2,200**

Lotus Pitcher in Delicia Citrus Pattern

Pitcher, 12" h., jug-type, "Bizarre" ware,
Trees & House patt., decorated w/wide bands of
narrow rings, decorated w/wide bands of
orange & black flanking a wide central
band w/green-roofed houses & black &
orange trees, marked, ca. 1930............. **$2,000**
Plate, 7 3/4" d., Broth patt., predominantly
orange w/bubbles & orange, purple &
blue cobwebs (few glaze scratches) **$230**
Plate, 9" d., "Bizarre" ware, Blue Chintz patt.,
decorated w/stylized flowers in green, blue
& pink against an ivory ground, marked....... **$650**
Plate, 9 3/4" d., Forest Glen patt., a stylized
cottage in a woodland scene in orange,
ivory & green, die-stamped "Clarice Cliff -
Newport Pottery - England"...................... **$950**
Plate, 10" d., "Fantasque" line, Autumn (Balloon Trees) patt. w/blue, yellow, green &
purple trees & orange striped border
bands, base stamped "Fantasque Hand
Painted Bizarre by Clarice Cliff Newport
Pottery England" **$1,725**
Sugar shaker, Autumn patt., sharply point-
ed conical form w/rows of small holes
pierced around the top, decorated in pas-
tel autumn colors, marked, 5 1/2" h. **$1,700**
Sugar shaker, "Bizarre" ware, Bonjour
shape, flattened egg-shaped body set on
two tiny log-form feet, Crocus patt., banded body w/a central row of stylized crocus blossoms, in yellow, blue, orange &
purple, stamped mark, 2 1/2" w., 5" h. **$900**
Sugar shaker, "Bizarre" ware, Crocus patt.,
sharply pointed conical form, decorated
w/blue, purple & orange crocus flowers,
marked, ca. 1930, 5 5/8" h. (chips on
base) **$600**

Clarice Cliff Bizarre Ware Tumbler

Tumbler, Bizarre Ware, slightly flaring cylindrical form, half-round stylized large blossoms along edge of rim in orange, pale green & yellow w/matching narrow bands around the inner rim, minor glaze nicks, 3 5/8" h. (ILLUS., previous page) **$115**

Tumbler, Sunray patt., conical form, polychrome decoration of a stylized sun, orange banding, marked, 3" h. **$800**

Vase, 5 1/4" h., "Bizarre" ware, Shape No. 341, squatty bulbous chalice-form, Delicia Citrus patt., bright fruits on a creamy ground (ILLUS. left w/cracker jar) **$900**

Vase, 8" h., "Bizarre" ware, Nasturtium patt., footed ovoid body w/a flaring rolled rim, decorated w/vivid orange, red & yellow blossoms w/black, red, yellow & green leaves atop a mottled caramel & tan ground against a white background, marked "Nasturtium - Bizarre by Clarice Cliff - Hand painted - England" **$900**

Vase, 8" h., "Bizarre" ware, Shape No. 362, ovoid upper body above a heavy ringed & waisted base, Delicia Citrus patt., brightly painted fruits on a cream ground (ILLUS. center w/cracker jar) **$900**

Crocus Pattern Vase

Vase, 8" h., "Bizarre" ware, Shape No. 386, swelled cylindrical base below the angled shoulder & tall gently flaring neck, Crocus patt., a yellow rim band & brown bottom section below a cluster of colorful crocus blossoms on a cream ground (ILLUS.) **$1,000**

Vase, 9" h., 4 3/4" d., "Bizarre" ware, baluster-shaped, Original Bizarre patt., a wide middle band of multicolored triangles flanked by a dark blue rim band & yellow & orange base bands, No. 264, ink mark (minor wear) **$2,500**

Vase, 9 1/2" h., 6 1/2" d., "Bizarre" ware, Isis shape, ovoid body tapering to a wide, flat rim, decorated in the Melon patt., bold stylized abstract fruits in dark red, blue, orange, green & yellow around the middle flanked by wide dark orange bands, ink mark **$3,200**

Vase, 10 7/8" h., "Bizarre" ware, My Garden patt., cylindrical form tapering to flared foot decorated w/h.p. relief-molded orange & yellow flowers & black leaves on

golden mushroom ground, shape No. 664, Wilkinson, Ltd. **$650**

Vase, 11 3/4" h., 10" d., "Bizarre" ware, Lotus shape, Geometric patt., urn-form, handled, decorated w/a wide maroon base band & wide green neck band flanking a wide central band of triangular devices in a row in cream, purple, blue, maroon & green, blue & cream rim bands & cream handles, marked **$2,900**

Vase, 12 1/4" h., gently flaring conical body on a wide round foot, molded in bold relief w/green & yellow budgie birds on a leafy branch against a light blue shaded to cream ground **$410**

Vases, 8" h., "Bizarre" ware, footed ovoid body w/flared rim, Crocus patt., orange, blue & purple crocuses, green, brown & yellow bands, small glaze chip, marked, pr. **$690**

Clewell Wares

Although Charles W. Clewell of Canton, Ohio, didn't operate a pottery, he is responsible for a category of fine art pottery through his development of a unique metal coating placed on pottery blanks obtained from Owens, Weller and others. By encasing objects in a thin metal shell, he produced copper- and bronze-finished ceramics. Later experiments led him to chemically treat the metal coating to attain the bluish green patinated effect associated with copper and bronze. Although he produced metal-coated pottery from 1902 until the mid-1950s, Clewell's production was quite limited, for he felt no one else could competently recreate his artwork, therefore operated a small shop with little help.

Clewell Wares Mark

Bowl-vase, a small footring supporting a wide bulbous body w/a short widely flared rim, fine bronzed & verdigris patina, incised "Clewell 417-2-G," 5 1/4" d., 4 1/2" h. **$495**

Clewell Presentation Mug

Mug, footed paneled ovoid form w/faux rivets along panels, presentation-type, panels on front read "APA - 1908," marked on base "Clewell Canton, O," 4 1/4" h. (ILLUS., previous page) $150

Vase, 3 3/8" h., bulbous body w/short molded rim, brown patina on upper half w/crusty green patina below, marked "Clewell" (minor scuffs) $252

Vase, 5 1/2" h., 7" d., copper-clad, squatty bulbous body tapering to a short cylindrical neck w/slightly flaring rim, loop handles from center of body to rim, incised "Clewell - 408-2-6," normal wear to fine bronze to verdigris patina, tight lines in copper on shoulder $788

Vase, 6 1/4" h., 3 1/2" d., simple ovoid body w/molded rim, copper-clad w/fine verdigris to bronze patina, some patination flakes to rim, incised "Clewell - 321 - 24" ... $619

Vase, 6 1/2" h., a wide round base tapering to a slender waisted body, deep red patina w/pale green patina band around the base, small glaze chips around base $287

Vase, 7" h., simple ovoid form tapering to a small flat mouth, overall shiny coppery patina, signed, light scratches & wear $374

Vase, 7 1/2" h., 3 1/2" d., ovoid body w/the rounded shoulder centering a small flaring neck, dark green verdigris shaded to dark reddish bronze patina, incised "Clewell - 351 - 215" $1,725

Vase, 7 1/2" h., 3 3/4" d., ovoid body w/the rounded shoulder centering a small flaring neck, overall shaded dark green to lighter green verdigris patina, couple of small patina flakes near base, incised "Clewell - 351- 6" $920

Vase, 7 3/4" h., bulbous base tapering to tall cylindrical neck w/flared rim, early 20th c., inscribed "Clewell 293-29" $575

Simple Elegant Clewell Vase

Vase, 7 3/4" h., flat-bottomed ovoid body w/wide shoulders tapering to a small trumpet mouth, fine overall bronze patina, incised "Clewell 351-258" (ILLUS.) $920

Clewell Vase with Vines & Berries

Vase, 8" h., cylindrical slightly flaring form molded in high relief w/vertical vines topped by leaves & berries, good original patina, minor lines (ILLUS.) $374

Vase, 8 1/2" h., 5" d., simple ovoid form tapering to a flat rim, deep reddish bronze & verdigris patina, pea-sized colored spot near base, incised "Clewell - 60- 215" $978

Vase, 9" h., 4 1/2" d., tall slender tapering urn-form body w/a flattened shoulder centering a short rolled neck flanked by small angled handles, bronze & verdigris patina, incised "C.W. Clewell - 520-220" (few patina chips on base) $1,125

Clewell Vase Clad on a Weller Vase

Vase, 9 5/8" h., slender ovoid body tapering to a trumpet neck, cladding on a Weller L'Art Nouveau vase molded w/an ear of corn design, base marked "Weller Art Nouveau," fine original patina (ILLUS.)...... $978

Vase, 10" h., tall baluster-form body, fine bronzed patina, No. 305-6, signed............. $862

Vase, 11" h., 7 3/4" d., copper-clad wide slightly flaring cylindrical body w/a narrow angled shoulder to the wide closed rim, unusual striated gold, green & copper patina, minor ceramic loss inside rim, incised "Clewell" $1,392

Vase, 11 1/4" h., 8 1/2" d., a large gently flaring cylindrical body w/a wide angled shoulder centering a low squatty neck, verdigris finish, signed $2,760

Vase, 14 1/2" h., 6 1/4" d., tall baluster-form copper-clad body w/flared rim on the short cylindrical neck, bronze to verdigris patina, small flakes to verdigris & some splits to copper on neck, incised "Clewell - 378 - 26" **$2,588**

Clifton Pottery

William A. Long, founder of the Lonhuda Pottery, joined Fred Tschirner, a chemist, to found the Clifton Art Pottery in Newark, New Jersey, in 1905. Crystal Patina was its first art pottery line and featured a subdued pale green crystalline glaze later also made in shades of yellow and tan. In 1906 its Indian Ware line, based on the pottery made by American Indians, was introduced. Other lines the Pottery produced include Tirrube and Robin's-egg Blue. Floor and wall tiles became the focus of production after 1911, and by 1914 the firm's name had changed to Clifton Porcelain Tile Company, which better reflected its production.

Clifton Crystal Patina Vase

Vase, 6 1/8" h., Crystal Patina line, footed squatty bulbous lower body tapering to a wide cylindrical neck w/a flaring rim, shaped light brown to pale green glaze w/long dark green streaks, incised company logo, dated 1906 (ILLUS.) **$288**

Clifton Vase in the Tirruba Line

Vase, 8 1/2" h., 5 1/4" d., Tirruba Line, footed bottle-form w/a wide squatty lower body tapering sharply to a flaring neck, matte red ground h.p. w/a white nasturtium blossom & pale green leaves up the side, stamped "Clifton - 140" (ILLUS.) **$374**

Clifton Indian Ware Gourd-form Vase

Vase, 11 1/2" h., Indian Ware, bulbous gourd-form body w/a tall tapering cylindrical neck, dark brown ground decorated around the bottom w/alternating ovals of tan & medium brown, marked "Middle Mississippi Valley - 231" (ILLUS.) **$690**

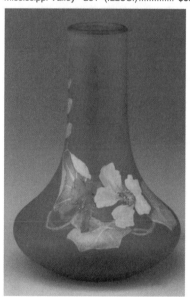

Clifton Vase with Nasturtium Blossoms

Vase, 12" h., 8 1/4" d., Tirruba Line, wide squatty bulbous base tapering sharply to a tall cylindrical neck, painted w/a large yellow & red nasturtium blossom & green leafy vine, marked "Clifton - Tirruba -254" (ILLUS.) **$805**

Coalport

Coalport Porcelain Works operated at Coalport, Shropshire, England, from about 1795 to 1926 and has operated at Stoke-on-Trent as Coalport China, Ltd., making bone china, since then.

Very Ornate Coalport Small Box

Box, cov., flat-bottomed spherical form, the domed cover w/a central "agate" panel surrounded by a gilt band enameled w/"ruby" jewels, radiating alternating cartouches of "agate" or turquoise "jewels," on an embossed gold ground w/overall tiny blue beading, each reserve against a pale blue band w/ornate gilt urn designs, the base w/matching decoration, interior & base in powdered gilt, dated 1893, green printed crown mark, overprinted gilt Chicago Exhibition mark, probably designed by T.J. Bott, 4 1/2" d. (ILLUS.) **$2,629**

Ornate Beaded Gold Coalport Ewer

Ewer, ring-footed baluster-form body tapering to a slender neck w/long arched spout

& ornate gold C-scroll handle, creamy white ground, the side painted w/a small oval lakeside landscape against a wide embossed gold band decorated overall w/graduated turquoise beading, gilt scroll & band trim, ca. 1900, green crowned mark, Registration No. 283672, 7 3/8" h. (ILLUS.).. **$956**

Very Ornate Coalport Loving Cup

Loving cup, three-handled, the tall domed, knopped & ringed pedestal base in cobalt blue w/ornate gold trim, supporting a large deep rounded trefoil bowl surrounded by three fancy gold C-scroll handles, the upper cobalt blue band centered by a small landscape medallion w/a lakeside view framed in gold & w/ornate gold scrolling above the creamy white lower body, green printed crowned mark, Pattern No. V5950, ca. 1900, 9" h. (ILLUS.) **$837**

Coalport China Canton Pattern Teapot

Teapot, cov., Canton patt., Kingsware line, footed squatty bulbous gently lobed body w/a wide mouth, domed cover w/arched loop finial, angled spout, C-scroll handle, part of the Wedgwood Group, England (ILLUS.).. **$90**

Ruby Ground Ornate Coalport Vase

Vase, 5 3/4" h., the short flaring pedestal base in gold w/turquoise beading supporting the wide squatty bulbous body w/a deep ruby red ground painted on the front w/a quatrefoil panel w/a lakeside landscape within a border band of ornate gilt scrolling, large angular gold shoulder handles, the wide short cream-ground neck & domed cover w/overall turquoise blue beading, ca. 1900, printed green crowned mark, Pattern No. V6677, mark of retailer Bailey, Banks & Biddle, Philadelphia (ILLUS.) **$1,434**

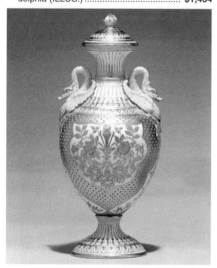

Outstanding Gold & Cream Coalport Vase

Vase, cov., 9 3/4" h., domed foot & short stem supporting the large ovoid body tapering to a trumpet neck w/domed cover & berry finial, cream ground, the gilt-trimmed cover above a collared ga-

drooned neck flanked by figural swan handles, the sides & central body decorated w/a meandering vine issuing cones, reserved on a shield-shaped embossed gold ground decorated w/graduated turquoise beading, ca. 1900, printed green crowned mark, Pattern No. V.2497 (ILLUS.) **$1,912**

Copeland & Spode

W.T. Copeland & Sons, Ltd., has operated the Spode Works at Stoke, England, from 1847 to the present. The name Spode was used on some of its productions. Its predecessor, Spode, was founded by Josiah Spode about 1784 and became Copeland & Garrett in 1843, continuing under that name until 1847. Listings dated prior to 1843 should be attributed to Spode.

Copeland & Spode Mark

Copeland Imari Pattern Compotes

Compotes, open, 9 1/4" d., Imari patt., the shallow round bowls w/three floral panels alternating w/cobalt blue & gold bands, pedestal base w/decorated panels on the round foot, one w/pinhead size flake, Copeland, 19th c., pr. (ILLUS.) **$440**

Ewers, large inverted pear-shaped body on a ringed stem & domed foot, tall reeded gilt scroll handle w/paired snakes & a Bacchic mask at the base & paired snakes at the top at the wide arched spout over the ringed cylindrical neck, overall cobalt blue ground, decorated overall in the Persian taste w/gold strapwork, pendent rosettes & trailing flowers all extensively trimmed w/enameled beads & jewels in white, ruby, blue & turquoise, Copeland, probably decorated by William Henry Goss, green printed marks, ca. 1855, 15 1/8" h., pr. (ILLUS., top next page) **$20,315**

Extraordinary Large Ornate Copeland Ewers

Platter, 17 1/2 x 22 1/2" oval, transfer design of flowers including chrysanthemums in blue, impressed Spode mark, first half 19th c. **$523**

Charming Colorful Copeland Salt Dip

Salt dip, triple, three deep rounded dishes joined across the top w/an arched three-part handle in white w/gold wrapped ribbon decor, each bowl decorated on the exterior in color w/a shell surrounded by entwined rose & cornflower garlands, each interior w/a berried laurel wreath, dated 1895, printed gold crowned Copeland mark, mark of retailer T. Goode & Son, London, 4" w. (ILLUS.) **$1,673**

Tea set: cov. teapot, cov. sugar bowl, creamer, eight 9" d. plates & eight cups & saucers; Classical Revival style, serving pieces of squatty bulbous oblong boat shape w/angled collars & inset domed covers w/button finials, pointed C-scroll handles, each piece decorated w/a dark cinnamon brown band painted w/gilt roses, marked "Spode - Copelands China - England - Tiffany & Co. - New York," ca. 1890s, one plate w/small flake, gilt wear to rims, teapot 5" h., the set (ILLUS.) **$715**

Copeland-Spode China Tea Set

Early Spode Porcelain Teawares

Tea set: cov. teapot & seven handled cups & saucers; the oval pot w/upright sides & a flat shoulder centered by a domed cover w/oval knob finial, serpentine spout & C-form handle, each piece decorated w/a wide orange-painted band trimmed w/stylized white flowerheads & bands of gilt leaves, Spode, Pattern No. 878, England, ca. 1820, some gilt wear, two saucers w/hairlines, the set (ILLUS. of part) **$405**

Sevres-style Copeland Teacup & Saucer

Teacup & saucer, footed deep rounded teacup decorated in the Sevres-style w/a cobalt blue ground centering a large oval reserve of colorful fruits framed by fancy gilt scrolling, matching saucer, printed green Copeland monogram marks, ca. 1870, saucer 5 1/2" d., set (ILLUS.) **$538**

Copeland-Spode Buttercup Teapot

Teapot, cov., Buttercup patt., squatty ribbed body w/concave ribbed shoulder & low domed cover w/blossom finial, straight ribbed spout & C-form handle, England, early 20th c. (ILLUS.) **$85**

Lovely Copeland Portrait Vases

Vases, cov., 11" h., a square foot & tapering pedestal in white w/heavy gold trim, the large ovoid body tapering to a short flaring neck w/domed cover & pointed knob finial, long low C-scroll handles from the shoulder to the vase, each painted on the front w/a large oval reserve portrait of an 18th c. beauty surrounded by a gold background painted overall w/meandering pink & green rose vines, neck & cover w/gold decoration matching the foot, printed green Copeland marks, ca. 1900, artist-signed, pr. (ILLUS.) **$1,793**

Cowan

R. Guy Cowan opened his first pottery studio in 1912 in Lakewood, Ohio. The pottery operated almost continuously, with the exception of a break during the First World War, at various locations in the Cleveland area until it was forced to close in 1931 due to financial difficulties.

Many of this century's finest artists began with Cowan and its associate, the Cleveland School of Art. This fine art pottery, particularly the designer pieces, are highly sought after by collectors.

Many people are unaware that it was due to R. Guy Cowan's perseverance and tireless work that art pottery is today considered an art form and found in many art museums.

Cowan Marks

Ashtray, model of a ram, green, designed by Edris Eckhardt, 5 1/4" l., 3 1/2" h. (ILLUS. lower left with chick ashtray/nut dish, bottom this column) **$225**

Ashtray, center relief-molded unicorn decoration, caramel glaze, designed by Waylande Gregory, w/footed foliate metal stand, Shape No. 925, 3/4 x 5 1/2" **$100**

Ashtray, three-section base w/figural leaping gazelle & foliage on edge, Oriental Red glaze, designed by Waylande Gregory, 5 3/4" h. (ILLUS. lower right with horse book end & boy & girl book ends, next column)... **$300**

Ashtray/nut dish, ivory glaze, Shape No. 769, 1" h... **$20**

Cowan Clown Ashtrays & Vases

Ashtray/nut dish, figural clown Periot, blue or ivory glaze, designed by Elizabeth Anderson, Shape No. 788, 2 1/2 x 3", each (ILLUS. lower center) **$130**

Cowan Ashtrays, Flower Frog & Vase

Ashtray/nut dish, model of a chick, green glaze, Shape No. 768, 3 1/2" h. (ILLUS. bottom center).. **$90**

Bookends, figural, model of a fish, Oriental Red glaze, Shape No. 863, 4 5/8" h., pr. ... **$800**

Bookends, figural Art Deco-style elephant, push & pull, tan glaze, designed by Thelma F. Winter, one Shape No. 840 & one Shape No. 841, 4 3/4" h., pr. **$800**

Cowan Bookends & Model of Horse

Bookends, figural, model of a seated polar bear, front paws near face, ivory glaze, designed by Margaret Postgate, 6" h., pr. (ILLUS. left)... **$1,200**

Bookends, figural, a nude kneeling boy & nude kneeling girl, each on oblong bases, creamy white glaze, designed by Frank N. Wilcox, Shape No. 519, Marks 8 & 9, ca. 1925, 6 1/2" h., pr. (ILLUS. with Cowan ashtray & kicking horse book end)... **$350**

Bookends, figural, a little girl standing wearing a large sunbonnet & full ruffled dress, verde green, designed by Kat. Barnes Jenkins, Shape No. 521, 7" h., pr. .. **$350**

Variety of Cowan Animal Pieces

Bookends, figural, model of a unicorn, front legs raised on relief-molded foliage base, orange glaze, designed by Waylande Gregory, Shape No. 961, mark No. 8, 7" h., pr. (ILLUS. left) **$1,200**

Bookends, figural, model of a ram, black, thick rectangular base w/slanted top, Shape No. E-3, designed by Waylande Gregory, 7 1/2" h., pr. **$1,800**

Elephant Bookends & Paperweights

Bookends, figural, modeled as a large rounded stylized elephant w/trunk curved under, standing on a stepped rectangular base, overall Oriental Red glaze, designed by Margaret Postgate, Shape No. E-2, 7 1/4" h., pr. (ILLUS. top center & lower left).. **$1,800**

Cowan Bookends & Ashtray

Bookends, model of a stylized horse, back legs raised in kicking position, black, designed by Waylande Gregory, Shape No. E-1, 9" h., pr. (ILLUS. of one, with ashtray & boy & girl book ends)......................... **$2,000**
Bowl, miniature, 2" d., footed, flared body, Shape No. 514, mark No. 5, orange lustre.. **$50**

Cowan Bowl & Vases

Bowl, 5 1/4" d., individual, green & black, designed by Arthur E. Baggs (ILLUS. right)... **$2,000**
Bowl, 7 1/2" w., octagonal, the alternating side panels hand-decorated w/floral design, brown & yellow glaze, Shape No. B-5-B... **$300**
Bowl, 2 1/2 x 9 1/4", Egyptian blue glaze, designed by R.G. Cowan, Shape No. B-12.. **$75**
Bowl, w/drip, 3 x 9 1/2", blue lustre finish, Shape No. 701-A..................................... **$100**
Bowl, 2 1/4 x 10 1/4", blue pearl finish........... **$100**
Bowl, 3 x 11 1/4", designed to imitate hand molding, two-tone blue glaze, Shape No. B-827.. **$225**
Bowl, 3 x 10 x 11 1/2", leaf design, ivory & green, designed by Waylande Gregory..... **$175**
Bowl, 3 x 9 1/4 x 12 1/4", copper crystal glaze, Shape No. B-785-A......................... **$125**
Bowl, 3 x 6 x 12 1/2" oblong, caramel w/light green glaze, Shape No. 683............ **$60**
Bowl, 2 3/4 x 11 1/2 x 15", Oriental Red glaze, designed by Waylande Gregory, Shape No. B-4...................................... **$225**
Bowl, 3 x 8 1/2 x 16 1/4", footed shallow form, flaring scalloped sides & rim, downcurved side handles, ivory exterior w/blue interior glaze, Shape No. 743-B............... **$125**
Bowl-vase, green & gold, Shape No. B-4, 11"... **$250**

Cowan Bust

Bust of a woman, close-cut hair in ringlets, original sculpture by Jose Martin, terra cotta, 13 1/2" h. (ILLUS.)........................ **$6,500**
Buttons, decorated w/various zodiac designs, by Paul Bogatay, 50 pcs................. **$500**
Candelabrum, "Pavlova," porcelain, two-light, Art Deco style, a footed squatty tapering central dish issuing at each side a stylized hand holding an upturned cornucopia-form candle socket, the center fitted w/a figure of a nude female dancer

standing on one leg w/her other leg raised, her torso arched over & holding a long swirled drapery, Special Ivory glaze, stamped mark, 10" l., 7" h. (chip under rim of one bobeche) **$525**

Candleholder, flaring base w/flattened rim, black & silver, Shape No. 870, 1 1/2" h. **$50**

Candleholder, figural, model of a Viking ship prow, green glaze, Shape No. 777, 5 1/4" h. **$35**

Candleholders, Etruscan, Oriental Red glaze, Shape No. S-6, 1 3/4" h., pr. **$60**

Candleholders, ivory glaze, Shape No. 692, 2 1/4" h., pr. **$25**

Candleholders, footed, designed by R.G. Cowan, ivory, Shape No. 811, 2 3/8" h., pr. **$35**

Candleholders, blue lustre finish, Shape No. 528, 3 1/2" h., pr. **$35**

Candleholders, semicircular wave design, white glaze, Shape No. 751, 4 3/4" h., pr. .. **$100**

Various Cowan Pieces

Candlestick, flared base below twisted column, blossom-form cup, green & orange drip glaze, Shape No. 625-A, 7 3/4" h. (ILLUS. far right) **$100**

Candlestick, figural, Byzantine figure flanked by angels, golden yellow glaze, designed by R.G. Cowan, 9 1/4" h. (ILLUS. left) **$325**

Byzantine Angel Candlesticks

Candlestick, figural, Byzantine figure flanked by angels, salmon glaze, designed by R.G. Cowan, 9 1/4" h. (ILLUS. right) **$375**

Cowan Figural Nude Candlestick

Candlestick, two-light, large figural nude standing w/head tilted & holding a swirling drapery, flanked by blossom-form candle sockets supported by scrolled leaves at the base, matte ivory glaze, designed by R.G. Cowan, Shape No. 745, 7 1/2" w., 9 3/4" h. (ILLUS.) **$1,000**

Cowan Figural Nude Candlestick

Candlestick, figural, seminude female standing before figural branches on round base w/flared foot, one arm across her body & the other raised overhead, shaded tan & green glaze, designed by R.G. Cowan, Shape No. 744-R, 12 1/2" h. (ILLUS.) **$1,000**

Candlestick/bud vase, tapering cylindrical shape w/flared foot & rim, blue lustre, Shape 530-A, 7 1/2" h. $70
Candlesticks, curled form, royal blue, 1 1/2" h., pr. $75
Candlesticks, figural grape handles, ivory glaze, 4" h., pr. $85
Candlesticks, w/loop handle, green, Shape No. 781, 4" h., pr. $65
Candlesticks, figural sea horse w/flared base, green, Shape No. 716, 4 3/8" h., pr. $50
Candlesticks, "The Girl Reserve," designed by R.G. Cowan, medium blue, Shape No. 671, 5 1/2" h., pr. $275

Cowan Candlesticks & Vase

Candlesticks, model of a marlin on waveform base, verde green, designed by Waylande Gregory, 8" h., pr. (ILLUS. right) $1,250
Centerpiece set, 6 1/4" h. trumpet-form vase centered on 8" sq. base w/candle socket in each corner, Princess line, vase Shape No. V-1, Mark No. 8, candelabra Shape No. S-2, Mark No. 8, black matte, 2 pcs., together w/four nut dishes/open compotes, green glaze, Shape No. C-1, Mark No. 8, the set $500
Charger, "Polo" plate, incised scene w/polo players & flowers under a blazing sun, covered in a rare glossy brown & cafe-au-lait glaze, designed by Victor Schreckengost, mark Nos. 8 & 9, Shape No. X-48, impressed "V.S. - Cowan," 11 1/4" d. $800
Charger, wall plaque, yellow, 11 1/4" d........ $75
Charger, octagonal, hand-decorated by Thelma Frazier Winter, 13 1/4" $1,000
Cigarette holder, w/wave design, Oriental Red glaze, designed by Waylande Gregory, Shape No. 927-J, 3 1/4" $75
Cigarette/match holder, sea horse decoration, pink, No. 726, 3 1/2 x 4" $55
Cigarette/match holder, flared foot w/relief-molded sea horse decoration, orange glaze, Shape No. 72, 3 1/2" h. $35
Clip dish, green, 3 1/4" d. (part of desk set, Shape PB-1)... $25

Comport, footed, square, green & white glaze, Shape No. 951, 4 1/2" sq., 2 1/4" h.. $30
Console bowl, octagonal, stand-up-type, verde green, Shape No. 689, 3 x 8 x 8 1/2"... $70
Console bowl, footed, low rounded sides w/incurved rim, orange lustre, Shape No. 567-B, 2 3/4 x 9 3/4"............................... $40
Console bowl, footed, flaring fluted sides, white glaze exterior, blue glaze interior, Shape No. 713-A, 3 1/2 x 7 1/4 x 10 1/2" $75
Console bowl, April green, Shape No. B-1, 11 1/2" l., 2 1/4" h................................... $75
Console bowl, turquoise & dark matte blue, Shape No. 690, 3 1/2 x 8 x 16".................... $95
Console bowl, ivory & pink glaze, Shape No. 763, 3 1/4 x 9 x 16 1/2" $65
Console bowl, w/wave design, verde green, designed by Waylande Gregory, 2 3/4 x 9 x 17 1/2" $250
Console bowls, 3 3/4 x 4 1/2 x 11", two-handled, footed, widely flaring fluted sides, verde green, Shape No. 538, pr. $225
Console set: 6 1/2 x 10 1/2 x 17" bowl & pr. of candleholders; footed bowl w/figural bird handles, lobed sides, designed by Alexander Blazys, Shape No. 729, mottled blue glaze, the set............................ $425
Console set: 9" d. bowl & pair of 4" h. candleholders; ivory & purple glaze, Shape Nos. 733-A & 734.................................. $150

Cowan Decanters & Wine Cups

Decanter w/stopper, figural King of Clubs, a seated robed & bearded man w/a large crown on his head & holding a scepter, black glaze w/gold, designed by Waylande Gregory, Shape E-4, 10" h. (ILLUS. left) $750
Decanter w/stopper, figural Queen of Hearts, seated figure holding scepter & wearing crown, Oriental Red glaze, designed by Waylande Gregory, Shape No. E-5, 10 1/2" h. (ILLUS. right with King of Clubs decanter).. $700
Desk set, w/paper clip dish, Oriental Red glaze, Shape PB-1, 2 1/2 x 5 1/2", the set $175

Figurine, "Pierette," stylized figure of young woman wearing a short flaring skirt & holding a scarf behind her, russet & salmon glaze, designed by Elizabeth Anderson, Shape No. 792, 8 1/4" h. (ILLUS. center with polar bear book ends, top page 164) **$1,000**

Cowan Figurines & Flower Frog

Figurine, "Spanish Dancer," female, white, designed by Elizabeth Anderson, Shape No. 793, 8 1/2" h. (ILLUS. right) **$750**
Figurine, "Spanish Dancer," male, white, designed by Elizabeth Anderson, Shape No. 793, 8 3/4" h. (ILLUS. left) **$750**
Figurine, kneeling female nude, almond glaze, 9" h. **$325**

Russian Tambourine Player Figurine

Figurine, Russian peasant, "Tambourine Player," white crackle glaze, designed by Alexander Blazys, Shape No. 757-760, 9" h. (ILLUS.) **$750**
Figurine, "Persephone," standing female nude holding a long scarf out to one side and near her shoulder, ivory glaze, de-

signed by Waylande Gregory, Shape No. D-6, 15" h. **$2,750**
Figurine, "Nautch Dancer," female w/a flaring pleated skirt on rectangular base, semi-matte ivory glaze w/silver accents, incised "Waylande Gregory," impressed mark, 6 3/4 x 9 1/4", 17 3/4" h **$5,000**
Figurines, "Spanish Dancer," male & female figures h.p. in polychrome glazes, the male mark No. 9, Shape No. 794-D, 8 1/4" h. & the female mark No. 8, Shape No. 793-D, 8 1/2" h., designed by Elizabeth Anderson, impressed marks, pr...... **$1,500**
Finger bowl, Egyptian blue, Shape No. B-19, 3" **$75**
Flower frog, figural, Art Deco dancing nude woman leaning back w/one leg raised & the ends of a long scarf held in her outstretched hands, overall white glaze, impressed mark, 7 1/2" h. **$325**
Flower frog, figural, Art Deco nude scarf dancer, No. 35, ivory glaze, signed, 7 1/4" h. **$375**
Flower frog, figural, Art Deco style, two nude females partially draped in flowing scarves, each bending backward away from the other w/one hand holding the scarf behind each figure & their other hand joined, on an oval base w/flower holes, ivory glaze, designed by R.G. Cowan, Shape No. 685, 7 1/2" h. (ILLUS. lower right with "Repose" flower frog) **$600**

Flower Frogs No. 698 & "Awakening"

Flower frog, figural, Art Deco-style nude dancing woman in a curved pose, standing on one leg & trailing a long scarf, ivory glaze, designed by Walter Sinz, Shape No. 698, 6 1/2" h. (ILLUS. left with Awakening flower frog) **$175**
Flower frog, figural, "Awakening," an Art Deco woman draped in a flowing scarf standing & leaning backward w/her arms bent & her hands touching her shoulders, on a flower-form pedestal base, ivory glaze, designed by R.G. Cowan, Shape No. F-8, impressed mark, 1930s, 9" h. (ILLUS. right with flower frog No. 698) **$550-650**

Figural Nude with Scarf Flower Frog

Cowan Female Form Flower Frogs

Flower frog, figural, "Diver," waveform base w/tall wave supporting nude female figure, back arched & arms raised over head, ivory glaze, designed by R.G. Cowan, Shape No. 683, 8" h. (ILLUS. right) **$800**

Flower frog, figural, "Fan Dancer," a standing seminude Art Deco woman, posed w/one leg kicked to the back, her torso bent back w/one arm raised & curved overhead, the other arm curved around her waist holding a long feather fan, a long drapery hangs down the front from her waist, on a rounded incurved broad leaf cluster base, overall Original Ivory glaze, designed by R.G. Cowan, Shape No. 806, stamped mark, 4" w., 9 1/2" h. **$2,000**

Flower frog, figural, "Marching Girl," Art Deco style, a nude female partially draped w/a flowing scarf standing & leaning backward w/one hand on her hip & the other raising the scarf above her head, on an oblong serpentine-molded wave base w/flower holes, ivory glaze, designed by R.G. Cowan, Shape No. 680, 8" h. (ILLUS. lower left with "Repose" flower frog) **$325**

Flower frog, figural, nude female, one leg kneeling on thick round base, head bent to one side & looking upward, one arm resting on knee of bent leg w/the other hand near her foot, ivory glaze, designed by Walter Sinz, 6" h. (ILLUS. left with Diver flower frog) **$375**

Flower frog, figural, nude woman w/long flowing scarf, ivory, designed by R.G. Cowan, Shape No. 687, 11 3/4" h. (ILLUS., top next column) **$750**

Flower frog, figural, Pan sitting on large toadstool, ivory glaze, designed by W. Gregory, Shape No. F-9, 9" h. (ILLUS. with ram & chick ashtrays, page 164) **$650**

Various Cowan Flower Frogs

Flower frog, figural, "Repose," Art Deco style, a seminude sinewy woman standing & slightly curved backward, her arms away from her sides holding trailing drapery, in a cupped blossom-form base, ivory glaze, designed by R.G. Cowan, Shape No. 712, 6 1/2" h. (ILLUS. lower center) **$350**

Flower frog, figural, "Scarf Dancer," Art Deco-style nude dancing woman in a curved pose standing on one leg & holding the ends of a long scarf in her outstretched hands, ivory glaze, designed by R.G. Cowan, Shape No. 686, 7" h. (ILLUS. top with "Repose" flower frog) **$325**

"Swirl Dancer" Flower Frog

Flower frog, figural, "Swirl Dancer," Art Deco nude female dancer standing & leaning to the side, w/one hand on hip & the other holding a scarf which swirls about her, on a round lobed base w/flower holes, ivory glaze, designed by R.G. Cowan, Shape No. 720, 10" h. (ILLUS.) **$1,200**

Flower frog, figural, "Triumphant," figure of a standing seminude Art Deco woman w/one leg raised, leaning back w/one arm raised above her head & the other on her hip, a clinging drapery around her lower body, standing on a round incurved leaf cluster base, overall Original Ivory glaze, stamped mark, 4 1/2" w., 15" h. **$1,400**

Flower frog, figural, "Wreath Girl," figure of a woman standing on a blossom-form base & holding up the long tails of her flowing skirt, ivory glaze, designed by R.G. Cowan, Shape No. 721, 10" h. (ILLUS. center with Diver flower frog) **$650**

Flower frog, fluted flower-form base centered by relief-molded stalk & leaves supporting the figure of a female nude standing w/one leg bent, knee raised, leaning backward w/one arm raised overhead & the other resting on a curved leaf, ivory glaze, designed by R.G. Cowan, Shape No. F-812-X, 10 1/2" h. (ILLUS. center with Spanish Dancers) **$750**

Flower frog, model of a deer, designed by Waylande Gregory, ivory glaze, Shape No. F-905, 8 1/4" h. (ILLUS. right with unicorn book ends) **$450**

Flower frog, model of a flamingo, orange glaze, designed by Waylande Gregory, Shape No. D2-F, 11 3/4" h. (ILLUS.) **$700**

Flower frog, model of a reindeer, designed by Waylande Gregory, polychrome finish, Shape No. 903, 11" h. (ILLUS. center with unicorn book ends) **$1,500**

Flower frog, model of an artichoke, light green, Shape No. 775, 3" h. **$75**

Ginger jar, cov., blue lustre, Shape No. 513, 6 3/4" h. **$250**

Ginger jar, cov., orange lustre, Shape No. 583, 10" h. **$350**

Lamp, candlestick-form, a disk foot & spiral-twist standard w/a flaring molded socket fitted w/an electric bulb socket, overall marigold lustre glaze, impressed mark, 11" h. **$125**

Lamp, foliage decoration, 9" h. **$275**

Lamp, girl w/deer decoration, ivory, 18" h. **$550**

Lamp, moth decoration, blue, w/fittings, 13" h., overall 22" h. **$425**

Lamp base, Art Deco style, angular, green, designed by Waylande Gregory, Shape No. 821, 8 3/8" h. **$250**

Cowan Lamp Base

Lamp base, round domed base below modernist teardrop-shaped body decorated w/nude female figure, ivory & brown glaze, designed by Waylande Gregory, 11" h. (ILLUS.) **$1,250**

Bird on Wave Model

Model of bird on wave, Egyptian blue, designed by Alexander Blazys, Shape No. 749-A, 12" h. (ILLUS., previous page) **$1,250**

Model of elephant, standing on square plinth, head & trunk down, rich mottled Oriental Red glaze, designed by Margaret Postgate, ca. 1930, faint impressed mark on plinth & paper label reading "X869 Elephant designed by M....et P....," 10 1/2" h. **$2,500**

Model of horse, standing animal on an oblong base, Egyptian blue glaze, designed by Viktor Schreckengost, 7 3/4" h. (ILLUS. right with polar bear bookends, page 164) **$3,000**

Model of ram, Oriental Red glaze, designed by Edris Eckhart, 3 1/2" h. **$250**

Paperweight, figural, modeled as a large rounded stylized elephant w/trunk curved under, standing on a stepped rectangular base, ivory glaze, designed by Margaret Postgate, Shape No. D-3, 4 3/4" h. (ILLUS. lower center with elephant bookends, page 165) **$250**

Paperweight, figural, modeled as a large rounded stylized elephant w/trunk curved under, standing on a stepped rectangular base, blue glaze, designed by Margaret Postgate, Shape No. D-3, 4 3/4" h. (ILLUS. lower right with elephant bookends, page 165) **$300**

Paperweight, figural, modeled as a large rounded stylized elephant w/trunk curved under, standing on a stepped rectangular base, overall Oriental Red glaze, designed by Margaret Postgate, Shape No. D-3, 4 3/4" h. (ILLUS. top right with elephant bookends, page 165) **$350**

Pen base, maroon, Shape No. PB-2, 3 3/4" **$65**

Plaque, hand-decorated by Arthur E. Baggs, Egyptian blue, artist-signed "AEB," 2 1/2 x 12 1/2" **$2,200**

Plaque, seascape decoration, designed by Thelma Frazier Winter, 11 1/2" d. **$650**

Plaque, terradatol, designed by Alexander Blazys, Egyptian blue, Shape No. 739, 15 1/2" **$900**

Strawberry jar w/saucer, light green, designed by R.G. Cowan, Shape No. SJ-6, 6" h., 2 pcs. **$250**

Strawberry jar w/saucer, Oriental Red glaze, designed by R.G. Cowan, Shape No. SJ-1, mark No. 8, 7 1/2" h., 2 pcs. **$375**

Trivet, round, center portrait of young woman's face encircled by a floral border, white on blue ground, impressed mark & "Cowan," 6 5/8" d. (minor staining from usage) **$225**

Urn, classical form w/trumpet foot supporting a wide bulbous ribbed body w/a wide short cylindrical neck flanked by loop handles, overall Peacock blue glaze, stamped mark, 8" d., 9 1/2" h. **$90**

Urn, cov., black w/gold trim & figural grape cluster handles, Shape No. V-95, 10 1/4" h. (ILLUS., top next column) **$275**

Cowan Urn w/Figural Grape Handles

Cowan Lakeware Urn & Vases

Urn, Lakeware, blue, Shape V-102, 5 1/2" h. (ILLUS. left with vases) **$75**

Vase, 3 1/4" h., footed, baluster-form, Feu Rouge glaze, Shape No. 533 .... **$90**

Vase, 4" h., bulbous ovoid tapering to cylindrical neck, Jet Black glaze, Shape No. V-5 (ILLUS. center w/urn) **$250**

Vase, 4" h., waisted cylindrical body w/bulbous top & wide flaring rim, mottled orange glaze, Shape No. 630 (ILLUS. second from left w/No. 625-A candlestick, page 166) **$75**

Vase, 4 1/4" h., mottled green, Shape No. V-54 .... **$65**

Vase, 4 3/4" h., bulbous body w/horizontal ribbing, wide cylindrical neck, green glaze, Shape No. V-30 (ILLUS. lower left with clown ashtrays, page 164) **$50**

Vase, 4 3/4" h., bulbous body w/horizontal ribbing, wide cylindrical neck, mottled turquoise glaze, Shape No. V-30 .... **$75**

Vase, 4 3/4" h., waterfall, designed by Paul Bogatay, maroon, hand-decorated, Shape No. V-77 .... **$950**

Vase, 4 3/4" h., wide tapering cylindrical body, mottled orange, brown & rust, Shape No. V-34 (ILLUS. second from right w/No. 625-A candlestick, page 166) **$60**

Vase, 5" h., fan-shaped, designed by R.G. Cowan, golden yellow, Shape No. V-801 .... **$60**

Vase, 5 1/4" h., Lakeware, melon-lobed shape **$60**
Vase, 5 1/2" h., footed wide semi-ovoid body w/flaring rim, dark bluish green, Shape 575-A, mark No. 4 .... **$60**
Vase, 5 1/2" h., Lakeware, bulbous base w/wide shoulder tapering to wide cylindrical neck, blue glaze, Shape No. V-72 .... **$60**
Vase, 5 1/2" h., orange lustre, Shape No. 608 .... **$50**
Vase, 6 1/4" h., experimental, polychrome, designed by Arthur E. Baggs, Shape No. 15-A, artist signed "AEB" **$1,250**
Vase, 6 1/4" h., six-sided w/stepped neck, blue rainbow glaze, Shape No. 546 .... **$65**
Vase, bud, 6 1/4" h., flaring domed foot below ovoid body tapering to cylindrical neck w/flaring rim, plum glaze, Shape No. 916 ..... **$75**
Vase, 6 1/2" h., blue & green, Shape No. V-55 .... **$95**

Cowan Decorated Vases

Vase, 6 1/2" h., bulbous body w/short molded rim, black w/Egyptian blue bands & center decoration, designed by Whitney Atchley, Shape No. V-38 (ILLUS. right).... **$1,600**
Vase, 6 1/2" h., footed, squatty bulbous base w/trumpet-form neck, flattened sides w/notched corners, green glaze, Shape No. V-649-A (ILLUS. right w/urn, page 171) **$100**
Vase, 6 1/2" h., mottled dark blue & green, Shape No. V-55 .... **$125**
Vase, 6 1/2" h., spherical body w/flaring cylindrical neck flanked by scroll handles, Egyptian blue, designed by Viktor Schreckengost, Shape No. V-99 (ILLUS. center w/bowl, page 165) **$375**
Vase, 6 1/2" h., wide bulbous body, yellow glaze, Shape V-91 .... **$200**
Vase, cov., 6 1/2" h., wide bulbous body, blue glaze, Shape V-91 .... **$200**
Vase, 6 5/8" h., bright yellow glaze, Shape No. 797 .... **$75**
Vase, 6 3/4" h., footed bulbous ovoid body w/wide tapering cylindrical neck, Jet Black glaze, Shape V-25 .... **$325**
Vase, 7" h., fan-shaped w/scalloped foot & domed base decorated w/relief-molded sea horse decoration, pink glaze, Shape No. 715-A **$50**
Vase, 7" h., footed bulbous base, the narrow shoulder tapering to a tall wide cylindrical neck, Oriental Red glaze, Shape No. V-79 .... **$190**
Vase, 7" h., Lakeware, bulbous base w/trumpet-form neck, Oriental Red glaze, Shape No. V-75 .... **$125**

Vase, bud, 7" h., blue lustre glaze **$65**
Vase, 7 1/4" h., footed slender ovoid body w/flaring rim, Oriental Red glaze, Shape No. V-12 .... **$150**
Vase, 7 1/2" h., baluster-form w/trumpet-form neck, blue rainbow lustre, Shape No. 631 .... **$75**
Vase, 7 1/2" h., flared foot below paneled ovoid body, orange lustre glaze, Shape No. 691-A, mark No. 6 .... **$75**
Vase, 7 1/2" h., footed, tapering cylindrical body, green drip over yellow glaze, Shape No. 591, 8" h. (ILLUS. far right with clown ashtrays, page 164) **$300**
Vase, 7 1/2" h., tall slender ovoid body w/short cylindrical neck, orange lustre, Shape No. 552 (ILLUS. lower right with chick & ram ashtrays, page 164) **$80**
Vase, 5 1/4 x 7 3/4", flared tulip-shaped body, squared feet, blue **$70**
Vase, 8" h., blue lustre, Shape No. 615 .... **$75**
Vase, 8" h., bulbous body tapering to cylindrical neck w/flaring rim, verde green, Shape No. V-932 .... **$150**
Vase, 8" h., bulbous body tapering to cylindrical neck w/flaring rim, gold, Shape No. V-932 (ILLUS. far left w/No. 625-A candlestick, page 166) **$175**
Vase, 8" h., bulbous body tapering to cylindrical neck w/flaring rim, Feu Rouge (red) glaze, Shape No. V-932 .... **$250**
Vase, 8" h., bulbous body tapering to cylindrical neck w/flaring rim, black drip over Feu Rouge (red) glaze Shape No. V-932 (ILLUS. top with clown ashtrays, page 164) **$325**
Vase, 8" h., cylindrical body, black w/overall turquoise blue decoration, triple-signed (ILLUS. left with bulbous vase, previous column) **$750**
Vase, 8" h., footed bulbous body w/trumpet-form neck, yellow shading to green drip glaze, Shape No. 627 (ILLUS. top center w/No. 625-A candlestick, page 166) **$225**
Vase, 10 1/2" h., footed bulbous ovoid body, Star patt., decorated w/relief-molded foliage, orange glaze, designed by Waylande Gregory, Shape V-32, mark No. 8 & 9 .... **$450**
Vase, 13 1/2" h., baluster-form body w/flaring rim, light blue glaze, Shape No. 563 (ILLUS. left w/marlin candlesticks, page 167) **$400**
Wine cups, Oriental Red glaze, Shape No. X-17, 2 1/2" h., each (ILLUS. of two, front left with decanter, page 167) **$35**

Czechoslovakian

Czechoslovakia did not exist until the end of World War I in 1918. The country was put together with parts of Austria, Bohemia and Hungary as a reward for the help of the Czechs and the Slovaks in winning the war. In 1993 Czechoslovakia split and became two countries: the Czech Republic and the Slovak Republic. Items are highly collectible because the country was in existence only 75 years. For a more thorough study of the subject, refer to the following books: Made in Czechoslovakia Books 1 and 2 by Ruth

Various J. Mrazek Pieces

A. *Forsythe;* Czechoslovakian Glass & Collectibles Books I and II *by Dale & Dian Barta and Helen M. Rose and* Czechoslovakian Perfume Bottles and Boudoir Accessories *by Jacquelyne Y. Jones North.*

Bell, w/original pottery heart clapper, geometric patt. on black ground, J. Mrazek, Peasant Art Industries, 4 1/4" h. (ILLUS. front row, left w/various J. Mrazek pieces, top of page) **$150**
Biscuit jar, w/rattan handle, decorated w/orange flower, 7" h. **$125**
Book ends, in the form of Indian heads, pr.... **$125**
Cache pot, decorated w/cherries, 4 1/2" h....... **$65**
Cigarette box, white, w/horse finial, 4" h. **$150**
Console bowl, footed, lilac, purple & green, Eichwald, 6" h. **$150**
Creamer, decorated w/orange cherries, 4 1/2" h.. **$55**
Creamer, w/handle in the form of a cat, white iridescent, 4" h. **$65**
Flower frog, round, w/airbrushed roses around middle **$150**
Humidor, cov., ovoid shape, geometric patt. on light green sponge ground, knobbed lid, J. Mrazek, Peasant Art Industries, 7 1/2" h. (ILLUS. back row, right w/various J. Mrazek pieces, top of page) **$375**

Model of bulldog, white w/brown & black splotches, 7" h. **$135**

Model of Toucan

Model of toucan, bird w/large yellow beak perches on black base, white body w/green, blue, yellow & red detail, 8" h. (ILLUS.)... **$750**
Mug, "Monte Carlo" patt., 1/2 liter **$40**

Czechoslovakian Pitchers & Vases

Hand-painted Pitcher

Pitcher, bulbous form w/short circular base, C-scroll handle, h.p. w/decoration of large flower on front & back w/green leaves as accents, "BATNA," Ditmar-Urbach (ILLUS.) $350

Pitcher, 1-liter, bulbous body w/flaring cylindrical neck, short base & S-scroll applied handle, h.p. decoration of orange, blue & black ellipses, green leaves & orange trim, LOSTRO (ILLUS. second from right w/other pitcher & vases, bottom previous page) $150

Pitcher, 1-liter, cov., ovoid body w/cylindrical neck, short base & C-scroll applied handle, h.p. overall floral decoration (ILLUS. second from left w/other pitcher & vases, bottom previous page) $125

Pitcher, 4" h., spherical form, geometric design on yellow sponge ground, J. Mrazek, Peasant Art Industries (ILLUS. front row, center w/various J. Mrazek pieces, top page 173) $175

Pitcher, 6" h., figural, in the form of a girl holding flowers, orange & white, Erphila $85

Cat Pitcher

Pitcher, 8" h., figural, in the form of a seated cat w/head turned to side, tail forms handle, one ear forms spout, cream w/red & black accents, imported by Eberling & Reuss (Erphila) (ILLUS.) $950

Pitcher, cover & underplate, 9" h., decorated on front w/orange flower w/green leaves, 3 pcs. $150

Plate, 6 1/2" h., geometric patt. on orange sponge ground, J. Mrazek, Peasant Art Industries (ILLUS. back row, center w/various J. Mrazek pieces, top page 173) $55

Plate, 9 1/2" d., white w/border decorated w/images of lobster, crab & shrimp $45

Plate, 12" d., cheese & crackers, white w/green airbrushed lines in several places, center w/figural multicolored rooster & holes for toothpicks $125

Salt & pepper shakers, "Monte Carlo" patt., pr. $30

Toby, Mr. Bumble, Erphila, 3 1/4" h. $45

Vase, 4 1/2" h., cylindrical form, geometric design on light green sponge ground, J. Mrazek, Peasant Art Industries, 7 1/2" h. (ILLUS. front row, right w/various J. Mrazek pieces, top of page 173) $110

Vase, 7" h., fan-shaped, w/multicolored h.p. slip decoration $195

Vase, 7" h., segmented ovoid form w/flaring rim & base, h.p. overall floral decoration (ILLUS. far right w/other vase & pitchers, bottom of page 173) $175

Vase, 7 1/2" h., waisted cylindrical form, geometric patt. on orange sponge ground, J. Mrazek, Peasant Art Industries (ILLUS. back row, left w/various J. Mrazek pieces, top of page 173) $275

Vase, 8" h., bulbous form w/short flared neck, short circular base, two side loop handles, airbrushed in purple & red (ILLUS. far left w/other vase & pitchers, bottom of page 173) $150

Vase, 8" h., two-handled, brown & yellow w/image of cottage on front $55

Vase, 8" h., white matte finish w/decoration of woman's head at base $175

Wall pocket, decorated w/orange flower, 7" h. $65

Dedham & Chelsea Keramic Art Works

This pottery was organized in 1866 by Alexander W. Robertson in Chelsea, Massachusetts, and became A.W. & H. Robertson in 1868. In 1872, the name was changed to Chelsea Keramic Art Works and in 1891 to Chelsea Pottery, U.S.A. About 1895, the pottery was moved to Dedham, Massachusetts, and was renamed Dedham Pottery. Production ceased in 1943. High-fired colored wares and crackle ware were specialties. The rabbit is said to have been the most popular decoration on crackle ware in blue.

Since 1977, the Potting Shed, Concord, Massachusetts, has produced quality reproductions of early Dedham wares. These pieces are carefully marked to avoid confusion with original examples.

Dedham & Chelsea Keramic Art Works
Marks

Dedham Pottery Rabbit Pattern Bowl

Bowl, 9" d., 3 1/2" h., Rabbit patt., base marked "Registered," 1929-43 (ILLUS.)..... **$288**

Dedham Rabbit Celery Tray

Celery tray, oval, Rabbit patt., base marked "Registered," 1929-43, 6 1/4 x 9 3/4" (ILLUS.)............................... **$240**

Dedham Horse Chestnut Creamer

Creamer, squatty bulbous shape, Horse Chestnut patt., base marked "Registered," 1929-43, 4 1/2" d., 3 1/4" h. (ILLUS.) **$640**

Dedham Five-sided Rabbit Dish

Dish, five-sided shallow form, Rabbit patt., base marked "Registered," 1929-43, 7 1/2" w., 1 1/2" h. (ILLUS.)....................... **$360**

Dedham Elephant Marmalade Jar

Marmalade jar, cov., barrel-shaped, Elephant patt., blue mark on base, cover w/3" slice off edge, 4" d., 3 3/4" h. (ILLUS.) **$403**
Plate, 4 3/8" d., butter size, Swan patt. **$259**

Dedham Duck Pattern Plate

Plate, 6" d., Duck patt., base marked "Registered," 1929-43, two rim hairlines (ILLUS.).... **$96**
Plate, 6 1/8" d., bread & butter size, Horse Chestnut patt.. **$144**
Plate, 7 1/2" d., salad size, Lobster patt........ **$288**

Dedham Turkey Pattern Plate

Plate, 8 1/2" d., Turkey patt., base marked "Registered," 1929-43 (ILLUS.)................. **$270**

Dedham Horse Chestnut Plate

Plate, 9 3/4" d., Horse Chestnut patt., impressed rabbit mark (ILLUS.)....................... **$60**

Rare Dedham Rabbit Pattern Tureen

Pair of Dedham Flower-decorated Plates

Plates, 6 1/4" d., unknown flower design, base marked "Registered," 1929-43, & impressed rabbit mark (ILLUS.) **$345**

Small Chelsea Keramic Art Vase

Dedham Elephant Pattern Sugar Bowl

Sugar bowl, cov., squatty bulbous shaped w/wide flat rim, wide flattened cover w/button finial, Elephant patt., 2" slice off side of cover, in-the-making mark on rim, 4" d., 3" h. (ILLUS.) **$345**

Tureen, cov., footed squatty bulbous oblong shaped w/small buttress end handles, domed cover w/figural rabbit finial, two bands of Rabbit patt. decoration, small chip inside rim, 7 1/2 x 11", 8" h. (ILLUS., top of page) **$2,185**

Vase, 3 3/4" h., 4 1/4" w., flattened pillow-shape on scroll feet, the sides carved in relief w/blue violets & green leaves on a bottle green ground, stamped "CKAW" & artist-signed "TT" or "TM," Chelsea Keramic Art Works (ILLUS., next column) **$881**

Experimental Robertson Dedham Vase

Vase, 7 1/2" h., 4 1/2" d., simple ovoid shape w/a short cylindrical neck, experimental design covered in a matte green orange-peel glaze, by Hugh Robertson, firing lines in the base incised mark "Dedham Pottery - HCR" (ILLUS.) **$1,998**

Derby & Royal Crown Derby

William Duesbury, in partnership with John and Christopher Heath, established the Derby Porcelain Works in Derby, England about 1750. Duesbury soon bought out his partners and in 1770 purchased the Chelsea factory and six years later, the Bow works. Duesbury was succeeded by his son and grandson. Robert Bloor purchased the business about 1814 and managed successfully until illness in 1828 left him unable to exercise control. The "Bloor" Period, however, extends from 1814 until 1848, when the factory closed. Former Derby workmen then resumed porcelain manufacture in another factory and this nucleus eventually united with a new and distinct venture in 1878 which, after 1890, was known as Royal Crown Derby.

A variety of anchor and crown marks have been used since the 18th century.

Derby & Royal Crown Derby Marks

Royal Crown Derby Imari-style Candlesticks

Candlesticks, decorated in the Imari taste, squared foot w/incurved sides & a dolphin head at each corner, tapering to a tall baluster stem supporting a squatty socket w/a widely flaring dished bobeche, in shades of white, brick red, cobalt blue & gold, Royal Crown Derby mark, 10 1/2" h., pr. (ILLUS.)................. **$1,093**

Creamer, helmet-shaped, flattened rim & naturalistically colored twig handle, painted on the front w/a bouquet of summer flowers & on the back w/honeysuckle, w/floral sprigs on the rim & foot, ca. 1760, 5 1/8" h. (tiny chips) **$1,265**

Cup & saucer, cylindrical cup w/angled handle, painted in the "Japan" patt. in a bright Imari palette, Bloor era, ca. 1815-30, cup 2 3/4" h..................... **$161**

Dessert dish, lozenge-shaped, the central oval panel painted w/two huntsmen & hounds within a gilt frame & a wide gilt foliate border at the lobed rim, probably painted by William Cotton, ca. 1815, crowned crossed batons & D in iron-red, painted initial I or number 7, 11 1/4" l. (slight rubbing) **$1,380**

Dessert service: platter, 12 1/4" l., 5 dessert plates, 7" d., & small sauce boat; in the Imari palette, early 20th c., the set **$525-550**

Dinner service: 12 dinner plates, six luncheon plates, five bread & butter plates, three large soup bowls, two small soup bowls, five cups & saucers, five oval vegetable bowls, four crescent-shaped bone dishes, two oval platters, one oval open vegetable dish, a cov. cigarette box & an English saucer in a similar design; composed of several very similar Imari patterns w/different factory marks, in shades of brick red, cobalt blue, white & gold, Royal Crown Derby, second quarter 20th c., the set (ILLUS., bottom of page) **$2,300**

Dish, cov., Imari pattern, w/dome-shaped lid w/gilt handle, early 20th c., 4 1/2" h., 8 3/4" d..................................... **$532**

Large Royal Crown Derby Dinner Service in Imari Patterns

Royal Crown Derby Tea Set

Figure group, "Tithe Pig," modeled w/the farmer's wife offering her baby to the black-clad parson, in lieu of the piglet held by her husband, all standing before a leafy tree on a grassy mound base w/a further piglet, a basket of eggs & a wheat sheaf, ca. 1770, 7 1/4" h. (some minor chips & restoration, fine hairline in base) **$862**

Jar, cov., globular form, floral decoration in colored enamels & gilt, ca. 1890, 12" h. **$1,150**

Plates, 9" d., Imari patt., early 20th c., set of four **$553**

Tea set: cov. teapot, cov. sugar bowl & creamer; oval cylindrical bodies, each decorated in an Imari-style design w/stylized Oriental blossoms in rust red w/green leaves against an oval black-ground center reserve w/gilt trim & rust red-outlined blossoms, a black-ground rim band w/gilt leafy bands & rust blossoms, Royal Crown Derby, ca. 1850, teapot 5 3/4" h., the set (ILLUS., top of page) **$525-550**

Vase, 8 1/4" h., bottle form, enamel & gilt-decorated w/fruits, flowers & foliage, ca. 1887 .... **$403**

Dorothy Doughty Birds

These magnificent porcelain birds were created by the talented artist Dorothy Doughty for the Royal Worcester Porcelain Factory in Worcester, England, beginning in 1935. They are life-sized, beautifully colored and crafted with the greatest artistry.

Dorothy Doughty Blue Tits & Pussy Willow

Blue Tits, "Blue Tit, Parvs Caer Olevs and Pussy Willow," signed & w/Royal Worcester mark, ca. 1964, pr. (ILLUS.) **$2,415**

Handsome Royal Crown Derby Tray

Tray, rectangular w/cut corners & rounded tab end handles, an ornate Imari-style design w/large stylized rust red Oriental blossoms w/scrolls over black & gold leaves on two sides & fan-shaped black-ground reserves at the ends, one w/birds in a tree, the other w/flowers, overall white ground w/outlined blossoms & leaves, black-ground border band w/gold & rust red leaves & blossoms, Royal Crown Derby, ca. 1850, 12 1/2 x 19" (ILLUS.) **$1,325-1,350**

Cactus Wrens & Prickly Pear Cactus

Cactus Wrens, "Cactus Wren Heleodyles Brunneicapillus Coues: & Prickly Pear," on stands, signed & w/Royal Worcester mark, ca. 1965, 11" h., pr. (ILLUS.) **$2,358**

Mockingbird & Myrtle Warbler Doughty Figurines

Extinct Carolina Paroquet

Carolina Paroquet, "Extinct Carolina Paroquet, Con Ucop sis Carolinensis," signed & w/Royal Worcester mark, 18" l., 6 1/2" h. (ILLUS.) **$1,380**

Cerulean Warblers, "Cerulean Warbler, Dendroica Cerulia and Maple," signed & w/Royal Worcester mark, in original fitted case, ca. 1965, 8 1/4" h., pr. (ILLUS. of one, below with Little Downy Woodpecker)... **$1,725**

King Fisher & Autumn Beech

King Fisher, "King Fisher, Alcedo Ispida and Autumn Beech," Model No. 3395, signed & w/Royal Worcester mark, in original fitted case, ca. 1964, 12 1/2" w., 12" h. (ILLUS.) **$1,610**

Little Downy Woodpeckers, "Little Downy Woodpecker, Dendrocopus Pubescens and Pecan," signed & w/Royal Worcester mark, in original fitted case, ca. 1967, 11 1/4" h., pr. (ILLUS. of one, above with Cerulean Warbler, left column) **$3,220**

Mockingbird, "Mocking-Bird, Mimus Polyglottis," signed & w/Royal Worcester mark, ca. 1964, 11" h. (ILLUS. left with Myrtle Warbler, top of page) **$3,220**

Myrtle Warbler, "Myrtle Warbler, Dendrocia Coronata Coronata," signed & w/Royal Worcester mark, ca. 1958, one blossom reattached, 10" h. (ILLUS. right with Mockingbird, top of page) **$1,150**

Cerulean Warbler & Little Downy Woodpecker

Male & Female Red Cardinals

Red Cardinals, "Red Cardinal, Richmonde-
na Cardinalis," signed & w/Royal
Worcester mark, male w/two leaves detached, female w/three leaves detached,
12" h., pr. (ILLUS.) **$2,760**

Doulton & Royal Doulton

*Doulton & Co., Ltd., was founded in Lambeth,
London, in about 1858. It was operated there
until 1956 and often incorporated the words
"Doulton" and "Lambeth" in its marks. Pinder,
Bourne & Co., Burslem was purchased by the
Doultons in 1878 and in 1882 became Doulton &
Co., Ltd. It added porcelain to its earthenware
production in 1884. The "Royal Doulton" mark
has been used since 1902 by this factory, which is
still in operation. Character jugs and figurines
are commanding great attention from collectors
at the present time.*

*John Doulton, the founder, was born in 1793.
He became an apprentice at the age of 12 to a potter in south London. Five years later he was
employed in another small pottery near Lambeth.
His two sons, John and Henry, subsequently
joined their father in 1830 in a partnership he
had formed with the name of Doulton & Watts.
Watts retired in 1864 and the partnership was
dissolved. Henry formed a new company that
traded as Doulton & Co.*

*In the early 1870s the proprietor of the Pinder
Bourne Co., located in Burslem, Staffordshire,
offered Henry a partnership. The Pinder Bourne
Co. was purchased by Henry in 1878 and became
part of Doulton & Co. in 1882.*

*With the passage of time the demand for the
Lambeth industrial and decorative stoneware
declined whereas demand for the Burslem manufactured and decorated bone china wares
increased.*

*Doulton & Co. was incorporated as a limited
liability company in 1899. In 1901 the company
was allowed to use the word "Royal" on its trademarks by Royal Charter. The well known "lion on
crown" logo came into use in 1902. In 2000 the
logo was changed on the company's advertising*

*literature to one showing a more stylized lion's
head in profile.*

*Today Royal Doulton is one of the world's lead-
ing manufacturers and distributors of premium
grade ceramic tabletop wares and collectibles.
The Doulton Group comprises Minton, Royal
Albert, Caithness Glass, Holland Studio Craft
and Royal Doulton. Royal Crown Derby was part
of the group from 1971 until 2000 when it became
an independent company. These companies market collectibles using their own brand names.*

Royal Doulton Mark

Animals & Birds

Bird, Bullfinch, blue & pale blue feathers,
red breast, HN 2551, 1941-46, 5 1/2" h. **$80**
Cat, Persian Cat, seated, black & white, HN
999, 1930-85, 5" h. **$115**
Cat, seated animal, red "Flambé" glaze,
1977-96, 11" h. **$248**

Siamese Cat

Cat, Siamese, seated, glossy cream &
black, DA 129, 4" h. (ILLUS.) **$30**
Cat, Siamese Cat, standing, cream & black,
HN 2660, 1960-85, 5" h. **$125**
Dog, Airedale Terrier, Ch. "Cotsford Top-
sail," standing, dark brown & black, light
brown underbody, HN 1024, 1931-68,
4" h. **$275**
Dog, Airedale Terrier, K 5, 1931-55,
1 1/4 x 2 1/4" **$275**
Dog, Alsatian, "Benign of Picardy," dark
brown, HN 1117, 1937-68, 4 1/2" **$250**
Dog, American Great Dane, light brown, HN
2602, 1941-60, 6 1/2" h. **$650**
Dog, Boxer, Champion "Warlord of Maze-
laine," golden brown coat w/white bib, HN
2643, 1952-85, 6 1/2" h. **$145**

Dog, Bull Terrier, K 14, lying, white, 1940-59, 1 1/4 x 2 3/4"................................... **$325**

Dog, Bulldog, HN 1044, brown & white, 1931-68, 3 1/4" h.............................. **$250**

Dog, Bulldog, HN 1047, standing, brown & white, 1931-38, 3 1/4"............................. **$215**

Dog, Bulldog, HN 1074, standing, white & brown, 1932-85, 3 1/4"........................ **$195**

Dog, Bulldog, K 1, seated, tan w/brown patches, 1931-77, 2 1/2"........................ **$95**

Dog, Bulldog Puppy, K 2, seated, tan w/brown patches, 1931-77, 2".................... **$85**

Dog, character dog yawning, white w/brown patches over ears & eyes, black patches on back, HN 1099, 1934-85, 4" h. **$75**

Dog, Chow (Shibu Ino), K 15, golden, 1940-77, 2 1/2"............................. **$135**

Dog, Cocker Spaniel, Ch. "Lucky Star of Ware," black coat w/grey markings, HN 1021, 1931-68, 3 1/2" h. **$195**

Dog, Cocker Spaniel, golden w/dark brown patches, HN 1187, 1937-69, 5"................ **$125**

Dog, Cocker Spaniel, liver & white, 1931-60, HN 1002, 6 1/2" h..................... **$575**

Dog, Cocker Spaniel, "Lucky Star of Ware," black coat w/grey markings, HN 1020, 1981-85, 5"................................ **$175**

Dog, Cocker Spaniel, seated, K9A, golden brown w/black highlights, 1931-77, 2 1/2" h................................ **$95**

Dog, Cocker Spaniel w/pheasant, seated, white coat w/black markings, HN 1137, 1937-66, 6 1/2 x 7 3/4"..................... **$375**

Dog, Cocker Spaniel w/pheasant, seated, white coat w/dark brown markings, red & brown pheasant, HN 1029, 1931-68, 3 1/2" h..................................... **$215**

Dog, Cocker Spaniel w/Pheasant, seated, white coat w/dark brown markings, red, brown & green pheasant, HN 1062, 1931-68, 3 1/2".......................... **$215**

Dog, Cocker Spaniel, white w/black markings, HN 1078, 1932-68, 3" h................... **$175**

Dog, Cocker Spaniel, white w/black markings, HN 1109, 1937-85, 5".................... **$140**

Dog, Cocker Spaniel, white w/light brown patches, HN 1037, 1931-68, 3 1/2".......... **$175**

Dog, Collie, Ch. "Ashstead Applause," dark & light brown coat, white chest, shoulder & feet, HN 1057, 1931-60, 7 1/2" h. **$750**

Dog, Collie, dark & light brown coat, white chest, shoulders & feet, HN 1059, 1931-85, 3 1/2"................................ **$195**

Dog, Collie, dark & light brown coat, white chest, shoulders & feet, medium, HN 1058, 1931-85, 5"............................. **$185**

Dog, Dalmatian, "Goworth Victor," white w/black spots, black ears, HN 1113, 1937-85, 5 1/2"......................... **$225**

Dog, Dalmatian, "Goworth Victor," white w/black spots, black ears, HN 1114, 1937-68, 4 1/4"......................... **$375**

Dog, Doberman Pinscher, Ch. "Rancho Dobe's Storm," black w/brown feet & chin, HN 2645, 1955-85, 6 1/4" **$165**

Dog, Dog of Fo, Flambé, RDICC, Model 2957, 1981, 5 1/4" h..................... **$215**

Dog, English Setter, Ch. "Maesydd Mustard," off-white coat w/black highlights, HN 1051, 1931-68, 4" h. **$215**

Dog, English Setter, "Maesydd Mustard," off-white coat w/black highlights, HN 1050, 1931-85, 5 1/4" h. **$135**

Dog, English Setter w/pheasant, grey w/black markings, reddish brown bird, yellowish brown leaves on base, HN 2529, 1939-85, 8" h. **$515**

Dog, Fox Terrier, K 8, seated, white w/brown & black patches, 1931-77, 2 1/2".. **$90**

Dog, Foxhound, K 7, seated, white w/brown & black patches, 1931-77, 2 1/2" **$110**

Dog, French Poodle, HN 2631, white w/pink, grey & black markings, 1952-85, 5 1/4" h.................................. **$195**

Dog, Great Dane, "Rebeller of Ouborough," light brown, HN 2562, 191-52, 4 1/2"........ **$725**

Dog, Greyhound, standing, golden brown w/dark brown markings, cream chest & feet, HN 1065, 1931-55, 8 1/2" h. **$1,150**

Dog, Greyhound, white w/dark brown patches, HN 1077, 1932-55, 4 1/2" **$575**

Dog, Irish Setter, Ch. "Pat O'Moy," HN 1056, 1931-68, 6" l., 4" h. **$225**

Dog, Irish Setter, Ch. "Pat O'Moy," reddish brown, HN 1054, 1931-60, 7 1/2" h. **$725**

Dog, Irish Setter, "Pat O'Moy," reddish brown, HN 1055, 1931-85, 5" **$175**

Dog, Labrador, "Bumblikite of Mansergh," black, HN 2667, 1967-85, 5 1/4"............. **$145**

Dog, Labrador, standing, black, DA 145, 1990-present, 5" h. **$55**

Golden Labrador

Dog, Labrador, standing, golden, DA 145, 1990-present, 5" h. (ILLUS.) **$55**

Dog, Pekinese, Ch. "Biddee of Ifield," golden w/black highlights, HN 1012, 1931-85, 3"..................................... **$95**

Dog, Rough-haired Terrier, Ch. "Crackley Startler," white w/black & brown markings, HN 1014, 1931-85, 3 3/4" h. **$125**

Dog, Scottish Terrier, Ch. "Albourne Arthur," black, HN 1015, 1931-60, 5".............. **$315**

Dog, Scottish Terrier, Ch. "Albourne Arthur," black, HN 1016, 1931-85, 3 1/2"............. **$175**

Dog, Scottish Terrier, seated, black & white, K 18, 1940-77, 2 1/4 x 2 3/4" **$125**

Dog, Sealyham, Ch. "Scotia Stylist," white, HN 1031, 1931-55, 4" **$425**

Dog, Springer Spaniel, "Dry Toast," white coat w/brown markings, HN 2517, 1938-55, 3 3/4"..................................... **$175**

Dog, Springer Spaniel, white w/black markings, HN 1078, 1932-68, 3"....................... **$150**

Dog, St. Bernard, lying, brown & cream, K 19, 1940-77, 1 1/2 x 2 1/2"..................... **$105**

Dogs, Cocker Spaniels sleeping, white dog w/brown markings & golden brown dog, HN 2590, 1941-69, 1 3/4" h. **$105**

Dogs, Terrier Puppies in a Basket, three white puppies w/light & dark brown markings, brown basket, HN 2588, 1941-85, 3" h. $105

Duck, Drake, standing, green, brown & white, HN 807, 1923-77, 2 1/2" h. $105

Duck, Drake, standing, white, HN 806, 1923-68, 2 1/2" h. $105

Elephant, trunk in salute, grey w/black, HN 2644, 1952-85, 4 1/4". $175

Horse, Punch Peon, Chestnut Shire, bay w/white markings on legs, HN 2623, 1950-60, 7 1/2" h. $750

Horses, Chestnut Mare and Foal, chestnut mare w/white stockings, fawn-colored foal w/white stockings, HN 2522, 1938-60, 6 1/2" h. $695

Kitten, licking hind paw, brown & white, HN 2580, 2 1/4". $75

Kitten, looking up, tan & white, HN 2584, 1941-85, 2". $75

Kitten, on hind legs, light brown & black on white, HN 2582, 1941-85, 2 3/4". $75

Kitten, sleeping, brown & white, HN 2581, 1941-85, 1 1/2". $75

Monkey, Langur Monkey, long-haired brown & white coat, HN 2657, 1960-69, 4 1/2" h. $255

Penguin, grey & white w/black tips, K 22, 1940-68, 1 3/4". $195

Shetland Pony

Pony, Shetland Pony (woolly Shetland mare), glossy brown, DA 47, 1989 to present, 5 3/4" (ILLUS.) $45

Tiger, crouching, brown w/dark brown stripes, HN 225, 1920-36, 2 x 9 1/2" $575

Tiger on a Rock, brown, grey rock, HN 2639, 1952-92, 10 1/4 x 12". $1,150

Beatrix Potter

The John Beswick factory in Longton, Stoke on Trent, celebrated its 100th anniversary in 1994. Originally, it produced earthenware household items and decorative ornaments. With the passage of time, the product line became more diverse and the decorations more ornate and attractive. Moreover, small domestic, farmyard and wild animal figurines were added to the product lines. Beswick was a family-owned and family-run pottery. As the owners neared retirement, they realized there were no next of kin to carry on the business. They sold the company to Royal Doulton in 1969.

Beatrix Potter is known the world over. Generations of children since the early 1900s have been fascinated by the antics of her coterie of small animals in her series of illustrated children's "Tales of Peter Rabbit and Friends." These storybook characters have been produced as small china figurines since the 1920s, but it was not until 1947 that Beswick gained copyright approval from the Frederick Warne Co., the Peter Rabbit book publisher, to manufacture and market them. Upon acquisition of the manufacturing rights, Royal Doulton continued to promote and sell the Beatrix Potter figures using the Beswick trademark until 1989, when it switched to a "Royal Albert" underprint. Royal Albert was another of its famous product lines and had greater brand recognition in the United States. The backstamp change was not well received by the global collector community. Within a decade, the Beswick backstamp was reintroduced and used on the Beatrix Potter figurines until the end of 2002, when the Warne license expired. The old Beswick factory was closed.

All the Beatrix Potter figurines were assigned a "P" or production model number. Although these "P" numbers do not appear on the figures themselves, they are used extensively by collectors to uniquely identify a particular figure.

Many varieties of backstamp exist. They indicate a period of manufacture and influence secondary market values. The basic types of backstamp are shown. If collectible subtypes exist, a range of market values is given for the basic type. Many special backstamps were used in the 1990s to promote sales. These details are outside the scope of this compendium.

Basic Beatrix Potter Backstamps

Amiable Guinea Pig, P2061, tan jacket, brown line backstamp, 1967-83 .... $350

Amiable Guinea Pig Figure

Amiable Guinea Pig, P2061, tan jacket, gold circle or oval backstamp, 1967-83 (ILLUS.) $700

And This Pig Had None, P3319, Beswick Made in England backstamp, 1992-98 .... **$50**

And This Pig Had None Figure

And This Pig Had None, P3319, crown backstamp, 1992-98 (ILLUS.) **$60**
Anna Maria, P1851, brown line backstamp, 1963-83 .... **$225**

Anna Maria Figure

Anna Maria, P1851, gold circle/oval backstamp, 1963-83 (ILLUS.) **$500**

Appley Dappley

Appley Dappley, P2333, bottle in, brown line backstamp, 1975-2002 (ILLUS.) **$70**

Appley Dappley, P2333, bottle in, crown backstamp, 1975-2002 (ILLUS.) **$35**
Aunt Pettitoes, P2276, brown line backstamp, 1970-93 .... **$75**
Aunt Pettitoes, P2276, crown backstamp, 1970-93 .... **$75**

Aunt Pettitoes Figure

Aunt Pettitoes, P2276, gold circle/oval backstamp, 1970-93 (ILLUS.) **$650**
Benjamin Bunny, P1105, ears in, shoes in, Beswick Ware backstamp, 1980-2000 (ILLUS.) **$35**
Benjamin Bunny, P1105, ears in, shoes in, crown backstamp, 1980-2000 (ILLUS.) **$35**

Benjamin Bunny Figure

Benjamin Bunny, P1105, ears in, shoes in, gold circle/oval backstamp, 1980-2000 (ILLUS.) **$80**
Benjamin Bunny, P1105, ears in, shoes in, John Beswick script backstamp, 1980-2000 (ILLUS.) **$175**

Benjamin Bunny Sat on a Bank

Benjamin Bunny Sat on a Bank, P2803, head down, brown jacket, brown line backstamp, 1983-85 (ILLUS.) **$105**
Cecily Parsley, P1941, brown line backstamp, 1965-93 .... **$125**
Cecily Parsley, P1941, crown backstamp, 1965-93 .... **$50**

Cecily Parsley Figure

Cecily Parsley, P1941, gold circle/oval backstamp, 1965-93 (ILLUS.) **$300**

Christmas Stocking Figural Group

Christmas Stocking, P3257, crown backstamp, 1991-94 (ILLUS.) **$250**
Cousin Ribby, P2284, brown line backstamp, 1970-93 .... **$65**
Cousin Ribby, P2284, crown backstamp, 1970-93 .... **$75**

Cousin Ribby Figure

Cousin Ribby, P2284, gold circle/oval backstamp, 1970-93 (ILLUS.) **$625**
Fierce Bad Rabbit, P2586, feet in, light brown rabbit, brown line backstamp, 1980-97 (ILLUS.) **$100**

Fierce Bad Rabbit Figure

Fierce Bad Rabbit, P2586, feet in, light brown rabbit, crown backstamp, 1980-97 (ILLUS.).. **$50**
Fierce Bad Rabbit, P2586, feet in, light brown rabbit, John Beswick script backstamp, 1980-97 (ILLUS.) **$150**
Flopsy, Mopsy & Cottontail, P1274, brown line backstamp, 1954-97 .... **$95**
Flopsy, Mopsy & Cottontail, P1274, crown backstamp, 1954-97 .... **$40**
Flopsy, Mopsy & Cottontail, P1274, gold circle/oval backstamp, 1954-97 .... **$350**

Flopsy, Mopsy & Cottontail

Flopsy, Mopsy & Cottontail, P1274, John
Beswick script backstamp, 1954-97
(ILLUS.) **$150**
Foxy Whiskered Gentleman, P1277, Be-
swick Made in England backstamp,
1954-2002 .... **$35**
Foxy Whiskered Gentleman, P1277,
brown line backstamp, 1954-2002 .... **$90**

Foxy Whiskered Gentleman

Foxy Whiskered Gentleman, P1277,
crown backstamp, 1954-2002 (ILLUS.)........ **$50**
Foxy Whiskered Gentleman, P1277, gold
circle/oval backstamp, 1954-2002 .... **$350**
Foxy Whiskered Gentleman, P1277, John
Beswick script backstamp, 1954-2002 ...... **$165**

Gentleman Mouse Made a Bow

Gentleman Mouse Made a Bow, P3200,
crown backstamp, 1990-96 (ILLUS.)............ **$78**

Goody & Timmy Tiptoes

Goody & Timmy Tiptoes, P2957, brown
line backstamp, 1986-96 (ILLUS.) **$300**
Goody & Timmy Tiptoes, P2957, crown
backstamp, 1986-96 .... **$100**
Goody Tiptoes, P1675, brown line backs-
tamp, 1961-67 .... **$75**
Goody Tiptoes, P1675, crown backstamp,
1961-67 .... **$45**

Goody Tiptoes Figure

Goody Tiptoes, P1675, gold circle/oval
backstamp, 1961-67 (ILLUS.).................... **$300**
Hunca Munca, P1198, Beswick Made in
England backstamp, 1951-2000 .... **$35**
Hunca Munca, P1198, brown line backs-
tamp, 1951-2000 .... **$75**

Hunca Munca Figure

Hunca Munca, P1198, crown backstamp,
1951-2000 (ILLUS., previous page) $45
Hunca Munca, P1198, gold circle/oval
backstamp, 1951-2000 .... $350
Hunca Munca, P1198, John Beswick script
backstamp, 1951-2000 .... $165

Hunca Munca Spills the Beads

Hunca Munca Spills the Beads, P3288,
crown backstamp, 1992-96 (ILLUS.)............ $70
Hunca Munca Sweeping, P2584, brown
dustpan, Beswick Made in England back-
stamp, 1977-2002 .... $35
Hunca Munca Sweeping, P2584, brown
dustpan, brown line backstamp, 1977-
2002 .... $90

Hunca Munca Sweeping

Hunca Munca Sweeping, P2584, brown
dustpan, crown backstamp, 1977-2002
(ILLUS.)... $35
Hunca Munca Sweeping, P2584, brown
dustpan, John Beswick script backstamp,
1977-2002 .... $150

Jemima Puddle-Duck

Jemima Puddle-Duck, P1092, yellow scarf
clip, Beswick Made in England backs-
tamp, 1948-2002 (ILLUS.) $35
Jemima Puddle-Duck, P1092, yellow scarf
clip, brown line backstamp, 1948-2002 ...... $80
Jemima Puddle-Duck, P1092, yellow scarf
clip, crown backstamp, 1948-2002 .... $50
Jemima Puddle-Duck, P1092, yellow scarf
clip, gold circle/oval backstamp, 1948-
2002 .... $250
Jemima Puddle-Duck, P1092, yellow scarf
clip, John Beswick script backstamp,
1948-2002 .... $145

Jemima Puddle-Duck Made a Feather Nest

Jemima Puddle-Duck Made a Feather
Nest, P2823, brown line backstamp,
1983-97 (ILLUS.) $60
Jemima Puddle-Duck Made a Feather
Nest, P2823, crown backstamp, 1983-97
.... $40
Jemima Puddle-Duck Made a Feather
Nest, P2823, John Beswick script backs-
tamp, 1983-97 .... $150
Jemima Puddle-Duck with Foxy Whis-
kered Gentleman, P3193, Beswick
Made in England backstamp, 1990-99 .... $80

Jemima Puddle-Duck with Foxy Whiskered Gentleman

Jemima Puddle-Duck with Foxy Whiskered Gentleman, P3193, crown backstamp, 1990-99 (ILLUS.).............................. **$85**

Jeremy Fisher Catches a Fish

Jeremy Fisher Catches a Fish, P3919, Beswick Made in England backstamp, 1999-2002 (ILLUS.)...................................... **$65**

John Joiner Figure

John Joiner, P2965, crown backstamp, 1990-97 (ILLUS.)...................................... **$55**
Lady Mouse, P1183, Beswick Made in England backstamp, 1950-2000 .... **$35**
Lady Mouse, P1183, brown line backstamp, 1950-2000 .... **$85**

Lady Mouse Figure

Lady Mouse, P1183, crown backstamp, 1950-2000 (ILLUS.) **$55**
Lady Mouse, P1183, gold circle/oval backstamp, 1950-2000 .... **$200-350**

Lady Mouse Made a Curtsey

Lady Mouse Made a Curtsy, P3220, crown backstamp, 1990-97 (ILLUS.) **$45**
Little Pig Robinson Spying, P3031, brown line backstamp, 1987-93 .... **$250**

Little Pig Robinson Spying

Little Pig Robinson Spying, P3031, crown backstamp, 1987-93 (ILLUS., previous page) **$125**

Miss Dormouse Figure

Miss Dormouse, P3251, crown backstamp, 1991-95 (ILLUS.) **$90**
Mr. Alderman Ptolemy, P2424, brown line backstamp, 1973-97 .... **$175**

Mr. Alderman Ptolemy

Mr. Alderman Ptolemy, P2424, crown backstamp, 1973-97 (ILLUS.) **$65**
Mr. Benjamin Bunny, P1940, pipe in, lilac jacket, Beswick Made in Endland backstamp, 1975-2000 .... **$35**

Mr. Benjamin Bunny

Mr. Benjamin Bunny, P1940, pipe in, lilac jacket, brown line backstamp, 1975-2000 (ILLUS.) **$75**
Mr. Benjamin Bunny, P1940, pipe in, lilac jacket, crown backstamp, 1975-2000 .... **$40**
Mr. Benjamin Bunny, P1940, pipe in, lilac jacket, John Beswick script backstamp, 1975-2000 .... **$125**

Mr. Benjamin Bunny & Peter Rabbit

Mr. Benjamin Bunny & Peter Rabbit, P2509, brown line backstamp, 1975-95 (ILLUS.) **$195**
Mr. Benjamin Bunny & Peter Rabbit, P2509, crown backstamp, 1975-95 .... **$95**
Mr. Jeremy Fisher, P1157, large spots on head, striped legs, Beswick Made in-England backstamp, 1950-2002 .... **$35**
Mr. Jeremy Fisher, P1157, large spots on head, striped legs, brown line backstamp, 1950-2002 .... **$70**

Mr. Jeremy Fisher

Mr. Jeremy Fisher, P1157, large spots on head, striped legs, crown backstamp, 1950-2002 (ILLUS.) **$35**
Mr. Jeremy Fisher, P1157, large spots on head, striped legs, gold circle/oval backstamp, 1950-2002 .... **$425**
Mr. Todd, P3091, crown backstamp, 1988-93 .... **$125**

Mr. Todd Figure

Mr. Todd, P3091, John Beswick script
backstamp, 1988-93 (ILLUS.) **$275**
Mrs. Rabbit, P1200, umbrella in, Beswick
Made in England backstamp, 1975-2002 .... **$35**
Mrs. Rabbit, P1200, umbrella in, brown line
backstamp, 1975-2002 .... **$70**

Mrs. Rabbit Figure

Mrs. Rabbit, P1200, umbrella in, crown
backstamp, 1975-2002 (ILLUS.) **$45**
Mrs. Rabbit, P1200, umbrella in, John Beswick script backstamp, 1975-2002 .... **$100**

Mrs. Rabbit & Bunnies

Mrs. Rabbit & Bunnies, P2543, brown line
backstamp, 1976-97 (ILLUS.) **$100**
Mrs. Rabbit & Bunnies, P2543, crown
backstamp, 1976-97 .... **$60**
Mrs. Rabbit & Bunnies, P2543, John Be-
swick script backstamp, 1976-97 .... **$145**

Mrs. Rabbit Cooking

Mrs. Rabbit Cooking, P3278, Beswick
Made in England backstamp, 1992-99
(ILLUS.)... **$45**
Mrs. Rabbit Cooking, P3278, crown back-
stamp, 1992-99 .... **$35**
Mrs. Rabbit & Peter, P3646, Beswick Made
in England backstamp, 1997-2002 .... **$60**

Mrs. Rabbit & Peter

Mrs. Rabbit & Peter, P3646, crown backs-
tamp, 1997-2002 (ILLUS.) **$55**
Mrs. Tiggy-Winkle, P1107, plaid dress, Beswick Made in England, backstamp,
1972-2000 .... **$35**
Mrs. Tiggy-Winkle, P1107, plaid dress,
brown line backstamp, 1972-2000 .... **$100**

Mrs. Tiggy-Winkle

Mrs. Tiggy-Winkle, P1107, plaid dress, crown backstamp, 1972-2000 (ILLUS.)........ **$35**
Mrs. Tiggy-Winkle, P1107, plaid dress, gold circle/oval backstamp, 1972-2000 ..... **$225**
Mrs. Tiggy-Winkle, P1107, plaid dress, John Beswick script backstamp, 1972-2000 .... **$140**

Mrs. Tittlemouse

Mrs. Tittlemouse, P4015, Beswick Made in England backstamp, 2000-2002 (ILLUS.) **$50**

No More Twist

No More Twist, P3325, crown backstamp, 1992-97 (ILLUS.)... **$65**

Old Mr. Brown, P1796, brown owl, brown line backstamp, 1963-99 .... **$75**

Old Mr. Brown Figure

Old Mr. Brown, P1796, brown owl, gold circle/oval backstamp, 1963-99 (ILLUS.)....... **$200**

The Old Woman Who Lived in a Shoe Knitting

Old Woman Who Lived in a Shoe Knitting (The), P2804, Beswick Made in England backstamp, 1983-2002 (ILLUS.)................. **$35**
Old Woman Who Lived in a Shoe Knitting (The), P2804, brown line backstamp, 1983-2002... **$225**
Old Woman Who Lived in a Shoe Knitting (The), P2804, crown backstamp, 1983-2002 .... **$40**

Peter Ate a Radish

Peter Ate a Radish, P3533, crown backstamp, 1995-98 (ILLUS.)............................. **$35**
Peter Rabbit, P1098, brown line backstamp, 1948-80 .... **$110**

Peter with Daffodils

Peter Rabbit Figure

Peter Rabbit, P1098, gold circle/oval backstamp, 1948-80 (ILLUS.)........................... **$300**
Peter Rabbit, P1098, light blue jacket, Beswick Made in England backstamp, 1980-2002 .... **$35**

Peter with Postbag

Peter with Postbag, P3591, crown backstamp, 1996-2002 (ILLUS.) **$40**
Pickles, P2324, brown line backstamp, 1971-82 .... **$425**

Peter Rabbit in Light Blue Jacket

Peter Rabbit, P1098, light blue jacket, brown line backstamp, 1980-2002 (ILLUS.) **$70**
Peter Rabbit, P1098, light blue jacket, crown backstamp, 1980-2002 .... **$35**
Peter Rabbit, P1098, light blue jacket, John Beswick script backstamp, 1980-2002 ...... **$135**
Peter with Daffodils, P3597, Beswick Made in England backstamp, 1996-99 (ILLUS., top next column) **$45**
Peter with Daffodils, P3597, crown backstamp, 1996-99 .... **$40**
Peter with Postbag, P3591, Beswick Made in England backstamp, 1996-2002 .... **$45**

Pickles Figure

Pickles, P2324, gold circle/oval backstamp, 1971-82 (ILLUS.) **$650**

Black-colored Pig-Wig

Pig-Wig, P2381, black pig, brown line backstamp, 1972-98 (ILLUS.) **$550**
Pig-Wig, P2381, grey pig, gold circle/oval backstamp, 1972-98 .... **very rare**
Pigling Bland, P1365, lilac jacket, Beswick Made in England backstamp, 1975-98 .... **$55**

Pigling Bland

Pigling Bland, P1365, lilac jacket, brown line backstamp, 1975-98 (ILLUS.) **$70**
Pigling Bland, P1365, lilac jacket, crown backstamp, 1975-98 .... **$55**

Poorly Peter Rabbit

Poorly Peter Rabbit, P2560, brown line backstamp, 1976-97 (ILLUS.) **$120**
Poorly Peter Rabbit, P2560, crown backstamp, 1976-97 .... **$55**
Poorly Peter Rabbit, P2560, John Beswick script backstamp, 1976-97 .... **$145**

Ribby & the Patty Pan

Ribby & the Patty Pan, P3280, crown backstamp, 1992-98 (ILLUS.)............................. **$50**

Simpkin Figure

Simpkin, P2508, brown line backstamp, 1975-83 (ILLUS.) **$600**

Sir Isaac Newton

Sir Isaac Newton, P2425, brown line backstamp, 1973-84 (ILLUS.)........................... **$450**

Squirrel Nutkin

Squirrel Nutkin, P1102, red-brown squirrel,
brown line backstamp, 1983-89 (ILLUS.)..... **$95**
Squirrel Nutkin, P1102, red-brown squirrel,
gold circle/oval backstamp, 1983-89... **$250-300**

Susan Figure

Susan, P2716, brown line backstamp,
1983-89 (ILLUS.)..................................... **$300**
Susan, P2716, crown backstamp, 1983-89 .. **$250**
Tabitha Twitchit & Miss Moppet, P2544,
brown line backstamp, 1976-93 .... **$235**

Tabitha Twitchit & Miss Moppet

Tabitha Twitchit & Miss Moppet, P2544,
crown backstamp, 1976-93 (ILLUS.) **$125**
Tabitha Twitchit & Miss Moppet, P2544,
John Beswick script backstamp, 1976-93
.... **$300**
Tailor of Gloucester, P1108, Beswick
Made in England backstamp, 1949-2002 .... **$35**
Tailor of Gloucester, P1108, brown line
backstamp, 1949-2002 .... **$65**
Tailor of Gloucester, P1108, crown backs-
tamp, 1949-2002 .... **$35**
Tailor of Gloucester, P1108, gold circle
backstamp, 1949-2002 .... **$325**
Tailor of Gloucester, P1108, gold oval
backstamp, 1949-2 .... **$200**

Tailor of Gloucester

Tailor of Gloucester, P1108, John Beswick
script backstamp, 1949-2002 (ILLUS.) **$100**
Timmy Tiptoes, P1101, brown line backs-
tamp, 1948-80 .... **$125**

Timmy Tiptoes

Timmy Tiptoes, P1101, gold circle/oval
backstamp, 1948-80 (ILLUS.).................... **$265**

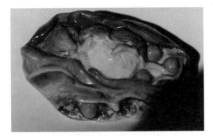

Timmy Willie Sleeping

Timmy Willie Sleeping, P2996, brown line
backstamp, 1986-96 (ILLUS.) **$225**
Timmy Willie Sleeping, P2996, crown
backstamp, 1986-96 .... **$65**
Tom Kitten, P1100, light blue suit, Beswick
Made in England backstamp, 1980-99 .... **$35**
Tom Kitten, P1100, light blue suit, brown
line backstamp, 1980-99 .... **$90**

Tom Kitten Figure

Tom Kitten, P1100, light blue suit, crown
backstamp, 1980-99 (ILLUS.) **$35**
Tom Kitten, P1100, light blue suit, John Beswick script backstamp, 1980-99 .... **$120**

Tommy Brock Figure

Tommy Brock, P1348, large eye patch,
spade handle in, Beswick Made in En-
gland backstamp, 1975-2002 (ILLUS.) **$35**
Tommy Brock, P1348, large eye patch,
spade handle in, brown line backstamp,
1975-2002 .... **$65**
Tommy Brock, P1348, large eye patch,
spade handle in, crown backstamp,
1975-2002 .... **$40**
Tommy Brock, P1348, large eye patch,
spade handle in, John Beswick script
backstamp, 1975-2002 .... **$120**

Yock-Yock in the Tub

Yock-Yock in the Tub, P3946, Beswick
Made in England backstamp, 2000-02
(ILLUS.).. **$60**

Bunnykins Figurines
Ace, DB 42, white & blue, 1986-89 .... **$250**
Airman, DB 199, limited edition of 5000,
1999 .... **$75**
Angel, DB 196, white & yellow, 1999 to
present **$45**
Astro, DB 20, white, red & blue, 1983-88 ...... **$155**
Aussie, DB 58, gold & green, 1988 .... **$750**

Bunnykins Australian Digger

Australian Digger, DB 248, brown, yellow
webbing, edition limited to 2001 (ILLUS.) .. **$125**

Banjo Player, DB 182, white & red striped blazer, black trousers, yellow straw hat, 1999, limited edition of 2,500 .... **$150**

Basket Ball Players, DB 208, limited edition of 2,500, the set (sold only in set of 5) .. **$625**

Bathtime, DB 148, white bathrobe w/grey trim, yellow towel & duck, 1994-97 .... **$50**

Be Prepared, DB 56, dark green & grey, 1987-96 .... **$60**

Bedtime, DB 55, blue & white striped pajamas, 1987-98 .... **$40**

Bedtime, DB 79, third variation, light blue & white, 1988 .... **$850**

Billie and Buntie Bunnykins Sleigh Ride, DB 4, blue, maroon & yellow, 1972-97 .... **$45**

Billie Bunnykins Cooling Off, DB 3, burgundy, yellow & greenish grey, 1972-87 .... **$185**

Bowler, DB 145, white, beige & black, 1994, limited edition of 1,000 .... **$265**

Boy Skater, second variation, DB 187, blue jacket, white trousers, red boots, 1998, limited edition of 2,500 .... **$55**

Bridesmaid, DB 173, yellow dress, dark yellow flowers, 1997-99 .... **$40**

Brownie, DB 61, brown uniform, yellow tie, 1987-93 .... **$75**

Business Man, DB 203, 1999, limited edition of 5,000 .... **$85**

Captain Cook, DB 251, dark blue & yellow, 2002, limited edition of 2,500 .... **$150**

Carol Singer Bunnykins

Carol Singer, DB 104, dark green, red, yellow & white, 1991, USA Backstamp, limited edition of 300 (ILLUS.) **$400**

Cavalier, DB 179, red tunic, white collar, black trousers & hat, yellow cape, light brown boots, 1998, limited edition of 2,500 .... **$265**

Cheerleader, DB 142, second variation, yellow, 1994, limited edition of 1,000 .... **$225**

Bunnykins Christmas Surprise

Christmas Surprise, DB 146, cream & red, 1994-2000 (ILLUS.) **$50**

Clarinet Player, DB 184, blue & white striped jacket, grey trousers, yellow straw hat, 1999, limited edition of 2,500 .... **$150**

Clown, DB 129, white costume w/red stars & black pompons, black ruff around neck, 1992, limited edition of 250 .... **$1,500**

Cook, DB 85, white & green, 1990-94 .... **$85**

Cowboy, DB 201, 1999, limited edition of 2,500 .... **$125**

Cymbals, DB 25, red, blue uniform & yellow cymbals, from the Oompah Band series, 1990, limited edition of 250 .... **$525**

Cymbals, DB 88, blue coat, 1990, limited edition of 250 .... **$525**

Day Trip, DB 260, two Bunnykins in green sports car, 2002, limited edition of 1,500 .... **$175**

Doctor, DB 181, white lab coat & shirt, dark blue trousers, black shoes, white & blue striped tie, 1998-2000 .... **$45**

Dollie Bunnykins Playtime, DB 8, white dress w/pink design, doll w/blue dress, 1972-93 .... **$45**

Dollie Bunnykins Playtime, DB 80, white & yellow, 1988, by Holmes, limited edition of 250 .... **$225**

Dollie Bunnykins Playtime, DB 80, white & yellow, 1988, by Strawbridge & Clothier, limited edition of 250 .... **$225**

Double Bass Player, DB 185, green & yellow striped trousers, 1999, limited edition of 2,500 .... **$125**

Drum-Major, DB 109, dark green, red & yellow, Oompah Band series, 1991, limited edition of 200 .... **$525**

Drum-Major, DB 90, blue & yellow uniform, Oompah Band series, 1990, limited edition of 250 .... **$525**

Drummer, DB 250, black & white striped jacket, 2002, limited edition of 2,500 .... **$175**

Drummer, DB 26B, blue, yellow, red & cream, Oompah Band series, 1984-90 ..... **$120**

Flamenco Dancer, DB 256, yellow & black, 2002, limited distribution **$50**

Easter Greetings Bunnykins

Easter Greetings, DB 149, yellow, white & green, 1995-99 (ILLUS.) **$45**
English Athlete, DB 216, white, red trim, 2000, limited edition of 2,500 .... **$110**
Family Photograph, DB 1, blue, white, burgundy & grey, 1972-88............................ **$115**
Father, DB 154, red & white striped blazer, creamy yellow trousers, Bunnykins of the Year series, 1996.. **$75**

Bunnykins Footballer

Footballer, DB 119, red, 1991, limited edition of 250 (ILLUS.).................................... **$650**
Footballer, DB 123, blue & white, 1991, limited edition of 250.................................... **$650**
Fortune Teller, DB 218, red, black & yellow, white ball, produced only in 2001................ **$55**

Father Christmas Limited Edition

Father Christmas, DB 237, white trimmed red cloak, 2000, limited edition of 2,500 (ILLUS.).. **$95**
Federation, DB 224, blue, Australian flag, limited edition of 2,500 .... **$165**
Fireman, DB 183, red jacket & helmet, black trousers, yellow boots, 1998, limited edition of 3,500..................................... **$75**
Fisherman, DB 170, blue hat & trousers, light yellow sweater, black wellingtons, 1997-2000.. **$45**

Bunnykins Friar Tuck

Friar Tuck, DB 246, brown w/green, 2001 (ILLUS.).. **$60**
Girl Skater, DB 153, green coat w/white trim, pink dress, blue books, yellow skates, 1995-97 .... **$45**
Goalkeeper, DB 118, red & black, 1991, special edition of 250 .... **$650**

Goalkeeper, DB 122, grey & black, 1991, limited edition of 250 .... $650

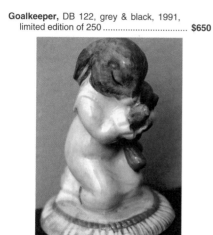

Bunnykins Goodnight

Goodnight, DB 157, pink nightgown, reddish brown Teddy, blue & white base, 1995-99 (ILLUS.).. $45
Groom, DB 102, grey & burgundy, 1991-2001 .... $45
Gymnasts, DB 207, 1999, limited edition of 2,500, the set (sold only in set of 5) $625
Happy Birthday, DB 21, red coat, blue trimmed white tablecloth, 1983-97 .... $50
Harry, DB 73, blue, brown, white & yellow, 1988-93.. $85
Harry the Herald, DB 49, maroon, white & tan, Royal Family series, 1986-90............. $155
Home Run, DB 43, blue, yellow & white, 1986-93.. $90
Ice Cream, DB 82, white, blue & green, 1990-93.. $200
Irishman, DB 178, green w/shamrocks, 1998, limited edition of 2,500 .... $225
Jester, DB 161, red, green & yellow, 1995, limited edition of 1,500 .... $495
Jogging, DB 22, yellow, blue & white, 1983-89 .... $115
John Bull, DB 134, grey, yellow, red, white & blue Union Jack waistcoat, 1993, limited edition of 1,000................................... $550
Judge, DB 188, red & white, 1999, RDICC exclusive $80
Juggler, DB 164, blue suit, black pompons, white ruff, 1996, limited edition of 1,500..... $395
King John, DB 45, red, yellow & blue, Royal Family series, 1986-90............................ $135
King Richard, DB 258, grey w/yellow trim, grey/green cloak, 2002............................. $60
Lawyer, DB 214, black robe, white wig, 2000, RDICC exclusive $60
Little Bo Peep, DB 220, yellow & orange dress, 2000 .... $60
Little Jack Horner, DB 221, maroon & yellow, 2000.. $60
Little Miss Muffet, DB 240, blue dress, green tuffet, 2002..................................... $60
Magician, DB 126, black suit, yellow shirt, yellow table cloth, 1992, limited edition of 1,500 .... $375

Maid Marion, DB 245, pink, yellow & green, 2001 .... $60
Mary, Mary, Quite Contrary, DB 247, pink, 2002.. $55
Mermaid, DB 263, 2003, limited edition of 3,000.. $125
Milkman, DB 125, white, green & grey, 1992, limited edition of 1,000 .... $750
Morris Dancer, DB 204, multicolored, 1999, limited edition of 2,000 .... $45
Mother and Baby, DB 167, brown, light pink dress, red shoes, yellow blanket, 1997-2000 .... $45
Mother's Day, DB 155, brown & blue, 1995-2000 .... $45
Mountie, Sergeant, DB 136, red coat w/yellow stripes on sleeve, blue & brown, 1993, limited edition of 250 .... $1,500
Mr. Bunnybeat Strumming, Music Box, DB 38, pink, white, yellow, 1987-89.......... $355
Mr. Bunnykins at the Easter Parade, DB 51, blue tie & hat band, maroon coat, light grey trousers, pink ribbon on package, 1986 .... $850
Mr. Punch, DB 234, blue, red, yellow stripes, 2002, limited edition of 2,500 ...... $180
Mrs. Bunnykins at the Easter Parade, DB 52, maroon dress, white collar, blue bow on bonnet, multicolored bows on packages, 1986 .... $950
Mrs. Bunnykins Clean Sweep, DB 6, blue & white, 1972-91 .... $75
New Baby, DB 158, blue dress w/white trim, white cradle, pink pillow, yellow blanket, 1995-99.. $45

Bunnykins Nurse with Green Cross

Nurse, DB 74B, dark & light blue & white, green cross, 1994-2000 (ILLUS.)................ $40
Olympic, DB 28A, white & blue, 1984-88 ..... $195
On Line, DB 238, pink & blue, 2001, limited edition of 2,500 .... $135
Oompah Band, DB 23, 24, 25, 26B, 27, red, 1990, the set $650
Out for a Duck, DB 150, white, beige & green, 1995, limited edition of 1,250........ $315
Paperboy, DB 77, green, yellow, red & white, 1989-93 .... $105

Pilgrim, DB 212, tableau, brown & green, 1999, limited edition of 2,500 .... **$125**
Policeman, DB 64, dark blue uniform, 1988-2000 .... **$45**

Bunnykins Postman

Postman, DB 76, dark blue & red, 1989-93 (ILLUS.)... **$120**
Prince Frederick, DB 94, red, blue & yellow, Royal family series, 1990, limited edition of 250.. **$465**
Princess Beatrice, DB 47, pale green, Royal Family series, 1986-90 .... **$105**
Queen Sophie, DB 46, blue & red, Royal Family series, 1986-90............................. **$145**

Rainy Day Bunnykins

Rainy Day, DB 147, yellow coat & hat, blue trousers, black boots, 1994-97 (ILLUS.) **$40**
Rise and Shine, DB 11, maroon, yellow & blue, 1973-88 .... **$125**
Robin Hood resin stand, for Robin Hood Collection, brown & green, 2001 .... **$60**
Runners, DB 205, 1999, limited edition of 2,500, the set (sold only in set of 5) **$625**

Sandcastle Money Box, DB 228, 2002, to mark the 30th anniversary of Bunnykins figures **$225**

Santa Bunnykins Happy Christmas

Santa, DB 17, red, white & brown, 1981-96 (ILLUS.)... **$45**

Santa Music Box

Santa, Music Box, DB 34, red, white, brown, 1988-91 (ILLUS.)........................... **$215**
Saxophone Player, DB 186, navy & white striped shirt, blue vest, black trousers, 1999, limited edition of 2,500 .... **$180**
Schoolboy, DB 66, blue, white & grey, 1988-91... **$155**
Scotsman (The), DB 180, dark blue jacket & hat, red & yellow kilt, white shirt, sporran & socks, black shoes, 1998, limited edition of 2,500 .... **$185**
Sheriff of Nottingham, DB 265, red cross on white apron, blue cloak, 2002 .... **$65**
Sightseer, DB 215, pink dress, 2000.............. **$50**
Sleighride, DB 4, 1972-91 .... **$45**

Soccer Player, DB 123, dark blue & white, 1991, limited edition of 250 .... **$650**

Sousaphone, DB 105, dark green, red & yellow, Oompah Band series, 1991, limited edition of 200 .... **$500**

Sousaphone, DB 86, blue uniform & yellow sousaphone, Oompha Band series, 1990, limited edition of 250 .... **$500**

Stopwatch, DB 253, green & yellow, produced only in 2002 .... **$55**

Storytime, DB 9, white dress w/blue design & pink dress, 1972-97 .... **$45**

Sundial, DB 213, red, blue & white, produced only in 2000 .... **$50**

Susan as Queen of the May

Susan Bunnykins as Queen of the May, DB 83, white polka dot dress w/blue, brown chair, 1990-91 (ILLUS.) **$165**

Sweetheart, DB 130, yellow sweater, blue trousers, red heart, 1992-97 .... **$50**

Swimmers, DB 206, 1999, limited edition of 2,500, the set (sold only in set of 5) **$625**

Tally Ho!, DB 12, burgundy, yellow, blue, white & green, 1973-88 .... **$105**

Tally Ho!, Music Box, DB 33A, maroon coat, yellow jumper, 1984-93 .... **$255**

Tennis, DB 277, tableau, issued in a pair w/Strawberries, 2003, limited edition of 3,000, pr. **$150**

Touchdown, DB 100 (University of Indiana), white & red, 1990, limited edition of 200 .... **$625**

Touchdown, DB 29B (Boston College), maroon & gold, 1985, limited edition of 50... **$2,000**

Touchdown, DB 97 (University of Michigan), yellow & blue, 1990, limited edition of 200 .... **$625**

Touchdown, DB 99 (Notre Dame), green & yellow, 1990, limited edition of 200 .... **$625**

Town Crier, DB 259, black, red & yellow, 2002, limited edition of 2,500 .... **$175**

Trumpet Player, DB 210, green striped coat, 2000, limited edition of 2,500 .... **$175**

Trumpeter, DB 24, red, blue & yellow, Oompah Band series, 1984-90 .... **$105**

Tyrolean Dancer, DB 246, black & white, 2001 .... **$60**

Uncle Sam, DB 50, blue, red & white, 1986 to present... **$45**

Waltzing Matilda, DB 236, yellow, red jacket, brown hat, 2001, limited edition of 2,001 .... **$225**

Welsh Lady, DB 172, light pink & yellow dress, black hat, 1997, limited edition of 2,500 .... **$225**

Will Scarlet, DB 264, green & orange, 2002 .... **$60**

With Love, DB 269, tinged yellow, w/engraveable nameplate, 2002 .... **$65**

Bunnykins Series

Bunnykins Aussie Explorer Teapot

Teapot, cov., Aussie Explorer patt., designed by Shane Ridge, limited edition of 2,500, introduced in 1996 (ILLUS.) **$225**

Two Views of the Bunnykins Geisha Girl Teapot

Teapot, cov., figural Geisha Girl model, designed by Martyn Alcock, limited edition of 2,500, introduced in 1998 (ILLUS. of two views, bottom previous page)............. **$225**

Bunnykins Lady of the Manor Teapot

Teapot, cov., figural Lady of the Manor, designed by Shane Ridge, limited edition of 1,500, introduced in 2003 (ILLUS.) **$300**

Bunnykins Lord of the Manor Teapot

Teapot, cov., Lord of the Manor patt., designed by Shane Ridge, limited edition of 1,500, introduced in 2003 (ILLUS.) **$300**

Bunnykins USA President Teapot

Teapot, cov., USA President model, designed by Shane Ridge, limited edition of 2,500, introduced in 1995 (ILLUS.)............ **$250**

Character Jugs

Anne Boleyn

Anne Boleyn, large, D 6644, 7 1/4" h. (ILLUS.) **$85**

Anne of Cleves

Anne of Cleves, large, D 6653, 7 1/4" h. (ILLUS.)... **$240**
Antony & Cleopatra, large, D 6728, 7 1/4" h... **$95**

Aramis

Aramis, large, D 6441, 7 1/4" h. (ILLUS., previous page) **$90**
Aramis, miniature, D 6508, 2 1/2" h. **$45**

Bacchus, large, D 6499, 7" h. (ILLUS.) **$60**
Bacchus, miniature, D 6521, 2 1/2" h. **$35**
Baseball Player, small, D 6878, 4 1/4" h. **$115**

'Ard of 'Earing

'Ard of 'Earing, large, D 6588, 7 1/2" h. (ILLUS.) **$1,250**

Beefeater

Beefeater, large, D 6206, 6 1/2" h. (ILLUS.) .. **$125**
Beefeater, small, D 6233, 3 1/4" h. **$35**
Ben Franklin, small, D 6695, 4" h. **$90**

'Arriet

'Arriet, large, D 6208, 6 1/2" h. (ILLUS.) **$65**
'Arriet, tiny, D 6256, 1 1/4" h. **$150**
'Arry, large, D 6207, 6 1/2" h. **$185**
'Arry, tiny, D 6255, 1 1/2" h. **$150**
Athos, small, D 6452, 3 3/4" h. **$50**
Auld Mac, miniature, D 6253, 2 1/4" h. **$40**
Auld Mac "A," large, D 5823, 6 1/4" h. **$60**

Blacksmith

Blacksmith, D 6571, large, 7" h. (ILLUS.) **$90**
Bootmaker, small, D 6579, 4" h. **$65**
Busker (The), large, D 6775, 6 1/2" h. **$85**
Buzfuz, small, D 5838, 4" h. **$55**
Cap'n Cuttle, mid, D 5842, 5 1/2" h. **$75**
Capt. Ahab, large, D 6500, 7" h. **$90**
Capt. Ahab, small, D 6506, 4" h. **$65**

Bacchus

Capt. Henry Morgan

Capt. Henry Morgan, large, 6 3/4" h. (ILLUS., previous page) **$115**
Capt Henry Morgan, miniature, 2 1/4" h. **$40**

Capt Hook

Capt Hook, large, D 6597, 7 1/4" h. (ILLUS.) .. **$500**
Capt. Hook, small, D 660, 4" h. **$350**
Cardinal (The), small, D 6033, 3 1/2" h. **$60**
Cardinal (The), tiny, D 6258, 1 1/2" h. **$165**

Catherine Howard

Catherine Howard, large, D 6645, 7" h. (ILLUS.) **$115**

Catherine of Aragon

Catherine of Aragon, large, D 6643, 7" h. (ILLUS.) **$85**

Catherine Parr

Catherine Parr, large, D 6664, 6 3/4" h. (ILLUS.) **$220**
Cavalier (The), large, D 6114, 7" h. **$105**
Cavalier (The), small, D 6173, 3 1/4" h. **$50**
City Gent, large, D 6815, 7" h. **$140**
Cliff Cornell, large, variation 2, dark blue suit, red tie w/cream polka dots, 9" h. **$250**

Cliff Cornell Toby Jugs

Cliff Cornell, large, variation No. 1, light brown suit, brown & cream striped tie, 9" h. (ILLUS. left) **$450**
Cliff Cornell, large, variation No. 3, dark brown suit, green, black & blue designed tie, 9" h. (ILLUS. right) **$750**
Cliff Cornell, small, variation No. 1, light brown suit, brown & cream striped tie, 5" h. **$1,500**
Cliff Cornell, small, variation No. 2, blue suit, 5" h. **$3,500**
Cliff Cornell, small, variation No. 3, dark brown suit, 5" h. **$250**
Clown w/red hair (The), large, D 5610, 7 1/2" h. **$2,750**

Clown with White Hair

Falstaff

Clown w/white hair (The), large, D 6322,
7 1/2" h. (ILLUS.) **$1,000**
Collector (The), large, D 6796, 7" h. **$165**
Davy Crockett & Santa Anna, large, D
6729, 7" h. **$150**
Dick Turpin, horse handle, large, D 6528,
7" h. **$80**
Dick Turpin, horse handle, miniature, D
6542, 2 1/4" h. **$35**
Dick Turpin, miniature, D 6128, 2 1/4" h. **$35**
Dick Turpin, pistol handle, small, D 5618,
3 1/2" h. **$35**
Dick Turpin "A," pistol handle, D 5485,
6 1/2" h. **$125**
Dick Whittington, large, D 6375, 6 1/2" h. **$350**

The Fortune Teller

Fortune Teller (The), large, D 6497,
6 3/4" h. (ILLUS.) **$550**
Fortune Teller (The), small, D 6503,
3 3/4" h. **$250**
Friar Tuck, large, D 6321, 7" h. **$450**
Gaoler, small, D 6577, 3 3/4" h. **$55**

Don Quixote

Don Quixote, large, D 6455, 7 1/4" h.
(ILLUS.) **$60**
Drake, small, D 6174, 3 1/4" h. **$55**
Falconer (The), miniature, D 6547, 2 3/4" h. **$35**
Falconer (The), small, D 6540, 3 3/4" h. **$50**
Falstaff, large, D 6287, 6" h. (ILLUS., top
next column) **$65**
Farmer John, large, D 5788, 6 1/2" h. **$125**
Farmer John, small, D 5789, 3 1/4" h. **$65**
Fat Boy, mid, D 5840, 5" h. **$125**
Fat Boy, miniature, D 6139, 2 1/2" h. **$45**

The Gardener

Gardener (The), large, D 6630, 7 3/4" h. (ILLUS, previous page) **$115**
General Gordon, large, D 6869, 7 1/4" h. **$225**
Genie, large, D 6892, 7" h. **$175**
George Washington, large, D 6669, 7 1/2" h. **$145**

George Washington

George Washington and George III, large, D 6749, 7 1/4" h. (ILLUS. of Washington side) **$125**

Gladiator

Gladiator, large, D 6650, 7 3/4" h. (ILLUS.)... **$600**
Gladiator, small, D 6553, 4 1/4" h. **$350**
Gone Away, miniature, D 6545, 2 1/2" h. **$35**
Gone Away, small, D 6538, 3 3/4" h. **$45**
Granny, large, D 5521, 6 1/4" h. **$55**
Granny, miniature, D 6520, 2 1/4" h. **$55**

Groucho Marx

Groucho Marx, large, D 6710, 7" h. (ILLUS.) **$155**

The Guardsman

Guardsman (The), large, D 6568, 6 3/4" h. (ILLUS.)... **$95**

Gulliver

Gulliver, large, D 6560, 7 1/2" h. (ILLUS.)..... **$700**
Gulliver, miniature, D 6566, 2 1/2" h. **$375**
Gunsmith, small, D 6580, 3 1/2" h. **$80**

Hamlet

Hamlet, large, D 6672, 7 1/4" h. (ILLUS.) **$150**
Happy John "A," large, D 6031, 8 1/2" h. **$85**

Henry V, flag decal, large, variation No. 3, D
6671, 7 1/4" h.. **$90**

Henry VIII

Henry VIII, large, D 6642, 6 1/2" h. (ILLUS.) .. **$105**

Izaac Walton Character Jug

Izaac Walton, large, D 6404, 7" h. (ILLUS.)..... **$65**

Jane Seymour

Jane Seymour, large, D 6646, 7 1/4" h.
(ILLUS.)... **$100**
Jester, seated, medium, D 6910, 5" h............ **$145**
Jester, small, D 5556, 3 1/8" h......................... **$45**
Jockey, large, D 6625, 7 3/4" h. **$150**
John Barleycorn, small, D 5735, 3 1/2" h. **$70**

John Doulton, small, two o'clock, D 6656,
4 1/4" h.. **$40**

John Peel

John Peel, large, D 5612, 6 1/2" h. (ILLUS.) .. **$115**
John Peel, tiny, D 6259, 1 1/4" h. **$125**
John Shorter, small, D 6880, 4 1/4" h. **$85**

Johnny Appleseed

Johnny Appleseed, large, D 6372, 6" h.
(ILLUS.).. **$325**
Juggler (The), large, D 6835, 6 1/2" h. **$125**
King Charles I, large, D 6917, 7" h. **$275**

The Lawyer

Lawyer (The), large, D6498, 7" h. (ILLUS.) **$90**
Lawyer (The), small, D 6504, 4" h. **$40**

Leprechaun, large, D 6847, 7 1/2" h. **$125**
Little Mester Museum Piece, large, D 6819, 6 3/4" h. **$115**
Lobster Man, large, D 6617, 7 1/2" h. **$65**
London 'Bobby' (The), large, D 6744, 7" h. .. **$100**
Long John Silver, miniature, D 6512, 2 1/2" h. **$40**

Lord Nelson

Lord Nelson, large, D 6336, 7" h. (ILLUS.) ... **$315**

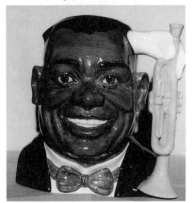

Louis Armstrong

Louis Armstrong, large, D 6707, 7 1/2" h. (ILLUS.) **$185**

Lumberjack

Lumberjack, large, D 6610, 7 1/4" h. (ILLUS.) **$90**

Macbeth, large, D 6667, 7 1/4" h. **$90**

Mad Hatter

Mad Hatter, large, D 6598, 7 1/4" h. (ILLUS.) .. **$165**
Mark Twain, small, D 6694, 4" h. **$65**
Mephistopheles, large, w/verse, D 5757, 7" h. **$2,250**
Mephistopheles "A," small, two-faced, w/verse, D 5758, 3 3/4" h. **$850**

Merlin

Merlin, large, D 6529, 7 1/4" h. (ILLUS.) **$85**
Merlin, small, D 6536, 3 3/4" h. **$40**
Mine Host, miniature, D 6513, 2 1/2" h. **$40**
Mr. Micawber, mid, D 5843, 5 1/2" h. **$130**

Mr. Pickwick

Mr. Pickwick, large, D 6060, 5 1/2" h. (ILLUS.) **$105**

Mr. Pickwick, tiny, D 6260, 1 1/4" h.............. $110
Mr. Quaker, large, D 6738, 7 1/2" h. $650
Neptune, small, D 6552, 3 3/4" h. $40

Parson Brown

Parson Brown "A," large, D 5486, 6 1/2" h.
(ILLUS.).. $125
Pearly King, large, D 6760, 6 3/4" h............. $125
Pearly Queen, large, D 6759, 7" h................ $115
Pied Piper, large, D 6403, 7" h. $75
Poacher (The), variation 2, large, D 6429,
7" h.. $80
Punch & Judy Man, large, D 6590, 7" h. $675
Queen Victoria, small, D 6913, 3 1/2" h. $165
Red Queen (The), large, D 6777, 7 1/4" h. $125

Night Watchman

Night Watchman, large, D 6569, 7" h.
(ILLUS.).. $130
North American Indian, small, D 6614,
4 1/4" h... $45
Old Charley, large, D 5420, 5 1/2" h............... $65

Old King Cole

Old King Cole, large, D 6036, 5 3/4" h.
(ILLUS.).. $230
Old Salt, large, D 6551, 7 1/2" h. $125

The Ringmaster

Ringmaster (The), large, D 6863, 7 1/2" h.
(ILLUS.).. $150

Paddy

Paddy, large, D 5753, 6" h. (ILLUS.).............. $120
Paddy, tiny, D 6145, 1 1/4" h. $45

Rip Van Winkle

Rip Van Winkle, large, D 6438, 6 1/2" h.
(ILLUS.).. $115

Robin Hood

Robin Hood, 2nd version, large, D 6527,
7 1/2" h. (ILLUS. left)................................... **$65**
Robin Hood, 2nd version, small, D 6234,
3 1/4" h. (ILLUS. right) **$55**

Robinson Crusoe

Robinson Crusoe, large, D 6532, 7 1/2" h.
(ILLUS.)... **$140**
Robinson Crusoe, miniature, D 6546,
2 3/4" h.. **$40**
Romeo, large, D 6670, 7 1/2" h...................... **$75**
Ronald Reagan, large, D 6718, 7 3/4" h........ **$750**

Sairey Gamp

Sairey Gamp, large, No. 5451, 6 1/4" h.
(ILLUS.).. **$65**

Sairey Gamp, tiny, D 6146, 1 1/4" h. **$60**
Sam Johnson, large, D 6289, 6 1/4" h. **$245**

Sam Weller

Sam Weller, large, D 6064, 6 1/2" h.
(ILLUS.)... **$80**
Sam Weller, tiny, D 6147, 1 1/4" h................... **$40**
Sancho Pança, large, D 6456, 6 1/2" h. **$85**

Santa Claus w/Doll & Drum Handle

Santa Claus, doll & drum handle, large, D
6668, 7 1/2" h. (ILLUS.) **$145**
Santa Claus, plain handle, large, D 6704,
7 1/2" h. **$125**

Scaramouche

Scaramouche, large, first version, D 6558,
7" h. (ILLUS.) **$825**

Simon the Cellarer, large, D 5504, 6 1/2" h.
.... **$110**
Simon the Cellarer, small, D 5616, 3 1/2" h.
.... **$40**

Simple Simon

Simple Simon, large, D 6374, 7" h. (ILLUS.) .. **$475**
Sir Francis Drake, large, D 6805, 7" h. **$105**

Sir Thomas More

Sir Thomas More, large, D 6792, 6 3/4" h.
(ILLUS.).. **$210**

The Sleuth

Sleuth (The), large, D 6631, 7" h. (ILLUS.)...... **$65**

St. George

St. George, large, D 6618, 7 1/2" h. (ILLUS.) .. **$175**
Tam O'Shanter, miniature, D 6640,
2 1/2" h.. **$40**
Toby Philpots, large, D 5736, 6 1/4" h. **$105**

Tony Weller

Tony Weller, large, D 5531, 6 1/2" h.
(ILLUS.).. **$105**
Touchstone, large, D 5613, 7" h. **$245**
Town Crier, large, D 6530, 7" h. **$175**

Ugly Duchess

Ugly Duchess, large, D 6599, 6 3/4" h.
(ILLUS.).. **$625**

Uncle Tom Cobbleigh, large, D 6337, 7" h. .. $275

Veteran Motorist

Veteran Motorist, large, D 6633, 7 1/2" h.
(ILLUS.).. $85

The Walrus & Carpenter

Walrus & Carpenter (The), large, D 6600,
7 1/4" h. (ILLUS.) $165

Shakespeare

William Shakespeare, large, D 6689,
7 3/4" h. (ILLUS.) $125

Winston Churchill, style 1, large, D 6907,
Union Jack & bulldog handle, 7" h. $325

Yachtsman

Yachtsman, large, D 6626, 8" h. (ILLUS.)
.... $145

Figurines

Abdullah, HN 2104, multicolored, 1953-62
.... $425

Ace (The), HN 3398, white, 1991-95 .... $195

Adele, HN 2480, flowered white dress,
1987-92... $175

Affection, HN 2236, purple, 1962-94............ $115

Afternoon Tea, HN 1747, pink & blue,
1935-82.. $475

Ajax, HN 2908, red, green & gold, 1980, lim-
ited edition of 950.................................... $475

Alexandra, HN 2398, patterned green
dress, yellow cape, 1970-76 .... $215

Alison, HN 2336, blue & white, 1966-92........ $175

Amy, HN 3316, blue & rose, Figure of the
Year series, 1991.................................... $950

An Old King, HN 2134, purple, red, green &
brown, 1954-92.. $450

Anna, HN 2802, purple & white, Kate
Greenaway Series, 1976-82 .... $225

Anne Boleyn, HN 3232, red & grey, 1990,
limited edition of 9,500............................. $550

April, HN 2708, white dress w/flowers,
Flower of the Month series, 1987.............. $225

Aragorn, HN 2916, tan, 1981-84 .... $140

Artful Dodger, M 55, black & brown, Dickens Miniatures Series, 1932-83 .... $75

As Good As New, HN 2971, blue, green
and tan, 1982-85...................................... $150

Ascot, HN 2356, green dress w/yellow
shawl, 1968-95... $200

Auctioneer (The), HN 2988, black, grey &
brown, 1986, R.D.I.C.C. Series (ILLUS.,
top next page) $195

August, HN 3165, white & blue dress
w/poppies, Flower of the Month Series,
1987 .... $275

Autumn Breezes, HN 1911, green & pink,
1939-76.. $325

Autumn Breezes, HN 1913, green dress,
blue jacket, 1939-71................................. $275

Autumn Breezes, HN 1934, red, 1940-97
.... $375

The Auctioneer

Autumn Breezes

Autumn Breezes, HN 2131, orange, yellow
& black, 1990-94 (ILLUS.) **$250**
Autumn Breezes, HN 2147, black & white,
1955-71 .... **$350**
Autumntime, HN 3231, golden brown,
R.D.I.C.C. Four Seasons Series (Style
Four), 1989... **$175**
Babie, HN 1679, green dress, 1935-92........... **$70**
Ballad Seller, HN 2266, pink, 1968-73 .... **$250**

Ballerina, HN 2116, lavender, 1953-73 .... **$425**
Balloon Man (The), HN 1954, black & grey,
1940 to present **$240**
Balloon Seller (The), HN 583, green shawl,
cream dress, 1923-49 .... **$950**
Basket Weaver (The), HN 2245, pale blue
& yellow, 1959-62 .... **$450**
Beachcomber, HN 2487, matte, purple &
grey, 1973-76... **$215**
Beat You To It, HN 2871, pink, gold & blue,
1980-87... **$475**

Bedtime

Bedtime, HN 1978, white w/black base,
1945-97 (ILLUS.) **$80**
Bedtime Story, HN 2059, pink, white, yel-
low & blue, 1950-98 .... **$330**
Belle, HN 2340, green dress, 1968-88............ **$70**
Belle O' the Ball, HN 1997, red & white,
1947-79 .... **$350**
Bernice, HN 2071, pink & red, 1951-53...... **$1,050**
Bess, HN 2003, purple cloak, 1947-50 .... **$850**
Biddy, HN 1513, red dress, blue shawl,
1932-51 .... **$180**
Biddy Penny Farthing, HN 1843, green &
lavender, 1938 to present **$300**
Bill Sykes, M 54, black & brown, 1932-81....... **$65**
Blacksmith of Williamsburg, HN 2240,
white shirt, brown hat, 1960-83................. **$225**
Blithe Morning, HN 2021, mauve & pink
dress, 1949-71 .... **$295**
Blithe Morning, HN 2065, blue & pink
dress, 1949-71 .... **$325**
Blithe Morning, HN 2065, red dress, 1950-
73.. **$225**
Bluebeard, HN 2105, purple, green &
brown, 1953-92 .... **$450**
Bo Peep, HN 1811, orange dress, green
hat, 1937-95... **$115**
Boatman (The), HN 2417, yellow, 1971-87 ... **$250**
Bonnie Lassie, HN 1626, red dress, 1934-
53.. **$575**
Boy from Williamsburg, HN 2183, blue &
pink, 1969-83 .... **$215**
Bride (The), HN 2166, pale pink dress,
1956-76.. **$175**
Bride (The), HN 2873, white w/gold trim,
1980-89.. **$175**

Bride (The), HN 3284, style 4, white, 1990-97 .... $175
Bridesmaid, M 30, pink & lavender, 1932-45 ..... $450
Bridesmaid (The Little), HN 2196, white dress, pink trim, 1960-76 .... $105
Bridesmaid (The Little), M 12, multicolor gown, 1932-45 ..... $425
Bridget, HN 2070, green, brown & lavender, 1951-73 ..... $280
Broken Lance (The), HN 2041, blue, red & yellow, 1949-75 ..... $450
Bunny, HN 2214, turquoise, 1960-75 ..... $200
Bunny's Bedtime, HN 3370, pale blue, pink ribbon, 1991, RDICC Series, limited edition of 9,500 ..... $175
Buttercup, HN 2309, green dress w/yellow sleeves, 1964-97 ..... $185
Buz Fuz, M 53, black & red, 1932-83 ..... $65
Camellia, HN 2222, pink, 1960-71 ..... $225
Captain Cook, HN 2889, black & cream, 1980-84 ..... $425
Captain Cuttle, M 77, yellow & black, 1939-82 ..... $65
Captain (The), HN 2260, black & white, 1965-82 ..... $225
Carol, HN 2961, white, 1982-95 ..... $180
Carolyn, HN 2112, white & green flowered dress, 1953-65 ..... $300
Carpet Seller (The), HN 1464 (hand open), green & orange, 1929-? $275
Carpet Seller (The), HN 1464A, (hand closed), green & orange, 1931-69 ..... $225
Carpet Seller (The), HN 2776, Flambé, 1990 to present $400
Catherine, HN 3044, white, 1985-96 ..... $75
Catherine of Aragon, HN 3233, green, blue & white dress, 1990, limited edition of 9,500 ..... $695
Cavalier, HN 2716, brown & green, 1976-82 .. $265
Centurian, HN 2726, grey & purple, 1982-84 ..... $225

Child from Williamsburg, HN 2154, blue dress, 1964-83 ..... $150
China Repairer, HN 2943, blue, white & tan, 1983-88 ..... $205
Chloe, HN 1765, blue, 1936-50 ..... $450
Christine, HN 2792, flowered blue & white dress, 1978-98 ..... $255
Christmas Morn, HN 1992, red & white, 1947-96 ..... $175

Christmas Parcels

Christmas Parcels, HN 2851, black, 1978-82 (ILLUS.) $225
Christmas Time, HN 2110, red w/white frills, 1953-67 ..... $545

Cissie

Cissie, HN 1809, pink dress, 1937-93 (ILLUS.) $100
Claire, HN 3209, red, 1990-92 ..... $175
Claribel, HN 1951, red dress, 1940-49 ..... $400
Clarinda, HN 2724, blue & white dress, 1975-81 ..... $175
Clarissa, HN 2345, green dress, 1968-81 ..... $185

Charlotte

Charlotte, HN 3813, brown figure, ivory dress, 1996-97 (ILLUS.) $225
Chief (The), HN 2892, gold, 1979-88 ..... $225

Clown (The), HN 2890, gold & grey, 1979-88 .... **$425**
Coachman, HN 2282, purple, grey & blue, 1963-71 .... **$575**
Cookie, HN 2218, pink & white,1958-75 .... **$125**
Coralie, HN 2307, yellow dress, 1964-88 .... **$95**
Country Lass (A), HN 1991A, blue, brown & white, 1975-81 .... **$210**
Cup O' Tea, HN 2322, dark blue & grey, 1964-83 .... **$175**
Curly Locks, HN 2049, pink flowered dress,1949-53 .... **$225**
Daffy Down Dilly, HN 1712, green dress, 1935-75 .... **$375**
Dainty May, M 67, pink skirt, blue over-dress, 1935-49 .... **$625**

Daisy

Daisy, HN 3805, ivory & gold, Charleston series, 1996-97 (ILLUS.) **$250**
Darling, HN 1319, white w/black base, 1929-59 .... **$175**
Darling, HN 1985, white nightshirt, 1946-97 .... **$90**
David Copperfield, M 88, black & tan, Dickens Miniatures Series, 1949-83 .... **$65**
Deborah, HN 2701, green & white, 1983-84 .... **$175**
Delight, HN 1772, red dress, 1936-67 .... **$225**
Delphine, HN 2136, blue & lavender, 1954-67 .... **$400**
Diana, HN 1986, red, 1946-75 .... **$175**
Discovery, HN 3428, matte white, 1992 .... **$125**
Duchess of York (The), HN 3086, cream, 1986, limited edition of 1,500 .... **$750**
Duke of Edinburgh (The), HN 2386, black & gold, 1981, limited edition of 1,500 .... **$425**
Dulcie, HN 2305, blue, 1981-84 .... **$225**
Easter Day, HN 1976, white dress, blue flowers, 1945-51 .... **$650**
Easter Day, HN 2039, multicolored, 1949-69 .... **$425**
Elegance, HN 2264, green dress, 1961-85 .... **$230**
Eliza, HN 2543, gold, Haute Ensemble Series, 1974-79 .... **$300**
Eliza, HN 3179, red & lilac, 1988-92 .... **$175**

Ellen

Ellen, HN 3816, ivory & light blue dress, 1996-97 (ILLUS.) **$160**
Elyse, HN 2429, blue dress, 1972-95 .... **$225**
Embroidering, HN 2855, grey dress, 1980-90 .... **$275**
Emily, HN 3204, style 2, white & blue, 1989-93 .... **$135**
Enchantment, HN 2178, blue, 1957-82 .... **$135**
Ermine Coat (The), HN 1981, white & red, 1945-67 .... **$365**
Eventide, HN 2814, blue, white, red, yellow & green, 1977-91 .... **$275**
Fagin, M 49, brown, 1932-83 .... **$65**
Fair Lady, HN 2193, green, 1963-96 .... **$125**
Fair Lady, HN 2832, red gown, green sleeves, 1977-96 .... **$205**
Fair Lady, HN 2835, coral pink, 1977-96 ...... **$225**
Fair Maiden, HN 2211, green dress, yellow sleeves, 1967-94 .... **$80**
Fair Maiden, HN 2434, red gown, 1983-94 ..... **$75**
Falstaff, HN 2054, red jacket, brown belt & boots, 1950-92 .... **$140**
Falstaff, HN 3236, brown, yellow & lavender, 1989-90 .... **$50**
Farmer's Wife, HN 2069, red, green & brown, 1951-55 .... **$250**
Fat Boy, M 44, blue & white, 1932-83 .... **$65**
Fatboy (The), HN 2096, blue & cream, 1952-67 .... **$375**
Favourite (The), HN 2249, blue & white, 1960-90 .... **$205**
Fiona, HN 2694, red & white, 1974-81 .... **$175**
First Dance, HN 2803, pale blue dress, 1977-92 .... **$225**
First Prize, HN 3911, white shirt, brown jodhpurs, black hat, dark blue coat, 1997-99 .... **$135**
First Steps, HN 2242, blue & yellow, 1959-65 .... **$475**
First Waltz, HN 2862, red dress, 1979-83 ..... **$275**
Fleur, HN 2368, green dress, 1968-95 .... **$165**
Flirtation, HN 3071, pale blue, 1985-95 .... **$215**
Flora, HN 2349, brown & white, 1966-73 .... **$225**
Flower Seller's Children, HN 1342, purple, red & yellow, 1929-93 .... **$575**

Foaming Quart (The), HN 2162, brown,
1955-92 .... **$125**

Fond Farewell

Fond Farewell, HN 3815, red, 1997-99
(ILLUS.) **$225**

Fortune Teller

Fortune Teller, HN 2159, multicolor, 1955-
67 (ILLUS.) **$550**
Forty Winks, HN 1974, green & tan, 1945-
73 .... **$295**
Four O'Clock, HN 1760, modeled by Leslie
Harradine, 1936-49 (ILLUS., top next col-
umn) **$2,000**
Fragrance, HN 2334, blue, 1966 to present .. **$225**
Francine, HN 2422, green & white dress,
1972-81 .... **$105**
French Peasant, HN 2075, brown & green,
1951-55 .... **$575**
Friar Tuck, HN 2143, brown, 1954-65 .... **$595**
Frodo, HN 2912, black & white, Middle
Earth Series, 1980-84 .... **$175**

Rare Four O'Clock Doulton Figurine

Gaffer (The), HN 2053, green & brown,
1950-59 .... **$425**
Gamekeeper (The), HN 2879, green, black
& tan, 1984-92 .... **$250**
Gandalf, HN 2911, green & white, Middle
Earth Series, 1980-84 .... **$275**
Geisha (The), HN 3229, Flambé, RDICC,
1989 .... **$315**
Genevieve, HN 1962, red, 1941-75 .... **$325**
Genie (The), HN 2989, blue, 1983-90 .... **$185**
Genie (The), HN 2999, Flambé, 1989-95 ...... **$350**
George Washington at Prayer, HN 2861,
blue & tan, 1977, limited edition of 750... **$2,750**
Gillian, HN 3042, green, 1984-91 .... **$125**
Gimli, HN 2922, brown & blue, Middle Earth
Series, 1981-84 .... **$235**
Giselle, The Forest Glade, HN 2140, white
& blue, 1954-65 .... **$425**
Golfer, HN 2992, blue, white & pale brown,
1988-91 .... **$275**
Good King Wenceslas, HN 2118, brown &
purple, 1953-76 .... **$275**
Good Morning, HN 2671, blue, pink &
brown matte, 1974-76 .... **$175**
Goody Two Shoes, M 80, blue skirt, red
overdress, 1939-49 .... **$115**
Graduate (The), HN 3017, male, black &
grey, 1984-92 .... **$215**
Grand Manner, HN 2723, lavender-yellow,
1975-81 .... **$245**
Granny's Shawl, HN 1647, red cape, 1934-
49 .... **$625**
Gypsy Dance, HN 2230, lavender dress,
1959-71 .... **$275**
Happy Anniversary, HN 3097, style one,
purple & white, 1987-93 .... **$205**
Harlequin, HN 2186, blue, 1957-69 .... **$425**

Harmony

Harmony, HN 2824, grey dress, 1978-84 (ILLUS.)... $225

Hazel, HN 1797, orange & green dress, 1936-49... $550

He Loves Me, HN 2046, flowered pink dress, 1949-62 .... $250

Her Ladyship, HN 1977, red & cream, 1945-59 .... $425

Hilary, HN 2335, blue dress, 1967-81............ $195

Home Again, HN 2167, red & white, 1956-95 .... $175

Homecoming (The), HN 3295, blue, pink & green, 1990, limited edition of 9,500, Children of the Blitz series $325

Honey, HN 1909, pink, 1939-49................... $525

Hornpipe (The), HN 2161, blue jacket, blue & white striped trousers, 1955-62 .... $750

HRH Prince Phillip, Duke of Edinburgh, HN 2386, black & gold, 1981, limited edition of 1,500 .... $463

HRH the Prince of Wales, HN 2883, purple, white & black, limited edition of 1,500, 1981 .... $450

Huntsman (The), HN 2492, grey coat, cream pants, black hat & boots, 1974-79 (ILLUS., top next column) $325

Ibrahim, HN 2095, brown & yellow, 1952-55 .... $625

Innocence, HN 2842, red, 1979-83 .... $205

Invitation, HN 2170, pink, 1956-75 .... $215

Irene, HN 1621, pale yellow dress, 1934-51 .... $525

Isadora, HN 2938, lavender, 1986-92 .... $350

Ivy, HN 1768, pink hat, lavender dress, 1936-79 .... $105

Jack, HN 2060, green, white & black, 1950-71 .... $175

Jacqueline, HN 2001, pink dress, 1947-51 .... $800

Jane, HN 2806, yellow dress, 1983-86 .... $300

The Huntsman

Jane, HN 3260, green, blue & yellow, 1990-95 .... $275

Janet, HN 1537, red dress, 1932-95 .... $125

Janet, M 69, pale green skirt, green overdress, 1936-49 .... $425

Janet, HN 1916, pink & blue, 1939-49 .... $350

Janice, HN 2022, green dress, 1949-55 .... $715

Janine, HN 2461, turquoise & white, 1971-95 .... $275

Jennifer, HN 2392, blue dress, 1981-92 .... $295

Jersey Milkmaid (The), HN 2057, blue, white & red, 1950-59 .... $325

Jester (A), HN 2016, pink, purple & orange, 1949-97 .... $325

Jill, HN 2061, pink & white, 1950-71 .... $175

Joan, HN 2023, blue, 1949-59 .... $225

Joker (The), HN 2252, white, 1990-92 .... $250

Judge (The), HN 2443, red & white, 1972-76 .... $250

Judge (The), HN 2443A, gloss, red & white, 1976-92 .... $260

Judith, HN 2089, red & blue, 1952-59 .... $405

Judith, HN 2278, yellow, 1986-89 .... $225

Julia, HN 2705, gold, 1975-90 .... $265

June, HN 2991, lavender & red, 1988-94 ..... $235

Karen, HN 1994, red dress, 1947-55 .... $450

Karen, HN 2388, style two, red & white, 1982 to present $350

Kate, HN 2789, white dress, 1978-87 .... $150

Kathleen, HN 3100, purple, cream & pink, 1986 .... $275

Katrina, HN 2327, red, 1967-69 .... $275

Kelly, HN 2478, white w/blue flowers, 1985-92 .... $220

Kirsty, HN 3213, red, 1988-97 .... $175

Ko-Ko, HN 2898, yellow & blue, 1980-85 ..... $650

L'Ambitieuse, HN 3359, rose & pale blue, 1991, RDICC, limited edition of 5,000....... $350

La Sylphide, HN 2138, white dress, 1954-65 .... $475

Lady April, HN 1958, red dress, 1940-49 ..... $425

Lady of the Georgian Period (A), HN 41, gold & blue, 1914-38.............................. $3,000

Lambing Time

Lambing Time, HN 1890, light brown, 1938-80 (ILLUS.)..................................... **$175**
Last Waltz, HN 2315, apricot dress, 1967-93 .... **$145**
Laura, HN 3136, dark blue & white, 1988 ...... **$225**
Leading Lady, HN 2269, blue & yellow, 1965-76 .... **$205**
Legolas, HN 2917, cream & tan, Middle Earth Series, 1981-84 .... **$205**
Lights Out, HN 2662, blue trousers & yellow spotted shirt, 1965-69 .... **$235**
Lilac Time, HN 2137, red, 1954-69................ **$385**
Lisa, HN 2394, yellow & lilac, 1983-90.......... **$175**
Little Boy Blue, HN 2062, blue, 1950-73 ...... **$175**
Lizzie, HN 2749, green, white & red, 1988-91 .... **$205**
Lorna, HN 2311, green dress, apricot shawl, 1965-85... **$175**
Love Letter, HN 2149, pink & blue dress, 1958-76... **$375**
Lucy Locket, HN 524, yellow dress, 1921-49 .... **$775**
Lynne, HN 2329, green dress, 1971-96........ **$175**
Madonna of the Square, HN 2034, light green-blue, 1949-51.............................. **$1,100**
Margaret, HN 1989, red & green, 1947-49 .... **$500**
Marguerite, HN 1928, pink dress, 1940-49.... **$600**
Marietta, HN 1341, black & red, 1929-49.... **$1,650**
Marjorie, HN 2788, blue & white dress, 1980-84... **$325**
Mary, HN 3375, blue & white, Figure of the Year Series, 1992 .... **$575**
Mary, Mary, HN 2044, pink, Nursery Rhymes Series, 1949-73.......................... **$225**
Masque, HN 2554, hand holds wand of mask, 1973-82.. **$315**
Mayor (The), HN 2280, red & white, 1963-71 .... **$275**
Melissa, HN 2467, purple & cream, 1981 to present **$250**
Melody, HN 2202, blue & peach, 1957-62 .... **$285**
Meriel, HN 1931, pink dress, 1940-49........ **$1,650**

Michelle, HN 2234, green, 1967-94.............. **$175**
Midsummer Noon, HN 2033, pink, 1949-55
.... **$700**
Minuet, HN 2019, white dress, floral print, 1949-71... **$285**
Miss Fortune, HN 1897, blue & white shawl, pink dress, 1938-49 .... **$1,000**
Monica, HN 1467, flowered purple dress, 1931-95... **$125**
Monica, M 66, shaded pink skirt, blue blouse, 1935-49 .... **$750**
Mr. Micawber, HN 1895, brown, black & tan, 1938-52... **$525**
Mr. Pickwick, HN 1894, blue, tan & cream, Dickens Series, 1938-42........................ **$475**
My Love, HN 2339, white w/red rose, 1969-97 .... **$225**
News vendor, HN 2891, gold & grey, 1986, limited edition of 2,500............................ **$225**
Newsboy, HN 2244, green, brown & blue, 1959-65... **$425**
Nicola, HN 2839, flowered lavender dress, 1978-95... **$275**
Nina, HN 2347, matte blue, 1969-76............. **$135**
Ninette, HN 2379, yellow & cream, 1971-97
.... **$225**
Noelle, HN 2179, orange, white & black, 1957-67... **$450**

Old Country Roses

Old Country Roses, HN 3692, red, 1995-99 (ILLUS.)... **$360**
Old King Cole, HN 2217, brown, yellow & white, 1963-67 .... **$625**
Old Meg, HN 2494, blue & grey matte finish, 1974-76... **$215**
Olga, HN 2463, turquoise & gold, 1972-75 .... **$195**
Oliver Twist, M 89, black & tan, Dickens Miniatures Series, 1949-83...................... **$65**
Omar Khayyam, HN 2247, brown, 1965-83
.... **$195**
Once Upon a Time, HN 2047, pink dotted dress, 1949-55.. **$475**
Orange Lady (The), HN 1953, light green dress, green shawl, 1940-75................... **$315**
Orange Vendor (An), HN 1966, purple cloak, 1941-49... **$950**

Owd Willum, HN 2042, green & brown, 1949-73 .... **$225**

Paisley Shawl, HN 1392, white dress, red shawl, 1930-49 .... **$450**

Paisley Shawl, M 4, green dress, dark green shawl, black bonnet w/red feather & ribbons, 1932-45 .... **$375**

Pamela, HN 3223, style 2, white & blue, 1989-89 .... **$225**

Pantalettes, HN 1362, green & blue, 1929-38 .... **$625**

Pantalettes, M 16, red skirt, red tie on hat, 1932-45 .... **$425**

Parisian, HN 2445, blue & grey, matte glaze,1972-75 .... **$150**

Partners, HN 3119, black, blue & grey, 1990-92 .... **$265**

Paula, HN 3234, white & blue, 1990-96 .... **$195**

Pauline, HN 2441, peach, 1984-1989 .... **$250**

Pearly Boy, HN 2035, reddish brown, 1949-59 .... **$195**

Pearly Girl, HN 1483, red jacket, 1931-49 ..... **$325**

Pecksniff, HN 2098, black & brown, 1952-67 .... **$375**

Peggy, HN 2038, red dress, green trim, 1949-79 .... **$125**

Penelope, HN 1901, red dress, 1939-75 .... **$375**

Penny, HN 2338, green & white dress, 1968-95 .... **$75**

Pensive, HN 3109, white w/yellow flowers on skirt, 1986-88 .... **$175**

Pied Piper (The), HN 2102, brown cloak, grey hat & boots, 1953-76 .... **$275**

Piper (The), HN 2907, green, 1980-92 .... **$350**

Polka (The), HN 2156, pale pink dress, 1955-69 .... **$295**

Polly, HN 3178, green & lavender, 1988-91 .. **$215**

Polly Peachum, HN 550, red dress, 1922-49 .... **$750**

Polly Peachum, M 21, red gown, 1932-45 .... **$600**

Premiere, HN 2343, hand holds cloak, green dress, 1969-79 .... **$195**

Pride & Joy, HN 2945, brown, gold & green, RDICC, 1984 (ILLUS.) **$275**

Priscilla, M 24, red, 1932-45 .... **$600**

Promenade, HN 2076, blue & orange, 1951-53 .... **$2,250**

Prue, HN 1996, red, white & black, 1947-55 .... **$550**

Puppetmaker, HN 2253, green, brown & red, 1962-73 .... **$475**

Queen Anne, HN 3141, green, red & white, 1989, Queens of the Realm Series, limited edition of 500 .... **$400**

Queen Elizabeth I, HN 3099, red & gold, 1987, Queens of the Realm Series, limited edition of 5,000 .... **$650**

Queen of the Ice, HN 2435, cream, Enchantment Series, 1983-86 .... **$195**

Rachel, HN 2919, gold & green, 1981-84 ..... **$215**

Rebecca, HN 2805, pale blue & lavender, 1980-96 .... **$450**

Regal Lady, HN 2709, turquoise & cream, 1975-83 .... **$195**

Rosabell, HN 1620, red & green, 1934-38 .... **$1,400**

Rosamund, M 32, yellow dress tinged w/blue, 1932-45 .... **$950**

Rosemary

Rosemary, HN 3698, mauve & yellow, 1995-97 (ILLUS.) **$315**

Rowena, HN 2077, red, 1951-55 .... **$750**

Sabbath Morn, HN 1982, red, 1945-1959 ..... **$295**

Sailor's Holiday, HN 2442, apricot jacket, 1972-79 .... **$295**

Sairey Gamp, HN 2100, white dress, green cape, 1952-67 .... **$475**

Salome, HN 3267, red, blue, lavender & green, 1990, limited edition of 1,000 .... **$950**

Sam Weller, M 48, yellow & brown, 1932-81 .... **$65**

Samwise, HN 2925, black & brown, Middle Earth Series, 1982-84 .... **$725**

Sandra, HN 2275, gold, 1969-97 .... **$225**

Sara, HN 2265, red & white, 1981-97 .... **$275**

Schoolmarm, HN 2223, 1958-81 .... **$275**

Secret Thoughts, HN 2382, green 1971-88 .... **$195**

Sharon, HN 3047, white, 1984-95 .... **$90**

Pride & Joy

The Shepherd

Shepherd (The), HN 1975, light brown, 1945-75 (ILLUS.)..................................... **$205**
Shore Leave, HN 2254, 1965-79................. **$295**
Silks and Ribbons, HN 2017, green, red & white dress, 1949 to present..................... **$225**
Simone, HN 2378, green dress, 1971-81 ...... **$135**
Sir Edward, HN 2370, red & grey, 1979, limited edition of 500..................................... **$550**
Skater (The), HN 3439, red, 1992-97 .... **$250**

Sleeping Beauty

Sleeping Beauty, HN 3079, green, 1987-89 (ILLUS.)... **$225**
Sleepyhead, HN 2114, 1953-55 .... **$2,250**
Soiree, HN 2312, white dress, green overskirt, 1967-84 .... **$175**
Solitude, HN 2810, cream, blue & orange, 1977-1983 .... **$325**

Sophie, HN 3257, blue & red, 1990-92 .... **$225**
Southern Belle, HN 2229, red & cream, 1958-97... **$350**
Spring, HN 2085, 1952-59 .... **$395**
Spring Flower, HN 1807, green skirt, greyblue overskirt, 1937-59 .... **$525**
Spring Morning, HN 1922, green coat, 1940-73... **$225**
Spring Morning, HN 1922, pink & blue, 1940-73... **$225**

Spring Walk

Spring Walk, HN 3120, blue, 1990-92 (ILLUS.)... **$305**
St. George, HN 2051, 1950-85 .... **$475**
St. George, HN 2067, purple, red & orange blanket, 1950-76 .... **$2,250**
Stiggins, M 50, black suit, 1932-1982 .... **$65**
Stop Press, HN 2683, brown, blue & white, 1977-81... **$175**
Summer, HN 2086, red gown, 1952-59 .... **$450**
Summer's Day, HN 2181, 1957-62 .... **$275**
Summertime, HN 3137, white & blue, 1987, RDICC Series **$225**
Sunday Morning, HN 2184, red & brown, 1963-69... **$425**
Susan, HN 2952, blue, black & pink, 1982-93... **$250**
Suzette, HN 2026, 1949-59 .... **$475**
Sweet Anne, HN 1330, red, pink & yellow skirt, 1929-49 .... **$325**
Sweet Anne, HN 1496, pink & purple dress & hat, 1932-67 .... **$275**
Sweet April, HN 2215, pink dress, 1965-67 .... **$425**
Sweet Dreams, HN 2380, multicolored, 1971-90... **$150**
Sweet Lavender, HN 1373, green, red & black, 1930-49 .... **$1,250**
Sweet Seventeen, HN 2734, white w/gold trim, 1975-93 .... **$195**
Sweet Sixteen, HN 2231, 1958-65 .... **$375**
Sweet Suzy, HN 1918, 1939-49 .... **$950**
Sweet & Twenty, HN 1298, red & pink dress, 1928-69 .... **$365**
Sweeting, HN 1935, pink dress, 1940-73 ...... **$135**
Teatime, HN 2255, 1972-95 .... **$250**

Teresa, HN 1682, red and brown, 1935-49
.... **$1,375**

Thanks Doc

Thanks Doc, HN 2731, white & brown,
1975-90 (ILLUS.)...................................... **$225**
This Little Pig, HN 1793, red robe, 1936-95 .... **$85**
Tiny Tim, HN 539, black, brown & blue,
1922-32 .... **$75**
Tootles, HN 1680, pink, 1935-75 .... **$105**
Top O' The Hill, HN 1833, green & blue
dress, 1937-71 .... **$275**

Top 'O The Hill

Top 'O The Hill, HN 2126, mauve & green,
1988, miniature (ILLUS.) **$125**
Town Crier, HN 2119, 1953-76..................... **$275**
Toymaker (The), HN 2250, brown & red,
1959-73 .... **$425**
Treasure Island, HN 2243, 1962-75.............. **$215**

Tumbler, HN 3183, pink & yellow, 1989-91 ... **$225**
Tuppence a Bag, HN 2320, green dress,
blue shawl, 1968-95................................... **$225**
Uriah Heep, HN 554, black jacket & trou-
sers, 1923-39... **$525**
Valerie, HN 2107, red gown w/white apron,
1953-95... **$95**
Vanity, HN 2475, red, 1973-1992 .... **$125**
Veneta, HN 2722, green & white, 1974-81 .... **$165**
Veronica, HN 3205, style 3, white & pink,
1989-92... **$165**
Victoria, HN 2471, patterned pink dress,
1973 to present....................................... **$295**
Victorian Lady (A), HN 728, red skirt, pur-
ple shawl, 1925-52.................................... **$495**
Victorian Lady (A), M 1, red-tinged dress,
light green shawl, 1932-45........................ **$500**
Virginia, HN 1693, yellow dress, 1935-49
.... **$1,300**
Wendy, HN 2109, blue dress, 1953-95............ **$80**
Willy-Won't-He, HN 2150, red, green, blue
& white, 1955-59 .... **$235**
Windflower, M 79, blue & green, 1939-49
.... **$1,250**
Winter, HN 2088, shaded blue skirt, 1952-
59... **$415**
Winter's Walk (A), HN 3052, pale blue &
white, 1987-95 .... **$250**

Wintertime

Wintertime, HN 3060, 1985, RDICC
(ILLUS.)... **$325**
Wizard (The), HN 2877, blue w/black &
white hat, 1979 to present......................... **$295**
Writing, HN 3049, flowered yellow dress,
1986, limited edition of 750, Gentle Arts
Series.. **$1,150**
Young Dreams, HN 3176, pink, 1988-92 ...... **$175**

Young Master, HN 2872, purple, grey & brown, 1980-89 .... **$250**
Yvonne, HN 3038, turquoise, 1987-92 .... **$155**

Miscellaneous

Shylock Baby Feeding Plate

Baby feeding plate, Dickens Ware, pale yellow rim & interior color scene of "Shylock," brown printed backstamp, early 20th c., 8 1/2" d. (ILLUS.)...................... **$75-100**
Bowl, 8" d., The Gleaners series **$185**
Bowl, 8 1/2" h., Gallent Fishers series **$200**
Bowl, 8 7/8" d., 3 3/4" h., wide shallow rounded form, interior w/transfer-printed polychrome fox hunt scenes, green vintage border w/gilt trim, early 20th c. **$125**
Bowl, 9" d., 4 1/8" h., Coaching Days series, street scenes **$125**
Cabinet plates, 10 1/4" d., each w/a different English garden view within a narrow acid-etched gilt border, transfer-printed & painted by J. Price, ca. 1928, artist-signed, green printed lion, crown & circle mark, impressed year letters, painted pattern numbers "H3587," set of 12 .... **$2,750**
Candlestick, "Old Moreton" series, low flaring round foot & slightly swelled cylindrical shaft below widely flaring flattened socket rim, color transfer of 16th c. gentleman titled "Old Moreton," impressed "7277," 6 3/8" h. **$80**

Tony Weller Dickens Ware Charger

Charger, Dickens Ware, round, color scene of Tony Weller, early 20th c., 13 1/2" d. (ILLUS.)... **$200-300**
Charger, Shakespeare Series, scene from "A Midsummer Night's Dream," 12 5/8" d. **$65**

Royal Doulton Charger

Charger, central scene of a lady riding horse sidesaddle w/hound racing alongside, in yellow, brown, green, black & white, border band of dark green stylized grapevine, marked "George Morland #1784," 14" d. (ILLUS.) **$125**
Chocolate set: 8" h. cov. chocolate pot, 6 1/2" h. cov. water pot, creamer, sugar bowl & eight cups & saucers; bone china, each enamel decorated w/relief-molded fox in various poses, crop-form handles, 20th c., England, the set **$650**
Chop plate, round w/flanged rim, "Old Moreton" series, black transfer-printed design decorated in polychrome, a large center interior scene titled "Queen Elizabeth at Old Moreton 1589," early 20th c., 12 3/4" d... **$85**

Fine Small Doulton Sung Ware Compote

Compote, cov., 2 3/4" h., Sung Ware, flaring octagonal low pedestal base supporting the wide rounded octagonal bowl w/a conforming fitted domed cover, a mottled Flambé glaze in shades of dark & light blue & deep red, Flambé & Sung marks, decorated by Noke & Moore, early 20th c. (ILLUS.)... **$690**
Cracker jar, cov., Gallant Fisher, Isaac Walton Ware, signed "NOKE" **$175**
Dish, round w/flattened fluted rim w/gold edging around a floral band, center

scene of romantic couples in a land-scape, transfer-printed blue on white, late 19th c., 5 1/2" d. **$45**
Dish, oval, Old English scene "The Glean-ers," 9 x 11 1/4, 2 1/8" h. **$55**
Ewers, Carrara ware, bulbous body w/a tan ground decorated w/life-sized pink wild roses w/enameled white highlights, gold molded leaf & florals, grey rim & ornate handle, marked "Doulton Carrara Lam-beth," 11 1/2" h., pr. **$375**
Fish plates, 10" d., each transfer-printed in blue & white w/a different fish, late 19th c., set of 12 .... **$400**

Yellow Ginger Jar with Bird & Flowers

Ginger jar, cov., bulbous nearly spherical body w/a domed cover, bright yellow ground painted in colorful enamels w/a long-tailed bird-of-paradise flying among stylized pendent flowers & fruiting branches, Model No. 1256C, date code for December 1925, 10 3/4" h. (ILLUS.).. **$1,315**
Humidor, cov., mottled brown leaves on a mottled light brown ground w/light blue to white sponge pattern, green band on lid & shoulder, metal finial & tongue on lid, "Patent No. 194168," has mark "Royal Doulton England" & #8846, 6" h. **$100**
Humidor, cov., Sung Ware, flambé glaze, figural elephant finial, artist-initialed **$2,400**

Royal Doulton Humidor with Landscape

Humidor, cov., thin footring on slightly swelled cylindrical body w/wide flat rim, inset metal-fitted patented cover, h.p. w/a continuous stylized landscape scene, impressed mark, early 20th c., 5 3/4" h. (ILLUS.) **$207**

Scarce Silicon Ware Doulton Owl Jar

Jar, cov., Silicon Ware, stylized model of a bulbous owl, the domed head forming the cover, the head w/finely incised & enam-eled light blue & white feathers around the dark blue-ringed white eyes, the body w/stylized blossom-like designs across the breast in dark & light blue, white & cream, further blue & white scaled feath-ers across the back, a dark buff ground, Doulton Lambeth - Silicon logo, some very minor nicks, 7 5/8" h. (ILLUS.) **$1,093**
Jar, cov., Rouge Flambé, footed squatty bulbous body w/a wide low-domed cover, scattered black splotches on crimson red ground, by Noke, fully stamped, 3 1/4" d., 2 3/4" h. **$358**

Classical Doulton-Lambeth Jardiniere

Jardiniere & pedestal, heavy pottery, large hexagonal urn-form jardiniere w/the side panels molded in relief w/classical designs of white putti playing musical instruments among leafy scrolls against a blue ground, dark brown borders & pale yellow rim, the conforming paneled pedestal w/matching decoration, top of jardiniere stamped "Doulton - Lambeth," restoration around rim of jardiniere, few small chips on pedestal, late 19th c., jardiniere 18 1/4" w., 15 1/2" h., pedestal 13" w., 20 1/2" h., 2 pcs. (ILLUS.) **$2,530**

Lamp base, slender ovoid ceramic body w/a tapering neck supporting electric lamp fittings, base decorated w/daffodils in greens, blue, white & yellow, fine brass round base mount w/a ring on the backs of four tiny figural turtles resting on a round disk on small ball feet, early 20th c., overall 28 1/2" h. (minor damage to body) **$325**

Loving cup, stoneware, cylindrical body w/low tapering base & wide short flaring rim, the wide tooled central band in band w/enameled floral designs in white & green flanked by thin brown stripes, three applied ear-form loop handles, handles, top & base in blue, marked "Doulton Lambeth," 6 1/8" h. **$275**

Loving cup, stoneware, three-handled cylindrical form w/a sterling silver rim band, a dark brown glaze band below the rim, most of the body w/a tan glaze, molded around the sides w/three white relief groups of bicycle riders, each titled either "Path," "Military," or "Road," late 19th c., base incised "8238," 5 1/2" h. **$275**

Large Rouge Flambé Leaping Salmon

Model of a salmon, Rouge Flambé, the leaping fish glazed in dark red shading to black, Model No. 666, early 20th c., 12 1/2" h. (ILLUS.) **$638**

Mug, stoneware, tall slender & slightly tapering sides w/a sterling silver rim band, the upper third w/a dark brown glaze, the lower section w/a tan glaze, the upper band molded in relief w/a large scrolling ribbon band reading "Speed Wheel," the

lower sides w/three white relief groups of bicycle racers each titled either "Path," "Military," or "Road," base incised "1957," late 19th c., 6" h. **$275**

Dutch Series Party Set

Party set: rectangular plate & squared cup; Series Wares, Dutch Series, scenes of Dutch people at the waterfront around the sides, ca. 1920, the set (ILLUS.) **$200**

Pitcher, jug-form, Kingsware, "Memories" design w/twelve faces shown, ca. 1920..... **$600**

Pitcher, Juliet, scene from Shakespeare's Romeo & Juliet **$150**

Pitcher, 5 1/2" h., brightly colored rose design on a salmon pink background, angled handle, mottling on the collar & base rim, gold trim, Doulton, Burslem, artist-signed **$150**

Pitcher, 5 1/2" h., Jackdaw of Rheims scene **$150**

Pitcher, 5 1/2" h., stoneware, bulbous form, the tan ground incised w/playful cats, the shoulder & neck glazed w/cobalt blue strap work, decorated by Hannah Barlow, impressed Doulton Lambeth mark, late 19th c. **$750**

Series Ware Pitcher with Old Bob Scene

Pitcher, 7 3/4" h., Series Ware, Old English Coaching Scenes, yellow ground w/figure of elderly man in long overcoat, stagecoach design rim band, inside of rim printed in black "Old Bob Ye Guard," ca. 1953-67 (ILLUS.) **$173**

Lambethware-style Limited-edition Jug

Pitcher, jug-form, 8 3/4" h., Lambethware
style & color, Doulton Archives series,
blue tracery on tan body, limited edition
of 100, 2002 (ILLUS.).............................. **$1,000**
Pitcher, 9" h., stoneware, bulbous ovoid
body tapering to a cylindrical neck
w/pinched spout, C-form handle, the upper half w/a dark brown glaze over a tan
glaze on the lower half, lower half applied
w/white relief designs including a windmill, dogs chasing deer, men drinking,
etc., Model No. 6859, Doulton, Lambeth
mark, late 19th c.. **$125**
Pitcher, 9 1/4" h., Shakespeare character
series, standing portrait of Sir John Falstaff, tall waisted cylindrical form w/high
arched spout, printed around the bottom
border "A Tapster is a Good Trade," early
20th c. **$150**

Hannah Barlow Lambethware Pitcher

Pitcher, 11" h., Hannah Barlow Doulton
Lambethware, design of hounds chasing
fox, 1875, vertical hairline crack (ILLUS.)
.... **$1,250**
Pitcher, 11" h., Poplars at Sunset patt. **$175**

Limited Edition Planter

Planter, ovoid form w/flat rim, short foot,
decorated w/design of ferns or oak
leaves on tan ground, Lambethware style
& colors, Doulton Archives series, limited
edition of 100, 2002 (ILLUS.).................... **$800**

"Robin Hood" Series Plate

Plate, 7 1/2" sq., "Robin Hood" series (Friar
Tuck Joins Robin Hood), natural-colored
scene of Robin Hood & Friar Tuck stand-
ing & talking under large tree (ILLUS.)......... **$85**

"The Cup That Cheers" Series Ware Plate

Plate, 9" d., Series Ware, Sayings Ware Series, "The Cup That Cheers," center bust

portrait of an elderly woman drinking tea, band of teacups around the rim, ca. 1907 (ILLUS.)... **$300**

Plate, 9 1/8" d., Peony patt., dark blue floral center w/rectangular panels around the border, trimmed w/reddish rust & beige, ca. 1900 .... **$65**

Plate, 9 1/2" d., Gallant Fishers series, Izaac Walton Ware, signed "NOKE"............ **$75**

Plate, 10" d., rack-type, Mr. Micawber **$75**

Plate, 10" d., rack-type, Old Jarvey **$75**

Plate, 10" d., rack-type, The Parson **$75**

Plate, 10 1/4" d., Bradley Golfers, "All Fools Are Not Knaves...,"................................... **$150**

Plate, 10 1/4" d., Old English scenes, "The Gleaners" **$65**

Plate, 10 1/4" d., "The Gypsies" **$65**

Plate, 10 1/2" d., blue transfer w/center portrait of Shakespeare, border w/twelve characters from his plays **$75**

Plate, 10 1/2" d., blue transfer w/central portrait of Dickens, border w/eleven of the Doulton characters used on various wares, unmarked.. **$75**

Plate, 10 1/2" d., overall decoration of Aesthetic Movement florals in green & blue, marked w/lion & crown, "Royal Doulton, England, Cyprus" **$75**

Plate, 10 1/2" d., rack-type, The Mayor........... **$75**

Plate, 10 1/2" d., rack-type, The Squire **$75**

Plate, 10 3/4" d., blue transfer w/Burns portrait in center, border shows characters such as Tam-O-Shanter, Highland Mary & others.. **$75**

Plates, 10 1/4" d., series-type, color transfer-printed scenes on a tan speckled ground, one titled "The Battle," the other "The Press Gang," pr. **$150**

Plates, 9" d., each h.p. w/different type of game bird including ducks, pheasant & quail, gold encrusted rims, artist signed "S. Wilson," purple stamped label w/impressed "Doulton," set of 6......................... **$425**

Plates, dessert, 8 3/4" d., raised gilt enamel scrolls, floral & diapered cartouches, on a pale blue ground, ca. 1920, set of 15 .... **$1,300**

Plates, 7 5/8" sq., creamware, transfer-decorated scenes, ca. 1900, set of 6.............. **$110**

Plates, 8" d., Coaching Days series, includes three scenes, "Boarding the Coach," "The Journey" & "Farewell," polychrome transfer decoration, early 20th c., set of 12..................................... **$413**

Plates, 9" d., slightly dished w/scalloped rim, gilt-trimmed rim w/polychrome leafy vines bordering brown enameled Shakespearean sites, retailed by Theodore B. Starr, New York City, Doulton, Burslem, late 19th c., set of 12.................. **$450**

Plates, 10 1/4" d., each w/a central rosette, the border elaborately gilded & enameled in the Art Nouveau style w/displaying peacocks, spade ornaments & trailing berried branches, the outer paneled blue border gilded w/beaded flowers, dated 1902, retailed by Tiffany & Co., New York, set of 4 .... **$1,500**

Platter, 17 1/2" l., oval, Imari patt., ca. 1860s **$1,000**

Doulton Stoneware Soap Dish

Soap dish, stoneware, oblong w/large brown & lavender flying insect molded along one side of the dark blue glazed dish, impressed markings on base for Wright's Coal Tar Soap, 4 1/4 x 5 3/4", 1 1/2" h. (ILLUS.) **$150**

Welsh Ladies Series Sugar Bowl

Sugar bowl, cov., Series Ware, Welsh Ladies Series, long straight-sided oval body w/angled end handles & flattened shoulder centering a flat covers w/peaked finial, scenes of Welsh ladies around the sides, introduced in 1906 (ILLUS.)............. **$300**

Tea set: cov. teapot, open sugar & creamer; Cockerel patt., the teapot modeled as a rooster, the sugar bowl as a hen & the creamer as a chick, introduced ca. 1935, the set (ILLUS., top next page).............. **$2,500**

Tea set: cov. teapot, open sugar & creamer; Kingsware, each piece w/a different embossed figural scene, introduced in 1902, the set (ILLUS., middle next page) **$750**

Tea set: large cov. teapot, small cov. teapot, cov. sugar bowl & creamer; Hunting Ware line, dark brown shaded to tan ground decorated w/applied relief-molded English hunting scenes, Doulton-Lambeth marks, ca. 1905, the set (ILLUS., bottom next page)..................................... **$600**

Unusual Cockerel Royal Doulton Tea Set

Early Royal Doulton Kingsware Tea Set

Doulton-Lambeth Hunting Ware Tea Set

Under the Greenwood Tree Tea Tile

Tea tile, oval, Series Ware, Under the Greenwood Tree Series, color scene of Robin Hood seated under a tree watching archers in the distance, "Lincoln The Forest of Sherwood" around the rim, introduced in 1914 (ILLUS.) **$250**

Rare Royal Doulton Bone China Teapot

Teapot, cov., bone china, hand-painted w/images of exotic birds & heavy gilt scroll trim, painted by Joseph Birbeck, ca. 1910 (ILLUS.) **$2,000**

Royal Doulton Bone China Teapot with Gilt Floral Decoration

Teapot, cov., bone china, wide squatty bulbous body w/a long angled spout, forked C-form handle & low domed cover w/button finial, decorated overall w/floral gilding, ca. 1923 (ILLUS.) **$500**

Beswick Figural Panda Teapot

Teapot, cov., Beswick Ware, figural Panda, introduced in 1989 (ILLUS.) **$300**

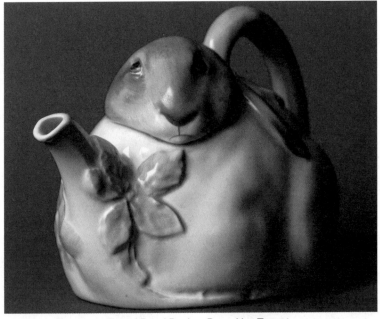

Figural Royal Doulton Bunnykins Teapot

Teapot, cov., Bunnykins Series, model of a large rabbit, designed by Charles Noke, introduced in 1939 (ILLUS.) **$3,000**

Early Bunnykins Casino Pattern Teapot

Teapot, cov., Bunnykins Series, wide short cylindrical body w/angled spout & angled handle, Casino patt., introduced in 1937 (ILLUS.)... **$750**

Royal Doulton Cadogan Teapot

Teapot, cov., Cadogan-style pot, decorated in the Crows patt., ca. 1907 (ILLUS.)...... **$2,000**

Doulton-Lambeth Faience Teapot

Teapot, cov., faience, rounded cylindrical body w/long serpentine spout, C-scroll handle & metal rim & hinged cover, stylized floral decoration, Doulton-Lambeth, ca. 1900 (ILLUS.)................... **$1,000**

Teapot, cov., figural Cowboy and Indian model, designed by Anthony Cartlidge, limited edition of 1,500, introduced in 2002 (ILLUS. of both sides, top of next page)... **$300**

Teapot, cov., figural, crouching camel w/a heavy load, the Arab driver pulling from behind & forming the handle, ruby glaze, designed by the Moore Brothers, apparently made by Doulton, Doulton-Lambeth, ca. 1877 (ILLUS., middle next page)... **$5,000**

Both Sides of the Cowboy & Indian Figural Teapot

Early Rare Figural Cameo Teapot

Modern Royal Doulton Falstaff Teapot

Teapot, cov., figural Falstaff model, 1989 (ILLUS.).. **$175**

Modern Long John Silver Doulton Teapot

Teapot, cov., figural Long John Silver w/parrot, 1989 (ILLUS.)............................. **$165**

Two Views of the Norman & Saxon Royal Doulton Teapot

Teapot, cov., figural Norman and Saxon model, designed by Anthony Cartlidge, limited edition of 1,500, introduced in 2003 (ILLUS. of both sides) **$300**

Royal Doulton Old Salt Teapot

Teapot, cov., figural Old Salt model, the body in the image of a sailor mending a net, a mermaid forming the handle, designed by William K. Harper, introduced in 1989 (ILLUS.).. **$300**

Early Royal Doulton Old Charley Teapot

Teapot, cov., figural Old Charley model, designed by Charles Noke, introduced in 1939 (ILLUS.)... **$2,000**

Two Views of the Doulton Pirate and Captain Teapot

Both Sides of the Doulton Policeman & Felon Teapot

Teapot, cov., figural Pirate and Captain model, designed by Anthony Cartlidge, limited edition of 1,500, introduced in 2003 (ILLUS. of both sides, bottom previous page) **$300**

Teapot, cov., figural Policeman and Felon model, designed by Anthony Cartlidge, limited edition of 1,500, introduced in 2002 (ILLUS. of both sides, top of page) ... **$300**

Teapot, cov., figural Sairey Gamp model, designed by Charles Noke, introduced in 1939 (ILLUS., to the right)...................... **$2,000**

Teapot, cov., figural Sodden and Sobriety model, designed by Anthony Cartlidge, limited edition of 1,500, introduced in 2003 (ILLUS. of both sides, bottom of page) **$300**

Early Royal Doulton Sairey Gamp Teapot

Front & Back of the Sodden & Sobriety Figural Teapot

Early Royal Doulton Tony Weller Teapot

Teapot, cov., figural Tony Weller model, designed by Charles Noke, introduced in 1939 (ILLUS.)... **$2,000**

Early Royal Doulton Floral Teapot

Teapot, cov., footed wide squatty bulbous body w/a wide flat neck & inset cover w/button finial, serpentine spout & C-form handle, decorated w/floral clusters, England, early 20th c. (ILLUS.) **$90**

Royal Doulton Teapot with Band of Polar Bears

Teapot, cov., footed very wide squatty low body tapering to a flat rim & conical cover w/disk finial, short angled spout & loop handle, overall crackled background w/a center band of walking polar bears, ca. 1920s (ILLUS.)... **$90**

Early Royal Doulton Kingsware Dame Pattern Teapot

Teapot, cov., Kingsware line, Dame patt. w/motto around base, introduced in 1901 (ILLUS.)... **$1,000**

Teapot, cov., Kingsware line, self-pouring style, relief-molded half-length portraits on side, J.J. Royle's Patent design, ca. 1900 (ILLUS., bottom of page)............... **$2,000**

Doulton Self-Pouring Kingsware Patent Teapot

Rare Doulton-Lambeth Marqueterie Teapot with Scene

Royal Doulton Kingsware Witch Teapot

Teapot, cov., Kingsware line, Witch patt., introduced in 1902 (ILLUS.) **$500**

Royal Doulton Morrisian Ware Teapot

Teapot, cov., Morrisian Ware, footed wide urn-shaped body w/a squared handle & serpentine spout, design of a dancing lady, ca. 1900 (ILLUS.) **$1,000**
Teapot, cov., Nightwatchman scene............. **$125**

Rare Doulton Marqueterie Ware Teapot

Teapot, cov., Marqueterie Ware, diamond lattice & swirl overall design, Doulton-Lambeth, ca. 1890 (ILLUS.) **$4,000**
Teapot, cov., Marqueterie Ware, low rectangular shape w/straight spout & angled loop handle, large design reserve w/scene of a child against a swirled background, Doulton-Lambeth, painted by Ada Dennis, ca. 1893 (ILLUS., top of page) **$5,000**

Royal Doulton Old Leeds Spray Pattern Teapot

Teapot, cov., Old Leeds Spray patt., squatty octagonal body, angled spout & squared handle, England, ca. 1912 (ILLUS.)........... **$100**

Royal Doulton Athens Series Teapot

Doulton Titanian Ware Bird of Paradise Teapot

Teapot, cov., Series Ware, low wide body decorated w/Grecian figures, from the Athens Series, introduced in 1910 (ILLUS., previous page) **$600**
Teapot, cov., Series Ware, Queen Elizabeth at Moreton Hall series **$125**

Doulton-Lambeth Teapot with Scene

Teapot, cov., stoneware, tapering cylindrical body w/flaring rim, angled spout, large rectangular panel w/scene of Bladud, the founder of the City of Bath, made for R.S. Carey, Bath, Doulton-Lambeth, ca. 1894 (ILLUS.) **$750**
Teapot, cov., Titanian Ware, Bird of Paradise patt., introduced in 1919 (ILLUS., top of page) **$800**

Babes in the Wood Tray

Tray, oblong, flattened diamond shape w/rounded corners, Babes in the Wood series, center design of woman followed by girl holding woman's cloak, 13 1/2" l. (ILLUS.) **$1,000**
Tureens, cov., earthernware sauce tureens, "Raby" patt., w/cobalt floral motif & gilt accents, each w/small matching ladle, ca. 1900, 6" h., 8 3/4" l., pr. **$225**
Tyg (three-handled drinking vessel), waisted cylindrical shape decorated w/applied figures & animals in relief, Sheffield silver rim band marked "Maypin and Webb," Doulton, Lambeth, late 19th - early 20th c., 4 3/4" d., 6 1/2" h. **$175**

Lovely Royal Doulton Covered Urn

Urn, cov., tall slender ovoid body raised on a ribbed & gadrooned gold & Kelly green pedestal base w/square foot & flanked by long gold full-length handles, tapering to a ringed & ribbed cylindrical neck w/flaring rim fitted w/a high Gothic spire-form cover, finely h.p. w/a colorful scene of highland cattle against a purplish mountain backdrop, glossy glaze, artist-signed by S. Kelsall, small professional repair to handle & pedestal, ca. 1910, 32" h. (ILLUS.) **$2,500**

Miniature Doulton Titanian Ware Vase

Vase, miniature, 3 3/8" h., Titanian Ware, flat-bottomed wide bulbous ovoid body tapering to a wide flat mouth, overall shaded glossy green to dark blue glaze, Titanian backstamp (ILLUS.) **$173**

Small Doulton Titanian Ware Vase

Vase, 3 1/2" h., 4" d., Titanian Ware, footed bulbous slightly tapering body w/a flattened shoulder centering a short flaring neck, soft celadon green ground decorated w/a small brown & white bird on a flowering branch, decorated by H. Allen, marked "Royal Doulton Flambé - Titanian - Young White-Throat" (ILLUS.) **$489**

Small Doulton Rouge Flambé Vase

Vase, 4" h., Rouge Flambé, footed squatty bulbous body tapering sharply to a two-lobed upright rim, red ground & veining down through a dark ground, marked w/Flambé insignia (ILLUS.) **$138**

Silver-overlaid Rouge Flambé Vase

Royal Doulton "Babes in Woods" Seriesware Vases

Vase, 4 1/8" h., Rouge Flambé, wide squatty bulbous form tapering to a tiny flared neck, the deep red background decorated w/silver overlay, a thin medial band below undulating silver leafy vines below a pierced Greek key neck band & silver-covered neck, silver marked by the Gorham Mfg. Co., one silver leaf missing, some minor glaze rubs, early 20th c. (ILLUS.)................ **$460**

Doulton Lambeth Stoneware Vase

Vase, 5 1/4" h., 3 1/8" d., stoneware, footed ovoid body w/short tapering neck, grey ground w/an incised design of pointed panels framing stylized leafy scrolls in brown, green & light blue, artist-signed by Arthur Beeve, Doulton, Lambeth (ILLUS.) **$175**

Vase, 5 1/2" h., Sung Ware, bulbous ovoid body tapering to a short cylindrical neck, a Flambé glossy glaze in red mottled w/dark green & gold, signatures of decorators Noke & Moore, early 20th c., base chip (ILLUS., top next column).................. **$173**

Doulton Sung Ware Vase

Vase, 5 3/4" h., 3 3/4" d., baluster-form w/short flaring neck, slip-decorated in color w/celadon green fish & kelp on a dark brown ground, stamped "Doulton-Lambeth - 1883 - GTH - WP (?) - 593" **$350**

Doulton Shaded Blue Titanian Vase

Vase, 5 7/8" h., Titanian Ware, footed ovoid body w/a short flaring neck, overall glossy shaded dark to teal blue crystalline glaze, Titanian logo mark on base, early 20th c. (ILLUS., previous page)......... $230

Vase, 6" h., "Babes in Woods" Seriesware, bulbous base, short slightly bulbous neck w/flat rim, decorated w/blue & white scene of young woman at snowy gate, printed green mark, early 20th c. (ILLUS. front row, left w/other Seriesware vases, top of page)... $431

Vase, 6" h., 3" d., Sung Ware, footed simple ovoid body tapering to a small trumpet neck, bright red & blue Flambé glaze, marked "Royal Doulton - Flambé - Sung - Noke" $250

Barlow-decorated Doulton Stoneware Vase

Vase, 6 3/8" h., stoneware, a small round foot supporting the wide ovoid body tapering to a short wide & deeply rolled neck, a wide body band in cream incised w/cattle in a meadow, the cobalt blue shoulder decorated w/incised pale blue scrolls, the lower body & foot w/lappet bands in cobalt blue, pale blue & brown, decorated by Hannah Barlow, 1887, Doulton-Lambeth, small glaze nick on top edge of rim (ILLUS.)............................... $1,093

Vase, 6 1/2" h., "Babes in Woods" Seriesware, ovoid form tapering to ring foot & flaring rim, decorated w/blue & white scene of woman w/basket at snowy gate, printed green mark, early 20th c. (ILLUS. front row, right w/other Seriesware vases, top of page) $633

Vase, 6 1/2" h., "Babes in Woods" Seriesware, tapering rectangular arched shape w/rounded edges, gilt flat rim & foot, gilt angular handles, decorated

w/blue & white winter scene of woman carrying basket, printed green mark, early 20th c. (ILLUS. front row, center w/other Seriesware vases, top of page 235) $690

Vase, 6 3/4" h., wide shoulder tapering toward the base, extended neck, decorated w/white daffodils w/blue centers outlined w/white slip on a mottled light olive green ground, impressed mark "t - 1898" & inscribed "MW".. $150

Vase, 7" h., "Babes in Woods" Seriesware, cylindrical shape w/slightly flaring rim, ruffled foot & small gilt angled handles near base, decorated w/blue & white scene of bonneted woman & child holding basket, printed green mark, early 20th c. (ILLUS. back row, right w/other Seriesware vases, top of page 235) $748

Vase, 7" h., Flambé Ware, footed wide bulbous body w/wide shoulder tapering to short cylindrical neck w/molded rim, rich red glaze w/swirling mottled grey, black, blue & cream, artist-signed, Charles Noke, ink stamp & Doulton paster on bottom $350

Doulton Rouge Flambé Vase

Vase, 7" h., 4 1/4" d., Rouge Flambé, footed ovoid body w/the wide shoulder tapering to a small, short rolled neck, black silhouetted desert landscape against the crimson red ground, shallow scratch, stamped "ROYAL DOULTON - FLAMBÉ - MADE IN ENGLAND" (ILLUS.) $250

Vase, 7 3/4" h., Art Deco style baluster-form decorated w/alternating vertical green & black panels, horizontal black & white panels on shoulder, impressed "Royal Doulton Lambeth England," "8190" w/"S" in black slip, artist's monogram incised in bottom $400

Vase, 10 3/4" h., stoneware-faience, Lambethware, tapering cylindrical shape w/vibrant reddish color decorated w/designs of birds in three roundels & scroll design overall, mottled metallic colored neck, ca. 1880 (ILLUS., next page).......................... $425

Lambethware Vase with Metallic Neck

Vase, 11" h., baluster form, the shoulder tapering to a tall wide cylindrical neck w/flat rim, the center w/sgraffito continuous scene depicting eight deer in blue, black or brown, by Hannah Barlow, the dark brown neck & shoulder decorated w/raised scrolled designs in gold & swags of white beads, beaded bands flanking the center scene, the dark brown base w/raised gold lines, impressed "Doulton - Lambeth - England" & incised artist's initials **$1,250**

Tall-necked Doulton Stoneware Vase

Vase, 11 1/4" h., stoneware, a round short pedestal foot supporting a nearly spherical lower body below the very tall slender tapering neck w/a flared rim, the lower body divided into large oval cobalt blue panels decorated w/ornate light green & white scrolls, another small blue band near the top of the neck, the background in mottled brown & moss green, Doulton-Lambeth, No. 8413 (ILLUS.) **$196**
Vase, 11 1/4" h., tall slender baluster-form w/flaring domed foot & waisted short wide-

ly flaring neck, the neck & foot in cobalt w/lacy gilt decoration, the body w/a creamy ground decorated w/scattered clusters of colorful flowers, Doulton-Burslem mark & incised "Lambeth - Doulton - Faience L6339," ca. 1882 .... **$225**

Vase with Special Rouge Flambé Glaze

Vase, 11 1/4" h., 4 3/4" d., Rouge Flambé, slightly flaring rounded cylindrical form w/a rounded shoulder to the short flaring neck, an experimental swirling deep red & black glaze, marked on the bottom "Royal Doulton Flambé - 26 - AERO G. - Taylor - 11.2.69 - Flambé" (ILLUS.) **$460**

Scenic Doulton Rouge Flambé Vase

Vase, 11 1/2" h., Rouge Flambé, wide bulbous baluster form tapering to a wide flat mouth, decorated w/a black silhouetted Arabian landscape w/men on camels, marked on the bottom "Royal Doulton Flambé," early 20th c. (ILLUS.) **$1,200-1,800**

Babes in the Wood Baluster-form Vase

Vase, 11 1/2" h., tall slender baluster-form w/cylindrical neck & flat rim, Babes in the Wood series, design of woman sheltering child in wintry landscape (ILLUS.)............. **$750**

Doulton Natural Foliage Ware Vase

Vase, 12 1/4" h., Natural Foliage Ware, tall baluster-form body w/a short neck w/cupped rim, mottled streaky yellowish tan & brown ground decorated w/long branches of mottled dark blue & green leaves, Doulton-Lambeth, Shape No. 6768 (ILLUS.).. **$230**
Vase, 12 1/2" h., Sung Ware, very wide bulbous ovoid body w/narrow cylindrical neck, stylized red, green & purple cherry blossoms interspersed w/lustered green, blue, red & tan drip glazes, decorated by Charles Noke, "Sung" & "Noke" in black slip & "7163," "4," & "46" impressed on bottom (restored drill hole in bottom) **$1,600**
Vase, 16" h., 6" d., tall baluster-form body w/a waisted tall trumpet neck w/scalloped rim, dark blue ground decorated around the body w/brown, pale green & light blue acanthus leaves & pods, decorated by Eliza Simmance, stamped mark "Doulton - Lambeth - England - 461" & initials, late 19th c. (ILLUS., top next column).............. **$920**

Handsome Large Doulton Lambeth Vase

Vase, 17" h., "Babes in Woods" Seriesware, slightly ovoid cylindrical body w/ring foot & rim, decorated w/blue & white scene of woman looking back at child, who is holding the train of her cloak, printed green mark, early 20th c. (ILLUS. back row, center w/other Seriesware vases, top of page 235).. **$1,380**

Pair of Doulton Vases

Vases, bulbous body w/foliate motifs, flared neck decorated w/stylized leaves & jewelwork, raised pedestal base, all-over green tones on deep brown ground accented by beige & brown, underside impressed w/marks & numbers "Doulton Lambeth, mm, 1870, CL, EAS - 318," ca. 1880-1895, 7 1/4" h., pr. (ILLUS.).............. **$350**

Pair of Babes in the Wood Vases

Vases, 9 1/2" h., bulbous form w/flaring neck, Babes in the Wood series, one w/design of girl looking into woman's basket, the other w/girl holding the hem of woman's cloak, pr. (ILLUS.)............... **$2,500**

Vases, 13 1/4" h., "Babes in Woods" Seriesware, tapering ovoid body, tapering shoulder, ruffled foot, short flaring cylindrical neck, slender gilt handles, decorated w/blue & white winter scene of young woman & child walking along path, printed green mark, early 20th c., pr. (ILLUS. of both, back row, far left w/other Seriesware vases)...................................... **$2,070**

Wash bowl & pitcher set, deep rounded wide bowl & tall slightly tapering tankard-form pitcher w/gently arched rim & angled handle, blue, white & gold-trimmed Art Nouveau-style "Aubrey" patt., ca. 1910, bowl 16" d., pitcher 13 1/2" h., the set **$450**

Wash bowl & pitcher set, Royal Mail series, early English coaching scenes around the sides of each, four in polychrome, early 20th c., bowl 11 7/8" d., pitcher 7 3/8" h., pr. **$225**

Doulton Aubrey Pattern Wash Set

Washbowl & pitcher set, Aubrey patt., the deep wide rounded bowl & tall tapering cylindrical tankard pitcher w/a swelled rim & short rounded rim spout, long angled handle, a light blue Art Nouveau design composed of stylized rounded blossoms & long undulating stems & leaves, geometric border bands, ca. 1910, very minor wear & tiny glaze nicks on rim of bowl, pitcher 12 3/4" h., the set (ILLUS.) ... **$460**

Whiskey jug w/figural stopper, "Kingsware," bulbous ovoid body w/a loop shoulder handle, the body in overall dark brown, the stopper in the shape of a stout 18th c. man wearing a tricorn hat & painted in polychrome, 8 1/4" h. **$135**

Whiskey jug w/stopper, stoneware, advertising-type, bulbous ovoid body w/a wide shoulder centered by a small cylindrical neck w/tiny knobbed stopper, small loop shoulder handle, brown neck & handle shaded to tan below, the front w/applied ship & label reading "Special Highland Whiskey" in olive green & cream, stopper w/"Dewar's Whiskey," 7 1/8" h. **$115**

Fiesta (Homer Laughlin China Co. -HLC)

Fiesta dinnerware was made by the Homer Laughlin China Company of Newell, West Virginia, from the 1930s until the early 1970s. The brilliant colors of this inexpensive pottery have attracted numerous collectors. On February 28, 1986, Laughlin reintroduced the popular Fiesta line with minor changes in the shapes of a few pieces and a contemporary color range. The effect of this new production on the Fiesta collecting market is yet to be determined.

Fiesta Mark

Ashtray chartreuse **$55**
Ashtray cobalt blue **$45**
Ashtray ivory.. **$45**
Ashtray red... **$45**
Ashtray turquoise **$35**
Ashtray yellow.. **$35**
Bowl, cream soup cobalt blue **$45**
Bowl, cream soup forest green...................... **$60**
Bowl, cream soup ivory **$45**
Bowl, cream soup red................................... **$45**
Bowl, cream soup turquoise **$30**
Bowl, cream soup yellow............................... **$30**
Bowl, dessert, 6" d. ivory **$40**
Bowl, dessert, 6" d. turquoise **$30**
Bowl, dessert, 6" d. cobalt blue **$40**
Bowl, dessert, 6" d. red................................. **$40**
Bowl, dessert, 6" d. yellow............................ **$30**
Bowl, individual fruit, 5 1/2" d. chartreuse **$35**
Bowl, individual fruit, 5 1/2" d. ivory **$25**
Bowl, individual fruit, 5 1/2" d. turquoise **$20**
Bowl, individual fruit, 5 1/2" d. yellow............ **$20**
Bowl, nappy, 8 1/2" d. ivory **$45**
Bowl, nappy, 8 1/2" d. turquoise **$30**
Bowl, nappy, 8 1/2" d. red............................... **$45**
Bowl, nappy, 8 1/2" d. yellow **$30**
Bowl, nappy, 8 1/2" d. cobalt blue................... **$45**
Bowl, nappy, 9 1/2" d. ivory **$60**
Bowl, nappy, 9 1/2" d. turquoise **$55**
Bowl, nappy, 9 1/2" d. cobalt blue................... **$60**
Bowl, nappy, 9 1/2" d. red............................... **$60**
Bowl, nappy, 9 1/2" d. yellow **$55**
Bowl, salad, large, footed cobalt blue.......... **$350**
Bowl, salad, large, footed red..................... **$350**
Bowl, salad, large, footed turquoise **$275**
Bowl, salad, large, footed yellow **$275**
Candleholders, bulb-type, pr. cobalt blue ... **$120**
Candleholders, bulb-type, pr. ivory **$120**
Candleholders, bulb-type, pr. red............... **$120**
Candleholders, bulb-type, pr. turquoise **$80**
Candleholders, bulb-type, pr. yellow............. **$80**
Carafe, cov. cobalt blue............................... **$275**
Carafe, cov. ivory.. **$275**
Carafe, cov. red... **$275**
Carafe, cov. turquoise **$250**
Carafe, cov. yellow **$250**
Casserole, cov., two-handled, 10" d. cobalt blue **$180**
Casserole, cov., two-handled, 10" d. ivory .. **$180**

Casserole, cov., two-handled, 10" d. red..... $180
Casserole, cov., two-handled, 10" d. tur-
quoise.. $150
Casserole, cov., two-handled, 10" d. yel-
low... $150
Coffeepot, cov. cobalt blue $230
Coffeepot, cov. ivory $230
Coffeepot, cov. red...................................... $230
Coffeepot, cov. turquoise $180
Coffeepot, cov. yellow.................................. $180
Coffeepot, cov., demitasse, stick handle
cobalt blue... $500
Coffeepot, cov., demitasse, stick handle
ivory.. $500
Coffeepot, cov., demitasse, stick handle
red.. $500
Coffeepot, cov., demitasse, stick handle
turquoise $400
Coffeepot, cov., demitasse, stick handle
yellow $400
Compote, 12" d., low, footed cobalt blue $180
Compote, 12" d., low, footed ivory $180
Compote, 12" d., low, footed red $180
Compote, 12" d., low, footed turquoise $160
Compote, 12" d., low, footed yellow $160
Compote, sweetmeat, high stand cobalt
blue $125
Compote, sweetmeat, high stand ivory $125
Compote, sweetmeat, high stand red $125
Compote, sweetmeat, high stand tur-
quoise... $95
Compote, sweetmeat, high stand yellow....... $95
Creamer cobalt blue...................................... $25
Creamer ivory.. $25
Creamer red.. $25
Creamer turquoise $20
Creamer yellow $20
Cup, demitasse, stick handle cobalt blue $80
Cup, demitasse, stick handle ivory $80
Cup, demitasse, stick handle red $80
Cup, demitasse, stick handle turquoise........ $70
Cup, demitasse, stick handle yellow $70
Cup, ring handle cobalt blue $25
Cup, ring handle ivory................................... $25
Cup, ring handle red $25
Cup, ring handle turquoise............................ $15
Cup, ring handle yellow $15
Cup & saucer, demitasse, stick handle
cobalt blue... $95
Cup & saucer, demitasse, stick handle
ivory.. $95
Cup & saucer, demitasse, stick handle
red.. $95
Cup & saucer, demitasse, stick handle
turquoise $85
Cup & saucer, demitasse, stick handle
yellow $85
Cup & saucer, ring handle cobalt blue.......... $27
Cup & saucer, ring handle ivory.................... $27
Cup & saucer, ring handle medium green $70
Cup & saucer, ring handle red...................... $27
Cup & saucer, ring handle turquoise $17
Cup & saucer, ring handle yellow $17
Egg cup cobalt blue $60
Egg cup ivory $60
Egg cup red $60
Egg cup turquoise... $55
Egg cup yellow.. $55
Fork (Kitchen Kraft) cobalt blue................... $150

Fork (Kitchen Kraft) light green................... $150
Fork (Kitchen Kraft) red............................... $150
Fork (Kitchen Kraft) yellow......................... $150
Gravy boat cobalt blue $60
Gravy boat forest green................................ $60
Gravy boat ivory $60
Gravy boat medium green............................. $200
Gravy boat red.. $60
Gravy boat turquoise $40
Gravy boat yellow.. $40
Marmalade jar, cov. cobalt blue................... $365
Marmalade jar, cov. ivory............................. $365
Marmalade jar, cov. red................................ $365
Marmalade jar, cov. turquoise $350
Marmalade jar, cov. yellow $350
Mixing bowl, nest-type, size No. 1, 5" d.
cobalt blue... $275
Mixing bowl, nest-type, size No. 1, 5" d.
ivory.. $275
Mixing bowl, nest-type, size No. 1, 5" d.
red.. $275
Mixing bowl, nest-type, size No. 1, 5" d.
turquoise $220
Mixing bowl, nest-type, size No. 1, 5" d.
yellow $220
Mixing bowl, nest-type, size No. 2, 6" d.
cobalt blue... $125
Mixing bowl, nest-type, size No. 2, 6" d.
ivory.. $125
Mixing bowl, nest-type, size No. 2, 6" d.
red.. $125
Mixing bowl, nest-type, size No. 2, 6" d.
turquoise $100
Mixing bowl, nest-type, size No. 2, 6" d.
yellow $100
Mixing bowl, nest-type, size No. 3, 7" d.
cobalt blue... $125
Mixing bowl, nest-type, size No. 3, 7" d.
ivory.. $125
Mixing bowl, nest-type, size No. 3, 7" d.
red.. $125
Mixing bowl, nest-type, size No. 3, 7" d.
turquoise $110
Mixing bowl, nest-type, size No. 3, 7" d.
yellow $110
Mixing bowl, nest-type, size No. 4, 8" d.
cobalt blue... $150
Mixing bowl, nest-type, size No. 4, 8" d.
ivory.. $150
Mixing bowl, nest-type, size No. 4, 8" d.
red.. $150
Mixing bowl, nest-type, size No. 4, 8" d.
turquoise $110
Mixing bowl, nest-type, size No. 4, 8" d.
yellow $110
Mixing bowl, nest-type, size No. 5, 9" d.
cobalt blue... $190
Mixing bowl, nest-type, size No. 5, 9" d.
ivory.. $190
Mixing bowl, nest-type, size No. 5, 9" d.
red.. $190
Mixing bowl, nest-type, size No. 5, 9" d.
turquoise $175
Mixing bowl, nest-type, size No. 5, 9" d.
yellow $175
Mixing bowl, nest-type, size No. 6, 10" d.
cobalt blue... $260
Mixing bowl, nest-type, size No. 6, 10" d.
ivory $260

Rare Fiesta Onion Soup Bowl

Mixing bowl, nest-type, size No. 6, 10" d. red **$260**
Mixing bowl, nest-type, size No. 6, 10" d. turquoise **$230**
Mixing bowl, nest-type, size No. 6, 10" d. yellow **$230**
Mixing bowl, nest-type, size No. 7, 11 1/2" d. cobalt blue **$400**
Mixing bowl, nest-type, size No. 7, 11 1/2" d. ivory **$400**
Mixing bowl, nest-type, size No. 7, 11 1/2" d. red.. **$400**
Mixing bowl, nest-type, size No. 7, 11 1/2" d. turquoise **$325**
Mixing bowl, nest-type, size No. 7, 11 1/2" d. yellow....................................... **$325**
Mug, Tom & Jerry style cobalt blue **$70**
Mug, Tom & Jerry style ivory/gold................. **$70**
Mug, Tom & Jerry style red **$70**
Mug, Tom & Jerry style turquoise **$50**
Mug, Tom & Jerry style yellow **$50**
Mustard jar, cov. cobalt blue........................ **$250**
Mustard jar, cov. ivory.................................. **$250**
Mustard jar, cov. light green **$240**
Mustard jar, cov. red.................................... **$250**
Mustard jar, cov. turquoise **$240**
Mustard jar, cov. yellow **$240**
Onion soup bowl, cov. turquoise (ILLUS., top of page)...................................... **$8,000**
Pie server (Kitchen Kraft) cobalt blue **$150**
Pie server (Kitchen Kraft) light green........... **$150**
Pie server (Kitchen Kraft) red **$150**
Pie server (Kitchen Kraft) yellow................... **$150**
Pitcher, water, disc-type chartreuse **$200**
Pitcher, water, disc-type cobalt blue **$150**
Pitcher, water, disc-type forest green **$200**
Pitcher, water, disc-type ivory..................... **$150**
Pitcher, water, disc-type medium green ... **$1,500**
Pitcher, water, disc-type red **$150**
Pitcher, water, disc-type turquoise.............. **$100**
Pitcher, water, disc-type yellow **$100**
Plate, 10" d. cobalt blue **$35**
Plate, 10" d. ivory **$35**
Plate, 10" d. light green **$30**
Plate, 10" d. medium green............................ **$125**
Plate, 10" d. red.. **$35**
Plate, 10" d. turquoise **$30**

Plate, 10" d. yellow... **$30**
Plate, 6" d. cobalt blue **$5**
Plate, 6" d. ivory.. **$5**
Plate, 6" d. red.. **$5**
Plate, 6" d. turquoise....................................... **$4**
Plate, 6" d. yellow.. **$4**
Plate, 7" d. cobalt blue **$8**
Plate, 7" d. ivory.. **$8**
Plate, 7" d. red **$8**
Plate, 7" d. turquoise....................................... **$7**
Plate, 7" d. yellow.. **$7**
Plate, 9" d. cobalt blue **$15**
Plate, 9" d. ivory **$15**
Plate, 9" d. red **$15**
Plate, 9" d. turquoise **$10**
Plate, 9" d. yellow... **$10**
Plate, chop, 13" d. cobalt blue........................ **$45**
Plate, chop, 13" d. ivory **$45**
Plate, chop, 13" d. red.................................... **$45**
Plate, chop, 13" d. turquoise **$45**
Plate, chop, 13" d. yellow **$40**
Plate, chop, 15" d. cobalt blue........................ **$90**
Plate, chop, 15" d. ivory **$90**
Plate, chop, 15" d. red.................................... **$90**
Plate, chop, 15" d. turquoise **$70**
Plate, chop, 15" d. yellow **$70**
Plate, grill, 10 1/2" d. cobalt blue.................... **$40**
Plate, grill, 10 1/2" d. ivory **$40**
Plate, grill, 10 1/2" d. red................................ **$40**
Plate, grill, 10 1/2" d. rose.............................. **$35**
Plate, grill, 10 1/2" d. turquoise **$35**
Plate, grill, 10 1/2" d. yellow **$35**
Platter, 12" oval cobalt blue **$50**
Platter, 12" oval ivory...................................... **$50**
Platter, 12" oval red **$50**
Platter, 12" oval turquoise............................... **$40**
Platter, 12" oval yellow **$40**
Relish tray w/five inserts cobalt blue **$355**
Relish tray w/five inserts ivory.................... **$355**
Relish tray w/five inserts red **$355**
Relish tray w/five inserts turquoise............. **$310**
Relish tray w/five inserts yellow **$310**
Salt & pepper shakers, pr. cobalt blue.......... **$25**
Salt & pepper shakers, pr. ivory.................... **$25**
Salt & pepper shakers, pr. red **$25**
Salt & pepper shakers, pr. turquoise **$22**
Salt & pepper shakers, pr. yellow **$22**

Soup plate, rimmed, 8" d. ivory $50
Soup plate, rimmed, 8" d. red......................... $50
Soup plate, rimmed, 8" d. turquoise $35
Soup plate, rimmed, 8" d. yellow $35
Sugar bowl, cov. cobalt blue........................... $60
Sugar bowl, cov. ivory.................................... $60
Sugar bowl, cov. medium green $225
Sugar bowl, cov. red..................................... $50
Sugar bowl, cov. turquoise $50
Sugar bowl, cov. yellow $50
Teapot, cov., large size (8 cup) cobalt blue
.... $250
Teapot, cov., large size (8 cup) ivory $250
Teapot, cov., large size (8 cup) light green .. $210
Teapot, cov., large size (8 cup) medium
green.. $1,200+
Teapot, cov., large size (8 cup) red $250
Teapot, cov., large size (8 cup) turquoise.... $250
Teapot, cov., large size (8 cup) yellow........ $210

Fiesta Teapot in Cobalt Blue

Teapot, cov., medium size (6 cup) cobalt
blue (ILLUS.)... $200
Teapot, cov., medium size (6 cup) ivory $200
Teapot, cov., medium size (6 cup) medi-
um green.. $1,198
Teapot, cov., medium size (6 cup) red $200
Teapot, cov., medium size (6 cup) tur-
quoise.. $150
Teapot, cov., medium size (6 cup) yellow ... $150
Tumbler, water, 10 oz. cobalt blue................. $80
Tumbler, water, 10 oz. ivory........................... $80
Tumbler, water, 10 oz. red $80
Tumbler, water, 10 oz. turquoise.................... $70
Tumbler, water, 10 oz. yellow $70
Utility tray cobalt blue.................................... $45
Utility tray ivory... $45
Utility tray red.. $45
Utility tray turquoise $45
Utility tray yellow $40
Vase, 8" h. cobalt blue................................. $650
Vase, 8" h. ivory $650
Vase, 8" h. red... $650
Vase, 8" h. turquoise.................................... $600
Vase, 8" h. yellow $600
Vase, bud, 6 1/2" h. cobalt blue $100
Vase, bud, 6 1/2" h. ivory $100
Vase, bud, 6 1/2" h. red $100
Vase, bud, 6 1/2" h. turquoise........................ $75
Vase, bud, 6 1/2" h. yellow $75

Florence Ceramics

Some of the finest figurines and artwares were produced between 1940 and 1962 by the Florence

Ceramics Company of Pasadena, California. Florence Ward began working with ceramics following the death of her son, Jack, in 1939.

Mrs. Ward had not worked with clay before her involvement with classes at the Pasadena Hobby School. After study and firsthand experience, she began production in her garage, using a kiln located outside the garage to conform with city regulations. The years 1942-44 were considered her "garage" period.

In 1944 Florence Ceramics moved to a small plant in Pasadena, employing fifty-four employees and receiving orders of $250,000 per year. In 1948 it was again necessary to move to a larger facility in the area with the most up-to-date equipment. The number of employees increased to more than 100. Within five years Florence Ceramics was considered one of the finest producers of semi-porcelain figurines and artwares.

Florence created a wide range of items including figurines, lamps, picture frames, planters and models of animals and birds. It was her extensive line of women in beautiful gowns and gentlemen in fine clothes that gave her the most pleasure and was the foundation of her business. Two of her most popular lines of figurines were inspired by the famous 1860 Godey's Ladies' Book and by famous artists from the Old Master group. In the mid-1950s two bird lines were produced for several years. One of the bird lines was designed by Don Winton and the other was a line of contemporary sculpted bird and animal figures designed by the well-known sculptor Betty Davenport Ford.

There were several unsuccessful contemporary artware lines produced for a short time. The Driftware line consisted of modern freeform bowls and accessories. The Floraline was a rococo line with overglazed decoration. The Gourmet Pottery, a division of Florence Ceramics Company, produced accessory serving pieces under the name of Scandia and Sierra.

Florence products were manufactured in the traditional porcelain process with a second firing at a higher temperature after the glaze had been applied. Many pieces had overglaze paint decoration and clay ruffles, roses and lace dipped in slip prior to the third firing.

Florence Marks

Figures

"Amber," brown hair, pink ruffled long
dress & large bonnet, right arm bent &
holding a pink parasol at right shoulder,
left arm extended w/fingers touching her
dress, articulated fingers, 9 1/4" h. **$425-475**
"Amelia," Godey lady, 8 1/4" h. **$175-225**

Florence "Angel," Downcast Eyes

"**Angel**," downcast eyes, yellow hair, arms bent across upper body, part of angel's wings showing, white robe w/gold trimmed rope sash, cuffs & collar, gold & brown ribbon sticker, 7" h. (ILLUS.) **$50-75**

"**Anita**," standing w/right arm bent, palm extended near waist, left arm almost straight down at side, gold brocade long dress w/short sleeves & fitted waist, articulated fingers, 15" h. **$1,500-2,000**

"**Annabel**," Godey lady, standing w/right arm bent & carrying a basket of flowers, left arm in outward position, long full jacket w/gold trim, large hat, articulated fingers, 8 " h. **$400-450**

Early "Annabelle" Florence Piece

"**Annabelle**," woman standing wearing a large dished hat & long flaring coat w/ruffled collar over a long striped dress, arms extended w/articulated hands, bird perched on her right hand (ILLUS.)..... **$450-500**

"**Ballet**," 7" h. **$225-250**

"**Barbara**," girl standing wearing a large picture hat & long dress w/puffed sleeves, holding a basket of flowers, 6" h. **$75-100**

Rare Birthday Girl Figure

"**Birthday Girl**," standing w/her arms bent & hands close together, wearing a long flaring aqua gown, 9 3/4" h. (ILLUS.) **$750-825**

"**Blynkyn**," young girl standing in long pink nightgown, holding a doll at her side, 5" h.. **$150-200**

"**Bride**," porcelain veil, 8 1/2" h. **$1,000-1,250**

"**Butch**," boy w/hands in pockets, 5" h. .. **$100-125**

"**Camille**," figure of standing woman wearing white dress trimmed in gold, shawl over both arms, triangular hat w/applied pink rose, ribbon tied to right side of neck, articulated hands, no lace, 8 1/2" h. ... **$125-150**

"**Camille**," woman standing & wearing white dress trimmed in gold, shawl over both arms made entirely of hand-dipped lace, brown hair, white triangular hat w/applied pink rose, ribbon tied to right side of neck, two hands, 8 1/2" h. **$300-50**

"**Carol**," girl standing wearing a high-front bonnet & jacket w/tiered shoulders above a widely flaring dress over tiered pantaloons, 7 3/4" h. **$200-250**

"**Caroline**," brocade fabric dress, 15" h. **$3,500-4,500**

"**Catherine**," seated on an open-backed settee, no hat variation, 7 3/4" l., 6 3/4" h. **$650-700**

"**Charles**," man standing & wearing 18th c. attire w/a long cape, 8" h. **$150-175**

"**Charmaine**," woman holding a parasol, wearing ruffled long dress, large hat w/flowers, w/articulated hands, 8 1/2" h. **$250-350**

"**Chinese girl**," standing wearing a flaring jacket applied w/roses & long flaring pants, 7 3/4" h............................... **$100-125**

"The Christening" Figure Group

"Christening (The)," woman w/dress trimmed in lace at neck, sleeves & front of dress holding an infant in a long white christening dress, articulated fingers, 10" h. (ILLUS.) **$2,000-2,500**

"Cindy," young woman standing in long flaring gown, arms bent & away from the body, 8" h. **$225-300**

"Clarissa," woman in full-sleeved jacket & long swirled & pleated skirt, bonnet & holding a muff in right hand, left hand on her shoulder, articulated hand, 7 3/4" h. **$175-200**

"Claudia," ruffled dress w/lace trim, lace shawl on shoulders, large hat, articulated hands, 8 1/4" h. **$250-275**

Florence "Cleopatra" Figure

"Cleopatra," exotic figure in flowing blended blue robes, standing on square base, 12" h. (ILLUS.) **$1,200-1,250**

"Colleen," woman standing w/head slightly turned to left, right hand behind back & left

arm to the front w/articulated hand, long wind-blown dress w/white collar, bonnet w/ribbon tied under chin, 8" h. **$150-200**

Florence Figure of "Darleen"

"Darleen," standing w/head tilted, brown hair w/curls & roses at neck, long dress w/white underskirt, white lace trim on bodice & extending to bottom of dress, right arm bent & holding an open parasol at right shoulder, left arm at waist, articulated fingers, 8 1/4" h. (ILLUS.).......... **$600-650**

"Dear Ruth," lady on bench, 7 1/2" h. **$1,500-1,750**

"Denise," off-the-shoulder white dress w/gold trim extending down the dress front, violet overskirt, brown hair w/roses, both arms bent at waist w/right hand holding a closed fan, articulated fingers, 10" h.. **$500-650**

"Diane," woman in Victorian costume wearing a high rounded bonnet w/feather & a high-collared long coat opening over a ruffled dress, one arm down at side holding a muff, articulated hands, 8" h. **$225-275**

Rare Dora Lee Figure

"**Dora Lee,**" woman wearing a long widely flaring & swirling royal red gown, a small round hat on her head w/a ribbon, arms away from the body, 9 1/2" h. (ILLUS., previous page).................................... **$750-900**

"**Edward,**" man in late Victorian costume sitting in an armchair, holding his bowler hat on one knee, 7" h. **$200-250**

Rare Variation of "Elizabeth"

"**Elizabeth,**" woman in 18th c. costume w/a wide flaring aqua gown w/half-sleeves & a lace-trimmed bodice, long curls down her neck, seated on a white settee, rare white settee variation, 7" w., 8 1/4" h. (ILLUS.) **$1,200-1,400**

"**Eve,**" woman standing wearing a long slightly flaring gown, one hand holding up the front hem to expose lace-trimmed petticoat, other hand at shoulder, lace-trimmed collar & cuffs on half-sleeves, 8 1/2" h. **$200-225**

Variation of "Fair Lady" Figure

"**Fair Lady,**" woman in Gay Nineties gown standing on scrolled base decorated w/a small basket of strewn flowers across the front, royal red dress w/ornate white lace collar, upswept brown hair w/roses, arms away from body w/articulated fingers, 11 1/2" h. (ILLUS.) **$1,750-2,000**

Rare "Georgia" in Brocade Gown

"**Georgia,**" woman standing wearing a long wide real brocade fabric gown, her hands lifting sides of gown at the front, 12" h. (ILLUS.)... **$1,500-2,000**

Florence "Her Majesty" Figure

"**Her Majesty,**" woman in 18th c.-style long dress w/long sleeves, fitted bodice w/standup collar, white w/gold trim, 7" h. (ILLUS.)... **$175-200**

"Jeannette," Godey lady, rose colored full-skirted dress w/peplum, white collar, flower at neck, left hand holding hat w/bow, right hand holding parasol, 7 3/4" h...... **$125-150**

"John Alden," man dressed in dark grey kneebritches, light grey coat, shoes & large brim hat & holding a gun, 9 1/4" h. **$175-200**

"Joyce," woman wearing full off-the-shoulder gown w/shoulder ruffles, a wide-brimmed picture hat, arms away at the front, 8 1/2" h..................................... **$325-350**

Florence "Karen" Figure

"Karen," woman in late Victorian costume, wearing a narrow-waisted fur-trimmed half-length coat over a widely flaring gown, small fur-trimmed hat, w/arms away from body, articulated fingers, 8 1/2" h. (ILLUS.) **$1,250-1,500**

"Lady Diana" with Plain Cuffs

"Lady Diana," woman stepping forward w/her arms away from her body, wearing

flowers in her piled hair & a low-cut narrow lilac gown w/a flaring lacy collar, tight waist & overgown pulled into a bustle, the half-length sleeves w/plain cuffs, 10" h. (ILLUS.)... **$500-575**

"Leading Man," man standing w/right leg in front of left, royal red knee britches, white stockings w/gold-trimmed shoes, knee-length coat w/lacy jabot at neck, left arm bent at elbow & raised upward, left arm extended outward holding a scroll, black hair, 10 1/4" h..................................... **$300-350**

Florence "Linda Lou" Figure

"Linda Lou," girl standing wearing a long full green dress w/peplum & long sleeves, holding a bouquet of flowers to her cheek, a high-fronted bonnet on her head, 7 3/4" h. (ILLUS.) **$100-125**

Rare "Little Princess" Figure

"Little Princess," girl standing in a long-sleeved very wide 17th c. farthingale gown, her hair in long curls, arms outstretched to edges of gown, 8 1/2" h. (ILLUS.) ... **$1,000-1,250**

Florence "Love Letter" Figurine

"Love Letter," woman standing reading a small letter, her hair piled on her head, wearing an off-the-shoulder long gown w/lace bands, 12" h. (ILLUS.) **$1,500-,750**
"Marc Antony," Roman warrior wearing helmet, breastplate, white short garment & long flowing cape, one sandaled leg resting on a rectangular block on a square base, 13" h. **$750-1,000**
"Marie Antoinette," woman in ornate 18th c. gown, her hair piled high & trimmed w/flowers, high lace collar & wide rounded gown w/center flower-trimmed drapes opening over tiered lace panels, arms in front, one holding a closed fan, smaller skirt style, 10" h. **$225-250**

Florence "Marilyn" Figure

"Marilyn," woman standing wearing 18th-c. moss green gown w/half-length sleeves w/lace cuffs & large balloon gathers at the waist above the long flaring gown, carrying a basket over one arm, 8 1/2" h. (ILLUS.) **$350-400**
"Mary," woman seated in balloon-back armchair, wearing a large picture hat, gown w/lace jabot & long sleeves, her hands in lap & on chair arm, 7 1/2" h. **$600-625**
"Melanie," Godey lady, wearing a close-fitting bonnet & long-sleeved long coat over a wide dress, arms at her sides, 7 1/2" h. **$100-125**
"Mikado," very tall Japanese man wearing small round cap, floor-length long-sleeved jacket above draped lower garment on round base, 15" h **$300-350**
"Our Lady of Grace," Madonna figure wearing long cloak w/gathered arms over long gown, on rounded domed base, 10 3/4" h **$175-200**

"Pamela" with Bonnet & Basket

"Pamela," girl standing wearing a flower-trimmed bonnet & long swirling short-sleeved dress, a basket of flowers in one hand, 7 1/2" h. (ILLUS.) **$450-475**
"Peter," man standing wearing Victorian frock coat over lacy cravat, one leg to side & leaning on a scroll pedestal w/a hand holding his top hat, 9 1/4" h. **$225-250**
"Prima Donna," woman in ornate 18th c. costume, her hair piled high & trimmed w/flowers, wearing a wide gown w/upright lacy collar, long ruffle-edged sleeves, the front of the gown formed by wide drapes opening over a tiered lacy underskirt, arms away from front, 10" h. **$550-625**
"Reggie," boy standing wearing Victorian outfit, Eton jacket & vest & long pants, scrolls at the side bottom, 7" h **$225-250**

"Rhett," man standing in front of low wood fence, right hand on vest, left hand in pocket, white ruffled shirt trimmed in color, flaring frock coat, 9" h. **$175-200**

"Sally," woman wearing Victorian outfit, high rounded bonnet tied w/bow, simple ruffled collar & long-sleeved coat over wide swirled & ruffled gown, both hands at sides, 6 3/4" h. **$125-150**

"Scarlett," Godey lady, wearing royal red dress & bonnet, right hand holding a muff near face, left hand holding handbag, articulated hands showing, 8 3/4" h. **$250-300**

"Story Hour," seated mother & girl, woman reading book held in left hand, wearing rose dress w/lace at neck, roses in her hair, & girl w/blonde hair w/right arm on bench, wearing ruffled lace short-sleeved white dress w/blue & pink trim, no little boy, 8" l., 6 3/4" h. **$800-850**

"Susan/Susann," woman standing in simple off-the-shoulder Victorian gown, hair pulled back w/long side curls & cluster of flowers, one hand holding up side of dress, other arm holding basket of flowers to her side, 9" h. **$300-350**

"Tess," woman standing wearing long dress w/lace ruffle at neckline, large picture hat, arms away w/one hand holding edge of skirt up over shoe, 7 1/4" h. ... **$250-300**

"Victor," man w/head tilted wearing a Victorian outfit, holding top hat in right hand, frock coat over long pants, swirling long cape, 9 1/4" h. **$175-225**

"Victoria," woman in Victorian dress seated on serpentine-back tufted Victorian settee, variation w/no bonnet, rose red gown w/ruffle-trimmed panels at waist, ruffled hem trim, arms away, 8 1/4" l., 7" h. .. **$325-350**

"Virginia" Figure with No Lace

"Virginia," woman standing wearing a wide picture hat & off-the-shoulder gown, variation w/no lace at collar or sleeves, long flaring & tiered rose red gown, 9" h. (ILLUS.).. **$900-1,000**

"Wynkin," boy toddler wearing long blue pajamas & holding a Teddy bear, 5 1/2" h.. **$150-200**

"Yvonne," woman standing wearing Victorian outfit, small ribbon-trimmed bonnet, long-sleeved jacket w/peplum over long wide dress, articulated hands w/one arm out & other one holding a small ribbon-trimmed box, 8 3/4" h........................ **$275-300**

Other Items

Bust, "American Lady," heavy lace trim, 7 3/4" h... **$350-400**

Bust, "Gigi," 10" h. **$175-200**

Bust, "Modern Girl," 9 1/2" h. **$100-125**

Bust, "Shen," Chinese woman w/wide upright scrolling headdress, scroll-trimmed jacket, 7 1/2" h. **$175-200**

Flower holder, "Beth," woman standing in a dirndl-style dress & holding up one corner of her long apron, holder at the back, 7 1/2" h... **$50-75**

Flower holder, "Chinese Boy," holder at the back, 7 3/4 .... **$40-50**

Flower holder, "Chinese Child/Girl," bamboo-form holder at side, 7" h.............. **$100-125**

Flower holder, "Jerry," young man standing in white suit trimmed in blue, pink tie, holding a white bass fiddle trimmed w/gold, 7 3/4" h. **$175-200**

Flower holder, "Molly," standing girl wearing long gown w/short ruffled sleeves at shoulder, standing beside a large cylinder vase embossed w/leafy boughs, 6 1/2" h... **$35-40**

Flower holder, "Sally," girl standing wearing long-sleeved long dress swirled to the side, hands to her side, one hand holding large picture hat, holder at the back, 6" h. **$35-40**

Head vase, "Fern," girl wearing wide lightly ruffled hat & dress w/small ruffled collar & wide ruffles at the shoulders, 7" h. **$125-150**

TV lamp, "Dear Ruth," 9" h. **$800-1,000**

Flow Blue

Flow Blue ironstone and semi-porcelain was manufactured mainly in England during the second half of the 19th century. The early ironstone was produced by many of the well known English potters and was either transfer-printed or hand-painted (brush stroke). The bulk of the ware was exported to the United States or Canada.

The "flow" or running quality of the cobalt blue designs was the result of introducing certain chemicals into the kiln during the final firing. Some patterns are so "flown" that it is difficult to ascertain the design. The transfers were of several types: Asian, Scenic, Marble or Floral.

The earliest Flow Blue ironstone patterns were produced during the period between about 1840 and 1860. After the Civil War Flow Blue went out of style for some years but was again manufactured and exported to the United States beginning about the 1880s and continuing through the turn of the century. These later Flow Blue designs are on a semi-porcelain body rather than heavier ironstone and the designs are mainly florals. Also see Antique Trader Pottery & Porcelain Ceramics Price Guide, 3rd Edition.

ABBEY (George Jones & Sons, ca. 1900)
Beeker, 3 1/2" d., 4" h. $55
Bowl, 8" d., 4 1/2" h... $85
Bowl, 9" d., 4 1/2" h... $95
Hot water pot, 6" h. $125

Abbey Punch Bowl

Punch bowl, 10 1/2" d., 6" h. (ILLUS.)........... $750
Shredded wheat dish, 6 1/4" l., 5" w.............. $65

ABBEY (Petrus Regout Co., Maastricht, Holland, date unknown)

Abbey Cup & Saucer

Farmer's cup & saucer, oversized, cup
    5" d., 4" h. & saucer, 8" d. (ILLUS.).............. $75

ABERDEEN (Bourne & Leigh), ca. 1900, Floral,
Butter pat, 3 1/2" d. $40

ACME (Sampson Hancock & Sons, ca. 1900)
Plate, 9" d., five-sided $55

Acme Plate

Plate, 9" d., scalloped (ILLUS.) $55

ADDERLEY (Doulton & Company, ca. 1886), Floral
Vegetable bowl, open, round, 8 1/2" d.,
    2 3/4" h... $125

ALASKA (W.H. Grindley & Company, ca. 1891)
Bowl, berry, 5" d. $45
Creamer, 5 1/4 h. $200
Plate, 10" d., scalloped $95
Platter, 14" l. $250
Soup plate w/flanged rim, 9" d...................... $90

ALBANY (Johnson Bros., ca. 1900)
Plate, salad/dessert, 8" d. $45
Tea cup & saucer, cup, 2 1/2" h., 3 1/2" d,
    saucer, 6" d. $85

ALBANY (W.H. Grindley & Company, ca. 1899)
Butter pat, 3 1/2" d. $40
Plate, bread, 6 1/2 d....................................... $40

Albany Platter

Platter, 14 1/2" l. (ILLUS.).............................. $275

ALTHEA (Podmore, Walker & Company, ca. 1834-1859)

Althea Coffeepot

Coffeepot, cov., 11" d. (ILLUS.)..................... $650
Creamer, 6" h... $250
Sugar, cov., footed, two-handled, 7" h.......... $250
Tea cup & saucer, cup, 4" d., 2 1/2" h., saucer, 5 3/4" d... $125

ALTON (W.H. Grindley & Co., ca. 1891)

Alton Platter

Platter, 18" l. (ILLUS.) $325

AMOUR (Societé Céramique, Dutch, ca. 1865)

Amour Footed Compote

Compote, footed, two-handled, 10" d.
(ILLUS.)... $375

ANDORRA (Johnson Bros., ca. 1901)

Andorra Vegetable Bowl

Vegetable bowl, open, round, 9 1/2" d.
(ILLUS.)... $165

ANEMONE (Lockhart & Arthur, ca. 1855)

Plate, 10 1/4" d... $75
Platter, 16" l. $250

ARGYLE (W.H. Grindley & Co., ca. 1896)

Argyle Platter

Platter, 16" l. (ILLUS.)................................... $350
Platter, 18" l. $450

ARUNDEL (Doulton & Co., ca. 1891)

Ginger jar, cov., 8" h...................................... $295

Arundel Pitcher

Pitcher, 8" h. (ILLUS.).................................... $325

Ten-piece Atlas Wash Set

ASHBURTON (W.H. Grindley & Co., ca.1891)
Plate, salad/dessert, 8" d. $55
Plate, luncheon, 9" d. $60
Plate, dinner, 10" d. $75
Platter, 12" l. $125
Platter, 14" l. $225

Ashburton Platter

Platter, 16" l. (ILLUS.) $275
Platter, 18" l. $300
Sauce ladle, 7" l. $295

ATALANTA (Wedgwood & Company, ca. 1900)

Atalanta Platter

Platter, 14" l. (ILLUS.) $175

ATLAS (W.H. Grindley and Co., ca. 1891)
Wash set: 13" h. x 10 1/2" w. pitcher, 15" d. wash bowl, cov. chamber pot, 13" h. cov. slop jar, soap dish without drainer, 4 1/2" h. shaving mug, 6" h. toothbrush holder; set of 10 (ILLUS., top of page)...... **$2,800**

AULD LANG SYNE (Rowland & Marcellus, ca. 1891) - miscellaneous
Cup & saucer, farmer's, cup 5 1/2" d., 3 1/2" h., saucer, 7 1/2" d.......................... $195

BALTIC (W.H. Grindley & Company, ca. 1891)
Compote, w/pedestal, 9 1/2" d., 3 1/4" h. $300
Creamer, 3 1/2" h.. $225
Gravy boat, 7" l. $125
Plate, dinner, 10" d... $75
Sugar bowl, cov., 4 1/2" h. $275
Teapot, cov., , 5 1/2" h. $575

BAMBOO (Samuel Alcock & Co., ca. 1845)
Soup tureen, cov. $650

BEAUFORT (W.H. Grindley & Co., ca. 1903)
Platter, oval, 14" l. (ILLUS.,, top next page) .. $225
Sugar bowl, cov., 7" handle to handle, 4" h. .. $250
Underplate, for cov. butter, two-handled, 9" d.. $125

BELMONT (Alfred Meakin, ca. 1891)
Teapot, cov., , 8 1/2" handle to spout, 6" h. $300

BELMONT (J.H. Weatherby & Sons, ca. 1892)
Plate, luncheon, 9" d. $65
Plate, dinner, 10" d... $75

BIMRAH (Flacket, Toft & Robinson, ca. 1857)
Covered vegetable, 10 1/2 x 12 1/4" handle to handle, 8" h. $400

BLUE BELL (Dillwyn-Swansea, Welsh, ca. 1840)
Syrup pitcher w/pewter lid, 8 1/2" h $700

14" Oval Beaufort Platter

BLUE DANUBE (Johnson Bros., ca. 1900)
Creamer, 4" h. $175

Blue Danube Luncheon Plate

Plate, luncheon, 9" d. (ILLUS.) $80
Plate, dinner, 10" d. $75
Soup bowl, luncheon, open, 9" d. $65
Soup tureen, cov., oval $475
Sugar, cov., 5" h. $175
Tea cup & saucer $85

BOLINGBROKE (The), (Ridgways, ca. 1909)

The Bolingbroke Platter

Platter, 13" l. (ILLUS.) $250

BOUQUET (Henry Alcock & Co., ca. 1895)

Bouquet Vegetable Dish

Vegetable dish, cov., footed, 12" l. (ILLUS.)
.... $225

BRAZIL (W.H. Grindley & Company, ca. 1891)

Brazil Sugar Bowl

Sugar bowl, cov., 5" h. $175

BRITISH SCENERY (Davenport & Co., ca. 1856)
Charger, 13" d. $350

British Scenery Platter

Platter, 19" l. (ILLUS.) **$350**
Vegetable bowl, oval, 10" l., 3 1/2" h............. **$250**

BURMESE (Thomas Rathbone & Co., ca. 1912)
Serving dish, rectangular, pierced, two-handled, 13 1/2" l., 9" w. **$200**

CALICO (Warwick China Co., American, ca. 1887-1910, aka Daisy Chain)

Calico Tankard-type Pitcher

Pitcher, 7 1/2" h., 9" w. (ILLUS.) **$350**

CAMBRIDGE (Alfred Meakin, ca. 1891)
Platter, 14" l. **$225**
Relish dish, oval, 8 1/2" l................................ **$85**

CANNISTER (maker unknown, marked "Germany," ca. 1891) - Miscellaneous (These cannisters, spice jars & kitchen items were made for export. They arrived without the name of the intended contents i.e. "Tea" or "Sugar." Machines were used to print the name after arrival. They were also in different shapes & languages.)

Sugar Canister

Canister, cov., marked "Sugar," 6" d., 8" h. (ILLUS.)... **$145**
Spice jar, cov., 5" h.. **$75**

CASHMERE (Francis Morley, ca. 1850)
Plate, 10 1/2" d. (ILLUS. left, bottom of page).. **$175**
Underplate, 8" d. (ILLUS. right, bottom of page).. **$175**

Cashmere Plate & Underplate

Chu-San Razor Box

CECIL (Thomas Till & Son, ca. 1891)
Bone dish, crescent-shaped........................... $55
Plate, bread, 6" d.. $35

CHINESE (Thomas Dimmock & Co., ca. 1845)
Tea set: cov. teapot, oversized cov. sugar & creamer; Primary body shape, teapot 9" h., the set $1,500

CHING (William Davenport, ca. 1840)
Plate, 9" d., twelve-sided, paneled $125

CHISWICK (Wood & Baggaley, ca. 1850)

Chiswick Cheese Stand

Cheese stand, 12" d. (ILLUS.)....................... $225

CHRYSANTHEMUM (Myott, Son & Co., ca. 1907)
Platter, 14" l. $200

CHU-SAN (John Meir & Son, ca. 1840)
Razor box, cov., 3 x 7 1/2" (ILLUS., top of page)... $250

CHUSAN (Francis Morley & Co., ca. 1850)
Comport, 9" d. $450

CHUSAN (J. Clementson, ca. 1840)

Clementson Chusan Pattern Flow Blue Teapot

Teapot, cov., Long Hexagon body shape (ILLUS.).. $650

CLARENCE (W.H. Grindley & Co., ca. 1900)

Clarence Platter

Platter, 16" l. (ILLUS.).................................... $250

CLAYTON (Johnson Bros., ca. 1902)
Chamber set: pitcher & bowl, chamber pot, shaving mug & small water pitcher; the set $1,500
Chamber set: pitcher & bowl, chamber pot, toothbrush holder & shaving mug; the set $1,500
Platter, 16" l. $250

Clayton Soup Plate

Soup plate w/flanged rim, luncheon, 9" d.
(ILLUS.).. $85
Vegetable dish, open, oval, 9" l.................... $125

CLYTIE (Wedgwood & Co., ca. 1908)
Plate, dinner, 10" d., w/turkey design............. $150
Platter, 19" l., w/turkey design $1,000

COLONIAL (J. & G. Meakin, ca. 1891)
Butter pat, 3 1/2" d. $40
Vegetable bowl, open, oval, 9" l.................... $125

CONWAY (New Wharf Pottery & Co., ca. 1891)

Conway Vegetable Bowl

Vegetable bowl, open, round, 9 1/2" d.
(ILLUS.).. $85

DAISY (Burgess & Leigh, ca. 1897)

Daisy Soup Plate

Soup plate w/flanged rim, 9" d. (ILLUS.) $65

DELFT (Minton, ca. 1893)

Delft Oyster Plate

Oyster plate, 10" d. (ILLUS.) $185

Delft Platter

Platter, 14" l. (ILLUS.) $175

The Sterling China Co. Fish Set

DERBY (W.H. Grindley, ca. 1891) - Floral (this is a "polychrome" pattern)
Plate, 9" d. **$65**

Derby Platter

Platter, 14" l. (ILLUS.) **$225**
Soup plate w/flanged rim, 9" d. **$85**
Vegetable dish, cov., 12" l., 7" h. **$225**

DOT FLOWER (Unknown, ca. 1840) - Brush-stroke
Creamer, 5" h. **$275**

ECLIPSE (Johnson Bros., ca. 1891)
Demitasse cup & saucer, cup 2 1/2" h.,
    saucer 4 1/2" d. **$125**
Plate, 9" d. **$80**
Vegetable bowl, cov. **$250**

EGERTON (Doulton & Co., Ltd., ca. 1905)
Cheese dish, 10" d. **$325**
Plate, 8 1/2" d. **$55**
Plate, 9 1/2" d. **$65**
Plate, 10 1/2" d. **$75**
Platter, 12" l. **$125**
Platter, 16" l. **$250**
Platter, 18" l. **$300**
Soup plate w/flanged rim, 10 1/2" d. **$75**

EUPHRATES (W. Ridgway, ca. 1840)

Egerton Covered Vegetable

Vegetable dish, cov., 13" w., 6 1/2" h.
    (ILLUS.) **$225**

ENGLISH ROSE (Unknown, ca. 1891)

English Rose Soup Plate

Soup plate w/flanged rim, 9" d. (ILLUS.) **$75**

ETON (Till & Sons, ca. 1880)
Platter, 16" l. **$300**

Euphrates Pattern Flow Blue Teapot

Teapot, cov., Sixteen Panel Ridged body
　shape (ILLUS.) **$500**

EUPHRATES (William Ridgway, ca. 1834)
Teapot, 10" w., 8 1/2" h. **$650**

EXCELSIOR (Thomas Fell, ca. 1850)
Platter, 20" l., w/meat well **$675**

**FAIRY VILLAS III (William Adams & Co.,
ca. 1891) - this has same Oriental scene
in center as Fairy Villas II, but floral border is same as Fairy Villas I**
Plate, 8" d. **$60**
Plate, 10 1/4" d. **$85**
Platter, 16" l. **$250**

FISH SET (Sterling China Co., ca. 1900)
Platter, 10 plates & sauce boat; 21" oval
　platter, 10" d. plates, sauce boat w/dou-
　ble spout & attached underplate, the set
　(ILLUS., top previous page) **$950**

**FLENSBURG (James Edwards, England,
ca. 1847)**

*Flensburg Pattern Flow Blue
Teapot by Edwards*

Teapot, cov., Six Sided Primary body shape
　(ILLUS.) **$450**

FLORA (Thomas Walker, ca. 1845)

Flora Plate

Plate, 10 1/2" d. (ILLUS.) **$125**

**FLORAL GAUDY (Mellor & Venables,
England, ca. 1849)**

Mellor & Venables Floral Gaudy Teapot

Teapot, cov., free-hand, Vertical Panel
　Gothic body shape (ILLUS.)...................... **$650**

FLORIDA (Ford & Sons, ca. 1891)
Plate, 10 1/4" d. **$100**

Florida Platter

Platter, 17" l. (ILLUS.) **$375**
Vegetable dish, cov., 12" w., 7" h. **$225**

FLORIDA (Johnson Bros., ca. 1900)
Egg cup, 3 1/2" h. **$150**

Pitcher, 7" h. $325
Plate, 10" d. $115
Platter, 14" l. $250

FORMOSA (T.J. & J. Mayer, ca. 1850)
Platter, 19" l. $800

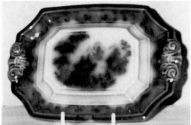

Formosa Undertray to Sauce Boat

Underplate to sauce boat, rectangular,
5 1/2 x 8 1/2" (ILLUS.)................................. $250

FORMOSA (W. Ridgway, England, ca. 1840s)

Formosa Pattern Flow Blue Teapot

Teapot, cov., Flat Panel Primary body
shape (ILLUS.) $600

GAINSBOROUGH (Ridgways, ca. 1905)
Creamer, 4" h. $200
Platter, 14" l. $225
Sugar, cov., 5" h. $225

GALLEON (Doulton & Co., ca. 1891)

Galleon Footed Pitcher

Pitcher, 6 7/8" h., footed, one side reading
"Those who have mony are troubled
about it. Those who have none are troubled without it" and the other side reading
"The pleasure of doing good is the only
one that never wears out" (ILLUS.)........... $475

GAUDY FLORAL (B. & B., ca. 1830)

Tall Gaudy Floral Flow Blue Teapot

Teapot, cov., Tall Eighteen Panel Fluted
body shape (ILLUS.) $750

GAUDY (Mellor, Venables & Co., ca. 1840)

Gaudy Flow Blue Teapot

Teapot, cov., Classic Gothic shape (ILLUS.)
.... $750-850

GEISHA (Upper Hanley Potteries, ca. 1901)
Plate, 9 1/4" d. $85

GENOA (J. & G. Meakin, ca. 1900)
Pitcher, 6" h. $165

GEORGIA (Johnson Bros., ca. 1903)
Pitcher, 5" h. $150

Godwin No. 26 Partial Child's Tea Set

Plate, 9" d. $80
Platter, 14" l. $250

GERANIUM (Doulton & Co., ca. 1890s)
Bowl, 10" l., heavily gilded, scalloped, foot-
ed $250

GIRONDE (W.H. Grindley & Co., ca. 1891)
Gravy boat, 6 1/2" l. $150
Plate, 10 1/4" d., 14-sided $75
Platter, 20" l. $475
Potato/vegetable dish, individual size,
6" w. $120

GIRTON (W.H. Grindley & Co., ca. 1891)
Pitcher, 8 1/2" h. $350
Plate, 10" d. $95

Girton Platter

Platter, 18" l. (ILLUS.) $450

GLADYS (New Wharf Pottery, ca. 1891)
Butter pat, 3 3/4" d. $45

GLOIRE DE DIJON (Doulton & Co., ca. 1895)

Gloire de Dijon Pitcher

Pitcher, belonging to pitcher/bowl wash set
(ILLUS.) $350

GODWIN NO. 26 (J. & R. Godwin, ca. 1834) - this pattern is found in child's tea set, not always marked; when it is, it's marked only w/"Godwin No. 26"
Tea set, child's: 3 3/4" h. cov. teapot,
2 3/4" h. creamer, 4" d. x 2 3/4" h. waste
bowl; partial set (ILLUS., top of page) $675

GRACE (W. H. Grindley & Co., ca. 1897)
Butter pat, 3 1/2" d. $60
Platter, 16" l. $300

Heath's Flower Creamer & Sugar

GRECIAN SCROLL (T.J. and J. Mayer, ca. 1850)

Grecian Scroll Teapot

Teapot, 10" h. (ILLUS.) **$695**

HADDON (W. H. Grindley & Co., ca. 1891)
Butter pat, 3 1/2" d. **$45**
Butter w/insert, cov. **$275**
Plate, 9" d. **$65**
Plate, 10" d. **$75**
Platter, 12" l. **$150**

Haddon Tree Platter with Meat Well

Platter w/meat well, 22" l. (ILLUS.) **$750**
Vegetable bowl, cov., round, 11" d.,
  6 1/2" h. **$200**

Vegetable bowl, open, oval, 9" d. **$125**

HEATH'S FLOWER (Thomas Heath, ca. 1830, brush stroke)
Creamer & cov. sugar, 5" h. creamer, 6" h.
  sugar (ILLUS., top of page)....................... **$725**

Heath's Flower Plate

Plate, 9 1/2" d., 12-sided (ILLUS.) **$125**
Platter, 13 1/2" l. **$225**

HOLLAND (Johnson Bros., ca. 1891)
Gravy boat, 6 1/2" l....................................... **$150**
Soup bowl, open, 8" d. **$85**
Vegetable dish, cov., footed, 12" l.,
  6 1/2" h. **$225**

HONC (Petrus Regout, ca. 1858)

Honc Bedpan

Bedpan (ILLUS., previous page)................ **$1,000**

INDIAN (F. & R. Pratt, ca. 1850)

Indian Flow Blue Pattern Teapot

Teapot, cov., Inverted Diamond body shape
(ILLUS.)... **$650**

INDIAN JAR (Jacob & Thomas Furnival, ca. 1843)

Creamer, 4 1/2" h.. **$250**
Sauce tureen, cov.. **$325**

1840s Indian Jar Pattern Flow Blue Teapot

Teapot, cov., Twelve Panel Ridged body
shape (ILLUS.)... **$650**

IRIS (Arthur J. Wilkinson, ca. 1907, slate/navy blue color)

Plate, 10" d... **$65**
Vegetable bowl, cov., 7 1/2" d...................... **$175**

IVANHOE (Wedgwood & Co., ca. 1900, each size plate has a different scene from the book)

Plate, 9 1/2" d... **$125**

Ivanhoe Plate

Plate, 10 1/2" d. (ILLUS.) **$150**
Soup tureen w/underplate, cov.................... **$575**

IVY (Unknown, ca. 1880)

Pitcher, 8" h.. **$175**

IVY (Wm. Davenport, ca. 1844)

Platter, 22" l., w/meat well **$875**

JANETTE (W. H. Grindley & Co., ca. 1897)

Plate, 10" d... **$90**
Platter, 14" l. **$200**
Vegetable tureen, cov. **$250**

JAPAN FLOWERS (Charles Meigh, ca. 1845)

Foot bath, oval... **$2,400**
Syrup pitcher, 10" h. **$575**

JEDDO (W. Adams & Co., ca. 1893)

Platter, 16" l. **$375**

JENNY LIND (Arthur J. Wilkinson, ca. 1895)

Cup & saucer, cup 3 1/2" d., saucer
5 3/4" d... **$85**
Plate, 6" d... **$45**

JEWEL (Johnson Bros., ca. 1900)

Bone dish **$65**

KENWORTH (Johnson Bros., ca. 1900)

Berry bowl, 5" d.. **$45**
Plate, 10" d... **$75**
Soup bowl, open, 9" d. **$65**

KIRKEE (John Meir & Son, ca. 1861)

Creamer, 5" h.. **$325**

KNOX (New Wharf Pottery & Co., ca. 1891)

Plate, 7" d... **$48**
Platter, 12" l. **$125**
Tea cup & saucer, cup 4" h., 3 1/2" d., sau-
cer 6" d... **$85**

KYBER (Wm. Adams & Co., ca. 1891)

Plate, 9" d... **$85**

12-Sided Kyber Plate

Plate, 10" d., 12-sided (ILLUS.)....................... $95
Platter, 16" l. $275

LA BELLE, LOVELY LADIES (Wheeling Pottery Co., American, ca. 1900)

LaBelle Portrait Plate

Portrait plate, 13" d. (ILLUS.)....................... $495

LA BELLE (Wheeling Pottery Co., American, ca. 1893-1900)

Charger, 13" d... $350

LaBelle Ring-handled Dish

Ring-handled dish, 11" l., 10 1/2" w.
(ILLUS.).. $325

LAHORE (Thomas Phillips & Son, ca. 1840)

Pitcher, 7" h. $375

LAKEWOOD (Wood & Sons, ca. 1900)

Butter pat, 3 1/2" d. $40
Gravy boat w/underplate $165

Lakewood Dinner Plate

Plate, 10" d. (ILLUS.) $100
Soup tureen, cov. $375
Tea cup & saucer, cup 4" h., 3 1/2" d., saucer 6" d.. $85

LANCASTER (New Wharf Pottery & Co., ca. 1891)

Butter pat, 3 1/2" d. $40

New Wharf Pottery Lancaster Pattern Teapot

Teapot, cov., squatty bulbous unnamed body shape (ILLUS.).................................. $500

LAZULI (James Edwards, ca. 1842)

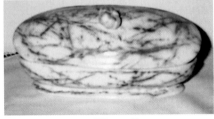

Lazuli Razor Box

Razor box, 9" w. (ILLUS.)............................. $275

Marlborough Graduated Pitchers

LORNE (W.H. Grindley & Co., ca. 1900)
Bowl, berry, 5" d... $45
Platter, 12" l. $165

MANHATTAN (Henry Alcock & Co., ca. 1900)
Bowl, berry, 5" d.. $45
Butter dish w/insert, cov............................... $250
Cake plate, two-handled $175
Plate, 8" d.. $45
Plate, 9" d.. $55
Platter, 14" l. $175
Platter, 16" l. $225
Soup plate w/flanged rim, 9" d....................... $65
Tea cup & saucer $65
Tea set: teapot, sugar & creamer; the set...... $900
Vegetable dish, cov., footed......................... $250

MARIE (W. H. Grindley & Co., ca. 1891)
Pitcher, 7" h. $275
Plate, 10 1/4" d.. $75

MARLBOROUGH (W. H. Grindley & Co., ca. 1891)
Butter pat, 3 1/2" d. $45
Pitcher, 6" h. (ILLUS. right, top of page)........ $225
Pitcher, 8" d. (ILLUS. middle, top of page)
.... $250
Pitcher, 10" h. (ILLUS. left, top of page) $300

Marlborough Open Vegetable Bowl

Vegetable bowl, open, oval, 9" l. (ILLUS.) **$125**

MARTHA WASHINGTON (Unknown, ca. 1900 aka "Chain of States")
Plate, 9" d.. $95

MEISSEN (F.A. Mehlem, German, ca. 1891)

Meissen Vegetable Bowl

Vegetable bowl, open, 10" d. (ILLUS.)............ **$95**

MELBOURNE (W.H. Grindley & Co., ca. 1891)
Bowl, berry, 5" d.. $45
Butter pat, 3 1/2" d. $55
Cake plate, 12" d., two-handled.................... $165
Plate, 6" d.. $45
Plate, 8" d.. $50
Plate, 9" d.. $65

Melbourne Dinner Plate

Plate, 10" d. (ILLUS.) $75
Platter, 14" l. $225

Platter, 16" l. $295
Platter, 18" l. $350

Melbourne Soup Tureen

Soup tureen, cov., oval, footed, 14" l.,
7 1/2" h. (ILLUS.) $650
Vegetable bowl, cov., oval $250
Vegetable bowl, open, round $125

MELROSE (Doulton & Co., ca. 1891)
Plate, 10 1/4" d. $65
Platter, 20" l. $350

MIKADO (A.J. Wilkinson, ca. 1896)

Mikado Dinner Plate

Plate, 10 1/2" d. (ILLUS.) $75
Platter, 18" l. $325
Soup plate w/flanged rim, 10 1/2" d. $65

MILTON (Poutney & Co. - Bristol Pottery, ca. 1886)

Milton Luncheon Plate

Plate, 9" d. (ILLUS.) $55
Plate, 10" d. $65

Platter, 18" l. $275
Sauce boat w/ladle & underplate, cov.,
oval, footed $350

MODERNA (J. & G. Meakin, ca. 1891)
Toothbrush holder, 5" h. $175

Washbowl in Moderna Pattern

Washbowl, belonging to pitcher & bowl set,
15" d. (ILLUS.) $500

MONGOLIA (Johnson Bros., ca. 1900)
Plate, 10" d. $90
Vegetable dish, cov. $25

MONGOLIAN (F. & W., Unknown, mid-to-late Victorian)
Charger, 14" d. $400

Mongolian Gravy Boat

Gravy boat, footed (ILLUS.) $195

MONTANA (Johnson Bros., ca. 1900)

Montana Luncheon Plate

Plate, 9" d. (ILLUS., previous page)................ $65
Vegetable dish, cov....................................... $225

MOORISH PALACES (James Kent, Old Foley Pottery, ca. 1910)

Morrish Palaces Plate

Bowl, 10 1/2" d. (ILLUS.) $175

MORNING GLORY (Elsmore & Forster, ca. 1853-71, brush-stroke)

Morning Glory Cup & Saucèr

Cup & saucer, no handle (ILLUS.) $150

MURIEL (Upper Hanley Pottery, ca. 1895)

Muriel Platter

Platter, 14" l. (ILLUS.) $250

NANKIN (Mellor, Venables & Co. or Thomas Walker, ca. 1845)

Plate from Nankin Tea Set

Tea set: teapot, oversized cov. sugar, creamer, 6 cups w/no handles & 6 saucers, 6 9" d. plates; Primary body style, the set (ILLUS. of plate).......................... **$2,500**

NON PAREIL (Burgess & Leigh - Middleport Potteries, ca. 1891)
Butter pat $55
Platter, 16" l. $350
Soup plate w/flanged rim, 9" d...................... $95

NORMANDY (Johnson Bros., ca. 1900)
Bowl, berry, 5" d. $45
Butter pat, 3 1/2" d. $55
Plate, 9" d.. $65

Normandy Soup Plate

Soup plate w/flanged rim, 10" d. (ILLUS.) $95

OLD CURIOSITY SHOP (Ridgways, ca. 1910)

Old Curiosity Shop Platter

Minton & Co. Flow Blue Tea Set

Platter, 16" l. (ILLUS., previous page) **$295**
Vegetable bowl, open, oval, 10" l. **$125**

ORCHID (John Maddock & Sons, ca. 1896)
Platter, 16" l. **$250**
Platter, 18" l. **$275**

ORIENTAL (Samuel Alcock & Co., ca. 1840)
Plate, 9 1/2" d. **$125**
Plate, 10 1/2" d. **$175**
Platter, 16" l. **$450**

Paisley Platters, Bone Dishes, Gravy

Platter, 20" l. (ILLUS. upper right, above) **$350**
Relish dish, 9" l. **$125**
Soup tureen, cov., round **$450**

PEKIN (Johnson Bros., ca. 1891)

Pekin Dinner Plate

Plate, 10" d. (ILLUS.) **$75**

PEONY (Minton & Co., ca. 1875-1891)
Tea set: cov. teapot, open sugar, creamer,
    cup & saucer, tray; the teapot
    6 1/2" h. x 9 1/2" w. from spout to handle,

Oriental Underplate

Underplate, two-handled w/reticulated tab
    handles, 13" d. (ILLUS.) **$450**

ORMONDE (Alfred Meakin, ca. 1891)
Plate, 8" d. **$45**
Plate, 10 1/4" d. **$65**

PAISLEY (Mercer Pottery Co., American, ca. 1890)
Bone dish, crescent-shaped (ILLUS. lower
    left, top next column) **$85**
Gravy boat (ILLUS. lower right, top next col-
    umn) **$150**

the sugar 2 1/2" h. x 5 1/2" w. from handle to handle, the creamer 2 1/2" h. x 4 1/2" w. from spout to handle, the cup 3" d. x 2 1/2" h., the saucer 5" d., the tab-handled tray 14 1/2" sq., only marked "Minton" w/crown above it, no patt. name, the set (ILLUS., top of page) **$1,200**

PERSIAN SPRAY (Doulton & Co., ca. 1885)
Bowl, 8" d. **$165**
Compote, 9" d. **$250**
Teapot, self-pouring **$475**

PERSIAN SPRIGS (J. & M.P. Bell & Co., Scottish, ca. 1853)

PLYMOUTH (New Wharf Pottery & Co., ca. 1891)

Plymouth Dinner Plate

Plate, 10" d. (ILLUS.) **$65**
Tea cup & saucer **$65**

POPPY (Doulton & Co., ca. 1902)
Jardiniere, 10" h. **$450**

POPPY (W. H. Grindley & Co., ca. 1891)

Poppy Dinner Plate

Plate, 10" d. (ILLUS.) **$100**

PORTMAN (W. H. Grindley & Co., ca. 1891)
Creamer, 4 1/2" h. **$175**
Fruit compote, w/pedestal, 10" d. x 4 1/2" h. .. **$350**

Portman Platter

Platter, 14" l. (ILLUS.) **$225**
Sugar, cov., 5 1/2" h. **$250**

QUEBEC (Paul Utzschneider, German, ca. 1891)

Quebec Plate

Plate, 10" d. (ILLUS.) **$75**

RALEIGH (Burgess & Leigh, ca. 1906)
Egg cup **$150**

Raleigh Gravy Boat

Gravy boat, 6 1/2" l. (ILLUS.) **$150**

REBECCA (George Jones & Sons, ca. 1900)

Rebecca Luncheon Plate

Plate, 9" d. (ILLUS.) **$65**

REEDS & FLOWERS (Unknown, ca. 1855, brush-stroke)

Reeds & Flowers Soup Plate

Soup plate w/flanged rim, 10 1/2" d.
(ILLUS.) **$150**

REGALIA (Thomas Hughes, ca. 1895)
Vegetable dish, cov. **$225**

REGENT (Johnson Bros., ca. 1910)
Plate, 8" d. **$45**
Plate, 9" d. **$55**
Plate, 10" d. **$65**
Platter, 18" l. **$250**
Tea cup & saucer **$65**
Tea set: cov. teapot, sugar & creamer; the
set **$750**

RHODES (possibly Samuel Ford & Co., ca. 1898-1929)

Rhodes 8" Plate

Plate, 8" d., marked "S.F. & Co." (ILLUS.) **$50**

RICHMOND I (Ford & Sons, ca. 1900)

Richmond Soup

Rim soup, flanged edge, 10" d. (ILLUS.)....... **$100**

RICHMOND (Johnson Bros., ca. 1900) - Floral

Richmond 8" Plate

Plate, 8" d. (ILLUS.) **$65**
Platter, 16" l. **$275**
Vegetable dish, open, 9" d. **$175**

RIO (Pountney & Co., Ltd., ca. 1893)
Platter, 13" l. **$200**
Vegetable dish, open, 10" d. **$150**

ROSE (Bourne & Leigh, ca. 1910)
Candlesticks, 5" h., pr. **$350**

ROSE & VINE (David Methven & Sons, ca. 1847)

Bowl in Rose & Vine Pattern

Bowl, 10 1/2" d. (ILLUS., previous page)....... **$175**

ROSES (Unknown, ca. 1850)

Large Platter in Roses Pattern

Platter, 17 x 22", only has mark "F.B. Roses" & impressed mark "Newstone," which was used by Spode & Co. after 1830 (ILLUS.)... **$650**

ROSEVILLE (John Maddock & Sons, ca. 1891)

Roseville Celery Dish

Celery dish, 11" l. (ILLUS.)........................... **$125**

ROYAL BLUE (Balmoral) (Burgess & Campbell, American, ca. 1880)

Butter dish, cov. **$225**

SCINDE (J. & G. Alcock, ca. 1840)

Scinde Jam Jar

Jam jar w/attached tray, w/lion's head handles, only one of its kind (ILLUS.) **$6,000**

Scinde Platter

Platter, 18" l. (ILLUS.)................................... **$750**

Scinde Teapot

Teapot, primary body style, 9" h. (ILLUS.)..... **$900**

SEVILLE (New Wharf Pottery & Co., ca. 1891)

Seville Dinner Plate

Plate, 10" d. (ILLUS.) **$75**

SHANGHAI (W.E. Corn, ca. 1900)

Shanghai Dinner Plate

Plate, 10" d. (ILLUS.) **$75**

SHUSAN (F. & R. Pratt & Co., ca. 1855)

Shusan Dinner Plate

Plate, 10 1/2" d. (ILLUS.) **$125**

SLOE BLOSSOM (William Ridgway & Co., ca. 1830)

Sloe Blossom Waste Jar

Waste jar, part of dresser set (ILLUS.) **$750**

Sloe Blossom Water Pitcher

Water pitcher, 7 1/2" h. (ILLUS.) **$475**

SOBRAON (Samuel Alcock & Co., ca.1850)

Platter, 20" l., w/meat well & tree **$1,400**

Soup tureen, cov. **$1,200**

SPINACH (Brushstroke, maker unknown)

Waste bowl, 5" d. **$125**

SPINACH (Libertas, Prussian, ca. 1900, brush-painted) (Also Turkey Feather or Oatmeal)

Bowl, 6 1/2" d., 3 1/2" h. (ILLUS. rear w/smaller bowls) **$95**

Spinach Pattern Bowls in Two Sizes

Bowls, 3 1/2" d., 2" h., each (ILLUS. fore-ground w/larger bowl) **$65**

SPRING (Thomas Rathbone & Co., ca. 1900)

Teapot in Spring Pattern

Teapot, 6" h., 10" w. from spout to handle (ILLUS., previous page) **$200**

STEERS (Doulton & Co., ca. 1900)
Serving set: 20" l. platter & twelve 10" d. plates; the set... **$2,800**

STRAWBERRY (J. Furnival & Co., ca. 1850)

Strawberry Pattern Flow Blue Teapot

Teapot, cov., freehand, Cockscomb Handle body shape, also found in flow mulberry (ILLUS.)... **$950**

STRAWBERRY (Thomas Walker, ca. 1856)
Creamer, w/cockscomb handle, 5 1/4" h. **$500**

STRAWBERRY (Unknown, ca. 1840s, brush-stroke & polychrome)

Rim Soup Bowl in Strawberry Pattern

Rim soup bowl, w/flanged edge, 10 1/2" d. (ILLUS.).. **$175**

SYRIAN (W. H. Grindley & Co., ca. 1892)

Syrian Chamber Pot

Chamber pot, cov., 11" w., 7" h. (ILLUS.) **$325**

TEMPLE (Podmore, Walker, ca. 1849)

Temple Pattern Flow Blue Teapot

Teapot, cov., Oval body shape (ILLUS.)........ **$800**

Temple Pattern Teapot in Varied Shape

Teapot, cov., Twelve Panel Bulbous body shape (ILLUS.).. **$750**

TOGO (F. Winkle & Co., ca. 1900) (Also known as Colonial)

Chamber pot $250
Pitcher, 7" h. $150

TOKIO (Johnson Bros., ca. 1900)

Tokio Luncheon Plate

Plate, 9" d. (ILLUS.) $55

TONQUIN (Wm. Adams & Son, ca. 1845)

Creamer, 6" h. $375
Rim soup, w/flanged edge, 9" d. $125

Tonquin Pattern Flow Blue Teapot

Teapot, cov., Full Panel Gothic body shape
(ILLUS.) $650

TOURAINE (Henry Alcock & Co., ca. 1898)

Butter dish, cov. $250
Cake plate, w/tab handles, 9 1/2" d. $175

Alcock Touraine Pattern Flow Blue Teapot

Teapot, cov., fluted urn-form unnamed body
shape (ILLUS.) $750
Vegetable bowl, individual size, 5 1/2" w. $100

TOURAINE (Stanley Potteries, England - modern)

Teapot, cov., fluted urn-form unnamed body shape, modern reproduction by the Stanley Potteries, England $75

TOURAINE (Stanley Pottery Co., ca. 1898)

Dinner service: eleven 10" d. dinner plates, six soup plates, four small plain edge cereal bowls, eight 8" d. salad plates, 18 dessert plates, 16 dessert bowls, 16 teacups & 25 saucers, ten bread & butter plates, eight crescent-shaped bone dishes, round sauce bowl, paneled round sauce bowl, open oval 8 1/2" l. vegetable dish, slightly larger open oval vegetable dish, two oval 17" l. meat platters, four ovoid open vegetable bowls, one slightly smaller open vegetable dish, two handled cov. sugar bowls (repaired handles), 4 1/2" h. creamer & 5" h. pitcher, the set (ILLUS., below) $3,450

Large Stanley Pottery Touraine Pattern Flow Blue Dinner Service

TRILBY (Wood & Sons, ca. 1891)

Trilby Cake Plate

Cake plate, w/tab handles, made for export for "Holmes Luce & Co., Boston, Mass.," to be given away w/each purchase of furniture, the name of the company printed on front, 10 1/2" d. (ILLUS.) **$150**

TROY (Charles Meigh, ca. 1840)
Teapot **$475**

TULIP (Copeland & Garrett, ca. 1845)

Tulip Fruit Compote

Fruit compote, footed, 10" d., 6" h. (ILLUS.) .. **$550**

TURKEY (Cauldon, Ltd., ca. 1905)

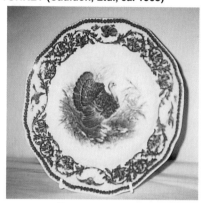

Turkey Dinner Plate

Plate, 10 1/2" d. (ILLUS.) **$150**

TURKEY (Doulton & Co., ca. 1900) (Doulton produced more than one design with a turkey)
Platter, 24" l. (ILLUS., bottom of page) **$1,200**

TURKEY (marked "La Belle China W.P." for La Belle China Co. & Wheeling Pottery Co. of Wheeling, West Virginia, when they merged; American, ca. 1893-1903)
Serving set: 18" l. platter & twelve 10" d. plates; the set **$1,800**

TURKEY (Ridgways, ca. 1900)
Turkey set: platter, 22" l., & 12 dinner plates, 10" d.; the set **$2,500**

TYROLEAN (Ridgway, ca. 1850)
Charger, 12 1/2" d. **$175**

VERMONT (Burgess & Leigh, ca. 1895)
Plate, 10" d. **$95**

Very Large Doulton Turkey Platter

VERMONT (Burgess & Leigh, ca. 1895)
Sauceboat w/underplate, 9" l., 5" h. **$275**

Vermont Pattern Flow Blue Teapot

Teapot, cov., ribbed pear-shaped unnamed
body (ILLUS.) **$450**

VERONA (Wood & Sons, ca. 1891)
Plate, 10" d. **$95**

VIRGINIA (John Maddock & Sons, ca. 1891)

Virginia Platter

Platter, 16" l. (ILLUS.) **$275**

WATER NYMPH (Josiah Wedgwood, ca. 1872)
Bowl, footed, 8" d., 5" h. **$195**

WATTEAU (Doulton & Co., ca. 1891)
Oil lamp, converted to electric, 26" h. **$850**

Watteau Dinner Plate

Plate, 10 1/2" d. (ILLUS.) **$95**

WAVERLY (John Maddock & Son, ca. 1891)

Waverly Platter

Platter, 16" l. (ILLUS.) **$275**

WENTWORTH (J. & G. Meakin, ca. 1907)
Butter pat, 3 1/2" d. **$40**

Wentworth Dinner Plate

Plate, 10" d. (ILLUS.) **$65**
Vegetable bowl, cov., 12" l., 6 1/2" h. **$175**

Fulper Pottery

The Fulper Pottery was founded in Flemington, New Jersey, in 1805 and operated until 1935, although operations were curtailed in 1929 when its main plant was destroyed by fire. The name was changed in 1929 to Stangl Pottery, which continued in operation until July of 1978, when Pfaltzgraff, a division of Susquehanna Broadcasting Company of York, Pennsylvania, purchased the assets of the Stangl Pottery, including the name.

Fulper Marks

Center bowl, "Effigy Bowl," a round disk base supporting a cluster of four stylized ancient squatting figures supporting a wide shallow bowl w/rolled sides, frothy ivory over matte mustard yellow glaze, ink racetrack mark, 10 1/2" d., 6 1/2" h. **$978**

Fulper Scarab Beetle Flower Frog

Flower frog, figural, model of a large oval scarab beetle, nice matte green glaze, unmarked, 3 1/4" l., 1 1/2" h. (ILLUS.) **$150**

Fulper Pottery Copper Dust Jug

Jug, bulbous ovoid body w/a wide shoulder centered by a short cylindrical neck, a high arched handle from base of neck to edge of shoulder, Copper Dust Crystalline glaze, small in-the-making grinding chip on base, incised racetrack mark, 7 3/4" d., overall 11 1/2" h. (ILLUS.)........ **$2,760**
Lamp, table model, a wide pottery mushroom-shaped shade w/a fine Leopard Skin Crystalline glaze, the border pierced w/clusters of small openings centered by a large triangular opening, all inset w/leaded slag glass pieces, on a widely flaring matching pottery pedestal base, original sockets & switch, hairline in a ceramic bridge between the two pieces of slag glass, rectangular ink mark on both pieces, shade 15 1/4" d., overall 18 1/2" h. (ILLUS., top next column) **$10,925**

Fine Fulper Pottery Table Lamp

Lamp, table model, wide mushroom-shaped pottery shade w/a brown, celadon green & blue glaze, pierced around the border w/heart-shaped & geometric openings inset w/green & amber slag glass, on a widely flaring pottery pedestal base w/a Cucumber Green matte glaze, both parts w/a rectangular ink mark, shade 17" d., overall 21 1/2" h. **$17,250**
Urn, bulbous ovoid form tapering to a wide short cylindrical neck w/thick rim, horizontal loop handles at the shoulder, hammered texture under a Leopard Skin crystalline glaze, ink racetrack mark, 11 1/2" d., 12 1/4" h. (small abraded area on one handle) **$2,185**

Squatty Copper Dust Fulper Vase

Vase, 4 3/4" h., 5 3/4" d., wide low squatty lower body w/a wide tapering shoulder to the wide flat mouth flanked by squared scroll handles, Copper Dust Crystalline glaze, incised racetrack mark (ILLUS.) **$575**

Bulbous Fulper Copper Dust Vase

Vase, 5 1/2" h., 5" d., bulbous ovoid body tapering to a low wide molded mouth, Copper Dust Crystalline glaze, raised racetrack mark (ILLUS.) **$1,035**

Cucumber Glaze Squatty Fulper Vase

Vase, 6" h., 8 1/2" d., footed wide squatty bulbous body w/a short wide cylindrical neck surrounded by three short loop handles, Cucumber Crystalline glaze, raised racetrack mark (ILLUS.) **$1,150**

Bulbous Cafe-au-Lait Fulper Vase

Vase, 7" h., 9 1/2" d., wide squatty bulbous tapering form w/a flat closed rim flanked by square buttressed handles, cafe-au-lait glaze, rectangular ink mark (ILLUS.) **$748**

Fulper Corseted Vase with Fine Glaze

Vase, 7 1/2" h., 4" d., corseted cylindrical body, dripping frothy ivory, blue & mahogany flambé glaze, rectangular ink mark (ILLUS.) **$1,035**

Fulper Vase with Blue-Amber Glaze

Vase, 7 1/2" h., 6" d., bulbous ovoid gourd-form body w/a slightly tapering cylindrical neck flanked by curved handles to the shoulder, blue & amber Crystalline glaze, incised racetrack mark (ILLUS.) **$546**

Vase, 8" h., 4" d., bottle-form, bulbous ovoid body tapering to a tall stick neck wrapped w/a stylized salamander, green & blue flambé glaze, rectangular ink mark **$748**

Vase, 8" h., 4" w., Vasekraft line, square tapering lower body below square flat sides, a stylized embossed coat-of-arms at the top of each side, Flemington Green Flambé glaze, rectangular ink mark (ILLUS., top next page) **$1,035**

Fulper Vasekraft Flambé-glazed Vase

Vase, 8" h., 5 1/2" d., a small pedestal foot below the very wide bulbous body tapering sharply to a shoulder molded w/three small, short cylindrical necks centered by a larger cylindrical neck, mahogany, ivory & turquoise flambé semi-matte glaze, incised racetrack mark **$805**

Vase, 8" h., 6" d., footed squatty wide body tapering sharply to a cylindrical neck w/flared rim, overall Mirror Black crystalline flambé glaze, incised racetrack mark .. **$575**

Vase, 8" h., 8" d., wide bulbous ovoid body w/the shoulder centered by a short cylindrical neck, a frothy gunmetal & blue flambé glaze over a Famille Rose ground, raised racetrack mark **$1,093**

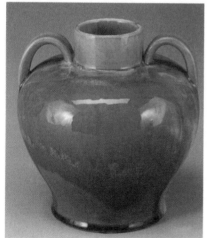

Aqua & Olive Flambé Fulper Vase

Vase, 8 1/2" h., 8" d., very wide bulbous ovoid body w/a wide shoulder centered by a short cylindrical neck flanked by

arched shoulder handles, aqua & olive Flambé glaze, raised racetrack mark (ILLUS.) **$460**

Vase, 9 1/2" h., 6" d., bulbous baluster-form body w/a short trumpet neck, mirrored Cat's-eye flambé glaze, ink racetrack mark **$633**

Fulper Vase with Frothy Blue Glaze

Vase, 9 1/2" h., 7" d., wide heavy baluster-form body, fine frothy turquoise blue glaze, ink racetrack mark (ILLUS.) **$489**

Grey to Blue Flambé-glazed Fulper Vase

Vase, 10" h., 7" d., wide squatty rounded lower body below the wide steeply tapering cylindrical sides flanked by long flattened & angled handles, mouse grey to dark blue flambé glaze, raised racetrack mark (ILLUS.) **$805**

Elegant Ivory Flambé & Yellow Fulper Vase

Vase, 10 1/2" h., 4 1/2" d., simple tall baluster-form body, Ivory Flambé glaze dripping over a mustard yellow matte ground, ink racetrack mark (ILLUS.) **$805**

Leopard Skin Glazed Fulper Vase

Vase, 11" h., 4 3/4" d., tall gently tapering cylindrical body w/a flat mouth flanked by long squared buttressed handles, fine Leopard Skin Crystalline glaze, rectangular ink mark (ILLUS.) **$1,093**

Vase, 11 1/2" h., 9" d., footed baluster-form body w/flaring rim, molded w/vertical low ribs forming panels up the sides, fine mirrored Cat's-eye flambé glaze, raised racetrack mark (ILLUS., top next column) **$4,025**

Fulper Vase with Cat's-eye Glaze

Fulper "Cattail" Pattern Vase

Vase, 12 3/4" h., 4 3/4" d., "Cattail" patt., tall cylindrical form molded overall w/cattails, Leopard Skin crystalline glaze, minor burst bubble at rim, rectangular ink mark (ILLUS.)... **$4,025**

Rare Fulper Cattail Flambé-glazed Vase

Vase, 13" h., 4 3/4" d., tall slightly tapering cylindrical body molded in relief overall in cattails, glossy bluish grey & Moss Flambé glaze, rectangular ink mark (ILLUS., previous page) **$4,313**

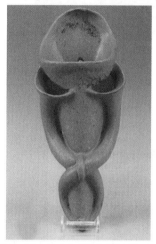

Matte Blue Fulper Triple Wall Pocket

Wall pocket, triple, a central tapering cone w/a high upturned back rim flanked down the sides w/smaller entwined open-topped cones, matte blue glaze, remnant of rectangular ink mark, 11 1/2" h. (ILLUS.)..................................... **$374**

Gallé Pottery

Fine pottery was made by Emile Gallé, the multitalented French designer and artisan who is also famous for his glass and furniture. The pottery is relatively scarce.

Gallé Pottery Mark

Candlesticks, figural, in the form of a seated roaring lion wearing a crown that forms the socket, a large shield at the front decorated w/a thistle & other floral decoration in grey, black & red on a light blue ground w/gilt trim, signed, late 19th c., repairs, 8" h., pr..................................... **$575**

Dish, foliate-shaped bowl, the interior painted in naturalistic colors w/wildflowers in front of a shore landscape, gilded rim, base w/red stamp mark, late 19th c., 10 1/4" w. (restored)................................. **$316**

Ewer, squatty bulbous body centering a very tall slender cylindrical neck, a long curved handle from the rim to the side of the shoulder, one side decorated w/a modeled mushroom-shaped flower, the opposite

Unusual Modeled Gallé Pottery Ewer

decorated w/a great raised blue & brown grasshopper, background w/splashes of blue, yellow, gold, rust & brown, signed on the bottom "E G Déposé" & signed "E Gallé Nancy," some very minor crazing to glaze, 9 1/4" h. (ILLUS.)........................... **$1,495**

Model of cat, seated w/head turned facing the viewer, bulging eyes w/smiling expression, glazed in white & decorated w/scattered ringed dots & heart-like devices, signed, ca. 1890, 13" h. **$3,600**

Gallé Cat with Flowers & Stripes

Model of cat, seated w/head turned facing the viewer, bulging eyes w/smiling expression, glazed in white & decorated w/pale lavender bands & reddish orange

Rare Gallé Planter with Barnyard Scene

& green floral clusters, a painted neck chain w/a locket holding a dog portrait, minor chips to paws & one ear, ca. 1895, 12 3/8" h. (ILLUS.) **$5,700**

Model of dog, seated Boston Terrier-like animal facing the viewer, open front legs, bulging eyes & angry expression, painted in white w/scattered ringed dots & heart-like devices, signed, ca. 1890, 12 5/8" h. **$6,000**

Model of owl, faience, molded in full relief, perched owl w/glass eyes, glazed in shades of grey & amber on russet base, inscribed **$3,737**

Planter, long flat-sided oval shaped w/curved top opening, raised on short flat legs, the front colorfully painted w/a scene of a rooster, hen & chicks in a farmyard, artist-signed, the reverse painted w/an interior scene of a barn w/hay, wheelbarrow, broom, etc., molded ring end handles, signed on the base w/a raised "E.G." Gallé signature & "244 - 3931," late 19th c., couple of small glaze imperfections & losses, 4 1/2 x 11 1/2", 7" h. (ILLUS., top of page) **$2,013**

Vase, 7" h., 4 1/2 x 11 1/2", long flat-sided oval form w/a long rectangular mouth flanked by lion heads w/ring handles, raised on four scroll feet, one side h.p. w/a colorful scene of a hen & rooster w/four chicks & a ladder, the other side w/a scene of a chicken w/wheelbarrow & broom on hay, base impressed w/lozenge mark "E.G.," mold number 244, artist-signed, late 19th c. **$518**

Rare Gallé Figural Wall Pocket

Wall pocket, round w/a large relief-molded crescent man-in-the-moon face around the border, the background h.p. Italianate seascape, signed "E. Gallé à Nancy 195" & molded "EG" w/a Cross of Lorraine & "Mode...et décor dép...," ca. 1890s, 14" w., 13 1/2" h. (ILLUS.).......... **$5,736**

Gaudy Dutch

This name is applied to English earthenware with designs copied from Oriental patterns. Production began in the 18th century. These copies flooded into this country in the early 19th century. The incorporation of the word "Dutch" derives from the fact that it was the Dutch who first brought the Oriental wares into Europe. The ware was not, as often erroneously reported, made specifically for the Pennsylvania Dutch.

Cup & saucer, handleless, Single Rose patt., orange, green, yellow & blue, early 19th c. (minor enamel flaking on cup) **$550**

Cup & saucer, handleless, War Bonnet patt., orange, green, blue & yellow, early 19th c. (harline & minor stain in cup) **$495**

Gaudy Welsh

This is a name for wares made in England for the American market about 1830 to 1860, with some examples dating much later. Decorated with Imari-style flower patterns, often highlighted with copper lustre, it should not be confused with Gaudy Dutch wares, the colors of which differ somewhat.

Cups & saucers, handleless, paneled rim, Urn patt., pink, orange, green cobalt blue & lustre trim, 19th c., set of 6 (some minor staining) **$715**

Plates, 8 1/2" d., paneled rim, Urn patt., pink, orange, green cobalt blue & lustre trim, 19th c., set of 6 (three w/light stain-ing) **$715**

Geisha Girl Wares

Geisha Girl Porcelain features scenes of Japanese women in colorful kimonos along with the flora and architecture of turn-of-the-century Japan. Although bearing an Oriental motif, the wares were produced for Western use in dinnerware and household accessory forms favored during the late 1800s through the early 1940s. There was minimal production during the Occupied Japan period. Less ornate wares were distributed through gift shops and catalogs during the 1960s-70s; some of these are believed to have been manufactured in Hong Kong. Beware overly ornate items with fake Nippon marks that are in current production today, imported from China. More than a hundred porcelain manufacturers and decorating houses were involved with production of these wares during their heyday.

Prices cited here are for excellent to mint condition items. Enamel wear, flaking, hairlines or missing parts all serve to lower the value of an item. Prices in your area may vary.

More than 275 Geisha Girl Porcelain patterns and pattern variations have been catalogued; others are still coming to light.

The most common patterns include:

Bamboo Tree

Battledore

Child Reaching for Butterfly

Fan series

Garden Bench series

Geisha in Sampan series

Meeting series

Parasol series

Pointing series

The rarest patterns include:

... And They're Off

Bellflower

Bicycle Race

Capricious

Elegance in Motion

Fishing series

Foreign Garden

In Flight

Steamboat

The most popular patterns include:

Boat Festival

Butterfly Dancers

By Land and By Sea

Cloud series

Courtesan Processional

Dragonboat

Small Sounds of Summer

So Big

Temple A

A complete listing of patterns and their descriptions can be found in The Collector's Encyclopedia of Geisha Girl Porcelain. *Additional patterns discovered since publication of the book are documented in* The Geisha Girl Porcelain Newsletter.

References: Litts, E., Collector's Encyclopedia of Geisha Girl Porcelain, *Collector Books, 1988;* Geisha Girl Porcelain Newsletter, *P.O. Box 3394, Morris Plains, NJ 07950.*

Bowl, 4 1/2" d., 1 1/4" h., rice, Garden Party patt., multicolor border **$15**

Bowl, 7" d., Garden Bench C patt., tri-foot-ed, rose, cobalt blue border w/gold em-bellishments **$45**

Bowl, 8 1/2" d., Drum D patt., pale cobalt blue border, signed "Kutani" **$55**

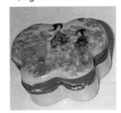

Geisha Girl Butterfly Trinket Box

Box, cov., trinket, Temple B patt., butterfly-shaped, red-orange border, marked "Ja-pan," rare, 2 3/4 x 2 x 1 1/4" (ILLUS.) **$25**

Box, manicure, Lady in Kaga patt., red bor-der, 2 1/2" d. **$15**

Butter pat, Lantern Processional patt., red-orange border w/gold lacing **$15**

Geisha Temple A Candlesticks

Candlesticks, Temple A patt., multicolor border, Noritake's green M-in-wreath Nippon mark, 5 3/4" h., pr. (ILLUS.) **$175**

Celery set (child's): master plus six salts; Flower Gathering A patt., pine green border w/white dots **$45**

Geisha Parasol F Chocolate Pot

Chocolate pot, cov., Parasol F patt., cobalt blue border w/gold lacing, unusual spout, 8 1/2" h. (ILLUS.) **$125**

Chocolate pot, Parasol C patt., red border w/gold buds, marked "Japan," 9 1/2" h. **$45**

Cup & saucer, bouillon w/lid, Pointing D patt., black border, signed in Japanese "Tashiro".. **$45**

Cup & saucer, child's demitasse, Torii patt., gold border, marked "Made in Japan" **$15**

Cup & saucer, cocoa, Bamboo Trellis patt., wavy red border w/gold lacing...................... **$18**

Cup & saucer, tea, four decorative reserves including Meeting & Parasol patts., ornate all-over design...................................... **$25**

Cup & saucer, tea, Parasol C patt., red border, marked "Japan"...................................... **$10**

Dish, Fan F patt., footed sherbet, red-orange border... **$35**

Dish, Garden Bench F patt., figural leaf shape, ornate multicolor border & highly gilded decoration... **$25**

Geisha Girl Dresser Tray

Dresser tray, rectangular, Blind Man's Bluff patt., designs in floral medallions on cobalt blue ground, 11 1/2 x 8" (ILLUS.)......... **$85**

Egg cup, double, Playing Catch patt., red border... **$18**

Geisha Girl Hanging Match Holder

Match holder, Temple B patt., hanging type, red-orange border, unusual divided style, 3 5/8 x 5" (ILLUS.) **$65**

Mustard jar w/lid & spoon, Lunchtime patt., blue-green border, marked "Made in Japan" **$30**

Geisha Girl Temple A Perfume Bottle

Perfume bottle, Temple A patt., multicolor border, R K Nippon mark, 4 1/2" h. (ILLUS.) **$95**

Small Geisha Girl Pitcher

Pitcher, 4 5/8" h., 7" spout to handle, Gardening patt., ornately molded bottom, swirl fluted body, gold striations & buds over red-orange border, signed in Japanese "Made in Japan by Kato" (ILLUS.)....... **$55**

Geisha Girl Plate

Plate, 7 1/4" d., Parasol patt. variant, dark green border w/unusual raised white enamel detailing **$15**

Plate, 8 1/2" d., Child Reaching for Butterfly patt., red-orange border............................... **$15**

Geisha Girl Music Recital B Plate

Plate, 8 1/2" h., Music Recital B patt., cobalt blue border w/gold lacing (ILLUS.)............... **$28**

Platter, 10" l., Duck Watching A patt., gold border, marked "Made in Japan".................. **$35**

Geisha Girl Ring Tree

Ring tree, Temple B patt., red-orange border w/interior gold lacing, signed "Kutani," 2 3/4" h., 3 1/2" d. (ILLUS.) **$35**

Salt & pepper shakers, Lantern Boy patt., pine green border, 2 3/4" h., pr. **$15**

Two Geisha Girl Fan A Sauce Dishes

Sauce dish, Fan A patt., refined, detailed & unusual underglaze blue, signed in Japanese, 2 5/8" d., 1" h. (ILLUS. of two)............ **$30**

Sugar & creamer, Chinese Coin patt., signed "Terazawa" **$45**

Geisha Girl Carp Sugar Shaker

Sugar shaker, Carp patt., red-orange border, floriate foot w/gold lacing, gold line around neck, gold star on top (ILLUS.)........ **$65**

Geisha Parasol B Pattern Tea Caddy

Tea caddy, cov., Parasol B patt., cobalt blue, scalloped border w/gold, missing interior lid, 4" h. (ILLUS.) **$28**

Teapot, cov., Battledore patt., apple green border.. **$35**

Teapot, cov., Bow B patt. in reserve on floral backdrop, cobalt blue border w/gold striping, gold upper edge & spout rim **$45**

Teapot, cov., Dragonboat patt., red & cobalt blue border w/gold lacing, swirl ribbed body **$40**

Toothpick holder, Carp A patt., three-sided, red border w/interior gold lacing............. **$25**

Tray, dual-handled, Parasol G patt., gold embellished red-orange border w/ornate interior framing, signed in Japanese "Nagoya Mukomatsu sei," 10 x 13 1/4" **$80**

Geisha Gardening Pattern Vase

Vase, 6 3/4" h., Gardening patt., red border w/interior band of gold lacing (ILLUS., previous page) **$28**

Gouda

While tin-enameled earthenware has been made in Gouda, Holland since the early 1600s, the productions of modern factories are attracting increasing collector attention. The art pottery of Gouda is easily recognized by its brightly colored peasant-style decoration, with some types having achieved a cloisonné effect. Pottery workshops located in or near Gouda include Regina, Zenith, Plazuid, Schoonhoven, Arnhem and others. Their wide range of production included utilitarian wares as well as vases, miniatures and large outdoor garden ornaments.

Gouda Pottery Marks

Colorful Gouda Astra Vase

Vase, 7 1/4" h., bulbous ovoid body tapering to a tall slender flaring trumpet neck, decorated in a bold colorful stylized design reminiscent of an Oriental carpet in shades of brick red, yellow, white, dark blue & turquoise blue, marked "Gouda - Holland - Astra" (ILLUS.)........................... **$138**

Gouda Vase with Stylized Flowers

Vase, 7 5/8" h., bulbous ovoid body tapering to a small bulbed neck w/flat rim, bold

simple stylized floral design on a ground consisting of alternating orange & green triangles separated by blue, marked "Archipel Holland" w/other marks (ILLUS.) **$127**

Gouda Vase with Tall Flowering Stems

Vase, 7 7/8" h., footed squatty compressed lower body tapering to a tall gently flaring neck, tall swirling leafy stems w/blue bellflowers up the neck, cobalt blue lower body, marked "Gouda Holland 617/2/278," restored base chip (ILLUS.) **$100-150**

Tall Stylized Floral Gouda Vase

Vase, 12 1/2" h., flaring foot below the sharply flaring body w/a wide rounded shoulder centering a trumpet-form neck, decorated w/bold stylized florals in shades of orange, dark blue & green, marked "Anemoon Holland 23.E - 21," minor glaze bubbling (ILLUS.) **$184**

Grueby

Some fine art pottery was produced by the Grueby Faience and Tile Company, established in Boston in 1891. Choice pieces were created with molded designs on a semi-porcelain body. The ware is marked and often bears the initials of the decorators. The pottery closed in 1907.

GRUEBY

Grueby Pottery Mark

Small Cylindrical Grueby Bowl

Bowl, 3" d., 4 1/4" h., a small footring supporting the deep vertical & slightly uneven sides, wide flat rim, dappled green matte glaze, impressed mark, two pinhead-sized glaze pops (ILLUS.)................ **$805**

Wide Shallow Blue Grueby Bowl

Bowl, 5 3/8" d., 1 7/8" h., wide low rounded sides & a wide flat molded rim, overall medium-dark blue matte glaze, impressed mark (ILLUS.).............................. **$345**

Yellow & Brown Grueby Candlestick

Candlestick, a wide flat dished base w/low vertical sides, centered by a tapering ringed shaft w/an ovoid socket w/a flattened flared rim, mottled yellow & brown matte glaze, circular tulip-style insignia, No. 227, glazed-over chip at top rim, 5 3/8" h. (ILLUS.) **$460**

Plaque, rectangular, architectural-type, carved & modeled w/a family of elephants in black against a bluish grey ground, mounted in a black box frame, two firing lines in body, restoration to one, small chip to one corner, stamped mark, 14 x 23" (ILLUS., bottom of page)
.... **$9,775**

Large Grueby Plaque with Elephant Family

Grueby Tile with White Rabbit & Shrub

Tile, square, a large white rabbit crouched behind a small stylized leafy shrub in white, both outlined in dark blue against a pale blue ground, impressed tulip-style mark, burst glaze bubbles, some small edge nicks, 3 7/8" w. (ILLUS.).................... **$690**

Grueby Vase with Broad Green Leaves

Vase, 5 1/2" h., 4 1/2" d., bulbous ovoid body w/a wide rolled rim, crisply tooled w/broad leaves up the sides, covered in a leathery dark green glaze, some high-point nicks, circular mark (ILLUS.) **$2,875**

Yellow Grueby Vase with Buds & Leaves

Vase, 6 1/4" h., squatty bulbous form w/a wide flat mouth, molded around the shoulder w/seven flower buds alternating w/seven wide leaves down the sides, mottled matte yellow glaze, unmarked, restoration to center of base, ca. 1908 (ILLUS.)... **$5,288**

Green Grueby Leaves & Buds Vase

Vase, 7 1/2" h., 4 1/2" d., ovoid body taper-ing to a wide gently flaring neck, tooled & applied w/rounded leaves around the low-er half w/four buds up the sides, medium matte green glaze, small nick to one leaf edge, mark obscured by glaze (ILLUS.)... **$2,875**

Rare Large Grueby Vase with Leaves

Vase, 12 1/2" h., 8 1/4" d., rare large form w/bulbous body centered by a flaring cy-lindrical neck, tooled & applied w/large

wide pointed overlapping leaves, fine organic matte green glaze, couple of very
minor edge nicks, by Marie Seaman,
stamped round mark (ILLUS.) **$11,500**

Hall China

*Founded in 1903 in East Liverpool, Ohio, this
still-operating company at first produced mostly
utilitarian wares. It was in 1911 that Robert T.
Hall, son of the company founder, developed a
special single-fire, lead-free glaze that proved to
be strong, hard and nonporous. In the 1920s the
firm became well known for its extensive line of
teapots (still a major product), and in 1932 it
introduced kitchenwares, followed by dinnerwares in 1936 and refrigerator wares in 1938.*

*The imaginative designs and wide range of
glaze colors and decal decorations have led to the
growing appeal of Hall wares with collectors,
especially people who like Art Deco and Art Moderne design. One of the firm's most famous patterns was the "Autumn Leaf" line, produced as
premiums for the Jewel Tea Company. For listings of this ware see "Jewel Tea Autumn Leaf."*

*Helpful books on Hall include The Collector's
Guide to Hall China by Margaret & Kenn Whit-
myer, and Superior Quality Hall China - A Guide
for Collectors by Harvey Duke (An ELO Book,
1977).*

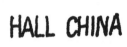

HALL CHINA **(HALL)**

MADE IN U.S.A.

Hall Marks

Baker, French Fluted shape, Silhouette
patt. $30
Baker, French Fluted shape, Yellow Rose
patt. $25

Five Band Batter Bowl

Batter bowl, Five Band shape, Chinese
Red (ILLUS.) $95
Batter jug, Sundial shape, Blue Garden
patt. $250
Bean pot, cov., New England shape, No.
488 patt. $275
Bean pot, cov., one handle, orange $55

Pert Shape Bean Pot

Bean pot, cov., Sani-Grid (Pert) shape, Chi-
nese Red (ILLUS.) $100
Bean pot, cov., tab-handled, Sani-Grid
(Pert) shape, Rose Parade patt. $115
Bowl, 6" d., Medallion shape, Silhouette
patt. $23
Bowl, 6" d., Radiance shape, No. 4, Crocus
patt. $25

Casserole with Chrome Base

Casserole, cov., Art Deco w/chrome reticulated handled base (ILLUS.) $75
Casserole, cov., Five Band shape, Flamin-
go patt. $75
Casserole, cov., Medallion shape, Silhou-
ette patt. $60
Coffeepot, cov., Drip-O-Lator, Waverly
shape $35
Coffeepot, cov., drip-type, all-china, Jordan
shape, Morning Glory patt. $275

Crocus Pattern Coffeepot

Coffeepot, cov., drip-type, all-china, Kadota shape, Crocus patt. (ILLUS., previous page) $350

Ansel Shape Tricolator Coffeepot

Coffeepot, cov., Tricolator, Ansel shape, yellow art glaze (ILLUS.) $75
Coffeepot, cov., Tricolator, Coffee Queen, Chinese Red $55

Coffee Queen Tricolator Coffeepot

Coffeepot, cov., Tricolator, Coffee Queen, yellow (ILLUS.) $35

Meadow Flower Cookie Jar

Cookie jar, cov., Five Band shape, Meadow Flower patt. (ILLUS.) $325
Cookie jar, cov., Owl, brown glaze $120
Cookie jar, cov., Red Poppy patt. $500
Cookie jar, cov., Sundial shape, Blue Blossom patt. $400

Custard cup, straight-sided, Rose White patt. $25
Custard cup, Thick Rim shape, Meadow Flower patt. $35

Radiance Shape Drip Jar

Drip jar, cov., Radiance shape, Chinese Red (ILLUS.) $60
Drip jar, cov., Thick Rim shape, Royal Rose patt. $25

Fantasy Leftover

Leftover, cov., Zephyr shape, Fantasy patt. (ILLUS.) $225
Mixing bowl, Thick Rim shape, Royal Rose patt., 8 1/2" d. $30
Mug, beverage, Silhouette patt. $60
Mug, flagon shape, Monk patt. $45

Irish Coffee Mug

Mug, Irish coffee, footed, pale yellow, 6" h. (ILLUS.) $15

Hall Ball-type Pitcher

Pitcher, ball shape, No. 3, orchid (ILLUS.) **$85**
Pitcher, ball shape, Royal Rose patt............... **$95**
Pitcher, cov., jug-type, Radiance shape,
No. 4, No. 488 patt.................................... **$195**
Pitcher, jug-type, Doughnut shape, cobalt
blue **$75**

Doughnut-shape Jug-type Pitcher

Pitcher, jug-type, large, Doughnut shape,
Chinese Red (ILLUS.)................................ **$135**
Pitcher, jug-type, Loop-handle, Blue Blos-
som patt. **$195**
Salt & pepper shakers, Medallion line, let-
tuce green, pr. **$85**
Salt & pepper shakers, Novelty Radiance
shape, Orange Poppy patt., pr. **$95**

Pert Salt & Pepper Shakers

Salt & pepper shakers, Sani-Grid (Pert)
shape, Chinese Red, pr. (ILLUS.)............... **$35**

Hall Adele Shape Teapot

Teapot, cov., Adele shape, Art Deco style,
Olive Green (ILLUS.) **$200**
Teapot, cov., Airflow shape, Chinese Red..... **$130**
Teapot, cov., Airflow shape, Cobalt Blue
w/gold trim, 6-cup..................................... **$100**
Teapot, cov., Aladdin shape, Cobalt Blue
w/gold trim, 6-cup..................................... **$125**

Hall Automobile Shape Teapot

Teapot, cov., Automobile shape, Chinese
Red (ILLUS.)... **$800**
Teapot, cov., Baltimore shape, Ivory Gold
Label line.. **$125**
Teapot, cov., Basket shape, Cadet Blue
w/platinum decoration **$150**

Basket Shape Chinese Red Teapot

Teapot, cov., Basket shape, Chinese Red
(ILLUS.)... **$300**
Teapot, cov., Basket shape, Warm Yellow **$175**
Teapot, cov., Basketball shape, Cobalt Blue
.... **$600**

Birdcage Teapot with "Gold Special" Decoration

Teapot, cov., Birdcage shape, Canary Yellow w/"Gold Special" decoration (ILLUS.) .. **$500**

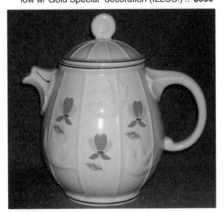

Special Birdcage Autumn Leaf Hall Teapot

Teapot, cov., Birdcage shape, Jewel Tea Autumn Leaf patt., specially produced for the Autumn Leaf Club in 1995 (ILLUS.) **$150**
Teapot, cov., Boston shape, Cobalt Blue w/gold Trailing Aster design, 6-cup **$150**
Teapot, cov., Bowknot shape, Victorian line, Pink **$50**
Teapot, cov., Cleveland shape, Warm Yellow... **$60**
Teapot, cov., Connie shape, Victorian line, Green, 6-cup **$45**
Teapot, cov., Cube shape, Emerald Green.... **$100**

Hall Cube Teapot in Green

Teapot, cov., Cube shape, short squared body w/overall green glaze, marked "The Cube" w/listing of design & patent numbers, licensed by Cube Teapots, Ltd., Leicester, England, ca. 1930s, East Liverpool, Ohio (ILLUS.) **$50**

Hall Reissued Donut Shape Teapot

Teapot, cov., Donut shape, Autumn Leaf patt., 1993 reissue (ILLUS.) **$150**
Teapot, cov., Donut shape, Chinese Red...... **$500**

Rare Orange Poppy Pattern Donut Shape Teapot

Teapot, cov., Donut shape, Orange Poppy patt. (ILLUS.)... **$450**

Commemorative Hall Donut Teapot

Teapot, cov., Donut shape, part of a limited edition produced for the East Liverpool High School Alumni Assoc., No. 2 of 16, 1997 (ILLUS.)... **$100**

Hall Cameo Rose Pattern Teapot on E-Shape Dinnerware Body

Teapot, cov., E-Shape Dinnerware, Cameo Rose patt. (ILLUS.) **$75**

Teapot, cov., Flare-Ware line, Gold Lace design... **$60**

Football Commemorative Teapot

Teapot, cov., Football shape, commemorative, "Hall 200 Haul, East Liverpool, Ohio" Ivory (ILLUS.) **$125**

Hall White French Shape 1-Cup Teapot

Teapot, cov., French shape, white, 1-cup size (ILLUS.) **$50**

Hall Globe No-Drip Pink Teapot

Teapot, cov., Globe No-Drip patt., dark pink w/standard gold decoration (ILLUS.) **$90**

Teapot, cov., Lipton Tea shape, Light Yellow... **$60**

Mustard Yellow Lipton Tea Shape Teapot

Teapot, cov., Lipton Tea shape, Mustard Yellow (ILLUS.)... **$40**

Los Angeles Teapot in Cobalt

Teapot, cov., Los Angeles shape, Cobalt Blue w/Standard Gold trim (ILLUS.)............. **$75**

Hall "McCormick Teahouse" Teapot

Teapot, cov., "McCormick Teahouse" design, upright rectangular cottage-form w/color transfer-printed design of an early English teahouse, 1985 (ILLUS.) **$75**

Miniature Hall China Aladdin Teapot

Teapot, cov., miniature, Aladdin shape, light blue glaze, unmarked, overall 7" l., 5" h. (ILLUS.).. **$15**

Moderne Teapot in Marine Blue

Teapot, cov., Moderne shape, Marine Blue (ILLUS.).. **$85**
Teapot, cov., New York shape, Red Poppy patt. **$125-150**
Teapot, cov., New York shape, Wild Poppy patt., 4-cup **$320-355**
Teapot, cov., Plume shape, Victorian line, Pink **$40**
Teapot, cov., Rhythm shape, Cobalt Blue...... **$180**

Rutherford Ribbed Chinese Red Teapot

Teapot, cov., Rutherford shape, ribbed, Chinese Red (ILLUS.) **$250**
Teapot, cov., Star shape, Cobalt Blue **$145**
Teapot, cov., Star shape, Cobalt Blue w/Standard Gold decoration **$125**

Tea-for-Two Teapot in Pink & Gold

Teapot, cov., Tea-for-Two shape, Pink w/gold decoration (ILLUS.)........................ **$150**
Teapot, cov., Tea-for-Two shape, Stock Brown w/gold decoration........................... **$100**
Teapot, cov., Thorley series, Apple shape, Black w/gold decoration **$95**
Vase, bud, No. 631 1/2, maroon....................... **$15**
Vase, bud, No. 641, canary yellow.................. **$10**

Blue Garden Water Bottle

Water bottle, cov., refrigerator ware line, Zephyr shape, Blue Garden patt. (ILLUS.).. **$650**

Hampshire Pottery

Hampshire Pottery was made in Keene, New Hampshire, where several potteries operated as far back as the late 18th century. The pottery now known as Hampshire Pottery was established by J.S. Taft shortly after 1870. Various types of wares, including Art Pottery, were produced through the years. Taft's brother-in-law, Cadmon Robertson, joined the firm in 1904 and was responsible for developing more than 900 glaze formulas while in charge of all manufacturing. His death in 1914 created problems for the firm, and Taft sold out to George Morton in 1916. Closed during part of World War I, the pottery was later reopened by Morton for a short time and manufactured white hotel china. From 1919 to 1921, mosaic floor tiles became the main production. All production ceased in 1923.

Hampshire Marks

Low Squatty Hampshire Bowl

Bowl, 2 1/4" h., wide flattened cushion-form body w/slightly raised flat mouth, molded around the top w/alternating knobs & swastikas under a mottled dark green glaze, short, tight rim line, impressed mark (ILLUS.).. **$207**

Green Melon-shaped Hampshire Pitcher

Pitcher, 8" h., bulbous ovoid melon shaped w/large leaves forming the neck & pointed spout, vine handle, overall green matte glaze, unmarked (ILLUS.) **$288**

Hampshire Vase with Streaky Glaze

Vase, 7 1/4" h., very slightly swelling cylindrical body w/a low wide ringed neck, overall mottled & streaky dark blue & pink matte drip glaze, designed by Cadmon Robertson, company logo, Shape No. 106, some grinding chips around the base (ILLUS.) **$690**

Bulbous Bluish Green Hampshire Vase

Vase, 4" h., 5" d., wide bulbous shape w/a wide short flat-rimmed neck, overall fine bluish green feathered glaze, marked (ILLUS.) **$558**

Peacock-glazed Hampshire Vase

Vase, 7 1/2" h., very slightly swelling cylindrical body w/a lightly molded wave-like band just below the low wide ringed neck, overall two-tone "peacock" glaze, designed by Cadmon Robertson, company logo, Shape No. 105 (ILLUS.) **$690**

Hampshire Vase with Brownish Glaze

Vase, 6 1/4" h., bulbous ovoid body w/a wide tapering neck, overall brownish grey matte glaze, marked (ILLUS.) **$441**

Fine Hampshire Vase with Leathery Glaze

Vase, 8 3/4" h., 9 3/4" d., very wide squatty bulbous shaped w/a rounded shoulder centering a short wide neck w/flat rim,

fine leathery green & blue matte glaze,
incised mark (ILLUS.)............................ **$2,703**

Harker Pottery

Harker Pottery was in business for more than 100 years (1840-1972) in the East Liverpool area of eastern Ohio. One of the oldest potteries in Ohio, it advertised itself as one of the oldest in America. The pottery produced numerous lines that are favorites of collectors.

Some of their most popular lines were intended for oven to table use and were marked with BAKERITE, COLUMBIA BAKERITE, HOTOVEN, OVENWARE, Bungalow Ware, Cameo Ware, White Rose Carv-Kraft (for Montgomery War) and Harkerware Stone China / Stone Ware brand names.

Harker also made Reproduction Rockingham, Royal Gadroon, Pate sur Pate, Windsong, and many souvenir items and a line designed by Russel Wright that have gained popularity with collectors.

Like many pottery manufacturers, Harker reused popular decal patterns on several ware shapes. Harker was marketed under more than 200 backstamps in its history.

Advertising, Novelty & Souvenir Pieces

Harker Advertising Ashtray

Ashtray, advertising Fontainebleau Hotel, dark blue glaze w/white lettering (ILLUS.)
.... **$8-12**
Ashtrays, w/advertising, each..................... **$5-10**

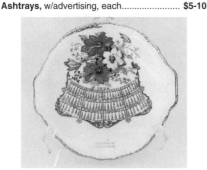

Harker 1929 Calendar Plate

Calendar plates, 1907 to 1930, later dates of lower value, each (ILLUS. of 1929 plate) **$25-35**

Souvenir plates, 6" d., 1890-1930, each ... **$20-50**
Souvenir plates, 6" to 10", 1950-1972, each **$5-20**
Tea tile, eight-sided.................................. **$25-75**
Tea tile, "Townsend Plan"........................ **$3-50**

Autumn Leaf

Harker made some Autumn Leaf for Jewel Tea before Hall China received the exclusive contract. The ware and decal are somewhat finer than that used by Hall China. Although some Autumn Leaf was unmarked, most was produced under the Columbia Chinaware (Statue of Liberty in color) trademark. Generally, prices for Harker Autumn Leaf are relatively high.

Cake plate, Virginia shape.................... **$200-250**
Casserole, cov... **$75-100**
Creamer, Empress shape...................... **$175-225**
Tumbler, handled.................................... **$150-200**

BakeRite, HotOven

Harker was one of the first American potteries to produce pottery that could go from the oven to the table. Most of this ware, made from the late 1920s to the late 1950s, features brightly colored decals that are popular with collectors today. Prices can vary widely, depending upon the decal pattern. Among the most popular designs are Countryside, Ruffled Tulip, Mallow, Red Apple, Silhouette, Jewel Weed, Carnivale, Crayon Apple, Whistling Teapots, Amy, Fire in the Fireplace, Lisa, Oriental Poppy, Ivy, Petit Point, and Pastel Posies. We will list examples of some of these patterns here.

Ivy Pattern

Grease jar, cov., D'Ware shape (ILLUS. left with other Ivy pieces, top next page) **$20-30**
Pie baker (ILLUS. second from right with other Ivy pattern pieces, top next page)
.... **$12-20**
Pitcher, jug-type, round (ILLUS. right with other Ivy pieces, top next page) **$4**
Plate, 10" d., dinner, plain round (ILLUS. second from left other Ivy pieces, top next page)... **$5-10**
Spoon, serving (ILLUS. center with other Ivy pieces, top next page)...................... **$15-20**

Mallow Pattern

Creamer, cov., paneled Ohio jug shape (ILLUS. top right with other Mallow pieces)... **$35-45**

Harker Mallow Pattern Pieces

Harker Ivy Pattern Pieces

Custard cup (ILLUS. top left with other Mallow pieces, previous page)....................... **$8-12**

Mixing bowl, 9" d. (ILLUS. bottom right with other Mallow pattern pieces, previous page)...................... **$25-30**

Mixing bowl, 9" d., w/rim spout (ILLUS. bottom left other Mallow pattern pieces, previous page)............................ **$25-35**

Modern Age/Modern Tulip

This shape was created to celebrate Harker's 100 year anniversary. Hollowware pieces had surface etching on the body of the pieces resembling arrow shafts and fletchings (feathers) and with lids having the distinctive "Life-Saver" finials. This shape was manufactured with many decal patterns, including Red Apple, Tulip Bouquet, Silhouette, Cactus, Emmy, Shadow Rose, Southern Rose, Petit Point, English Ivy, Calico (Gingham), Tulip and Modern Tulip, to name a few.

Bowl, utility, 4" d., Zephyr shape (ILLUS. middle row, second from left)...................... **$3-5**

Bowl, utility, 5" d............................. **$4-8**

Cake plate **$12-18**

Cookie jar, cov. (ILLUS. bottom row).......... **$20-30**

Creamer (ILLUS. top row center, next column)... **$3-5**

Custard cup, individual, Zephyr shape (ILLUS. second row, second from right, next column) **$4-6**

Pie baker (ILLUS. top right, left, next column).. **$18-24**

Modern Age/Modern Tulip Pieces

Pitcher, cov., square, jug-type (ILLUS. top row, right, next column)........................... **$35-40**

Plate, 6" d., plain round (ILLUS. middle row, far right).. **$2-4**

Rolling pin, 14 3/4" l. (ILLUS., bottom of page).. **$50-75**

Sugar bowl, cov.. **$8-12**

Petit Point Pattern

Batter set: two covered Ohio Jugs, lifter & Virginia utility plate; the set **$80-110**

Modern Tulip Rolling Pin

Various Petit Point Pattern Pieces

Bean pot, individual (ILLUS. top row, center front with other Petit Point pieces, top of page) **$5-8**

Bowl, utility, 4" **$10-15**

Bowls, utility, 3" to 5" d., nesting-type, Zephyr shape, each (ILLUS. of 3" d. size, bottom, second from left with other Petit Point pieces, top of page) **$10-15**

Bowls, mixing, 10" to 12" d., nesting-type, Zephyr shape, each (ILLUS. of 10" bowl, bottom row center with other Petit Point pieces, top of page) **$20-40**

Butter dish, cov., 1 lb. **$50-60**

Cake/cheese plate, round **$20-25**

Casserole, cov. (ILLUS. top row, far left with other Petit Point pieces, top of page) **$30-40**

Cheese bowl, cov., Zephyr shape **$30-40**

Coffeepot, ball finial on cover **$50-60**

Cookie jar, cov., Modern Age shape **$40-50**

Cookie jar, cov., round................................ **$35-45**

Cup & saucer, plain round **$10-15**

Custard cup, individual................................. **$4-6**

Custard cup set: six cups in a rack; the set **$50-60**

Grease/drips jar, cov., D'Ware shape........ **$15-20**

Grease/drips jar, cov., Skyscraper shape **$15-20**

Mixing bowl, w/pouring lip, 10" d............... **$40-50**

Ohio jug, cov., pitcher-shaped, paneled shape, medium...................................... **$35-45**

Pie baker **$15-25**

Pitcher, cov., jug-shape, Hi-rise shape, Gem Clay Forming Company -NOTE: No "Skyscraper" shape in pitchers or teapots. **$40-50**

Pitcher, jug-shape, square body **$40-50**

Plate, 6" d., plain round **$3-5**

Plate, 8" d., plain round **$4-6**

Plate, 10" d., dinner, plain round (ILLUS. middle row, right with other Petit Point pieces)... **$5-8**

Salad fork, (ILLUS. bottom row, front right with other Petit Point pieces)................... **$12-18**

Salt & pepper shakers, Skyscraper shape, 4 1/2" h., pr. (ILLUS., top next column)... **$20-25**

Scoop **$60-75**

Petit Point Hi-Rise Shape Shakers

Teapot, ball finial on cover.......................... **$35-45**

Trivet (tea tile), octagonal, (ILLUS. top row, center back, with other Petit Point pieces, top of page)... **$25-35**

Utility plate, Virginia shape, 12" w. **$15-20**

Red Apple I & Red Apple II Patterns

Red Apple I is the continuous (multiple fruits, Harker advertised as "Orchard Pattern") decal and Red Apple II (advertised as "Colorful Fruit") is the large decal.

Bowl, utility, 4" d., Red Apple I patt., Zephyr shape (ILLUS. front row, second from left with other Red Apple pieces)................. **$10-15**

Various Red Apple Pieces

Casserole, ball finial on cover, Red Apple I patt., Zephyr shape (ILLUS. far right with other Red Apple pieces) **$30-40**

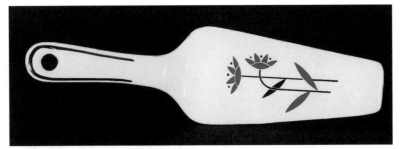

Red Deco Dahlia Pattern Lifter

Red Apple II Swirl Shape Plate

Plate, 7" d., Red Apple II patt., Shell shape (ILLUS.) **$10-15**

Plate, 10" d., dinner, plain round, Red Apple II patt. (ILLUS. second from left with other Red Apple pieces) **$10-15**

Salt & pepper shakers, Red Apple II patt., Skyscraper shape, pr. **$20-25**

Teapot, cov., Red Apple II patt., Zephyr shape (ILLUS. far left with other Red Apple pieces) **$50**

Other Patterns

Bean pot, Calico Tulip patt. **$8-12**

Harker Monterey Cup & Saucer

Cup & saucer, Monterey patt. (ILLUS.) **$12-18**

Lifter, cake or pie, Red Deco Dahlia patt., 9" l. (ILLUS., top of page) **$15-20**

Ohio jug, cov., paneled pitcher-shape, Silhouette patt., medium **$35-45**

Pitcher, cov., jug-type, Red Deco Dahlia patt., Hi-Rise style, GC shape **$45-60**

Utility plate, Calico Tulip patt., Virginia shape, 12" w. **$12-20**

Cameoware

This process was used by Bennett Pottery in Baltimore and when Bennett closed in 1936, the patent holder brought the process to Harker. Harker made Cameoware from about 1940-1948 in the Dainty Flower pattern with its design etched through to the white body. This is Harker's most widely collected pattern. The heaviest production was in blue with pink the next most popular color. Harker also made Dainty Flower in yellow, teal, gray, pumpkin, chartreuse and black but in much smaller quantities. These latter colors are the most rare and command the highest prices which greatly exceed those for blue and pink pieces.

About 1950 Harker made the "White Rose Carv-Kraft" pattern (in blue and pink) exclusively for Montgomery Ward. Though not as common as "Dainty Flower," "White Rose" has its own devoted fans.

Cameoware Pieces

Ashtray, Dainty Flower patt., blue, Modern Age shape (ILLUS. far left with other Dainty Flower & Pear pattern pieces) **$18-24**

Berry set: square serving bowl & six small dishes; Dainty Flower patt., blue, the set **$35-50**

Harker Cameoware Collection

A Variety of Dainty Flower Pieces

Bowl, 5" sq., berry or fruit, Dainty Flower patt., blue (ILLUS. top, far right with other blue Dainty Flower pieces).......................... **$5-8**

Bowl, 7" sq., cereal, Dainty Flower patt., blue **$10-12**

Bowl, 8" sq., soup, Dainty Flower patt., blue (ILLUS. bottom with other blue Dainty Flower pieces).. **$10-18**

Bowl,, 9 1/2" d., Pear patt., Shell shape, blue (ILLUS. front center with ashtray).... **$20-30**

Casserole, cover w/ball finial, Dainty Flower patt., blue **$20-30**

Coffeepot, cov., Dainty Flower patt., blue.. **$50-60**

Coffeepot, cov., Dainty Flower patt., pink... **$50-60**

Cookie jar, cov., Dainty Flower patt., Zephyr shape, blue (ILLUS. far right with Dainty Flower ashtray)..................................... **$35-45**

Creamer, round, Dainty Flower patt., blue, Shell shape **$10-15**

Cup & saucer, Dainty Flower patt., blue, Shell shape **$5-10**

Cup & saucer demitasse, Dainty Flower patt., blue **$12-18**

Cup & saucer demitasse, Dainty Flower patt., pink.. **$25-35**

Custard cup, Dainty Flower patt., blue or pink, each.. **$3-5**

Fork or spoon, serving-type, Dainty Flower patt., blue or pink, each........................... **$12-18**

Gravy boat, Dainty Flower patt., blue or pink, each.. **$10-15**

Grease/drips jar, cov., Dainty Flower patt., D'Ware shape, blue or pink.................... **$25-35**

Grease/drips jar, cov., Dainty Flower patt., Skyscraper shape, blue or pink , each.... **$20-25**

Hot water baby feeder, metal reservoir, various animal designs, blue or pink, each **$60-75**

Lifter, pie or cake, Dainty Flower patt., blue or pink, each **$12-19**

Mixing bowl, 9"-12" d., nesting-type, Dainty Flower patt., blue or pink, each.............. **$25-45**

Pitcher, cov., jug-type, Dainty Flower patt., Hi-Rise style, GC shape, blue................ **$50-70**

Pitcher, cov., jug-type, Dainty Flower patt., Round Body shape, blue........................ **$35-45**

Pitcher, cov., jug-type, White Rose patt., Carv-Kraft line, Round Body shape, blue **$40-50**

Pitcher, jug-type, Dainty Flower patt., Round Body shape, yellow (ILLUS. second from left with various colored Cameoware collection, top of page)................ **$50-75**

Pitcher, jug-type, Dainty Flower patt., Square Body shape, blue........................ **$35-45**

Pitcher, jug-type, Dainty Flower patt., Square Body shape, pink........................ **$50-75**

Plate, 6" d., Swirl shape **$5-8**

Plate, 6" sq., Dainty Flower, blue (ILLUS. top row, far left with other blue Dainty Flower pieces, top of page)........................ **$2-4**

Plate, 7" d., Dainty Flower patt., Shell shape, blue (ILLUS. back row, left with blue Dainty Flower ashtray, previous column)... **$3-5**

Plate, 7" sq., Dainty Flower patt., blue or pink, each.. **$4-6**

Plate, 9" sq., Dainty Flower patt., blue or pink, each.. **$4-6**

Platter, 12" l., rectangular, Dainty Flower patt., Virginia shape, pink (ILLUS. second from right with various colored Cameoware collection, top of page) **$25**

Platter, 14" l., oval, plain, Dainty Flower patt., blue or pink, each........................... **$25-35**

Rolling pin, Dainty Flower patt., blue or pink, each.. **$60-75**

Salt & pepper shakers, Dainty Flower patt., D'Ware shape, teal, pr. (ILLUS. far right with various colored Cameoware collection, top of page)..................................... **$50-60**

Salt & pepper shakers, Dainty Flower patt., D'Ware shape, yellow, pr. (ILLUS. left with various colored Cameoware collection, top previous page)............................ **$30-40**

Salt & pepper shakers, Dainty Flower patt., Modern Age shape, blue or pink, pr. **$8-12**

Salt & pepper shakers, Dainty Flower patt., Skyscraper shape, blue, pr. (ILLUS. top row, center front with other blue Dainty Flower pieces, previous page) **$15-20**

Sugar bowl, cov., square, tab handles, Dainty Flower patt., blue **$10-15**

Sugar bowl, cov., square, tab handles, Dainty Flower patt., pink.......................... **$20-25**

Sugar bowl, cover w/ball finial, round, Dainty Flower patt., Shell shape, blue.............. **$8-12**

Teapot, cov., Dainty Flower patt., blue....... **$35-45**

Teapot, cov., Dainty Flower patt., pink....... **$40-50**

Trivet (tea tile), Dainty Flower patt., blue **$15-25**

Trivet (tea tile), Dainty Flower patt., pink **$20-25**

Utility plate, square, Virginia shape........... **$15-20**

Vegetable bowl, 9" sq., Dainty Flower patt., blue **$12-15**

Vegetable dish, cov., tab handles, Dainty Flower patt., blue.................................... **$40-50**

Vegetable dish, cov., tab handles, Dainty Flower patt., pink.................................... **$50-60**

Children's Ware

Harker's Kiddo sets came in pink and blue with etched classic designs. The mugs had a toy soldier and a circus elephant on either side. Plates might have a duck with an umbrella, a bear with a ballon or a goat on a pull cart, facing either right or left. Related bowls might have a kitten or what looks like an early Donald Duck. Hot water feeder baby dishes were made with cavorting lambs, double ducks, bunny butts and baby ducks, all of which were made in blue or pink. Harker also made demitasse-style cups & saucers with baby ducks in both colors, though these are more rare.

Bowl, various animal designs, blue or pink, each **$20-25**

Hot water baby feeder, ceramic reservoir, various animal designs, blue or pink, each **$40-50**

Mug from Kiddo Set

Mug, elephant & toy soldier decorations, pink, 3" h. (ILLUS. of elephant side) **$12-15**

Child's Mug & Plate

Mug, toy soldier decoration, blue, 3" h. (ILLUS. front with plate) **$12-15**

Plate, Teddy bear w/balloon decoration, blue (ILLUS. w/toy soldier mug)............. **$20-30**

Gadroon and Royal Gadroon

This shape, with its distintive scalloped edge, was extremely popular and was produced in several glaze colors, with the classic Chesterton grey and Corinthian green (which commands slightly higher prices) presenting an especially elegant table setting. Pate sur pate, though frequently used, is only one of several marks found on this ware. The Royal Gadroon shape was also decorated with numerous colorful decals, including Bridal Rose, Shadow Rose, Royal Rose, Wild Rose, Currier & Ives, Godey, Game Birds, Morning Glories, Violets and White Thistle (silk screened on yellow and pink glazed ware).

Gadroon

Bowl, berry or fruit.. **$2-4**

Harker Chesterton Collection

Bowl, cereal/soup, lug handles (ILLUS. middle right with Chesterton collection) **$3-5**

Cake set: 10" lug-handled cake plate, six dessert plates & lifter; 8 pcs................... **$25-35**

Creamer (ILLUS. front right with Chesterton collection)... **$4-8**

Cup & saucer (ILLUS. middle left with Chesterton collection) **$7-10**

Harker Royal Gadroon Pieces

Fork, serving **$10-15**
Gravy boat (ILLUS. middle row, center with
Chesterton collection, previous page)......... **$5-8**
Gravy underplate (relish/pickle dish), ... **$3-5**
Lifter, cake or pie **$10-15**
Luncheon set: 7" sq. plate w/cup ring &
matching cup; 2 pcs. **$8-12**
Plate, 7" sq., salad (ILLUS. rear right with
Chesterton collection, previous page)......... **$3-5**
Plate, 9" d., dinner (ILLUS. left rear with
Chesterton collection, previous page)......... **$4-6**
Platter, 12" l., oval..................................... **$10-12**
Platter, 13" l., oval..................................... **$10-12**
Salt & pepper shakers, pr............................ **$4-8**
Soup plate, flat rim..................................... **$6-9**
Spoon, serving.. **$8-12**
Sugar bowl, cov. (ILLUS. front left with
Chesterton collection) **$5-8**
Teapot, cov. **$30-40**
Vegetable dish, cover w/lug handles.......... **$10-15**

Royal Gadroon
Bowl, 4 1/2" d., berry or fruit, Cortland
(a.k.a. St. John's Wort) patt. (ILLUS.
middle row, center, with other Royal Ga-
droon pieces, top of page) **$4-6**
Cake plate, Old Rose (a.k.a.Wild Rose)
patt., 10" d. (ILLUS. bottom row, left with
Royal Gadroon pieces, top of page) **$8-10**
Cake set: 9" or 10" d. cake plate w/six 6" d.
matching serving plates & cake lifter;
Currier & Ives patt., 8 pcs....................... **$25-45**
Plate, 6" d., luncheon, Bermuda patt.
(ILLUS. top row, right with other Royal
Gadroon pieces, top of page).................... **$3-5**
Plate, 6" d., luncheon, Pheasants patt.
(ILLUS. middle row, right with other Roy-
al Gadroon pieces, top of page)................. **$3-5**

Plate, 9" d., dinner, Magnolia patt., w/gray
band (ILLUS. top row, center with other
Royal Gadroon pieces, top of page) **$5-8**
Plate, 9" d., dinner, Violets patt. (ILLUS. top
row, left with other Royal Gadroon piec-
es, top of page)....................................... **$8-10**
Platter, 15" l., oval, Vintage (Grapes) patt.
(ILLUS. middle row, left with other Royal
Gadroon pieces, top of page) **$35-50**
Rolling pin, depending on the decal & scar-
city can vary greatly in price................. **$35-150**
Teapot, cov., Ivy Vine patt. (ILLUS. bottom
row, right with other Royal Gadroon piec-
es, top of page)....................................... **$35-45**

Royal Gadroon (decal decorations)
Bowl, cereal/soup, lug handles, Vintage
patt. (ILLUS. bottom row, center with
Royal Gadroon pieces, top of page) **$5-10**

Later Intaglios
*This is the technical name for the process used
to make Cameo and more modern patterns in the
1960s and 1970s. Although highly popular during their time and quite plentiful on the market
today, these patterns are not generally in high
demand and prices reflect this. Colors include
celadon green, blue, yellow, orange, black and
pink cocoa. Some patterns that command higher
prices include Brown-Eyed Susan and Wild Rice
(in blue, gray & salmon). Modern Intaglio pattern
names include Cock 0' Morn, Rooster, Coronet,
Star-Life, Sun-Glo, Everglades, Rose on Cameo
Blue, Mosaic, Patio, Country Cousins, Provincial,
Petite Fleurs, White Daisy, Spring Time, Snow
Leaf, Bamboo, Fruit, Wheat, Vintage I & II (a.k.a.
Grapes), Orchard, Daisy Lane, Viking, Rocaille,
Alpine, Fern, Lotus, Ivy Wreath, Spanish Gold,
Acorns, Wreath and Russel Wright White Clover.*

Creamer & sugar bowl, pr. **$8-20**
Cup & saucer **$4-8**
Plate, dinner... **$3-10**
Platter 11" or 13"....................................... **$10-20**

Reproduction Rockingham
*Harker Reproduction Rockingham was made
in the early 1960s. This line included hound-handled pitchers (the only pieces actually made in the
mid-19th century), hound-handled mugs, Jolly
Roger jugs*, Daniel Boone jugs*, ashtrays, Armed
Forces logo plates and ashtrays, soap dishes, candleholders (for rhw hound-handled mugs),
tobacco leaf candy dish/ashtrays, Rebecca at the
Well teapots, tidbit trays, Give Us This Day Our
Daily Bread plates, octagonal trivets, a 7 1/2" h.
bald eagle figure, 6" l. skillet spoon holders
(unmarked), Jolly Roger pipes (extremely rare),
and even a rolling pin (only found to date).
Colors included brown, gold (honey brown), and
bottle green and a light creamy brown trivets and
soap dishes have also turned up. Because some
pieces have a date of "1840" and are not marked
as reproductions, some confusion has resulted,
but modern pieces should not confuse anyone
familiar with mid-19th century wares and their
glazes.*

**(Harker called this "jugs" but they were really
mugs.)*

Ashtray (candy dish), model of a leaf, brown $12-18

Ashtray (candy dish), model of a leaf, honey brown or bottle green, each............... $20-30

Bread tray, bottle green $30-40

Bread tray, brown $15-20

Bread tray, honey brown (gold) $20-25

Jug (mug), figural Daniel Boone head, bottle green $30-40

Jug (mug), figural Daniel Boone head, brown $18-24

Jug (mug), figural Daniel Boone head, honey brown.. $18-24

Jug (mug), figural Jolly Roger head, bottle green $25-35

Jug (mug), figural Jolly Roger head, brown $18-24

Jug (mug), figural Jolly Roger head, honey brown $20-30

Mug, figural hound handle, bottle green...... $25-35

Mug, figural hound handle, brown $15-20

Mug, figural hound handle, honey brown $20-30

Pitcher, jug-type w/figural hound handle, bottle green $65-80

Hound-handled Pitcher

Pitcher, jug-type w/figural hound handle, brown (ILLUS.) $35-40

Pitcher, jug-type w/figural hound handle, honey brown.. $50-60

Plate, relief-molded American eagle (Great Seal of the U.S.), brown $5-8

Plate, relief-molded American eagle (Great Seal of the U.S.), honey brown or bottle green, each $18-24

Stone China

This heavy ware, with its solid pink, blue, white or yellow glazes over a gray body, was manufacturered in the 1960s and 1970s. The glaze was mixed with tiny metallic chips, which many collectors call "Oatmeal." Later Harker created hand-decorated designs using the intaglio process to create several designs such as Seafare, Peacock Alley, MacIntosh and Acorns, to name a few.

Values listed here are for pieces in any of the four solid colors.

Bowl, 5" or 6" round, each $3-5

Bowl, 7" or 8" round, each $8-12

Butter dish, cov. $18-24

Casserole, cov.. $20-30

Coffeepot, cov., jug-style.......................... $30-40

Cookie jar, cov... $30-50

Creamer, ... $5-8

Cruet set: two handled jugs w/covers;, "O" for oil & "V" for vinegar, pr...................... $20-30

Cup & saucer $3-5

Pitcher with stopper lid, jug-type $25-35

Plate, 8" d... $2-4

Platter, 11" oval $5-8

Rolling pin $150-200

Tidbit tray, three-tier................................. $15-25

Tahiti

This labor intensive and hand-decorated line has gained popularity with collectors in recent years.

Tahiti Ashtray and Shakers

Ashtray, w/metal stand (ILLUS. right with Tahiti salt & pepper shakers) $15-20

Creamer, ... $10-12

Plate, 10" d.. $7-10

Plate, 6" d... $6-10

Salt & pepper shakers, pr. (ILLUS. left w/Tahiti ashtray)..................................... $18-24

Sugar bowl, cov... $15-20

Woodsong

Another latecomer to the Harker line, this unique ware was impressed with maple leaves and made in honey brown (gold), bottle green, grey, and white.

Coffeepot, cov., jug-style, 10" h. $25-40

Harker Woodsong Divided Dish

Dish, divided, 12" l. (ILLUS.)....................... $35-45

Teapot, cov., 9" l. $75-90

Teapots- Miscellaneous

Pink Dainty Flower Teapot

Teapot, cov., Pink Dainty Flower patt., cylindrical body tapering in at shoulder, angled handle, serpentine spout, stepped base, pink w/cream-colored stylized floral design on body, cream finial on lid & line decoration on rim, part of Cameoware line, ca. 1935 (ILLUS.) **$40**

Harker Teapot in Pink Luster

Teapot, cov., Pink Luster patt., spherical body w/C-form handle & short serpentine spout, metallic lustre glaze in pink w/black highlights on rim, finial & lid, ca. 1900 (ILLUS.) **$40**

Harker's Rebecca at the Well Rockingham Reproduction Teapot

Teapot, cov., Rebecca at the Well patt., cylindrical body tapering in at shoulder, short foot & neck, domed inset lid w/turned finial, C-scroll handle w/thumbrest, turned serpentine spout, brown body embossed w/scene of Rebecca at the Well, part of Harker's line of Rockingham reproductions, the date of 1840 on bottom referring to the year Harker Pottery opened, ca. 1960 (ILLUS.) **$40**

Harker Red Apple Pattern Teapot

Teapot, cov., Red Apple patt., Zephyr shape, cylindrical body, angled handle, serpentine spout, stepped base, a horizontal band of decoration just below shoulder consisting of red apples & yellow pears w/green leaves & blue shading, red highlights on rim, lid, finial & spout, oven-to-table ware, ca. 1930 (ILLUS.) **$45**

Tulip Bouquet Teapot by Harker

Teapot, cov., Tulip Bouquet patt., Royal Gadroon shape, squatty lobed bulbous body w/piecrust rim, short foot, ribbed C-scroll handle & slightly serpentine spout, the conforming lid w/applied scroll loop handle, the body, spout & lid decorated w/small flowers in shades of turquoise, pink, blue, purple & orange w/green leaves on white ground, ca. 1940 (ILLUS.) **$20**

Vintage Pattern Teapot on Royal Gadroon Shape

Teapot, cov., Vintage patt., Royal Gadroon shape, squatty lobed bulbous body w/piecrust rim, short foot, ribbed C-scroll handle & slightly serpentine spout, the conforming lid w/applied scroll loop handle, the body & lid decorated w/horizontal bands of entwined grapevines w/purple fruit, the finial, spout & handle accented w/green line decoration, ca. 1940 (ILLUS.) **$25**

Haviland

Haviland porcelain was originated by Americans in Limoges, France, shortly before the mid-19th century and continues in production. Some Haviland was made by Theodore Haviland in the United States during the last World War. Numerous other factories also made china in Limoges. Also see LIMOGES.

Haviland Marks

Ashtray, rectangular, white w/gold Embassy eagle, 3 x 5"... $45
Baker, oblong open bowl shape, unglazed bottom, Schleiger 33, Blank 19................... $85
Basket, mixed floral decoration w/blue trim, Blank No. 1130, 5 x 7 1/2"...................... $154
Beaner, open, oval, Schleiger 876, 3 1/2 x 5"... $45
Bonbon plate, w/three dividers, h.p., H & Co, 9 1/2" d.. $175
Bone dish, Schleiger 72, decorated w/roses & green flowers............................ $30
Bone dishes, No. 146 patt., Blank No. 133, set of 4.. $100
Bouillon cup & saucer, Drop Rose patt., Schleiger 55C, pale pink............................ $125
Bouillon cup & saucer, Ranson blank, Schleiger 42A, flared shape decorated w/pink roses.. $50
Bouillon cups & saucers, No. 72 patt., Blank No. 22, ten sets............................. $550
Bouillon w/saucer, cov., Marseilles blank, decorated w/blue flowers, H & Co............... $75
Bowl, 9 1/2" d., soup, cobalt & gold w/floral center, Theodore Haviland.................... $125
Bowl, 10" d., 3" h., salad, Schleiger 19, Silver Anniversary.. $225
Bowl, 8 3/8 x 10 3/8", 3 1/2" h., Christmas Rose patt., Blank No. 418...................... $425
Broth bowl & underplate, No. 448, 2 pcs..... $110
Butter dish, cov., No. 133 patt....................... $145
Butter dish, cov., No. 271A patt., Blank No. 213.. $145

Butter pat, Schleiger 271A, decorated w/blue flowers & pink roses, 3"................... $25
Cake plate, square, CFH/GDM, decorated w/spray of yellow wildflowers, 9" sq........... $85
Cake plate, handled, 87C patt., Blank No. 2, 10 1/2" d.. $125
Cake plate, handled, No. 1 Ranson blank, patt. No. 228, 10 3/4" d.............................. $95
Cake plate, handled, No. 72 patt., Blank No. 22.. $175
Cake plate, handled, Ranson blank No. 1..... $125
Candleholders, Swirl patt., decorated w/dainty roses, pr................................... $135
Candlesticks, Marseille blank, h.p. floral decoration, 6 3/4" h., pr........................... $275
Celery tray, Schleiger 150, Harrison Rose, decorated w/small pink roses, 12" l. $125
Celery tray, Baltimore Rose patt., Blank No. 207, 5 5/8 x 12".. $275
Celery tray, Blank No. 305, titled "Her Majesty," 13" l. $145
Cereal, Schleiger 57A, Ranson blank, decorated w/pink roses & blue scrolls, 6 x 2" $32
Cheese dish w/underplate, CFH/GDM, straight sides, high dome w/flat top, small hole in top near handle, decorated w/blue flowers & gold trim..................................... $250
Chocolate cup & saucer, No. 72A................. $45
Chocolate pot, Autumn Leaf patt., 9" h........ $325
Chocolate pot, cov., scallop & scroll mold w/floral decoration & gold trim, marked "Haviland Limoges, France," 9" h. $275
Chocolate set: cov. pot & eight cups & saucers; decorated w/pink & blue flowers w/green stems, Blank No. 1, the set......... $650
Chocolate set: cov. pot & eight cups & saucers; Schleiger 235B, decorated w/pink & green flowers & gold trim........................ $750
Chocolate set: tall tapering pot & six tall cups & saucers; Albany patt., white w/narrow floral rim bands & gold trim, late 19th - early 20th c., the set (ILLUS., bottom of page)..................................... $450-650
Coffee set: cov. coffeepot, creamer, sugar bowl & twelve cups & saucers; Ranson blank No. 1, the set................................... $950
Coffeepot, cov., demitasse, Osier, Blank No. 211, impressed "Haviland & Co. - Limoges - France" & English mark $195

Haviland Albany Pattern Chocolate Set

Coffeepot, cov., Old Wedding Ring patt.,
white w/gold trim, Old H & Co $225
Coffeepot, cov., Paradise, blue edge
w/decoration of birds, Theodore Havi-
land, 8" h... $225
Coffeepot, cov., Schleiger 98, Cloverleaf,
9" h... $450
Coffeepot, cov., Sylvia patt., 1950s.............. $225
Comport, divided, shell-shaped, white
w/green trim, full-bodied red lobster at
center, non-factory decor of red, green &
black.. $450

Footed Comport with Reticulated Rim

Comport, pedestal on three feet w/ornate
gold shell design, top w/reticulated edge,
peach & gold design around base & top,
9" d. (ILLUS.) $595
Comport, round, English, shaped like regu-
lar pedestal comport without pedestal,
Schleiger 56 variation, decorated w/lav-
ender flowers, 9" d. $125
Comport, Meadow Visitors patt., smooth
blank, 5 1/8" h., 9 7/8" d. $225
Cracker jar, cov., floral decoration, cobalt,
gold & blue bells, 1900 & decorator's
marks $550
Cracker jar, cov., Marseille blank $450
Cream soup w/underplate, Schleiger 31,
Ranson blank, decorated w/pink roses,
5" d. bowl, 2 pcs....................................... $55
Creamer, Schleiger 146, commonly known
as Apple Blossom, Theodore Haviland,
4"... $60
Creamer, Moss Rose patt., gold trim,
5 1/2" h. $50
Creamer & open sugar, dessert, Cloverleaf
patt., Schleiger 98, pr. $145
Creamer & open sugar, Ranson blank,
Drop Rose patt., w/very ornate gold trim,
pr. $695
Creamer & sugar, Schleiger 223A, Blank 1,
decorated w/pink flowers, pr. $125
Creamer & sugar bowl, Mont Mery
patt., ca. 1953, pr. $125
Cup & saucer, coffee, Schleiger 39D, dec-
orated w/pink roses & gold trim................... $55
Cup & saucer, demitasse, Arcadia, bird
patt. $45
Cup & saucer, tea, Schleiger 19, white
w/gold trim.. $45
Cup & saucer, breakfast, Moss Rose patt.
w/gold trim... $55

Cup & saucer, demitasse, Papillon Butterfly
patt., floral by Pallandre $75
Cup & saucer, Moss Rose patt., "Haviland
& Co. - Limoges - France" $45
Cup & saucer, Rosalinde patt. $45

Meadow Visitors Cup & Saucer

Cups & saucers, Papillon butterfly handles
w/Meadow Visitors decoration, six sets
(ILLUS. of one set).................................... $900
Cuspidor, smooth blank, bands of roses
decorating rim & body, 6 1/2" h.................. $350
Cuspidor, Moss Rose patt., smooth blank,
8" d., 3 1/4" h. $450
Dessert set: 8 1/2 x 15" tray & four 7 1/4"
dishes; Osier Blank No. 637, fruit & floral
decoration, the set $325
Dessert set: 9 x 15" oblong tray w/twelve 7"
square matching plates; centers decorated w/Meadow Visitors patt. & bordered in
rich cobalt blue w/gold trim, commis-
sioned for Mrs. Wm. A. Wilson, 13 pcs. ... $2,000

Haviland Dinnerware in Blank No. 5

Dinner service: service for eight w/five-
piece place settings & additional bowls,
pitcher, gravy boat & other pieces; mostly Blank No. 5 w/delicate pink floral decoration, late 19th - early 20th c., 54 pcs.
(ILLUS. of part)........................... $1,000-1,200

*Haviland Dinner Service in the
Albany Pattern*

Dinner service: twelve 8-piece place settings w/additional open & cov. vegetable

dishes & oval platter; Albany patt., white w/narrow floral rim bands & gold trim, late 19th - early 20th c., the set (ILLUS.) **$800-1,000**

Haviland Scenic Dish

Dish, shell-shaped, incurved rim opposite pointed rim, h.p. scene of artist's waterside studio, decorated by Theodore Davis, front initialed "D," back w/presidential seal & artist's signature, part of Hayes presidential service, 8 x 9 1/2" (ILLUS.) **$2,000**
Dresser tray, h.p. floral decoration, 1892 mark **$125**
Egg cup, footed, No. 69 patt. on blank No. 1 .... **$65**
Egg cups, footed, No. 72 patt., Blank No. 22, pr. **$150**
Fish set: 23" l. platter & six 9" d. plates; each w/different fish scene, dark orange & gold borders, Blank No. 1009, 7 pcs.... **$1,250**

Plate from Fish Set

Fish set: 22" l. oval platter & twelve 8 1/2" d. plates; each piece w/a different fish in the center, the border in two shades of green design w/gold trim, h.p. scenes by L. Martin, mark of Theodore Haviland, 13 pcs. (ILLUS. of plate) **$2,750**
Fish set: 23 1/4" l. platter & twelve 7 3/8" plates; Empress Eugenie patt., No. 453, Blank No. 7, 13 pcs. **$3,500**
Gravy boat, No. 761 .... **$95**

Gravy boat w/attached underplate, No. 98 patt., Blank No. 24 .... **$145**
Gravy boat w/attached underplate, Schleiger 46, Ranson blank, decorated w/pink & blue flowers **$125**

Haviland Hair Receiver

Hair receiver, cov., squatty round body on three gold feet, h.p. overall w/small flowers in blues & greens w/gold trim, mark of Charles Field Haviland (ILLUS.) **$150**
Honey dish, 4" d., bowl-form, Schleiger 33, decorated w/white flowers, pink shading **$25**
Ice cream set: tray & 6 individual plates; Old Pansy patt. on Torse blank, 7 pcs. **$395**
Jam jar w/underplate, cov., Christmas Rose patt. **$795**
Jam jar w/underplate, cov., No. 577 patt., smooth blank.. **$325**
Match box, gold trim, 1882 & decorator's marks **$175**

Haviland Mayonnaise

Mayonnaise bowl w/attached underplate, decorated w/pink wild roses touched w/yellow, Schleiger 141D, 5" d. (ILLUS.) **$145**
Mayonnaise bowl w/underplate, leaf-shaped, Blank No. 271A **$175**
Muffin server, No. 31 patt., Blank No. 24...... **$275**
Mustache cup & saucer, No. 270A patt., Blank No. 16 .... **$225**
Mustard pot, cov., No. 266 patt. on Blank No. 9 .... **$225**
Mustard pot w/attached underplate, cov., CFH/GDM, copper color w/gold floral design overall, cov. w/spoon slot, 2 1/2 x 4" .. **$225**
Nut dish, footed, No. 1070A patt. **$55**
Olive dish, No. 257 patt................................... **$85**
Oyster plate, Ranson blank, Schleiger 42A, decorated w/pink roses **$175**

Haviland Oyster Plate

Oyster plate, six clam-shaped sections w/round center section for sauce, white, 8" d. (ILLUS.) **$175**

Oyster plate, The Princess patt., Schleiger 57C, 9 1/2" d. **$195**

Oyster plates, four-well, all white w/relief-molded scrolled design, 7 1/2" d., pr. **$250**

Oyster plates, five-well, 72C patt., Blank No. 17, center indent for sauce, 9" d., pr. .. **$450**

Oyster scoop, oyster-shaped, CFH/GDM, h.p., 1 3/4 x 2 1/5" **$65**

Oyster tureen, Henri II Blank, decorated by Dammouse **$850**

Pancake server, decorated w/yellow flowers w/pale green stems, smooth blank, 1892 & decorator marks **$165**

Pickle dish, shell-shaped w/gold trim, leaf mold, 8 3/4" l. **$65**

Pin box, cov., oblong, ornate scrolled base & rim, loop finial on h.p. floral decorated lid, marked "H & Co. L. France," 4" l. **$175**

Pin tray, rectangular, open handles, decorated w/pink roses, Blank 1, Schleiger 251, 3 x 5" **$125**

Pitcher, syrup-type, Schleiger 144, decorated w/pink roses & green scrolls **$145**

Pitcher, 7" h., milk, Schleiger 98, Blank 12, Cloverleaf patt. **$195**

Pitcher, 7" h., milk-type, tankard style w/tapering cylindrical white body w/a large relief-molded anchor under the heavy rope-twist loop handle, bright gold trim, old Haviland & Co. mark (ILLUS.) **$1,165**

Pitcher, 8 3/8" h., Ivy patt. w/gold trim **$175**

Pitcher, 8 5/8" h., Art Deco stylized figural "Farewell" cat in yellow & white, base inscribed "Theodore Haviland Limoges/France Copyright Depose" & "E.M. Sandoz sc" **$1,250**

Pitcher, 8 5/8" h., Ranson blank No. 1 .... **$250**

Haviland Lemonade Pitcher

Pitcher, 9" h., lemonade-type, Schleiger 1026B variation, Blank 117, decorated w/lavender flowers & brushed gold trim, Theodore Haviland (ILLUS.) **$250**

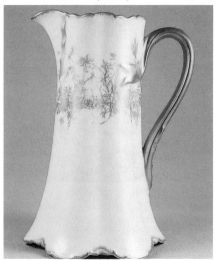

Gold-decorated Lemonade Pitcher

Pitcher, 9" h., tankard-shaped lemonade-type, Ranson blank, delicate floral band around the upper body trimmed in gold,

Pitcher with Anchor in Relief

gold handle & trim bands, factory-decorated, Haviland & Co. mark (ILLUS.).......... $250

Pitcher, 9 1/2" h., No. 279 patt., Blank No. 643 .... $225

Place setting: dinner, salad, bread & butter plates, cup & saucer; w/scalloped double gold edge, Schleiger 91A $135

Plate, dinner, No. 72.......... $40

Plate, dinner, No. 9 patt., set of 10 .... $300

Plate, dinner, Rosalinde patt. $32

Plate, Partridge in a Pear Tree from 12 Days of Christmas series, 1970 .... $75

Plate, ice cream, 5" l., leaf-shaped w/handle, cobalt & gold.......... $125

Paisley Pattern Plate

Plate, bread & butter, 6 1/2" d., Paisley patt., smooth blanks w/gold edge, brownish red ground w/flowers in yellow, bright blue, green & white border design w/yellow flowers & bright blue leaves, turquoise scroll trim, Haviland & Co. mark (ILLUS.).......... $26

Plate, bread & butter, 6 1/2" d., Schleiger 340, decorated w/pink roses & blue scrolls $28

Plate, coupe salad, 7 1/2" d., Baltimore Rose patt, Blank No. 207, set of 8 .... $600

Plate, 8 1/2" d., cobalt & gold Pallandre patt. .. $175

Plate with Draped Pink Roses

Plate, luncheon, 8 1/2" d., smooth edge, design on border of draped pink roses, Schleiger 152, Theodore Haviland (ILLUS.) $28

Plate, 7 1/2 x 8 1/2", heart-shaped, Baltimore Rose patt. $275

Plate, 9 1/2" d., scalloped edge, cobalt & gold w/floral center.......... $225

Plate, dinner, 9 1/2" d., Dammouse antique rose w/gold medallion & flowers $180

Plate, dinner, 9 1/2" d., Feu de Four, Poppy & Seeds $125

Plate, dinner, 9 1/2" d., Schleiger 19, Silver Anniversary.......... $35

Plate, dinner, 9 1/2" d., Schleiger 29-K, decorated w/pink flowers & gold trim $40

Plate, 9 3/4" d., portrait of woman in forest scene, artist-signed, Blank No. 116 .... $125

Plate, dinner, 10" d., Schleiger 150, known as Harrison Rose, decorated w/small pink & yellow roses $30

Plate, 10 1/2" d., service, Blank 20, white w/gold trim.......... $45

Plate, chop, 11 1/4" d., 33A patt., Blank No. 19.......... $125

Plate, chop, 12" d., Schleiger 233, The Norma, decorated w/small pink & yellow flowers.......... $125

Plates, luncheon, 8 3/8" d., Club Ware, Meadow Visitors patt. & various fruits, set of 8.......... $280

Platter, 16" l., rectangular, Marseilles, Schleiger 9.......... $125

Platter, 12 1/4 x 18" oval, Moss Rose patt. w/blue trim, smooth blank $150

Platter, 14 x 20", Ranson blank No. 1.......... $275

Pudding set, Schleiger 24, white w/gold trim, complete w/unglazed insert & undertray.......... $475

Punch bowl, Baltimore Rose patt.......... $2,000

Punch cup, tapering scalloped pedestal foot supporting wide shallow cup bowl, decorated w/flowers in shades of green w/some pink flowers & green leaves, variation of Schleiger No. 249B on Blank 17, Haviland & Co. mark, 4" h.......... $75

Ramekins & underplates, Ranson Blank No. 1, set of 12.......... $540

Relish, oval, Schleiger 570, two-tone green flowers, gold edge, 8" l.......... $45

Salad plate, bean-shaped, variation of Schleiger 1190, decorated w/orange flowers & gold trim, 4 1/2 x 9" $95

Salt, CFH/GDM, h.p. flowers, 1 1/2 x 3/4".......... $45

Salt, Schleiger 31, decorated w/pink roses & gold trim, 2 x 1".......... $65

Sauce tureen w/attached underplate, cov., No. 146 patt., Blank No. 133, 7" d. underplate, bowl 5 1/4" d. $145

Sauce tureen w/attached undertray, cov., oval, Schleiger 619, green design w/gold trim, Theodore Haviland.......... $145

Double-spouted Sauceboat & Tray

Sauceboat & undertray, footed double-spouted boat-shaped sauceboat w/looped side handles w/molded rope trim, matching dished undertray, heavy gold trim on white, old Haviland & Co. mark, 2 pcs. (ILLUS., previous page)......... **$150**

Serving bowl, Schleiger 235B, 12" d., 2" h. .. **$195**

Multifloral Serving Dish

Serving dish, quatrefoil form, Multifloral patt., Old H & Co, 9" sq., 2" h. (ILLUS.) **$125**

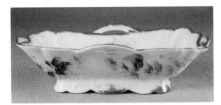

Haviland Serving Dish with Poppies

Serving dish, scalloped rectangular form w/a scalloped foot ring below the flaring side w/low open side handles, decorated w/pale yellowish green to dark green poppies & pale pink shadows, gold trim, variation of Schleiger No. 665, Haviland & Co. mark, 8 x 10" (ILLUS.)...................... **$225**

Serving plate, blue & burgundy Art Deco decoration, black ground, "Haviland & Co. - Limoges - France," 10 1/2" d. **$95**

Sipper dishes, Meadow Visitors patt., smooth blank, 4 3/4" d., set of 8................. **$176**

Sorbet, footed, w/gold embossed trim, Schleiger 276 .... **$65**

Soup bowls, No. 271A patt., Blank No. 213, set of 8 .... **$280**

Soup plate w/flanged rim, No. 761................. **$35**

Soup tureen, cov., pink Drop Rose patt., on Blank No. 22.. **$895**

Soup tureen, round, Ranson blank, Schleiger 29M, decorated w/tiny blue flowers.. **$350**

Sugar bowl, cov., large cylindrical form w/small loop side handles & inset flat cover w/arched handle, white ground decorated w/sprays of pink daisies touched w/yellow & greyish brown leaves, variation of Schleiger No. 1311, 1 lb. size, Charles Field Haviland, marked "CFH/GDM" (ILLUS., top next column) **$75**

Haviland Covered Sugar Bowl

Tea caddy, cov., Ranson blank **$325**

Tea set: cov. teapot, creamer & sugar bowl; floral & leaf mold w/gold trim, 3 pcs. **$450**

Tea set: small cov. teapot, creamer & sugar bowl, six cups & saucers; No. 19 patt., 15 pcs. **$700**

Tea & toast set: scalloped plate & cup; Marseilles blank, decorated w/pink roses, H & Co **$175**

Tea & toast tray & cup, No. 482 patt., Blank No. 208, pr. **$275**

Tea tray, round, Schleiger 29A, decorated w/pink flowers, unglazed bottom, 16" d. **$275**

Butterfly-handled Cup and Saucer

Teacup & saucer, cup w/tapering cylindrical bowl & figural butterfly handle, h.p. grey band design on rim & border, Haviland & Co. (ILLUS.)................................... **$125**

Teapot, cov., 4-cup, CFG/GDM, white w/gold, ribbon handle................................ **$225**

Teapot, cov., Henri II blank w/gold & silver decoration **$275**

Squatty Haviland Porcelain Teapot

Teapot, cov., wide squatty bulbous tapering sides w/a flat rim, low domed cover w/arched finial, upright serpentine spout & C-scroll handle, white w/gold trim & thin

yellow leaftip bands around the rim &
cover, double Haviland mark, ca. 1900
(ILLUS.).. **$75**

Toothbrush box, cov., Moss Rose patt.
w/gold trim, smooth blank, ca. 1860s-
70s, 8" l. **$225**

Vases, 15" h., Terra Cotta, brown w/white
water lily & large green leaves in relief,
Haviland & Co, pr..................................... **$4,500**

Vegetable dish, oval, Schleiger 142A, decorated w/pink daisy-like flowers, blue
fences & scrolls, gold trim, Theodore
Haviland, 8 x 10"...................................... **$85**

Vegetable dish, cov., Marseille patt., Blank
No. 9, 9 1/2" l. **$145**

Vegetable dish, cov., decorated w/small orange roses, Blank No. 24, 10" d. **$145**

Wash pitcher, Moss Rose patt. w/gold trim,
smooth blank, 12" h. **$350**

Waste bowl, Schleiger 233A, The Norma,
decorated w/tiny pink & yellow flowers &
gold daubs, 5 x 3" **$47**

Head Vase Planters

*Head Vase Planters were most popular and
most abundant during the 1950s. Whereas some
could be found prior to this period, the majority
were Japanese imports and a direct product of
Japan's postwar industrial boom. Sizes, shapes,
styles and quality varied according to importer.
American manufacturers did produce some head
vase planters during this time, but high quality
standards and production costs made it hard to
compete with the less expensive imports.*

Ardalt, No. 6039, Madonna w/both hands
holding roses, pastel coloring in glossy
bisque, planter, paper label, 6" h. **$30**

Ardco, No. C1248, high bouffant hair, dark
green dress, earrings, necklace, paper
label, 5 1/2" h. **$75**

"Lita" Head Vase

Betty Lou Nichols, "Lita," redheaded woman in black off-the-shoulder dress w/red-
orange flowers, wide-brimmed black hat,
eyes closed, rare, 8" h. (ILLUS.) **$850**

Betty Lou Nichols, "Mary Lou," woman
w/brown hair wearing grey dress w/brown
crisscross ribbon at throat, brimmed hat
matches ribbon color, closed eyes, 8" h.
(ILLUS., top next column) **$600**

Betty Lou Nichols Head Vase

"Mary Lou" Head Vase

Betty Lou Nichols, "Mary Lou," woman
w/dark hair wearing blue & white plaid
dress w/fancy ruffled high-button shawl
collar, w/white-brimmed hat w/hat band in
matching blue & white plaid, 8" h. (ILLUS.)
.... **$650**

Brinn, No. TP2071, molded blonde hair,
painted eyes, earrings, right hand near
face, 6" h. **$125**

California Pastels Head Vase

California Pastels, Kaye No. 601, woman in flowered off-the-shoulder grey, pink, black & yellow dress & turban-style blue, yellow, green & pink hat w/big pink rose at front, 10 1/2" h. (ILLUS., previous page) **$300**

Inarco, King w/full grey beard, red, yellow & black w/gold trim, 4 3/4" h. (small base flake) **$100**

"Mitzie Gaynor" Head Vase Planter

Inarco, No. 2968, "Mitzie Gaynor," woman wearing white flower in upswept hair, posed w/hand under chin, 6 3/4" h. (ILLUS.) **$750**

Woman with Heart Necklace

Inarco, No. 5626, blonde w/red bow in hair & red fingernails, wearing heart necklace and pearl earrings, posed w/hand touching lips, 7" h. (ILLUS.) **$1,800**

Inarco, No. E1062, head turned to the right, gold clasps on black gown, earrings, necklace, closed eyes w/big lashes, paper label & stamp, 1963, 5 1/4" h. **$125**

Inarco, No. E1062, ringlet hair, earrings, closed eyes w/big lashes, black gloved right hand holding gilt decorated fan under right cheek, paper label & stamp, 1963, 6" h. **$225**

Inarco, No. E1611, closed eyes w/big lashes, earrings, gold painted bracelet, left hand under face on right, 1964, 5 1/2" h. **$600**

Inarco, No. E1756, "Lady Aileen," gold & green tiara & matching painted necklace, paper label, 5 1/2" h. **$275**

Inarco, No. E1852, Jackie Kennedy wearing black dress & glove w/hand to cheek, paper label, 6" h. **$350**

Inarco, No. E193/M, applied pink rose in hair, light green dress, earrings, necklace, right hand on cheek, closed eyes w/big lashes, 1961, 5 1/2" h. **$100**

Inarco, No. E2254, black dress, pearl finish on hair, earrings, necklace, closed eyes w/big lashes, paper label, 6" h. **$100**

Inarco, No. E2322, black dress, black open-edged hat w/white ribbon, gloved hand by right cheek, earrings, necklace, paper label, 7 1/4" h. **$250**

Inarco, No. E2523, child w/blue scarf & dress, pigtails, painted eyes, high gloss, stamped, 5 1/2" h. **$70**

Inarco, No. E2735, soldier boy w/bayonet, closed eyes, stamped, 5 3/4" h. **$55**

Inarco, No. E5624, pink hat & blue dress, earrings, painted eyes, paper label & stamp, 5 1/2" h. **$200**

Inarco, No. E779, applied blonde hair & peach rose, peach dress, earrings, necklace, right hand by cheek, paper label & stamp, 1962, 6" h. **$125**

Inarco, No. E969/S, mint green hat & dress, painted closed eyes w/big lashes, 1963, 4 1/2" h. **$65**

Doll-like Head Vase

Japan, doll-like form dressed like Russian peasant w/babushka, red, blue & green, 8 1/4" h. (ILLUS.) **$100**

Japan, No. 2261, black dress w/white collar, black bow in blonde hair, painted eyes, earrings, glazed finish, 7" h. **$275**

Japan, woman w/platinum blonde hair w/black bow, wearing black ribbon choker w/white flower around neck, eyes closed, rare, 5 1/2" h. (ILLUS., next page) **$550**

Lefton, No. 1086, white iridescent blouse, necklace, paper label, 6" h. **$150**

Lefton, No. 1343A, applied flowers on large brimmed hat & collar, painted features, raised right hand, paper label, glossy finish, 6" h. **$105**

Head Vase Made in Japan

Lefton, No. 2536, flower in hair, painted earrings & necklace, gloved right hand under chin, 5 1/4" h. **$80**

Lefton, No. 2796, blue blouse, blue sash on head, paper label, 6" h. **$100**

Lefton, No. 2796, pink blouse, pink sash on head, paper label, 6" h. **$100**

Lefton, No. 4596, green hat, scarf & coat, earrings, painted eyes, black gloved hand under cheek, partial Lefton's label, 5 1/2" h. **$95**

Lefton, No. 611B, Lefton paper label & Geo. Z. Lefton stamp, bird on pink floral hat, high collar, closed painted eyes, glossy finish, 6 1/4" h. **$70**

Manchu, Ceramic Arts Studio of Madison, Wisconsin, 7 1/2" h. **$150**

Napco, No. A5120, large pink hat, fur-trimmed pink dress w/blue daisy, closed eyes w/big lashes, paper label, 5" h. **$75**

Napco, No. A5120, orange bonnet w/bow & matching lace-trimmed dress, paper label, 5 1/4" h. **$80**

Napco, No. C1775A, green striped hat w/bow on top right, jeweled green dress, hand by cheek, big lashes, stamped, 1956, 7 1/4" h. .. **$150**

Napco, No. C2589A, wearing black dress & feather hat, gold painted earring, closed eyes w/big lashes, right hand under right side of chin, bracelet, paper label & stamp, 1956, 5" h. **$65**

Napco, No. C2632C, large lavender hat w/dark trim, matching lavender dress, hand to hat, earring in exposed ear, 7" h. .. **$165**

Napco, No. C2633C, black hat & dress, gold dots on white hat bow, earrings, necklace, closed eyes w/big lashes, 1956, 5 1/2" h. **$85**

Napco, No. C2634B, baby w/white bonnet, paper label, 5 1/2" h. **$55**

Napco, No. C2636B, flat white hat w/gold trim, dark green dress, left hand under chin, earrings, necklace, closed eyes w/big lashes, paper label, 1956, 6" h. **$125**

Napco, No. C2637C, white round flat hat, black dress, hand under left cheek, painted eyes, earrings, necklace, paper label & stamp, 1956, 7" h. **$225**

Napco, No. C2638C, earrings, painted eyes, molded necklace, stamped, 1956, 6" h. **$100**

Napco, No. C3205B, wearing crown of gold & white flowers, necklace, paper label, 5 1/2" h. **$80**

Napco, No. C3815, gold & white trim on blue hat, blue high collar jacket, earrings, closed eyes w/big lashes, paper label, 1959, 5 1/2" h. **$85**

Napco, No. C3959A, blue hat w/bow & high collar blouse, real lashes, earrings, paper label, 5 1/2" h. **$75**

Napco, No. C4556C, child wearing green hat, painted eyes, glossy finish, partial paper label, impressed, 1960, 5 1/4" h. **$75**

Napco, No. CX2707, Christmas girl, green w/red trimmed hat & dress, painted eyes, right hand under cheek, paper label & stamp, 1957, 5 1/2" h. **$85**

Napco, No. CX2708, Christmas girl, holly sprigs in hat, painted cross necklace, gloved right hand away from face, closed eyes w/big lashes, paper label & stamp, 1957, 6" h. **$300**

Napco, No. CX2709A, Christmas child in fur-trimmed hat & coat, holding song book, painted eyes, paper label & stamp, 1957, 3 1/2" h. (worn paint on back near base) **$75**

Napcoware, No. 8494, gold bow in long hair, gold dress w/white collar, left earring, painted eyes, 7 1/4" h. **$225**

Napcoware, No. C6428, three flowers on neck of blue gown, dark gloved hand on left cheek, earrings, closed eyes w/big lashes, stamped mark, 5 1/2" h. **$125**

Napcoware, No. C6429, molded bouffant hair, white floral collar on blue gown, closed eyes w/big lashes, earrings, dark blue glove, hand by cheek, 7" h. **$250**

Napcoware, No. C6985, green dress w/center jewel, closed eyes w/big lashes, earrings, necklace, 8 1/2" h. **$350**

Napcoware, No. C7472, dark blue blouse, necklace & earrings, paper label, 6" h. **$85**

Napcoware, No. C7473, head turned to right, applied floral decoration on right shoulder, earrings, necklace, painted eyes, 7 3/4" h. **$165**

Napcoware, No. C8493, long hair off to right side, gold bow & dress w/white collar, earring in left ear, painted eyes, 6" h. .. **$100**

Relpo, No. 2004, green dress & hair bow, painted eyes, earrings, paper label & stamp, 7" h. **$250**

Relpo, No. 2089, Marilyn, grey bow in hair on right, black halter dress, earrings, painted eyes, open lips, paper label & stamp, 7" h. (chip on top of bow, minor paint wear on chin & left cheek) **$3,000**

Relpo, No. 5634, Christmas girl, hood w/holly, fur-trimmed coat, painted eyes, gloved hand near face, Sampson Import Co., impressed, 1965, 7 1/2" h. **$200**

Relpo, No. K1175M, wearing hat & matching dress, w/hands folded under chin, open eyes, earrings, necklace, 5 1/2" h. **$110**

Relpo, No. K1633, Japan, black dress w/white decoration, gloved right hand touching chin & cheek, earring, necklace, painted eyes, 7" h. **$200**

Relpo, No. K1662, floral molded green & lavender hat & green dress, painted eyes, earrings, necklace, paper label & stamp, 6" h. **$175**

Relpo, No. K1696, wearing green bow in hair & matching top, earrings, necklace, paper label, 5 1/2" h. **$100**

Woman in Green

Relpo, No. K1835, blonde woman in pale green brimmed hat w/darker green bow, in dark green coat w/beige fur-like collar, 7 1/2" h. (ILLUS.) **$425**

Relpo, No. K1836, Japan, white hat w/blue edge & bow, blue dress w/white trim, painted eyes, right earring, 6 1/2" h. **$500**

Relpo, No. K1932, black bows in hair & black high collar dress, earrings, painted eyes, paper label & stamp, 5 1/2" h. **$225**

Rare Head Vase Planter

Royal Crown, blonde in white sundress/swimsuit & black floppy-brimmed hat w/white sunglasses sitting on brim, very rare, 7" h. (ILLUS.) **$2,500**

Ruben, multicolored clown in green & yellow, closed eyes, 5" h. **$35**

Ruben, No. 4123, white ruffled black dress, earrings, necklace, painted eyes, impression & paper label, 7" h. **$75**

Ruben, No. 4129, blonde ponytails, painted eyes, earrings, necklace, paper label, 5 1/2" h.. **$110**

Ruben, No. 4185, braided blonde hair w/flower, green dress w/high white collar, impressed mark, 5 1/2" h. **$110**

Ruben, No. 484, heart-shaped grey hat, necklace, earrings, paper label, 5 3/4" h.... **$150**

Ruben, No. 531, Japan, Lucy in top hat w/horse neck piece, shades of grey, stamped & painted lashes, flake in tie end, 7 1/2" h. **$450**

Rubens, No. 531, Japan, Lucy in top hat w/horse neck piece, yellow & green w/glazed finish, stamped & painted lashes, 7 1/2" h... **$450**

Ucagco, baby dressed in blue bonnet trimmed w/lace & blue bib, paper label, 6" h.. **$45**

"Heads Up" Head Vase Planter

United Design, Abigail 1953 "Heads Up," Cameo Girl series, blonde in pink & white dress & white brimmed hat & gloves, wearing pearl earrings & necklace, holds miniature version of similar design in hand, collector's edition of 500, made for 10th annual Head Vase Convention (ILLUS.)...... **$350**

Commemorative Head Vase Planter

United Design, Judith "Smart Shopper," Cameo Girl series, blonde in leopard print coat, black gloves & black brimmed hat trimmed in white, w/six-sided open box w/miniature head vase inside, limited edition of 500, commemorative piece for the 11th annual Head Vase Convention, 5 3/4" h. (ILLUS.) **$300**

Velco, No. 3688, Japan, pink hair bow & dress, w/hand at cheek, paper label, 5 1/2" h. (missing one earring) **$110**

Velco, No. 3749, white bow on grey hat, black dress, rhinestone earrings, closed eyes w/big lashes, left hand near chin, paper label & stamp, 5 3/4" h. **$125**

Carmen Miranda-style Head Vase

Miscellaneous, stylized black Carmen Miranda-like woman in pink & yellow dress w/fruit, unmarked, 7 3/4" h. (ILLUS.) **$300**

Miscellaneous, woman in off-the-shoulder lime green dress, eyes closed, unmarked, 7 1/2" h. (ILLUS., top next column) **$150**

Woman in Green Dress Head Vase

Historical & Commemorative Wares

Numerous potteries, especially in England and the United States, made various porcelain and earthenware pieces to commemorate people, places and events. Scarce English historical wares with American views command highest prices. Objects are listed here alphabetically by title of the view.

Most pieces listed here will date between about 1820 and 1850. The maker's name is noted at the end of the entry.

Almshouse, Boston tureen & cover, flowers within medallions border, dark blue, footed deep ovoid body w/wide angled rim, domed cover & scroll end handles, Ridgway, 12 3/4" l., 9 1/2" h. (two hairlines in base, chip on inside edge of cover) **$3,300**

Almshouse, New York platter, vine border, dark blue, Ridgway, 16 1/2" l. **$1,100-1,200**

Mayer, ca. 1830, 17 1/8" l. (ILLUS., bottom of page) **$5,600**

Arms of Delaware Platter

Group of Historical Cups Plates & a Toddy Plate

Arms of Delaware platter, trumpet flower & vine border, dark blue, Thomas **Arms of Rhode Island plate,** flowers & vines border, dark blue, T. Mayer, minor glaze scratches, 8 1/2" d. **$750-775**

Baltimore & Ohio Railroad, level (The) plate, shell border, dark blue, E. Wood, 10 1/8" d. (stains, minor roughness on table ring) **$990**

Battle of Bunker Hill platter, vine border, dark blue, R. Stevenson, 10 1/4 x 13" **$8,625**

Scarce Boston Mails Wash Set

Boston Mails wash set: 13 1/4" d. wash bowl (under rim chips & crack), 12" pitcher (base chip), 6" h. chamber pot & cover (base crack), 7 1/4" l. toothbrush box base; black scenes of the gentleman's or ladies' cabins, J. & T. Edwards, the set (ILLUS.) **$920**

Boston State House basket & undertray, flowers & leaves border, basket w/reticulated sides & scalloped flaring rim, dark blue, J. Rogers, basket 6 1/2 x 9 1/4", the set (hairline cracks) **$2,760**

Boston State House dish, flowers & leaves on flanged rim, deep sides, dark blue, J. Rogers, 12 3/4" d. (minor glaze scratches) **$2,070**

Boston State House pitcher, Rose Border series, fully opened roses w/leaves border, dark blue, Stubbs, 6" h. (small chip on handle) **$978**

Boston State House sauce tureen, cover & undertray, flowers & leaves border, pedestal base w/upward looped handles, high domed cover, dark blue, J. Rogers, tureen 7 1/4 x 8 1/4", the set **$3,738**

Cadmus Historical Cup Plate

Cadmus (so-called) cup plate, trefoil border, dark blue, Wood, tiny spot of glaze wear on rim, 3 11/16" d. (ILLUS.) **$275**

Cadmus (so-called) plate, shell border, irregular center, dark blue, Wood, 10" d. (light scratches) **$500-600**

Capitol, Washington (The) serving bowl, vine border, embossed white rim, dark blue, Stevenson, 11" d. (glaze imperfections) **$2,645**

Castle Garden, Battery, New York cup plate, trefoil separated by knobs border, dark blue, 3 3/4" d., E. Wood (ILLUS. bottom row right with other cup plates, top of previous page) **$303**

Christianburg Danish Settlement on the Gold Coast, Africa platter, shell border, well-and-tree center, dark blue, E. Wood, 18 3/4" l. (minor glaze imperfections)...... **$3,220**

City Hall, New York plate, flowers within medallions border, medium blue, J. & W. Ridgway, 9 3/4" d. **$150-200**

City Hotel, New York plate, oak leaf border, double portrait reserves at border of Washington & Lafayette, inset view of the Entrance to the Erie Canal, dark blue, R. Stevenson, 8 1/2" d. (minor scratching) **$4,600**

Columbia College, New York plate, acorn & oak leaves border, portrait medallion at rim of "President Washington," inset of "View of the Aqueduct Bridge at Rochester," dark blue, R. Stevenson, 7 1/2" d. (minor scratches) **$8,625**

Commodore MacDonnough's Victory plate, shell border, dark blue, E. Wood, 8 3/8" d. **$350-375**

Commodore MacDonnough's Victory tea set, shell border, dark blue, cov. teapot, cov. sugar bowl & creamer, E. Wood, teapot 7 1/2 x 11", the set **$1,275-1,325**

Court House, Baltimore plate, fruit & flowers border, dark blue, Henshall, Williamson & Co., 8 1/2" d. (light wear, hairline) ... **$470**

Dam & Water Works (The), Philadelphia (Sidewheel Steamboat) plate, fruit & flowers border, dark blue, Henshall, Williamson & Co., 9 7/8" d. **$646**

Dix Cove on the Gold Coast, Africa soup tureen, cov., dark blue, shell border, irregular center, pedestal base, loop end handles, E. Wood, 11 x 15" (interior staining)... **$4,888**

Doctor Syntax Amused with Pat in the Pond platter, flowers & scrolls border, dark blue, E. Wood, 14 1/4 x 19" (glaze scratches, scattered minor staining) **$1,840**

East View of LaGrange, the residence of the Marquis La Fayette plate, dark blue, floral border, E. Wood, 9 1/4" d. **$300-350**

Entrance of the Erie Canal into the Hudson at Albany - View of the Aqueduct Bridge at Little Falls pitcher, floral border, dark blue, E. Wood, excellent condition, 6" h. **$1,500-1,725**

Esplanade and Castle Garden, New York - Almshouse, Boston pitcher, vine border, dark blue, R. Stevenson, 10" h. **$2,300**

Esplanade and Castle Garden, New York platter, vine border, dark blue, R. Stevenson, minor glaze scratches, 14 1/2 x 18 1/2".................................... **$5,750**

Franklin (Tomb) cup & saucer, handleless, floral border, dark blue, E. & G. Phillips, Longport **$385**

Pink Historical Staffordshire Teapot

Fulton's Steamboat on the Hudson - Ship Cadmus teapot & cover, the squatty bulbous body w/a serpentine spout & C-scroll handle, white ground transfer-printed in rusty pink w/a scene on each side, the low domed cover & button finial w/further transfer scenes, pink lustre band trim on the rim, handle & spout, Staffordshire, England, ca. 1830-50, restoration to the base, end of spout & cover, 6" h. (ILLUS.) **$303**

Fulton's Steamboat soup plate, floral border, dark blue, unknown maker, 10 1/4" d. (minor scratches & rim chips) **$875-900**

Harper's Ferry, U.S. platter, flowers, shells & scrolls border, scalloped rim, red, Adams, 15 3/8" l. **$440**

Highlands, Hudson River platter, shell border, dark blue, E. Wood, minor roughness on interior rim, 10 x 12 3/4" **$3,335**

Insane Asylum, New York - New York City Hall pitcher, vine border, dark blue, footed bulbous body w/high arched spout & arched handle, Stevenson, 9" h. (minor stains & wear w/some crazing in bottom) **$1,100**

Junction of the Sacandaga and Hudson Rivers platter, floral & scroll border, dark blue, Stevenson, 14 1/4" l. ... **$1,950-2,000**

Lafayette at Franklin's Tomb coffeepot, floral border, tall footed ovoid body w/flared rim & domed cover, dark blue, Wood, 11 3/4" h. **$4,875-5,000**

Lake George, State of New York platter, shell border, dark blue, E. Wood, 16 1/2" l. (very minor glaze scratches).... **$2,585**

Landing of General Lafayette at Castle Garden, New York, 16 August 1824 plate, primrose & dogwood border, dark blue, Clews, 8 7/8" d. **$300-350**

Landing of General Lafayette at Castle Garden, New York, 16 August 1824 pepper pot, floral & vine border, dark blue, 4 5/8" h., Clews (shallow chip & flakes on domed top) **$2,750**

Landing of General Lafayette at Castle Garden, New York, 16 August 1824 pitcher, floral & vine border, jug-type, dark blue, Clews, 6 1/4" h. **$1,750-1,850**

Landing of General Lafayette at Castle Garden, New York, 16 August 1824 platter, floral & vine border, dark blue, Clews, 15 1/4" l. **$2,000-2,200**

Landing of General Lafayette at Castle Garden, New York, 16 August 1824 platter, floral & vine border, dark blue, Clews, 19" l. **$3,000-3,200**

Landing of General Lafayette at Castle Garden, New York, 16 August 1824 sauce tureen, cover & underplate, floral & vine border, dark blue, Clews, tureen 8 3/8" l., undertray 9 7/8" l., the set **$1,975-2,200**

Landing of General Lafayette at Castle Garden, New York, 16 August 1824 sugar bowl & cover, floral & vine border, dark blue, deep boat-shaped form w/flared rim & domed cover, Clews, 6 1/4" h. **$600-700**

Landing of General Lafayette at Castle Garden, New York, 16 August 1824 tureen, cover & ladle, floral & vine border, dark blue, 11" l., 10" h., Clews **$5,000-6,000**

Landing of the Fathers at Plymouth, Dec. 22, 1620 cup plate, scrolls & leaves border, dark blue, 3 3/4" d., E. Wood (ILLUS. bottom row left with other cup plates, top of page 314) **$523**

Marine Hospital, Louisville, Kentucky plate, shell border, dark blue, irregular center, E. Wood, 9 1/4" d. **$325-375**

Mendenhall Ferry platter, spread eagle border, dark blue, J. Stubbs, minor glaze scratches, 13 3/4 x 16 3/4" **$2,185**

Mount Vernon, The Seat of the Late Gen'l. Washington tea set: cov. teapot, cov. sugar bowl, creamer, waste bowl & handleless cup & saucer; large flowers border, dark blue, unknown maker, teapot, 10" l., 5" h., the set **$3,800-4,000**

Park Theatre, New York bowl, oak leaf border, dark blue, R. Stevenson, 8 3/4" d. **$2,500-2,600**

Park Theatre, New York plate, oak leaf border, four portrait medallions at the border of Jefferson, Washington, Lafayette & Clinton, inset of the Aqueduct Bridge at Little Falls, dark blue, R. Stevenson, 10" d. **$3,700-3,800**

Pass in the Catskill Mountains undertray, shell border, circular center, dark blue, E. Wood, 8" l. (minor scratches, edge roughness) **$440**

Peace and Plenty plate, dark blue, wide band of fruit & flowers border, Clews, 8 7/8" d., ... **$325-350**

Pennsylvania Hospital Platter

Pennsylvania Hospital, Philadelphia platter, flowers within medallions border, Beauties of America series, dark blue, Ridgway, few minor scratches, 14 1/8 x 18 3/8" (ILLUS.) **$1,880**

Quebec vegetable dish, cov., shell border, footed square form w/domed cover & floriform finial, dark blue, E. Wood, 9 1/2" w. **$2,150-2,250**

Sandusky (Ohio) platter, floral border, medium dark blue, harbor scene w/steamship "Henry Clay" & other ships, shoreline in background w/several buildings, unmarked Clews, two small blurred areas in transfer, 16 1/2" l. **$4,600-4,700**

State House, Boston platter, spread-eagle border, dark blue, Stubbs, 14 3/4" l. **$1,250-1,300**

States series pitcher, building, two wings, water in foreground, border w/names of fifteen states in festoons separated by five-point stars border, dark blue, Clews, 6 3/4" h. (minor interior staining) **$975-1,000**

States series plate, two-story building w/curved drive, border w/names of fifteen states in festoons separated by five-point stars border, dark blue, Clews, 7 3/4" d. **$330-350**

States series platter, mansion, foreground a lake w/swans, names of states in festoons separated by five-point stars border, dark blue, Clews, ca. 1830, 16 3/4" l., ... **$2,280**

Table Rock, Niagara plate, shell border - circular center, dark blue, E. Wood, 10 1/8" d. **$500-550**

Tappen Zee from Greensburg, New York vegetable bowl, oblong, shell border, dark blue, E. Wood, 8" l. **$935**

Upper Ferry Bridge over the River Schuylkill platter, spread-eagle border, dark blue, Stubbs, 15 1/2 x 18 3/4" ... **$700-750**

View of Pittsburgh platter, floral & scrolled leaves border, brown, Clews, 16 1/8 x 19 5/8" **$3,525**

Washington Standing at Tomb, scroll in hand waste bowl, floral border, dark blue, E. Wood, 6 1/4" d., 3 1/4" h. **$750-860**

West Point Military Academy basket & undertray, reticulated basket & undertray, fruit & flowers border, Celtic China, dark blue, E. Wood, undertray 11 1/2" l., 2 pcs. **$3,750-3,850**

West Point Military Academy platter, shell border, dark blue, E. Wood, 9 1/4 x 11 3/4" (minor glaze scratches) **$2,760**

Winter View of Pittsfield, Massachusetts platter, vignette views & flowers border, dark blue, Clews, glaze scratches, 14 x 16 1/2" **$3,450**

Winter View of Pittsfield, Massachusetts toddy plate, full border w/three medallions, dark blue, 4 5/8" d.,flake on table ring, Clews (ILLUS. top row left with cup plates) **$440**

Woodlands Near Philadelphia cup plate, partial leaf border, dark blue, E. Wood, 3 3/16" d. (ILLUS. top row right with other cup plates) **$330**

Hummel Figurines & Collectibles

The Goebel Company of Oeslau, Germany, first produced these porcelain figurines in 1934, having obtained the rights to adapt the beautiful pastel sketches of children by Sister Maria Innocentia (Berta) Hummel. Every design by the Goebel artisans was approved by the nun until her death in 1946. Although not antique, these figurines with the "M.I. Hummel" signature, especially those bearing the Goebel Company factory mark used from 1934 and into the early 1940s, are being sought by collectors, although interest may have peaked some years ago. A good reference is Luckey's Hummel Figurines & Plates, Identification and Value Guide by Carl F. Luckey (Krause Publications). Trademarks: TMK 1 - Crown - 1934-1950TMK 2 - Full Bee - 1940-1959TMK 3 - Stylized Bee - 1958-1972TMK 4 - Three Line Mark - 1964-1972TMK 5 - Last Bee - 1970-1980TMK 6 - Missing Bee - 1979-1991TMK 7 - Hummel Mark - 1991-1999TMK 8 - Goebel Bee - 2000-

Hummel Marks

A Fair Measure, #345, 4 3/4" h., new style, Trademark 5 .... **$350-450**
A Stitch in Time, #255, 6 3/4" h., Trademark 3 .... **$550-800**

A Stitch in Time

A Stitch in Time, #255, 6 3/4" h., Trademark 6 (ILLUS.)...................................... **$300**
Accordion boy, #185, 5 1/2" h., Trademark 2 .... **$425**
Adoration, #23/I, 6 1/4" h., Trademark 6 .... **$430**
Adoration, #23/I, 6 1/4" h., Trademark 2 .... **$600-800**
Advent Boy with Horse candleholder, #117, 3 1/2" h., Trademark 4 .... **$100-125**
Advent Girl with Fir Tree candlestick, #116, 3 1/2" h., Trademark 2 .... **$150-200**
Adventure Bound, #347, 7 1/4 x 8", Trademark 5 .... **$5,000-6,000**
Angel at Prayer font, #91/A, 4 3/4" h., Trademark 2.................................... **$200-260**

Angel Cloud font, #206, 2 1/4 x 4 3/4", Trademark 2.. **$250-350**
Angel Duet, #261, 5" h., Trademark 5.......... **$270**
Angel Duet font, #146, 2 x 4 3/4", Trademark 3... **$250-275**
Angel Lights candleholder, #241, 8 1/3 x 10 1/3", Trademark 5 .... **$400-500**
Angel Serenade, #214D (angel standing), color decoration, part of Nativity set, 3" h., Trademark 2 .... **$125-145**
Angel Serenade with lamb, #83, 5 1/2" h, Trademark 5.................................... **$240**
Angel with Accordion, #238/B, 2 1/2" h., Trademark 4.................................... **$125**
Angel with Lute candleholder, #III/38/I, 2 1/2" h., Trademark 2 .... **$250-300**
Angel with Trumpet, #238/C, 2 1/2" h., Trademark 4.................................... **$125**
Angelic Song, #144, 4" h., Trademark 1....... **$550**
Apple Tree Boy, #142/3/0, 4" h., Trademark 2... **$300-350**
Apple Tree Boy, #142/I, 6" h., Trademark 5 .... **$400-450**
Apple Tree Boy, #142, 6" h., Trademark 2 .... **$600-700**
Apple Tree Boy & Apple Tree Girl book ends, 5 1/4" h., Trademark 3, pr............. **$425**
Apple Tree Boy table lamp, #230, 7 1/2" h., Trademark 3 .... **$375-400**
Apple Tree Girl, #141/3/0, 4 1/4" h., Trademark 6... **$150**
Apple Tree Girl table lamp, #229, 7 1/2" h., Trademark 2............................... **$900-1,000**
Artist (The), #304, 5 1/2" h., Trademark 3 .... **$2,000-3,000**
Auf Wiedersehen, #153/0, 5 3/4" h., Trademark 6... **$255**
Autumn Harvest, #355, 4 3/4" h., Trademark 6... **$250**
Ba-Bee Ring plaque, #30/B, boy, 5" d., Trademark 2.................................... **$350-450**
Ba-Bee Rings plaques, #30A & #30B, boy & girl, 5" d., Trademark 2, pr.............. **$250-350**
Baker, #128, 4 3/4" h., Trademark 5............. **$245**
Band Leader, #129, 4 1/4", Trademark 2 ...... **$425**
Barnyard Hero, #195, 4" h., Trademark 5..... **$200**
Bashful, #377, 4 3/4" h., Trademark 5.... **$400-600**
Be Patient, #197/2/0, 4 1/4" h., Trademark 2 .... **$400-500**
Be Patient, #197/I, 6 1/4" h., Trademark 2 .... **$550-650**
Begging His Share, #9, 5 1/2" h., Trademark 1 .... **$750-900**
Big Housecleaning, #363, 4" h., Trademark 4.. **$1,500-2,500**
Bird Duet, #169, 4" h., Trademark 4...... **$225-250**
Bird Watcher, #300, 5" h., Trademark 5 .... **$255**
Birthday Serenade, #218/2/0, 4" h., Trademark 6... **$185**
Birthday Serenade, #218/2/0, reverse mold, 4 1/4" h., Trademark 3 .... **$400-450**
Blessed Child (Infant of Krumbad), #78/III, 5 1/4" h., Trademark 3 .... **$75-100**
Blessed Event, #333, 5 1/2" h., Trademark 6 .... **$365**
Book Worm, #3/I, 5 1/2" h., Trademark 3 .... **$600-700**
Book Worm, #3/III, 9 1/2" h., Trademark 3 .... **$1,600-1,800**

Botanist (The), #351, 4 1/4" h., Trademark 6 .... **$200**
Boy with Toothache, #217, 5 1/2" h., Trademark 2 .... **$400-600**
Boy with Toothache, #217, 5 1/2" h., Trademark 6 .... **$225**
Call to Glory (Fahnentager), #739/I, 5 3/4" h., first issue 1994, three flags included **$265**
Carnival, #328, 5 3/4" h., Trademark 6 .... **$235**
Celestial Musician, #188, 7" h., Trademark 2 .... **$850-1,100**
Chef, Hello, #124/0, 6" h., Trademark 6 .... **$240**
Chick Girl, #57/0, 3 1/2" h., Trademark 2 .... **$310-375**
Chick Girl candy dish, #57/III, old style, 5 1/4" h., Trademark 3 .... **$300-350**
Chick Girl candy dish, #III/57, 5 1/4" h., Trademark 2 .... **$580-650**
Chicken Licken, #385, 4 3/4" h., Trademark 5 .... **$350-400**
Child in Bed plaque, #137/B, 2 3/4" d., Trademark 2 .... **$250-350**
Chimney Sweep, #12/1, 6 1/2" h., Trademark 2 .... **$475**
Christmas Song, #343, 6 1/2" h., Trademark 6 .... **$240**
Cinderella, #337, new style, eyes closed, 5 1/2" h., Trademark 5 .... **$250-300**
Close Harmony, #336, 5 1/2" h., Trademark 5 .... **$365-395**
Coffee Break, #409, 4 1/4" h., 1984, exclusive special edition No. 8 for Members of the Goebel Collectors' Club **$300**
Confidentially, #314, 5 1/2" h., Trademark 3 .... **$1,000-1,500**
Congratulations, #17/0, early version, no socks, 6" h., Trademark 2 .... **$450-550**
Congratulations, #17/0, newer version, w/socks, 6 1/4" h., Trademark 3 .... **$250-300**
Coquettes, #179, 5" h., Trademark 6 .... **$325**
Cow (Ox), #214/K, Nativity set piece, 6 1/2" l., Trademark 2 .... **$160**
Crossroads, #331, 6 3/4" h., Trademark 2 .... **$4,000-5,000**
Culprits, #56A, 6 1/4" h., Trademark 2 ... **$375-425**
Daddy's Girl, #371, 4 3/4" h.,Trademark 6 .... **$250**
Dealer display plaque, #187 (Moon Top), 4 x 5 1/2", Trademark 4 .... **$375-475**
Doctor, #127, 4 3/4" h., Trademark 2 ..... **$300-350**
Doll Bath, #319, 5 1/4" h., Trademark 3 .... **$750-1,000**
Doll Mother, #67, 4 3/4" h., Trademark 2 .... **$600-700**
Duet, #130, 5 1/4" h., Trademark 3 .... **$450-475**
Easter Greetings, #378, 5" h., Trademark 5 .. **$245**
Evening Prayer (Abengebet), #495, 4" h., first issue 1992 .... **$110**
Eventide, #99, 4 3/4" h., Trademark 5 .... **$400-500**
Fair Measure, #345, 6" h., Trademark 5 .... **$365**
Farewell, #65/I, 4 3/4" h., Trademark 3 ... **$350-450**
Farm Boy, #66, 5 1/4" h., Trademark 3 .. **$300-325**
Favorite Pet, #361, 4 1/2" h., Trademark 6 ... **$320**
Feathered Friends, #344, 4 3/4" h., Trademark 5 .... **$350-400**
Feeding Time, #199/0, 4 1/4" h., Trademark 3 .... **$300-350**
Feeding Time, #199, 5 3/4" h., Trademark 2 .... **$525-625**

Festival Harmony, #173/0, 8", Trademark 6 .. **$355**
Festival Harmony, #172/II, angel w/mandolin, 11" h., Trademark 3 .... **$700-800**
Flitting Butterfly plaque, #139, 2 1/2 x 2 1/2", Trademark 1 .... **$350-550**

Flower Madonna Hummel in Color

Flower Madonna, #10/I, color, 8 1/4" h., Trademark 3 (ILLUS.) **$575-675**
Flower Madonna, #10/I, white, 9 1/2" h., Trademark 1 .... **$500-600**
Flower Vender, #381, 5 1/4" h., Trademark 6 .... **$275**
Follow the Leader, #369, 7" h., Trademark 4 .... **$1,350-1,400**
For Father, #87, 5 1/2" h., Trademark 4 .... **$325-350**
For Father, #87, 5 1/2" h., Trademark 2 .... **$400-530**
For Mother, #257, 5 1/4" h., Trademark 3 .... **$700-800**
For Mother, #257, 5 1/4" h., Trademark 6 ..... **$225**
Forest Shrine, #183, 9" h., Trademark 6 ...... **$625**
Friends, #136/I, 5 3/8" h., Trademark 6 .... **$225**
Friends, #136/V, 10 3/4" h., Trademark 2 .... **$2,000-3,000**
Gift from a Friend (Aus Nachbars Garten), #485, 5 1/4" h., exclusive edition 1991/92 M.I. Hummel Club, original box.... **$275**
Girl with Doll, #239B, 3 1/2" h., Trademark 4 .... **$100-200**
Globe Trotter, #79, 5" h., Trademark 2 .... **$350-450**
Globe Trotter, #79, 5" h., Trademark 1 .... **$500-750**
Going to Grandma's, #52/0, 4 3/4" h., Trademark 1 .... **$750-1,000**
Going to Grandma's, #52/I, 6" h., Trademark 2 .... **$550-650**
Good Friends, 4" h., Trademark 4 .... **$350-400**
Good Friends table lamp, #228, 7 1/2" h., Trademark 3 .... **$550-650**
Good Hunting, #307, 5 1/4" h., Trademark 6 .... **$300-325**
Good Shepherd, #42/0, 6 1/4" h., Trademark 2 .... **$500-550**
Goose Girl, #47/3/0, 4" h., Trademark 3 .... **$250-350**
Goose Girl, #47/3/0, 4 1/4" h., Trademark 6 .... **$185**

Goose Girl, #47/II, 7 12/" h., Trademark 5
.... $450-500
Goose Girl, #47/II, 7 1/2" h., Trademark 2
.... $700-900
Happiness, #86, 4 3/4" h., Trademark 1
.... $400-500
Happy Birthday, #176, 5 1/3" h., Trademark 1 .... $1,150
Happy Days, #150/0, 5 1/4" h., Trademark 5 .... $325-350
Happy Pastime, #69, 3 1/2" h., Trademark 3 .... $350-450
Happy Traveler, #109/0, 5" h., Trademark 2
.... $275-350
Hear Ye, Hear Ye, #15/0, 5" h., Trademark 5 .... $225
Hear Ye, Hear Ye, #15/I, 6" h., Trademark 1
.... $1,600-1,700
Heavenly Lullaby, #262, 3 1/2 x 5", Trademark 4 .... $600-700
Heavenly Protection, #88/II, 9 1/4" h., Trademark 3 .... $1,000-1,200
Heavenly Protection, #88, 9 1/4" h., Trademark 2 .... $1,300-1,600
Home From Market, #198/I, 5 3/4" h., Trademark 4 .... $375-400
I'm Carefree, #633, 4 3/4" h., signature on back, first issue 1994 .... $875
Joyful, #53, 4" h., Trademark 1 .... $350-450
Joyful candy box, #III/53, 6 1/4" h., Trademark 2 .... $475-500
Joyous News, #27/3, 4 1/4 x 4 3/4", Trademark 1 .... $2,000
Jubilee, #416, 6 1/4" h., 1980, 50 years, M.I. Hummel Figurines 1935-1985, "The Love Lives On" $475
Just Resting, #112/I, 5" h., Trademark 2
.... $400-600
Just Resting table lamp, #II/112, 7 1/2" h., Trademark 3 .... $375-525
Kiss Me, w/socks, 6" h., Trademark 4 ..... $400-450
Knit One, Purl One, #432, 3" h., Trademark 5 .... $130
Knitting Lesson, #256, 7 1/2" h., Trademark 5 .... $550-650
Latest News, #184, inscribed "Munchener Presse," 5 1/4" h., Trademark 3 .... $425-500
Let's Sing ashtray, #114, 3 1/2 x 6 3/4", Trademark 4 .... $250-350
Little Bookkeeper, #306, 4 3/4" h., Trademark 3 .... $1,000+
Little Bookkeeper, #306, 4 3/4" h., Trademark 4 .... $425
Little Drummer, #240, 4 1/4" h., Trademark 3 .... $245-260
Little Fiddler, #2/0, 6" h., Trademark 3 .. $350-400
Little Gabriel, #32/0, 5" h., Trademark 3
.... $250-300
Little Goat Herder, #200/I, 5 1/2" h, Trademark 5 .... $275
Little Hiker, #16/2/0, 4 1/4" h., Trademark 2
.... $250-350
Little Nurse, #376, 4" h., Trademark 6 .... $270
Little Pharmacist, #322, 6" h., Trademark 6 .. $265
Little Sleeper, #171/4/0, 3" h., Trademark 6 .. $115
Little Sweeper, #171, 4 1/2" h., Trademark 5 .... $200-250
Lost Sheep, #68/0, 5 1/2" h., Trademark 2
.... $325-350
Madonna plaque, #48/II, 4 3/4 x 6", Trademark 2 .... $375-525

Make a Wish (Die Pusteblume), #475, 4 1/2" h., Trademark 6 .... $225
Max & Moritz, #123, 5 1/4" h., Trademark 5 .. $265
Merry Wanderer, #11/2/0, 4 1/4" h., Trademark 1 .... $450-550
Merry Wanderer plaque, #92, 4 3/4 x 5 1/8", Trademark 3 .... $250-350
Mischief Maker, #342, 5" h., Trademark 5.... $345
Mother's Helper, #133, 5" h., Trademark 4... $275
Mountaineer, #315, 5 1/4" h., Trademark 4
.... $400-450
On Holiday, #350, 4 1/4" h., Trademark 6..... $165
Out of Danger, #56/B, 6 1/2" h., Trademark 6 .... $335
Photographer (The), #178, 4 3/4" h., Trademark 5 .... $345-370
Pigtails, #2052, 3 1/4" h., M.I. Hummel Club Membership Year, 1999/2000, original box $75
Playmates, #58/I, 4 1/2" h., Trademark 3
.... $400-500
Postman, #119, 5" h., Trademark 3 .... $300
Prayer Before Battle, #20, 4 1/4" h., Trademark 1 .... $650
Puppy Love, #1, 5" h., Trademark 6 .... $325
Retreat to Safety plaque, #126, 4 3/4 x 5", Trademark 3 .... $250-350

Ride Into Christmas Hummel Figurine

Ride into Christmas, #396, 5 3/4" h., Trademark 6 .... $525
Ride into Christmas, #396, 5 3/4" h., Trademark 4 .... $2,000-2,500
Ring Around the Rosie, #348, 6 3/4" h., Trademark 5 .... $3,200

Saint George

Saint George, #55, 6 3/4" h., Trademark 6
(ILLUS.)... **$350**
School Boy, #82/2/0, 4" h., Trademark 2
.... **$400-500**
School Boy, #82/II, 7 1/2" h., Trademark 5
.... **$550-650**
School Girl, #81/0, 5 1/4" h., Trademark 5
.... **$300-400**
School Girls, #177, 9 1/2" h., Trademark 2
.... **$3,000-4,000**
Sensitive Hunter, #6/0, 4 3/4" h., Trademark 3... **$350-450**
Sensitive Hunter, #6, 4 3/4" h., Trademark 1... **$850-1,000**
Serenade, #85/0, 4 3/4" h., Trademark 3...... **$200**
She Loves Me, She Loves Me Not!, #174, 4 1/4" h., Trademark 6 .... **$225**
Shepherd's Boy, #64, 5 1/2" h., Trademark 2.. **$450-550**
Shining Light, #358, 2 3/4" h., Trademark 5 .. **$100**
Signs of Spring, #203/2/0, 4" h., Trademark 4.. **$425-525**
Silent Night candleholder, #54, 5 1/2" l., 4 3/4" h., Trademark 1 .... **$1,100**
Sing Along (Auf los geht's los), #433, 4 1/2" h., Trademark 6 .... **$315**
Singing Lesson, #63, 2 3/4" h., Trademark 3... **$200-300**
Sister, #98/2/0, 4 3/4" h., Trademark 6 .... **$155**
Skier, #59, 5 1/4" h., Trademark 3 .... **$400-500**
Sleep Tight (Schlaf gut), #424, 4 3/4" h., Trademark 6... **$240**
Smart Little Sister, #436, 4 3/4" h., Trademark 4.. **$400-500**
Soldier Boy, #332, red cap, 6" h., Trademark 4... **$650**
Soloist, #135, 4 3/4" h., Trademark 2 .... **$325**
Sound of the Trumpet, #457, 3" h., Trademark 6... **$110**
Spring Cheer, #72, 5" h., Trademark 5 .. **$250-300**
Spring Dance, #353/0, 5 1/2" h., Trademark 6... **$365**
St. George, #55, 6 3/4" h., Trademark 5. **$400-450**
Standing Boy plaque, #168, 4 1/8 x 5 1/2", Trademark 2................................... **$800-900**

Star Gazer

Star Gazer, #132, 4 3/4" h., Trademark 3
(ILLUS.)... **$350**
Stormy Weather, 71, 6 1/4" h., Trademark 3 (ILLUS., top next column) **$900-1,000**
Storybook Time (Marchenstude), #458, 5" h., First Issue 1992 .... **$445**
Street Singer, #131, 5 1/2" h., Trademark 3 .... **$325**

Trademark 3 Stormy Weather Hummel

Strolling Along, #5, 4 3/4" h., Trademark 2
.... **$750-950**
Supreme Protection, #364, 9 1/4" h., 1984, "1909-1984, In Celebration of the 75th Anniversary of the Birth of Sister M.I. Hummel" **$375**
Surprise, #94/I, 5 1/2" h., Trademark 3 .. **$450-550**
Sweet Greetings, #352, 4 1/4" h., Trademark 6... **$200**
Telling Her Secret, #196/0, 5 1/4" h., Trademark 5... **$365**
To Market, #49/3/0, 4" h., Trademark 1 .. **$500-650**
To Market, 6 1/4" h., Trademark 1.... **$1,400-1,700**
Trumpet Boy, #97, 4 3/4" h., Trademark 2
.... **$300-400**
Trumpet Boy, #97, 4 3/4" h., Trademark 6.... **$145**
Tuneful Goodnight plaque, #180, 4 3/4 x 5", Trademark 3 .... **$300-400**
Two Hands, One Treat (Rechts oder links?), #493, 4" h., 1991-99, M.I. Hummel Club.. **$125**
Umbrella Boy, #152/0 A, 5" h., Trademark 3... **$1,000-1,200**
Umbrella Boy, #152, 8" h., Trademark 2
.... **$2,400-2,900**
Umbrella Girl, #152/B, 8" h., Trademark 2
.... **$2,200-2,700**
Valentine Gift, #387, 5 3/4" h., 1972, exclusive special edition No. 1 for members of the Goebel Collectors' Club **$575**
Village Boy, #51/3/0, 4" h., Trademark 1
.... **$350-450**
Village Boy, #51/I, 7 1/4" h., Trademark 3
.... **$550-650**
Visiting an Invalid, #382, 5" h., Trademark 4... **$1,000-1,500**
Volunteers, #50/0, 5 1/2" h., Trademark 3
.... **$455-480**
Waiter, #154/0, 6" h., Trademark 2........ **$375-475**
Wash Day, #321, 5 3/4" h., Trademark 3
.... **$750-1,000**
Watchful Angel, #194, 6 1/2" h., Trademark 3... **$600-700**

Wayside Devotion, #28/II, 7 1/2" h., Trademark 1 .... **$1,500**
Wayside Devotion, #28/III, 8 3/4" h., Trademark 2................................. **$1,000-1,200**
Wayside Harmony, #111/3/0, 3 3/4" h., Trademark 3....................................... **$200-300**
We Congratulate, #220/2/0, 4" h., Trademark 2... **$475-575**
Weary Wanderer, #204, 6" h., Trademark 4 .... **$400-500**
What Now?, #422, 5 3/4" h., 1983, exclusive special edition No. 7 for members of the Goebel Collectors' Club **$375**
Whitsuntide, #163, 6 1/2" h., Trademark 6 ... **$325**
Whitsuntide, #163, 7 1/4" h., Trademark 1 .... **$1,000-1,200**
Worship, #84, 5" h., Trademark 1.......... **$475-625**
Worship, #84/V, 13" h., Trademark 4 .... **$1,250-1,350**

Imari

This is a multicolor ware that originated in Japan, was copied by the Chinese, and imitated by English and European potteries. It was decorated in overglaze enamel and underglaze-blue. Made in Hizen Province and Arita, much of it was exported through the port of Imari in Japan. Imari often has brocade patterns.

Large Colorful Imari Covered Jar

Jar, cov., large bulbous ovoid body w/a short cylindrical neck fitted w/a high domed cover w/large knob finial, the cover w/scenes of birds & flowers, the sides decorated w/cartouches showing birds in flight above flowering branches in garden fences, worn gilt, restoration to finial, chip

on inner cover rim, small chips on inner jar mouth, ca. 1870, 16 1/2" h. (ILLUS.) **$500**
Umbrella stand, tall cylindrical form, bands of stylized leaves & blossoms around the top & base, the center decorated overall w/traditional stylized flowers & birds in a garden setting, Japan, late 19th c., 23 1/4" h... **$1,610**

Elaborately Mounted Imari Vase

Vase & clock, 20 1/2" h., the large ovoid covered jar w/bold designs in rust red & cobalt blue on white fitted at the front w/an French clock within a bronze dore fruit & leaf mount, the vase fitted into an ornate scroll-cast bronze dore base & large high scrolled handles, the vase & cover rims w/bronze dore mounts & a pineapple finial, clock marked "Rue Caummet, No. 42, Paris," France, ca. 1870 (ILLUS.)..................................... **$850-950**

Ironstone

The first successful ironstone was patented in 1813 by C.J. Mason in England. The body contains iron slag incorporated with the clay. Other potters imitated Mason's ware, and today much hard, thick ware is lumped under the term ironstone. Earlier it was called by various names, including graniteware. Both plain white and decorated wares were made throughout the 19th century. Tea Leaf Lustre ironstone was made by several firms.

General

Cabinet plates, each w/a scalloped rim, "Japan" patt., floral border & center, painted in the Imari palette, Hick & Meigh, England, ca. 1830, 10 3/8" d., pr. (one w/hairline) **$235**
Cabinet plates, each w/a scrolling gilt floral border w/alternating cartouches of birds & flowers, centered by a coat-of-arms, Ashworth, England, ca. 1875, set of 8 (normal surface scratches) **$365**

Two Views of a White Ironstone Cookie Plate

Cookie plate, oval, footed, New York shape, all-white, J. Clementson, ca. 1858, 10" l. (ILLUS. of two views) **$130-150**

Ironstone Ceres Pattern Cup & Saucer

Cup & saucer, handleless, Ceres shape, all-white, Elsmore & Forster, ca. 1859 (ILLUS.) **$55-65**

Cups & saucers, handleless, "gaudy" Blackberry patt. in underglaze-blue trimmed w/yellow & orange enamel & lustre, E. Walley mark, ca. 1850, some variation, set of 10 .... **$1,375**

Dessert service: 10 5/8" l. shaped dish, 5 3/4" h. open compote, four 10" l. leaf-shaped dishes & fourteen 9 1/4" d. plates; Imari-style designs w/shaped edges & deep green borders, Mason's, mid-19th c., the set **$3,680**

Dinner service: child's size; Moss Rose patt., by G. Scott, 16 pcs. (a few w/light discoloration, one inner lid chip) **$625**

Full Ribbed Ironstone Egg Cup

Egg cup, Full Ribbed, all-white, J.W. Pankhurst, ca. 1855, 2 1/4" h. (ILLUS.)... **$85-100**

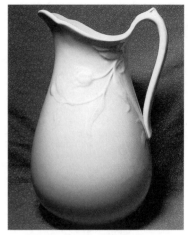

White Ironstone Tulip Ewer

Ewer, floral decoration on side, C-scroll handle, Tulip, Powell & Bishop, ca. 1870, 13" h. (ILLUS.) **$250-300**

Hyacinth Pattern Gravy Boat

Gravy boat, footed, C-scroll handle, Hyacinth patt., all-white, Wedgwood, ca. 1860s (ILLUS.) **$40-50**

Gravy boat, Long Octagon shape, all-white, ca. 1847, T.J. & J. Mayer **$125-140**

Fig/Union White Ironstone Mug

Mug, footed, C-scroll handle, Fig/Union shape, all-white, Davenport, ca. 1856, 3" h. (ILLUS.) **$175-200**

Mug, Gothic patt., all-white, ca. 1840s, James Edwards **$120-130**

Hyacinth Ironstone Cider Mug

Mug, large mug for cider, w/C-scroll handle, floral design on side, Hyacinth patt., all-white, Wedgwood, ca. 1860s, 4" h. (ILLUS.) **$90-105**

Pitcher, 9 3/4" h., footed wide squatty bulbous body molded w/wide ribs & tapering to a wide mouth w/arched spout, high arched C-scroll handle, transfer decoration of birds in flowering trees & foliage w/polychrome enamel, mark of Ashworth Bros., England, ca. 1890 .... **$303**

Pitcher, 9 3/4" h., table-type, Grape Octagon shape, all-white, Pearson & Hancock **$150-180**

Plate, 8" d., twelve-sided, "gaudy" Bittersweet patt. w/underglaze flow blue & copper luster, impressed "Real Ironstone" (light stains).................................... **$83**

Plate, 8 3/8" w., paneled shape, "gaudy" freehand Strawberry patt., underglaze-blue w/green & two shades of red enamel & copper lustre trim, mid-19th c. **$385**

Plate, 8 1/2" d., "gaudy" decoration, vintage grape vine design painted in underglaze-blue, black, ochre & two shades of green (wear, crazing) **$110**

Plate, 8 1/2" d., "gaudy" style, center w/urn in flow blue w/pink & red flowers & copper lustre highlights (stains) **$110**

Plate, 8 3/4" w., "gaudy" Strawberry patt., paneled shape w/underglaze-blue trimmed w/red, pink, green & copper lustre, impressed mark, mid-19th c................ **$138**

Plate, 9 1/4" w., paneled shape, "gaudy" freehand Morning Glory patt., underglaze-blue trimmed w/two shades of green, red & black enamel, mid-19th c. **$303**

Plate, 9 1/2" d., Bordered Hyacinth/Lily shape, all-white, ca. 1860, W. & E. Corn **$50-65**

Plate, 9 1/2" d., Flora shape, all-white, Wedgwood & Co., ca. 1860 (ILLUS., top next column)... **$65-75**

Plate, 9 1/2" w., paneled sides, "gaudy" Floral Urn freehand patt., underglaze-blue & green & trimmed w/two shades of red enamel & copper lustre, mid-19th c. (light stains, tiny enamel flake)........................... **$330**

Plate, 9 5/8" d., "gaudy" Blackberry patt., underglaze-blue & black trimmed w/red, yellow & copper lustre, impressed "E. Walley - Niagara Shape," 1850s **$193**

Flora White Ironstone Plate

Plate, 10" d., Trent shape, all-white, John Alcock, ca. 1855 .... **$50-65**

Plate, 10 1/4" d., New York shape, all-white, ca. 1858, J. Clementson.............. **$50-65**

Plate, 10 1/4" d., twelve-sided "gaudy" style w/strawberries, pink flowers & underglaze flow blue leaves.............................. **$248**

Plate, 10 1/2" d., Fig shape, all-white, ca. 1856, Davenport/Wedgwood **$60-75**

Plates, 8 1/2" d., decorated w/floral motif in blue & rust, marked "Ashworth Brothers Hanley," England, ca. 1890, set of 9......... **$134**

Plates, 9 5/8" d., paneled edge, central transfer-printed garden landscape w/urn of flowers, flower & scroll border, Florilla patt., purple highlighted w/yellow, green, blue & red enamel, mid-19th c., set of 6 (stains) **$138**

Plates, 10 1/2" d., scalloped flanged rim, overall Imari-style transfer decoration in polychrome trimmed w/gold, mid-19th c., pr.. **$303**

Platter, oval, 10" l., President shape, all-white, John Edwards............................... **$30-40**

Platter, 13 1/2" l., octagonal, "gaudy" Strawberry patt., underglaze-blue w/red, pink & green enamel & luster trim, wear, stains & some enamel flaking **$770**

Platter, 13 1/2" l., rectangular w/cut corners, "gaudy" freehand Morning Glory patt., underglaze-blue trimmed w/two shades of green, red & black, mid-19th c. (old red flaking, minor stains).................... **$385**

Platter, 11 3/8 x 14 1/8", rectangular, romantic transfer scene of a lakeside cabin w/boaters, marked "Cat, Albion" & "Turnbull, Stepney," light blue, mid-19th c......... **$121**

Platter, 14 3/4" oval, "gaudy," blue transfer-printed War Bonnet patt. trimmed in red, orange & yellow, marked "Ironstone China," mid-19th c. (wear, scratches) **$165**

Platter, 15 3/4" l., rectangular w/cut corners, Florentine patt., light blue, T. Mayer, mid-19th c. (internal hairline) **$110**

Platter, 16" l., eight-sided oblong, Fig/Union shape, all-white, Wedgwood, ca. 1856 (ILLUS., top next page)...................... **$155-175**

Platter, oval, 16" l., Corn & Oats shape, all-white, Davenport/Wedgwood................. **$65-75**

Fig/Union White Ironstone Platter

Platter, rectangular, 16" l., Rolling Star shape, all-white, James Edwards.......... **$90-100**

Platter, 16 1/4" l., oval w/lightly scalloped rim, "gaudy" freehand Strawberry patt., underglaze black, mid-19th c. (small chips on one corner) **$413**

Platter, 18 1/2" l., Indiana patt., ca. 1880, Wedgwood **$196**

Platter, 16 x 21", well-and-tree-type, oval, Rural Scenery patt., broad floral border surrounding a meadow landscape w/figures & animals, Davewell & Goodfellow, England (chips on foot, hairline)................. **$440**

Platter, 21 1/4" l., oval w/flanged rim, the center transfer-printed w/a large landscape scene of a dog holding a stick on the bank of a river w/figures rowing a boat, the river flanked by trees & a country house in the distance, wide floral border, blue & white, back w/printed mark of a ribbon-tied banner inscribed "British Views," mid-19th c.................................... **$1,265**

Platter, 22" l., oval, polychrome floral decoration w/gilt trim, Stokes Works mark on base, 19th c.. **$863**

Platters, 8 1/4 x 10 1/2" & 10 1/2 x 13 1/4", oval, each decorated w/a scrolling gilt floral border w/alternating cartouches of birds & flowers, centered by a coat-of-arms, Ashworth, England, ca. 1875, pr. (normal surface scratches)......................... **$300**

Punch bowl, footed deep rounded bowl, floral embellishments around the rim & base, twig urn w/flowers & bird at center & sides, in shades of cobalt blue, yellow, pink, orange & green w/gilt highlights, mid-19th c., 14 1/4" d., 6 1/2" h.............. **$1,035**

Punch bowl, footed, New York shape, all-white, J. Clementson, ca. 1858, 15" d. (ILLUS., top next column) **$450-500**

Relish dish, 1851 Shell shape, all-white, ca. 1851, T. & R. Boote **$100-125**

Relish dish, Berlin Swirl, all-white, ca. 1856, Mayer & Elliot............................... **$65-75**

Relish dish, elongated shell form, Cameo Gothic, all-white, James Edwards, ca. 1850s, 8" l. (ILLUS., next column) **$100-125**

Relish dish, mitten-shaped, Moss Rose patt., marked "C.P.W." (some faded gold trim) **$55**

Relish dish, plain, oval w/two tab handles, all-white, ca. 1870s, Wood, Son & Co. **$20-30**

New York Ironstone Punch Bowl

Cameo Gothic Ironstone Relish

Various Red Cliff Pieces

Salt & pepper shakers, Boote's 1851 shape, all-white, ca. 1960s, Red Cliff, 4" h., pr. (ILLUS. far right & far left, top of page) **$50-60**

White Ironstone Sardine Box

Sardine box, cov., rectangular, all-white, image of sardine on front, lid w/ribbed design curving up to finial-type handle, unmarked, ca. 1870s (ILLUS.) **$170-190**

Sauce ladle, Moss Rose patt. **$110**

Sauce tureen, cov., oblong form, decorated in color w/the Japanese Garden patt., molded butterfly handles & finial, England, 19th c., 5 3/4" h. **$173**

Pie Crust Three-Piece Soap Box

Soap box, cover & liner, Pie Crust/Blanket Stitch, all-white, J. & G. Meakin, ca. 1880 (ILLUS.) **$50-75**

Soap box, cover & liner, plain oval, all-white, ca. 1872-87, Thomas Elsmore & Son, 3 pcs. **$40-45**

Soap box, cover & liner, President shape, all-white, John Edwards, 3 pcs **$120-130**

Soap dish, open, plain hollow rectangular body w/drain holes in well & one on side for cleaning, all-white, various potters..... **$20-30**

Soup plate, flanged paneled rim, Paradise patt., purple floral transfer design w/polychrome trim, mid-19th c., 10 1/2" w. **$83**

Soup plate, Sharon Arch shape, all-white, Davenport, 9 1/2" d. **$50-60**

Soup tureen, cover, ladle & underplate, Stafford shape, all-white, ca. 1854, S. Alcock & Co., 4 pcs. **$750-800**

Soup tureen, undertray, cover & ladle, Vista England patt., footed deep tureen, grape leaf & vine border, cranberry, tray 14 3/4" l., tureen 10 1/2" h., the set........... **$605**

Sugar bowl, cov., Favorite shape, Moss Rose patt., Grindley (glaze flake on cover rim).. **$180**

Syrup pitcher, w/pewter lid, Lily of the Valley patt., all-white, James Edwards, ca. 1859, 6" h... **$475-510**

Alcock's Pear White Ironstone Teapot

Teapot, cov., all-white, Alcock's Pear shape, by John Alcock, England, ca. 1860 (ILLUS.)...................................... **$125-150**

Alternate Panels Ironstone Teapot

Three Boote's 1851 Shape Pieces

Teapot, cov., all-white, Alternate Panels shape, unknown potter, England, mid-19th c. (ILLUS., previous page) **$125-150**

Teapot, cov., all-white, Boote's 1851 shape, adult size, by T. & R. Boote, England, ca. 1851 (ILLUS. left with other Boote's 1851 pieces, top of page)............................. **$300-325**

Teapot, cov., all-white, Boote's 1851 shape, child's size, by T. & R. Boote, England, ca. 1851 (ILLUS. center with other Boote's 1851 pieces, top of page) **$200-250**

Teapot, cov., all-white, Boote's 1851 shape cov. creamer, a ca. 1960s reproduction by Red Cliff, based on the early shape (ILLUS. right with other Boote's 1851 pieces, top of page)................................ **$35-45**

Edwards Lily of the Valley Teapot

Inverted Diamond Ironstone Teapot

Teapot, cov., all-white, Inverted Diamond shape, by T. J. & J. Mayer, England, ca. 1840s (ILLUS.).................................... **$250-300**

Teapot, cov., all-white, Lily of the Valley shape, by James Edwards, England, ca. 1860s (ILLUS., top next column)......... **$200-225**

Ironstone Loop & Dot Shape Teapot

Teapot, cov., all-white, Loop & Dot shape, by E. & C. Challinor, England, ca. 1865 (ILLUS.)... **$190-210**

Edwards Pedestaled Gothic Teapot

Teapot, cov., all-white, Pedestaled Gothic shape, by James Edwards, England, ca. 1845 (ILLUS.)...................................... **$300-325**

Plain Seashore White Ironstone Teapot

Teapot, cov., all-white, Plain Seashore shape, molded dolphin on handle & finial, by W. & E. Corn, ca. 1885 (ILLUS.) **$125-150**

Red Cliff Sydenham Shape White Teapot

Teapot, cov., all-white Sydenham shape, copy of Victorian ironstone original design, produced by Hall China for Red Cliff, ca. 1960s (ILLUS.) **$95**

Red Cliff Grape Leaf Pattern Teapot

Teapot, cov., all-white tall paneled & tapering body w/domed cover, molded Grape Leaf patt., produced by Hall China for Red Cliff, ca. 1960s (ILLUS.) **$150**

White Ironstone Tulip Shape Teapot

Teapot, cov., all-white, Tulip shape, by Elsmore & Forster, England, ca. 1855 (ILLUS.)... **$200-225**

Blue-trimmed Tulip Shape Teapot

Teapot, cov., all-white, Tulip shape, trimmed in blue, by Elsmore & Forster, England, ca. 1855 (ILLUS.)................ **$290-320**

White Ironstone Tuscan Shape Teapot

Teapot, cov., all-white, Tuscan shape, by John Edwards, England, ca. 1853 (ILLUS.) **$150-175**

Wheat & Clover Ironstone Teapot

Teapot, cov., all-white, Wheat & Clover shape, by Turner & Tompkinson, England, ca. 1860s (ILLUS.).............. **$220-250**

Virginia Shape White Ironstone Teapot

Teapot, cov., all-white, Virginia shape, by Brougham & Mayer, England, ca. 1855 (ILLUS.).. **$200-230**

Early Sebring China Company Teapot

Teapot, cov., bulbous ovoid body molded down the sides w/fanned devices forming a panel printed w/a large floral cluster, tall serpentine spout, C-scroll handle, domed cover w/arched loop finial, Sebring China Co., East Liverpool, Ohio, ca. 1890s (ILLUS.) **$75**

Western Shape Child's Teapot

Teapot, cov., all-white, Western shape, child's size, by J.F., ca. 1860 (ILLUS.) **$175-200**

Burford Brothers Decorated Teapot

Teapot, cov., bulbous ovoid body w/a wide cylindrical neck, embossed w/a long trailing floral vine, domed cover w/arched finial, upright spout, C-form handle, decorated w/gold lustre bands, Burford Brothers, East Liverpool, Ohio, ca. 1890s (ILLUS., previous page) **$70**

Ott & Brewer Ironstone Teapot

Teapot, cov., bulbous tapering ovoid body w/a flared rim, domed cover w/bar handle, serpentine spout, C-scroll handle, decorated w/a long delicate flowering vine design, Ott & Brewer, Trenton, New Jersey, ca. 1870-80 (ILLUS.) **$75**

Inverted Diamond Ironstone Teapot

Teapot, cov., footed, facet effect design, Inverted Diamond, all-white, T.J. & J. Mayer, ca. 1845, 8 1/2" h. (ILLUS.)..... **$225-250**

Teapot, cov., "gaudy" strawberry design, paneled body w/a domed cover w/blossom finial, decorated w/blue flowers, red & green strawberries & gilt trim, ca. 1850, 9 3/4" h. (nick) **$2,300**

Teapot, cov., Memnon shape, six panels w/branch handle & bud finial, all-

white, ca. 1850s, John Meir & Son, 8 3/4" h... **$175-200**

Teapot, cov., tall tapering paneled form w/angled handle & inset high domed cover w/floret finial, "gaudy" Strawberry patt. w/large blossoms highlighted w/flowing blue & copper lustre, mid-19th c., 9" h. (minor flake on spout, reglued finial)....... **$1,375**

Teapot w/hinged metal cover, spherical body, Moss Rose patt., Knowles, Taylor & Knowles (small interior pit & stain, inside rim roughness) **$170**

Sevres Shape Ironstone Brush Box

Toothbrush box, cov., Sevres shape, all-white, John Edwards, ca. 1860s, 8 1/2" l. (ILLUS.).. **$90-120**

Toothbrush vase, cylindrical w/ruffled rim, Moss Rose patt., Alfred Meakin (worn lustre) **$130**

Vegetable dish, cov., Scotia (Poppy) shape, oval, all-white, ca. 1870, F. Jones & Co., 9" l.. **$100-120**

Washbowl & pitcher, miniature, Classic Gothic shape, all-white, Red Cliff, ca. 1960s, overall 4 1/2" h. (ILLUS. second from right w/salt & pepper shakers, top of page 325).. **$50-75**

Washbowl & pitcher, miniature, Fig (registered Union shape), all-white, Red Cliff, ca. 1960s, overall 3 1/2" h. (ILLUS. second from left w/salt & pepper shakers, top of page 325).................................... **$50-75**

Washbowl & pitcher, miniature, Sydenham shape, all-white, Red Cliff, ca. 1960s, overall 4 1/2" h. (ILLUS. center w/salt & pepper shakers, top of page 325)......... **$80-100**

Washbowl & pitcher, "Tudor" patt., transfer-printed overall w/stylized floral medallions, branches & berries in lilac on an ivory ground, William Brownfield & Sons, 1871-91, bowl 15" d., overall 10" h., 2 pcs. **$287**

Tea Leaf Ironstone

Butter dish, cover & insert, Basketweave patt., A. Shaw (tiny glaze flaw inside) **$425**

Butter dish, cover & insert, Lion's Head patt., Mellor Taylor (minor wear & crazing).. **$200**

Cake plate, Daisy & Tulip patt., Wedgwood & Co. **$130**

Cake plate, Prairie Flowers patt., gold Tea Leaf, Powell & Bishop.............................. **$130**

Chamber pot, open, Daisy n' Chain patt., Wilkinson... **$110**

Coffeepot, cov., Lily-of-the-Valley patt., Anthony Shaw (small under rim chip on cover)... **$275**

Compote, open, 9 1/4" sq., Square Ridged patt., Wedgwood & Co. **$325**

Compote, open, domed foot below the ringed stem supporting the wide shallow round bowl w/rolled rim, Edge Malkin **$550**

Compote, open, round, small low round foot below the wide shallow round bowl, T. Furnival **$195**

Creamer, Chelsea patt., Alfred Meakin, 5" h. **$90**

Creamer, Favorite patt., Grindley.................... **$90**

Creamer, Victory patt., Edwards, 5" h. (Some lustre wear)..................................... **$100**

Creamer & cov. sugar bowl, Simple Pear patt., Alfred Meakin, pr. (lustre wear) **$340**

Cup & saucer, handled, white body, Edge Malkin.. **$50**

Gravy boat, Lily of the Valley patt., Anthony Shaw **$325**

Gravy boat & undertray, Chelsea patt., Alfred Meakin, 2 pcs.................................... **$160**

Pitcher, water, Little Cable patt., square shape, T. Furnival **$200**

Pitcher, 6 3/4" h., Favorite patt., Grindley...... **$155**

Pitcher, 8" h., Hawthorn patt., A. Wilkinson **$95**

Pitcher, 8 1/2" h., Chelsea patt., Alfred Meakin (potting flaw under base rim) **$350**

Pitcher, 8 1/2" h., Daisy n' Chain patt., Wilkinson.. **$125**

Posset cup, Lily-of-the-Valley patt., Anthony Shaw **$275-300**

Punch bowl, footed, deep rounded bowl w/flared rim, H. Burgess........................ **$1,100**

Relish dish, mitten-shaped, A. Wilkinson (slight crazing)... **$95**

Sauce dish, Lily of the Valley patt., Anthony Shaw **$50**

Sauce ladle, Alfred Meakin **$250**

Sauce ladle, Cable patt., A. Shaw **$255**

Sauce tureen, cover & undertray, Cable patt., Anthony Shaw, 3 pcs. **$120**

Shaving mug, Maidenhair Fern patt., Wilkinson (some lustre touch-up).............. **$400**

Shaving mug, Scroll patt., Alfred Meakin **$110**

Soap dish, cover & drainer, Simple Square patt., Wedgwood & Co. **$150**

Soap dish, cover & insert, Chinese patt., Anthony Shaw (small flakes & hairline)...... **$250**

Soup tureen, cover, ladle & undertray, Bullet patt., Red Cliff, ca. 1970, the set...... **$175**

Soup tureen, cover, ladle & undertray, Scroll patt., Alfred Meakin (hairline in cover) **$440**

Sugar bowl, cov., Lily-of-the-Valley patt., Anthony Shaw.. **$275**

Teapot, Cable patt., T. Furnival...................... **$90**

Teapot, cov., Fig Cousin patt., pink lustre trim, Davenport (lid crazing, small flake inside cover) **$300**

Teapot, cov., Pagoda patt., H. Burgess, 8 3/4" h.. **$275**

Teapot, cov., Square Ridged patt., H. Burgess (minor potting flaw) **$80**

Toothbrush vase, Chelsea patt., ovoid shape, Alfred Meakin (moderate glaze & lustre wear) **$275**

Toothbrush vase, Maidenhair Fern patt., ovoid body w/fluted rim, A. Wilkinson (chip on upper rim)................................. **$500**

Toothbrush vase, Square Ridged patt., Wedgwood & Co.. **$225**

Toothbrush vase & undertray, Fig Cousin patt., pink lustre trim, Davenport (minor crazing).. **$2,300**

Vegetable dish, cov., Hexagon patt., Anthony Shaw, 13" w. **$75**

Vegetable dish, cov., oval, Coronet patt., W. & E. Corn, 12" l. (very minor crazing)..... **$70**

Vegetable dish, cov., round, Cable patt., Anthony Shaw, 11 1/2" d. **$175**

Washbowl & pitcher, Pagoda patt., H. Burgess, the set (base rim glaze flakes, tiny body nick).. **$300**

Tea Leaf Variants

Brush box, cov., oblong, Grape Octagon shape, copper lustre band decoration, E. Walley (small inside rim chip) **$200**

Butter dish, cover & insert, Twelve-Panelled shape, copper lustre band trim, Livesley & Powell (slight roughness inside cover) **$175**

Cake plate, Berry Cluster patt., cobalt blue & lustre band decoration, Jacob Furnival... **$275**

Cake plate, Rose patt., Washington shape, Powell & Bishop.. **$325**

Chamber pot, open, Grape Octagon shape, lustre band trim, E. Walley **$130**

Compote, open, 9" h., tall paneled pedestal w/large paneled bowl flanked by scroll handles below the wide flaring rim w/flat molded edge, copper lustre band decoration, Livesley & Powell **$625**

Creamer, Morning Glory patt., Portland shape, Elsmore & Forster, 6" h. **$175**

Creamer, Teaberry patt., Grand Loop shape, J. Furnival..................................... **$375**

Mug, child's, Morning Glory patt., unmarked (professional repair to rim hairline) **$425**

Pitcher, 8 1/2" h., Teaberry patt., Heavy Square shape, Clementson Bros. **$500**

Punch bowl, pedestal foot below the wide squatty rounded bowl w/a widely flaring rim, copper lustre primrose scroll decorated around the sides & inner rim, Livesley & Powell **$600**

Relish dish, mitten-shape, Teaberry patt., Elegance shape, Clementson Bros. (one small pinprick, worn lustre) **$500**

Sauce tureen, cover, ladle & undertray, Nautilus shape, copper lustre band decoration, J. Clementson (hairlines, cover chip) **$650**

Soap dish, cov., Grape Octagon patt., copper lustre band decoration, unmarked (bottom inside rim flakes)......................... **$210**

Sugar bowl, cov., Cockscomb shape, pedestal base, copper lustre & cobalt blue band trim, J. Furnival **$475**

Sugar bowl, cov., Panelled Grape shape, lustre band & cobalt sprig decoration......... **$200**

Sugar bowl, cov., Pinwheel patt., Full Panelled Gothic shape **$125**

Sugar bowl, cov., Teaberry patt., Beaded Band shape, Clementson Bros. **$180**

Teapot, cov., Ceres shape, lustre trim, Elsmore & Forster....................................... **$600**

Teapot, cov., Pinwheel patt., Grape Octagon shape **$375**

Teapot, cov., Wrapped Sydenham shape, copper lustre band decoration, E. Walley (slight crazing)... **$160**

Water pitcher, lustre band trim, New York shape, J. Clementson (very slight lustre wear)... **$150**

Jasper Ware (Non-Wedgwood)

Jasper ware is fine-grained, exceedingly hard stoneware made by including barium sulphate in the clay. It was first devised by Josiah Wedgwood, who utilized it for the body of many of his fine cameo blue-and-white and green-and-white pieces. It was subsequently produced by other potters in England and Germany, notably William Adams & Sons, and is in production at the present. Also see WEDGWOOD - JASPER.

Box, cov., miniature, round w/ringed foot, fitted flat cover w/slightly flared rim, the top w/a white relief bust of an Art Nouveau woman w/flowing hair, blue glossy ground, 2 1/2" d. **$45-55**

Box, cov., deep round blue jasper base raised on four small tab feet, the sides decorated in white relief w/leafy swags & ribbons, the slightly domed cover w/four small rim tabs decorated w/a blue border band w/white relief blossom & leaf band around a central medallion w/a brown ground & a white relief group of musicians, Germany, ca. 1910, 2 3/4" d., 3 3/4" h. **$200-250**

German Jasper Ware Plaque with Cupid

Plaque, round, green ground w/a white relief center scene of Cupid holding a broken arrow w/a heart at his side, scrolling leaf border, Germany, 5 3/8" d. (ILLUS.) **$75-85**

Fisherman Jasper Ware Plaque

Plaque, round, pierced to hang, green ground w/a white relief central scene of a standing fisherman smoking & holding the end of a long coil of rope in his hand, a crate & post behind him, a white relief wide border band of wrapped cattails, Germany, early 20th c., 6 1/4" d. (ILLUS.) .. **$145**

Plaque, oval, white relief scene of seminude water sprite on a black ground, Limoges, France, early 20th c., unframed, 5 x 7 3/4"....................................... **$350**

Plaque, rectangular, white relief classical beauty w/a tambourine on a blue ground, Limoges, France, late 19th - early 20th c., framed, plaque 6 x 10"...................... **$225-250**

Vase, 6" h., white relief scene of women, royal blue ground, Schafer & Vater, Germany **$175-200**

German Jasper Ware Jam Jar

Jam jar, cov., cylindrical waisted form w/scalloped rim & inset domed cover w/button finial, blue ground decorated w/two classical female figures, Schafer & Vater, Germany, 3 3/4" d., 5 1/4" h. (ILLUS.) **$125-150**

Plaque, oblong, white relief Native American chief w/full headdress, titled "Painted Horse," w/border of owls, green ground, small **$125-150**

Jewel Tea Autumn Leaf

Although not antique, this ware has a devoted following. The Hall China Company of East Liverpool, Ohio, made the first pieces of Autumn Leaf pattern ware to be given as premiums by the Jewel Tea Company in 1933. The premiums were an immediate success and thousands of new customers, all eager to acquire a piece of the durable Autumn Leaf pattern ware, began purchasing Jewel Tea products. Although decorate linens, glasswares and tinware, we include only the Hall China Company items in our listing.

Autumn Leaf Bean Pot

Bean pot, one-handled, 2 1/4 qt. (ILLUS.)..... **$950**
Bowl, ceral, 6 1/2" d. **$12**
Bowl, flat soup, 8 1/2" **$20**
Bowl, salad, 9" d. **$30**

Jewel Tea Butter Dish

Butter dish, one-handled, 2 1/4 qt. (ILLUS.)
.... **$1,400**

Butter Dish with Butterfly Handle

Butter dish, one-handled, 2 1/4 qt. (ILLUS.)
.... **$1,800**

Drip-type Coffee maker

Coffee maker, one-handled, 2 1/4 qt.
(ILLUS.)... **$325**

Autumn Leaf Electric Percolator

Coffeepot, one-handled, 2 1/4 qt. (ILLUS.) ... **$300**
Cup & saucer **$14**
French baker, swirled soufflé-style, 2 pt.
.... **$120-130**
Gravy boat & undertray, the set **$50**
Mixing bowl, 7" d., part of set **$20**
Pickle dish (gravy undertray) **$25**
Pie baker, 10" d. **$35**
Plate, 10" d., dinner **$14**
Salt & pepper shakers, bell-shaped, miniature size, pr. **$35**
Salt & pepper shakers, regular size, bell-shaped, pr. **$500**

Hall Jewel Tea Autumn Leaf Aladdin Teapot

Teapot, cov., Aladdin shape, (ILLUS.) **$75**
Teapot, cov., Newport shape w/gold trim,
1978 version **$200**

Newport Autumn Leaf Teapot

Teapot, cov., Newport shape w/gold trim
(ILLUS.).. **$250**
Vegetable bowl, 10 1/2" oval **$30**

Kitchen & Serving Accessories

Cow Creamers

Bennington Pottery Cow Creamer

Bennington pottery, platform-type, Rockingham glaze, rare, missing lid, chip on
one horn, tail repair, expect damage as
this creamer is a rare find in any condi-
tion, 5 x 7" (ILLUS.)............................ **$450-550**

Bisque Cow Creamer

Bisque porcelain, highly textured bisque
body, black spots, pink bow, w/yellow bell
at neck, all glazed, "Japan" paper label,
4 1/4 x 5 3/4" (ILLUS.) **$20-24**

Black Ceramic Cow Creamer

Ceramic, black high-gloss glaze over red
clay pottery, highly detailed, cold-painted features, maker unknown, 5 x 5 1/2"
(ILLUS.).. **$39-44**

Blue Painted Japanese Cow Creamer

Ceramic, blue painted flowers on both
sides, molded green bell around neck,
flowers in various colors, ink stamped
"Japan" on bottom, 5 1/4 x 7 3/4" (ILLUS)
.... **$32-35**

Blue Polka-dotted Cow Creamer

Ceramic, blue polka-dots on white glazed
pottery, molded bell at neck, eyes accented w/long lashes, unmarked, maker
unknown, 5 1/2 x 5 3/4" (ILLUS.)............ **$49-55**

Brahma Cow Creamer

Ceramic, Brahma, laying down, black at
top, graduating to reddish brown over
cream pottery, highly glazed, unglazed
bottom, very unusual, maker unknown,
3 3/4 x 8 3/4" (ILLUS.) **$39-45**

Walking Brahma Bull Creamer

Ceramic, Brahma, walking, head raised,
shaded brown to white, made in Japan
stamped mark, 5 1/4" l., 3 1/4" h.
(ILLUS.) **$19-25**

Brown & White Cow Creamer

Ceramic, brown markings on white glazed ceramic, h.p. eyes, tail curls down & connects to back hind leg forming handle, unmarked, 4 x 7" (ILLUS.)...................... **$21-24**

Common Cow Creamer

Ceramic, brown markings over highly glazed white ceramic, ink stamped number "B544" underneath, common, 3 1/2 x 5 3/4" (ILLUS.)............................ **$22-26**

Brown & White Bull Creamer

Ceramic, bull, brown & white, grey hooves & facial shading, tail curls under to form handle, ink stamped "K393," maker unknown, 4 1/2 x 7 3/4" (ILLUS.) **$29-35**

Grouping of Bull Creamers

Ceramic, bull creamers, also found w/matching salt & pepper shakers, stamped "Made in Japan," also "Occupied Japan," 3 x 3", each (ILLUS.) **$19-24**
Ceramic, bull creamers, also found w/matching salt & pepper shakers, stamped "Made in Japan," also "Occupied Japan," larger sizes, each **$24-35**

Cow Creamer Bust

Ceramic, bust-form, brown markings on white w/pink ears, cheeks & mouth, bulging eyes, yellow horns & bell at neck, commonly found in various other animal shapes, h.p. marked "Japan," 4 x 4" (ILLUS.) **$24-28**

Artmark Originals Cow Creamer

Ceramic, bust-form, dark brown w/lighter brown paint-dripping effects, gold highlights on tips of horns, lashes & bell, bottom red & gold foil paper label, h.p., "Artmark Originals, Japan," 3 1/2 x 5 3/4" (ILLUS.)................................... **$25-29**

Smiling Cow Creamer

Ceramic, bust-form, golden ringlets & horns at crown, molded blue bell about the neck, black markings, highly detailed smiling features, ink stamped "M6149 Japan," original price 49 cents, 4 x 4 1/4" (ILLUS.)................................... **$49-55**

Comical Cow Creamer

Ceramic, comical, pink on white, ink stamped "Japan" on bottom, original ink stamp price of 19 cents on bottom of hoof, 4 x 5" (ILLUS.) **$19-24**

Dark Brown Walking Cow Creamer

Ceramic, dark brown over red clay, highly glazed, w/gold accents about the feet & eyes, light brown drippings of paint at opening, missing paper label, Japan, 4 1/2 x 5 1/2" (ILLUS.) **$19-23**

Cow Creamer with Shamrocks

Ceramic, dark green shamrocks on white glaze, tail curls underneath to form han-

dle, marked "Cream" on front side, un-
marked, 5 x 8" (ILLUS.)........................... **$40-45**

Blue Floral Cow Creamer

Ceramic, dark & light blue flowers on white
glaze, w/blue nose & ears, tail curled up
over back to form handle, "Cream"
stamped on one side, bottom ink stamp
"E-3801," 4 1/4 x 7" (ILLUS.).................. **$39-46**

Flat-Bottomed Cow Creamer

Ceramic, flat bottom, turquoise spots on
cream glazed pottery w/brown accents,
molded bell at neck, rouge painted jaw
area, unmarked, unglazed bottom,
5 1/2 x 7" (ILLUS.)................................. **$65-69**

Handpainted Cow Creamer

Ceramic, h.p. floral on white, molded bell at
neck, many found with "Souvenir" label
from places visited, Japan, 3 1/4 x 5 1/4"
(ILLUS.).. **$14-19**

Holly Ross Cow Creamer

Ceramic, h.p. flower on one side, bud on
reverse, facial features, hooves & ribbon
in gold, w/gold under glaze bottom
marks, artist signed "Holly Ross, LaAn-
na, PA. Made in the Poconos," 5 x 7 1/2"
(ILLUS.) **$39-45**

Otagiri Cow Creamer

Ceramic, h.p., w/gold foil label "M O C Japan, Otagiri 1981," embossed underneath, foil label on side, "Handpainted,"

still being produced, common, by Otagiri,
3 x 5 1/2" (ILLUS.) **$12-15**

Black Cow Creamer

Ceramic, highly-glazed black over red clay,
cold-painted features in pink, blue &
gold, pottery bell w/painted flower attached by metal chain, original lid w/tip
of tail ornamental to top, unmarked,
5 1/2 x 6" (ILLUS.)................................... **$34-39**

Sponged Design Cow Creamer

Ceramic, laying down, legs tucked underneath, dark green sponging over brown,
yellow & cream glazed pottery, "Made in
Japan" bottom ink stamp, rare sponged
design, 3 1/2 x 7 1/4" (ILLUS.).............. **$95-100**

Brown & White Cow Creamer

Ceramic, light brown over white, sometimes
mistaken as the popular "Elsie"
creamer, h.p. dark green garland at neck &
bow on tail, black hooves, eyes shut w/fine
lashes, unmarked, 6 x 6" (ILLUS.)............ **$25-29**

Tan & White Japanese Cow Creamer

Ceramic, light tan over white, high glaze,
large black painted eyes & hooves, bottom ink stamp "B588," "Japan,"
3 3/4 x 5 3/4" (ILLUS.) **$14-19**

Black & White Lustre-glazed Creamer

Ceramic, lustreware, walking cow in white
w/black spots & lutres glaze, red stamp
"Handpainted Japan" w/clover & an "H" in

the center, mark of Hotta Yu Shoten & Co., closed in 1947, 7 1/2" l., 5 1/4" h. (ILLUS.).................. **$74-80**

Peach Lustre Walking Cow Creamer

Ceramic, lustreware, walking cow w/overall peach lustre glaze, red stamp "Hand-painted - Made in Japan" w/crown & leaves in the center, gold tail & horns, 7 1/4" l., 5" h. (ILLUS.) **$79-90**

Calico Cow Creamer

Ceramic, lying down, dark blue on white, "Milk" stamped on one side, bottom ink stamp "Calico Burleigh Staffordshire England," new, still in production, 3 x 7 1/4" (ILLUS.)... **$35-39**

Cow Creamer with Eyes Shut

Ceramic, lying down, eyes shut, yellow crown, pink nose, highlighted in brown on white glazed pottery, tail curled up to form handle loop over rear, impressed branding iron marking "R" within a "G" on back side, unglazed pottery bottom, maker unknown, 5 x 6 1/2" (ILLUS.) **$42-45**

Black & White Lustre Cow Creamer

Ceramic, lying down, feet tucked under, lustreware w/black spots & gold accented horns, red ink stamp "Made in Japan," 4 x 6" (ILLUS.)....................................... **$27-32**

Handpainted Japanese Cow Creamer

Ceramic, lying down, red dotted flowers on white w/dark green tail, hooves & crest, pink nose & ribbon, bottom marking "Hand Painted Japan," 1950-60, 4 x 6 1/2" (ILLUS.)................................. **$24-29**

Miniature Japanese Cow Creamer

Ceramic, miniature, h.p. flower on each side, stamped "Japan" on front hooves, 2 1/4 x 3 1/2" (ILLUS.) **$16-20**

Orange & White Cow Creamer

Ceramic, orange spots on both sides over white, black tail & facial features, unmarked, 1960 (ILLUS.)........................... **$19-24**

Petite Cow Creamer

Ceramic, petite, decorated w/flowers on white glaze, molded bell at neck, unmarked, Japan, 4 1/2 x 4 3/4" (ILLUS.) **$16-19**

Mottled Pink Cow Creamer

Ceramic, pink mottled high glaze, grey base, horns & tail, black ink stamp "Made in Japan" w/flower in middle, very unusual, 4 1/2 x 6 1/4" (ILLUS.)....................... **$49-55**

Gold Accented Cow Creamer Pitcher

Ceramic, pitcher, black high gloss w/22 kt. gold detailed accents, bottom stamped in gold "Pearl China Co., hand decorated, 22 kt. Gold, U.S.A.," impressed "#635," larger than usual cow creamer, 6 1/2 x 6 1/2" (ILLUS.)... **$29-35**

Kenmar Purple Cow Creamer

Ceramic, purple glazed, small tin bell attached at neck w/fine wire, gold foil label marked "Kenmar, Japan," various colors, common, mint w/bell, 4 1/2 x 6 1/2" (ILLUS.) **$25-29**

Cow Creamer w/Pink Flowers

Ceramic, reddish brown on cream, pink flowers at base, unmarked, w/flat bottom base, 1950-60, 3 3/4 x 5 1/2" (ILLUS.).... **$19-25**

Common Japanese Cow Creamer

Ceramic, reddish brown over cream, Japanese, mass-produced before, during & after the war, found in many sizes, colors & various markings, common, 3 1/2 x 5 1/4" (ILLUS.)............................. **$25-28**

Brown Cow Creamer & Sugar Set

Ceramic, set: cow creamer & cov. sugar; brown markings over white, large prominent eyes, molded bells at neck, standing cow creamer, lying down sugar w/lid, tail curls up to form handle on lid of sugar, unmarked, 1950, creamer 5 1/4 x 5 1/2" h., sugar 4 3/4 x 6", the set (ILLUS.) **$42-49**

Purple Cow Creamer & Sugar Set

Ceramic, set: cow creamer & cov. sugar; purple accents on white, sugar has satin ribbon on head, sold by Norcrest China Co., unmarked, "Japan," common, also found w/matching salt & pepper shakers, creamer 6 x 4 3/4" h., sugar 3 x 4 3/4", the complete set (ILLUS.) **$29-35**

Cow Creamer & Sugar

Ceramic, set: cow creamer, cov. sugar, salt & pepper; grey & black markings on white, highly glazed, removable salt & pepper heads, warehouse find, "Japan" stamped, mint in box, 5 x 5", the set (ILLUS. of part w/creamer on right)................................. **$39-44**

Handpainted Creamer & Sugar Set

Ceramic, set: creamer & cov. sugar; purple over white glaze, large pink flared nostrils, yellow horns, hooves & tails, tails curl up over backs to form handles, ink stamp "52/270" under glaze, foil gold & black paper stickers "Made in Japan," marked "Thames, Handpainted," found w/matching salt & pepper, complete, mint, creamer 5 x 5 1/2", sugar 4 1/2 x 6", the set (ILLUS.)...................... **$45-49**

Creamer from Purple Cow Set

Ceramic, set: creamer & matching cov. sugar; purple over white glaze, yellow horns & molded bell at neck, "Japan" paper label, 1950-60, both 4 1/2 x 4 1/2", the set (ILLUS. of creamer only)......................... **$29-32**

Purple Cow Set with Original Tag

Ceramic, set: creamer & matching cov. sugar; purple & pale pink glaze, original paper hang tag w/ Purple Cow rhyme, horns, hooves & bells w/gold trim, 1940-50, creamer 5" l., 4 1/2" h., the set (ILLUS.)... **$65-79**

Blue Tulip Decorated Cow Creamer

Ceramic, sitting, blue tulips on white glaze, bottom ink stamp "Japan" under glaze, 1950-60, common, 3 3/4 x 4" (ILLUS.) .. **$14-19**

Kent Ceramic Cow Creamer

Ceramic, sitting, brown w/white spots, gold molded bell around neck, tail curled up connecting at back of neck to form handle, bottom impressed stamp "Kent," 5 1/4 x 6" (ILLUS.).................................. **$24-29**

Sitting Bust Cow Creamer

Ceramic, sitting bust, reddish brown, bottom ink stamp "Made in Japan," 3 1/2 x 3 3/4" (ILLUS.)............................. **$29-35**

Sitting Cow Creamer w/Flowers

Ceramic, sitting, flowers on both sides over deep yellow chrome, enhanced gold highlights around features, no bottom markings, 4 3/4 x 6 1/2" (ILLUS.) **$39-45**

Sitting Cow Creamer

Ceramic, sitting, mottled brown on white pottery, yellow tail forming handle, found w/many other color variations, top of head is both opening & pouring vessel, unmarked (ILLUS.).................................. **$14-19**

Japanese Ceramic Cow Creamer

Ceramic, small, blue, w/molded green bell around neck, "Made in Japan" ink stamp underneath, 3 1/2 x 5" (ILLUS.) **$30-35**

Nashville Souvenir Cow Creamer

Ceramic, souvenir-type from Nashville, Tennessee, Music City, U.S.A., usually gold in color, found w/all states printed on side, paper label "Made in Japan," common, 3 1/2 x 5" (ILLUS.) **$14-19**

Early 1940s Cow Creamer

Ceramic, two large black spots on cream w/black hooves, unmarked, early 1940s, formerly used as a planter, also found in brown on cream, 5 1/2 x 7" (ILLUS.)....... **$39-45**

Simple Brown-spotted Cow Creamer

Ceramic, very simple in form & markings w/five light spots about body, horns & hooves highlighted in brown, paper label missing, 4 1/4 x 5 3/4" (ILLUS.) **$24-29**

Cow Creamer w/Pink & Grey Transfers

Ceramic, w/pink & grey flower transfer on both sides & gold hooves, found in various floral designs, unmarked, 5 1/2 x 7" (ILLUS.)... **$39-45**

Czech Creamer with Molded Flowers

Czechoslovakian pottery, reclining, tan shading to white glossy glaze, the sides deeply embossed w/flowers, made in Czechoslovakia mark on bottom, 6 1/4" l., 3 3/4" h. (ILLUS.) **$60-75**

Seated Brown-spotted Czech Creamer

Czechoslovakian pottery, sitting, orange spots on white porcelain, black tail, circle black ink stamp "Made in Czechoslovakia," 4 3/4 x 5 3/4" (ILLUS., previous page)....... **$75-78**

Czechoslovakian Cow Creamer

Czechoslovakian pottery, sitting, orange w/black ears & tail, dime size circle black ink stamp "Made in Czechoslovakia," minor paint wear, 4 3/4 x 5 3/4" (ILLUS.).... **$59-65**

Delft Faience Cow Creamer

Delft faience, exceptional blue coloring, windmill scene on front side, unmarked, 4 1/4 x 6 1/2" (ILLUS.)........................ **$124-130**

Delft Pottery Cow Creamer

Delft pottery, handpainted, light blue w/darker blue accents, signed by the artist, lidded opening, unusual that tail doesn't form handle, bottom marking under glaze "Made in Holland," mint, 3 3/4 x 6" (ILLUS.).............................. **$129-135**
Delft pottery, painted & lightly glazed porcelain, cow dressed in assorted men's clothing, either sitting or standing, rare & very desirable **$165-179**

Rare Marked Elsie the Cow Creamer

Elsie the Cow, standing w/head up, molded daisy chain around her neck, two-tone beige glaze, original foil label reads "Elsie - Copyright T.B.C.," 6" l., 5 1/2" h. (ILLUS.) **$234-245**

German Orange Bust-form Creamer

German china, bust w/deep orange glaze, marked "MW Co. - Made in Germany," 3 1/4" w., 3 3/4" h. (ILLUS.) **$74-79**

Standing Cow Creamer w/Infant

German china, standing in upright position, reddish brown cow wearing a white & blue dress, holding an infant in a blanket, bottom circular ink stamp "Made in Germany," rare, 3 3/4" w., 5 3/4" h. (ILLUS.) **$400-475**

German Porcelain Cow Creamer

German porcelain, brown markings over white, black highlights on tail, hooves & horns, unmarked, 4 1/2 x 5 1/2" (ILLUS.) **$48-52**

Brown & Cream German Cow Creamer

German porcelain, brown on cream porcelain, black accented tail, horns & hooves, red ink stamped "Germany," 3 1/2 x 5" (ILLUS.)... **$55-59**

German Green Reclining Cow Creamer

German porcelain, lying, w/tail curled up to form handle, impressed "Germany 1391" on back side, unusual light green color, mint, 3 1/2 x 7 1/2" (ILLUS.)............... **$114-120**

Miniature German Cow Creamer

German porcelain, miniature, grey/black on fine white porcelain, impressed on back "Germany," 2 5/8 x 3 5/8" (ILLUS.) **$45-55**

German Porcelain Standing Creamer

German porcelain, reddish brown graduating to white on softly glazed fine porcelain, extremely detailed features, impressed on reverse side "Germany 8610," 7 1/2" h., 4 3/4" l. (ILLUS.) **$75-82**

Goebel China Cow Creamer

Goebel china, brown markings on cream glazed ceramic, tin gold bell on string, tail curls under to form handle, unmarked, opening 2 1/4", 3 3/4 x 5 3/4" (ILLUS.).... **$32-36**

Brown-spotted Goebel Cow Creamer

Goebel china, brown markings on white, original tin bell on cord, full "Bee" blue ink stamp, "Germany," 5 x 7 1/2" (ILLUS.).... **$74-79**

Ironstone China Cow Creamer

Ironstone china, lying, w/legs tucked under, burgundy floral transfer on both sides, backstamp reads "Charlotte Royal Crownford Ironstone England," commonly found mold w/markings of different companies in various colors, marked "Made in England," 3 1/2 x 7" (ILLUS.) ... **$39-45**

Black Platform-Style Cow Creamer

Jackfield pottery, high-gloss black glaze over red clay w/gold trim, on platform w/lid, Shropshire, England, 4 1/2 x 6 1/4" (ILLUS.)... **$139-145**

Jackfield Cow Creamer

Jackfield pottery, platform base, high-gloss black glaze over red clay, gold details, w/original lid, Shropshire, England, 5 x 7 1/4" (ILLUS.) **$195-225**

Rare Jell-O Sebastian Cow Creamer

Jell-O model, white glaze printed w/colorful fruits on each side, produced by Sebastian of Marblehead, Massachusetts, 7" l., 5 1/4" h. (ILLUS.) **$345-375**

Limoges Porcelain Cow Creamer

Limoges porcelain, solid white, highly glazed, stamped in green ink inside top opening "Limoges, France," common mold, used for some souvenir items, 4 1/2 x 6 1/2" (ILLUS.) **$25-29**

Rare Occupied Japan Cow Creamer

Occupied Japan china, lying down, legs folded underneath, irregular spots, graduating colors of greens & brown on cream, ink stamped "Made in Occupied Japan," rare, mint, 5 1/4 x 7" (ILLUS.) **$69-75**

Occupied Japan Cow Creamer

Occupied Japan china, various dark brown markings, white background, glazed, tail curls up to form handle, found w/many different Japan stamps, common, prices depend on bottom markings, largest size 5 x 8" (ILLUS.) **$35-39**

Japanese Cow Creamer w/Lacy Collar

Porcelain, grey on white w/gold accents, very delicate & lacy collar around neck w/bell attached, eyes shut, red ink stamp "Japan" on hoof, 3 3/4 x 4 1/2" (ILLUS.) **$21-24**

German Porcelain Cow Creamer

Porcelain, white, tail & horns missing black cold-paint due to wear, "Germany" impressed on back underneath, 4 3/4 x 7" (ILLUS.) **$64-69**

Brown Pottery Cow Creamer

Pottery, medium brown sponged markings, blue molded bell at neck, unmarked, 1970-80, 4 1/2 x 6" (ILLUS.) **$12-17**

Pottery Cow Creamer

Pottery, pink accents on cream, green dots around neck forming a bow, lock handle tail, unmarked, 3 1/2 x 5" (ILLUS.) **$14-19**

Fine Early Staffordshire Cow Creamer

Staffordshire pottery, cov., platform-type, sponged dark brown & orange over white pottery, milkmaid seated on green base, facing forward, ca. 1810-20, 6 1/2" l. (ILLUS.) **$1,200-1,400**

Early Cow & Calf Spatterware Creamer

Staffordshire pottery, cov., spatterware, bands of black & yellow spatter along the body, feeding calf below also w/black & brown spots, on an oval platform base w/blue & green edge bands, England, ca. 1800, tail repaired (ILLUS.).......... **$1,200-1,325**

Purple Sponged Cow Creamer

Staffordshire pottery, cov., sponged purple lustre over cream glazed pottery, orange backstamp "Old Staffordshire Ware, England," 1910-20, small chip on ear, 6 1/2" l. (ILLUS.) **$165-179**

Staffordshire pottery, cov., standing, sponged in manganese & yellow, milkmaid seated performing her task at oblong platform base, facing left, ca. 1780, repair, 6 3/4" l. **$1,400-1,800**

Later Staffordshire Cow Creamer

Staffordshire pottery, pink floral transfer on white, w/yellow bell at neck, unmarked, England, 20th c., 5 x 8" (ILLUS.) **$80-95**

Old Staffordshire Spotted Cow Creamer

Staffordshire pottery, platform-type, reddish brown spots over white, embossed green flower on platform, w/original lid, early, dates from 1870, minor paint loss to be expected, 4 1/2 x 6 1/2" (ILLUS.) **$225-250**

Staffordshire solid agate, cov., body, two legs & suckling calf w/brown & ochre striations, the group modeled standing on a domed rectangular plain creamware base, the cover applied w/a creamware flower-form knop, ca. 1775, 8" l. (restoration to front of base, cover, calf's legs, horns & tail, tiny glaze chips) **$2,875**

English Sterling Silver Cow Creamer

Sterling silver, cov., ornate flowers around lid w/fly perched on top, marks "RC" w/"M" in a shield, lion w/raised paw facing left, leopard's head, letter "e," English, ca. 1960, still being produced, expect to pay more for earlier versions, 5.2 oz., 4 x 6" (ILLUS.) **$500-700**

White Lusterware Cow Creamer

White lustreware china, w/gold horns & tail, opening highlighted in gold, unmarked, mint, 4 3/4 x 6 1/2" (ILLUS.) **$74-79**
Yellowware pottery, cov., standing on a platform, lid w/little or no repair, similar to the Bennington cow creamer, very rare **$1,500-2,000**

Egg Cups

Ceramic egg cups were a common breakfast table accessory beginning about the mid-19th century and were used for serving soft-boiled eggs. Ceramics egg "hoops" or "rings" were used for many years before the cup-form became common. Egg cups continue to be produced today, and modern novelty and souvenir types are especially collectible.

The descriptions and values listed here were provided by collector Dr. Joan M. George, who notes that values for older egg cups are based on their marks, rarity and recent sales results.

Bucket-style, blue monogram "EIIR," for Queen Elizabeth II, England, 1950s **$22**
Bucket-style, commemorates death of Princess Diana, England, 1997.................... **$35**
Bucket-style, souvenir of Portsmouth, England w/picture of the HMS Victory, England, 1996 .... **$8**

English Gollywog Egg Cup

Bucket-type, colored design of a Gollywog pointing to a stove, Robertsons & Sons, England, ca. 1960s (ILLUS.) **$35**

Bjorn Wiinblad Designed Egg Cup

Bucket-type, colorful stylized modernistic design, Bjorn Wiinblad, Rosenthal, Germany, 1985 (ILLUS.).................................. **$45**
Double, decorated w/a chick & a green stripe, Roseville Pottery, ca. 1919 .... **$250**
Double, Garland patt., dark red flower on a grey ground, Stangl Pottery, ca. 1960s....... **$20**
Double, Luckenbach Line, pennant w/logo, unmarked, American-made......................... **$50**
Double, Mexicana patt. by Homer Laughlin, ca. 1930s **$40**

Singapore Bird Pattern Egg Cup

Double, Singapore Bird patt., Oriental-style design of birds & flowering branches on a celadon green ground, Adams, England, ca. 1950s (ILLUS.)........................ **$25**
Double, souvenir of Caesar's Palace, Las Vegas, Nevada, brown design, 1993 .... **$18**

Early Staffordshire Egg Hoop

Hoop-style, green transfer-printed design of people & houses, Staffordshire, England, 19th c. (ILLUS.) **$65**
Hoop-style, white decorated w/green garland band & gilt scrolls, Haviland, Limoges, France, 1990s **$85**

W.H. Goss Crest Egg Cup

Single, banner w/crest marked "Ye Ancient Port of Seaford," W.H. Goss, England, 1930s (ILLUS.) **$20**

French Bart Simpson Egg Cup

Single, Bart Simpson bust, yellow w/blue base, France, 1997, large (ILLUS.) **$25**
Single, Bayeux Tapestry, white ground w/a picture showing a portion of the tapestry, Limoges, France, 1998 .... **$15**

French Bellhop Egg Cup

Single, bellhop wearing blue hat & coat, cigarette in his mouth, France, ca. 1920 (ILLUS.) **$70**

Rare Betty Boop Egg Cup

Single, Betty Boop head, red dress, grey lustre hair, Germany, ca. 1930s (ILLUS.) .. **$300**

Minton Blue Delft Pattern Egg Cup

Single, blue floral Delft patt., gold band trim, Minton, England, 1990s (ILLUS., previous page) **$55**

Single, Booth's "Pompadour" patt., multicolored flowers, Silicon China, England, ca. 1920s **$30**

New York-Brooklyn Bridge Egg Cup

Figural Bugs Bunny Egg Cup

Single, Bugs Bunny head, grey & white, part of a set including Tweety Bird, Tasmanian Devil & Sylvester the Cat, unmarked, large size, 1980s, each (ILLUS.) **$25**

Souvenir Cup with Dutch Children

Handled Quaker Oats Man Egg Cup

Single, bust of the Quaker Oats Man, handled, tall, England, 1920s (ILLUS.) **$65**

Single, CAAC insignia of star & wings, small, current, China **$12**

Single, color copy of the Mona Lisa on a white cup, unmarked, France, 1998............ **$10**

Single, color scene of bridge w/"New York & Brooklyn Bridge," Germany, early 20th c. (ILLUS., top next column) **$35**

Single, color scene of Dutch children around the sides, printed in gold at the top "Souvenir Holland," unmarked, 1930s (ILLUS., middle next column)...................... **$32**

Early Goebel Boy's Head Egg Cup

Single, comical boy's head, painted features, high collar below chin, Goebel, Germany, ca. 1930s (ILLUS.) **$140**

Goebel Girl's Head Egg Cup

Single, comical girl's head, painted features, ruffled collar & pink hair band, Goebel, Germany, ca. 1930s (ILLUS.)....... **$140**

Single, commemorates the wedding of Princess Grace & Prince Rainier of Monaco, France, 1956.. **$95**

Charles & Diana Divorce Egg Cup

Single, commemorating the divorce of Prince Charles & Princess Diana, Coronet Pottery, England, 1996 (ILLUS.) **$30**

Rare Baby Doll Figural Egg Cup

Single, cov., baby doll head & shoulders painted in natural colors form the top, the footed base shows the hands & feet, unmarked, probably American-made, ca. 1930s, rare (ILLUS. of base)...................... **$150**

Single, cov., full-figure English Beefeater guard, England, 1999................................. **$15**

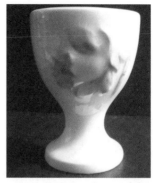

Goebel Daffodil Egg Cup from Series

Single, daffodil blossom, one of an annual series of flowers, birds & animals by Goebel of Germany, 1982 (ILLUS.) **$25**

Single, dark blue jasper ware w/white coat-of-arms of the Dominion of Canada, England, ca. 1950....................................... **$40**

Single, decorated by hand w/blue scroll arches trimmed w/gold, Davenport, England, 1887 .... **$85**

Meissen Blue Orchid Egg Cup

Single, deeply scalloped rim, Blue Orchid patt., Meissen, Germany, 1988 (ILLUS.) **$95**

French Faience Egg Cup

Single, faience, h.p. w/colorful blue & yellow florals & scrolls, France, ca. 1920s (ILLUS., previous page) $45
Single, figural Swee'pea, from Popeye cartoons, KFS Vandor Imports, Japan, 1980, large size $55
Single, figural ugly man's face in grey clay, large nose & blue & white eyes, England, 1999 .... $15
Single, flow blue Watteau patt., two figures in landscape having a picnic, Doulton, Ltd., England, ca. 1900 .... $85

Figural Staffordshire Egg Cup

Single, "Ham and Eggs," model of a pig seated at a table that forms the egg cup, Staffordshire bone china, England, ca. 1980s (ILLUS.) $35

Early Mintons Floral Egg Cup

Single, hand-decorated w/a colorful floral & geometric border band above floral garlands, Mintons, England, ca. 1890s (ILLUS.) $50
Single, hand-decorated w/a face, Desimone, Italy, ca. 1980s $40

Harrod's Bear Egg Cup

Single, Harrod's bear mascot, standing wearing trademark green Harrod's sweater, tall, England, 1999 (ILLUS.) $35

Unusual Humpty Dumpty Egg Cup

Single, Humpty Dumpty body in blue, sitting on a wall titled "Humpty Dumpty Egg Cup," egg would form the head, unmarked, ca. 1920s (ILLUS.) $45

Jemima Puddleduck Egg Cup

Single, Jemima Puddleduck standing beside a bush-form cup, one from a set of Beatrix Potter characters, Enesco, 1999, each (ILLUS., previous page) **$35**

Single, King Edward VII coronation commemorative, portrait wearing crown, England, 1901 .... **$85**

Single, King George V of England coronation commemorative, England, 1911........... **$65**

Royal Albert, England Egg Cup

Single, Lady Carlyle patt., decorated w/large clusters of flowers below a scalloped pink rim band, Royal Albert, England, ca. 1950s (ILLUS.) **$35**

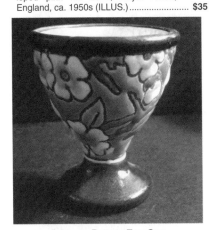

Longwy Pottery Egg Cup

Single, large bright pink blossoms & branches on a light blue ground w/dark blue foot & rim, Longwy, France, ca. 1920s (ILLUS.) **$60**

Single, lightly scalloped rim, colorful design of exotic bird & flowering branches, one of a series representing the months, marked "MARZ - Hutschenreuther," Germany, 1980s (ILLUS., top next column)....... **$25**

Single, Marilyn Monroe picture transfer-printed on hollow cup, England, 2002 .... **$15**

Hutschenreuther "March" Egg Cup

Rare Early Minnie Mouse Egg Cup

Single, Minnie Mouse, pointed nose & large ears, wearing orange skirt & blue blouse on a green base, Japan, ca. 1930s (ILLUS.) **$55**

Modern Cow-form Egg Cup

Single, model of a cow, round, painted black & white over green grass, Knobler, U.S., 1987 (ILLUS.).................................... **$15**

Single, model of a lion supporting the cup on its back, tan lustre glaze, Royal Fenton, Staffordshire, England, ca. 1930s **$25**

Single, model of a peacock, colorful bird supporting the cup on its back, Sarreguemines, France, ca. 1930s **$50**

Unusual Train Egg Cup - Whistle

Single, model of a train engine w/whistle at end, marked "Foreign" in a circle on the base, Germany, ca. 1920s (ILLUS.)........... **$175**

Figural Noah's Ark Egg Cup

Single, model of Noah's Ark w/cup on the roof, England, ca. 1920s (ILLUS.)............... **$75**

Single, Muppets, either Statler, Waldorf, Sam or Zoot, American-made, 1981, each **$50**

Royal Doulton Nanking Egg Cup

Single, Nanking patt., band of stylized colorful flowers & blue ribbons, Royal Doulton, England, ca. 1930s (ILLUS.)................. **$28**

Single, Niagara Falls picture titled "Niagara Falls Prospect Point Canada," Japan, 1930s **$28**

Royal Doulton Egg Cup in Orange

Single, orange rim band of stylized floral panels above floral sprigs, gold rim band, Royal Doulton, England, ca. 1930s (ILLUS.) **$35**

Mintons Egg Cup

Single, overall dark blue branching design on exterior & interior, gold rim stripes, Mintons, England, ca. 1910 (ILLUS.).......... **$50**

Torquay Pottery Egg Cup

Single, painted sea gull & "Torquay" on a dark blue ground, Torquay, England, 1985 (ILLUS.)... **$35**

Royal Delft Floral-Painted Egg Cup

Single, painted w/small stylized blue flower sprigs, Royal Delft, Germany, 1967 (ILLUS.) $55

Single, picture of Queen Elizabeth of England as a child, England, 1937 .... $90

Early Tower of London Egg Cup

Single, pink lustre ground around a white reserve w/a black transfer-printed scene of the Tower of London, Germany, early 20th c. (ILLUS.) $25

Smiling Policeman Egg Cup

Single, policeman, smiling & wearing a helmet w/a chin strap, unmarked, ca. 1930 (ILLUS.) $40

Early Figural Popeye Egg Cup

Single, Popeye full-figure, standing wearing a white suit w/blue trim & anchors, Japan, 1930s (ILLUS.) $125

Blessed Mother Shrine Souvenir

Single, portrait of the Virgin Mary, Blessed Mother Shrine, marked "Present from Carfin" (Scotland), made in Czechoslovakia, 1930s (ILLUS.) $35

Single, Prince Charles, "Spitting Image," Luck & Flaw, England, 1980s $55

Single, Prince William birth commemorative, family portrait, Coronet, England, 1982 .... $30

Single, Queen Elizabeth II 70th birthday commemorative, England, 1996 .... $25

Single, Queen Elizabeth II Golden Jubilee commemorative w/portrait & royal crest, England, 2002 .... $25

Single, Queen Mary of England coronation commemorative, mate to George V cup, England, 1911 .... $50

Single, Rhodes, Greece, white w/picture, 2000 .... $6

Modern Wedgwood Egg Cup

Single, rim band in blue & gold w/tiny red blossoms, Wedgwood, England, 1990s (ILLUS.).. **$25**

Single, Royal Copenhagen "Flora Danica" patt., hand-painted, Denmark, current **$475**

Single, Royal Doulton example decorated w/roses & gold garlands, England, 1927...... **$50**

The Drunk Figural Egg Cup

Single, The Drunk, silly face of a man w/half-closed eyes & tongue hanging out, unmarked, ca. 1930s (ILLUS.)................... **$75**

Single, Union Pacific Railroad "Winged Streamline" design, Scammell China, 1930s.. **$65**

Chintz "Welbech" Pattern Egg Cup

Single, Royal Winton Chintz "Welbech" patt., England, 1999 (ILLUS.)...................... **$35**

Single, "Running Legs," white cup attached to legs w/yellow shoes, Carlton Ware, England, 1970s **$40**

Single, scalloped bottom, black transfer-printed scene of "Porta Nigra, Tier," oldest city in Germany, Germany, 1998............ **$15**

Egg Cup Decorated with Chickens

Single, upper section decorated in color w/scenes of chickens, yellow foot, gold rim bands, unmarked, 1930s (ILLUS.)........ **$35**

Single, white ground w/a flag in an oval, titled "Nova Scotia," Canada, 2001................. **$7**

Rare Disney Snow White Egg Cup

Single, Snow White, standing beside cup marked w/her name, Walt Disney Enterprises, part of a set, Japan, 1937 (ILLUS.)... **$225**

Winston Churchill-VE Day Egg Cup

Single, Winston Churchill portrait against the Union Jack, commemorates 50th Anniversary of VE Day, Norwich Bone China, England, 1995 (ILLUS.) **$55**

Shy Lady Egg Cup by Goebel

Single, woman w/center-parted brown hair pulled into a bun, shy smile & side-glancing eyes, yellow bow at neck, Goebel, Germany, ca. 1930s (ILLUS.) **$140**

Egg Timers

A little glass tube filled with sand and attached to a figural base measuring between 3" and 5" in height was once a commonplace kitchen item. Although egg timers were originally used to time a 3-minute egg, some were used to limit the length of a telephone call as a cost saving measure.

Many beautiful timers were produced in Germany in the 1920s and later in Japan, reaching their heyday in the 1940s. These small egg timers were commonly made in a variety of shapes in bisque, china, chalkware, cast iron, tin, brass, wood or plastic.

Egg timers had long been considered an essential kitchen tool until, in the 1920s and 1930s, a German pottery company, W. Goebel, introduced figural egg timers. Goebel crafted miniature china figurines with attached glass vials. After the Great Depression, Japanese companies introduced less detailed timers. The Goebel figural egg timers are set apart by their trademark, delicate painting and distinctive clothes. It is best to purchase egg timers with their original tube, but the condition of the figure is most important in setting prices.

Goebel Baker Egg Timer

Baker, ceramic, Goebel (ILLUS.) **$50**

Goebel Bears Egg Timer

Bears, ceramic, brown & tan, white base, Goebel (ILLUS.) **$75**

Bellhop, ceramic, Oriental, wearing red outfit, marked "Germany" **$35**

Bird, ceramic, sitting on nest, wearing white bonnet w/green ribbon, Josef Originals sticker **$35**

Bird & Egg Near Stump Egg Timer

Bird, ceramic, standing next to stump w/egg at base, shades of brown w/green grassy base & leaves on stump, Japan (ILLUS.) **$50**

Black Baby Egg Timer

Black baby, ceramic, sitting w/left arm holding timer (ILLUS.) **$75**

Black chef, ceramic, sitting w/arm up holding timer, variety of sizes, Germany **$65-95**

Black Chef with Fish Egg Timer

Black chef, ceramic, standing w/large fish, timer in fish's mouth, Germany, 4 3/4" h. (ILLUS.).. **$125**

Black Chef w/Frying Pan Egg Timer

Black chef with frying pan, composition, Japan (ILLUS.)... **$85**

Bo-Peep Egg Timer

Bo-Peep, ceramic, "Bo-Peep" on base, Japan (ILLUS.).. **$85**

Boy, ceramic, holding rifle, marked "Germany"... **$35**
Boy, ceramic, skiing pose, marked "Germany," 3" h.. **$35**

Wooden Cat Egg Timer

Cat, wooden, black cat w/yellow eyes & red collar on domed yellow base, timer lifts out of back (ILLUS.).................................... **$25**
Chef, ceramic, holding blue spoon, marked "Germany".. **$50**
Chef, ceramic, winking, white w/black shoes & trim, turning figure on its head activates sand, 4" h... **$35**
Chef, composition board, black chef holding platter of chicken, w/pot holder hooks.......... **$25**
Chef, composition, w/cake, Germany **$65**

Egg Timer with Chef Holding Egg

Chef, porcelain, white & blue, holding reddish orange egg, supporting timer, Germany (ILLUS.)... **$50**
Chef, wood, "Time Your Egg"........................... **$20**
Chick, ceramic, white, yellow & purple chick, marked "Japan"................................. **$35**
Chick with cap, ceramic, Josef Originals........ **$35**
Chicken, ceramic, white w/black wings & tail feathers, marked "Germany" **$50**
Chicken, on nest, green plastic, England, 2 1/2" h.. **$20**

Goebel Chimney Sweep Egg Timer

Chimney sweep, ceramic, Goebel, Germany (ILLUS.) **$50**

Chimney sweep, ceramic, wearing black outfit w/top hat, carrying ladder, Germany **$50**

Clockman Planter

Clock, ceramic, clock face, w/man's plaid suit & tie below, w/planter in back, Japan (ILLUS.) **$25**

Clown Egg Timer

Clown, ceramic, Germany (ILLUS.) **$95**

Clown on phone, ceramic, standing, full-figured, Japan **$48**

Colonial lady with bonnet, ceramic, variety of dresses & colors, Germany, 3 3/4" h., each **$48**

Colonial man, ceramic, yellow & white, Japan **$48**

Dog, ceramic, Dachshund, red w/hole in back for timer, label on back reads "Shorty Timer" **$35**

Lustreware Dog

Dog, ceramic, lustre ware, white w/brown ears & tail, Japan **$50**

Dog, ceramic, Pekingese, standing brown & white dog, marked "Germany" **$48**

Dog Egg Timer

Dog, ceramic, sitting, white w/brown tail & ears, timer in head, Germany (ILLUS.) **$50**

Dogs, ceramic, Scotties, brown, standing facing each other holding timer in paws, marked "Germany" **$75**

Duck, wood, hanging-type, duck sitting on green egg, marked "Germany" **$25**

Dutch boy, ceramic, wearing blue & white sailor outfit, Germany, small **$35**

Dutch boy, ceramic, yellow pants, brown shoes, hat, scarf, Japan **$35**

Dutch Boy Egg Timer

Dutch boy, composition, blue pants & hat, red shirt, white tie w/blue polka dots, Germany (ILLUS.) **$35**

Goebel Dutch Boy & Girl Egg Timer

Dutch boy & girl, ceramic, double-type, timer marked w/3-, 4- & 5-minute intervals, Goebel, Germany, 1953 (ILLUS.) **$75**
Dutch girl, ceramic, talking on telephone, Japan **$35**
Dutch girl, ceramic, w/red heart on apron, Germany **$35**
Dutch girl w/flowers, chalkware, walking, unmarked, 4 1/2" h. **$50**
Elephant, ceramic, white, sitting w/timer in upraised trunk, marked "Germany" **$50**

Elf by Well Egg Timer

Elf by well, ceramic, Manorware, England (ILLUS.) **$25**

English Bobby Egg Timer

English Bobby, ceramic, Germany (ILLUS.) **$75**

Lustreware Fish Egg Timer

Fish, ceramic, lustre ware, burgundy, yellow & green, Germany (ILLUS.) **$65**

Fisherman Egg Timer

Fisherman, ceramic, standing, wearing brown jacket & hat, tall black boots, carrying a large white fish on his shoulders, timer attached to mouth of fish, Germany (ILLUS.) **$85**

Friar Tuck, ceramic, single, Goebel, Germany, 4" h. $48

Frog, ceramic, multicolored frog sitting on egg, marked "Japan" $50

Gollywog, bisque, England $165

Happy the Dwarf, ceramic, from "Snow White & the Seven Dwarfs," Maw Co., England $75

Honey bear, ceramic, brown & white, w/timer in mouth made to resemble milk bottle, Cardinal China Co., No. 1152 .... $48

House with clock face, ceramic, yellow & gold, Japan... $25

Huckleberry Finn, ceramic, sitting in front of post, Japan $100

Humpty Dumpty, ceramic, wearing hat & bow tie, turn onto head to activate sand, marked "California Cleminsons".................. $35

Indian Egg Timer

Indian, ceramic, kneeling, white, wearing headdress w/red, blue & green feathers, holding timer in one hand, marked "Germany," rare (ILLUS.) $150

Leprechaun, glazed chalkware, sitting on wishing well, "Porkush" on front base, marked "Manorware," England.................... $25

Lighthouse, ceramic, blue, cream & orange lustre ware, Germany, 4 1/2" h. $50

Little Boy Egg Timer

Little boy, ceramic, standing wearing black shorts & shoes & large red bow tie, Germany (ILLUS.)... $50

Little girl on phone, ceramic, sitting w/legs outstretched, pink dress, Germany $50

Goebel Little Girl & Chick Egg Timer

Little girl with chick on her toes, ceramic, Goebel, Germany (ILLUS.).................... $125

Mammy, tin lithographed, mammy cooking on gas stove, w/pot holder hooks, unmarked, 7 3/4" h...................................... $125

Minuteman, ceramic, holding rifle & leaning against stone wall, "Kitchen Independence" on front base, marked "Enesco" & "Japan".. $30

Mother Rabbit Egg Timer

Mother rabbit, ceramic, holding carrot w/basket, Japan (ILLUS.)............................. $48

Mouse Chef Egg Timer

Mouse, ceramic, sitting & holding timer, brown w/white apron marked "Chef" in red letters, Josef Originals (ILLUS.)............. $35

Mrs. Claus Egg Timer

Mrs. Claus, ceramic, in yellow dress w/green collar, cuffs & hem, w/red bag full of gifts & black bag w/timer (ILLUS.) **$50**
Newspaper boy, ceramic, Japan, 3 1/4" h. **$48**
Oliver Twist, ceramic, wearing red pants & vest, brown jacket, black hat, marked "Germany" **$75**

Goebel Owl Egg Timer

Owl, ceramic, Goebel, Germany (ILLUS.) **$50**
Parlor maid with cat, ceramic, Japan **$50**
Penguin, glazed chalkware, standing on green & white base w/"Bagnor Regis" painted on front, marked "Manorware, England" **$35**

Rabbit with Carrot Egg Timer

Rabbit, ceramic, sitting, white w/red jacket, holding carrot that supports the timer, Germany (ILLUS.) **$50**
Rabbit with floppy ears, ceramic, standing, tan, Germany **$50**

Rabbits, ceramic, double-type, various color combinations, Goebel, Germany, 4" h. **$50**
Rooster, wood, multicolored, standing on thick base **$25**

Sailboat Lustre-glazed Egg Timer

Sailboat, ceramic, lustre ware, tan boat w/white sails, Germany (ILLUS.) **$50**
Sailboat with sailor, ceramic, lustre ware, Germany **$50**
Santa Claus, ceramic, sitting, unmarked **$50**
Scotsman with bagpipes, plastic, England, 4 1/2" h. **$28**

Sea Gull Egg Timer

Sea gull, ceramic, timer in beak, Germany (ILLUS.) **$50**

Sea Gull Egg Timer with Bottle Opener

Sea gull, iron, white & tan bird w/red beak & legs, on black & white branch that is also a bottle opener (ILLUS.) **$20**

Swiss woman, ceramic, w/multicolored
striped apron, marked "Germany" **$50**
Telephone, ceramic, black, Japan **$25**
Vegetable person, ceramic, Japan **$95-125**
Veggie man or woman, bisque, Japan,
4 1/2" h., each **$95-125**

Waiter Egg Timer

Waiter, ceramic, standing next to ovoid
holder for timer, black & white, Germany
(ILLUS.) **$50**
Welsh woman, ceramic, Germany,
4 1/2" h. **$35**

Windmill with Pigs Egg Timer

Windmill, ceramic, w/pigs on base, Japan,
3 3/4" h. (ILLUS.) **$65**

Napkin Dolls

Figure of angel, blonde, wearing blue &
white dress w/gold trim, holding maroon
flowers w/green leaves, gold halo on
head, two slits in shoulders for napkins to
form "wings," 5 3/8" h. **$100-135**
Figure of bartender/waiter, w/black mus-
tache, red & white checked apron, black
bow tie & shoes, holds a tray that serves
as candleholder, foil sticker w/"Viking
Handmade, Made in Japan," w/matching
salt & pepper shakers, 8 3/4" h. (ILLUS.,
top next column) **$135-140**
Figure of genie, dressed in white robes
trimmed in gold, jewel-decorated turban,
holds a gold lantern, label reads "Genie
at Your Service," Enesco, 8" h. **$100-135**

Bartender/Waiter Napkin Doll & Shakers

Byron Molds Napkin Doll

Figure of girl holding flowers, red hair,
yellow dress w/matching hair bow, arms
clutch flowers to chest, marked "copy-
right Byron Molds," 8 1/2" h. (ILLUS.) **$55-75**

Atlantic Mold Napkin Doll

Figure of girl holding lily, mouth open as if
singing, brown bobbed hair w/yellow
headband, bright yellow dress w/green
leaf design, holds a blue lily in arms, Atlantic Mold, 11" h. (ILLUS.) **$50-65**

Figure of "Miss Versatility," woman in red & white dress w/red scallop trim & matching red picture hat that serves as candleholder, one hand held behind back, California Originals, 13" h............................ **$60-75**

Figure of Santa Claus, in red suit w/black belt & shoes, toothpick holes in hat, marked "Japan," w/a "Sage Store" label, 6 3/4" h... **$95-150**

Woman in Hat Napkin Holder

Holt Howard Napkin Doll

Figure of "Sunbonnet Miss," red-haired little girl in yellow dress w/white shoulder ruffle, matching yellow picture hat w/pink rose serves as candleholder, one hand pats hair, other arm is extended, marked "© Holt Howard 1958" (ILLUS.) **$135-165**

Holland Mold Napkin Holder

Figure of woman w/daisy, black hair w/bangs, dressed in blue & white dress & long white gloves, one hand fixes daisy behind ear, ca. 1958, marked "Holland Mold," 7 1/4" h.. **$75-95**

Napkin Holder/Toothpick Holder

Figure of woman holding tray, blonde, wearing black off-the-shoulder dress, one hand on hip, other holding pink covered tray, the lid w/holes to hold toothpicks, 8 1/2" h. (ILLUS.) **$75-95**

Figure of woman in hat, in dress w/yellow drop waist & purple skirt, yellow & purple hat w/upturned brim, marked "Cal. Cer. Mold," 12 1/2" h. (ILLUS., top next column).. **$65-85**

Napkin Doll Holding Fan

Figure of woman w/fan, in 18th-c. white dress w/blue trim on bodice & sleeves & blue bows on front of dress & in her dark hair, one hand holds up white fan w/blue trim, marked "Jam. Calif. ©" (ILLUS., previous page)... **$55-65**

Figure of woman w/poodle, blonde, dressed in pink dress trimmed in black, matching hat serves as candleholder, blue jeweled eyes, crystal jeweled necklace & red jewel on finger, holds a white poodle, marked "Kreiss & Co.," 10 3/4" h. **$115-135**

Figure of woman w/toothpick tray, bobbed hair, white dress w/yellow scalloped trim, holds oblong toothpick tray attached at waist, 10 3/4" h. **$60-75**

Woman with Bird Napkin Doll

Figure of woman w/toothpick tray, brown hair, green lustre dress decorated w/pink roses, one arm holds a toothpick tray w/similar decoration on her head, pink bird perches on other arm, 10 1/2" h. (ILLUS.)................................. **$75-95**

Model of rooster, black w/yellow & white trim, red comb & wattle, yellow beak & feet, paper label w/"Made in Japan," 10 1/4" h. **$35-45**

Pie Birds

A pie bird can be described as a small, hollow device, usually between 3 1/2" to 6" long, glazed inside and vented from the top. Its function is to raise the crust of a pie to allow steam to escape, thus preventing juices from bubbling over onto the oven floor while providing a flaky, dry crust.

Originally, in the 1880s, pie birds were funnel-shaped vents used by the English for their meat pies. Not until the turn of the 20th century did figurals appear, first in the form of birds, followed by elephants, chefs, etc. By the 1930s, many shapes were found in America.

Today the market is flooded with many reproductions and newly created pie birds, usually in many whimsical shapes and subjects. It is best to purchase from knowledgeable dealers and fellow collectors.

Advertising, "Kirkbrights China Stores Stockton on Tees," ceramic, white, England.. **$60**

Advertising, "Lightning Pie Funnel England," ceramic, white, England.................. **$75**

Advertising, "Paulden's Crockery Department Stretford Road," ceramic, white, England.. **$50**

Advertising, "Roe's Patent Rosebud," ceramic, England, 1910-30............................. **$50**

Advertising, "Rowland's Hygienic Patent," ceramic, England, 1910-30......................... **$50**

Advertising, "Sequel...Porcelain," ceramic, white, England **$35**

Advertising, "The Gourmet Crust Holder & Vent, Challis' Patent," ceramic, white, England.. **$75**

Advertising, "The Grimmage Purfection Pie Funnel," ceramic, England, 1910-30........... **$35**

Bird, ceramic, black on white base, yellow feet & beak, Nutbrown, England **$25**

Camark Pottery Pie Bird in Blue

Bird, ceramic, Camark Pottery, Camden, Ark., ca. 1950s-60s, depending on color, 6 1/2" h. (ILLUS.) **$125-400**

Half-doll Style Pie Bird

Bird, ceramic, half-doll style, blue & yellow on conical base, USA (ILLUS.) **$350**

Bird, ceramic, "Midwinter," black, England **$35**

Bird, ceramic, orange, Sunglow, England, ca. 1950s **$65**

Sunglow Pie Bird

Bird, ceramic, tan glaze, Sunglow, England (ILLUS.).. **$50**

Rare Bird on Nest Pie Bird

Bird on nest w/babies, ceramic, Artisian Galleries, Fort Dodge, Iowa (ILLUS.).. **$400-700**

Two-headed Pie Bird

Bird, ceramic, two-headed, Barn Pottery, Devon, England (ILLUS.) **$50**

Black Chef with Blue Smock

Black chef, ceramic, full-figured, blue smock, "Pie-Aire," USA, w/original tag (ILLUS.).. **$125**
Black chef, ceramic, full-figured, green smock, "Pie-Aire," USA **$175**

Rowe Pottery Pie Bird

Bird, ceramic, two-piece w/detachable base, 1992, Rowe Pottery (ILLUS.) **$25**
Bird, ceramic, w/flowers, Chic Pottery, ca. 1930s-60s, hard to find **$175**
Bird, pottery, "Scipio Creek Pottery, Hanni-bal, MO" **$15**

Black Chef w/Gold Spoon Pie Bird

Black chef, ceramic, w/gold spoon, white w/red trim (ILLUS.)................................... **$250**

Jackie Sammond Pie Bird & Owl

Blackbird, ceramic, 3" h., Jackie Sammond, early 1970s (ILLUS. right with owl) **$75**
Blackbird, ceramic, England............................ **$25**
Blackbird, ceramic, for child's pie, 2 3/4" **$95**

Stylized English Blackbird

Blackbird, ceramic, simple stylized shape w/brown beak, ca. 1930s-40s, English (ILLUS.).. **$150**

Very Large Black Pie Bird

Blackbird, ceramic, very large, 2 1/2" w x 5" h., English (ILLUS.) **$75**
Blackbird, ceramic, w/yellow trim on brown base **$65**

Wide-Mouth Blackbird Pie Bird

Blackbird, ceramic, wide mouth, yellow beak, fat, English (ILLUS.)......................... **$150**
Blackbird, clay w/black & yellow glaze, ca. 1960s-70s.. **$35**
Blackbird, red clay w/black glaze, ca. 1930s-40s.. **$35**
Bluebird, ceramic, Japan, post-1960............... **$35**
Chef, ceramic, "A Lorrie Design, Japan," Josef Originals, 1980s **$85**

"Benny the Baker" Pie Bird

Chef, ceramic, "Benny the Baker," w/tools & box, Cardinal China Co., USA (ILLUS.) **$125**
Chef, ceramic, half-figure, all-white, England **$65**

"Pie-Aire" Chefs

Chef, ceramic, "Pie-Aire," solid color, green, red or yellow, each (ILLUS.) **$125**
Chef, ceramic, "Servex Oven China, Bohemia, Guaranteed Heatproof, RD 17494 Aus., RD 4098 N.Z.," Australia, 4 5/8" h. ... **$100**

Holland Servex Chef Pie Bird

Chef, ceramic, white w/black buttons, "The Servex Chef" in black letters on hat, marked "Holland" inside (ILLUS.).............. **$100**

Cherry, apple & peach, ceramic, ca. 1950s, in original box, set of three **$350-450**

Chick with Dust Cap

Chick, ceramic, w/dust cap, Josef Originals (ILLUS.).. **$65**

Chick, ceramic, yellow w/pink lips, Josef Originals.. **$40**

Rare Donald Duck Pie Bird

Donald Duck, ceramic, "Walt Disney" marked on one side & "Donald Duck" on the other, rare (ILLUS.).......................... **$1,000**

Welsh Dragon Pie Birds

Dragon, ceramic, Creiciau Pottery, Wales, United Kingdom, each (ILLUS.) **$125**

English Dragon Pie Birds

Dragons, ceramic, various shapes & colors, 1980s-1990s, England, each (ILLUS. of three).. **$50**

Brown English Duck Pie Bird

Duck, ceramic, brown w/white & yellow beak, black trim, white base, England (ILLUS.)... **$95**

Duck, ceramic, pink, blue or yellow, full-bodied, USA, each **$50**

Pink English Duch Head Pie Bird

Duck head, ceramic, pink, England (ILLUS.) **$95**

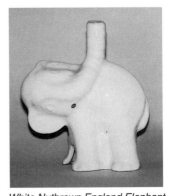

White Nutbrown England Elephant

Elephant, all-white w/trunk up, Nutbrown, England (ILLUS.) **$50**

Dutch Girl Multipurpose Pie Bird

Dutch girl, ceramic, doubles as pie vent, measuring spoon holder and/or receptacles for scouring pads & soap, Cardinal China, rare (ILLUS.) **$100-135**
Dwarf Dopey, ceramic, Disney **$300-450**

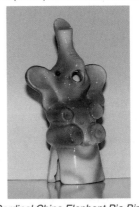

Cardinal China Elephant Pie Bird

Elephant, ceramic, grey & pink w/swirled pink base, Cardinal China Co., USA (ILLUS.) **$175**
Elephant, ceramic, white, ca. 1930s **$125**

Grey Nutbrown, England Elephant

Elephant, all-grey w/trunk up, ca. 1930s, Nutbrown, England (ILLUS.) **$200**

"Fred the Flour Grader" Pie Bird

"Fred the Flour Grader," ceramic, black & white, from Homepride Flour, ca. 1978 (ILLUS.) **$65-100**

Charles & Diana Funnel-shaped Pie Bird

Funnel-shaped, ceramic, white w/blue transfer-printed image of Prince Charles & Princess Diana above "Charles and Diana 1981" (ILLUS.)...................................... **$45**

Granny Pie Baker

Granny, ceramic, "Pie Baker," figure of woman holding bowl, Josef Originals (ILLUS.) **$65-95**

Kookaburra Pie Bird

Kookaburra, ceramic, light blue, Australia (ILLUS.).. **$195**

Luzianne Mammy Pie Baker

Luzianne Mammy, ceramic, black woman dressed in yellow shirt & green skirt, carrying a red tray w/coffee service, white turban on head (ILLUS.) **$65**

Multipurpose Mammy Pie Bird

Mammy, ceramic, doubles as pie vent, measuring spoon holder, and/or receptacles for scouring pads & soap (ILLUS.) **$75**

Clarice Cliff Mushroom Pie Bird

Mushroom, ceramic, white w/brown & green trim, designed by Clarice Cliff, ca. 1930s, England (ILLUS.)........................ **$85-95**

Mushroom-shaped Pie Bird

Mushroom-shaped, ceramic, England
(ILLUS.) **$300-450**

Rare Pie Boy Pie Bird

"Pie Boy," ceramic, white w/black & green
trim, Squire Pottery of California, USA,
rare (ILLUS.) **$350-500**

Josef Originals Owl

Owl, ceramic, "A Lorrie Design, Japan," Josef Originals, 1980s (ILLUS.) **$175-295**
Owl, ceramic, Jackie Sammond, USA. ca.
1970s (ILLUS. left with blackbird) **$125**

Josef "Pie Chef"

"Pie Chef," ceramic, Josef Originals **$65-95**
"Pie-Chic," ceramic, given as premium in
Pillsbury Flour, USA **$35-65**

Peasant Woman Pie Baker

Peasant woman, ceramic, brown glaze,
1960s-70s (ILLUS.) **$75**

Marion Drake Rooster Pie Bird

Rooster, ceramic, Marion Drake, white
w/black, red & yellow trim on brown base
(ILLUS.) **$50**

Pearl China Rooster

Rooster, ceramic, white w/tan trim, Pearl China, USA, depending on coloration (ILLUS.) **$100-350**

Rooster "Patrick" Pie Bird

Rooster "Patrick," ceramic, many color variations, California Cleminsons, USA, each (ILLUS.) **$35-75**

Rare Brown "Patrick" Pie Bird

Rooster "Patrick," ceramic, tan w/brown trim, California Cleminsons, USA, rare (ILLUS.).. **$175**

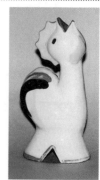

Cleminsons Rooster Pie Bird

Rooster "Patrick," ceramic, white w/pink & burgundy trim, thin line around base, California Cleminsons, rare (ILLUS.)................ **$85**

Green Songbird Pie Bird

Songbird, ceramic, beige, green, blue & pink variations, USA, each (ILLUS.) **$50**

Chic Pottery Black Songbird

Songbird, ceramic, black w/gold beak, feet & trim, Chic Pottery (ILLUS.).............. **$100-125**

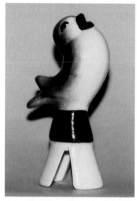

Puff-chested Songbird Pie Bird

Songbird, ceramic, lavender & brown trim, puff-chested, ca. 1940s (ILLUS.) **$300-400**
Songbird, ceramic, yellow, USA **$125**

Thistle-shaped Pie Bird

Thistle-shaped, ceramic, blue, England (ILLUS.) **$125**
Unusual pie vent, ceramic, "The Bleriot Pie Divider," white, 1910-20 .... **$450**

Yankee Pie Bird with Package

Yankee pie bird, ceramic, Millford, New Hampshire, ca. 1960s, w/original package (ILLUS.) **$35**

Reamers

Floral Ceramic Reamer

One-piece, saucer shape w/lipped spout and shell-form handle, white ground w/pink & magenta flowers, green leaves & gold bead trim, marked "Hand Painted Japan" (ILLUS.) **$150-175**

Reamer with Lattice Strainer

One-piece, saucer shape w/spout & side handle, round seed dam w/lattice strainer, white ground w/design of red cherries & green leaves, gold trim, 3" h. (ILLUS.) **$85-115**

Gold-trimmed Reamer

One-piece, saucer shape, white w/gold trim, w/figures of tree, swan, butterfly & flowerpot, marked "Made In France - Limoges France," 3 1/2" d. (ILLUS.) **$75-95**

Hall Ceramic Reamer

One-piece, simple round shape w/lip & side tab handle, green outside, white inside, marked "Hall," 6" h. (ILLUS.).............. **$550-600**

Souvenir Ceramic Reamer

One-piece, souvenir, saucer shape w/spout & side handle, blue, rust & cream, w/painted image of Victorian woman w/parasol on one side of bowl & mass of flowers on the other, marked "Made in England, A Present From Dobercourt," 3 1/4" d. (ILLUS.) **$85-125**

Three-piece, teapot shape, orange & white w/gold trim, cone sits under gold-handled lid, 3 1/2" h. **$50-60**

Three-piece w/tray, ceramic w/sterling silver trim, white ground w/orange flowers, green leaves, rust trim, marked "France," 5" h. **$225-250**

Two-piece, figure of duck w/white lustre body, blue head, orange beak, yellow top knot, marked "Made In Japan," 2 3/4" h. **$35-50**

Oriental Man's Head Reamer

Two-piece, in the shape of an Oriental man's head, w/collar as base, hat as lid/reamer, light blue w/dark grey highlights, incised "9496," 5 3/4" h. (ILLUS.) **$125-150**

Two-piece, model of lemon slice, yellow w/green handle, marked "Japan," 6 3/4" h... **$35-45**

Reamer with Basketweave Design

Two-piece, pitcher shape w/C-form handle, basketweave design in dark green w/orange & maroon flowers & light green leaves, yellow top & cone, black trim, marked "Maramotoware Hand Painted Japan," 4" h. (ILLUS.) **$40-50**

Squat Pitcher-form Reamer

Two-piece, squat pitcher form w/lip & circular handle, white ground w/maroon & yellow flower design, gold trim, marked "Hand Painted Japan," 3 3/4" h. (ILLUS.)............ **$75-95**

Tall Pitcher-form Reamer

Two-piece, tall pitcher form w/lip, C-form handle & short outcurved base, pale pink ground w/painted floral decoration in pinks, blues, yellows & greens, thin green rim decoration, marked "Pantry Bak-In Ware by Crooksville," 8 1/4" h. (ILLUS.) **$125-175**

Two-piece, teapot shape on three legs, white ground w/color photograph of Westminster Abbey, marked "Foreign," 3 1/2" h. **$100-125**

Figural Painted Ceramic Reamer

Two-piece, teapot shape, with earthtone & purple pansy-type flowers on white ground, green lustre trim on handle & rim of body, lid & spout, ribbed lid w/holes for liquid to pass through, reamer in the form of a head with yellow ribbed cone hat, marked "Made in Japan," 6" h. (ILLUS.) **$75-125**

String Holders

String holders were standard equipment for general stores, bakeries and homes before the use of paper bags, tape and staples became prevalent. Decorative string holders, mostly chalkware, first became popular during the late 1930s and 1940s. They were mass-produced and sold in five-and-dime stores like Woolworth's and Kresge's. Ceramic string holders became available in the late 1940s through the 1950s. It is much more difficult to find a chalkware string holder in excellent condition, while the sturdier ceramics maintain a higher quality over time.

Apple, ceramic, handmade, 1947 .... **$35**
Apple w/face, ceramic, "PY" **$95**
Apple with berries, chalkware, common......... **$20**

Apple with Worm String Holder

Apple with worm, chalkware, "Willie the Worm," ca. 1948, Miller Studio (ILLUS.) **$35**

Art Deco Woman String Holder

Art Deco woman, chalkware, green beret & scarf (ILLUS.).. **$95**
Baby, chalkware, frowning **$125**
Balloon, ceramic, variety of colors, each **$25**
Bananas, chalkware, ca. 1980s-present **$25**

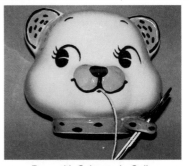

Bear with Scissors In Collar

Bear, w/scissors in collar, ceramic, Japan (ILLUS.).. **$25**
Betty Boop, chalkware, original **$400**
Bird, ceramic, green, "Arthur Wood, England," also found in blue & brown.............. **$15**

"String Swallow" Bird String Holder

Bird, ceramic, in birdhouse, "String Swallow" (ILLUS.).. **$35**
Bird, ceramic, yellow bird on green nest, embossed "String Nest Pull," Cardinal China, U.S.A. **$35**

Bird, chalkware, peeking out of birdhouse **$125**
Bird & birdhouse, wood & metal **$25**

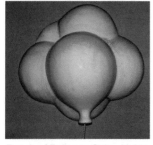

Bird in Birdcage String Holder

Bird in birdcage, chalkware (ILLUS.) **$75**
Bird on birdhouse, chalkware, cardboard,
"Early Bird," bobs up & down when string
is pulled, handmade **$25**
Bird on branch, ceramic, Royal Copley **$30**
Bird on nest, ceramic, countertop-type, Jo-
sef Originals **$35**

Boy with Tilted Cap

Boy, w/tilted cap, chalkware (ILLUS.) **$65**
Boy, w/top hat and pipe, eyes to side, chalk-
ware **$30**
Brother Jacob and Sister Isabel, chalk-
ware, newer vintage, each **$50**

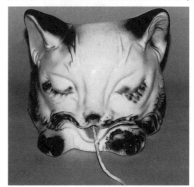

Bunch of Balloons String Holder

Bunch of balloons, ceramic, green, pink &
blue, ca. 1983, Fitz & Floyd (ILLUS.) **$25**
Butler, ceramic, black man w/white lips &
eyebrows, Japan, hard to find **$150**

Cabbage String Holder

Cabbage, ceramic, Japan (ILLUS.) **$85**
Campbell Soup boy, chalkware, face only ... **$175**

Black Cat with Gold Bow

Cat, ceramic, black w/gold bow, handmade
(ILLUS.) **$25**
Cat, ceramic, climbing a ball of string **$50**
Cat, ceramic, full-figured w/flowers & scis-
sors **$25**

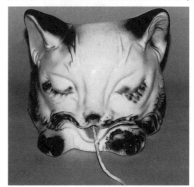

"Knitter's Pal" String Holder

Cat, ceramic, "Knitter's Pal" (ILLUS.) **$25**

Cat, ceramic, w/matching wall pocket **$50**

Cat with Plaid Collar String Holder

Cat, ceramic, w/plaid collar, space for scissors, Japan (ILLUS.) **$25**
Cat, ceramic, w/scissors in collar, "Babbacombe Pottery, England" **$20**
Cat, ceramic, white face w/pink & black polka dot collar **$35**

Cat Face String Holder

Cat, ceramic, white, w/large green eyes, scissors hang on bow (ILLUS.) **$25**

Cat with Ball of String Holder

Cat, ceramic, white, full-figured on top of ball of string (ILLUS.) **$35**

Cat on Ball of String String Holder

Cat, chalkware, grinning, on a ball of string, Miller Studio, 1952 (ILLUS.) **$30**
Cat, chalkware, w/bow, holding ball of string **$25**
Chef, ceramic, "Gift Ideas Creation, Phila., Pa.," w/scissors in head **$25**

Chef with Rosy Cheeks

Chef, ceramic, w/rosy cheeks, marked "Japan" (ILLUS.).. **$28**

Chef, chalkware, baby face w/chef's hat........ **$100**

Chef with Spoon & Box String Holder

Chef, chalkware, full-figured black chef w/spoon & blue box (ILLUS.) **$95**

Chef, chalkware, "Little Chef," Miller Studio **$95**

Chef with Black Face

Chef, chalkware, black face, white hat (ILLUS.) **$95**

Chef, chalkware, chubby-faced, "By Bello, 1949," rare **$250**

Chef with Bushy Eyebrows

Chef, chalkware, unusual version of chef w/bushy eyebrows (ILLUS.) **$75**

Common Chef Head String Holder

Chef, chalkware, common (ILLUS.) **$35**

Chef with Large Hat

Chef, chalkware, w/large hat facing left (ILLUS.)... **$75**

Chef with a Bottle

Chef w/bottle & glass, ceramic, full-figured, Japan (ILLUS.) **$85**

Bunch of Cherries String Holder

Cherries, chalkware, bunch on leafy stem (ILLUS.) **$150**
Chicken, ceramic, "Quimper of France," found in several patterns, still in production **$50**
Chicken, ceramic, unmarked **$35**

Chipmunk String Holder

Chipmunk's head, ceramic, white & brown, red & white striped hat & bow, bow holds scissors, Japan (ILLUS.) **$35**
Clown, ceramic, full-figured, "Pierrot," hand holds scissors **$65**

Jo-Jo the Clown String Holder

Clown, chalkware, "Jo-Jo," ca. 1948, Miller Studio (ILLUS.) **$150**
Crock, ceramic, "Kitchen String," by Burleigh Ironstone, Staffordshire, England, w/scissors in top **$25**

"The Darned String Caddy"

"Darned String Caddy (The)," ceramic, marked "Fitz & Floyd, MCMLXXVI" (ILLUS.) **$20**
Delicious apple, chalkware, w/stem & leaves **$20**
Dog, ceramic, "Bonzo," comic character dog w/bee on chest **$75**

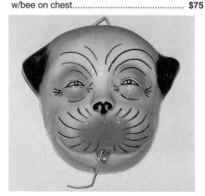

Bonzo Face String Holder

Dog, ceramic, Bonzo face,comic character dog, marked "Japan," rare (ILLUS., previous page) **$275**

Ceramic Boxer String Holder

Dog, ceramic, Boxer (ILLUS.) **$75**
Dog, ceramic, Collie, "Royal Trico," Japan **$85**
Dog, ceramic, full-figured Shaggy Dog, w/scissors as glasses, marked "Babbacombe Pottery, England" **$20**
Dog, ceramic, German Shepherd, "Royal Trico, Japan" **$75**

Dog String Holder

Dog, ceramic (ILLUS.) **$50**

Scottie String Holder

Dog, ceramic, Scottie, marked "Royal Trico, Japan" (ILLUS.) **$75**

Dog, ceramic, w/diamond-shaped eyes **$65**
Dog, ceramic, w/puffed cheeks **$25**
Dog, chalkware, Bulldog w/studded collar, ca. 1933 .... **$85**

Dog with Chef's Hat String Holder

Dog, chalkware, w/chef's hat, "Conovers Original" (ILLUS.) **$250**

Westie with Bow String Holder

Dog, chalkware, Westie, bow at neck (ILLUS.) **$85**

Westie with Studded Collar

Dog, chalkware, Westie, white w/studded color (ILLUS.) **$75**

Dog, wood, "Sandy Twine Holder," body is ball of string.. **$20**

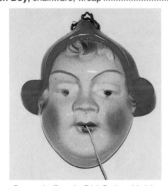

Dog with Black Eye

Dog w/black eye, ceramic, w/scissors holder in collar, right eye only circled in black, England (ILLUS.)... **$25**
Dove, ceramic, Japan...................................... **$25**
Dutch Boy, chalkware, w/cap **$75**

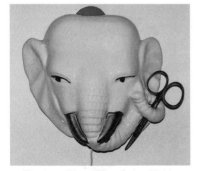

Ceramic Dutch Girl String Holder

Dutch Girl, ceramic, head only, Japan (ILLUS.) **$25**
Dutch Girl, chalkware, head only, w/large hat **$45**
Elephant, ceramic, "Hoffritz, England" **$20**
Elephant, ceramic, marked "Babbacombe Pottery, England," scissors as glasses **$20**

Elephant Pincushion-String Holder

Elephant, ceramic, white w/gold tusks, pincushion on head, Japan (ILLUS.)................. **$28**

Father Christmas String Holder

Father Christmas, ceramic, Japan (ILLUS.) **$95**
Flowerpot, ceramic, yellow, w/measuring spoon holder **$50**

Chalkware Chef String Holder

French chef, chalkware, w/scarf around neck (ILLUS.).. **$85**
Funnel-shaped, w/thistle or cat & ball, ceramic **$45**
Gourd, chalkware.. **$50**
Granny, ceramic, full-figured, top of nose holds scissors that look like glasses **$25**

Granny in Rocking Chair String Holder

Granny in rocking chair, ceramic, marked "PY," Japan (ILLUS., previous page) **$65**

Humpty Dumpty, ceramic, sitting on wall, white & yellow (ILLUS.) **$35**

Grapes String Holder

Grapes, chalkware, bunch (ILLUS.) **$50**
Green pepper, ceramic, Lego sticker **$50**

Indian in Headdress String Holder

Indian w/headdress, chalkware, brightly colored (ILLUS.) **$100**
Iron w/flowers, ceramic **$45**
Ladybug, chalkware **$85**

Puffed Heart String Holder

Heart, ceramic, puffed, heart reads "You'll always have a 'pull' with me!" California Cleminsons (ILLUS.) **$35**

Cleminsons House String Holder

Latchstring house, ceramic, California Cleminsons (ILLUS.) **$50**

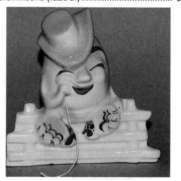

Humpty Dumpty String Holder

Lemon String Holder

Lemon, ceramic, Japan (ILLUS.) **$50**

Little Bo Peep String Holder

Little Bo Peep, ceramic, white w/red & blue trim, marked "Japan" (ILLUS.) **$85**
Little Red Riding Hood, chalkware, head wearing hood... **$150**

Mammy Holding Flowers

Mammy, chalkware, full-figured, holding flowers, marked "MAPCO" (ILLUS.)............. **$95**
Mammy, chalkware, head only, marked "Ty-Me" on neck **$125**

Loverbirds String Holder

Lovebirds, ceramic, Morton Pottery (ILLUS.) **$35**
Maid, ceramic, Sarsaparilla, 1984 .... **$35**
Mammy, ceramic, full-figured, plaid & polka dot dress, Japan **$60**

"Genuine Rockalite" Mammy

Mammy, chalkware, head only, w/polka-dot bandana, marked "Genuine Rockalite," made in Canada (ILLUS.) **$125**
Mammy, cloth-faced, "Simone," includes card that reads "I'm smiling Jane, so glad I came to tie your things, with nice white strings," rare **$95**

Mammy String Holder

Mammy, ceramic, full-figured, w/arms up & scissors in pocket (ILLUS.) **$100**

Coconut Mammy

Mammy, coconut, w/red and blue floral scarf (ILLUS., previous page) **$20**
Mammy, felt, head only, w/plastic rolling eyes.. **$35**
Man, ceramic, head only, drunk, designed by & marked "Elsa" on back, Pfaltzgraff, York, Pennsylvania **$50**

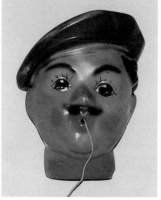

Gigolo Man String Holder

Man, chalkware, head only, marked across collar "Just a Gigolo" (ILLUS.)..................... **$50**
Mexican man, chalkware, head only, common **$30**

Mexican Man with Flowered Hat

Mexican man, chalkware, head only, flower-trimmed hat (ILLUS.) **$60**
Mexican woman, chalkware, head only, w/braids & sombrero **$95**
Monkey, chalkware, sitting on ball of string, found in various colors **$95**
Mouse, ceramic, countertop-type, Josef Originals sticker... **$25**
Mouse, ceramic, England................................ **$20**
Oriental man, ceramic, w/coolie hat, Abingdon Pottery **$250**
Owl, Babbacombe Pottery, England **$20**
Owl, ceramic, full-figured, Josef Originals **$20**

Pancho Villa String Holder

Pancho Villa, chalkware (ILLUS.)................... **$95**
Parrot, chalkware, brightly colored **$85**
Peach, ceramic **$25**
Pear, chalkware.. **$20**

Peasant Woman Knitting String Holder

Peasant woman, ceramic, full-figured, knitting sock, sticker reads "Wayne of Hollywood" (ILLUS.).. **$85**
Penguin, ceramic, full-figured w/scissors holder in beak, marked "Arthur Wood, England" **$35**

Floral Decorated Pig String Holder

Pig, ceramic, white w/red & yellow flowers & green leaves decoration, scissors holder on back near tail, Arthur Wood, England (ILLUS.).. **$25**

Pineapple, chalkware, "Prince Pineapple," by Miller Studio **$95**

Tomato String Holder

Tomato chef, ceramic, eyes closed, "Japan" **$50**

Porter String Holder

Porter, clay, without teeth, marked "Fredericksburg Art Pottery, U.S.A." (ILLUS.) **$95**
Prayer lady, ceramic, by Enesco **$95**
Rooster, porcelain, head only, Royal Bayreuth **$225**
Sailor Boy, chalkware **$85**
Sailor Girl (Rosie the Riveter), chalkware ... **$145**

Woman in Flowered Dress String Holder

Woman, ceramic, full-figured, blue dress w/white & red flowers, Japan (ILLUS.) **$50**
Woman, ceramic, head only, arched eyebrows **$95**

Snail String Holder

Snail, ceramic, dark brown (ILLUS.) **$20**
Soldier, chalkware, head only, w/hat **$30**
Southern gentleman with ladies, ceramic **$35**
Strawberry, chalkware, w/white flower, green leaves & no stem **$45**
Susie Sunfish, chalkware, Miller Studio, 1948 .... **$95**
Teapot, ceramic, w/parakeet, Japan **$35**
Teddy bear, ceramic, brown, hole for scissors in bow at neck, marked "Babbacombe Pottery, England" **$20**
Thatched-roof cottage, ceramic **$25**
Tom cat, ceramic, "Takahashi, San Francisco," Japan **$25**
Tomato, ceramic (ILLUS., top next column) **$35**
Tomato, chalkware **$35**

Chalkware, Cardboard & Cloth String Holder

Woman's face, chalkware on cardboard box w/cloth bonnet (ILLUS.) **$50**
Young black girl, ceramic, w/surprised look, Japan **$100**

Kutani

This is a Japanese ware from the area of Kutani, a name meaning "nine valleys" where porcelain was made as early as about 1675. The early wares are referred to as "Ko-Kutani" and "Ao-Ko Kutani."

Centerpiece, a wide shallow ceramic bowl h.p. w/round panels depicting figures, birds & fowl, fitted w/a pierced bronze rim band w/ring handles & supported on a round gilt-bronze base w/figural elephant head feet, late 19th c., 14 1/2" d., 6" h. (ILLUS., bottom of page) **$1,380**

Fancy Kutani Covered Bowl

Bowl, cov., 14" l., 9 1/2" h., squatty bulbous base w/a short wide rolled rim supporting a domed cover w/figural foo lion finial, crouching lion shoulder handles, white panels on the sides of the base & cover delicately painted w/flowers & birds in flight in pale greens & earth tones, fancy deep red ground w/ornate gilt trim, signed under base, small cracks at rim, normal wear, ca. 1880 (ILLUS.) **$863**

Fancy Japanese Dragon Teapot

Teapot, cov., ovoid white body w/fancy moriage decoration w/an undulating dragon body continuing up onto the domed cover to form the dragon head finial, the dragon body handle continuing into the body & ending in a painted dragon head, a tall dragon head spout, in shades of red, brown & white, marked "Kutani China - Japan," ca. 1920s (ILLUS.) **$85**

Fine Bronze-mounted Kutani Bowl

Geisha Girl Teapot with Unusual Pink Background

Teapot, cov., pedestal base supporting the wide squatty body w/a short wide neck, serpentine spout & C-scroll handle, low domed cover w/pointed finial, Fan Dance A & Flower Gathering A patterns in reserves, unusual pink background, gold border, signed "Kutani," Japan, first quarter 20th c., 5" h. (ILLUS.) **$95**

Footed Kutani Teapot in So Big Pattern

dle, low domed cover w/knob finial, hand-painted So Big patt., geometric pine green & red border w/gold trim, signed "Kutani," Japan, late 19th - early 20th c., overall 8" l., 5" h. (ILLUS.)........................... **$60**

Decorative Japanese Kutani Teapot

Teapot, cov., round scalloped foot below the wide ovoid body tapering to a short neck w/high domed cover w/figural butterfly finial, serpentine spout, ornate C-scroll handle, completely hand-painted w/Japanese Geisha, red & gold borders, signed "Watayasu Sei," Japan, late 19th - early 20th c., 6" h. (ILLUS.) **$75**

Teapot, cov., three-footed squatty bulbous body w/serpentine spout & C-form han-

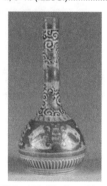

Kutani Bottle-form Vase

Vase, 9 1/2" h., bottle-form, bulbous spherical base w/a tall stick neck, decorated w/stylized colorful butterflies & gold scrolls on a deep red ground, marked on the base, late 19th c. (ILLUS.) **$240**

Lenox

The Ceramic Art Company was established at Trenton, New Jersey, in 1889 by Jonathan Coxon and Walter Scott Lenox. In addition to true porcelain, it also made a Belleek-type ware. Renamed Lenox Company in 1906, it is still in operation today.

Lenox China Mark

Fine Lenox Painted Tankard Pitcher

Pitcher, 13" h., tankard-type, footed tall gently tapering cylindrical sides w/a scalloped rim & large arched rim spout, fancy C-scroll handle, h.p. w/large red cherry on a leafy branch, pale yellow to brick-red handle, artist-signed, early 20th c. (ILLUS.) **$196**

Fine CAC-Lenox Cabinet Plate

Plate, 10 3/8" d., cabinet-type, a wide maroon rim band decorated w/ornate gilt floral swags & scrolls, the center h.p. w/a bust portrait of a lovely maiden w/long brown hair holding a cluster of pink roses, Ceramic Art Company monogram & Lenox wreath mark, artist-signed, ca. 1903-07 (ILLUS.).. **$1,434**

Sunday Brunch Lenox China Teapot

Teapot, cov., Butler's Pantry Series, Sunday Brunch design, tapering cylindrical ruffled form, undecorated, modern (ILLUS.) **$45**

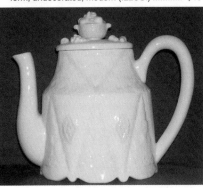

Lenox Teapot in Butler's Pantry Series

Teapot, cov., Butler's Pantry Series, tapering cylindrical form w/molded V-shaped panels, undecorated, modern (ILLUS.)........ **$45**

Modern Lenox Christmas Tree Teapot

Teapot, cov., Christmas Tree patt., figural decorated tree, modern (ILLUS.) **$75**

Lenox Summer Enchantment Teapot

& vine decoration, modern (ILLUS., top of
page) **$75**

Limoges

*Limoges is the generic name for hard paste
porcelain that was produced in one of the Limoges
factories in the Limoges region of France during
the 19th and 20th centuries. There are more than
400 different factory identification marks, the
Haviland factory marks being some of the most
familiar. Dinnerware was commonly decorated by
the transfer method and then exported to the
United States.*

*Decorative pieces were hand painted by a fac-
tory artist or were imported to the United States
as blank pieces of porcelain. At the turn of the
20th century, thousands of undecorated Limoges
blanks poured into the United States, where any
of the more than 25,000 American porcelain
painters decorated them. Today hand-painted
decorative pieces are considered fine art. Limoges
is not to be confused with American Limoges.
(The series on collecting Limoges by Debby
DeBay, Living With Limoges, Antique Limoges at
Home and Collecting Limoges Boxes to Vases are
excellent reference books.)*

Newer Lenox Garden Party Teapot

Teapot, cov., Garden Party patt., Butler's
Pantry series, modern (ILLUS.) **$45**

New Lenox China Pumpkin Teapot

Teapot, cov., pumpkin-shaped, molded
scrolling leaf panels alternating w/plain
panels, vine finial, produced in 2004
(ILLUS.) **$75**

Teapot, cov., Summer Enchantment patt.,
footed squatty spherical body w/serpen-
tine spout, C-form handle & domed cover
w/figural butterfly finial, colorful butterfly

Limoges Cache Pot

Cache pot, underglaze factory mark in
green "W.G.&Co." (William Guérin),
12" h. (ILLUS.) **$1,500**

Cake plate, h.p. in the Pickard factory, underglaze factory mark "B&C France," 11 1/2" d. $600

Cake plate on pedestal, h.p., underglaze factory mark in green "T&V Limoges France Depose" (Tressemann & Vogt), 4 x 12" $395

Candlesticks, h.p. roses, heavy gold, underglaze factory mark in green "T&V," 16" h., pr. $600

Chalice, h.p. violets, underglaze factory mark "J.P.L. France" (Jean Pouyat), 10 1/2" h. $700

Charger, dramatic h.p. roses on dark ground, gold scroll on rim, underglaze factory mark in green "AK [over] D France" (A. Klingenberg), 15" d. $1,000

Charger, h.p. all over w/light roses, underglaze factory mark in green "AK [over] D France," 15" d. $1,000

Limoges Charger with Red Roses

France" (J. Pouyat), ca. 1891-19332, 14 1/2" d. (ILLUS.) $1,200

Cheese dish, cov., rare domed style, h.p., underglaze factory mark in green "J.P.L France," 7" h. $400

Chocolate set: 10 1/2" h. bulbous covered pot & four matching cups & saucers; h.p. purple violets, underglaze green factory mark "T&V - Limoges, France" (Tressemann & Vogt), ca. 1892-1907, the set (ILLUS., bottom of page)....................... $2,000

Chocolate set: 10 1/2" pot, six cups & saucers; h.p. & signed by factory artist "Magne," underglaze factory mark in green "T&V Limoges France," decorating factory mark "All Over Hand Painted" in red banner, the set $3,500

Chocolate set: 12 1/5" pot, 5 cups & saucers, 14" oval tray; h.p., underglaze factory mark in green "J.P.L. France," (Jean Pouyat-Limoges) the set $3,000

Chocolate set: 12" pot, two cups, 12" tray; h.p., underglaze factory mark in green "J.P.L. France" (Jean Pouyat, Limoges), the set $1,500

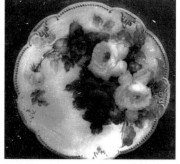

Limoges Charger with Dark Roses

Charger, h.p. w/dark flowers on light ground, underglaze factory mark in green "AK [over] D France," (Klingenberg), 15" d. (ILLUS.) $1,000

Charger, round w/gold scroll border & large h.p. red roses by an amateur artist, underglaze green factory mark "J.P.L. -

Chocolate Set with Violets

Rose-decorated Limoges Dresser Set

red roses, underglaze green mark "W.G. & Co. - France" (William Guerin), ca. 1891-1900, the set (ILLUS., top of page) **$1,500**

Dresser set: tray, cov. jar & hair receiver; h.p. by amateur artist, underglaze factory mark in green "W.G.&Co., France" (William Guérin), the set **$500**

Limoges Floral-decorated Compote

Compote, open, 10" d., 9" h., h.p. large pink flowers & green leaves on a shaded brown to yellow ground, underglaze green factory mark "H& Co. - L./France" (Haviland & Co.), amateur artist's signature "Andrew," ca. 1888-1896 (ILLUS.) **$950**

Cracker jar, cov., barrel-shaped, h.p. large roses, h.p., underglaze mark in green "T&V Limoges France," 7 1/2" h. **$325**

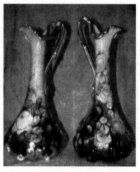

Rare Pair of Limoges Ewers

Ewers, h.p. by unknown amateur artist, underglaze factory mark in green "W.G.&Co.," rare pair, 15 1/4" h., pr. (ILLUS.) **$2,500**

Squatty Cracker Jar with Roses

Cracker jar, cov., wide squatty bulbous shape w/inset cover w/gold finial & gold loop handles, h.p. pink & yellow roses, underglaze green factory mark "T&V Limoges France," (Tressemann & Vogt), ca. 1907-1919, 9" w., 6 1/2" h. (ILLUS.) **$650**

Cup & saucer, tea/toast, underglaze factory mark in green "T&V Limoges," 9" d. **$200**

Dresser set: cov. rectangular box on small tray, small cov. round jar, cov. powder jar, kidney-shaped tray; all h.p. w/pink &

Limoges Ferner with Purple Violets

Ferner, squatty bulbous body scalloped rim & large gold scroll feet, h.p. purple violets & green leaves, underglaze green factory mark "Elite - L. France" (Bawo & Dotter), after 1900-1912, 11 1/2" l., 8" h. (ILLUS.) **$900**

Ice cream set: serving dish & 12 individual dishes in original presentation case; cobalt & gold, two Haviland marks, ca. 1888-1896, the set **$3,500**

Limoges Jardiniere with Red Roses

Jardiniere, bulbous body w/a wide flat gold rim, gold scroll handle & scroll feet, h.p. large dark red roses, underglaze green factory mark "D&Co." (Delinieres & Co.), ca. 1894-1900, 10 1/2" h. (ILLUS.) **$4,000**

Lion Head-handled Jardiniere

Jardiniere, bulbous body w/wide flat gold rim & ornate lion head handles, on a separate base w/scroll & paw feet, h.p. large pink roses, underglaze green factory marks "D&Co." (R. Delinières), , ca. 1894-1900, 11 1/2" h. (ILLUS.) **$3,500**

Jardiniere, fluted pedestal base, fluted handles, h. p. large roses & leaves, underglaze factory mark in green "J.P.L. France" w/anchor, 12 x 14" **$2,500**

Jardiniere, footed, h.p. & artist signed "H.E. Page," dated 1897, underglaze factory mark in green "Limoges France" w/anchor (probably A. Lanternier), 10" h. **$3,000**

Jardiniere, footed, ornate handles, cherub decoration, underglaze factory mark in green "D&Co." (R. Délinieres), 11" h....... **$3,000**

Jardiniere, footed, side handles at top, deeply scalloped rim, large h.p. roses, underglaze factory mark in green "T&V France," (Tressemann & Vogt) very rare blank, 11 1/2" h. **$2,000**

Jardiniere, on original base, lion head handles, h.p. roses & detail, underglaze factory mark in green "D&Co." (R. Delinières), 12 x 14" **$4,500**

Jardiniere, on original base, no handles, bold floral decoration, underglaze factory mark in green "D&Co.," (R. Delinieres) 11 x 12".. **$2,500**

Jardiniere, original base, elephant head handles, raised gold paste trim, large h.p. roses, underglaze factory mark in green "J.P.L.," 11 1/5" h. **$3,000**

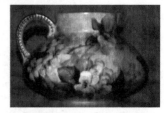

Small Limoges Cider Pitcher

Pitcher, cider, 7" h., squatty bulbous body, overall florals h.p. by amateur artist "E. Miler," underglaze factory mark in green "J.P.L. France" (ILLUS.) **$600**

Limoges Cider Pitcher with Roses

Pitcher, cider, 10 1/2" h., h.p. large deep pink roses & gold trim, signed by factory artist "Roby," underglaze factory mark in green "T&V France," "T&V" decorating mark in purple (ILLUS.) **$1,500**

Tall Grape-decorated Pitcher

Pitcher, 15" h., tankard-type, h.p. red & purple grape clusters & leaves, underglaze green factory mark "W.G. & Co. - Limoges, France" (William Guerin), ca. 1900-1932 (ILLUS.)............................. **$900**

Planter, h.p. w/vibrant chrysanthemums, gilt handles & four feet, underglaze factory mark in green "D&Co.," 8 x 12 1/2" **$2,000**

Planter, no base, h.p. roses, underglaze factory mark in green "W.G.&Co.," 14" h. **$2,500**

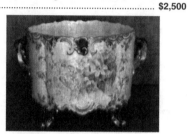

Unusual Limoges Planter

Planter, tall, unusual blank, h.p. florals & ornate gold trim, underglaze factory mark in green "D&Co.," 9 x 9 1/2" (ILLUS.) **$2,000**

Planter or jardiniere, large h.p. roses & leaves, blank attributed to the d'Albis & Romanet Factory, swan handles, overglaze factory decorating mark in red "Elite Works," (Bawo & Dotter) 8 x 10".... **$1,500**

Plaque, h.p. interior scene w/people, underglaze factory mark in green "Limoges France," overglaze decorating mark in red "Limoges France," artist signed "Dubois," pierced factory holes in back for hanging, 14" d. **$2,500**

Plaque, oval w/ornate molded rim & scroll end handles, h.p. florals trimmed in heavy gold, underglaze factory mark "Limoges" in star (Coiffe), 13 1/4" h. **$1,200**

Fine Limoges Plaque

Plaque, rectangular, h.p. scene of a young mother holding her child in her lap, underglaze green factory mark "T&V Limoges France," signed on back "Mother to

Marud," ca. 1892-1907, ornate gold frame, image 22 x 26" (ILLUS.) **$10,000**

Plate, 10 1/2" d., heavy gold rim & h.p. roses, underglaze factory mark in green "J.P.L. France," overglaze factory decorating mark w/pink & green wreath **$225**

Cobalt Blue Dessert Plate from Set

Plates, 6" w., dessert, squared shape in cobalt blue w/raised gold paste trim, underglaze green factory mark "AL" w/anchor & "Limoges, France" (Lanternier), ca. 1891-1914, overglaze blue factory decorating studio mark "Limoges, France" in a double circle, Lanternier, ca. 1891-1914, import mark "WL Helm & Graff," set of 8 (ILLUS. of one)..................................... **$1,200**

Plates, red & gold, underglaze factory mark in green "GDA," overglaze decorating mark in red "GDA" (Gérard Dufraisseix and Abbot), set of 12 .... **$3,000**

Platter, 18" l., game-type, h.p. game birds & florals signed by factory artist "Dubois," "Limoges France" & star, Flambeau studio decorating mark **$2,000**

Powder jar, cov., h.p. roses w/heavy gold, underglaze mark in green "T&V," 5 1/2 x 6 1/2".. **$550**

Limoges Punch Bowl with Roses

Punch bowl & undertray, rare mammoth blank w/three gold feet, h.p. w/dramatic roses by unknown artist, underglaze factory mark in green "J.P.L. France," 13 x 26", 2 pcs. (ILLUS.)........................ **$5,500**

Punch set: bowl, 18" tray, cups; factory-decorated h.p. roses & heavy gilt, all factory artist signed "Aubin," underglaze factory mark in green "T&V Limoges France," factory decorating mark in grey "L.R.L.," the set **$6,500**

Limoges Set with Teapot, Cups & Saucers & Tray

Punch set: bowl, base, tray, cups; h.p. at White's Art Co., Chicago, underglaze factory mark in green "D&Co.," rare, the set **$5,500**

Punch set: bowl w/original base, tray, cups; h.p. by unknown artist w/dark grapes & heavy gilt, underglaze factory mark in green "T&V Limoges France," the set **$3,500**

Seafood set: platter, 14 1/2" gravy boat, plates; h.p. w/image of lobster & signed by factory artist "Dubois," "Limoges France" mark w/star, Flambeau studio decorating mark, rare, the set **$4,000**

(Wm. Guerin), before 1891, rare red overglaze factory decorating studido mark "W.G. & Co. France," before 1891, very rare blank, color & mark, the set (ILLUS. of tureen)... **$4,500**

Tea set: cov. teapot, cov. sugar, creamer, tray; unusual pot on pedestal w/roses, artist signed "C. Wynn" & dated 1901, the set **$1,000**

Tea set: cov. teapot, cups & saucers & round tray; tall urn-form teapot & tall conical cups, each piece h.p. w/bands of pink roses & green leaves, green factory mark "France - PM - De M Limoges" (Mavaleix mark 1), ca. 1908-14, the set (ILLUS., top of page)................................. **$600**

Blue Limoges Soup Tureen from Set

Soup tureen set: cov. tureen & eight matching bowls;, squatty bulbous oblong shape w/swirled ribs on base & domed cover, gold scroll end handles & dolphin finial, scroll-molded base, h.p. ocean blue ground w/gold leafy sprigs, underglaze green factory mark "W.G. & Co. France"

Rose-decorated Teapot, Cups & Saucers & Dessert Plates

Tea set: cov. teapot, four cups & saucers & four dessert plates; squatty bulbous teapot w/gold C-form handle & loop finial on domed cover, serpentine spout, each piece h.p. w/bands composed of pairs of pink roses & green leafage, factory mark of Jean Pouyat, Limoges, France, 1891-1932, the set (ILLUS.)............................... **$700**

GDA Limoges Tea Set on Tray

Tea set: one-cup cov. teapot, open sugar, creamer & oblong tray; each piece painted w/colorful roses, a gold wave scroll band around the teapot & creamer neck, gold loop handles & teapot finial, marks of Gérard, Dufraisseix & Abbot, Limoges, France, ca. 1900-41, the set (ILLUS.)........ **$900**

Six-cup Limoges Teapot From Set

Tea set: six-cup cov. footed spherical teapot w/a low scalloped rim, domed cover w/loop finial, serpentine spout & C-scroll handle, h.p. w/lovely shaded red & pink roses & green leaves, gold trim, matching four-cup teapot, cov. sugar, creamer, cups & saucers & an 18" l. double-handled tray, France, late 19th c., the set (ILLUS. of six-cup teapot) **$1,400-2,000**

Elegant Gold & White Limoges Tea Set on Tray

Tea set: tall cov. teapot, cov. sugar bowl, creamer, six cups & saucers & a tray; the tall tapering teapot in white w/a scroll gold band around the neck below a wide gold rim band, matching band design on the other pieces, gold handles, spouts & covers, marks for Blakeman & Henderson, Limoges, France, ca. 1890s, teapot 6" h., the set (ILLUS.)............................. **$1,500**

Tall Teapot from Three-Piece Set

Tea set: tall cov. teapot, cov. sugar & creamer; teapot w/wide rounded bottom & tall tapering sides, each piece in white w/heavy gold trim on spout, handles, rims & finials, green factory mark "France P.M. deM - Limoges," decorator mark of "Coronet France - Borgfeldt," ca. 1908-14, the set (ILLUS. of teapot)................... **$350**

Tressemann & Vogt Limoges Teapot

Teapot, cov., bulbous tapering ovoid body w/long serpentine spout, high C-form handle & low domed cover w/loop finial, white w/simple trim, mark of Tressemann & Vogt, Limoges, ca. 1900 (ILLUS.) **$200**

Ornately Decorated Limoges Teapot

Teapot, cov., bulbous tapering ribbed body w/wide domed cover w/fancy loop finial, gold serpentine spout & C-scroll handle, star mark of the Coiffe factory & Flambeau China mark of decorating firm, also a Haviland & Co. mark, France, early 20th c. (ILLUS.).. **$100**

Pretty Tressemann & Vogt Teapot

Teapot, cov., squatty bulbous footed body w/domed cover w/double-loop gold finial, serpentine spout, gold C-form handle, h.p. w/swags of roses, factory mark of Tressemann & Vogt, Limoges, France, ca. 1892-1907, 4" h. (ILLUS.) **$400**

Teapot, cov., tall cylindrical body w/a long serpentine spout, C-form handle & domed cover w/knob finial, decorated w/an oval reverse & a border band of grapevines, Bernadaud & Company, France, early 20th c. (ILLUS., bottom of page) **$85**

Guerin Gold & White Limoges Teapot

Teapot, cov., wide flat bottom w/tapering cylindrical sides & flat rim, slightly domed cover w/pointed disk finial, angled handle, serpentine spout, white w/gold bands & scrollwork around the neck & a gold finial, spout & handle, marks of Wm. Guerin & Co., Limoges, France, ca. 1891-1932 (ILLUS.) **$150**

White & Gold Limoges Teapot

Teapot, cov., wide squatty bulbous body w/low domed cover & knob finial, C-form handle, serpentine spout, white w/gold bands on the spout, rim & handle, marks of Tressemann & Vogt, Limoges, France, ca. 1907-1919, four-cup size (ILLUS.) **$150**

Tile, h.p. porcelain, artist signed "Ann" & dated 1898, underglaze factory mark in green "T&V Limoges, France," 14 x 17" **$2,500**

Tile, h.p. porcelain of woman & cherub, underglaze factory mark in green "T&V France," 11 x 14" **$3,000**

Simple Limoges Porcelain Teapot

Teapot, cov., wide bulbous body w/a long gold spout & C-form handle, domed cover w/pointed disk finial, marks of B & H Limoges, France & Legrand, Limoges, ca. 1920 (ILLUS.) **$50**

Bernadaud & Co. Limoges Teapot

Limoges Tray with Rare Scenic Decoration

Tray, 18" l., oval, rare central color balcony scene of a Blackamoor speaking with an older man & a young woman, encircled by heavy & ornate rasied gold paste w/enameling, underglaze green factory mark "T&V Limoges, France - Déposé" (Tressemann & Vogt), ca. 1907-1919 (ILLUS.) **$4,000**

Tureen, cov., squatty bulbous form w/domed cover, loop end handles & scrolled base & feet, h.p. w/berries, artist signed "Andrew," underglaze factory mark in green "P&P" (Paroutaud Frères), 8 x 9" **$1,500**

Urn, w/original stopper, tall slender ovoid body w/split handles, h.p. florals, underglaze factory mark in green "W.G.&Co., Limoges, France," 14" h. **$2,000**

Squatty Rose-decorated Limoges Vase

Vase, 6" h., 9" d., wide squatty bulbous form w/small flaring neck, overall h.p. red, white & yellow roses & green leaves, underglaze green factory mark "T&V Limoges France," ca. 1892-1907 (ILLUS.) **$900**

Vase, 8" h., 13 1/2" d., low squatty round body w/a short rolled neck, h.p. roses, underglaze factory mark in green "T&V Limoges France" & artist signed "Vera Gray," unusual shape & size **$3,000**

Limoges Vase with Lady & Harp Scene

Vase, 12" h., unique ovoid body w/double handles & scrolled base, finely h.p. scene of woman playing a harp, underglaze green factory mark "J.P.L. - Limoges" (Jean Pouyat), amateur artist's signature "L. M. Cowgill," ca. 1890-1932 (ILLUS.).. **$2,500**

Vase, 12 1/2" h., large ovoid body w/a short flared neck & w/separate original base, h.p. w/large red & pin rosees & green leaves, underglaze factory mark in green "J.P.L.," unusual **$2,500**

Vase, 14" h., one of a pair h.p. in a factory in Chicago w/image of woman known to be a factory model in the early 20th c., underglaze mark in green "J.P.L. France," each **$3,500**

Vase, 14" h., tapering waisted conical body, factory h.p. w/ roses & artist signed "Rouncon," underglaze mark in green "PBM DE M Limoges, France" (Malaleix), overglaze decorating mark in green "Coronet" in crown **$3,000**

Vase, 14" h., unique lion head handles, h.p. by "Mrs CW Lamson, Erie, PA," dated March 16, 1901, underglaze factory mark in green "D&Co." **$2,500**

Unusual Tall Five-sided Limoges Vase

Vase, 15 1/2" h., tall five-paneled ovoid body w/paneled foot & short flaring neck, large h.p. red roses & green leaves around sides & interior of rim, underglaze green factory mark "B&C - France" (Bernardaud & Co.," amateur artist's signature "Hicks K," ca. 1900-1914 (ILLUS.)... **$4,000**

Liverpool Pitcher with American Ship

Pitcher, 8 1/2" h., jug-type, decorated w/black transfer-printed scenes w/some hand-tinting & gilt trim, one side w/a sailing ship under full sail & flying an American flag, the other side w/a circular medallion enclosing a Latin inscription, all surrounded by circles w/the names of the first 13 states, tight crow's-foot in the base, early 19th c. (ILLUS.) **$1,725**

One of Two Tall Limoges Vases

Vase, 22" h., tall slender ovoid body bolted on a pedestal base & w/a slender trumpet neck w/rolled rim, raised gold trim, one of a pair, h.p. w/roses & enameled w/raised gilt, underglaze factory mark in green "W.G.&Co.," ca. 1891-1900, each (ILLUS. of one) **$4,000**

Liverpool

Liverpool is most often used as a generic term for fine earthenware products, usually of cream-ware or pearlware, produced at numerous potteries in this English city during the late 18th and early 19th centuries. Many examples, especially pitchers, were decorated with transfer-printed patriotic designs aimed specifically at the American buying public.

Rare Boston Fusiliers Liverpool Pitcher

Pitcher, 9 1/2" h., jug-type, decorated w/black transfer-printed scenes w/some hand-tinting & gilt trim, the front w/a large oval wreath medallion topped by Masonic devices & enclosing a full-length portrait of an officer in full uniform & holding the Massachusetts state flag, the border band inscribed "Aut Vincere Aut Mori - Success to the Independent Boston Fusiliers, Incorporated July 4th, 18787 - America Fore Ever...," the reverse w/an oval design w/the allegorical figures of Liberty, Justice & Peace above the inscription "United We Stand - Divided We Fall," a wreath above the figures includes 16 stars surmounted by an American flag, a floral design below the spout, base chip, very minor discoloration & enamel loss, rare design (ILLUS.) **$11,163**

Two Views of an Early Liverpool Pitcher with the Ship Nancy of Boston

Washington Memorial Liverpool Pitcher

Pitcher, 10 1/4" h., jug-type, decorated w/black transfer-printed scenes, the front w/a large oval memorial scene w/weeping willows flanking a monument to George Washington w/a mourning figure below, a ribbon across the top inscribed "Washington In Glory" & a bottom ribbon w/"America In Tears," the back w/a scene of an American ship under full sail, a spread-winged American eagle below the spout, imperfections, early 19th c. (ILLUS.) **$1,293**

Pitcher, 11" h., jug-type, decorated w/black transfer-printed scenes w/some hand-tinting & gilt trim, one side w/a large grouping of Masonic symbols between pillars, the other side w/a ship under full sail flying an American flag & titled "Nancy of Boston," decorated under the spout w/the figure of a standing woman leaning on a large anchor below a wreath w/the inscription "Edward and Nancy Staples," accompanied by a letter giving the history of the ship, ca. 1806, wear, base hairline & repaired spout (ILLUS., top of page) **$3,450**

Lladró

Spain's famed Lladró porcelain manufactory creates both limited- and non-limited-edition figurines as well as other porcelains. The classic simple beauty of the figures and their subdued coloring make them readily recognizable and they have an enthusiastic following.

Lady Swinging Golf Club Lladró Figure

Lady Swinging Golf Club, No. 6689, 14 1/2" h. (ILLUS.) **$115**

Lladró Mother & Child Figurine

Mother & child, tall slender mother looking down at her child wearing a blue night-gown, 14" h. (ILLUS.) **$316**

Tall Mother & Infant Lladró Figurine

Mother & infant, matte finish, a young mother wearing a long mottled blue robe & holding her infant close to her face, No. 2429, 18 1/4" h. (ILLUS.) **$259**

Longwy

This faience factory was established in 1798 in the town of Longwy, France and is noted for its enameled pottery, which resembles cloisonné. Utilitarian wares were the first production here, but by the 1870s an Oriental-style art pottery that imitated cloisonné was created through the use of heavy enamels in relief. By 1912, a modern Art Deco style became part of Longwy's production; these wares, together with the Oriental-style pieces, have made this art pottery popular with

collectors today. As interest in Art Deco has soared in recent years, values of Longwy's mod-ern-style wares have risen sharply.

Bright Floral-decorated Longwy Compote

Compote, 13 1/4" d., 5 1/2" h., flattened paneled foot below a band of blue beads supporting the widely flaring paneled bowl, overall bright polychrome floral de-sign in pinks, greens & dark blue inside the bowl & on the foot, turquoise blue bowl exterior, stamped & numbered, ear-ly 20th c. (ILLUS.) **$431**

Cup & saucer, decorated w/overall vibrant colored stylized flowers, ink stamp marks, rim chips on both pieces, cup 2 1/4" h., the set **$70-80**

Art Deco Longwy Tile

Tile, square, decorated in bold colors w/a stylized Art Deco woman in a garden, a deep brick red ground w/the woman in purple, white & black w/a yellow & white landscape w/purple, pink, white & black trees, marked "Longwy France Primav-era," 8" w. (ILLUS.) **$400-500**

Vase, 11 3/4" h., flared neck on a round flat-tened body raised on an oval foot, the ex-terior w/turquoise blue crackle glaze, base w/a green ink stamp mark "Primav-era Longwy France," after 1913 .... **$250-275**

Vase, 12 1/2" h., tapering ovoid body w/everted lip, molded w/a mythological ram & bird w/two female nudes amid a stylized landscape, covered in ivory, tur-quoise blue, cobalt blue, purple & black

glaze, green printed mark "Primavera -
Longwy - France," ca. 1925 .... **$2,600-2,700**
Vase, 22" h., ten sided melon-form body
w/stepped tapering neck & circular foot,
molded w/stylized teal & pink berries on
black vines reserved on a crackled ivory
ground, sawtooth border at neck & cobalt
glazed rim & foot, ca. 1925, printed "So-
ciete Des Faienceries - Longwy - France"
.... **$2,250-2,500**

Three Lotus Ware Columbia Bowls

Bowl, 6 1/2" d., 4 1/2" h., Columbia design, pinched ovoid shaped w/applied
flowers & filigreed medallions on the
sides (ILLUS. left with two other Colum-
bia bowls) **$300-450**

Doughnut-shaped Longwy Wine Flask

Wine flask, footed, doughnut-shaped
w/open center, tapering to a cylindrical
neck w/a pointed rim spout, arched turquoise blue ropetwist handle, decorated
w/ornate exotic birds & flowers in bright
shades of pink, blue, green, purple, yellow & brown, stamped on base "Longwy
- 1115 - 16 - D486," 6 1/2" w., 11 1/2" h.
(ILLUS.).. **$259**

Fine Lotus Ware Decorated Shell Bowl

Bowl, 10" w., Shell design, rough shell embossing on the outsides w/blue & pink
blush trim, smooth shell interior, red
along inside edge, blue & pink blush, h.p.
scene in the bottom of a sailing ship &
gulls on rough seas crashing on a rocky
shoreline (ILLUS.)............................... **$600-800**

Lotus Ware - Knowles, Taylor & Knowles (KT&K)

*Knowles, Taylor & Knowles made Lotus Ware
(bone china) for a very short time. Reference books
differ on the starting date but it ranges between
1889 and 1892. There is agreement that production of the ware ceased sometime in 1896. KT&K
tried to make Lotus Ware again in 1904 but it
proved too costly and was soon abandoned. Many
pieces of this ware were hand-painted and hand-
decorated. Lotus Ware rivaled some of the finest
European decorated bone china in quality and
refinement of decoration and artwork. KT&K
employed skilled artists, whose work is highly
prized to this day by knowledgeable collectors.*

Bowl, 4 3/4" d., 4 1/2" h., Columbia design, plain ovoid sides w/wide crimped
rim (ILLUS. center with two other Co-
lumbia bowls) **$300-400**
Bowl, 6 1/2" d., 4" h., Columbia design,
pinched ovoid body w/crimped rim & filigreed medallions on the sides (ILLUS.
right with two other Columbia bowls) .. **$200-300**

Lotus Ware Cracker Jar & Tuscan Vase

Cracker jar, cov., all-white, barrel-shaped
body w/a low flared & scalloped rim,

domed inset cover w/button finial, applied
w/flowers, branches, vines & berries,
6 1/2" h. (ILLUS. right with Tuscan Vase)
.... **$200-350**

Two Lotus Ware Chestnut Creamers

Creamer, Chestnut design, all-white w/twig
handle, 3 1/2" h. (ILLUS. left with other
Chestnut creamer) **$150-200**
Creamer, Chestnut design, pale blue background, painted in gold below the spout
w/the initials "JMD," h.p. purple violets
& green leaves on the sides, 3 1/2" h.
(ILLUS. right with other Chestnut cream-
er)... **$225-250**

Lotus Ware Souvenir-type After-dinner Cup &
Saucer

Cup, after-dinner style, cylindrical cup w/a
green transfer design titled "Holyrood
Castle," 2 3/4" h. (ILLUS. right with
matching saucer)................................. **$75-100**

Mecca After-dinner Cup & Saucer & a Globe
Cup & Saucer

Cup & saucer, after-dinner style, Mecca
design, all-white, cylindrical cup w/an-
gled handle, lightly molded matching
saucer, saucer 3" d., cup 2 3/8" h., the
set (ILLUS. left with Globe cup & saucer)
.... **$75-125**

Lotus Cup & Saucer with Frog Scene

Cup & saucer, cylindrical cup w/ruffled rim,
decorated in color w/a scene of a frog
seated under an umbrella & fishing, titled,
"Oregon Webfoot," w/a lotus pad-
shaped saucer, saucer 4 3/4" d., cup
2 1/4" d., 1 5/8" h. (ILLUS.)................. **$125-150**
Cup & saucer, Globe design, footed wide
shallow cup & shallow saucer, saucer
6" d., cup 4 1/2" d., 1 1/2" h., the set
(ILLUS. right with Mecca after-dinner
cup & saucer)...................................... **$75-125**

Two Lotus Ware Star Design
Cups & Saucers

Cup & saucer, Star design, all-white, cup
3 1/2" d., 1 5/8" h. (ILLUS. left with decorated Star design cup & saucer) **$75-100**
Cup & saucer, Star design, h.p. w/pink,
blue & yellow flowers, cup 3 1/2" d.,
1 5/8" h. (ILLUS. right with plain Star de-
sign cup & saucer) **$100-125**

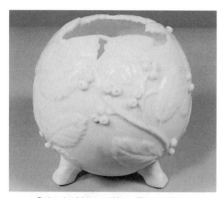

Spherical Lotus Ware Flower Bowl

Flower bowl, footed spherical form w/a pierced closed rim, applied w/berries & leaves around the sides, 3 3/4" d., 4 1/2" h. (ILLUS.) **$250-300**

Ornate Lotus Ware Deccan Jar

Jar, cov., Deccan Jar (a.k.a. Luxor Jar), all-white footed bulbous body decorated w/four filigreed medallions & applied tear-drops & beaded strings, matching pierced cover (ILLUS.) **$400-600**

Lotus Ware Ivica Jar, Globe Pitcher & Thebian Vase

Jar, Ivica Jar, footed bulbous ovoid body w/a closed rim, large gold beads around the foot & rim, h.p. pink & white flowers & green leaves around the sides, missing

the cover, 4 5/8" h. (ILLUS. left with a Globe pitcher & Thebian Vase).......... **$250-350**

Two White Lotus Ware Nappies & a Salt Dip

Nappy, scalloped oblong four-lobed all-white shape, twig feet, 4 x 5 1/8" (ILLUS. right with larger nappy & salt dip)....... **$100-125**
Nappy, scalloped oblong four-lobed all-white shape, twig feet, 4 x 7" (ILLUS. left with smaller nappy & salt dip) **$100-125**

Decorated Globe Jug Pitcher

Pitcher, 3 1/8" h., 4 1/4" d., jug-style, Globe design, squatty bulbous body w/a wide low rim & spout, gold forked handle, bisque finish, the sides h.p. w/pink & yellow flowers & blue & green leaves all outlined in gold (ILLUS.) **$125-150**
Pitcher, 5" h., 7" d., jug-type, Globe design, squatty bulbous body w/a wide low flaring rim & spout, gold forked handle, the sides h.p. w/burgundy & yellow roses (ILLUS. right with Ivica jar and Thebian Vase, previous column) **$400-600**

Non-Bone China Leaf Design Pitcher

Pitcher, 6 1/4" h., 7 1/2" d., jug-style, Leaf design, all-white, squatty bulbous body lightly embossed w/a leaf design, made

from a Lotus Ware mold but not bone china (ILLUS.) **$45-60**
Salt dip individual size, all-white, rounded scalloped shape, 1 1/2" d., 1/2" h. (ILLUS. in front of smaller nappy, page 397) **$30-50**
Saucer, shallow dished form, four panels printed in green "Holyrood Commandery - No. 32 - K.T. - Cleveland, Ohio 1899," 4 7/8" d. (ILLUS. left with matching after-dinner cup, page 396) **$50-75**

Non-Bone China Teapot from Lotus Mold

Gold-decorated Lotus Ware Sugar Bowl

Sugar bowl, cov., squatty bulbous body w/a domed cover & button finial, angled handle, molded gadroon body design, highlighted over overall w/gold, 6" l., 4" h. (ILLUS.) **$100-125**

Three Lotus Ware Shell-shaped Trays

Tray, shell-shaped, raised base, white ground w/a delicate brown vine decoration & gilt trim, 4 3/8" w., 4" h. (ILLUS. left front with two other shell-shaped trays) **$100-125**
Tray, shell-shaped, raised base, pale yellow blush ground decorated w/a band of small blue flowers & pink ribbons, gold trim, 5 3/8" w., 5" h. (ILLUS. right with two other shell-shaped trays) **$125-150**
Tray, shell-shaped, raised three-twig base, all-white, 8 1/2" w., 8" h. (ILLUS. left behind small shell-shaped tray) **$200-250**

Three Piece Lotus Ware Valiniennes Tea Set

Tea set: cov. teapot, cov. sugar bowl & creamer; Valinciennes design, each piece h.p. w/violets in panels between light purple applied fishnet, twig handles, creamer (some damage) 4" l., 3 1/8" h., sugar 5 1/2" l., 3 3/4" h., teapot 7" l., 4 1/4" h., the set (ILLUS.) **$475-600**

Violet-decorated Lotus Ware Valinciennes Tea Set

Tea set: cov. teapot, cov. sugar bowl & creamer; Valinciennes design, each piece h.p. w/violets, twig handles, creamer (some damage) 4" l., 3 1/8" h., sugar 5 1/2" l., 3 3/4" h., teapot 7" l., 4 1/4" h., the set (ILLUS.) **$300-400**
Teapot, cov., squatty bulbous body w/swirled ribbing, domed cover w/knob finial, short spout & angled handle, blue blush ground h.p. w/pink & blue flowers on a brown transfer, gold-sponged throat & cover, from a Lotus Ware mold but not bone china, 7 1/2" l., 5" h. (ILLUS., top next column) **$75-85**

Cremoniam & Parmian Lotus Vases

Vase, 6" h., Cremoniam shape, all-white ovoid body tapering to a molded flaring neck flanked by small ring handles (ILLUS. right with Parmian vase, previous page) **$150-200**

Two Lotus Ware Grecian Vases

Vase, 6" h., Grecian design, ewer-form w/bulbous tapering ovoid body, pointed upright spout & angled white handle, embossed base & neck, the lower body h.p. w/pink & yellow flowers (ILLUS. left with other Grecian vase) **$150-200**
Vase, 6" h., Grecian design, ewer-form w/bulbous tapering ovoid body, pointed upright spout & angled gold handle, embossed neck trimmed in gold, the lower pale blue body h.p. w/tiny blue flowers (ILLUS. right with other Grecian vase) **$150-200**
Vase, 8" h., Tuscan Vase, all-white, wide cylindrical body on three large ball feet, applied morning glory blossoms, vines & bugs (ILLUS. left with cracker jar) **$500-750**
Vase, 8 1/4" h., Thebian shape, double-gourd form w/angular handles from rim to shoulder, bisque finish in pale yellow h.p. w/pink & yellow flowers (ILLUS. center with Ivica jar & Globe pitcher) **$400-600**
Vase, 10" h., Parmian shape, all-white, ruffled foot & bulbous nearly spherical body w/a tall slender cylindrical embossed neck w/flared rim, asymetric wine-like handles down around the neck (ILLUS. left with Cremoniam vase) **$200-300**

Lustre Wares

Lustred wares in imitation of copper, gold, silver and other colors were produced in England in the early 19th century and onward. Gold, copper or platinum oxides were painted on glazed objects that were then fired, giving them a lustred effect. Various forms of lustre wares include plain lustre, with the entire object coated to obtain a metallic effect, bands of lustre decoration and painted lustre designs. Particularly appealing is the pink or purple "splash lustre" sometimes referred to as "Sunderland" lustre in the mistaken belief it was confined to the production of Sunderland-area potteries. Objects decorated in silver lustre by the "resist" process, wherein parts of the objects to be left free from lustre decoration were treated with wax, are referred to as "silver resist."

Copper

Pepper pot, cov., bulbous body on short foot w/round base, waisted neck tapering to domed lid w/finial, decorated w/light rust band w/pink lustre foliage & blue berries, 4 1/8" h. **$165**
Pitcher, 4 1/2" h., ribbed body, scrolled handle & molded fan spout, white neck w/red, green & pink lustre strawberries, base has a starch blue band **$55**
Salt, open, squat bulbous body on flared foot w/round base, ring rim on top, decorated w/blue band of pink lustre foliage & pale yellow berries, 2" h. (minor interior wear) **$110**

Silver & Silver Resist

Tea service: cov. teapot, cov. sugar bowl, milk jug & three larger jugs; teapot, sugar bowl, milk jug & larger jug in silver lustre w/floral decoration, another jug w/enamel floral decoration in blues & reds on cream ground beneath silver-lustre neck, spout & handle, & one copper lustre jug w/spout in form of bear's head & dolphin form handle, decorated w/red, yellow, pink & green flowers & leaves on blue ground; Staffordshire, ca. 1820, tallest jug 8 7/8" h., the set (chips, hairline, restuck handle) **$1,560**

Sunderland Pink & Others

Pitcher, 7" h., jug-form, black transfer-printed w/two oval reserves, one "Captain Hull of the Constitution" & the other "Pike - be always ready to die for your country," pink lustre trim, early 19th c. (imperfections) **$5,750**
Pitcher, 8" h., Sunderland lustre pitcher w/dark red transfer of ship, verse & two sailors w/"Mariners Arms," h.p. enamel in red, green, yellow & blue (spout has minor wear) **$770**
Pitcher, 8 1/2" h., pearlware, satyr head spout, pink lustre h.p. w/pink queen's roses in blue, green & orange, w/a scene of three sailing ships, verse & "David & Elizabeth Buchannan" (minor flaking, in-the-making hairline on handle) **$1,320**
Pitcher, 8 3/4" h., jug-form, black transfer-printed design of the farmer's arms flanked by a farmer & wife surrounded by various symbols in a landscape, the other side w/an inspirational verse, oval reserve below the spout signed "Mary Hayward Farmer Sandhurft Kent," polychrome trim, highlighted w/pink lustre trim & florals, early 19th c. (imperfections) **$1,150**
Pitcher, 9 3/8" h., jug-form, bulbous cream-colored body decorated w/vignettes on each side, one side w/a polychrome-trimmed black transfer-printed scene of a British sailing ship & a verse in a cartouche reading "May Peace and Plenty On Our Nation Smile and Trade with Commerce Bless the British Isle," the other side w/a verse in a floral wreath, under the spout is "The Sailor's Tear" beneath a printed Mariner's Compass flanked by

British ships, red, green & yellow trim, pink lustre squiggles around the sides, early 19th c., imperfections **$646**

Pitcher, 9 3/8" h., jug-form, the bulbous body decorated on the sides w/large banded reserves, one w/a black transfer-printed figural scene titled "The Sailor's Farewell," the other one w/a sailor's verse, a large panel under the spout inscribed "George Henry Page - Born Sept. 7th 1800 - Charlotte Page - Born Feb. 7th 1802," w/a whimsical puzzle verse, wide Sunderland pink lustre bands around the top & base, polychrome trim in yellow & green, early 19th c., imperfections **$3,290**

Pitcher, 10 1/8" h., jug-form, wide bulbous body decorated w/large black transfer-printed reserves on the sides, one titled "A West View of the Iron Bridge over the Wear under the Patronage of R. Burdon Esq. M.P.," the reverse w/an inspirational verse in a floral wreath, a pouring handle under the spout centering a black transfer-printed sailing ship & an inscription "Arther Rutter 1840," overall spattered pink lustre decoration, minor imperfections **$1,645**

Pitchers, 7 3/8" h., jug-type, bulbous body tapering to a short neck w/large rim spout, angled handle, pink lustre band trim, each transfer-printed in puce w/figural designs, one side w/a standing American Indian & large eagle flanking an American flag above a banner reading "Success to the United States of America," the reverse w/"Peace, Plenty and Independence" & depicting a star & ribbon wreath w/the names of New York & ten other states all surmounted by a large eagle & American flag & flanked by allegorical figures of Peace & Plenty, a foliate geometric design beneath the spout, early 19th c., imperfections, pr. **$2,233**

Majolica

Majolica, a tin-enameled glazed pottery, has been produced for centuries. It originally took its name from the island of Majorca, a source of figuline (potter's clay). Subsequently it was widely produced in England, Europe and the United States. Etruscan majolica, now avidly sought, was made by Griffen, Smith & Hill, Phoenixville, Pa., in the last quarter of the 19th century. Most majolica advertised today is 19th or 20th century. Once scorned by most collectors, interest in this colorful ware so popular during the Victorian era has now revived and prices have risen dramatically in the past few years.

Etruscan

Bread tray, Oak Leaf patt., pink edge, 12" l. (ILLUS. bottom row, right, with other Etruscan plates & trays)................................. **$358**

Butter pat, Begonia Leaf on Wicker patt. (minor rim nick) **$110**

Butter pat, Shell & Seaweed patt. w/seaweed... **$193**

Cake plate, Napkin patt., pink & white napkin on yellow ground w/cobalt blue border (handle repaired)... **$330**

Cake stand, Maple Leaves patt., white ground.. **$138**

Cake stand, Morning Glory patt., rare cobalt blue morning glories, 8" d., 4" h. **$385**

Cake stand, Morning Glory patt., yellow morning glories, 8" d., 4" h....................... **$275**

Rare Etruscan Cheese Dish

Cheese dish, cov., Lily, Fern & Floral patt., high domed cover w/large green leaves & yellow blossoms w/a bud finial on a white ground, wide base flange w/further leaves, very minor hairline in cover, 11 1/4" d., 6" h. (ILLUS.)...................... **$1,925**

Cup & saucer, Shell & Seaweed patt. **$220**

Mug, Oak Leaf & Acorn patt......................... **$121**

Mug, Water Lily patt. **$121**

Plate, 8" d., Bamboo patt. **$220**

Grouping of Etruscan Plates & More

Plate, 9" d., Cauliflower patt. (ILLUS. top row, left, with other Etruscan plates & trays).. **$150-225**

Plate, 9" d., Classical Dog patt...................... **$275**

Plate, 9" d., Classical line, Dog patt., green center w/pink border band (ILLUS. center row, right, with other Etruscan plates & trays).. **$110**

Plate, 9" d., Maple Leaf on Basketweave pat., large green leaf on pale yellow & pink ground (ILLUS. center row, left, with other Etruscan plates & trays).................. **$193**

Plate, 9" d., Maple Leaves patt., on pink background, rim nick (ILLUS. top row, center, with other Etruscan plates & trays) **$138**

Plate, 9" d., Maple Leaves patt., pink ground, great color **$303**

Plate, 9" d., Overlapping Begonia Leaf patt. (ILLUS. center row, middle, with other Etruscan plates & trays) **$110**

Plate, 9" d., Strawberry & Apple patt., white ground (ILLUS. top row, right, with other Etruscan plates & trays) **$110**

Shell & Seaweed Plates & Platter

Plates, 7" d., Shell & Seaweed patt., set of 3 (ILLUS. of one, bottom row right with other Shell & Seaweed pieces) **$440**

Plates, 8" d., Shell & Seaweed patt., nick to one, set of 4 (ILLUS. of one, bottom row left with other Shell & Seaweed pieces) **$715**

Platter, Geranium patt., large leaf w/twig handles **$220**

Platter, 14" l., Shell & Seaweed patt. (ILLUS. top row with Shell & Seaweed plates) **$495**

Scarce Etruscan Sardine Box

Sardine box, cov., Water Lily patt., rectangular base w/molded white water lilies & green leaves on a pink ground w/a brown ropetwist border band, the rectangular flat-topped cover w/matching decor & a figural swan finial, professional restorations, 2 pcs. (ILLUS.) **$825**

Sauce dishes, shell-shaped, natural colors, pr. **$358**

Syrup pitcher w/hinged pewter cap, Rose patt., w/butterfly spout **$138**

Syrup pitcher w/hinged pewter cap, Sunflower patt., white ground **$440**

Etruscan Cauliflower Pattern Teapot

Teapot, cov., Cauliflower patt., the body molded as a head of cauliflower in creamy white & dark green, green spout & handle, marked on bottom, Griffin, Smith & Hill, Phoenixville, Pennsylvania, late 19th c., minor roughness on interior rim, interior rim chip on cover, 5 1/2" h. (ILLUS.) **$374**

American Shell & Seaweed Teapot

Teapot, cov., Shell & Seaweed patt., spherical body molded as large shells trimmed w/seaweed, mottled green coral-form handle & spout, mottled pink, brown & green cover w/shell finial, Griffin, Smith & Hill, Phoenixville, Pennsylvania, late 19th c., 10" l., 6 1/2" h. (ILLUS.) **$525-575**

Tray, Geranium patt., white flowers & green leaves on a light yellow ground, brown branch handles, 10 x 12 1/2" (ILLUS. bottom row, left, with other Etruscan plates & trays) **$238**

Tray, oval, Grape patt., grape clusters & leaves on tan ground, entwined vine brown border band (ILLUS. bottom row, center, with other Etruscan plates & trays) **$220**

General

Basket, Bird, Fan & Floral patt., oblong shape pinched in at the center & joined by an arched handle, pinks & greens w/cobalt blue trim, 11" l., 8" h. **$413**

Box, cov., round, pale turquoise ground molded w/flying birds in dark green flanking a central brown twig handle, Joseph Holdcroft, England, 4 1/2" d. **$715**

Bread tray, oblong, Napkin patt., woven napkin design in center in brown & yellow, yellow rope border band, rim embossed "Eat Thy Bread With Thankfulness," 15" l. **$413**

Bread tray, oval, Begonia Leaf patt. w/mottled cobalt blue, green, pink & yellow leaves in center, brown border embossed "Eat Thy Bread With Thankfulness," 13" l. $303

Bread tray, oval, New England Aster patt., dark pink blossoms & green leaves on a cream ground, green border embossed "Eat To Live Not Live To Eat"............. $330

Bread tray, oval, Wheat patt., brown center, green leaves & yellow wheat, brown border band embossed "Eat Thy Bread With Thankfulness," 13" l. $303

Lovely Majolica Bust of a Young Boy

Bust of a young boy, the realistically modeled and colored bust show the smiling youth wearing a brown cockade hat w/purple bow, a shirt w/a large ruffled white collar, blue inner jacket & lavender outer jacket trimmed along the edge w/ball-shaped tassels, Brothers Urbach, Germany, 19th c., minor glaze loss, 19" h. (ILLUS.) $748

Cake stand, on three knob feet, Pond Lily patt., 9" d. $165

Cake stand, round w/low pedestal, Bird in Flight patt., large brown bird on a pale blue pebbled ground, pink blossoms around rim, Joseph Holdcroft, England, 9 1/2" d. $220

Centerpiece, figural, a large wide shallow bowl w/green interior & wide rolled rim molded by a band of blue shells, raised on a leaf-cast pedestal supported by two winged cupids resting on a shell-molded round base, Hugo Lonitz & Co., Germany, late 19th c., 16" w., 20" h. (various professional repairs to high points) $2,475

French Fern Pattern Cheese Keeper

Cheese keeper, cov., Fern patt., tall cylindrical cover w/a flat top, the sides molded w/large green fern leaves on a brown ground, the cover w/water lily pads & a blossom finial, base w/green ferns on the flanged rim, France, late 19th c., minor nicks to cover finial, rim chip on cover, 11 1/2" h. (ILLUS.) $880

Large Thos. Forester Cheese Dish

Cheese keeper, cov., high domed cover w/branch handle, molded overall w/birds, flowers, leaves & branches in white, yellow, brown & green, flanged rim on base, Thomas Forester & Sons, England, late 19th c., professional repair on base, 11" h. (ILLUS.) $2,200

George Jones Pansy Pattern Cheese Dish

Cheese keeper, cov., Pansy patt., wide cylindrical cover w/flat top, pink blossoms on green leafy vines around the sides against a cobalt blue ground, George Jones, England, late 19th c., professional repair to cover handle, base 10 1/4" d., overall 7 1/2" h. (ILLUS.) $3,850

Cheese keeper, cov., Pansy patt., wide cylindrical cover w/flat top, yellow blossoms on green leafy vines around the sides against a cobalt blue ground, George Jones, England, late 19th c., base 10 1/4" d., overall 7 1/2" h. **$5,500**

Compote, open, 9" d., low pedestal, Floral & Pinwheel patt., deep red blossoms & brown stems on cream & pale green ground, Samuel Lear, England, late 19th c. **$248**

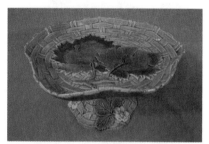

Victoria Pottery Majolica Compote

Compote, open, 9" d., 5" h., Basketweave & Maple Leaf patt., wide gently fluted shallow bowl w/a turquoise basketweave design & large brown & green leaves, turquoise basketweave pedestal w/green leaves & white blossoms, Victoria Pottery Co. (ILLUS.) **$605**

Compote, open, 9 1/2" d., Begonia Leaf patt., unmarked **$132**

Condiment server, four shell-shaped lobes in alternating pink & pale green centered by a shell handle, 9" l. **$358**

Unusual Minton Majolica Creambowls

Creambowls, figural, a large naturalistic nautilus shell bowl supported on a pedestal composed of entwined dolphins & green seaweed, on a round disk-form gadrooned green oval foot, Minton, England, Model No. 902, date code for 1862, overall 9" h., pr. (ILLUS.) **$3,824**

Cup & saucer, Pineapple patt., nice color **$275**

Unique Elephant Majolica Dish

Dish, cov., figural, a model of a large grey elephant walking & carrying a black trainer & large brown & white howdah on its back, Hugo Lonitz & Co., Germany, late 19th c., 10" l., 9" h. (ILLUS.) **$935**

Brownfield Blackberry Egg Basket

Egg basket, the oval basket w/vertical sides molded in relief w/blackberries on leafy blossoming vines against a yellow basketweave ground, cobalt blue upper border, double bamboo-form arched handle from side to side, the interior fitted w/six holes to support eggs, Brownfield, England, late 19th c., 11 1/2" l., 6 1/2" h. (ILLUS.) **$990**

Egg server, rounded basket-form frame decorated w/red blossoms & green leaves on a cream ground around the sides, holds six egg cups, S. Fielding & Co., England, late 19th c. (professional repair to base of egg cups) **$468**

George Jones Game Dish

Game dish, cov., deep oval form, the base molded w/upright green leaves & ferns on a brown ground, yellow rope band around rim centered by a dead game bird in brown & yellow on green ferns on a brown ground, George Jones, England, 11" l. (ILLUS.).. **$1,100**

Holdcroft Blackamoor Garden Seat

Garden seat, figural, Blackamoor patt., three mottled green & brown bun feet supporting a base w/a cobalt blue border band supporting a brown mound issuing the figural pedestal composed of a full-figure Blackamoor youth seated among green & brown cattails, the top composed of a flattened cobalt blue cushion-form seat w/yellow ropetwist border, professional restoration to the seat, Holdcroft, England, late 19th c., overall 17 1/2" h. (ILLUS.).. **$6,050**

Humidor, cov., figural, model of a large fat green frog wearing a red smoking jacket, Europe, late 19th c., 6 1/2" h. **$468**

Jam pot, cov., cylindrical, Strawberry patt., molded green leaves & red berries around the sides, berry finial, Brownfield & Son, England, late 19th c...................... **$143**

Rare George Jones Jardiniere

Jardiniere, footed bell-form bowl w/flared yellow rim, the sides in turquoise blue molded w/water lilies, cattails & a bird in shades of green, white, brown & black, George Jones, England, late 19th c., professional hairline repair, 17" d., 15 1/2" h. (ILLUS.).. **$6,050**

Rare Stork Jardiniere-Stand

Jardiniere-stand, figural, a model of a very tall stork in grey, black, white & gold standing holding a fish in its beak, a flaring cylindrical container behind it formed as a cluster of cattails & leaves, Hugo Lonitz, late 19th c., repairs to stork body & beak & tips of cattails, fine detail (ILLUS.) **$8,800**

Unusual Majolica Marmalade Pot

Marmalade pot, cov., Apple Blossom patt., the high domed top w/spoon opening molded w/a brown branch handle & pink blossoms & green leaves on a turquoise ground, the base w/a turquoise ground banded w/brown wicker design & a flanged rim w/further blossoms & leaves, George Jones, England, late 19th c., interior rim chips on rim of cover, 5" h. (ILLUS.)..................................... **$2,475**

Mug, Bird in Flight & Water Lily patt., green leaves w/brown & yellow bird on a cobalt blue ground, high relief, 4 1/4" h. **$358**

Nut Serving Tray with Squirrel

Nut serving tray, wide, shallow, rounded tray w/large green leaves & brown twigs on a turquoise ground, a figural brown squirrel w/nut seated at the rim, George Jones, England, late 19th c., repair to tail, 10 1/2" w. (ILLUS.).................................. **$1,100**

Paperweight, slab-type, rectangular, relief-molded brown owl on branch against a pale green ground, Mayer, late 19th c. **$138**

Pitcher, 6" h., Fish on Waves with Shell patt. **$275**

Colorful Majolica Pitcher with Parrot

Pitcher, 6 1/2" h., 4" d., slightly tapering cylindrical body w/angled handle, molded w/narrow bands flanking a parrot-like bird on leafy branches, in mottled shades of brown, green, yellow & pink, late 19th c. (ILLUS.)... **$175-225**

Pitcher, 6 3/4" h., Stork in March patt., brown & white bird on pale blue ground w/cobalt blue rim & base bands, angled branch handle, George Jones, England **$2,200**

Pitcher, 7" h., Eagle with Rabbit patt., footed w/flat round sides, cobalt blue ground... **$165**

Pitcher, 7 1/4" h., Wheat patt., cylindrical sides molded w/long green leaves & yellow green on a pink ground, ribbon-wrapped brown handle, George Jones, England... **$4,400**

Pitcher, 8 1/2" h., Ram patt., lavender top, great color... **$303**

Pitcher, 9" h., Bird's Nest patt., branch handle, probably American-made (minor hairline) **$440**

Pitcher, 9" h., figural, white swan forms the top of the body w/the neck curving down to form handle, lower ovoid body in cobalt blue w/green leaves, John Bevington, England, late 19th c. **$1,100**

Pitcher, 10" h., figural, model of mother monkey holding her baby, French, late 19th c. **$275**

Pitcher, 10 1/2" h., figural, model of standing pig dressed as waiter, Frie Onnaing, France, late 19th c. **$605**

Pitcher, 12" h., Chrysanthemum patt., Avalon Faience mark of the Chesapeake Pottery, Baltimore, Maryland, late 19th c. **$66**

Pitcher w/hinged pewter cover, 9 1/2" h., Dogwood patt., mottled brown & green ground... **$385**

French Majolica Plaque with Cherries

Plaque, round, molded & applied in full-relief w/red cherries, green leaves & brown branches on a shaded brown to pale blue ground, France, late 19th c., 12 3/8" d. (ILLUS.)... **$225-275**

Plate, 7 3/4" d., Strawberry patt., large green leaves w/pink blossoms & berries on a brown ground.................................. **$154**

Plate, 8 3/4" d., Bellflower patt., pink & white blossoms & green leaves on a cobalt blue ground... **$248**

Plate, 9" d., Pineapple patt., George Jones, England, late 19th c. (very minor rim glaze nick)... **$605**

Plate, 9" d., Summer Sun patt., sun face molded in the center surrounded by a bird, butterfly & grapes, in golden yellows & brown... **$275**

Plate, 9 1/2" d., Fern & Floral patt., cobalt blue ground & pink Greek key border band... **$248**

Plates, 8 1/2" d., Overlapping Begonia Leaf patt., dark green w/dark pink borders, set of 4... **$605**

Platter, 11" l., oblong w/scalloped rim, Dog & Doghouse patt., dark brown, green & cream... **$275**

Platter, 13" l., oval, molded flowers & berries on a pale blue ground around the sides, pink ribbon border & bow handles, mottled dark green center, George Jones, England (hairline) **$1,980**

Salt dip, figural, large green & pink shell supported atop a green dolphin on an oval foot, 4 3/4" h. **$374**

Sauce dish, Strawberry patt., round, w/scalloped rim molded w/pink blossoms, green leaves on turquoise ground in sides, George Jones, England, 5" d. **$440**

Strawberry server, Napkin & Strawberry patt., oblong, shallow dish molded w/a creamy napkin & green strawberry leaves, inset at each end, one holding the small pink w/green leaves creamer, the other the matching open sugar, George Jones, England, 15" l., the set **$1,430**

Strawberry spoon, green w/pink blossom in bowl & on handle, George Jones, England, 7 1/2" l. **$605**

Sweet meat dish, figural, modeled as a young girl seated on the side of a rowboat, a fishing net draped along the side, Europe, 19th c., 9" l., 7" h. **$385**

Syrup pitcher w/hinged pewter cover, Floral & Basket patt., great color, 4 3/4" h. **$385**

Syrup pitcher w/hinged pewter cover, molded floral design, Edwin Bennett Pottery, Baltimore, Maryland, late 19th c. **$154**

Tea set: Bamboo & Fern patt., cov. teapot, cov. sugar bowl & creamer; each body molded as a cluster of yellow bamboo w/long green fern leaves wrapping around the lower body, Wardle & Co., England, late 19th c., minor nicks on teapot, mismatched sugar cover, the set (ILLUS. right with Daisy pattern set) **$308**

Fine George Jones Basketweave & Floral Tea Set

Tea set: Basketweave & Floral patt., cov. teapot, cov. sugar bowl, creamer, two cups & saucers & oblong handled tray; serving pieces w/tapering ovoid bodies molded around the bottom w/bands of tan basketweave below a cobalt blue upper body molded w/branches of pink blossoms & green leaves, domed covers w/arched twig handles, brown branch handles & spout, George Jones, England, late 19th c., professional repair to sugar cover rim, one cup & saucer repaired, teapot cover not perfect fit, tray 19 1/2" l., teapot 7" h., the set (ILLUS.)... **$3,640**

Tea set: Basketweave & Floral patt., cov. teapot, cov. sugar bowl & creamer; wide

squatty bulbous molded pale blue basketweave bodies decorated w/branches of pink blossoms & green leaves, brown branch handles, flattened covers w/white blossom finials, probably England, late 19th c., rim chip on creamer, the set (ILLUS. right with Floral Branch pattern tea set) **$196**

Bird & Fan and Cranes Pattern Tea Sets

Tea set: Bird & Fan patt., cov. teapot, cov. sugar bowl & creamer; spherical bodies molded w/colorful fans, each w/a flying bird against a pebbled pale yellow background, brown branch handles & spout, probably England, late 19th c., minor spout chip on teapot, the set (ILLUS. left with Cranes pattern tea set) **$308**

Tea set: Bird & Fan patt., cov. teapot, cov. sugar bowl & creamer; spherical body molded w/an open white fan w/flying blue, red & yellow bird, flanked by pink blossoms, all on a pale blue ground, branch spout & handles, Fielding, England, late 19th c., chip on sugar cover, the set (ILLUS. right with Wedgwood Cauliflower tea set) **$392**

Tea set: Blackberry & Basketweave patt., cov. teapot, cov. sugar bowl & creamer; each piece w/a spherical body molded on the lower half w/a band of tan basketweave, the upper half in cobalt blue molded w/blackberry vines in pink & green, brown branch handles & spout, mottled basketweave covers w/ring finials, probably England, late 19th c., the set (ILLUS. right with Oriental pattern tea set) **$364**

Cauliflower & Bird and Fan Majolica Tea Sets

Tea set: Cauliflower patt., cov. teapot, cov. sugar bowl & creamer; each piece modeled as a white head of cauliflower w/wide green leaves, Josiah Wedgwood,

England, late 19th c., minor spout nicks on teapot, teapot 6" h., the set (ILLUS. left with Bird & Fan tea set w/pale blue ground).. **$924**

Tea set: cov. teapot, open sugar & creamer, water server, milk pitcher, tray & two cups & saucers; embossed stylized Oriental design of pink blossoms & green leaves among brown angular lines on a cream ground, brown bamboo-form handles, Brownhills Pottery Co., England, late 19th c., the set.................................... **$440**

Tea set: Cranes patt., cov. teapot, cov. sugar bowl & creamer; spherical bodies molded around the lower half w/a yellow basketweave design, the wide upper band w/a pale blue ground molded w/bands of brown flying cranes, brown twig handles & spout, probably England, late 19th c., minor glaze nicks, the set (ILLUS. right with Bird & Fan pattern tea set with yellow ground) **$168**

Daisy Pattern & Bamboo & Fern Pattern Majolica Tea Sets

Tea set: Daisy patt., cov. teapot, cov. sugar bowl & creamer; each piece w/a hexagonal body in dark brown, the panels molded w/large white & yellow daisy blossoms & green leaves, angled green branch handles & spout, figural flower cover finials, mark of the Victoria Pottery Company, late 19th c., professional spout repair on creamer, the set (ILLUS. left with Bamboo & Fern pattern set)....................... **$784**

Teapot, cov., Chinaman patt., modeled as a rotund seated Chinese man holding a large brown dramatic mask to one side, the mask issuing a green & yellow spout, a rope handle at his other side, his head forming the cover, shown wearing a pale blue jacket w/small red, green & white blossoms & dark green pants & brown shoes, Model No. 1838, Mintons, England, date code for 1874, 8 1/4" h. (ILLUS. far right with two other majolica teapots)... **$4,465**

Teapot, cov., figural Monkey model, made by Minton, reissue of Victorian original, limited edition of 1,793, introduced in 1993 (ILLUS., top next column) **$850**

Teapot, cov., Gondolier patt., the body modeled as an elongated Chinese gondola-style sailing ship w/tall upturned stern & bow, the bow forming the spout, the body of the pot composed of the molded brown cargo, white sail & triangu-

Minton Reissue of Monkey Teapot

lar panels of light blue sky between the rigging ropes, a rigging rope connecting the top of the sail w/the top of the stern, the figure of a bent-over Chinese man forming the finial on the cover, Model No. 3520/30, George Jones, England, diamond registry date of 1876, 12 1/2" h. (ILLUS. center top with two other majolica teapots, previous column) **$32,900**

English Japonisme Majolica Teapot

Teapot, cov., Japonisme style, a flattened demi-lune form in turquoise blue, the flat cover w/a small squared finial, straight angled spout & simple C-form handle, the shoulder molded w/a stylized fret design, the sides molded w/an Oriental figure preparing tea in a garden & a large stylized blossom on a leafy stem, England, possibly by Joseph Holdcroft or Samuel Lear, ca. 1880, 9 3/4" l. (ILLUS.) **$2,271**

Figural Lemon Mintons Teapot

Teapot, cov., Lemon patt., model of a large yellow lemon w/molded green leaves around the sides & forming the base, green stem spout & handle, cover modeled as an inverted mushroom, Mintons, England, date code for 1873, Shape No. 643, 7" l., 4 1/2" h. (ILLUS.) **$8,800**

Teapot, cov., Mintons Fish patt., figural, limited edition produced by Royal Doulton, 20th c. **$616**

Monkey on Coconut Figural Teapot

Teapot, cov., Monkey & Coconut patt., modeled as a large cobalt blue coconut w/green leaves & a dark grey figure of a monkey seated at the top end above the brown branch handle, brown branch spout, small cover w/figural pink bud & green leaves, J. Roth, England, late 19th c., 10" l., 7 1/4" h. (ILLUS.)...................... **$3,696**

Mintons Monkey & Coconut Figural Teapot

Teapot, cov., Monkey & Coconut patt., the body modeled as a large mustard yellow coconut w/the figure of a seated brown monkey at one end grasping the nut, wearing a black jacket w/dark red blossoms & green leaves, the grey head w/pale green knob finial forming the cover, molded green leaves below the curved brown bamboo-form spout, the tail of the monkey forming the handle, Mintons, England, third quarter 19th c., minor hairline in spout, 8 1/2" l., 6" h. (ILLUS.) **$6,440**

Teapot, cov., Monkey & Coconut patt., the bulbous body modeled as a seated grey monkey wearing a dark blue outfit w/large pink polka dots, its arms & legs wrapped around a large mustard yellow coconut w/green leaves, the stem forming the spout, the monkey's head &

Three Rare Victorian Figural Majolica Teapots

shoulders forming the cover w/a blue knob finial, Model No. 1844, Mintons, England, date letter for 1874, 9" h. (ILLUS. far left with two other majolica teapots) **$8,225**

New Minton Figural Tortoise Teapot

Teapot, cov., Tortoise patt., produced by Minton, limited edition of 2,500, introduced in 1999 (ILLUS.).............................. **$750**

Extraordinary Mintons Majolica Teapot

Teapot, cov., Vulture & Snake patt., an elaborately modeled design w/a large standing vulture w/a yellow & black body & pink neck & head grasping the head &

body of a large writhing green snake, both on a rockwork base, Model No. 1851, designed by H.H. Crealock, Mintons, England, dated ca. 1872, 8 3/8" h. (ILLUS.).. **$89,625**

Tray, oval, Butterfly & Orchid patt., large white, pink & green blossoms & green leaves & large black & brown butterflies against a dark brown ground, George Jones, England, late 19th c., 11" l. **$2,420**

Tray, rectangular w/rounded corners, Leaf patt., molded oak leaf & acorn end handles, mottled dark green, pink & yellow w/cobalt blue accents, 10" l....................... **$303**

Holdcroft Banana Plant Umbrella Stand

Umbrella stand, Banana Plant design, tall upright triangular form, the front sides molded in bold relief w/a cluster of tall wide green & yellow leaves & leafy branches w/molded bulbous brown fruit, turquoise blue background & a bark-textured pale greenish brown band at the rim & base, Joseph Holdcroft, England, ca. 1880, overall 21 1/4" h. (ILLUS.) **$3,346**

Very Rare Bear Umbrella Stand

Umbrella stand, figural, a model of a large standing brown bear snarling & holding a large wooden log bar, molded leafy

branches forming the square rockwork base, Brownfield & Son, England, late 19th c., very rare, professional repair to oak leaves & feet, 34" h. (ILLUS.)......... **$11,000**

Minton Vase with Daisy-like Flowers

Vase, 6 3/4" h., footed wide bulbous ovoid body tapering to a short flaring cylindrical neck w/a gold rim band flanked by loop handles, molded w/clusters of white & yellow daisy-like flowers on the sides above a yellow basketweave band around the base, Minton, England, No. 1316, second half 19th c., minor nicks on flowers (ILLUS.) **$770**

Vase, 7" h., baluster-form body w/flaring rim, angled branch handles, brown ground molded w/large pink morning glory blossoms & green leafy vines, Brownfield & Son, England, late 19th c............... **$303**

Wall pocket, a long cartouche-form backplate in brown molded w/red & green Christmas holly, a long yellow wicker basket holder at the center, T.C. Brown, Westhead, Moore & Co., England, late 19th c., 10 1/2" l. **$660**

Wall pockets, Palissy Ware, molded as brown branches of green oak leaves & acorns, each w/a model of a lizard on the front, Thomas Sergent, 12" l., pr. (one w/professional repair to rim, other w/repair to lizard's head)............................... **$2,530**

Marblehead

This pottery was organized in 1904 by Dr. Herbert J. Hall as a therapeutic aid to patients in a sanitarium he ran in Marblehead, Massachusetts. It was later separated from the sanitarium and directed by Arthur E. Baggs, a fine artist and designer, who bought out the factory in 1916 and operated it until its closing in 1936. Most wares were hand-thrown and decorated and carry the company mark of a stylized sailing vessel flanked by the letters "M" and "P."

Marblehead Mark

Marblehead Tankard Pitcher with Flowers

Pitcher, 8 3/4" h., 5 1/2" d., tankard-type, tall corseted body w/a flat mouth & small rim spout, angled side handle, incised panels down the sides incorporating stylized flower blossoms in brown, green & indigo on a speckled matte green ground, stamped ship mark & initials of artist Hannah Tutt (ILLUS.)..................................... **$5,750**

Marblehead Mini Vase with Grapes

Vase, miniature, 3 1/2" h., 3" d., bulbous squatty ovoid body w/a wide flat mouth, decorated around the rim w/dark blue grapes & leaves against a speckled grey ground, impressed ship mark (ILLUS.) ... **$2,300**

Floral-decorated Marblehead Vase

Vase, 4 1/8" h., small tapering ovoid body w/a wide flat mouth, decorated w/six stylized flowers in green & rust up around the sides against an oatmeal yellow ground, by Hannah Tutt, impressed logo (ILLUS.) **$2,415**

Marblehead Vase with Carved Geese

Vase, 6" h., 5 1/2" d., wide squatty gourd-form tapering to a wide flat mouth, carved in relief around the top w/a continuous band of stylized flying geese in black against a dark green matte ground, unmarked (ILLUS.)..................................... **$2,875**

Extremely Rare Marblehead Vase

Vase, 7 1/4" h., swelled cylindrical body tapering to a wide flat mouth, the sides w/tall narrow vertical panels divided by narrow black stripes, each panel topped by a stylized brown flowerhead w/yellow center, against a matte green ground, decorated by Hanna Tutt, ca. 1908 (ILLUS.)..................................... **$50,190**

Simple Dark Blue Marblehead Vase

Vase, 7 3/4" h., gently tapering cylindrical body w/a thin flared mouth, red clay covered in a mottled blue matte glaze, impressed mark (ILLUS.) **$403**

Martin Brothers

Martinware, the term used for this pottery, dates from 1873 and is the product of the Martin brothers—Robert, Wallace, Edwin, Walter and Charles—often considered the first British studio potters. From first to final stages, their hand-thrown pottery was completely the work of the team. The early wares may be simple and conventional, but the Martin brothers built up their reputation by producing ornately engraved, incised or carved designs as well as rather bizarre figural wares. The amusing face-jugs are considered some of their finest work. After 1910, the work of the pottery declined and can be considered finished by 1915, though some attempts were made to fire pottery as late as the 1920s.

Martin Brothers Mark

Dish, figural, the oblong form w/a crouching, grinning gargoyle at one end, the body forming the open dish composed of two tiered dishes, the neck & body w/fine incised lines to resemble hair, unglazed clay, very small edge nicks, signed "Martin Bros. - London & Southall - 4-1894," 5 1/2" l., 2 3/4" h. **$1,875-1,950**

Jar, cov., figural, modeled as a large comical bird w/a rounded oversized head w/droopy beak & sleepy eyes, bulbous body & thick legs w/wide webbed feet, on a round platform base, dark brown, black & tan glazing, firing crack in body secured at factory w/beeswax, incised "R.W. Martin - London & Southall," 5 1/2" w., 11 1/2" h. **$10,500-11,500**

Jar, cov., modeled as a grotesque bird w/a bulbous oversized head w/large beak & sleepy expression, feathers in green, light blue & black, marked "Martin Bros -

London + Southall - 6-1897," oval base mounted on oval ebonized wooden base, 1897, 10" h. **$13,500**

Fine Martin Brothers Face Pitcher

Pitcher, jug-form, 8" h., a spherical body molded in relief on each side w/a round smiling face w/curly molded hair, short neck w/pinched spout at one side of the top, loop handle from neck rim to shoulder, glazed in dark & warm browns, incised "R.W. Martin Bros. - London - Southall," 1870-80 (ILLUS.) **$7,050**

Pitcher, 9" h., salt-glazed stoneware, a footed ovoid body tapering to a high widely flaring & pinched neck, D-form strap handle, finely incised & decorated w/birds nestled amid branches, glazed in shades of brown, green & rust against a blue striped ground, marked "6-1-2 - 1-8-50 - Martin Bros London & Southall," 1902 .... **$1,500-2,000**

Vase, 10 1/4" h., 6" d., wide ovoid body w/a short cylindrical neck, incised overall w/a design of stylized scrolling leafy vines & blossoms in sand, dark & light brown, marked "27.3.84 - R.W. Martin & Bros. - London & Southall," 1884 .... **$1,100-1,200**

Massier (Clement)

Clement Massier was a French artist potter who worked in the late 19th and early 20th centuries creating exquisite earthenware items with lustre decoration.

Massier Mark

Charger, round, slightly dished form, overall Mediterranean bay scene w/large pine trees in the right foreground, fine lustred gold on burgundy glazes, impressed "CLEMENT MASSIER - GOLFE JUAN," 13" d. **$1,425-1,450**

Vase, 3 7/8" h., simple ovoid form w/flat rim, clam & seaweed decoration in brilliant metallic glaze, marked "C.M. Golfe Juan A.M." **$525-550**

Clement Massier Vase with Buckeyes

Vase, 5" h., footed squatty bulbous lower body w/a tall cylindrical neck, decorated w/buckeyes beneath the iridescent metallic glaze, incised mark "Clement Massier" & impressed "Juan Golf AM," few burst glaze bubbles (ILLUS.)...................... **$345**
Vase, 6 3/4" h., 2 1/2" d., bud-type, bottle-shaped, bulbous ovoid body tapering to a very tall slender "stick" neck, decorated w/a design of mistletoe in a silky red, gold & green iridescent glaze, unmarked.... **$225-250**

Urn-form Massier Vase with Tulips

Vase, 6 3/4" h., 3" d., tall ovoid urn-form w/squared shoulder handles, painted tulips in burgundy on a purple & greenish gold iridescent ground, signed "Clement Massier - Golfe-Juan AM" (ILLUS.) **$489**

McCoy

Collectors are now seeking the art wares of two McCoy potteries. One was founded in Roseville, Ohio, in the late 19th century as the J.W. McCoy Pottery, subsequently becoming Brush-McCoy Pottery Co., later Brush Pottery. The other was also founded in Roseville in 1910 as Nelson McCoy Sanitary Stoneware Co., later becoming Nelson McCoy Pottery. In 1967 the pottery was sold to D.T. Chase of the Mount Clemens Pottery Co., who sold his interest to the Lancaster Colony Corp. in 1974. The pottery shop closed in 1985. Cookie jars are especially collectible today.

A helpful reference book is The Collector's Encyclopedia of McCoy Pottery, by the Huxfords (Collector Books), and by Harold Nichols (Nichols Publishing, 1987).

McCoy Mark

McCoy Seaman's Bank

Bank, figural seaman w/sack over shoulder, white, blue & black, 5 3/4" h. (ILLUS.) **$115-130**
Book ends, decorated w/swallows, ca. 1956, 5 1/2 x 6" **$200-250**
Book ends, model of violin, ca. 1959, 10" h., pr. **$100-150**
Cache pot, double w/applied bird, ca. 1949, 10 1/2" l. **$35-45**

Astronaut Cookie Jar

Cookie jar, Astronaut, 1963, good gold trim
(ILLUS., previous page) **$500-800**

Bunch of Bananas Cookie Jar

Cookie jar, Bunch of Bananas, ca. 1948
(ILLUS.).. **$150-250**

Freddie the Gleep Cookie Jar

Cookie jar, Freddie the Gleep, 1974
(ILLUS.)... **$350-400**
Cookie jar, Garbage Can, ca. 1978........... **$30-40**
Cookie jar, heart-shaped, Hobnail line, ca.
1940... **$300-350**
Cookie jar, Hobby Horse, ca. 1948 .... **$100-150**

Chipmunk Cookie Jar

Cookie jar, Chipmunk, ca. 1960 (ILLUS.)
.... **$100-125**

McCoy Indian Head Cookie Jar

Cookie jar, Indian Head, ca. 1954 (ILLUS.)... **$633**

Christmas Tree Cookie Jar

Cookie jar, Christmas Tree, ca. 1959
(ILLUS.) .... **$1,000+**
Cookie jar, Corn (ear of corn), ca. 1958
.... **$150-175**

Two Kittens in a Basket Cookie Jar

Cookie jar, Kittens in a Basket, ca. 1950s
(ILLUS.)... **$500-600**

Koala Bear Cookie Jar

Cookie jar, Koala Bear, ca. 1983 (ILLUS.)
.... **$125-150**
Cookie jar, Mr. & Mrs. Owl, ca. 1952......... **$75-95**
Cookie jar, Teepee, 1956-59 .... **$403**
Cookie jar, Tomato, ca. 1964 .... **$60-70**

Yellow Mouse Cookie Jar

Cookie jar, Yellow Mouse, ca. 1978
(ILLUS.)... **$35-45**
Figurine, head of witch, ca. early 1940s,
3" h... **$400-600**
Iced tea server, El Rancho Bar-B-Que
line, ca. 1960, 11 1/2" h. **$250-300**
Jardiniere, Loy-Nel-Art line, wide bulbous
shape w/a wide molded flat rim, painted
w/large orange tulips & green leaves on a
shaded dark brown ground,
unmarked, ca. 1905, 6 1/2" h. **$173**

McCoy Quilted Pattern Jardiniere

Jardiniere, Quilted patt., glossy glaze, deep
aqua, marked, 1954, 10 1/2" d., 7 1/2" h.
(ILLUS.)... **$144**
Jardiniere, swallows decoration, ca. late
1930s, 7" h. **$90-125**
Jardiniere, fish decoration, ca. 1958,
7 1/2" h.. **$350-400**

Leaves & Berries Jardiniere & Pedestal

Jardiniere & pedestal base, Leaves & Berries design, ca. 1930s, overall 21" h., 2
pcs. (ILLUS.)..................................... **$250-350**

Sand Butterfly Jardiniere & Pedestal

Jardiniere & pedestal base, sand butterfly
decoration, shaded brown & green
ground, overall 21" h., 2 pc. (ILLUS.).. **$250-350**
Jardiniere & pedestal base, ring
design, ca. 1930s, overall 29" h., 2 pcs.
.... **$450-550**

McCoy Cowboy Boots Lamp

Lamp w/original shade, model of pair of cowboy boots base, original shade, ca. 1956 (ILLUS.)..................................... **$150-200**

Model of Angelfish

Model of angelfish, aqua, ca. early 1940s, Cope design, 6" h. (ILLUS.) **$300-400**
Model of cat, ca. 1940s, 3" h. **$300-400**

Large Oil Jar

Oil jar, bulbous ovoid body w/slightly flaring rim, angled shoulder handles, shaded blue, ca. 1930s, 15" h. (ILLUS.)......... **$250-300**
Oil jar, bulbous ovoid body w/slightly flaring rim, angled shoulder handles, red sponged glaze, 18" h. **$300-400**
Pitcher, embossed w/parading ducks, ca. 1930s, 4 pt. **$90-125**
Pitcher, 7" h., Donkey, marked "NM," early 1940s **$300-350**
Pitcher, 10" h., Butterfly line **$150-225**
Pitcher-vase, 7" h., figural parrot, ca. 1952 .... **$200-225**

Rare Madonna Planter

Planter, figural, Madonna, white, ca. 1960s, rare, 6" h. (ILLUS.)............................. **$200-250**
Planter, model of baby scale, ca. 1954, 5 x 5 1/2"... **$35-50**
Planter, model of backward bird, ca. early 1940s, 4" h. **$60-70**

Figural Bear Planter

Planter, model of bear w/ball, yellow w/black trim, red ball, 1940s-50s, 5 1/2 x 7" (ILLUS.) **$100-125**
Planter, model of carriage w/umbrella, ca. 1955, 8 x 9"..................................... **$150-200**
Planter, model of Cope monkey head, 5 1/2" h.. **$100-200**

Fish Planter

Planter, model of fish, green, ca. 1955,
7 x 12" (ILLUS.)............................ **$1,000-1,200**
Planter, model of lemon, ca. 1953,
5 x 6 1/2" **$100-125**

1950s Liberty Bell McCoy Planter

Planter, model of Liberty Bell, cold painted
black bell, base embossed "4th July
1776," 8 1/4 x 10" (ILLUS.) **$350-400**
Planter, model of pomegranate, ca. 1953,
5 x 6 1/2" **$125-150**
Planter, model of rooster on wheel of
wheelbarrow, ca. 1955, 10 1/2" l. **$100-125**
Planter, model of snowman, ca. 1940s,
4 x 6".. **$70-90**
Planter, model of stork, ca. 1956, blue &
pink, 7 x 7 1/2" **$75-100**
Planter, model of "stretch" dachshund,
8 1/4" l. **$150-175**
Planter, model of trolley car, ca. 1954,
3 3/4 x 7"... **$50-60**
Planter, model of wagon wheel, ca. 1954,
8" h... **$30-40**
Planter, Plow Boy, ca. 1955, 7 x 8"......... **$100-125**
Planter, rectangular, relief-molded golf
scene, ca. 1957, 4 x 6"...................... **$150-200**
Planting dish, model of swan, ca. 1955,
10 1/2" l. **$350-400**
Planting dish, rectangular, front w/five re-
lief-molded Scottie dog heads, white,
brown & green, ca. 1949, 8" l................. **$50-60**
Platter, 14" l., Butterfly line, ca. 1940s
.... **$250-600**

Porch Jar

Porch jar, wide tapering cylindrical body
w/ribbed base, embossed leaf & berry
decoration below rim, green, marked
"NM," ca. 1940s, 9 1/2 x 11" (ILLUS.)
.... **$200-250**
Spoon rest, Butterfly line, ca. 1953,
4 x 7 1/2"... **$90-125**
Sprinkler, model of turtle, green w/yellow
trim, ca. 1950, 5 1/2 x 10".................... **$80-100**
Tea set: cov. teapot, creamer & open sugar
bowl; Pine Cone patt., ca. 1946, 3 pcs.
.... **$75-100**

McCoy Pottery Shaded Brown Teapot

Teapot, cov., spherical body w/molded
rings around the bottom, short spout,
squared handle, low domed cover
w/pointed loop finial, shaded brown
glaze, ca. 1948 (ILLUS.) **$25**

McCoy Strawberry Country Teapot

Teapot, cov., Strawberry Country patt.,
heavy cylindrical white body w/short

spout & C-form handle, printed w/a cluster of strawberries, blossoms & leaves, flat green cover w/knob finial, 1970s (ILLUS.) **$25**

McCoy Fireplace TV Lamp

TV lamp, model of fireplace, ca. 1950s, 6 x 9" (ILLUS.)...................................... **$75-100**

Umbrella Stand with Leaf Design

Umbrella stand, cylindrical w/applied handles, ribbed panels alternating w/embossed leaf design panels, glossy brown glaze, ca. 1940s, 19" h. (ILLUS.) **$250-350**
Vase, 6" h., footed, heart-shape w/embossed roses, ca. 1940s **$60-80**
Vase, 6" h., Hobnail line, Castlegate shape, ca. early 1940s..................... **$150-200**
Vase, 6 1/2" h., figural tulip, ca. 1953..... **$100-125**
Vase, 8" h., figural chrysanthemum, ca. 1950 .... **$100-125**
Vase, 8" h., footed bulbous base w/trumpet-form neck & scrolled handles, embossed peacock decoration, ca. 1948 .... **$40-60**
Vase, 8 1/4" h., figural magnolia, pink, white, brown & green, ca. 1953 (ILLUS., top next column).................................. **$250-300**
Vase, 8 1/2" h., figural wide lily-form, white, brown & green, ca. 1956 .... **$100-125**

McCoy Magnolia Vase

Fawn Vase

Vase, 9" h., boot-shaped w/figural fawn & foliage, chartreuse w/green, ca. 1954 (ILLUS.)... **$100-125**
Vase, 10" h., 13 1/2" w., Blades of Grass, fan-shaped....................................... **$175-225**
Vase, 12" h., strap, double handled, ca. 1947... **$80-110**
Vase, 14" h., Antique Curio line, ca. 1962. **$75-100**
Vase, 14" h., figural seated cat, matte black, ca. 1960................................. **$200-250**
Vase, 14 1/2" h., Tall Fan, ca. 1954 .... **$150-200**

Butterfly Line Wall Pocket

Wall pocket, Butterfly line, aqua blue, marked "NM," ca. 1940s, 6 x 7" (ILLUS., previous page) $450-550

McCoy Clown Wall Pocket

Wall pocket, figural, clown, white w/red & black trim, ca. 1940s, 8" l. (ILLUS.)..... $100-150
Wall pocket, model of apple, ca. early 1950s, 6 x 7" $200-225
Wall pocket, model of bellows, ca. mid-1950s, 9 1/2" l. $90-110
Wall pocket, model of bird bath, late 1940s, 5 x 6 1/2" $90-110
Wall pocket, model of cuckoo clock, plus chains & weights, ca. mid-1950s, 8" l.
.... $200-225
Wall pocket, model of fan, blue, mid-1950s, 8 x 8 1/2" $75-90
Wall pocket, model of lovebirds on trivet, ca. early 1950s, 8 1/2" l. $75-90
Wall pocket, model of pear, ca. early 1950s, 6 x 7" $200-225

Meissen

The secret of true hard paste porcelain, known long before to the Chinese, was "discovered" accidentally in Meissen, Germany by J.F. Bottger, an alchemist working with E.W. Tschirnhausen. The first European true porcelain was made in the Meissen Porcelain Works, organized about 1709. Meissen marks have been widely copied by other factories. Some pieces listed here are recent.

Meissen Mark

Elaborate Meissen Victorian Centerpiece

Centerpiece, allegorical, the flaring reticulated oblong top base w/open end handles decorated overall w/encrusted colorful flowers & green leaves among gilt-trimmed scrolls, raised on an ornate flower-encrusted pedestal w/a flower-painted scrolled cartouche above a group of children representing the Four Seasons around the scrolled base, blue crossed-swords mark, modeled by Leuteritz, ca. 1880, overall 17 3/8" h. (ILLUS.)............. $7,768
Dinner service: ten 10" d. dinner plates, nine cups & saucers, eight cream soup bowls & eight underplates; Blue Onion patt., all marked w/the blue crossed swords, 19th c., the set (ILLUS. of part, top next page)....................................... $1,725

Mother & Children Figure Group

Figure group, a young mother in 18th c. costume seated holding her bare-bottomed toddler across her lap w/a switch to spank it in her other hand, her young daughter pulling at her arm to dissuade her, on a round molded & gilt-trimmed base, blue crossed-swords mark, late 19th c., 10 1/4" h. (ILLUS.) $3,585

Meissen Blue Onion Pattern Dinner Service

Satirical Figure of Baron Munchhaussen

Meissen Figure of Young Boy Drinking

Figures of child, blond boy wearing white nightgown, blue socks & tan slippers, holding blue & white bowl or cup to lips, a horse toy on its back behind him, under-glaze blue crossed sword mark, 20th c., 7 1/2" h. (ILLUS.) **$1,035**

Figurine, Baron Munchhaussen, in a satiri-cal pose dressed as a cavalry office riding on the full moon, on a stepped eb-onized wood base, blue crossed-swords mark, signed by Alexander Struck, ca. 1941, 13 1/4" h. (ILLUS., next column) ... **$5,975**

Plate, 9" d., a small h.p. round central scene in color showing a half-nude Classical male holding a wreath above the head of a half-nude woman, a narrow reticulated outer border band enclosing a wide co-balt blue ground ornately decorated w/delicate gold, blue crossed-swords mark, titled "Le Printemps - Watteau," ca. 1900 (ILLUS., bottom next column) **$1,691**

Lovely Meissen Plate with Center Scene

Meissen Cup & Saucer with City View

Teacup & saucer, the cup w/a cobalt blue ground painted on the side w/a large oblong reserve w/a color scene of a church in Dresden, bordered in gold scrolls, the matching cup w/three oblong reserves painted w/colorful floral bouquets outlined w/gold scrolls, scene titled "Kathol Kirche zu Dresden," blue crossed-swords mark, ca. 1850 (ILLUS.) **$1,076**

Teapot, cov., bulbous tapering body w/a foliage-molded wishbone handle & bird's-head spout, the body w/a yellow background painted on each side w/a black-outlined cartouche containing a waterway landscape scene of merchants at various pursuits by barrels, sacks & figures on horseback & boating, low domed cover w/pale red figural strawberry finial flanked by cartouches, further gold, puce & iron-red trim on the spout & handle, blue crossed-swords mark & impressed number, ca. 1740, 3 5/8" h. **$4,183**

Meissen Teapot with Landscape Scenes

Teapot, cov., slightly squatty nearly spherical body w/a molded fish-form spout & London-shape handle w/shell design, h.p. on each side in color w/a landscape w/cow & sheep framed by trellis & blossom bands, blue crossed-swords mark, ca. 1795, hairline in base (ILLUS.) **$748**

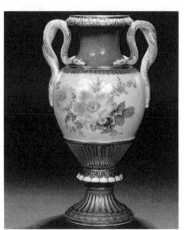

Small Early Meissen Porcelain Teapot

Teapot, cov., nearly spherical slightly tapering body decorated w/a robin's-egg blue ground, the flat cover w/a gold knob finial, short curved shoulder spout & pointed arch handle, each side centered by a h.p. color scene of merchants haggling at quayside within a gold border, the cover w/two smaller views, "indianische Blumen" design under spout & on handle, blue crossed-swords mark, 1735-40, overall 4 1/4" l., 4 1/4" h. (ILLUS.) **$4,780**

Fancy Floral-decorated Meissen Urn

Urn, a flaring gadrooned foot joined by a white-beaded disk to the large ovoid urn-form body w/gold gadrooning around the lower portion below the wide white central band h.p. w/a large bouquet of colorful flowers, the tapering neck in deep pink below the heavy gold rolled & gadrooned rim, white & gold entwined serpent handles at each side, blue crossed-swords mark, late 19th c., 11" h. (ILLUS.) **$518**

Pair of Extremely Ornate Meissen Potpourri Vases

orful flowers & fruits, the flaring pedestal base trimmed in gold & green & mounted on one side w/the figure of a small putto or nymph, after a model by J.J. Kandler, blue crossed-swords mark, ca. 1900, pr. (ILLUS., top of page)............................. **$10,755**

Mettlach

Ceramics with the name Mettlach were produced by Villeroy & Boch and other potteries in the Mettlach area of Germany. Villeroy and Boch's finest years of production are thought to be from about 1890 to 1910. Also see STEINS.

Mettlach Mark

Cobalt Blue Meissen Vase with Putti

Vase, 6 5/8" h., footed bottle-form body tapering to a ringed neck w/a widely flaring rim, cobalt blue ground enameled in white in the Limoges style w/a pair of amorous putti sitting on a leafy branch, one extending a floral wreath to a third in flight releasing a dove, gold banding at the foot, neck ring & rim, blue crossed-swords mark, probably designed by E.A. Leuteritz, ca. 1880 (ILLUS.).................. **$2,868**

Vases, cov., 29 7/8" h., potpourri-type, ornate Rococo style, each domed & pierced cover surmounted by a large bouquet of realistic flowers, the bulbous inverted pear-shaped body w/front & back panels finely decorated w/colorful floral bouquets, the sides very ornately encrusted w/a wide variety of large, col-

Charger, gilt bronze-mounted, large round shallow dish w/the colorful Golden Pheasant & Flowers design in the center, the wide border decorated w/colorful flowers & butterflies, decorated by M. Hein, the back signed & numbered, dated 1887, No. 1676, the gilt-bronze rim band w/scrolling leaf & blossom handles, raised on a base w/four scrolled feet joined by floral swags, 23 1/2" d., 7 1/4" h. (ILLUS. of two views, top next page)... **$4,140**

Cracker jar, cov., wide, squatty, bulbous body w/a silver plate rim, flat cover w/turned finial & swing handle, mosaic decoration of narrow geometric bands in shades of dark blue, tan, brown & white above a wider base band w/stylized flowering branches, tan ground, No. 1332, 5" d... **$575**

Lovely Mettlach Gilt Bronze-Mounted Charger

Large Mettlach Drinking Set Decorated with German City Crests

Drinking set: tall tapering cylindrical tankard pitcher w/hinged pewter cover & twelve cylindrical beakers; paint-underglaze decoration, the pitcher decorated w/tan bands at the top & base, a large black Prussian eagle at the front w/bands featuring the crests of various German cities above & below, each beaker decorated w/a different German city crest below a border band naming the city, pitcher No. 2893-1200 & beakers No. 2327-1200, beakers 1/4 L , pitcher 3 1/4 L, the set (ILLUS., center of page) **$1,811**

Flowerpot, a narrow footring below the wide cylindrical body w/a slightly flared rim, the sides divided into panels etched w/color scenes of Cavaliers drinking, white lappet band around the rim, No. 2170, 6" h. **$374**

Jardiniere, Aesthetic Movement-style, the round disk foot w/a molded leaftip band supporting the wide compressed rounded lower body decorated w/oblong panels w/stylized flowers below wide slightly tapering sides below the low rounded leaftip rim, leafy C-scroll handles at the lower body each mounted by a figure of a putto playing a mandolin, the sides decorated w/a continuous frieze of Renaissance era beauties in a garden among

Lovely Mettlach Aesthetic Jardiniere

fruiting trees all painted in shades of blue & brown, No. 1355, ca. 1880, signed by Warth, 16 3/8" d., 23" h. (ILLUS.) **$4,183**

Jardiniere, Art Nouveau design, low narrow oblong form w/rounded tapering sides raised on low brackets, the flat rim w/stepped ends, decorated w/an etched design of panels formed by brown lattice & bars against a tan ground w/clusters of green buds, No. 2980, 14" l., 5" h. **$460**

Mettlach Phanolith Jardiniere

Jardiniere, Phanolith type, a wide disk foot supporting the wide cylindrical body w/a flared rim, dark blue ground decorated w/applied white relief mythological figures & pale green florals around the sides, incised mark, 8" h. (ILLUS.)............. **$690**

Mantel garniture: clock in urn & pair of matching side urns; the large baluster-form central urn w/a mosaic design of stylized floral & leaf panels in alternating cream w/green & tan & rust red w/tan, brown & green, the flared neck w/tan ground & floral swags, raised on a high gilt-metal plinth w/a scroll-cast footed base, gilt-metal serpent-form shoulder handles & a scalloped metal rim band & gadrooned domed cover w/leaf bud finial, a clock set into one side within a brass bezel, the matching shorter urns w/similar gilt-metal details, shorter urns 15 1/2", tallest urn 19" h., the set (ILLUS., bottom of page)... **$3,565**

Pilsner Beaker with the Munich Child

Pilsner beaker, a flaring foot supporting a tall gently flaring bowl, the sides decorated in color w/a scene of the Munich Child framed by brick red & deep yellow bands on a creamy ground, No. 2775-1014, 1/2 L (ILLUS.)... **$432**

Unique Mettlach Garniture Set

Art Nouveau-style Mettlach Pitcher

Pitcher, 5 1/2" h., bulbous octagonal lower body tapering to tall cylindrical sides w/a wide long angled spout & angled handle, stylized Art Nouveau decorated in deep gold & dark blue w/stylized fruiting trees up the sides & geometric panels around the lower body, marked "Mettlach Reg. US Pat. Off. - Made in Germany," ca. 1920s (ILLUS.) **$115**

Art Nouveau Floral Mettlach Planter

Planter, Art Nouveau-style, oblong scrolling base band below the squatty bulbous body tapering to a scalloped gadrooned rim w/six C-scroll handles curving down from the rim to the shoulder, the body in dark blue etched & decorated overall w/stylized six-petaled dark & light blue flowers w/brown centers, the border bands in pale green & dark brown, No. 2417, 10 x 16 1/2", 8" h. (ILLUS.) **$1,150**

Mettlach Snow White & Dwarfs Plaque

Plaque, an etched color scene of Snow White & the Seven Dwarfs against a dark blue ground, decorated by H. Schlitt, mi-

nor gold wear, No. 2148, 17" d. (ILLUS.) **$1,116**

Mettlach Woman & Roses Plaque

Plaque, Art Nouveau design, a large etched bust portrait of an Art Nouveau woman on the left sniffing large tan roses on dark green leafy stems, tan border band decorated w/dark green & rust red leaf devices, No. 2544, pierced to hang, 20" d. (ILLUS.) **$863**

Phanolith Plaque with Figures

Plaque, phanolith, a dark green ground decorated in white relief w/three seminude classical water nymphs & flying birds, No. 7043, pierced to hang, 21" d. (ILLUS.) **$719**

Plaques, each etched w/a colorful scene of figures from Germanic folklore, one showing Siegfried & Gertrude, the other Lohengrin's Ankunst, No. 3163 & No. 3165, 17" d., each (ILLUS. of both, top next page) **$1,840**

Plaques, etched designs, each centered by a bust portrait of a Renaissance woman wearing a large feathered hat, in natural tones & dark blue, dark pink & white against a pale blue ground, the wide border band w/overall stylized scrolling leaves in brown, tan & blue on a dark blue ground, No. 1424 & 1425, pierced to hang, 15 1/2" d., facing pr. **$1,035**

Two Mettlach Folklore Plaques

Mettlach Punch Bowl Set

Punch bowl, cover & underplate, a footed bulbous squatty bowl w/a short wide cylindrical neck & low domed cover w/leaf loop finial, large loop shoulder handles w/satyr mask terminals, red foot, body & neck bands, the body band decorated w/a continuous white relief scene of dancing peasants, the background body in a putty color, No. 2087, 8 L, the set (ILLUS.) **$1,208**

Tobacco jar, cov., barrel-shaped, an etched design w/repeating pairs of large herringbone panels in dark blue & dark red separated by horizontal & vertical white bands w/"Tabac" in black, four alternate white panels etched w/an outlined figure of a man smoking a pipe above another panel w/a dark blue, dark red & dotted black checkerboard design w/another white band w/"Tabac," domed cover w/checkerboard panels & white knob, very rare, No. 4504, 6 1/2" h. **$719**

Two Small Mettlach Vases

Vase, 5 1/4" h., ovoid body w/a short rolled neck, white ground transfer-printed & hand-enameled w/an overall design of crosses alternating w/florets in shades

of green, yellow & red, No. 1016-3058 (ILLUS. right with other Mettlach vase) **$242**

Vase, 6" h., wide ovoid body w/a narrow shoulder to the low flared neck, glazed in relief w/an Oriental-style decoration, a dark red ground w/lappet bands around the base & shoulder & a narrow center band flanked by opposing pairs of ornate lappets, all in shades of dark blue, pink & green, No. 1596 (ILLUS. left with other Mettlach vase)... **$242**

Mettlach Vase with Poppies

Vase, 7" h., bulbous ovoid body tapering to a bulbed neck w/narrow scalloped rim, a dark blue ground etched overall w/an Art Nouveau design w/clusters of large deep pink poppy blossoms & a narrow pale blue ribbon band, tiny pink leaf designs scattered around the sides & neck, No. 2434 (ILLUS.)... **$460**

Vase, 7" h., mosaic decoration on a brick red ground, a funnel foot w/dark blue band & leaf tips below the wide ovoid body decorated w/bands of tiny florets flanking the wide center band w/vertical almond-form devices w/scroll leaves in dark blue & stylized four-petal designs in tan & slate blue, short flaring neck w/band of tiny beads, No. 1573 .... **$311**

Vase, 9" h., bulbous ovoid form w/a dark blue ground decorated in mosaic w/scattered pink & pale blue three-petal blossoms & tiny blue bead blossoms, a brick red neck band decorated w/a band of applied dark blue beads, No. 2868 .... **$288**

Unusual Mettlach Vase in Red & Green

Vase, 9 1/2" h., flat-bottomed bulbous lower body tapering to a wide cylindrical neck, painted under glaze w/green hops & leaves against a deep red ground, overall slightly iridescent glaze, No. 2541 (ILLUS.) **$253**

Mettlach Vase with Germanic Maidens

Vase, 12 3/4" h., a tapering foot below the wide squatty compressed lower body tapering to the tall ringed & flaring cylindrical upper body, the lower body & foot w/etched stylized bands in shades of brown, tan, white & green, the upper body w/a dark brown ground decorated on each side w/an etched keyhole-shaped panel featuring a full-length color portrait of a Germanic maiden, decorated by Gorig, No. 1749 (ILLUS.) **$284**
Vase, 13 1/2" h., tall cylindrical body raised on small scroll legs, Oriental landscape scene, a dark brown matte ground molded in relief w/pairs of geese in white, brown & greyish blue on brown rockwork, tall golden brown bamboo stocks behind

them & pale blue water in front of them, No. 1515 (one leg repaired) **$719**
Vase, 16 1/2" h., Art Nouveau design, baluster-form body tapering to a tall cylindrical neck w/flared rim, slender serpentine handles from rim to shoulder, decorated w/a glossy moss green glaze w/dark green handles & base bands, the neck & shoulder molded in low relief w/suspended fuchsia blossoms, No. 2731 .... **$891**
Vases, 10" h., a low, round foot supporting a tall, squared body w/a short flaring neck, each side w/a large oblong mosaic panel filled w/arabesque entwined scrolls in white, light blue, green & gold w/a maroon almond-form central reserve, dark blue borders, No. 2032, pr. **$1,093**

One of Two Red Mettlach Vases

Vases, 13 1/2" h., tall ovoid body w/long elephant head figural handles, etched & glazed to resemble Oriental cloisonné, the bright red ground decorated w/zigzag bands & stylized flowers & leafy scrolls in shades of blue, white, green & purple, No. 1870 (ILLUS. of one) **$575**

Minton

The Minton factory in England was established by Thomas Minton in 1793. The factory made earthenware, especially the blue-printed variety, and Thomas Minton is sometimes credited with the invention of the blue "Willow" pattern. For a time majolica and tiles were also important parts of production, but bone china soon became the principal ware. Mintons, Ltd., continues in operation today. Also see MAJOLICA.

Minton Marks

Ornate Sèvres-style Mintons Bowl

Ornate Sèvres-style Bottle Cooler

Bottle cooler, Sèvres-style, footed wide & deep cylindrical form w/a ring-molded wide flat rim, gilt-trimmed scroll handles, the lower body in turquoise blue decorated w/a band of tall gold leaves, a narrow shoulder band in blue decorated w/Classical figural reserves in white on black framed by gilt scrolls, narrower white bands w/delicate florals flanking it, based on a piece from a service made for Catherine the Great of Russia, gold crowned globe mark, ca. 1906, 7 1/2" h. (ILLUS.) **$9,560**

Bowl, 9 1/2" d., Sèvres-style, a low footring below the wide rounded upright sides w/a wide flat rim, turquoise blue ground decorated on the front & back w/a large oval reserve of colorful exotic birds framed w/ornate gilt oak leaf banding & swags, gilt line rim & interior gilt dentil band, based on a service made by Sèvres for the Prince of Rohan, gold crowned globe mark, ca. 1900 (ILLUS., top of page) **$2,629**

Bowl, majolica, deep, rounded, molded & ribbed yellow basketweave exterior w/a band of wide overlapping green leaves around the rim, turquoise interior, shape No. 582, date code for 1865, mint **$495**

Mintons Charger with Scene of Artemis

Charger, round, finely painted w/a celestial view of the nude Artemis standing before a tree w/a net ensnaring flying putti, one putto captured & tucked in her side satchel, in pastel colors, painted & impressed mark, decorated by Louis Marc Solon, 1872, 11 7/8" d. (ILLUS.) **$5,736**

Unusual Minton Chestnut Server

Chestnut server, majolica, shell-form dish w/scalloped flanged rim molded w/green leaves on brown, large arching green & pink leaves & figural chestnut cover half the turquoise blue bowl, shape No. 494, date code for 1862, 9 1/2" w. (ILLUS.) **$1,540**

Ewer, majolica, monumental piece, large figural handle of a mermaid w/braided hair & fish scale vest & tail reaching down & entwining w/the horns of a bold relief satyr's head, the large wide curved spout above a neck molded in a ruffled pink shell & green leaf design above the bulbous lower portion, which features a full-figure putto at the rim opposite the handle, large green garland bands divide the lower body into panels molded in white relief w/a classical woman & putti against a tan ground, short swirled brown pedestal on the round foot w/a yellow shell-molded edge band, date code for 1871, shape No. 1290, mint, overall 16" w., 21" h. **$55,000**

Rare Mintons Pate-sur-Pate Pilgrim Bottle

Pilgrim bottle, pate-sure-pate, the footed flattened round body topped by a cylindrical neck w/flared rim flanked by small gold loop shoulder handles, dark chocolate brown ground, a large round front reserve w/a border of pale blue bands w/a top bow centered by a green leaftip band, the center in cobalt blue decorated in white slip relief w/a seated Bacchante resting w/a wine ewer in her lap, spilling fruit & an upturned jug at her feet, gold crowned globe mark, decorated by Frederick Alfred Rhead, ca. 1875, 10" h. (ILLUS.) **$8,365**

Minton Majolica Garden Seat

Garden seat, majolica, large ovoid form w/a flaring, lightly ruffled top, cobalt blue w/a large turquoise blue ribbon & bow around the neck above a large suspended branch of pink & white flowers & green leaves, shape No. 2367, date code for 1881, 17" h. (ILLUS.) **$2,750**

Humidor, cov., majolica, figural, a cylindrical tall coil of yellow rope forming the body, a large seated figure of a sailor drinking from a mug on the flat top, shape No. 716, 9" h. **$2,200**

Jardiniere, majolica, large bulbous urn top w/a flaring cobalt blue neck, the turquoise sides molded w/two large bold-relief lion masks supporting green swags molded w/colorful fruit, nuts & wheat, floral rosettes w/pink ribbons & bows alternate w/the lion masks, on a pedestal molded w/green leaves above the round turquoise foot w/a golden brown lappet band, date code for 1869, 15" d., 14 1/2" h. **$3,300**

Mintons Art of Union Commemorative Plate

Plate, 9 3/4" d., "Act of Union" commemorative, the wide deep pink border decorated w/three long reserves decorated w/plants representing England (roses), Scotland (thistles) & Ireland (shamrocks) all bordered in gilt floral scrolls, the white center h.p. w/the large entwined monogram "VR" for Queen Victoria below a small crown, representing the Union of Great Britain, dated 1874, impressed uppercase mark (ILLUS.) **$3,107**

Minton Sevres-style Individual Tea Set

Salt dip, master size, majolica, model of a small tapering cylindrical basket in yellow w/a large square tab at one rim, turquoise interior, date code for 1872, 5" h. **$193**

Salt dip, master size, majolica, oblong four-lobed form w/pink interior & cobalt blue exterior on a green foot, date code for 1862, 5" l., 2 1/2" h. **$330**

Tea set: individual-size, cov. teapot, cov. sugar bowl, creamer, handled cup & rounded triangular undertray; Sevres-style, each piece in white painted w/a band of pink rose blossoms between turquoise "jeweled" gilt chains, lavender edge bands, Pattern No. A1213, date code for 1853, tray 11 1/4" w., the set (ILLUS., top of page) **$2,868**

harebell swags, Paris Exhibition model w/dated ribbon for 1878, impressed date cypher for 1877, printed gold Prince of Wales feathers mark, saucer 5 1/2" d., pr. (ILLUS.) **$478**

Toby jugs, majolica, figural Barrister & Lady, stocky figures in colorful 18th c. attire, great detail, 11 1/2" h., pr. (minor professional rim repair) **$2,750**

Elegant Mintons Pate-sur-Pate Vase

Vase, 8 1/2" h., pate-sure-pate, a gently swelled cylindrical body w/a narrow flat shoulder centering a short molded neck, dark chocolate brown ground finely painted & hand-tooled in white relief slip w/a standing nymph attended by two grief-stricken putti, beneath a ribbon-tied laurel swag, the neck & shoulder trimmed w/a gold scale design, gold crowned globe mark, Shape No. 2443, signed by Alboo-in Birks, ca. 1900 (ILLUS.) **$4,780**

Vincennes-style Mintons Teacup & Saucer

Teacup & saucer, Vincennes-style, a footed deep rounded bowl & matching dished saucer, white ground decorated w/round reserves in deep rose featuring putti among clouds, each surrounded by a gold beaded border & joined by gold

Elegant Pair of Minton Turquoise Cloisonné-style Vases

Minton Art Nouveau-style Vases

Vases, 9 1/2" h., 4" d., Art Nouveau style, tall slender ovoid body tapering to a small flat mouth, each decorated in the squee-zebag style in a Secessionist design of undulating ribbons up around the sides highlighted w/stylized clusters of bubble-like devices, one in deep purple, dark blue & green, the other in deep red, maroon & white & green, one w/restoration to the base & small rim chip, stamped "Minton Ltd. - No. 1" (ILLUS.).................... **$805**

Vases, 10" h., decorated to resemble Oriental cloisonné, gold ring-footed bottle form w/tall slender tapering neck, turquoise blue ground decorated around the lower body w/an ornate band of stylized scrolls & leaves in shades of dark blue, brick red, white & pale green, a lappet band in white, blue & green on the upper neck below the

gold rim, each mounted on the side w/a large scarab beetle in similar colors, Shape No. 1644, designed by Christopher Dresser, puce printed crowned globe mark, dated 1974, pr. (ILLUS., top of page)... **$19,120**

One of Two Large Sèvres-style Vases

Vases, Sèvres classical style, a square foot & tapering ringed pedestal supporting the wide bulbous ovoid body tapering to a cy-lindrical neck w/a flared rim, molded gold rope swags around the neck & down the sides, dark green & gold on the base & lower body, the main body in white h.p. overall w/large colorful swags of flowers & leaves, a green band & bow at the top of the neck, ca. 1855, 12 5/8" h., pr. (ILLUS. of one)... **$6,573**

Mocha Canister, Mug & Pitcher

Mocha

Mocha decoration is found on basically utilitarian creamware or yellowware articles and is achieved by a simple chemical reaction. A color pigment of brown, blue, green or black is given an acid nature by infusion of tobacco or hops. When this acid nature colorant is applied in blobs to an alkaline ground color, it reacts by spreading in feathery seaweed designs. This type of decoration is usually accompanied by horizontal bands of light color slip. Produced in numerous Staffordshire potteries from the late 18th until the late 19th centuries, its name is derived from the similar markings found on mocha quartz. In addition to the seaweed decoration, mocha wares are also seen with Earthworm and Cat's Eye patterns or a marbleized effect.

Bowl, 6" d., 3 1/4" h., footed deep rounded shape w/a flat rim, an upper wide salmon red band outlined in black & decorated w/black seaweed design, England, mid-19th c. (one minor footring chip, hairline) **$353**

Canister, cov., wide cylindrical body w/incised lines near the top, domed cover w/disk finial, yellowware decorated around the middle w/thin dark brown bands flanking a wide white band w/blue seaweed designs, matching design on the cover, professional restoration to chipping & glaze flaking in the cover, tight full-length line through body, 19th c., 8" h. (ILLUS. center with mocha mug & pitcher, top of page).. **$220**

Mocha Chamber Pot with Earthworm Pattern

Chamber pot, pearlware, footed squatty bulbous form w/a flared flattened rim, C-form handle, dark brown upper & lower bands decorated in the Cat's-eye patt., the wider

central grey band decorated w/Earthworm patt. in blue, ochre & white, one rim chip, faint spider crack in base, ca. 1830, 11 3/8" d., 5 3/4" h. (ILLUS.) **$1,410**

Flowerpot & undertray, slightly tapering cylindrical body w/narrow flanged rim, conforming undertray, the pot & tray each w/bands of mottled green & brown encrusting below bands of blue & brown slip w/black slip-inlaid beading, probably Yorkshire, England, ca. 1800, 6 3/4" h., 2 pcs. (one area of glaze & slip loss on pot, numerous glaze flakes on interior & base, hairlines) **$940**

Jar, cov., small footed baluster-form w/a domed cover & knob finial, the base w/a dark reddish brown band above a wide light brown band decorated w/black seaweed design, England, early 19th c., 3 1/4" h. (cracks)..................... **$1,116**

Mocha Jar with Seaweed Decoration

Jar, cov., yellowware, cylindrical w/thin incised rings around the lower body, a white & brown central band decorated w/black seaweed decoration, domed cover w/button finial decorated w/another brown seaweed-decorated band, ca. 1850, tight hairline, minor flake under cover, 4 1/2" h. (ILLUS.) **$242**

Mixing bowl, small foot below the deep rounded sides w/a wide rolled rim, yellowware decorated under the rim w/a wide white band flanked by thin blue bands & decorated w/dark navy blue seaweed design, late 19th - early 20th c., 12" d., 5 3/4" h. (overall very tight age lines) **$330**

Rare Mocha Earthworm Child's Mug

Mug, child's, yellow-glazed earthenware, cylindrical w/C-scroll handle, green ground decorated w/a bold black & white Earthworm patt., thin white & black rim & base bands, partial impressed mark on base, chips to base edge, glaze wear on rim, early 19th c., 2 5/8" h. (ILLUS.)........ **$2,938**

Mug, cylindrical w/applied strap handle, dark yellow base & rim bands outlined in black & flanking the wide center band decorated w/bands of black inlaid rouletting & engine turning in a block checked design, England, ca. 1790, 6" h. (stress cracks at rim)... **$881**

Mug, cylindrical w/applied strap handle, pale yellow base & rim bands outlined in black, the main body decorated overall w/random splashes of slip in bluish grey, white & black on a deep rust red background, England, ca. 1790, 5 7/8" h. (minor rim chip restoration)...................... **$2,115**

Mug, cylindrical w/applied strap handle, upper & lower bands in dark olive green & brown flanking central bands of S-curved engine turning, half-pint, England, ca. 1800, 3 3/4" h. (minor lines in base) **$470**

Mug, cylindrical w/molded base band & C-form handle, yellowware w/thin brown bands flanking a wide white band decorated w/blue seaweed designs, professional restoration to the replaced handle, glaze age crazing, 19th c., 3 3/4" h. (ILLUS. left with mocha canister & pitcher, top of previous page) **$358**

Mug, porter-type, short cylindrical shape w/flared base, applied strap handle w/foliate terminals, dark brown rim & base bands, the putty-colored body decorated w/a painted random design of brown, white & black short slip trailings or dashes, England, ca. 1830, 3 1/8" h. (one hairline) **$999**

Scarce Mocha Seaweed Mustard Jar

Mustard jar, cov., pearlware, footed bulbous ovoid body tapering to a flat rim, domed cover w/spoon notch & knob finial, C-form handle, dark brown body & cover bands each decorated in the black seaweed decoration, finial repair, small rim & base chips, early 19th c., 3 1/2" h. (ILLUS.).. **$1,645**

Pitcher, 7" h., wide cylindrical lower body tapering to a cylindrical neck w/pinched rim spout, C-form handle, yellowware decorated w/pair of thin brown bands flanking a wide white band decorated w/blue seaweed design, surface roughness at spout under the glaze, 19th c. (ILLUS. right with mocha mug & canister)............................ **$495**

Mocha Seaweed Decor Salt Dip

Salt dip, pearlware, footed wide squatty bulbous form w/a slightly flared rim, dark brown body band decorated in the black seaweed decoration, white foot, thin black & green rim bands, cracked, rim chip, early 19th c., 2 3/4" d. (ILLUS.)........ **$558**

Tea caddy, wide cylindrical body w/an angled shoulder to a short cylindrical neck, green reeded bands around the shoulder & base, the shoulder & body decorated in marbleized slip in white, brown & ochre, England, late 18th - early 19th c., 4 1/2" h. (repair to rim) **$1,645**

Waste bowl, footed w/flaring flat sides, blue background w/blue Earthworm patt. band, early 19th c., 5" d., 2 1/2" h. (hairlines in bottom)..................................... **$330**

Moorcroft

William Moorcroft became a designer for James Macintyre & Co. in 1897 and was put in charge of the art pottery production there. Moorcroft developed a number of popular designs, including Florian Ware, while with Macintyre and continued with that firm until 1913, when it discontinued the production of art pottery.

After leaving Macintyre in 1913, Moorcroft set up his own pottery in Burslem, where he continued producing the art wares he had designed earlier, introducing new patterns as well. After William's death in 1945, the pottery was operated by his son, Walter.

MOORCROFT *Moorcroft*

Moorcroft Marks

Extremely Rare Silver-mounted Claremont Coffee Service

Moorcroft Claremont Pattern Bowl

Bowl, 8 1/4" d., 3 3/4" h., Claremont patt., wide shallow form, the interior decorated w/large mushrooms in shades of maroon & light green against a shaded midnight blue & dark green ground, Moorcroft-Burslem mark & William Moorcroft signature, professionally repaired (ILLUS.) **$345**

Box, cov., Dawn patt., footed wide squatty bulbous body topped by a low-domed inset cover w/button finial, decorated around the body w/a stylized hilly landscape w/trees below a border band of small overlapping scales, similar scene around the cover, a slightly crystalline glaze in shades of dark & light blue, green, white & rose, impressed "Moorcroft - Made in England" on base & painted initials of William Moorcroft, faint overall crazing, 6 1/4" d., 4" h. (ILLUS.)
.... **$2,300**

Coffee service: tall ovoid cov. coffeepot, cov. sugar bowl & creamer; Claremont patt., each piece decorated w/large mushrooms in shades of blues, greens & deep maroon against a shaded blue ground, each silver-mounted around the rim & base w/a band of sterling silver blossoms, made for Shreve & Co., San Francisco & so marked, silver stamped "Shreve & Co. - Sterling," ca. 1905, coffeepot 9 3/4" h., the set (ILLUS., top of page).. **$16,800**

Cracker jar, cov., Pomegranate patt., barrel-shaped body w/a silver plate rim, cover & swing bail handle, in shades of cobalt blue, deep red, mustard yellow & green, marked "Moorcroft - Burslem - 102" w/Moorcroft signature, restoration around base, ca. 1916, 5 1/4" d., 9 1/2" h. (ILLUS., top next page)
.... **$489**

Lamp, baluster-form body decorated in the Springtime Flowers patt. on a cream to cobalt blue ground, fitted on a round brass foot & w/a pierced cap & electric fitting, body 10" h. **$990**

Fine Moorcroft Dawn Pattern Box

Moorcroft Pomegranate Cracker Jar

Miniature Moorcroft Orchids Vase

Small Dark Blue Moorcroft Vase

Vase, miniature, 2 7/8" h., footed wide & low squatty body centered by a short flaring neck, overall mottled dark blue lustre glaze, impressed "Moorcroft M82 - Made in England" (ILLUS.) **$173**

Moorcroft Anemones Table Lamp

Lamp, table model, Anemones patt., footed ovoid body tapering to a wide flat mouth w/electrical fittings, the foot in dark blue, the body in a shaded pale yellow decorated w/large blue, white & pink blossoms & green leaves, stamped mark & original paper label, early 20th c., base 10" h., overall 19" h. (ILLUS.)............................... **$523**

Vase, miniature, 2 5/8" h., Orchids patt., footed very wide squatty bulbous body centered by a short flaring neck, painted w/vivid deep rose & dark blue orchids & yellow & green leaves on a cobalt blue ground, marked (ILLUS., top next column)... **$230**

Miniature Moorcroft Grape & Leaf Vase

Vase, 3" h., miniature, Grape & Leaf patt., footed nearly spherical body w/a small short flared neck, a large green shaded to maroon leaf in front of a large cluster of dark blue red-tinted grapes on a dark blue ground, W. Moorcroft signature, ca. 1930s, some glaze anomalies & slight crazing, a few glaze pops (ILLUS.)............ **$196**

Miniature Moorcroft Florian Ware Vase

Vase, miniature, 3 1/2" h., Florian Ware, a wide flat-bottomed squatty ovoid body w/a wide shoulder centering a small trumpet neck, a white ground decorated w/a band of large blue poppies on delicate pale green leafy stems, dark blue interior, MacIntyre era, No. 63, ca. 1898-1905, mild crazing (ILLUS.).................. **$1,265**

Small Moorcroft Hibiscus Vase

Vase, 5 1/8" h., Hibiscus patt., footed bulbous ovoid body tapering to a widely flaring trumpet neck, a large pink blossom & green leaves on a dark green ground, marked w/partial paper label, few minor glaze pits (ILLUS.)............................ **$184**

Moorcroft Blackberry Pattern Vase

Vase, 7" h., Blackberry patt., baluster-form body w/a short, wide rolled neck, large mottled deep red & green leaves & clusters of large dark purple berries around the shoulder against a mottled brown & dark blue & green ground, impressed mark & facsimile signature, faint crazing (ILLUS.)... **$575**

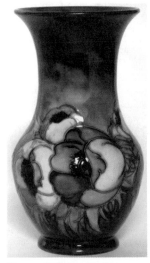

Moorcroft Vase with Anemones

Vase, 10" h., ovoid base w/long neck & flaring rim, decorated w/band of anemones on cobalt blue & green ground, facsimile signature & impressed factory mark, W.M. script (ILLUS.)................................. **$805**

Morton Potteries

A total of six potteries were in operation at various times in Morton, Illinois, from 1877 to 1976. All traced their origins from the Morton Brick and Tile Company begun in 1877 by six Rapp brothers who came to America in the early 1870s to escape forced military service under Kaiser Wilhelm I. Sons, nephews and cousins of the founding fathers were responsible for the continuation of the pottery industry in Morton as a result of buyouts or the establishment of new and separate operations. The potteries are listed chronologically by beginning dates.

Morton's natural clay deposits were ideal for the Rapps' venture into pottery production. Local clay was used until it was depleted in 1940. That clay fired out to a golden ecru color. After 1940, clay was imported from South Carolina and Indiana. It fired out snow white. The differences in clay allow one to easily date production at the Morton potteries. Only a few items were marked by any of the potteries. Occasionally, paper labels were used, but most of those have long disappeared. Glaze is sometimes a determinant. Early glazes were Rockingham brown, green and cobalt blue, or transparent, to produce yellowware. In the '20s and '30s colorful drip glazes were used. In the later years solid pastel and Deco colors were in vogue.

Most of Morton's potteries were short-lived, operating for twenty years or less. Their products are elusive. However, Morton Pottery Company was in operation for fifty-four years, and its products appear regularly in today's secondary market.

Rapp Brothers Brick & Tile Company & Morton Pottery Works (1877-1915) - Morton Earthenware Company (1915-1917)

Baker, deep, yellowware, 10" d. $125
Bank, figural acorn, brown Rockingham glaze, no advertising $50
Churn, mottled brown Rockingham glaze, 4 gal. $250

Rapp Bros. Green-glazed Creamer

Creamer, waisted cylindrical form w/molded bark & flowers under a dark green glaze, 5" h. (ILLUS.) $50

Rapp Brothers Jardiniere

Jardiniere, tapering cylindrical form, embossed leaf design, green, 7" d. (ILLUS.) $50
Lapel button, model of an elephant w/embossed "GOP" on side, dark brown glaze, 1 1/8 x 1 3/4" $95

Rapp Bros. Turk's Turban Mold

Mold, food, Turk's turban shape, field tile clay w/dark brown glaze, 7" d. (ILLUS.) $80
Mug, cylindrical, w/lightly molded lappet rim band, brown Rockingham glaze, 3 1/4" h., each (ILLUS. left & center, bottom of page) $55
Mug, cylindrical, yellowware, 2 3/4" h. (ILLUS. right with other mugs, bottom of page) $80

Bison Paperweight

Paperweight, model of a bison, advertises Rock Sand Company, brown Rockingham glaze, 2 7/8" l. (ILLUS.) $70

Three Rapp Brothers Mugs

Rapp Brothers Dutch Jug Pitcher

Pitcher, jug-type, milk (Dutch jug), brown Rockingham glaze, 3 1/2 pt. (ILLUS.) **$80**

Cliftwood Figure of a Billiken

Figure of a Billiken, seated, dark brown Rockingham glaze, 10 1/2" h. (ILLUS.)...... **$125**
Flower frog, figural turtle, holes pierced on back, bluish mulberry drip glaze, 4" l. **$30**

Rapp Bros. Sauerkraut Crock

Sauerkraut crock, cover/press, impressed mark, dark brown glaze, 4 gal., rare, 11" h. (ILLUS.) **$175**
Stein, barrel-shaped w/"Trinke was klar ist und rede was wahr ist" embossed around rim & base, green, 1 pt.................................. **$65**
Teapot, cov., acorn-shaped, mottled brown Rockingham glaze, 3 3/4 cup size **$90**

Cliftwood Art Potteries, Inc. (1920-1940)

Cliftwood Art Deco Lamp Base

Lamp base, Art Deco style, spherical body on four square legs, pinkish orchid drip glaze, base 4" h. (ILLUS.)........................... **$50**

Figural Cow Creamer

Creamer, figural cow, standing, tail forms handle, chocolate brown drip glaze, 3 3/4 x 6" (ILLUS.).................................... **$100**

Lamp Base with Sailing Ships

Lamp base, waisted cylindrical form w/a stepped shoulder, embossed panels around the sides showing a sailing ship, herbage green glaze, round metal foot, 11" h. (ILLUS.) **$70**

Cliftwood Model of a Bison

Model of bison, natural colors of light & dark brown, 9 1/2" l., 6 1/2" h. (ILLUS.)...... **$200**

Cliftwood Deco Vase with Drip Glaze

Vase, 8" h., Art Deco style, square gently flaring sides w/a widely flared rim, chocolate brown drip glaze (ILLUS.) **$75**

Cliftwood Model of German Shepherd

Model of dog, German shepherd, reclining, white, 8 1/2" l., 6" h. (ILLUS.) **$75**
Model of elephant, standing, chocolate brown drip glaze, 7 1/4 x 13 1/2" **$125**

Cliftwood Vase with Chain Design

Vase, 10" h., footed, slightly flaring cylindrical body w/rounded base & shoulder w/a flat mouth, lightly embossed vertical chain bands, matte orchid glaze (ILLUS.) **$80**
Vase, 16" h., footed baluster-form body w/flat rim, No. 114, bluish grey drip glaze **$85**
Vase, 18 1/4" h., urn form w/figural snakes swallowing fish handles, No. 132, chocolate brown drip glaze.................................. **$150**
Wall pocket, bullet-shaped w/handle on each side, matte turquoise & ivory glaze, 5" w., 7 1/2" h. **$70**
Wall pocket, elongated bell shape, No. 123, matte green glaze, 3 1/3" w., 8 3/4" h. **$50**

Cliftwood Model of a Frog

Model of frog, seated, glass eyes, shaded green to white glaze, 5" h. (ILLUS.) **$50**
Model of lioness, standing, chocolate brown drip glaze, 16" h., 5" h. **$95**

Morton Pottery Company (1922-1976)
Bank, figural, cat, sitting, yellow & white, 8 1/2" h... **$60**
Bank, figural, hen on nest, white w/red cold painted comb, black feather detail, yellow beak, 4" h... **$50**

Bank, figural, house, shoe-shaped, yellow
w/green roof, 6 1/2" h. **$40**
Bank, figural, Little Brown Church,
2 5/8 x 3 5/8", 3 3/4" h. **$30**

Morton Pottery Teddy Bear Bank

Bank, figural, Teddy bear, seated w/legs
outstretched, brown, pink, blue & black
on white, 8" h. (ILLUS.) **$50**

Morton Pottery Canister Set

Canister set: marked "Coffee," "Flour,"
"Sugar" & "Tea;" white cylindrical base
w/yellow hat-shaped lid w/high button
handle, 9" & 10" h., the set (ILLUS.) **$55**
Cookie jar, cov., baby bird in blue & yellow
spray over white **$60**
Cookie jar, cov., basket of fruit, green or
brown basket w/colored fruit, No. 3720,
each **$50**

Panda Bear Cookie Jar

Cookie jar, cov., panda bear, black & white,
front paws crossed (ILLUS.) **$80**
Creamer & sugar bowl, model of chicken &
rooster, black & white w/cold-painted red
comb, pr. **$55**

Morton Pottery Egg Tray

Egg tray, hexagonal cluster of eggs & half-
round eggs w/a figural chick in the center,
12" w. (ILLUS.) **$45**
Figure of John F. Kennedy, Jr., standing
on square base, right hand to head in salute position, gold paint trim, rare version,
7" h. **$125**
Grass grower, bisque, bust of "Jiggs," the
comic strip character, 5" h. **$35**
Grass grower, bisque, model of a standing
pig, 7 1/2" l., 3 3/4" h. **$20**
Head vase, woman w/1920s hairstyle, wide
brim hat, white matte glaze **$75**
Head vase, woman w/1940s hairstyle, pill
box hat, blue matte glaze **$65**
Head vase, woman w/upswept hairstyle,
white w/red lips, bow in hair & heart-
shaped locket **$40**

Morton Pottery Jardiniere

Jardiniere, squared form w/swelled sides,
low rectangular mouth, tab side handles,
small block feet, pink ground w/em-
bossed floral sprig in blue & green,
4 1/2" h. (ILLUS.) **$30**

Morton Kerosene Lamp

Lamp, kerosene, brass fixture w/glass
chimney, cylindrical body w/ribbed base

& relief-molded swag design, white glaze (ILLUS.).. **$70**

Morton Davy Crockett Lamp & Shade

Lamp, table, figural Davy Crockett w/bear beside tree, original shade (ILLUS.)........... **$200**

Dog with Pheasant Lamp Base

Lamp base, model of a black & white dog w/brown pheasant in mouth, relief-molded brown & green grassy base, double opening in planter, 5 x 10", 8 1/4" h. (ILLUS.) **$125**

Morton Pottery Bird Planter

Planter, model of a bird w/bright colors of yellow, blue, orange & red on a green grassy base, 5" h. (ILLUS.)......................... **$24**

Morton Rooster on Rockers Planter

Planter, model of a rooster on rockers, yellow & pink sprayed glaze w/h.p. black & red trim, 4 1/2" h. (ILLUS.) **$30**

Boston Terrier Planter

Planter, model of Boston terrier, sitting, black & white (ILLUS.) **$30**

Kitten & Fish Bowl TV Lamp

TV lamp, figural, black kitten seated on chartreuse stump base reaching for glass fish bowl, 9" h. (ILLUS.) **$75**

Vase, model of a tree trunk, matte green glaze, No. 260... **$30**

Morton Santa Claus Punch Set

Morton Heart-shaped Vase

Vase, 12" h., model of a large & small red heart on an oval base, rare (ILLUS.)............ **$70**

Christmas Novelties

Figural Santa Claus Head Cigarette Box

Cigarette box, cov., figural Santa Claus head, hat cover becomes ashtray, cold painted red hat (ILLUS.)............................. **$50**
Lollipop tree, w/holes to insert lollipops, green bisque, 9 1/4" h. **$60**
Model of a sleigh, Victorian style, white w/h.p. holly & berries, No. 3015 .... **$40**
Model of a sleigh, Victorian-style, red paint, No. 772.. **$45**
Nut dish, oval, stylized Santa face, red background, rare, 2 1/2 x 3" (ILLUS. left, top next column)... **$30**
Nut dish, oval, stylized Santa face, white background, rare, 2 1/2 x 3" (ILLUS. right, top next column)................................. **$30**

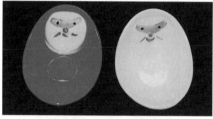

Morton Santa Nut Dishes

Plate, 8", figural Santa Claus face, h.p. white w/blue eyes, pink cheeks, hat cold painted red.. **$50**
Plate, 12", figural Santa Claus face, white w/blue eyes, pink cheeks, hat cold painted red.. **$95**
Punch set: punch bowl & 8 punch cups; figural Santa Claus head, white w/pink trim, green stone eyes, 9 pcs. (ILLUS. of part, top of page)... **$295**

Midwest Potteries, Inc. (1940-1944)

Midwest Leaping Deer Book Ends

Book ends, Art Deco style, a stylized leaping deer against an upright disc, round foot, blue glaze, 7 3/4" h., pr. (ILLUS.)......... **$40**
Figure of baseball player, batter, grey uniform, 7 1/4" h. **$300**
Figure of baseball player, catcher, white uniform, 6 3/4" h....................................... **$300**

Figure of baseball player, umpire, black uniform, 6 1/4" h. **$300**

Model of deer w/antlers, white w/gold trim, 12" h. **$50**

Model of swan, large stylized bird w/tall upright curved & flared wings, long neck turned to back, dark brown & yellow drip glaze, 8" h. (ILLUS.)..................................... **$30**

Midwest Potteries Ducks

Model of ducks, three attached in graduated sizes, white w/yellow trim, 6" l. (ILLUS.) **$36**

Model of flamingo, brownish green spray glaze, 10 1/2" h. **$50**

Midwest Potteries Golden Pheasants

Models of golden pheasants, white w/gold trim, male 4 3/4" h., female 4 1/2" h., pr. (ILLUS.)... **$45**

Midwest Potteries Hen & Rooster

Models of hen & rooster, white w/cold painted red & yellow trim, hen 7" h., rooster 8" h., pr. (ILLUS.)............................ **$50**

Midwest Potteries Flying Fish

Model of flying fish, stylized form in leaping pose, white glaze, 9 1/4" h. (ILLUS.)...... **$45**

Pitcher, 4 1/2" h., figural, seated cow, brown & white drip glaze............................ **$30**

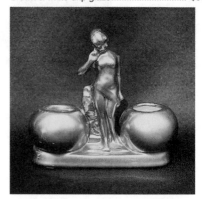

Midwest Potteries Deco-style Planter

Planter, figural, Art Deco style, standing draped nude woman flanked by globeshaped planters, platinum glaze, 5 3/4" l., 5 1/2" h. (ILLUS.) **$55**

Midwest Potteries Swan Model

Calico Cat & Gingham Dog Planters

Planter, figural, Calico Cat, yellow & blue spatter on white, 7 1/2" h. (ILLUS. right, above) **$30**
Planter, figural, Gingham Dog, blue & yellow spatter on white, 7 1/2" h. (ILLUS. left with Calico Cat, above) **$30**

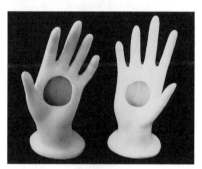

Midwest Potteries Hand Vases

American Art Potteries (1947-1963)

Midwest Potteries Owl TV Lamp

TV lamp, model of an owl w/spread wings, sprayed brown on white ground, green eyes, 12" h. (ILLUS.).................................... **$95**
Vase, 4 1/2" h., bud-type, model of an open hand, white matte glaze (ILLUS. right, top next column).. **$25**
Vase, 4 1/2" h., bud-type, model of open hand, turquoise matte glaze (ILLUS. left, top next column).. **$25**

American Art Candlestick

Candlestick, three-light, open doughnut-shaped ring fitted w/three sockets, wide round foot, dark bluish green glaze, No. 140J, 7 1/2" w., 6 1/2" h. (ILLUS.)............... **$35**

Double Cornucopia Table Lamp

Lamp, table, double cornucopia form, white w/gold trim, 13" h. (ILLUS.) **$50**

Lamp, table, figural, stylized crouching panther on a tall tree trunk, rose & black spray glaze, 11 1/2" h. (ILLUS.) **$60**

American Art Bird on Stump Model

Model of bird on stump, white w/gold trim, 7" h. (ILLUS.) **$25**

Model of cockatoo on stump, natural colors, No. 315, 7" h. **$30**

French Poodle Table Lamp

Lamp, table, figural, model of a seated French poodle, black ground w/sprayed pink on bands of curls, 15" h. (ILLUS.) **$70**

Rearing Horse by American Art

Model of horse, rearing position, brown & green spray glaze (ILLUS.) **$25**

Model of pig, black w/white band, No. 89, 5 1/2" h. **$45**

Crouching Panther Table Lamp

Chunky Pony Figural Planter

Planter, figural, model of a chunky standing pony, dark streaky mauve & pink spray glaze, sticker on side, No. 49, 5 1/4" l., 4 3/4" h. (ILLUS.) **$15**

Bird on Stump Planter

Planter, figural, model of a long-tailed bird perched on a stump, green & brown spray glaze, 7" h. (ILLUS.) **$20**

Recumbent Deer Figural Planter

Planter, figural, model of a recumbent deer w/head turned over shoulder, green & brown spray glaze, 5" h. (ILLUS.) **$20**

Doe and Fawn Figural Planter

Planter, figural, model of a standing doe bending her head down to her reclining fawn, mottled brown glaze, No. 322J, 7 1/4" h. (ILLUS.) **$25**
Planter, figural, model of a swordfish, blue & mauve spray glaze, No. 307P, 7 1/2 x 11" **$25**
TV lamp, figural, model of a standing doe bending her head down to her reclining fawn, mottled brown glaze, No. 322J, 7 1/4" h. **$50**
Vase, 8" h., ewer-form, blue & mauve glaze w/gold trim, No. 209G **$35**

Vase, 10 1/2" h., double cornucopia form, white w/gold trim, No. 208B **$30**
Vase, 12" h., octagonal, pink & mauve spray glaze, No. 214G **$25**
Wall pocket, figural, model of a dustpan, white w/h.p. underglaze decoration, No. 81C **$24**
Wall pocket, figural, model of a red apple on a green leaf, No. 127N **$20**
Wall pocket, figural, model of a teapot, white w/h.p. underglaze decoration, No. 79C **$24**
Window sill box, arched diamond design, green & pink spray glaze, No. 32I, 3 1/2 x 4 x 10" **$30**
Window sill box, white w/h.p. ivy, No. 25D, 2 1/2 x 4 x 13" **$30**

Newcomb College

This pottery was established in the art department of Newcomb College, New Orleans, Louisiana, in 1897. Each piece was hand-thrown and bore the potter's mark & decorator's monogram on the base. It was always a studio business and never operated as a factory. Its pieces are, therefore, scarce, with the early wares being eagerly sought. The pottery closed in 1940.

Newcomb College Pottery Mark

Small Squatty Newcomb College Bowl

Bowl, 2 1/2" h., wide squatty flat-bottomed form tapering to a wide flat rim, dark blue ground molded w/a band of light blue spaced blossoms around the shoulder, decorated by Sadie Irvine, potted by Joseph Meyer, 1926 (ILLUS.) **$1,610**

Newcomb Bowl with Pink Blossoms

Bowl, 5 1/4" d., 2 7/8" h., footed wide low compressed lower body below a wide steeply tapering shoulder to the wide flat mouth, the shoulder decorated w/clusters of pale pink blossoms below leafy green stems against a dark blue ground, the lower body in medium blue, decorated by Henrietta Bailey, potted by Joseph Meyer, dated 1920 (ILLUS.)......................... **$1,840**

Bulbous Newcomb Jar with Trees

Jar, cov., wide bulbous ovoid body tapering to a flat mouth flanked by large thick loop shoulder handles in dark blue, flattened inside cover w/a dark blue knob finial, decorated around the sides w/groups of tall slender trees in dark blue w/a leafy canopy at the top, impressed logo, date code for 1910, unobtrusive overall crazing, tiny nick on lower edge of cover, 4 7/8" h. (ILLUS.) **$3,680**

Scarce Newcomb Jar with Live Oaks

Jar, cov., wide bulbous ovoid body tapering to a flat rim w/a low domed cover w/disk finial, carved decoration of live oaks & Spanish moss in dark blue & pale green on a denim blue ground, matte glaze, decorated by A.F. Simpson, 1929, original paper label, 4 1/2" d., 5" h. (ILLUS.).. **$8,625**

Rare Set of Newcomb College Mugs with Blossoms

Mugs, tankard-type, tapering cylindrical form w/thick angled handle in dark blue, painted w/large stylized saracena blossoms & undulating leaves in brushed light blue over white against a dark blue ground, incised base rings, decorated by Marie de Hoa LeBlanc, potted by Joseph Meyer, glossy glaze, 1901, 5 1/4" h., set of 4 (ILLUS.).. **$9,488**

Newcomb Tankard Pitcher with Flowers

Pitcher, 7 1/2" h., 5 1/2" d., tankard-type, tapering cylindrical body w/a rim spout & long angled dark blue handle, decorated w/large open medium blue tulip blossoms on tall green leafy stems, dark blue top band, panels of tiny dark blue horizontal striping between each set of leaves, glossy glaze, painted by Elizabeth Rogers, potted by Joseph Meyer, ca. 1900 (ILLUS.)... **$5,750**

Teapot, cov., "Solitaire," wide squatty bulbous body w/a short angled spout, low slightly tapering cover w/knob finial, C-form handle, rare early high-glaze shaded green, potted by Joseph Fortune Meyer, decorated by Irene Borden Keep, fully signed & numbered, 1901, 4" h. (ILLUS., next page)...................... **$2,300**

Rare High-glaze Newcomb College Teapot

Dark Blue & Pink Spanish Moss Vase

Vase, miniature, 3 7/8" h., flat-bottomed wide ovoid body w/a wide short cylindrical neck, a very dark blue & green Spanish moss in oak trees design against a pink ground, decorated by Sadie Irvine, potted by Jonathan Hunt, dated 1929 (ILLUS.) **$2,300**

Newcomb Tyg with Motto Band

Tyg (three-handled mug), motto-type, wide tapering cylindrical body flanked by three long C-form handles, each panel modeled w/grape clusters & vines in shaded blue, a continuous band around the base w/phrase "Till Love and Life Are One - Live and Love," glossy glaze, decorated by Sadie Irvine, potted by Joseph Meyer, dated 1909, 6" d., 4 3/4" h. (ILLUS.) **$5,865**

Small Moss, Oaks & Moon Newcomb Vase

Vase, 4" h., wide flat-bottomed bulbous ovoid form tapering to a wide low molded rim, dark blue Spanish moss in oaks decoration against a pale blue sky w/a pale yellow full moon, decorated by Sadie Irvine, potted by Kenneth Smith, dated 1933 (ILLUS.) **$2,875**

Miniature Glossy Newcomb College Vase

Vase, miniature, 3 1/4" h., glossy glaze, bulbous nearly spherical body w/the creamy yellow sides incised w/vertical stripes, the shoulder incised w/overlapping cobalt blue scales outlined in pale green, a short wide cobalt blue rim, decorated by Sadie Irvine, potted by Kenneth Smith, dated 1933 (ILLUS.) **$2,070**

Small Squatty Floral Band Newcomb Vase

Vase, 4 3/4" h., footed wide squatty bulbous body tapering to a short tapering cylindrical neck, incised around the wide shoulder w/a continuous band of large white blossoms & green leaves against the mottled dark blue matte ground, decorated by Anna Frances Simpson, dated 1916 (ILLUS., previous page) **$2,645**

Newcomb Vase with Berries & Leaves

Vase, 8" h., slightly swelled cylindrical form w/a rounded shoulder tapering to a short cylindrical neck, molded w/pale blue leaves & berry clusters drooping down from the rim against a shaded dark blue matte ground, potter Joseph Meyer, Shape No. 250, 1923 (ILLUS.).............. **$3,220**

Squatty Bulbous Floral Newcomb Vase

Vase, 5 1/4" h., footed wide squatty bulbous form tapering to a wide flat mouth, deeply carved around the shoulder w/a wide band of large stylized white blossoms & green leaves above a dark blue matte ground, potter Joseph Meyer, ca. 1925, professionally repaired rim chip (ILLUS.)............ **$1,150**

Very Rare Tulip-decorated Newcomb Vase

Vase, 8 1/4" h., baluster-form body w/a wide low mouth, modeled w/large dark blue tulip blossoms on tall dark green leafy stems around the sides against a white ground, glossy glaze, painted by Harriet Joor, ca. 1900 (ILLUS.)........................ **$21,850**

Extremely Rare Early Newcomb Vase

Vase, 5 1/2" h., 7 1/4" d., a wide low squatty bulbous body w/a wide shoulder tapering to a tiny cylindrical neck, finely painted w/a repeating design of large blue irises & stylized scrolling foliage, highlighted w/dark mustard yellow including a band of small irises around the small neck, glossy glaze, painted by Elizabeth Goelet Rogers, potted by Joseph Meyer, dated 1898 (ILLUS.)...................................... **$19,550**

Niloak Pottery

This pottery was made in Benton, Arkansas, and featured hand-thrown varicolored swirled clay decoration in objects of classic forms. Designated Mission Ware, this line is the most desirable of Niloak's production, which began early in this century. Less expensive to produce, the cast

Hywood Line, finished with either high gloss or semi-matte glazes, was introduced during the Depression of the 1930s. The pottery ceased operation about 1946.

ΝΙᴄΟΑᏥ

Niloak Pottery Mark

Bowl, 5" d., Mission Ware, squatty rounded base tapering slightly to the wide, flat rim, swirled red, brown, cream & blue clays, marked **$175-200**
Bowl, 6 3/4" d., 3" h., Mission Ware, wide, deep rounded form w/a flat mouth, swirled dark blue, light blue, dark brown, cream & reddish brown clays, impressed mark, paper label **$175-200**
Box, cov., Mission Ware, squatty bulbous body & high squatty mushroom-shaped cover, swirled dark brown, reddish brown, tan & blue clays, impressed mark, 4" h. **$1,035**

Niloak Mission Ware Jardiniere

Jardiniere, Mission Ware, wide slightly swelled cylindrical form, swirled brown, blue & tan clays, stamped mark, 7" d., 7" h. (ILLUS.) **$411**
Jug, spherical body w/flat bottom, a pointed loop handle on the shoulder opposite a short, round spout, overall mottled golden tan & green matte glaze, ink mark, 6" h. **$225-250**
Lamp base, Mission Ware, tapered ovoid form w/flared round base, swirled marbleized clays in red, blue, cream & taupe, two-socket fixture, early 20th c., 10 1/4" h. **$375-400**
Puff box, cov., Mission Ware, footed wide, squatty, bulbous body w/a low rim & flat inset cover w/pointed finial, swirled dark brown, tan & dark blue clays, 4" h. **$575**
Vase, 3 1/2" h., miniature, Mission Ware, ovoid form tapering gently to a wide flat mouth, swirled light & dark blue, tan & light brown clays, minute flakes **$242**
Vase, 3 1/2" h., miniature, Mission Ware, wide ovoid form tapering to a heavy molded rim, swirled dark & light brown, dark blue, cream & reddish brown clays, impressed mark **$150**

Vase, 5" h., 6" d., Mission Ware, flat-bottomed wide bulbous form curving to a wide flat rim, swirled dark & light brown, cream, reddish brown & blue clays, impressed mark **$265**
Vase, 6" h., Mission Ware, simple baluster form w/a wide closed rim, swirled red, cream & grey clays, impressed mark **$200-250**
Vase, 6" h., Mission Ware, wide cylindrical form rounded at the base & top rim, bold swirled bands of dark blue, reddish brown & dark & light brown clays, impressed mark **$403**
Vase, 7 1/4" h., Mission Ware, simple cylindrical form, fine swirls of dark blue, cream & dark brown clays, early impressed mark w/patent pending wording **$633**
Vase, 8 1/4" h., Mission Ware, tall ovoid form tapering gently to flat rim, unusual decoration of overall incised squiggles in a tan matte glaze over a dark brown base, paper label **$1,150**
Vase, 8 3/4" h., Mission Ware, large bulbous ovoid body tapering to a short slightly rolled neck, swirled dark & light brown clays, rare ink stamp mark **$1,093**
Vase, 10" h., Mission Ware, tall simple cylindrical form, bold swirls of medium blue, dark & light brown, cream & reddish brown clays, impressed mark **$288**

Tall Niloak Mission Ware Vase

Vase, 10" h., 5" d., footed w/bulbous lower body w/sharp shoulder tapering to a tall cylindrical neck, swirled dark teal & brown clays, minute inside rim flecks, stamped mark (ILLUS.) **$294**
Vase, 11" h., Mission Ware, tall baluste form w/widely flaring flattened neck, bold squiggly swirls of blue, cream, reddish brown, dark & light brown clays, impressed mark **$500**
Vase, 12 1/4" h., footed bulbous body tapering to a tall flaring trumpet neck, overall dark matte blue glaze, impressed mark **$748**

Nippon

"Nippon" is a term used to describe a wide range of porcelain wares produced in Japan from the late 19th century until about 1921. It was in 1891 that the United States implemented the McKinley Tariff Act, which required that all wares exported to the United States carry a marking indicating their country of origin. The Japanese chose to use "Nippon," their name for Japan. In 1921 the import laws were revised and the words "Made in" had to be added to the markings. Japan was also required to replace the "Nippon" with the English name "Japan" on all wares sent to the United States.

Many Japanese factories produced Nippon porcelain, much of it hand-painted with ornate floral or landscape decoration and heavy gold decoration, applied beading and slip-trailed designs referred to as "moriage." We indicate the specific marking used on a piece, when known, at the end of each listing. Be aware that a number of Nippon markings have been reproduced and used on new porcelain wares.

Important reference books on Nippon include: The Collector's Encyclopedia of Nippon Porcelain, Series One through Five, *by Joan F. Van Patten (Collector Books, Paducah, Kentucky) and* The Wonderful World of Nippon Porcelain, 1891-1921 *by Kathy Wojciechowski (Schiffer Publishing, Ltd., Atglen, Pennsylvania).*

Bowl, squatty round body on short feet, slightly lobed flat rim, ornate C-scroll side handles, h.p. floral design in pale pinks & greens, w/moriage scrolling decoration on handles, feet, around base & at inter-vals on body, blue maple leaf mark, 7 1/2" d. (ILLUS. front row, far right w/other h.p. Nippon pieces, bottom of page)... **$115**

Bowl, 8 1/2" d., three-handled, decorated w/a scene of a sailing ship w/palm trees & ruins on the shore, green "M" in wreath mark.. **$144**

Bowl, 10" d., low sides, three-footed, decorated w/large open roses, blue maple leaf mark... **$56**

Box, cov., squatty round form on footring, decorated around sides & rim of lid w/h.p. floral design in blue & pink, w/transfer portrait in center of lid, 4 1/2" d. (ILLUS. front row, second from right w/other Nippon pieces, top next page)....................... **$104**

Nippon Scenic Chamberstick

Chamberstick, saucer-form base decorated w/scene of house by lake w/trees & mountains, natural colors, green "M" in wreath mark, 4 1/4" d., 2" h. (ILLUS.) **$100-125**

Hand Painted Nippon Pieces

Various Nippon Ceramic Pieces

Chocolate set: cov. pot & six cups & saucers; an Art Deco-style mold copied from R.S. Prussia wares, painted w/open roses, green "I&E" wreath mark, pot 8" h., the set **$280**

Condensed milk container, cylindrical, decorated w/gilt scrolls & florals, green "M" in wreath mark, 5 1/2" h.......................... **$67**

Dresser tray & tumbler, h.p. Egyptian scene w/enameled rim, 2 pcs. **$112**

Rose-decorated Nippon Chocolate Set

Chocolate set: cov. tall ovoid pot & 12 cups & saucers; each piece h.p. w/large yellow, red & lavender roses & green leaves on a shaded brown to cream ground, marked, pot 7 3/4" h., the set (ILLUS.)....... **$173**

Rare Noritake Molded Owl Humidor

Humidor, cov., cylindrical body w/a flared rim, wide domed cover w/large knob finial, decorated w/a large relief-molded owl in brown, black & white perched on a leafy oak tree branch, on shaded yellow to orange & brown ground, tiny flakes inside rim & cover, green "M" in Wreath mark, 7" h. (ILLUS.) **$748**

Swan & Lake Scene Nippon Chocolate Set

Chocolate set: tall tankard cov. pot w/ornate loop handle & five tall cups & saucers; each piece h.p. w/a lakeside scene of swimming swans w/trees in the foreground, Nippon mark, pot 8" h., the set (ILLUS.)..................................... **$173**

A Large Grouping of Fine Varied Nippon Pieces

Hand Painted Nippon Humidor

Humidor, cov., cylindrical form, moriage decorated w/h.p. scene of white owl on branch, distant mountains in background, in browns & buffs, blue maple leaf mark, 6" h. (ILLUS.) **$3,565**

Humidor, cov., hexagonal barrel-shaped body & conforming domed cover w/a large squared knob finial, the sides h.p. w/a continuous rural landscape w/large trees in the foreground, a paneled geometric rim band, the cover w/a similar landscape, green "M" in Wreath Nippon mark, 6 1/2" h. (ILLUS., top next column) **$230**

Nippon Humidor with Landscape Scene

Humidor, cov., squared form, decorated w/four scenic panels of sailboats, green "M" in wreath mark, 4 1/2" h **$308**

Muffineer, a tapering paneled body w/molded & slightly swirled ribbing to a rounded shoulder & flat top pierced w/small holes, a C-form handle, the white ground decorated around the base w/a gold band & fine gold scrolls against thin blue panels, the upper half h.p. w/large gilt scrolls w/tiny pink blossoms & blue panels, blue "Maple Leaf" mark, 4 3/4" h. (ILLUS. bottom row, far right, with other Nippon pieces, top of page) **$69**

Mug, h.p. landscape scene w/embossed rim & handle w/raised enameling, green "M" in wreath mark, 5 1/2" h. **$112**

Nappy, souvenir, trefoil shape w/ornate gilt scroll decoration & h.p. pink roses framing scene of U.S. Capitol in center, gilt scroll ring handle at side, green maple leaf mark, rare, 6 1/2" w. (ILLUS. front row, center w/other Nippon pieces, page 451) **$115**

Nut tray, molded in relief w/beechnuts painted in natural colors, green "M" in wreath mark, 8" l. **$78**

Pitcher, tankard, 13" h., tapering cylindrical form, slightly scalloped rim w/high arched spout, C-scroll handle, decorated w/h.p. pink roses, pale green leaves & gilt ferns on gilt-decorated cobalt ground (ILLUS. front row, far left w/other h.p. Nippon pieces, page 450) **$460**

Pitcher, tankard, 13 1/2" h., cylindrical shape on short squatty bulbous base, flaring to scalloped rim w/arched spout, D-form handle, decorated w/h.p. pink floral design in oval gilt medallion, w/gilt scrolling & bead decoration overall on body of pale aqua, cream, cobalt & deep reddish brown (ILLUS. back row, far right w/other h.p. Nippon pieces, page 450) **$374**

Powder box, cov., three small peg feet supporting the wide squatty bulbous body & fitted domed cover, white ground decorated around the base w/very ornate delicate gilt floral scrolls, matching gold decor on the cover centered by red roses, green "Maple Leaf" mark, 6" d. (ILLUS. bottom row, second from right with various other Nippon pieces, previous page) **$138**

Tankard, cylindrical, finely painted gold-decorated rim & base, applied scroll handle, blue maple leaf mark, 13" h. (minor gold loss) **$345**

Floral-decorated Nippon Tea Set

Tea set: cov. teapot, cov. sugar bowl, creamer & six cups & saucers; bulbous bodies on the serving pieces, each h.p. w/stylized pink & yellow floral border bands w/green leaves & gilt trim, unmarked, early 20th c., the set (ILLUS.) **$150**

Nippon Teapot with Birds in a Tree

Teapot, cov., bulbous ovoid body w/a serpentine spout, C-scroll handle & low domed cover w/gold loop finial, decorated w/colorful birds in a blossoming tree, "M" in Wreath mark, ca. 1911 (ILLUS.) **$40**

Noritake-Nippon Porcelain Teapot

Teapot, cov., footed wide squatty bulbous body w/a high domed cover w/button finial, short spout & C-form handle, decorated around the top & cover w/ornate gold scrolls & delicate roses, early Noritake-Nippon mark, ca. 1910-20 (ILLUS.) **$50**

Vase, 7" h., a tapering cylindrical lower body flaring into a large bulbous upper body centered by a short gold-decorated neck w/pointed sides & integral high arched gold handles down to the shoulder, the pastel lavender to cream ground ornately decorated overall w/large Coralene clusters of pink & deep rose blossoms & green leaves outlined in gold, 1909 patent mark (ILLUS. bottom row, second from left with various Nippon pieces, top of page 452) **$460**

Brown Nippon Vase with Castle Scene

Vase, 8" h., footed wide cylindrical body w/a wide shoulder tapering to a short neck w/rolled rim, pointed scroll shoulder handles, dark brown ground decorated on the front w/a stylized landscape showing a castle above a forest of trees in shades of brown, green, pale yellow & blue, a brown & white slip Greek key band near the base & around the base of the decorated neck, blue "Maple Leaf" mark (ILLUS.) **$127**

Vase, 8 1/4" h., slightly waisted cylindrical form, w/h.p. scene of ships at sail in still waters against pastel ground & sky, decorated w/bands of scrolled moriage lace, enameled jewels & iridescent abalone applications, blue "M" in wreath mark **$431**

Vase, 8 1/2" h., slightly waisted cylindrical form, the body decorated w/h.p. pastoral scene & gilt floral designs, the shoulder w/horizontal panel h.p. w/pink & yellow enameled blossoms against deeper rose ground & gilt borders (ILLUS. back row, right w/other Nippon pieces, top of page 451) **$230**

Vase, 9" h., Art Deco form w/"coraline" decoration of lotus leaves & flowers, marked in magenta "KinRan - U.S. Patent Feb. 9, 1909" (minor loss to beading) **$661**

Vase, 9 1/4" h., slightly ovoid form on footring, tapering shoulder w/cylindrical neck w/slightly flaring rim, the body decorated w/h.p. scene of lone traveler in pastoral setting, the shoulder & rim decorated w/stylized floral & geometric designs, two raised enamel handles (ILLUS. front row, second from left w/other Nippon pieces, top of page 451) **$86**

Vase, 9 1/2" h., tall six-sided form w/bamboo-style handles, the body w/panels of h.p. pastoral scenes against cobalt ground decorated w/ornate gilt scroll designs overall, indistinguishable mark (ILLUS. front row, second from right w/other h.p. Nippon pieces, top of page 450) **$345**

Nippon Vase with Bands of Large Roses

Vase, 10" h., a tall ovoid body tapering to a small trumpet neck flanked by arched gold shoulder handles, the shaded grey to white ground h.p. around the base & shoulder w/large clusters of yellow & pink roses & pale green leaves w/gold highlights, blue "Maple Leaf" mark (ILLUS.) **$316**

Vase, 10" h., baluster form, disk foot, cylindrical neck w/short flaring rim, decorated w/h.p. scene of palm trees on island w/ships at sea and mountains in the distance, the neck decorated w/band of scrolling floral enamel designs, green "M" in wreath mark (ILLUS. front row, far right w/other Nippon pieces, top of page 451) ... **$173**

Vase, 10 1/4" h., tapering cylindrical form on footring, w/ruffled flaring rim, the body decorated w/raised brickwork design in deep greens, rectangular panels around sides decorated w/h.p. scenes in pastel colors, narrow panels of moriage extending from top of body to rim at intervals (ILLUS. front row, far left w/other Nippon pieces, top of page 451) **$201**

Blue & Gold Nippon Vase with Roses

Vase, 9 3/4" h., raised disk foot below the wide gently tapering cylindrical body topped by a deep rounded cupped neck flanked by angled gold handles, a medium blue ground decorated on the body w/a pair of gold leafy bands also enclosing a large oval reserve, the reserve & space between the bands h.p. w/a continuous lakeside landscape featuring large red roses in the foreground, a white band just below the neck trimmed w/gilt florals & further gilt florals on the blue neck, green "M" in Wreath mark (ILLUS.) **$230**

Vase with Ornate Gilt Decoration

Vase, 10 1/4" h., 5" d., baluster-form body raised on a scalloped flaring foot & tapering to a flaring pointed lobed rim, long slender S-scroll handles up the sides, decorated overall w/heavy gold stylized leaves & berries on vines, blue maple leaf mark (ILLUS., previous page) **$175**

Nippon Vase with Delicate Gold & Florals

Vase, 10 3/4" h., a low four-lobed gold foot below the tall cylindrical body w/a swelled shoulder ring & low rounded shoulder centering a short ringed neck, four upright scroll handles around the top of the shoulder, the sides w/a white ground decorated w/delicate gold pendants, jewels & swags surrounding a large shield-shaped reserve bordered in gold & salmon pink & enclosing a cluster of salmon pink peony blossoms & green leaves, green "M" in Wreath mark (ILLUS.) **$196**

Vase, 12" h., ovoid form w/short neck & flaring ruffled rim, slightly scalloped base, open scroll handles holding ring bases, w/h.p. decoration of pink & rose flowers & green leaves against pastel ground decorated w/raised enameled gilt scroll designs, blue maple leaf mark (ILLUS. back row, center w/other h.p. Nippon pieces, top of page 450) **$2,530**

Vase, 13" h., 7" d., finely painted landscape w/heavy etched gold decoration of flowers & striped band, probably studio decorated, green "M" in wreath mark **$489**

Vase, 16" h., cylindrical form w/ring neck, overall decoration of h.p. flowers in shades of pink, green leaves & gilt raised leafy scrolls on dark green ground (ILLUS. back row, far left w/other h.p. Nippon pieces, top of page 450) **$460**

Wall plaque, h.p. scene of palm trees & sailboats, pierced for hanging **$101**

Wall plaque, oval, decorated w/scene of sailboat docked at waterside cottage h.p. in pastel shades, the rim w/border of styl-

ized floral & leaf design, 10" l. (ILLUS. front row, center w/other h.p. Nippon pieces, top of page 450) **$316**

Wall plaque, round, decorated w/relief molded scene of a squirrel w/nut set against background of trees & water in pastel shades of green, yellow & blue, 10 3/4" d. (ILLUS. back row, left w/other Nippon pieces, top of page 451) **$719**

Wall plaque, round, pierced to hang, h.p. w/an expansive landscape w/groves of trees in meadows sloping down to a river, mountains in the distance, in shades of dark & light green, purple, lavender, pink & white, blue "M" in Wreath mark, 10" d. (ILLUS. front row, far left with various other Nippon pieces, top of page 452)..... **$100-200**

Wall plaque, pierced to hang, round, molded in relief w/a lion & lioness in a rocky landscape, natural coloration, green "M" in wreath mark, 10 1/2" d. (ILLUS. back row, far right with various other Nippon pieces, top of page 452) **$475-575**

Wall plaque, pierced to hang, round, a relief-molded bellowing bull elk in the foreground w/a painted lakeside landscape in the background, green "M" in Wreath mark, 11" d. (ILLUS. back row, second from right with various Nippon pieces, top of page 452)..................................... **$400-600**

Hand Painted Nippon Wine Jug

Wine jug, cov., bulbous base tapering to short neck & flared rim, decorated w/h.p. scene of owl on branch against blue sky w/white clouds, this decoration extending to lid, applied moriage decorated C-form handle, in asymmetrical woven split bamboo basket frame, green "M" in wreath mark, 8" h. (ILLUS.) **$1,150**

Wine jugs w/original bulbous stoppers, a bulbous ovoid body tapering to a short flared neck & arched brown handle, fitted w/a bulbous stopper, each h.p. around the base & shoulder w/a black band highlighted by black & white shields flanked by pairs of small seated green lions, a similar band around each stopper, the wide body band decorated w/a continuous panoramic landscape scene w/a flowering tree in the foreground and a pathway w/cottage & clumps of trees behind, a lake & mountains in the background, all in shades of green, pale blue, white & black, blue "Maple Leaf" mark, 9 1/2" h., matched pair, each (ILLUS. top row, far left with various other Nippon pieces, top of page 452)....................... **$1,610**

Noritake

Noritake china, still in production in Japan, has been exported in large quantities to this country since early in the last century. Although the Noritake Company first registered in 1904, it did not use "Noritake" as part of its backstamp until 1918. Interest in Noritake has escalated as collectors now seek out pieces made between the "Nippon" era and World War II (1921-41). The Azalea pattern is also popular with collectors.

Noritake Mark

Ashtray, center Queen of Clubs decoration, 4" w. **$38**
Ashtray, figural polar bear, blue ground, 4 1/4" d., 2 1/2" h....................................... **$250**
Ashtray, center Indian head decoration, 5 1/2" w. **$275**
Ashtray, figural nude woman seated at edge of lustered flower form tray, 7" w.... **$1,050**

Noritake Basket with Flowers

Basket, oblong w/center handle, gold lustre ground, interior w/center stylized floral decoration & geometric design in each corner & around rim, 7 3/4" l., 3" h. (ILLUS.) **$85**
Basket, Roseara patt. **$60**
Basket-bowl, footed, petal-shaped rim, 6 1/2" w. **$110**
Basket-vase, 7 1/2" h. **$115**
Berry set: master bowl & 6 sauce dishes; decal & h.p. purple orchids, green leaves & pods decoration on green ground, 7 pcs... **$70**

Bonbon, raised gold decoration, 6 1/4" w........ **$25**
Bonbon dish, Azalea patt............................... **$40**

Noritake Scenic Bowl

Bowl, 6" sq., flanged rim w/pierced handles, orange lustre ground decorated w/h.p. scene w/large tree in foreground (ILLUS.) **$85**

Art Deco Bowl

Bowl, 6 1/2" d., 2" h., fluted sides of alternating light & dark grey panels w/pointed rims, center w/Art Deco floral decoration (ILLUS.)... **$160**
Bowl, 7" w., square w/incurved sides, three-footed, interior w/relief-molded filbert nuts in brown trimmed w/h.p. autumn leaves.. **$85**

Art Deco Checkerboard & Roses Bowl

Bowl, 8 3/4" d., 2" h., Art Deco-style orange
& white checkerboard ground decorated
w/stylized dark brown roses & leaves outlined in grey & grey stems (ILLUS., previ-
ous page) $270
Bowl, 9" d., footed, scenic interior decora-
tion, lustre finish exterior $45
Bowl, shell-shaped, three-footed, Tree in
Meadow patt. $160
Bowl, soup, Azalea patt. $30
Butter dish, cover & drain insert, Azalea
patt., 3 pcs. $80
Cake plate, Sheridan patt., 9 3/4" d. $20

Noritake Oriental Scene Cake Plate

Cake plate, rectangular, open-handled, turquoise border w/oval center Oriental
scene on black ground, 10" l. (ILLUS.) $140
Cake plate, open-handled, Tree in Meadow
patt. $35
Cake set: 10" d. handled master cake plate
& 6 serving plates; fruit bowl medallions
centers, blue lustre rims, 7 pcs. $80
Cake set: 14 x 6 1/4" oblong tray w/pierced
handles & six 6 1/2" d. serving plates;
white w/pale green & gold floral border, 7
pcs. $90
Candlesticks, Indian motif decoration,
3 1/4" h., pr. $160
Candy dish, octagonal, Tree in Meadow
patt. $60
Candy dish, cov., figural bird finial, scal-
loped rim, blue lustre finish, 6 1/2 x 7 1/4" $90
Celery set: celery tray & 6 individual salt
dips, decal & h.p. florals & butterflies dec-
oration, 7 pcs. $90
Celery tray, Azalea patt. $50

Figural Swan Cigarette Holder

Cigarette holder, footed, figural swan, orange lustre w/black neck & head, black
outlining on wing feathers & tail, 3" w.,
4 1/2" h. (ILLUS.) $310
Cigarette holder, bell-shaped w/bird finial,
5" h. $375

Cigarette Holder with Golfing Scene

Cigarette holder/playing card holder,
pedestal foot, gold lustre ground decorated w/scene of golfer, 4" h. (ILLUS.) $300

Cigarette Jar in Art Deco Style

Cigarette jar, cov., bell-shaped cover w/bird
finial, Art Deco-style silhouetted scenic
decoration of woman in chair & man
standing, both holding cigarettes,
4 3/4" h., 3 1/2" d. (ILLUS.) $575
Coffee set: cov. coffeepot, creamer, cov.
sugar bowl & four cups & saucers; greyish blue butterfly, pink florals & grey
leaves decoration, 11 pcs. $255
Cologne bottle w/flower cluster stopper,
Art Deco man wearing checkered cape,
lustered sides, 6 3/4" h. $470

Cologne bottle w/stopper, two-handled, Art Deco woman decoration...................... **$780**

Noritake Condiment Set

Condiment set: cov. mustard jar & pr. salt & pepper shakers on handled tray; blue lustre w/tops decorated w/flowers, 7" w. tray, the set (ILLUS.)................................ **$120**

Noritake Figural Condiment Set

Condiment set: cov. mustard jar & pr. salt & pepper shakers on handled tray; bulbous blue lustre mustard jar w/red rosebud finial, green leaves, ovoid shakers w/clown head tops, red, blue, orange & white lustre, blue lustre tray, 7" l., the set (ILLUS.)... **$630**

Condiment set: cov. mustard jar & pr. salt & pepper shakers on handled tray; lustre borders & tops, 5 1/2" w. tray, the set **$75**

Noritake Cracker Jar with Lake Scene

Cracker jar, cov., footed spherical body decorated w/a black band w/white swords & shields design & center oval yellow medallion w/scene of white sailboat on lake, white clouds in distance & blue stylized tree in foreground, black &

white geometric design bands around rim & cover edge, orange lustre ground, 7" h. (ILLUS.)... **$210**

Creamer, Azalea patt. **$25**

Creamer, Tree in Meadow patt. **$20**

Creamer & cov. sugar bowl, Azalea patt., pr.. **$75**

Creamer & cov. sugar bowl, blue scenic decoration, brown borders, pr. **$65**

Creamer & Sugar in Art Deco Style

Creamer & open sugar bowl, Art Deco-style checked decoration in black, blue, brown & white, orange lustre interior basket-shaped sugar bowl w/overhead handle, creamer 3" h., sugar bowl 4 1/2" h., pr. (ILLUS.) **$125**

Scenic Berry Creamer & Sugar Shaker

Creamer & sugar shaker, berry set-type, decorated w/a scene of a gondola, orange lustre ground, 6 1/2" h., pr. (ILLUS.) **$85**

Scenic Creamer & Sugar Shaker Set

Creamer & sugar shaker, berry set-type, orange lustre interior, scenic decoration w/cottage, bridge & trees above floral cluster, blue lustre ground, 6 1/2" h., pr. (ILLUS.).. **$85**

Creamer & sugar shaker, berry set-type, raised gold decoration, 5 3/4" h. creamer & 6 1/4" h. sugar shaker, pr. **$80**

Noritake Floral Cruet Set

Cruet set w/original stoppers, the two conjoined globular bottles set at angles & joined w/a handle at the shoulder, shaded orange lustre ground decorated w/green & yellow clover leaves & stems, 6" l., 3 1/2" h. (ILLUS.) **$130**
Cup & saucer, demitasse, Tree in Meadow patt. **$25**
Cup & saucer, Tree in Meadow patt. **$20**
Desk set: heart-shaped tray w/pen rack at front & two cov. jars w/floral finials; decal & h.p. florals, 6 1/2" w. **$385**
Dinner bell, figural Chinaman, 3 1/2" h. **$250**
Dish, blue lustre trim, 5" sq. **$20**
Dresser box, cov., figural woman on lid, lustre finish, 5" h. **$770**
Figurine, maiden carrying a bundle of sticks on her head **$55**
Fish plates, h.p. & decal w/h.p. center fish decoration, gold borders, 8 1/2" d., pr. **$125**
Flower holder, model of bird on stump, base pierced w/four flower holes, 4 1/2" h. **$95**

Hair Receiver in Art Deco Style

Hair receiver, cov., Art Deco style, geometric design on gold lustre ground, 3 1/2" d. (ILLUS.) **$190**
Humidor, cov., model of an owl w/head as cover, lustre finish, 7" h. **$770**
Humidor, cov., relief-molded & h.p. horse head, 7" h. **$575**
Humidor, cov., four panels of decal & h.p. yellow roses & black leaves on orange ground within h.p. black oval borders, 7 1/2" h. **$350**
Inkwell, model of an owl, Art Deco style, 3 1/2" h. **$260**

Melon-shaped Jam Jar Set

Jam jar, cover & underplate, melon-shaped, pink ground w/grey leaves, handle & leaf-shaped underplate, 5 3/4" l., 4 1/4" h., the set (ILLUS.) **$115**
Lemon plate, Azalea patt. **$35**
Lobster set: sauce bowl, underplate & ladle; molded lotus form, petals w/highlights & lobster decoration on 10 3/4" d. underplate **$210**
Marmalade jar, cover, underplate & ladle, flower bud finial, 5 1/4" h. **$80**
Mayonnaise set, Azalea patt., 3 pcs. **$70**
Night light, figural woman, 9 1/4" h., 2 pc. . **$4,400**
Nut bowl, tri-lobed bowl w/figural squirrel seated at side eating nut, 7 1/2" w. **$125**
Nut bowl, molded nut shell form w/three relief-molded nuts & side h.p. w/walnuts & green ferns decoration **$85**
Nut set: 6" d. bowl shaped like open chestnut & six 2" d. nut dishes; earthtone ground w/h.p. nuts & leaves, the set **$135**
Plate, 6 1/2" d., Azalea patt. **$15**
Plate, 6 1/2" d., Tree in Meadow patt. **$15**
Plate, 7 1/2" d., Azalea patt. **$15**
Plate, dinner, Azalea patt. **$40**
Platter, 10" l., Tree in Meadow patt. **$50**
Platter, 14" l., Tree in Meadow patt. **$55**
Powder box, cov., figural, an Art Deco-style female figure on a chair in colors of orange, black, green, white & brown w/a lustre finish, 1930s, 4 1/4 x 5", 7" h. **$6,800**
Powder box, cov., figural bird finial, 3 1/2" d. **$110**
Powder box, cov., Art Deco decoration, 4" d. **$440**

Noritake Disc-form Powder Puff Box

Powder puff box, cov., disc-form, stylized floral decoration in red, blue, white & black on a white iridized ground w/blue lustre border, 4" d. (ILLUS.) **$160**

Relish dish, Azalea patt., 8" l. $25
Ring holder, model of a hand $40
Salt & pepper shakers, Tree in Meadow
patt., pr. $20
Sauce dish, Azalea patt. $25
Shaving mug, landscape scene w/tree,
birds & moon decoration $70
Smoke set: handled tray, cigar & cigarette
jars & match holder; cigars, cigarettes &
matchsticks decoration, the set $365

Noritake Double Spoon Holder

Spoon holder, double tray-form, oblong
shape w/gold angular center handle, orange lustre interior, exterior decorated
w/flowers & butterfly on black ground,
6 1/2" l., 2 1/2" h. (ILLUS.) $90
Sugar bowl, cov., Azalea patt. $60
Sugar shaker, lavender & gold decoration,
blue lustre trim $40
Syrup jug, Azalea patt. $70
Tea strainer w/footed rest, cov., Azalea
patt. decal & h.p. red roses & gold trim on
green ground, 2 pcs. $120

Crinoline Lady Noritake Teapot

Teapot, cov., Crinoline Lady patt., bulbous
slightly tapering body w/C-form handle &
long serpentine spout, domed cover
w/knob finial, Victorian lady in a garden
against a blue background, Noritake mark
"38.016 DS," 5 1/2" l., 3 3/4" h. (ILLUS.) $175

Figural Noritake Oriental Man Teapot

Teapot, cov., figural, model of a short
stocky Oriental man wearing a blue robe,
one arm extended to the side forming the
spout, the other hand holding the end of
a brown branch that continues to form the
handle, black hair w/topknot forms the
cover, Noritake mark "M1J," 8 1/2" l.,
5 3/4" h. (ILLUS.) $40

Noritake Teapot with Stylized Flowers

Teapot, cov., footed bulbous ovoid body
w/angled green shoulder & domed cover
w/oval loop finial, C-scroll handle & long
serpentine spout, large stylized blossoms
on a slender leafy tree, in shades of blue,
purple, green & brown, Noritake mark
"27.1 DS," 8 1/4" l., 5 3/4" h. (ILLUS.) $45

Noritake Pattern #16034 Teapot

Teapot, cov., Gold & White Pattern No.
16034, squatty bulbous body w/long spout
& pointed angled handle, domed cover
w/pointed handle, band of gold decoration
around upper half, marked "Noritake -
Made in Japan - #16034," ca. 1920s-30s,
8 1/4" l., 4 1/2" h. (ILLUS.) $30-35

Noritake China Howo Pattern Teapot

Teapot, cov., Howo patt., spherical body
w/serpentine spout & hooked loop handle,
domed cover w/knob finial, marked "Nori-

take - Made in Japan," ca. 1930s, 9 1/2" l.,
6 1/2" h. (ILLUS.) **$85-95**

Squatty Noritake Howo Pattern Teapot

Teapot, cov., Howo patt., squatty bulbous body w/serpentine spout & C-form handle, low domed cover w/arched loop handle, marked "Noritake - Howo - Made in Japan," ca. 1930s, 8" l., 4 1/2" h. (ILLUS.) **$55-65**

Noritake Indian Pattern Teapot

Teapot, cov., Indian patt., wide squatty bulbous body w/small rim spout, inset red cover w/cylindrical finial, bent bamboo swing bail handle, the white sides decorated w/Native American-style stick-like figures, Noritake mark "50.3DS," 6" l., 3 1/2" h. (ILLUS.) **$95**

Lovely Noritake Iris Pattern Teapot

Teapot, cov., Iris patt., Art Deco style, tall gently flaring body w/angled handle, tall angled spout, angled shoulder & peaked cover w/open diamond-shaped finial, blue iris & green leaves design, Noritake mark "54DS," 7 1/4" h. (ILLUS.) **$130**

Rare Noritake Lady & Bird Teapot

Teapot, cov., Lady & Bird in Garden patt., tall footed urn-form body w/long serpentine spout, tall arched black-trimmed blue handle, domed cover in red w/black urn-shaped finial, dark blue background w/an Art Deco-style scene of a crinolined lady holding a bird in one hand w/a birdcage in front of her, in shades of yellow, green, black, white, light blue & orange, Noritake mark "27.1 DS," 6 3/4" l., 6 1/4" h. (ILLUS.) .. **$645**

Deep Red Oriental Scene Teapot

Teapot, cov., tall footed urn-form body w/long serpentine spout, tall arched gold handle, domed cover w/gold urn-shaped finial, dark red background w/an Oriental scene decoration w/a figure standing looking out to a sailing ship & island, panel w/stylized florals, in shades of black, white, turquoise blue & gold, Noritake mark "27.1 DS," 6 1/2" l., 6 1/4" h. (ILLUS.) $160

Toast rack, two-slice, blue & yellow decoration $45

Tray, pierced handles, decal & h.p. fruit border, lustre center, 11" w. $80

Long Floral-decorated Noritake Tray

Tray, rectangular, pierced end handles, floral decoration on white ground, green edge trim w/brown trim on handles, 17 1/2" l. (ILLUS.) $90

Scenic Noritake Vase with Grape Handles

Vase, 4 1/4" h., 5 1/4" d., footed bulbous body w/figural leaf & grape cluster handles, gold & blue lustre ground decorated w/scene of trees & children (ILLUS.) $365

Vase, 5 1/2" h., orange & gold rim & handles, h.p. tree & cottage lakeside scene $80

Noritake Fan-shaped Vase

Vase, 6 1/2" h., footed, fan-shaped, colorful Art Deco floral design on orange ground (ILLUS.) $205

Vase, 7" h., fan-shaped w/ruffled rim, fruit & vines decoration, green & blue base $90

Unusual Noritake Butterfly Vase

Vase, 8" h., footed ovoid body w/squared rim handles, butterfly decoration on shaded & streaked blue & orange ground (ILLUS.) $250

Noritake Vase with Stylized Flowers

Vase, 8 1/4" h., 5 1/4" d., footed ovoid body w/scalloped rim & scrolled rim handles, blue interior, exterior base w/blue, brown & black vertical lines on white, black band on upper body decorated w/stylized flowers in yellow, purple, brown & blue w/green & brown leaves (ILLUS.) $660

Vase, 8 1/4" h., Indian motif & lustre decoration $140

Vase, 8 1/2" h., bulbous body, Tree in Meadow patt. $90

Vegetable bowl, open, round, Tree in Meadow patt. $30

Vegetable dish, cov., round, Azalea patt. $75

Scenic Noritake Wall Plaque

Wall plaque, pierced to hang, silhouetted Art Deco-style scene of woman in gown w/full ruffled skirt, sitting on couch & holding mirror, white lustre ground, 8 3/4" d. (ILLUS.).. **$840**

Wall plaque, pierced to hang, relief-molded & h.p. double Indian portraits, 10 1/2" d..... **$650**

Wall pocket, double, conical two-part form w/arched backplate, decorated w/an exotic blue & yellow bird among branches of red & blue stylized blossoms against a cream ground, purple lustre rim band, 8" l. **$165**

Wall pocket, trumpet-form, wide upper band decorated w/an autumn sunset scene, lavender lustre rim band & base, 8 1/4" l. **$90**

Wall pocket, double, relief-molded floral cresting backplate, stylized florals & bird of paradise decoration, lustre border, 8" l. .. **$200**

Wall pocket, single, h.p. tree & cottage lakeside scene on blue lustered ground, 8" h.. **$90**

Waste bowl, Azalea patt. **$55**

North Dakota School of Mines

All pottery produced at the University of North Dakota School of Mines was made from North Dakota clay. In 1910, the University hired Margaret Kelly Cable to teach pottery making, and she remained at the school until her retirement. Julia Mattson and Margaret Pachl also served as instructors between 1923 and 1970. Designs and glazes varied through the years ranging from the Art Nouveau to modern styles. Pieces were marked "University of North Dakota - Grand Forks, N.D. - Made at School of Mines, N.D." within a circle and also signed by the students until 1963. Since that time, the pieces bear only the students' signatures. Items signed "Huck" are by the artist Flora Huckfield and were made between 1923 and 1949.

North Dakota School of Mines Mark

North Dakota Covered Wagon Bowl-Vase

Bowl-vase, wide squatty spherical form w/low molded flat mouth, "Covered Wagon" patt., a wide incised band of oxendrawn wagons around the shoulder, matte dark brown glaze w/darker brown highlights, by Margaret Cable, ink mark, signed, titled & numbered "186," 7 1/4" d., 6 1/2" h. (ILLUS.) **$1,093**

Pink-striped North Dakota Vase

Vase, 4 3/8" h., wide flat-bottomed short bulbous body w/a wide rounded shoulder tapering to the flat mouth, a dark blue ground decorated w/a repeating design of pink stripes w/a ring at each end alternating w/pink stripes w/the two rings at the center, short medium blue bars alternating w/pink stripes at the rim & base, decorated by Beverly Bushaw, 1937, ink stamp mark, light crazing (ILLUS.).......... **$1,725**

North Dakota School of Mines Vase

Vase, 5 5/8" h., bulbous ovoid body tapering to a wide flat mouth, carved jack-in-the-pulpit blossoms around the sides in brown highlighted w/black slip, stamped mark on the base & incised "Flower-Jack-in-the-Pulpit - Huck 74 A," short tight line at rim professionally repaired (ILLUS., previous page) $863

the craft will ever see. The majority of his works were hand-thrown, exceedingly thin-walled items, some of which have a crushed or folded appearance. He considered himself the foremost potter in the world and declined to sell much of his production, instead accumulating a great horde to leave as a legacy to his children. In 1972 this collection was purchased for resale by an antiques dealer.

GEO. E. OHR

BILOXI, MISS.

Ohr Pottery Marks

Ohr Bisque Clay Bowl-Vase

Bowl-vase, footed squatty body w/deeply indented & folded sides below a flattened rounded shoulder, bisque red clay, script signature, 5" d., 3 3/4" h. (ILLUS.) **$2,875**

North Dakota Vase with Bentonite Glaze

Vase, 7 3/8" h., flat-bottomed swelled cylindrical body w/a wide flat molded mouth, Bentonite glaze, a brown ground decorated w/a large very dark brown stylized flowering cactus, dark brown rim band, decorated by J. Mattson, No. 1023 (ILLUS.).... **$2,760**

North Dakota Floral-striped Vase

Vase, 11 1/8" h., gently swelled cylindrical body w/a narrow rounded shoulder to the low flaring neck, decorated around the sides w/stripes composed of large mustard yellow blossoms & dark green leaves against a pale yellow ground, decorated by L. Thorne & Huckfield, Shape No. 576, chip & areas of fired-on red glaze (ILLUS.) **$575**

Ohr (George) Pottery

George Ohr, the eccentric potter of Biloxi, Mississippi, worked from about 1883 to 1906. Some think him to be one of the most expert throwers

Small Pinched Black Ohr Pitcher

Pitcher, 2 1/2" h., 4 1/4" l., a round foot below the body pulled & pinched into a large spout opposite a thin, pointed finform handle, rolled rim, speckled gunmetal glaze, repairs to handle & rim edge, stamped "G.E. OHR - Biloxi, Miss." (ILLUS.) **$5,463**

Extremely Rare George Ohr Pottery Teapot

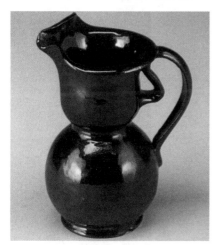

Double-bulb Black Ohr Pitcher

Pitcher, 5 1/2" h., 3 3/4" d., footed spherical lower body w/a small waist below the deep cupped upper body w/a flaring rim & wide folded rim spout, arched loop handle, mirror black & eggplant glazed, stamped "G.E. OHR - Biloxi, Miss." (ILLUS.) **$6,325**

Small George Ohr Pottery Teapot

Teapot, cov., a cylindrical slightly waisted body w/a flattened shoulder centering a short cylindrical neck, serpentine spout & long C-form handle, small inset cover w/large mushroom knop, covered overall in a green speckled glossy glaze, stamped "GEO. E. OHR/BILOXI, MISS.," minor restoration to spout, rim & cover, 6 1/2" l., 4 1/4" h. (ILLUS.) **$5,581**

Teapot, cov., a large size pot w/a footring supporting the wide squatty bulbous body tapering to a cupped neck w/inset flat cover, long serpentine spout & simple C-form handle, covered in a spectacular white, red & pink glaze sponged on an amber ground, stamped "G.E. OHR/ Biloxi, Miss.," late 19th - early 20th c., 12 1/2" l., 5 1/2" h. (ILLUS., top of page) **$55,813**

Miniature Ohr Vase in Raspberry & Amber

Vase, 3 1/4" h., 3" d., wide domed base w/medial ring below the trumpet-form neck w/pinched & twisted rim, overall raspberry & amber glossy glaze, stamped "GEO. E. OHR," tight line in the base (ILLUS.) **$1,955**

Small Bisque Twisted Ohr Vase

Vase, 3 3/4" h., 4" d., bulbous squatty form w/a deep in-body twist around the center, bisque red clay fired to a dark brown sheen, stamped "GEO. OHR" (ILLUS.)
.... **$2,760**

Squatty Twisted-neck Ohr Vase

Vase, 4 3/4" h., 3 3/4" d., wide squatty bulbous lower body centered by a cylindrical deeply twisted neck w/a bulbed top w/a flaring crimped rim, gunmetal black glaze, stamped "GEO. E. OHR - Biloxi, Miss.," minute rim nick & small kiln kiss (ILLUS.)... **$5,463**

Footed Shaker-style Ohr Vase

Vase, 4 3/4" h., 2 1/4" d., footed shaker-style body tapering to a tiny flared mouth, overall mottled forest green glossy glaze, stamped "G.E. OHR - BILOXI," touch-up to rim, minor base abrasion (ILLUS.)
.... **$3,105**

Ohr Vase with Rare Volcanic Glaze

Vase, 6" h., 2 3/4" d., bulbous ovoid lower body tapering to a waisted neck w/cylindrical top, overall unusual raspberry & white volcanic glaze on a glossy blue ground, stamped "G.E. OHR - Biloxi, Miss.," underglaze firing line inside neck (ILLUS.)... **$14,950**

Old Ivory

Old Ivory china was produced in Silesia, Germany, in the late 1800s and takes its name from the soft white background coloring. A wide range of table pieces was made with the various patterns, usually identified by a number rather than a name.

The following prices are averages for Old Ivory at this time. Rare patterns will command higher prices, and there is some variance in prices geographically. These prices are also based on the item being perfect. Cups are measured across the top opening.

Basket, handled, No. U2 Deco blank **$450**
Berry set: 10 1/2" master bowl & six small berries; No. 7 Clairon blank, the set **$300**
Berry set: 9 1/2" master bowl & six small berries; No. 12 Clairon blank, the set **$350**
Berry set: 10 1/2" d. master bowl & six small berries; No. 15 Clairon blank, the set **$285**
Berry set: 9 1/2" master bowl & six small berries; No. 84 Empire blank, the set **$250**
Bonbon, inside handle, No. 62 Florette blank, rare, 6" l. **$500**
Bone dish, No. 16, Worcester blank, rare **$400**
Bouillon cup & saucer, No. 16 Clairon blank, 3 1/2" d. **$250**
Bowl, 5 1/2" d., No. 7 Clairon blank **$45**
Bowl, 5 1/2" d., waste, No. 11 Clairon blank .. **$285**

No. 84 Worchester Bowl

Bowl, 5 1/2" d., waste, No. 84 Worchester blank (ILLUS.) **$300**
Bowl, 6" d., cereal, No. 76 Louis XVI blank **$95**
Bowl, 6 1/2" d., No. 22 Clairon blank **$150**

No. 28 Alice Bowl

Bowl, 7" d., whipped cream, No. 28 Alice blank (ILLUS.) **$325**
Bowl, 9" d., No. 34 Empire blank **$175**
Bowl, 9" d., No. 69 Florette blank **$200**
Bowl, 9" d., No. 200 Deco blank **$100**
Bowl, 10" d., No. 5 Elysee blank................... **$350**
Bowl, 10" d., No. 10 Clairon blank **$200**
Bowl, 10" d., No. 11 Clairon blank **$100**
Bowl, 10" d., No. 16 Clairon blank **$100**

Bowl, 10" d., No. 73 Empire blank **$250**

Old Ivory Bun Tray

Bun tray, oval w/open handles, No. 122 Alice blank, 10" l. (ILLUS.) **$300**
Butter pat, No. 15 Mignon blank, 3 1/4" d. **$150**
Cake plate, tab-handled, No. U15 Florette blank, 9 1/2" d. **$200**
Cake plate, open-handled, No. 200 Deco blank, 9 1/2" h. **$100**
Cake plate, open-handled, No. 10 Clairon blank, 10 1/2" d. **$125**
Cake plate, open-handled, No. 17 Clairon blank, 10 1/2" d. **$450**
Cake plate, tab-handled, No. 57 Florette blank, 10 1/2" d. **$300**
Cake plate, tab-handled, No. 137 Rivoli blank, 10 1/2" d. **$200**

No. 204 Deco Cake Plate

Cake plate, w/open handles, No. 204 Deco blank, 10" d. (ILLUS.) **$300**

Florette Cake Plate

Cake plate, tab-handled, No. 75 Florette blank (ILLUS.) **$250-300**

No. 44 Florette Blank Pieces

Pieces from No. 12 Clairon Cake Set

Cake set: 11" d. serving plate & 5 individual plates; No. 12 Clairon blank, the set (ILLUS. of two pieces) **$450**

Cake set: 10 1/2" d. cake plate & six small serving plates; No. 69 Florette blank, the set **$450**

Celery dish, No. 12 Clairon blank, 11 1/2" l. .. **$200**

Celery dish, No. 22 Clairon blank, 11 1/4" l. .. **$300**

Celery dish, No. 28 Clairon blank, 11 1/4" l. .. **$150**

Center bowl, No. 84 Deco Variant blank, 12 1/2" d. **$500**

Charger, No. 8 Clairon blank, 13 1/2" d. **$385**

No. 90 Clairon Charger

Charger, No. 90 Clairon blank, 13 1/2" d. (ILLUS.) **$500**

Charger, No. 16 Clairon blank, 13" d. **$300**

Charger, 13 1/2" l., No. 75 Alice blank **$400**

Charger, No. 44 Florette blank (ILLUS. back row, w/Florette pieces, top of page) **$500-650**

Chocolate pot, cov., No. 44 Florette blank, rare, 9 1/2" h. (ILLUS. far right w/Florette pieces) **$600-700**

Chocolate pot, No. 118 Empire blank, rare, 9 1/2" h. **$600**

Chocolate set, No. 22 Clairon blank, rare, 7-pc. set **$2,500**

Chocolate set: 9 1/2" h. cov. pot & six cups & saucers; No. 53 Empire blank, rare, the set **$1,500**

Chocolate set: 9 1/2" h. cov. pot & six cups & saucers; No. 75 Empire blank, the set.... **$900**

Chocolate set, No. 200 Deco blank, 7 pcs.... **$600**

Chowder cup & saucer, No. U29 Eglantine blank, 4" d. **$300**

Cider cup & saucer, No. 16 Clairon blank, 3" d. **$150**

Coffeepot, cov., No. 84 Deco variant blank, 9" h. **$1,200**

Empire Blank Demitasse Coffeepot

Coffeepot, cov., demitasse, No. 123 Empire blank (ILLUS.) **$500-650**

Compote, 9" d., open, No. U11 Alice blank, rare **$600**

Cracker jar, No. 11 Clairon blank, 8 1/2" h. **$400**

No. U15 Florette Sugar & Creamer

Cracker jar, No. 120 Clairon blank, rare, 8 1/2" h. **$800**
Cracker jar, cov., No. 33 Empire blank, 5 1/2" h. **$500**
Cracker jar, cov., No. 39 Empire blank, very rare, 5 1/2" h. **$1,200**
Cracker jar, cov., No. 15 Clairon blank, 8 1/2" h. **$500**
Cracker jar, No. 44 Florette blank (ILLUS. far left w/Florette pieces) **$850-1,000**

Creamer & cov. sugar bowl, No. U15 Florette blank, 4" h., pr. (ILLUS., top of page) **$250**
Creamer & cov. sugar bowl, No. 16 Deco blank variant, 6" h., pr. **$400**

No. 53 Empire Sugar & Creamer

Creamer & cov. sugar bowl, No. 53 Empire blank, 4" h., pr. (ILLUS.) **$500**
Creamer & cov. sugar bowl, No. 122 Alice blank, pr. **$250**
Creamer & cov. sugar bowl, No. 11 Clairon blank, 5 1/2" h., pr. **$150**
Creamer & cov. sugar bowl, No. 202 Deco blank, pr. **$165**
Creamer & cov. sugar bowl, service size, No. 84 Deco variant blank, pr. **$400**
Creamer & cov. sugar bowl, service size, No. U17 Eglantine blank, pr. **$500**
Creamer & cov. sugar bowl, No. 39 Empire blank, rare, 3 1/2" & 5 1/2" h., pr. **$600**
Creamer & cov. sugar bowl, No. 99 Empire blank, rare, 5 1/2" h., pr. **$500**

No. 75 Deco Variant Creamer

Creamer, No. 75 Deco blank variant, service, 5 1/2" h. (ILLUS.) **$195**
Creamer & cov. sugar bowl, No. 4 Elysee blank, 4" h., pr. **$300**
Creamer & cov. sugar bowl, No. 10 Clairon blank, 4" h., pr. **$175**

Louis XVI Blank Creamer & Sugar

Creamer & cov. sugar bowl, No. 76 Louis XVI blank, rare, pr. (ILLUS., bottom previous page).. **$350-450**

No. 4 Elysee Chocolate Cup & Saucer

Cup & saucer, chocolate, No. 4 Elysee blank, 2 1/2" d. (ILLUS.)............................. **$250**
Cup & saucer, demi, No. 10 Clairon blank, 2 1/2" d... **$135**
Cup & saucer, No. 15 Clairon blank, 3 1/2" d.. **$50**
Cup & saucer, No. 22 Clairon blank, very rare, 3 3/4" d... **$500**
Cup & saucer, bouillon, No. 27 Alice blank, rare, 3 1/2" d.. **$450**
Cup & saucer, cov., bouillon-type, No. 73 Alice blank, rare, 3 1/2" d. **$400**
Cup & saucer, No. 99 Empire blank, rare, 3 1/2" d... **$450**
Cup & saucer, No. 114 Clairon blank, very rare, 3 1/2" d.. **$400**
Cup & saucer, No. 204 Deco blank, scarce, 3 3/4" d... **$175**
Cup & saucer, No. U30 Alice variant blank w/Y border... **$65-75**
Cup & saucer, No. 16 Clairon blank, 3 1/4" d... **$75**

No. 90 Clairon Blank Cup & Saucer

Cup & saucer, No. 90 Clairon blank (ILLUS.)
.... **$75-95**
Cup & saucer, No. 203 Deco blank, 3 1/4" d... **$95**
Cup & saucer, No. 82 Empire blank........... **$75-95**
Cup & saucer, No. 84 Empire blank, 3 1/4" d... **$65**
Cup & saucer, 5 o'clock-type, No. 28 Empire blank, 3" d. **$85**

Florette Blank Cup & Saucer

Cup & saucer, No. 62 Florette blank (ILLUS.).. **$200-250**
Demitasse cup & saucer, No. 16 Clairon blank, 2 1/2" d. **$125**
Demitasse cup & saucer, No. 22 Clairon blank, 2 1/2" d. **$250**

Deco Variant Cup & Saucer & Teapot

Demitasse cup & saucer, No. 75 Deco variant blank (ILLUS. left) **$125-140**
Demitasse cup & saucer, No. 5 Elysee blank, rare, 2 1/2" d..................... **$200**
Demitasse pot, No. 16 Clairon blank, 7 1/2" h. **$500**
Demitasse pot, No. 97 Clairon blank, very rare, 7 1/2" h. **$2,000**
Demitasse pot, cov., No. 73 Clairon blank, 7 1/2" h.. **$650**
Demitasse pot, cov., No. 33 Empire blank, 7 1/2" h.. **$500**
Demitasse pot, No. 44 Florette blank (ILLUS. front, second from right w/Florette pieces, above)............................ **$800-900**
Demitasse pot, cov., No. 62 Florette blank, very rare, 7 1/2" h. **$1,200**
Demitasse set: 7 1/2" pot & 4 cups & saucers; No. 15 Clairon blank (ILLUS., top next page)...................................... **$1,200**
Demitasse set: 7 1/2" pot & 4 cups & saucers; No. U22 Eglantine blank **$1,800**
Dish, tri-lobed, No. 202 Deco blank, 6" w. **$95**
Dish, tri-lobed, No. 204 Rivoli blank, 6" w. **$175**
Dresser tray, No. 122 Clairon blank, 11 1/2" l.. **$300**
Dresser tray, No. 90 Clairon blank, 11 1/2" l.. **$350**
Dresser tray, No. 34 Empire blank............... **$250**
Egg cup, No. 84 Eglantine blank, very rare, 2 1/2" h.. **$500**

No. 15 Clairon Demitasse Set

Eglantine Blank Ice Cream Bowl

Jam jar, cov., No. 200 Deco blank, 3 1/2" h.
(ILLUS.)... **$400**
Mayonnaise set: dish & underplate; No. 10
Empire blank, 6 1/2" l., the set.................. **$275**
Mayonnaise set: dish & underplate; No. 84
Empire blank, 6 1/2", the set..................... **$265**
Muffineer, No. 73 Louis XVI blank, 4" h. **$485**

Louis XVI Muffineer & Salt & Peppers

Ice cream bowl, No. 6 Eglantine blank
(ILLUS.)... **$300-400**
Jam dish, individual, No. 28 Alice blank **$150**
Jam jar, cov., No. 137 Deco blank, 3 1/2" h. .. **$400**

Muffineer, No. 84 Louis XVI blank (ILLUS.
left)... **$350-450**
Mustache cup & saucer, No. 4 Elysee
blank, 3 1/2" d. **$500**
Mustache cup & saucer, No. 16 Clairon
blank, 3 1/2" d. **$300**
Mustard pot, cov., No. 12 Clairon blank,
3 3/4" h... **$425**
Mustard pot, cov., No. 84 Carmen blank,
3 3/4" h... **$325**
Mustard pot, cov., No. 200 Deco blank,
3 3/4" h... **$450**
Nappy, No. 65 Clairon blank, rare, 6" l. **$550**
Olive dish, No. 17 Clairon blank, 6 1/2" l...... **$400**
Olive dish, No. 20 Florette blank, rare,
6 1/2" l.. **$225**
Olive dish, No. 75 Empire blank, 6 1/2" l........ **$75**
Pickle dish, No. 32 Empire blank, 8 1/2" l. **$75**
Pickle dish, No. 84 Empire blank, 8 1/2" l. **$85**
Pin tray, No. U22 Eglantine blank................. **$350**

No. 200 Deco Jam Jar

Acanthus Blank Water Pitcher

Pitcher, water, No. 84 Acanthus blank
(ILLUS.)..................................... **$1,000-1,200**
Pitcher, 8" h., water, No. 11 Acanthus blank
.... **$1,200**
Plate, 6 1/2" d., No. 121 Alice blank................ $50
Plate, luncheon, 8 1/2" d., No. U30 Alice
blank $20
Plate, 8 1/2" d., No. 60 Alice blank.................. $85
Plate, 9 1/2" d., No. U30 Alice blank $100
Plate, 6 1/2" d., No. 10 Clairon blank $45
Plate, 7 1/2" d., No. 12 Clairon blank $85
Plate, 7 1/2" d., No. 119 Clairon blank, rare ... $250
Plate, 8 1/2" d., No. 8 Clairon blank $85
Plate, 8 1/2" d., luncheon, No. 73 Clairon
blank.. $90
Plate, 9 1/2" d., dinner, No. 21 Clairon
blank, rare $350
Plate, 9 3/4" d., dinner, No. 16 Clairon blank .. $200
Plate, 10" d., No. 16 Clairon blank, open-
handled $100
Plate, 6 1/2" d., No. U4 Deco blank................. $40
Plate, 8 1/2" d., No. 200 Deco blank $75
Plate, 7 1/2" d., No. 4 Elysee blank................ $65

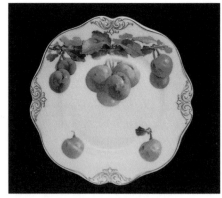

Rare No. 99 Empire Plate

Plate, 7 1/2" d., No. 99 Empire blank, rare
(ILLUS.)... $300
Plate, 7 1/2" d., No. 107 Empire blank, rare ... $250
Plate, 7 3/4" d., No. 84 Empire blank $65
Plate, 8 1/2" d., No. 15 Empire blank $75

Plate, 8 1/2'"d., No. 53 Empire blank **$125**
Plate, 9 1/2" d., dinner, No. 40 Empire
blank, rare.. **$300**
Plate, 9 3/4" d., dinner, No. 34 Empire blank .. **$300**
Plate, 9 1/2" d., tab handle, No. U16 Flor-
ette blank **$350**
Plate, 8 1/2" d., luncheon, No. 76 Louis XVI
blank **$150**

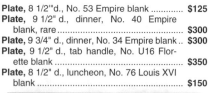

No. U26 Mignon Dinner Plate

Plate, 9 3/4" d., dinner, No. U26 Mignon
blank (ILLUS.)... **$385**
Plates, 6 1/4" d., No. 40, set of 5 .... **$200**

No. 34 Alice Platter

Platter, 21" l., No. 34 Alice blank (ILLUS.).. **$1,000**
Platter, 11 1/2" l., No. 22 Clairon blank......... **$400**
Porringer, No. 39 Empire blank, very rare,
6 1/4" h.. **$900**
Porringer, No. 82 Empire blank, 6 1/4" d. **$200**
Powder jar, cov., No. U22 Eglantine blank,
rare.. **$450**
Powder jar, No. 84 Deco blank variant,
scarce **$400**
Ramekin & underplate, No. 11 Quadrille
blank, rare, 4 1/2" d., 2 pcs....................... **$500**
Salt & pepper shakers, No. 44 Florette
blank (ILLUS. second from left w/Florette
pieces).. **$150-250**
Salt & pepper shakers, No. 15 Louis XVI
blank, 2 3/4" h., pr. (ILLUS. right w/muff-
ineer)... **$125**
Salt & pepper shakers, No. 76 Louis XVI
blank, 2 3/4" h., pr..................................... **$200**
Shaving mug, No. 22 Clairon blank, rare,
3 1/4" h.. **$1,000**

Soup tureen, cov., No. 84 Deco variant blank, rare, 13" l. **$2,500**
Spoon rest, No. 200 Deco blank, 8 3/4" l. **$250**
Spoon rest, lay-down type, No. 204 Deco blank, 8 1/4" l. **$250**

No. 29 Carmen Spooner

Spooner, No. 29 Carmen blank, 4" h. (ILLUS.) **$400**
Spooner, No. 40 Carmen blank, 4" h. **$400**
Tazza, No. U2 Rivoli blank, rare, 9" d. **$600**
Tea cup & saucer, No. 4 Elysee blank, 3 1/4" d. **$95**
Tea tile, No. 11 Alice blank, 6" d. **$250**
Tea tile, No. 15 Alice blank, 6" sq. **$225**

Old Ivory Teapot Decorated in Beige

Teapot, cov., Alice blank, bulbous body tapering to neck w/short lip, angled handle, short curving spout, domed lid w/finial, decorated w/line decoration & roses in shades of beige & brown, Hermann Ohme, Germany, 7" h. (ILLUS.) **$500**

Child's Old Ivory Alice Teapot

Teapot, cov., child's, Alice blank, bulbous body tapering in to neck w/slightly flaring lip, short foot, angled handle, slightly curving spout, inset domed lid w/finial, body decorated w/pale pink roses & green leaves, clear glaze, marked "Alice," Hermann Ohme, Germany, 4" h. (ILLUS.) **$75**

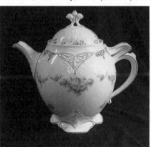

Old Ivory Clairon Teapot

Teapot, cov., Clairon blank, almost spherical ovoid body on short quatrefoil base, C-form handle w/separate thumbrest applied to body above it, short curved spout, domed lid w/cutout trefoil finial, the body decorated w/sprigs & garland of pink roses & green leaves, line decoration highlighting the shoulder, foot, handle, spout & finial, Hermann Ohme, Germany, 8" h. (ILLUS.) **$250**

Two Sizes of Old Ivory Deco Teapots

Teapot, cov., Deco blank, nearly cylindrical body on short foot, w/tapering shoulder, angled handle, graceful curving spout, flat lid w/finial, Hermann Ohme, Germany, different sizes, each (ILLUS. of two, bottom of previous page) **$500**

Small Deco Variant Teapot

Teapot, cov., Deco Variant blank, cylindrical body on short foot, short tapering shoulder, angled handle, curving spout, flat lid w/cutout angled finial, decorated w/line decoration & daisies in shades of white, beige & brown, Hermann Ohme, Germany, 5 1/2" h. (ILLUS.)................................. **$450**

Old Ivory Melon-shaped Teapot

Teapot, cov., melon-lobed bulbous body on short quatrefoil foot, short flaring neck, domed lobed lid w/finial in the shape of a melon/gourd stem, C-form handle, serpentine spout, the body & lid decorated w/delicate blue & yellow floral designs, the spout & rim w/gold line decoration, Hermann Ohme, Germany, 7 1/2" h. (ILLUS.) .. **$250**

Old Ivory Mignon Teapot

Teapot, cov., Mignon blank, lobed bulbous body on ruffled foot, short flaring neck w/ruffled rim, peaked lid w/ornate cutout finial, ornate C-scroll handle w/thumbrest & serpentine spout, the body & lid decorated w/embossed decoration & sprigs of delicate green flowers & leaves, gold highlights on foot, rim, spout & handle, Hermann Ohme, Germany, 8" h. (ILLUS.)........ **$135**

Old Ivory Rivoli Teapot

Teapot, cov., Rivoli blank, hexagonal body on short foot, angled handle, long curved spout, slightly domed lid w/cutout pointed finial, clear glaze, hand-painted decoration of purple violets & green leaves, gold highlights, Hermann Ohme, Germany, 7 1/2" h. (ILLUS.) **$475**

Old Ivory Swirl Teapot

Teapot, cov., Swirl blank, footed bulbous body w/delicate swirled ribs, flaring lip, domed lid w/finial, applied ribbed scroll loop handle w/thumbrest, serpentine spout, clear glaze, the body decorated w/large wine-colored floral design, the lid & spout w/wine-colored floral sprigs, the finial, rim, handle & base highlighted in gold, Hermann Ohme, Germany, 8 1/2" h. (ILLUS.) **$250**
Teapot, cov., No. 204 Deco blank, 5 1/2" h. **$700**
Teapot, cov., No. 200 Deco blank, 8 1/2" l. ... **$500**
Teapot, cov., No. 75 Deco variant blank (ILLUS. right w/demitasse cup & saucer) **$500-600**
Toothpick holder, No. 15 Clairon blank, 2 1/4" h... **$295**
Toothpick holder, No. 73 Clairon blank, 2 1/4" h... **$340**
Toothpick holder, No. 121 Quadrille blank, 2 1/4" h... **$325**

Vase, 9" h., No. U12 blank $1,700
Vase, 5" h., No. 134 Deco variant blank $385
Vegetable dish, cov., No. 15 Clairon blank,
10 1/2" l. $1,000
Vegetable dish, cov., No. 16 Clairon blank,
10 1/2" l. $1,500

Old Ivory Covered Vegetable Dish

Vegetable dish, No. 28 blank, 10 1/2" l.
(ILLUS.) $1,500
Vegetable dish, cov., No. 75 Rivoli blank,
10 1/2" l. $1,500
Vegetable dish, cov., No. 84 Carmen
blank, 10 1/2" l. $1,300
Waste bowl, No. 28 Worcester blank, 5" d. ... $295

Owens

Owens pottery was the product of the J.B. Owens Pottery Company, which operated in Ohio from 1890 to 1929. In 1891 it located in Zanesville and produced art pottery from 1896, introducing "Utopian" wares as its first art pottery. The company switched to tile after 1907. Efforts to rebuild after the factory burned in 1928 failed, and the company closed in 1929.

Owens Pottery Mark

Owens Utopian Jug with Ear of Corn

Jug, Utopian Line, bulbous body w/an integral arched loop handle across the top to the upright cylindrical neck w/a tiny spout, decorated w/a large yellow ear of corn w/green leaves against a dark

brown ground, painted by Tot Steele, impressed mark, Shape No. 1266, 7 1/2" h.
(ILLUS.) $259

Rare Owens Utopian Kerosene Lamp

Lamp, kerosene-type, Utopian Ware, the base composed of a tall baluster-form vase h.p. w/a profile bust portrait of a Native American woman titled "Gentle Bird - Flatheads," in dark brown, black & dark green on a shaded dark brown to green ground, fitted into a scroll-cast & footed cast metal base, a copper band supporting the font fitted into the top, w/early burner & cased amber ball shade & clear chimney, painted by Mae Timberlake, bottom of lamp w/Utopian mark, 13 7/8" h. (ILLUS.) $4,025

Tall Owens Mug with Indian Portrait

Mug, Lightweight Line, flaring ringed base & tall slightly tapering cylindrical sides, large angled handle, h.p. large bust portrait of a Native American Chief by Albert Haubrich, Shape No. 830, completely oversprayed, indicating some restoration, 7 5/8" h. (ILLUS.) $431

Bulbous Utopian Vase with Pansies

Vase, 4 1/8" h., Utopian Line, bulbous ovoid body w/a wide shoulder centered by a short ringed neck, h.p. w/yellow & orange pansies against a shaded dark to light brown ground, decorated by Tot Steele, marked on base "J.B. Owens Utopian - 1110" (ILLUS.)... **$161**

Copper-clad Owens Pottery Vase

Vase, 5 3/4" h., copper-clad, wide bulbous ovoid body w/a scalloped base & four tab feet, a tiny cylindrical neck w/a flared rim, the sides incised w/large balloon-like panels outlined in double lines, marked w/an "N" inside & circle & the date 1905 (ILLUS.).. **$500**

Owens Utopian Vase with Roses

Vase, 5 7/8" h., Utopian line, gently flaring cylindrical body w/a wide slightly rounded shoulder centering a small trumpet neck, decorated w/large deep red & pink wild roses & green leaves on a dark brown shaded to dark gold ground, artist-initials, some dry crazing (ILLUS.)........................ **$173**

Rare Owens Matte Green Pine Cone Vase

Vase, 6 1/2" h., wide bulbous ovoid body w/a wide rounded shoulder centered by a small rolled neck, molded w/four small open twisted twig handles around the neck continuing to relief-molded pine cones amid long pine needles, overall deep green matte glaze, impressed Owens mark, Shape No. 326 (ILLUS.) **$1,093**

Green Matte Owens Pottery Vase

Vase, 8 7/8" h., squatty bulbous lower body w/four buttress feet, a double-ringed neck w/widely flaring rim, overall matte green glaze, marked, minor nicks on feet (ILLUS.).. **$500**

Vase, 10 1/4" h., Utopian Ware, cylindrical body w/a wide flattened shoulder centered by a tiny neck, decorated w/dark orange nasturtium blossoms & long green leafy stems against a dark to medium brown ground, impressed "Owens 1010" (ILLUS., top next page)............................. **$259**

Utopian Vase with Nasturtiums

Fine Utopian Portrait Vase

Vase, 10 1/2" h., 5 1/2" d., Utopian Line, tall swelled cylindrical form w/a flat mouth, h.p. w/a half-length bust portrait of a Native American titled "Sanches Apache," dark brown, reddish brown, cream & black on a shaded brown to tan ground, by artist A.F. Best, some glaze lifting, early 20th c. (ILLUS.)................... **$2,530**

Tall Owens Utopian Vase with Roses

Vase, 11" h., simple footed tall ovoid body w/a tiny neck, h.p. w/large yellowish orange roses & green leafy stems against a shaded dark brown to green ground, Owens Utopian logo, artist-signed (ILLUS.)... **$460**
Vase, 11 3/4" h., footed large bulbous ovoid body tapering to a tiny cylindrical neck, pierced w/rectangles on the shoulder, rectangular relief panels w/stylized swans on the sides, matte green glaze, impressed "Owens 1025"....................... **$1,495**

Tall Slender Owens Lotus Ware Vase

Vase, 14" h., Lotus Ware, a tall slender baluster-form body, h.p. w/pale white & blue pansies around the middle against a blue shaded to white ground, Owens mark, Shape No. 016 (ILLUS.)............................. **$460**

Parian

Parian is unglazed porcelain in the biscuit stage, and takes its name from its resemblance to Parian marble used for statuary. Parian wares were made in this country and abroad through much of the last century and continue to be made.

Bust of Charles Dickens, mounted on a waisted circular socle, England, 19th c., 15 1/2" h... **$575**
Bust of Charles Sumner, mounted on a raised socle base, impressed title, verse & manufacturer's mark of Robinson & Leadbeater, England, ca. 1880, 12 7/8" h... **$345**
Bust of Clytie, mounted on a round waisted socle, England, 19th c., 10 3/4" h. **$200-250**
Bust of General Robert E. Lee, mounted on a raised circular plinth, sculpted by Roland Morris, manufactured by James & Thomas Berington, impressed marks & title, England, ca. 1870, 12 3/4" h. **$675-725**
Bust of Shakespeare, bearded man wearing cord-tied collared shirt & cloak, on a socle base, name impressed on the back, 19th c., 8" h. **$125-175**
Busts of Mozart & Beethoven, each mounted on a raised circular plinth, each titled, attributed to Robinson & Leadbeater, England, ca. 1880, 11 1/4" h., pr.
.... **$750-850**

Parian Figure Group of "The Two Wellers"

Figure group, "The Two Wellers," based on Dickens' characters, Sam & Tony Weller, shown seated beside a round tavern table, on an oblong plinth base, small chip to the cup on the table, England, late 19th - early 20th c., 7 1/2 x 10 1/2", 12" h. (ILLUS.) **$259**

Figure of fisherman, modeled as a scantily clad male holding a net, England, 19th c., 22 2/12" h. **$1,150**

Figure of "The Greek Slave," a standing nude woman leaning on a low draped column, on a ribbed socle base, modeled by Richard Cook after original statue by Hiram Powers, impressed mark "RC 17," mid-19th c., 13" h. **$805**

Figure of woman, the kneeling maiden wearing a simple costume, her hands clasped in her lap, raised on a separate molded circular base, impressed marks of the Gustafsberg factory, Sweden, late 19th c., overall 16 1/2" h., 2 pcs. **$575**

Figure of woman gathering wheat, full-length figure of woman in long skirt holding small pot & sickle, on round base, 21 3/4" h. (narrow piece of sickle is missing) **$660**

Figures, each molded as a child in a different pose, each seated on a trunk, England, 19th c., 13 1/4" h., pr. **$1,265**

Figural Owl Match Holder

Match holder, figural, two owls snuggled together on a tree branch w/a small stump in front for the matches, inscribed across the front of the platform base "Match Making," English registry mark for 1871, 5 3/8" w., 7 3/4" h. (ILLUS.) **$195**

Paris & Old Paris

China known by the generic name of "Paris" and "Old Paris" was made by several Parisian factories from the 18th through the 19th century; some of it is marked and some is not. Much of it was handsomely decorated.

Delicate Old Paris Cachepot & Drain Plate

Cachepot & drain plate, in the Louis XVI style, the round disk-form gold-banded drain plate supporting the trumpet-form pot w/a white ground finely decorated w/delicate gold florals & swags & deep red & blue scrolls, blue underglaze "A" mark under plate, late 18th c., 7 3/4" d., overall 8 1/4" h., the set (ILLUS.) **$1,380**

Old Paris Cup & Saucer with Children

Cup & saucer, the cylindrical cup in white w/a grisaille scene of children in 18th c. attire holding a rooster, gold edge banding & handle, matching saucer w/a scene of a seated girl, workshop of Le Petit Carousel, last quarter 18th c., restoration to handle, saucer 6" d., cup 4" h., the set (ILLUS.) **$575**

Very Ornate Paris Potpourri Jars

Paris Porcelain Incense Burners

Incense burners, figural, one modeled as a seated knight wearing a maroon outfit trimmed in gold, the other as a Medieval lady wearing a long maroon gown & long green robe, each on a rectangular platform base w/black marbleizing about the gilt-trimmed white scroll base, Franed, second quarter 19th c., 6 x 7", 10 1/4" h., pr. (ILLUS.) **$575**

Inkstand, figural, four gold paw feet supporting a gold-banded oval base mounted by the white figure of Cupid holding a garland of flowers & seated on rockwork next to the inkwell formed by a deep flaring basket w/a short oval basket beside it, a gold cylindrical quill holder behind him, the edge of the stand inscribed in gold script w/a couplet by Voltaire, perhaps Dagoty, ca. 1810, 6" h. (ILLUS.) **$1,016**

Potpourri jars, cov., a cubical form fitted w/a square tapering cover w/block finial, gold dentil bands around the top & base w/gold corner bands ending in figural swan feet, each side panel w/a dark blue ground h.p. w/a large oval reserve decorated w/a colorful bouquet of flowers outlined in delicate gilt floral borders, possibly Jacob Petite, 19th c., some damage to gallery, one w/a body crack, 5" sq., 7" h., pr. (ILLUS., top of page) **$575**

Gold & White Paris Porcelain Tea Set

Tea set: cov. teapot, cov. sugar bowl, creamer & two handled cups & saucers; each w/a squatty bulbous body w/alternating narrow stripes of gold & white, teapot & sugar w/flanged & scalloped rims molded w/shells & inset covers w/acorn finial, the other pieces w/the same design, France, first half 19th c., teapot 6 1/2" h., the set (ILLUS.) **$2,760**

Old Paris Figural Inkstand with Cupid

Pair of Fine Paris Porcelain Vases

Vases, 6 1/2" h., rhyton-form terminating in a figural eagle head, raised on an oblong scroll-molded platform base, the cornucopia-form body in celeste blue w/a gilt-bordered white reserve h.p. w/colorful flowers, the rim & eagle trimmed in gold, the base in pink w/gold trim, France, late 19th c., pr. (ILLUS.).................................... **$633**

Vases, 17 1/4" h., footed tall ovoid body tapering to a trumpet neck, the shoulders mounted w/large figural white goat-head handles, the sides & shoulders ornately trimmed w/applied blue flowers & green leaves all trimmed in gold, the front white panel h.p. w/a colorful bouquet of flowers, late 19th c., restoration & repairs to rim & handles, pr. (ILLUS.) **$748**

Wine glass cooler, oval squatty rounded form w/a deeply scalloped rim forming rests for the feet of the wine glasses, gold-trimmed cattail end handles, the sides h.p. w/a continuous band of delicate vining flowers between gold borders, the lower body w/scattered tiny flowers, gold rim & foot band, two variant iron-red stenciled crowned "M" marks for Monsieur's Factory, ca. 1790, 13 1/4" l. (ILLUS., bottom of page)....................... **$7,768**

Large Elaborate Old Paris Vases

Rare 18th Century Old Paris Wine Glass Cooler

Paul Revere Pottery

This pottery was established in Boston, Massachusetts, in 1906, by a group of philanthropists seeking to establish better conditions for underprivileged young girls of the area. Edith Brown served as supervisor of the small "Saturday Evening Girls" Club" pottery operation, which was moved, in 1912, to a house close to the Old North Church where Paul Revere's signal lanterns had been placed. The wares were mostly hand decorated in mineral colors, and both sgraffito and molded decorations were employed. Although it became popular, it was never a profitable operation and always depended on financial contributions to operate. After the death of Edith Brown in 1932, the pottery foundered and finally closed in 1942.

Breakfast set: child's, 7 1/2" d. plate & 3 5/8" h. mug; each h.p. w/a circle enclosing a picture of a white rabbit lying on a green grassy mound, white & blue outer bands, initialed by the artist, early 20th c., the set (ILLUS.)............... **$1,116**

Paul Revere Marks

Paul Revere Jardiniere with Lotus Band

Jardiniere, wide bulbous squatty body w/a closed rim, yellow ground w/a wide rim band in cuerda seca w/black-outlined white lotus blossoms trimmed w/yellow, stamped mark, firing lines around rim & base, two restored rim chips, 9" d., 7" h. (ILLUS.)............... **$1,495**

Plate, 7 5/8" d., decorated w/incised geese in mottled green on a speckled blue ground, painted mark "S.E.G. 6-13," & artist's initials "I.G.," ca. 1913................... **$489**

Paul Revere Bowl with Greek Key Rim

Bowl, 6" d., 3" h., deep rounded sides w/a wide flat rim, brown semi-matte ground decorated around the rim w/a cuerda seca band of Greek key in taupe & ivory on white, signed "SEG - 10.12 - FL" (ILLUS.)
.... **$1,116**

Paul Revere Dinner Plate with Lotus

Plate, dinner, 10" d., dark greyish blue ground decorated around the rim in cuerda seca w/a band of stylized white lotus blossoms, signed "SEG - AM - 11-14," rim bruise, small chips to footring (ILLUS.) **$646**

Vase, 6 1/4" h., 3 3/4" d., simple ovoid body w/a wide flat rim, dark bluish grey lower body, a wide shoulder band in cuerda seca decorated w/a band of stylized oak leaves & acorns in green, brown & pale blue, inkstamped "SEG - AM - 12-17," 1917 (ILLUS., next page)...................... **$4,025**

Paul Revere Child's Breakfast Set

Fine Paul Revere Vase with Oak Leaves

Pennsbury Pottery

Henry Below and his wife, Lee, founded the Pennsbury Pottery in Morrisville, Pennsylvania, in 1950. The Belows chose the name because William Penn's home was nearby. Lee, a talented artist who designed the well-known Rooster pattern, almost the entire output of folk art designs and the Pennsylvania German blue and white hand-painted dinnerware, had been affiliated with Stangl Pottery of Trenton, New Jersey. Mr. Below had learned pottery making in Germany and became an expert in mold making and ceramic engineering. He, too, had been associated with Stangl Pottery, and when he and Lee opened Pennsbury Pottery, several workers from Stangl joined the Belows. Mr. Below's death in 1959 was unexpected, and Mrs. Below passed away in 1968 after a long illness. Pennsbury filed for bankruptcy in October 1970. In 1971 the pottery was destroyed by fire.

During Pennsbury's production years, an earthenware with a high temperature firing was used. Most of the designs are a sgraffito-type similar to Stangl's products. The most popular coloring, a characteristic of Pennsbury, is the smear-type glaze of light brown after the sgraffito technique has been used. Birds are usually marked by hand and most often include the name of the bird. Dinnerware followed and then art pieces, ashtrays and teapots. The first dinnerware line was Black Rooster, followed by Red Rooster. There was also a line known as Blue Dowry, which had the same decorations as the brown folk art pattern but done in cobalt.

Pennsbury Pottery Marks

Advertising display sign, 4 1/4 x 4 3/4"
.... **$125-150**
Canister, cov., Black Rooster patt., w/black rooster finial, front reads "Flour," 9" h.
.... **$125-175**
Casserole & cover in metal stand, Rooster patt. **$40-50**
Cookie jar, cov., Rooster patt. **$50-70**
Desk basket, Two Women Under Tree patt., 5" h. **$15-20**
Letter holder, Pennsylvania Dutch patt., 5 1/4 x 7 1/4" **$30-40**
Model of a hen, painted in blues & white, 10 1/2" h. **$125-150**
Model of a hen, realistically molded & decorated in reds, blues & greens, 10 1/2" h.
.... **$175-200**
Model of a rooster, realistically painted in reds, blues & greens, signed, 11 3/4" h.
.... **$175-200**
Model of a rooster, the large bird realistically molded & decorated in black & white, marked, 11 5/8" h. **$200-250**
Model of bird, Crested Chickadee, blue, No. 101, 4" h. **$75-100**
Model of bird, Wren, No. 109, 3" h. **$60-70**
Model of chickadee, head down, on irregular base, model No. 111, signed "R.B.," 3 1/2" h. **$100-125**
Mug, beer-type, Barber Shop Quartet patt.
.... **$15-25**

Amish Pattern Beer Mug

Mug, beer, Amish patt., dark brown rim & bottom w/dark brown applied handle, 5" h. (ILLUS.) **$15-25**
Oil & vinegar cruets w/stoppers, figural Amish man & woman heads, pr. **$35-45**

Commemorative Pie Plate

Pie plate, Dutch Haven commemorative, birds & heart in center, inscribed around the rim "When it comes to Shoo-Fly Pie - Grandma sure knew how - t'is the Kind of Dish she used - Dutch Haven does it now," 9" d. (ILLUS.)............................ **$90-100**
Pitcher, 5" h., Delft Toleware patt., fruit & leaves, white body w/fruit & leaves outlined in blue, blue inside......................... **$40-50**

Amish Pattern Pitcher

Pitcher, 7 1/4" h., Amish patt. w/interlocked pretzels on reverse (ILLUS.) **$50-75**

Small Black Rooster Plate

Plate, 6" d., Black Rooster patt. (ILLUS.).... **$30-40**
Plate, 8" d., Courting Buggy patt. **$30-40**

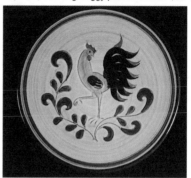

Large Red Rooster Pattern Plate

Plate, 10" d., Red Rooster patt. (ILLUS.).... **$50-60**
Platter, fish-type, 10 x 17"........................ **$75-100**
Relish tray, Black Rooster patt., five-section, each w/different scene, Christmas-tree shape, 14 1/2" l., 11" w **$110-130**
Salt & pepper shakers, figural head of Amish man & Amish woman, pr............. **$25-35**
Teapot, cov., Rooster patt........................ **$35-45**

Commemorative Plaque

Wall plaque, commemorative, "What Giffs, what ouches you?," reverse marked "NFBPWC Philadelphia, PA 1960," drilled for hanging, 4" d. (ILLUS.)............ **$20-30**

Plaque with Rooster

Wall plaque, Rooster patt., "When the cock crows the night is all," drilled for hanging, 4" d. (ILLUS., previous page) **$20-30**

"It is Whole Empty" Plaque

Wall plaque, shows woman holding Pennsbury cookie jar, marked "It is Whole Empty," drilled for hanging, 4" d. (ILLUS.) **$20-30**

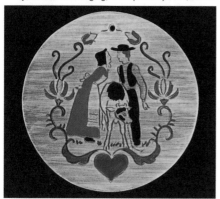

Amish Man & Woman Kissing Plaque

Wall plaque, Amish man & woman kissing over cow, drilled for hanging, 8" d. (ILLUS.) **$25-35**

Donkey & Clown Wall Pocket

Wall pocket, donkey & clown w/dark green border, ivory center, 6 1/2" sq. (ILLUS.) **$100-125**

Peters & Reed

In 1897 John D. Peters and Adam Reed formed a partnership to produce flowerpots in Zanesville, Ohio. Formally incorporated as Peters and Reed in 1901, this type of production was the mainstay until after 1907, when they gradually expanded into the art pottery field. Frank Ferrell, a former designer at the Weller Pottery, developed the "Moss Aztec" line while associated with Peters and Reed, and other art lines followed. Although unmarked, attribution is not difficult once familiar with the various lines. In 1921, Peters and Reed became Zane Pottery, which continued in production until 1941.

Peters & Reed Mark

Marbleized Peters & Reed Candlesticks

Candlesticks, squatty shouldered base we/tall slender tapering paneled sides, marbleized brown, green, yellow & black glossy glaze, glaze bubbles, flakes on edges, unmarked, 10 1/4" h., pr. (ILLUS.) **$147**

Jardiniere, Moss Aztec line, wide tapering ovoid form w/a wide flat mouth above a molded band of poppy blossoms & four wide buttress panels down the sides, minor chips & nicks, signed, 13" d., 9 3/4" h. **$460**

Pitcher, 11 3/4" h., tankard-type, tall tapering form w/ri spout & D-form handle, overall streaky brown & black glossy glaze & large sprigged-on grapevine & clusters (ILLUS., next page) **$173**

Tall Cylindrical Peters & Reed Pitcher

Peters & Reed Small Landsun Vase

Vase, 18" h., floor-type, tall slightly waisted cylindrical form w/a flaring rim, molded around the top w/large stylized blossoms on slender stems slightly spiraling down the sides, dark green matte glaze w/clay showing through, unsigned **$546**

Pewabic

Mary Chase Perry (Stratton) and Horace J. Caulkins were partners in this Detroit, Michigan, pottery. Established in 1903, Pewabic Pottery evolved from their Revelation Pottery, "Pewabic" meaning "clay with copper color" in the language of Michigan's Chippewa Indians. Caulkins attended to the clay formulas and Mary Perry Stratton was artistic creator of forms & glaze formulas, eventually developing a wide range of colors for her finely textured glazes. The pottery's reputation for fine wares and architectural tiles enabled it to survive the Depression years of the 1930s. After Caulkins died in 1923, Mrs. Stratton continued to be active in the pottery until her death, at age 94, in 1961. Her contributions to the art pottery field are numerous.

Tall Footed Peters & Reed Pitcher

Pitcher, 13 1/2" h., tankard-type, footed body w/swelled base band below the tall cylindrical sides ending in a scalloped rim w/a high arched spout, pierced C-scroll handle, streaky dark brown & black glossy glaze trimmed w/sprigged-on grape clusters & grapevine (ILLUS.) **$219**

Vase, 5" h., Landsun Line, flared foot & widely flaring trumpet-form body, decorated w/a band of upright swirled & pointed dark brown leaf-like devices around the bottom overlapping a band of transparent brown leaves over a dark green & yellow ground, unmarked, some small base chips (ILLUS., top next column) **$81**

Vase, 12" h., Landsun line, tall slender cylindrical body w/a flared base, streaky pale green, brown & blue banded glaze, ca. 1922, light crazing.................................... **$115**

Pewabic Pottery Mark

Small Blue Pewabic Bowl

Bowl, 3" d., small round foot supporting the deep wide bell-formed bowl, a medium blue glaze applied over an iridescent yellowish green glossy glaze, round logo, some areas of thin glaze near the rim (ILLUS.) **$374**

Pewabic Commemorative Paperweight

Paperweight, round disk-type, presentation-type, the center carved w/a city skyline along a lake incised "Detroit" in shades of dark iridescent bluish green & brown, the outer brown border band incised "GFWC - 1935," 3" d. (ILLUS.) **$173**

Pewabic Paperweight with Fish

Paperweight, square tile-form, incised w/a large light brown fish against a mottled blue & green ground, circular seal mark, 2 3/4" w. (ILLUS.) **$58**

Rare Pewabic Plate with Rabbits

Plate, dinner, 9 1/4" d., a crackle ivory ground decorated in squeezebag w/a border band w/pairs of facing white rabbits alternating w/a green tree or shrub, outlined in black, stamped company name, few minor glaze nicks (ILLUS.) **$2,875**

Squatty Experimental Pewabic Vase

Vase, experimental-type, a crimped uneven foot below the wide squatty disk-form body tapering sharply to a wide short cylindrical neck, a mottled white neck band above the dark rusty brown drippy glaze covering the sides, oak leaf mark & round paper label, some burst air bubbles & a base chip (ILLUS.) **$431**

Pewabic Stacked Pots-style Vase

Vase, stacked pots-style, composed of three small sharply tapering ovoid pots w/small mouths clustered together & topped in the center by a single matching pot, overall glossy grey glaze, unmarked (ILLUS.) **$138**

Miniature White & Blue Pewabic Vase

Vase, miniature, 2 3/4" h., baluster-form body w/a widely flaring trumpet neck, a drippy white & brown glaze around the neck & shoulder above a very dark blue mottled glaze on the lower body, round company sticker, very minor base grinding (ILLUS.) **$633**

Miniature Pewabic Vase in Drippy Black

Vase, miniature, 3 1/8" h., simple ovoid body w/a short wide neck, a drippy black glaze covering most of the lustrous grey base glaze, impressed round mark, flat chip on base (ILLUS.) **$460**

Small Experimental Pewabic Vase

Vase, miniature, 3 1/8" h., wide ovoid body w/a wide shoulder to the short, wide flat mouth, experimental type w/a drippy dark brown glaze down from the top over a moss green ground, incised mark & round paper label (ILLUS.) **$1,380**

Colorful Mottled Pewabic Vase

Vase, 4 7/8" h., a wide flat base below wide gently flaring short cylindrical sides w/a wide tapering shoulder to a short flat neck, glossy glaze w/mottled cream, brick red & shades of green, unmarked, two chips at the base (ILLUS.) **$374**

Mottled Blue Pewabic Vase

Vase, 6 3/4" h., footed wide ovoid body w/a wide shoulder to the short flaring neck, mottled & swirled iridescent glaze in shades of dark & lighter blue, impressed logo (ILLUS.) **$1,035**

Pewabic Vase with Stylized Flowers

Vase, 7" h., wide cylindrical body w/a tapering rounded shoulder to the wide short cylindrical mouth, glossy glaze h.p. w/a repeating design of clusters of round brick-red stylized flowers on slender leafy stems against a mustard yellow ground, dark bands at the neck & base, round company sticker (ILLUS.) **$1,150**
Vase, 7 1/8" h., footed spherical body w/a short flaring neck, overall dark blue matte glaze w/silvery iridescent patches, impressed twice w/logo (ILLUS., next page) **$690**

Spherical Dark Blue Pewabic Vase

Phoenix Bird & Flying Turkey Porcelain

The phoenix bird, a symbol of immortality and spiritual rebirth, has been handed down through Egyptian mythology as a bird that consumed itself by fire after 500 years and then rose again, renewed, from its ashes. This bird has been used to decorate Japanese porcelain designed for export for more than 100 years. The pattern incorporates a blue design of the bird, variously known as the "Flying Phoenix," the "Flying Turkey" or the "Ho-o," stamped on a white ground. It became popular with collectors because of the abundant supply resulting from the long period of time the ware was produced. Pieces can be found marked with Japanese characters, with a "Nippon" mark, a "Made in Japan" mark or an "Occupied Japan" mark. Although there are several variations to the pattern and border, we have grouped them together since values seem to be quite comparable. Later pieces have more modern shapes than older pieces. A similar design, made by Takahaski, is no longer in production either. The standard reference for this category is Phoenix Bird Chinaware *by Joan Collett Oates.*

Berry server, style "B," w/seven drain holes, 6" d.	$145
Bouillon cup & saucer, cov.	$45
Butter pat	$15
Cann, w/handle, straight sides	$25
Casserole, style #1, small oval	$75
Celery, style #1, 13 1/2" l.	$125
Cheese & cracker plate, tiered, style A	$135
Chocolate pot, style #1, 8 3/4" h., 5 1/4" d.	$125
Chocolate pot, style #2, scalloped body & base	$140
Chocolate set: style #1 pot w/five demi cups & saucers; the set	$150
Coffeepot, cov., style No. 1	$65
Coffeepot, cov., style No. 6	$75
Condensed milk jar, cov., style No. 1	$85
Cracker jar, cov., style No. 3	$165
Cup & saucer	$7
Espresso cup & saucer	$15
Gravy boat, style No. 6	$55
Gravy boat and underplate, style No. 6, the set	$75

Hot water pot cov., style No. 4	$55
Ice cream dish, w/inverted scallops, 7" l.	$55
Lemonade glass, w/flared top	$45
Lemonade pitcher	$145
Mustard jar, cover & attached underplate, style No. 12, the set	$55
Pancake, cov., w/two steam holes	$135
Plate, 7 1/4" d.	$7
Plate, 8 1/2" d., luncheon	$15
Platter, 12" l., oval, scalloped edge	$65
Platter, 16 1/8" l., scalloped rim	$95
Ramekin, style "A"	$22
Ramekin, style "B"	$18
Reamer, two-piece	$195
Relish, style No. 12, double handles, 10" l.	$145
Rice tureen, style No. 3-A	$75
Salt dip, style No. 3, three round feet (Book IV)	$18
Sauce boat with handle, spout & underplate, style No. 2,	$65
Syrup, cov., style No.12	$65
Syrup, cov., style No. 13	$55

Modern Phoenix (T-Bird) Teapot

Teapot, cov., Modern Phoenix (T-Bird) patt., upright square body w/angled spout, flat cover w/loop handle, swing bail bamboo handle, marked w/a small square & seven Japanese characters, post-1970, 6" l., 6 3/4" h. (ILLUS.) $30

Phoenix Bird Teapot Found in Three Sizes

Teapot, cov., Phoenix Bird patt., bulbous body w/a narrow shoulder & wide flat rim, long serpentine spout & angled D-form handle, low domed cover w/knob finial, marked "Made in Japan" within a double circle, largest of three sizes, 8" l., 5 1/2" h. (ILLUS.) $35

Rattan-handled Phoenix Bird Teapot

Teapot, cov., Phoenix Bird patt., bulbous body w/a serpentine spout, overhead woven rattan swing bail handle (ILLUS.) **$35-55**

Phoenix Bird Wicker-handled Teapot

Teapot, cov., Phoenix Bird patt., bulbous body w/serpentine spout & domed cover w/knob finial, overhead swing bail handle of blue bands of wicker woven w/uncolored wicker, marked w/six Japanese characters, ca. 1920s-30s, 5 1/4" h. (ILLUS. with liner) **$45**

Large Modern Phoenix Bird Teapot

Teapot, cov., Phoenix Bird patt., bulbous nearly spherical body w/a flat rim, upright serpentine spout, woven wicker swing bail handle, w/original liner, extra large size, marked "Made in Japan" in a black square, post-1970, 8" l., 5 5/8" h. (ILLUS.) **$45**

English Phoenix Bird Pattern Teapot

Teapot, cov., Phoenix Bird patt., earthenware, bulbous tapering paneled body w/a flared rim, pointed angled handle, long serpentine spout, pyramidal cover w/square pointed finial, marked w/a crown above "Myott Son & Co. - England - Satsuma," ca. 1930s, 8 3/8" l., 5 3/4" h. (ILLUS.) **$65**

Extra Large Phoenix Bird Teapot

Teapot, cov., Phoenix Bird patt., extra large nearly spherical body w/upright serpentine spout & a D-form handle molded to resemble bamboo, originally came w/a liner, unmarked, ca. 1920s-30s, 9 1/2" l., 5 3/4" h. (ILLUS.) **$35**

Bulbous Phoenix Bird Pattern Teapot

Teapot, cov., Phoenix Bird patt., footed bulbous body w/a serpentine spout & heavy ring handle w/small thumbrest, low domed cover w/knob finial, marked "Made in Japan," ca. 1920s-30s, 7 1/2" l., 4 1/2" h. (ILLUS., previous page) **$30**

Extra Large Phoenix Bird Teapot

Teapot, cov., Phoenix Bird patt., footed bulbous lower body & wide tapering shoulder w/a non-traditional design, long serpentine spout, angled handle w/small thumbrest, inset tapering cover w/knob finial, marked w/an "S" enclosed in a bulb above "Made in Japan," ca. 1920s-30s, extra large size, 10" l., 6 1/2" h. (ILLUS.) **$70**

Delicate, Quality Phoenix Bird Teapot

Teapot, cov., Phoenix Bird patt., scalloped round foot supporting the wide squatty bulbous body w/a short spout & large ring handle, inset cover w/squared loop handle, delicate & fine quality, unmarked, ca. 1920s-30s, 7 3/4" l., 4 3/8" h. (ILLUS.) **$55**

Phoenix Bird HO-O Border Teapot

Teapot, cov., Phoenix Bird patt., squatty bulbous body w/low domed cover & knob finial, ring handle & short spout, w/HO-O

heart-like variant border design, unmarked, 7 1/2" l., 4 3/4" h. (ILLUS.) **$45-50**

Phoenix Bird Teapot with Less Vinework

Teapot, cov., Phoenix Bird patt., squatty bulbous body w/low domed cover & knob finial, long serpentine spout, C-form handle, less vinework in the background design, originally came w/a strainer, unmarked, 7 3/4" l., 5" h. (ILLUS.) **$35-45**

Wicker-handled Phoenix Bird Teapot

Teapot, cov., Phoenix Bird patt., squatty bulbous body w/serpentine spout, early overhead swing bail handle in woven wicker, marked w/three small triangles, each enclosing a Japanese character w/three additional characters below, originally came w/strainer, 6 3/4" l., 5" h. (ILLUS.) **$45-55**

Phoenix Bird Stack-set Teapot

Two Upright Waisted Phoenix Bird Teapots

Teapot, cov., Phoenix Bird patt., stack-set, squatty bulbous pot w/a long serpentine spout & C-form handle, stacked top w/a creamer topped by a cov. sugar, mark of a small flower w/a "T" inside & "Japan," ca. 1920s-30s, overall 5 3/4" h. (ILLUS., previous page) **$65**

Teapot, cov., Phoenix Bird patt., tall tapering waisted body w/upright shaped spout & pointed loop handle, low domed cover w/button finial, marked w/a four-petaled flower on stem & "Japan," ca. 1920s-30s, 6 3/4" l., 5 1/2" h. (ILLUS. left with matching smaller teapot) **$35**

Teapot, cov., Phoenix Bird patt., tall tapering waisted body w/upright shaped spout & pointed loop handle, low domed cover w/button finial, marked w/a four-petaled flower on stem & "Japan," ca. 1920s-30s, 6 1/4" l., 4 1/4" h. (ILLUS. right with matching larger teapot, top of page) **$40**

Phoenix Bird with Circle-Border K Teapot

Teapot, cov., Phoenix Bird patt. w/Circle-Border K, bulbous body w/a flat rim, serpentine spout, C-form handle, domed cover w/knob finial, unmarked, originally came w/strainer, ca. 1920s-30s, 8 1/4" l., 6 3/4" h. (ILLUS.) **$40**

Finely Decorated Phoenix Bird Teapot

Teapot, cov., Phoenix Bird patt., tapering waisted cylindrical body w/upright serpentine spout & high loop handle, low domed cover w/small loop finial, fine overall decoration, marked w/three Japanese characters above "Japan," ca. 1920s-30s, overall 7" l., 5 1/8" h. (ILLUS.) **$65**

"M in Wreath" Marked Teapot

Teapot, cov., Phoenix Bird patt., wide squatty bulbous body w/serpentine spout & D-form handle, low domed cover w/knob finial, "M in Wreath" Morimura Bros. mark & "Japan," ca. 1930s, 7 3/8" l., 3 3/4" h. (ILLUS.) **$20**

Pisgah Forest Pottery

Walter Stephen experimented with making pottery with his parents in Tennessee shortly after 1900 . After their deaths in 1910, he eventually moved to the foot of Mt. Pisgah in North Carolina, where he became a partner of C.P. Ryman. Together they built a kiln and a shop, but this partnership was dissolved in 1916. During 1920 Stephen again began to experiment with pottery, and by 1926 he had his own pottery and equipment. Pieces are usually marked and may also be signed "W. Stephen" and dated. Walter Stephen died in 1961, but work at the pottery continues, although on a part-time basis.

Pisgah Forest Marks

Bowl-vase, wide, spherical body w/the wide, round shoulder centered by a short cylindrical neck, amber glaze w/white & blue crystals, raised Stephen mark, dated 1947, 5 3/4" d., 5" h.............................. **$385**

Pisgah Forest Crackled Glaze Jug

Jug, ovoid body tapering to a very small mouth & strap shoulder handle, dark purplish brown crackled glaze, glaze bursts, marked & dated 1934, 6 1/2" d., 10" h. (ILLUS.)... **$264**
Teapot, cov., spherical form w/inset cover w/button finial, short, cylindrical spout & D-form shoulder handle, fine Chinese blue glaze w/red, green & blue highlights, raised mark, 8" w. **$231**
Vase, 12 1/4" h., 8" d., Cameo Ware, wide bulbous baluster form w/a wide cylindrical neck flanked by arched shoulder handles, dark blue upper half w/white relief design of the twelve signs of the Zodiac around a center band, lighter blue lower half, potter mark & 1931 date, special gift order (ILLUS., top next column).... **$1,500-2,500**
Vase, 4" h., 5 1/2" d., wide, squatty, bulbous body w/the shoulder sloping to a low,

molded, wide mouth, overall streaky white & blue crystalline exterior glaze, raised potter's mark, 1948 .... **$605**

Rare Pisgah Forest Cameo Ware Vase

Vase, 4 1/2" h., 6" d., wide, bulbous form w/a wide, short, flat neck, overall white crystalline exterior glaze, raised potter's mark, 1942.. **$330**
Vase, 5" h., 4 3/4" d., wide, squatty, bulbous lower body tapering to a cylindrical neck w/rolled rim, white & amber glaze w/blue crystals, raised potter mark, dated 1940.... **$358**
Vase, 6 1/2" h., 4" d., simple baluster form w/a short, wide, flaring neck, fine amber glaze w/tightly packed white & dark blue crystals, raised potter mark, dated 1940 ... **$660**

Pisgah Pottery Vase with Mottled Glaze

Vase, 6 1/2" h., 4 1/2" d., ovoid body w/a short, wide flared neck, overall mottled purple & turquoise semi-matte glaze, raised potter mark & dated 1931 (ILLUS.).. **$499**
Vase, 6 1/2" h., 4 1/2" d., tall, deeply corseted form w/a wide, flaring mouth, amber glaze w/grey crystals, raised potter mark & illegible date.. **$413**
Vase, 7" h., 4" d., ovoid body tapering to a cylindrical neck, brown & amber flambé glaze w/clusters of large blue crystals, grinding chip at base, embossed mark **$605**
Vase, 7 1/2" h., 4 3/4" d., baluster form tapering to a short, wide, rolled neck, amber flambé glaze w/a few blue crystals,

raised Pisgah Forest mark & illegible
date $523

Trumpet-form Pisgah Forest Vase

Vase, 7 3/4" h., trumpet-form, fine blue & white crystalline glaze on the exterior, pink interior, impressed mark (ILLUS.)....... $460
Vase, 7 3/4" h., 4 1/4" d., baluster form w/flared neck, overall streaky blue, green & white crystalline glaze, raised potter's mark, 1949 .... $495
Vase, 7 3/4" h., 4 3/4" d., wide baluster-form body tapering to a short, wide, flaring neck, amber glaze w/white & blue large crystals around the lower half, raised Stephen mark, dated 1949 .... $770
Vase, 8" h., 5 1/4" d., wide bottle form w/bulbous, tapering body below a tall, waisted, cylindrical neck, overall white glaze w/white crystals, raised potter mark & dated 1941 .... $715

Purinton

The Purinton Pottery Company was founded in Shippenville, Pennsylvania, in 1941 by Bernard S. Purinton. Earlier, beginning in 1936, Mr. Purinton started a smaller pottery operation in Wellsville, Ohio, but by 1941, wanting to expand, he chose the site near Shippenville, where a large, new plant was constructed.

Most of Purinton's products were cast and then hand-painted with a variety of colorful patterns by local people trained at the factory. One of its best known and most popular designs was Peasant Ware, originally introduced at the Wellsville plant in the 1930s. Until the plant was finally closed in 1959, the company continued to produce a colorful, hand-decorated range of tablewares, kitchenwares, vases and novelty items.

Basket planter, Palm Tree, no cutout, 6 1/4" h.. $299
Beer mug, Palm Tree, purple intaglio, 16 oz., 4 3/4" h. $380
Butter dish, tab handle, 6 1/2" l. $80
Candy dish, w/loop handle $65
Carafe, Cactus Flower, two-handled, 7 1/2" h. $264
Children's cereal bowl, w/puppy, 5 1/4" d. $179
Chop plate, Crescent, footed, 12" d. $249

Chop plate, Fruits Blessing, signed by Dorothy Purinton, footed, some for meat, 12" d. (one chip)..................................... $501
Coffee carafe, Autumn Leaves...................... $39
Coffee mug, 12 oz.. $80
Coffee server, TST shaped, w/lid, 10 1/2" $555
Coffeepot, cov., eight-cup $75
Cookie jar, rooster.. $335
Diamond grill platter, oblong, 12" l............... $46
Dinner plate, signed by Dorothy Purinton, w/cabin & trees, 9 3/4" d. $1,031
Dutch jug, w/ice lip, Cactus, 2 pint $362
Dutch jug, w/ice lip, Red Ribbon Flower, 2 pint.. $1,226
Honey jug, Holly, loop handle, 6 1/4" h. $480
Honey jug, Palm Tree, loop handle, 6 1/4" h.. $130
Honey jug, Pear, loop handle, 6 1/4" h......... $155
Jam/jelly, tab handle.................................... $54
Oil & vinegar cruet set, tall, 9 1/2" h. $125
Pig bank, blue.. $19
Planter, Napco, Yellow Intaglio, rectangular, 6" l... $23
Rebecca jug, Starflower, 7 1/2" h. $255
Roll tray, oblong $50
Rum jug planter, 6 1/2" h. $61
Salt & pepper set, Old Salt & wife.............. $85
Salt & pepper set, shake-n-pour type, bulbous, 4 1/2" h. $71
Spaghetti bowl, 14 1/5" d............................ $205
Sprinkler, w/red tulips, 5 1/2" h. $114
Sugar/creamer set, Cactus Flower (sugar some damage).. $238
Tumblers, 12 oz... $20
Winged grease jar $96

Brown Intaglio
Beanpot, individual $46
Beverage pitcher, 42 oz., 6 1/4" h. $59
Candleholder, round, 5" d., 2 1/2" h............. $90
Candy dish, w/loop handle $37
Canister set, apartment size $128
Coffeepot, cov., 8 cup $26
Cookie jar, cov., wide oval, 9 1/2" $50
Decanter $30
Dutch jug, w/ice lip, 5 pint,.......................... $60
Range grease jar, cov., oval $47
Range grease & salt & pepper set $60
Spaghetti bowl, 14 1/2" d............................. $72
Tumbler, 12 oz... $38

Chartreuse
Cup & saucer $14
Range salt & pepper shakers, 4" h............. $128
Rum jug, loop handle, cutouts...................... $136

Fruit
Cookie jar, cov., wide oval, 9 1/2" $51
Flour canister, cov., round, wood lid, 8" h. $89
Oil & vinegar set, conical shaped $77
Sugar canister, cov., round, wood lid, 8" h. $50
Tea 'n' toast plate, Wellsville Pear, 8 1/2" d... $18

Heather
Kent jug, bulbous body, 4 1/2" h. $45
Pickle dish, 6" l.. $20

Maywood
Casserole, cov., 9" l..................................... $30
Cereal bowl, 5 1/2" d.................................... $13

Jam/jelly, tab handle $53
Wallpocket, 3 1/2" h. (small hairline) $105

Ming Tree
Cereal bowl, 5 1/4" d. $43
Chop plate, footed, 12" d. $250
Fruit bowl, footed, 12" d. $230

Mountain Rose
Kent jug $32
Meat platter, oblong, 12" $179
Sugar/creamer set, 4-petal $74

Normandy
Candy dish, w/loop handle $52
Casserole, cov., 9" l. $36
Fruit bowl, footed, 12" d. $41
Mini jug salt & pepper set, 2 1/5" h. $18
Winged vase, bulbous, 6" h. $25

Other Intaglios
Chop plate, turquoise, footed, 12" d. $125
Dinner plate, turquoise, 9 3/4" d. $24
Salt & pepper set, turquoise, stacking-type,
2 1/4" h. $43

Peasant Garden
Grill platter, oblong, 12" l. $257
Roll tray, oblong $61

Pennsylvania Dutch
Chop plate, footed, 12" d. $130
Dutch jug, 5 pint, ice lip $511
Meat platter, oblong, 12" $46
Mini jug salt & pepper set $108
Sandwich tray, w/metal handle, 12" d. $180

Petals
Juice mug, 6 oz. $53
Kent jug, bulbous, 4 1/2" h. $164

Provincial Fruit
Dessert bowl, 4" d. $24
Meat platter, oblong, 12" $150

Red Ivy
Mini sugar, 2" h. $31
Range grease, cov., oval $26
Range salt & pepper, 4" h. $27

Saraband
Beanpot, cov., individual, 3 1/4" h. $44
Dinner plate, 9 1/2" d. $13
Jam/jelly, tab handle $82
Kent jug, bulbous body, 4 1/2" h. $108
Meat platter, oblong, 12" d. $35
Tea 'n' toast, w/cup $19

Seaform
Sugar/creamer set, w/tray, 5" h. $123

Quimper

This French earthenware pottery has been made in France since the end of the 17th century and is still in production today. Because the colorful decoration on this ware, predominantly of Breton peasant figures, is all hand-painted and each piece is unique, it has become increasingly popular with collectors in recent years. Most pieces offered today date from about the mid-19th century to the present. Modern potteries continue

to operate today, with contemporary examples available in gift shops.

The standard reference in this field is Quimper Pottery A French Folk Art Faience by Sandra V. Bondhus (privately printed, 1981).

Quimper Marks

Baby's feeding pitcher, 4 1/2" h., tiny spout, decorated w/only a flower garland band, unsigned, 19th c., excellent $150
Basket, exterior w/raised basketweave design, interior w/image of peasant woman w/flower sprays, "HB Quimper - x364," 8 1/4 x 7", 6" h., mint $325
Bell, bagpipe shape w/original unglazed clapper, "Ivoire Corbeille" patt., bust portrait of man on front, half sunburst w/sponged circlets design on reverse, "HenRiot Quimper 73," 3 1/4" h., mint $75
Book ends, Modern Movement-style girl toddlers hold onto brown sponged wall as they attempt their first steps, both wearing white caps & navy dresses, one w/yellow checked apron, one w/pink checked apron, "HenRiot Quimper 136" & artist "J.E. Sevellec," 5 1/2" h., excellent, pr. $550

Quimper Card Tray

Card tray, rococo amorphous form, "decor riche" patt., center decorated w/pair of Breton musicians surrounded by flower sprays of wild gorse & broom, "HenRiot Quimper 148," 13 x 10 1/2", mint (ILLUS.) .. $350
Charger, w/image of woman in profile holding flower, framed by flower garland band, "HR" mark only, early, 11" d. (slight wear on outer edge) $100
Cigarette box, cov., image of woman w/flower branches on lid, geometric patt. on base, "HenRiot Quimper 116," 4 1/2" l., 3 1/4" w., mint $100

Coffee Set with Music Theme

Cigarette holder/ashtray, figural, yellow-glazed Modern Movement form of woman wearing turquoise polka dotted blouse & red striped apron & holding double baskets w/holes on top for cigarettes, molded indentation on base forming ashtray, "HB Quimper 605," 8 1/2" h., mint **$400**

Coffee set: 9 1/4" h. cov. coffeepot, creamer & cov. sugar; each decorated w/different Breton musician & very richly ornamented "Rouenesque" border, "HB Quimper 15," excellent, the set (ILLUS., top of page) **$525**

Cup & saucer, "croisille" style, the 4" lip-to-handle cup decorated w/image of seated woman in trefoil cartouche w/"tennis ball" latticework trim, 5" d. saucer, "HR Quimper," mint, pr. **$50**

Dish, divided, double bagpipe shape, "decor riche" patt., bow & twisted knot handles, each division featuring peasant couple standing beneath sprigs of Breton wildflowers, 13 1/2" l., 11" w., excellent (ILLUS., next column) **$550**

Dish, fish shape, center w/design of woman wearing the costume of La Rochelle & surrounded by flower branches, "La Rochelle HenRiot Quimper 137," pierced for hanging, 10" l., 4 1/2" w., mint **$85**

Divided Dish

Doll chamber pot, decorated w/floral band on outside & eye painted on bottom of interior, "HenRiot Quimper 115," 2 1/2" l. from lip to handle tip, mint **$35**

Doll dish set: 4" d. cov. tureen, 4" d. charger, 3" l. gravy boat, two 2 3/4" d. plates & two 1 3/4" d. plates; each w/decoration of sailboat on waves, creamy buff glaze & rose pink sponged border, unsigned, attributable to HenRiot, excellent, set of eight (ILLUS., bottom of page) **$125**

Doll's Dish Set

Quimper Inkwell & Plate

Doll plate, red & blue striped pinwheel geometric patt., "HenRiot Quimper France 115," 1 3/4" d., mint (glaze skips) **$35**

Doll plate, Modern Movement colors w/geometric stylized flower patt. in brown, yellow, blue & rose red, "HenRiot Quimper 106," 2 3/4" d., mint **$30**

Egg cup, figural, in the form of a yellowsponged chick w/blue feathers, w/attached 3 1/2" d. underdish, "HB Quimper," mint **$50**

Figure by "Fanch," wearing pantaloons & playing flute, Modern Movement colors, "HenRiot Quimper France 597," 3 1/2" h., mint **$175**

Figure group, Modern Movement bride & groom by artist Fanch, from "Noce Bigoudenne" group, the bride wears white dress & loaf coif painted w/yellow "embroidery" work, the groom a dark navy suit & red tie, "HB Quimper," mint **$200**

Figure group, Modern Movement-style dancing couple posed so woman's flaring skirt shows off decorative trim on hem, "HenRiot Quimper 78" & artist "R. Micheau-Vernez," 12 1/2" h., mint **$450**

Figure of St. Anne w/child Mary, "HenRiot Quimper France 127," 5 1/2" h., mint **$95**

Figure of St. Yves, the patron saint of lawyers wears legal garb of the period, "HenRiot Quimper," 4 3/4" h., mint **$100**

Figure of woman w/cane, Modern Movement-style figure of elderly woman in polka dotted blue shawl & green & orange striped apron leaning on cane, artist "L.H. Nicot" embossed on base, "Henriot Quimper 136," 8" h., mint **$325**

Holy water font, base w/figure of the Christ Child holding a cross in relief, the top adorned w/image of eye of God enclosed within radiant sun & two stars, Modern Movement colors, "HB Quimper 119," 5 1/2" l., mint **$150**

Inkwell, cov., in the form of a Breton hat, w/original inset & lid w/acorn finial, scene on lid of seated woman w/basket of eggs at her side, "HenRiot Quimper France 72," 5 1/2" w., mint (ILLUS. left, w/plate, top of page) **$175**

Inkwell, cov., square w/cut corners, design of peasant man w/flowers & red S-link chain border, w/original inset & lid, "HB Quimper 497," 3 1/2" sq., excellent **$150**

Quimper Inkwell & Pen Tray

Inkwell w/pen tray, cov., oblong, w/four feet & center apron, "demi-fantasie" patt., scene on front of Bretonne woman balancing milk pail on her head surrounded by flowering branches & lattice work, original inset & knobbed lid, "HenRiot Quimper France 99," excellent (ILLUS.) **$275**

Cradle-shaped Jardiniere

Jardiniere, cradle shape on four tiny feet,
double knobs at four upper corners,
w/scene of peasant couple executed in
the "demi-fantasie" style, back panel dis-
playing full-blown red & yellow rose set in
flower branch, "HR Quimper," 7 1/4" l.,
mint (ILLUS., previous page) $675

Quimper Crown-shaped Jardiniere

Jardiniere, crown shape, "decor riche"
patt. w/seated couple facing each other
on front, back w/Crest of Brittany held by
lions, "HenRiot Quimper 23," 11 1/2" l.,
one handle professionally restored
(ILLUS.) $650

Jardiniere with Ropetwist Handles

Jardiniere, octagonal shape w/country
French geometric patt., blue sponged
ropetwist handles, unsigned, 19th c., ex-
cellent, 12" l. (ILLUS.) $300

Handled "Decor Riche" Jardiniere

Jardiniere, oval shape w/cutout rim, short
oval outcurved base, dainty scroll handles, "decor riche" patt., main cartouche
shows seated woman holding a jug, reverse features crowned Crest of Brittany, "HB Quimper," 12 1/2 l., 7" h., mint
(ILLUS.) $500
Jardiniere, oval w/scalloped rim, footed, flat
ring handles, "decor riche" patt., image of
seated musician on front, "HB Quimper
128," 9" l., mint (ILLUS., top next column)
.... $325

Scalloped-rim Jardiniere

Knife rest, figural, Modern Movement-style
form of reclining woman w/her head on
her hands & her elbows extended, "Hen-
Riot Quimper" and mark of artist C. Mail-
lard, 4" l., mint $100
Knife rests, tricorner shape, each decorat-
ed w/images of peasant figure & flower
branches, HB Quimper "xo" mark, excel-
lent overall, 3" l., six pcs. $100

"Ivoire Corbeille" Liqueur Set

Liqueur set: barrel keg w/original wooden
spigot, wooden stand & six original small
handled cups; "Ivoire Corbeille" patt.
w/bust portrait of woman in profile on side
of keg, "HenRiot Quimper," mint, the set
(ILLUS.).. $150

Quimper Liquor Set

Liquor set: 7" d. tray, 6" h. cov. decanter &
four 1" h. handleless cups; figure of traditional peasant woman adorning decanter, a bold daisy patt. covering the
tray, each cup w/flower spray on front,

"Decor Riche" Pattern Plates

"HenRiot Quimper France 75," mint, the set (ILLUS.) **$175**
Match holder, wall-mounted type, pocket features image of peasant woman w/flowers, back panel has lattice & dot geometric design, "HR Quimper," 3 x 2 1/2", mint **$150**
Model of swan, figure of seated peasant lad holding pipe is depicted on swan's breast, "HenRiot Quimper France 89," 4" h., 4 3/4" l., mint **$120**

Artist-signed Flower Holder

Pique fleurs (flower holder), figural, Modern Movement-style image of a kneeling Bigoudenne lifting a basket of flowers, the basket w/holes for flower stems, "HenRiot Quimper" and signature of artist C.H. Maillard on base, 8" h., 9" l., mint (ILLUS.) **$750**
Pitcher, 2 1/2" h., child-size, decorated w/image of Breton man & flowers, "Made in France 12" beneath handle, "HenRiot," mint **$65**
Pitcher, 3" h., Odetta gresware w/concentric double diamond patt. in white & rich brown on navy blue/cobalt ground, "HB Quimper Odetta 494," mint (ILLUS. top right, w/other Odetta pitchers, top next column) **$150**
Pitcher, 3 3/4" h., Odetta gresware w/concentric double diamond patt. in white & rich brown on navy blue/cobalt ground, "HB Quimper Odetta 424," mint (ILLUS.

bottom right, w/other Odetta pitchers, top next column) **$150**
Pitcher, 6" h., decorated w/scene of Breton man & flowers, concentric bands of yellow & blue on border, "HenRiot Quimper France 115," mint **$65**

Odetta Gresware Pitchers

Pitcher, 9 1/2" h., Odetta gresware w/a rich deep chocolate brown glaze over a light tan matte glaze "biscuit," bold geometric patt., "HB Quimper Odetta 423-1081+," mint (ILLUS. left, w/other Odetta pitchers) **$300**
Plate, 6" d., w/pie crust rim, center shows woman standing in profile w/one hand tucked into apron pocket, flower garland border w/blue sponged edges, "HenRiot Quimper France 72," mint (ILLUS. right, w/inkwell) **$150**
Plate, 8 3/4" d., "decor riche" patt. w/unusual scene of a Breton knight, Bertrand Duguesclin, "HR Quimper," mint (ILLUS. right, w/peasant plate, top of page) **$525**
Plate, 9" d., yellow glaze w/row of French houses w/a fountain in front & trees on either side of homes, clouds in sky, "HB Quimper France 176," mint **$75**
Plate, 9 1/2" d., "decor riche" patt. w/scalloped border & pair of nicely detailed peasant folk, "HR Quimper," mint (ILLUS. left, w/Breton knight plate, top of page) **$350**

Pair of Matched Plates

Plate in "Botanique" Pattern

Plate, 9 1/2" d., First Period Porquier Beau, "Botanique" patt., decorated w/spray of yellow narcissus & snail, signed w/intersecting "PB" mark in blue, mint (ILLUS.) **$1,150**

First Period Porquier Beau Plate

Plate, 9 1/2" d., First Period Porquier Beau, entitled "Ramasseur de goemon-Guisseny," scene of fisherman on shoreline

holding a pike, w/Crest of Brittany above him in acanthus border, signed w/intersecting "PB" and name of scene, mint (ILLUS.) **$1,250**

Plate, 9 3/4" d., "Broderie Bretonne" geometric patt., ten-pointed star on metallic gold background glaze, intricate raised-to-the-touch heart-shaped patterns in border, "HB Quimper P.F. 163 D 708," mint **$100**

Plates, 7 1/2" d., pale blue sponged ruffled rims, center display of seated peasant man on one, seated peasant woman on other, "HB" mark only, 19th c., mint, pr. (ILLUS., top of page) **$300**

Plates, 8 1/2" d., "demi-fantasie" patt., w/different Breton peasant on each, marked w/"HenRiot Quimper France" and various two-digit numbers, mint, set of 5, each (ILLUS., top next page) **$100**

Platter with Courting Scene

Platter, 12" l., 8 1/2" w., oval, "decor riche" patt., center showing courting scene of young Breton couple seated beneath canopy of trees, "HB Quimper," excellent (ILLUS.) **$550**

Platter, 13" l., 10" w., rectangular w/cut corners, decorated w/image of open basket w/bouquet of flowers, corners w/black ermine tails, "HenRiot Quimper France," excellent **$150**

Set of Five Peasant Plates

Oval Platter with Peasant Couple

Platter, 14 1/2" l., 11" w., oval, scene of peasant couple & "a la touche" flower garland band, "HB" mark only, 19th c., mint (ILLUS.) **$175**

"Croisille" Pattern Platter

Platter, 15" l., 10" w., ovoid, in the "croisille" style w/alternating panels of stylized dogwood blossom, finely detailed couple posed in conversation in the center, "HenRiot Quimper France 162," mint (ILLUS.) **$450**

Wedding Procession Platter

Platter, 19" l., 8 1/2" w., oblong shape in Modern Movement Celtic style, center depicting wedding procession walking on path from building in distance, "HenRiot Quimper 72," pierced for hanging, mint (ILLUS.) **$425**

"Ivoire Corbeille" Fish Platter

Platter, 20 3/4" l., 10" w., oval fish platter, "Ivoire Corbeille" patt. w/portrait busts of young Breton couple framed w/Celtic motifs, "HenRiot Quimper," pierced for hanging, mint (ILLUS.) **$300**

Porringer, traditional decoration of peasant woman & flowers, blue sponged tab handles, "HenRiot Quimper France," 5 1/2" handle to handle, mint.................................. **$25**

Salt, open oval w/yellow glaze & flower sprig patt. on sides, "HenRiot Quimper," 2" l., mint **$25**

Salt, pepper & mustard set, "Ivoire Corbeille" patt. "menagere," acorn-shaped mustard pot w/figural twig handle & tiny acorn on lid & bust portrait of young peasant girl on the side, salt & pepper are attached open compartments w/twig feet, "HenRiot Quimper," 5 1/2" l., 5" h., mint..... **$100**

Tea set: 7" h. cov. teapot, creamer, five cups & six saucers; traditional peasant patt., decorative scalloped borders, "HR Quimper," excellent (ILLUS., middle of page)... **$750**

Scalloped Tea Set

Elaborate Henriot Quimper "Decor Riche" Tea Set

HR Quimper Tea Set with Lobed Bodies

Tea set: cov. teapot, cov. sugar bowl, creamer & six cups & saucers; Rococo Louis XV-style swirl-molded bodies, all decorated in the "decor riche" patt., each piece w/a color portrait of a Breton peasant w/two musicians on the teapot, dark blue leafy scroll border bands, mark of HenRiot, Quimper, designed by artist LeBorgne, mint except for one glaze fleck on one cup handle, early 20th c., the set (ILLUS., bottom of previous page) **$2,800**

Tea set: cov. teapot, creamer, five cups & saucers & an extra saucer; each piece w/a lobed body, each painted w/a figure of a Breton peasant woman or man, stylized floral wreath borders in dark blue, orange & green, ornate blue C-scroll handle on the teapot, mark of HR Quimper, France, early 20th c., teapot 7" h., the set (ILLUS., top of page) **$550**

Tobacco jar, cov., figural, Modern Movement style, in the form of a Bretonne woman w/Quimper coif & "embroidery" detailing on blouse & sleeves, the top lifting off at elbow level, by Andre Galland, "HenRiot Quimper A.G. 161," 7" h., mint.... **$400**

Tray, pyrographic wooden tray by Paul Fouillen, w/scene depicting interior of cottage where woman serves meal from Quimper cov. tureen, "Fouillen" signature on front & his trademark logo on back, excellent painting w/vibrant colors, 7 1/4 x 14 3/4" **$325**

Tray, yellow glaze w/multicolor ropetwist handles, center featuring a pitcher-toting woman wearing the headdress of Cherbourg flanked by floral designs, HenRiot made-on-commission example, signed only "Cherbourg," 12 x 8", mint (ILLUS.) ... **$175**

Tumbler/beaker, w/traditional design of Breton woman & flowers, "HenRiot Quimper France 124," 4 1/2" h., mint.......... **$65**

Tureen w/attached underplate, cov., oval shape, the lid decorated w/image of peasant woman w/flower sprays & seashell finial, sides adorned w/garlands of flowers, "HenRiot Quimper France 101," 6" l., 4" h., excellent **$200**

Vase, 3 1/2" h., 5 1/2" w., fan shape, front decorated w/image of peasant man flanked by flower branches, back w/flower sprig & four blue dots, feet are molded butterflies sponged in blue, "HenRiot Quimper," mint **$150**

Vase, 7 1/2" h., 9" w., Modern Movement style, bust portrait of Breton man framed in triangular cartouche on front, the reverse w/stone church w/trees & grassy slope, "Quimper" in blue on base, artist "P. Fouillen" signature beside figure of the man, mint **$400**

Tray with Ropetwist Handles

"Broderie Bretonne" Vase

Vase, 8 1/2" h., cylindrical form tapering in at top & in to short base, "Broderie Bretonne" patt., w/scene of standing peasants, a woman knitting, a man smoking a pipe, raised-to-the-touch Breton embroidery work on the sides, "HB Quimper," mint (ILLUS., previous page) **$350**

"Decor Riche" Double Vase

Vase, 9" h., "Decor Riche," donut shape divided at top center w/separate openings on each side of division, four short outcurved feet, "decor riche" patt., decorated w/cartouches featuring woman holding basket & man playing flute flanking one w/view of the city of Quimper reflected in the Odet River, reverse side decorated w/multicolor flower garland, dragon-like side handles, mint (ILLUS.) **$1,800**

Quimper "Demi-fantasie" Vase

Vase, 15" h., slightly ovoid cylindrical body, flaring to narrow neck w/outcurved rim, side loop handles, "demi-fantasie" patt., portly man smokes pipe on front panel, reverse shows bold double daisy w/wheat flower spray, "HenRiot Quimper France 73," mint (ILLUS.) **$300**

Vases, 6" h., matched pair, bagpipe shape, "Demi-fantasie" patt., decorated w/images of man playing horn & woman holding distaff of flax, "HR Quimper," excellent, pr. **$375**

Wall pocket, bagpipe shape w/double blue bows, decorated w/image of peasant man holding walking stick & posed in an open field, "HB Quimper" beneath figure, 5 1/2" l., mint **$100**

R.S. Prussia & Related Wares

Ornately decorated china marked "R.S. Prussia" and "R.S. Germany" continues to grow in popularity. According to the Third Series of Mary Frank Gaston's Encyclopedia of R.S. Prussia (Collector Books, Paducah, Kentucky), these marks were used by the Reinhold Schlegelmilch porcelain factories located in Suhl in the Germanic regions known as "Prussia" prior to World War I, and in Tillowitz, Silesia, which became part of Poland after World War II. Other marks sought by collectors include "R.S. Suhl," "R.S." steeple or church marks, and "R.S. Poland."

The Suhl factory was founded by Reinhold Schlegelmilch in 1869 and closed in 1917. The Tillowitz factory was established in 1895 by Erhard Schlegelmilch, Reinhold's son. This china customarily bears the phrase "R.S. Germany" and "R.S. Tillowitz." The Tillowitz factory closed in 1945, but it was reopened for a few years under Polish administration.

Prices are high and collectors should beware of the forgeries that sometimes find their way onto the market. Mold names and numbers are taken from Mary Frank Gaston's books on R.S. Prussia.

The "Prussia" and "R.S. Suhl" marks have been reproduced, so buy with care. Later copies of these marks are well done, but quality of porcelain is inferior to the production in the 1890-1920 era.

Collectors are also interested in the porcelain products made by the Erdmann Schlegelmilch factory. This factory was founded by three brothers in Suhl in 1861. They named the factory in honor of their father, Erdmann Schlegelmilch. A variety of marks incorporating the "E.S." initials were used. The factory closed circa 1935. The Erdmann Schlegelmilch factory was an earlier and entirely separate business from the Reinhold Schlegelmilch factory. The two were not related to each other.

R.S. Prussia & Related Marks

R.S. Germany

Berry set: 9" master bowl & six matching 5 1/2" sauce dishes, Iris mold, decorated w/large red roses, 7 pcs. **$500-550**

Bowl, 8" h., handled, decorated w/scene of two colorful parrots, green highlights .. **$275-325**

Bowl, 10" d., decorated w/wild roses, raspberries & blueberries, glossy glaze **$125-175**

Bowl, 10 1/2", handled, Lebrun portrait, Tiffany finish, artist's palette, paintbrush **$1,800-2,000**

Bowl, large, Lettuce mold, floral decoration. lustre finish **$300-350**

R.S. Germany Cake Plate

Cake plate, double-pierced small gold side handles, decorated w/a scene of a maiden near a cottage at the edge of a dark forest, 10" d. (ILLUS.) **$275-325**

Coffeepot, cov., demitasse, Ribbon & Jewel mold, rose garland decoration **$400-450**

Creamer, Mold 640, decorated w/roses, gold trim on ruffled rim & ornate handle .. **$35-50**

R.S. Germany Cup & Saucer

Cup & saucer, decorated w/blue, black & white bands on beige lustre ground, cup w/center silhouette of Art Deco woman in blue dancing w/blue scarf, cup 3 1/2" d., 2 1/4" h., saucer 5 3/4" d. (ILLUS.) **$100-150**

Cup & saucer, demitasse, ornate handle, eight-footed **$75-100**

Gravy boat w/underplate, poppy decoration **$75-100**

Mustard jar, cov., calla lily decoration **$65-100**

Pitcher, 9" h., Mold 343, floral decoration w/overall gilt tracery on cobalt blue (red castle mark) **$700-800**

Plate, 7 1/4" d., poppy decoration **$30-50**

Plate, 8" d., decorated w/scene of colorful parrots, gold rim **$250-300**

Salad set, 10 1/2" d. lettuce bowl & six 8" d. matching plates, Mold 12, Iris decoration on pearl lustre finish, 7 pcs. **$300-350**

Toothpick holder, two-handled, decorated w/roses & gold trim, artist-signed **$75-125**

Tray, handled, decorated w/large white & green poppies, 15 1/4" l. **$275-300**

R.S. Prussia

Bell, tall trumpet-form ruffled body w/twig handle, decorated w/small purple flowers & green leaves on white ground, unmarked, 3 1/2" l. **$300-350**

Berry set: 11" d. master bowl & five 4" d. sauce dishes; Mold 155, each decorated w/a Sheepherder landscape scene w/cottage & flowering trees & shrubs, the set (ILLUS., top of next page) **$1,250-1,650**

Berry set: master bowl & six sauce dishes; five-lobed, floral relief rim w/forget-me-nots & water lilies decoration, artist-signed, 7 pcs. **$400-450**

Berry set: master bowl & six sauce dishes; Ribbon & Jewel mold (Mold 18) w/Melon Eaters decoration, 7 pcs. (ILLUS., middle next page) **$3,500-3,800**

Bowl, 7" d., decorated w/roses, satin finish **$150-200**

Bowl, 9 3/4" d., Iris variant mold, rosette center & pale green floral decoration .. **$250-300**

Bowl, 10" d., floral decoration in black & gold **$150-175**

Bowl, 10" d., Iris mold, Spring Season portrait decoration **$2,400-2,600**

Bowl, 10" d., Mold 202, gold beaded rim, double swans center scene in shades of beige & white, unmarked **$200-225**

Summer Season Portrait Bowl

Bowl, 10" d., Mold 85, Summer Season portrait w/mill scene in background (ILLUS.) **$2,200-2,600**

Sheepherder Prussia Berry Set

Ribbon & Jewel Melon Eaters Berry Set

Bowl, 10 1/4" d., center decoration of pink roses w/pearlized finish, border in shades of lavender & blue w/satin finish, lavish gold trim (unlisted mold)............ **$400-450**

Bowl, 10 1/4" d., Mold 251, apple blossom decoration, satin finish **$250-300**

Bowl, 10 1/2" d., Countess Potocka portrait decoration, heavy gold trim.......... **$4,000-4,300**

Bowl, 10 1/2" d., decorated w/pink roses & carnations on white shaded to peach ground, iridescent Tiffany finish **$595**

Bowl, 10 1/2" d., decorated w/scene of Dice Throwers, red trim........................... **$900-1,200**

Bowl, 10 1/2" d., handled, four-lobed, decorated w/Art Nouveau relief-molded scrolls & colorful sprays on shaded green ground... **$200-250**

Bowl, 10 1/2" d., Iris mold, poppy decoration **$350-400**

Bowl, 10 1/2" d., Mold 101, Tiffany finish around rim, orchid & cream trim on molded border blossoms, central bouquet of

pink, yellow & white roses w/green leaves **$250-300**

Ornate Mold 211 Bowl with Roses

Bowl, 10 1/2" d., Mold 211, deeply fluted scalloped border, decorated w/large roses

in pink, white & yellow, shadow flowers & blue trim around border (ILLUS.) **$250-300**
Bowl, 10 1/2" d., Point & Clover mold (Mold 82), decorated w/forget-me-nots & roses, satin finish, artist-signed **$300-350**
Bowl, 10 1/2" d., Point & Clover mold (Mold 82), decorated w/pink roses & green leaves w/shadow flowers & a Tiffany finish **$250-300**

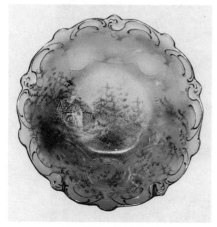

Rare "Tapestry" Bowl

Bowl, 10 3/4" d., Mold 217, "tapestry" center mill scene, gilt scroll border (ILLUS.) **$1,100-1,400**
Bowl, 11" d., 3" h., Sunflower mold, satin finish **$450-500**
Bowl, 11" d., Mold 155, Sheepherder scene decoration in shades of green w/gold & pink **$350-400**
Bowl, 11" d., Mold 22, four large jewels, satin finish **$250-300**

Man in the Mountain Prussia Bowl

Bowl, 11" d., Mold 304, gilt scroll border, overall color scene of the Man in the Mountain (ILLUS.) **$550-600**
Bowl, 11" d., 3" h., Fishscale mold, decorated w/white lilies on purple & orange lustre ground, artist-signed **$325-375**

Bowl, 15" d., Icicle mold (Mold 7), Snow Bird decoration, scenic reserves around the rim, very rare **$12,000-14,000**
Bread tray, Mold 428, wide oval form w/low flared sides w/a narrow flanged rim, pierced end rim handles, decorated w/a large cluster of roses in peach, pink & green, traces of gold edging, 9 x 12 1/2" **$175-225**
Butter dish, cover & insert, Mold 51, floral decoration, unmarked **$200-250**

Cake Plate with Dice Players

Cake plate, Ribbon & Jewel mold (Mold 18), open-handled, heavy gold border around florals framing the keyhole scene of Dice Players, 9" d. (ILLUS.) **$1,000-1,200**

Floral Decorated Cake Plate

Cake plate, open handled, decorated w/pink & white flowers, green leaves, pink & yellow ground, gold trim, 9 3/4" d. (ILLUS.) **$225**
Cake plate, open-handled, Fleur-de-Lis mold, Spring Season portrait, 9 3/4" d. **$1,300-1,600**
Cake plate, open-handled, Mold 155, hanging basket decoration, 10" d. **$325-350**
Cake plate, open-handled, Mold 259, decorated w/pink & yellow roses, pearl button finish, 10" d. **$350-400**

Lebrun-decorated Chocolate Set

Cake plate, open-handled, Fleur-de-Lis mold, decorated w/a castle scene in rust, gold, lavender & yellow, 10 1/4" d. **$1,000-1,300**

Cake plate, open-handled, Medallion mold, center Flora portrait, Tiffany finish w/four cupid medallions, unmarked, 10 1/2" d. **$900-1,000**

Cake plate, Iris mold, yellow poppy decoration, 11" d. **$250-300**

Cake plate, open-handled, Carnation mold (Mold 28), dark pink roses against teal & green w/gold trim, 11" d. **$250-300**

Cake plate, open-handled, modified Fleur-de-Lis mold, floral decoration, beaded, satin finish, artist-signed, 11" d. **$175-225**

Cake plate, Hidden Image mold, light blue highlights, 11 1/2" d. **$450-500**

Cake plate, open handles, Mold 256, satin ground decorated w/flowers in blue, pink & white w/gold trim, 11 1/2" d. **$120-150**

Cake plate, open-handled, Mold 330, decorated w/snapdragons on pastel ground, artist-signed, 11 1/2" d. **$350-375**

Cake plate, open-handled, Mold 343, Winter figural portrait in keyhole medallion, cobalt blue inner border, gold outer border, 12 1/2" d. **$400-450**

Cake plate, Bow-tie mold, pink & gold **$500-600**

Cake plate, open-handled, Carnation mold, decorated w/multicolored roses **$300-350**

Celery dish, Carnation mold, carnations & pink roses decoration on white shaded to peach ground, iridescent Tiffany finish, 9" l. **$375**

Celery dish, Hidden Image mold, colored hair, 5 x 12" **$400-450**

Celery dish, Mold 25, oblong, pearlized finish w/Surreal Dogwood blossoms w/gold trim, 6 x 12 1/4" **$75-125**

Celery tray, Mold 254, decorated w/green & pink roses, lavish gold tracery, artist-signed, 12" l. **$275-325**

Celery tray, Ribbon & Jewel mold (Mold 18), pink roses & white snowball blos-

soms within a wide cobalt blue border w/gilt trim, 12" l. **$250-300**

Celery tray, Mold 255, decorated w/Surreal Dogwood decoration, pearlized lustre finish, artist-signed, 12 1/4" l. **$200-225**

Celery tray, open-handled, decorated w/soft pink & white flower center w/lily-of-the-valley, embossed edge of ferns & pastel colors w/gold highlights, 12 1/2" l. **$200-250**

Celery tray, Carnation mold, decorated w/pink & yellow flowers on lavender satin finish, 6 1/2 x 13 1/4" **$300-350**

Centerpiece bowl, Carnation mold, decorated w/pink & yellow roses, 15 1/2" d. **$2,300-2,600**

Chocolate cup & saucer, decorated w/castle scene... **$125-150**

Chocolate pot, cov., Carnation mold (Mold 526), pink background & pink roses w/gold-trimmed leaves & blossoms & ornate gold handle, 12" h. **$400-500**

Chocolate pot, cov., Icicle mold (Mold 641), rosebush decoration, 10" h. **$300-400**

Chocolate pot, cov., Ribbon & Jewel mold (Mold 645), Dice Players scene, jeweled trim, 11" h.. **$2,000-2,300**

Chocolate pot, cov., Hidden Image mold, image on both sides, light green, 9 3/4" h. **$1,000-1,100**

Chocolate pot, cov., peacock & pine trees decoration **$650-750**

Chocolate pot, cov., Swag & Tassel mold, decorated w/scene of sheepherder & swallows... **$900-1,000**

Chocolate set: cov. pot & four cups & saucers; sunflower decoration, the set **$700-750**

Chocolate set: 10" h. cov. chocolate pot & four cups & saucers; Mold 729, pansy decoration w/gold trim, the set **$900-975**

Chocolate set: 10" h. cov. chocolate pot & four cups & saucers; Ribbon and Jewel mold, scene of Dice Throwers decoration on pot & single Melon Eater scene on cups, the set................................. **$4,500-5,000**

Melon Eaters Creamer & Sugar

Chocolate set: tankard-style cov. pot & six cups & saucers; Mold 510, laurel chain decoration, the set **$1,000-1,300**
Chocolate set: 10" h. cov. chocolate pot & six cups & saucers; Mold 517, Madame Lebrun portrait decoration, the set (ILLUS., top of previous page)
.... **$7,500-8,200**
Coffeepot, cov., Mold 517, raised floral designs as part of border, unmarked **$250-300**
Cracker jar, cov., Mold 540a, beige satin ground w/floral decoration in orchid, yellow & gold, 9 1/2" w. handle to handle, overall 5 1/2" h. **$300-350**
Cracker jar, cov., Mold 634, molded feet, surreal dogwood blossoms decoration on pearlized lustre finish, 8" d., 6 1/2" h.
.... **$250-300**
Cracker jar, cov., Mold 704, grape leaf decoration, 7" h. **$450-500**
Cracker jar, cov., decorated w/hanging basket of flowers, satin finish, 6 x 9 1/2"
.... **$325-375**
Cracker jar, cov., Hidden Image mold, image on both sides, green mum decoration **$900-1,000**
Cracker jar, cov., Lebrun portrait decoration, no hat, satin finish **$1,500-2,000**
Creamer & cov. sugar bowl, floral decoration, green highlights, pr. **$125-150**
Creamer & cov. sugar bowl, Mold 505, pink & yellow roses, pr. **$125-175**
Creamer & cov. sugar bowl, Ribbon & Jewel mold, single Melon Eaters decoration, pr. (ILLUS., top of page) **$1,500-1,800**
Creamer & cov. sugar bowl, satin finish, Tiffany trim, pr. **$175-200**
Cup & saucer, decorated w/pink roses, peg feet & scalloped rim, cup 1 3/4" h., saucer 4 1/4" d., pr. **$125-175**
Dessert set: 9 1/2" d. cake plate & six 7" d. individual plates; Carnation mold, decorated w/carnations, pink & white roses, iridescent Tiffany finish on pale green, the set **$995**
Dessert set: pedestal cup & saucer, oversized creamer & sugar bowl, two 9 3/4" d., handled plates, eleven 7 1/4" d. plates, nine cups & saucers; plain mold,

decoration w/pink poppies w/tints of aqua, yellow & purple, all pieces are matching, the set......................... **$2,200-2,500**
Dresser tray, decorated w/mill scene, shaded green ground, 7 x 11" **$350-450**
Dresser tray, Icicle mold, scenic decoration, Man in the Mountain, 7 x 11 1/2"
.... **$600-700**
Ferner, six vertical ribs, scalloped, decorated w/lilies-of-the-valley on shaded pastel ground, artist-signed, 3 7/8 x 8 1/4"
.... **$200-250**
Hair receiver, cov., Mold 814, Surreal Dogwood decoration **$150-175**
Match holder w/striker, floral decoration
.... **$100-125**
Model of a lady's slipper, embossed scrolling on instep & heel & embossed feather on one side of slipper, a dotted medallion w/roses & lily-of-the-valley on the other, shaded turquoise blue w/fancy rim trimmed w/gold, 8" l. **$250-300**
Mug, Lily mold, Lebrun portrait decoration (no hat)................................ **$200-250**
Mug, rose decoration on pink satin finish **$125-175**
Mustache cup, Mold 502....................... **$250-300**
Mustard pot, cov., Mold 509a, decorated w/white flowers, glossy light green ground... **$150-175**
Mustard pot, cov., Mold 521, pink rose decoration, satin finish **$150-200**
Nut bowl, footed, Point & Clover mold, decorated w/ten roses in shades of salmon, yellow & rose against a pink, green & gold lustre-finished ground, 6 1/2" d.
.... **$150-200**
Nut dish, Carnation mold (Mold 28), floral decoration w/pearlized finish **$200-250**
Pin dish, cov., Hidden Image mold, floral decoration, 2 3/4 x 4 3/4" **$350-450**
Pitcher, tankard, 12 1/4" h., Mold 569, rare Bird of Paradise decoration w/shaded gold & light green in the lower half, white above, gold trim, only one known (ILLUS., next page)................. **$17,000-20,000**
Pitcher, tankard, 12 1/2" h., Carnation mold (Mold 526), Summer Season decoration, pink border trim (ILLUS., next page)
.... **$7,000-8,000**

Unique Bird of Paradise Pitcher

Carnation - Summer Season Pitcher

Carnation Mold Pitcher with Roses

Pitcher, tankard, 13" h., Carnation mold (Mold 526), decorated w/clusters of dark pink & creamy white roses w/a shaded dark green ground & pale green molded blossoms (ILLUS.) **$1,000-1,200**

Pitcher, cider, 7" h., iris decoration w/green & gold background **$250-300**

Pitcher, lemonade, 6" h., Mold 501, relief-molded turquoise blue on white w/pink Surreal blossoms & fans around scalloped top & base, unmarked **$250-300**

Pitcher, tankard, 10" h., Mold 584, decorated w/hanging basket of pink & white roses **$700-750**

Pitcher, tankard, 11" h., Carnation Mold, overall decoration of pink poppies & carnations, white ground, iridescent Tiffany finish **$1,100**

R.S. Prussia Tankard Pitchers

Pitcher, tankard, 12" h., Mold 538, decorated w/Melon Eaters scene (ILLUS. left, bottom previous page) **$3,500-4,000**
Pitcher, tankard, 13" h., decorated w/poppies **$600-650**
Pitcher, tankard, 13" h., decorated w/scene of Old Man in Mountain & swans on lake (ILLUS. right w/other tankard pitcher, bottom previous page) **$4,000-4,500**
Pitcher, tankard, 13 1/4" h., Stippled Floral mold (Mold 525), roses decoration, unmarked **$625-675**
Pitcher, tankard, 13 1/2" h., Carnation Mold, pink poppy decoration, green ground **$750-850**
Pitcher, water, 8 3/4" h., Carnation mold **$660**
Plaque, decorated w/scene of woman w/dog, 9 1/4 x 13" **$2,000-2,500**
Plate, 7" d., Fleur-de-Lis mold, Summer Season portrait decoration **$450-500**
Plate, 7 1/2" d., Carnation mold, decorated w/pink roses, lavender ground, satin finish **$200-250**
Plate, 7 1/2" d., Carnation mold, decorated w/pink roses, pink ground, unmarked **$175**
Plate, 7 3/4" d., Medallion mold (Mold 14), Snowbird decoration, landscape scenes in medallions, black rim band **$1,800-2,200**
Plate, 8 1/2" d., Gibson Girl portrait decoration, maroon bonnet **$500-550**
Plate, 8 1/2" d., Medallion mold (Mold 14), Reflecting Lilies patt. **$125-150**
Plate, 8 1/2" d., Mold 261, Ostrich decoration **$2,000-2,500**
Plate, 8 1/2" d., Mold 263, pink & white roses decoration............................... **$175-200**
Plate, 8 1/2" d., Mold 300, beaded gold band around the lobed rim, Old Mill Scene decoration in center against a shaded dark green to yellow & blue ground **$150-200**
Plate, 8 3/4" d., Mold 278, center decoration of pink poppies on white ground, green border... **$150-175**

Rare Spring Keyhole Portrait Plate

Plate, 9" d., Mold 343, Spring figural scenic decoration in keyhole medallion, iridescent Tiffany purple finish at base of figure, heavy gold around portrait decoration w/small pink roses against a deep red ground (ILLUS.) **$1,800-2,100**
Plate, 9 3/4" d., Icicle mold, swan decoration **$800-900**
Plate, 11" d., decorated w/carnations & roses w/gold trim, white shading to peach ground, iridescent Tiffany finish (slight gold wear)... **$250**
Plate, 11" d., Point & Clover mold, Melon Eater decoration.............................. **$900-1,100**

Rare Madame Recamier Plate

Plate, 12" d., Lily mold (Mold 29), Madame Recamier portrait, dark blue Tiffany bronze finish in border panels (ILLUS.) **$3,000-4,000**
Plate, dessert, Mold 506, branches of pink roses & green leaves against a shaded bluish green to white ground w/shadow flowers & satin finish **$100-125**
Relish dish, Iris mold (Mold 25), oval w/scalloped sides & end loop handles, Spring Season portrait surrounded by dark border w/iris, 4 1/2 x 9 1/2" **$1,200-1,400**

Mold 91 Rose-decorated Plate

Plate, 8 3/4" d., Mold 91, yellow roses decoration on pink ground, shiny yellow border (ILLUS.)...................................... **$150-200**

Relish dish, Fleur-de-Lis mold, basket of flowers decoration w/shadow flowers, 8" l. **$100-125**
Relish dish, scene of masted ship, 4 1/2 x 9 1/2" **$250-300**
Relish dish, Icicle mold, scene of swans on lake...................................... **$450-500**
Relish dish, Mold 82, decorated w/forget-me-nots & multicolored carnations, six jeweled domes **$125-175**
Shaving mug, Hidden Image mold, floral decoration **$175-225**
Spooner/vase, Mold 502, three-handled, decorated w/delicate roses & gold trim, unsigned, 4 1/4" h. **$75-100**
Syrup pitcher, Mold 512, dogwood & pine decoration **$175**
Syrup pitcher & underplate, Mold 507, white & pink roses on a shaded brown to pale yellow ground, 2 pcs.................... **$200-250**
Tea set: child's, cov. teapot & four cups & saucers; decorated w/roses, the set **$650-700**
Tea set: cov. teapot, creamer & cov. sugar bowl; floral decoration, the set **$300-350**
Tea set: cov. teapot, creamer & cov. sugar bowl; mill & castle scene, shaded brown ground, 3 pcs. **$900-1,000**
Tea set: cov. teapot, creamer & cov. sugar bowl; pedestal base, scene of Colonial children, 3 pcs. **$600-700**
Tea strainer, floral decoration............... **$200-250**
Toothpick holder, ribbed hexagonal shape w/two handles, decorated w/colorful roses **$265-300**
Toothpick holder, Stippled Floral mold (Mold 23), white floral decoration **$150-175**
Toothpick holder, three-handled, decorated w/white daisies on blue ground, gold handles & trim on top **$150-175**
Toothpick holder, urn-shaped, floral decoration, molded star mark **$150-175**
Tray, pierced handles, Mold 82, decorated w/full blossom red & pink roses, gold Royal Vienna mark, 8 x 11 1/8"......... **$250-300**
Tray, rectangular, pierced handles, Mold 404, decorated w/pink & white roses, Tiffany border w/gold clover leaves........ **$250-300**
Vase, 4" h., salesman's sample, handled, Mold 914, decorated w/large lilies & green foliage, raised beading around shoulder, gold handles, shaded green ground, artist-signed **$150-175**
Vase, 4 1/2" h., Mold 910, decorated w/pink roses, satin finish w/iridescent Tiffany finish around base................................... **$250-275**
Vase, 5 1/2" h., cottage & mill scene decoration, cobalt trim................................. **$550-650**
Vase, 6 1/4" h., castle scene decoration, brown tones w/jewels......................... **$450-500**
Vase, 6 1/4" h., decorated w/brown & cream shadow flowers **$75-100**

Vase, 6 1/4" h., decorated w/mill scene, brown w/jewels.................................... **$450-500**
Vase, 8" h., cylindrical body w/incurved angled shoulder handles, decorated w/parrots on white satin ground, unmarked **$2,200-2,600**

R.S. Prussia Vases with Animals

Vase, 8" h., ovoid body w/wide shoulder tapering to cylindrical neck w/flared rim, decorated w/scene of black swans (ILLUS. left) **$1,200-1,500**
Vase, 10" h., ovoid body decorated w/scene of two tigers, pastel satin finish (ILLUS. right)...................................... **$5,500-7,000**

R.S. Prussia Ovoid Vase w/Parrots

Vase, two-handled, tall, slender, ovoid body w/colorful scene of two parrots, shaded brown foliage, unmarked (ILLUS.) **$1,800-2,000**

Rare Melon Eaters Vases

Vases, 11 3/4" h., Mold 901, footed, slightly tapering cylindrical bodies w/high, flaring, cupped, deeply fluted necks w/jewels, beading & jewels around the shoulders & feet, ornate scrolled gilt handles, Melon Eaters decoration against shaded dark green ground, each (ILLUS. of pair) **$1,600-2,000**

Other Marks

Bowl, 10" d., Cabbage mold w/center rose decoration (R.S. Tillowitz) **$250-300**
Bowl, 10" d., shallow w/very ornate, large Flora portrait, front pose past waist, floral garland, veiling, four different cameo por-

traits of Flora, wide Tiffany border, lavish gold (E.S. Prov. Saxe) **$1,100-1,300**
Chocolate pot, cov., Art Nouveau decoration, glossy finish (R.S. Tillowitz - Silesia) **$55**
Chocolate pot, cov., lemon yellow ground w/Art Deco decoration & gold trim (R.S. Tillowitz - Silesia) **$150**
Coffee set: 6 5/8" l., 3 1/4" d., cov. ovoid coffeepot & two cups & saucers; each piece decorated w/a color oval reserve w/a different romantic scene within a thin gilt border & a deep burgundy panel against a creamy white ground trimmed w/gilt scrolls, a wide red & narrow dark green border band on each, saucers 2 3/4" d., cups 2 1/4" h., blue beehive & R.S. Suhl marks, the set (ILLUS., bottom of page) **$650**
Fernery, pedestal base, decorated w/pink & white roses, mother-of-pearl finish (R.S. Poland) **$450**
Match holder, hanging-type on attached backplate decorated w/a scene of a man w/mug of beer & pipe (E.S. Prov. Saxe) **$175-200**
Plate, 7" d., scene of girl w/rose, trimmed w/gold flowers, beading & a burgundy border **$100-125**
Plate, 7 3/4" d., Sunflower mold, rose pink & yellow roses w/Tiffany finish (Wheelock Prussia) **$125-150**
Plate, 8" d., peafowl decoration (R.S. Tillowitz - Silesia) **$150-200**
Plate, 10 1/2" d., lovely center portrait of Madame DuBarry, four cameos in different poses on a deep burgundy lustre border band (E.W. Prov. Saxe) **$500-600**
Relish dish, woman's portrait w/shadow flowers & vine border on green ground, 8" l. (E.S. Germany Royal Saxe) **$100-125**

R.S. Suhl Coffee Set with Romantic Scenes

R.S. Poland Center-handle Server

Server, center handle w/three loops, dished paneled base w/a lightly scalloped rim, lavender & pink roses & green leaves on a pale creamy green ground & gilt border trim, 11" d., 8" h., R.S. Poland (ILLUS.) **$500-550**

E. Schlegelmilch Handled Server

Server, center-handled, decorated w/orange, white & pink poppies on a shaded bluish grey ground, w/a narrow gilt border band, 8 1/2" d., 3 3/4" h., E. Schlegelmilch - Thuringia (ILLUS.) **$100-150**
Tray, rectangular, open-handled, bright colored bird decoration, 5 x 14" (R.S. Tillowitz) **$75-100**
Vase, miniature, 3 1/2" h., cylindrical body w/a rounded shoulder tapering to a tiny rolled neck, decorated w/a colored scene of crowned cranes (R.S. Poland) **$375-425**
Vase, 6 3/8" h., 3" d., wide, ovoid, shouldered body tapering to slender, flaring cylindrical neck, Melon Eaters decoration surrounded by gold border w/reverse decorated w/heart-shaped area w/dainty pink roses on pastel ground, two-thirds of vase covered in purplish lustre w/fine gold leaves & flowers overall, neck in off white w/fine gold floral decoration, artist-signed in gold, Red Crown "Viersa" mark, Suhl or Tillowitz (ILLUS., top next column) **$350-400**

Melon Eaters Vase

Vase, 7" h., footed urn form w/scrolled handles, decorated w/scene of two geese, R.S. Poland **$1,500-1,800**
Vase, 7 1/2" h., wide, squatty, bulbous base tapering sharply to a tall, slender, cylindrical neck w/an upturned four-lobed rim, long slender gold handles from rim to shoulder, decorated w/a center reserve of a standing Art Nouveau maiden w/her hands behind her head & a peacock behind her framed by delicate gold scrolls & beading & floral bouquets, all on a pearl lustre ground (Prov. Saxe - E.W. Germany) **$375-425**

Tall Ovoid R.S. Suhl Vase

Vase, 9" h., 3" d., tall, slender, ovoid body tapering to a tall, slender trumpet neck, a wide band around the body decorated w/a colored scene of The Melon Eaters between narrow gold & white bands, the neck & lower body in deep rose decorated w/gilt leaf sprigs, R.S. Suhl (ILLUS.) **$800-1,000**

Vase, 9 1/4" h., gently tapering cylindrical body w/a wide, cupped, scalloped gilt rim, pierced gold serpentine handles from rim to center of sides, decorated around the body w/large blossoms in purple, pink, yellow & green on a shaded brownish green ground (Prove. Saxe) **$125-150**

Vase, 9 1/2" h., portrait of "Lady with Swallows," gold beading, turquoise on white ground (Prov. Saxe - E.S. Germany) **$500-550**

Vase, 10" h., gold Rococo handles, scene of sleeping maiden w/cherub decoration (E.S. Royal Saxe).............................. **$350-400**

Vase, 13 1/2" h., portrait of "Lady with Swallows," gold beaded frame, green pearl lustre finish w/gold trim (Prov. Saxe - E.S. Germany) **$600-650**

Vase, 13 1/2" h., twisted gold handles, portrait of "Goddess of Fire," iridescent burgundy & opalescent colors w/lavish gold trim (Prov. Saxe, E.S. Germany)........ **$650-700**

R.S. Poland Landscape Vase

Vases, 10" h., gently swelled body tapering to narrow rounded shoulders & a short, flaring, scalloped neck, ornate C-scroll gilt shoulder handles, gold neck band, the body decorated w/a colored scene of a sheepherder leading his flock toward a mill in the background, trees overhead, the second identical except w/a cottage scene, R.S. Poland, pr. (ILLUS. of one) **$1,350-1,400**

Red Wing

Various potteries operated in Red Wing, Minnesota, from 1868, the most successful being the Red Wing Stoneware Co., organized in 1877. Merged with other local potteries through the years, it became known as Red Wing Union Stoneware Co. in 1906, and was one of the largest

producers of utilitarian stoneware items in the United States. After a decline in the popularity of stoneware products, an art pottery line was introduced to compensate for the loss. This was reflected in a new name for the company, Red Wing Potteries, Inc., in 1936. Stoneware production ceased entirely in 1947, but vases, planters, cookie jars and dinnerwares of art pottery quality continued in production until 1967, when the pottery ceased operation altogether.

Red Wing Marks

Art Pottery

Ash receiver, figural, model of a pelican, turquoise, embossed "Red Wing, USA," No. 880 .... **$195**

Basket with 75th Anniversary Seal

Basket, yellow & grey, embossed "Red Wing USA," No. 348, w/75th anniversary seal (ILLUS.).. **$65**

Cookie jar, cov., Carousel shape, white, blue, red & brown, h.p., very rare, 8 1/2 x 8"... **$575**

Cookie jar, cov., grape design, royal blue, 10" h.. **$220**

Cookie Jar with Peasants Design

Cookie jar, cov., Labriego design decorated w/incised dancing peasants, h.p., green, red & yellow, no markings, 9 1/2" h. (ILLUS., previous page) $100
Figures of cowboy & cowgirl, fully decorated, 11" h., pr. $500
Planter, hanging-type, No. M-1487 .... $45

Planter in the Form of a Stove

Planter, in the form of a stove, green & cream, No. 765, 8" h. (ILLUS.) $55

Planter in the Form of a Log

Planter, in the form of a white birch log, no markings, 11" l. (ILLUS.) $110
Vase, deer decoration, No. 1120 .... $60
Vase, figural elephant handle, ivory ground, matte finish, Rum Rill mark $140
Vase, No. 1079, blue glaze $65
Vase, No. 839, blue glaze $100
Vase, 7" h., expanding cylinder w/squared handles rising from narrow shoulder to mouth, No. 163-7, grey & tan glaze $100
Vase, 7" h., No. 1509-7, black satin matte glaze.. $35
Vase, 9" h., ribbed, No. 637 .... $45
Vase, 9 1/2" h., No. M1442-9 1/2, Colonial buff & salmon $65
Vase, 10" h., No. 902-10, lustre Dubonnet..... $100
Vase, 11" h., No. 1377/11, green & yellow glaze.. $75
Wall pocket, No. M 1630, brown glaze, 10" h. $80

Brushed & Glazed Wares
Vase, leaf decoration, buff & green, No. 1166 .... $35
Vase, 7" h., bulbous body tapering to a short cylindrical neck, angled handles, decorated w/acorn & oak leaf design, dark & light green, No. 149-7.............................. $165

Vase, 8" h., flower design decoration, green & mauve, No. 1107 (minor base flake) $75

Matte Green & White Cemetery Vase

Vase, 10" h., cemetery vase, green & white, no markings (ILLUS.)................................. $125
Vase, 15" h., swelling cylindrical body tapering to a flat rim, angled shoulder handles, green & yellow, No. 186-15...................... $145

Convention Commemoratives
Bowl, 1980 Red Wing Collectors Society commemorative $800
Cookie jar, 1996 Red Wing Collectors Society commemorative, grey line $120
Crock, 1977 Red Wing Collectors Society commemorative, salt glaze $2,250

Commemorative Ball Lock Jar

Jar, cov., ball lock, 2002 Red Wing Collectors Society 25th anniversary commemorative, white glaze (ILLUS.)........................ $90
Mug, 1982 Red Wing Collectors Society commemorative, cherry band $750
Planter, 1995 Red Wing Collectors Society commemorative, in the form of a giraffe
.... $105

Poultry waterer, 1993 Red Wing Collectors Society commemorative, bell-shaped w/saucer.. $110

Dinnerwares & Novelties

Ash receiver, figural, model of a seated donkey w/mouth wide open, green glaze $195

Red Wing Bob White Casserole

Casserole, cov., Bob White patt., 4 qt. (ILLUS.).. $50
Celery dish, Flight patt. $175
Cocktail tray, Bob White patt. $40
Coffeepot, cov., Village Green line................. $35
Cookie jar, cov., Bob White patt. $60

Rare "Pretty Red Wing" Wing Ashtray

Ashtray, earthenware, "Pretty Red Wing" style, model of a large red-glazed wing embossed w/a bust profile of an Indian maiden (ILLUS.) $400-450

Red Wing Dutch Girl Cookie Jar

Beverage server w/stopper, Bob White patt. $75
Beverage server w/stopper, Smart Set patt. $180
Bowl, berry, Bob White patt. $8
Bowl, berry, Capistrano patt............................. $9
Bowl, berry, Tampico patt. $10
Bowl, cereal, Bob White patt.......................... $25
Bowl, cereal, Tampico patt.............................. $15
Bowl, salad, Random Harvest patt., large....... $40
Bowl, soup, Bob White patt............................ $20
Bowl, salad, 12" d., Capistrano patt................ $75
Bowl, salad, 12" d., Tampico patt. $85
Bread tray, Round Up patt............................ $200
Bread tray, rectangular, Bob White patt., 24" l. $100
Butter dish, cov., Bob White patt., 1/4 lb. $75
Butter warmer, Bob White patt....................... $95
Candlesticks, Magnolia patt., pr.................... $50
Carafe, cov., Bob White patt. $185
Casserole, Bob White patt., 2 qt. $40
Casserole, cov., French-style w/stick handle, Town & Country patt., peach glaze $95
Casserole, cov., Smart Set patt., 2 qt. $68

Cookie jar, cov., figural Katrina (Dutch girl), yellow glaze (ILLUS.)................................. $100
Cookie jar, cov., figural monk, blue glaze...... $100
Cookie jar, cov., side handle & side top, red glaze $225
Creamer, Bob White patt. $25
Cruets w/stoppers, Bob White patt., pr. $175
Cruets w/stoppers in metal rack, Bob White patt., the set.................................. $325
Cup & saucer, Bob White patt........................ $9
Cup & saucer, Capistrano patt. $13
French bread tray, Bob White patt., 24" l. $90
Gravy boat, cov., Bob White patt..................... $55
Gravy boat w/stand, Tampico patt., 2 pcs...... $60
Hor d'oeuvres holder, Bob White patt., model of a bird pierced for picks................. $50
Mug, Bob White patt....................................... $80
Pitcher, jug-type, Tampico patt., 2 qt.............. $65
Pitcher, 12" h., Round Up patt...................... $210
Pitcher, water, Bob White patt., 60 oz. $50
Plate, salad, Flight patt................................. $60
Plate, 6 1/2" d., Capistrano patt. $5
Plate, 6 1/2" d., Tampico patt........................... $7
Plate, bread & butter, 6 1/2" d., Bob White patt.. $6
Plate, 8" d., Bob White patt. $8
Plate, 8 1/2" d., Tampico patt.......................... $12

Plate, 10 1/2" d., Capistrano patt. $10
Plate, 10 1/2" d., Tampico patt. $14
Plate, dinner, 10 1/2" d., Bob White patt. $13
Platter, 13" oval, Bob White patt. $85
Platter, 20" l., Bob White patt. $100
Platter w/metal rack, Bob White patt., large, 2 pcs. $160
Relish, Bob White patt., three-part $70
Relish, Bob White patt., two-part $45
Relish, Tampico patt., 13" l. $35
Salt & pepper shakers, figural bird, Bob White patt., pr. $35
Salt & pepper shakers, figural pitcher, jug-type w/ice lip, red, Rum Rill mark, pr. $45
Salt & pepper shakers, figural Schmoo, bronze glaze, pr. $95
Salt & pepper shakers, figural Schmoo, cinnamon glaze, Rum Rill mark, pr. $65
Syrup pitcher, Town & Country patt., blue glaze $75
Teapot, cov., Village Green patt. $60
Teapot, cover & stand, Bob White patt., the set $140
Tidbit tray, Random Harvest patt., original paper label $27
Tray on warmer, Smart Set patt., large, 2 pcs. $145
Vegetable dish, open, divided, Capistrano patt. $24
Vegetable dish, open, divided, Smart Set patt. $65
Vegetable dish, open, divided, Tampico patt. $45

Specialty Items

Book, "The Clay Giants," 1st edition, history, stoneware of Red Wing, rare, mint, 1977 .... $175
Book, "The Clay Giants," 3rd edition, history w/price guide, stoneware of Red Wing, mint, 1987 .... $160
Bottle, w/iron bailed stopper, amber, embossed "Red Wing Brewing Co., Red Wing, Minn.," rare, 14" h. $105
Gunny sack, 100 pounds flour, "Red Wing, Minn." $85
Yard stick, advertising Hi-Park Guernsey Milk, Red Wing, Minn. $45

Stoneware & Utility Wares

Bean pot, cov., white & brown glaze, advertising, "Christmas Greetings from Christle's Cash Store, Brillion, Wis.," rare $145
Bean pot, cov., white & brown glaze, advertising "Geo. C. Radloff, Farmersburg, Iowa" $115
Bean pot, cov., white & brown glaze, advertising "Peter Bootzin, Medford, Wis.".......... $125
Bean pot, cov., white & brown glazes, wire handles, marked "Red Wing Union Stoneware" $115
Beater jar, cylindrical, Sponge Band line $325
Beater jar, cylindrical w/a molded rim, white glaze w/blue bands & advertising in a rectangle on front $200
Beater jar, white glaze w/blue band, advertising "Klatt & Stueber, Clyman, Wis." $200
Beater jar, white glaze w/blue band, advertising "Schulenburg & Thom, Wells, Minn." $200

Bowl, 8" d., spongeware paneled, advertising "Swanson & Nelson, Chisago City" [sic], very rare $250
Bowl, Sponge Band line, South Dakota advertising in bottom, No. 7 .... $285
Bowl, 4" d., spongeband, deep, rounded form $575

Small Blue & White Greek Key Bowl

Bowl, 6" d., embossed Greek Key patt., pale blue on white glaze (ILLUS.) $125-145
Bowl, 6" d., spongeware paneled, advertising "Muscodo Spring Green, Boscobel, Wis.," rare $195

White-glazed Bowl with Pink & Blue Bands

Bowl, 7" d., deep rounded & ribbed sides, white-glazed & decorated w/pale pink & blue bands (ILLUS.) $75-125
Bowl, 7" d., Dunlap, brown & white glaze, advertising "Columbia Metal Products Co., Chicago, Ill." $45
Bowl, 7" d., "Milk Pan Bowl," white glaze, embossed "RWS Co." on bottom $95
Bowl, 9" d., Gray Line (Sponge Band) ware, deep rounded & ribbed sides w/a narrow sponged orange band flanked by thin blue bands (ILLUS., top next page) $175-225
Butter crock, blue sponge glaze, no markings $325
Butter crock, white glaze, 4" wing mark, "20 lbs" stamped above wing, very rare $1,100
Churn, w/pottery lid, white glaze, 4" wing mark, blue oval pottery stamp below wing, 2 gal. $500
Churn, w/pottery lid, white glaze, 4" wing mark, blue oval pottery stamp below wing, 4 gal. $395

Large Gray Line (Sponge Band) Bowl

Churn, w/pottery lid & wooden dasher, white glaze, 4" wing mark, blue oval pottery stamp below wing, 5 gal..................... **$450**

Churn, w/pottery lid, white glaze, 4" wing mark, blue oval pottery stamp above wing, 6 gal... **$595**

Churn w/wooden lid & dasher, swelled cylindrical body, Union Stoneware Co., large wing mark, 3 gal............................... **$325**

Churn w/wooden lid & dasher, swelled cylindrical body w/eared handles & a molded rim, white-glazed, blue birch leaves over oval & "4," Union Stoneware Co., Red Wing, Minnesota, 4 gal., 20" h........... **$325**

Churn w/wooden lid & dasher, swelled cylindrical body w/eared handles & a molded rim, white-glazed, large wing mark w/oval wing stamp below, 2 gal................. **$350**

Red Wing Stoneware Iced Tea Cooler

Cooler, cov., iced tea, white glaze, wire handles, no wing, 5 gal. (ILLUS.).............. **$500**

Crock, white-glazed, big wing mark, 1 gal. **$500**

Crock, white glaze, embossed on base "Minnesota Stoneware, Red Wing, Minn.," no wing, 1 gal................................. **$75**

Crock, w/molded rim, white-glazed, large "2" over double birch leaves & oval

marks, Red Wing Union Stoneware, 2 gal., 9 3/4" d.. **$85**

Crock, white glaze, two "elephant ears," oval Union Stoneware Co. stamp in blue, 2 gal. **$125**

Crock, w/eared handles & molded rim, cobalt blue hand-decorated leaf below a "5," grey salt glaze, sidewall stamp, 5 gal. .. **$850**

Crock, w/eared handles, white glaze, stamped 4" wing mark, Red Wing oval stamp, 13" d., 6 gal. **$95**

Crock, salt glaze, cobalt blue "butterfly" design, rare, 8 gal. **$3,000**

Crock, cov., white glaze, small wing, blue oval stamp below wing, bailed handles, 15 gal. **$185**

Crock, cov., white glaze, bail handles, 4" wing mark, blue oval stamp below wing, 25 gal. **$300**

Crock, cov., white glaze, bail handles, 4" wing mark, blue oval stamp below wing, 30 gal. **$500**

Crock, white-glazed, 6" l. wing mark, 40 gal. **$1,200**

Crock, white-glazed, large wing mark, 50 gal. **$2,400**

Crock, white glaze, advertising "Ev-Re-Day Oleomargarine, Wisconsin Butterine Co.," no wing, 2 qt...................................... **$75**

Fruit jar, cov., white glaze, blue or black stamp, "Stone - Mason Fruit Jar - Union Stoneware Co. - Red Wing, Minn.," very rare, 1 gal... **$1,100**

Fruit Jar with Screw-on Lid

Fruit jar, screw-on metal lid, cylindrical w/tapering shoulder, white-glazed, black stamp reads "Stone - Mason Fruit Jar - Union Stoneware Co. - Red Wing, Minn.," 2 qt. (ILLUS., previous page) **$275**
Jar, cov., applesauce, white glaze, bail handles, ball lock, oval Union Stoneware stamp, 3 gal... **$325**
Jar, steam table jar, white glaze, cobalt blue #5 stamp, no wing....................................... **$50**
Jar, cov., white-glazed, ball lock, 4" wing over Red Wing oval stamp mark, 5 gal. **$325**

Red Wing 3 Gal. Birch Leaves Jug

Jug, beehive shape, white glaze, two birch leaves, Union Stoneware Co. oval stamp, 3 gal. (ILLUS.)... **$425**

Minnesota Stoneware Brown Jug

Jug, beehive-shaped, overall dark brown glaze, mark on bottom for the Minnesota Stoneware Company, 1/2 gal. (ILLUS.) .. **$75-95**
Jug, brown glaze, embossed "Minnesota Stoneware, Red Wing" on base, 1 gal. **$95**
Jug, syrup, white glaze, cone-shaped top, embossed "Minnesota Stoneware Co." on base, 1 gal... **$75**

3-Gallon Beehive Jug with Leaves

Jug, beehive-shaped, white w/printed blue size number, double birch leaves & oval Union Stoneware Co. mark, 3 gal. (ILLUS.)... **$400-450**
Jug, w/white-glazed shoulder, 4" wing above Red Wing oval mark, 3 gal............. **$125**

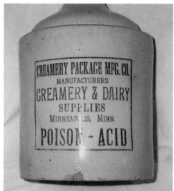

Red Wing Advertising Jug

Jug, white glaze, advertising "Creamery Package Mfg. Co. - Manufacturers - Creamery & Dairy Supplies - Minneapolis, Minn. - Poison - Acid," 1 gal. (ILLUS.) .. **$195**
Jug, brown- & white-glazed shoulder, 4" wing mark, 2 gal. **$600**

Rare Red Wing Jug

Jug, beehive-shaped, small cylindrical neck, dark blue printed diamond w/Iowa advertising above the blue double birch leaf mark, 5 gal. (ILLUS., previous page) $2,900

Jug, beehive-shaped, white-glazed, w/Portland, Oregon advertising, 5 gal. $950

Red Wing 5-Gallon Marked Jug

Jug, shoulder-style, cylindrical body w/rounded shoulder & small neck, white glaze, printed blue size number, oval Red Wing Union Stoneware mark & a 4" red wing, 5 gal., 18" h. (ILLUS.) $173

Jug, white-glazed shoulder, 4" wing mark, blue oval stamp, 5 gal. $125

Jug, beehive shape, Albany slip, North Star Stoneware, large embossed star on base, very rare, 1 qt. $275

Jug, w/a salt-glazed body & tapering rounded brown-glazed shoulder & neck, oval printed panel w/liquor advertising, 2 qt. $1,200

Jug, white glaze, advertising "Ladner Brothers Wines & Liquors, Red Wing, Minn.," 2 qt. $500

Red Wing Stoneware "Koverwate"

"Koverwate" (crock cover-weight designed to keep the contents submerged under preserving liquid; bottom & side holes allowed brine to come to the top), white glaze, stamped "Koverwate - Red Wing, Minn.," 15 gal., 13 3/4" d. (ILLUS.) $295

Rare Sleepy Eye Advertising Verse Mug

Mug, Sleepy eye verse-type, cylindrical white glazed form w/double blue bands flanking Sleepy Eye advertising, a bust of Chief Sleepy Eye & a verse (ILLUS.) $2,500-2,800

Red Wing Packing Jar with Cover & Seal

Packing jar, cov., cylindrical w/rounded shoulder & cylindrical neck w/original ball-lock sealing mechanism & wire bail handle w/wooden grip, white glaze, a script "3" above the 4" red wing & oval Red Wing Union Stoneware marks, 3 gal. (ILLUS.).. $275-325

Poultry feeder, KoRec chicken feeder, white glaze, 1 gal., 2 pcs.......................... $175

Poultry waterer, w/end opening, "Eureka"-style, marked around opening "Patd. April 7, 1885," Red Wing marking on bottom.. $250

Refrigerator jar, stacking-type, short form w/a molded rim, white-glazed w/narrow blue bands & "Red Wing Refrigerator Jar" on the side, 5 1/2" d. $225

Salt box, cov., hanging-type, grey line **$1,800**
Trivet, advertising Minnesota Centennial
1858-1958 .... **$95**
Water cooler, cov., w/spigot, bail handles,
white glaze, 4" wing mark, blue oval Red
Wing stamp below wing, 3 gal. **$950**
Water cooler, cov., w/spigot, bail handles,
white glaze, two birch leaves, no oval
stamp, 4 gal. **$750**
Water cooler, cov., white-glazed, side han-
dles, large wing mark, 5 gal. **$850**
Water cooler, cov., w/spigot, bail handles,
white glaze, 4" wing mark, blue oval Red
Wing stamp below wing, 6 gal. **$850**
Water cooler, cov., w/spigot, bail handles,
white glaze, 4" wing mark, blue oval Red
Wing stamp below wing, 10 gal. **$1,200**

Redware

*Red earthenware pottery was made in the
American colonies from the late 1600s. Bowls,
crocks and all types of utilitarian wares were
turned out in great abundance to supplement the
pewter and handmade treenware. The ready
availability of the clay, the same used in making
bricks and roof tiles, accounted for the vast production. The lead-glazed redware retained its
reddish color, although a variety of colors could
be obtained by adding various metals to the glaze.
Interesting effects occurred accidentally through
unsuspected impurities in the clay or uneven temperatures in the firing kiln, which sometimes
resulted in streaks or mottled splotches.*

*Redware pottery was seldom marked by the
maker.*

Apple butter jar, bulbous ovoid body w/a
wide flat thin molded rim, fine mottled
brownish green alkaline glaze, probably
New York state origin, excellent
condition, ca. 1830, 6" h. **$275**

Scarce Redware Butter Churn

Butter churn, ovoid form w/two sides handles, partial brown glaze, incised decoration of star punch, swag & waves in eight
horizontal rows, possibly Maine, 19th c.,

chips, cracks & missing pieces, overall
14 1/2" h. (ILLUS.) **$2,588**
Crock, bulbous ovoid form w/flat flaring rim,
eared handles & incised lines, glaze
w/dark brown daubs in vertical rows
around the sides, 19th c., 8 5/8" h. (edge
chips, hairline) **$660**

Rare Signed Redware Crock

Crock, wide ovoid body w/a wide flat rim,
interior brown glaze, exterior w/incised
line at shoulder above stamped mark of
Benjamin Dodge, Portland, Maine, 19th
c., one small rim chip, 7 1/4" d., 8 1/4" h.
(ILLUS.) **$1,898**
Dish, shallow round form, reddish brown in-
terior glaze, probably made in Pennsylvania, 19th c., 8" d., 1 3/4" h. (minor sur-
face wear) **$55**
Flowerpot, tapering cylindrical form w/flat
molded rim, unglazed, impressed mark of
A. Wilcox, West Bloomfield, New
York, ca. 1850, 6 1/4" h. (dime-sized chip
at rim) **$110**
Food mold, Turk's turban form, mottled red
& brown alkaline glaze, ca. 1850,
9 1/2" d., 3" h. (couple of surface chips
on exterior) **$44**
Food mold, Turk's turban form, brown pep-
pered alkaline glaze, attributed to the Wilcox factory, West Bloomfield, New York,
early 19th c., 10 1/2" d., 3 3/4" h. (minor
surface wear at bottom) **$44**

Maine Redware Jar with Cover

Jar, cov., ovoid body tapering to a dish rim supporting the flat cover w/knob finial, orange & green splotchy glaze, probably John Safford, Maine, 19th c., incised on base "203," 5 1/2" h. (ILLUS., previous page).. $240

Jar, cylindrical w/narrow angled shoulder to flaring rim, black brush marks starting at shoulder & running downward, incised rings around top & center, glaze stopping short of base, 19th c., 8 1/2" h. (edge chips)... $281

Jar, footed bulbous ovoid body tapering to a wide flat flared neck, applied eared handles, incised linear bands on neck & shoulder, dark brown splotches on a dark orangish red ground, eastern United States, early 19th c., 10 1/4" h. (glaze wear on rim & handle edges, few base chips).. $470

Jug, ovoid body tapering to a small cylindrical neck, applied strap handle, reddish glaze w/green highlights, three incised shoulder rings, probably John Safford, Maine, 19th c., 6" h. $575

Jug, ovoid body tapering to a short cylindrical banded neck, remnants of applied handle, dark brown & green glaze, branded across the front by the maker, John M. Safford, Maine, 19th c., 7" h. $805

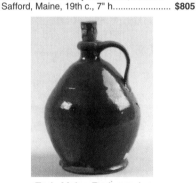

Early Maine Redware Jug

Jug, ovoid body tapering sharply to a small neck w/molded rim & applied strap handle, nice red & green speckled glaze, Norcross-type shape, Maine, 19th c., some chips & hairline, 8 1/2" h. (ILLUS.) $1,035

Redware Milk Bowl with Sponging

Milk bowl, deep flat angled sides w/molded flat rim, dark brown sponged bands up the exterior & around the rim, leadglazed, 19th c., 11" d. (ILLUS.) $288

Model of a lion, seated hollow-molded animal w/open front legs, on a thin rectangular base, black mica glaze w/painted red mouth & yellow eyes, base painted yellow & orange, 19th c., 6 3/4 x 11", 14" h. (few chips, tail handmade replacement) $1,210

Mug, very tall slender cylindrical form w/C-form handle, overall brick red alkaline glaze, unsigned but attributed to the redware factory in Bergholtz, New York, ca. 1860, 10" h. (minor chipping at base & rim)... $99

Preserve jar, cov., flat-bottomed cylindrical form curving up to a wide flat cupped mouth w/an inset flat cover w/button finial, fine burnt orange peppered glaze, attributed to the Wilcox factory, Bloomfield or Morganville, New York, ca. 1840, 8" h. (surface wear on rim chip, few surface chips at base, rim chipping on cover) $165

Early Redware Salt Dip

Salt dip, round foot & short wide stem supporting a deep rounded bowl w/flat rim, mottled brown alkaline glaze, ca. 1850, excellent condition, 2 1/4" h. (ILLUS.)......... $66

Stew pot, cov., ovoid body tapering to a flared rim, applied side strap handle, inset flat cover w/ringed knob finial, brownish red glaze, five incised shoulder lines, bottom incised "703," cover impressed "John Safford 2d - 703," shoulder also incised w/maker's mark, Maine, 19th c., 7" h. (chip to rim, some bottom roughness) $1,600

Redware Teapot Glazed in Drippy Blue

Teapot, cov., wide slightly waisted cylindrical body w/a thin shoulder & low flat neck, serpentine spout & C-scroll handle, inset cover w/button finial, ivory-colored base clay covered in a mottled runny dark blue, the base & interior glazed in dark

reddish brown, 19th c., minor glaze
flakes on spout, 5 1/2" h. (ILLUS.) **$138**

Rockingham Wares

*The Marquis of Rockingham first established
an earthenware pottery in the Yorkshire district
of England around 1745, and it was occupied
afterwards by various potters. The well-known
mottled brown Rockingham glaze was introduced
about 1788 by the Brameld Brothers and became
immediately popular. It was during the 1820s
that the production of true porcelain began at the
factory, and it continued to be made until the firm
closed in 1842. Since that time the so-called Rockingham glaze has been used by various potters in
England and the United States, including some
famous wares produced in Bennington, Vermont.
Very similar glazes were also used by potteries in
other areas of the United States including Ohio
and Indiana, but only wares specifically attributed to Bennington should use that name. The following listings will include mainly wares
featuring the dark brown mottled glaze produced
at various sites here and abroad.*

Bowl, 10 1/2" d., 3" h., flat bottomed w/deep
canted sides, yellowware w/overall dark
mottled brown glaze, molded ribbing on
exterior bottom, late 19th - early 20th c.,
excellent condition..................................... **$66**
Bowl, 11" d., 5" h., small footring below the
wide deep rounded sides w/a thick molded & rolled rim, the exterior molded w/a
repeating design of columns, yellowware
w/overall dark brown mottled glaze, late

19th - early 20th c. (minor surface wear,
small shallow stone ping on interior)........... **$99**
Bowl, 11 1/2" d., 3 3/4" h., footring below
the wide rounded bowl w/a flaring rolled
rim, yellowware w/overall dark mottled
brown glaze, molded pattern of columns
around the sides, late 19th c. (short hairline at rim extending from worn small
chip) **$44**
Coffeepot, cov., miniature, tapering cylin-
drical body w/a large rim spout & angled
handle, inset cover w/knob finial, yellowware w/overall dark brown mottled glaze,
uncommon form, late 19th c., 4 1/2" h. **$358**
Creamer, footring below the bulbous ovoid
body tapering to a curved rim w/broad
upright spout & C-scroll handle, each
side molded in relief w/a fancy scrolled
oval frame enclosing the bust profile of a
man, yellowware w/very dark brown mot-
tled glaze, late 19th c., 4 1/2" h................. **$121**
Creamer, tapering ovoid body w/an undulating rim & wide arched spout, C-scroll
handle, yellowware w/overall mottled
dark brown Rockingham glaze, 19th c.,
5 1/2" h. (ILLUS. left with hound-handled
pitcher, bottom of page) **$44**
Flask, flattened ovoid body w/small neck,
yellowware molded in relief w/an oval reserve enclosing a half-length portrait of a
man snorting snuff on each side, overall
dark mottled brown Rockingham glaze,
possibly Bennington, Vermont, or East
Liverpool, Ohio, excellent condition, first
half 19th c., 7 1/2" h. (ILLUS., next page)
.... **$248**

Rockingham Creamer & Hound-handled Pitcher

Early Flask with Scene of Man Taking Snuff

Early Rockingham Ware Foot Warmer

Foot warmer, wide flattened half-round form w/two molded indentations on the top for feet, a small spout at the top end, overall mottled brown glaze, American-made, ca. 1860, underside crazing, small flakes in the glaze, 7" w., 10" h. (ILLUS.) $230

Mug, waisted cylindrical form w/molded base band, C-form strap handle, yellowware w/finely mottled dark brown glaze, excellent condition, late 19th c., 3 1/2" h. $77

Mug, cylindrical w/molded base band, C-form handle, yellowware w/boldly spotted overall mottled brown glaze, excellent condition, late 19th c., 3 3/4" h. $358

Pie plate, round flat-bottomed form w/canted sides, yellowware w/overall light mottled brown glaze, late 19th c., 9 1/2" d. (minor glaze crazing on bottom, rim chip) $33

Pie plate, round flat-bottomed form w/canted sides, yellowware w/overall finely speckled dark mottled brown glaze, late 19th c., 9 1/2" d. (tight clay separation line down from rim from firing)...................... $66

Pie plate, round flat-bottomed form w/canted sides, yellowware w/overall bold dark mottled brown glaze, late 19th c.,

9 3/4" d. (surface wear at bottom edge, minor glaze wear on interior) $44

Pie plate, round flat-bottomed form w/canted sides, yellowware w/overall dark mottled brown glaze, late 19th c., 9 3/4" d. (minor glaze wear on bottom) $66

Pie plate, round flat-bottomed form w/canted sides, yellowware w/overall boldly spotted dark mottled brown glaze, late 19th c., 10 1/4" d. (minor surface wear on bottom, tight hairline from rim into bottom)... $55

Pie plate, round flat-bottomed form w/canted sides, yellowware w/overall bold dark mottled brown glaze, late 19th c., 10 3/4" d. (very tight hairline down from rim to center bottom).................................. $22

Hound-handled Molded Rockingham Pitcher

Pitcher, 6 1/2" h., hound-handled, flat-bottomed swelled cylindrical body w/a flattened shoulder to the neck w/a wide arched spout, the body molded in relief w/a continuous hound & deer hunting scene, molded vine band around the neck, yellowware w/overall dark brown Rockingham glaze, possibly West Troy Factory, Troy, New York, ca. 1860, excellent condition (ILLUS.)......................... $275

Rockingham Pitcher with Hunting Scene

Pitcher, 6 1/2" h., hound-handled, wide bulbous body w/a flattened shoulder to the wide flared neck & wide arched spout, relief-molded w/stag hunting scene, overall very dark brown glaze, possibly Bennington, Vermont, ca. 1850 (ILLUS.) $144

Pitcher, 8" h., footed paneled body w/large pointed petals at the bottom of each side panel, shaped rim w/wide arched spout, C-scroll handle, yellowware w/overall dark mottled brown glaze, 19th c. (very minor chip at rim) **$66**

Pitcher, 8 1/4" h., cylindrical w/a molded design of a peacock & palm trees on each side, yellowware w/overall dark brown mottled glaze, excellent condition, late 19th c. **$88**

Pitcher, 8 1/2" h., hound-handled, footed baluster-form body w/a wide arched spout, the body deeply molded w/a design of hanging dead game including ducks, rabbits & a fox, yellowware w/overall dark brown mottled Rockingham glaze, few minor glaze wear spots, rare design, mid-19th c. (ILLUS. right with creamer) **$248**

Hound-handled Rockingham Pitcher

Pitcher, 9 1/2" h., yellowware w/overall mottled dark brown glaze, molded hound handle, wide baluster form shape molded in relief w/eight panels of hanging game & fowl, a molded eagle under the wide spout, minor hairline in bottom, minor glaze wear, ca. 1850 (ILLUS.).................. **$121**

Platter, 9 1/2 x 12 1/2", wide rectangular form w/canted corners & shallow angled sides, yellowware w/overall finely mottled dark brown glaze, 19th c. (some glaze wear & surface scratching from use)......... **$176**

Rockingham Rebecca at the Well Teapot

Teapot, cov., footed ovoid body w/swan's-neck spout & C-form handle, domed cover w/bud-form finial, mottled brown glaze w/relief-molded scene of Rebecca at the well, early 20th c., Ohio, 8 1/2" h. (ILLUS.) **$200**

Rockingham Gothic Arch Tobacco Jar

Tobacco jar, cov., wide molded base below the paneled body w/a large Gothic arch in each panel, wide rolled rim & inset cover w/knob handle, molded leaf scroll side handles, overall dark brown mottled glaze, attributed to Bennington, Vermont, ca. 1847-58, some nicks on top rim, cover replaced, 8" w., 8 1/2" h. (ILLUS.)................. **$288**

Unusual Rockingham Washboard

Washboard, rectangular wooden frame enclosing a yellowware washboard w/a mottled brown glaze, minor glaze wear, overall wear to frame, ca. 1880, 25" h. (ILLUS.).. **$550**

Rookwood

Considered America's foremost art pottery, the Rookwood Pottery Company was established in Cincinnati, Ohio, in 1880 by Mrs. Maria Nichols Longworth Storer. To accurately record its development, each piece carried the Rookwood insignia or mark, was dated, and, if individually decorated, was usually signed by the artist. The pottery remained in Cincinnati until 1959, when it was sold to Herschede Hall Clock Company and moved to Starkville, Mississippi, where it continued in operation until 1967.

A private company is now producing a limited variety of pieces using original Rookwood molds.

Rookwood Mark

Early Silver-overlaid Rookwood Basket

Basket, squatty rounded shape w/the sides folded up and the ends pulled out, a broad peaked handle from side to side, Standard glaze decorated w/yellow flowers & buds & large green leaves against a shaded dark to light brown ground, decorated w/silver overlay in a leafy scroll design around the ends, rim & handle, silver marked by the Gorham Mfg. Co., breaks & losses to silver, 1893, Harriet Wilcox, 7 x 10 1/2" (ILLUS.) **$2,185**

Ewer, short squatty bulbous body tapering to a flared & pinched rim, small loop shoulder handle, Standard glaze, decorated w/yellow & brown pansies on a mottled tan & green ground, fine overall crazing, 1892, Harriet Straefer, 3 3/4" h..... **$345**

Humidor Decorated by Maria Nichols

Humidor, cov., Limoges-style decoration, round foot below the four-sided rounded body w/a flattened domed cover, painted

w/an overall design of spiders & bats on a mottled tan, rust, blue & white ground, glaze bubble under outer lid, 1882, Maria Longworth Nichols, 6" w., 6" h. (ILLUS.) **$2,185**

Rookwood Standard Glaze Humidor

Humidor, cov., wide gently tapering cylindrical body w/a low flaring serpentine rim & inside flat cover w/knob finial, Standard glaze, decorated w/a scene of two Native American dancers against a dark brown to brownish green ground, 1893, Harriet Wilcox, 6 1/2" d., 6 1/2" h. (ILLUS.) **$1,115**

Early Standard Glaze Humidor

Humidor, cov., wide slightly tapering cylindrical form w/a low cupped rim around the inset flattened cover w/a button finial, Standard glaze, decorated around the sides w/orange nicotiana blossoms & green leaves against a shaded gold to moss green ground, hairline inside cover, 1893, Bruce Horsfall, 6" d., 6 1/4" h. (ILLUS.) **$575**

Mug, tankard-type, base band & tall tapering cylindrical sides w/an angled handle, Standard glaze, decorated w/a three-quarters length portrait of a Native American, Chief Mountain (Big Brave) - Blackfeet, against a dark green to golden yellow ground, 1899, Grace Young, 6 1/2" d., 7 1/2" h. (ILLUS., next page) **$4,600**

Tall Rookwood Mug with Portrait

Paperweight, model of a seated squirrel on a half-round log, bluish green matte glaze, No. 6025, 1928, 4 1/4" h................ **$303**

Pitcher, 10" h., 5" d., tankard-type, a base band below the tall tapering slender body w/a small rim spout & squared handle, Standard glaze decorated w/a school of green fish against a shaded yellow to orange ground, further decorated w/silver overlay pierced scrolls around the base & a grapevine around the rim, a silver-clad handle, silver marked by the Gorham

Tall Rookwood Silver-overlaid Pitcher

Mfg. Co., 1894, Matthew Daly (ILLUS.) **$3,335**

Plaque, long horizontal rectangular form, decorated w/a misty lakeside landscape w/trees in the foreground, in shades of dark & light green, blue, grey & lavender, in a wide flat oak frame, 1922, E. Timothy Hurley, glaze miss, plaque 4 x 8" (ILLUS., bottom of page) **$4,313**

Lovely Rookwood Porcelain Landscape Plaque

Fine Meadow Landscape Plaque

Plaque, rectangular, Vellum glaze, a verdant landscape w/a large meadow in the foreground & a small river & trees in the distance, shades of green, grey, blue & white, original wide flat oak frame, 1915, Kate Van Horn, 8 3/4 x 11" (ILLUS., top of page) **$6,325**

Platter, 6 x 10 1/4", oblong undulating organic shaped w/a low upright edge, Standard glaze, decorated w/leafy strawberry vines on a light green ground, uncrazed, 1892, Edward Abel..................................... **$805**

Unusual Rookwood Turkish Teapot

Teapot, cov., tall Turkish-style pot, a narrow footring supporting the bulbous ovoid lower body tapering sharply to a tall cylindrical neck w/a domed cap cover & gold button finial, tall slender serpentine spout joined to the neck w/a delicate S-scroll bracket, long arched handle from the top of the neck to the shoulder, creamy ground h.p. on one side w/a scene of a blue frog seated on shore & holding a fishing pole, the reverse decorated w/a scene of sandcrabs, in shades of dark blue, tan & dark blue w/ornate gold trim, dull semi-matte glaze, mark attributed to M.L. Nichols, dated 1883, 11" h. (ILLUS.)
.... **$1,725**

Standard Glaze Rookwood Teapot

Teapot, cov., footed wide squatty bulbous body w/a short angled spout, flat rim w/low domed cover sprig finial, an arched real bamboo swing bail handle, Standard Glaze, decorated w/dark golden yellow leafy & flowering branches on a shaded brown to dark green to mustard yellow ground, Shape No. 404W, 1894, Josephine Zettel, 7" l., 4" h. (ILLUS.)................ **$881**

Trivet, round, embossed w/a large bird among bare branches, matte light yellow glaze on an ivory ground, 1929, 5 1/2" d. .. **$403**

Lovely Iris Glaze Vase with Leaves

Vase, 6 1/2" h., 3 3/4" d., ovoid body tapering to a short cylindrical neck, Iris glaze, decorated w/yellowish amber maple leaves against a dark grey shaded to pale yellow ground, overall crazing, No. 1905E, 1903, Irene Bishop (ILLUS.) **$1,725**

Sea Green Glazed Vase with Flowers

Vase, 6 3/4" h., 5" d., ovoid body tapering to a wide flat mouth flanked by small loop handles, Sea Green glaze, decorated w/large brown & cream flowers on dark green stems against a dark blue to green ground, No. 604D, 1902, Sallie Toohey (ILLUS.)... **$3,738**

Vase, 7" h., slightly swelled cylindrical form tapering to a short flared neck, Standard glaze, decorated w/yellow narcissus against a dark brown to green to yellow ground, a few scratches, 1894, Lenore Asbury... **$546**

Vase, 7" h., 3" d., slightly swelled cylindrical form w/a narrow shoulder tapering to a

short rolled neck, Green Vellum glaze, stylized scenic w/a bird's-eye view of an arid landscape w/a cobalt blue river, No. 904E, 1911, Sara Sax............................ **$6,900**

Rookwood Sea Green Vase with Cranes

Vase, 7 1/4" h., 3" d., footring below the slightly swelled cylindrical body w/a narrow shoulder to the thick flared rim, Sea Green glaze, decorated w/three standing cranes in black, white & a touch of red, among tall dark green grasses, against a dark green to pale yellowish green ground, small firing line at rim, 1894, Matthew Daley (ILLUS.)................................ **$4,313**

Elegant Scenic Vellum Rookwood Vase

Vase, 7 1/2" h., 3 1/2" d., cylindrical w/incurved flat wide mouth, Vellum glaze, scenic design elegantly painted w/flying Canada geese above stalks of bamboo against a dark blue to cream to green ground, no crazing, 1911, No. 952E, Kataro Shirayamadani (ILLUS.) **$8,625**

Vase, 7 1/2" h., 4" d., footed swelling cylindrical body w/a wide closed rim, Wax Matte glaze, decorated around the upper body w/a wreath of blue dogwood blossoms & green leaves against a shaded purple to blue butterfat ground, No. 1779, 1925, Margaret McDonald **$1,495**

Vase, 8 1/4" h., 3 3/4" d., slightly waisted cylindrical form w/a flat rim, Standard glaze, decorated w/large yellow tulips & green leaves against a shaded black to green to orange ground, No. 950D, 1905, Caroline Steinle... **$748**

Vase, 8 1/2" h., 3 3/4" d., slightly tapering ovoid form w/a small flat mouth, Vellum glaze, a scenic design w/a large leafy tree beside a pond w/trees in the distance, in shades of greens, creams & peach, very light crazing, 1916, No. 2033E, Elizabeth McDermott **$4,600**

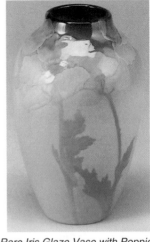

Rare Iris Glaze Vase with Poppies

Vase, 10 1/2" h., 4 1/4" d., slightly swelled cylindrical form w/a flat closed rim, Carved Matte glaze, deeply modeled around the top w/oak branches & acorns in green, brown & burgundy on a brown butterfat ground, No. 951C, 1905, Rose Fechheimer... **$3,220**

Vase, 10 1/2" h., 5 1/2" d., ovoid body tapering to a wide flat mouth, Incised Matte glaze, molded around the shoulder w/bright red fruit & green & purple leaves on a shaded deep purple to umber butterfat ground, No. 943C, 1918, Elizabeth Lincoln.. **$3,450**

Rookwood Venetian Harbor Scene Vase

Vase, 9 1/2" h., tall slightly swelled cylindrical body w/a narrow shoulder to a short neck w/molded flat rim, Vellum glaze, decorated w/a continuous Venetian glaze in shades of blue, green, black & brown, crazing, 1922, Carl Schmidt (ILLUS.) **$3,450**

Vase, 9 1/2" h., 6" d., simple ovoid body tapering to a flat rim, Iris glaze, decorated w/large mauve poppies w/yellow centers on pale green leafy stems against a shaded mauve to pale yellowish green ground, Pan American Exposition paper label, No. 900B, 1900, O.G. Reed (ILLUS., top next column)... **$9,775**

Vase, 10" h., 3 1/4" h., footed slender baluster-form body w/a widely flaring trumpet rim, Jewel Porcelain, decorated w/long green leafy vines of orange trumpet flowers against a light yellow ground, 1923, No. 2545C, Sara Sax **$3,335**

Jewel Porcelain Vase with Magnolias

Vase, 11" h., 7 1/2" d., footed cylindrical form w/a rounded base & shoulder centered by a flat mouth, Jewel Porcelain, decorated w/smeary branches of large pink & grey magnolia blossoms on an ivory ground, No. 2581, 1923, William Hentschel (ILLUS.)................................. **$4,025**

Vase, 11 3/4" h., 5" d., slightly swelling cylindrical body w/a wide flat mouth, Incised Matte glaze, decorated w/a stylized pattern around the shoulder in red & turquoise over a purple butterfat ground, No. 2039C, 1915, William Hentschel **$3,450**

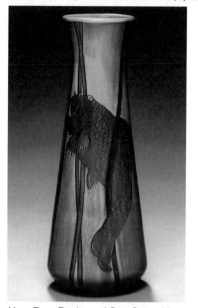

Very Rare Rookwood Sea Green Vase

Vase, 12 7/8" h., slender tapering cylindrical form w/a flaring rim, Sea Green glaze, decorated w/a large fish swimming among sea grass, in shades of green against a pale yellow ground, 1899, Albert Valentien (ILLUS.)...................... **$17,925**

Extraordinary Rookwood Portrait Vase

Vase, 16" h., 15" w., pillow-type, wide flattened & rounded form w/a narrow pinched-in rim, Standard glaze, decorat-

ed w/a large bust portrait of the Native American Chief Hollow Horn Bear - Sioux, against a shaded dark brown to orange & green ground, 1900, Matthew Daley (ILLUS.) **$74,750**

Very Early Rookwood Vase

Vase, 23 1/2" h., 11" d., broad ovoid body tapering to a wide cylindrical neck w/a flared rim, Limoges-style, the body decorated w/a continuous Japanese-inspired scene of birds perched on blossoming branches against a tan ground highlighted w/brown & white, the neck in dark green w/a gold rim, 1883, Albert Valentien (ILLUS.).. **$5,750**

Rose Medallion & Rose Canton

The lovely Chinese ware known as Rose Medallion was made through the past century and into the present one. It features alternating panels of people and flowers or insects, with most pieces having four medallions with a central rose or peony medallion. The ware is called Rose Canton if florals and birds or insects fill all the panels. Unless otherwise noted, our listing is for Rose Medallion ware.

Rose Medallion Pitcher & Covered Vegetable Dishes

Pitcher, 6 3/4" h., flat-bottomed bulbous ovoid body tapering to a wide arched spout & arched loop handle, alternating panels of figures & birds among flowers, some gilt wear, late 19th c. (ILLUS. left with pair of vegetable dishes) **$805**

Fine Rose Medallion Punch Bowl

Punch bowl, deep rounded sides, decorated around the exterior & interior w/alternating panels featuring domestic scenes or birds in gardens, border band of alternating floral panels, w/a carved wood stand, ca. 1800, 15 1/4" d., 6 1/4" h. (ILLUS.) **$1,265**

Tall Rose Medallion Vase

Vase, 25" h., traditional form w/swelled cylindrical body tapering to a tall cylindrical neck w/a wide flattened rim, gilt figural foo dogs & salamanders at the shoulder, decorated w/large alternating figural & flower & butterfly panels, chip on bottom of base, late 19th c. (ILLUS.) **$920**

Rose Medallion Vegetable Dish

Vegetable dish, cov., rectangular notched corners, the domed cover w/a large figural fruit finial & alternating panels of Chinese figures on parquet floors & bird, butterflies & flowers, interior of bottom w/matching design centering a bird perched on flowering branches w/a butterfly against a conforming ground w/a wide gold rim, the sides of the base w/four red & green floral sprays, heavy gilt wear, small chips to interior & base rim, ca. 1880, 10 x 10 3/4", 6 3/4" h. (ILLUS.) **$920**
Vegetable dishes, cov., low oval form w/a wide flattened flanged rim w/serpentine edge, low domed cover w/pine cone finial, decorated w/floral panels, 8 1/2 x 11", 4" h., pr. (ILLUS. right with pitcher) **$690**

Roseville

Roseville Pottery Company operated in Zanesville, Ohio, from 1898 to 1954, having been in business for six years prior to that in Muskingum County, Ohio. Art wares similar to those of Owens and Weller Potteries were produced. Items listed here are by patterns or lines.

Roseville Mark

Apple Blossom (1948)
White apple blossoms in relief on blue, green or pink ground; brown tree branch handles.

Blue Fanned Apple Blossom Basket

Basket, flattened fan-shaped body w/widely flaring arched rim, high round overhead branch handle, blue ground, No. 309-8", 8" h. (ILLUS.) **$175-275**

Green Fanned Apple Blossom Basket

Basket, flattened fan-shaped body w/widely flaring arched rim, high round overhead branch handle, green ground, No. 309-8", 8" h. (ILLUS.) **$150**

Tall Green Apple Blossom Ewer

Ewer, tall, footed, slender ovoid body w/a tall arched spout & branch handle, green ground, No. 318-15", 15" h. (ILLUS.) **$374**

Jardiniere & pedestal base, green ground, jardiniere, No. 302-8", 8" h., pedestal, No. 305-8", 24 1/2" h., 2 pcs. (minor flake on foot of jardiniere) **$690**

Teapot, cov., blue ground, No. 371-P **$300**

Teapot, cov., pink ground, No. 371-P **$250**

Long Green Apple Blossom Basket

Basket, footed, long narrow body, low overhead branch handle, green ground, No. 310-10", 11 1/2" l., 10" h. (ILLUS.) **$316**

Spherical Green Apple Blossom Vase

Vase, 6" h., spherical body w/asymmetrical rim & handles, green ground, chips under base, No. 342-6" (ILLUS.) **$173**

Apple Blossom Round Candlesticks

Candlesticks, footed, spherical form w/small branch handles, green ground, No. 351-2", 2" h., pr. (ILLUS.) **$92**

Cylindrical Green Apple Blossom Vase

Vase, 9 1/2" h., 5" d., asymmetrical handles, cylindrical w/disc base, green ground, No. 387-9" (ILLUS.) **$184**

Blue Apple Blossom Vase

Vase, 10" h., wide flaring foot w/base handles, trumpet-form body, blue ground, No. 388-10" (ILLUS.).................................. **$184**

Pink Cylindrical Apple Blossom Vase

Vase, 10" h., swelled cylindrical body w/shaped rim, disk base w/handles up the sides, pink ground, No. 389-10" (ILLUS.) **$140-180**

Footed Cylindrical Apple Blossom Vase

Vase, 10" h., swelled cylindrical body w/shaped rim, disk base w/handles up the sides, green ground, No. 389-10" (ILLUS.)
.... **$184**

Blue Apple Blossom Floor Vase

Vase, 15" h., floor type, double base handles, short globular base, long cylindrical neck, blue ground, No. 392-15" (ILLUS.)... **$518**
Wall pocket, conical w/overhead branch handle, stepped rim, green ground, No. 366-8", 8" h. **$230**

Pink Apple Blossom Wall Pocket

Wall pocket, conical w/overhead branch handle, stepped rim, pink ground, No. 366-8", 8" h. (ILLUS.)................................ **$230**

Baneda (1933)
Band of embossed pods, blossoms and leaves on green or raspberry pink ground.

Fine Footed Green Baneda Jardiniere

Jardiniere, footed, wide bulbous body w/wide flat mouth, two-handled, green ground, No. 626-5", 5" h. (ILLUS., previous page) **$690**

Vase, 4" h., footed bulbous body w/incurved flat rim, flat shoulder handles, raspberry pink ground, No. 587-4" **$288**

Footed Bulbous Green Baneda Vase

Small & Large Baneda Vases

Vase, 5" h., footed, pear-shaped w/small loop handles near rim, green ground, No. 601-5" (ILLUS. left) **$345**

Small Footed Bulbous Baneda Vase

Vase, 6 1/4" h., footed bulbous body w/short slightly flaring rim, small loop shoulder handles, raspberry pink ground, light glaze crazing, No. 591-6" (ILLUS.) **$489**

Footed Bulbous Pink Baneda Vase

Vase, 6" h., bulbous body w/slightly flaring rim, small loop shoulder handles, raspberry pink ground, gold Roseville sticker, glaze bruise inside one handle, minor glaze bursts, No. 591-6" (ILLUS.) **$316**

Vase, 6" h., bulbous body w/slightly flaring rim, small loop shoulder handles, green ground, No. 591-6" (ILLUS., top next column) **$500**

Fine Raspberry Pink Baneda Vase

Vase, 7" h., footed wide cylindrical body tapering to short wide cylindrical neck, small loop handles, raspberry pink ground, No. 592-7" (ILLUS.) **$575**

Cylindrical Pink Baneda Vase

Vase, 7 1/4" h., footed, swelled cylindrical body tapering to a short, wide, cylindrical neck flanked by small down-curved loop handles, raspberry pink ground, minor glaze skips, No. 590-7" (ILLUS.) **$350-450**

Raspberry Pink Bulbous Baneda Vase

Vase, 8" h., footed, globular w/shoulder handles, raspberry pink ground, small gold foil sticker, repair at base, No. 595-8" (ILLUS.) **$431**
Vase, 9" h., cylindrical w/short collared neck, handles rising from shoulder to beneath rim, green ground, No. 594-9" (ILLUS. right with small vase, previous page) **$1,150**
Vase, 9" h., cylindrical w/short collared neck, handles rising from shoulder to beneath rim, green ground, No. 594-9" (ILLUS., top next column) **$1,610**
Vase, 12" h., expanding cylinder w/small rim handles, green ground, No. 599-12" **$575**

Large Green Baneda Vase

Bittersweet (1940)

Orange bittersweet pods and green leaves on a grey blending to rose, yellow with terra cotta, rose with green or solid green bark-textured ground; brown branch handles.

Basket w/pointed overhead handle, asymmetrical scalloped rim, grey ground, No. 808-6", 6" h. **$115**
Book ends, handles, grey ground, No. 859, 5 1/2" h., pr. **$144**
Ewer, grey ground, No. 816-8", 8" h. **$173**
Teapot, cov., yellow ground, No. 871-P **$225**

Yellow Bittersweet Wall Pocket

Wall pocket, curving conical form w/overhead handle continuing to one side, yellow ground, No. 866-7", 7 1/2" h. (ILLUS.) .. **$288**

Blackberry (1933)

Band of relief clusters of blackberries with vines and ivory leaves accented in green and terra cotta on a green textured ground.

Blackberry Candleholders & Other Pieces

Candleholders, tapering domed base below a tall socket flanked by small open handles, No. 1086, 4 1/2" h., pr. (ILLUS. bottom left, top of page) **$748**
Console bowl, rectangular w/small handles, No. 228-10", 3 1/2 x 13" (ILLUS. top with candleholders, top of page) **$460**
Vase, 4" h., two-handled, bulbous, No. 567-4" **$500**
Vase, 5" h., loop handles at midsection, bulbous base tapering to wide cylindrical neck, No. 570-5" (ILLUS. bottom right with candleholders, top of page) **$748**
Vase, 6" h., wide flaring lower body w/a wide slightly tapering upper body flanked by small loop handles at the rim, No. 572-6" **$431**
Vase, 6" h., globular w/tiny rim handles, No. 574-6" **$690**
Vase, 8" h., handles at mid-section, slightly globular base & wide neck, No. 575-8" (bruise on one handle) **$500**

Bleeding Heart (1938)
Pink blossoms and green leaves on shaded blue, green or pink ground.

Jardiniere, green ground, No. 651-6", 6" h. **$150-250**
Vase, 5" h., footed trumpet-form w/angled side handles, pink ground, No. 962-5" **$144**

Bushberry (1948)
Berries and leaves on blue, green or russet bark-textured ground; brown or green branch handles.

Green Bushberry Hanging Basket

Basket, hanging type w/original chains, green ground, pin nick on body, No. 465-5", 7" d. (ILLUS.) **$173**

Bushberry Basket with Branch Handle

Basket, footed bulbous body w/wide uneven rim, long angular overhead branch handle, green ground, No. 370-8", 8" h. (ILLUS.) **$196**
Basket w/asymmetrical overhead handle, blue ground, No. 370-8", 8 1/2" h. **$259**

Green Bushberry Bookends

Bookends, green ground, No. 9, pr. (ILLUS.) **$200-300**

Bushberry Console Bowl & Flower Frog

Console bowl & flower frog, long, narrow boat-shaped bowl raised on a low forked branch pedestal forming pointed end handles & raised on an oval foot, No. 45 flower frog w/round low pedestal base, topped by a leaf & high curved & pointed open branch handle, green ground, bowl No. 1-10", 10" l., 2 pcs. (ILLUS.) **$259**
Ewer, cut-out rim, green ground, No. 3-15", 15" h. **$690**

Blue Bushberry Jardiniere

Jardiniere, 3" h., small side handles, globular, blue ground, No. 657-3" (ILLUS.) **$138**
Teapot, cov., blue ground, No. 2 .... **$250-350**
Teapot, cov., russet ground, No. 2 .... **$150-250**
Vase, 14 1/2" h., tall ovoid body w/an upward pointed handle at one side & a small downward pointed handle on the other side, blue ground, No. 39-14" **$460**

Tall Bushberry Blue Floor Vase

Vase, 18" h., floor type, footed baluster-form body w/angled branch shoulder handles,

blue ground, two small chips to outer rim edge, No. 41-18" (ILLUS.) **$403**
Vases, bud, 7 1/2" h., cylindrical body, asymmetrical base handles, russet ground, No. 152-7", pr. **$374**
Wall pocket, high-low handles, blue ground, No. 1291-8", 8" h. **$431**

Carnelian I (1915-27)
Matte smooth glaze with a combination of two colors or two shades of the same color with the darker dripping over the lighter tone. Generally in colors of blue, pink and green.

Bowl, 9" d., 3" h., two-handled, canted sides, pink & grey, No. 164-7" **$104**
Ewer, footed bulbous ovoid body w/a short neck & wide arched spout, long loop handle, pink & grey, No. 1312-10", 10" h. **$259**
Plate, footed wide flattened round shape, green, 158-12", 12 1/2" d. **$300-400**
Vase, double bud, 5" h., gate-form, olive green & blue-green, No. 56-5" **$115**
Vase, 7" h., double gourd-form w/wide neck & flaring rim, ornate pointed & scrolled handles from mid-section of base to below rim, light & dark green, No. 310-7" **$144**

Carnelian II (1915-31)
Intermingled colors, some with a drip effect, giving a textured surface appearance. Colors similar to Carnelian I.

Candleholders, angular pyramidal base flanked by low open handles, rectangular socket, mottled pink & purple, No. 1064-3", 3 1/2" h., pr. **$173**
Wall pocket, widely flaring peaked rim above a ringed neck & bullet-form base, straight handles from bottom of rim to the sides, mottled pink & purple, No. 1253-8", 8" l. **$374**

Cherry Blossom (1933)
Sprigs of cherry blossoms, green leaves and twigs with pink fence against a combed blue-green ground or creamy ivory fence against a terra cotta ground shading to dark brown.

Terra Cotta Cherry Blossom Bowl-Vase

Bowl-vase, wide, squatty, bulbous body tapering to a wide, flat, molded mouth flanked by small loop handles, terra cotta ground, partial triangular sticker, No. 350-5", 5" h. (ILLUS.) **$259**

Pink & Blue Cherry Blossom Bowl-Vase

Bowl-vase, wide, squatty, bulbous body tapering to a wide, flat, molded mouth flanked by small loop handles, pink & blue ground, blisters in the flowers, No. 350-5", 5" h. (ILLUS.)............................ **$288**

Cherry Blossom Flowerpot

Flowerpot, footed wide slightly flaring cylindrical shape w/small loop handles at the rim, terra cotta ground, No. 239-5", 5" h. (ILLUS.).. **$288**

Bulbous Cherry Blossom Jardiniere

Jardiniere, squatty bulbous body w/a wide molded rim flanked by small loop handles, terra cotta ground, No. 627-5", 5" h. (ILLUS.).. **$316**
Lamp, footed spherical vase body w/a short neck flanked by small loop handles, a low domed cap at the top for wiring, shaded yellowish green, experimental, repaired chip on base, No. 625-8", 9" h. (ILLUS., top of next column).................................... **$863**

Experimental Cherry Blossom Lamp

Small Squatty Cherry Blossom Vase

Vase, 4" h., compressed squatty bulbous body w/a short, slightly flared neck flanked by small loop handles, pink & blue ground, some peppering in glaze, No. 617-3 1/2" (ILLUS.)............................ **$316**

Terra Cotta Cherry Blossom 5" Vase

Vase, 5" h., bulbous ovoid body tapering to a small molded mouth flanked by small loop handles, terra cotta ground, No. 618-5" (ILLUS.)... **$288**

Pink & Blue Cherry Blossom 5" Vase

Vase, 5" h., bulbous ovoid body tapering to a small molded mouth flanked by small loop handles, pink & blue ground, No. 618-5" (ILLUS.) **$431**

Pink & Blue Cherry Blossom Ovoid Vase

Vase, 5" h., wide ovoid body tapering to a wide, slightly rolled mouth flanked by small loop handles, pink & blue ground, No. 619-5" (ILLUS.) **$375-400**

Terra Cotta 5" Cherry Blossom Vase

Vase, 5" h., wide ovoid body tapering to a wide slightly rolled mouth flanked by small loop handles, terra cotta ground, No. 619-5" (ILLUS.) **$259**

Bulbous 6" Cherry Blossom Vase

Vase, 6" h., bulbous body, shoulder tapering to wide molded mouth, small loop shoulder handles, terra cotta ground, unmarked, No. 621-6" (ILLUS.) **$259**

Ovoid Cherry Blossom Vase

Vase, 7" h., ovoid body tapering to a small rolled mouth flanked by small loop shoulder handles, silver Roseville sticker, terra cotta ground, No. 622-7" (ILLUS.) **$288**

Pink-Blue Ovoid Cherry Blossom Vase

Vase, 7" h., ovoid body w/tiny shoulder handles, pink & blue ground, No. 623-7" (ILLUS., previous page) **$403**

Ovoid Cherry Blossom Vase

Vase, 7" h., ovoid body w/tiny shoulder handles, terra cotta ground, unmarked, No. 623-7" (ILLUS.) **$374**

Cylindrical Cherry Blossom Vase

Vase, 7 1/2" h., footed cylindrical body w/small loop handles near the rim, pink & blue ground, No. 620-7" (ILLUS.).............. **$403**

Tall Cherry Blossom Vase

Vase, 10" h., slender ovoid body w/wide cylindrical neck, loop handles from

shoulder to middle of neck, terra cotta ground, small glaze miss on rim, No. 626-10" (ILLUS.) **$500**

Vase, 15" h., floor-type, bulbous ovoid w/wide molded mouth, small loop shoulder handles, terra cotta to brown ground, No. 628-15" (bruise to base rim)........... **$1,495**

Chloron (1907)

Molded in high relief in the manner of early Roman and Greek artifacts. Solid matte green glaze, sometimes combined with ivory. Very similar in form to Egypto.

Rare Chloron Fish-form Candlestick

Candleholder, chamberstick-type, oblong shallow fish-form base w/flat upright fish-tail handle at one end, the shaft molded as upright folded green leaves around a bud-form candlesocket, No. 341-7", 7" h. (ILLUS.)... **$1,093**

Unusual Bubbled Chloron Vase

Vase, 8" h., wide squatty bulbous lower body w/overall large bubble-like raised design tapering to a ribbed neck flaring to a lobed, cupped rim w/low ruffled rim, uncommon & intricate Chloron inkstamp mark, bruise & nick at rim, No. 23-8" (ILLUS.)................. **$489**

Clemana (1934)

Stylized blossoms with embossed latticework and basketweave on blue, green or tan ground.

Three Blue Clemana Vases

Vase, 6" h., footed spherical body w/a wide flat mouth flanked by small angled tab handles, blue ground, small flakes on handles, No. 280-6" (ILLUS. center with other Clemana vases, top of page)............ **$201**

Vase, 6" h., swelled cylindrical body w/a small flat mouth, small angled handles at the shoulders, tan ground, No. 749-6" **$230**

Vase, 6 1/2" h., footed gently flaring cylindrical body w/a wide flat rim, small angled shoulder handles, green ground, No. 750-6"... **$374**

Vase, 7 1/2" h., ovoid body tapering to a short cylindrical neck, small pointed shoulder handles, tan ground, No. 752-7" .. **$173**

Vase, 8 1/2" h., trumpet foot below the wide gently flaring cylindrical body flanked by small pointed handles near the base, blue ground, No. 753-8" (ILLUS. left with spherical vase, top of page)....................... **$230**

Vase, 10" h., footed slightly swelled cylindrical body w/a short wide neck, small pointed shoulder handles, blue ground, No. 757-10" (ILLUS. right with spherical vase, top of page) **$259**

Clematis (1944)

Clematis blossoms and heart-shaped green leaves against a vertically textured ground, white blossoms on blue, rose-pink blossoms on green and ivory blossoms on golden brown.

Blue Clematis Hanging Basket

Basket, hanging type, blue ground, no chains, No. 470-5", 5" h. (ILLUS.)....... **$100-150**

Brown Clematis Basket with High Handle

Basket, waisted cylindrical body w/a high rounded arch overhead handle w/forked ends at each side, brown ground, No. 387-7" (ILLUS.)... **$173**

Large Blue Clematis Basket

Basket w/high overhead handle, pedestal base, blue ground, No. 389-10", 10" h. (ILLUS.)... **$150-200**

Green Clematis Long Console Bowl

Console bowl, long, low, narrow oblong form w/upright tiered sides & rim, pointed end handles, green ground w/pink blossoms, No. 458-10", 10" l. (ILLUS.) **$100-150**

Clematis Brown Creamer & Sugar

Creamer & open sugar bowl, brown ground, Nos. 5-C & 5-S, pr. (ILLUS.) **$69**

Brown Clematis Cookie Jar

Cookie jar, cov., brown ground, tiny glazed pit in body, No. 3-8", 8" h. (ILLUS.) **$250-300**

Tall Blue Clematis Ewer

Ewer, footed squatty bulbous lower body tapering sharply to a tall forked neck w/a very tall arched spout, long pointed handle from rim to shoulder, blue ground, No. 17-10", 10 1/2" h. (ILLUS.) **$125-175**

Blue Clematis Cornucopia-Vase

Cornucopia-vase, flattened fanned & tiered sides w/angular handle at the front, resting on a rectangular base, blue ground, No. 193-6", 6" h. (ILLUS.) **$75-85**

Cornucopia-vase, flattened fanned & tiered sides w/angular handle at the front, resting on a rectangular base, green ground w/pink blossom, No. 193-6", 6" h. **$65-75**

Brown Clematis Ewer

Ewer, footed squatty bulbous lower body tapering sharply to a tall forked neck w/a very tall arched spout, long pointed handle from rim to shoulder, brown ground w/creamy yellow flowers, No. 17-10", 10 1/2" h. (ILLUS.) **$150-200**

Pale Green Clematis Ewer

Ewer, footed squatty bulbous lower body tapering sharply to a tall forked neck w/a very tall arched spout, long pointed handle from rim to shoulder, shaded pale green ground w/white flowers, No. 17-10", 10 1/2" h. (ILLUS.) **$104**

Teapot, cov., brown ground, No. 5, 7" h. **$150-200**

Teapot, cov., green ground, No. 5 .... **$150-200**

Green & Pink Clematis Vase

Vase, 8" h., footed bulbous ovoid body tapering to a short cylindrical neck flanked by pointed shoulder handles, green ground w/pink blossoms, No. 107-8" (ILLUS.) **$161**

Tall Green & Pink Clematis Vase

Vase, 10 1/4" h., footed tall ovoid body w/a wide flat mouth flanked by small pointed loop handles, green ground w/pink flowers, No. 111-10" (ILLUS.) **$138**

White & Blue Clematis Vase

Vase, 12 1/2" h., tall gently swelled cylindrical body w/a flat mouth, open angled handles near the rim, blue ground, No. 112-12" (ILLUS.) **$150-200**

Vase, 15" h., footed tall waisted cylindrical form w/flaring rim flanked by long pierced pointed handles, blue ground, No. 114-15" (minor base chip) **$250-350**

Columbine (1940s)

Columbine blossoms and foliage on shaded ground, yellow blossoms on blue, pink blossoms on pink shaded to green, and blue blossoms on tan shaded to green.

Basket, elaborate handle rising from midsection, tan ground, No. 365-7", 7" h. **$115**

Basket, asymmetrical overhead handle, blue ground, No. 367-10", 10" h. **$288**

Jardiniere, squatty body w/small handles at shoulder, tan ground, No. 655-4", 4" h. **$115**

Vase, 7" h., footed tall waisted form w/fanned rim, pointed angled handles at the lower body, tan ground, No. 16-7" **$115**

Corinthian (1923)

Deeply fluted ivory and green body below a continuous band of molded grapevine, fruit, foliage and florals in naturalistic colors, narrow ivory and green molded border at the rim.

Footed 7" Corinthian Vase

Vase, 7" h., footed, swelled cylindrical sides w/molded neck band & flaring rim band, old gift shop sticker, slight firing line at base, No. 216-7" (ILLUS., previous page) .. **$150**

Cosmos (1940)
Embossed blossoms against a wavy horizontal ridged band on a textured ground, ivory band with yellow and orchid blossoms on blue, blue band with white, and orchid blossoms on green or tan.

Small Green Cosmos Jardiniere

Jardiniere, wide ovoid body w/small arched side handles & a wide upright scalloped rim, green ground, No. 649-3" (ILLUS.) **$104**

Flared Rectangular Blue Cosmos Vase

Vase, 8 1/2" h., rectangular foot below the wide waisted rectangular body w/a flaring crenelated rim, low arch handles down the sides, blue ground, No. 950-8" (ILLUS.) **$230**

Dahlrose (1924-28)
Band of ivory daisy-like blossoms and green leaves against a mottled tan ground.

Small Dahlrose Candleholders

Candleholders, angular handles rising from low slightly domed base, No. 1069-3", 3" h., pr. (ILLUS.) **$150-250**

Oval Dahlrose Center Bowl

Center bowl, 11" l., footed oval squatty bulbous body tapering to a wide flared rim, angular end handles from rim to shoulder, No. 180-8" (ILLUS.) **$260-290**

Center bowl, 11" l., footed oval squatty bulbous body tapering to a wide flared rim, angular end handles from rim to shoulder, No. 180-8" (ILLUS. center with chamberstick & jardiniere, top next page) **$288**

Chamberstick, domed oval base w/an off-center swelled cylindrical stem flanked by asymmetrical loop handles, No. 77-7", 7 1/2" h. (ILLUS. right with other Dahlrose pieces, top next page) **$316**

Jardiniere, bulbous slightly squatty body w/a molded rim & tiny rim handles, No. 614-7", 7" d., 4" h. (ILLUS. left with other Dahlrose pieces, top next page) **$230**

Small Spherical Dahlrose Jardiniere

Jardiniere, footed spherical body w/a wide low rolled neck flanked by small pointed handles, No. 614-4", 4 1/4" h. (ILLUS.) **$173**

Jardiniere, footed, bulbous form w/a thick molded rim flanked by tiny squared rim handles, No. 614-6", 6" h. (ILLUS., next page) **$161**

Vase, triple bud, 6" h., a domed round base w/a swelled cylindrical central shaft joined by floral panels to outcurved squared side holders, No. 76-6" **$250-300**

Dahlrose Chamberstick, Center Bowl & Jardiniere

Bulbous Dahlrose Jardiniere

Vase, 6" h., cylindrical form w/small pointed handles at the shoulder, No. 363-6".......... **$104**

Wide Bulbous Dahlrose Vase

Vase, 6" h., squatty bulbous body tapering to wide rolled rim, tiny angled handles from shoulder to rim, No. 364-6" (ILLUS.) **$161**

Vase, 6" h., 8" l., flattened pillow-type, tall upright rectangular form w/small angled handles at the top ends, black paper label, No. 358-8" (ILLUS., below) **$489**

Dahlrose Rectangular Pillow Vase

Rare Square Dahlrose Vase

Vase, 6 1/8" h., square flared foot below the slightly tapering square body w/a wide sharply flaring neck, black paper label, No. 372-6" (ILLUS.) **$748**

Roseville Dahlrose Bud Vase

Vase, bud, 8" h., slender swelled body w/flaring base & rolled rim, angled buttress side handles w/blossoms, black paper label, No. 78-8" (ILLUS.).............. **$175-200**

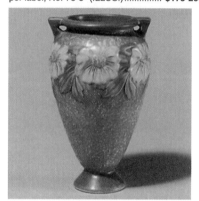

Footed Ovoid Dahlrose Vase

Vase, 8" h., small conical foot supporting the bulbous ovoid body w/a wide molded mouth flanked by tiny pointed shoulder handles, No. 365-8" (ILLUS.).................... **$230**

Bulbous Dahlrose Vase

Vase, 8" h., footed, bulbous lower body w/a slightly tapering upper half below the molded incurved mouth, angled handles from the rim to the shoulder, No. 367-8" (ILLUS.).).. **$150-200**
Vase, 12" h., footed wide ovoid body w/wide flaring rim, angled handles from shoulder to rim, No. 370-12"..................................... **$690**

Dawn (1937)
Incised spidery flowers on green ground with blue-violet tinted blossoms, pink or yellow ground with blue-green blossoms, all with yellow centers.

Rose bowl, squatty spherical body w/tab handles at sides, square base, yellow ground, No. 316-6", 6" d. **$230**
Vase, 6" h., semi-ovoid form, tab handles at rim, square foot, pink ground, No. 827-6" .. **$230**
Vase, 8" h., slender cylinder w/tab handles below rim, square foot, pink ground, No. 828-8" **$230**

Dogwood I - Smooth (1916-19)
White dogwood blossoms and brown branches against a smooth green ground.

Basket, wide bulbous body w/a heavy arched branch handle across the top w/forked ends, 6" h. **$288**
Basket, low widely flaring body w/incurved rim, a high arched & pointed handle from rim to rim, w/flower frog, 7" h. **$230**
Basket, ovoid body w/an arched & forked handle across the top, 9" h. **$316**

Bulbous Dogwood I Jardiniere

Jardiniere, bulbous cylindrical form w/wide flat closed rim, No. 590-9", 9 1/2" h. (ILLUS.) **$173**

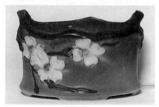

Dogwood I Planter Tub

Planter tub, oval w/upright sides, small
branch handles at rim ends, 4 x 7"
(ILLUS.) **$259**
Planter tub, oval w/upright undulating
rounded sides, 11 1/4" l., 6" h. **$350-400**
Vase, 8" h., ovoid body tapering to wide cylindrical neck, No. 135-8" **$230**

Large Dogwood I Vase

Vase, 14 1/2" h., tall ovoid form tapering to
a flat mouth, openwork branches just below the rim, a bruise on one side, some
minor glaze pits, No. 140-15" (ILLUS.) **$431**

Dogwood II - Textured (1926)
White dogwood blossoms and brown branches
against a textured green ground.

Bowl, 9" d., wide flattened squatty form
w/heavy molded rim, No. 150-9" **$115**
Vase, 7 1/4" h., footed bulbous ovoid body
tapering to a low wide rolled mouth, No.
301-7" **$200-275**

Donatello (1915)
Deeply fluted ivory and green body with wide
tan band embossed with cherubs at various pur-
suits in pastoral settings.

Wide, Low Donatello Bowl

Bowl, 8 1/2" d., 3 1/2" h., wide, low, cylindrical form, No. 238-7" (ILLUS.) **$125-150**

Large Squatty Donatello Jardiniere

Jardiniere, wide bulbous squatty form w/a
wide flaring short neck, No. 579-12",
12" h. (ILLUS.) **$374**

Large Donatello Jardiniere & Pedestal

Jardiniere & pedestal base, 12" h. jardiniere, No. 579-12", overall 34" h., 2 pcs.
(ILLUS.) **$1,000-1,200**

Donatello 10" Wall Pocket

Wall pocket, bullet-shaped w/arched backplate, No. 1202-10", 10" h. (ILLUS.) **$184**

Three Fine Roseville Falline Vases

Falline (1933)

Curving panels topped by a semi-scallop separated by vertical pea pod decorations; blended backgrounds of tan shading to green and blue or tan shading to darker brown.

Vase, 6" h., footed, cylindrical, w/large loop handles from midsection to rim, tan shading to brown, No. 642-6" (ILLUS. right with other Falline vases, top of page) **$633**

Vase, 6" h., globular body w/a narrow swelled shoulder below the wide short cylindrical neck, C-scroll handles from the neck to the top of the body, green "pods" on a light shaded to dark brown ground, No. 644-6" (ILLUS. center with other Falline vases, top of page) **$690**

Globular Falline Vase in Tan & Brown

Rare Nearly Spherical Falline Vase

Vase, 6 1/4" h., nearly spherical body w/a rounded shoulder band below the slightly flaring cylindrical neck flanked by C-scroll handles, brown shaded to pale yellow & green, unmarked, No. 644-6" (ILLUS.) ... **$1,610**

Vase, 7" h., globular body tapering to stepped shoulder & wide cylindrical neck w/shoulder loop handles, shaded tan to brown ground, gold sticker on bottom, repair to top of one handle, small nick on other, No. 648-7" (ILLUS., next column) **$374**

Trumpet-form Falline Vase

Vase, 8 1/4" h., 6" d., footed trumpet form w/a widely flaring rim, low arched handles from under the rim to mid-body, tan shading to green & blue, No. 646-8" (ILLUS., previous page) **$1,495**

Falline Trumpet Vase in Tan & Brown

Vase, 8 1/4" h., 6" d., footed trumpet form w/a widely flaring rim, low arched handles from under the rim to mid-body, tan shading to brown, small gold sticker, No. 646-8" (ILLUS.) **$690**

Ribbed Falline Vase

Vase, 9" h., two large handles rising from midsection to neck, horizontally ribbed lower section, shaded brown, small body nick, edge of one handle professionally repaired, No. 652-9" (ILLUS.) **$460**

Vase, 9" h., two large handles rising from midsection to neck, horizontally ribbed lower section, tan shading to blue & green, No. 652-9" (ILLUS. left with other Falline vases) **$1,840**

Vase, 14" h., tall cylindrical body w/a flat mouth flanked by small loop handles, dark brown shading to tan w/pale green pods, small bruise on footring, unobtrusive firing separation under footring, No. 654-13 1/2" (ILLUS., top next column).... **$1,725**

Vase, 14" h., tall cylindrical body w/a flat mouth flanked by small loop handles, tan shading to green & blue, No. 654-13 1/2" **$2,990**

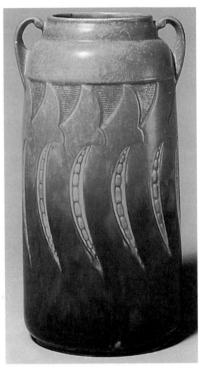

Tall Falline Vase in Shaded Brown

Rare Tall Falline Vase

Vase, 15" h., tall ovoid body w/stepped cylindrical neck flanked by curved handles, No. 655-15" (ILLUS.) **$4,025**

Ferella (1931)

Impressed shell design alternating with small cut-outs at top and base; mottled brown or turquoise and red glaze.

Ferella Bowl and Two Vases

Bowl, 8" d., sharply canted sides, low foot, turquoise & red glaze, No. 211-8" (ILLUS. center with smaller vases, top of page)... **$1,035**

Vase, 4" h., angular handles, short narrow neck, mottled brown glaze, No. 497-4" (ILLUS. left with Ferella bowl, top of page) **$500**

Vase, 4" h., angular handles, short narrow neck, turquoise & red glaze, No. 497-4" (ILLUS. right with Ferella bowl, top of page) **$546**

Vase, 6" h., handles rising from shoulder of compressed globular base to beneath the rim of the long tapering neck, mottled brown glaze, No. 502-6" (ILLUS. left with other brown vases, bottom of page) **$550-750**

Vase, 6" h., bulbous base w/canted shoulder flanked by small angular handles, wide cylindrical neck, mottled brown

glaze, No. 505-6" (ILLUS. right with other brown vases, bottom of page) **$550-750**

Vase, 9" h., flaring lower body w/an angled mid-shoulder tapering to the tall flared neck, long handles from the upper neck to the shoulders, mottled brown glaze, No. 510-9" (ILLUS. center with other brown vases, bottom of page)..... **$$1,250-1,500**

Foxglove (1940s)

Sprays of pink and white blossoms embossed against a shaded dark blue, green or pink matte-finish ground.

Basket w/circular overhead handle, footed conical body w/widely flaring rim, pink ground, No. 374-10", 10" h. **$230**

Ewer, wide squatty body w/a wide shoulder centered by a short split neck w/long angled spout & pointed loop handle, pink ground, No. 4-6 1/2", 6 1/2" h. **$200-250**

Ferella Mottled Brown Vases

Very Tall Pink Foxglove Ewer

Ewer, wide squatty base w/a very tall tapering body w/a split neck & high arched spout, long handle from rim to top of base, pink ground, No. 6-15", 15" h. (ILLUS.) **$500**

Foxglove 7" Pink Vase

Vase, 7" h., semi-ovoid w/long slender angled side handles, pink ground, No. 45-7" (ILLUS.) **$230**
Vase, 8 1/2" h., fan-shaped, handles rising from disk base to midsection, green & pink ground, No. 47-8" **$200-250**

Tall Green & Pink Foxglove Vase

Vase, 9" h., footed spherical body tapering to wide cylindrical neck w/flaring rim, small angled shoulder handles, green & pink ground No. 50-9" (ILLUS.) **$225-275**

Freesia (1945)

Trumpet-shaped blossoms and long slender green leaves against wavy impressed lines, white and lavender blossoms on blended green, white and yellow blossoms on shaded blue, or terra cotta and brown.

Freesia Basket with High Arched Handle

Basket, footed, flattened & flaring ovoid body w/a divided rim, long arched overhead handle, terra cotta ground, No. 390-7", 7" h. (ILLUS.) **$138**

Blue Freesia Console Set

Console Set: 10" d. footed squatty rounded bowl w/small angled side handles & a pair of short domed candleholders; blue ground, bowl No. 7-10", candleholders No. 1160-2", the set (ILLUS.) **$150**
Cookie jar, cov., bulbous ovoid body w/angled shoulder handles, slightly domed lid w/knob finial, green ground, No. 4-8", 8" h. **$546**

Short Terra Cotta Freesia Ewer

Ewer, footed, squatty body w/a wide shoulder tapering to a short split neck w/high arched spout, loop handle from rim to shoulder, terra cotta ground, No. 19-6", 6" h. (ILLUS., previous page) **$104**

Squatty Blue Freesia Ewer

Ewer, footed, squatty body w/a wide shoulder tapering to a short split neck w/high arched spout, loop handle from rim to shoulder, blue ground, No. 19-6", 6" h. (ILLUS.) **$115**

Ewer, disk foot & ringed base below the tall ovoid body w/a short split neck w/long arched spout & pointed loop handle, terra cotta ground, No. 21-15", 15" h. **$460**

Jardiniere, footed nearly spherical body w/a very wide flat mouth flanked by tiny rim handles, terra cotta ground, No. 669-6", 6". **$175-250**

One of a Pair of Blue Freesia Lamps

Lamps, pierced brass base supporting the tall ovoid body tapering to a trumpet neck, angled loop shoulder handles, blue ground, No. 127-12", 12" h., pr. (ILLUS. of one) **$546**

Tea set: cov. teapot, creamer & open sugar bowl, green ground, No. 6, 3 pcs. **$546**

Teapot, cov., blue ground, No. 6 .... **$200-250**

Teapot, cov., green ground, No. 6 .... **$150-250**

Teapot, cov., terra cotta ground, No. 6 ... **$150-250**

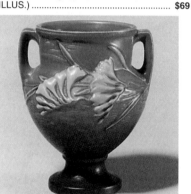

Bulbous Terra Cotta Freesia Urn-Vase

Urn-vase, footed, bulbous body w/a wide sloping shoulder to a wide flat mouth, angled loop handles at edges of shoulder, terra cotta ground, No. 463-5", 5" h. (ILLUS.) **$69**

Terra Cotta Freesia Urn-Vase

Urn-vase, two-handled, bulbous body tapering to wide cylindrical neck, terra cotta ground, No. 196-8", 8 1/2" h. (ILLUS.) **$140-160**

Very Rare Experimental Freesia Vase

Vase, experimental, swelled cylindrical body w/a wide flat mouth, curved loop handles at the upper sides, pastel shaded blue to yellow ground w/pink blossoms (ILLUS., previous page)................ **$4,600**

Blue Freesia 6" Vase

Vase, 6" h., baluster-form w/flat mouth & pointed angled handles, blue ground, No. 117-6".. **$150**

Blue Freesia Vase No. 118-6"

Vase, 6 1/4" h., footed, squatty, bulbous base w/wide cylindrical neck, large angled base handles, blue ground, No. 118-6" (ILLUS.) **$104**

Freesia Vase with Tall Cylindrical Neck

Vase, 7" h., footed disk-form base w/angular base handles below the tall cylindrical neck, blue ground, No. 119-7" (ILLUS.)..... **$115**

Blue Freesia Bud Vase

Vase, bud, 7" h., handles rising from compressed globular base, long slender tapering neck, blue ground, No. 195-7" (ILLUS.) **$115**

Blue Footed Ovoid Freesia Vase

Vase, 8" h., footed, ovoid body flanked by D-form handles, blue ground, No. 121-8" (ILLUS.).. **$115**

Blue Footed Freesia Vase

Vase, 9 1/2" h., a short ringed pedestal base supporting a flaring half-round body w/an angled shoulder tapering slightly to a tall, wide cylindrical neck, down-curved angled loop handles from center of neck to rim of lower shoulder, blue ground, No. 123-9 (ILLUS., previous page) **$115**

Blue Freesia Wall Pocket

Wall pocket, waisted long body w/small angled side handles, blue ground, small glazed-over chip, No. 1296-8", 8 1/2" h. (ILLUS.).. **$138**

8" Freesia Terra Cotta Wall Pocket

Wall pocket, waisted long body w/small angled side handles, terra cotta ground, No. 1296-8", 8 1/2" h. (ILLUS.) **$161**

Fuchsia (1939)
Coral pink fuchsia blossoms and green leaves against a background of blue shading to yellow, green shading to terra cotta, or terra cotta shading to gold.

Basket, footed inverted bell-form body w/overhead handle, terra cotta ground, No. 351-10", 10" h. **$374**

Basket w/flower frog, a short pedestal foot supporting a wide squatty half-round body w/small half-round tabs on two sides of the incurved rim, a high round handle joining the two other edges, green ground, No. 350-8", 8" h. **$325-350**

Console bowl, footed low oblong boat-shaped form w/under-rim end loop handles, blue ground, No. 353-14", 15 1/2" l. .... **$200 - 225**

Ewer, footed rounded lower body w/a wide shoulder tapering to a tall neck w/a high upright spout & long handle from rim to shoulder, terra cotta ground, No. 902-10", 10" h. **$316**

Ewer, footed rounded lower body w/a wide shoulder tapering to a tall neck w/a high upright spout & long handle from rim to shoulder, blue ground, No. 902-10", 10" h. **$345**

Jardiniere, footed spherical body w/short wide neck flanked by small angled handles, terra cotta ground, No. 645-3", 3" h. **$81**

Vase, 7" h., bulbous base tapering to flaring rim, large loop handles from shoulder to below rim, terra cotta ground, No. 895-7" .. **$230**

Vase, 9" h., footed cylindrical form w/wide flaring rim & large C-form handles, terra cotta ground, No. 900-9" **$259**

Vase, 9" h., footed cylindrical form w/wide flaring rim & large C-form handles, green ground, No. 900-9" **$288**

Wall pocket, two-handled bullet shape w/fanned rim, terra cotta ground, No. 1282-8", 8 1/2" h. **$345**

Fudji (1904)
Same technique as Rozane Woodland. Sometimes trimmed w/dots & studs & wavy lines. Matte-finished ground. Detailed decorations are in high gloss.Kovel-See Rozane Woodland--when the dots were omitted, it was called Fujiyama or Rozane Fudji.

Fine Early Roseville Fudji Vase

Vase, 6 1/2" h., upright squared & twisted form tapering to a small low flared mouth, decorated w/a dark brown chrysanthemum on a tall green leafy stem against a dark brown to pale green ground, marked, minor expert repair at rim (ILLUS.).............. **$863**

Futura (1928)
Varied line with shapes ranging from Art Deco geometrics to futuristic. Matte glaze is typical although an occasional piece may be high gloss.

Three Futura Blue-Green Vases

Bowl, 4" h., square inverted pyramidal bowl supported between four open buttress legs on a square base, yellow speckled w/green matte glaze, No. 189-4-6" **$1,265**

Candleholders, shaped square base rising to square candle nozzle, relief-molded stylized green vine & foliage on sandy beige ground, No. 1073-4", 4" h., pr.......... **$460**

Console bowl, cut-out base, sharply canted sides w/embossed stylized floral design, No. 196-5-6 1/2" , 12" l., 5" h. **$748**

Vase, 6" h., 3 1/2" d., cylindrical body swelling to wider bands at the top & base, long pierced angled handles down the sides, apricot w/green bands & handles, No. 381-6".. **$403**

Vase, 6" h., upright squared buttressed form, terra cotta & gold, No. 423-6", paper label **$500-600**

Small Mug-style Futura Vase

Vase, 6" h., 3 1/2" d., cylindrical body swelling to wider bands at the top & base, long pierced angled handles down the sides, tan w/dark blue bands & handles, No. 381-6" (ILLUS.) **$460**

Vase, 7" h., spherical top w/large pointed dark blue & green leaves curving up the sides, resting on a gently sloped rectangular foot, shaded blue & green blue ground, No. 387-7" (ILLUS. center with other blue-green vases, top of page)...... **$1,093**

Spherical Futura Footed Vase

Vase, 7" h., spherical top w/large pointed dark blue & green leaves curving up the sides, resting on a gently sloped rectangular foot, shaded blue & green blue ground, No. 387-7" (ILLUS.) **$1,093**

Vase, 8" h., upright rectangular form on rectangular foot, stepped neck, long square handles, grey & pink ground, No. 386-8" **$748**

Futura Pink Twist 8" Vase

Vase, 8" h., square, slightly tapering body twisting toward the rim, pink ground, No. 425-8" (ILLUS., previous page)................. **$431**

Futura Ovoid Thistle Vase

Vase, 8" h., semi-ovoid, flaring foot, flat closed handles from midsection to neck, molded trailing thistles on side, purple & mauve, No. 427-8" (ILLUS.)...................... **$805**

Cone-shaped Roseville Futura Vase

Vase, 8 1/4" h., 5" d., conical body on flat disk base, buttressed sides, orange w/green buttresses & blue base, No. 401-8" (ILLUS.) **$690**

Vase, 10" h., compressed globular base supporting long flaring squared neck, elongated triangular design on each side, blue & green, No. 392-10" (ILLUS. left with spherical blue-green vase) **$800-1,000**

Vase, 10" h., footed tall tapering ringed body w/a short flaring neck, shaded bluish green glossy glaze, No. 434-10" (ILLUS. right with spherical blue-green vase)........ **$2,760**

Rare Tall Futura Vase

Vase, 14" h., 5 1/2" d., two large handles at lower half, squat stacked base & faceted squared neck, matte glaze in three shades of brown, No. 411-14" (ILLUS.).. **$4,312**

Colorful Futura Wall Pocket

Wall pocket, canted sides, angular rim handles, geometric design in blue, yellow, green & lavender on brown ground, No. 1261-8", 6" w., 8 1/4" h. (ILLUS.)........ **$400-600**

Gardenia (1940s)
Large white gardenia blossoms and green leaves over a textured impressed band on a shaded green, grey or tan ground.

Large Green Gardenia Basket

Basket, widely flaring fan-shaped body w/high circular arched handle enclosing the body, green ground, No. 609-10", 10" h. (ILLUS.) **$175**
Book ends, green ground, No. 659, 5 1/2" h., pr.. **$200-250**

Small Gardenia Candleholders

Candleholders, small domed shape, green ground, No. 651-2", 2" h., pr. (ILLUS.) **$81**
Ewer, footed ovoid body tapering to a tall slender neck w/upright arched spout, loop handle from neck to shoulder, grey ground, No. 617-10", 10" h. **$175-200**
Jardiniere & pedestal base, grey ground, No. 605-8", 24 1/2" h., 2 pcs. **$920**
Vase, 8" h., handles rising from base to mid-section, cylindrical body, tan ground, No. 683-8" **$173**

Imperial II (1924)
Much variation within the line. There is no common characteristic, although many pieces are heavily glazed, and colors tend to run and blend.

Small Bulbous Imperial II Vase

Vase, 6" h., bulbous ovoid tapering body w/wide banding, thin flat rolled rim, mot-

tled purple & yellow glaze, marked w/a gold foil label, No. 469-6" (ILLUS.) **$316**

Globular Deep Rose Imperial II Vase

Vase, 7" h., globular body tapering to a wide tapering neck w/horizontal ribbing, mottled dark rose glaze, No. 471-7" (ILLUS.) .. **$690**

Wide Squatty Blue Imperial II Vase

Vase, 7" h., wide squatty hemispherical turquoise blue body w/a wide gently sloping shoulder centering a cylindrical neck w/a band of molded inverted-comma designs in mottled yellow & white, No. 474-7" (ILLUS.) **$288**

Wide Handled Imperial II Vase

Vase, 8 1/8" h., two handles at shoulder, expanding cylinder w/light horizontal ribbing around lower quarter of body, slightly crystalline rust over caramel matte glaze, No. 478-8" (ILLUS., previous page) **$431**

Handsome Dark Blue Imperial II Vase

Vase, 9 1/2" h., baluster form w/short wide cylindrical neck w/wave-like band, cobalt blue ground, No. 477-9 1/2" (ILLUS.)...... **$1,265**

Rare Mottled Imperial II Wall Pocket

Wall pocket, canted sides w/rounded bottom, horizontal wide ribbing at base & narrow ribbing at midsection, green & pale lavender mottled glaze, No. 1263, 6 1/2" h. (ILLUS.) **$920**

Ixia (1930s)

Embossed spray of tiny bell-shaped flowers and slender leaves, white blossoms on pink ground, lavender blossoms on green or yellow ground.

Long Ixia Centerpiece with Candleholders

Centerpiece, one-piece console set w/six candleholders attached to center bowl,

yellow shaded to brown ground, minor firing separation at base end, No. 328-11 1/2", 13" l. (ILLUS.) **$518**

Jonquil (1931)

White jonquil blossoms and green leaves in relief against textured tan ground, green lining.

Jardiniere, bulbous form w/wide flat mouth flanked by tiny loop handles, No. 621-7", 7" d.. **$316**
Jardiniere & pedestal, jardiniere No. 621-10" & pedestal No. 621-18-10", overall 29" h.. **$1,725**
Strawberry jar, flaring cylindrical form w/wide central vase flanked on opposing sides by small tapering vases, opposing pair of handles down the other two sides, on a saucer base, No. 96-7", 7 1/4" h. **$633**

Rare Jonquil Strawberry Jar & Plate

Strawberry jar & underplate, the wide ovoid body w/flat rim pierced around the top w/four wide projecting openings alternating w/clusters of flowers, separate underplate, No. 97-6", 2 pcs. (ILLUS.)........ **$3,105**
Vase, 3" h., wide, low, squatty, tapering, cylindrical body w/wide flat mouth, inverted D-form loop handles from rim to edge of base, No. 523-3" **$175-275**
Vase, 4" h., bulbous spherical form, downturned loop handles from rim to shoulder, No. 524-4" (ILLUS. center with other Jonquil vases, top next page) **$230**

Small Tapering Jonquil Vase

Vase, 4 1/2" h., footed, wide, tapering cylindrical body w/a flat rim flanked by small loop handles, No. 539-4" (ILLUS.) **$150**

Three Jonquil Vases

Vase, 5 1/2" h., spherical w/a wide flat rim flanked by small pointed loop handles, No. 542-5 1/2" (ILLUS. left with other Jonquil vases, top of page) .... **$300 - 400**

Small Bulbous Jonquil Vase

Vase, 6" h., footed, bulbous body w/a short wide cylindrical neck flanked by small loop handles, No. 538-6" (ILLUS.) **$316**

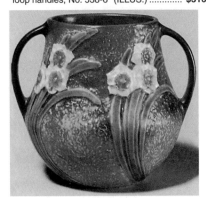

Jonquil Vase No. 526-6 1/2"

Vase, 6 1/2" h., bulbous base w/wide, slightly tapering sides to a wide flat mouth, curved handles from rim to midsection, No. 526-61/2" (ILLUS.) **$374**

Vase, 6 1/2" h., wide bulbous body tapering to flat rim, C-form handles, No. 543-6 1/2" **$403**

Slender Jonquil Bud Vase

Vase, bud, 7" h., swelled base & a tall slender tapering body w/a widely flaring trumpet mouth, low arched handles from edge of base to part way up the sides, No. 102-7" (ILLUS.) **$546**

Vase, 9 1/2" h., bulbous base tapering slightly to wide cylindrical neck, loop handles at midsection, No. 544-9" (ILLUS. right with other Jonquil vases, top of page) **$805**

Juvenile (1916 on)

Transfer-printed and painted on creamware with nursery rhyme characters, cute animals and other motifs appealing to children.

Two-handled Juvenile Line Mug

Mug, two-handled, Sunbonnet Girl design,
2 7/8" h. (ILLUS.) **$173**

Laurel (1934)
Laurel branch and berries in low relief with reeded panels at the sides. Glazed in deep yellow, green shading to cream or terra cotta.

Bowl, 6" d., squatty bulbous body w/incurved rim & angled shoulder handles, terra cotta ground, No. 250-6 1/4".............. **$345**

Laurel Terra Cotta Vase

Vase, 6" h., cylindrical w/stepped rounded shoulder flanked by low curved shoulder handles, terra cotta ground, No. 668-6" (ILLUS.)... **$230**
Vase, 6" h., tapering cylinder w/wide mouth, closed angular handles at shoulder, green ground, No. 667-6"......................... **$259**
Vase, 7 1/4" h., tapering cylinder w/pierced angular handles at midsection, green ground, No. 671-7 1/4" **$316**

Luffa (1934)
Relief-molded ivy leaves and blossoms on shaded brown or green wavy horizontal ridges.

Spherical Luffa Jardiniere

Jardiniere, brown ground, spherical w/a wide flat mouth flanked by tiny angled

handles, brown ground, No. 631-7", 7"
(ILLUS.).. **$201**

Rare Tall Luffa Jardiniere & Pedestal

Jardiniere & pedestal, large bulbous jardiniere w/small angled rim handles, pedestal w/widely flaring base tapering to a cylindrical column w/raised platform top, green ground, No. 631-10", overall 28" h. (ILLUS.).. **$1,725**

Luffa Lamp Base with No Fittings

Lamp base, footed bulbous body w/a narrow rounded shoulder centered by a flattened closed top flanked by small angled shoulder handles, brown ground, lamp No. 7005, no electric fittings, 9 3/4" h. (ILLUS.)..................................... **$345**

Vase, 6" h., tapering cylindrical body w/angled handles from shoulder to rim, green ground, No. 683-6" **$230**

Small Spherical Luffa Vase

Vase, 6" h., nearly spherical body tapering slightly to a wide, flat mouth flanked by tiny pointed rim handles, green ground, small gold sticker, No. 255-6" (ILLUS.) **$345**
Vase, 6" h., tapering cylindrical body w/angled handles from shoulder to rim, brown ground, No. 683-6" **$230**

Brown Luffa Vase No. 684-6"

Vase, 6 1/4" h., swelled cylindrical body tapering slightly to a flat mouth flanked by pointed rim handles, brown ground, No. 684-6" (ILLUS.) **$230**

Green Luffa Vase No. 684-6"

Vase, 6 1/4" h., swelled cylindrical body tapering slightly to a flat mouth flanked by

pointed rim handles, green ground, No. 684-6" (ILLUS.) **$259**
Vase, 7" h., ovoid body w/small angled handles from shoulder to rim, brown ground, No. 685-7" **$258**
Vase, 8" h., footed widely swelling ovoid body w/a wide shoulder to the short cylindrical neck flanked by low angled handles, brown ground, No. 689-8" **$345**
Vase, 8 1/2" h., ovoid body tapering slightly to a low cylindrical neck flanked by small angled handles, green ground, No. 687-8" **$258**

Very Tall Luffa Vase

Vase, 14 1/2" h., footed, tall, swelled, cylindrical body w/a wide flaring mouth flanked by small pointed rim handles, green ground, No. 692-14" (ILLUS.) **$690**

Luffa Brown Wall Pocket

Wall pocket, long ovoid form w/arched & flaring rim flanked by tiny angled handles, brown ground, No. 1272-8", 8" h. (ILLUS.) **$575**

Magnolia (1943)

Large white blossoms with rose centers and black stems in relief against a blue, green or tan textured ground.

Ashtray, two-handled, low bowl form, tan ground, No. 28, 7" d., 2" h........................... **$46**

Basket, large fan-shaped body w/a wide, low & pointed overhead handle, tan ground, No. 385-10", 10" h.......................... $230
Basket, large fan-shaped body w/a wide, low & pointed overhead handle, blue ground, No. 385-10", 10" h.................. $250-300

Blue Magnolia Basket

Basket w/ornate overhead handle, blue ground, No. 383-7" (ILLUS.) $230
Console set: low, narrow, long bowl w/painted end handles & a pair of low candleholders w/curved pointed handles; green ground, bowl No. 450-10", candle-holders No. 1156-2", the set $225-250

Tan Magnolia Cookie Jar

Cookie jar, cov., shoulder handles, tan ground, No. 2-8, overall 10" h. (ILLUS.) $200-300

Green Magnolia Cookie Jar

Cookie jar, cov., shoulder handles, green ground, No. 2-8, overall 10" h. (ILLUS.)..... $207

Blue Magnolia Cornucopia-Vase

Cornucopia-vase, blue ground, No. 184-6", 6" h. (ILLUS.) $81

Very Tall Magnolia Ewer

Ewer, wide, squatty base tapering sharply to a slender neck w/a divided rim w/a high, long, arched spout, angled shoulder handle, tan ground, No. 15-15", 15" h. (ILLUS.).. $345
Jardiniere & pedestal, blue ground, No. 665-10", jardiniere 10" h., 30 1/4" h., 2 pcs. $1,000-1,500

Ball-shaped Blue Magnolia Pitcher

Pitcher, cider, 7" h., ball-shaped w/pointed arch handle, blue ground, No. 1327 (ILLUS.) **$259**

Long Magnolia Planter in Tan

Planter, long rectangular shape, two-handled, tan ground, No. 389-8", 8" l. (ILLUS.)... **$90-115**
Teapot, cov., green ground, No. 4 .... **$350-400**
Teapot, cov., tan ground, No. 4............... **$250-350**

Experimental Blue Magnolia Vase

Vase, experimental, bulbous nearly spherical body w/small loop handles on shoulder, shaded light blue ground w/white blossoms & brown branches (ILLUS.)..... **$4,025**

Large Blue Magnolia Vase

Vase, 9" h., footed wide ovoid body w/a wide flat shoulder & flat mouth, long angled shoulder handles down the sides, blue ground, glaze chip on shoulder, No. 94-9" (ILLUS.) **$150**

Unusual Tan Magnolia Vase

Vase, 9 1/4" h., footed, wide, half-round lower body w/a wide, flat shoulder centered by a large trumpet neck, large pointed angular handles from top of base to center of neck, tan ground, No. 93-9" (ILLUS.).. **$104**

Magnolia Vase with Unusual Shape

Vase, 9 1/4" h., footed, wide, half-round lower body w/a wide, flat shoulder centered by a large trumpet neck, large pointed angular handles from top of base to center of neck, blue ground, chips under the base, No. 93-9" (ILLUS.) **$138**

Unusual Green Magnolia Vase

Vase, 9 1/4" h., footed, wide, half-round lower body w/a wide, flat shoulder centered by a large trumpet neck, large pointed angular handles from top of base to center of neck, green ground, No. 93-9" (ILLUS.) $138

Large Tan Magnolia Vase

Vase, 14" h., footed tall ovoid body w/angled shoulder handles, tan ground, No. 97-14" (ILLUS.) $374

Large Green Magnolia Floor Vase

Vase, floor type, 18 1/2" h., footed, large ovoid body w/a thin flared mouth & pointed shoulder handles, green ground, No. 100-18" (ILLUS.) $500

Matt Green (before 1916)

Matte green glaze on smoking set, jardinieres, fern dishes, hanging baskets, planters, some smooth with no pattern, some embossed with leaves or children's faces spaced evenly around the top.

Wide Squatty Matt Green Bowl

Bowl, 13" d., 8 1/2" h., footed, wide, squatty, rounded body w/a wide thick rolled rim flanked by loop shoulder handles, original paper label, No. 456-9" (ILLUS.) $230

Matt Green Gate-form Double Bud Vase

Vase, double bud, 5" h., 8" w., fluted columns joined by a gate, No. 7 (ILLUS.) $115

Paneled 10" Matt Green Wall Pocket

Wall pocket, tapering half-round three-paneled body below the high stepped & arched backplate w/hanging hole, No. 1211-10", 10" l. (ILLUS.) $345

Paneled & Impressed Wall Pocket

Wall pocket, tapering half-round three-paneled body w/impressed dotted triangles at the top of each panel below the high stepped & arched backplate w/another impressed triangle & a long hanging hole, 10 1/4 l. (ILLUS.) $316

Floral-embossed Matt Green Wall Pocket

Wall pocket, long, round trumpet-form body lightly embossed w/blossoms on stems, the high arched backplate pierced w/oblong openings & a hanging hole, 4 3/4" w., 11 1/4" l. (ILLUS.) **$403**

Ming Tree (1949)
High gloss glaze in mint green, turquoise, or white is decorated with Ming branch; handles are formed from gnarled branches.

Basket w/overhead branch handle, ruffled rim, white ground, No. 509-12", 13" h. **$201**

Tall Curved Ming Tree Basket

Basket w/overhead branch handle, curved body w/asymmetrical rim, green ground, No. 510-14", 14 1/2" (ILLUS.) **$200-225**
Ewer, white ground, No. 516-10", 10" h. **$100-150**
Vase, 6 1/2" h., single branch handle, white ground, No. 572-6" **$50-100**
Wall pocket, overhead branch handle, blue ground, No. 566-8", 8 1/2" h. **$173**

Moderne (1930s)
Art Deco-style rounded and angular shapes trimmed with an embossed panel of vertical lines and modified swirls and circles, white trimmed with terra cotta, medium blue with white, and turquoise with a burnished antique gold.

Moderne Pattern Turquoise Compote

Compote, 5" h., open stem, turquoise, No. 295-6 (ILLUS.) **$196**

Morning Glory (1935)
Delicately colored blossoms and twining vines in white or green with blue.

Flaring Morning Glory Vase

Vase, 5 1/4" h., footed, flaring sides w/small angled handles at midsection, white ground, No. 723-5" (ILLUS.) **$300-400**
Vase, 7" h., footed flattened fanned shape w/angular handles at the bottom, white ground, No. 120-7" (ILLUS. right with other Morning Glory vases, top next page)..... **$374**
Vase, 8 1/2" h., trumpet-shaped handles at base, green ground, No. 726-8" **$633**
Vase, 8 1/2" h., trumpet-shaped handles at base, white ground, No. 726-8" (ILLUS. left with other Morning Glory vases, top next page) **$600-800**

Three Morning Glory Vases

(ILLUS. center with Moss bowl-vase and vase, top next page) **$259**

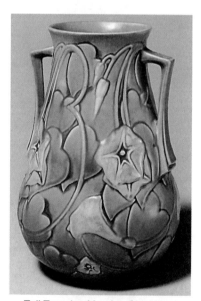

Tall Tapering Morning Glory Vase

Vase, 10 1/2" h., bulbous base tapering to wide molded rim, two-handled, white ground, No. 730-10" (ILLUS.) **$1,495**

Moss (1930s)

Green moss hanging over brown branch with green leaves; backgrounds are pink, ivory or tan shading to blue.

Bowl-vase, spherical body w/a wide flat mouth, small angular handles rising from base to mid-section, ivory, No. 290-6", 6" h. (ILLUS. left with console bowl and vase, top next page) **$345**

Console bowl, oval w/shaped rim & angled end handles, pink shading to green ground, No. 293-10", 10 1/2" l., 3" h.

Rare Moss Jardiniere & Pedestal

Jardiniere & pedestal base, tan to blue ground, No. 635-10", 29" h., 2 pcs. (ILLUS.) **$3,738**

Vase, 6" h., footed flaring lower body below cylindrical sides, large open angular handles, pink & green ground, No. 774-6" **$201**

Vase, 7" h., flattened fan shape w/angular handles down the side, blue ground, partial foil label, No. 778-7" (ILLUS. right with Moss bowl-vase and console bowl, top next page) **$200-250**

Mostique (1915)

Indian designs of stylized flowers and arrowhead leaves, slip decorated on bisque, glazed interiors. Occasional bowl glazed on outside as well.

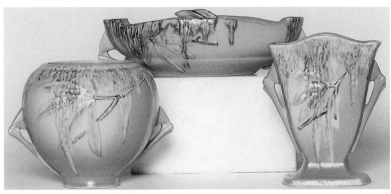

Moss Bowl-Vase, Console Bowl & Vase

Mostique Vase with Tall Leaves & Flower

Vase, 6" h., gently tapering cylindrical body w/a flared flat mouth, heavy dark green bands around the base & rim w/a pair of light green leaves flanking a white four-petal diamond-shaped blossom on two sides, tan ground, some small base chips, No. 3-6" (ILLUS.) **$230**

Geometric Green Mostique Vase

Vase, 8" h., swelled base below tall cylindrical sides w/a wide flat mouth, narrow dark green incised bands around the base & top, two sides of the top incised w/a dark green & red fanned diamond design above dark green angular panels all on a pale green ground, small rim chip, No. 8-8" (ILLUS.) **$259**

Mostique 8" Vase with White Blossom

Vase, 8" h., gently swelled cylindrical form w/flat closed rim, a white four-petal diamond-form blossom above three angular green leaves around the sides, No. 10-8" (ILLUS.) **$374**

Flaring Mostique Vase in Grey & Blue

Vase, 8 1/4" h., waisted cylinder w/wide flaring mouth, large handles rising from above base to midsection, geometric design, dark blue, brick red & white on a grey ground, No. 532-8" (ILLUS.) **$230**

Cylindrical Mostique Vase with Leaves

Vase, 10" h., cylindrical w/wide closed mouth, dark green incised rings around the base & light green matching rings around the top, decorated w/a dark green square enclosing a square white blossom & suspending a pale green sprig of incised leaves, light tan ground, N0. 15-10" (ILLUS.)...................................... **$460**

Baluster Mostique Vase with Flowers

Vase, 10" h., baluster-form body w/thin incised dark green rings around the base & the neck, the sides incised w/large stylized pairs of green leaves centering a dark green & deep red blossom bud, light tan ground, No. 18-10" (ILLUS.) **$316**

Simple Waisted Cylindrical Mostique Vase

Vase, 10 1/4" h., tall waisted cylindrical body w/widely flaring rim, band of yellow spearpoint on green shafts up around the sides alternating w/small blue triangles on a grey ground, No. 164-10" (ILLUS.)
.... **$161**

Unusual Mostique Window Box

Window box, long narrow upright rectangular shape, the long sides w/dark green incised bands along the top rim & down sides, the top center w/two squared four-petal blossoms in pink & white above three dark green triangular leaves, pale green ground, 5 1/2 x 11", 6" h. (ILLUS.) **$805**

Panel (Rosecraft Panel 1920)
Background colors are dark green or dark brown; decorations embossed within the recessed panels are of natural or stylized floral arrangements or female nudes.

Bowl, 9" d., wide flat bottom w/low incurved sides, pink & light green floral panels on a dark green ground, marked............. **$125-200**
Vase, 6" h., fan-shaped body w/wide disk foot, female nudes in panels, orange on dark brown ground...................................... **$431**

Rosecraft Panel Fan Vase with Nudes

Vase, 8" h., flattened fan-shaped bowl on a short knob pedestal on flaring round foot, nudes in panels, orange on a dark brown ground (ILLUS.) **$700-800**
Vase, 11" h., footed conical form w/long low angular handles from rim down sides, nude in panel, dark brown ground, No. 298-11" (ILLUS., next page) **$1,380**

Rare Rosecraft Panel Vase with Nudes

Panel Wall Pocket with Nude

Wall pocket, conical form w/ruffled rim flanked by cut-out panels, nude decoration in orange, dark brown ground, repair to lip, 7" h. (ILLUS.) **$316**

Rosecraft Panel Wall Pocket with Leaves

Wall pocket, wide conical shape w/rounded end, leaves in panel, brown ground, 9" h. (ILLUS.) **$431**

Rosecraft Panel Floral Window Box

Window box, long narrow rectangular shape w/three panels on each long side, swirling flower & leaf design, light green on dark green ground, 6 x 12" (ILLUS.) **$460**

Peony (1942)
Floral arrangement of white or dark yellow blossoms with green leaves on textured, shaded backgrounds in yellow with mixed green and brown, pink with blue, and solid green.

Basket, hanging-type, bulbous wide body w/a wide flat molded rim flanked by small loop handles, yellow blossoms on mixed green & brown ground, No. 467-5" **$150-250**
Console bowl, long, narrow, oblong form w/arched sides & stepped flaring end above tiny pointed handles, gold ground, No. 432-12", 12" l. **$200-225**
Cornucopia-vase, pink & green ground, No. 171-8", 8" h. **$104**
Model of a conch shell, gold ground, No. 436, 9 1/2" w. **$175-200**

Peony Conch Shell

Model of a conch shell, pale yellow blossom on pink shaded to blue ground, No. 436, 9 1/2" w. (ILLUS.) **$173**
Teapot, cov., gold ground, No. 3 .... **$200-250**
Teapot, cov., green ground, No. 3 .... **$150-225**
Vase, 8" h., footed, large ovoid body tapering to a low flared mouth, pointed shoulder handles, deep pink shaded to green ground w/yellow flowers, No. 63-8" (ILLUS., top next page) **$115**

Peony Shaded Pink to Green 8" Vase

Vase, 18" h., floor type, round domed foot & tall ovoid body w/a wide flared rim, pointed angular shoulder handles, pink shaded to green ground w/yellow flowers, No. 70-18" (ILLUS.) **$460**

Green Peony 18" Floor Vase

Vase, 18" h., floor type, round domed foot & tall, ovoid body w/a wide, flared rim, pointed angular shoulder handles, green ground, No. 70-18" (ILLUS.) **$500**

Wall pocket, bullet-shaped w/widely flaring deeply ruffled rim, two side handles, white blossoms on green ground, No. 1293-8", 8" **$230**

Gold Peony Tall Vase

Vase, 12 1/2" h., footed tall ovoid body tapering to a short flared neck flanked by pointed loop handles, gold ground, No. 67-12" (ILLUS.) **$288**

Pine Cone (1935 & 1953)

Realistic embossed brown pine cones and green pine needles on shaded blue, brown or green ground. (Pink is extremely rare.)

Ashtray, blue ground, No. 25 .... **$201**

Almond-shaped Pine Cone Ashtray

Ashtray, almond-shaped w/long pine needles curving around one end, green ground, No. 499, 4 1/2" l. (ILLUS.) **$81**

Pink to Green Peony Floor Vase

Basket, w/overhead branch handle, asymmetrical fanned & pleated body, blue ground, No. 408-6", 6 1/2" h........................ **$374**

Fanned & Pleated Pine Cone Basket

Basket, w/overhead branch handle, asymmetrical fanned & pleated body, brown ground, No. 408-6", 6 1/2" h. (ILLUS.) **$489**
Basket, long boat-shaped body w/long arched overhead branch handle, raised on short peg feet, 12" l. **$201**
Bowl, 4" d., bulbous spherical body w/incurved rim, green ground, No. 278-4"........ **$207**

Squatty Bulbous Pine Cone Bowl

Bowl, 4" d., squatty bulbous spherical body w/closed rim, blue ground, No. 278-4" (ILLUS.).. **$288**
Bowl, 6" d., wide low form w/incurved sides & small angled twig handles, green shaded to cream, No. 425-6" **$276**

Single Blue Pink Cone Candleholder

Candleholder, flat disc base supporting candle nozzle in the form of a pine cone

flanked by needles on one side & branch handle on the other, blue ground, No. 112-3", 3" h. (ILLUS.)................................ **$161**

Pine Cone Triple Candleholder

Candleholder, triple, domed round base w/an open high arched pine needle & branch supporting three graduated cupform sockets, green ground, No. 1106-5 1/2", 5 1/2" h. (ILLUS.).......................... **$173**

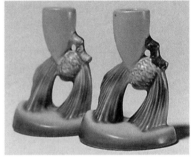

Pine Cone Pine Sprig Candleholders

Candleholders, oblong base supporting two thick pine needle clusters & a pine cone w/small branch supporting the egg-shaped candle socket, green ground, No. 451-4", 4" h., pr. (ILLUS.)......................... **$230**

Simple Brown Pine Cone Candlesticks

Candlesticks, wide round foot tapering to a tall cylindrical socket w/slightly flared rim, brown ground, No. 1099-4 1/2", 4 1/2" h., pr. (ILLUS.) **$288**

Small Spherical Pine Cone Jardiniere

Jardiniere, spherical w/two twig handles, brown ground, No. 632-3", 3" h. (ILLUS.) .. **$173**

Blue Pine Cone Cornucopia-Vase

Cornucopia-vase, blue ground, couple of very minor glaze pits, No. 126-6", 6" h. (ILLUS.).. **$196**

Small Brown Pine Cone Jardiniere

Jardiniere, footed wide squatty bulbous body w/a wide flat mouth, small asymmetrical twig handles, brown ground, No. 632-4", 4" h. (ILLUS.)................................ **$259**

Brown Pine Cone Cornucopia-Vase

Cornucopia-vase, brown ground, some minor glaze peppering, No. 126-6", 6" h. (ILLUS.).. **$184**

Large Blue Pine Cone Jardiniere

Jardiniere, blue ground, 632-10", 10" h. (ILLUS.)... **$900-1,200**
Match holder, upright oval form, brown ground, No. 498, 3" h. (ILLUS. center with ewer and vase)................................. **$288**

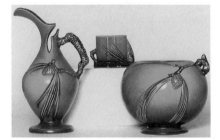

Brown Pine Cone Ewer, Match Holder & Vase

Ewer, footed ovoid body tapering to a split neck w/a high arched spout, branch handle, brown ground, No. 909-10", 10" h. (ILLUS. left with match holder and vase) ... **$805**
Flowerpot & saucer, brown ground, No. 633-5", 5" h. **$316**

Blue Pine Cone Footed Mug

Mug, footed, blue ground, few minor glaze puckers, No. 960-4", 4" h. (ILLUS., previous page) **$316**

Brown Pine Cone Pattern Mug

Mug, footed, brown ground, No. 960-4", 4" h. **$316**

Large Ovoid Pine Cone Pitcher

Pitcher, 9 1/2" h., ovoid, small branch handle, brown ground, very slight glaze peppering, No. 708-9" (ILLUS.) **$633**

Tall Fanned Pine Cone Pitcher

Pitcher, 10 1/2" h., upright curved & fanned body w/long branch & sprig handle from rim to base, green ground, No. 485-10" (ILLUS.) **$460**

Pitcher w/ice lip, 8" h., footed wide spherical body w/curved rim & squared spout, brown ground, No. 1321 .... **$460**

Oblong Pine Cone Planter

Planter, oval upright sides w/flaring arched serpentine rim, an openwork pine needle & cone handle at one end & a small twig handle at the other, some glaze discoloration, few pinpoint glaze dimples, brown ground, No. 457-7", 4 1/2" h. (ILLUS.) **$207**

Blue Cupped Pine Cone Planter

Planter, a deep cup-shaped bowl set off-center on an oval foot w/a pine cone & pine needle handle extending from base to rim, another sprig on pine needles molded into the lower body, blue ground, No. 124-5", 5" h. (ILLUS.) **$288**

Cup-shaped Pine Cone Planter

Planter, deep cup-shaped bowl set off-center on an oval foot w/a pine cone & pine needle handle extending from base to rim, another sprig on pine needles molded into the lower body, green ground, No. 124-5", 5" h. (ILLUS.) **$173**

Vase, 6" h., 6 1/2" d., footed spherical body w/closed rim, small branch handle at one side of rim, brown ground, No. 261-6", 6" d. (ILLUS. right with ewer and match holder) **$300-325**

Footed Brown Pine Cone Vase

Vase, 6" h., footed bulbous base w/wide cylindrical neck, handles from shoulder to mid-section of neck, brown ground, No. 839-6" (ILLUS.) **$230**

Blue Footed Bulbous Pine Cone Vase

Vase, 6" h., footed bulbous base w/wide cylindrical neck, handles from shoulder to midsection of neck, blue ground, No. 839-6" (ILLUS.) **$316**

Cylindrical Pine Cone Vase

Vase, 6 1/2" h., wide cylindrical body w/flaring rim, asymmetrical handles, brown ground, No. 838-6" (ILLUS.) **$259**

Vase, bud, 7" h., green ground, No. 112-7" ... **$173**

Brown Pine Cone Waisted Shape Vase

Vase, 7" h., footed waisted cylindrical body tapering to slightly flaring rim, asymmetric handles, brown ground, No. 840-7" (ILLUS.) **$259**

Handled Cylindrical Pine Cone Blue Vase

Vase, 7" h., footed gently flaring cylindrical body w/a flaring wide rim flanked by large angular branch handles, blue ground, No. 907-7" (ILLUS.) **$316**

Green Flattened Pine Cone Vase

Vase, 7 1/4" h., long oval base supporting a tall flattened & fanned body w/asymmetrical twig handles & a large molded pine cone & needle sprigs across the front, green ground, No. 121-7" (ILLUS.) **$207**

Footed Flattened & Fanned Pine Cone Vase

Vase, 7 1/4" h., long oval base supporting a tall flattened & fanned body w/asymmetrical twig handles & a large molded pine cone & needle sprigs across the front, brown ground, No. 121-7" (ILLUS.)............ **$345**

No. 479-7" Pine Cone Bud Vase

Vase, bud, 7 3/4" h., round disk foot w/upright slender ovoid body w/sprig handle from side to foot, brown ground, No. 479-7", 1950s version of No. 112-7" (ILLUS.)... **$259**

Slender Blue Pine Cone No. 479 Vase

Vase, bud, 7 3/4" h., round disk foot w/upright slender ovoid body w/sprig handle from side to foot, blue ground, No. 479-7", 1950s version of No. 112-7" (ILLUS.)... **$403**

Green Handled Cylindrical Pine Cone Vase

Vase, 7 1/2" h., two-handled, footed wide cylinder w/flat rim & small asymmetrical handles, green ground, No. 704-7" (ILLUS.)
.... **$196**

Vase, 8 1/2" h., pillow-type, wide flattened bulbous body w/asymmetrical branch handles, green ground, No. 114-8" (ground flake on base)............................ **$374**

Footed Cylindrical Pine Cone Vase

Vase, 7 1/2" h., two-handled, footed wide cylinder w/flat rim & small asymmetrical handles, silver foil label, brown ground, No. 704-7" (ILLUS.).................................. **$316**

Brown Pine Cone Pillow-type Vase

Vase, 8 1/2" h., pillow-type, wide flattened bulbous body w/asymmetrical branch handles, brown ground, gold foil label, No. 114-8" (ILLUS.) **$374**

Horn-shaped Blue Pine Cone Vase

Vase, 8 1/2" h., horn-shaped w/fanned & pleated rim, pine needles & cone-form handle from base of oval foot to midsection, blue ground, No. 490-8" (ILLUS.)....... **$431**

Pine Cone Vase with Unusual Rim

Vase, 10" h., footed, two-handled bulbous body tapering to wide tall cylindrical neck w/irregular cut-out rim, brown ground, tiny nick on cut-out rim, No. 848-10" (ILLUS.).... **$403**

Large Footed Cylindrical Pine Cone Vase

Vase, 10" h., foot w/flaring ringed short pedestal supporting a wide cylindrical body w/a nearly flat wide rim, long angular handles down the sides, brown ground, No. 910-10" (ILLUS.)................................. **$633**
Vase, 10 1/2" h., footed expanding cylinder w/wide flat mouth flanked by small twig

handles, brown ground, No. 709-10"
.... **$400-500**

Fine Blue Pine Cone Footed Vase

Vase, 10 1/2" h., footed expanding cylinder w/wide flat mouth flanked by small twig handles, blue ground, No. 709-10" (ILLUS.)... **$748**

Tall Green Pine Cone Vase

Vase, 12" h., tall tapering corseted form w/asymmetric branch handles, green ground, No. 712-12" (ILLUS.) **$431**
Vase, 12" h., tall tapering corseted form w/asymmetric branch handles, brown ground, No. 712-12"................................. **$431**

Tall Tapering Blue Pine Cone Vase

Vase, 12" h., tall tapering corseted form w/asymmetric branch handles, blue ground, No. 712-12" (ILLUS., previous page) **$748**

Green Double Pine Cone Wall Pocket

Wall pocket, double, two flaring conical containers joined by an arched pine cone & needle top handle, green ground, silver Roseville paper label, No. 1273-8", 8 1/2" h. (ILLUS.) **$460**

Wall pocket, bucket-shaped, green ground, No. 1283-9", 9" h. **$850-950**

Wall shelf, brown ground, No. 1-5 x 8", 5" w., 8" h. **$374**

Poppy (1930s)
Shaded backgrounds of blue or pink with decoration of poppy flower and green leaves.

Large Pink Roseville Poppy Basket

Basket, wide trumpet-form w/high & wide arched handle, pink ground, glaze skip on the handle, No. 347-10", 10" h. (ILLUS.)... **$316**

Ewer, footed gently flaring cylindrical body w/a cut-out lip w/arched spout, C-form handle, pink ground, No. 876-10", 10" h. **$450-550**

Rare Tall Poppy Ewer

Ewer, very tall slender ovoid body w/a split neck & high arched spout, C-scroll handle, pink ground, foil label, No. 880-18", 18" h. (ILLUS.) **$550-650**

Small Pink Poppy Jardiniere

Jardiniere, footed, squatty, spherical body w/a wide, flat mouth flanked by tiny handles at rim, pink ground, No. 642-3", 3 1/2" h. (ILLUS.) **$104**

Grey to Yellow Poppy Jardiniere

Jardiniere, footed, wide, bulbous, ovoid body w/a very wide flat mouth flanked by tiny C-scroll handles, grey shaded to yellow ground, No. 642-6", 6" h. (ILLUS.)....... **$161**

Green to Pink Poppy Jardiniere

Jardiniere, footed, wide, bulbous, ovoid body w/a very wide, flat mouth flanked by tiny C-scroll handles, green shaded to pink ground, No. 642-6", 6" h. (ILLUS.)...... **$184**

Vase, 10" h., two-handled, semi-ovoid, cutout rim, pink ground, No. 875-10" **$300-400**

Tall Grey Poppy Vase

Vase, 15" h., footed squatty lower body tapering to tall cylindrical sides w/a flared rim, small C-scroll lower shoulder handles, grey ground, No. 878-15" (ILLUS.)
.... **$450-550**

Pink Poppy Tall Floor Vase

Vase, 18 1/4" h., floor type, footed, tall, ovoid body w/a closed mouth & C-scroll shoulder handles, pink ground, No. 879-18" (ILLUS.) **$1,200-1,400**

Rozane (1900)

Dark blended backgrounds; slip decorated underglaze artware.

Tall Rozane Tankard Pitcher with Grapes

Pitcher, 14" h., tankard-type, flaring base & tall slightly tapering sides w/a pinched rim spout & long, low C-form handle, decorated w/a dark bluish black grape cluster & dark green leaves down from the rim on a dark green shaded to gold to brown ground, Royal Rozane mark, nominal overall glaze crazing, decorated by Walter Myers (ILLUS.) **$259**

Small Rozane Vase with Clover

Vase, 4" h., wide bulbous baluster-form body tapering to a tiny rolled neck, decorated w/orange clover blossoms & green leaves on a dark shaded brown ground, artist-initials, glaze inclusion, few minor glaze pits (ILLUS.)..................................... **$104**

Unusual Silhouette Basket

handle, florals, brown ground, No. 710-10", 10" h. (ILLUS.)..................................... **$104**
Basket w/asymmetrical rim & overhead handle, florals, tan, No. 709-8", 8" h. **$127**

Exceptional Large Rozane Royal Vase

Vase, 23 3/8" h., tall ovoid body w/a narrow rounded shoulder & a wide low flat neck, decorated w/life-sized yellow irises, buds & dark green leaves on a shaded dark brown ground, Rozane Royal mark, signed by Walter Myers (ILLUS.) **$10,063**

Silhouette (1950)
Recessed area silhouettes nature study or female nudes. Colors are rose, turquoise, tan and white with turquoise.

Basket, flaring cylinder w/pointed overhead handle, florals, turquoise blue, No. 708-6", 6" h. **$173**

Brown Silhouette Basket with Florals

Basket, curved rim & asymmetrical handle, florals, brown ground, No. 710-10", 10" h. (ILLUS.)... **$259**
Basket, rectangular wedge-shaped foot supporting a squared football-form body w/curved rim, overhead asymmetrical

Brown Silhouette Console Set

Console set: long, narrow, footed, rectangular console bowl & a pair of short tapering candleholders; brown ground, florals, candleholders No. 751-3", bowl No. 730-10", bowl 10" l., the set (ILLUS.)................ **$115**
Ewer, rectangular foot supporting sharply tapering slender squared sides ending in an upright rolled spout, pointed long handle, florals, brown ground, No. 717-10", 10" h. **$200-300**
Vase, 7" h., fan-shaped, nude woman, brown ground, No. 783-7" **$230**

Footed Urn-form Silhouette Vase

Vase, 8" h., urn-form tapering ovoid body raised on four angled feet on a round disc base, wide, slightly flaring mouth, female nude, brown ground, No. 763-8" (ILLUS.) .. **$460**

Turquoise Blue Silhouette Vase with Nude

Vase, 10" h., small open handles between square base & waisted cylindrical body, shaped rim, female nudes, turquoise ground, No. 787-10" (ILLUS.) **$750-850**

Snowberry (1946)

Brown branch with small white berries and green leaves embossed over spider-web design in various background colors (blue, green and rose).

Blue Fan-shaped Snowberry Basket

Basket, footed, fan-shaped body w/wide looped & pointed handle, shaded blue ground, No. 1BK-7", 7" h. (ILLUS.) **$150-175**

Shaded Rose Snowberry Basket

Basket, round foot below the wide, flattened ovoid body w/a downswept rim, asymmetrical overhead handle, shaded rose ground, No. 1BK-8", 8" h. (ILLUS.) **$250-275**

10" Green Snowberry Basket

Basket, wide, round foot tapering to a flaring, cylindrical body w/a steeply angled rim, curved overhead handle, shaded green ground, No. 1BK-10", 10" h. (ILLUS.)... **$161**

Shaded Green Snowberry Console Bowl

Console bowl, boat-shaped, pointed end handles, shaded green ground, No. 1BL2-12", 12" l. (ILLUS.)............................. **$92**

Shaded Rose Snowberry Console Bowl

Console bowl, boat-shaped, pointed end handles, shaded rose ground, No. 1BL2-12", 15" l. (ILLUS.) **$100-150**

Bulbous Blue Snowberry Jardiniere

Jardiniere, wide bulbous body w/a wide flat mouth flanked by small angled shoulder

handles, shaded blue ground, No. 1J-6",
6" h. (ILLUS.) **$200-300**

6" Bulbous Rose Snowberry Jardiniere

Jardiniere, wide, bulbous body w/a wide, flat mouth flanked by small angled shoulder handles, shaded rose ground, No. 1J-6", 6" h. (ILLUS.) **$104**

Green Snowberry Rose Bowl

Rose bowl, bulbous body tapering to a four-notch mouth flanked by small pointed shoulder handles, shaded green ground, No. 1RB-5", 5" h. (ILLUS.) **$100-130**
Teapot, cov., shaded green ground, No. 1TP.. **$200-250**

Crescent-shaped Snowberry Pillow Vase

Vase, 6 1/2" h., pillow type w/crescent-shaped body w/wedge-form foot, asymmetrical side handles, shaded green ground, No. 1FH-6" (ILLUS.)..................... **$115**

Snowberry Shaded Rose Bud Vase

Vase, 7 1/2" h., bud, rectangular foot tapering to a tall, slender, flaring body w/angled rim, asymmetrical pointed loop handles at the base, shaded rose ground, No. 1V1-7" (ILLUS.) **$104**

Tall-necked Blue Snowberry Vase

Vase, 7 1/2" h., bulbous base w/tall cylindrical neck, pointed shoulder handles, shaded blue ground, No. 1V2-7" (ILLUS.) .. **$104**
Vase, 9" h., large round disk foot supporting a tall cylindrical body w/a flared rim, down-turned pointed handles just above the foot, shaded green ground, No. 1V1-9".. **$150-200**

Green Snowberry 9" Vase

Vase, 9" h., base handles, shaded green ground, No. 1V1-9" (ILLUS.)..................... **$150**

Shaded Rose 10" Snowberry Vase

Vase, 10" h., footed, bulbous lower body below a wide, cylindrical neck w/flaring rim, pointed handles from middle of neck to shoulder, shaded rose ground, No. 1V2-10" (ILLUS.) **$161**

Shaded Rose Baluster Snowberry Vase

Vase, 12 1/2" h., footed, tall, baluster-form body w/flaring rim, pointed angled handles at sides, shaded rose ground, No. IVI-12" (ILLUS.) **$200-300**

Tall Blue Snowberry Vase

Vase, 12 1/2" h., conical base tapering to a tall, fanned body w/a flaring stepped rim, pointed handles at the lower body, shaded blue ground, No. 1V2-12" (ILLUS.) **$230**

Pink Snowberry Wall Pocket

Wall pocket, wide, half-round form tapering to a pointed base, low angled handles along the lower sides, shaded rose ground, No. 1WP-8", 8" w., 5 1/2" h. (ILLUS.) **$200-300**

Green Snowberry Window Box

Window box, long, rectangular form w/pointed end handles, shaded green ground, No. 1WX-8", 8" l. (ILLUS.) **$150-200**

Sunflower (1930)

Tall stems support yellow sunflowers whose blooms form a repetitive band. Textured background shades from tan to dark green at base.

Bowl, 7 1/2" d., wide squatty form w/wide flat rim, No. 208-5" (ILLUS. right with Sunflower vases, top next page) **$805**
Console bowl, elongated low diamond form w/loop end handles, 12 1/2" l., 3" h. **$920**

Very Large Sunflower Jardiniere

Jardiniere, large, bulbous form w/a ringed rim around the wide, flat mouth, No. 619-12", 12" h. (ILLUS.) **$3,000-4,000**

Sunflower Bowl and Vases

Spherical Sunflower Urn-Vase

Urn-vase, nearly spherical w/short wide neck, No. 489-7", 7" h. (ILLUS.)................ **$978**

Fine Sunflower Jardiniere & Pedestal

Jardiniere & pedestal, jardiniere No. 619-10", 10" h., overall 29" h., 2 pcs. (ILLUS.)
.... **$4,140**

Urn-vase, nearly spherical w/closed rim flanked by tiny rim handles, 4" h. (ILLUS. left with Sunflower bowl and vase, top of page) **$575**

Roseville Sunflower Vase

Vase, 5" h., swelled cylindrical body w/long side handles & flat rim. No. 512-5" (ILLUS.).. **$575**

Small Spherical Sunflower Vase

Vase, 4" h., spherical body tapering to a wide, low, flared rim flanked by rounded loop shoulder handles, original foil sticker, No. 566-4" (ILLUS.) **$450-550**

Swelled Cylindrical Sunflower Vase

Vase, 6 1/4" h., slightly swelled & flaring cylindrical body w/a wide, short, slightly flaring neck flanked by tiny loop handles, No. 494-6" (ILLUS.) **$575**

Wide Cylindrical Sunflower Vase

Vase, 5" h., wide, flat base w/gently flaring cylindrical sides & a rounded shoulder to the wide closed mouth, No. 486-5" (ILLUS.) **$863**

Sunflower Vase with Bulbous Base

Vase, 8" h., bulbous base, wide tapering cylindrical neck, No. 490-8" (ILLUS.).......... **$1,093**

Nearly Spherical Sunflower Vase

Vase, 6" h., bulbous, nearly spherical body, wide shoulder tapering to a short cylindrical neck, No. 488-6" (ILLUS.) **$900-1,000**

Ovoid Sunflower Vase

Vase, 8 1/4" h., ovoid body w/a widely flaring rim flanked by small loop handles, No. 491-8" (ILLUS.) **$1,035**

Vase, 9" h., bulbous base w/wide cylindrical neck, small loop handles, No. 493-9" (ILLUS. center with bowl and urn-vase, top of page 584) **$1,495**

Cylindrical Sunflower Vase

Vase, 10" h., swelled cylindrical body w/tiny shoulder handles, No. 492-10" (ILLUS.) **$920**

Rare Sunflower Wall Pocket

Wall pocket, bucket-form w/pierced double-arch top handle, No. 1265-7", 7" h. (ILLUS.)... **$1,380**

Teasel (1936)
Embossed decorations of long stems gracefully curving with delicate spider-like pods. Colors and glaze treatments vary from monochrome matte to crystalline. Colors are beige to tan, medium blue highlighted with gold, pale blue, and deep rose (possibly others).

Footed Squatty Teasel Bowl

Bowl, 4" d., low pedestal foot below the wide, squatty, bulbous body w/a closed rim, tiny pointed side handles, pale blue ground, No. 342-4" (ILLUS.) **$175-200**
Vase, 8" h., closed handles at shoulder, low foot, beige shading to tan, No. 884-8" **$259**

Deep Rose Teasel Vase

Vase, 9" h., closed handles at base, flaring mouth, deep rose, No. 886-9" (ILLUS.)
.... **$100-150**

Thorn Apple (1930s)
White trumpet flower with leaves reverses to thorny pod with leaves. Colors are shaded blue, brown and pink.

Low Rounded Blue Thorn Apple Bowl

Bowl, 5" d., wide, squatty, rounded form w/wide, flat rim flanked by tiny angled rim handles, shaded blue ground, No. 306-5" (ILLUS.)... **$104**

Thorn Apple Blue Bowl-Vase

Bowl-vase, footed, spherical form w/three openings & buttressed handles, shaded blue ground, No. 305-6", 10" w., 6 1/4" h. (ILLUS.)... **$173**

Thorn Apple Brown Centerpiece

Centerpiece, long, narrow, rectangular foot supporting short, slender trumpet-form candle sockets at each end centered by a half-round spherical bowl resting on a large leaf cluster, shaded brown ground, No. 313, 11" l., 4 1/2" h. (ILLUS.) **$325-400**

Upright Flattened Thorn Apple Vase

Vase, 6" h., round disk foot supporting a wide, flattened, vertical body w/stepped sides & rim, angled handles at the base, shaded brown ground, No. 812-6" (ILLUS.) **$150-175**

Thorn Apple Triple Wall Pocket

Wall pocket, triple, white blossom & green leaf across top, shaded pink ground w/large green leaf, repair to lower portion, No. 1280-8", 8" h. **$345**

Tourmaline (1933)

Although the semi-gloss medium blue, highlighted around the rim with lighter high gloss and gold effect seems to be accepted as the standard Tourmaline glaze, the catalogue definitely shows this and two other types as well. One is a

mottled overall turquoise, the other a mottled salmon that appears to be lined in the high gloss but with no overrun to the outside.

Blue Tourmaline Urn-Vase

Urn-vase, round pedestal foot below the bulbous ribbed lower body below wide, slightly flaring cylindrical sides flanked by long angled handles, mottled blue ground, unnumbered, 6 1/4" h. (ILLUS.).... **$104**

Drippy Turquoise Tourmaline Vase

Vase, 7" h., footed, swelled, cylindrical body tapering to a short, wide neck w/flared rim, drippy mottled turquoise, No. A-308-7" (ILLUS.) **$104**

Turquoise to Pink Tourmaline Vase

Vase, 7" h., footed, swelled, cylindrical body tapering to a short, wide neck w/flared rim, turquoise shading to mottled pink, No. A-308-7" (ILLUS.) **$104**

Mottled Blue Roseville Tourmaline Vase

Vase, 8 1/4" h., base handles, bulbous tapering to flared rim, mottled blue, No. A-332-8" (ILLUS.) **$127**

Tuscany (1928)

Marble-like finish most often found in a shiny pink, sometimes in matte grey, more rarely in a dull turquoise. Suggestion of leaves and berries, usually at the base of handles, are the only decorations.

Flower arranger vase, flaring oval foot w/ringed stem supporting a flattened urn-form body w/loop handles on the shoulder pierced w/holes, mottled pink ground, No. 69-5", 5 1/2" h. **$81**

Lamp, table model, upright flat three-sided vase No. 343-7" fitted on a squared gilt-metal base, pink, overall 9" h. **$150-200**

Vase, 4" h., 6 1/2" w., bowl-form, footed widely flaring trumpet-form w/open handles from under rim to the foot, grey, No. 67-4" **$92**

Vase, 5" h., footed wide squatty bulbous body tapering sharply to a flat mouth, loop handles from rim to shoulder, grey, No. 341-5" **$144**

Three-sided Tuscany Vase

Vase, 7" h., upright flat three-sided shape, two-handled, pink, No. 343-7" (ILLUS.) **$173**

Wall pocket, conical w/wide flaring half-round ringed rim, loop handles at sides molded w/small purple grape clusters & pale green leaves, pink, No. 1254-7", 7" h. **$288**

Pink Tuscany 8" Wall Pocket

Wall pocket, long open handles, rounded rim, mottled pink glaze, paper label, short hairline from mounting hole to rim, No. 1255-8", 8" h. (ILLUS.) **$173**

Vista (1920s)

Embossed green coconut palm trees & lavender blue pool against grey ground.

Undulating Cylindrical Vista Basket

Basket, undulating cylindrical form w/flaring rim, pointed overhead handle, unmarked, some touched-up rim chips, 10" h. (ILLUS.) **$403**

Ovoid Vista Basket with Arched Handle

Basket, footed, slender, ovoid body, unmarked, high arched overhead handle, rim chip, tiny base chips, 12" h. (ILLUS.)... **$403**

28" Vista Jardiniere & Pedestal

Jardiniere & pedestal, 9 1/2" h. jardiniere on a flaring pedestal base, jardiniere No. 589-9", chip on top of pedestal, overall 28" h., 2 pcs. (ILLUS.).............................. **$1,610**

Vista Vase with Flaring Foot

Vase, 9 3/4" h., cylindrical body tapering to flared base, flattened shoulder w/flat molded mouth, unmarked, No. 127-10" (ILLUS.).. **$633**

Rare Vista Wall Pocket

Wall pocket, ovoid bullet shape w/a high arched backplate, glaze chip on back, 9 1/2" h. (ILLUS.).. **$690**

Water Lily (1943)

Water lily and pad in various color combinations: tan to brown with yellow lily, blue with white lily, pink to green with pink lily.

Light Blue Water Lily Basket

Basket, cylindrical, w/widely flaring rim, pointed overhead handle, pale blue ground, No. 380-8", 8" h. (ILLUS.)............. **$150**
Basket, trumpet-shaped w/widely flaring rim, high arched & pointed handle across the top & under the rims, pink to green ground, No. 380-8", 8" h. **$150-200**
Basket, conch shell-shaped w/high arched handle, tan shaded to brown ground, No. 381-10", 10" h. **$288**

Unusual Brown Water Lily Basket

Basket, round foot supporting a wide, flattened, ovoid body w/the serpentine rim pulled up into a tall, curved three-tier section at one end, asymmetrical overhead handle, tan shaded to brown ground, No. 382-12", 12" h. (ILLUS.)..................... **$250-350**
Console set: 14" l. bowl w/large pointed end handles, shaped sides, & pr. of 2" h. candleholders, pink shading to green ground, bowl No. 444-14", 14" l., candleholders No. 1154-2", the set **$288**

Cookie jar, cov., angular handles, pink shading to green ground, No. 1-8", 8" h..... **$403**

Ewer, squatty flared bottom tapering to a tall split neck w/high arched spout & high pointed loop handle, blended blue ground, No. 10-6", 6" h. (ILLUS.)............... **$92**

Water Lily Blue Cornucopia-Vase

Cornucopia-vase, large water lily blossom applied at base, pale blue ground, No. 177-6", 6" h. (ILLUS.).......................... **$100-150**

Tall Water Lily Ewer

Ewer, disk foot below a bulbous, ovoid body tapering to a divided rim w/a long upright arched spout, large angular shoulder handle, light blue ground, No. 12-15", 15" h. (ILLUS.) **$400-500**

Tan to Brown Water Lily Ewer

Ewer, squatty, flared bottom tapering to a tall split neck w/high arched spout & high pointed loop handle, tan to brown ground, No. 10-6", 6" h. (ILLUS.) **$100-125**

Small Blue Water Lily Jardiniere

Jardiniere, squatty, bulbous lower body w/low, wide, cylindrical sides to an in-curved rim, small angled handles from rim to lower body, pale blue ground, No. 663-4", 4" h. (ILLUS.)........................ **$100-150**

Large Blue Water Lily Conch Shell

Model of a conch shell, shaded blue ground, No. 438-8", 8" l. (ILLUS.) **$150-200**

Blue Water Lily Pattern Ewer

Bulbous Blue Water Lily Vase

Vase, 8 1/4" h., footed, bulbous, ovoid body w/a short, wide, cylindrical neck flanked by angular handles, pale blue ground, No. 77-8" (ILLUS.)................................ **$175-225**

No. 80-10" Water Lily Vase

Vase, 10 1/4" h., low foot below the widely flaring flattened lower body tapering to a tall waisted neck w/flaring rim, large angled handles from center of neck to edge of lower body, tan shading to brown ground, No. 80-10" (ILLUS.).............. **$200-300**

Footed Ovoid Blue Water Lily Vase

Vase, 9" h., footed, ovoid body w/wide, flat mouth, the sides w/pointed downswept handles, pale blue ground, No. 78-9" (ILLUS.) **$175-250**

Water Lily Footed Cylindrical Vase

Vase, 14" h., wide disk foot below the tall, gently flaring, cylindrical body, long curved handles from mid-body to the foot, tan shading to brown ground, No. 82-14" (ILLUS.).................................. **$250-300**

Pink Shaded to Green Water Lily Vase

Vase, 9" h., footed, ovoid body w/wide, flat mouth, the sides w/pointed downswept handles, pink shaded to green ground, No. 78-9" (ILLUS.)................................ **$250-350**

Brown Water Lily 15 1/2" Floor Vase

Vase, 15 1/2" h., round, stepped foot below the tall, ovoid body w/a closed mouth flanked by angular shoulder handles, tan shading to brown ground, No. 83-15" (ILLUS., previous page) **$350-450**

Water Lily 15 1/2" Floor Vase

Vase, 15 1/2" h., round stepped foot below the tall ovoid body w/a closed mouth flanked by angular shoulder handles, pale blue ground, glaze nick on a petal, firing separations & blistering on flower centers, No. 83-15" (ILLUS.) **$460**

Tall Brown Water Lily Floor Vase

Vase, 16 1/4" h., floor type, footed, tall, ovoid body w/swelled shoulder & short, wide neck, angled handles from shoulder

to mid-body, shaded tan to brown ground, No. 84-16" (ILLUS.) **$250-350**

White Rose (1940s)

White roses and green leaves against a vertically combed ground of blended blue, brown shading to green, or pink shading to green.

Large Blue White Rose Basket

Basket, footed, widely flaring fanned body w/downswept rim, sweeping handle rising from base to rim at opposite side, blended blue ground, No. 364-12", 12 1/2" h. (ILLUS.) **$275-325**

White Rose Pink to Green Candleholders

Candleholders, two-handled, low, pink shading to green ground, No. 1141-2", 2" h., pr. (ILLUS.) **$104**

Spherical Blue Water Lily Jardiniere

Jardiniere, spherical w/wide notched rim flanked by small shoulder loop handles, blended blue ground, No. 653-10", 10" h. (ILLUS.)... **$200-250**
Tea set: cov. teapot, sugar bowl & creamer; brown shading to green ground, Nos. 1T, 1S, 1C, 3 pcs. **$489**

White Rose Brown & Green Urn-Vase

Urn-vase, pedestal base below the wide, bulbous, ovoid body w/a wide cylindrical neck w/a notched rim, curved handles from rim to shoulder, brown shaded to green ground, No. 147-8", 8" h. (ILLUS.) **$150-175**

White Rose Brown & Green 9" Vase

Vase, 9" h., footed, wide, tapering, cylindrical body w/large handles from foot to shoulder, notched rim, brown shading to green ground, No. 986-9" (ILLUS.) **$150-250**

White Rose Pink & Green 8 1/2" h. Vase

Vase, 8 1/2" h., small footring below a squatty, bulbous base & tall, wide, cylindrical body w/notched flat rim, long loop handles from rim to edge of base, pink shading to green ground, No. 985-8" (ILLUS.) **$150-200**

Tall Ovoid Pink & Green White Rose Vase

Vase, 12 1/2" h., tall, ovoid body tapering to a notched rim flanked by angled shoulder handles, pink shading to green ground, No. 991-12" (ILLUS.) **$250-350**

Brown & Green White Rose Vase

Vase, 8 1/2" h., small footring below a squatty bulbous base & tall, wide, cylindrical body w/notched flat rim, long loop handles from rim to edge of base, brown shading to green ground, No. 985-8" (ILLUS.) **$127**

White Rose 18 1/2" Floor Vase

Vase, 18 1/2" h., floor type, tall ovoid body tapering to a low notched rim, large looped shoulder handles, brown shaded to green ground, No. 994-18" (ILLUS.) **$403**

Wincraft (1948)

Revived shapes from older lines such as Pine Cone, Bushberry, Cremona, Primrose and others. Vases with animal motifs, contemporary shapes in high gloss of blue, tan, lime and green.

Long, Low Tan Wincraft Basket

Basket, rectangular foot supporting very long, narrow, arched boat-shaped body, long, low overhead handle, berries & foliage in relief on glossy brown shading to tan ground, No. 209-12", 12" h. (ILLUS.)
.... **$150-200**

Large Blue Wincraft Basket

Basket, rectangular concave foot supporting fanned body w/divided arched rim, high overhead handle forming two loop handles to one side, glossy blue ground, No. 210-12", 12" h. (ILLUS.) **$200-250**

Low Oblong Wincraft Bowl

Bowl, 8" l., low foot supporting the low, oblong, two-lobed bowl w/pointed end tab handles, glossy green ground, No. 226-8" (ILLUS.) **$100-150**

Blue Domed Wincraft Creamer & Sugar

Creamer & open sugar bowl, flat-bottomed domed shape w/cylindrical neck, small angled loop handles, glossy blue ground, No. 250C & 250S, 2 1/2" & 3 1/2" h., pr. (ILLUS.) **$100-150**

Blue Wincraft Bell-form Ewer

Ewer, bell-form body below a tall neck w/upright tall spout & angled shoulder handle, glossy blue ground, No. 216-8", 8" h. (ILLUS.) **$104**

Green & Brown Wincraft Flowerpot

Flowerpot, thin disk foot & widely flaring flat sides, glossy green to brown ground, No. 256-5", 5" h. (ILLUS.) **$92**

Glossy Blue Wincraft Flowerpot

Flowerpot, thin disk foot & widely flaring flat sides, glossy green to brown ground, glossy blue ground, No. 256-5", 5" h. (ILLUS.) **$80**

Tea set: cov. teapot, creamer & sugar bowl; white floral decoration in relief on glossy tan ground, No. 271, 3 pcs......................... **$201**
Teapot, cov., brown & yellow ground, No. 271-P.. **$100-150**

Wincraft Football-form Vase

Vase, 6" h., a square foot supporting a nearly horizontal football form w/integral fin-like handles at each end, glossy brown to tan ground, No. 241-6" (ILLUS.) **$100-150**
Vase, 7" h., square, paneled sides w/swirled Art Deco style design in relief on glossy yellow and tan ground, No. 274-7"...... **$100-200**

Tall Tan Wincraft Vase

Vase, 10" h., ovoid base & long cylindrical neck w/wedge-shaped closed handle on one side & long closed column-form handle on the other, shaded tan ground, No. 284-10" (ILLUS.) **$150-200**

Cylindrical Wincraft Green Vase

Vase, 10" h., cylindrical w/flat disk base, relief arrowroot leaf & blossom decoration on glossy green ground, No. 285-10" (ILLUS.) **$175-200**

Box-like Wincraft Wall Pocket

Wall pocket, rectangular box-like holder w/horizontal ribbing & ivy leaves as rim handle, glossy light green to brown ground, No. 266-4", 8 1/2" h. (ILLUS.) **$173**

Windsor (1931)

Brown or blue mottled glaze, some with leaves, vines and ferns, some with a repetitive band arrangement of small squares and rectangles in yellow and green.

Elegant Lamp with Windsor Glaze

Lamp, tall baluster-form base w/shaded reddish brown to brown Windsor glaze, fitted on a round cast-metal openwork base w/a shell & scroll design & a matching top fitting rim, pottery section 8 7/8" h. (ILLUS.).. **$633**

Spherical Windsor Vase with Ferns

Vase, 7 1/8" h., large spherical body tapering to a wide short flaring neck w/slender curved handles from rim to shoulder, stylized ferns against mottled blue ground, No. 551-7", chip on back edge of one handle (ILLUS.) **$633**

Scarce Windsor Vase with Blossoms

Vase, 8 1/2" h., two-handled cylindrical body w/low flat rim, decorated w/thin straight green stems suspending a long leaf & small yellow blossoms around the

shoulder on a mottled blue ground, w/a small black Roseville sticker, No. 552-8" (ILLUS.) **$978**

Wisteria (1933)

Lavender wisteria blossoms and green vines against a roughly textured brown shading to deep blue ground or brown shading to yellow and green; rarely found in only brown.

Low Squatty Wisteria Bowl

Bowl, 6 1/2" d., 2 1/2" h., wide, low, flaring, squatty form w/a wide, closed rim, brown shaded to yellow & green ground, unmarked (ILLUS.) **$150-200**

Bowl & flower frog, 6 1/2" d., 3" h., sharply flaring low rounded sides w/a closed rim, brown ground (ILLUS. center with bowl-vase and vase, bottom of page) **$374**

Small Wisteria Bowl-Vase

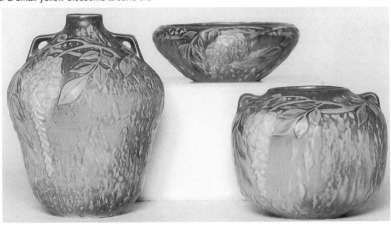

Wisteria Bowl and Vases

Bowl-vase, squatty, bulbous form tapering sharply to a flat mouth flanked by small loop handles, brown & blue ground, No. 242-4", 4" h. (ILLUS., previous page) **$431**

4" Spherical Wisteria Bowl-Vase

Bowl-vase, bulbous, spherical form tapering to a small, flat mouth flanked by tiny rounded shoulder handles, brown shading to yellow & green ground, No. 632-4", 4" h. (ILLUS.) **$316**
Bowl-vase, bulbous spherical form tapering to a small flat mouth flanked by tiny shoulder handles, brown shading to yellow & green ground, No. 632-5", 5" h. (ILLUS. right with bowl and vase, bottom of previous page).............................. **$450-500**

Small Wisteria Bowl-Vase

Bowl-vase, bulbous spherical form tapering to a small flat mouth flanked by tiny shoulder handles, brown shaded to yellow & green ground, No. 632-5", 5" h. (ILLUS.) **$450-550**

Bulbous Spherical Wisteria Bowl-Vase

Bowl-vase, bulbous, spherical form tapering to a small, flat mouth flanked by tiny shoulder handles, brown shading to yellow & green ground, No. 632-5", 5" h. (ILLUS.) **$450-500**

9 1/2" Wisteria Console Bowl

Console bowl, narrow, oblong form w/upright sides & small pointed end handles, brown ground, No. 243-5 x 9", 9 1/2" l. (ILLUS.)... **$345**
Vase, 4" h., squatty, angular handles on sharply canted shoulder, brown ground, No. 629-4" **$345**

Squatty Tapering Wisteria Vase

Vase, 4" h., squatty, w/angular handles on sharply canted shoulder, blue ground, gold triangular sticker, No. 629-4" (ILLUS.)... **$500-700**

Tapering Ovoid Small Wisteria Vase

Vase, 6" h., ovoid body tapering to short, cylindrical neck flanked by small loop handles, blue ground, No. 631-6" (ILLUS.)
.... **$546**

Squatty and Tall Wisteria Vases

Rare Ovoid 6 1/2" Wisteria Vase

Vase, 6 1/2" h., 4" d., bulbous, ovoid body w/a wide shoulder tapering up to a small mouth, small angled shoulder handles, mottled blue & yellow ground, No. 630-6" (ILLUS.).. **$748**

Globular 6 1/2" Wisteria Vase

Vase, 6 1/2" h., globular w/small, flat mouth & tiny angular shoulder handles, brown shaded to green & yellow ground, No. 637-6 1/2" (ILLUS.) **$575**
Vase, 6 1/2" h., globular w/small flat mouth & tiny angular shoulder handles, brown to blue ground, No. 637-6 1/2" (ILLUS. left with tall vase, top of page) **$1,035**

Bulbous Waisted Wisteria Vase

Vase, 7" h., bulbous waisted ovoid body w/small pointed shoulder handles, brown ground, No. 634-7" (ILLUS.) **$633**
Vase, 8" h., pear-shaped body w/short cylindrical neck & tiny angled shoulder handles, brown shading to yellow & green ground, No. 636-8" (ILLUS. left with bowl and bowl-vase)... **$633**

8" Brown Shaded to Yellow Wisteria Vase

Vase, 8" h., 6 1/2" d., wide, tapering, cylindrical body w/small angled handles flanking the flat rim, brown shaded to yellow & green ground, No. 633-8" (ILLUS.) **$575**

Tapering Cylindrical Wisteria Vase

Vase, 8" h., 6 1/2" d., wide, tapering, cylindrical body w/small angled handles flanking the flat rim, blue ground, No. 633-8" (ILLUS.)... **$1,265**

Ovoid Wisteria Vase with Tall Neck

Vase, 9 1/2" h., cylindrical ovoid body w/angular handles rising from shoulder to midsection of slender cylindrical neck, brown shaded to yellow & green ground, No. 638-9" (ILLUS.)... **$690**

Rare Flaring Wisteria Vase

Vase, 8 1/2" h., flaring foot tapering to the gently flaring body bulging slightly below the flat rim, short handles from lower body to foot, brown shading to yellow & green ground, No. 635-8" (ILLUS.) **$575**

Cylindrical 10" Wisteria Vase

Vase, 10" h., cylindrical body w/closed rim, angled shoulder handles, brown shaded to yellow & green ground, silver foil sticker, No. 639-10" (ILLUS.) **$500**

Rare Flaring Blue Wisteria Vase

Vase, 8 1/2" h., flaring foot tapering to the gently flaring body bulging slightly below the flat rim, short handles from lower body to foot, brown shading to yellow & green ground, gold foil label, blue ground, No. 635-8" (ILLUS.) **$1,035**

Tall Wisteria Vase with Small Handles

Vase, 10" h., cylindrical body w/closed rim, angled shoulder handles, brown to blue ground, silver foil Roseville label, No. 639-10" (ILLUS., previous page & right with squatty vase, page 598) **$1,495**

Fine Flaring Wisteria Vase

Vase, 10 1/4" h., bulbous lower body tapering sharply to a tall trumpet neck, angled handles from center of neck to lower body, brown ground, No. 682-10" (ILLUS.) **$1,035**

Rare Tall Wisteria Vase

Vase, 15" h., bottle-shaped w/angular handles at shoulder, blue ground, No. 641-15" (ILLUS.) **$2,530**

Zephyr Lily (1946)

Tall lilies and slender leaves adorn swirl-textured backgrounds of Bermuda Blue, Evergreen and Sienna Tan.

Basket, footed flaring rectangular body w/upcurved rim & long asymmetrical handle, green ground, No. 394-8", 8" h........... **$173**

Green Zephyr Lily Basket

Basket, footed, cylindrical body flaring slightly to an ornate cut rim w/low, wide overhead handle, green ground, No. 395-10", 10" h. (ILLUS.) **$161**

Basket, footed cylindrical body flaring slightly to an ornate cut rim w/low wide overhead handle, blue ground, No. 395-10", 10" h. **$230**

Green Zephyr Lily Bookends

Bookends, green ground, No. 16, 5 1/2" h., pr. (ILLUS.) **$173**

Blue Zephyr Lily Cookie Jar

Cookie jar, cov., blue ground, No. 5-8", 10" h. (ILLUS.) **$288**

Green & Brown Zephyr Lily Cornucopia

Cornucopia-vase, green shaded to brown
ground, No. 204-8" 8 1/2" h. (ILLUS.)
.... **$100-150**

Zephyr Lily Creamer & Open Sugar Set

Creamer & open sugar bowl, brown shaded to green ground, Nos. 7C & 7S, pr.
(ILLUS.) **$125-150**
Ewer, footed baluster-form w/a tall neck
w/tall forked rim & upright spout, handle
from rim to shoulder, terra cotta ground,
No. 24-15", 15" h. **$460**
Jardiniere, terra cotta ground, No. 671-8",
8" h. (minor touch-up on foot rim) **$259**

Blue Zephyr Lily Tea Set

Tea set: cov. teapot, creamer & open sugar
bowl; No. 7T, 7C & 7S, blue ground, 3
pcs. (ILLUS.) **$550-600**
Teapot, cov., blue ground, No. 7T **$250-350**
Teapot, cov., green ground, No. 7T **$100-200**
Teapot, cov., terra cotta ground, No. 7T . **$200-250**
Tray, leaf-shaped, terra cotta ground, No.
477-12", 14 1/2" l. **$115**
Urn-vase, two-handled, green ground, No.
202-8", 8 1/2" h. (ILLUS., top next col-
umn) **$173**

Zephyr Lily Urn-Vase in Green

Trumpet-form Zephyr Lily 9" Vase

Vase, 9" h., round, flaring foot tapering to a
tall trumpet-form body, short angled handles at base, green ground, No. 136-9"
(ILLUS.).. **$161**

Tall Terra Cotta Zephyr Lily Vase

Vase, 10" h., bulbous base tapering to a tall
trumpet neck, low curved handles at center of the sides, terra cotta ground, No.
137-10" (ILLUS.) **$150-200**

Tall Green Zephyr Lily Vase

Vase, 12 1/2" h., handles rising from shoulder of compressed globular base to middle of slender neck w/flaring mouth, green ground, No. 140-12" (ILLUS.) ... **$200-250**
Vase, 12 1/2" h., handles rising from shoulder of compressed globular base to middle of slender neck w/flaring mouth, terra cotta & green ground, No. 140-12" **$276**

Royal Bayreuth

Good china in numerous patterns and designs has been made at the Royal Bayreuth factory in Tettau, Germany since 1794. Listings below are by the company's lines, plus miscellaneous pieces. Interest in this china remains at a peak and prices continue to rise. Pieces listed carry the company's blue mark except where noted otherwise.

Among the important reference books in this field are Royal Bayreuth - A Collectors' Guide and Royal Bayreuth - A Collectors' Guide - Book II by Mary McCaslin (see Special Contributors list).

Royal Bayreuth Mark

Devil & Cards
Ashtray **$125-150**

Devil & Cards Candy Dish

Candy dish, shallow paneled dish composed of playing cards w/a figural seated devil handle, 6 1/2" w. (ILLUS.) **$288**
Creamer, figural red devil, 3 1/2" h. **$300-350**
Plate, 6" d. **$400-500**
Salt shaker **$150-175**
Sugar bowl, cov. **$350-400**

Mother-of-Pearl
Compote, open, decorated w/roses, pearlized finish, small **$50**

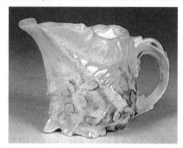

Figural Spiky Shell Creamer

Creamer, figural Spiky Shell patt., pale lavender & pink highlights (ILLUS.) **$81**
Cup & saucer, demitasse, footed, figural Spiky Shell patt., pearlized finish **$125-150**
Hatpin holder, figural poppy mold, pearlized white finish **$550-600**
Pitcher, milk, boot-shaped, figural Spiky Shell patt., pearlized finish, 5 1/2" h.... **$325-375**
Toothpick holder, Spiky Shell patt........ **$110-125**

Rose Tapestry
Basket, two-color roses, 3" h. **$300-350**
Cake plate, pierced gold handles, three-color roses, 10 1/2" d............................. **$500-600**

Rare Rose Tapestry Centerpiece Bowl

Centerpiece bowl, a large squatty bulbous lobed body decorated w/roses & a scene of a garden wall above deep red dot & blue bands around the lower body & pedestal base, mounted w/an ornate gilt-brass pierced rim w/winged putti masks, scrolled dolphin handles & on a pierced, domed scroll base, 18 1/2" w., 13 1/2" h. (ILLUS.).. **$978**
Chocolate set: cov. chocolate pot w/four matching cups & saucers, three-color roses, 9 pcs................................. **$2,200-2,600**

Creamer & cov. sugar bowl, two-color roses, pr. **$500-550**

Two-piece Rose Tapestry Dresser Set

Dresser set: 10" rectangular tray & cov. hair receiver; three-color roses decoration, blue marks, the set (ILLUS.) **$460**

Hatpin holder, small red roses at top & base, large yellow roses on body, reticulated base, gold trim, 4 1/2" h. **$450-500**

Humidor, cov., three-color roses, 7" h. **$600-650**

Model of a Victorian woman's high-heeled shoe, three-color roses **$400-450**

Pitcher, 5" h., wide cylindrical body tapering slightly toward rim, three-color roses, 24 oz. **$350-400**

Tray, rectangular, with short rim, three-color roses, 11 1/2 x 8" **$500-600**

Tomato Items

Tomato creamer, cov., large **$150-200**

Tomato Creamer & Sugar Bowl

Tomato creamer & cov. sugar bowl, creamer 3" d., 3" h., sugar bowl 3 1/2" d., 4" h., pr. (ILLUS.) **$115**

Tomato plate, 5 1/2" d., ring-handled, figural lettuce leaf w/molded yellow flowers **$30-35**

Tomato plate, 7" d., ring-handled, figural lettuce leaf w/molded yellow flowers **$40**

Tomato salt & pepper shakers, pr. **$125-150**

Miscellaneous

Ashtray, figural lobster **$125-150**

Ashtray, scenic decoration of Dutch woman w/basket, 5 1/2" d. **$50-75**

Basket, miniature, scene w/cows, unmarked **$70**

Basket, handled, boy & donkey decoration, artist-signed, 5 3/4" h. **$150-175**

Bell, peacock decoration, 2 1/2" d., 3" h. **$300**

Royal Bayreuth Musicians Berry Set

Berry set: 9 3/4" d. bowl & five 5" d. sauce dishes; Peasant Musicians decoration, 6 pcs. (ILLUS.) **$250-300**

Bowl, 5 3/4" d., nursery rhyme scene w/Jack & Jill **$125-175**

Royal Bayreuth Bowl with Roses

Bowl, 10 1/2" d., scalloped rim & molded interior lobes, decorated w/scattered pink roses & green leaves w/a satin finish, blue mark (ILLUS.) **$115**

Royal Bayreuth Heart-shaped Box

Box, cov., heart-shaped, decorated w/scene of two brown & white cows & trees in pasture, green & yellow background, unmarked, 2 x 3 1/4", 1 1/2" h. (ILLUS.) **$75-100**

Royal Bayreuth Charger with Grapes

Charger, round w/lightly scalloped rim stenciled w/gilt sprigs, decorated w/large clusters of deep red & green grapes on a shaded pale green to white ground, blue mark, 13" d. (ILLUS.) $92
Creamer, figural black cat $200-300
Creamer, figural duck............................ $250-300
Creamer, figural fish head, grey.................... $250
Creamer, figural grape cluster, light green..... $125
Creamer, figural monkey, green............. $500-550
Creamer, figural oak leaf, white w/orchid highlights.. $250-300
Creamer, figural snake......................... $750-1,000
Creamer, figural watermelon.................. $300-350
Creamer, "Huntsman," scene of hunter & dogs, small flying bird on flared rim, 4" h.
.... $100-125
Creamer, pasture scene w/cows & trees, 3 1/4" h... $75-100
Creamer, crowing rooster & hen decoration, 4 1/4" h.. $125-175
Creamer & cov. sugar bowl, figural rooster, pr.. $300-350
Creamer & open sugar bowl, figural poppy, white satin finish, pr...................... $500-550

Pitcher with Musicians Scene

Pitcher, milk, Goose Girl decoration...... $150-175
Pitcher, milk, 5 1/2" h., figural fish head
.... $300-400

Squatty Royal Bayreuth Ewer with Cows

Ewer, squatty bulbous form w/a flat cylindrical body band & wide flattened shoulder centered by a short cylindrical neck w/angled handle, green shoulder & lower body, side band decorated w/a continuous scene of cows in a landscape in shades of rust, green, brown & black, blue mark, 5" h. (ILLUS.)........................... $104
Gravy boat w/attached liner, decorated w/multicolored floral sprays, gadrooned border, gold trim, cream ground.................. $60
Hair receiver, cov., three-footed, scene of dog beside hunter shooting ducks $250-300
Match holder w/striker, decorated water scene w/brown "Shadow Trees" & boats on orange & gold ground, unmarked, 3 1/4" d., 2 1/2" h................................ $75-100
Model of a man's shoe, black oxford..... $250-300
Pitcher, 3 1/2" h., 2 1/4" d., scene of musicians, one playing bass & one w/mandolin, unmarked (ILLUS., top next column)...... $65
Pitcher, squatty, 5" h., 5" d., decorated w/hunting scene $100-125
Pitcher, 7 1/2" h., w/orange, cream & green bands, applied handle $150-200
Pitcher, milk, figural oak leaf.................. $500-600

Royal Bayreuth Figural Apple Pitcher

Pitcher, water, 6" h., figural apple (ILLUS.)
.... $600-700

Figural Sunflower Pitcher

Pitcher, water, 6 1/2" h., figural sunflower (ILLUS.)...................................... $4,000-4,500

Royal Bayreuth Child's Tea Set

ed w/a scene of children playing, the set (ILLUS., top of page)......................... **$750-850**

Royal Bayreuth "Tapestry" Tea Set

Tea set: cov. teapot, cov. sugar bowl & creamer; each w/a squatty bulbous body & gold handles, "Tapestry" decoration of white mums & purple violets on a pale blue ground, blue mark, Germany, early 20th c., teapot 7" l., the set (ILLUS.).......... **$460**

Tea set: cov. teapot, cov. sugar bowl & creamer; ovoid bodies, the sugar & creamer w/C-scroll handles, the teapot w/overhead fixed handle & serpentine spout, each piece decorated w/a colorful fairy tale scene, the set (ILLUS., bottom of page)... **$350-400**

Royal Bayreuth Elk Water Pitcher

Pitcher, water, 7" h., figural elk (ILLUS.)
.... **$300-400**

Plate, 8 1/2" d., scene of man fishing............ **$135**

Plate, 9 1/2" d., "tapestry," landscape scene w/deer by a river................................ **$250-300**

Tea set: child's, cov. teapot, cov. sugar, creamer, two plates, & two cups & saucers; ovoid bodies, each piece decorat-

Royal Bayreuth Fairy Tale Tea Set

Tray with Girl & Geese Scene

Toothpick holder, decorated w/scene of girl w/two chickens **$150-200**
Toothpick holder, three-handled, harvest scene decoration **$150-200**
Toothpick holder, two-handled, four-footed, scene of horsemen, unmarked **$75-125**
Tray, decorated w/scene of girl w/geese, molded rim w/gold trim, 9 x 12 1/4" (ILLUS., top of page) **$400-450**
Tray, "tapestry," scene of train on bridge over raging river, 7 3/4 x 11" **$700-800**
Tureen, figural, in the form of a rose on short petal feet, 6" w., 2 3/4" h. **$450-550**

Vase, 4" h., ovoid body w/a tiny, short flaring neck, "tapestry," scene of two cows, one black & one tan **$425-475**

Small Royal Bayreuth Vase with Cows

Vase, 4 1/2" h., footed ovoid body tapering to a short flaring neck, decoration of cows watering w/mountains in the distance, in shades of purple, lavender, green, orange, brown & black, blue mark (ILLUS.) **$92**
Vase, bud, 4 3/4" h., "tapestry," rounded body w/a thin tall neck, Lady & Prince scenic decoration **$150-200**
Vase, 5" h., "tapestry," decoration of cockfight against scenic ground **$135-175**
Vase, 6" h., "tapestry," decorated w/a scene of an elk & three hounds in a river **$425-475**

Miniature Royal Bayreuth Spouted Vase

Vase, miniature, 3" h., 3 1/2" d., spherical body w/two flaring spouts at the top centered by a small loop handle, Cavalier Musicians decoration (ILLUS.) **$75-125**
Vase, 3 1/4" d., footed, baluster-form body w/angled shoulder handles, short cylindrical silver rim, Cavalier Musicians scene on grey ground **$75-125**

Royal Bayreuth Skiff with Sail Vase

Vase, 7" h., footed cylindrical form w/trumpet-form rim, central color band w/Skiff with Sail decoration, gold band borders trimmed w/delicate gilt stencil bands & gilt floral stencils around the lower body, a pale blue ground & shaded brown foot, blue mark (ILLUS.).................................. **$92**

Vase, 8" h., colorful "tapestry" portrait of girl & pony on blue ground...................... **$375-425**

Tall Royal Bayreuth Cavaliers Vase

Vase, 9" h., tall waisted cylindrical shape w/a flaring ruffled rim, three angular green scrolled branch handles around the sides, the main body in dark green, a color top band in the Toasting Cavalier design, blue mark (ILLUS.) **$184**

Vase, 11 1/2" h., polar bear scene **$900-1,100**

Vase, double-bud, ovoid body w/two angled short flaring necks joined by a small handle, scene of Dutch children.............. **$100-150**

Royal Bonn & Bonn

Bonn and subsequently Royal Bonn china were produced in Bonn, Germany, in a manufactory established in 1755. Later wares made there are often marked "Mehlem" or bear the initials "FM" or a castle mark. Most wares were of the hand-painted type. Clock cases were also made in Bonn.

Royal Bonn & Bonn Mark

Centerpiece, bowl form, h.p w/flowers outlined in raised gold against a matte cream ground, brushed gold rims, late 19th c., 13 1/2" l., 6" h. **$400**

Clock, mantel-type, upright ornately scroll-molded case w/a scroll cartouche crest above the round enameled dial w/Arabic numerals & a gilt-metal bezel, waisted scroll-molded sides & floral & scrolling leaf-decorated lower front, on mold hoof feet, late 19th - early 20th c., 15 1/2" h **$1,035**

Ewer, slender ovoid shouldered body tapering to a short slender neck w/a tall upright petal-form spout & a high arched gilt handle, the cream ground decorated w/polychrome flowers & gilt trim, late 19th c., 12 1/2" h. **$110**

Royal Bonn Royal Dutch Line Vase

Vase, miniature, 3 3/4" h., Old Dutch Line, spherical body w/a small trumpet neck, decorated around the shoulder w/a band of colorful stylized blossoms in pink, white & brick red on a dark green & blue ground, white & yellow leafy stems up from the lower body against a dark brown ground, marked "Royal Bonn - Old Dutch - 7 3091/3 319," late 19th c. (ILLUS.) **$115**

Another Royal Bonn Old Dutch Vase

Vase, miniature, 3 3/4" h., Old Dutch Line, spherical body w/a small trumpet neck, decorated w/a wide central band featuring an undulating thin green-striped ribbon entwined w/matching arches, against a dark brown ground w/deep purple leaf clusters, the shoulder w/a band of repeating arches in brown, yellow & dark blue below a thin dark blue band & the dark green & yellow neck, a matching arched band around the base, marked "Royal Bonn - Germany - Old Dutch - D60," late 19th c. (ILLUS.) **$100-150**

Vase, 8 1/4" h., spherical body w/a short cylindrical neck, decorated w/a painted central vignette of a female surrounded by a floral landscape, printed mark, ca. 1900 .... **$575**

Vase, 8 1/2" h., tapering cylindrical body w/a short flaring neck, overall sand tapestry decoration, four tall arch-topped narrow panels w/a cream ground decorated w/multicolored scrolls & blossoms, dividing bands in dark maroon w/gold trim & patterned gold around the shoulder & neck, a narrow & white chain band around the base, one in gold on maroon, the other w/maroon on green, marked, ca. 1890 .... **$330**

Pair of Royal Bonn Vases with Pastoral Scenes of Watering Cattle

Vases, 11 1/2" h., ovoid form w/short neck & flaring lobed rim, studio decorated in the round w/h.p. scenes of cattle standing in shallow stream, w/trees & foliage in background & foreground, low hills in the distance, artist signed "J. Sticher," marked "Royal Bonn," Germany, late 19th c., pr. (ILLUS.) **$2,300**

Pair of Royal Bonn "Tapestry" Vases

Vases, 12" h., "tapestry-type," ovoid body tapering to a tall cylindrical neck, h.p. overall w/an exotic woodland scene w/large colorful blossoms under a textured surface, marked on bottom, late 19th c., pr. (ILLUS.) **$575**

Pair of Royal Bonn Portrait Vases

Vases, 14" h., cylindrical form tapering out to rounded shoulder w/short flaring neck, each w/h.p. scene of young woman w/flowing brown hair picking flowers in meadow w/trees & distant hills in background, one wearing green skirt & pink & white blouse, the other w/a white sleeveless dress w/green apron, the meadow in shades of yellow & light yellow-green, the base & neck of each turquoise w/gilt decoration, artist signed indistinguishably, printed marks, Germany, early 20th c., pr. (ILLUS.) **$1,725**

Royal Copenhagen

Although the Royal Copenhagen factory in Denmark has been in business for over 200 years, very little has been written about it. That is not to say the very beautiful porcelain it produces is not easily recognizable. Besides producing gorgeous dinnerware, such as "Blue Fluted" and "Flora Danica," it produced - and still does - wonderful figurines depicting animals and people. The company employs talented artists as both modelers and painters. Once you become familiar with the colors, glazes and beauty of these figurines, you will have no trouble recognizing them at a glance.

Collecting these magnificent figurines seems as popular now as in the past. As with most objects, and certainly true of these figurines, value will depend on the complexity, size, age and rarity of the piece. There is other Danish porcelain on the market today, but the Royal Copenhagen figurines can readily be recognized by the mark on the bottom with the three dark blue wavy lines. Accept no imitations!

Girl Feeding Calf Figure Group

Royal Copenhagen Mark

Royal Copenhagen Harvest Group

Figure group, Harvest Group, young farmer & farm girl standing close together, each leaning on a hoe, No. 1300, small, 4" w., 7 1/2" h. (ILLUS.) **$250**

Boy with Teddy Bear Figure Group

Figure group, boy & Teddy bear, toddler standing wearing blue romper, holding tan bear behind him, No. 3468, 3 1/2" w., 7" h. (ILLUS.) **$150**
Figure group, girl feeding calf, a farm girl bending over to feed a calf from a pail, green oblong base, No. 779, 6 1/2" l., 6 1/2" h. (ILLUS., top next column) **$250**
Figure group, Hans Clodhopper, boy seated astride a billy goat, No. 1228, 5 1/2" l., 6 3/4" h. **$175**

Shepherd Boy and Dog

Figure group, shepherd boy w/dog, standing boy wearing cap & long blanket cloak, No. 782, 3 1/2" w., 7 1/2" h. (ILLUS., previous page).. **$175**

Faun on Tortoise Figure Group

Figure group, young faun seated astride a large tortoise, No. 858, 3 1/2" l., 4" h. (ILLUS.)... **$145**

Young Children & Puppy Figure Group

Figure group, young girl & boy hugging brown puppy, No. 707, 5 1/2" l., 5 3/4" h. (ILLUS.)... **$250**

Figure of a boy, February Boy Juggler, standing wearing a top hat & holding a baton to juggle, No. 4524, 6 1/2" h. **$150**

Royal Copenhagen Sandman Figure

Figure of boy, Sandman (Wee-Willie-Winkie), standing on white square stepped base & leaning on an umbrella, holding another, dressed in grey, No. 1145, 6" h. (ILLUS.) **$75**

Royal Copenhagen Sandman Figure

Figure of boy, Sandman (Wee-Willie-Winkie,) standing wearing a long white nightgown & pointed blue cap, a closed umbrella under one arm, opening a brown vial in his hands, No. 1145, 6 3/4" h. (ILLUS.)....................................... **$75**

Royal Copenhagen Boy on Gourd

Figure of boy on gourd, young barefoot boy wearing white shirt & blue overalls seated astride a large green gourd, No. 4539, 4 1/4 x 4 1/2" (ILLUS.) **$75**

Figure of Young Man Eating Lunch

Figure of young man eating lunch, reclining position, eating from a lunch box, No. 865, 7" l., 4" h. (ILLUS., previous page)..... **$150**
Model of bird, Budgie on Gourd, white bird w/blue trim on dark blue gourd, No. 4682, 4 x 5 1/2" **$125**

Model of a Fat Robin

Model of bird, Fat Robin, rounded baby robin in blue, white & rust red, No. 2266, 3" h. (ILLUS.) **$55**

Royal Copenhagen Model of a Grebe

Model of bird, Grebe, handsome swimming bird w/blue crest & grey & white body, No. 3263, 7" l., 4" h. (ILLUS.) **$95**

Royal Copenhagen Icelandic Falcon

Model of bird, Icelandic Falcon, large bird w/speckled bluish grey & white feathers, No. 263, 8 1/2" l., 11" h. (ILLUS.)............... **$350**
Model of birds, pair of blue, white & grey finches perched close together, No. 1189, 5" l., 2" h. (ILLUS., top next column) **$45**

Model of Finches

Royal Copenhagen Cow & Calf

Model of cow & calf, Mother cow licking calf nestled against her, white w/shaded grey & black spots, No. 800, 5 x 11" (ILLUS.)..... **$250**

Royal Copenhagen Great Dane

Model of dog, Great Dane, large recumbent dog in tan w/black striping, No. 1679, 9" l., 4" h. (ILLUS.) **$175**
Model of dog, Male Boxer, standing, white & shaded tan & grey w/black face, No. 3634, 5 1/2 x 7" **$95**

Royal Copenhagen Elephant

Model of elephant, walking w/head & trunk raised & mouth open, No. 2998, small size, 6" l., 5" h. (ILLUS.)............................... **$65**

Royal Copenhagen Elk

Model of elk, (moose), reclining position, shaded grey & white w/white antlers, No. 2813, 9 x 10" (ILLUS.)................................. **$300**

Royal Copenhagen Lioness

Model of lioness, recumbent animal, No. 804, 12" l., 6 1/2" h. (ILLUS.) **$200**

Royal Copenhagen Mink

Model of mink, white w/black eyes & brown nose, No. 4654, 3 3/4 x 7" (ILLUS.) **$175**

Royal Copenhagen Monkey Figure

Model of monkey, seated animal w/head tilted to side, No. 1444, 3" w., 5" h. (ILLUS.).. **$95**

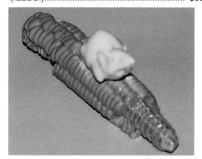

Mouse on Ear of Corn Figure

Model of mouse, white & pink mouse perched on an ear of brown corn, No. 512, 5" l., 2" h. (ILLUS.) **$48**

Royal Copenhagen Panda Figure

Model of panda, seated eating bamboo, No. 662, 5 1/2" w., 7" h. (ILLUS.)............... **$175**

Royal Copenhagen Penguins

Model of penguins, two birds seated side by side, No. 1190, 4" h. (ILLUS.) **$75**
Model of piglets, pair of piglets fused together, white w/grey spots, pink snout, No. 683, 2 1/2 x 4 1/2" **$75**

Small Royal Copenhagen Rabbit

Model of rabbit, seated upright eating leaf,
No. 1019, small size, 3 1/2" h. (ILLUS.) **$48**

Royal Copenhagen Sea Lion

Model of sea lion, head raised, shades of
tan & grey, No. 265, 7 x 12" (ILLUS.) **$275**

Royal Copenhagen Rose Bowl

Rose bowl, squatty spherical form w/wide
flat mouth, dark blue ground painted
w/large white blossoms & green leaves,
No. 424, 8" d., 6" h. (ILLUS.) **$125**

Royal Copley

Royal Copley was a trade name used by the Spaulding China Company of Sebring, Ohio, during the 1940s and 1950s for a variety of ceramic figurines, planters and other decorative pieces. Similar Spaulding pieces were also produced under the trade name "Royal Windsor," or carried the Spaulding China mark.

Dime stores generally featured the Royal Copley line, with Spaulding's other lines available in more upscale outlets.

The Spaulding China Company ended production in 1957, but for the next two years other potteries finished production of its outstanding orders. Today these originally inexpensive wares are developing a dedicated collector following thanks to their whimsically appealing designs.

Figurines

Airedale Figurine

Airedale, seated, brown & white, 6 1/2" h.
(ILLUS.) **$40-45**
Blackamoor Man & Blackamoor Woman,
kneeling, 8 1/2" h., pr. (ILLUS., top next
page) **$100-120**
Cockatoos, 7 1/4" h. **$50-60**
Cocker Spaniel, 6 1/4" h. **$35-40**
Deer & Fawn, 8 1/2" h. **$60-70**
Dog, 6 1/2" h. **$30-35**
Dog, 8" h. **$40-45**
Hen & Rooster, large, Royal Copley mark,
7" & 8" h., pr. **$100-130**
Hen & Rooster, Royal Windsor mark, 6 1/2"
& 7" h., pr. **$120-140**
Hen & Rooster, small, Royal Copley mark,
6" & 6 1/2" h., pr. **$90-100**
Kingfishers, 5" h. **$40-50**
Mallard Duck, 7" h. **$40-45**

Oriental Boy & Girl Figurines

Blackamoor Man & Woman Figures

Oriental Boy & Oriental Girl, standing, 7 1/2" h., pr. (ILLUS., previous page)...... **$35-55**
Parrots, 8" h. **$35-45**
Sea Gulls, 8" h. **$35-55**

Thrushes, 6 1/2" h. **$20-25**
Titmouse, 8" h. **$25-35**
Wrens, 6 1/4" h. **$20-25**

Planters

Spaniel Pup with Collar Figurine

Spaniel Pup with Collar, 6" h. (ILLUS.)..... **$40-45**
Swallow with extended wings, 7" h. **$110-130**
Swallows on Double Stump, 7 1/2" h., pr.
.... **$120-140**

Large Kneeling Angel Planter

Angel, large, kneeling, blue robe, 8" h. (ILLUS.).. **$70-85**

Angel on Star Planter

Angel on Star, white relief figure on creamy
  yellow ground, 6 3/4" h. (ILLUS.) $30-40
Apple and Finch, 6 1/2" h. $50-60
Balinese Girl, 8 1/2" h. $50-60
Bare Shoulder Lady head vase, 6" h. $70-80
Big Hat Chinese Boy & Girl, 7 1/2" h., pr. . $50-60
Blackamoor Prince head vase, 8" h. $35-45
Cinderella's Coach, 6" h., 3 1/4" h. $25-30

Dog with Raised Paw Planter

Dog with Raised Paw, 7 1/2" h. (ILLUS.)... $70-80
Dog with Suitcase (Skip), 7" h. $50-55
Dogwood, oval, 3 1/2" h. $30-35
Dogwood, small, 4 1/2" h. $25-30
Duck with Mailbox, 6 3/4" h. $70-80
Duck with Wheelbarrow, 3 3/4" h. $20-25
Dutch Boy & Girl with Buckets, 6 1/4" h.,
  pr. $60-85
Elephant, large, 7 1/2" h. $35-40

Royal Copley Clown Planter

Clown, 8 1/4" h. (ILLUS.) **$120-145**
Cocker Spaniel, 8" h. $30-35
Deer & Doe, 7 1/2" h. $20-25

Elf and Shoe Planter

Elf and Shoe, 6" h. (ILLUS.) $60-70
Elf and Stump, 6" h. $50-60

Doe & Fawn Head Planter

Doe & Fawn Head, rectangular log-form
  planter, 5 1/4" h. (ILLUS.) **$50-60**

Fancy Finch on Tree Stump Planter

Fancy Finch on Tree Stump, red, white & black bird perched on brown leafy branch beside white planter, 7 1/2" h. (ILLUS., previous page) **$90-100**
Fighting Cock, 6 1/2" h. **$60-70**
Girl Leaning on Barrel & Boy Leaning on Barrel, 6 1/4" h., pr. **$50-60**

Girl on Wheelbarrow Planter

Girl on Wheelbarrow, 7" h. (ILLUS.) **$50-55**
Goldfinch on Stump, 6 1/2" h. **$50-60**
High Tail Rooster, 7 3/4" h. **$60-70**

Horse Head with Mane Planter

Horse Head with Flying Mane, 8" h. (ILLUS.) **$35-55**

Kitten and Book Planter

Kitten and Book, 6 1/2" h. (ILLUS.) **$45-55**

Kitten in Picnic Basket, 8" h. **$70-80**

Kitten on Cowboy Boot Planter

Kitten on Cowboy Boot, 7 1/2" h. (ILLUS.) **$65-70**
Mallard Drake, sitting, 5 1/4" h. **$50-55**
Mallard Duck, standing, 8" h. **$20-25**
Mallard Duck on Stump, 8" h. **$35-45**
Mature Wood Duck, 7 1/4" h. **$35-45**
Nuthatch, 5 1/2" h. **$30-35**
Oriental Boy with Basket on Back & Oriental Girl with Basket on Back, 8" h., pr. **$140-150**

Palomino Horse Head Planter

Palomino Horse Head, 6 1/4" h. (ILLUS.).. **$50-60**
Peter Rabbit, 6 1/2" h. **$90-100**

Reclining Poodle Planter

Poodle, reclining, white w/black nose & eyes, 8" l. (ILLUS., previous page) **$80-90**
Poodle with Bow, posing, 5 1/4" h. **$80-90**

Ribbed Star Royal Windsor Planter

Ribbed Star, all-white, "Royal Windsor" sticker, 4 3/4" h. (ILLUS.) **$35-40**

Stuffed Animal Dog Planter

Stuffed Animal Dog, white & brown, 5 1/2" h. (ILLUS.) **$70-80**

Stuffed Animal Elephant Planter

Stuffed Animal Elephant, pale green & white, 6 1/2" h. (ILLUS.) **$90-100**
Stuffed Animal Rooster, pale green & white, 6" h. (ILLUS., top next column)..... **$80-90**
Tanagers, 6 1/4" h. **$30-40**
Teddy Bear, 6 1/4" h. **$35-45**

Stuffed Animal Rooster Planter

Teddy Bear, white, 8" h. **$85-100**
Teddy Bear in Picnic Basket, 8" h. **$80-100**

Rare Teddy Bear with Concertina

Teddy Bear with Concertina, rare, 7 1/4" h. (ILLUS.) **$120-145**
Teddy Bear with Mandolin, 6 3/4" h. **$60-85**

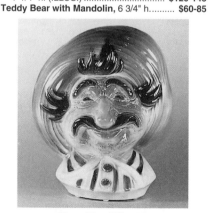

Tony Head Planter

Tony Head, man wearing large blue hat, 8 1/4" h. (ILLUS.) **$60-85**
Wide Brim Hat Boy & Wide Brim Hat Girl, 7 1/4" h., pr. **$100-110**
Woodpeckers, 6 1/4" h. **$30-40**

Miscellaneous

Leaping Salmon Ashtray

Ashtray, Leaping Salmon, oblong boat-shaped bowl w/figural salmon on rim, 5 x 6 1/4" (ILLUS.)................................... **$35-45**

Bow Tie Pig Bank

Bank, Bow Tie Pig, standing, wearing green bow tie & blue outfit, 6 1/4" h. (ILLUS.)... **$85-95**
Bank, Teddy Bear, 7 1/2" h. **$120-140**

Barber Pole Blade Bank

Blade bank, model of a barber pole in red & white w/"Blades" on the side, 6 1/4" h. (ILLUS.)... **$80-90**
Pitcher, Floral Beauty, 8" h. **$80-95**
Smoking set, models of ducks, 3" & 4" h., 3 pcs. **$70-85**
Vase, 5 3/4" h., Fish, open center............. **$55-70**

Happy Anniversary Vase

Vase, 6" h., upright rectangular form w/flaring serpentine rim, dark blue centered by a large white panel decorated w/wedding bells & bluebirds & "Happy Anniversary" in gold (ILLUS.) **$60-70**
Vase, 6 1/4" h., footed pillow-shape, ivy decoration **$25-30**
Vase, 7" h., Carol's Corsage **$30-40**
Vase, 7 1/4" h., Deer, open center **$40-45**
Vase, 7 1/4" h., Flying Bird, open center **$55-60**
Vase, 8 1/4" h., Dogwood........................... **$35-45**
Vases, 8 1/4" h., cornucopia-shaped w/decal decoration, pr. **$60-70**
Wall plaque-planters, Hen & Rooster, 6 3/4" h., pr. **$140-170**

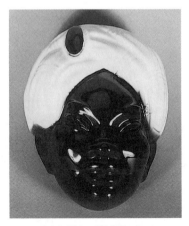

Island Man Wall Pocket

Wall pocket, Island Man, black head wearing white turban, 8" h. (ILLUS.)........... **$150-170**
Wall pocket, Salt Box, 5 1/2" h.................. **$70-80**
Wall pocket, Spice Box, 5 1/2" h. **$90-100**
Wall pocket, Straw Hat, large, 7" h. **$85-95**

Royal Dux

This factory in Bohemia was noted for the figural porcelain wares in the Art Nouveau style it exported around the turn of the 20th century. Other notable figural pieces were produced through the 1930s. The factory was nationalized after World War II.

Royal Dux Marks

Two Shepherds Resting at Rock

Young Woman Embracing Young Man

Figure of Boy on Donkey

Figure group, two shepherds, the man sitting on rock w/legs crossed & about to blow into primitive pipe, the woman standing next to him holding crook, polychrome decoration in shades of buff, applied pink triangle mark, early 20th c., 21 1/2" h. (ILLUS.) **$1,035**

Figure group, young hunter wearing primitive tunic & sandals, carrying quiver & laden w/dead fowl embraces young barefoot woman, polychrome decoration in olive greens & buffs, applied pink triangle mark, first half 20th c., 22" h. (ILLUS., top next column) **$1,150**

Figure of boy on donkey, the boy wearing apricot trousers & matching brimmed hat & pale olive shirt, bare feet, sitting astride saddled white donkey, both looking to side, applied pink triangle mark, first half 20th c., 14 1/4" h. (ILLUS.) **$518**

Figure of Woman Reading Book

Figure of woman, sitting on rock-form base & reading book, wearing off-the-shoulder reddish brown top & draping long olive green skirt, applied pink triangle mark, first half 20th c., 19" h. (ILLUS.) **$1,093**

Pair of Royal Dux Shepherds

Figures of shepherds, the young woman standing w/lamb, the young man w/goat, each w/h.p. features & wearing apricot & pale olive green clothes, each on paneled base, applied pink triangle mark, first half 20th c., 20 1/2" h., pr. (ILLUS.) **$1,725**

Royal Dux Shepherds

Woman with Water Jars

Figure of woman, w/h.p. features, wearing turban-style headdress & olive green tunic w/sleeves rolled up above elbows, holding water jar in each hand, a mug hanging from her sash belt, on base decorated w/leaves, applied pink triangle mark, first half 20th c., 23" h. (ILLUS.) **$920**

Figures of shepherds, w/h.p. features, the young woman wearing apricot dress & pale olive turban-style headdress, holding kid in her arms, w/two other kids at her feet, the young man wearing short apricot tunic w/sheepskin & green hat, holding panpipe as if about to play, two lambs at his feet, each on oval base, applied pink triangle mark, mid-20th c., 17" h., pr. (ILLUS.) **$1,955**

Figures of Water Carriers

Figures of water carriers, the young man wearing apricot turban-style headdress & pale olive tunic belted w/apricot sash, holding large handled earthenware jar in both hands as if pouring contents out, the young woman wearing a pale pink veil-type headdress & pale olive gown w/apricot sash, holding handle of earthenware jar on ground at her feet, each on oval base w/pale pink floral trim, applied pink triangle mark, early 20th c., 20" h., pr. (ILLUS.).................................... **$1,265**

Pair of Figures Carrying Baskets

Figures of woman & man, the woman wearing mid-calf-length apricot dress & pale olive short-sleeved blouse, the man wearing apricot trousers & matching brimmed hat & pale olive long-sleeved shirt, each w/one hand on hip, the other steadying a large empty basket on shoulder, each on oval base, applied pink triangle marks, first half 20th c., 16" h., pr. (ILLUS.)... **$805**

Figures of Women in Classical Dress

Figures of women, wearing classical dress in shades of olive green & pale pink & peach, one posed as if playing cymbals, the other arching back as if dancing, holding hem of gown out in dramatic pose, each on oval bases trimmed w/scroll design, applied pink triangle mark, early 20th c., some minor professional repair, 22" h., pr. (ILLUS.) **$1,610**

Royal Dux Vases with Vines & Fruit

Vases, 19" h., Art Nouveau style, tall ovoid body on a squared foot, molded in bold relief w/undulating foliage & fruit, the ivory ground highlighted w/dark gold, pink triangle mark, early 20th c., bases drilled for lamp adaptation, pr. (ILLUS.)............. **$1,380**

Four Fancy Royal Vienna Cabinet Plates

Royal Vienna

The second factory in Europe to make hard paste porcelain was established in Vienna in 1719 by Claud Innocentius de Paquier. The factory underwent various changes of administration through the years and finally closed in 1865. Since then, however, the porcelain has been reproduced by various factories in Austria and Germany, many of which have also reproduced the early beehive mark. Early pieces, naturally, bring far higher prices than the later ones or the reproductions.

Royal Vienna Mark

Plate, 9 1/2" d., cabinet-type, a colorful h.p. central scene of four classical ladies seated w/cherubs representing Venus & her attendants, wide border in white decorated w/alternating arched panels in ornate gold & red, blue beehive mark, titled in German on the back (ILLUS. second from right with three other Royal Vienna plates, top of page) **$845**

Plate, 9 1/2" d., cabinet-type, the center h.p. w/a bust profile portrait of a lovely young woman w/long brown hair wearing a red cap, wide gold border band decorated w/small oval medallions alternating w/green arches w/gilt florals , overall blue dotting on the gold ground, blue beehive mark, titled in German on the back, several tiny beads missing (ILLUS. far right with three other Royal Vienna plates, top of page) **$1,208**

Marie Antoinette Royal Vienna Plate

Plate, 9 1/2" d., cabinet-type, a central color bust portrait of Marie Antoinette, signed by Wagner, the cobalt blue border band ornately decorated w/gold panels, scrolls & florals (ILLUS.)..................................... **$1,150**

Plate, 9 1/2" d., cabinet-type, a colorful h.p. central landscape scene of a lady playing a mandolin while looking down at children, dark red border band w/ornate gold scrolls, artist-signed, blue beehive mark (ILLUS. left with three other Royal Vienna plates, top of page) **$725**

Lovely Royal Vienna Portrait Plate

Plate, 9 1/2" d., cabinet-type, the center w/a finely painted bust portrait of a Renaissance era noblewoman w/a feathered headdress, the cobalt blue border band ornately decorated w/undulating panels of fancy florals, mounted in a deep gilt-wood shadowbox frame lined in deep red velvet, overall 16" sq. (ILLUS. of plate) **$1,725**

Royal Vienna Marie Antoinette Plate

Plate, 9 3/4" d., cabinet-type, central color portrait of Queen Marie Antoinette in 18th c. attire w/white hair & wearing a fancy plumed hat against a greyish cream ground, the wide ornate border w/a cobalt blue & light green ground heavily decorated w/gold florals, blue beehive mark & retailer's mark "Ovington Bros. Co." (ILLUS.)...................... **$1,000-1,500**
Plate, 10 1/4" d., cabinet-type, the center w/a small color bust portrait of a pretty brown-haired lady, the wide background in cobalt blue decorated w/ornate decorative gold sprigs & panels, artist-signed, blue beehive mark (ILLUS. second from left with three other Royal Vienna plates) .. **$604**

Ornate Royal Vienna Urn, Cover & Stand

Urn, cover & stand, the domed stand on shaped gold tab feet & a gold border, the cobalt blue ground ornately decorated w/overall bands of delicate floral vines centering a round reserve h.p. in color w/a scene of a Greek god & goddess, the urn w/a tapering pedestal below the wide urn-form body, cobalt blue ground decorated overall w/gold bands & ornate delicate leafy vines, a large central oval reserve h.p. in color w/a group of Greek gods & goddesses, long angled gold handles flanking the shoulder & the tapering domed cover w/a pointed gold finial

& h.p. w/another color reserve, late 19th - early 20th c., overall 21 1/4" h., the set (ILLUS.)... **$5,581**

Royal Worcester

This porcelain has been made by the Royal Worcester Porcelain Co. at Worcester, England, from 1862 to the present. Royal Worcester is distinguished from wares made at Worcester between 1751 and 1862, which are referred to only as Worcester by collectors.

Royal Worcester Marks

Candlesticks, figural seated boy & girl w/h.p. features, each dressed in pale peach & white, leaning against tree trunk forms that make up candlesticks, printed marks, late 19th c., 9" h., pr. (ILLUS. back row, left w/other Royal Worcester pieces, top next page)............................. **$690**
Cracker jar, cov., ovoid melon-lobed body & disk lid decorated w/h.p. florals in pastel shades on ivory ground, gilt trim, the lid w/gilt handle, printed purple mark, late 19th c., 7 1/2" h. (ILLUS. front row, second from left w/other Royal Worcester pieces, top next page)............................. **$288**

Fine Royal Worcester Cracker Jar

Cracker jar, cov., spherical melon-lobed body w/flattened cover & gold branch handle, cream ground painted w/flowering vines in shades of deep rose, pink, brown & green, all trimmed w/gold, ca. 1889, 6 1/2" d., 7" h. (ILLUS.)................... **$325**
Ewer, bulbous form bisected w/gilt horizontal band, short gilt ring foot, long slender neck w/gilt ring at base & gilt trim at rim, arched spout, applied gilt C-scroll handle w/embossed scroll designs, h.p. floral decoration in pale pinks & greens on ivory ground, marked "Royal Worcester," late 19th c., 10" h. (ILLUS. front row, far right w/other Royal Worcester pieces, top next page)... **$431**

Various Royal Worcester Pieces

Floral-decorated Royal Worcester Ewer

Ewer, tapering bulbous body w/a wide upright spout, an unusual gold figural ram's head & scroll handle, the creamy ground h.p. w/a tall bouquet of mums in shades of orange, pink, blue & green trimmed in gold, gold base & rim bands, magenta mark, Shape No. 1255, 9" h. (ILLUS.) **$288**

Game set: twelve 9" d. scallop-edged plates, 13 x 17 1/2" oval platter w/molded bird head & wings end handles, 7 1/2" h. cov. sauce tureen w/molded bird head & wings end handles, two 5 x 7" oval dishes w/molded bird head & wings end handles, 5 x 8" scallop-handled serving dish; each piece h.p. in color w/a different game bird, very ornate delicate floral border band, each piece marked & dated 1889, the set (ILLUS., bottom of page)... **$4,600**

Jug, bulbous shape tapering to flared scalloped rim w/arched spout, applied gilt ribbed angular handle, applied figural salamander & gilt band at neck on cream-colored embossed basketweave ground, marked "Royal Worcester," late 19th c., 5 1/2" h. (ILLUS. front row, second from right w/other Royal Worcester pieces, top of page) **$345**

Truly Extraordinary Royal Worcester Game Set

Hand-painted Royal Worcester Plate

Outstanding Royal Worcester Flask

Pilgrim flask, an oblong flaring oval foot below the large flattened round body topped by a short conical reticulated neck, four gold square pegs around the outer edge alternating w/panels of turquoise strapwork, the double-walled sides decorated in the Persian taste w/a central rosette & radiating pierced concentric bands, the peripheral band enriched w/a ribbon enameled w/turquoise & white "jewels," magenta mark, by George Owen, ca. 1890, 6" h. (ILLUS.) **$14,340**

Plate, 10 3/4" d., h.p. English village scene w/road & trees in the foreground, artist-signed, dated 1953 (ILLUS., top next column) **$225-275**

Fine Royal Worcester Dinner Plates

Plates, 10 1/2" d., dinner, a broad salmon pink border w/swags of two-color gold featuring antique vases, white center, ca. 1900, set of 12 (ILLUS.) **$1,380**

Rare Royal Worcester Aesthetic Movement Figural Teapot

Teapot, cov., Aesthetic Movement figural design, molded on one side as a late Victorian Aesthetic dandy wearing a large sunflower, one arm & bent wrist forming the spout, his other arm the handle, the reverse modeled as his female counterpart wearing a large lily, each wearing a dark green shirt w/white collar & a dark pink hat in the spirit of Oscar Wilde, inscribed on the bottom "Fearful consequences, through the laws of natural selection and evolution of living up to one's teapot," signed "Budge," marked & w/date code for 1882, 6" h. (ILLUS. of both sides) **$11,163**

Fine Royal Worcester Dragon Teapot

Teapot, cov., Oriental design w/squared block-style body in turquoise blue molded on the sides w/a flying bird in green, yellow, tan & pink w/pink & green floral bands, the flattened shoulders w/an impressed Greek key design, flat square cover w/pyramidal finial, squared curved corner spout w/the end opening formed by the head of a black dragon whose slender body arches across the top to form the handle, late 19th c., minor professional repair to spout, 7 1/2" h. (ILLUS.) **$3,360**

Rare Reticulated Royal Worcester Pot

Teapot, cov., spherical white body w/an elaborate overall reticulated outer layer composed of fine honeycomb, diamonds & rings, the low domed cover, C-form handle & shaped spout all w/further reticulation, the cover w/a spire finial & applied pale turquoise beaded chain trim also used on the handle & spout, crafted by George Owen, impressed factory mark, ca. 1890 (ILLUS.) **$4,780**

Urn, cov., spherical shape w/long cylindrical neck, figural bronze serpent handles, flared foot, reticulated rim & applied embossed foliage, h.p. features, marked w/purple "Royal Worcester" crown & "1168," 19th c., 15" h. (ILLUS. front row, far left w/other Royal Worcester pieces) **$1,955**

Fine Royal Worcester Ovoid Vase

Vase, 7 1/8" h., footed ovoid body w/reticulated small panels & motifs on the shoulder below the slender trumpet-form neck w/reticulated scrolls at the base, pointed angled shoulder handles, the foot in gold w/white beading, the lower body w/gilt-bordered gadrooning on the ivory body h.p. w/swags of deep pink & yellow roses suspended from ornately gilt scroll panels, gilt lattice panels on the upper shoulder & up the neck, the reticulated section trimmed in pale blue, magenta mark, Shape No. 1575, probably by George Owen & Henry Chair, retailer mark of Tiffany & Co., New York, dated 1897 (ILLUS.) **$6,573**

Vase, 12" h., bulbous form on short tapered gilt foot w/rickrack design, slender fluted gilt neck below gilt reticulated everted rim, small ring scroll gilt handles, the body w/h.p. floral decoration in pinks & green on ivory ground, marked "Royal Worcester," late 19th c. (ILLUS. back row, right w/other Royal Worcester pieces, top of page 624) **$633**

Ornate Bottle-form Royal Worcester Vase

Vase, cov., 14 1/2" h., bottle-form, a flaring foot in dark brown decorated w/a band of delicate gold arches, the bulbous creamy body decorated w/white pate-sur-pate blossoms & long gold leaves, a tall cylindrical reticulated brown neck w/molded gold band, the bulbous creamy a spiral band, the flared rim supporting the reticulated domed brown cover w/a pointed finial & fancy gold trim, grotesque scrolled dragon gold shoulder handles, professional cover repair, magenta mark, Shape No. 1168, late 19th c. (ILLUS., previous page) **$748**

Russel Wright Designs

The innovative dinnerware designed by Russel Wright and produced by various companies beginning in the late 1930s was an immediate success with a society that was turning to a more casual and informal lifestyle. His designs, with their flowing lines and unconventional shapes, were produced in many different colors, which allowed a hostess to arrange creative tables.

Although not antique, these designs, which we list here by line and manufacturer, are highly collectible. In addition to dinnerwares, Wright was also known as a trendsetter in the design of furniture, glassware, lamps, fabric and a multitude of other household goods.

Russel Wright Marks

American Modern (Steubenville Pottery Co.)

Baker, glacier blue, small $55
Baker, granite grey, small $25
Bowl, child's, black chutney $100
Bowl, child's, chartreuse $100
Bowl, fruit, lug handle, cedar green $30

Group of American Modern Pieces

Bowl, fruit, lug handle, chartreuse (ILLUS. left) $20
Bowl, fruit, lug handle, glacier blue $40
Bowl, salad, cedar green $100

Bowl, salad, white $165
Bowl, soup, lug handle, bean brown $35
Butter dish, cov., granite grey $255
Butter dish, cov., white................................ $365
Carafe, granite grey (no stopper) $200
Carafe w/stopper, bean brown..................... $500
Casserole, cov., stick handle, black chutney $40

Black Chutney Celery Tray

Celery tray, black chutney, 13" l. (ILLUS.) $30
Coaster, granite grey $20
Coaster, white.. $30
Coffee cup cover, black chutney $175
Coffee cup cover, coral................................ $175
Coffeepot, cov., after dinner, chartreuse $120
Coffeepot, cov., after dinner, coral $120
Coffeepot, cov., after dinner, granite grey $120
Coffeepot, cov., black chutney $250
Coffeepot, cov., cedar green $275
Coffeepot, cov., seafoam blue...................... $275
Creamer, cedar green.................................... $30
Creamer, white... $35
Cup & saucer, coffee, cantaloupe $40
Cup & saucer, coffee, seafoam blue $27
Cup & saucer, demitasse, cantaloupe $60
Cup & saucer, demitasse, chartreuse $30
Gravy boat, chartreuse.................................. $20
Gravy liner/pickle dish, seafoam blue........... $25
Gravy liner/pickle dish, white....................... $45
Hostess plate, chartreuse $60
Hostess plate & cup, cedar green, pr............ $90

American Modern Hostess Set

Hostess plate & cup, white, pr. (ILLUS.) $150
Ice box jar, cov., black chutney $225
Ice box jar, cov., coral $225
Mug (tumbler), black chutney......................... $90
Mug (tumbler), cedar green $100
Pitcher, cov., water, cedar green................ $400+
Pitcher, cov., water, white........................... $500+
Pitcher, water, 12" h., bean brown $150
Pitcher, water, 12" h., granite grey $85

Pitcher, water, 12" h., seafoam blue............. $125
Plate, bread & butter, 6 1/4" d., coral $6
Plate, salad, 8" d., seafoam blue..................... $18
Plate, salad, 8" d., white................................... $25
Plate, dinner, 10" d., cantaloupe $40
Plate, dinner, 10" d., granite grey $20
Plate, chop, 13" sq., chartreuse $30
Plate, chop, 13" sq., seafoam blue.................. $50
Plate, child's, coral $60
Plate, child's, seafoam blue............................ $75
Platter, 13 3/4" l., oblong, granite grey............ $30
Platter, 13 3/4" l., oblong, white $65
Ramekin, cov., individual, bean brown $250
Ramekin, cov., individual, granite grey $170
Relish dish, divided, raffia handle, coral....... $175
Relish dish, divided, raffia handle, white....... $300
Relish rosette, granite grey........................... $200
Relish rosette, seafoam blue $250
Salad fork & spoon, coral, pr........................ $150
Salad fork & spoon, white, pr. $300
Sauceboat, bean brown.................................. $75
Sauceboat, coral.. $40
Shaker, single, chartreuse $8
Shaker, single, glacier blue............................. $20
Stack server, cov., cedar green (ILLUS.
  back, with fruit bowl)................................... $300
Stack server, cov., chartreuse....................... $250
Stack server, cov., granite grey..................... $250
Sugar bowl, cov., chartreuse........................... $20
Sugar bowl, cov., granite grey......................... $20
Teapot, cov., cedar green $150
Teapot, cov., seafoam blue............................ $135
Tumbler, child's, cedar green $140
Tumbler, child's, granite grey........................ $125
Vegetable bowl, cov., cedar green, 12" l........ $75
Vegetable bowl, cov., coral, 12" l. $40
Vegetable dish, open, divided, black chut-
  ney $110
Vegetable dish, open, divided, cedar green
  (ILLUS. right front, with fruit bowl)............. $130
Vegetable dish, open, oval, cantaloupe,
  10" l. $75
Vegetable dish, open, oval, granite grey,
  10" l. $25

Casual China (Iroquois China Co.)

Bowl, 5" d., cereal, ripe apricot $15
Bowl, 5 1/2" d., fruit, ice blue, 9 1/2 oz. $15
Bowl, 5 3/4" d., fruit, oyster grey..................... $20
Bowl, 10" d., salad, pink sherbet, 52 oz.......... $40
Butter dish, cov., brick red, 1/4 lb. .... $1,000+
Butter dish, cov., white, 1/2 lb..................... $150
Butter dish, cov., pink sherbet $75
Carafe, charcoal.. $350
Carafe, oyster grey..................................... $900+

Rare Oyster Grey Casual China Carafe

Carafe, oyster grey, rare color (ILLUS.)....... $900+
Casserole, cov., lettuce green, 8" d., 2 qt....... $75
Casserole, deep tureen, lemon yellow $250
Casserole, deep tureen, white..................... $260
Coffeepot, cov., nutmeg brown $140
Coffeepot, cov., oyster grey (ILLUS. right,
  bottom of page)... $225
Coffeepot, cov., sugar white......................... $200

Casual Creamer, Pitcher & Coffeepot

Rare Mustard Gold Creamer & Sugar

Coffeepot, cov., after dinner, avocado yellow **$135**
Coffeepot, cov., after dinner, lemon yellow ... **$125**
Cover for 4 qt. casserole, oyster grey **$45**
Cover for cereal/soup bowl, nutmeg brown **$30**
Cover for vegetable bowl, open/divided, ice blue **$35**
Cover for water pitcher, ripe apricot **$60**
Creamer, family-style, oyster grey (ILLUS. left w/coffeepot & pitcher, bottom previous page) **$55**
Creamer, family-style, pink sherbet **$40**
Creamer, stacking-type, ice blue **$20**
Creamer & cov. sugar bowl, redesigned, mustard gold (color produced only one year), the set (ILLUS., top of page) **$100**
Cup & saucer, coffee, original, oyster grey (ILLUS. front center w/other cups & saucers & shakers, below) **$30**
Cup & saucer, coffee, redesigned, charcoal **$25**
Cup & saucer, coffee, redesigned, lemon yellow **$25**
Cup & saucer, original, avocado yellow **$20**
Cup & saucer, tea, original design, lemon yellow (ILLUS. front left with other cups & saucers & shakers, below) **$60-85**

Gravy, redesigned w/cover which becomes stand, sugar white **$250**
Gravy bowl, 5 1/4", 12 oz. **$40**
Gravy stand, ice blue **$40**
Gravy stand, oyster grey **$70**
Gravy w/attached stand, avocado yellow **$100**
Gravy w/attached stand, nutmeg brown **$125**
Gumbo soup bowl, cantaloupe, 21 oz. **$60**
Gumbo soup bowl, charcoal, 21 oz. **$50**
Gumbo soup bowl, ice blue, 21 oz. **$40**
Hostess set: plate w/well & matching cup; sugar white, 2 pcs. **$90**

Rare Casual China Charcoal Mug
Mug, original, charcoal, rare (ILLUS.) **$400**

Three Casual China Original Mugs
Mug, original design, ice blue (ILLUS. center with two other mugs) **$60-85**
Mug, original design, pink sherbet (ILLUS. left with two other mugs) **$60-85**
Mug, original design, ripe apricot (ILLUS. right with two other mugs) **$60-85**

Casual Cups & Saucers & Shakers

Cup & saucer, demitasse, avocado yellow (ILLUS. front left w/other cups & saucers & shakers) **$150-175**
Cup & saucer, demitasse, pink sherbet **$175**
Cup & saucer, demitasse, sugar white **$225**
Gravy, redesigned w/cover which becomes stand, ripe apricot **$185**

Mug, original design, sugar white,........... $175-200
Mug, restyled, aqua...................................... $225
Mug, restyled, ice blue $100
Pepper mill, lemon yellow............................ $300+
Pitcher, cov., charcoal, 1 1/2 qt. $200
Pitcher, cov., ice blue, 1 1/2 qt...................... $150
Pitcher, nutmeg brown................................. $200
Pitcher, redesigned, ripe apricot (ILLUS. center with creamer & coffeepot, previous page) $200
Plate, bread & butter, 6 1/2" d., lettuce green.. $10
Plate, salad, 7 1/2" d. $15
Plate, luncheon, 9 1/2" d., pink sherbet........... $17
Plate, dinner, 10" d., oyster grey $25
Plate, chop, 13 7/8" d., ice blue........................ $50
Plate, chop, 13 7/8" d., parsley green $65
Platter, 10 1/4" oval, individual, lettuce green.. $50
Platter, 12 3/4" oval, brick red.......................... $90
Platter, 12 3/4" oval, parsley green.................. $40
Platter, 14 1/2" oval, sugar white $45
Salt & pepper shakers, stacking-type, ice blue, pr... $25
Salt & pepper shakers, stacking-type, oyster grey, pr. (ILLUS. right rear, with cups & saucers).. $60
Salt & pepper shakers, stacking-type, parsley green, pr. $60
Salt shaker & pepper mill, redesigned, lemon yellow, pr. (ILLUS. left rear, with cups & saucers, previous page).............. $500+
Soup, 11 1/2 oz.. $30
Soup, cov., redesigned, 18 oz........................ $30
Sugar, redesigned, aqua.............................. $150
Sugar, redesigned, brick red........................ $225+
Sugar, stacking-type, pink sherbet................. $15
Sugar, stacking-type, sugar white, family size.. $40
Teapot, cov., redesigned, aqua................ $2,500+

Casual Redesigned Ripe Apricot Teapot

Teapot, cov., redesigned, ripe apricot, mid-1950s (ILLUS.).................................... $150-175
Tumbler, iced tea, Pinch patt., seafoam blue, Imperial Glass Co., 14 oz. $50
Tumbler, water, Pinch patt., ruby red, Imperial Glass Co., 11 oz................................ $125+
Vegetable dish, open, cantaloupe, 10" d. $85
Vegetable dish, open, cantaloupe, 8 1/8", 36 oz. $60
Vegetable dish, open, nutmeg brown, 8 1/8", 36 oz. $35
Vegetable dish, open or divided (casserole), 10", sugar white $60

Iroquois Casual Cookware

Casserole, 3 qt. .... $225+
Dutch oven .... $500+
Fry pan, cov. .... $500+
Sauce pan, cov. .... $500+
Serving tray, electric, 12 3/4 x 17 1/2" ..... $2,000+

Knowles Esquire Line (Edwin M. Knowles China Co.)

Knowles Esquire Grass Pattern Pitcher

Pitcher, water, Grass patt., pink, unusual (ILLUS.)... $225+

Residential Pattern (Plastic tablewares by Northern)

Plastic Residential Pattern Tumblers

Tumbler, red or blue, each (ILLUS. of two) $50

Sterling Line (Sterling China Co.)

Sterling China Gray Creamer

Creamer, gray (ILLUS.).................................... $50

Satsuma

These decorated wares have been produced in Japan since the end of the 18th century. The early pieces are scarce and high-priced. Later Satsuma wares are plentiful and, with prices rising, are also becoming highly collectible.

Fine Satsuma Plate and Vases

(ILLUS. left with a dessert plate, top of page)... **$748**

Finely Decorated Satsuma Jar

Jar, cov., bulbous ovoid body w/the shoulder tapering to a short rolled neck & domed cover w/a gold pointed button finial, the sides h.p. w/a wide continuous band showing scenes of children involved in various activities, pink shoulder & cover decorated w/ornate cloud designs w/gold trim, late 19th - early 20th c., unmarked, 6" h. (ILLUS.) **$403**

Plates, 7 1/2" d., dessert, each finely painted w/landscapes & figures w/Mt. Fuji in the background, Meiji period, ca. 1920, set of 6 (ILLUS. of one at right with two vases, top of page)........................... **$748**

Vase, 25" h., floor-type, footed baluster form w/a tall neck w/widely flared ruffled rim & foo dog & ring shoulder handles, dark blue background painted w/pink & blue blossoms & surrounded a large panel showing two Geisha against a dark gold ground, unmarked, ca. 1900 (ILLUS., top next column)........................... **$250-300**

Vases, 7 1/4" h., simple ovoid form w/a flat gold mouth, each h.p. in color w/family scenes of mothers & children in front of a red house, flowering trees, waters & mountains in the distance, some gilt wear, signed, Meiji period, ca. 1900, pr.

Large Decorative Satsuma Floor Vase

Schafer & Vater

Founded in Rudolstadt, Thuringia, Germany in 1890, the Schafer and Vater Porcelain Factory specialized in decorative pieces of porcelain usually in white or colored bisque. It produced many novelty figural items such as creamers, toothpick holders, boxes and hatpin holders, and also a line of jasper ware with white relief decoration in imitation of the famous Wedgwood jasper wares. The firm also decorated whiteware blanks.

The company ceased production in 1962, and collectors now seek out its charming pieces, which may be marked with a crown over a starburst containing the script letter "R."

Schafer & Vater Mark

Bottle, figural, a figure of a male golfer in color & wearing a white outfit w/knickers & a cap leaning over a large brown flat-sided round flask w/a short neck projecting at an angle, the flask inscribed "Golf and Good Spirits Make a Good Highball," 4 1/2" h. (missing stopper) **$322**

Bottle, figural, a skeleton standing enveloped in a sheet marked on the front "Gift!" (Poison), white w/brown trim, No. 6109, 9 1/2" h. **$334**

Bottle, figural, large rounded head of a young man w/wild hair wearing an inverted funnel for a hat, the funnel inscribed "Nurnberger Trichter," overall glossy washed blue glaze, No. 6218, 8" h. **$403**

Bottle set: figural bottle, six cups & tray; bottle in the form of a comical short, fat doctor w/curled wig standing beside a large upright syringe, six small cylindrical cups w/names of medicines around the base resting on a round tray, pointed tip of syringe forms bottle stopper, overall glossy washed blue glaze, bottle 9 3/4" h., the set **$575**

Figural Chinese Man Creamer

Creamer, figural, in the form of a Chinese man wearing a long orange robe, holding a large white goose by the feet while it tries to fly away, thus forming the spout w/the open beak for pouring, the man's long black pigtail forming the handle, unmarked, 2 1/4" w., 4" h. (ILLUS.) **$135**

Figurines, Sun Ladies & Moon Men, two w/a smiling cream-colored sun head on the body of a seated late-Victorian woman, one w/her arms away from her body, wearing a black jacket, white dress & red slippers w/a red handbag in her lap, the other w/a matching outfit but playing a banjo; the three men w/a cream crescent moon head, one head smoking a pipe & attached to the body of a reclining late-Victorian man wearing a short white coat w/black collar & white knee breeches, a second man wearing a similar outfit but kneeling & holding out a bouquet w/one hand & a pink hat in the other, the third man reclining on his stomach w/his lower legs in the air, No. 3150 through 3155,

3 1/2 to 4 1/2" l., the set of 5 (two women w/minor chip repairs)............................. **$1,380**

Schafer & Vater Sugar Shaker

Sugar shaker w/original metal top, bisque, a slender waisted cylindrical white form w/a band of embossed scrolls around the wide bottom & a molded lappet band at the top, the body molded in relief w/figures of Grecian women tinted grey w/an altar in pink & foliage in green, 3 1/4" d., 6 1/8" h. (ILLUS.)...................... **$135**

Tea set: cov. teapot, cov. sugar bowl, creamer & two cups & saucers; figural, all in pink bisque w/grey-green trim, the teapot body formed by the wide deep skirt of a woman, a slender ribbed spout at the front, the cover formed by the torso of the woman wearing a ruffled collar & balloon sleeves, a tall ribbon on her head, the handle formed by a slender, elongated figure of a bent-over gentleman wearing a tall top hat, the figural sugar bowl in the form of a similar lady but w/small scroll handles at the sides, the open creamer in the form of a wide skirt w/the handle in the form of the bent-over gentleman, each cup w/a gentleman handle & on a ruffled saucer, all pieces w/molded ornate scrolls & swags, No. 3861, 3862 & 3863, 4" to 7" h., the set (few small chips, repaired lines) **$834**

Sèvres & Sèvres-Style

Some of the most desirable porcelain ever produced was made at the Sèvres factory, originally established at Vincennes, France, and transferred, through permission of Madame de Pompadour, to Sèvres as the Royal Manufactory about the middle of the 18th century. King Louis XV took sole responsibility for the works in 1759, when production of hard paste wares began. Between 1850 and 1900, many biscuit and soft-paste pieces were made again. Fine early pieces are scarce and high-priced. Many of those available today are late productions. The various Sèvres marks have been copied, and pieces listed as "Sèvres-Style" are similar to actual Sèvres wares but not necessarily from that factory. Three of the many Sèvres marks are illustrated here.

Sèvres marks

Bowl, 9 1/4" d., a footring below the wide flaring rounded & lobed sides, white ground painted on the exterior w/three different musical trophies alternating w/three gilt sprigs of fruiting vine below a blue foliate scroll border, the interior w/a colorful garland of flowers, second half 18th c. **$3,000**

Fine Casket-form Sèvres-style Box

Box, cov., casket-form, the low rectangular serpentine sides supported on ornate gold scrolled corner legs, the dark blue sides h.p. w/oval reserves w/colorful florals framed by ornate gilt scrolls, the hinged & low domed cover also in dark blue w/a large white reserve w/floral clusters & vines framing a central panel decorated w/a couple in 18th c. costume, pseudo-Sèvres marks, late 19th c., 6 1/2" h. (ILLUS.) **$3,220**

Ornate Sèvres-style Bowl in Gilt-bronze Frame

Center bowl, Sèvres-style, gilt-bronze mounted, the long oval shallow bowl w/a dark blue exterior centering a large oval reserve w/a color scene of 18th c. lovers in a landscape, framed by ornate gold leafy vines, the white interiors decorated w/floral designs, a beaded gilt-brown rim band & slender inward-scrolled end handles connecting to the pedestal base w/scrolls raised on an oblong platform w/scroll feet, late 19th c., overall 20" l. (ILLUS.) **$2,875**

Fine Sèvres-Style Centerpiece Bowl

Centerpiece bowl, in the Louis XVI taste, a celeste blue wide border w/gilt floral sprig band around the center painted w/a colorful scene of 18th c. peasant figures, mounted in a gilt-brass framework w/scroll handles & scroll feet joined by floral swags, pseudo-Sèvres interlaced Ls mark on base, late 19th c., 16 1/2" w., 6" h. (ILLUS.) **$690**

Cup & saucer, footed slightly swelled cylindrical cup & deep dished saucer, the cup decorated en grisaille w/a reserve of a cupid reclining on clouds & holding a vine of grapes, surrounded by gilt edging on a trelliswork & bird's-eye decorated ground, the saucer w/a similar design w/two reserves of marshal trophies flanking a central scrolling foliate medallion, Sèvres mark & date code for 1770, cup 3 1/8" h., the set **$3,600**

Garniture set: centerpiece & a pair of cov. vases; the vases w/ovoid bodies w/flaring necks ending in flattened dome lids w/pinecone finials, on slender ringed flaring pedestals on gilt bronze rectangular plinths w/bracket feet, the necks w/pierced gilt decorative band joined to gilt scroll handles mounted to shoulders, the body decorated w/h.p. romantic scenes in pastel shades on emerald green ground framed in raised gilt scroll & bead design, the wide bowl-form centerpiece w/matching pierced gilt rim & handles attached at rim & scrolling to base of bowl, bowl w/matching decoration & raised on a matching pedestal base, artist signed "Poylet," lids marked "Chateau de Longpre" w/"S" in diamond & "France," ca. 1900, centerpiece 17" w., vases 18" h., the set (ILLUS., top next page) **$3,450**

Bronze-mounted Sèvres-style Jardiniere

Jardiniere, Sèvres-style, gilt bronze-mounted, a wide low squatty bowl decorated

Artist-signed Sèvres Garniture Set

w/upper & lower dark blue bands w/gilt stripes & floral clusters, a white central band h.p. w/playful putti alternating w/lion face masks, metal rim band joining arched scroll handles continuing down to the ornate scrolled metal platform raised on claw feet, ca. 1870, 11 1/2 x 26 1/2", 13 1/2" h. (ILLUS.) **$1,725**

Jardinieres, Sèvres-style, gilt bronze-mounted, a footed wide cylindrical body w/a dark blue ground, one side h.p. w/a large rectangular reserve of 18th c. figures in a woodland, the other side w/a large floral reserve, gold borders & lacy scrolls, metal rim band joined to lion mask & ring side handles continuing to the round base on ornate scrolled feet, blue interlaced "L"s mark, late 19th c., 10 1/2" d., 10 1/2" h., pr. (ILLUS., bottom of page) **$5,060**

Pitcher w/hinged cover, 5 1/8" h., a silver-gilt footring supporting the bulbous body tapering to a cylindrical neck w/a rim spout, large loop handle, the cover attached w/later silver-gilt French mounts, white ground painted around the neck & cover w/garlands of flowers suspended from a gilt foliate & laurel wreath border &

narrow claret-ground band at the rim, Sèvres mark & date code for 1760 .... **$1,800**

Salt dips, triple, three slightly flaring cylindrical cups forming three lobes joined across the top w/a triple-loop handle, white ground, molded gilt-trimmed ribbons topped by a bow knop on the handle, the sides painted near the rim w/thin gold & green leaf bands, Sèvres mark & date code for 1778, 3 1/2" h., pr. **$960**

Serving dish, cover & underplate, deep round base w/D-form loop side handles, white ground finely painted overall w/bowknotted festoons of colorful flowers, foliate-entwined handles, cover w/twig finial, Sèvres mark & date code for 1760, underplate 8 1/4" d., the set **$2,700**

Serving dish, cover & undertray, deep round bowl-form w/side loop handles, low domed cover w/gilt-trimmed scroll handle, Bleu Celeste ground painted en grisaille w/panels of cherubs among clouds & marshal trophies reserved within a gilt-edged berried laurel wreath border on the blue white-dotted ground, Sèvres mark & date code for 1770, oval undertray 7 1/8" l., the set **$10,200**

Very Fine Blue Sèvres-style Bronze-mounted Jardinieres

Bleu Nouveau Gilt-decorated Sevres Tea Set

Tea set: cov. teapot, cov. sugar bowl, creamer & one cup & saucer; dark Bleu Nouveau ground, the serving pieces w/bulbous ovoid bodies, each piece decorated w/gilt leaf band around the base & a band of stylized blossoms & leaves around the shoulder, further leaf band & gilt line decoration on each piece, various decorator & potter marks, France, mid-19th c., teapot 6 1/4" h., the set (ILLUS.) **$2,271**

Sevres-style Tea Set with Spurious Factory Marks

Tea set: cov. teapot, cov. sugar bowl, creamer, two cups & saucers & an undertray; Sevres-style, the serving pieces w/bulbous ovoid bodies tapering to flat mouths & domed covers w/fluted pointed finials, each w/a cobalt blue ground centered on the front w/a large rounded gold-bordered reserve featuring a bust portrait of a court beauty of the late 18th c., the four-lobed tray centered by a color half-length portrait of Louis XVI, each piece further trimmed w/ornate delicate gold scrolls, spurious Sevres & chateau marks, France, early 20th c., tray 11 7/8" w., the set (ILLUS. of part) **$2,350**

Fine Sévres-style Porcelain Tea Set with a Pink Ground

Tea set: tete-a-tete style, cov. teapot, cov. sugar bowl, creamer, two cylindrical cups & saucers & a scalloped round footed undertray; Sevres-style, teapot w/ovoid body, creamer w/tapering ovoid body raised on four gold legs, cylindrical sugar bowl, all w/a pink ground elaborately painted w/overall bands of long gold arabesques highlighted w/delicate turquoise blue, deep red & pink "jeweling," spurious gilt interlaced Ls mark, France, mid- to late 19th c., undertray 8 7/8" d., the set (ILLUS., top of page)............................. **$3,760**

Sévres-Style Decorated Teapot

Teapot, cov., cylindrical body w/flat shoulder centering a short neck & low domed cover w/pointed knob finial, curved rim spout & C-scroll handle, turquoise blue ground decorated on one side w/a vignette in color of a barefoot boy playing the flute w/a dog at his feet, the other side w/a colorful bouquet of flowers within a gilt scroll border, teapot 18th c., the decoration added later, spurious blue Sévres interlaced Ls mark, 5" h. (ILLUS.) **$598**

Urn, cov., Sèvres-style, gilt bronze-mounted, a gilt-bronze notch-cornered foot below the cobalt blue ringed pedestal w/ornate gilt scrolls below the tall urn-form body supported on gilt-bronze leaves, the main body h.p. w/a continuous color scene of a semi-nude maiden frolicking w/putti in a garden setting, the shoulder cast w/a nar-

Very Elaborate Classical-style Urn

row metal band w/one side featuring frolicking putti, the other side w/a putto drawing a sword, the tapering cobalt blue neck & domed cover w/ornate gilt scrolling, upright gilt-bronze scroll shoulder handles & a gilt-bronze flame finial on the cover, late 19th c., overall 25 1/4" h. (ILLUS.) **$3,346**

One of Two Sèvres Japanese Taste Vases

Vases, 13 1/8" h., simple ovoid body tapering to a tall trumpet neck, decorated in the Japanese taste to resemble cloisonné, the dark blue ground h.p. w/large purple peonies & rust-colored leafy stems, delicate white blossoms & stems around the neck, Sèvres factory marks, ca. 1875-80, pr. (ILLUS. of one) **$4,780**

Shawnee

The Shawnee Pottery Company of Zanesville, Ohio, opened its doors for operation in 1936 and, sadly, closed in 1961. The pottery was inexpensive for its quality and was readily purchased at dime stores as well as department stores. Sears, Roebuck and Co., Butler Bros., Woolworth's and S. Kresge were just a few of the companies that were longtime retailers of this fine pottery.

Shawnee Pottery Company had a wide array of merchandise to offer, from knickknacks to dinnerware, although Shawnee is quite often associated with colorful pig cookie jars and the dazzling "Corn King" line of dinnerware. Planters, miniatures, cookie jars and Corn King pieces are much in demand by today's avid collectors. Factory seconds were purchased by outside decorators and trimmed with gold, decals and unusual hand painting, which makes those pieces extremely desirable in today's market and enhances the value considerably.

Shawnee Pottery has become the most sought-after pottery in today's collectible market.

Reference books available are Mark E. Supnick's book Collecting Shawnee Pottery, The Collector's Guide to Shawnee Pottery *by Duane and Janice Vanderbilt or* Shawnee Pottery - An Identification & Value Guide *by Jim and Bev Mangus.*

Shawnee Mark

Shawnee Figural Ashtrays

Ashtray, figural kingfisher, parrot, bird, fish, terrier or owl, marked "U.S.A.," dusty rose, turquoise, old ivory, white or burgundy, 3" h., each (ILLUS. of fish, kingfisher & bird).. **$45-50**

Figural Howdy Doody Bank

Bank, figural Howdy Doody riding a pig, marked "Bob Smith U.S.A.," 6 3/4" h. (ILLUS.) **$450-475**

Rare Shawnee Batter Pitcher

Batter pitcher, Pennsylvania Dutch patt., marked "U.S.A.," rare, 34" h. (ILLUS.) **$750-900**

Shawnee Figural Book Ends

Book ends, figural, full figure of a man at potter's wheel, brown, marked "Crafted by Shawnee Potteries Zanesville, Ohio 1960," 9" h., pr. (ILLUS.)..................... **$400-500**
Cookie jar, cov., figural fruit basket, marked "Shawnee U.S.A. 84," 8 1/2" h............. **$75-100**
Cookie jar, cov., figural Jo-Jo the clown, marked "Shawnee U.S.A. 12," *repro-duction alert, 9" h. **$125-150**

Jumbo (Lucky) Elephant Cookie Jar

Cookie jar, cov., figural Jumbo (Lucky) elephant, decal decoration & gold trim, marked "U.S.A.," 11 3/4" h. (ILLUS.)... **$400-450**

Cookie jar, cov., figural Smiley Pig, shamrock decoration, marked "U.S.A.," 11 1/4" h. **$195-225**

Figural Elephant Creamer

Creamer, figural elephant, w/gold decoration & decals, marked "Patented U.S.A.," 4 3/4" h. (ILLUS.) **$175-200**

Pitcher, 7 1/2" h., figural Boy Blue, gold trim, marked "Shawnee U.S.A. 46" **$225-250**

Pitcher, 7 1/2" h., figural Chanticleer rooster, marked "Patented Chanticleer U.S.A." **$50-65**

Shawnee Clown Planter

Planter, figural clown w/blocks, marked "Shawnee U.S.A.," 4 1/2" h. (ILLUS.) ... **$85-100**

Planters, models of train engine, coal car, boxcar & caboose, blue, yellow, green & butterscotch, decorated, Nos. 550, 551, 552, 553, 4 pcs. **$85-100**

Salt & pepper shakers, figural cottage, pr. **$200-250**

Winnie Pig Cookie Jar

Cookie jar, cov., figural Winnie Pig, w/peach collar, marked "Patented Winnie U.S.A.," 11 3/4" h. (ILLUS.) **$250-275**

Pennsylvania Dutch Creamer & Sugar Bowl

Creamer, ball-type, Pennsylvania Dutch style, marked "U.S.A. 12," 4 1/2" h. (ILLUS. right) **$50-65**

Figural Smiley & Winnie Shakers

Yellow & Blue Shawnee Elephant Teapots

Salt & pepper shakers, figural Smiley Pig &
Winnie Pig, clover blossom decoration,
3", pr. (ILLUS., previous page)............... **$65-85**
Salt & pepper shakers, figural Smiley Pig &
Winnie Pig, clover blossom decoration,
5" h., pr... **$175-200**
Salt & pepper shakers, figural Smiley Pig &
Winnie Pig, heart decoration, 5", pr. ... **$100-125**

Shawnee Figural Elephant Teapot

Clover Blossom Shawnee Teapot

Teapot, cov., Clover Blossom patt., embossed decoration, marked "U.S.A.," 6-
cup, 6 1/2" h. (ILLUS.)......................... **$125-150**
Teapot, cov., figural Elephant patt., blue or
yellow glaze, marked "U.S.A.," 6 1/2" h.,
each (ILLUS., top of page).................. **$150-200**
Teapot, cov., figural Elephant patt., green
glaze, marked "U.S.A.," 6 1/2" h. **$175-225**
Teapot, cov., figural elephant w/burgundy,
green & brown h.p. on white ground,
marked "U.S.A.," 6 1/2" h. (ILLUS., top
next column)..................................... **$200-225**
Teapot, cov., figural Granny Ann, air-
brushed decoration w/blue apron & burgundy shawl, marked "Patented Granny
Ann U.S.A.," each (ILLUS., last next col-
umn).. **$500-650**

Rare Airbrushed Granny Ann Teapot

Shawnee Granny Ann Teapot

Teapot, cov., figural Granny Ann, green apron & shawl w/burgundy & yellow trim, w/gold decal shawl & trim, marked "Patented Granny Ann U.S.A." (ILLUS.).... **$400-450**

Tom the Piper's Son Teapot

Teapot, cov., figural Tom the Piper's Son, white body w/h.p. trim, marked "Tom the Piper's Son patented U.S.A. 44," 7" h. (ILLUS.)... **$65-85**
Teapot, cov., figural Tom the Piper's Son, white body w/h.p. trim w/patches & gold trim, marked "Tom the Piper's Son patented U.S.A. 44," 7" h. **$175-200**
Teapot, cov., Flower & Fern patt., 5-cup size, 5 1/4" h. **$30-35**
Teapot, cov., Flower & Fern patt., gold-trimmed, 5-cup size, 5 1/4" h. **$75-85**

Horizontal Ribbed Shawnee Teapot

Teapot, cov., Horizontal Ribbed patt., h.p. floral vine decoration, marked "U.S.A.," 6" h. (ILLUS.) **$35-45**
Teapot, cov., Horizontal Ribbed patt., w/gold trim & depending on the h.p. decoration, marked "U.S.A.," 6" h. **$65-85**
Teapot, cov., Laurel Wreath patt., 6 3/4" h. **$30-35**

Shawnee Pennsylvania Dutch Teapot

Teapot, cov., Pennsylvania Dutch patt., marked "U.S.A. 10," 10 oz., two-cup size, also found in 14 oz., 18 oz., 27 oz. & 30 oz. sizes, each (ILLUS. of 10 oz. size) **$50-65**

Shawnee Rosette Pattern Teapot

Teapot, cov., Rosette patt., yellow glaze, marked "U.S.A.," 6" h. (ILLUS.) **$20-25**
Teapot, cov., Snowflake patt., 5-cup size, 5 1/2" h.. **$30-35**

Gold-trimmed Sunflower Shawnee Teapot

Teapot, cov., Sunflower patt., gold-trimmed, marked "U.S.A.," 30 oz., 6 1/4" h. (ILLUS.)................................. **$125-175**
Teapot, cov., Sunflower patt., marked "U.S.A.," 30 oz., 6 1/4" h. **$65-85**

Swirl Pattern Teapot by Shawnee

Teapot, cov., Swirl patt., turquoise blue glaze, marked "U.S.A.," 6 1/2" h. (ILLUS.) **$25-30**

Scotty Dog Wall Pocket

Wall pocket, Scotty dog head, green, burgundy, cobalt, yellow or white, unmarked, 9 1/2" h. (ILLUS.) **$45-55**

Wall pocket, Sunflower patt., marked "U.S.A.," 6 3/4" h. **$40-50**

Shelley China

Members of the Shelley family were in the pottery business in England as early as the 18th century. In 1872 Joseph Shelley formed a partnership with James Wileman of Wileman & Co. who operated the Foley China Works. The Wileman & Co. name was used for the firm for the next fifty years, and between 1890 and 1910 the words "The Foley" appeared above conjoined "WC" initials.

Beginning in 1910 the Shelley family name in a shield appeared on wares, although the firm's official name was still Wileman & Co. The company's name was finally changed to Shelley in 1925 and then Shelley China Ltd. after 1965. The firm changed hands in the 1960s and became part of the Doulton Group in 1971.

At first only average quality earthenwares were produced, but in the late 1890s new shapes and better quality decorations were used.

Bone china was introduced at Shelley before World War I, and these fine dinnerwares became very popular in the United States and are

increasingly popular today with collectors. Thin "eggshell china" teawares, miniatures and souvenir items were widely marketed during the 1920s and 1930s and are sought-after today.

Shelley Mark

Shelley Begonia Teapot in Dainty Big Floral Shape

Teapot, cov., Dainty Big Floral Shape, Begonia patt. No. 13427, from the Best Ware group, 1943 (ILLUS.) **$180-280**

Shelley Capper's Strawberry Teapot in Dainty Big Floral Shape

Teapot, cov., Dainty Big Floral Shape, Capper's Strawberry patt. No. 2396, from the Seconds group, 1959 (ILLUS.) **$200-300**

Trailing Violets Teapot in Dainty Kettle Garlands Shape

Teapot, cov., Dainty Kettle Garlands Shape, Trailing Violets patt. No. 9056, shaded style, from the Best Ware group, 1897 (ILLUS.) **$180-380**

Shelley Regency Teapot in Dainty Plain Shape

Teapot, cov., Dainty Plain Shape, Regency patt. No. 785, from the Special group, 1945 (ILLUS.)..................................... **$150-250**

Shelley Thistle Teapot in Dainty Shape

Teapot, cov., Dainty Shape, Thistle patt. No. 13829, from the Best Ware group, 1955 (ILLUS.)..................................... **$200-300**

Shelley Rosebud Teapot in Dainty Repeat Shape

Teapot, cov., Dainty Repeat Shape, Rosebud patt. No. 13426, from the Best Ware group, 1943 (ILLUS.).......................... **$250-350**

Undecorated Dainty Shape Teapot

Teapot, cov., Dainty Shape, undecorated, ca. 1912-25, overall 7 1/8" l., 4" h. (ILLUS.) **$100-150**

Dainty Shape Teapot with Pink Roses Pattern No. 7447

Teapot, cov., Dainty Shape, Wileman & Co., patt. No. 7447, introduced in 1896, designed by William Morris, shape continued in production until factory closing in 1966 (ILLUS.)................................ **$300-350**

Her Majesty Teapot in Dainty Shape by Shelley

Teapot, cov., Dainty Scenic Shape, Her Majesty (tractor) patt., from the Souvenir Ware group, 1920 (ILLUS.) **$50-150**

Dainty Shape Teapot with Floral Pattern No. 9056

Teapot, cov., Dainty Shape, Wileman & Co., patt. No. 9056, 1896-1966, 5 1/2" h. (ILLUS., previous page) **$300-600**

Popular Shelley Dainty Blue Teapot

Teapot, cov., Dainty Shape, Dainty Blue patt., the original & most sought-after Shelley design, 1896-1966+ (ILLUS.) .. **$500-600**

Wileman Jungle Print Tall Teapot

Teapot, cov., Daisy Shape, Jungle Print patt., Wileman & Co., 1885-1914, 7 1/4" l., 6 1/8" h. (ILLUS.) **$400-600**

Dorothy Teapot with Tea Tile

Teapot, cov., Dorothy Shape, patt. No. 8063, w/matching tea tile w/earlier Wileman backstamp, teapot overall 9 5/8" l., 6 1/4" h., the set (ILLUS.) **$200-500**

Empire Shape Teapot with Bold Red & Blue Florals

Teapot, cov., Empire Shape, patt. Wileman & Co., No. 0888, shape introduced in 1893 (ILLUS.) **$600-900**

Empire Shape Spano Lustra Teapot by Wileman

Teapot, cov., Empire Shape, Spano Lustra patt., Wileman & Co., 1893-1912, 5" h. (ILLUS.) **$300-600**

Shelley Blue Duchess Teapot in Gainsborough Shape

Teapot, cov., Gainsborough Shape, Blue Duchess patt. No. 13403, Elegant style, from the Best Ware group, 1943 (ILLUS.) **$100-200**

Gainsborough Drifting Leaves Teapot

Teapot, cov., Gainsborough Shape, Drifting Leaves patt. No. 13848, from the Contemporary group, 1957 (ILLUS.) **$80-150**

Wileman Gainsborough Teapot with Delicate Florals

Teapot, cov., Gainsborough Shape, Wileman & Co., unnumbered floral patt., introduced in 1900 (ILLUS.) **$300-600**

Globe Teapot with Flower Basket

Shelley Bluebell Wood Teapot

Teapot, cov., Globe Shape, Bluebell Wood patt. No. 12108, Scenic style, from the Best Ware group, 1932 (ILLUS.)......... **$100-200**

Teapot, cov., Globe Shape, white ground decorated w/a colorful basket of flowers, undated (ILLUS.).................................. **$100-200**

Shelley Daffodil Time Teapot

Teapot, cov., Globe Shape, Daffodil Time patt. No. 13370, Scenic style, from the Best Ware group, 1942 (ILLUS.)......... **$100-200**

Green Daisy Teapot in Henley Shape

Teapot, cov., Henley Shape, Chintz Green Daisy patt. No. 13450, from the Best Ware group, 1943 (ILLUS.)................. **$200-300**

Marguerite Teapot & Other Pieces in Henley Shape

Teapot, cov., Henley Shape, Marguerite patt. No. 13688, Chintz style, from the Best Ware group, 1949, teapot only (ILLUS. w/stand & sugar & creamer - add at least $100 for stand & about $150 for sugar & creamer) **$150-250**

Rare Early Imperial Shape Wileman Teapot

Teapot, cov., Imperial Shape, Wileman & Co., first introduced w/an Intarsio patt. in the 1890s, this example w/a Shelley backstamp, patt. No. 7666, ca. 1910 (ILLUS.) **$1,500-2,000**

Shelley Chintz Blue Daisy Teapot & Other Pieces in Mayfair Shape

Teapot, cov., Mayfair Shape, Chintz Blue Daisy patt. No. 14268, from the Best Ware group, 1964 (ILLUS. w/stand & sugar & creamer - add at least $100 for stand & about $150 for sugar & creamer) **$150-250**

Art Deco Mode Shape with Blocks Pattern

Teapot, cov., Mode Shape, Art Deco design, Blocks patt., 1929-1934 (ILLUS.)
.... **$600-900**

Shelley Teapot in New York Shape

Teapot, cov., New York Shape, Plain style, white w/green trim on rim, handle, finial & spout, from the Best Ware group, 1940, teapot only (ILLUS. w/stand - add at least $100 for stand).................................... **$50-150**

Mode Art Deco Pot with Pink Florals

Teapot, cov., Mode Shape, floral decoration w/pink blossoms, light blue trim, factory second, 1929-34, 9 1/8" l., 4 7/8" h. (ILLUS.) **$350-500**

Saltcoats Crest on New York Teapot

Teapot, cov., New York Shape, Saltcoats Crested design, 1890-1905, overall 5 3/4" l., 4" h. (ILLUS.) **$70-100**

New York Shape Floral Decor Teapot

Teapot, cov., New York Shape, decorated w/delicate bands of colorful flowers, 1890-1905 (ILLUS.)........................... **$150-250**

New York Teapot with Blue Sprigs

Teapot, cov., New York Shape, scattered blue floral sprigs, 1890-1905 (ILLUS.) .. **$75-125**

Shelley London Crested Teapot in New York Shape

Teapot, cov., New York Shape, London patt., Crested style, from the Souvenir Ware group, 1910 (ILLUS.).................. **$50-150**

Rare & Unusual Oriental Shape Teapot

Shelley Poppies Teapot, Cup & Saucer in Princess Shape

Teapot, cov., Oriental Shape, Intarsio decoration, Wileman & Co., patt. No. 3081,
short production period, 1899 (ILLUS.,
previous page) **$1,200-1,500**

Teapot, cov., Princess Shape, Poppies, orange patt. No. 12227, Floral style, from
the Best Ware group, 1933, teapot only
(ILLUS. w/matching cup & saucer, top of
page) **$350-550**

Black Cloisonne Teapot & Other Pieces in Queen Anne Shape

Teapot, cov., Queen Anne Shape, Black Cloisonne patt. No. 8321, Chintz style, from the Best Ware
group, 1910, teapot only (ILLUS. w/stand & other pieces - add at least $100 for stand)... **$500-700**

Blue Iris Teapots of Various Sizes in Queen Anne Shape by Shelley

Teapot, cov., Queen Anne Shape, Blue Iris patt. No. 11561, Floral style, from the Best Ware group,
1919, various sizes, each (ILLUS. of various sizes) **$300-400**

Fine Wileman Shell Shape Teapot

Teapot, cov., Shell Shape, Wileman & Co., patt. No. 5137, introduced in 1891 (ILLUS.).. **$500-600**

Basket of Fruit Teapot in Tulip Shape

Teapot, cov., Tulip Shape, Basket of Fruit patt. No. 8204, Floral style from the Stenciled group, 1918 (ILLUS.)................ **$120-160**

Slipware

This term refers to ceramics, primarily redware, decorated by the application of slip (semiliquid paste made of clay). Such wares were made for decades in England and Germany and elsewhere on the Continent, and in the Pennsylvania Dutch country and elsewhere in the United States. Today, contemporary copies of early Slipware items are featured in numerous decorator magazines and offered for sale in gift catalogs.

Tall Teapot Made for Ideal China Co.

Teapot, cov., tall trumpet shape w/ring handle & finial, made for the Ideal China Co., Canada, registration number 781613, overall 7 1/4" h. (ILLUS.).................... **$250-400**

Bowl, 11" d., 3" h., wide shallow rounded form, redware w/applied light brown interior glaze decorated w/several yellow slip wavy bands around the interior sides, unglazed exterior, found in Pennsylvania, excellent condition, ca. 1870 (ILLUS. right with sgraffito charger, bottom of page)... **$1,073**

Yellow Slip-decorated Bowl & Sgraffito Charger

Slipware Star Flower Bowl & Line-decorated Dish

Bowl, 13" d., 4 3/4" h., flat bottom w/steeply angled sides & molded flat rim, the interior slip-decorated in yellow w/a large eight-point star flower surrounded by tiny blossoms in the bottom, the sides w/a row of tiny blossoms below a bold beaded swag band below an upper band of large seven-point star flowers alternating w/tiny dotted blossoms, small nick, flakes to rim & base, 19th c. (ILLUS. right with slipware dish, top of page) **$431**

Charger, large shallow round form w/wide flanged rim, redware decorated w/concentric bands of squiggle slip decoration & a central long stylized leafy branch, Pennsylvania, 19th c., 11 5/8" d............. **$1,195**

Rare Early Slipware Sgraffito Charger

Charger, round w/wide flanged rim, redware w/overall white interior glaze decorated in sgraffito w/a central large image in green, yellow & brown slip of Benjamin Franklin seated in a ladder-back armchair, surrounded by an incised verse in the Pennsylvania Dutch dialect that roughly translates "Work hard when you are a youth and after you are grown keep it up regardless of how hard the work is," wide flange decorated w/stylized flowers & leaves in yellow, green & brown, ca.

1779, early repair to a glued crack, 12" d. (ILLUS.)... **$2,530**

Dated Slipware Charger with Bird

Charger, round w/wide gently sloped sides, the bottom interior w/a large slip-quilled black outlined bird w/cream dashes below the date "1822," thin cream border bands flanking a dark green squiggle band, Pennsylvania, 12 1/4" d. (ILLUS.)
.... **$3,107**

Charger, wide round shallow form, redware w/sgraffito decoration of tulips, leaves & a central flowerhead in the applied interior glazes of yellow, orange, brown & green, Pennsylvania origin, extensive wear & chipping to surface, very old hairline at rim, ca. 1800, 12" d. (ILLUS. left with slipware bowl, previous page) **$3,740**

Charger, wide shallow round form, tooled coggled rim, yellow slip loop bands above the script name "Jackson," probably a commemorative for President Andrew Jackson, typical Connecticut form, ca. 1830, 14" d. (some staining & surface chipping around rim) **$3,850**

Dish, round shallow form w/a coggled rim, the interior slip-decorated in yellow w/triple short S-scroll bands flanking straight bands, each composed of four lines, all centered by a long wavy four-line band, Pennsylvania, 19th c., rim chips,

11 1/2" d. (ILLUS. left with star flower bowl).. **$805**

Spatterware

This ceramic ware takes its name from the "spattered" decoration, in various colors, generally used to trim pieces handpainted with rustic center designs of flowers, birds, houses, etc. Popular in the early 19th century, most was imported from England.

Related wares, called "stick spatter," had freehand designs applied with pieces of cut sponge attached to sticks, hence the name. Examples date from the 19th and early 20th century and were produced in England, Europe and America.

Some early spatter-decorated wares were marked by the manufacturers, but not many. Twentieth century reproductions are also sometimes marked, including those produced by Boleslaw Cybis.

Cup, handleless, Tree Trunk patt. in black w/green spatter leaves, purple spatter background, first half 19th c. (minor stains, crow's foot) **$303**

Spatterware Miniature Cup & Various Plates

Cup, miniature, handleless, footed w/flat flaring sides, Beehive patt., a yellow beehive surrounded by green spatter below a red spatter rim band, hairlines (ILLUS. front row, center w/spatter plates & platter) **$2,530**

Early Spatterware Plates & Teapots

Cup plate, paneled edge, the center w/a small transfer-printed spread-winged eagle atop a flower urn w/some hand-coloring, a two-tone blue spatter border band, impressed on the back "Warranted," early 19th c., 3 3/4" w. (ILLUS. front row center w/spatterware teapots & plates) **$300-600**

Early Child's Spatterware Tea Set

Cup & saucer, handleless, Four Petal Flower patt. in red & green, heavily sponged red & blue spatter background, first half 19th c. (minor stains in cup) **$468**

Plate, 7 1/2" d., paneled rim, Fort patt. in grey, green, black & red, blue spatter background, first half 19th c. (minor knife scratches, flake on table ring) **$303**

Plate, 8 1/4" d., Rainbow spatter in a bold four-color pinwheel design, yellow, green, red & dark brown w/green center, edge w/faint feather molding, first half 19th c. (hairlines, overall stains & flakes) **$9,900**

Plate, 8 1/4" d., round, Rainbow patt., a central bull's-eye design w/bands of dark brown & lavender, the border band w/alternating stripes of dark brown & lavender (ILLUS. front row, right, with miniature spatter cup & other plates, top of page) **$1,840**

Plate, 9 1/2" d., Peafowl patt. in red, green & blue, blue spatter border, first half 19th c. (stains, mostly on back, flake & rim repair) **$303**

Platter, 12 x 15 1/2", octagonal, Peafowl patt., a large central bird in deep red, blue, green & black, overall red spatter background, impressed "Adams" mark on the back, a few faint knife scratches (ILLUS. back row left, with miniature cup & other spatterware plates, top of page)
.... **$3,680**

Sauce dish, round w/flanged rim, Thistle patt., a red blossom & green leaves within a blue spatter background, 5 1/8" d. (ILLUS. front row left with miniature spatter cup & other plates, top of page) **$259**

Soup plate, paneled flanged rim, Tulip patt. h.p. in red, blue, green & black, a wide red spatter border, impressed number on the back, 10 1/2" w. (ILLUS. back row right, with other spatterware plates & teapots, top of page) **$2,185**

Soup plate, round w/flanged rim, Peafowl patt., a central bird in deep red, blue, yellow & black, overall light green spatter background, short hairline, 10" d. (ILLUS. back row right with miniature cup & other spatterware plates, top of page) **$633**

Sugar bowl, cov., footed bulbous body w/a low-domed fitted cover w/knob finial, vertical rim strap handles, Rose patt. in red & green, brown spatter background, first half 19th c., 4 1/4" d. (interior stains) **$468**

Sugar bowl, cov., footed squatty bulbous form w/rolled rim & inset cover w/knob finial, Rainbow spatter in alternating blue & green stripes up the sides, first half 19th c., 4 3/4" d., 4 1/2" h. (repairs to base & rim) **$330**

Tea set: child's, cov. teapot, cov. sugar bowl, two handleless cups & saucers; Fort patt., the teapot & sugar w/footed squatty bulbous bodies w/wide tapering paneled shoulders supporting domed covers w/button finials, teapot w/serpentine spout & C-scroll handle, sugar w/rolled tab handles, each piece w/a blue spatter ground centered by a painted fort building in black & brown w/green trees, England, ca. 1830, spout & rim flake on teapot, hairline on base of sugar, one cup w/repaired rim, teapot 4 3/8" h., the set (ILLUS., top of page) **$825**

Child's Green Spatterware Tea Set

Tea set: child's size, two cov. teapots, two cov. sugar bowls, two creamers, four handleless cups & one saucer; Peafowl patt., teapots & sugars w/footed squatty bulbous bodies w/flaring necks & inset domed covers w/pointed knob finials, each piece decorated w/a green spatter center band decorated w/a yellow, red & blue peafowl, similar designs w/slightly varying colors, England, ca. 1830, some damage & repair, teapots 4 1/4" h., the set (ILLUS. of part, previous page) **$1,610**

Teapot, cov., footed squatty bulbous body w/serpentine spout & C-scroll handle, Peafowl patt., a long slender bird in dark yellow, blue & red against a banded green spatter ground, some repair on inner rim flange, 6" h. (ILLUS. bottom row, left, with other spatter teapot & plates, top previous page) **$1,840**

Teapot, cov., miniature, Peafowl patt., a large bird on the side in red, dark blue, green & black against a greenish blue spatter background, early 19th c., 3 5/8" h. (ILLUS. front row, right, with other spatterware teapot & plates, top previous page) **$748**

Teapot, cov., Peafowl patt., footed squatty bulbous body tapering to a flaring rolled neck, long shaped spout & C-scroll handle, low domed cover w/button finial, a light green spatter band around the shoulder above a large h.p. blue, yellow, red & black peafowl, England, ca. 1830, 6" h. (lid slightly undersized & different green, small flake on inner flange) **$1,840**

Teapot, cov., Rainbow patt., flat-bottomed slightly tapering bulbous body w/an incurved shoulder tapering to a flat rim, long shaped spout & C-scroll handle, low domed cover w/button finial, decorated w/green spatter around the shoulder & vertical alternating stripes of red & green spatter around the body, England, ca. 1830, 7" h. (repaired spout & cover, additional flaking on cover) **$633**

Rare Yellow Spatterware Teapot

Teapot, cov., Thistle patt., a flared base tapering to a wide bulbous ovoid body tapering to a cylindrical neck w/flat rim, serpentine spout & C-form handle, low domed

cover w/button finial, bright yellow spatter ground centered by a large red & green thistle design, end of spout damaged, English-made, ca. 1830, 7" h. (ILLUS.) **$4,140**

Teapot, cov., Thumbprint patt., footed wide paneled body w/a squatty bulbous lower section below sides tapering to a flared rim, shaped spout & pointed scroll handle, domed cover w/pagoda finial, dark blue spatter background w/large black spatter overall thumbprints, England, ca. 1825-30, 7 1/2" h. (light overall stains w/a repaired spout & cover)............................. **$690**

Toddy plate, round, Schoolhouse patt., a dark blue building in the center surrounded by green & brown spatter, a red spatter border band, 5 7/8" d. (ILLUS. back row, left, with other spatterware plates & teapots, top previous page) **$2,645**

Spongeware

Spongeware's designs were spattered, sponged or daubed on in colors, sometimes with a piece of cloth. Blue on white was the most common type, but mottled tans, browns and greens on yellowware were also popular. Spongeware generally has an overall pattern with a coarser look than Spatterware, to which it is loosely related. These wares were extensively produced in England and America well into the 20th century.

White-banded Blue Spongeware Bowl

Bowl, 8 3/4" d., 3 1/2" h., three bands of blue on white sponging alternating w/two narrow white bands, minor surface wear, late 19th - early 20th c. (ILLUS.) **$88**

Blue-sponged Butter Crock

Butter crock, wide flat-bottomed cylindrical form, overall dark blue sponging on white w/the printed word "Butter," excellent condition, 6 1/2" d., 4 1/4" h. (ILLUS.)........ **$143**

Chamber Set in Cream with Blue Sponging

jar w/cover; cream background w/overall coarse blue sponging, minor losses to pitcher, late 19th - early 20th c., pitcher 10" h., the set (ILLUS., top of page) **$546**

Dark Blue Sponged Charger

Charger, round dished form w/overall dark blue sponging on white, minor wear, late 19th c., 10 1/8" d. (ILLUS.) **$173**

Blue Spongeware Covered Canister

Canister, cov., cylindrical w/molded rim & inset flat cover, light blue fine overall sponging on cream, very tight hairline through bottom, stack mark on cover, late 19th - early 20th c., 7" h. (ILLUS.).............. **$303**

Spongeware Creamer with Molded Design

Creamer, bulbous wide body tapering to a wide cylindrical neck w/wide spout & loop handle w/pointed thumb rest, the lower body molded in relief w/a scene of a heron holding a snake in its beak in a garden setting, dark blue overall sponging on white, late 19th - early 20th c., 5 1/2" h. (ILLUS.).. **$495**

Creamer, footed bulbous ovoid body w/a rim spout & C-form handle, overall light blue sponging on white, 3 3/4" h. (some very minor spout roughness) **$220**

Miniature Blue Sponged Chamber Pot

Chamber pot, miniature, cream w/overall light blue sponging, ca. 1900, 1 1/2" h. (ILLUS.).. **$88**

Chamber set: washbowl & pitcher, round soap dish, shaving mug & master waste

Rare Blue Spongeware Harvest Jug

Harvest jug, beehive-shaped w/high arched handle across the top above the short angled shoulder spout & round raised back shoulder opening, overall heavy blue sponging on white w/the incised & blue-tinted name "A. Noland," long U-shaped glued crack on the back, rare, ca. 1860, 13" h. (ILLUS.) **$688**

Master potty (slop jar), wide baluster-form body tapering to a flat rim w/a stepped domed cover w/button finial, small vertical loop handles at upper sides, overall dense dark blue sponging on white w/two narrow white bands flanking a dark blue band near the base, excellent condition, late 19th - early 20th c., 13" h. **$963**

Mug, bulbous ovoid body w/small C-form handle, bands of dark blue sponging on white around the rim & base, a relief-molded geometric design around the center of the body, 3" h. (one minor glaze flake on rim) **$165**

Spongeware Pitcher with Pointed Handle

Pitcher, 6 1/2" h., cylindrical body w/molded rim & pointed rim spout, pointed scroll loop handle, overall dark blue sponging on white, minor interior stains, late 19th - early 20th c. (ILLUS.) **$201**

Pitcher, 8 3/4" h., cylindrical body w/a flat rim & small pointed spout, large C-form handle, overall dense dark blue sponging on white, surface chip at side of base

(ILLUS. far right with three other sponged pitchers, top next page) **$132**

Pitcher, 8 3/4" h., ovoid body w/a flat rim & small pinched spout, long molded C-form handle, a plain band around the rim & bottom, the wide center section & the handle decorated w/a finely textured dense dark blue sponging on white w/a thin accent line at the top & bottom of sponging, late 19th - early 20th c. (minor age crazing & staining) **$413**

Pitcher, 9" h., cylindrical body w/a flat rim & large pointed spout, small C-form handle, overall medium blue dense sponging on white w/a blue accent band at the rim, faint hairline from rim at left side of spout, couple of interior glaze flakes (ILLUS. far left with three other sponged pitchers, top next page) **$176**

Blue Sponge Banded Pitcher

Pitcher, 9" h., cylindrical body w/a flat rim & large pointed spout, small C-form handle, overall coarse banded blue sponging on white, early 20th c. (ILLUS.) **$403**

Pitcher, 9" h., cylindrical body w/flat rim & large pointed spout, large C-form handle, overall medium blue repeating leaf-like sponged rows on white, very minor glaze flake on right side of spout (ILLUS. second from right with three other sponged pitchers, top next page) **$209**

Pitcher with Medium Blue Sponging

Four 9" Blue-sponged Pitchers

Group of Four Spongeware Pitchers

Pitcher, 9" h., cylindrical body w/flat rim & pointed spout, squared loop handle, overall fine medium blue sponging on white, flake on base, early 20th c. (ILLUS., previous page) **$288**

Pitcher, 9" h., cylindrical body w/swelled band near the bottom, rim spout & angled handle, very dark blue overall sponging in an unusual triangular leaf-like design on white, one minor interior rim chip (ILLUS. second from right with three other 9" pitchers, top of page)... **$605**

Pitcher, 9" h., cylindrical w/a flat rim & pinched spout, C-form handle, dark blue overall coarse sponging on white, late 19th - early 20th c. (tight hairline down from rim, minor flake at end of spout, minor use staining).. **$176**

Pitcher, 9" h., cylindrical w/a flat rim & pinched spout, C-form handle, medium blue finely mottled overall sponging on white, late 19th - early 20th c. (professional restoration to spout chip) **$132**

Pitcher, 9" h., cylindrical w/rim spout & C-form handle, dark blue large "chicken wire" design sponging on white, interior rim chip, small hairline left of spout, few glaze flakes (ILLUS. second from left with three other 9" pitchers. top of page).......... **$220**

Pitcher, 9" h., cylindrical w/rim spout & C-form handle, medium blue repeating wavy vertical bands of sponging on white, interior rim flake near spout (ILLUS. far left with three other spongeware 9" pitchers. top of page).. **$275**

Pitcher, 9" h., paneled cylindrical form w/rim spout & C-form handle, all over scattered large blue dot sponging on

white, professional restoration to a large chip at spout & a couple of interior glaze flakes at rim, overall glaze crazing, late 19th - early 20th c. (ILLUS. second from left with three larger sponged pitchers, second from top).. **$143**

Spongeware Pitcher with Chicken Wire Design

Pitcher, 9" h., slightly tapering cylindrical body w/pointed rim spout & small C-form handle, overall blue on white "chicken wire" design, tight T-shaped hairline in bottom rim up into the sides, late 19th - early 20th c. (ILLUS.) **$165**

Wavy Navy Blue Spongeware Pitcher

Pitcher, 9" h., slightly tapering cylindrical body w/pointed rim spout & small C-form handle, dark overall navy blue on white wavy design, hairline from rim near handle, late 19th - early 20th c. (ILLUS.) **$176**

Pitcher, 9" h., slightly tapering cylindrical body w/rim spout & C-form handle, medium blue vertical stripes of rounded sponging on white, three faint hairlines at rim, minor spout glaze flake (ILLUS. far right with three other 9" pitchers) **$468**

Spongeware Pitcher with Angled Handle

Pitcher, 9" h., swelled bottom below the cylindrical body w/a pointed rim spout & angled loop handle, overall blue sponging on white, minor glaze flake at spout, late 19th - early 20th c. (ILLUS.) **$303**

Boldly Sponged Blue & White Pitcher

Pitcher, 9" h., tall slightly tapering cylindrical body w/a molded rim w/pointed spout, C-form long handle, overall bold blue sponging on white, minor crazing in glaze, late 19th - early 20th c. (ILLUS.) **$303**

Nice Uhl Pottery Spongeware Pitcher

Pitcher, 9 1/2" h., bulbous ovoid body tapering to a cylindrical neck, pinched spout & long C-form handle, overall medium blue sponging on white, marked on the base by the Uhl Pottery Co., Huntingburg, Indiana, early 20th c., excellent condition (ILLUS.) **$303**

Blue Sponged Oblong Platter

Spongeware Spittoon, Teapot & Washbowl

Platter, oblong shape, overall fine dark blue sponging on white, late 19th c., 10 1/4 x 13 3/4" (ILLUS., previous page) ... **$173**

Spongeware Combination Salt & Pepper

Salt & pepper shaker, one-piece, ovoid body divided into two halves w/two short spouts w/metal caps, overall blue & brown sponging on white, some small cap dents, excellent condition, early 20th c., 3" h. (ILLUS.) **$154**

Spittoon, footed bulbous rounded body tapering to a widely flaring rim, grey ground w/molded overall basketweave design decorated w/scattered bold dark blue sponging, few glaze flakes, small tight hairline at rim, 8" d., 5" h. (ILLUS. right with spongeware teapot & washbowl, top of page) **$66**

Syrup jug, advertising-type, bulbous beehive-shaped w/short rim spout & wire bail handle w/black turned wood grip, overall blue sponging w/lower oval reserve stenciled "Grandmother's Maple Syrup of 50 Years Ago," relief-molded vine design around top half, bottom molded in relief "Mfg'd by N. Weeks - Style XXX Pat. Pending - Akron, O.," surface chips on spout, late 19th - early 20th c., 5 1/4" h. (ILLUS., top next column) **$495**

Teapot or pipkin, cov., wide bulbous slightly tapering cylindrical body w/a low flared rim w/spout, small C-form handle, white w/overall light blue "chicken wire" design sponging on white, minor glaze crazing, glaze flake at spout, unusual form, late 19th c., 5 3/4" h. (ILLUS. left with spongeware spittoon & washbowl, top of page) **$1,265**

Small Advertising Sponged Syrup Jug

Rare Blue Spongeware Toothbrush Vase

Toothbrush vase, footed baluster-form, wide dark blue on white sponged bands alternating w/two narrow white bands, excellent condition, late 19th - early 20th c., 5" h. (ILLUS.) **$440**

Umbrella stand, tall cylindrical form, decorated w/four wide bands of fine banded blue sponging on white, sponged bands separated by three bands composed of two white bands flanking a narrow blue center band, late 19th - early 20th c., excellent condition, 20 1/2" h. **$770**

Vegetable or loaf dish, shallow oblong form w/arched ends & flaring sides, overall very dense dark blue sponging on white, late 19th c., 9 1/4" l., 2" h. (minor glaze fleck imperfection on exterior) **$99**

Washbowl, footed deep rounded flaring sides w/rolled rim, white ground decorated w/dark blue sponging around the top & base, the center w/two plain white bands flanking a dark blue band, full-length tight glued crack, late 19th - early 20th c., 14" d., 4 1/2" h. (ILLUS. center with spongeware teapot & spittoon).......... **$121**

Blue Sponged Washbowl & Pitcher Set

Washbowl & pitcher, bulbous ovoid pitcher tapering to a wide flaring neck, C-scroll handle, matching bowl w/rolled rim, the pitcher w/overall coarse blue sponging on white w/a wide band in blue & white around the bottom, sponged rim & base bands on the bowl flank the wide blue & white bands, attributed to Red Wing, Minnesota, early 20th c., minor hairline & glaze flake on pitcher, pitcher 12" h. (ILLUS.) **$633**

Blue Spongeware Pig Whimsey Figure

Whimsey, model of a standing pig, white Bristol glaze w/scattered blue spots, some surface chipping, ca. 1990, 5" l. (ILLUS.) **$303**

Staffordshire Figures

Small figures and groups made of pottery were produced by the majority of the Staffordshire, England potters in the 19th century and were used as mantel decorations or "chimney ornaments," as they were sometimes called. Pairs of dogs were favorites and were turned out by the carload, and 19th-century pieces are still available. Well-painted reproductions also abound, and collectors are urged to exercise caution before investing.

Chimney vase, figural, model of a boy kneeling at the right & wearing a pink & green outfit, feeding a white & gold swan to the left, tree trunk vase at back center, decorated in pink, orange & yellow coleslaw, 19th c., 5 1/8" h **$495**

Chimney vase, figural, model of a family of three white swans w/gilt trim, tree trunk vase at back w/orange interior & light blue coleslaw foliage, 19th c., 5" h **$275**

Chimney vases, figural, one w/a standing sheep in white w/sanded coat & long tail & other w/standing matching ram, each standing in front of a tree trunk vase w/coleslaw foliage, oval bases painted red, yellow & green, mid-19th c., 5 1/8" h., facing pair (repair, minor edge damage).................................... **$303**

Staffordshire Spaniels & an Equestrian Group

Dogs, Spaniels, seated position looking at viewer, white w/large rust red spots, yellow chain collars & black face details, hairlines & minor flaking, 7 5/8" h., pr. (ILLUS. left & right w/sportsman equestrian group) **$316**

Equestrian group, a sportsman wearing a brown jacket & black boots mounted on a tan horse, green & brown mounted background base, hairlines, 7" h. (ILLUS. center with pair of spotted Spaniels)............... **$345**

Equestrian group, a young boy wearing a bright red skirted outfit standing in front of a white horse upon which is seated a young girl in a white dress & hat, said to represent Prince Albert & Princess Victoria, children of Queen Victorian, mid-19th c., 12 3/4" h. **$316**

Three Staffordshire Figure Groups

Figure group, a young woman standing & holding a jug at her side, wearing a feathered hat, pink blouse & dotted white dress, a spotted white lamb lying at her feet, applied coleslaw trim, oblong gilt-lined base, 1 3/4 x 3", 6 1/2" h. (ILLUS. center with figures of children on goats, top of page) **$132**

Figure groups, one w/a boy wearing a white outfit seated on a large white goat, the other w/a matching girl, oval gilt-lined bases, girl w/chip on back base, 3 1/4 x 7", 12 1/2" h., facing pr. (ILLUS. left & right with small figure group of standing girl, top of page) **$1,760**

Staffordshire Hens on Nests

Hen on nest, bisque hen trimmed w/grey w/red comb & wattle on amber glazed basketweave base, late 19th c., 9" l. (ILLUS. top right w/other hens on nests) **$748**

Hen on nest, bisque hen trimmed w/grey w/red wattle on custard glazed basketweave base, mid to late 19th c., 11" l. (ILLUS. top left w/other hens on nests)...... **$748**

Hen on nest, h.p. grey hen w/darker grey trim & black w/red comb & wattle on yellow gold glazed basketweave base, 19th c., 9" l. (ILLUS. bottom left w/other hens on nests) **$748**

Hen on nest, hen h.p. in shades of browns & greys, w/red comb & wattle on amber gold glazed basketweave base, 19th c., 9" l. (ILLUS. bottom right w/other hens on nests) **$978**

Staffordshire Leaping Deer Spill Vases

Spill vases, figural, a leaping red & white stag above a spotted hound, all mounted on a green & brown stump-form base w/a central stump vase, 9" l., 11" h., opposing pr. (ILLUS.)...................................... **$316**

Staffordshire Transfer Wares

The process of transfer-printing designs on earthenwares developed in England in the late 18th century, and by the mid-19th century most common ceramic wares were decorated in this manner, most often with romantic European or Oriental landscape scenes, animals or flowers. The earliest such wares were printed in dark blue, but a little later light blue, pink, purple, red, black, green and brown were used. A majority of these wares were produced at various English potteries right up until the turn of the 20th century, but French and other European firms also made similar pieces and all are quite collectible. The best reference on this area is Petra Williams' book Staffordshire Romantic Transfer Patterns - Cup Plates and Early Victorian China *(Fountain House East, 1978).*

Two Early Staffordshire Transfer-printed Platters

Platter, 12 x 15" oval, Bologna patt. by Adams, blue, ca. 1830s (knife marks w/light staining)... **$330**

Platter, 15 3/4" l., long octagonal shape, the center w/a romantic European landscape, the border design of flowering vines, dark mulberry grey, Rhone patt., Thomas, John & Joseph Mayer, ca. 1843-55 (ILLUS. right with Japan Flowers platter, top of page)............................ **$259**

Platter, 17" l., oval w/gently scalloped rim, the center w/a large urn of flowers in the foreground & an exotic garden in the background, four small scenic panels around the rim alternating w/long scroll & floral panels, deep rose on white, Japan Flowers patt., Ridgway, Morley, Wear & Company, ca. 1836-42 (ILLUS. left with Rhone pattern platter, top of page) **$259**

#18," first quarter 19th c. (ILLUS., below) **$1,150**

Early Dark Blue Stubbs Platter

Platter, 16 x 19 1/2" oval, Parisian Chateau patt. by R. Hall, brown, ca. 1840s (rim wear).. **$605**

Large Mulberry Vdina Platter

Platter, 17 1/2" l., octagonal, the center w/a large exotic mountainous landscape, the border band w/scroll-bordered panels of large roses, dark greyish mulberry on white, Vdina patt., Joseph Clementson, ca. 1845-64 (ILLUS.) **$460**

Platter, 15 1/4 x 18 1/4" oval, the oval center decorated w/a large cluster of fruit, the wide body band decorated w/large clusters of flowers alternating w/scrolled panels, early deep blue, back marked "Stubbs

Aesthetic Movement Style Soup Plates

Soup plates, round, Aesthetic Movement style, a Japonesque design w/a large fan w/ribbons in the center, the border band w/arched panels of Oriental motifs, dark blue on white, Browne-Westhead, Moore & Co., England, ca. 1875, 10" d., set of 9 (ILLUS.).. **$230**

Sugar bowl, cov., deep bulbous boat-form w/small tab handle & flaring collar, high domed cover w/floral finial, dark blue scene of a man pulled on a low sled by two galloping horses, deer & woods in the backgrounde, thistle design on the cover, England, ca. 1830, 6 1/2" h. **$770**

English Victorian Staffordshire Tea Set

Tea set: cov. teapot, cov. sugar bowl, creamer, two handled cups & saucers & a large undertray; each serving piece of upright diamond shape, each wide side panel decorated w/overall small salmon-colored flowers separated by a narrow panel decorated w/stylized black cranes, blue & black floral neck border, mark of Powell & Bishop, England, second half 19th c., minor gilt wear, small flake on teapot spout, tray 14 x 21 1/2", teapot 5" h., the set (ILLUS.)................................ **$330**

Stangl Pottery

Johann Martin Stangl, who first came to work for the Fulper Pottery in 1910 as a ceramic chemist and plant superintendent, acquired a financial interest and became president of the company in 1926. The name of the firm was changed to Stangl Pottery in 1929 and at that time much of the production was devoted to a high grade dinnerware to enable the company to survive the Depression years. One of the earliest solid-color dinnerware patterns was its Colonial line, introduced in 1926. In the 1930s it was joined by the Americana pattern. After 1942 these early patterns were followed by a wide range of hand-decorated patterns featuring flowers and fruits, with a few decorated with animals or human figures.

Around 1940 a very limited edition of porcelain birds, patterned after the illustrations in John James Audubon's "Birds of America," was issued. Stangl subsequently began production of less expensive ceramic birds, which proved to be popular during the war years 1940-46. Each bird was handpainted and well marked with impressed, painted or stamped numerals indicating the species and the size.

All operations ceased at the Trenton, New Jersey, plant in 1978.

Two reference books collectors will find helpful are The Collectors Handbook of Stangl Pottery by Norma Rehl (The Democrat Press, 1979), and

Stangl Pottery by Harvey Duke (Wallace-Homestead, 1994).

Stangl Mark

Birds

Audubon Warbler, pair, No. 3756-D, 7 3/4" h. **$425**

Two Stangl Bluebird Figures

Bluebird, No. 3276-S, 5" h. (ILLUS. right with Bluebirds) **$125**
Bluebirds (double), No. 3276-D, 8 1/2" h. (ILLUS. left with single Bluebird figure) **$250**
Bobolink, No. 3595, 4 3/4" h. **$300**
Canary, Blue Flower, No. 3747, 6 1/4" h. **$210**
Cardinal (female), pine cones, No. 3444, 6" h. **$125**
Chat (Carolina Wren), No. 3590, 4 1/4" h. **$260**
Cliff Swallow, No. 3852, 3 1/4" h. **$150**
Cockatoo, large, No. 3584, 11 3/8" h. **$395**
Duck, flying, No. 3443, 9" **$331**
Parakeets, No. 3582D, blue/green, 7" h., pr. **$325**

Two Stangl Pheasant Cock Figures

Pheasant Cock, No. 3492, 11" l., the set (ILLUS. of two)................................. **$250-300**
Red-Headed Woodpeckers, double, ornate leaf & blossom branches on a white oval base, one reglued leaf, more ornate than usual model, 7 1/2" w., 7 1/2" h. **$4,406**
Red-Headed Woodpeckers, No. 3752-D, 7 3/4" h., pr. **$495**
Redstarts, No. 3490-D, 9" h., pr. **$325**
Rooster, No. 3445, 9" h. **$250**
Scissor-Tailed Flycatcher, No. 3757, 11" h. **$895**

Wrens, No. 3401-D, 8", pr. **$75**

Other Wares

Stangl Charger with Painted Tulip

Charger, round, h.p. in the Pennsylvania Dutch style w/a large stylized yellow, brown & green tulip, pale green & yellow banded border, marked, No. 3319, 14 1/2" d. (ILLUS.) **$100-200**

Squatty Tangerine Stangl Vase

Vase, 4 7/8" h., squatty bulbous form tapering to a short flared neck flanked by shoulder handles, tangerine glaze h.p. w/green leaves & black seed pods, ca. 1931, small glaze nick on handles (ILLUS.) **$115**

Stangl Tropical Ware Decorated Vase

Vase, 7 1/4" h., bulbous double-gourd form w/flared neck, deep orange ground applied around the sides w/blue S-scrolls, Tropical Ware line, ca. 1935, Shape 2024-7", impressed mark (ILLUS.) **$345**

Steins

Colorful 19th Century Faience Stein

Faience, cylindrical, h.p. around the sides w/oblong deep rose panels each w/a colorful flower, a background of small blue stars & small colored blossoms, Erfurt, domed pewter cover w/ball thumbrest, cover hinge a replacement, ca. 1870, 1 L, 11" h. (ILLUS.) **$817**

Hauber & Reuther, pottery, etched color decoration of a trumpeter on horseback, ringed & domed pewter cover, .5 L (ILLUS. center with two other Hauber & Reuther steins) **$247**

Three Colorful Hauber & Reuther Steins

Hauber & Reuther, pottery, etched color decoration of men bowling, high ringed & pointed dome cover, No. 175, .5 L (ILLUS. left with two other Hauber & Reuther steins) **$277**

Hauber & Reuther, pottery, etched colorful design of people rowing in a boat, peaked & domed pewter cover, No. 446,

.5 L (ILLUS. right with two other Hauber &
Reuther steins).. **$261**

Three Tall Colorful Mettlach Steins

Mettlach, No. 2176-1055, painted-under-
glaze (PUG) w/a colorful festive scene,
signed by artist H. Schlitt, domed pewter
cover, 2.1 L (ILLUS. center with two other
tall Mettlach steins) **$524**

Mettlach, No. 2261-1012, PUG, a colorful
scene of Germans meeting Romans, artist H. Schlitt, domed pewter cover, 2.25 L
(ILLUS. left with two other tall Mettlach
steins) **$564**

Lovely Meissen Porcelain Stein

Meissen porcelain, cylindrical w/a hinged
porcelain cover, the front w/a large four-
lobed reserve painted in full color w/an
elaborate battle scene w/men on horseback, the cobalt blue background completely covered w/ornate gold leafy
scrolls, blue Crossed Swords mark, 19th
c., .25 L, 5 1/4" h. (ILLUS.)..................... **$4,649**

Two Mettlach Steins with Pointed Covers

Mettlach, No. 2382, etched color design of
an armored knight in a tavern, titled "The
Thirsty Rider," pointed roof-style pottery
cover, hairline repair in rear, 1 L (ILLUS.
left with Mettlach No. 2580) **$544**

Mettlach, No. 2430, etched color scene of a
Cavalier seated on the edge of a tavern
table, inlaid cover, 3 L (ILLUS. right with
two other tall Mettlach steins) **$1,208**

Mettlach, No. 2580, etched scene of a knight
& village people, DeKannenburg, pointed
pottery roof-style cover, 1 L (ILLUS. right
with Mettlach No. 2382 stein)................. **$1,032**

Bismarck & Comic Scene Mettlachs

Mettlach, No. 1794, etched portrait of Otto
von Bismarck, inlaid cover, .5 L (ILLUS.
left with Mettlach No. 2880 stein).............. **$506**

Mettlach, No. 2880, etched scene of men pouring water down a sleeping man's shirt, artist F. Quidenus, inlaid cover, 1 L (ILLUS. right with No. 1794 Bismarck stein, previous page)............................... **$357**

Large Mettlach Faience Stein

Mettlach, No. 5102, faience, footed tall baluster-form body w/a flaring neck, domed hinged pewter cover w/ball thumbrest, h.p. w/shades of dark blue w/a portrait of a man in Renaissance dress holding a goblet, blue scalloped band trim, .5 L (ILLUS.).......................... **$1,265**

Pewter, footed bulbous body w/a low domed hinged cover, the front cast in relief w/a horned devil head, pewter cover, marked "Riceszinn 559," Germany, 19th c., .5 L (ILLUS. right with two other pewter steins, below)...................................... **$193**

Three Old European Pewter Steins

Pewter, round domed foot & cylindrical plain sides w/a flattened domed cover, cover etched w/"FWF 1827," touch marks under cover, minor dents & scratches, Europe, 1 L (ILLUS. left with two other pewter steins) **$190**

Pewter, three ringed ball feet supporting the cylindrical body w/cartouches above each foot & a large engraved crest on the front, stepped & domed cover, pewter lid w/coin in center, marked "F. Samesson Stockholm Hvit Metall," Sweden, 19th c., 1 L (ILLUS. center with two other pewter steins, previous column)........................... **$144**

Regimental, pottery, tall ringed cylindrical body w/a flaring base, the wide center band painted w/a soldier on horseback above a small bust portrait, four side scenes & roster, domed pewter cover w/eagle thumblift, marked "2 Comp. Hannov. Train Batl. Nr. 10 Hannover 1909-11," dent to finial, .5 L, 13 1/2" h. (ILLUS. right with other Regimental stein) **$725**

Two German Regimental Steins

Regimental, pottery, tall ringed cylindrical body w/a flaring base, the wide center band decorated w/German sailors & naval symbols, two side scenes & roster, marked "S.M.S. Rheiland 1908-11," domed pewter cover w/figural eagle thumblift w/inset Stanhope, 1 L, 14 1/2" h. (ILLUS. left with other Regimental stein) **$1,328**

Stoneware

Stoneware is essentially a vitreous pottery, impervious to water even in its unglazed state, that has been produced by potteries all over the world for centuries. Utilitarian wares such as crocks, jugs, churns and the like were the most common productions in the numerous potteries that sprang into existence in the United States during the 19th century. These items were often enhanced by the application of a cobalt blue oxide decoration. In addition to the coarse, primarily salt-glazed stonewares, there are other categories of stoneware known by such special names as basalt, jasper and others.

der loops, design fry on blue, large, long stack mark in the back design, surface wear at base & bail handle, use staining, ca. 1850, 1 gal., 9" h. (ILLUS.)...... **$880**

Bottle, figural, model of a recumbent pig, decorated w/cobalt blue spots & accents on the face, unsigned, two flakes, wear on ears & snout, late 19th - early 20th c., 6 1/8" l. **$978**

Rare Early Stoneware Anchovy Jar

Anchovy jar, wide cylindrical body w/angled shoulder to a wide molded mouth, blue-trimmed impressed swimming fish & balloon design all around the shoulder, attributed to Old Bridge, New Jersey potter, in-the-making dark clay color, rare, ca. 1810, 1 qt., 6 1/2" h. (ILLUS.) **$743**

Bank, figural, reclining cat w/head raised & back leg lifted & scratching its side, realistic molded fur & details, overall mottled brown Rockingham glaze, probably 20th c., 6" h. **$44**

Small Churn with Clover Decoration

Butter churn, swelled cylindrical body tapering to a thick molded mouth flanked by eared handles, cobalt blue slip-quilled large three-leaf clover design below the blue-tinted impressed mark of S. L. Pewtress & Co., Fairhaven, Connecticut & a size number, design fry, uncommon small size, ca. 1880, 2 gal., 12" h. (ILLUS.).. **$358**

Cowden & Wilcox Early Batter Jug

Batter jug, wide ovoid body tapering to a short, wide cylindrical neck, short angled shoulder spout, shoulder loops for holding the wire bail handle w/turned wood grip, cobalt blue brushed drooping flower below the impressed mark of Cowden & Wilcox, Harrisburg, Pennsylvania, on the back, brushed plume accents at spout & shoul-

Rare Early Iowa Stoneware Butter Churn

Butter churn, tall slightly tapering cylindrical body w/a flared molded rim & eared handles, cobalt blue brushed long stylized floral design at the top below the impressed mark "Cedar Falls, Iowa - 6," probably by Martin White, ca. 1865, crack on reverse w/minor losses, 6 gal., 17 1/4" h. (ILLUS.) **$2,875**

Churn with Paddletail Bird & Flowers

Butter churn, slightly ovoid body w/a molded rim & eared handles, slip-quilled cobalt blue large paddletail bird perched on a long flowering stem, fine shading & detail, impressed mark of N.A. White & Son, Utica, New York, chip at front & right ear professionally repaired, tight short hairline from rim on back, ca. 1870, 3 gal., 15" h. (ILLUS.) **$9,900**

Churn with Less Detailed Bird & Flower

Butter churn, slightly ovoid body w/a molded rim & eared handles, slip-quilled cobalt blue large paddletail bird perched on a long flowering stem, impressed mark of N.A. White & Son, Utica, New York, chip at leaf ear professionally restored, ca. 1870, 3 gal., 16" h. (ILLUS.)................... **$2,420**

Butter Churn with Large Stylized Flower

Butter churn, tall slightly ovoid body w/molded rim & eared handles, cobalt blue large slip-quilled bull's-eye flower design, impressed mark of New York Stoneware Co., Fort Edward, New York, ca. 1880, 5 gal., 17 1/2" h. (ILLUS.) **$330**

Nice Covered Cake Crock with Flowers

Cake crock, cov., eared handles, large cobalt blue brushed flower & leaves band around the sides, flat cover w/brushed blue leaves, unsigned, couple of rim chips, extensive knob chipping on cover, ca. 1850, 2 gal., 11" d., 7" h. (ILLUS.) **$688**

Early Cream Pot with Script Name

Cream pot, ovoid body w/a wide cylindrical neck & flat rim flanked by eared handles, double stamped "2" above a cobalt blue script "Butter" on one side & "Dolly" on the other side, probably New York state, ca. 1840, professional restoration to a hairline, 2 gal., 10 1/2" h. (ILLUS.) **$798**

Cream Pot with Bold Blue Flowers

Cream pot, ovoid form w/a molded rim & eared handles, slip-quilled large cobalt

blue blossoms on leafy stems below the number "3," impressed mark of T. Harrington, Lyons, New York, washed in blue, ca. 1850, 3 gal., 12" h. (ILLUS.)..... **$2,200**

Unsigned Flower-decorated Small Crock

Crock, flat-bottomed wide ovoid body tapering to a flattened molded wide mouth, light cobalt blue large brushed tulip above leaves design, unsigned but probably Pennsylvania origin, minor glaze burn or cinnamon clay color occurred in the making, minor surface wear & use staining on the back, ca. 1850, 1 pt., 5 1/4" h. (ILLUS.) **$688**

Crock, bulbous ovoid body w/a wide slightly flared mouth flanked by eared handles, large brushed cobalt blue tulip design below the impressed mark of C. Hart & Co., Ogdensburg, New York, & impressed number, some glaze spider cracks & crazing on back, ca. 1855, 2 gal., 10" h. (ILLUS. right with two other New York state crocks, bottom of page)................... **$220**

Crock, bulbous ovoid body w/a wide slightly flared mouth flanked by eared handles, cobalt blue slip-quilled antler design below a number, impressed mark of John B. Caire & Co., Pokeepsie (sic), New York, very tight hairline behind one handle, X-shaped body spider crack by other, heavy wear to interior brown Albany slip glaze, fairly uncommon maker, ca. 1850, 3 gal., 10" h. (ILLUS. left with two other New York state crocks, bottom of page).... **$220**

Three Early Crocks from New York State

Crock, cylindrical w/thick molded rim & eared handles, cobalt blue slip-quilled design of a flying bird chasing a butterfly, unsigned, probably New York state origin, surface chipping on inner & outer rim, two hairlines extending from rim at front & back of left handle, ca. 1880, 3 gal., 10 1/2" h. $495

Crock, bulbous ovoid body w/a wide slightly flared mouth flanked by eared handles, cobalt blue large brushed stylized flower & stem below the blue-trimmed impressed mark "Manufactured for and Sold by Chapman & Thorp, Oxford, NY," rare mark, probably Albany area, cinnamon-colored glaze, stack marks, 3 gal., 12 1/2" h. (ILLUS. center with two other New York state crocks, bottom of previous page) $743

Advertising Crock with Large Hen

Crock, advertising-type, cylindrical w/molded rim & eared handles, slip-quilled cobalt blue large hen pecking at corn, impressed advertising for Cornells & Mumford, Providence, Rhode Island, above a "2", unsigned Norton of Bennington pieces, ca. 1865, 2 gal., 9 1/2" h. (ILLUS.) $3,300

Unique Crock with a Camel Scene

Crock, wide cylindrical form w/molded rim & eared handles, cobalt-blue slip-quilled

decoration of a standing camel w/palm trees & a pyramid in the distance, impressed mark of Wm. A. Macquoid & Co., Little Wst. 12th St., New York, New York, small rim chip on front, tight full-length hairline on back, ca. 1870, 1 1/2 gal., 10" h. (ILLUS.) $12,650

Fat Bird & Leaf Decor on Three-gallon Crock

Crock, cylindrical w/molded rim & eared handles, cobalt blue slip-quilled fat bird w/head up perched on a small leafy sprig, impressed mark "Ottman Bros. & Co. - Fort Edward, NY - 3," professional restoration to full-length hairline on front, ca. 1870, 3 gal., 10" h. (ILLUS.) $209

Bennington Crock with Slender Bird

Crock, cylindrical w/molded rim & eared handle, dark cobalt blue slip-quilled slender bird w/crest perched on a leafy sprig design below the impressed mark "E. & L. P. Norton - Bennington, VT - 3," small stone ping in the design w/minor stain, stabilized long hairline from rim on the back, ca. 1880, 3 gal., 10 1/2" h. (ILLUS.)
.... $633

Boldly Decorated John Bell Crock

Crock, cov., ovoid w/eared handles & a wide molded rim, heavy brushed cobalt blue bands of leafy flowering vines around the sides & on the cover, also blue-slip date "1874" under each handle, impressed mark of John Bell, Waynesboro, Pennsylvania, tightly glued hairline behind right handle, small piece reglued, ca. 1874, 4 gal., 13" h. (ILLUS.) **$11,550**

Two-Gallon Jar with Large Flower

Jar, cylindrical tapering to a short upright rim & eared handles, slip-quilled cobalt blue large stylized flower & leaves w/a number "2" beside them, impressed mark of F. Stetzenmeyer & G. Goetzman, Rochester, New York, washed in blue, very tight line through bottom, surface chip at base of right handle, ca. 1857, 2 gal., 11" h. (ILLUS.) **$1,430**

Crock with Very Rare Decoration

Crock, cylindrical w/eared handles & molded rim, slip-quilled cobalt blue extremely detailed scene of a large reclining stag & fence in the foreground & a large house & tree in the distance, impressed mark of J. & E. Norton, Bennington, Vermont, & a "5," minor surface chipping to rim interior, very tight minor hairline in left handle, ca. 1855, 5 gal., 13" h. (ILLUS.) **$23,650**

Cortland, New York Jug with Starburst Design

Jug, cylindrical body w/rounded shoulder tapering to a molded mouth, applied strap handle, unusual bold slip-quilled cobalt blue four-petal starburst w/arrows & dots design, impressed mark of Cortland, New York, minor glaze wear, surface chip on back base, ca. 1860, 1 gal., 11" h. (ILLUS.) **$578**

blue slip-quilled long parrot perched on a vertical leafy sprig below the impressed mark "F.B. Norton and Co. - Worcester, Mass. - 2," excellent condition, ca. 1870, 2 gal., 13 1/2" h. (ILLUS.) **$1,485**

Jug with a Large Stylized Flower

Advertising Jug Made in Lyons, New York

Jug, flat-bottomed beehive shape w/small mouth & strap handle, advertising-type w/brushed cobalt blue inscription reading "R.H. Gilgallon - Scranton - Pa" & "2," made by Co-operative Pottery Co., Lyons, New York, cinnamon clay color in the making & some staining from use, ca. 1890, 2 gal., 12 1/2" h. (ILLUS.)................ **$275**

Jug, ovoid body tapering to a small molded mouth, slip-quilled cobalt blue large eight-petalled flower blossom w/fine shading & the number "2" above it, impressed mark of N. Clark & Co., Rochester, New York, washed in blue, couple of minor stack marks, ca. 1850, 2 gal., 14 1/2" h. (ILLUS.) **$3,520**

Jug, flat-bottomed beehive shape w/small cylindrical mouth & strap handle, impressed mark reading "Wm. Radam's Microbe Killer Co.," trimmed in blue, ca. 1890-1900, 10 3/8" h. **$96**

Rare Early "Brandy" Keg

F.B. Norton Jug with Parrot Design

Jug, cylindrical body tapering to a small molded mouth & strap handle, cobalt

Keg, barrel-shaped, molded pairs of horizontal bands trimmed in cobalt blue, top band hand-incised "BRANDY" trimmed in blue, the center band incised w/a scene of a rowboat & oars trimmed in blue, impressed mark of Tyler & Dillon, Albany, New York, chip on left to edge, hairline across from chip, short-lived pottery, ca. 1825, 2 gal., 13 1/2" h. (ILLUS.)............. **$5,500**

Stoneware Milk Pan with Plume Decor

Milk pan, deep slightly flaring cylindrical sides w/a molded rim & pinched spout, decorated w/five small brushed cobalt blue plumes around the sides & three dashes under the spout, unsigned, size designation tooled just below the spout, X-shaped hairline at the base w/a grease stain, ca. 1850, 1 1/2 gal., 11 1/2" d., 6" h. (ILLUS.) **$330**

Brown-glazed Stoneware Pitcher

Pitcher, 8 1/2" h., footed bulbous body tapering to a tall neck w/molded rim & deeply molded spout, strap handle, unsigned, overall dark brown alkaline glaze, some very minor surface chipping at the back rim, ca. 1870, 1/2 gal. (ILLUS.) **$303**

Small Stoneware Begging Spaniel Figure

Model of a dog, seated begging spaniel in cream w/dark bluish green applied accents under the Bristol glaze, probably from Ohio, possibly early 20th c., minor surface wear, 5 1/2" h. (ILLUS.)................ **$495**

Tall Stoneware Pitcher with Cherries

Pitcher, 10" h., ovoid body tapering to a wide cylindrical neck w/pinched spout, impressed 3/4 capacity mark below the spout & above a cobalt blue brushed cluster of cherries decoration, unsigned but probably from New Jersey or Pennsylvania, glaze burn & mottled clay color, ca. 1850 (ILLUS.)............................ **$990**

Preserve jar, cov., cylindrical body tapering to a wide, low cupped rim w/inset flat cover w/button finial, overall mottled dark green alkaline glaze, unsigned, ca. 1860, excellent condition, 1 qt., 5 3/4" h. **$55**

Preserve jar, advertising-type, gently swelled cylindrical form tapering to a molded rim, cobalt blue brushed double plain bands & a squiggle band around the top & a single plain band around the base, the whole center of the side stenciled in cobalt blue w/inscription reading "From Ood's Hardpan Crockery - Lockhaven, PA," the oversized "C" & "Y" in "Crockery" flanking the center part of the inscription, a stenciled size number flanked by leafy scrolls below the inscription, unknown maker, excellent condition, ca. 1870, 2 gal., 11 1/2" h. **$1,705**

Preserve jar, tapering cylindrical form w/molded rim & eared handles, slip-quilled cobalt blue swimming fish, impressed mark of H.M. Whitman, Havana, New York, trimmed in blue, w/original hand-wrought iron lid, ca. 1860, 1 gal., 9" h. (ILLUS.) **$7,425**

Preserve Jar with Nice Incised Flowers

Preserve jar, cylindrical tapering slightly to an upright rim & eared handles, finely incised design of large double pod-like flowers on leafy stems washed w/cobalt blue, impressed mark of J.M. Mott & Co., Ithaca, New York, washed w/blue, minor staining, ca. 1855, 2 gal., 11" h. (ILLUS.) **$3,630**

Preserve Jar with Blue Inscription

Preserve jar, cov., cylindrical body tapering to a flaring flat neck & inset cover w/disk finial, large cobalt blue slip-quilled "2 Quarts" in script below a round blue-trimmed tooled & impressed circle mark for a Cortland, New York factory, ca. 1860, 2 qt., 7 1/2" h. (ILLUS.) **$303**

Rare Fish-decorated Preserve Jar

Preserve Jar with Rare Long Horn Cow

Preserve jar, cov., tapering cylindrical form w/eared handles & short flared rim w/inset cover, slip-quilled cobalt blue scene of a Texas Long Horn steer, impressed mark of Cowden & Wilcox, Harrisburg, Pennsylvania, & a "3," over-glazed in the making, ca. 1870, 3 gal., 12 1/2" h. (ILLUS.) **$14,300**

Bennington Preserve Jar with Stag

Preserve jar, cylindrical tapering body w/a molded rim & eared handles, slip-quilled cobalt blue elaborate scene of a large reclining stag w/fences & fir trees, impressed mark of J. & E. Norton, Bennington, Vermont, washed in blue, surface wear at rim interior, few glaze flakes, ca. 1855, 4 gal., 14 1/2" h. (ILLUS.)............. **$9,350**

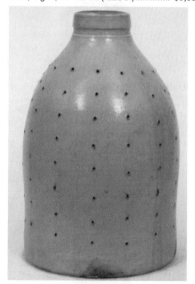

Unusual Stoneware Strainer-Jug

Strainer-jug, cylindrical body tapering to a short wide molded mouth, no handle, pierced overall w/strips of small holes down the sides, possibly an oyster strainer, unmarked, stack marks at base, some minor use staining, ca. 1870, 2 gal., 13 1/2" h. (ILLUS.) **$358**

Water cooler, cov., wide cylindrical form relief-molded around the sides w/a scene

of an elk in a forest setting, overall cobalt blue glaze, pine boughs & cones around the cover, metal spigot at the front base, minor chips under the cover, late 19th - early 20th c., 14 3/4" h. **$345**

Unusual Decorative Stoneware Water Cooler

Water cooler, wide disk foot supporting a wide tapering bulbous urn-form body w/loop shoulder handles, incised large addorsed perched birds trimmed in cobalt blue, brushed cobalt decoration of dots, lines & sprig bands around the neck & shoulder, the back w/a brushed cobalt blue double flower in a pot, mark of the Somerset Potters Works, Massachusetts, kiln burn on front, glued crack on front, in-the-making chip out of bung hole frame, ca. 1870, 3 gal., 15" h. (ILLUS.).... **$3,960**

Water Cooler with a Plump Bird

Water cooler, wide ovoid body w/bung hole at bottom front, eared handles, short cylindrical neck w/molded rim, slip-quilled cobalt blue large plump bird perched on a

scrolled branch, fine detail, impressed
mark of O.L. & A.K. Ballard, Burlington,
Vermont, couple of very tight hairlines
from rim, few glaze spiders & flakes, professional restoration to chip at bung
hole, ca. 1870, 6 gal., 15" h. (ILLUS.) **$2,640**

Teco Pottery

*Teco Pottery was actually the line of art pottery
introduced by the American Terra Cotta and
Ceramic Company of Terra Cotta (Crystal Lake),
Illinois, in 1902. Founded by William D. Gates in
1881, American Terra Cotta originally produced
only bricks and drain tile. Because of superior
facilities for experimentation, including a chemical laboratory, the company was able to develop
an art pottery line, favoring a matte green glaze
in the earlier years but eventually achieving a
wide range of colors including a metallic lustre
glaze and a crystalline glaze. Although some
hand-thrown pottery was made, Gates favored a
molded ware because it was less expensive to produce. By 1923, Teco Pottery was no longer being
made, and in 1930 American Terra Cotta and
Ceramic Company was sold. A book on the topic
is* Teco: Art Pottery of the Prairie School, *by
Sharon S. Darling (Erie Art Museum, 1990).*

Teco Mark

Vase, 5 1/4" h., 3" w., ovoid body framed by
low integral buttress handles up the sides
& joining the short cylindrical neck,
smooth matte green glaze, stamped
mark **$1,410**

Squatty Teco Vase with Loop Handles

Vase, 5 1/2" h., 8 1/2" l., squatty bulbous
oblong form w/the sides pulled up to form
integral loop handles flowing into the
widely flaring rim of the short flaring neck,
overall smooth matte green glaze,
stamped mark (ILLUS.) **$1,998**
Vase, 6 3/4" h., 5 1/2" d., bulbous double-
gourd body w/four heavy curved &
squared handles from the base to the
wide flat mouth, designed by W.B.

Teco Double Gourd Handled Vase

Mundie, charcoal matte green glaze,
stamped mark (ILLUS.) **$4,313**

Unusual Glossy Crystalline Teco Vase

Vase, 11 1/4" h., footed bulbous bottle-form
body w/tall gently flaring neck, glossy
crystalline glaze in swirled deep reds &
black, unmarked, tiny stilt pull on base
(ILLUS.) **$748**

Extremely Rare Figural Teco Vase

Vase, 22 5/8" h., rare design reminiscent of Van Briggle's "Lorelei" vase, the top mounted by a finely modeled nude wrapping backward around the small opening, the tall slender slightly swelled cylindrical body also molded w/a leafy vine down around the sides, all w/a mottled green glaze, stamped mark & No. 228, figure & one large leaf at top broken off & professionally restored (ILLUS., previous page) **$24,150**

Tiffany Pottery

In 1902 Louis C. Tiffany expanded Tiffany Studios to include ceramics, enamels, gold, silver and gemstones. Tiffany pottery was usually molded rather than wheel-thrown, but it was carefully finished by hand. A limited amount was produced until about 1914. It is scarce.

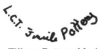

Tiffany Pottery Mark

Tiffany Favrile Vases

Vase, 6 3/4" h., Favrile bronze pottery type, cylindrical shape w/molded flowers & stems in relief, signed on bottom "LCT" conjoined & "BP197" w/"L," ca. 1910-14 (ILLUS. left w/Tiffany Favrile plant-form vase) **$2,358**

Vase, 6 3/4" h., Favrile, plant form, bulbous base w/three handles forming stems of leaves that form neck of vase, glazed in cream, shades of green & black, signed on base "Tiffany Favrile Pottery P1014" & "LCT" conjoined w/"L," ca. 1910 (ILLUS. right w/Tiffany Favrile bronze pottery vase) **$8,913**

Tiles

Tiles have been made by potteries in the United States and abroad for many years. Apart from small tea tiles used on tables, there are also decorative tiles for fireplaces, floors and walls. This is where present collector interest lies, especially in the late 19th century American-made art pottery tiles.

American Encaustic Tile Tableau

American Encaustic Tiling Co., Los Angeles, California, branch, a vertical rectangular tableau composed of twenty-four 4" tiles depicting white water lily blossoms w/purple & green leaves floating on mottled pale blue & brown water, factory closed in 1929, mounted on plywood, 17 x 25" (ILLUS.) **$978**

Rare Arketex Corp. Tile

Arketex Corp., Brazil, Indiana, square boldly molded in high-relief w/a stylized grotesque face of a cougar, mottled gold w/blue highlights & cobalt blue border (ILLUS.) **$995**

Long Tile with Galleons at Sea

Cambridge Art Pottery Portrait Tile

Cambridge Art Pottery, Cambridge, Ohio, square, molded in low-relief w/a realistic bust profile of a pretty young Victorian lady w/sausage curls, signed on back, very minor back edge nicks, 6" sq. (ILLUS.) **$138**

Cook Pottery Co., Trenton, New Jersey (attributed), rectangular, a detailed incised & glazed seascape w/two large galleons under full sail in the foreground, smaller ships in the distance, a crystalline glaze in shades of brown, mustard yellow, brick red, black, pale blue & green, black slip mark on the back "Delft," minor edge chips, early 20th c., overall 4 1/8 x 8 3/8" (ILLUS., top of page) **$690**

Hartford Faience Company, Hartford, Connecticut, rectangular, entitled "Eventide," showing a half-length portrait of a pretty young woman holding a cluster of flowers, golden hair & dark blue cloak, brown & green rockwork background & blue sky, molded grout lines, cement covering on the back, right upper corner broken & repaired, framed, 8 x 13" (ILLUS., below) **$5,290**

Hartford Faience Portrait Tile

Pair of International Tile Co. Tiles

International Tile and Trim Co., Brooklyn, New York, square, a facing pair, one w/a low-relief bust profile portrait of a beaded cavalier, the other w/a bust portrait of a young woman wearing a simple bonnet, overall glossy golden glaze, impressed marks on back, few small chips to one, firing line in rear on other, 6" w., pr. (ILLUS.) **$230**

Large Framed Owens Seascape Tile

Arts & Crafts Landscape Tile by Mosaic

Mosaic Tile Co., Zanesville, Ohio, square, Arts & Crafts landscape of leafy trees w/a cottage in the distance, in pastel colors of turquoise blue, lavender, deep purple, pink & creamy yellow, impressed mark, in old frame & mounting, unobtrusive nicks on back edge, 6" w. (ILLUS.) **$575**

Owens (J.B.) Pottery, Zanesville, Ohio, large rectangular plaque-type, raised line seascape showing two galleons sailing on churning sea composed of various shades of green, billowing white & lavender clouds in the blue sky, impressed marks on back, in a new wide flat black wood frame, small edge chips covered by frame, couple of nearly invisible pinpoint nicks to raised lines, early 20th c., 11 7/8 x 17 1/2" (ILLUS., top of page) **$4,830**

Harris Strong Sailboats Tile Tableau

Strong (Harris G.), long rectangular tableau composed of 12 square tiles, forming a Modernistic stylized seascape w/racing sailboats on choppy water in shades of moss green, lavender, deep purple, light blue, white & dark brown, original wooden frame, overall 12 x 35 1/2" (ILLUS., bottom previous page) **$345**

Framed Harris Strong Tile Tableaux

Strong (Harris G.), two matching tableaux, the first comprised of twelve tiles forming a scene of natives in colorful outfits seated beneath umbrellas, the second, also w/twelve tiles, showing a scene of water buffalo lying outside a thatched hut, labels read "High Fired Hand Painted Ceramic Tiles by Harris G. Strong," framed, each 18 x 24", pr. (ILLUS.) **$1,035**

One of Two Trent Tile Scenic Sets

Trent Tile Co., Trenton, New Jersey, rectangular, sets of three square tiles forming

a scene, one showing three Classical maidens reclining in a woodland, the other showing a Classical maiden reaching up to pick cherries, overall shaded mulberry glossy glaze, each in a new wide black wood frame, impressed marks, some minor chips on high points & edges, each tile 6" sq., two sets (ILLUS. of one set) **$863**

Torquay Pottery

In the second half of the 19th century several art potteries were established in the South Devon region of England to take advantage of a belt of fine red clay there. The coastal town of Torquay gives its name to this range of wares, which often featured incised sgraffito decoration or colorful country-style decoration with mottos.

The most notable potteries operating in the Torquay area were the Watcombe Pottery, The Torquay Terra-cotta Company and the Aller Vale Art Pottery, which merged with Watcombe Pottery in 1901 and continued production until 1962. Other firms whose wares are collectible include Longpark Pottery and The Devonmoor Art Pottery.

Early wares feature unglazed terra cotta items in the Victorian taste including classical busts, statuary and vases and some painted and glazed wares including examples with a celeste blue interior or highlights. In addition to sgraffito designs, other decorations included flowers, Barbotine glazes, Devon pixies framed in leafy scrolls and grotesque figures of cats, dogs and other fanciful animals, produced in the 1890s.

The dozen or so potteries flourishing in the region at the turn of the 20th century introduced their most popular product, Motto Wares, which became the bread and butter line of the local industry. The most popular patterns in this line included Cottage, Black and Colored Cockerels and Scandy, based on Scandinavian rosemaling designs. Most of the mottoes were written in English, with a few in Welsh. On early examples the sayings were often in Devonian dialect. These Motto Wares were sold for years at area seaside resorts and other tourist areas, with some pieces exported to Australia, Canada and, to a lesser extent, the United States. In addition to standard size teawares and novelties, some miniatures and even oversized pieces were offered.

Production at the potteries stopped during World War II, and some of the plants were destroyed in enemy raids. The Watcombe Pottery became Royal Watcombe after the war, and Longpark also started up again but produced simpler patterns. The Dartmouth Pottery, started in 1947, produced cottages similar to those made at Watcombe and also developed a line of figural animals, banks and novelty jugs. The Babbacombe Pottery (1950-59) and St. Marychurch Pottery (ca. 1962-69) were the last two firms to turn out Motto Wares, but these later designs were painted on and the pieces were lighter in color, with less detailing.

Many books on the various potteries are available, and information can be obtained from the products manager of the North American Torquay Society.

Torquay Pottery Marks

Smaller "Lakes" Teapot by Watcombe

Teapot, cov., faience "Lakes" decoration, very wide sharply tapering cylindrical body w/small inset cover w/knob finial, a very popular pattern in England but seldom offered in the U.S., Watcombe Pottery, 6" l., 4" h. (ILLUS.) **$165**

Watcombe Faience "Lakes" Teapot

Teapot, cov., faience "Lakes" decoration, wide tapering cylindrical body w/small inset cover w/knob finial, a very popular pattern in England but seldom offered in the U.S., Watcombe Pottery, 7" l., 4" h. (ILLUS.) **$195**

Royal Torquay Rosy Sunset Ships Teapot

Teapot, cov., faience Rosy Sunset Ships patt., flat-bottomed wide tapering cylindrical body w/angled shoulder & conical cover w/knob finial, decorated w/a scene

of sailing ships at sunset, Royal Torquay Pottery, 4 7/8" l., 3 1/2" h. (ILLUS.).............. **$95**

Rare Aller Vale Miniature Teapot

Teapot, cov., miniature, colored scrolling B-1 decoration, Aller Vale Pottery, 5 1/4" l., 3 1/2" h. (ILLUS.) **$350-400**

Miniature Longpark Crocus Teapot

Teapot, cov., miniature, Crocus patt., wide low tapering cylindrical body w/wide shoulder tapering to conical cover w/knob finial, straight spout, C-form handle, Longpark Pottery, 4 1/4" l., 2 1/2" h. (ILLUS.) **$250**

Mini Royal Watcombe Sailing Ship Teapot

Teapot, cov., miniature, Sailing Ship patt., spherical body w/angled spout, C-form handle & inset cover w/knob finial, Royal Watcombe Pottery, 4 7/8" l., 3" h. (ILLUS.)
.... **$180-250**

Miniature Black Cockerel Teapot

Teapot, cov., Motto Ware, Black Cockerel patt., miniature size, wide squatty bulbous tapering body w/angled spout & C-form handle, conical cover w/button finial, reads "Duee drink a cup a tay," Longpark Pottery, 4 1/2" l., 2 1/2" h. (ILLUS.) **$250-295**

Small Blue Spikey Tail Cockerel Teapot

Teapot, cov., Motto Ware, Blue Spikey Tail Cockerel patt., wide squatty body w/inset domed cover w/knob finial, angled spout & high C-form handle, reads: "Guid morn!," Aller Vale Pottery, small size (ILLUS.) **$125**

Blue-Tailed Cockerel Pattern Teapot

Teapot, cov., Motto Ware, Blue-Tailed Cockerel patt., squatty bulbous tapering body w/wide mouth & inset cover w/button finial, reads: "Ye may get better cheer but no' wi' better heart. Guid morn," Aller Vale Pottery, 7 1/2" l., 4" h. (ILLUS.) ... **$150-175**

Longpark Brown Cockerel Motto Ware Teapot

Teapot, cov., Motto Ware, Brown Cockerel patt., wide squatty bulbous body w/short spout, C-form handle, tapering cover w/pointed finial, motto reads "Dawntee be fraid out now," Longpark Pottery (ILLUS.) **$195-225**

Unusual Cat Pattern Aller Vale Teapot

Teapot, cov., Motto Ware, Cat patt., wide bulbous body w/inset cover w/knob finial, comical stylized cat on a green background, reads "The Midnight Warbler," Aller Vale Pottery, 6 7/8" l., 4 1/8" h. (ILLUS.) .. **$425**

Old English Cock Fight Faience Teapot

Teapot, cov., Motto Ware, Cock Fight patt., faience, wide flat bottom w/slightly tapering cylindrical sides & narrow angled shoulder, inset cover w/knob finial, reads: "Old English Cock Fight," Watcombe Pottery, 6 1/2" l., 4 1/4" h. (ILLUS.) **$295**

Colored Cockerel Longpark Motto Ware Teapot

Teapot, cov., Motto Ware, Colored Cockerel patt., footed deep half-round body w/curved shoulder to wide flat rim & inset flat cover w/button finial, C-form handle & upright spout, motto reads "Duee drink a cup a tay," Longpark Pottery (ILLUS.) .. **$125-150**

Colored Cockerel Longpark Teapot

Teapot, cov., Motto Ware, Colored Cockerel patt., ovoid body w/long serpentine spout & C-form handle, conical cover w/pointed finial, reads "We'el tak a cup o' kindness fer Auld Lang Syne," Longpark Pottery, 5 1/4" w., 6" h. (ILLUS.) **$125-150**

Rare Colored Cockerel Christmas Gift Teapot

Rare Large Longpark Motto Ware Teapot with the Colored Cockerel Pattern

Teapot, cov., Motto Ware, Colored Cockerel patt., special Christmas gift presentation piece, inscription reads: "To Mother - From Florrie - Xmas 1928 - Tak yourself a nice cup of tay," Longpark Pottery, very rare, 8" l., 5 1/2" h. (ILLUS. of both sides, top of page) **$350**

Teapot, cov., Motto Ware, Colored Cockerel patt., very large & rare design, wide low tapering cylindrical body w/an angled shoulder decorated w/a band of dots, conical cover w/button finial, short spout & large C-scroll handle, long motto reads "May we all in travelling thro this so called vale of tears - Find ever true and constant friends to share the cup that cheers," some professional restoration, Longpark Pottery, 9" l., 5" h. (ILLUS. of both sides, second from top) **$350**

Toy Size Cottage Pattern Teapot

Teapot, cov., Motto Ware, Cottage patt., toy size, footed spherical body w/an angled spout, C-form handle & small cover w/knob finial, reads "For my dolly," Royal Watcombe Pottery, 4 7/8" l., 3 1/4" h. (ILLUS.) **$175-200**

Rare Watcombe Colored Cockerel Teapot

Teapot, cov., Motto Ware, Colored Cockerel w/mottled blue wing patt., reads "Cum me artiez an 'ave a cup o tay," Watcombe Pottery, rare, 7 1/2" l., 5" h. (ILLUS.) **$250**

Motto Ware Gray Cockerel Teapot

Teapot, cov., Motto Ware, Gray Cockerel patt., footed spherical body w/a serpentine spout, C-form handle & small cover w/knob finial, reads "Good morning," Watcombe Pottery, 7 7/8" l., 4 3/4" h. (ILLUS.) **$275**

Watcombe Faience Cock Fight Teapot

Teapot, cov., Motto Ware, Old English Cock Fight patt., faience decoration, wide slightly tapering cylindrical body w/serpentine spout & long C-form handle, small inset cover w/knob finial, rim reads "The English Cock," Watcombe Pottery, 6 1/2" l., 4 1/4" h. (ILLUS.) **$250-300**

Watcombe Lindisfarne Castle Teapot

Teapot, cov., Motto Ware, scene of Lindisfarne Castle, miniature, faience decoration, spherical body w/angled spout, C-form handle, small cover w/knob finial, reads "Lindisfarne Castle - Holy Island," Royal Watcombe Pottery, 4 3/4" l., 3" h. (ILLUS.).. **$180-200**

Watcombe Green Motto Ware Teapot

Teapot, cov., Motto Ware, wide flat-bottomed tapering cylindrical shape w/angled shoulder to a flat mouth w/a tapering cover w/double-knob finial, straight spout, C-form handle, reads "Du'ee drink a cup ov tay," green glaze, Watcombe Pottery, 6 1/2" w., 3 1/2" h. (ILLUS.) ... **$125-150**
Teapot, cov., souvenir ware, Sea Gull patt., miniature, spherical body w/a serpentine spout, C-form handle & small cover w/knob finial, reads "Lands End," Royal Watcombe Pottery, 4 7/8" l., 3" h. (ILLUS.) **$180-200**

Small Souvenir Sea Gull Pattern Teapot

Rare Tiny Mini Aller Vale Teapot

Teapot, cov., tiny miniature size, early Forget-Me-Not h.p. decoration, white clay, Aller Vale Pottery, ca. 1890s, rare (ILLUS.) **$200**

Cockerel Pattern
Curling iron tile, Black Cockerel patt., Motto Ware, "O list to me ye ladies fair - and when ye wish to curl your hair - For the safety of your domicile - Pray place your lamp upon this tile," Longpark Torquay mark, scarce, ca. 1903-09, 5 x 7 1/4" **$198**

Hot water pot, cov., Black Cockerel patt., Motto Ware, "Good Morning - Life is a struggle Not a race - A wise man keeps an even pace," Aller Vale mark, ca. 1902-24, overall 7 1/4" h. **$176**
Mug, miniature, Colored Cockerel patt., Motto Ware, "If you can't fly - climb," Longpark Torquay impressed mark, scarce, ca. 1910, 1 5/8" h. **$95**
Vase, 5 3/4" h., Black Cockerel patt., four spouts, Motto Ware, "May you never find a mouse in your cupboard with tears in its eyes," desirable motto, Longpark Torquay early mark, ca. 1904-18 .... **$279**

Cottage Pattern
Bowl, 4" d., 3 1/2" h., four-handled, Motto Ware, in Devon dialect, "Come an' zee us in the zummer," Crown Dorset Pottery, ca. 1915..................................... **$134**
Coffeepot, cov., long spout, Motto Ware, "Gude things be scarce take care of me," Watcombe Torquay mark, ca. 1925-35, 7" h.. **$151**
Creamer, miniature, Motto Ware, "Isle of Wight - Fresh from the cow," Royal Watcombe circle mark, ca. 1950, 1 3/4" h.......... **$41**

Molded Cottageware Pieces

Cup & saucer, Molded Cottageware, details in relief w/sponged details in rose, green & yellow, Torquay Pottery Co., ca. 1918-24, scarce, saucer 5 1/4" d., cup 3" h., the set (ILLUS. left & right) **$63**

Dog bowl, Motto Ware, "Love Me - Love My Dog," lovely calligraphy & "Tintern," Longpark Torquay, England mark, ca. 1930s, 5 5/8" w. **$175**

Humidor, cov., Motto Ware, "When work is done the pipe don't shun," painted Watcombe mark, ca. 1901-20, overall 5 1/4" h. **$165**

Pin dish, round, Motto Ware, "I'll take care ov the pins," Longpark Torquay, ca. 1918-30, 3 1/8" d. **$45**

Cottage Motto Ware Pitcher

Pitcher, 5 1/4" h., 4" d., Motto Ware, wide ovoid body tapering to a flat rim w/spout, brown loop handle, inscribed "If you can't be easy, Be as easy as you can" (ILLUS.) **$110-120**

Plate, 6 3/4" d., Molded Cottageware, cottage scene w/thatched roof, sponged design of flowers & trees w/windows & door slip-lined, Torquay Pottery Co. impressed mark, scarce, ca. 1908-15 (ILLUS. center with cups & saucers) **$82**

Shaving mug, Motto Ware, "A hair on the head is worth two on the chin," Watcombe Torquay, England mark, ca. 1925-35 (tiny sealed hairline).................... **$151**

Teapot, cov., Molded Cottageware, colorful sponge-decorated design, large & heavy, Torquay Pottery Co. mark, ca. 1905-20, overall 9 1/4" l., 6 3/4" h. **$152**

Toast rack, four large tines, Motto Ware, "Crisp Toast" on front, "Truro" on short side, Watcombe Torquay, England impressed mark, ca. 1930, 5 1/4" l. **$178**

Scandy Pattern

Dresser tray, oval, Motto Ware, "A place for everything and everything in its place," Watcombe Torquay mark, ca. 1920s, 7 3/8 x 12" **$176**

Hot water-coffeepot, cov., Motto Ware, "May we be kind but not in words alone," many details, Aller Vale, ca. 1891-1910, overall 5" h. **$108**

Inkwell, Motto Ware, "Don't forget the dear ones far away," Watcombe mark, ca. 1920s, 2" h. **$61**

Match holder, Motto Ware, Devon dialect, "No place on earth so plaizes me - as this wan Babbacombe By-the-zay," Longpark Torquay mark, ca. 1903-09, 3 1/4" h. **$100**

Pitcher, 4 1/2" h., Motto Ware, "Another little drink won't do us any harm," Lemon & Crute Pottery, ca. 1920 (rim roughness, spout rub) **$53**

Plate, 5" d., Motto Ware, "Carry a vision in your heart," Watcombe Torquay impressed mark, ca. 1930 .... **$59**

Puzzle jug, Motto Ware, "Within this jug there is good liquor - Fit for Parson or for Vicar. But how to drink and not to spill - will try the utmost of your skill," Longpark, ca. 1920, 4 1/4" h. **$125**

Teapot, cov., Motto Ware, "Ye may get better cheer but no' wi' Better heart," Aller Vale mark, ca. 1891-1910, 6 3/4" l., 3 3/4" h. **$120**

Other Patterns

Torquay Pixie Design Ashtray

Ashtray, Motto Ware, long rectangular shape w/cigarette rests in each corner, creamer ground molded in the center w/an elfin figure in colorful clothes, inscribed "Lucky Devon Pixie," 3 x 5" (ILLUS.) **$60-70**
Basket, Art Nouveau swags, braided black handle, Barton Pottery, ca. 1922-38, overall 5" h. **$135**

Large Cockington Forge Bowl

Bowl, 12" d., Cockington Forge patt., round shallow form w/h.p. scene of the forge, inscribed at rim "Cockington Forge - Torquay," Devon Tors Pottery, ca. 1925-30 (ILLUS.) **$335**
Candlesticks, Primrose patt., Motto Ware, "Many are called but few get up" on one, the other w/"Be the day weary or be the day long - At last it ringeth to Evensong," H.M. Exeter Pottery mark, ca. 1920, 7" h., pr **$125**
Curling iron tile, Forget-me-not patt., Motto Ware, "O list to me ye ladies fair - And when Ye wish to curl your hair - For the safety of this domicile - Pray place your lamps upon this tile," Watcombe Torquay impressed mark, ca. 1920s, 5 1/2 x 7 3/4" **$140**
Humidor, cov., C3 Pattern, Motto Ware, "Help yersel tae a pipe o' bacca," early Scandy-type pattern, Watcombe mark, ca. 1910-20, overall 5" h. **$88**

Mug, commemorative, "Coronation of Queen Elizabeth - June 2, 1953," no mark, Sandygate Pottery, 2 3/4" h. **$50**

Sailboat Commemorative Mug

Mug, Sailboat patt., commemorative, "Barbara - Peace Celebrations - Bath - 1919," black sailboat w/rosy sunset background, Torquay Pottery Co. mark, 3 3/4" h. (ILLUS.) **$122**
Pitcher, 2 7/8" h., jug-form, Passion Flower patt., Motto Ware, green ground w/motto in a band between the flowers, "May all the hours be winged with joy," H.M. Exeter Pottery, ca. 1930 .... **$71**
Pitcher, 4 3/4" h., Pixie patt., three pixies in relief amid a colorful leafy scroll design, "Pixy fine - Pixy gay," scarce, impressed Aller Vale mark, ca. 1891-1910 .... **$350**
Scent bottle, Gardenia patt., black curled handle, Motto Ware, "A thing of beauty is a joy Forever - Gardenia Eau de Cologne - Toogoods - London - England," pink gardenia on blue ground, brass crown-form stopper, Watcombe, ca. 1930s, 5" h. **$151**
Scent bottle, Lavender patt., "Hill's English Lavender," marked "Genuine Devon Pottery - Made in England," still sealed, ca. 1930s, 2 1/2" h. **$50**
Scent bottle, Violets patt., curved lavender handle & motto "May the hinges of friendship Never go rusty," gold crown-form stopper, "Made in England" stamped mark, Watcombe, 1930s, 4" h. **$119**
Toby jug, inscribed "Peter Gurney from Widecombe Fair," Royal Torquay mark, ca. 1924-30, 2 3/4" h. **$80**
Toby jug, inscribed "Jan Stewer from Widecombe Fair," Royal Torquay, ca. 1924-30, 5 1/4" h. **$132**
Vase, 4 1/2" h., D1 Scroll patt., colorful leafy scrolls & geometric designs on a blue ground, scarce, Aller Vale, ca. 1890s
.... **$146**
Vase, 6 1/4" h., Moonlight Cottages patt., faience, two cottages on a blue ground, impressed Bovey mark, very unusual, ca. 1930 .... **$203**

Rare Cavalier Pattern Vase

Vase, 7 1/2" h., Cavalier patt., faience, two handles, large ovoid form w/wide flat mouth, decorated w/portrait of a Cavalier standing in a landscape, rare subject, Mosanic Pottery mark, Crown Dorset, rare, ca. 1910 (ILLUS.)............................... **$395**

Vase, 8" h., Persian patt., three handles, six colorful Persian flowers on a cream ground, very early pattern, Watcombe, ca. 1890s-1910 .... **$210**

Uhl Pottery

Original production of utilitarian wares began at Evansville, Indiana, in the 1850s and consisted mostly of jugs, jars, crocks and pieces for food preparation and preservation. In 1909, production was moved to Huntingburg, Indiana, where a more extensive variety of items was eventually produced including many novelty and advertising items that have become highly collectible. Following labor difficulties, the Uhl Pottery closed in 1944.

Unless it is marked or stamped, Uhl is difficult to identify except by someone with considerable experience. Marked pieces can have several styles of ink stamps and/or an incised number under glaze on the bottom. These numbers are die-cut and impressed in the glazed bottom. Some original molds were acquired by other potteries. Some production exists and should not be considered as Uhl. These may have numbers inscribed by hand with a stylus and are usually not glazed on the bottom.

Many examples have no mark or stamp and may not be bottom-glazed. This is especially true of many of the miniature pieces. If a piece has a "Meier's Wine" paper label, it was probably made by Uhl.

While many color variations exist, there are about nine basic colors: blue, white, black, rose or

pink, yellow, teal, purple, pumpkin and browns/tans. Blue, pink, teal and purple are currently the most sought after colors. Animal planters, vases, liquor/wine containers, pitchers, mugs, banks, kitchenware, bakeware, gardenware and custom-made advertising pieces exist.

Similar pieces by other manufacturers do exist. When placed side by side, a seasoned collector can recognize an authentic example of Uhl Pottery.

A Variety of Uhl Marks

Ashtray, #199, in the form of a dog lifting its leg at a hydrant, marked (ILLUS. top row, left w/Uhl Pottery pieces) **$550**
Ashtray, brown, American Legion emblem **$120**
Ashtray, green, hand-turned mark, 3" d. **$150**
Ashtray, round, black, unmarked.................... **$30**
Bank, figural, large grinning pig, yellow, unmarked.. **$400**
Bank, figural, medium-size grinning pig, white, painted circus theme, unmarked **$425**
Bean pot, brown/blue, marked "Boston Bean Pot".. **$170**
Bean pot, brown/tan, side handles, marked .. **$130**
Bowl, basketweave, blue, unmarked **$90**
Bowl, 5" d., picket fence **$50**
Bowl, 5" d., shouldered mixing bowl, unmarked.. **$140**
Bowl, 8" d., blue, marked "Boonville Implement Company" **$100**
Bowl, 8" d., luncheon, blue, marked **$70**
Bowl, 8" d., luncheon, green, unmarked......... **$40**
Canteen, commemorative of Uhl Collectors Society, 1988 .... **$275**
Canteen, miniature, blue, Meier Wine paper label **$50**
Casserole, cov., blue, #528 & marked............ **$60**
Churn, 3-gal., white, acorn mark.................... **$90**
Churn, 4-gal., cov., white, acorn mark, solid lid **$185**
Cookie jar, miniature, blue, unmarked.......... **$185**
Creamer, light tan, hand-turned square mark, 5 1/2" h... **$150**
Creamer & sugar, cov., robin's-egg blue, both w/hand-turned mark........................ **$475**
Flowerpot, ribbed, yellow, no attached saucer, unmarked, 6" **$25**
Funnel, brown, unmarked............................... **$22**
Jar, 1-gal., white, acorn mark........................ **$50**
Jar, 2-gal., white, acorn mark........................ **$55**
Jar, 3-gal., tan, Evansville, Ind., mark........... **$360**
Jar, 3-gal., white, acorn mark........................ **$75**
Jar, 6-gal., white, acorn mark........................ **$75**

Miscellaneous Uhl Containers

Jar, blue & white (ILLUS. middle row left w/Uhl containers) $65
Jar, cov., cottage cheese, white, metal lid embossed "UHL" $500
Jar, cov. (ILLUS. top row right w/miscellaneous Uhl containers) $75
Jug, 3-gal., light tan, Evansville, Ind., mark.... $360
Jug, 3-oz., miniature Egyptian, rose, marked #6 .... $35
Jug, 5-gal., blue/white, marked "Dillsboro Sanitarium, Dillsboro, Ind." $700
Jug, 5-gal., brown/white, acorn mark $70
Jug, 6-gal., light tan, Evansville, Ind., oval mark $120
Jug, blue Egyptian, marked #133.................... $45

Uhl Pottery Pieces

Jug, form of football, large, 5" l., rarer than smaller version (ILLUS. middle row, left w/Uhl Pottery pieces)............................... $225
Jug, form of softball, Meier's label, 3 3/8" d. (ILLUS. middle row, right w/Uhl Pottery pieces) $250
Jug, in the form of a football, large size, brown, unmarked...................................... $225
Jug, in the form of a football, small size, brown, unmarked.. $40
Jug, miniature acorn, marked "Acorn Wares" $70

Various Uhl Pottery Items

Jug, blue & white, "Colonial Mineral Springs, Martinsville, Indiana" (ILLUS. top left w/various Uhl Pottery items)....... $1,400
Jug, brown/white, "1939 Merry Christmas," marked $200
Jug, brown/white, miniature shoulder, front acorn mark $550

Various Uhl Mugs & Jugs

Jug, miniature, "Canadian Apple Blossom," 3 3/8" h. (ILLUS. bottom left w/various Uhl mugs & jugs).. $90
Jug, miniature, marked, 1" h. $100
Jug, miniature prunella, black, unmarked $35
Jug, miniature, "Pure Corn, Souvenir Lincoln Birthplace, Kentucky," 3" h. (ILLUS. bottom right w/various Uhl mugs & jugs) ... $225
Jug, red/green, "1940 Merry Christmas," marked "Uhl Pottery Company," 2 3/8" h. ... $225
Jug, "Season's Greetings, 1940-1941, Henderson, Kentucky," 6 5/8" h. (ILLUS. top row w/various Uhl mugs & jugs).......... $175

Lamp, Liberty Bell **$145**
Match holder, marked Uhl, 2 1/4" h. (ILLUS.
bottom row right w/miscellaneous Uhl
containers)... **$135**
Model of cat, potter's name engraved, un-
marked.. **$1,000**
Model of cowboy boot, marked (ILLUS.
bottom row, right w/Uhl Pottery pieces) **$150**
Model of dog & hydrant, similar to ashtray
#199, two separate pieces, no marks
(ILLUS. top row, center & right w/Uhl
Pottery pieces)... **$350**
Model of military boot, marked (ILLUS.
bottom row, center w/Uhl Pottery pieces) **$95**
Model of shoe, miniature woman's slipper,
blue, marked **$75**
Model of shoe, miniature woman's slipper,
marked (ILLUS. of two bottom row, left
w/Uhl Pottery pieces) **$130**
Model of shoe, miniature woman's slipper,
purple, marked.. **$100**
Model of shoes, tied baby shoes, pink, both
marked, pr. **$180**
Model of shoes, white, marked #2, pr. **$110**
Mug, barrel-shaped, blue & white, marked
"Dillsboro Sanitarium"............................... **$350**
Mug, "Chicco Beverage Co." (ILLUS. middle
row left w/various Uhl mugs & jugs) **$110**
Mug, "Chicco Beverage, Norristown" (ILLUS.
middle row right w/various Uhl mugs &
jugs)... **$110**
Mug, coffee, blue, marked............................... **$65**
Mug, coffee, pink, marked.............................. **$60**
Mug, "Homestead Hotel, No. 7 Water"
(ILLUS. bottom right w/various Uhl Pot-
tery items).. **$150**
Mug, "West Baden Springs Hotel" (ILLUS.
bottom left w/various Uhl Pottery items) **$145**
Orange blossom jar, #118 (ILLUS. top row
left w/miscellaneous Uhl containers)........... **$85**
Orange jar (ILLUS. middle row right w/mis-
cellaneous Uhl containers)......................... **$75**
Pepper shaker, dark blue, unmarked **$35**
Pepper shaker, light blue, unmarked............. **$35**
Pitcher, barrel-shaped, blue, marked.............. **$65**
Pitcher, barrel-shaped, brown, marked........... **$45**
Pitcher, barrel-shaped, brown, unmarked....... **$40**
Pitcher, bulbous grape, blue, #183................. **$80**
Pitcher, bulbous grape, pumpkin, #183 .... **$55**
Pitcher, globe-shaped, light blue, unmarked **$40**
Pitcher, Hall Boy, blue & white, unmarked.. **$1,500**
Pitcher, ice water, yellow, unmarked **$50**
Pitcher, miniature, blue, marked "Norris-
town, Tenn." **$180**
Pitcher, miniature, teal green, marked #28...... **$95**
Pitcher, squat grape, blue, unmarked........... **$160**

Plaque, Lincoln **$550**

Rare Uhl Plate

Plate, 6 3/4" d., stamped "Santa Claus, Indi-
ana," very rare, only three known to exist
(ILLUS.)... **$600+**
Salt & pepper shakers, pink, unmarked **$77**

Uhl Sand Jar

Sand jar, basketweave design, brushed
green or ivory, used to snuff cigarettes,
Item #530, 20" h., 10 1/2" d. (ILLUS.)
.... **$400-450**
Stein, 3-oz., miniature, brown, marked **$80**
Stein, 3-oz., miniature, teal green, marked.... **$140**
Stein, miniature, w/box, commemorative of
Uhl Collectors Society, 1987..................... **$500**
Syrup pitcher, cov., blue, marked................ **$180**
Teapot, 2-cup, blue, marked #131................ **$200**

Three Sizes of the Uhl Pottery Teapot

Teapot, cov., spherical body w/long serpentine spout, C-form handle, low rim w/inset flattened cover w/knob finial, one of three sizes made, marked w/the circle mark on the bottom & also usually an incised number, made in various colors including white, yellow, brown, at least three shades of blue, a scarce shade of green, dark blue, pink, teal, black or purple are most desirable today, value depends on color, large size, 8-cup (ILLUS. in dark blue at far right with other Uhl teapots, bottom previous page) $100

Teapot, cov., spherical body w/long serpentine spout, C-form handle, low rim w/inset flattened cover w/knob finial, one of three sizes made, marked w/the circle mark on the bottom & also usually an incised number, made in various colors including white, yellow, brown, at least three shades of blue, a scarce shade of green, dark blue, pink, teal, black or purple are most desirable today, value depends on color medium size, 4-cup (ILLUS. in light blue in the center with other Uhl teapots, bottom previous page) $125

Teapot, cov., spherical body w/long serpentine spout, C-form handle, low rim w/inset flattened cover w/knob finial, one of three sizes made, marked w/the circle mark on the bottom & also usually an incised number, made in various colors including white, yellow, brown, at least three shades of blue, a scarce shade of green, dark blue, pink, teal, black or purple are most desirable today, value depends on color, small size, 2-cup (ILLUS. in dark blue at far left with other Uhl teapots) $200

Thieves jar, miniature, black, #138 .... $105

Tulip bowl, yellow, marked #119 .... $70

Uhl Garden Urn

Urn, garden, Roman style, Old Ivory, two pieces, 19 x 12" (ILLUS.) $190

Vase, blue, hand-turned mark $700

Vase, blue, marked #158 .... $80

Vase, dark blue, marked #154 .... $90

Vase, plum, marked #156 .... $85

Vase, waisted form, "Merrill Park Florist, Battle Creek, Mich.," extremely rare (ILLUS. top right w/various Uhl Pottery items) .... price unknown

Vase, 3 5/8" h., marked "American Legion Huntingburg Post 221" on bottom (ILLUS. bottom row left w/miscellaneous Uhl containers) $250

Vase, 4 3/4" h., bud vase, #107, hard to find, price depends on color, w/blue & especially purple being most popular (ILLUS. center w/various Uhl vases) $45-75

Various Uhl Vases

Vase, 5" h., handled, #152, very hard to find, marked, price depends on color, w/blue & especially purple being most popular (ILLUS. bottom left w/various Uhl vases) $45-75

Vase, 5 1/4" h., fan-shaped w/scalloped rim, #157, hard to find, price depends on color, w/blue & especially purple being most popular (ILLUS. bottom right w/various Uhl vases) $55-75

Vase, 5 1/4" h., flaring ribbed neck, #158, incised, hard to find, price depends on color, w/blue & especially purple being most popular (ILLUS. top left w/various Uhl vases) $45-75

Vase, 5 1/4" h., side handles, #156, incised, hard to find, price depends on color, w/blue & especially purple being most popular (ILLUS. top right w/various Uhl vases) $45-75

Water cooler, 3-gal., cov., white, acorn mark $200

Water cooler, 5-gal., cov., white, acorn mark $225

Water cooler, 6-gal., blue & white, w/embossed polar bears $1,500

Van Briggle

The Van Briggle Pottery was established by Artus Van Briggle, who formerly worked for Rookwood Pottery, in Colorado Springs, Colorado, at the turn of the century. He died in 1904, but the pottery was carried on by his widow and others. From 1900 until 1920, the pieces were dated. It remains in production today, specializing in Art Pottery.

Early Van Briggle Pottery Mark

Van Briggle Puppy Bookends

Bookends, figural, a plump seated puppy on a rectangular block base, deep mulberry matte glaze w/dark blue on the puppy, marked, pr. (ILLUS.).............................. **$345**

Bowl, 8 3/4" d., 2 3/4" h., low incurved sides molded in relief w/four dragonflies, deep mulberry matte glaze, ca. 1920s............... **$345**

Bowl-vase, wide low squatty form w/a wide shoulder tapering to a wide flat mouth, molded overall w/large swirled pointed leaves, dark green matte glaze w/buff clay showing through, dated 1903, Shape No. 145, 4 1/2" d., 2" h................ **$2,185**

Bowl-vase, footed spherical body w/a wide flat mouth, embossed around the shoulder w/large heart-shaped leaves, fine leathery green & cobalt blue matte glaze, ca. 1908-11, 4 1/2" d., 4" h........... **$2,415**

Modern Van Briggle Native American Bust

Bust of Native American Chief, finely detailed, wearing a large feathered headdress, dark turquoise blue matte glaze, company logo on base w/"Van Briggle Colo. Springs Co. - Chief Two Moons - Cheyenne - Limited Edition No. 186 - 1979," 11 1/2" h. (ILLUS.) **$196**

Early Brown Van Briggle Candlestick

Candlestick, a round foot tapering to a tall slender cylindrical shaft supporting a wide cupped socket, overall mottled dark brown matte glaze, dated 1914, small grinding chips off the base, 8 5/8" h. (ILLUS.) **$546**

Lady of the Lake Console Bowl & Flower Frog

Console bowl & flower frog, "Lady of the Lake" design, a low undulating oblong bowl w/incurved sides, one end w/an angled rockwork ledge mounted w/the kneeling figure of a maiden looking down into the bowl, a round flower frog inside mounted w/the model of a turtle, shaded blue & turquoise blue matte glaze, each piece marked, some interior staining, bowl 9 7/8 x 14 3/4", 2 pcs. (ILLUS.) **$690**

Siren of the Sea Console Bowl & Frog

Console bowl & flower frog, "Siren of the Sea" design, turquoise blue matte glaze, a low footed & rounded shell-shaped bowl w/a full-length figure of a mermaid wrapping around the sides, a shell-form flower frog inside, frog 6" d., 2 3/4" h., bowl 8 x 13", 2 pcs. (ILLUS.) **$460**

Damsel of Damascus Van Briggle Lamp

Lamp, table-type, "Damsel of Damascus" design, a kneeling peasant woman holding an urn on one shoulder, urn holding electric fittings, on a domed rockwork base, overall black matte glaze, signed on base, w/newer shade not shown, base 10 5/8" h. (ILLUS., previous page)............ **$196**

Vase, 3 3/4" h., 4" d., squatty nearly spherical smooth form, green & raspberry matte glaze, dated 1903, Shape No. E209.. **$575**

Small Van Briggle Vase with Leaves

Vase, 4 1/4" h., squatty bulbous lower body tapering to a wide cylindrical neck w/a flat mouth, molded around the bottom w/large rounded leaves w/swirled stems up the sides, Mountain Craig Brown glaze w/green leaves (ILLUS.).................. **$104**

Vase, miniature, 4 1/4" h., 3" d., ovoid body tapering to a flat mouth, molded around & down the sides w/poppy pods on long stems, rare cobalt blue & yellow striated matte glaze, dated 1902, Shape No. 24... **$4,140**

Vase, 5" h., 4 1/4" d., bulbous ovoid body w/a wide flat mouth, molded around the top & down the sides w/Jugenstil-style irises, rare dark bluish-green leathery matte glaze, dated 1906, Shape No. 443.......... **$2,185**

Vase, 5 1/4" h., 5 3/4" d., wide squatty bulbous form w/a flat mouth, molded around the lower body w/stylized blossoms & leaves, mustard yellow matte glaze, ca. 1908-11, Shape No. 643...................... **$1,035**

Corseted Blue & Mulberry Van Briggle Vase

Vase, 6" h., ovoid corseted form w/a small flat mouth, lightly molded around the top

w/stylized three-petaled flowers in undulating panels, dark blue flowers against a dark mulberry matte ground, marked (ILLUS.).. **$173**

Vase, 6" h., 3 1/2" d., cylindrical lower half & a bulbous upper half w/a closed rim, molded around the top w/crocus blossoms, the stems curving down the sides, mustard yellow matte glaze, dated 1903, Shape No. 195...................................... **$2,415**

Vase, 6 1/2" h., 3 1/4" d., copper-clad, cylindrical lower body w/the top molded w/large stylized blossoms, the rim flanked by small loop handles, original patina, ca. 1908-11, Shape No. 521 ...... **$2,875**

Yellow "Dos Cabezas" Vase

Vase, 7 1/2" h., 4 3/4" d., "Dos Cabezas," ovoid body molded around the top w/two Art Nouveau maidens, unusual mustard yellow matte glaze, small flat chip in one fold, ca. 1908-11 (ILLUS.)...................... **$6,900**

Vase, 7 1/2" h., 6 1/4" d., bulbous ovoid body tapering to a wide short neck, embossed cornflowers & stems around the sides forming a ribbed effect, thick curdled brown matte glaze, dated 1907....... **$2,415**

Vase, 8" h., 3 1/2" d., simple tall ovoid body w/a tiny mouth flanked by small loop handles, overall blackish-green leathery matte glaze, dated 1903, Shape No. 192.......... **$1,610**

Green Dandelion Van Briggle Vase

Vase, 8 1/2" h., 7 1/2" d., tapering bulbous body w/a wide cupped rim w/a flat mouth, molded w/dandelion blossoms glazed in red w/leafy stems around the sides all on a chartreuse matte ground, dated 1904, Shape No. 137 (ILLUS.).......................... **$6,325**

Lorelei Vase in Dark Blue & Mulberry

Vase, 9 1/4" h., 4" d., "Lorelei," swelled cylindrical form w/a figure of a maiden draped around the rim, cobalt blue over a dark mulberry matte glaze, 1920-25, marked, overall crazing (ILLUS.)................ **$978**

Very Plain Mulberry Van Briggle Vase

Vase, 9 5/8" h., flat-bottomed completely smooth ovoid body tapering to a slender tall trumpet neck, overall deep mulberry matte glaze (ILLUS.) **$115**

Rare Van Briggle Green Poppy Vase

Vase, 9 3/4" h., 8" d., bulbous ovoid body tapering to a flat mouth, molded overall w/poppy blossoms on leafy stems, mottled red & sheer chartreuse matte glaze w/buff clay showing, dated 1903, Shape No. 143 (ILLUS.)................................... **$12,650**

Vase, 10 1/4" h., 4 1/2" d., swelled cylindrical form w/a short shoulder tapering to a low cylindrical neck, molded up around the sides w/curving poppy pods & leaves, sheer frothy lime green matte glaze w/tan clay showing through, dated 1903, Shape No. 173.. **$4,600**

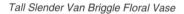

Tall Slender Van Briggle Floral Vase

Vase, 10 3/4" h., a tall very slender tapering cylindrical form, molded around the base w/scrolling leaves, slender stems up the sides w/tiny blossoms at the rim, shaded dark blue to pale green matte glaze, dated 1914, fine overall crazing (ILLUS.)........ **$690**

Fine Tall Blue Van Briggle Vase

Vase, 13 1/2" h., 5" d., a low swelled base below the slightly tapering cylindrical sides w/a small flat mouth, crisply molded w/tall irises & leaves, periwinkle blue leathery matte glaze, buff clay showing through, dated 1903, Shape No. 133 (ILLUS.)
.... **$10,350**

Vase, 15" h., 10" d., large ovoid body tapering to a small flared neck, overall frothy matte green glaze, dated 1905, Shape No. 978 .... **$2,645**

Vernon Kilns

The story of Vernon Kilns Pottery begins with the purchase by Mr. Faye Bennison of the Poxon China Company (Vernon Potteries) in July 1931. The Poxon family had run the pottery for a number of years in Vernon, California, but with the founding of Vernon Kilns, the product lines were greatly expanded.

Many innovative dinnerware lines and patterns were introduced during the 1930s, including designs by such noted American artists as Rockwell Kent and Don Blanding. In the early 1940s items were designed to tie in with Walt Disney's animated features "Fantasia" and "Dumbo." Various commemorative plates, including the popular "Bits" series, were also produced over a long period of time. Vernon Kilns was taken over by Metlox Potteries in 1958 and completely ceased production in 1960.

Vernon Kilns Mark

"Bits" Series

Plate, 8 1/2" d., Bits of Old New England Series, The Cove **$30**
Plate, 8 1/2" d., Bits of the California Missions Series, San Rafael Archangel **$40**
Plate, 8 1/2" d., Bits of the Old South Series, Cotton Patch **$40**
Plate, 8 1/2" d., Bits of the Old West Series, The Fleecing **$40**

Plate, chop, 14" d., Bits of the Old Southwest Series, Pueblo **$75**

Cities Series - 10 1/2" d.

Plate, "Atlanta, Georgia," maroon **$15-20**
Plate, "Augusta, Maine," blue **$15-20**

Dinnerwares

Bowl, chowder, tab handle, Gingham patt. . **$15-18**
Bowl, fruit, Native California patt. **$8-10**
Bowl, soup, Coronado patt. **$15-20**
Bowl, 8 1/2" d., soup, Bel Air patt. **$15-20**
Bowl, 13" d., salad, Homespun patt. **$75-85**
Bowl, Homespun patt. 1 pt........................... **$30-35**
Butter dish, cov., Casual California patt..... **$25-30**
Butter dish, cov., Tam O'Shanter patt........ **$45-50**
Butter dish, cov., Tickled Pink patt............. **$30-40**
Butter pat, individual, Organdie patt., 2 1/2" d... **$30-35**
Candleholders, teacup form w/metal fittings, Tam O'Shanter patt., pr........... **$100-125**
Casserole, cov., chicken pot pie, Gingham patt.. **$35-40**
Casserole, cov., Heavenly Days patt......... **$45-60**
Casserole, cov., individual, Organdie patt., 4" d.. **$30-35**
Casserole, cov., Tam O'Shanter patt. **$50-70**
Casserole, cov., Vernon's 1860s patt........ **$75-85**
Coaster, Gingham patt................................. **$25-30**
Coffee server w/stopper, carafe form, Tam O'Shanter patt...................................... **$60-70**
Coffeepot, cov., Heavenly Days patt., 8-cup **$65**
Coffeepot, Ultra California patt. **$80-100**
Creamer, Modern California patt................ **$10-15**
Creamer, Ultra patt. **$10-15**
Cup & saucer, after-dinner size, Early California patt., red or cobalt blue, each (ILLUS. front, bottom of page) **$25-30**
Cup & saucer, after-dinner size, Monterey patt... **$40-45**
Egg cup, Early California patt., turquoise (ILLUS. with Early California cups & saucers, bottom of page) **$20-25**

Early California Egg Cup & After Dinner Cups & Saucers

Organdie Flowerpot & Saucer

Flowerpot & saucer, Organdie patt., 4" d. (ILLUS.)... $50-60
Gravy boat, Gingham patt. $20-25
Gravy boat, Native California patt.................... $35
Mixing bowls, nesting set, Gingham patt., 5" to 9" d., five pcs. $175-200
Muffin cover, Early California patt., red, cover only... $125-150
Mug, Barkwood patt., 9 oz..................... $25
Mug, Homespun patt., 9 oz. $35-40
Pepper mill, Homespun patt................ $150-175
Pitcher, jug-form, bulb bottom, Tam O'Shanter patt., 1 pt.............................. $25-35

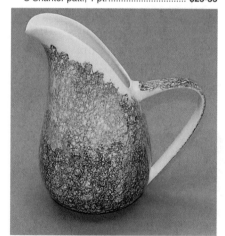

Hawaiian Coral Streamline Pitcher

Pitcher, Streamline shape, Hawaiian Coral patt., 1 qt. (ILLUS.).................................. $45-55
Pitcher, Streamline shape, Gingham patt., 2 qt. $50-75
Pitcher, 5" h., Streamline shape, Barkwood patt., 1/2 pt. $25-30
Plate, 6 1/2" d., bread & butter, Gingham patt... $5-10
Plate, 7 1/2" d., Frontier Days patt. $35-45
Plate, 7 1/2" d., salad, Tweed patt. $10-12

Coastline Series Florida Plate

Plate, 9 1/2" d., Coastline series, Florida patt., Turnbull design (ILLUS.)............ $100-125
Plate, 9 1/2" d., luncheon, Organdie patt. ... $10-12
Plate, 9 1/2" d., Native American series, Going to Town patt., Turnbull design...... $35-45
Plate, 9 1/2" d., Trader Vic patt.............. $100-125
Plate, 10 1/2" d., Casa California Hermosa patt., Turnbull design $25-30
Plate, 10 1/2" d., dinner, Calico patt................ $25
Plate, 10 1/2" d., Iris patt., Harry Bird design $50-60
Plate, chop, 12" d., Frontier Days patt. ... $150-175
Plate, chop, 12" d., Organdie patt. $25-30
Plate, chop, 14" d., Gingham patt. $35-40
Plate, 17" d., chop-type, Early California patt... $30-50
Platter, 12" d., round, Organdie patt. $20-25
Platter, 14" l., oval, Native California patt. .. $30-35
Relish dish, leaf-shaped, four-part, Native California patt... $50-75
Relish dish, single leaf shape, Monterey patt., 12" l.. $35-45
Salt & pepper shakers, large size, Tam O'Shanter patt., pr................................... $45-65
Salt & pepper shakers, Native California patt., pr.. $20
Salt & pepper shakers, regular size, Gingham patt., pr....................................... $20

Trumpet Flower Saucer

Saucer, Trumpet Flower patt., Harry Bird design (ILLUS.)...................................... $10-15

Spoon rest, Organdie patt. $75-85

Tweed Pattern Sugar Bowl

Sugar bowl, cov., Tweed patt. (ILLUS.)...... $30-35
Teacup & saucer, colossal size, Homespun
   patt., 15" d. saucer, 4 qt. $250-275
Teacup & saucer, jumbo size, Homespun
   patt. $45-55
Teacup & saucer, Ultra patt. $10-12
Teacup & saucer, Winchester '73 patt. $45-50

Santa Barbara Pattern Teapot

Teapot, cov., Santa Barbara patt. (ILLUS.)
   .... $75-95
Teapot, cov., Tam O'Shanter patt. $45-55
Tidbit, two-tier w/wooden handle, Home-
   spun patt. $30-35
Tumbler, Bel Air patt. $20-25
Tumbler, Homespun patt. $35
Tumbler, Tickled Pink patt. $20

Disney "Fantasia" & Other Items
Bowl, 6" d., chowder, Nutcracker patt. $50
Bowl, 8" d., soup, Flower Ballet patt. $50
Bowl, 8" l., No. 134, decorated figural bird . $75-85
Figure of Baby Weems, No. 37, 6" h. $150-175
Plate, 17" d., chop, Fantasia patt. .... $600+
Tray, hors d'oeuvre, May & Vieve Hamilton
   design, 16" d. $400-600
Vase, 4 1/2" h., Pine Cone patt., No. 5, ivory
   .... $95-125
Vase, 12" h., carved handles, May & Vieve
   Hamilton design .... $1,500+

Don Blanding Dinnerwares
Creamer, demitasse size, Hawaiian Flow-
   ers patt., blue $40-50
Cup & saucer, Coral Reef patt., blue $40-50
Platter, 16 1/2", Lei Lani patt. $200-250
Sugar bowl, cov., Coral Reef patt., blue..... $85-95
Sugar bowl, cov., Hawaiian Flowers patt.,
   blue $75-85
Tumbler, Hilo patt., #4, 5 1/2" h............. $125-150

Rockwell Kent Designs
Bowl, chowder, "Our America" series, coco-
   nut tree, blue $60-70
Creamer, regular, "Our America" series,
   houseboaters, brown $75-90
Cup & saucer, Moby Dick patt., maroon $45-50
Cup & saucer, Salamina patt. $50-60
Dinner service: four 9 1/2" d. luncheon
   plates, four 6 3/4" w. chowder bowls, four
   6 1/4" d. bread & butter plates, four cups
   & saucers, an 8" d. bowl & a 9" d. bowl;
   Salamina patt., ca. 1935, one chowder
   bowl repaired, the set (ILLUS. of part,
   bottom of page)..................................... $920

Portion of Rockwell Kent Salamina Pattern Dinner Service

Plate, 6 1/2" d., "Our America" series, steamship, blue **$45-50**
Plate, 6 1/2" d., Salamina patt. **$40**
Plate, 9 1/2" d., Moby Dick patt., blue **$110-145**
Plate, 17" d., chop, Salamina patt. **$400-500**
Sugar bowl, cov., Moby Dick patt., blue ... **$85-105**
Teapot, cov., Moby Dick patt., Rockwell Kent Designs, blue, 6-cup **$150-175**

States Map Series - 10 1/2" d.
Plate, Connecticut **$20**
Plate, Texas **$40-45**

States Picture Series - 10 1/2" d.
Plate, Alaska, blue... **$25**
Plate, North Dakota, multicolored.................... **$25**
Plate, Vermont, blue.................................... **$18-20**
Plate, Virginia, maroon............................... **$18-20**

Miscellaneous Commemoratives
Ashtray, Vermont...................................... **$15-20**
Cup & saucer, after-dinner size, Niagara Falls.. **$25**
Plate, 8 1/2" d., Memento Plate of factory **$75**

Christmas Tree Pattern Pieces

Plate, 10 1/2" d., Christmas Tree patt. (ILLUS. w/Christmas Tree teacup & saucer)... **$65-75**
Plate, 10 1/2" d., General MacArthur, brown **$20**
Plate, 10 1/2" d., Hollywood Stars, blue **$70-80**
Plate, 10 1/2" d., Knott's Berry Farm, California **$35**
Plate, 10 1/2" d., Notre Dame University, brown **$20-25**
Plate, 10 1/2" d., Old Man of the Mountain, New Hampshire...................................... **$20-25**
Plate, Postmasters Convention, showing buildings in Boston, border reading "Souvenir of the 48th National Convention of the National Association of Postmasters of the United States - Boston, Massachusetts, October 12-16, 1952," multicolor (ILLUS., top next column) **$30-35**
Plate, Statue of Liberty, multicolor.............. **$50-75**
Plates, 8 1/2" d., Cocktail Hour series, brown transfer, complete set of 8....... **$400-600**
Teacup & saucer, Christmas Tree (ILLUS. with Christmas Tree plate) **$30-35**

1952 Postmasters Convention Plate

Warwick

    Numerous collectors have turned their attention to the productions of the Warwick China Manufacturing Company that operated in Wheeling, West Virginia, from 1887 until 1951. Prime interest seems to lie in items produced before 1911 that were decorated with decal portraits of beautiful women, monks and Native Americans. Fraternal Order items, as well as floral and fruit decorated items, are also popular with collectors.

    Researcher John R. Rader, Sr. has recently determined that the famous "IOGA" and helmet mark was used by Warwick from April 1903 until December 1910. "Ioga" is a Native American word meaning "Beautiful."

Warwick Mark

Salesman's Sample Ashtray

Ashtray, salesman's sample, white trimmed in gold w/"Warwick China" in script & knight's helmet in black, no mark on back, ca. 1940s, 4 3/4" l., 3 1/2" w. (ILLUS.) **$75**

"June Bride" Sugar & Creamer

"Tudor Rose" Sugar & Creamer

Creamer & cov. sugar, white w/pink roses in "June Bride" decor patt., gold trim, marked w/Warwick knight's helmet, decor code A2003, ca. 1940s, creamer 4" h., sugar 3 1/2" d., pr. (ILLUS., top of page) **$55**

Creamer & cov. sugar, white w/red "Tudor Rose" decor patt. (rare), marked w/Warwick knight's helmet in green, ca. 1940s, creamer 4 1/2" h., sugar 5" d., pr. (ILLUS., second from top) **$95**

Ewer, brown, tan & cream w/gold rim, pink poppies, embossing around bottom, marked w/IOGA knight's helmet in green, decor code A-6, ca. 1905, 10" h. **$70**

Warwick Flow Blue Fern Dish

Fern dish, Pansy decor patt. in Flow Blue, gold trim & highlights, marked "Warwick China" in black, ca. 1896, 4 3/4" h., 7 1/2" d. (ILLUS.) **$475**

Warwick Ewer with Hazelnuts

Ewer, matte brown & tan w/hazelnuts, gold trim, marked w/IOGA knight's helmet in green, decor code M2, ca. 1908, 11" h. (ILLUS.) **$150**

Humidor with B.P.O.E. Elk Logo

Humidor, cov., brown & tan w/elk's head & clock, "Cigars" on back, marked w/IOGA knight's helmet in grey & "Warwick China" in black, decor code A-13 in red, scarce, ca. 1903, 6 1/2" h., 4 1/2" d. (ILLUS., previous page) **$260**

Mug, cylindrical, decorated w/the head of an elk & the "BPOE" emblem............................ **$45**

Pitcher, 6 1/2" h., lemonade shape, brown shaded to brown ground, color floral decoration, No. A-27 .... **$100**

Pitcher, 6 1/2" h., Tokio #3, brown shaded to brown ground, decorated w/color portrait of Native American, A-12 .... **$300**

Pitcher, 7" h., Tokio #2, overall white ground, color bird decoration, D-1.............. **$155**

Pitcher, 7 3/4" h., Tokio #1 shape, overall red ground w/color portrait of fisherman in yellow slicker, No. E-3 .... **$155**

Lemonade Pitcher with Woman

Pitcher, 9 3/4" h., lemonade shape, overall pink ground w/color "Gibson Girl" type bust portrait of a young woman w/dark hair in a bouffant style & holding purple flowers, No. H-1 (ILLUS.) **$265**

Pitcher, 10 1/4" h., monk decoration.............. **$165**

Game Bird Platter

Platter, 15" l., h.p. scene of game bird rooster & hen in field, gold rim, marked w/Warwick knight's helmet in green, signed "Real," ca. 1930s, rare (ILLUS.) **$325**

Platter in "June Bride" Pattern

Platter, 22" l., white w/small pink flowers & gold rim in "June Bride" decor patt., marked w/Warwick knight's helmet in maroon, decor code #B2062, ca. 1940s (ILLUS.) **$25**

Shaving mug, brown w/portrait of Cardinal, marked w/IOGA knight's helmet in green & "Warwick China" in black, decor code A-36 in red, ca. 1903, 3 1/2" d., 3 1/2" h. **$75**

Portrait Spirits Jug

Spirits jug, matte tan & brown w/woman in low-cut gown & flowing hair, marked w/IOGA knight's helmet in green, decor code M-1 in red, scarce, ca. 1908, 6 1/4" h. (ILLUS.) **$225**

Stein with Native American Chief

Shriner Tankard Set

Stein, brown & cream w/portrait of Native American chief in full bonnet, marked w/IOGA knight's helmet in green, ca. 1905, 5" h. (ILLUS., previous page) **$100**

VP Style Stein with Bulldog

Stein, VP style, brown & cream w/photographic transfer of bulldog, "Ch. I'Almassadeur," marked w/IOGA knight's helmet, decor code A-32, ca. 1906, 2 2/4" d., 4 1/2" h. (ILLUS.) **$75**

Tankard set: 9 3/4" h. tankard & six 4" h. steins; turquoise & salmon w/Shriner symbol near top & desert scene at bottom, marked w/IOGA knight's helmet in green, no decor code, ca. 1909, scarce, the set (ILLUS., top of page) **$925**

Teapot, cov., h.p. portrait, "Gibson Girl" decor, turquoise & pink, matte finish, signed "H. Richard Boehm," marked w/IOGA knight's helmet in green, decor code M5, rare in this color, ca. 1910, 7 1/2" h. **$425**

Vase, 4" h., Pansy shape, yellow shading to green ground, color portrait of Anna Potaka, K-1 .... **$200**

Vase, 4" h., Parisian shape, overall charcoal ground, color nude portrait signed "Carreno," No. C-1 .... **$500**

Vase, 4" h., Violet shape, brown shading to tan ground, color beechnut decoration, matte finish, M-2 (ILLUS., top next column) **$110**

Violet Vase with Beechnut

Vase, 4" h., Violet shape, overall charcoal ground, color floral decoration, C-6 .... **$130**

Warwick Violet Style Vase

Vase, 4" h., Violet style, brown & tan w/poppies, marked w/IOGA knight's helmet, decor code A-6 in red, scarce, ca. 1904 (ILLUS.) **$110**

Vase, 4 1/2" h., Dainty shape, brown shaded to brown ground, colored floral decoration, No. A-27 .... **$145**
Vase, 6" h., Narcis #3 shape, brown shaded to brown ground, decorated w/a fisherman wearing a yellow slicker, No. A-35 ..... **$165**
Vase, 6 1/2" h., Clytie shape, overall red ground w/poinsettia decoration, No. E-2.... **$210**
Vase, 6 1/2" h., Clytie shape, tan shaded to brown ground w/beechnut decoration, matte finish, No. M-2 .... **$250**
Vase, 6 1/2" h., Clytie style portrait vase, portrait of Madame Lebrun, red glaze, marked w/IOGA knight's helmet in grey, decor code I14 in red, rare, ca. 1908 .... **$290**
Vase, 6 1/2" h., Den shape, brown shaded to brown ground, pine cone decoration, No. A-64 .... **$250**
Vase, 6 3/4" h., Narcis #2 shape, overall red ground, color portrait of Princess Potaka, No. E-1 .... **$220**
Vase, 7" h., Albany shape, tan shading to tan ground, color nut decoration, matte finish, M-64 .... **$200**
Vase, 7 1/4" h., Cuba shape, brown shading to brown ground, color pine cone decoration, A-64 .... **$260**
Vase, 7 1/2" h., Verbena #2 shape, brown shaded to brown ground, adult portrait of Madame Lebrun, No. A-17 .... **$200**
Vase, 8" h., Carol shape, green shaded to green ground, red rose decoration, No. F-2 .... **$255**
Vase, 8" h., Carol shape, overall pink ground decorated w/a "Gibson Girl" type decoration w/portrait of a woman wearing a boa, No. H-1 .... **$300**
Vase, 8" h., Chicago shape, brown shaded to brown ground w/red & green floral decoration, No. A-40 .... **$210**
Vase, 8" h., Duchess shape, brown shading to brown ground, color floral decoration, A-27 .... **$155**
Vase, 8" h., Duchess shape, overall white ground w/color bird decoration, D-1 .... **$185**
Vase, 8" h., Grecian shape, brown shading to brown ground, color floral decoration, A-6 .... **$190**
Vase, 8" h., Rose shape, overall red ground w/color portrait of Madame Recamier, No. E-1 .... **$230**
Vase, 8 1/4" h., Narcis #1 shape, overall white ground w/color bird decoration, No. D-1 .... **$190**
Vase, 8 1/4" h., Victoria shape, overall red ground w/red poinsettia decoration, No. E-2... **$190**
Vase, 8 1/4" h., Victoria style, white w/gold rim, two herons, marked w/IOGA knight's helmet in grey, decor code D-1 in red, ca. 1909 .... **$190**
Vase, 9" h., Flower shape, green shaded to green ground, portrait of a young woman w/flowing red hair, No. M-1 .... **$200**
Vase, 9" h., Verbena #1 style, grey w/pink poppies & pink & white daisies, rim trimmed in gold, marked w/IOGA knight's helmet, decor code C-6 in red, ca. 1906 (ILLUS., top next column) **$160**

Warwick Verbena Style Vase

Vase, 9 1/4" h., brown shaded to brown ground, floral decoration, No. A-23 .... **$160**
Vase, 9 1/4" h., Windsor shape, brown shaded to brown ground, acorn decoration, No. A-67 .... **$290**

Penn Vase with Acorn Decoration

Vase, 9 1/2" h., Penn shape, brown shaded to brown ground, acorn decoration, No. A-64 (ILLUS.) **$175**
Vase, 9 1/2" h., Penn shape, overall green color w/no decoration, matte finish, No. M-6 .... **$270**
Vase, 9 1/2" h., Thelma style, pink w/h.p. "Gibson Girl" decal, signed "H. Richard Boehm," marked w/IOGA knight's helmet, decor code H-1, scarce, ca. 1909 ...... **$245**
Vase, 9 1/2" h., Verbenia #1 shape, brown shaded to brown ground, color floral decoration, No. A-6................................... **$165**
Vase, 9 3/4" h., Iris shape, brown shaded to brown ground, nut decoration, No. A-64 .... **$150**
Vase, 10" h., baluster shape w/scroll handles, brown w/pink roses, marked w/IOGA knight's helmet, decor code A-12 in red, scarce, ca. 1904 .... **$205**
Vase, 10" h., Flower shape, brown shaded to brown ground, color floral decoration, No. A-6... **$135**
Vase, 10" h., Henrietta shape, brown shaded to brown ground, color portrait of a seminude young woman, No. A-30 .... **$275**

Vase, 10" h., Magnolia style, grey w/picture of partially nude woman, signed "Carreno," marked w/IOGA knight's helmet, decor code #C-2 in red, ca. 1905 .... $850

Vase, 10" h., Roberta shape, brown shaded to brown ground, portrait of a monk, No. A-36....................... $205

Vase, 10" h., Royal #2 shape, brown shaded to brown ground, floral decoration, No. A-27....................... $210

Vase, 10" h., Virginia shape, overall pink ground, "Girls of the Mid West" type decoration w/portrait of a young woman w/a flower in her hair, No. H-1 .... $300

Vase with Woman with Hibiscus

Portrait Vase with Gypsy Girl

Vase, 10 1/4" h., Bouquet #2 portrait style in tan & brown, bust portrait of Gypsy girl in red dress & headscarf, marked w/IOGA knight's helmet in green, decor code M-1 in red, ca. 1908 (ILLUS.)........................... $240

Warwick Bouquet #2 Style Vase

Vase, 10 1/4" h., Bouquet #2 style in pink w/red, pink & white roses, marked w/IOGA knight's helmet in green, decor code H-4, ca. 1908 (ILLUS.) $190

Vase with Woman with Red Rose

Vase, 10 1/4" h., Bouquet #2 style, brown & cream w/decal portrait of young Victorian woman w/red rose in hair, marked w/IOGA knight's helmet in green, decor code A-17 in red, scarce, ca. 1907 (ILLUS.) $265

Vase, 10 1/4" h., Bouquet #2 style, brown & tan w/decal portrait of young Victorian woman w/hibiscus flower in hair, marked w/ IOGA knight's helmet in green, decor code A-17 in red, scarce, ca. 1907 (ILLUS., top next column)............................ $295

Vase with "Girls of the Mid West" Decor

Vase, 10 1/4" h., Bouquet #2 style, tan & brown matte w/"Girls of the Mid West" decor of hatted woman holding rose,

marked w/IOGA knight's helmet in green, decor code M1 in red, scarce, ca. 1909 (ILLUS.) **$305**
Vase, 10 1/4" h., Bouquet #2 style, white w/gold rim & two herons, marked w/IOGA knight's helmet in green, decor code D-1 in red, ca. 1909 .... **$190**
Vase, 10 1/4" h., Bouquet #2 style, white w/gold trim & portrait of Gypsy girl, marked w/IOGA knight's helmet in green, ca. 1908 .... **$220**
Vase, 10 1/4" h., Monroe style, brown & tan matte w/pine cones on branch, marked w/IOGA knight's helmet in green, decor code M-2, ca. 1909 .... **$150**
Vase, 10 1/4" h., Orchid shape, overall red ground, poinsettia decoration, No. E-2 ...... **$210**

Warwick Bouquet #2 Portrait Vase

Vase, 10 1/2" h., Bouquet #2 shape, brown shaded to brown ground, portrait of a young woman w/dark hair holding a branch w/white flowers, No. A-17 (ILLUS.) .. **$225**
Vase, 10 1/2" h., Clematis shape, tan shaded to tan ground w/nut decoration, matte finish, No. M-64 .... **$250**
Vase, 10 1/2" h., Magnolia shape, green shaded to green ground, color floral decoration, No. B-30 .... **$225**
Vase, 10 1/2" h., Monroe shape, overall pink ground, "Girls of the Mid West" type decoration w/portrait of a young woman wearing a large hat, No. H-1 .... **$275**
Vase, 11" h., Geran shape, overall charcoal ground w/red floral cluster, No. C-6 (ILLUS., top next column) **$230**
Vase, 11" h., Oriental shape, brown shading to brown ground, color floral decoration, A-21 .... **$240**
Vase, 11" h., Royal #1 shape, brown shaded to brown ground w/colored floral decoration, No. A-40 .... **$225**
Vase, 11 1/2" h., Bouquet #1 shape, brown shaded to brown ground, portrait of young woman wearing a pearl necklace, No. A-17 .... **$215**

Geran Shape Warwick Vase

Vase, 11 1/2" h., Chrysanthemum #3 shape, brown shaded to brown ground, color floral decoration, No. A-6 .... **$160**

Warwick Vase with Hibiscus Flower

Vase, 11 1/2" h., footed ovoid base angling to long narrow neck & flaring rim, slender graceful handles from base to top of neck, brown w/hibiscus flower, marked w/IOGA knight's helmet, decor code A27 in red, scarce, ca. 1904 (ILLUS.) **$200**
Vase, 11 1/2" h., Hibiscus shape, brown shaded to brown ground, large color scene of red & black & white setter dogs hunting, No. A-50 .... **$375**
Vase, 11 1/2" h., President shape, tan shaded to tan ground, acorn decoration, matte finish, No. M-4 .... **$220**
Vase, 11 1/2" h., Regency shape, brown shading to brown ground, color floral decoration, A-40 .... **$240**
Vase, 11 1/2" h., Roman shape, overall white ground, color bird decoration, D-1 .... **$220**
Vase, 11 1/2" h., Senator #3 shape, brown shading to brown ground, color floral decoration, A-6 .... **$165**

Bouquet Style Vase with Orchid

Vase, 11 3/4" h., Bouquet #1 style, brown & cream w/orchid in shades of pink, marked w/IOGA knight's helmet in green, decor code A-14, ca. 1904 (ILLUS.)........... **$190**

Egyptian Shape Vase with Flowers

Vase, 11 3/4" h., Egyptian shape, brown shaded to brown ground, red floral decoration, No. A-27 (ILLUS.)........................... **$245**

Vase, 11 3/4" h., Verona shape, overall white ground, color bird decoration, D-1 (ILLUS., top next column) **$205**

Vase, 11 7/8" h., Nasturtium shape, brown shading to brown ground, color floral decoration, A-40.. **$240**

Vase, 12" h., Bouquet #1 style, tall cylindrical form w/twig handles, colored transfer of a woman holding long-stemmed yellow roses, shaded ground **$225**

Vase, 12" h., Gem shape, brown shading to brown ground, color floral decoration, A-16.. **$190**

Vase, 12" h., Helene shape, color portrait of woman w/large hat, matte finish, M-1 .... **$255**

Vase, 12" h., Queen shape, overall charcoal ground, color floral decoration, No. C-6 ..... **$290**

Verona Shape Vase with Bird

Vase, 12 1/2" h., Alexandria shape, brown shaded to brown ground w/color floral decoration, No. A-40................................ **$275**

Warwick Vase with Poppies

Vase, 12 1/2" h., baluster form, brown w/pink poppies, marked w/IOGA knight's helmet in green, decor code A40, scarce, ca. 1904 (ILLUS.) **$200**

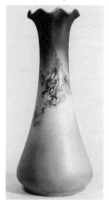

Vase with Hazelnuts

Vase, 13" h., Senator #2 style, brown & tan matte w/hazelnuts on branch, marked w/IOGA knight's helmet in green, decor code M-2 in red, ca. 1909 (ILLUS.)............ **$175**

Warwick Restaurant Soup Bowls

Vase, 13 1/2" h., Chrysanthemum #2 shape, overall charcoal ground decorated w/colored florals, No. C-6...................... **$145**

Vase, 13 1/2" h., Senator #2 shape, tan shading to brown ground, color portrait of a gypsy wearing scarf, matte finish, M-1.... **$190**

Vase, 15" h., A Beauty shape, brown shaded to brown ground w/red rose (American Beauty) decoration, No. A-20.................... **$300**

Vase, 15" h., A Beauty shape, white ground w/red rose (American Beauty) decoration, No. D-2... **$325**

Vase, 15" h., Princess shape, brown shading to brown ground, color floral decoration, A-27... **$350**

Vase, 15" h., Senator #1 shape, green shading to green ground, color acorn decoration, matte finish, M-4..................... **$200**

Vase, 15 1/2" h., Chrysanthemum #1 shape, overall red ground w/a Madame Lebrun child portrait, No. E-1 .... **$180**

Commercial China

Bowl, 4 1/4 x 10 1/4" oval, white ironstone w/green band, "Osiris" emblem.................... **$20**

Bowl, 3 3/4" d., soup, double-handled, white w/black & orange decorative band below rim & on handles, marked w/Warwick knight's helmet in green, ca. 1940s, each (ILLUS. of six, top of page)................... **$6**

Bowl, 5" d., white w/bands, star emblem w/"Bethlehem Chapter No. 14 O.E.S."......... **$15**

Butter pat, white w/"The Brass Rail" logo, 3" **$20**

knight's helmet, ca. 1937, 4 1/4" h. (ILLUS.).. **$21**

Warwick "Sumter Hospital" Creamer

Creamer, white w/two green bands & "Sumter Hospital" logo, 2 1/2" h. (ILLUS.).... **$22**

Cup, white w/"Johnny's" logo **$25**

Cup & saucer, brown wave decoration, Santone finish **$25**

Cup & saucer, white w/"Duckwall's" logo **$40**

Cup & saucer, white w/"Liggett's" logo............ **$20**

Cup & saucer, white w/"St. Gregory's" logo **$22**

Cup & saucer, white w/Crestwood pattern...... **$25**

Cup & saucer, white w/Dakota pattern............ **$20**

Mug, various decorations, marked w/Warwick knight's helmet in green, ca. 1940s, 3" d., 3 1/4" h., each **$9**

Mug, white w/green drape & emblem, "The Security Benefit Assoc.," 3 1/2" h. **$15**

Warwick Commercial Creamer

Creamer, white w/green tree & bands & "Camp Lone Tree," marked w/Warwick

Warwick "Duckwall's" Mustard Jar

Mustard jar, cov., white w/"Duckwall's" logo (ILLUS.).. **$28**

Plate, 6 1/4" d., white w/one green band, double headed eagle emblem w/"AASR 32" & "Valley of Wheeling" **$24**

4H Plate by Warwick

Plate, 7 1/4" d., white w/4H camp w/stream & trees in green, two green bands inside rim, marked w/Warwick knight's helmet in green, scarce, ca. 1944 (ILLUS.) **$25**
Plate, 9" d., white w/"Hotel Anthony" logo **$18**
Plate, 9" d., white w/black & red bands, "Masonic Temple of Austin" emblem................. **$18**
Plate, 10" d., white w/"compliments of Dine Furniture Company" **$40**
Plate, 10" d., white w/gold band, "Souvenir of Pleasanton" decal **$25**
Plate, 10 1/4" d., white w/"The Washington Duke" logo... **$35**

Warwick B&O Railroad Platter

Platter, 8 1/4" l., white w/22k gold decorative band on rim & B&O Railroad symbol, marked w/Warwick knight's helmet in green, ca. 1938 (ILLUS.).......................... **$175**

Wentworth Military Academy Platter

Platter, 15" l., white w/Wentworth Military Academy crest, maroon band inside rim, marked "Warwick China" in green, ca. 1930s (ILLUS.)... **$40**

Warwick "Sumter Hospital" Sugar Bowl

Sugar bowl, cov., white w/two green bands, "Sumter Hospital" logo, 3 3/4" h. (ILLUS.) **$25**
Syrup pitcher, cov., white w/"Johnny's" logo **$50**
Tray, oval, white w/"The Washington" logo, 3 1/2 x 9 3/4"...................................... **$30**

"Oakley's" Oval Vegetable Dish

Vegetable dish, individual, oval, white w/"Oakley's" logo (ILLUS.)......................... **$25**

Dinnerwares
Bowl, oval, Pattern No. 2000 .... **$25**
Cup & saucer, Pattern No. 9572, Silver Poppy decoration...................................... **$10**
Cup & saucer, Pattern No. 9903, Grey Blossom decoration **$18**
Cup & saucer, Pattern No. B-9551................. **$20**

Warwick Demitasse Cup & Saucer

Demitasse cup & saucer, Gray Blossom decor patt. w/platinum rim, saucer only marked w/Warwick knight's helmet in

gold w/patt. name "Gray Blossom - Pat.
#9903," ca. 1940, 2 1/4" h. cup, 5" d.
saucer, cup & saucer (ILLUS.) $26
Gravy boat w/underplate, Pattern No. B-
9289 .... $30
Pitcher, 8" h., buttermilk-type, white ground
w/floral decoration of small pink flowers $45
Pitcher, 8" h., milk-type, white ground w/flo-
ral decoration of blue forget-me-nots $35
Plate, 6 1/2" d., bread & butter, Pattern No.
9437-M, Windsor Maroon decoration $5
Plate, 6 1/2" d., bread & butter, Pattern No.
D-9351, platinum bands $20
Plate, 6 1/2" d., bread & butter, Pattern No.
E-9450 .... $15
Plate, 9" d., Pattern AB-9231 .... $8
Plate, 9" d., Pattern No. B-9059 .... $15
Plate, 9" d., Pattern No. C-9295, Bird of Par-
adise decoration w/two birds $12
Plate, 10" d., dinner, Pattern No. 9584, Bird
of Paradise decoration w/single bird $10
Plate, 10" d., Pattern No. 2098, Venetian
Rose decoration $10
Platter, 13" l., Pattern No. B-9272, coin gold
trim $40
Vegetable bowl, cov., Pattern No. 2001 .... $40
Vegetable bowl, handled, Pattern No. 2062 .... $30

Watt Pottery

*Founded in 1922, in Crooksville, Ohio, this pot-
tery continued in operation until the factory was
destroyed by fire in 1965. Although stoneware
crocks and jugs were the first wares produced, by
1935 sturdy kitchen items in yellowware were the
mainstay of production. Attractive lines like Kitch-
N-Queen (banded) wares and the hand-painted
Apple, Cherry and Pennsylvania Dutch (tulip) patterns were popular throughout the country. Today
these hand-painted utilitarian wares are "hot"
with collectors.*

A good reference book for collectors is Watt
Pottery, An Identification and Value Guide, *by
Sue and Dave Morris (Collector Books, 1993)*

Watt Pottery Mark

Baker, cov., Open Apple patt., No. 110,
8 1/2" d. $165
Baker, open, White Daisy patt., 7" $25
Baker, cov., Rooster patt., No. 67, 8 1/4" d. $85
Baker, cov., Apple patt., No. 96, 8 1/2" d.,
5 3/4" h. $55
Baker, Tear Drop patt., rectangular, No. 85,
9" w. (minor hairline in base) $210
Bean cup, Apple patt., individual, No. 75,
3 1/2" d. 2 1/4" h $155
Bean cup, Tear Drop patt., individual, No.
75, 3 1/2" d. 2 1/4" h $10
Bean pot, cov., two-handled, Star Flower
(four petal) patt., No. 76, 7 1/2" d., 6 1/2" h. $85
Bowl, 4 1/4" d., 2" h., Starflower (four-petal)
patt., ribbed, No. 04 .... $30

Watt Pottery Apple Pattern Bowls

Bowl, 4" d., 1 1/2" d., Apple patt., No. 602
(ILLUS. far left) $30
Bowl, 4 1/4" d., 2" h., Starflower (five-petal)
patt., ribbed, No. 04 .... $10
Bowl, 4 1/4" d., 2" h., Apple patt., ribbed,
No. 04 .... $20
Bowl, 5" d., Eagle patt., ribbed, No. 5 .... $75
Bowl, 5" d., individual cereal or salad, Apple
patt., No. 68 .... $40
Bowl, 5" d., 1 3/4" h., Tear Drop patt., No.
68 .... $30
Bowl, 5" d., 2" h., Apple patt., No. 603
(ILLUS. center left) $45
Bowl, cov., 5 " d., 2 1/2" h., Apple patt., No.
05 .... $35
Bowl, 5 1/2" d., 2" h., Reduced Decoration
Apple patt., No. 74 .... $20
Bowl, 5 3/4" d., Apple patt., No. 23 .... $18
Bowl, 5 3/4" d., Cut-Leaf Pansy (Rio Rose)
patt., No. 23 .... $15
Bowl, 6" d., 1 3/4" h., cereal or salad, Apple
patt., No. 94 .... $25
Bowl, 6" d., 1 3/4" h., cereal or salad, Au-
tumn Foliage patt., No. 94 .... $10
Bowl, 6" d., 2 1/2" h., Apple patt., No. 604
(ILLUS. center) $30
Bowl, cov., 7 1/2"d., Apple patt., w/Iowa ad-
vertising, No. 66 .... $60
Bowl, 8" d., Cross-Hatch Pansy (Old Pan-
sy) patt., small spaghetti, No. 44 .... $165
Bowl, 8" d., Cut-Leaf Pansy (Rio Rose)
patt., small spaghetti, No. 44 .... $15
Bowl, cov., 8 1/2" d., Butterfly patt., No. 67
(hairline in base) $375
Bowl, 9 1/2" d., 4" h., salad, Apple patt., No.
73 .... $20
Bowl, 10 3/4" d., 3 1/2" h., footed salad, Ap-
ple patt., No. 106 .... $125
Bowl, 11 3/4" d., 4" h., Apple (two-leaf)
patt., No. 55 .... $50

Two-leaf Apple Spaghetti Bowl

Bowl, 13" d., Apple (two-leaf) patt., spaghetti, No. 39 (ILLUS.) $60

Bowl, 13" d., Starflower (five-petal) patt., spaghetti, No. 39 .... **$25**

Canister, cov., Dutch Tulip patt., large, No. 72, 7 1/4" d., 9 1/2" h. (chip inside cover rim) **$195**

Canister, cov., Tear Drop patt., large, No. 72, 7 1/4" d., 9 1/2" h. **$200**

Casserole, cov., Apple patt., individual, French handled, No.18, 8" l. **$125**

Casserole, cov., Autumn Foliage patt., individual, French handled, No.18, 78" l. **$105**

Casserole, cov., Black Moonflower patt., individual, French handled, No. 18, 8" l. **$20**

Casserole, cov., Dutch Tulip patt., individual, French handled, tab handle on cover, No. 18, 8" l. **$95**

Casserole, cov., Raised Pansy patt., individual, French handled,No.18, 8" l. **$15**

Casserole, cov., Tear Drop patt., individual, French handled, No.18, 8" l. **$65**

Casserole, Morning Glory patt., cream-colored, No. 94, 8 1/2" d. (missing cover) **$95**

Casserole, cov., Apple patt., w/advertising, on metal stand, No. 96, 8 1/2" d., 5 1/2" h. **$65**

Casserole, cov., Double Apple patt., No. 96, 8 1/2" d., 5 1/2" h. **$95**

Chip-n-Dip set, Apple patt., No. 110 & 120 bowls, the set **$110**

Cookie jar, cov., Cross-Hatch Pansy (Old Pansy) patt., No. 21, 7 1/2" h. **$200**

Cookie jar, cov., Cut-Leaf Pansy (Rio Rose) patt., No. 21, 7 1/2" h. **$105**

Creamer, Apple (two-leaf) patt., No. 62, 4 1/4" h. **$55**

Creamer, Apple (two leaf) patt., No. 62 w/advertising, 4 1/4" h. **$55**

Autumn Foliage Creamer & Pitchers

Creamer, Autumn Foliage patt., No. 62, 4 1/4" h. (ILLUS. right w/Autumn Foliage pitchers) **$30-50**

Creamer, Double Apple patt., No. 62, 4 1/4" h. **$195**

Creamer, Dutch Tulip patt., No. 62, 4 1/4" h. .. **$115**

Creamer, Morning Glory patt., cream-colored, No. 97, 4 1/4" h. **$425**

Rooster Pattern Creamer & Pitchers

Creamer, Rooster patt., No. 62, 4 1/4" h. (ILLUS. left w/pitchers) **$125**

Cup & saucer, Cross-Hatch Pansy (Rio Rose) patt., No. 40, the set **$135**

Dip bowl, slanted sides, Autumn Foliage patt., No. 120, 5" d., 2" h. **$20**

Grease jar, cov., Apple patt., w/South Dakota advertising, No. 01, 5 1/2" h. **$200**

Mixing bowl, Double Apple patt., No. 64, 7 1/2" d., 5" h. **$50**

Tear Drop No. 64 Mixing Bowl

Mixing bowl, Tear Drop patt., No. 64, w/Minnesota advertising, 7 1/2" d., 5" h. (ILLUS.) **$40**

Mixing bowl, Pansy patt., ribbed, w/Minnesota advertising, No. 8, 8" d., 4 1/2" h. **$20**

Mixing bowl, Autumn Leaf patt., w/advertising, No. 9, 9" d., 5" h. **$40**

Mug, Star Flower (four-petal) patt., barrel-shaped, No. 501, 4 1/2" h. **$30**

Mug, Apple patt., cylindrical w/angled handle, No. 701, 3 3/4" h. **$300**

Mug, Apple patt., tapering cylindrical form, No. 121, 3 3/4" h. **$105**

Mug, Autumn Foliage patt., cylindrical waisted shape, No. 121, 3 3/4" h. **$75**

Pie plate, Apple patt., No. 33, 9" d. **$50**

Pie plate, Cross-Hatch Pansy (Old Pansy) patt., No. 33, 9" d. **$175**

Starflower Four-Petal No. 15 Pitcher

Pitcher, 5 1/2" h., Starflower (four-petal) patt., No. 15 (ILLUS.) **$30**

Pitcher, 6 1/2" h., Apple patt., w/advertising, No. 16 .... **$50**

Pitcher, 8" h., 8 1/2" d., refrigerator-type, square-shaped, Apple (two-leaf) patt., No. 69 .... **$300**

Pitcher, 5 1/2" h., Autumn Foliage patt., No. 15 (ILLUS. center w/Autumn Foliage creamer, previous page) $30
Pitcher, 5 1/2" h., Dutch Tulip patt., No. 15 ... $100
Pitcher, 5 1/2" h., Rooster patt., No. 15 (ILLUS. center w/Rooster creamer & pitcher, previous page) $65
Pitcher, 5 1/2" h., Tear Drop patt., No. 15 ...... $25
Pitcher, 5 1/2" h., Tulip patt., No. 15....... $400-500
Pitcher, 6 1/2" h., Autumn Foliage patt., No. 16 (ILLUS. left w/Autumn Foliage creamer, previous page) $30
Pitcher, 6 1/2" h., Cherries patt., No. 16 .... $65
Pitcher, 6 1/2" h., Dutch Tulip patt., No. 16 (rub on spout).. $50
Pitcher, 6 1/2" h., Rooster patt., No. 16 (ILLUS. right w/Rooster creamer & pitcher, previous page) $50-100
Pitcher, 7" h., 7 3/4" d., Cross-Hatch Pansy (Rio Rose), old style $175
Pitcher, 8" h., Apple patt., w/ice lip, No. 17 (nick on spout).. $85
Plate, 10" d., Cut-Leaf Pansy (Rio Rose) patt., No. 101.. $40

Pink on Black Moonflower Plate

Plate, 10" d., Moonflower patt., pink on black, No. 101 (ILLUS.)............................... $65
Plate, 10 1/2" d., divided, Dutch Tulip patt. $700
Platter, 12" d., Apple patt., No. 49 .... $105

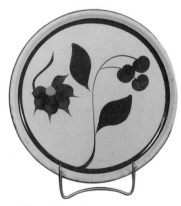

Watt Cherry Pattern 12" Platter

Platter, 12" d., Cherry patt., No. 49 (ILLUS.) $95
Platter, 12" d., Pansy patt., No. 49 .... $30
Platter, 15" d., Cherries patt., No. 31 .... $65
Platter, 15" d., Cross-Hatch Pansy (Rio Rose) patt., No. 31.................................... $105

Apple Hourglass Salt & Pepper Shakers

Salt & pepper shakers, Apple patt., hourglass shape, w/Iowa advertising, No. 117 & No. 118, pr. (ILLUS.) $145
Salt & pepper shakers, Autumn Foliage patt., hourglass shape, No. 117 & No. 118, pr.. $75
Salt & pepper shakers, Starflower (five-petal) patt., barrel-shaped, w/advertising, No. 45 & No. 46, 4" h., the set $35
Salt & pepper shakers, Tear Drop patt., barrel-shaped, No. 45 & No. 46, 4" h., pr. $265
Salt & pepper shakers, Tear Drop patt., hourglass shape, No. 117 & No. 118, each $135
Salt shaker, Cherries patt., barrel-shaped, No. 45, 4" h... $45
Sugar bowl, cov., Apple patt. w/advertising, No. 98 .... $170
Sugar bowl, cov., Autumn Foliage patt., No. 98.. $45
Sugar bowl, cov., Morning Glory patt., w/advertising, cream-colored, No. 98, 4 1/4" h.. $195

Watt Pottery Autumn Foliage Teapot

Teapot, cov., Autumn Foliage patt., No. 505, 9" w., 5 3/4" h. (ILLUS.) $650-750

Two Rare Apple Pattern Watt Teapots

Teapot, cov., Apple patt., No. 505, 5" h. (ILLUS. on left with other Apple teapot) .... **$2,800+**

Teapot, cov., Apple (three-leaf) patt., No. 112, rare, spout professionally repaired, 6" h. (ILLUS. right with other Apple teapot) **$1,400**

Wedgwood

Reference here is to the famous pottery established by Josiah Wedgwood in 1759 in England. Numerous types of wares have been produced through the years to the present.

WEDGWOOD

Early Wedgwood Mark

Basalt Ware

Potpourri jar, cov., footed bulbous nearly spherical body w/angled loop shoulder handles, fitted low domed cover pierced overall w/small holes & centered by a striped spherical knob, the black ground of the body ornately decorated w/enamel & gilt designs of exotic birds among flow-

ering vines, floral sprigs on the cover, impressed mark, finial possibly reglued, inner disk lid missing, ca. 1820, 13" h. (ILLUS. right with Basalt vase & Rosso Antico potpourri, bottom of page) **$3,055**

Wedgwood Decorated Basalt Teapot

Teapot, cov., baluster-form body tapering to a flat rim w/low domed cover & button knob, serpentine spout & C-form handle, the black ground h.p. overall w/large blossoms & leaves in shades of brick red, white & green, Josiah Wedgwood, late 18th - early 19th c., 6 3/4" h. (ILLUS.) **$1,495**

Wedgwood Basalt & Rosso Antico Pieces

Large Group of Crimson & Yellow Jasper Ware Piece

Teapot, cov., wide baluster-form body w/flat rim & low domed cover w/knob finial, shaped spout & C-scroll handle, black ground applied w/tall deep red Rosso Antico acanthus leaves & bellflowers around the sides, radiating applied leaves around the cover, impressed mark of Josiah Wedgwood, England, early 19th c., 7 1/4" h. (rim nick) **$743**

Vase, 15 1/4" h., exaggerated antique bottle-form shape, footed bulbous body tapering to a very slender neck supporting a very wide dished & stepped rim, a round loop shoulder handle, the black ground decorated w/iron-red Grecian figures & stylized decorative banding, impressed mark, early 19th c. (ILLUS. center with Basalt & Rosso Antico potpourri jars, bottom previous page).................. **$14,100**

Caneware

Teapot, cov., footed wide squatty body w/a low domed cover w/button finial, short gently arched spout & arched C-scroll handle, smear-glazed & applied around the middle w/a wide band of tight scrolls & leaftips in green, radiating spearpoints applied around cover, impressed mark of Josiah Wedgwood, England, 19th c., 4" h. (faint spider crack in base)............. **$2,432**

Jasper Ware

Bowl, cov., 5 1/8" d., footed wide cylindrical form w/a flattened cover & disk finial, crimson ground decorated w/panels of white relief classical figures alternating w/foliate vertical bars, impressed mark, ca. 1920 (ILLUS. bottom row, second from left, with large group of yellow & crimson Jasper Ware pieces, top of page).. **$1,880**

Candlesticks, flaring foot below the cylindrical shaft & wide cupped socket rim, yellow ground applied w/black relief classical figures & palm trees, an arabesque floral foot band & leaftip top band, stain to one socket rim, impressed marks, ca. 1930, 7 3/4" h., pr. (ILLUS. top row, far left with large grouping of crimson & yellow Jasper Ware. top of page)............... **$1,058**

Doorknob & escutcheon sets: two oval blue Jasper knobs each decorated w/a white relief figure of a Grecian woman within a white relief leaftip border band, w/pairs of fancy cast gilt-metal knob backplates & keyhole escutcheons, one handle cracked, 19th c., handle 1 5/8 x 2 1/2", 2 1/4" h., the set (ILLUS., top next page).... **$288**

Match box, cov., flared base & cylindrical sides w/a domed cover, crimson ground decorated w/applied white relief classical figures & a leaftip foot band, slight relief loss, impressed mark, ca. 1920, 2 3/4" h. (ILLUS. bottom row, second from right w/large grouping of crimson & yellow Jasper Ware pieces, top of page).......... **$1,880**

Early Jasper Portrait Medallion

Medallion, portrait-type, oval, blue ground w/a bold white relief bust portrait of Warren Hastings, Governor-General of India, the name & title impressed below the bust, modeled by John Flaxman Jr., impressed mark, mounted in an ebonized wood frame, ca. 1787, medallion 3 1/2 x 4 3/8" (ILLUS.) **$1,880**

Unusual Jasper Ware Doorknobs & Metal Fittings

Mustard pot on attached undertray, cov., the flaring dished undertray holding the wide short cylindrical pot w/a fitted domed silver plate cover, yellow ground applied w/black relief fruiting grapevine swags around the sides joined by small lion masks & rings, impressed mark, ca. 1930, rim chip on pot, interior stain, undertray rim restored, 4" h. (ILLUS. top row, second from right with the large grouping of crimson & yellow Jasper Ware pieces, top of page) **$323**

Pitcher, miniature, 3 7/8" h., ovoid body w/pinched rim spout & long C-form handle, crimson ground decorated in white relief w/classical figures alternating w/vertical scroll bands, ca. 1920 (ILLUS. bottom row, fourth from right with large group of crimson & yellow Jasper Ware pieces, top of page).................... **$1,528**

Pitcher, 4 3/4" h., jug-type, wide ovoid body w/a wide short cylindrical neck & arched spout, C-scroll handle, crimson ground decorated w/a band of white relief classical figures, the neck w/applied white swagging, ca. 1920, impressed mark, some relief loss (ILLUS. bottom row, third from left with large grouping of crimson & yellow Jasper Ware pieces, top of previous page) **$499**

Pitcher, 5 3/4" h., jug-type, wide ovoid body w/a short cylindrical neck & rim spout, C-scroll handle, yellow ground decorated w/black relief classical figures around the body, black relief swags around the neck, impressed mark, ca. 1930 (ILLUS. top row, third from right with large grouping of crimson & yellow Jasper Ware pieces, top of previous page) **$588**

Pitcher, 6 1/2" h., jug-type, wide ovoid body w/a short wide cylindrical neck & rim spout, C-scroll handles, crimson ground decorated w/a white relief band of classical figures, white relief swags around the neck, impressed mark, ca. 1920, shallow chip at side of spout (ILLUS. bottom row far left with large grouping of various crimson & yellow Jasper Ware pieces, top previous page) **$940**

Blue Jasper Ware Pitcher with Metal Lid

Pitcher, cov., 6 1/2" h., 3 3/4" d., slightly tapering cylindrical body w/loop handle & attached hinged metal lid, dark blue ground w/white relief Grecian figures around the bottom & a grapevine around the rim, marked "Wedgwood - England," late 19th - early 20th c. (ILLUS.)........ **$185-200**

Portland vase, classic design w/a wide ovoid body tapering to a trumpet-form neck flanked by arched handles, yellow ground decorated w/white relief classical scenes, impressed mark, ca. 1900, footrim & rim chip, areas of relief repair, 7" h. (ILLUS. top row, second from left with various other pieces of crimson & yellow Jasper Ware, top previous page) **$2,115**

Wedgwood Jasper Diceware Tea Set

Tea set: cov. teapot, cov. sugar bowl & creamer; Diceware patt., each piece w/a black ground w/applied white vinework framing engine-turned dicing w/yellow quatrefoils, Josiah Wedgwood, first half 19th c., footrim chip on teapot ground out, sugar bowl 4" h., teapot 3 7/8" h., the set (ILLUS.).. **$1,081**

Miniature Wedgwood Jasper Ware Tea Set

Tea set: miniature, cov. teapot, cov. sugar, creamer & oval tray; blue Jasper Ware, baluster-shaped pot & squatty bulbous sugar & creamer, all w/white relief Classical figures, modern, the set (ILLUS.) **$50**

Josiah Wedgwood Jasper Ware Teapot

Teapot, cov., squatty bulbous form in green w/white relief Classical figures, regular size (ILLUS.) **$65**

Vase, 5 1/2" h., round flaring foot below the flaring trumpet-form body, yellow ground decorated around the body w/blue relief classical figures highlighted by thin white bands, a band of blue relief palmette leaves around the foot, a blue relief nar-

row upper band w/a thin blue band near the rim, impressed mark, missing inner disk lid, restored chips below the base, 19th c. (ILLUS. top row, far right with the large group of crimson & yellow Jasper Ware pieces, top of page 709)................. **$940**

Vase, cov., 11" h., Classical urn-form, a wide round foot & short pedestal base supporting a short swelled lower body issuing large upturned loop handles, the wide gently flaring cylindrical sides w/a wide rolled rim, inset domed cover w/a pointed knob finial, crimson ground, the body decorated w/a continuous scene of white relief classical figures, the foot & lower body w/white relief pointed & fanned leaf & a lappet band, the rolled rim w/another lappet band & the cover w/long white relief acanthus leaves, impressed mark, hairlines in the cover, finial restoration at join, ca. 1920 (ILLUS. bottom row, far right with large group of various crimson & yellow Jasper Ware pieces, top of page 709) **$3,525**

Queensware

1940s Wedgwood Queens Ware Pot

Teapot, cov., footed squatty bulbous body in creamy white w/a short angled spout, upright squared handle & tapering domed cover w/knob finial, applied light blue grapevine band around shoulder & cover, marked "Wedgwood Embossed Queens Ware of Etruria & Barlaston," Josiah Wedgwood & Sons, England, ca. 1940, 8 3/4" l., 5" h. (ILLUS.) **$70**

Rosso Antico

Potpourri jar, cov., footed bulbous nearly spherical body w/angled loop shoulder handles, fitted low domed cover pierced overall w/small holes & centered by a striped spherical knob, the matte terra cotta body enameled w/scattered large colorful flowers & leaves, impressed mark, restored rim chip on cover, early 19th c. (ILLUS. left with Basalt potpourri jar & vase)............................. **$1,528**

Teapot, cov., squatty rounded shape w/nearly straight spout, flaring flanged front top rim & high angled handle, dark red ground applied w/Oriental-style white prunus blossoms & branches in relief, impressed mark of Josiah Wedgwood, England, early 19th c., 8 5/8" l. (nick to edge of spout)... **$1,175**

Teapot, cov., squatty rounded shape w/short slightly curved spout & high squared handle, dark red ground applied w/black bands of stylized Egyptian motifs & hieroglyphs, the slightly domed cover w/radiating fluting & a figural crocodile finial, impressed mark for Josiah Wedgwood, England, early 19th c., 4 1/2" h. (nicks to cover rim, restoration to finial, spout lip & handle, cover slightly misfit) **$881**

Miscellaneous

Bowl, 7 1/8" w., octagonal, Dragon Lustre, the exterior w/a mottled blue ground under the large entwined dragon, a light mother-of-pearl interior, No. Z4829, printed mark, ca. 1920, slight glaze scratches (ILLUS. second from left with other Lustre ware pieces, bottom of page)............... **$470**

Box, cov., Dragon Lustre, wide squatty bulbous base w/domed cover & knob finial, orangish red ground decorated w/an entwined gold dragon, mottled purple interior, printed mark, ca. 1920, 5" h. (ILLUS. second from right with other Lustre pieces, bottom of page) **$1,116**

Punch bowl, Butterfly Lustre, a wide flaring round foot below the wide rounded bowl, deep ruby luster on the exterior w/butterflies & insects, a mother-of-pearl interior w/butterflies, No. Z4827, printed mark, ca. 1920, very slight interior gilt wear, 11" d. (ILLUS. third from right with other pieces of Lustre ware, bottom of page)... **$2,820**

Modern Josiah Wedgwood Teapot

Teapot, cov., Mandarin patt., Queen's shape, Barleston, England, mid-20th c. (ILLUS.).. **$35**

Early Wedgwood Pearlware Tureen

Tureen, cov., pearlware, a long lightly fluted oval pedestal base w/gadrooned band below the deep oval body w/light fluting around the sides & upswept scrolled ends above the ropetwist end handles, the steeply domed fluted cover topped by a nude figure seated atop a recumbent horse, dark blue banded highlights, impressed mark, early 19th c., overall 16 1/2" l. (ILLUS.) **$1,554**

Vase, 8 1/2" h., Hummingbird Lustre, simple baluster shape w/a short flaring neck, mottled blue exterior ground decorated w/large hummingbirds, orangish red mottled interior, No. Z5294, printed mark, ca. 1920 (ILLUS. far right with other Lustre pieces, bottom of page) **$1,175**

Vase, 8 1/2" h., lustre-type in the "Daventry" patt., footed slender cylindrical body w/a narrow shoulder tapering to the trumpet-form neck, a plum-colored ground w/green-0utlined bands around the foot, center, shoulder & neck, the main background decorated w/stylized landscapes & florals trimmed in gold, No. Z5418, printed mark, ca. 1920 (ILLUS. far left with other Lustre pieces, bottom of page) **$3,290**

Grouping of Wedgwood Lustre Pieces

Nicely Hand Painted Wedgwood Vase

Vase, 12 3/4" h., china, footed slender ovoid body tapering to a widely flaring trumpet neck, a deep maroon lower body band trimmed overall w/delicate gilt flower sprigs, the wide white body band h.p. w/large leaf vines w/deep red, blue & yellow flowers, a gilt-trimmed maroon neck band below the white floral-decorated upper neck, marked (ILLUS.) **$196**

Weller

This pottery was made from 1872 to 1945 at a pottery established originally by Samuel A. Weller at Fultonham, Ohio, and moved in 1882 to Zanesville. Numerous lines were produced, and listings below are by pattern or line.

Reference books on Weller include The Collectors Encyclopedia of Weller Pottery by Sharon & Bob Huxford (Collector Books, 1979) and All About Weller by Ann Gilbert McDonald (Antique Publications, 1989).

WELLER

Weller Marks

Ardsley (1928)
Various shapes molded as cattails among rushes with water lilies at the bottom. Matte glaze.

Bulb bowl, lobed blossom form base w/leaf-form openwork top, pale green leaves on white, 4 7/8" h. **$69**

Vase, 9 1/2" h., bud-type, triple, four tall curved green leaves forming three small openings beside a tall molded blue iris blossom, molded green rockwork base **$431**

Aurelian (1898-1910)
Similar to Louwelsa line but with brighter colors and a glossy glaze. Features bright yellow/orange brush-applied background along with brown and yellow transparent glaze.

Aurelian Ewer with Yellow Roses

Ewer, a thin widely flaring disk-form base tapering sharply to a tall slender neck w/a tri-lobed flaring mouth, long S-scroll handle from the top rim to the base, shaded dark to light brown ground h.p. w/large yellow roses & green leaves around the lower body, decorated by Marie Rauchfuss, Aurelian-Weller mark, 9" h. (ILLUS.)... **$374**

Aurelian Jug with Golden Grapes

Jug, footed squatty bulbous body w/a short small rolled neck & C-form shoulder handle, h.p. golden grapes & dark green leaves on a shaded gold to black ground, impressed mark, initials of artist Helen Windle, 5" h. (ILLUS.) **$345**

Tall Aurelian Mug with Orange Fruits

Mug, flared ringed base below the tall slightly tapering sides, large C-form handle, h.p. large deep orange fruits & green leaves against a mottled gold & dark green & brown ground, decorated by Charles Chilcote, 6 1/2" h. (ILLUS.) **$173**

Small Squatty Aurelian Vase

Vase, 4 1/4" h., three flared knob feet supporting the squatty bulbous body tapering to a low three-lobed rolled rim, h.p. yellow carnations & green leaves on a dark blackish brown ground, Aurelian mark, some dry crazing (ILLUS.) **$184**

Aurelian Whiskey Jug with Grapes

Whiskey jug, footed nearly spherical body w/a short round shoulder spout & large arched handle across the top, h.p. w/large dark purple grapes & green leaves on a mottled yellow, dark brown & black ground, initialed by artist Frank Ferrell, 6 1/8" h. (ILLUS.).............................. **$259**

Baldin (about 1915-20)
Rustic designs with relief-molded apples and leaves on branches wrapped around each piece.

Bowl, 7" d., wide squatty bulbous form w/wide short flared rim, molded w/large pink & white apples, green leaves & brown branches on a dark blue ground...... **$201**

Blossom (mid-late 1930s)
Pale pink flowers & green leaves on a blue or green matte ground.

Jardiniere, footed bulbous body w/a wide rolled rim flanked by small loop shoulder handles, blue ground.................................... **$81**

Blue & Decorated Hudson (1919)
Handpainted lifelike sprays of fruit blossoms and flowers in shades of pink and blue on a rich dark blue ground.

Vase, 7 1/2" h., octagonal slightly flaring body tapering slightly at the top to a flat mouth, decorated w/a dark pink band & pink blossoms around the top, dark blue ground, impressed mark **$201**

Blue Louwelsa (ca. 1905)
A high-gloss line shading from medium blue to cobalt blue with underglaze slip decorations of fruits & florals and sometimes portraits. Decorated in shades of white, cobalt and light blue slip. Since few pieces were made, they are rare and sought after today.

Cylindrical Blue Louwelsa Vase

Vase, 5 1/8" h., simple cylindrical form, a dark blue ground h.p. w/large pansy-like blossoms in lavender, dark blue & black, impressed mark, glaze inclusion on back (ILLUS.).. **$431**

Tall Floral Blue Louwelsa Vase

Vase, 11 1/2" h., tall slender ovoid form tapering to a small molded flat mouth, dark blue shaded to lighter blue ground h.p. w/large stylized black, dark blue & light blue blossoms up the sides, repair to the rim (ILLUS., previous page) **$690**

Blue Ware (before 1920)
Classical relief-molded white or cream figures on a dark blue ground.

Vase, 12" h., cylindrical body w/closed-in rim, decorated w/a repeating scene of dancing maidens, trees & birds, narrow floral band below the rim **$288**
Vase, 12" h., slightly flaring cylindrical body w/a flared foot & flaring rim, decorated w/a repeating design of a tall cream-colored Grecian-style dancing woman holding aloft a cluster of grapes, shorter green trees & shrubs in the background, a band of rose cluster swags around the rim & a band of pink rose blossoms around the base **$230**

Bonito (1927-33)
Hand-painted florals and foliage in soft tones on cream ground. Quality of artwork greatly affects price.

Vase, 5" h., double-gourd form w/wide flat mouth, cream ground h.p. w/a large pink daisy-like flower & green leafy stem, impressed mark **$143**

Burnt Wood (1908)
Molded designs on an unglazed light tan ground with dark brown trim. Similar to Claywood but no vertical bands.

Unusual Tall Burnt Wood Vase

Vase, 15 1/2" h., a sharply tapering conical body below a wide shallow squared cupped rim supported on a winged scarab design, the body design showing the Three Wise Men on camelback following the Christmas star, some glaze misses inside the rim & some background unevenness (ILLUS.) **$805**

Coppertone (late 1920s)
Various shapes with an overall mottled bright green glaze on a "copper" glaze base. Some pieces with figural frog or fish handles. Models of frogs also included.

Cigarette or match holder, model of a lily pad bloom w/seated frog, 5 1/2" w., 4 1/2" h. **$201**
Console bowl & flower frog, shallow flaring & lobed bowl, molded, the rim at one end w/a model of a seated frog next to a water lily bud, a separate domed rockwork flower frog, flower frog 2 1/2" h., oval 10 1/2" l., 2" h., 2 pcs. **$550-750**
Model of a turtle, brown w/heavy green splotching, 6 1/2" l. **$460**

Rare Coppertone Bud Vase with Frog

Vase, bud, 9" h., 3 1/4" d., slender body w/flaring irregular rim, frog crawling up the side, mottled green & brown glaze (ILLUS.)... **$920**

Dickensware 2nd Line (early 1900s)
Various incised "sgraffito" designs, usually with a matte glaze. Quality of the artwork greatly affects price.

Dickensware II Chinaman Humidor

Humidor, cov., figural, model of a Chinese man's head, realistic coloring, two chips on edge of cover, 5 1/2" h. (ILLUS.) **$431**

Vase, 7" h., triangular baluster-form body flaring at the base, the flat molded mouth w/three tiny loop handles, streaky dark blue ground incised w/pink & dark blue fish, impressed mark **$311**

Dickensware 2nd Line Vase with Monk

Vase, 10 1/8" h., cylindrical w/a narrow angled shoulder to the flat low rounded rim, incised & colored portrait of a monk playing a flute, decorated by Anna Best, minor surface rubs (ILLUS.)........................... **$288**

Vase, 11" h., tall ovoid body tapering slightly to a molded mouth, incised decoration of a shepherd & his sheep walking toward a group of trees, shaded green to brown ground, matte glaze, impressed mark........ **$633**

Dresden (ca. 1907)
Simple forms with a blue or green matte ground slip-painted with dark blue Dutch scenes of windmills, sailboats or people, sometimes with a seascape in the distance.

Fine Dresden Vase with Windmill Scene

Vase, 10" h., simple cylindrical form, decorated w/a landscape with a Dutch windmill against a mottled blue over dark green ground, decorated by Levi Burgess, barely visible glaze line down from rim (ILLUS.)... **$575**

Eocean and Eocean Rose (1898-1925)
Early art line with various handpainted flowers on shaded grounds, usually with a clear glossy glaze. Quality of artwork varies greatly.

Fine Eocean Lamp Base with Birds

Lamp base, tall baluster form w/a cushion base, h.p. w/a pale tan crabapple bough w/pink & white blossoms descending from the rim & supporting two bluebirds against a shaded black body band, cast hole in base, Arthur Powell mark on base, slight overall crazing w/small glaze skip near base & rim, great color & composition, 15 1/4" h. (ILLUS.).................. **$1,610**

Dark Green Eocean Pitcher with Cherries

Pitcher, 6 1/4" h., a footed low wide cylindrical lower section w/a deep indented band joining it to the wide slightly tapering cylindrical upper body w/a wide rim spout & squared inverted D-form heavy handle from the side of the top to the side of the base, very dark green shaded to lighter green ground painted on the upper body w/dark red cherries & green leaves, marked, minor firing separations (ILLUS.) .. **$230**

Eocean Vase with Large Yellow Rose

Vase, 7 1/8" h., flaring cylindrical body w/a wide rounded shoulder tapering to a short molded neck, h.p. w/a large pale yellow rose & green leaves atop long thorny stems down the sides, on a dark greyish blue to pale blue ground, initialed by the artist (ILLUS.) **$345**

Eocean Vase with Yellow Irises

Vase, 7 7/8" h., a cushion foot tapering to a tall ovoid body w/a wide low flared mouth, a black shaded down to grey ground painted w/a tall cluster of yellow irises accented w/pink & green leaves, unmarked (ILLUS.) **$259**

Unusual Eocean Wine Carafe

Wine carafe, footed wide cylindrical body w/a narrow shoulder tapering to a wide cylindrical neck surrounded by six short integrated arched handles from the rim to the shoulder, dark green shaded to pale green ground, h.p. w/a large bunch of purple & green grapes w/leafy stems, deco-

rated by Frank Ferrell, marked on base, missing the cover, 11 1/2" h. (ILLUS.) **$575**

Etched Floral (ca. 1905)

Various simple shapes decorated with incised flowers or berries outlined in black and usually against solid backgrounds in green, orange, yellow, beige, or pink.

Rare Etched Floral Jardiniere & Pedestal

Jardiniere & pedestal, the wide bulbous ovoid body w/a wide flat closed mouth, decorated w/a wide incised rim band of half-round sunflowers & large green leaves above the pale yellow body, the matching tall waisted pedestal w/a flaring base w/a leaf-molded ruffled foot, a matching sunflower band above the foot, signed by Frank Ferrell, small chip on inside of jardiniere & some interior staining, overall 31 1/4" h., 2 pcs. (ILLUS.) **$2,070**

Etna (1906)

Colors similar to Early Eocean line, but designs are molded in low relief and colored.

Mug, tall tapering cylindrical form w/angled loop handle, dark blue to grey shaded background decorated w/large pink & deep pink mum blossoms on pale green stems, impressed marks, 5 1/4" h **$92**

Etna Vase with Dark Red Wild Roses

Vase, 5 1/2" h., a wide low squatty round base tapering sharply to a flaring neck, very dark green shaded to pale green ground painted w/dark maroon wild roses & dark green leaves, impressed Weller & Etna marks (ILLUS.).................................. **$150**

Vase, 6" h., wide squatty bulbous lower body centered by tapering sides to a flat mouth, shaded dark blue to grey ground painted w/large pink & purple blossoms on slender stems, impressed marks **$218**

Weller Etna Vase with Pink Blossoms

Vase, 9 3/4" h., slightly tapering cylindrical body flaring at the top, a black top shading down to dark grey & pale grey, painted w/large pink blossoms at the top & base joined by a slender green stem, Weller & Etna marks (ILLUS.).................... **$219**

Etna Vase Painted with Large Pink Poppy

Vase, 10" h., a slightly tapering cylindrical body w/a bulbous top centered by a short rolled neck, dark green shaded to pale green ground painted w/a large pink poppy blossom at the top w/green stems & leaves down the sides, marked, few underglaze color spots (ILLUS.).................... **$219**

Flemish (mid-teens to 1928)

Clusters of pink roses and green leaves, often against a molded light brown basketweave ground. Some pieces molded with fruit or small figural birds. Matte glaze.

Rare Flemish Towel Bar with Birds

Towel bar, narrow oblong back plate molded in relief w/a pair of bluebirds at the top center w/pale green vines around the edges & a cluster of deep red blossoms at the lower edge, a long round curve-ended bar from end to end, tiny handle nick, 12" l., 6" h. (ILLUS.)..................... **$1,610**

Floretta (ca. 1904)

An early line with various forms molded with clusters of various fruits or flowers against a dark brown, shaded brown or sometimes a dark grey to cream ground. Usually found with a glossy glaze but sometimes with a matte glaze.

Vase, 8" h., flat-bottomed ovoid form tapering sharply to a tiny flared neck, dark brown w/a central wide band of tan molded w/a large cluster of green grapes suspended below the neck, glossy glaze, impressed marks.. **$81**

Vase, 8" h., a wide flattened ovoid body tapering sharply to a tiny flared neck, dark brown glossy ground molded down from the neck w/a large cluster of dark purple grapes, impressed mark **$81**

Forest (mid-teens to 1928)

Realistically molded and painted forest scene.

Cylindrical Weller Forest Pitcher

Pitcher, 5 1/2" h., cylindrical w/small rim spout & branch handle, overall molded forest scene in color, chip at top of handle, marked on base (ILLUS.).................... **$173**

Tall Weller Forest Pattern Vase

Vase, 12" h., tall gently flaring waisted shape, woodland path through trees scene, some old glaze chips at rim (ILLUS.).. **$230**

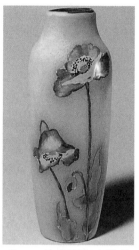

Large Scarce Fudzi Vase with Poppies

Garden Wares & Related Items

Between 1904 and 1948 the Weller Pottery Company manufactured a wide variety of garden items and related pieces such as planters. An especially wide selection of urns, birdbaths, figurines, fountains, sundials, toadstool seats and oil jars appeared in the 1920s and 1930s. The unique and whimsical human and animal figurals are among the desirable pieces on the market today.

Weller Forest Wall Pocket with Owl

Wall pocket, conical w/owl peering out of tree trunk, die-stamped twice "Weller," chips on back edge of top & back edge of hanging hole, some glaze skips, 5 1/2 x 11" (ILLUS.)..................................... **$207**

Fudzi (ca. 1905)

An early art line developed by Japanese artist Gazo Fudji. While the clay was still moist Fudji incised flowers and leaves with further dots of ornamentation and then colored the designs in rich orange, green or brown enamels. The background was left matte in softly shaded tones contrasting with the incised design.

Vase, 11 3/4" h., gently swelled cylindrical body tapering gently at the shoulder to a flat mouth, a tan shaded to pale blue ground incised w/large maroon & pale green poppy blossoms up the sides w/green leaves & buds near the base, unmarked (ILLUS., top next column) **$2,185**

Garden-style Hanging Basket with Birds

Basket, hanging-type, a wide rounded bowl form w/a narrow angled rim fitted w/hanging chains, all molded to resemble glossy green rockwork, four round holes spaced around the sides w/a model of a yellow & black goldfinch applied below each, tail repair to each bird, stress lines at each round hole, 9 1/2" d., 4 3/4" h. (ILLUS.)..... **$460**

Glendale (early to late 1920s)

Various relief-molded birds in their natural habitats, lifelike coloring.

Vase, 4 1/2" h., bulbous body, wooded scene of white wren in nest, unmarked...... **$201**

Wall pocket, cornucopia-form w/curved tall, arched & scalloped backplate pierced w/a hanging hole, the base molded w/a wren & its young on a flowering cherry blossom branch, unmarked, 6 1/2 x 12 1/2"............. **$374**

Greenbriar (early 1930s)

Hand-made shapes with green underglaze covered with flowing pink overglaze marbleized with maroon striping.

Gourd-shaped Greenbriar Vase

Vase, 8" h., double-lobed gourd-form graduated body w/a short wide gently flaring neck, some short firing separations at base (ILLUS.) $104

Greora (early 1930s)

Various shapes with a bicolor orange shaded to green glaze splashed overall with brighter green. Semigloss glaze.

Vases, 5" h., bulbous wide twisted body tapering slightly to a wide flat mouth, impressed mark, pr. $173
Wall pockets, arrowhead shape w/pointed overhead handle, marked, 10 3/8" h., pr.... $374

Hudson (1917-34)

Underglaze slip-painted decoration, "parchment-vellum" transparent glaze.

Pale Hudson Bowl-vase with Roses

Bowl-vase, 3 5/8" h., wide squatty bulbous body tapering to a wide flat mouth, a pale green to yellow ground decorated w/large yellow & white rose blossoms & green leaves, marked (ILLUS.) $173
Vase, 5 1/2" h., bulbous ovoid body w/a wide shoulder & short cylindrical neck, white shaded to green ground decorated w/large white daisies on pale green leafy stems, artist-signed, impressed mark $230
Vase, 5 1/2" h., wide bulbous body topped by a short cylindrical neck, creamy white shaded to pale green ground decorated w/large pale pink poppy-like blossoms on

green leafy stems, artist-signed, impressed mark $316

Hudson Vase with Colorful Flowers

Vase, 7" h., narrow flared foot supporting the swelled cylindrical body w/a widely flaring rim, dark blue shaded to lighter blue ground h.p. w/a cluster of five-petal white, pink, purple & blue blossoms on slender green stems, Weller mark & mark of artist Ruth Axline, small glaze miss at base (ILLUS.) $374

Hudson Vase with Prunus Branches

Vase, 7 3/4" h., footed bulbous ovoid body tapering to a cylindrical neck w/molded rim flanked by small angular shoulder handles, a deep tan shading to pale yellow ground decorated around the neck & shoulder w/black prunus branches w/white blossoms, decorated by Mae Timberlake, Weller mark (ILLUS.)............. $431

Weller Hudson Water Lily Vase

Vase, 7 3/4" h., footed ovoid body tapering to a wide short cylindrical neck w/molded rim flanked by angled handles from rim to shoulder, dark blue to pale yellow ground decorated w/a large white & green water lily w/a golden center & large lily pad leaves, signed by Mae Timberlake on side, some roughness at base (ILLUS., previous page) **$690**

Hudson Vase with Morning Glories

Vase, 8" h., simple swelled cylindrical form tapering to a wide flat mouth, shaded dark blue to dark grey ground decorated w/large blue & white morning glories on green leafy vines, decorated by Hester Pillsbury, marked on base (ILLUS.) **$1,150**
Vase, 9 1/2" h., cylindrical body w/a narrow rounded shoulder to a wide flat mouth, light moss green shaded to cream ground painted w/a repeating design of yellow & white daffodils on tall pale green leafy stems, impressed mark **$288**

Hudson Vase with Large Flower Cluster

Vase, 12" h., simple ovoid body tapering to a low widely flared neck, light blue shaded to pale pink ground h.p. w/a large cluster of pale pink, white & blue poppy-like blossoms on leafy stems, signed by Hester Pillsbury, drill hole in base removed part of the mark, few minor glaze inclusions (ILLUS.) **$920**

Hunter (before 1910)

Brown or green ground with under-the-glaze slip decoration of ducks, butterflies and probably other outdoor subjects. Signed only "HUNTER." High gloss glaze. Usually incised decoration.

Hunter Mug with Swimming Duck

Mug, wide ringed base below the tall slightly tapering cylindrical sides w/a flat mouth & large C-form handle, decorated w/a swimming brown & white duck against a mottled light green & brown shading to dark green ground, Hunter mark, roughness to rim, 6" h. (ILLUS.) **$259**

Rare Disk-form Hunter Vase with Fish

Vase, 1 1/4" h., 5" d., very low wide disk-form body w/a low molded central mouth, mottled green & yellow ground decorated w/a dark green & brown swimming fish, decorated by Edwin L. Pickens, Hunter mark on base, minor glaze inclusion & several pinpoint glaze pimples (ILLUS.) **$748**

Hunter Pillow Vase with Flying Duck

Vase, 5 1/4" h., pillow-type, a flattened bulbous oblong body tapering to a narrow flared oval mouth, decorated w/a large soaring duck in brown & white below a band of dark green stripes around the top, a shaded dark golden yellow to mottled green background, Hunter mark, some very minor glaze rubs on back (ILLUS.) **$518**

Jap Birdimal (1904)
Stylized Japanese-inspired figural bird or animal designs on various solid colored grounds.

Fine Jap Birdimal Umbrella Stand

Umbrella stand, gently swelled cylindrical form w/a swelling band below the wide low flaring neck, decorated w/slip-quilled landscape of tall dark blue trees in the foreground & smaller trees in the distance, all on a shaded medium to light blue ground w/a pale yellow moon, marked (ILLUS.).. **$920**

Juneau (ca. 1933)
Simple forms decorated with a glossy mottled drip glaze in red, yellow, blue or green with the drips forming pointed arrow-like designs.

Juneau Vase with Drippy Red Glaze

Vase, 10 1/4" h., footed bulbous ovoid body tapering to a wide cylindrical neck flanked by angled handles from the top rim to the shoulder, mottled deep red, pink & maroon drip glaze, marked, few tiny glaze indentations (ILLUS.) **$207**

Kenova (1920)
Simple shapes with a dark green or tan leather-like ground molded with raised designs, usually of roses or daisies but sometimes cameos of birds or women.

Rare Kenova Vase with Rose on Vine

Vase, 8" h., simple wide ovoid shape w/a wide flat mouth, molded w/a large red rose on a leafy green vine wrapping around the sides, Weller mark, museum label on the base, very rare (ILLUS.)...... **$1,150**

L'Art Nouveau (1903-04)
Various figural and floral-embossed Art Nouveau designs.

Vase, 11 1/2" h., tall four-sided slightly tapering body w/molded bands around the base & up each corner, flared four-lobed rim w/a large pansy-like blossom molded in each lobe, pale green matte ground & pink blossoms, impressed mark................ **$230**

Unusual Tall L'Art Nouveau Poppy Vase

Vase, 13 3/4" h., a compressed bulbous lower body w/tapering cylindrical sides up to a band of molded high-relief pink poppy blossoms below a small top band, shaded pale green background, impressed Weller mark, minor surface rubs (ILLUS.).. **$690**

Lorbeek (mid-1920s - 28)

Modernistic forms, usually geometric fan shapes, with a creamy white matte or glossy lavender pink glaze.

White Lorbeek Four-piece Console Set

Console set: 13 3/4" w. console bowl, 5" w. flower frog & a pair of low 2 1/2" h. candleholders; all w/a white glaze, some minor chips on bowl, the set (ILLUS.) **$259**

Louwelsa (1896-1924)

Handpainted underglaze slip decoration on dark brown shading to yellow ground; glossy yellow glaze.

Clock, abstract design case w/a large ruffled rounded crest above large C-scrolls flanking the round dial w/Arabic numerals, painted small berry decoration on the dark shaded brown ground, impressed "Louwelsa Weller 639," 6 1/2" h. (minute edge flake touch-up, non-working) **$219**

Ewer, footed bulbous ovoid body tapering to a tall slender neck w/a tri-form rim & wide spout, long S-scroll handle, shaded brown ground painted w/a yellow daffodil & long green leaves, 11" h. **$259**

Jug, footed large spherical body w/a small short spout on one shoulder & an arched loop handle across the top, painted w/cherries & green & yellow leaves on a shaded dark brown to dark gold ground, decorated by William Hall, impressed mark, 7 1/2" h. **$288**

Louwelsa Tall Mug with Cherries

Mug, tall slightly tapering cylindrical body w/a thick D-form handle, decorated w/dark red cherries & green leaves against a dark background, Louwelsa Weller logo & number 562, several glaze scratches, 5 3/4" h. (ILLUS.) **$127**

Small Squatty Louwelsa Pitcher

Pitcher, 5" d., three-footed wide squatty low body tapering to a short neck w/a wide arched spout & round loop handle, h.p. pink & deep red wild roses & green leaves on a shaded dark green ground, Louwelsa mark, some areas of dry glazing (ILLUS.) **$161**

Unusual Weller Louwelsa Pitcher-Jug

Pitcher, 10" h., jug-type, footed bulbous ovoid body tapering to a wide curved stove pipe-style cylindrical neck w/a second small cylindrical spout at the back of the neck above the C-form strap handle, decorated w/yellow cherries & green leaves w/some goldtone effect on a dark ground, Weller Louwelsa mark & "3 8," some minor in-the-making glaze flaws (ILLUS.) **$230**

Louwelsa Tankard with Indian Portrait

Pitcher, 16 3/4" h., tankard-type, stepped ringed foot below the tall slightly tapering cylindrical body w/small rim spout & large

C-form handle, h.p. bust portrait of a Native American warrior against a black to gold ground, decorated by Marie Rauchfuss, subject identified on the base as High Bear, Sioux Chief w/Weller Louwelsa marks, some restoration to sides, ca. 1905 (ILLUS.) **$920**

Small Louwelsa Vase with Wild Roses

Vase, 4" h., footed wide low squatty lower body tapering sharply to a tall widely flaring trumpet neck, decorated w/red & yellow wild roses & dark green leaves on a dark background, numbered "239-1" & artist-initialed for Lillie Mitchell, tiny base nick (ILLUS.) **$127**

Vase, bud, 9" h., widely flaring base tapering sharply to a tall slender trumpet neck w/flared rim, painted w/an orangish red wild rose blossom & green leaves on a dark brown ground, impressed "Weller Louwelsa F" (glaze flakes on rim) **$127**

Tall Louwelsa Vase with Orange Flowers

Vase, 13 1/2" h., tall slender swelled cylindrical body tapering to a short cylindrical neck, dark blackish brown shaded to green ground, h.p. w/large orange trumpet vine flowers on leafy stems, decorated by Amelia Brown Sprague, Weller Louwelsa mark on base, some small glaze bubbles (ILLUS.) **$460**

Vase, 14 1/8" h., tall cylindrical body w/a thin shoulder & low rolled mouth, dark brown shaded to tan & pale green ground, h.p. w/large green & orange clematis-like blossoms on leafy vines, decorated by Anna Fulton Best, im-

Tall Cylindrical Louwelsa Vase

pressed marks, tight hairline at the rim, some dry crazing (ILLUS.) **$230**

Manhattan (early 1930s-'34)
Simple modern shapes embossed with stylized leaves or leaves and blossoms and glazed in shades of green or brown.

Vase, 8" h., wide squatty rounded lower body tapering gently to wide cylindrical sides & a wide flat mouth, molded around the bottom w/three overlapping bands of short rounded leaves, molded ribs up the sides, light brown matte glaze.................... **$92**

Vase, 8 1/2" h., wide squatty rounded lower body tapering gently to wide cylindrical sides & a wide flat mouth, molded around the bottom w/three overlapping bands of short rounded leaves, molded ribs up the sides, mottled bluish green matte glaze..... **$230**

Marengo (1926)
A line of lustre-decorated wares with orange, lavender, blue, green or pink background painted with stylized trees and landscapes in darker colors.

Wall pocket, long conical shape in deep orange lustre decorated w/tall stylized trees & distant hills in dark reddish brown outlined w/white, 8 3/4" l. **$374**

Matt Green (ca. 1904)
Various shapes with slightly shaded dark green matte glaze and molded with leaves and other natural forms.

Matt Green Vase with Stylized Florals

Vase, 10 1/4" h., slightly waisted cylindrical body w/a flat rim, a repeating band of stylized looped scrolls around the top, the sides w/overall molded swirling stylized Art Nouveau florals, impressed mark (ILLUS., previous page) **$316**

Muskota (1915 - late 1920s)
Figural pieces with human figures, birds, animals or frogs. Matte glaze.

Figure, woman kneeling on a raised rock platform looking over the edge, decorated in pale green & brown, 8" h. (chip repair) **$230**

Scarce Muskota Kingfisher Fish Bowl Base

Fish bowl base, figural, a low oblong woodgrained base w/two short stumps rising from one end, one stump w/a white & blue Kingfisher perched on it, impressed Weller mark, repairs to beak & tail, 13 1/2" l., 11" h. (ILLUS.) **$500**

Flower frog, figural, a rounded pale green base w/block feet topped by two figures, a white standing boy nude except for a cloth around his waist that he holds out, the second nude boy kneeling & peering over the edge of the base, catalog model No. 109, 7" h. (near mint except for a firing line) **$518**

Muskota Figural Turtle Flower Frog

Flower frog, model of a green turtle w/a lily pad & white blossom on its back, impressed mark, small chip on side of lily pad, 9 1/2" l., 4 1/4" h. (ILLUS.) **$330**

Flower frog, model of a woodpecker in brown w/a blue head & black beak perched on a domed brown twisted root base w/two small stump openings, glossy glaze, 5 1/2" h. **$144**

Muskota Flower Frog with Two Ducks

Flower frog, model of two white ducks, one standing on the rim, the other below it swimming, pale green base, few minor glaze flakes, 5 1/2" h. (ILLUS.) **$288**

Paragon (1934)
A late Art Deco line composed of bowls, vases and candlesticks molded with stylized rounded blossoms hidden among a dense design of long pointed angular leaves. Glazed in magenta, gold, blue and a semi-gloss white.

Magenta Paragon Bowl

Bowl, 4 1/2" h., bulbous nearly spherical form w/a wide flat mouth, dark magenta glaze, Weller script mark (ILLUS.) **$127**

Perfecto (early 1900s)
Also known as "Matt Louwelsa." Predominantly sea green, blending into a delicate pink matte finish, unglazed painted decoration.

Vase, 4" h., small bulbous ovoid form tapering to a flat rim, shaded dark yellow lower body shading to creamy white & decorated around the middle w/a continuous band of thin branches w/light blue blossoms, impressed mark **$288**

Vase, 5 1/2" h., simple ovoid form tapering to a small slightly flared rim, pale purple ground painted w/small stylized pink blossoms on green stems, artist-signed **$288**

Weller Perfecto Vase with Irises

Vase, 7 1/4" h., gently swelled cylindrical body w/a narrow shoulder to the wide flat mouth, the pale blue ground decorated w/a tall cluster of dark blue & lavender irises & tall pale green leaves, painted by Dorothy England, impressed Weller mark, chip-bruise on rim (ILLUS.) **$345**

Roma (1912-late '20s)
Cream-colored ground decorated with embossed floral swags, bands or fruit clusters.

Vase, 6 1/4" h., upright rectangular fan-shaped sides w/an openwork rim joined by crossbars, pair of red blossoms & blue berry cluster on each side, pale green border bands **$52**

Wall pocket, conical, incised vertical lines & decorated w/roses & grape cluster near top, green leaves w/yellow center at base, cream ground, 8 1/4" h. **$92**

Scandia
A little known line composed of low bowls and vases with simple forms, each decorated with a creamy white vertical picket fence-like design against a black ground. Ca. 1915

A Pair of Weller Scandia Vases

Vases, 7 5/8" h., gently swelled cylindrical body w/flat rim, tight hairline from rim of one, pr. (ILLUS.) **$138**

Sicardo (1902-07)
Various shapes with iridescent glaze of metallic shadings in greens, blues, crimson, purple or

coppertone decorated with vines, flowers, stars or freeform geometric lines.

coppertone decorated with vines, flowers, stars or freeform geometric lines.

Unusual Sicardo Star-shaped Box

Box, cov., shaped as a five-pointed star w/a conforming cover w/knob finial, overall iridescent design of small stars, unmarked, cover restoration, some grinding chips on base, 2 1/2" w. (ILLUS.) **$403**

Unusual Lobed Sicardo Vase

Vase, 6 3/4" h., squatty tapering four-part melon-lobed lower body below the wide squatty lobed top, small pointed loop handles from upper lobes to lower sides, overall iridescent sunflowers & leaves design in shades of red, blue & green, impressed Weller mark & signed on the side (ILLUS.) **$2,645**

Sicardo Vase with Nasturtiums

Vase, 9 5/8" h., cylindrical w/a narrow rounded shoulder to the low flared mouth, overall design of stylized nasturtium blossoms & leaves in tones of gold, green, red & blue, some open pinpoint glaze bubbles in one area, signed on the side (ILLUS.) **$1,265**

Sicardo Vase with Spider Mum Design

Vase, 9 3/4" h., cylindrical w/a narrow rounded shoulder to the low flared mouth, overall design of stylized spider mums in tones of gold, green, red & blue, signed on the side (ILLUS.).................... **$1,840**

Very Rare Molded Sicardo Vase

Vase, 11" h., tall cylindrical lower body w/a bulbous shoulder centered by a small, short cylindrical neck, large relief-molded

nasturtium blossoms & leaves around the shoulder w/stems & buds down the sides, colorful iridescent glaze, signed on the side, rare form (ILLUS.) **$10,350**

Silvertone (1928)
Various flowers, fruits or butterflies molded on a pale purple-blue matte pebbled ground.

Vase, 6 1/2" h., tapering form w/small loop handles near the rim, molded w/decorated daisies & leaves, marked **$259**
Vase, 8" h., ovoid body tapering to a wide flat mouth flanked by small loop branch handles, molded w/yellow & maroon tulip blossoms & green leaves, marked **$283**
Vase, 10" h., footed bulbous lower body tapering to a tall cylindrical neck w/molded rim, long angled handles from the edge of the rim to the shoulder, molded large daisy-like flowers in white & pale pink on green leafy stems, lavender pebbled ground, stamped mark **$288**

Souevo (1907-10)
Unglazed redware bodies with glossy black interiors. The exterior decorated with black & white American Indian geometric designs.

Bulbous Weller Souevo Vase

Vase, 5 3/8" h., flat-bottomed wide bulbous ovoid body w/a rounded shoulder to the low molded rim band, black rim above a thin scalloped band, the body decorated w/a wide white band painted w/large black Native American-style geometric designs, some staining (ILLUS.) **$150**

Turada (1897)
Turada was an early ware used to produce lamps, mugs, vases & various other decorative items. The dark glossy background was glazed in shades of brown, orange, blue, olive green & claret and highlighted with applied bands of delicate ivory or white pierced scrolling. Pieces were often marked with the line name.

Bowl, cov., 6" d., wide half-round bowl in dark brown decorated w/blue flowers & ivory vines, the domed cover in ivory & blue w/a wide pierced scroll band flanked by raised scroll bands & topped w/a knop finial, impressed mark (repaired) **$201**

Velvetone (late 1920s)

Blended colors of green, pink, yellow, brown, green, matte glaze.

Pink to Green Velvetone Vase

Vase, 4 3/4" h., bulbous ovoid body tapering to a widely flaring ruffled rim, pale pink shaded to light green, incised mark (ILLUS.) $69

White & Decorated Hudson (1917-34)

A version of the Hudson line usually with dark colored floral designs against a creamy white ground.

White & Decorated Vase with Branches

Vase, 8 7/8" h., simple tall ovoid body w/a low rolled mouth, creamy ground h.p. w/continuous curving black branches w/small purple blossoms & pale green leaves, impressed mark, pinpoint rim nick (ILLUS.)... $316

Woodcraft (1917)

Rustic designs simulating the appearance of stumps, logs and tree trunks. Some pieces are adorned with owls, squirrels, dogs and other animals. Matte finish.

Mug, cylindrical tree trunk form w/three small molded foxes peeking out of trunk opening, double loop branch handle, large loop above smaller loop, 6" h. $431

Low Cylindrical Planter with Foxes

Planter, wide low cylindrical log form w/three small embossed foxes peeking out on front, flat rim, short tight hairline at rim, 7 1/2" d., 4 1/4" h. (ILLUS.) $250

Vase, bud, 10" h., cylindrical tree trunk form w/top opening & two short relief-molded branch openings down the sides, apple & leaves down the front............................. $80-100

Wall pocket, conical flattened form modeled as a tree trunk in green & brown w/entwined rose vine w/red flowers, an applied figural squirrel at the base, 9 1/2" h.. $345

Wall pocket, long flattened trumpet form molded as a tree trunk w/molded leaves near the base & a round opening showing the head of an owl near the top, 11" l. ... $374

Wheatley Pottery

Thomas J. Wheatley was one of the original founders of the art pottery movement in Cincinnati, Ohio, in the early 1880s. In 1879 the Cincinnati Art Pottery was formed, and after some legal problems it operated under the name T.J. Wheatley & Company. Its production featured Limoges-style handpainted decorations, and most pieces were carefully marked and often dated.

In 1882 Wheatley dissociated himself from the Cincinnati Art Pottery and opened another pottery, which was destroyed by fire in 1884. Around 1900 Wheatley finally resumed making art pottery in Cincinnati, and in 1903 he founded the Wheatley Pottery Company with a new partner, Isaac Kahn.

The new pottery from this company featured colored matte glazes over relief work designs; green, yellow and blue were the most often used colors. There were imitations of the well-known Grueby Pottery wares as well as artware, garden pottery and architectural pieces. Artwork was apparently not made much after 1907. This plant was destroyed by fire in 1910 but was rebuilt and run by Wheatley until his death in 1917. Wheatley artware was generally unmarked except for a paper label.

Wheatley Marks

Bowl, 6" d., 2 1/2" h., low, upright, corseted sides w/a wide incurved rim, embossed around the sides w/a band of short, upright, pointed, wide leaves, thick matte green glaze, illegible mark **$175-200**

Jardiniere, wide, thick, ovoid body w/a thick squared rim band joining four heavy squared buttresses down the sides, feathered matte green glaze, in the style of Teco, small chip on edge of foot, 9" d., 7" h. **$900-1,000**

Lamp base, thick, slightly tapering cylindrical body w/a wide squared rim band issuing four thick squared buttresses down the side, a copper tube running through the lower buttresses, fine feathered matte green glaze, unmarked, 8 1/2" d., 11" h. **$575-625**

Lamp base, wide, tapering double gourd-form body w/four heavy squared buttress handles from the top rim to the base, leathery matte green glaze, w/original oil font insert, several burst bubbles, incised "WP - 672," 10 1/2" d., 11 1/2" h. .. **$2,800-2,900**

Lamp base, wide, round flaring base tapering to a slender baluster-form standard, embossed oblong leaves around the foot w/the stems continuing up the standard, fine leathery matte green glaze, unmarked, 10" d., 16 1/4" h. **$1,575-1,650**

Vase, 5 1/2" h., 7" d., wide, bulbous form w/a wide rounded shoulder centered by a wide, flat molded mouth, deeply embossed w/a band of wide ribbed upright leaves alternating w/small buds, thick & frothy matte green glaze, incised "W-685" **$1,300-1,400**

Vase, 6" h., 5" d., wide ovoid body tapering slightly to a wide, flat mouth, embossed w/large upright arrowhead leaves around the sides, matte green glaze, incised "WP," several burst bubbles **$775-875**

Vase, 6 3/4" h., 5" d., ovoid shouldered form w/a short, wide neck & flat rim, molded w/a continuous vertical band of wide tapering ribbed leaves, mottled matte green glaze, several clay pimples, mark partially obscured **$950-1,050**

Vase, 7 1/4" h., 7 1/4" d., squatty bulbous body molded around the lower half w/a band of overlapping rounded, pointed leaves, the sides tapering to a cylindrical neck w/narrow molded rings, frothy light green & amber glaze, signed "WP" (several burst glaze bubbles)................ **$900-1,000**

Vase, 7 1/4" h., 9" d., a deep, thick rounded form w/a thick squared flat rim band issuing four heavy squared buttresses down the sides, flower dead-matte green glaze, marked "61" **$1,800-1,900**

Vase, 8 1/2" h., slightly ovoid body tapering to a wide flat mouth, the sides molded w/alternating upright pointed & rounded leaves, matte green glaze, several small chips on leaf edges **$975-1,075**

Vase, 10 1/4" h., 5" d., footed baluster-form body w/the shoulder issuing four long scrolled tendril-like handles to the rim, matte green glaze, marked **$1,025-1,100**

Vase, 10 1/2" h., four heavy square buttress feet tapering up the wide, slightly tapering cylindrical sides, wide molded mouth, overall matte green glaze, illegible mark, several small glaze chips on feet **$1,450-1,500**

Wheatley Vase with Ochre Glaze

Vase, 10 1/2" h., 8 1/2" d., architectural style w/wide bullet-form body supported by four buttressed feet & w/wide upright band of embossed leaves around the upper half, matte ochre glaze, chip on one foot, WP mark (ILLUS.)......................... **$1,150**

Vase, 11 1/2" h., slightly swelled cylindrical form w/a wide bulbed ring around the middle, wide flat rim, mottled matte green glaze w/incised geometric design, unmarked **$975-1,075**

Vase, 11 1/2" h., 9 1/4" d., small rectangular feet supporting the wide, tapering cylindrical body w/a wide, thick molded rim w/four projecting blocks above buttresses, pulled matte green glaze, base pierced w/five drainage holes in the making, signed, some minor glaze flecks, chips to feet **$2,100-2,200**

Vase, 12" h., 7 1/2" d., large, slightly tapering cylindrical form w/a thick rolled rim above a recessed neck band w/four small buttress handles, embossed around the sides w/large, rounded veined leaves alternating w/buds on the rim, curdled medium matte green glaze, marked "WP - C13," couple of burst bubbles **$2,700-2,800**

Vase, 12 1/2" h., 6" d., simple ovoid body tapering to a short cylindrical neck, the sides molded w/tall arrowroot leaves, medium matte green glaze, mark obscured (several clay pimples & burst bubbles) **$1,800-1,900**

Vase, 12 1/2" h., 9" d., wide baluster form w/wide cushion neck, in the style of Grueby's Kendrick vase, molded around the sides & neck w/wide leaves, fine frothy matte light brown glaze, small chip to edge of neck, remnants of paint ... **$3,500-3,600**

Vase, 13" h., 9" d., "Kendrick" style, large ovoid body w/a wide, squatty bulbed neck w/incurved rim, molded around the sides w/wide, tapering ribbed leaves w/matching shorter leaves around the neck, leathery green matte glaze, two small chips on side decoration, marked, after a model by G.P. Kendrick **$4,000-5,000**

Vase, 14 1/4" h., 8" d., based on a Teco form, a bulbous bottom tapering slightly to wide cylindrical body w/a four-scallop ring issuing four vine-like handles down the sides, frothy matte green glaze, incised "WP - 615" **$2,900-3,000**

Vase, 14 1/4" h., 8" d., footed bulbous base narrowing slightly to a tall, wide cylindrical neck flanked by four arched & webbed handles from the rim to the shoulder, leathery matte green glaze, incised "WP" (several burst bubbles, few glaze chips at rim, grinding chips to base) **$3,200-3,300**

Vase, 14 1/2" h., 9 1/4" h., footed, tapering, slightly ovoid body molded w/tall ribbed & pointed leaves up the sides alternating w/shorter leaves topped by projecting blocks embossed on the front w/small swastikas, frothy matte green glaze, no visible mark, several burst bubbles, touchups to two corners of cubes & tip of one leaf **$1,600-1,700**

Vase, 18 1/2" h., 10 1/2" d., tall paneled ovoid form w/a short rolled neck, each panel molded w/a tall serrated & veined leaf alternating w/a stem topped by a three-petal blossom, leathery matte green glaze, two glaze chips on ribs, incised "WP" **$4,000-4,200**

Vase, 20" h., 10" d., the tall, swelled cylindrical body tapering to a slightly bulbed cylindrical neck flanked by pointed tall buttress handles down the side, each w/a half-round cut-out, the body molded w/tall ribbed & pointed leaves alternating w/stylized blossom buds around the neck, dark leathery matte green glaze, mark obscured, long grinding chip on base **$4,500-5,500**

Wall pocket, half-round body composed of three wide, tapering leaf-form panels curled in at the top & alternating w/buds, a low arched backplate w/hanging hole, curdled medium matte green glaze, unmarked, 9 1/4" w., 8" h. **$675-725**

Willow Wares

This pseudo-Chinese pattern has been used by numerous firms throughout the years. The original design is attributed to Thomas Minton about 1780, and Thomas Turner is believed to have first produced the ware during his tenure at the Caughley works. The blue underglaze transfer print pattern has never been out of production since that time. An Oriental landscape incorporating a bridge, pagoda, trees, figures and birds supposedly tells the story of lovers fleeing a cruel father who wished to prevent their marriage. The gods, having pity on them, changed them into birds, enabling them to fly away and seek their happiness together.

Blue

Ashtray, figural whale, ca. 1960, Japan **$25-30**
Ashtray, unmarked, American **$15**
Bank, figural, stacked pigs, ca. 1960, Japan, 7" h. **$50-55**
Batter jug, frosted, Hazel Atlas Glass, 9" h. **$75-95**
Batter jug, Moriyama, Japan, 9 1/2" h. **$100-125**
Bell, modern, Enesco, Japan **$15**
Bone dish, ca. 1890, unmarked, England .. **$40-45**

Blue Willow Bone Dish

Bone dish, Buffalo Pottery, 6 1/2" l. (ILLUS.) **$60-70**
Bowl, 12 1/4" d., serving-type w/beaded rim **$50-75**
Bowl, berry, Allertons, England **$12-15**
Bowl, berry, Japan **$8**
Bowl, berry, milk glass, Hazel Atlas **$15**
Bowl, cereal, Royal China Co. **$11**
Bowl, individual, 5 1/4" oval, J. Maddock **$20**
Bowl, soup, 8" d., Japan **$18-20**
Bowl, soup w/flanged rim, 8 1/4" d., Royal China Co. **$10**
Bowl, 6 1/2 x 8 1/4", Ridgways, England **$45-50**
Bowl, salad, 10" d., Japan **$75**
Bowls, 8", 9 1/4" & 10 1/2" l., rectangular, stacking-type, Ridgways, set of 3 .... **$200**
Butter dish, in wood holder, 6" d. **$50-75**
Butter dish, cov., for stick, Japan, rectangular, 7" l. **$60-70**
Butter dish, cov., 8" d., England **$100**
Butter dish, drain & cover, Ridgways, 3 pcs. **$200**
Butter pat, Buffalo Pottery **$25**
Butter pat, Wood & Sons **$20**
Cake plate, Green & Co., 8" sq. **$40-45**
Canister, cov., round, tin, 5 3/4" h. **$20-25**

Blue Willow Coffee Canister

Canister, labeled "Coffee," marked "Willow," Australia, ca. 1920s, 5 3/4" h. (ILLUS., previous page) **$35-40**
Canister set: cov., "Coffee," "Flour," "Sugar," "Tea," barrel-shaped, ca. 1960s, Japan, the set **$275-300**
Chamber pot, Wedgwood, 9" d. **$175-200**
Charger, 11 3/4" d., Moriyama, Made in Japan **$65-85**
Charger, 12" d., Buffalo Pottery **$75-95**
Cheese dish, cov., rectangular, unmarked, England **$150**

Blue Willow Cheese Stand

Cheese stand, J. Meir & Sons, England, 8 1/2" d. (ILLUS.) **$175-200**
Condiment cruet set: cov. oil & vinegar & mustard cruet, salt & pepper; carousel-type base w/wooden handle, Japan, 7 1/2" h., the set **$175-200**

Blue Willow Cracker Jar

Cracker jar, cov., silver lid & handle, Minton, England, 5" h. (ILLUS.) **$175**
Creamer, Allerton, England **$40**

Blue Willow Cow-shaped Creamer

Creamer, cow-shaped, W. Kent, England, 1920s-50s (ILLUS.) **$250-300**
Creamer, individual, Shenango China Co... **$25-30**

Creamer, John Steventon **$30**

Blue Willow Figural Cow Creamer

Creamer w/original stopper, figural cow standing on oval base, mouth forms spout & tail forms handle, ca. 1850, unmarked, England, 7" l., 5" h. (ILLUS.) **$500-600**
Cruets w/original stoppers, oil & vinegar, Japan, 6" h., the set **$55**
Cup & saucer, Booth **$40-45**
Cup & saucer, Buffalo Pottery **$40-45**
Cup & saucer, child's, ca. 1900, unmarked, England **$50**
Cup & saucer, demitasse, Copeland, England **$40**
Cup & saucer, "For Auld Lang Syne," W. Adams, England, oversized **$100-125**
Cup & saucer, Japan **$10-15**
Drainer, butter, ca. 1890, England, 6" sq........ **$75**
Egg cup, Booths, England, 4" h. **$40-45**
Egg cup, Japan, 4" h. **$20-25**
Egg cup, Allerton, England, 4 1/2" h. **$40-45**
Ginger jar, cov., Japan, 5" h. **$30**
Ginger jar, cov., Mason's, 9" h. **$50-60**
Gravy boat, Buffalo Pottery **$65-75**

Blue Willow Gravy Boat

Gravy boat, ca. 1890, unmarked, England, 7" l. (ILLUS.) **$50-60**
Gravy boat w/attached underplate, double-spouted, Ridgways, England **$60-70**
Hot pot, electric, Japan, 6" h. **$75**
Invalid feeder, ca. 1860, unmarked, England **$150-175**
Knife rest, ca. 1860, unmarked, England .. **$85-95**
Ladle, pattern in bowl, unmarked, England, 6" l... **$125-135**
Ladle, pattern in bowl, floral handle, unmarked, England, 12" l. **$175-185**
Lamp, w/ceramic shade, Japan, 8" h. **$50**
Lamp, w/reflector plate, Japan, 8" h. **$60**
Lamp, Wedgwood, England, 10" h. **$200-225**
Lighter, teacup-shaped, Japan **$35-45**

Mug, "Farmer's," Japan, 4" h...................... **$18-20**

Blue Willow Mug

Mug, barrel-shaped mold, Granger & Worcester, England, ca. 1850, 4 1/4" h. (ILLUS.).. **$200-250**

Willow Ware Mug

Mug, Maling, England, 4 1/2" h. (ILLUS.)......... **$50**
Mustache cup & saucer, Hammersley & Co... **$125-150**

Blue Willow Mustard Pot

Mustard pot, cov., ca. 1870, unmarked, England, 3" h. (ILLUS.)............................... **$75-95**
Napkin holder, Japan.............................. **$40-50**

Blue Willow Nut Dish

Nut dish, scalloped shape, ca. 1900, 7" l. (ILLUS.).. **$75-85**
Pastry stand, three-tiered plates, Royal China Co., Sebring, Ohio, 13" h............. **$40-50**
Pepper pot, ca. 1870, England, 4" h. **$100-125**

Willow Ware Pepper Shaker

Pepper shaker, figural Toby, "Prestopan," unmarked, Scotland, 5 1/4" h. (ILLUS.)
.... **$250-275**

Blue Willow Pitcher

Pitcher, 5 1/2" h., Ridgway, England (ILLUS.).. **$65-75**

Buffalo Pottery Blue Willow Pitcher

Pitcher, cov., 5 1/2" h., Buffalo Pottery (ILLUS.)... **$150-175**
Pitcher, 6" h., scalloped rim, Allerton, England **$100**

Blue Willow "Chicago Jug"

Pitcher, 7" h., "Chicago Jug," ca. 1907, Buffalo Pottery, 3 pt. (ILLUS.).................. **$200-225**
Pitcher, 8" h., glass, Johnson Bros., England **$35-40**
Pitcher w/ice lip, 10" h., Japan **$100**

Blue Willow Place card Holder

Place card holder, unmarked, England, ca. 1870s, 2 1/2" d. (ILLUS.)...................... **$85-100**
Place mat, cloth, 16 x 12" **$18-20**
Plate, bread & butter, Allerton, England...... **$12-15**
Plate, bread & butter, Japan........................... **$5-7**
Plate, child's, 4 1/2" d., Japan **$10-15**
Plate, "Child's Day 1971," sandman w/willow umbrella, Wedgwood...................... **$50-60**
Plate, dinner, Booth's, England **$40-45**

Buffalo Blue Willow Dinner Plate

Plate, dinner, Buffalo Pottery, 1911 (ILLUS.)
.... **$30-35**
Plate, dinner, ca. 1870, unmarked, England
.... **$35-40**
Plate, dinner, Cambridge, blue patt. on clear glass.. **$40-50**

Plate, dinner, flow blue, Royal Doulton **$65-75**
Plate, dinner, Holland................................. **$18-20**
Plate, dinner, Japan **$10-15**
Plate, dinner, Mandarin patt., Copeland, England **$35-40**
Plate, dinner, modern, Royal Wessex............ **$6-8**
Plate, dinner, Paden City Pottery **$30-35**
Plate, dinner, restaurant ware, Jackson...... **$15-20**
Plate, dinner, Royal China Co..................... **$10-15**
Plate, dinner, scalloped rim, Allerton, England.. **$30-35**
Plate, grill, Allerton, England...................... **$45-50**
Plate, luncheon, Wedgwood, England **$20-25**
Plate, luncheon, Worcester patt. **$35-40**
Plate, 7 1/2" d., Arklow, Ireland...................... **$20**
Plate, 10" d., tin, ca. 1988, Robert Steffy **$10-12**
Plate, grill, 10" d., Japan **$18-20**
Plate, 10 1/4" d., paper, Fonda **$1-2**
Plate, grill, 10 1/2" d., Holland.................... **$18-20**

Blue Willow Wedgwood Platter

Platter, 9 x 11" l., rectangular, Wedgwood & Co., England (ILLUS.) **$100-125**
Platter, 8 1/2 x 11 1/2" l., oval, scalloped rim, Buffalo Pottery **$100-125**
Platter, 9 x 12" l., oval, American............... **$15-18**
Platter, 9 x 12" l., oval, Japan **$20-25**
Platter, 9 x 12" l., rectangular, Allerton, England **$150-175**
Platter, 11 x 14" l., oval, Johnson Bros., England **$50-60**
Platter, 11 x 14" l., rectangular, Buffalo Pottery **$150-175**
Platter, 11 x 14" l., rectangular, ca. 1880s, unmarked, England............................ **$150-175**
Platter, 15 x 19" l., rectangular, well & tree, ca. 1890, unmarked, England..... **$275-325**
Platter, 20 1/2" l., oval, English, late 19th - early 20th c. **$250-300**
Pudding mold, England, 4 1/2" h. **$35-40**

Willow Ware Punch Cup

Punch cup, pedestal foot, unmarked, England, ca. 1900, 3 1/2" h. (ILLUS., previous page) $40-50

Early Willow Leaf-shaped Relish Dish

Relish dish, leaf-shaped, ca. 1870, England (ILLUS.) $100-125

Blue Willow Salt Box

Salt box, cov., ca. 1960, wooden lid, Japan, 5 x 5" (ILLUS.) $150-200
Salt dip, master, pedestal base, unmarked, England, 2" h. $100-125
Salt & pepper shakers, Japan, pr. $30-35

Blue Willow Sauce Tureen

Sauce tureen, cov., England, ca. 1880s, 5" h. (ILLUS.) $125-150
Soup tureen, cov., ca. 1880, unmarked, England $350-400
Spoon rest, Japan $35-40
Sugar Barrel, cov., silver lid & handle, unmarked, England, ca. 1880s, 5" h. (ILLUS., top next column) $175
Sugar bowl, cov., Japan $20-25
Sugar bowl, cov., Ridgway, England $40-50
Tea set, child's, Japan, service for six in box $200-250

Blue Willow Sugar Barrel

Tea set, child's, tin, Ohio Art Co., Bryan, Ohio, service for four.......................... $100-125
Tea tile, ca. 1900, unmarked, England, 6" sq. $75
Tea tile, Minton, England, 6" sq. $75
Teapot, child's, Made in Occupied Japan... $35-40
Teapot, cov., ca. 1890, Royal Doulton.... $250-300
Teapot, cov., child's, Japan $25-30
Teapot, cov., Homer Laughlin.................... $75-85
Teapot, cov., round, Allerton, England.... $200-250

"Auld Lang Syne" Blue Willow Teapot

Teapot, cov., six-paneled squatty bulbous body on short feet, flat hexagonal neck & cover topped w/figural gold lion finial, gold beaded C-form handle, serpentine spout, embellished w/gold line decoration on feet, spout & lid, the sides of the neck reading "We'll tak a cup o' kindness yet, for days o' auld lang syne" in blue, made for Tiffany & Co., New York by Copeland China, England, ca. 1870s (ILLUS.) $200

Mintons Blue Willow Teapot

Teapot, cov., squatty bulbous body tapering to flaring asymmetrical neck, slightly domed cover w/trefoil finial, C-scroll handle, slightly serpentine spout, dark blue handle, spout & finial, Mintons, England, ca. 1900 (ILLUS.)................. $175-200

Royal Corona Ware Teapot

Teapot, cov., squatty ovoid body on short foot, flattened dome cover w/button finial, C-form handle, gently serpentine spout, dark blue spout, handle & finial, gold highlights, Royal Corona Ware, S. Hancock & Sons, England, early 20th c. (ILLUS.)... **$225-250**

Hammersley & Co. Blue Willow Teapot

Teapot, cov., squatty ovoid body on short foot, incurved neck, C-scroll handle, slightly serpentine spout, inset cover tapering to peaked circular finial, decorated w/bands of gold beading at shoulder & on cover, gold decoration on rim, handle, spout & finial, Hammersley & Co., England, ca. 1912-39 (ILLUS.)........... **$150-175**

Royal Worcester Blue Willow Teapot

Teapot, cov., squatty ovoid body tapering in at shoulder to gently peaked cover w/knob finial, straight spout, C-scroll handle, Royal Worcester porcelain, England, ca. 1920s (ILLUS.).............. **$150-175**

Doulton & Co. Blue Willow Teapot

Teapot, cov., squatty ovoid body tapering in at shoulder to short cylindrical neck, slightly tapering inset cover w/disk finial, angled handle, slightly curved spout, shoulder reads "We'll tak a cup o' kindness yet, for days o' auld lang syne," Doulton & Co., England, ca. 1882-91 (ILLUS.) **$200**

Miles Mason Blue Willow Teapot

Teapot, cov., squatty ovoid body tapering in at shoulder to short neck, C-scroll handle, slightly serpentine spout, tapering cover w/disk finial, embellished w/silver line decoration & band of silver grapevine decoration at shoulder & on cover, Miles Mason, England, ca. 1807-13 (ILLUS.) **$300-350**

Miniature Blue Willow Teapot

Teapot, cov., miniature, lobed ovoid body, domed inset cover w/finial, C-scroll handle, serpentine spout, gold line decoration on handle, spout, rim & finial, Windsor China, England, 3 3/4" h. (ILLUS.).... **$15-20**

Teapot, cov., individual, Moriyama, Japan, 4 1/2" h... **$75-100**

Teapot, cov., Sadler, 4 3/4" h. **$40-45**

Teapot, cov., enamelware, unmarked, 7" h. **$75-85**

Blue Willow Teapot & Trivet

Teapot, cover & trivet, spherical body on short tapering foot, short neck w/inset cover w/button finial, C-scroll handle, serpentine spout, on matching round trivet,

Grimwades, England, early 20th c., teapot 6" h., 2 pcs. (ILLUS.)..................... **$250-275**

"Yorkshire Relish" Tip Tray

Tip tray, "Yorkshire Relish," England, 4" d. (ILLUS.).. **$40-50**

Blue Willow Tip Tray

Tip tray, "Schweppes Lemon Squash," England, 4 1/2" d. (ILLUS.)......................... **$40-50**

Blue Willow Toby Jug

Toby jug, w/Blue Willow jacket, unmarked, England, 6" h. (ILLUS.) **$300-400**
Toby jug, w/Blue Willow jacket, W. Kent, England, 6" h.................................... **$300-400**
Toothbrush holder, Wedgwood, England, 5 1/4" h.. **$50-75**
Tray, round, brass, 6" d.................................... **$50**
Trivet, scalloped foot, Moriyama, very rare, 6"... **$50-75**
Vegetable bowl, open, Japan, 10 1/2" oval..... **$35**

Warmer for butter, round, holds candle, Japan... **$50-60**
Wash pitcher & bowl, ca. 1890, unmarked, England, the set................................. **$400-500**

Blue Willow Wash Bowl & Pitcher

Wash pitcher & bowl, Royal Doulton, the set (ILLUS.).. **$500-750**

Other Colors

Butter dish, rectangular, for stick, red, Japan, 7"... **$65-75**
Butter pat, red, Japan..................................... **$20**
Charger, brown, Buffalo China, 11" d. **$60-70**
Coffeepot, cov., ca. 1890, brown, unmarked, England, 8 3/4" h. **$175-200**

Purple Willow Ware Cup

Cup, purple, handleless, unmarked, England (ILLUS.)... **$50-75**
Cup & saucer, red, ca. 1930, Buffalo China **$30-35**
Egg cup, red, England, 4 1/2" h................. **$35-40**

Red Willow Ware Pitcher

Pitcher, 5" h., red, "Old Gustavsberg," Sweden (ILLUS.).. **$50-60**

Plate, 2 3/4" d., green, miniature, modern,
Coalport, England **$20-25**

Brown Willow Ware Child's Plate

Plate, 4 3/4" d., brown, child's, E.M. & Co.
(ILLUS.).. **$40-50**
Plate, 6" d., restaurant ware, brown, Buffalo
China... **$15**
Plate, 9" d., ca. 1890, brown, John Meir &
Son.. **$20-25**

Copeland Red Mandarin Pattern Plate

Plate, 9" d., Mandarin patt., red, Copeland
(ILLUS.).. **$35-40**
Plate, 9" d., purple, Britannia Pottery **$35-40**
Plate, bread & butter, 6" d., green, Japan ... **$18-20**
Plate, dinner, pink... **$10**
Plate, dinner, red, Japan **$15-20**
Plate, grill, 11 1/4" d., green, Royal Willow
China... **$25-30**
Platter, 9", brown, early, unmarked, En-
gland **$90-100**
Platter, 9", red, Petrus Regout, Holland..... **$35-45**
Platter, 9 1/4 x 11 1/4", rectangular, red, Al-
lerton, England **$150-175**
Platter, 11 x 19" l., rectangular, green, John
Steventon & Sons **$125-150**
Sugar bowl, red, Japan **$25-35**
Teapot, cov., purple, Britannia Pottery **$175-200**
Teapot, cov., red, child's, E.M. & Co., En-
gland **$125-150**
Teapot, cov., red, restaurant ware, Sterling
China... **$75-85**
Vegetable bowl, cov., round, green, Victo-
ria Porcelain **$100-125**
Vegetable bowl, red, Allertons, 7" d. **$50-60**
Vegetable bowl, red, cov., Japan, 10" d......... **$30**

Worcester

*The famed English factory was established in
1751 and produced porcelains. Earthenwares were
made in the 19th century. Its first period is known
as the "Dr. Wall" period; that from 1783 to 1792 as
the "Flight" period; that from 1792 to 1807 as the
"Barr and Flight & Barr" period. The firm became
Barr, Flight & Barr from 1807 to 1813; Flight,
Barr & Barr from 1813 to 1840; Chamberlain &
Co. from 1840 to 1852, and Kerr and Binns from
1852 to 1862. After 1862, the company became the
Worcester Royal Porcelain Company, Ltd., known
familiarly as Royal Worcester, which see. Also
included in the following listing are examples of
wares from the early Chamberlains and early
Grainger factories in Worcester.*

Marks

Bowl, 6 3/8" d., footed, deep, gently flaring
rounded sides, underglaze-blue fruits &
flowers exterior decoration, shaded crescent mark, 18th c. (glaze wear).......... **$175-200**
Dessert dish, oval, "Japan" patt., brightly
painted w/an Oriental river garden w/ex-
otic birds flying above a bridge, fencing,
rockwork & a pagoda, impressed
crowned Barr, Flight & Barr marks & red-
printed Royal Arms round address
mark, ca. 1810, 11 1/8" l. **$2,300-2,400**
Dessert dishes, shaped oval form, painted
w/a central arrangement of flowers amid
scattered flower sprays & sprigs within a
gilt gadrooned rim, impressed crowned
Flight, Barr & Barr mark, ca. 1820,
11 7/8" l., pr. (tiny rim chips) **$925-975**
Dishes, leaf & vine-shaped, molded w/two
overlapping leaves edged in green & pale
yellow w/puce veining, set w/a brown
twig handle, each dish painted in the center w/colorful flower sprays & sprigs, ca.
1765, 7 3/4" l., pr. (slight enamel rubbing)
.... **$4,300-4,400**
Egg drainer, the shallow pierced circular
bowl in gilt w/a flower sprig within a foliate
garland entwined about a narrow blue
band, the rim w/a narrow blue & gilt border & set w/a gilt foliate lug handle, underglaze-blue open crescent mark, ca.
1780, 3 1/2" d................................... **$450-475**
Finger bowl underplate, round w/lightly
scalloped rim, painted w/a spray of yellow, pink & orange flowers within four
flower & leaf sprigs at the rim, 1758-60,
5 3/4" d. **$850-875**
Pitcher, 5 1/2" h., milk, jug-form, "Japan"
patt., bulbous body raised on a circular
foot, brightly painted w/an Oriental river
garden w/exotic birds flying above a
bridge, fencing, rockwork & a pagoda, below a gilt gadrooned rim, Barr, Flight &
Barr, ca. 1810............................... **$2,600-2,700**

Part of Set of Worcester Dessert Plates

Pitcher, 9 3/8" h., jug-type, cabbage-leaf style w/mask spout, typically molded w/overlapping leaves & painted below the naturalistically colored mask spout w/the arms of Miss Barbara Band of Hurworth Manor, Darlington within an elaborate puce & gilt foliate & colorful floral cartouche, flanked by turquoise-ground puce scale panels pendent from an underglaze-blue & gilt border below the neck, the gilt dentil-edged rim w/a similar border suspended w/puce leaf swags, underglaze-blue open crescent mark, ca. 1770-75 .... **$10,000-11,000**

Plate, 7" d., scalloped rim, blue-scale-decorated, gilt-edged mirror & vase-shaped panels enclosing brightly colored flower sprays & sprigs, painted in the workshop of James Giles, ca. 1770, pseudo-seal underglaze-blue mark (slight wear) **$1,050-1,100**

Plate, 7" d., scalloped rim, painted w/a loose bouquet & sprigs of summer flowers within a gilt-edged rim, decorated in the workshop of James Giles, ca. 1770 (slight gilt rubbing) **$575-625**

Plate, 9" d., shaped rim, a central spray of blackberries surrounded by three exotic birds perched in branches at the gilt-edged rim, painted in the workshop of James Giles, 1768-70 (two minor shallow rim chips) **$2,9000-3,000**

Plates, 8 1/2" d., dessert, a wide border decorated w/scrolling vines, leaves & floral designs, Chamberlain's, ca. 1815, set of 7 .... **$525-575**

Plates, 8 1/2" d., dessert plates, w/wide border of scrolling vine, leaf & floral motifs, Chamberlains Worcester, ca. 1815, set of 7 (ILLUS. of four, top of page) **$500-800**

Platter, 10 1/8" l., oval, painted in the center in grey, iron-red, black & gold w/the Cookes crest of an armored arm holding a dagger & rising from a gilt battlemented coronet within a grey garter inscribed in black w/a motto, the cavetto & rim w/a wide gilt vermiculé border edged w/salmon-ground gilt-fretwork bands, impressed crowned Barr, Flight & Barr mark, ca. 1810 .... **$1,400-1,500**

Platter, 12 1/8" l., oval, "Royal Lily" patt., typically painted in underglaze-blue w/radiating foliate panels about a central blue & gilt oval medallion, the brown-edged rim w/a narrow blue & gilt chevron-patterned border, Flight & Barr marks, ca. 1795 .... **$450-500**

Platters, 10" l., oval, "Japan" patt., painted w/a border of flowering plants, fencing & rockwork in a colorful Imari palette within a gilt-edged rim, impressed crowned Flight, Barr & Barr mark, ca. 1815, pr. **$1,250-1,300**

Salad bowls or junket dishes, blue & white, the interior printed in underglaze-blue w/the "Pine Cone" patt. within a border of molded scallop shells printed w/further sprays of flowers & fruit beneath the shaped rim, the exterior printed w/three clusters of root vegetables, scattered insects & flower sprigs, ca. 1775, hatched crescent marks in underglaze-blue, 10 1/2" d., pr. **$1,400-1,500**

Soup tureen, cover & stand, each piece printed in underglaze-blue w/the "Pine Cone" patt. within a gadrooned border, the stand & quatrelobed tureen set w/shell-form handles, the cover w/a double bud knop, ca. 1775, hatched crescent mark in underglaze-blue, 12 1/2" w. across handles (very small chip to handle of stand) **$1,850-1,900**

Sweetmeat dish, "Bengal Tiger" patt., "Blind Earl" design, scalloped oval form, molded at each end w/a rose branch handle, painted in the center w/alternating panels of fabulous beasts & vases on tables within a cell-diaper border & gilt-edged rim, ca. 1770, 6 5/8" l. **$1,600-1,700**

Sweetmeat dish, "Blind Earl" patt., molded w/a twig handle issuing two sprays of rose leaves & two buds picked out in underglaze-blue, the ground also painted in blue w/scattered insects, all within a scalloped rim, ca. 1765, underglaze-blue open crescent mark, 6" d. (small chip to underside edge of rim) **$2,600-2,650**

Sweetmeat stand, shell form, the triangular base encrusted w/colorful, naturalistically molded shell, coral & seaweed supporting three tiers of three puce-edged shells w/gilt rims graduating in size & a circular shell above, each painted inside w/polychrome floral sprays, ca. 1770, 8 1/2" h. (some cracks & restorations) **$5,200-5,300**

Teacups & saucers, richly painted & gilt in underglaze-blue, iron-red, turquoise, green & pink w/a variation of the "Japan" patt., gilt line rims, impressed crown mark of Barr, Flight & Barr, ca. 1807, set of 6 .... **$700-750**

Teapot, cov., ovoid body, decorated w/scattered sprays of flowers beneath a gilt dentil-edged rim, the entwined handle & fluted spout decorated w/gilt dots & the domed cover w/an open flower knop, crossed swords & number 9 in underglaze-blue, 1770-75, 6 5/8" h. (knop repaired, minor chips on spout) **$800-850**

Tureens, cov., sauce-type, swelled oval body w/shell end handles & serpentine rim, domed cover w/artichoke finial, decorated in underglaze-blue w/panels of flowers & cells, pseudo-Chinese marks, 18th c., slight chips to one handle, 6 1/2" l., pr. **$2,000-2,200**

Yellow-Glazed Earthenware

In the past this early English ware was often referred to as "Canary Lustre," but recently a more accurate title has come into use.

Produced in the late 18th and early 19th centuries, pieces featured an overall yellow glaze, often decorated with silver or copper lustre designs or black, brown or red transfer-printed scenes. Most pieces are not marked.

Today the scarcity of examples in good condition keeps market prices high.

Creamer, urn shape w/molded ring handle, decorated w/black stripes & transfer of fishermen in front of gate house, 5 1/2" h. (colored-in rim flake) **$385**

Creamer, footed, tapering, bulbous body below the wide cylindrical neck w/pointed rim spout & C-scroll handle, yellow ground w/large round brick red h.p. blossoms & green leaves around the body & vining flowers & leaves around the neck, 3 1/2" h. (small chips) **$600-650**

Cup plate, decorated w/a polychrome bird perched on a branch w/green spatter foliage, early 19th c., 4 1/4" d. **$325-350**

Cup & saucer, handleless, each transfer-printed in brick red w/a fishing scene &

castle & windmill in background, all on the yellow ground **$500-600**

Cup & saucer, handleless, footed cup w/flaring sides & scalloped rim, matching deep saucer, each h.p. w/large rounded brick red blossoms alternating w/smaller blossom buds among green leaves, green rim bands **$1,100-1,200**

Cup & saucer, handleless, yellow ground transfer-printed in orange & brown w/a scene of a mother & children, early 19th c. **$325-375**

Flowerpot & saucer, tapering cylindrical pot w/rounded thick rim band, conforming deep saucer, each w/h.p. large stylized flowers, vines & leaves in red, green & wear, early 19th c., saucer 4 1/2" d., 1 1/4" h., pot 4 1/2" d., 4" h. **$1,100-1,200**

Garniture set: a pair of vases & a slightly taller vase; each of trumpet-form w/a flaring foot & widely flaring, flattened rim, decorated at the rim & base w/two thin brown stripes, the body decorated w/h.p. flower clusters on leafy vines around the sides, in red, brown & green, two vases 4 1/4" h., third one 4 7/8" h., the set (wear, repair, decoration slightly varies) **$1,450-1,550**

Mug, child's, cylindrical, russet transfer-printed design titled "A Rabbit For William," early 19th c., 2 1/2" h. (minor chips)` **$625-675**

Mug, child's, cylindrical, transfer-printed scene of a coach within an oval wreath w/inscription "A New Carriage For Ann," 2" h. **$475-525**

Mug, child's, cylindrical w/applied handle, decorated w/stylized multicolored flowers & leaves w/lustre trim, 2 1/4" h. **$800-900**

Mug, child's, cylindrical w/C-scroll leaf tip handle, the front w/a rectangular scroll-trimmed reddish brown transfer-printed cartouche enclosing the motto "My Son, if sinners entice thee, consent thou not lest disgrace come upon thee," 2 3/8" h. (small lip flakes) **$425-475**

Mug, child's, cylindrical, yellow ground h.p. w/a pink lustre cottage scene, applied handle, 2 1/2" h. **$350-400**

Mug, child's, cylindrical w/applied handle, the yellow ground decorated w/delicate sprigs of small brick red blossoms on leaf stems, green rim band, 3" h. **$750-800**

Mustard pot, cov., painted w/alternating zigzag bands of brown & red, ca. 1820-30, 2 7/8" h. **$2,500-3,000**

Pitcher, 4 3/4" h., mask form, the front molded in relief w/the face of a man w/flesh-toned skin, black hair & beard, the sides molded overall w/large rounded knobs painted brick red w/a green sprigged ground on the yellow ground, angled handle & gently flaring rim & spout w/green band **$950-1,000**

Pitcher, 7 1/4" h., ovoid, wide-lobed body tapering to a flat rim w/pointed spout & molded feather edging, C-form handle, sides h.p. w/large delicate stylized scrolling brown flowers & leaves w/brown band at rim, fine restoration along side of handle, few spots on spout rim, early 19th c. **$550-650**

Pitcher, 7 1/2" h., transfer-printed on each side w/octagonal panel of fruit & birds, inscribed & dated beneath spout in blue enamel "S.Gray:Hodnet, 1810" (rim chip) **$1,100-1,150**

Plate, 6 1/2" d., h.p. central design of stylized reddish orange blossoms & green leafy branches on a white ground, yellowglazed border band **$250-300**

Plate, 8 1/4" d., yellow ground w/the flanged rim embossed w/fruits & flowers painted in brick red & green, the center w/a large h.p. brick red blossom framed by smaller pointed blossoms & green leaves **$400-475**

Plate, 8 3/8" d., modeled as a leafy bunch of grapes resting in a basket, bright yellow, gold & green, ca. 1820-30 .... **$1,950-2,000**

Platter, 9 1/2 x 11", oval, w/gently scalloped rim, h.p. King's Rose center design in reddish orange, yellow & green, reticulated border w/yellow (hairline) **$825-875**

Soup plate w/flanged rim, the rim h.p. w/clusters of small brick red blossoms & . green leaves, the center h.p. w/large brick red pinwheel-form blossoms framed by smaller blossoms & green leaves, 8 1/4" d. **$2,800-2,900**

Whistle, model of a bird perched on a round base, the angled tail forming the blowhole, early 19th c., 3" h. (small flake near wing) **$375-425**

Yellowware

Yellowware is a form of utilitarian pottery produced in the United States and England from the early 19th century onward. Its body texture is less dense and vitreous (impervious to water) than stoneware. Most, but not all, yellowware is unmarked and its color varies from deep yellow to pale buff. In the late 19th and early 20th centuries bowls in graduated sizes were widely advertised. Still in production, yellowware is plentiful and still reasonably priced.

Simple Deep Yellowware Bowl

Bowl, 8 1/2" d., 4" h., small footring & deep bulbous rounded sides w/rolled rim, minor age crazing to glaze, probably early 20th c. (ILLUS.) **$33**

Candlesticks, a stepped rectangular foot below the round stem & deep cylindrical socket w/cupped rim, decorated overall w/a mottled yellow & dark green alkaline glaze, late 19th c., 6" h., pr. (minor age crazing) **$853**

Food mold, miniature, round domed shape w/the interior molded w/vertical wide ribs & a swirled design at the top, late 19th - early 20th c., 4 3/4" d., 2 3/4" h. (very minor staining) **$77**

Large Yellowware Mixing Bowl

Mixing bowl, footring below the deep flaring & rounded sides w/a molded rim band, decorative band composed of brown & white pinstripes, late 19th c., 14 1/2" d. (ILLUS.) **$106**

Yellowware Mug with Molded Flowers

Mug, cylindrical w/molded base below two thin molded bands, relief-molded wide band of flowers & leaves around the body below a thin beaded rim band, C-form strap handle, tan band of glaze around the rim, stained from use, 19th c., 3" h. (ILLUS.) **$77**

Zeisel (Eva) Designs

One of the most influential ceramic artists and designers of the 20th century, Eva Zeisel began her career in Europe as a young woman, eventually immigrating to the United States, where her unique, streamlined designs met with great success. Since the 1940s her work has been at the forefront of commercial ceramic design, and in recent decades she has designed in other media. Now in her ninth decade, she continues to be active and involved in the world of art and design.

Castleton - Museum Ware

Bowl, 11" d., salad, White $160
Bowl, 13" d., salad, French Garden $375

Castleton - Museum Ware Coffee Set

Coffeepot, cov., tall, slender form w/C-
scroll handle (ILLUS. second from left
w/coffee set)... $500
Coffeepot, cov., White $400-500
Creamer, handleless (ILLUS. second from
right w/coffee set)...................................... $300
Creamer, handleless, White.................. $150-175
Cup & saucer, flat, Mandalay $20
Cup & saucer, flat, White................................ $40
Cup & saucer (ILLUS. far left w/coffee set)
.... $150-200
Plate, 8 1/4" d., salad, White $30
Plate, 8 1/4" sq., salad, White $135
Plate, 8 1/4" sq., salad, Wisteria $18
Plate, 10 1/2" d., dinner, White........................ $50
Sugar, cov., handleless (ILLUS. far right
w/coffee set)... $250

Goss American - Wee Modern

Wee Modern Child's Plate

Child's plate (ILLUS.) $265

Hall China Company - Kitchenware

Golden Clover Cookie Jar

Cookie jar, cov., Golden Clover (ILLUS.) $65
Creamer, Tri-tone... $45
Marmite, Casual Living $30

Tri-tone Nested Mixing Bowls

Mixing bowls, nested, Tri-tone, set of 5
(ILLUS.).. $250
Refrigerator jug, cov., Casual Living $100
Refrigerator jug, cov., Tri-tone..................... $150

Casual Living Shakers

Shakers, Casual Living, set (ILLUS.).............. $40
Sugar, Tri-tone... $60

Tri-tone Teapot

Teapot, cov., 6-cup, Tri-tone, ca. 1954
(ILLUS.).. $85

Hallcraft by Hall China Co. - Tomorrow's Classic Shape

This shape was produced in plain white and with a variety of decal designs. A selection of the designs are listed here.

Black Satin
Cup & saucer, the set $25

Bouquet (blue floral decals)
Creamer, after-dinner size $55
Creamer $45
Onion soup, cov.. $100
Platter, 17 1/4" oval $60

Caprice (muted floral decals)
Bowl, fruit, 5 3/4" d.. $15
Celery dish $42
Gravy boat $40
Gravy ladle $50
Platter, 13" oval $40
Platter, 17 1/4" oval $50
Vegetable serving bowl, oval, 11 3/4" l......... $45

Classic White (no decals)
Ashtray $55
Creamer $55

Cup	$25
Cup & saucer, after dinner size, the set	$95
Gravy boat	$75
Gravy ladle	$100
Plate, 11" d., dinner......................................	$22
Saucer	$7
Teapot, cov.	$175

Dawn (mottled design)
Creamer, after dinner size $45

Fantasy (abstract black lines)
Creamer $45
Cup & saucer, the set.................................... $30
Egg cup $125
Plate, 6" d., bread & butter $10
Plate, 11" d., dinner....................................... $32
Platter, 15 1/8" oval....................................... $55
Sugar bowl, cov... $55
Vegetable serving bowl, oval, 11 3/4" l. $70

Frost Flowers (blue floral)
Creamer $30
Platter, 12 7/8" oval....................................... $40
Sugar bowl, cov... $35

Harlequin (pink & black abstract design)
Bowl, 6" d., cereal... $20
Plate, 6" d., bread & butter $10
Plate, 11" d., dinner....................................... $25
Platter, 12 7/8" oval....................................... $45
Salt & pepper shakers, the set $65
Vegetable serving bowl, oval, 11 3/4" l. $50

Holiday (red & black modern poinsettia design)
Ashtray $25
Plate, 11" d., dinner....................................... $23
Platter, 15 1/8" oval....................................... $45

Mulberry (literal mulberry design)
Bowl, 6" d., cereal... $17
Cup & saucer, the set.................................... $22
Plate, 11" d., dinner....................................... $25

Spring (modern floral design)
Teapot, cov. $155

Hallcraft - Century Dinnerware
Creamer, Fern.. $35
Cup & saucer, Garden of Eden $20
Gravy boat & ladle, Fern................................ $95

Fern Jug

Jug, Fern, 1 1/4 qt. (ILLUS.)	$60
Plate, 10" d., dinner, Sunglow.......................	$25
Platter, 15" l., White.....................................	$25
Relish, divided, White	$90
Sugar, cov., Fern	$35

White Vegetable Bowl

Vegetable bowl, 10 1/2" d., White (ILLUS.) $35

Hollydale

Hollydale Chop Plate

Chop plate, 14" l., brown (ILLUS.)................. $60
Creamer $62
Gravy bowl, bird-shape $85
Plate, 10 1/4" d., desert yellow....................... $30
Sauce dish, bird-shape, yellow/turquoise...... $200
Sugar, cov.. $62
Tureen & ladle, bird design, the set $300

Hyalyn "Z Ware"
Bowl, cereal, oxblood, commercial grade/restaurant ware................................ $40
Carafe, autumn gold..................................... $125

Satin Black "Z Ware" Coffee Server

Coffee server, cov., satin black w/white lid (ILLUS.)... $150

"Z Ware" Autumn Gold Compote

Compote, footed, autumn gold, 5" (ILLUS.)... **$350**
Creamer, handleless, autumn gold,
4 3/4" h... **$85**
Mug & saucer, olive green............................ **$145**

Johann Haviland
Bowl, fruit, Wedding Ring patt. **$12**
Coffeepot, cov., Eva White.............................. **$75**
Creamer & cov. sugar, Wedding Ring patt. **$60**
Creamer & sugar, Eva White, the set............. **$65**
Cup & saucer, Wedding Ring **$20**
Dinnerware set, Wedding Ring, 20-pc. ser-
vice for 4... **$200-250**
Plate, bread & butter, Wedding Ring patt. **$10**
Plate, 10 1/4" d., dinner, Wedding Ring **$18**
Platter, oval, Wedding Ring patt. **$60**
Sauce dish & underplate, Wheat **$50**
Serving bowl, round, Wedding Ring patt. **$40**

Johann Haviland

Blue Roses Teapot

Teapot, cov., Blue Roses patt., 1950s
(ILLUS.) **$65**

Johann Haviland
Tureen/vegetable bowl, cov., White **$80**

Monmouth Dinnerware
Butter pat, Pals, 4" **$25**
Creamer, Blueberry... **$35**
Creamer, Lacy Wings...................................... **$50**
Cup & saucer, Lacey Wings/Rosette................ **$5**

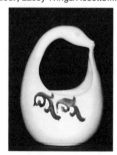

Goose-shaped Gravy Boat

Gravy boat, goose shape, Lacey Wings
(ILLUS.).. **$175**
Sauce dish, Pals... **$140**

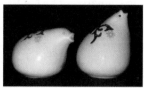

Lacey Wings Shakers

Shaker set, Lacey Wings, pr. (ILLUS.) **$65**
Sugar, cov., bird lid, Blueberry....................... **$25**

Monmouth Bird-shaped Sugar

Sugar, cov., bird lid, Lacey Wings (ILLUS.) **$50**

Lacey Wings Teapot with Bird Decoration

Teapot, cov., Lacey Wings patt., wire handle w/ceramic grip, Prairie Hen, w/bird
decoration, ca. 1952 (ILLUS.).................... **$150**

Pals Teapot

Teapot, cov., Pals patt., in the form of a stylized bird w/"dancing turnips" decoration,
ceramic ribbon handle, ca. 1952 (ILLUS.) .. **$375**

Vase, 7 1/2" h., perforated, Lacey Wings $85
Vegetable bowl, 9 1/2" d. $65

Norleans Dinnerware by Meito
(pieces marked "Made in Occupied Japan" are worth 25% more)

Fairfield Cup & Saucer

Cup & saucer, Fairfield (ILLUS.) $8
Cup & saucer, Livonia $12

Livonia Gravy Boat with Underliner

Gravy boat w/underliner, Livonia (ILLUS.) $65

Livonia Dinner Plate

Plate, dinner, Livonia (ILLUS.) $12
Plate, salad, Livonia $10
Service for six, Livonia, 36-piece set $200

Norleans Vegetable Bowl

Vegetable bowl, 12" oval, Livonia (ILLUS.) $55

Riverside

Riverside Bowl

Bowl, 8 1/2" d., celadon & moss yellow
   (ILLUS.).. $600
Creamer $175
Plate, dinner, yellow & olive green.................. $60

Riverside Vase in Rust

Vase, 4 1/2" h., rust (ILLUS.) $55

Schmid Dinnerware

Casserole, cov., bird lid, 9 1/2 x 8" $150

Schmid Dinnerware Coffeepot

Coffeepot, cov., Lacey Wings/Rosette
   (ILLUS.).. $125
Gravy or sauce server, Lacey Wings, 7" d. .. $175

Sunburst Mug

Mug, Sunburst (ILLUS.) $16

Schmid Dinnerware Pitcher

Pitcher, 10" h., Lacey Wings & Sunburst
(ILLUS.).. **$85**
Plate, 10 1/2" d., dinner, Lacey Wings/Sun-
burst **$25**

Schmid Bird-shaped Teapot

Teapot, cov., bird-shaped, rattan handle,
Lacey Wings, 1950s (ILLUS.) **$85**

Schramberg

Schramberg Triangular Ashtray

Ashtray, triangular, Gobelin 13 (ILLUS.)........ **$160**
Creamer, cov., Mondrian.............................. **$170**
Cup & saucer, Gobelin 13 .... **$75**

Gobelin 13 Covered Jar

Jar, cov., Gobelin 13, 5" (ILLUS.) **$375**

Mondrian Covered Jar

Jar, cov., terraced, Mondrian, 5" (ILLUS.)... **$1,000**
Jug, cover & undertray, hot water, Mondri-
an.. **$90**
Pitcher, 4 1/2" h., Mondrian **$225**
Plate, salad, matte grun (green)..................... **$20**
Plate, 7 1/2" d., dessert, Gobelin 13 .... **$60**

Mondrian Covered Sugar

Sugar, cov., Mondrian (ILLUS.) **$125**

Gobelin 13 Teapot

Teapot, cov., Gobelin 13 patt., Germany,
1930s (ILLUS.).. **$900**
Tray, Mondrian, 12"...................................... **$450**

Gobelin 8 Vase

Vase, 6" h., offset oval, Gobelin 8 (ILLUS.).... **$200**

Stratoware

Stratoware Candlestick

Candlestick, brown trim (ILLUS.) **$120**
Casserole, cov., beige & brown **$150**

Stratoware Cup & Saucer

Cup & saucer, gold interior (ILLUS.) **$50**
Plate, 11 1/2" d., yellow & green **$60**

Stratoware Refrigerator Jar

Refrigerator jar, cov., blue & beige
(ILLUS.)... **$200**

Stratoware Shakers

Shakers, green trim, pr. (ILLUS.)................... **$85**

Stratoware Covered Sugar

Sugar, cov., gold & beige (ILLUS.) **$70**

Town and Country Dinnerware - for Red Wing Potteries

Pieces are unmarked and must be identified by the unique shapes. Glaze colors include rust, gray, dusk blue, peach, chartreuse, sand, Ming green, bronze & white.

Baker, oval, dusk blue, 10 3/4" l. **$85**
Baker, oval, rust, 10 3/4" l.............................. **$85**
Bowl, 5 3/4" d., chili or cereal, bronze **$30**
Bowl, 5 3/4" d., chili or cereal, peach............. **$20**
Bowl, 5 3/4" d., chili or cereal, sand................ **$18**
Creamer, peach **$50**
Creamer, sand **$45**

Town and Country "Yawn" Creamer

Creamer, "yawn," bronze (ILLUS.)................. **$70**

Town and Country Mustard Jar

Town and Country Cruets

Cruets, dusk blue & peach, set (ILLUS.)........ **$130**
Cup & saucer, peach, the set........................... **$40**
Cup & saucer, rust, the set.............................. **$40**

Lazy Susan Relish Set

Lazy Susan relish set w/mustard jar
    (ILLUS.).. **$600**
Mixing bowl dusk blue................................... **$175**
Mixing bowl rust **$175**
Mustard jar, cover & ladle, dusk blue, the
    set (ILLUS., top of page)............................ **$250**
Pitcher, jug-type, chartreuse, 3 pt................. **$250**
Pitcher, jug-type, dusk blue, 3 pt. **$250**
Pitcher, jug-type, Ming green, 3 pt................ **$285**
Pitcher, jug-type, rust, 3 pt............................ **$250**
Pitcher, syrup, chartreuse (ILLUS., top next
    page)... **$135**
Pitcher, syrup, rust....................................... **$140**

Town and Country Syrup Pitcher

Plate, 8" d., salad, chartreuse **$30**
Plate, 8" d., salad, dusk blue............................ **$30**
Plate, 8" d., salad, sand **$30**
Plate, 10 1/2" d., dinner, bronze...................... **$55**
Plate, 10 1/2" d., dinner, gray........................... **$40**
Plate, 10 1/2" d., dinner, peach........................ **$45**
Plate, 10 1/2" d., dinner, rust............................ **$45**
Platter, 15" l., comma shape, dusk blue **$110**
Platter, 15" l., comma shape, rust................. **$110**

Large & Small "Schmoo" Shakers

Shaker, large "schmoo," Ming green (ILLUS.
    right w/small "schmoo" shaker).................... **$75**

Shaker, large "schmoo," rust $70
Shaker, small "schmoo," chartreuse $40
Shaker, small "schmoo," rust (ILLUS. left
  w/large "schmoo" shaker, previous page) $40

Salad Serving Spoons

Spoons, salad servers, white, the set
  (ILLUS.) $1,700
Sugar bowl, cov., charteuse $60
Sugar bowl, cov., dusk blue $60
Sugar bowl, cov., rust.................................... $60

Bronze Town and Country Teapot

Teapot, cov., ca. 1947, bronze (ILLUS.) $550

Town & Country Covered Soup Tureen

Tureen, cov., soup, sand (ILLUS.) $850

Watt Pottery

Watt Pottery Drip Glaze Bowl

Bowl, 8 1/4" d., blue drip glaze (ILLUS.) $25

Watt Pottery Carafe

Carafe, ribbon handle, Nassau (ILLUS.) $80
Chop tray, Mountain Road, 14 1/2" $210
Shaker set, hourglass shape, bisque $35
Teapot, cov., rattan handle, Animal Farm
  patt., ca. 1954 .... $650

Zsolnay

This pottery was made in Pecs, Hungary, in a factory founded in 1862 by Vilmos Zsolnay. Utilitarian earthenware was originally produced, but by the turn of the 20th century ornamental Art Nouveau-style wares with bright colors and lustre decoration were produced; these wares are especially sought today. Currently Zsolnay pieces are being made in a new factory.

 ZSOLNAY PÉCS

Zsolnay Marks

Zsolnay Domed Box

Box, cov., rectangular, w/domed lid, Ivory
  Ware medieval design w/later metallic
  eosin glaze, incised Zsolnay factory
  mark, unknown form number, ca. 1900,
  3 1/4" h. (ILLUS.) $400-600
Bust, "Luna" by Sandor Apati Abt, realistic
  portrait of woman w/long hair & closed
  eyes, various metallic eosin glazes, incised Zsolnay factory mark, incised form
  number 5494, exhibited at the Paris Exposition in 1900, ca. 1899, 11" h. (ILLUS.,
  top next page) $25,000-30,000

"Luna" Portrait Bust by Zsolnay

Zsolnay Polychrome Charger

Center bowl, oblong boat-shaped form, the top of one end w/a standing figural polar bear peering into water that forms the walls of the piece, waves & fish in relief, iridescent purple, blue & amber glaze w/matte lustre, convex round trademark stamp, early 20th c., chips on base, minor wear, 6 1/2 x 19", 9" h. **$690**

Centerpiece, figural, boat-shaped, a reticulated floral border on a boat-shaped vessel decorated w/stylized Oriental flowers in pink, teal & gold tones w/gilt highlights, mounted in an ormolu base w/patinated metal cherubs riding atop wavelike formations & driving a bridled swan at the front, w/seashell feet, impressed "Zsolnay 1211" & blue stamp marks, late 19th c., 13 1/2" l. (hairline) **$1,150**

Very Rare Large Zsolnay Plaque with Scene of Eve in the Garden

Charger, large round shallow form, h.p. w/a large scene of a nude Eve w/long brown hair in the Garden of Eden, a field of tall white lilies at one side & a group of large threatening snakes on the other, done in vibrant Eosin metallic colors of dark brown, tan, white, dark green & rose, painted by Sandor Apati Abt, 1899, h.p. Zsolnay logo on back w/other markings, cast holes in back for hanging, 14 3/4" d. (ILLUS.)... **$20,700**

Zsolnay Chalice

Chalice, organic form w/applied handles curving out connecting base to bowl, multi eosin glazes, printed Zsolnay Factory mark, incised form number 5668, ca. 1900, 6" h. (ILLUS.) **$1,500-2,000**

Charger, cream ground w/enameled polychrome flowers & leaves in the Iznik style copying designs from the 18th c., printed factory mark & incised form number 470, ca. 1875, 14 1/5" d. (ILLUS., top next column)...................................... **$750-900**

Zsolnay Armin Klein Charger

Charger, painted w/scene of peasants in folkloric costumes pressing grapes in a vineyard, design by Armin Klein, printed

Zsolnay factory mark, incised form number 470, ca. 1880, 15" d. (ILLUS.) **$1,500-2,000**

Ewer, spherical body and elongated neck fitted w/spout & handle, raised on pedestal base, all-over applied decoration, underside marked "Zsolnay 7," ca. 1830, 12" h. **$420**

Figure of woman, seated cloaked woman beside a large low tapering vessel, iridescent gold glaze, gilt stamp mark, early 20th c., 5 1/4" h. (minor glaze wear) **$374**

Figure of woman, partially clad reclining woman w/green, gold & pink lustre glaze, clothing & rectangular base a blue & green iridescent glaze, stamped company mark, 10" l. **$990**

Zsolnay Jardiniere

Jardiniere, realistic polychrome decoration of thistles & leaves, majolica glaze, incised Zsolnay Factory mark & form number 5454, ca. 1899, 18" h. (ILLUS.) **$5,000-7,000**

Zsolnay Tadé Sikorsky Jug

Jug, form designed by Tadé Sikorsky, shriveled glaze w/applied pierced decorations, incised Zsolnay factory mark & form number 1379, ca. 1885, 8" h. (ILLUS.) **$350-550**

Zsolnay Hungarian-style Jug

Jug, on circular base, C-scroll handle, typical Hungarian folkloric form w/cream ground & enameled polychrome flower & leaf decoration, incised Zsolnay Factory mark, incised form number 1157, ca. 1883, 11 1/2" h. (ILLUS.) **$550-650**

Zsolnay Lamp by Lajos Mack

Lamp, figural, Art Nouveau model of a woman in the style of Lolie Fuller, w/arms upraised & flowing hair, designed by Lajos Mack, mostly gold/green eosin glazes, round raised Zsolnay factory mark, incised form number 6324, ca. 1900, 22 1/2" h. (ILLUS.) **$20,000-25,000**

Zsolnay Miniature Pitcher

Pitcher, 4 1/2" h., miniature form, squatty footed base tapering to long cylindrical body, flared rim, handle formed by woman peering into the pitcher, exceptional eosin glazes, round raised Zsolnay Factory mark, incised form number 5956, ca. 1900 (ILLUS.).............................. **$2,250-2,750**
Pitcher, 9 1/2" h., slightly bulbous tankard shape w/angular handle, metallic eosin glazed decoration in the style of Loetz Bohemian glass, round raised Zsolnay factory mark, incised form number 8925, ca. 1918 .... **$7,500-9,500**
Pitcher, 12 3/4" h., crackled glaze, red color, modern design by Gabriella Törzsök, printed Zsolnay Factory mark, ca. 1959 .... **$300-500**

Zsolnay Dragon Motif Pitcher

Pitcher, 13" h., cov., decorative Ivory Ware lid, dragon form handle & spout, cream ground w/gilt trim, incised & applied dec-

oration of dragon & gargoyle copying 18th-c. designs, printed Zsolnay factory mark, incised form number 2994, ca. 1889 (ILLUS.) **$600-800**
Pitcher, 15 1/2" h., tapering tankard style w/C-scroll handle, overall high-relief decoration of oak leaves, acorns & large beetles, pale green eosin glaze, incised Zsolnay Factory mark & form number 4115, ca. 1893 .... **$4,500-5,500**

Zsolnay Cock-form Pitcher

Pitcher, 18" h., in the form of a crowing cock w/stylized feathers on oval base, open beak forms spout, pale green eosin glaze, incised Zsolnay factory mark, incised form number 1132, ca. 1903 (ILLUS.) **$4,000-5,000**

Zsolnay Puzzle Jug

Zsolnay Plaque-like Tile

Puzzle jug, shriveled yellow glaze w/applied stylized flowers & bird figure attached to C-scroll handle, based on 17th-c. designs, pierced neck & flowers, stepped circular base, incised factory mark & form number 547, ca. 1875, 9 1/2" h. (ILLUS., previous page)........ **$550-750**

Tile, rectangular plaque form w/oval cartouche w/relief decoration of idyllic setting w/Art Nouveau-style female dancer & Pan-like figures playing musical instruments, multicolored eosin glazes, designed by Lajos Mack, incised Zsolnay factory mark, incised form number 7892, ca. 1906, 8 1/4 x 10 3/4" (ILLUS., top of page)................................. **$7,500-9,500**

Tile, square, decorated w/flowers & leaves, green & gold eosin glazes, unmarked, unusual & rare, ca. 1900, 5" sq. (ILLUS.)
.... **$1,250-1,500**

Rare Zsolnay Umbrella Stand

Umbrella stand, tall, slightly waisted cylindrical form w/rolled rim, the sides decorated w/dark golden iridescent fish swimming in iridescent swirls of dark blue, purple & gold, impressed "Zsolnay - Pecs - 4036 - 21," ca. 1900, 26 3/4" h. (ILLUS.)
.... **$14,400**

Zsolnay Tile

Egyptian Decor Zsolnay Vase

Vase, 5" h., cylindrical, tapering out toward top, then in toward short neck w/small opening, Art Deco Egyptian decor, designed by Teréz Mattyasovszky-Zsolnay, printed Zsolnay factory mark, ca. 1915 (ILLUS.).. **$1,250-1,500**

Miniature Zsolnay Vase

Vase, miniature, 4" h., wide base tapering to ring foot & long neck, richly decorated w/Hungarian folkloric designs in gold & blue/green eosin glazes, incised Zsolnay factory mark, ca. 1912 (ILLUS.)
.... **$1,000-1,250**

Zsolnay Vase with Iridescent Eosin Glaze

Vase, 6 7/8" h., bulbous ovoid lower body tapering to a pinched center below the upright squared neck, iridescent Eosin glaze w/rust over brushed gold, marked w/raised wafer logo & impressed numbers "6035 - 23" (ILLUS.)........................... **$863**

Vase, earthenware, wide ovoid base w/broad flattened shoulder centered by a short cylindrical rim, decorated w/a caravan of men on camels carrying guns & spears, in an oasis w/palm trees, below a wavy edged border of scattered flower heads, iridescent red, brown & blue glaze, ca. 1900-10, molded factory seal, impressed "8868" & "19," imperfection at edge of foot, 8" w. **$2,300**

Miniature Footed Zsolnay Vase

Vase, miniature, 4 3/4" h., footed form w/ovoid body tapering to narrower neck, decorated w/Hungarian folkloric designs in metallic blue eosin glaze, incised Zsolnay Factory mark, ca. 1906 (ILLUS.)
.... **$750-1,000**

Zsolnay Vase with Sun & Trees

Vase, 8 1/2" h., slightly ovoid cylindrical shape, decorated w/idyllic view of trees, sun & road, metallic eosin glazes, round raised Zsolnay Factory mark, incised form number 6011, ca. 1906 (ILLUS.) **$12,500-15,000**

Vase, 9" h., baluster form w/figure of draped woman molded in full relief at shoulder, tall cylindrical neck w/flaring scalloped rim, metallic green & blue glaze, stamped company mark **$660**

Zsolnay Vase with Landscape Scene

Vase, 9 3/4" h., cylindrical body tapering to short, flared neck, painted w/landscape scene of trees, sunset, clouds & flowers, brilliant eosin glazes, round raised Zsolnay factory mark, incised form number 8196, ca. 1909 (ILLUS.) **$12,500-15,000**

Vase, 10" h., 5" d., tall slender ovoid body tapering to a flat rim, decorated w/ruby red pomegranate design against a nacreous eocin ground, die-stamped & wax-resist mark **$1,760**

Zsolnay Vase with Metallic Glaze

Vase, 10 1/2" h., freeform body w/quatrefoil opening, decorated w/relief & applied leaves & lilies, highly metallic silver/blue eosin glaze, printed Zsolnay Factory mark, incised form number 5424, ca. 1900 (ILLUS.) **$10,000-12,500**

Zsolnay Vase by Sándor Pillo-Hidasy

Vase, 10 3/4" h., ovoid body tapering in at neck, which tapers further to short molded rim, decorated w/three spotted leopards around body, silver metallic leaves w/red early Deco decorations, signed by Sándor Pillo-Hidasy, round raised Zsolnay factory mark, incised form number 8589, ca. 1912 (ILLUS.) **$20,000-25,000**

Vase, 11" h., figural, consists of three realistic owls in high relief, green/gold metallic eosin glaze, round raised Zsolnay Factory mark, incised form number 5236, ca. 1898 .... **$6,500-8,500**

Vase, 11" h., slightly swelled cylindrical lower body below a bulbed upper body & angled shoulder to the short flared neck, iridescent gold glaze w/purple & blue marbleized striations, impressed "Zsolnay - 7595" & gilt stamp mark, early 20th c. **$460**

body & neck, soft green/blue eosin glaze, incised Zsolnay Factory mark, incised form number 4626, ca. 1897 (ILLUS.) **$2,500-3,500**

Zsolnay Vase with Swirl Base

Vase, 12 1/4" h., swirl pattern ovoid base, long, slightly tapering cylindrical neck, scalloped rim, cream ground w/enameled painted flowers & leaves, gilt decoration, printed Zsolnay Factory mark, incised form number 3088, ca. 1885 (ILLUS.) **$400-600**

Hungarian Millennium Vase

Vase, 11 3/4" h., bulbous waisted form w/short bulbous applied feet, Hungarian Millennium decoration of painted stylized birds & flowers, round printed Zsolnay factory mark, incised form number 933, ca. 1882 (ILLUS.) **$2,500-3,500**

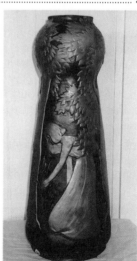

Lajos Mack Vase with Relief Design

Vase, 28" h., tapering cylindrical form w/squat ovoid neck, decorated w/relief design of figures in forest setting including Pan-like form, various eosin metallic glazes, designed by Lajos Mack, incised Zsolnay factory mark, incised form number 5902, ca. 1900 (ILLUS.)...... **$25,000-30,000**

Zsolnay Vase with Swirled Banding

Vase, 12" h., cylindrical footed body tapering to narrow neck w/highly stylized fluted lip, raised banding in swirl pattern around

GLOSSARY OF SELECTED CERAMICS TERMS

Abino Ware—A line produced by the Buffalo Pottery of Buffalo, New York. Introduced in 1911, this limited line featured mainly sailing ship scenes with a windmill on shore.

Agate Ware—An earthenware pottery featuring a mixture of natural colored clays giving a marbled effect. Popular in England in the 18th century.

Albany slip—A dark brown slip glaze used to line the interiors of most salt-glazed stoneware pottery. Named for a fine clay found near Albany, New York.

Albino line—A version of Griffen, Smith and Hill's Shell & Seaweed majolica pattern with an off-white overall color sometimes trimmed with gold or with pink or blue feathering.

Albion Ware—A line of majolica developed by Edwin Bennett in the 1890s. It featured colored liquid clays over a green clay body decorated with various scenes. Popular for jardinieres and pedestals.

Bas relief—Literally "low relief," referring to lightly molded decorations on ceramic pieces.

Bisquit—Unglazed porcelain left undecorated or sometimes trimmed with pastel colors. Also known as bisque.

Bocage—A background of flowering trees or vines often used as a backdrop for figural groups which were meant to be viewed from the front only.

Bone china—A porcelain body developed in England using the white ashes of bone. It has been the standard English porcelain ware since the early 19th century.

Coleslaw—A type of decoration used on ceramic figurines to imitate hair or fur. It is finely crumbled clay applied to the unfired piece and resembling coleslaw cabbage.

Crackled glaze—A glaze with an intentional network of fine lines produced by uneven contracting of the glaze after firing. First popular on Chinese wares.

Crazing—The fine network of cracks in a glaze produced by uneven contracting of the glaze after firing or later reheating of a piece during usage. An unintentional defect usually found on eathernwares.

Creamware—A light-colored fine earthenware developed in England in the late 18th century and used by numerous potters into the 19th century. Josiah Wedgwood marketed his version as Queensware.

Crystalline glaze—A glaze containing fine crystals resulting from the presence of mineral salts in the mixture. It was a popular glaze on American art pottery of the late 19th century and early 20th century.

Eared handles—Handles applied to ceramic pieces such as crocks. They are crescent or 'ear' shaped, hence the name.

Earthenware—A class of fine-grained porous pottery fired at relatively low temperature and then glazed. It produces a light and easily molded ware that was widely used by the potteries of Staffordshire, England in the late 18th and early 19th century.

Faience—A form of fine earthenware

featuring a tin glaze and originally inspired by Chinese porcelain. It includes early Dutch Delft ware and similar wares made in France, Germany and other areas of Europe.

Fairyland Lustre—A special line of decorated wares developed by Susannah 'Daisy' Makeig-Jones for the Josiah Wedgwood firm early in the 20th century. It featured fantastic or dreamlike scenes with fairies and elves in various colors and with a mother-of-pearl lustre glaze. Closely related to Dragon Lustre featuring designs with dragons.

Flambé glaze—A special type of glaze featuring splashed or streaked deep reds and purple, often dripping over another base color. Popular with some American art pottery makers but also used on porcelain wares.

Flint Enamel glaze—A version of the well known brown mottled Rockingham pottery glaze. It was developed by Lyman Fenton & Co. of Bennington, Vermont and patented in 1849. It featured streaks and flecks of green, orange, yellow and blue mixed with the mottled brown glaze.

Glaze—The general term for vitreous (glass-like) coating fired onto pottery and porcelain to produce an impervious surface and protect underglaze decoration.

Hard-paste—Refers to 'true' porcelain, a fine, white clay body developed by the Chinese and containing kaolin and petuntse or china stone. It is fired at a high temperature and glazed with powdered feldspar to produce a smooth, shiny glaze.

Lead glaze—A shiny glaze most often used on cheap redware pottery and produced using a dry powdered or liquid lead formula. Since it would be toxic, it was generally used on the exterior of utilitarian wares only

Lithophane—A panel of thin porcelain delicately molded with low-relief pattern or scenes which show up clearly when held to light. It was developed in Europe in the 19th century and was used for decorative panels or lamp shades and was later used in the bottom of some German and Japanese steins, mugs or cups.

Majolica—A type of tin-glazed earthenware pottery developed in Italy and named for the island of Majorca. It was revived in Europe and America in the late 19th century and usually featured brightly colored shiny glazes

Married—A close match or a duplicate of the original missing section or piece, such as a lid.

Mission Ware—A decorative line of pottery developed by the Niloak Pottery of Benton, Arkansas. It featured variously colored clays swirled together and was used to produce such decorative pieces as vases and candlesticks.

Moriage—Japanese term for the slip-trailed relief decorations used on various forms of porcelain and pottery. Flowers, beading and dragon decoration are typical examples.

Pâte-sur-pâte—French for 'paste on paste,' this refers to a decorative technique where layers of porcelain slip in white are layered on a darker background. Used on artware produced by firms like Minton, Ltd. of England.

Pearlware—A version of white colored creamware developed in England and widely used for inexpensive eathenwares in the late

18th and early 19th century. It has a pearly glaze, hence the name.

Pillow vase—a form of vase designed to resemble a flattened round or oblong pillow. Generally an upright form with flattened sides. A similar form is the Moon vase or flask, meant to resemble a full moon.

Porcelain—The general category of translucent, vitrified ceramics first developed by the Chinese and later widely produced in Europe and America. Hard-paste is 'true' porcelain, while soft-paste is an 'artificial' version developed to imitate hard-paste using other ingredients.

Pottery—The very general category of ceramics produced from various types of clay. It includes redware, yellowware, stoneware and various earthenwares. It is generally fired at a much lower temperature than porcelain.

PUG—An abbreviation for "printed under glaze," referring to colored decorations on pottery. Most often it is used in reference to decorations found on Mettlach pottery steins.

Relief-molding—A decorative technique, sometimes erroneously referred to as "blown-out," whereby designs are raised in bold relief against a background. The reverse side of such decoration is hollowed-out, giving the impression the design was produced by 'blowing' from the inside. Often used in reference to certain Nippon porcelain wares.

Rocaille—A French term meaning 'rockwork.' It generally refers to a decoration used for the bases of ceramic figurines.

Salt-glazed stoneware—A version of stoneware pottery where common rock salt is thrown in the kiln during firing and produces hard, shiny glaze like a thin coating of glass. A lightly pitted "orange peel" surface is sometimes the result of this technique.

Sanded—A type of finish usually on pottery wares. Unfired pieces are sprinkled or rolled in fine sand, which, when fired, gives the piece a sandy, rough surface texture.

Sang-de-boeuf—Literally French for "ox blood," it refers to a deep red glaze produced with copper oxide. It was first produced by the Chinese and imitated by European and American potters in the late 19th and early 20th century.

Sgrafitto—An Italian-inspired term for decorative designs scratched or cut through a layer of slip before firing. Generally used on earthenware forms and especially with the Pennsylvania-German potters of America.

Slip—The liquid form of clay, often used to decorate earthenware pieces in a process known as slip-trailing or slip-quilling.

Soft-paste—A term used to describe a certain type of porcelain body developed in Europe and England from the 16th to late 18th centuries. It was used to imitate true hard-paste porcelain developed by the Chinese but was produced using a white clay mixed with a grit or flux of bone ash or talc and fired at fairly low temperatures. The pieces are translucent, like hard-paste porcelain, but are not as durable. It should not be used when referring to earthenwares such as creamware or pearlware.

Sprigging—A term used to describe the ornamenting of ceramic pieces with applied relief decoration, such as blossoms, leaves or even figures.

Standard glaze—The most common form of glazing used on Rookwood

Pottery pieces. It is a clear, shiny glaze usually on pieces decorated with florals or portraits against a dark shaded backhground.

Stoneware—A class of hard, high-fired pottery usually made from dense grey clay and most often decorated with a salt glaze. American 19th century stoneware was often decorated with slip-quilled or hand-brushed cobalt blue decorations.

Tapestry ware—A form of late 19th century porcelain where the piece is impressed with an overall linen cloth texture before firing. The Royal Bayreuth firm is especially known for their fine "Rose Tapestry"

line wherein the finely textured ground is decorated with colored roses.

Tin glaze—A form of pottery glaze made opaque by the addition of tin oxide. It was used most notably on early Dutch Delft as well as other early faience and majolica wares.

Underglaze-blue—A cobalt blue produced with metallic oxides applied to an unfired clay body. Blue was one of the few colors which does not run or smear when ired at a high temperature. It was used by the Chinese on porcelain and later copied by firms such as Meissen.

APPENDIX I
CERAMICS CLUBS & ASSOCIATIONS

ABC Plates
 ABC Collectors' Circle
 67 Stevens Ave.
 Old Bridge, NJ 08857-2244

Abingdon Pottery Club
 210 Knox Hwy. 5
 Abingdon, IL 61410-9332

American Art Pottery Association
 P.O. Box 834
 Westport, MA 02790-0697
 www.amartpot.org/

American Ceramic Circle
 520 - 16th St.
 New York, NY 11215

Amphora Collectors Club
 129 Bathurst St.
 Toronto, Ontario
 CANADA M5V 2R2

Arkansas Pottery

National Society of Arkansas Pottery
 Collectors
 2006 Beckenham Cove
 Little Rock, AR 72212
 www.flash.net/~gemoore/nsapc.htm

Pottery Lovers Reunion
 4969 Hudson Dr.
 Stow, OH 44224

Bauer Pottery
 www.bauerpottery.com/

Belleek Collectors International Society
 9893 Georgetown Pike, Ste. 525
 Great Falls, VA 22066
 www.belleek:ie/collectors.com

Blue & White Pottery Club
 224 12th St. NW
 Cedar Rapids, IA 52405

Blue Ridge Collectors Club
 208 Harris St.
 Erwin, TN 37650
 (423) 743-9337

Carlton Ware Collectors International
 Carlton Works
 P.O. Box 161
 Sevenoaks, Kent, England
 TN15 6GA
 e-mail: cwciclub@aol.com

Ceramic Arts Studio Collectors
 P.O. Box 46
 Madison, WI 53701-0046
 www.ceramicartsstudio.com/

Chintz Connection
 P.O. Box 222
 Riverdale, MD 20738-0222

Clarice Cliff Collectors Club
 Fantasque House
 Tennis Drive, The Park

Nottingham NG7 1AE
UNITED KINGDOM
www.claricecliff.com/

Currier & Ives Dinnerware
Collectors Club
29470 Saxon Rd.
Toulon, IL 61438
www.royalchinaclub.com

Czechoslovakian Collectors Assoc.
P.O. Box 137
Hopeland, PA 17533

The Dedham Pottery Collectors Society
248 Highland St.
Dedham, MA 02026-5833
www.dedhampottery.com/

Delftware Collectors Association
P.O. Box 670673
Marietta, GA 30066
www.delftware.org/

Doulton & Royal Doulton
Northern California Doulton
Collectors Club
P.O. Box 214
Moraga, CA 94556
www.royaldoultonwest.com/

Royal Doulton International
Collectors Club
701 Cottontail Lane
Somerset, NJ 08873
www.royal-doulton.com/

Fiesta Collector's Club
P.O. Box 471
Valley City, OH 44280-0471
www.chinaspecialties.com/fiesta.html

Flow Blue International Collector's Club
P.O. Box 6664
Leawood, KS 66206
www.flowblue.org

Franciscan Pottery Collectors Society
500 S. Farrell Dr., #S-114
Palm Springs, CA 92264
www.gmcb.com/franciscan/

Frankoma Family Collectors Association
P.O. Box 32571
Oklahoma City, OK 73123
www.frankoma.org/

Gonder Collectors Club
3735 E. Rousay Dr.
Queen Creek, AZ 85242
e-mail:GonderNut@aol.com

Goss & Crested China Club
62 Murray Road
Horndean
Waterlooville, Hants. PO8 9JL
UNITED KINGDOM
www.gosschina.com/

Gouda Pottery
See Delftware Collectors Association

Haeger Pottery Collectors of America
5021 Toyon Way
Antioch, CA 94509-8426

Hall China Collector's Club
P.O. Box 360488
Cleveland, OH 44136-0488
www.chinaspecialties.com/hallnews.html

Haviland Collectors International
Foundation
P.O. Box 271383
Fort Collins, CO 80527
www.havilandcollectors.com/

Head Vases (Head Hunters Newsletter)
P.O. Box 83H
Scarsdale, NY 10583-8583

Hull Pottery Association
112 Park DeVille Dr.
Columbia, MO 65203
www.hullpotteryassociation.org <http://
hullpotteryassociation.org>

Homer Laughlin China Collectors
P.O. Box 1093
Corbin, KY 40702-1093
www.hlcca.org/

Illinois Pottery
Collectors of Illinois Pottery
& Stoneware
308 N. Jackson St.
Clinton, IL 61727-1320

Ironstone China

White Ironstone China Association
P.O. Box 855
Fairport, NY 14450-0855
www.whiteironstonechina.com/

Jewel Tea Autumn Leaf
National Autumn Leaf Collectors Club
P.O. Box 7929
Moreno Valley, CA 92552-7929
www.nalcc.org/

Majolica International Society
1275 First Ave., PBO 103
New York, NY 10021-5601
www.majolicasociety.com/

McCoy Pottery Collectors' Society
14 North Morris St.
Dover, NJ 07801
www.mccoypotterycollectorssociety.org

McCoy Pottery Collectors Connection
2210 Sherwin Dr.
Twinsburg, OH 44087
www.ohiopottery.com/mccoy/

Moorcroft Collectors Club
Sandbach Road
Burslem, Stoke-on-Trent ST6 2DG
UNITED KINGDOM
www.moorcroft.com/

Nippon Porcelain
International Nippon Collectors Club
1387 Lance Court
Carol Stream, IL 60188
www.nipponcollectorsclub.com

Lakes & Plains Nippon Collectors' Club
P.O. Box 230
Peotone, IL 60468-0230

New England Nippon Collectors Club
64 Burt Rd.
Springfield, MA 01118-1848

Sunshine State Nippon Collectors' Club
P.O. Box 425
Frostproof, FL 33843-0425

Noritake Collectors' Society
1237 Federal Ave. E.
Seattle, WA 98102-4329
www.noritakecollectors.com

North Dakota Pottery Collectors Society
P.O. Box 14
Beach, ND 58621-0014

Old Ivory China
Society for Old Ivory & Ohme Porcelains
700 High St.
Hicksville, OH 43526

Pewabic Pottery
10125 E. Jefferson Ave.
Detroit, MI 48214
www.pewabic.com/

Phoenix Bird Collectors of America
1107 Deerfield St.
Marshall, MI 49068

Pickard Collectors Club
300 E. Grove St.
Bloomington, IL 61701-5232

Porcelier Collectors Club
21 Tamarac Swamp Road
Wallingford, CT 06492-5529

Purinton Pottery
Purinton News & Views Newsletter
P.O. Box 153
Connellsville, PA 15425

Quimper Club International
5316 Seascape Lane
Plano, TX 75093
www.quimperclub.org/

Red Wing Collectors Society, Inc.
P.O. Box 50
Red Wing, MN 55066-0050
www.redwingcollectors.org

Royal Bayreuth International Collectors'
Society
P.O. Box 325
Orrville, OH 44667-0325

R.S. Prussia
International Association of
R.S. Prussia Collectors Inc.
P.O. Box 185
Lost Nation, IA 55254
www.rsprussia.com/

Shelley China
National Shelley China Club
591 W. 67th Ave.
Anchorage, AK 99518-1555
www.nationalshelleychinaclub.com

Southern Folk Pottery Collectors Society
220 Washington St.
Bennett, NC 27208

Staffordshire
The Transfer Ware Collectors Club
734 Torreya Court
Palo Alto, CA 94303
www.transcollectorsclub.org/

Stangl/Fulper Collectors Association
P.O. Box 538
Flemington, NJ 08822
www.stanglfulper.com/

Stoneware
American Stoneware Collectors Society
P.O. Box 281
Point Pleasant Beach, NJ 08742-0281

Susie Cooper Collectors Group
P.O. Box 7436
London N12 7QF
UNITED KINGDOM

Tea Leaf Club International
Maxine Johnson, Membership
P.O. Box 377
Belton, MO 64012

www.TeaLeafClub.com

Torquay Pottery
North American Torquay Society
214 N. Ronda Road.
McHenry, IL 60050
www.torquayus.org

Uhl Collectors Society, Inc.
3704 W. Old Road 64
Huntingburg, IN 47542
www.uhlcollectors.org/

Van Briggle Collectors Society
600 S. 21st St.
Colorado Springs, CO 80904
www.vanbriggle.com/

Wade Watch, Ltd.
8199 Pierson Court
Arvada, CO 80005
www.wadewatch.com/

Watt Collectors Association
1431 4th St. SW
P.M.B. 221
Mason City, IA 50401
server34.hypermart.net/wattcollectors/
watt.htm

Wedgwood International Seminar
22 De Savry Crescent
Toronto, Ontario

CANADA M45 2L2
www.w-i-s.org/

Wedgwood Society of Boston, Inc.
P.O. Box 215
Dedham, MA 02027-0215
htlp://www.angelfire.com/ma/wsb/
index.html

The Wedgwood Society of New York
5 Dogwood Ct.
Glen Head, NY 11545-2740
www.wsny.org/

Wedgwood Society of Washington, DC
3505 Stringfellow Court
Fairfax, VA 22033

Willow Wares
International Willow Collectors
503 Chestnut St.
Perkasie, PA 18944
www.willowcollectors.org/

Wisconsin Pottery Association
P.O. Box 8213
Madison, WI 53708-8213
www.wisconsinpottery.org/

Eva Zeisel Collectors Club
695 Monterey Blvd. #203
San Francisco, CA 94127
www.evazeisel.org/

APPENDIX II
Museums & Libraries with Ceramic Collections

CERAMICS (AMERICAN)

Everson Museum of Art of Syracuse &
Onondaga County
401 Harrison St.
Syracuse, NY 13202-3019
www.everson.org/

Museum of Ceramics at East Liverpool
400 E. 5th St.
East Liverpool, OH 43920-3134
www.ohiohistory.org/places/ceramics/

CERAMICS (AMERICAN ART POTTERY)

Cincinnati Art Museum
953 Eden Park
Cincinnati, OH 45202
www.cincinnatiartmuseum.com/

Newcomb College Art Gallery
Woldenberg Art Center
Newcomb College/Tulane University
1229 Broadway
New Orleans, LA 70118
www.newcomb.tulane.edu/

Zanesville Art Center
620 Military Rd.
Zanesville, OH 43701
www.zanesville.com

OTHER CERAMICS:

BENNINGTON

The Bennington Museum
West Main St.
Bennington, VT 05201
www.benningtonmuseum.com

CATALINA ISLAND POTTERY

Catalina Island Museum
P.O. Box 366
Avalon, CA 90704
www.catalina.com/museum

CHINESE EXPORT PORCELAIN

Peabody Essex Museum
East India Square
Salem, MA 01970
www.pem.org

CLEWELL POTTERY

Jesse Besser Museum
491 Johnson St.
Alpena, MI 49707
www.ogdennews.com/upnorth/
museum/home.htm

COWAN POTTERY

Cowan Pottery Museum at the Rocky River
Public Library
1600 Hampton Rd.
Rocky River, OH 44116-2699
www.rrpl.org/rrpl_cowan.stm

DEDHAM

Dedham Historical Society
612 High St.
Dedham, MA 02027-0125
www.dedhamhistorical.org

GEORGE OHR

Ohr/O'Keefe Museum of Art
136 G.E. Ohr St.
Biloxi, MS 39530
www.georgeohr.org/

PENNSYLVANIA GERMAN

Hershey Museum
170 W. Hersheypark Dr.
Hershey, PA 17033

ROSEVILLE POTTERY

Roseville Historical Society
91 Main St.
Roseville, OH 43777

www.netpluscom.com/~pchs/
rosevill.htm

SOUTHERN FOLK POTTERY

Museum of Southern Stoneware
River Market Antiques Mall
3226 Hamilton Rd.
Columbus, GA 31904

WEDGWOOD

Birmingham Museum of Art
2000 Eighth Ave. No.
Birmingham, AL 35203
www.artsbma.org/

GENERAL COLLECTIONS:

The Bayou Bend Collection
#1 Westcott
Houston, TX 77007
www.bayoubend.uh.edu

Greenfield Village and Henry Ford Museum
20900 Oakwood Blvd.
Dearborn, MI 48124-4088

Museum of Early Southern
Decorative Arts
924 Main St.
Winston Salem, NC 27101

Abby Aldrich Rockefeller Folk
Art Collection
England St.
Williamsburg, VA 23185

The Margaret Woodbury Strong Museum
700 Allen Creek Rd.
Rochester, NY 14618

Henry Francis DuPont Winterthur Museum
Winterthur, DE 19735
www.winterthur.org/

APPENDIX III
References to Pottery and Porcelain Marks

DeBolt's Dictionary of American Pottery
Marks—Whiteware & Porcelain
Gerald DeBolt
Collector Books,
Paducah, Kentucky, 1994

Encyclopaedia of British Pottery and
Porcelain Marks
Geoffrey A. Godden
Bonanza Books,
New York, New York, 1964

Encyclopedia of Marks on American,
English, and European Earthenware,
Ironstone and Stoneware
Arnold A. and Dorthy E. Kowalsky
Schiffer Publishing, Ltd.
Atglen, PA, 1999

Kovel's New Dictionary of Marks, Pottery &
Porcelain, 1850 to the Present
Ralph & Terry Kovel

Crown Publishers,
New York, New York, 1986

Lehner's Encyclopedia of U.S. Marks on
Pottery, Porcelain & Clay
Lois Lehner
Collector Books,
Paducah, Kentucky, 1988

Marks on German, Bohemian and Austrian
Porcelain, 1710 to
the Present
Robert E. Röntgen
Schiffer Publishing, Ltd.,
Atglen, Pennsylvania

Pictorial Guide to Pottery & Porcelain Marks
Chad Lage
Collector Books
Paducahy, Kentucky, 2004

APPENDIX IV
English Registry Marks

Since the early nineteenth century, the English have used a number of markings on most ceramics wares which can be very helpful in determining the approximate date a piece was produced.

The 'registry' mark can be considered an equivalant of the American patent number. This English numbering system continues in use today.

Beginning in 1842 and continuing until 1883, most pottery and porcelain pieces were printed or stamped with a diamond-shaped registry mark which was coded with numbers and letters indicating the type of material, parcel number of the piece and, most helpful, the day, month and year that the design or pattern was registered at the Public Record Office. Please note that a piece may have been produced a few years after the registration date itself.

Our Chart A here shows the format of the diamond registry mark used between 1842 and 1867. Accompanying it are listings of the corresponding month and year letters used during that period. In a second chart, Chart B, we show the version of the diamond mark used between 1868 and 1883 which depicts a slightly different arrangement. Keep in mind that this diamond registry mark was also used on metal, wood and glasswares. It is important to note that the top bubble with the Roman numeral indicates the material involved; pottery and porcelain will always be Numeral IV.

After 1884, the diamond mark was discontinued and instead just a registration number was printed on pieces. The abbreviation "Rd" for "Registration" appears before the number. We list here these design registry numbers by year with the number indicating the first number that was used in that year. For instance, design number 494010 would have been registered sometime in 1909.

CHART A

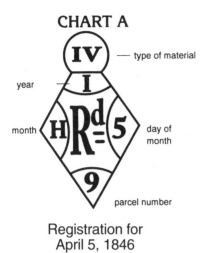

Registration for
April 5, 1846

CHART B

Registration for
August 6, 1871

LIST
Month of the Year of Registration

C—January	I—July
G—February	R—August
W—March	D—December
H—April	B—October
E—May	K—November
M—June	A—December

LIST
Year of Registration—1842-1867

1842—X	1851—P	1860—Z
1843—H	1852—D	1861—R
1844—C	1853—Y	1862—O
1845—A	1854—J	1863—G
1846—I	1855—E	1864—N
1847—F	1856—L	1865—W
1848—U	1857—K	1866—Q
1849—S	1858—B	1867—T
1850—V	1859—M	

LIST 3

Year of Registration — 1868-1883

1868—X	1874—U	1879—Y
1869—H	1875—S	1880—J
1870—C	1876—V	1881—E
1871—A	1877—P	1882—L
1872—I	1878—D	1883—K
1873—F		

LIST 4

DESIGN REGISTRY NUMBERS — 1884-1951

Jan. 1884—1	1907—493900	1929—742725
1885—20000	1908—518640	1930—751160
1886—40800	1909—535170	1931—760583
1887—64700	Sep. 1909—548919	1932—769670
1888—91800	Oct. 1909—548920	1933—779292
1889—117800	Jan. 1911—575817	1934—789019
1890—142300	1912—594195	1935—799097
1891—164000	1913—612431	1936—808794
1892—186400	1914—630190	1937—817293
1893—206100	1915—644935	1938—825231
1894—225000	1916—635521	1939—832610
1895—248200	1917—658988	1940—837520
1896—268800	1918—662872	1941—838590
1897—291400	1919—666128	1942—839230
Jan. 1898—311677	1920—673750	1943—839980
1899—332200	1921—680147	1944—841040
1900—351600	1922—687144	1945—842670
1901—368186	1923—694999	Jan. 1946—845550
1902—385180	1924—702671	1947—849730
1903—403200	1925—710165	1948—853260
1904—424400	1926—718057	1949—856999
1905—447800	1927—726330	1950—860854
1906—471860	1928—734370	1951—863970

INDEX